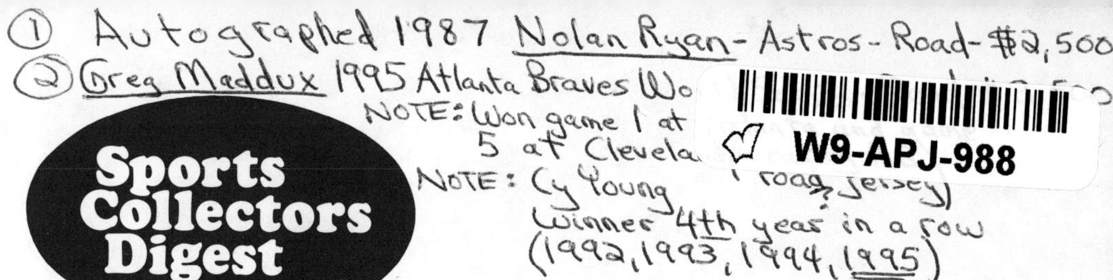

TEAM BASEBALLS

A comprehensive guide to the identification, authentication and value of autographed baseballs.

By Mark Allen Baker

Editor — Mark K. Larson

Photography by Mark Allen Baker and the National Baseball Hall of Fame & Library, Cooperstown, New York

---

Published by Krause Publications
700 E. State St.
Iola, Wis. 54990
(715) 445-2214

Library of Congress: 91-76401
ISBN: 0-87341-185-4

Printed in the United States of America.

Dedication

To Aaron, Elizabeth and Rebecca

Learn to seek your own truths and believe in your own dreams. I know dreams come true, as you are mine.

"Every time I sign a baseball, and there must have been thousands, I thank my luck that I wasn't born Coveleski or Wambsganss or Peckinpaugh."

Mel Ott

Contents

Dedication 2
Preface 4
Foreword 5
Chapter 1: Collecting Autographed Baseballs 10
Chapter 2: The History of Baseballs 17
Chapter 3: The History of Writing Materials 22
Chapter 4: Collection Organization, Display and Preservation 28
Chapter 5: Autographed Baseball Values 33
Chapter 6: Authenticity, Identification and Signature Variation 43
Chapter 7: How To Use This Book 50
Chapter 8: Acquiring Autographed Baseballs 56
1920s 59
1930s 101
1940s 143
1950s 186
1960s 229
1970s 283
1980s 349
1990s 419
Chapter 9: Autographed All-Star Baseballs (1933-1991) 433
Chapter 10: Single-Signature Baseballs 465
Chapter 11: Autographed Commemorative Baseballs 469
Chapter 12: Autographed Game Baseballs 479
Chapter 13: Autographed Celebrity Baseballs 482
Key Player Index 486
Supplements 529
Acknowledgements 538
Additional source material and notes 539
Selected bibliography 540

Preface

This book was a project that I and Krause Publications believed was greatly needed in the hobby, a multi-billion dollar hobby that now exceeds the revenues of many major corporations. The complexity and vastness of the subject, autographed team baseballs, warranted an independent source. The book's primary objective is to provide the collector with all the tools necessary to properly identify and appraise an autographed team or group baseball. Another goal, no less important, is to provide the hobbyist with useful information essential for maintaining, enhancing or preserving his collection.

Educating the collector is of paramount importance in Section One. Its topics include: The History of Baseball & Writing Materials, Organization & Display, Value and Collecting Hints. Included in this section are useful photographic examples to assist the collector in determining the condition of an autographed baseball — a key factor in setting the value of such an item.

The heart of the book is Section Two, which provides the information necessary to perform the book's primary task — to properly identify and appraise an autographed team or group baseball. Each team, by year, will be identified by players, listed alphabetically. Players who have appeared in less than 10 games are noted at the end, signifying their rarity as more obscure individuals. A list of key signatures, those players or managers who greatly enhance the value of the baseball, is also provided. Additional source data and estimated values will also be included. Of added interest, and provided in a similar format, are chapters discussing All-Star teams, commemorative events, celebrities, and individual autographed baseballs. A "Key Player Index" is provided at the end of the book to expedite the identification process. Collectors interested strictly in single-signed baseballs of players in the Baseball Hall of Fame should consider purchasing the "Sports Collectors Digest Baseball Autograph Handbook," second edition, also available from Krause Publications.

Collecting autographed baseballs has never been as popular as it is today, particularly the focus on the elite members of the Baseball Hall of Fame. Most autograph collecting has centered only around single signatures on baseballs. Thus, the value of these items has escalated beyond what is normally attainable to the average collector. Ironically, and almost inexplicable, has been the lack of interest in autographed team baseballs. It's astonishing that if I wanted to acquire the autographs of inductees Casey Stengel and Ernie Lombardi, in single signature form, it could cost at least $1,000. But to do so on a multiple-signature baseball may only cost $250. Equally astounding is the lack of interest in team baseballs from those teams which have had a monumental impact on our national pastime — "The Big Red Machine," "Murderers' Row" and "The Moustache Gang." Most expert collectors attribute this anomaly to the lack of a definitive guide on this area of collecting — a factor I hope will soon be dismisssed.

With this book collectors and dealers should be able to date, grade and identify, by players, an autographed team baseball. Add to this the factor of completeness, or the percentage of the team whose signatures appear on the baseball, and one should be able to properly access the item's value. To the novice collector, this task once seemed insurmountable. To the autograph expert it was tedious and time consuming. Now they both have a tool to facilitate these collecting needs, and with it perhaps a renewed interest in historic autographed team or group baseballs.

For those of you who have just ventured into this segment of the hobby, I hope you find this book useful and functional in building an outstanding collection.

Mark Allen Baker
P.O. Box 2492
Liverpool, N.Y. 13089

Foreword

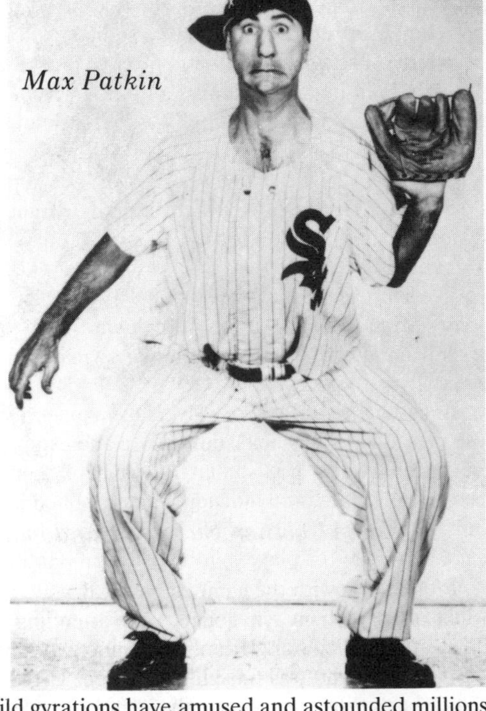
Max Patkin

Baseball has been an abundant provider, not only to the game's direct participants, but also to those who have resided on its periphery. This clandestine lot, who, without baseball, may have been fated an alternative and no doubt less enjoyable form of occupation, have made baseball their lives. Their abiding love for the game transcends their occupational purpose. Few, if any, will ever realize how they, as individuals, have touched the game and the souls of those who play it. They are the reseachers, trainers, equipment managers, announcers, entertainers and even collectors. Although the game may have gone on without them, it wouldn't have been the same. How can we say that the soul of the great game of baseball has not been touched by Pete Sheehy, Stephen Clark, Roger Angell, Bob Shepard or the gangly, six-foot-three "Clown Prince of Baseball," Max Patkin?

Although fans and collectors may wonder if the mystique and fun of the game is gone, there is Max Patkin. For nearly half a century Patkin has been the Charlie Chaplin of the baseball diamond. His accentuated facial features and wild gyrations have amused and astounded millions of baseball fans. He is the last link in a long line of ballpark entertainers, including the Brown's Arlie Latham and Germany Schaefer, Nick Altrock and Al Schacht.

Before bird-like baffoons traipsed through ballparks, there was Patkin. With no need for a costume, his physique precedes his personality. He often describes himself as "a lollipop stick with a nose." In fact, Bill Veeck once told Patkin that "it's as if someone put you together without the benefit of an instruction manual." Even when Patkin is in a conversation his image shows through - a myriad of motion often accompanying a priceless baseball tale.

Patkin's appearance in the 1988 movie "Bull Durham," with Kevin Costner and Tim Robbins, although legitimizing his skills as an actor, was the most natural part of the movie. His rigorous annual schedule of minor league ballparks visits makes him synonomous with the term minor league. Although the thickness of hotel walls seems to increase each passing year, the loneliness of the road doesn't stop baseball's last Clown Prince. It is as if Patkin, having taken the field with such immortals as Jackie Robinson, Joe DiMaggio and Jim Thorpe, is the last vigil to a game we once knew.

On behalf of the fans of the game,

Max:
Although you still believe there won't be a place for you in the Baseball Hall of Fame, the laughs and enjoyment you have given all of us has found a place in our hearts. And to tell you the truth, I'm not sure which I would rather have.

M.A.B.

Kevin Costner, Susan Sarandon and Max Patkin on the movie set.

I fell in love with the game of baseball while living in southwest Philadelphia. I was 8 years old when I went with my synagogue, while attending Hebrew school, to a Philadelphia Athletics game down at old Shibe Park. I can't remember who the opposing team was, but I do remember watching Ty Cobb, who was finishing his career at that time (1928), Eddie Collins and Tris Speaker. I remember sitting way, way up there in the bowels of the bleachers watching my first major league baseball game. That's when I fell in love with the sport. From that time on I began playing baseball in the sandlots and streets of Philadelphia. My parents, who were from Russia, didn't understand the game, but allowed me to play anyway. I just kept on playing and playing, right up until high school. My high school coach, seeing how hard I could throw, made me into a pitcher. From high school, I went to Brown Prep, hoping to land a scholarship with Temple or Villanova.

In 1941, however, along came the Chicago White Sox. I was signed by the team — and invited to spring training in Arkansas. Well, about five of their teams were training there at the time, I mean hundreds of players running around, only identified by the numbers on their back. I had a Waterloo contract at the time, which was a class D contract, and meant you were with some pretty fast company. What I remember most, however, was that they were releasing guys so fast your head would spin. A guy would pitch in just a few innings and if they didn't like what they saw they would give him a bus ticket home. You had to show something while you were out there on the field, and although I was a skinny six-foot-three-inch player, when I kicked my leg up during my pitching release, I could really let go of the ball; the team was impressed by the velocity of the pitches. However, the management, including Joe Brown Jr., thought I was kind of goofy-looking out there on the mound. Everyone was laughing at me when I was trying to be serious. I was a colorful character and I knew that this would help me a little bit, but I didn't think that it might ever hurt me. It's funny; in the big leagues they call this type of behavior "color," but in the minor leagues you're labeled a "clown."

In 1941, I was sold to the Wisconsin Rapids team, where I won 10 games and lost eight, with an earned run average of 3.94. An interesting event, however, came about at the end of the season.

Our team was already out of the pennant race and the Friday before Labor Day, I pitched a doubleheader against the Oshkosh team. I lost the first game, 1 to 0, and won the second, 1 to 0, but then on Monday (Labor Day), I pitched again, beating La Crosse, 3 to 2. Think of that — three games in three days, winning two out of the three, while striking out 27 men. Following this performance the media was calling me "The Iron Man of Baseball," after completing my 10th and final win of the season.

****

1941 Max Patkin

Wisconsin Rapids (Official Record)

G=32, CG =13, W=10, L=8, Pct.=.556, IP=178, AB=709, R=94,
H=170, ER=78, BB=95, HB=9, SO=134, WP=13, ERA=3.94

****

I wasn't moved up in 1942, because of my lack of pitching control, accompanied by an arm injury. Joining the Navy in 1942, I was quickly offered an opportunity to become a physical instructor. Following a few months in Maryland, I moved on to Great Lakes for five or six months, until the base commander said, "We can't have him as a physical instructor. Just look at him in that sailor suit." My 160 men used to laugh at me during drill sessions. So they stuck me on a "flat top" and shipped me overseas. On my way to the South Pacific I passed through Pearl Harbor. On the island they were looking for big league ballplayers to join some of the inner service teams. While waiting for my assignment, I told them I played professional baseball, and they took me off the ship and assigned me to one of the teams. This is how I met all the other ballplayers — Johnny Pesky, Schoolboy Rowe, Johnny Vander Meer, Mickey Vernon, Barney McCosky, and Pee Wee Reese, just to name a few.

Perhaps the most memorable inner service game came when I pitched against the Seventh Air Force. They were an unbelievable team, with Ferris Fain, Joe Gordon, Bob Dillinger, Mike McCormick and Joe DiMaggio. Imagine being a class D ballplayer pitching against all these great players. The first time I faced DiMaggio I struck him out. The next, well, look out; he clipped me for the longest home run drive I have ever seen. As DiMaggio trotted around the bases, I followed him with my hat sideways, matching the Yankee Clipper stride for stride. The whole team came out of the dugout to shake my hand, not DiMaggio's, who ended up sitting alone while his team walked me to the mound.

Following the war, I returned to Wilkes Barre of the class A Eastern League, primarily as a result of the strength of my showing in Hawaii. Following one game, the arm trouble returned, and I drew my release. My "strictly unintentional" reputation as a clown attracted many teams, who offered to hire me to do comedy bits during games. While performing in Harrisburg, Pa., in an exhibition game between the local class B team and the Cleveland Indians, I attracted the attention of Lou Boudreau. Boudreau was so enlightened by my performance that he called Bill Veeck, the owner of the Indians, who hired me sight unseen as a coach.

When Veeck called me into Cleveland, I thought he was just going to hire me to do the comedy routine for a day. I walked into his office and there were Lou Boudreau, Al Simmons and Tris Speaker, all chatting with Veeck. I guess the A's must have been in town and that's why Simmons was there. Veeck turns to me and says "I'm going to hire you as a coach. Lou wants you to coach first base for two innings of every ball game." I didn't realize it at the time, but Veeck was grooming me as a performer. Veeck even began booking me in various minor league ballparks during this time. Bill and I were always very close, right up until the day he died. We used to go out all the time socially because he loved having me around to make everyone laugh.

I always got along great with the ballplayers because they knew I was a baseball man. Lou Boudreau, Eddie Robinson, Bob Lemon, Red Embree, Mel Harder, all turned out to be great friends.

In 1946, Bob Feller began his barnstorming tours. Feller was so successful that he hired me in 1947. We toured the country for a month, playing some of the greatest teams imaginable, including the Kansas City Monarchs of the Negro Leagues. We never failed to fill the stands, especially when Feller and Satchel Paige would match up against each other. We had quite a ballclub, too, with players such as Ed Lopat, Jim Hegan, and Ralph Kiner.

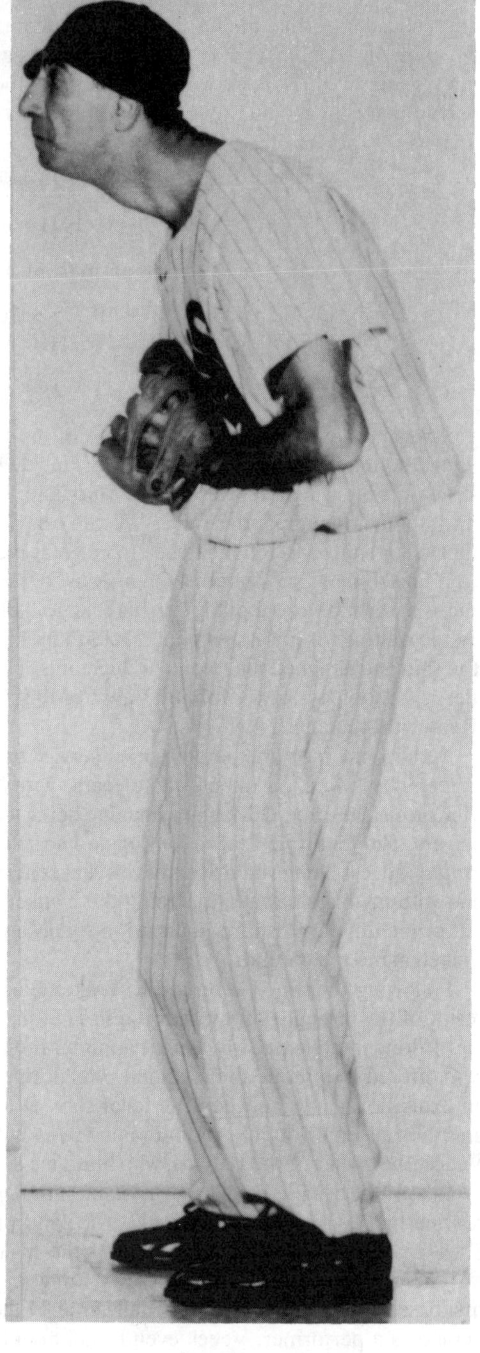

One of the funniest things I ever witnessed at a game took place during Feller's barnstorming tour. The club was in Tampico, Mexico, where a railroad track ran across the field. In the third inning, the train whistle blew, the gate opened in the left field wall, and a train began to move across the diamond. A ball was then hit to left field. Jeff Heath ran toward it, saw the ball was going to land on the flat cars, climbed up onto the car, caught the ball and then rode the train triumphantly out of the ballpark. It didn't mean anything to the fans that were there, because they were used to seeing the train exit from the wall, but to us it was unbelievably amusing.

A lot of funny things have happened to me. One in particular comes to mind. On a cool September evening in 1946, while I was in Washington D.C., I was coaching first base. During my usual routine, I kick some dirt, then fall completely backwards. Mickey Vernon, who wasn't playing that evening, came out of the dugout with a full bucket of flour mixed with water and popped it right on top of me. So here I am in front of only about 3,000 people, covered from head to toe with this thick white paste. Bill McGowan, who was a very strict umpire and not a big fan of my on-field antics, made me wipe up every bit of it. Needless to say, it took about 20 towels and 10 minutes of time to wipe the mess up. The toughest part was that the paste began to harden because it was so cold out.

But you talk about tough performances, and I think about the Sunday afternoon in Great Falls, Mont., when I played in front of only four people. Only four people, because that was the day in 1969 when man first set foot upon the moon. After the game, the general manager came up to me and said, "Max, I can't believe you worked that hard in front of only four people." To that I simply replied, "but they have never seen me before."

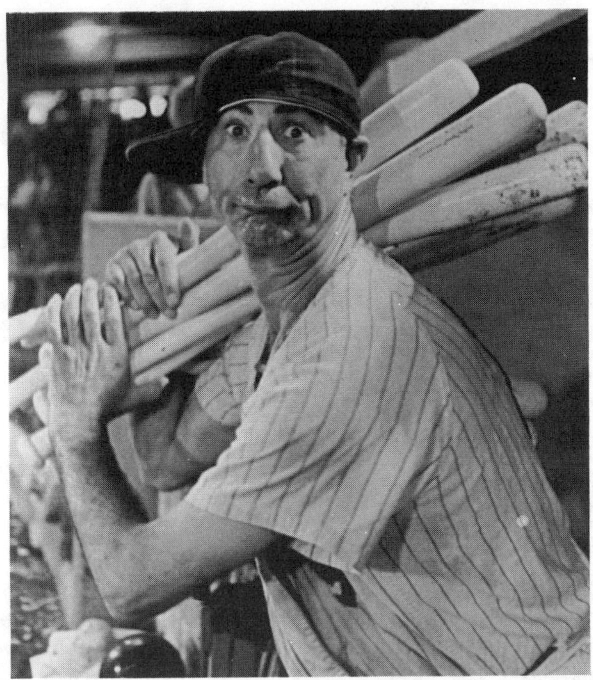

The baseball players of today are bigger and stronger; there is no getting away from that. However, what has really changed the game is the relief pitching. This is why Ted Williams will be the last .400 hitter. When you're paying a top relief pitcher a million dollars a year it's hard for a player to get that extra hit he needs to stay on target for such a milestone.

Baseball's mystique is in jeopardy today, primarily due to money — it's all money. The television media have become so powerful that they are beginning to control the game. As for the players today, they are not nearly as dedicated to the sport. In the old days they played for the love of the game. Today, it's the money. Many of the players even control the managers, telling them what to do. As for multi-year contracts, well, that's crazy, too. They defeat a player's incentive, unless, of course, it's time to renegotiate.

The most I ever charged for an autograph was one dollar, and that was only to recover some of my costs. Players charging twenty and thirty dollars for their signatures, not to mention varying the fee depending upon what they sign, is ridiculous.

In 1988, Ron Shelton, who was a writer and director, and, by the way, a former minor leaguer with the Baltimore Orioles, contacted me to request my appearance in his movie "Bull Durham." Ron claimed that during his years in the minor leagues I used to ask him to go out after the game, for no particular reason, other than to relax. Never forgetting how grateful he was for the invitation, he wrote me into the movie. What many don't realize is that in the original script I was suppossed to get killed. We even filmed the entire segment. My big scene was with Susan Sarandon, who plays Annie, who, by the way, is one of the nicest ladies you would ever want to meet. The scene before I got killed began in the nightclub, where I first introduced her to Crash Davis (Kevin Costner). She asks me why I go on all these years, and I tell her why. "I love the game of baseball, and I have no real close family, and when I die I am going to be cremated and leave my ashes to you, Annie. Please do me a favor and spread my ashes at home plate and save some of my ashes and put me in the rosin bag, because I always want to stay in the game." She reaches over and kisses me. Then I introduce her to Kevin. Costner is also a gentleman. In fact, when he first met me he said, "I've heard so much about you, and I'm so glad you're in this movie with us, because you're really baseball." In fact, I was the first person Costner ever directed. He helped on some of my scenes.

I'd love to get in the Hall of Fame someday. I know it's a dream, but once you get in there it gives you some status. It makes you feel that you will be remembered, and that perhaps there was joy in what you did. After 46 straight years of performing, I feel I have given something to the game of baseball — laughter, and that is the greatest thing in the world.

Max Patkin

Sept. 28, 1991

Collecting Autographed Baseballs

To comprehend why an individual collects autographed baseballs is to understand the game itself.

America's game

Baseball, America's game, has long been our release — a daily escape from an often monotonous lifestyle. It has been a mirror of our society, and thus a look into ourselves. For its fans, baseball has been a game that has gone beyond what has been asked of it. It has enriched our language and transcended our national boundaries. It has even broken the barriers of race, creed and class.

For those who follow it, baseball is more than just a game; it is a vestige to our youth, one of the few elements in our lives that somehow has remained consistent during our maturity. For how often are forgotten memories resurrected by the smell of fresh peanuts and popcorn at the ballpark?

As an anachronism, baseball has withstood the aftermath of time, survived only by the inconsistent definitions of an era's literary laureate. For it was Samuel L. Clemens (pseudonym, Mark Twain, and to my knowledge no relation to Roger) who declared:

> "Baseball is the very symbol, the outward and visible expression of the drive and push and rush and struggle of the raging, tearing, booming nineteenth century."

A century later, it was Roger Angell who stated:

> "Baseball is not life itself, although the resemblance keeps coming up. It's probably a good idea to keep the two sorted out, but old fans, if they're anything like me, can't help noticing how cunningly our game replicates the larger schedule, with its beguiling April optimism; the cheerful roughhouse of June; the grinding, serious, unending (surely) business of midsummer; the September settling of accounts, when hopes must be traded in for philosophies or brave smiles; and then the abrupt running down of autumn, when we wish for, almost demand, a prolonged and glittering final adventure just before the curtain."

Regardless of setting, if America survives anywhere as more than a memory, it is in the game of baseball. From Toronto's majestic SkyDome to the innocence of Cooperstown's Doubleday Field, the game is relentless in its mystique.

Although resistant to innovation, the game has faced changes, and when it has, it has done so noblely and without disregard to its origin. Like a respectful grandchild to its elders, baseball has learned to respect adversity, not dwell upon it. When compared to institutions of equal antiquity, baseball has transformed far less, its concept holding faithful to the game's creators.

"A simple piece of white ash from the timbers of upstate New York, trying to send two pieces of cowhide, with 108 stiches, 284 feet over an eight-foot wall."

— from the Sports Collectors Digest Baseball Autograph Handbook, second edition

Baseball signed by Bobby Thomson and Ralph Branca.

Most of us know where we were when President John F. Kennedy was assassinated, or when man first set foot on the moon. To understand a baseball fan is to accept that equal relevance is placed on the memories of "The Shot Heard 'Round the World" by Bobby Thomson, or a certain World Series home run by Kirk Gibson or Bill Mazeroski. These recollections have now become a part of our life's milestones. Baseball, as we often forget or simply don't want to be reminded of, was here first — We were born into it, grew up with it, and will grow old by it.

Collecting

Autographed baseball collectors, a subset of all baseball memorabilia enthusiasts, are identified primarily by the medium they choose to have signed. There seems to be a fascination about collecting autographed baseballs, an innate attraction that entices the collector and the signer. To the collector, it is playful, clean, compact, aesthetically appealing, and thus deserving of prominent display. To the signer, it is often an attribute of his profession, symbolic in its association with the game and his participation in it. To most, however, a baseball's innocence and simplicity is a testament to our youth. Perhaps this is why those individuals unaffiliated with the game derive so much pleasure in signing one.

Autographed baseball collections are often quite diverse, due to the distinct social, financial and occupational backgrounds of collectors. This vast spectrum of collecting has lent itself to specialization, not only because of economics, but also due to the limited availability of certain types of material. Specialization provides a focus for collectors, along with an ability to assess the economics, completeness and viability of a task.

****

Example:

Task:

A collector who wishes to obtain a baseball, signed by each player who has hit 500 or more home runs in the major leagues, realizes the following:

1. Number of signatures required for completion: 14
2. Number of living players to accomplish this task to date: 11 (Hank Aaron, Willie Mays, Frank Robinson, Harmon Killebrew, Reggie Jackson, Mike Schmidt, Mickey Mantle, Willie McCovey, Ted Williams, Ernie Banks, Eddie Mathews)
3. Number of deceased players who have accomplished task: 3 (Babe Ruth, Jimmie Foxx, Mel Ott)

Viability:

Unlikely; the chances of a collector purchasing the baseball necessary to begin the task, with only just the signatures of the three deceased players on it, is doubtful. A viable alternative task would be to obtain only the signatures of the living players who have accomplished this recognized milestone.

Estimated Value: $300 to $400

This is Reggie Jackson's signature.

Collector Classifications

Frequently, collectors will concentrate on a specific team, event, group or individual. There are many reasons for specializing in one of these four classifications of autographed baseballs. Most, however, center around a collector's affiliation with a particular player, group of players or team. The motivating factor behind the desire is often the sentimental satisfaction derived from owning these relics. In recent years, an increasing incentive has been the economic value associated with the acquisition of these souvenirs, a factor driven by the media, the influx of new collectors into the hobby, and the game itself. The collector, as an investor, is a topic unto itself, and ironically, written between the lines of these pages.

Collecting autographed baseballs can be segmented into four classifications:

1. Single-signature or signed baseballs (by those affiliated with the game)

A ball, most often an "Official League Baseball," signed by a particular player or individual. Most collectors desire the signature to be placed on the "sweet spot," centered at the shortest distance between the two seams of the baseball. On an "Official League Baseball" there is only one recognized sweet spot; the only other desired spot is occupied by a printed title (Official Ball, American or National League, etc....) and the signature of a baseball executive (league president, commissioner, etc....).

Examples: Baseball players, managers, executives, umpires, sportswriters, broadcasters, etc....

Ken Griffey and his son, Ken Jr., signed this ball.

2. Team- or group-signed baseballs

A ball, most often an "Official League Baseball," signed by a group of players affiliated with a particular team, event, or achievement. On a team baseball the sweet spot is often referred to as the "manager's spot," a space reserved for the manager's signature out of respect or protocol. If a manager is unrelated to the particular event or achievement, the signatures of the players of greatest notoriety are desired on the sweet spot.

Many teams may use the services of 50 or more players during a season, making the acquisition of a single baseball with every member's signature unlikely. Most team baseballs will reflect the current roster at the time of the signing. A team baseball will typically include an average of 26 signatures. The definition of a "team baseball" implies the inclusion of the entire starting lineup (8 or 9), star pitchers, and other "key" players or individuals associated with the team during the particular season.

Group-signed baseballs often center around events, such as an "Old-Timers' Day," or ceremonies honoring a particular individual, team or event. The combination of signatures, and their relationship to the particular event, are of paramount importance to the collector.

Examples: National or American League teams, "Old-Timers' Day" or "reunion" baseballs, a group of signatures (often acquired during a ceremony) that relate to a particular individual or event.

Participants in a 1933 world baseball tour signed this ball.

3. Commemorative, signed baseballs

A ball, most often an "Official League Baseball," signed by an individual or group of players affiliated with a particular achievement or milestone. Commemorative baseballs can be "limited editions," or those that have an acknowledged production or manufacturing amount. Commemorative, signed baseballs often acknowledge a particular milestone, such as a single baseball signed by all the living players to achieve 3,000 hits in the major leagues. Commemorative, signed baseballs are often unique, due to the limited production of the medium itself and the scarcity of the particular signatures in a certain form.

Examples: An "Official League All-Star Baseball" signed by a National League or American League team, the "3,000 Hit Club," the "500 Home Run Hitters," "Cy Young Award Winners," a baseball used in a game, signed and dated by the winning pitcher.

California Angels' Jim Abbott signed after his first major league victory.

This ball commemorates Sandy Koufax's June 4, 1964, no-hitter against Philadelphia.

This baseball, signed by tycoon Donald Trump, is an example of a ball autographed by someone unaffiliated with the game. Below, Richard Nixon throws out the first ball at a New York Yankees game. Most collectors prefer to have celebrities' individual signatures on the ball's sweet spot.

4. Single-signature or group-signed baseballs (by those unaffiliated with the game)

A ball, most often an "Official League Baseball," signed by a particular individual, or group, unaffiliated with the game. Most collectors prefer an individual signature to be placed on the sweet spot, or centered at the shortest distance between the two seams of the baseball, on the unprinted side. Examples that have entered the hobby in this form include single-signature baseballs of celebrities, presidents of the United States and entertainers. It is the only classification of autographed baseballs where the subject is secondary to the medium, and as such has a limited appeal.

Examples: presidents of the United States, rock 'n' roll bands, assorted politicians and entertainers.

This baseball, signed by the World Champion 1974 Oakland A's, is an example of an autographed team ball.

As a collector of autographed baseballs, you will undoubtedly fall into one or more of the classifications previously defined. As such, the primary variable that separates you from other collectors is the determination you exude in collecting. The first step toward being a better collector is education, a goal exemplified by the purchase of this book. In addition to the pursuit of hobby-related research materials, collectors are encouraged to exchange information with each other. As collectors, however, you should be realistic with your goals, personally and financially, never allowing either to strip the enjoyment you derive from the hobby.

Negro League autographed team baseballs, such as this one signed by the 1924 Negro World Champion Kansas City Monarchs, are very rare.

The History of Baseballs

From left: some minor leagues used seamless balls in the early 1890s; a 1876 "double eight" cover similar to that used today; a 1890 ball with different stitching. About six balls were used per game in the late 1800s.

Although the game has changed significantly since its inception, the ball has not. A century and a quarter later it is nine percent lighter, five percent smaller, cork centered instead of India-rubber centered, and has tighter stitching. More resilient than its predecessors, the ball also travels farther, primarily because the modern baseball undergoes far less wear and tear. Prior to 1920, baseballs were used until they were irretrievable; it was unheard of and considered wasteful if a home team supplied two dozen balls per game.

To enhance offensive play (worn balls were not as lively), accompanied by a concern for player safety (players couldn't see a discolored ball), the league stipulated the use of only clean and new baseballs in 1920.

In 1910, the league authorized the use of a cushioned cork center, instead of the rubber-centered ball, in part due to the league's depressed batting averages. The more lively cork-centered ball was introduced in time for the 1910 World Series. Additional changes in the makeup of the ball included variations in yarn styles and winding, raised and depressed stitching, and a cover switch from horsehide to cowhide (1974). The seemingly insignificant later changes were attributable to manufacturing technology, not to rules variations.

Several manufacturers made baseballs during the late 1800s, but the dominant firm was the A.J. Reach Co. of Philadelphia. The company founder, Al Reach, was a second baseman during the 1870s for the Athletics. Advanced machinery for manufacturing baseballs allowed Reach to make claims of superior durability. In the late 1800s, four to six balls was the average number used during a professional game. Generally, balls were removed from play only if they were severely damaged. Many of the damaged baseballs were reconditioned and sent to amateur leagues. Today, the average game life of a baseball is about five minutes; between 30 to 50 are used per game.

The growth of the game spurred equipment manufacture, and Reach's baseball production grew from 24 a day during the 1870s, to three to four million balls annually by 1900. Reach's partner, Benjamin F. Shibe, was responsible for much of the corporation's success; he invented the sophisticated machinery used to dominate baseball production for professional use. In 1909 Shibe also invented the cork-centered baseball. When this baseball was adopted by the American League, A.G. Spalding Brothers, Reach's major competitor, countered with a version for the National League.

The Official American League baseball, produced by the A.J. Reach Co., was patented April 6, 1909. The Official National League ball, produced by A.G. Spalding & Brothers, was patented Aug. 31, 1909. Both official baseballs were double stitched — the Spalding ball in red and black until 1933, and the A.J. Reach ball in red and blue until 1934. After the 1933 and 1934 seasons the stitching colors changed to the present color of red.

Examples of baseballs throughout history include a 1914 Official Federal League baseball; an experimental yellow baseball from a 1938 Brooklyn Dodgers' game; a Wilson-made Negro American League baseball.

Official league baseball manufacturers

American Association: Mahn (1882), Reach (1833 to 1891)
American League: Reach (1901 to 1974), Spalding (1975 to 1976), Rawlings (1977 to present)
Federal League: Victor
National League: Spalding (1876 to 1977), Rawlings (1978 to present)

During the turn of the century, professional baseballs were composed of a round rubber ball, one inch in diameter, layered with a half inch of wound woolen yarn, covered by a thin coating of glue. Two more layers of half-inch wollen yarn were then added, coated again by cement and covered by horsehide, stitched by hand with either red or black cotton thread.

The alum-tanned horsehide, made as white and as soft as possible, provided the outer coating of the baseball. One stretched horsehide during the early years was good for 18 to 20 covers. Perfectly-formed covers were then adhered manually by men astride a bench that incorporated a clamping device to tightly grasp the ball. Upon the cover's completion, an additional machine process-rolled the ball, guaranteeing roundness and smoothness. Once determined smooth, the ball was stamped with the official league designation and trademark, wrapped in tinfoil and tissue paper, and sealed in a box. A dozen Reach Official American League baseballs cost a club $15 in 1910.

"B.B. Johnson," referring to league President Ban Johnson, signed the ball above, a 1927 Official American League ball. At right is an Official National League ball with league President John A. Heydler's signature.

By 1973, the bulk of professional baseballs were made in Haiti, due to growing production costs. The manufacture shifted again in the 1990s, this time to Costa Rica. In 1972, Spalding's manufacturing cost had risen to $23 a dozen, or a dollar more than what the professional teams were paying for them. In 1971, major league baseball production was estimated at about 350,000 units annually, or an average of about 1,200 dozen per team. Due to the cost of importing horsehide, the cover material was substituted with cowhide in 1974.

Spalding eventually acquired Reach, although the name Reach remained on the American League baseball for years after. In 1970, Spalding became a subsidiary of the Toledo-based Questor Corp. Spalding, trying to ward off competition, acquired Rawlings, but lost an antitrust suit, forcing the company to sell the newly-acquired firm.

Rawlings, now a division of Figgie International Inc., is the exclusive manufacturer of major league baseballs under an agreement that lasts until 1996. Few realize that Rawlings made baseballs under the Spalding trademark from 1968 to 1974.

Rawlings produces baseballs meeting very demanding specifications, winding 300 yards of wool yarn and poly-cotton thread around the "pill," or cushioned cork center. Precise measurements of weight and circumference are attained prior to the application of the two pieces of cowhide manually sewn together with 106 stitches.

Following a final inspection, the balls are stamped with the manufacturer's name, registered trademark, patented type "cushioned cork center," patent number "17200" and the signature of the league president.

The most prominent identifier used to determine the age of modern baseballs is the signature of the league president stamped on one of the two sweet spots (post mid-1930s), or on the side (post 1920s). The first signature of a National League president to appear on a baseball was John A. Heydler's. Heydler's signature appeared primarily on the side of the baseball until the mid-1930s, when it was moved to the sweet spot. The first signature of an American League president to appear on a baseball was Ban B. Johnson's (early 1920s), in the form of "B.B. Johnson," and stamped on the side. The signature of Johnson's successor in 1927, Ernest S. Barnard, also appeared on the side. The first signature of an American League president to appear on the ball's sweet spot was William Harridge's (mid-1930s).

These official balls for the American and National leagues have various signatures for the different league presidents throughout history.

League presidents' signatures on Official League Baseballs

National

John A. Heydler:	Dec. 10, 1918	to	Dec. 11, 1934 *
Ford C. Frick:	Dec. 11, 1934	to	Oct. 8, 1951
Warren C. Giles:	Oct. 8, 1951	to	Dec. 31, 1969
Charles S. Feeney:	Jan. 1, 1970	to	Dec. 11, 1986
A. Bartlett Giamatti:	Dec. 12, 1986	to	Mar. 31, 1989
William D. White:	April 1, 1989	to	present

American

Byron B. Johnson:	April 24, 1901	to	Oct. 17, 1927 **
Ernest S. Barnard:	Oct. 31, 1927	to	May 27, 1931 **
William Harridge:	May 27, 1931	to	Jan. 31, 1959 *
Joseph E. Cronin:	Feb. 1, 1959	to	Dec. 31, 1973
Leland S. MacPhail Jr.:	Jan. 19, 1974	to	Dec. 31, 1983
Robert W. Brown:	Jan. 19, 1984	to	present

Notes:

** = Signature appears only on the side of an Official League Baseball.

* = Signature appears on the sweet spot and side of an Official League Baseball.

Rawlings made the 1989 World Series balls, while Wilson made a ball to commemorate competition between the United States and Russia. The ball at right was used in the 1984 Summer Olympics in Los Angeles.

Collectors can determine from the list of league presidents which deceased players could have signed a particular official baseball. Upon the departure of any league president, it is usually months before any official league baseballs appear with the successor's name.

Rawlings has also produced commemorative baseballs for many major events, including the Olympics, World Series, All-Star games, and even a salute to Comiskey Park. Since 1976, the company has produced an exclusive baseball for use in the World Series, each including a Major League Baseball World Series logo, with the signature of the commissioner replacing the league president's. Since 1979, the company has also released a special baseball for use in the All-Star game. It includes the official logo of the host city and the commissioner's signature. During the 1991 season, the Chicago White Sox used a special commemorative baseball for all the team's home games. This Official American League baseball only differs by the addition of a Comiskey Park logo, placed beneath the seam, directly underneath the signature of League President Bobby Brown. This is the first time in history, other than the World Series or All-Star games, that a commemorative ball was used in major league games.

3 The History of Writing Materials

Above are a Bic pen and a Sharpie, both used for autographs.

The knowledge of writing instruments and materials can not only enhance an autographed baseball collector's chance of obtaining a genuine signature, but can also provide him with additional information useful in dating and preserving a ball. As have most inventions, writing instruments have developed in many stages. Studying each evolutionary stage will eventually save collectors authentication time, and possible preservation costs. Although the Bible refers to the existence of ink in the Old Testament, the reference point for the autographed baseball collector begins with the use of iron gall inks, used into the 20th century.

Writing instruments

Historically, writing instruments are commonly divided into four categories: quills, durable pens, reservoir pens and pencils. Since the problems with quills and their eventual solutions led to the development of metal pens by the 19th century, quills are impertinent to the topic of autographed baseballs. Pencil, although a popular writing device since its "lead strip" discovery in 1564, was not an acceptable form for use on the material of a baseball. Limited adherence qualities and erasability limited pencil use for informal, non-permanent applications. Moreover, its use for even correspondence was precluded by the rules of etiquette. Although ink was a bit troublesome during its evolution, it was the favored and accepted medium.

The writing instruments of greatest interest to the autographed baseball collectors are durable and reservoir pens. The "steel pen," which was a durable pen, was fully accepted as a writing instrument by 1845, when the first acknowledged organized club, the New York Knickerbockers, was formed by one of its members, Alexander J. Cartwright.

DURABLE PENS

Steel, gold and glass pens are considered durable pens. The use of these pens began in the late 1700s, dominated the 1800s, and later gave way to the more practical reservoir pens. The durability of metal and glass logically replaced the quill, but still required an independent ink reservoir.

Durable steel tip pens were used for these presidential signatures.

Steel pen

Only isolated references to metallic pens were made before the end of the 18th century. The steel pen, with its conflicting date of origin, was successfully reintroduced in England in 1780. It was best described as a sheet of steel rolled in the form of a cylinder, with one end cut and trimmed to a point (similar to the quill). The seam, where both edges met, formed the slit of the pen. The first patent in England for metal pens was awarded in 1808 to Bryan Donkin. Machine-made pens were introduced in about 1822. A United States patent for a "metallic writing pen" was issued to Peregrine Williamson in 1809. Although the steel pen was commonplace by the mid 1840s, it wasn't until 1858, the year after Henry Chadwick invented the box score, that the first steel pen company was established in the United States by Richard Esterbrook Jr., a former pen salesman.

A steel pen can be readily discerned by examining strokes under magnification. In contrast to its predecessor, the quill, a steel pen is distinguished by the presence of "nib tracks," which are a result of the pen's point (nib), a metal slit, separating under pressure on the downstroke and digging into the material it is in contact with. Nib choices naturally and predictably effect the line quality in writing. Special types of steel pens produced distinctive line quality, due to the flow of ink into the nib. For example: the "stub pen" produced a slightly outlined, yet uniform, stroke that became lighter as the ink neared its end inside the nib. The stub pen, although of limited use in the 1870s, grew in popularity and represented about one third of the total pen consumption entering the 1930s.

Gold pen

The "gold pen," which was a method of giving quills a metalic cast by dipping them into a solution of nitromuriate of gold, was patented in 1818 by Charles Watt. It was a natural evolution to the guilding of quills to increase durability. Although the gold was useful in resisting the corrosive tendencies of acidic ink, the points still lacked sufficient hardness and quickly broke.

Glass pen

Glass was one of many materials experimented with in the making of pens, found as early as 1850. A United States patent of 1890 describes it as "a pen formed of a piece of round glass drawn out to a point and having grooves running spirally down the sloping sides and meeting at the point." Many early glass pens were sold as "marking pens," for writing on fabric, and used indelible inks. Its ink permanence was a favorable factor for an application, such as autographing a baseball, but the pen was never very plentiful and has been used in only isolated instances.

The demise of the durable pen was ironically attributed to its lack of extended durability. The problem was the frequent need to replenish the pen's ink source, requiring repeated dipping into the inkwell.

RESERVOIR PENS

Dip pen writing, produced by durable pens, identifies itself with words graduated in intensity, from dark to light, to dark again. This "ink failure," a key identification characteristic, acted as a stimulus for reservoir pen inventors.

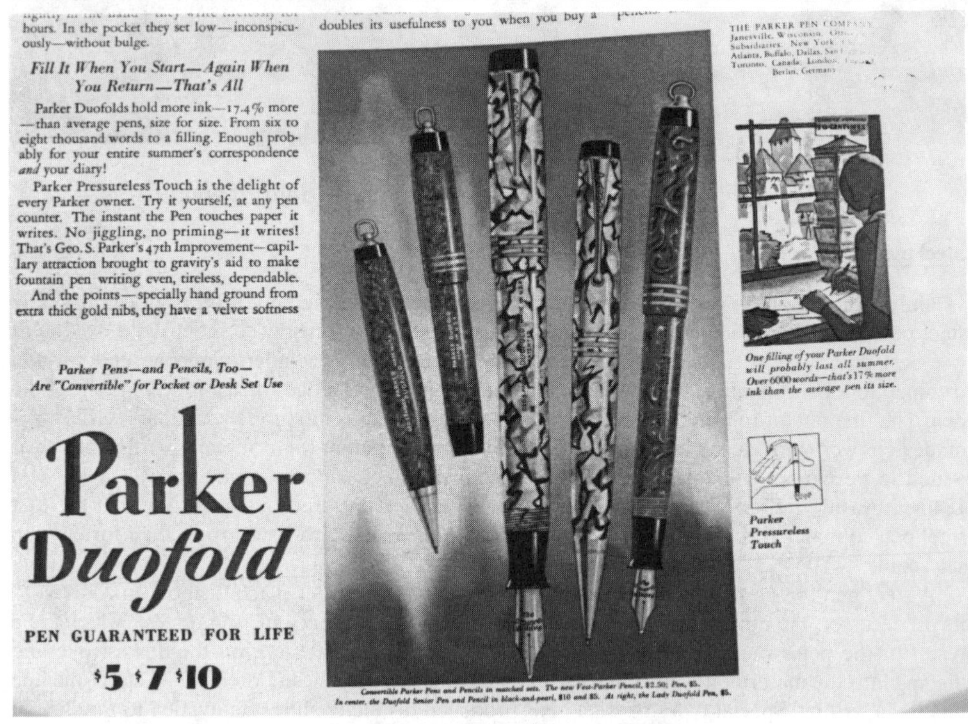

This is a 1930s ad for Parker Duofold fountain pens.

Fountain pen

Attempts to solve "ink failure" included a "solid ink" fountain pen, circa 1870s, that held a stick of concentrated ink which was dipped into water for writing. Fountain pen patents were profuse, being regularly advertised in periodicals by the 1870s. During this time "stylographic" pens also became popular. These pens had a plunger that was pushed back while writing, allowing ink to flow out. Stylographic pen writing is characterized by its thin strokes of uniform diameter. Interchangeable pen points allowed the user to vary the diameter of its strokes.

In 1864, Lewis E. Waterman marketed the first truly successful fountain pen. George S. Parker, seeing Waterman selling millions of pens annually, was enticed to establish his own company in 1888. With several patents improving ink feed design, Parker became the leading American fountain pen manufacturer by the end of the 1930s.

Ray Schalk's autograph to "Warren" is an example of a ballpoint pen signature on a flat item. Walter Johnson's signature at left was done by a steel tip pen.

Ballpoint pen

The highly successful fountain pen, with its numerous variations in style, was eventually displaced in the late 1940s by the ballpoint pen. Although ballpoint pen patents can be traced as far back as 1888, it wasn't until 1935 that two Czechoslovakians, Frank Klimes and Paul Eisner, began producing a modern-style ballpoint. Two Hungarian brothers, Ladislao and George Biro, also developed a rotatable ball pen in 1938. The Eberhard Faber Co. eventually obtained rights to it, and when the United States Army expressed interest in purchasing large quantities of the pen, Scheaffer outbid its competitors to share the American rights with Faber. The Biro pen became so popular that one American businessman marketed and sold almost 25,000 pens through Gimbel's department store in New York.

Early ballpoint writing is easily recognizable by its blotting and skipping. These characteristics were attributed to the ink, which was a dye solution in a base of oil, that, although smooth flowing, dried slowly. Additionally worth noting to autographed baseball collectors is the fading of the ink when exposed to light. This characteristic is most noticeable with those pens produced before 1954.

Most of the deficiencies in the ballpoint pen design were remedied by Parker's introduction of the "Jotter" in 1954. The Jotter, made entirely of stainless steel, wrote five times as long as its competitors. The pen also offered a variety of point sizes.

Parker also introduced the "Liquid Lead Pencil" in 1955. This pen contained a liquid graphite solution that was erasable. Failing to gain acceptance, this pen was phased out of production during the 1960s. Ironically, the Paper Mate division of the Gillette Co. introduced the "Eraser Mate" pen in April 1979, capturing what was thought to be a non-existent portion of the market.

Porous tip pens

The ballpoint pen began to face competition in the early 1940s, when a "pourous paint" pen, composed of fibrous materials acting like a nib and storing ink in a spongy material, began to be marketed. By the early 1950s these pens became known as "markers" and included airtight leakproof stems that fed ink into a felt wedge-shaped wick. After some Japanese enhancements, the pen was reintroduced and popularized around 1964. Additional varieties of colored inks were subsequently introduced, but many of the inks were not permanent and became badly faded after a few days of exposure to sunlight.

Sanford's "Sharpie," a highly water-resistant, permanent, large fiber tip marker that writes on virtually every surface, appeared in the mid-1970s. Although the marker was available in 1963 (black) and in 1964 (blue), it did not gain popularity until nearly a decade later. This writing device has become an ad hoc hobby standard due to its surface adherence and ease of use. But its deterioration qualities are still being examined. Tests conducted on an "Official League" baseball have shown major surface bleeding twice the thickness of the signature in less than five years. Additionally, expect minor discoloration and bleeding in less than six months, even if the baseball is stored in total darkness. Collectors are urged to avoid this pen for use on autographed baseballs, unless they are willing to accept the deterioration characteristics. Additionally, collectors tend to shy away from pens that produce large strokes because they impair character definition.

Several types of pens and ink were introduced in the 1980s, from gold and silver markers, to metallic inks. The market has been saturated with new writing instruments, most which have been used on the surface of a baseball. For many of these materials it is far too early to determine their deterioration characteristics. For collectors who are serious about preservation and safety, "material data sheets," or MSDSs, are available from every manufacturer. They clearly describe an ink's ingredients. All parents are urged to familiarize themselves with the safety hazzards of any ink that may come into contact with a child.

Pen and ink identification

Pen and ink are just a few of the elements that a collector has at his disposal to aid in the identification of an autographed baseball. Although more complex than dating a ball by its printed markings or by the player's name scrolled upon it, pen and ink identification can provide collectors with additional information useful in dating and authentication.

Since writing instruments have evolved over time, pen identification is an obvious adjunct to dating. From the steel and fountain pens, to the ballpoint and felt tip pens, each employs a distinctive stylographic variety.

Ink also has value in determining the age of writing. From iron gall ink varieties to nigrosine inks, each has specific properties that are quickly identified by a sample's reaction to chemical reagents. Alternative and more sophisticated forms of dating are available, but have limited application to autographed baseballs, since identification and authentication can be successfully completed by inexpensive and less complex methods.

To identify the writing device used on an autographed baseball, a collector should acquire a high-powered magnifying glass and, in conjunction with a good light source, carefully review the discernible signatures. Particular attention should be paid to beginning and ending strokes where immediate association with a writing instrument is most easily accomplished. This "Pen Identification Chart" should expedite your task.

These two markers are generally used for bats and pictures.

PEN IDENTIFICATION CHART

Origin Date	Writing device	Characteristics/Comments
Early 1950s	Porous tip pens	Porous material tips, in a variety of shapes and sizes. Relatively uniform line width, lack "nib tracks" or roller marks. Ending strokes often appear dry. "Sharpie" popular mid-1970s, although available in late 1960s. Some permanent markers will evidence bleeding. Early felt-tip markers badly fade.
Mid-1940s	Ballpoint pen	Distinctive line appearance due to ink and ball combination. Produces line of even width. Early samples will exhibit blotting, skipping and fading. Recent pen varieties produce more free-flowing ink.
1884 *	Fountain pen	Continuous ink flow. Contrast between upstrokes and heavier downstrokes.
1870s	Stylographic pen	Continuous ink flow. Uniform width on upstrokes and downstrokes.
1858**	Steel pen	Nib tracks evident, indentation may be possible. Dip pen writing characteristics. Stub pen; more shaded strokes, distinguishable on tops of rounded letters. Dip pen writing characteristics. Double line pen; dual line effect. Dip pen writing characteristics.

Notes:

** = Esterbrook, U.S. manufactured.
* = Waterman manufactured.

Collection Organization, Display and Preservation

This custom-built cabinet holds 25 autographed team baseballs.

Organization, storage and display

Collectors take tremendous pride in displaying their collections, large or small, flat or round. It is in the collector's best interest to properly display, store and organize his collectibles; a haphazard approach to any of these factors could have a devastating impact on an item. For example, an autographed baseball left in direct sunlight, unprotected from ultraviolet radiation, for an extended period of time, will soon become discolored. Its signatures will show advanced signs of fading and deterioration.

Any item not being displayed should be properly stored. Proper storage is a necessary form of preservation, and a cost-effective investment. Collectors are encouraged to pursue preservation with the same vigilance in which they pursue acquisition.

As a collection grows, organization increases in importance. Although there is no set format

Ball holders can be round or square.

for filing systems, collectors should choose one that is flexible to their needs, yet specific in terms of acquisition information. There is nothing more frustrating to a collector than not being able to identify the background of an acquisition, particularly if the authenticity is questioned. Collectors are urged to detail the following information: name or description of the item, acquisition date, important or unique information or comments about the piece (team baseballs should list players), condition, purchase price, seller information (name, address, phone) and return policy.

For example:

Acquisition: 1965 New York Yankees team ball; acquisition date: 1/23/85

Purchase Price: $450; Condition: Excellent; Official League Baseball

Comments:
19 signatures, slight smudge in Tony Kubek's signature. Players include Joe Pepitone, Bobby Richardson, Tony Kubek, Clete Boyer, Hector Lopez, Tom Tresh, Mickey Mantle, Elston Howard, Phil Linz, Ray Barker, Roger Repoz, Horace Clarke, Roger Maris, Mel Stottlemyre, Whitey Ford, Al Downing, Pedro Ramos, Jim Bouton and Johnny Keane.

Seller: Baker Enterprises, P.O. Box 2492, Liverpool, N.Y. 13089 (90-day return policy).

Although it may seem tedious to list each signature on a baseball, it can be particularly useful for research purposes. Additionally, if a collector acquired a particular autograph on a ball during a baseball card star show, a clipping of an advertisement promoting the event may also be worth saving for reference. Collectors may find it useful to purchase a small, lockable filing cabinet to store reference materials, catalogs, related articles or even their collections.

Many collectors choose to store valuable portions of their collections in safe-deposit boxes at their local banks. Autographed baseballs are not as conveniently stored as other flat collectibles, so larger, more expensive safe-deposit boxes will probably be required. Fireproof cabinets and safes are also cost-effective alternatives for storage. For very large collections that collectors choose to keep at their fingertips, I recommend a quality, infrared home security system. Another habit that is particularly helpful, and a requirement of most insurance policies, is photographing your collection. Photographs can bypass unneeded handling of a collectible and provide an instant compact reference of an item.

Most collectors store autographed baseballs in round or square ball holders, which cost collectors between $1 and $1.25 each, if purchased by the case. One manufacturer offers a square holder that contains ultraviolet light screening materials. Although it's a bit expensive, ($12 each, if purchased by the dozen) it could be cost-effective. Ultraviolet radiation can have devastating deterioration effects on a baseball; its prevention should therefore be of paramount importance to collectors. Most of these storage devices are available at local hobby stores, or via mail order. Little is known about the long-term preservation capabilities of the inexpensive holders. Some collectors choose the square holders because of their stacking capability. Others favor the round holders because the baseball has restricted movement. Collectors should be wary of all types of storage materials, unless a clear description of the item's material content and preservation capabilities are available. I favor any storage device that has minimal contact with the autographed baseball and provides the greatest protection from all environmental deterioration factors. If an autographed baseball is openly displayed and in contact with sunlight, a storage device that obviates ultraviolet radiation is a must.

Since the deterioration characteristics of many new inks are unknown, it is suggested that collection pieces should never touch other baseballs while being stored or displayed. Routine inspections of items are advised to avoid any potential preservation problems. Collectors who ignore preservation must face the associated risks.

Although it is common for museums and libraries to mark items with acquisition numbers, this is not a procedure recommended for the average collector. The provenance of an item is important, but proper cataloging should be sufficient for the average collector. Acquisition numbers should be limited to institutions, with very large collections, where permanent collections and donations necessitate such. Collectors should not alter a piece in any way. Retracing signatures, adding signatures, or attempts to alter a baseball's surface can have devastating effects on preservation, and value.

Display

Part of a collector's gratification in collecting autographed baseballs is the display, as best exemplified by the National Baseball Hall of Fame in Cooperstown, N.Y. Each exhibit there attempts to educate the collector by bringing him back in time. Few people realize the amount of time and associated expenses spent in creating such spectacular exhibits.

If a trip to Cooperstown is impractical, then a visit to a local library or museum might provide you with enough inspiration to properly display your collection. Also, many local baseball card and memorabilia shops, and even sports restaurants or bars, have learned the value of proper and enticing displays.

When creating a display, put yourself in the viewer's shoes. Clearly identify each item and its significance. It's frustrating for a viewer to see an item, but not understand the importance of the display. Unless a common theme exists between the items being displayed, or there is a chronological order exemplified, general collections or unrelated collectibles can be very confusing to the viewer.

How a collection of autographed baseballs is displayed is very important. Most display cases vary in size, style, and accessibility. Older collectors often modified existing display materials to suit the peculiar display needs of autographed baseballs. In recent years, manufacturers, especially those of plastic materials, have acknowledged the market by offering a variety of wall-mounted display cases. These cases, in several sizes, are becoming more accessible to collectors through advertisements in hobby periodicals, such as Sports Collectors Digest. Autographed team or group baseballs are commonly displayed with the most prominent signatures emphasized, a task not required with a single-signed baseball. Multi-signature baseballs typically have four autographed surfaces, and thus are best displayed in cases that allow for viewing from different directions.

Properly lighting a display can be difficult. Most collectors know the potential hazzards of direct sunlight, or constant artificial lighting. Florescent lighting is common, but, if not properly filtered of harmful rays, may damage a piece over time. If built-in display lighting is an option, collectors should realize the heat generated by the light will affect the humidity in the case and

The Baseball Hall of Fame features autographed World Series balls.

possibly the items inside. External, indirect lighting, properly filtered, and not focused right on the display, is most common.

Preservation

Preservation most often implies paper-based collectibles, primarily because of age. But the preservation of certain materials relating to the game is still being understood. Autographed baseballs do deteriorate, by many of the same factors which affect paper. Typical causes of autographed baseball deterioration include the collector, environmental elements, such as light, temperature, and humidity, and the baseball's own material characteristics. To avoid these causes of deterioration, a chart of hints and suggestions has been provided.

****

Autographed Baseball Preservation
Hints & Suggestions

The Collector

* Frequently inspect your collection for signs of deterioration.
* If an autographed baseball shows excessive signs of deterioration, seek the assistance of a professional conservator.
* Avoid excessive handling.
* Display and storage cabinets should be designed and purchased to accommodate your specific size, weight and ventilation needs.
* Never retrace over a faded signature or add any markings.

Environmental elements

* Never display an item in direct sunlight.

This display is featured in Bleachers, a sports bar in Liverpool, N.Y.

* Properly screen all light sources from ultraviolet radiation found in sunlight and florescent light.
* Incandescent lighting poses no threat in the generation of ultraviolet radiation, but it can generate excessive heat. Suggested lighting is an incandescent 100-watt bulb, indirectly focused from a distance no closer than three feet.
* Recommended storage and display conditions are 65 to 70 degrees, with a relative humidity of about 50 percent.
* Keep your collection area dry and properly ventilated.
* Avoid smoking, eating or drinking near valuable autographed baseballs.
* Use only acid-free archival supplies for storage.

The baseball

* Avoid contact with alien surfaces; when one type of material touches another, a chemical reaction occurs.
* Never attempt to preserve a baseball by adding a substance to its surface.
* Only use "Official League" baseballs for autograph purposes.
* Use only high-grade inks. Cheaper inks can spread, flake, or fade.
* Inspect a baseball's surface, prior to autographing, for signs of defective manufacture.

****

The fate of your collection is in your own hands. To budget a percentage of your acquisition funds for preservation is to protect your initial investment. Many autographed baseballs have been ruined by collector neglect. That is a grave injustice not only to the collector, but to the game. The Baseball Hall of Fame depends on donations from collectors to add to the museum. Hobbyists' collections far exceed what is generally available for public viewing. Thus, we must commit ourselves to the preservation of the past, for the sake of the future.

Autographed Baseball Values

How does a collector or dealer put a value on an autographed team baseball? Is a player's signature worth more money if it is on an Official League baseball? Is a 1957 Yankees team baseball still worth money even if it's missing Mickey Mantle's autograph?

There are six key factors that affect the value of authentic autographed baseballs — ball type; medium or writing material; completeness; condition; scarcity and demand; and signature form, style and placement. To a dealer, understanding these factors assures proper pricing and identification. To a collector, these elements are paramount in determining the investment potential of a particular item. In recent years, the tremendous growth in the hobby has started to impact the casual collector, who is now becoming more aware of its economic rewards.

A quick glimpse into the pages of this book provides a plethora of ways to collect autographed baseballs. Novice collectors are no longer complacent with a their idols' signatures placed randomly on the first convenient baseball in sight. Instead, the maturing market for autographed baseballs has taught us the importance of the writing device used to sign the sphere, the desired location of the signature on it and the particular type of ball preferred by the hobby. All of this is an attempt to preserve the value of the baseball.

As the market for autographed baseballs grows, so does the number of periodicals aimed at addressing the collectors' needs. These resource materials are increasing the education level in the market at an astounding rate, giving hobbyists an instant knowledge base to build upon. Beginning collectors, who possess advanced skills compared to their predecessors, are now better positioned to accurately assess the value of an autographed baseball, and build a more cost-effective collection. The impact of this knowledge has created a more competitive market.

A knowledgeable collector base can add significantly to the market value of particular items. For example, the growing interest in single-signed baseballs of every member of the Baseball Hall of Fame not only yielded quick and substantial price increases, but an innumerable amount of price guides, newsletters and periodicals.

The lack of substantial interest in autographed team baseballs is primarily attributed to the absence of information necessary to properly identify, grade and value the item. This book should help revitalize collector interest in this limited collectible and bring currently undervalued autographed team baseballs back into proper market perspective.

Price guides, despite their comprehensiveness, lend themselves to the subjective opinions of their users. A value factor, such as condition, will forever yield substantially different viewpoints from its assessors. The many attempts by collector organizations to standardize this subjectivity is applauded, but only if it is done with the collectors' best interest in mind.

Moreover, collectors are realizing the value in specialization. The framework of specialization is conducive economically and mentally. Too often collectors approach the hobby randomly, spending a lot of money on items of little interest. Specialization concentrates a knowledge base, and because its boundaries are specific, the collector's awareness is gratified by a percentage of completeness. For example, collectors wishing to complete a single baseball with the signatures of all living players with more than 300 career wins realize that, as of the date of this printing, there are eight left, out of 20 players who have accomplished this feat.

Quality is of paramount importance to any autographed baseball collector or dealer because value is primarily impacted by the quality of an item. A purchaser should be fully aware of any factor that affects the quality. For the autographed team baseball collector, these factors include ball type (official or unofficial); signature form, style and placement; medium (writing device); scarcity and demand; completeness (percentage of team); and condition.

Care should also be taken in evaluating the authenticity of the autographs on a team baseball, and the genuineness of the item on which the signatures appear. I once saw what appeared to be an authentic Jimmie Foxx signature on a group baseball, but after careful inspection I noticed one small problem. Although the signature was on an "Official League" baseball, the league president's signature on the ball was Leland MacPhail's. However, he didn't obtain that position until six-and-a-half years after Foxx's death.

Popularity breeds price escalation, as exemplified best perhaps by the dynamic growth in collecting of at least one single-signature baseball of every member of the Baseball Hall of Fame. Because the average single-signature baseball from this prestigious group has surpassed $1,800, the general collector has given up hopes of this impossible achievement, purely for economic reasons. Many novice collectors fail to realize that this task, if achievable, will cost more than $350,000. These costs are why so many collectors are turning to various niches of the hobby where the market has not met its true potential. One such area is autographed team baseballs. For comparison purposes, a look at the economic differential is offered below.

****

SINGLE-SIGNATURE BASEBALLS VERSUS TEAM BASEBALLS

TYPE: Single-signed baseballs

Player	price
Gil Hodges	$523
Pee Wee Reese	$24
Duke Snider	$26
Roy Campanella	$1,955
Don Drysdale	$20
Sandy Koufax	$30
	Total $2,578

TYPE: 1957 Brooklyn Dodgers team baseball

Players:

Gil Hodges, Pee Wee Reese, Duke Snider, Roy Campanella, Don Drysdale and Sandy Koufax, plus 18 others.

Total $500

Source: the Sports Collectors Digest Baseball Autograph Handbook, second edition, 1991

****

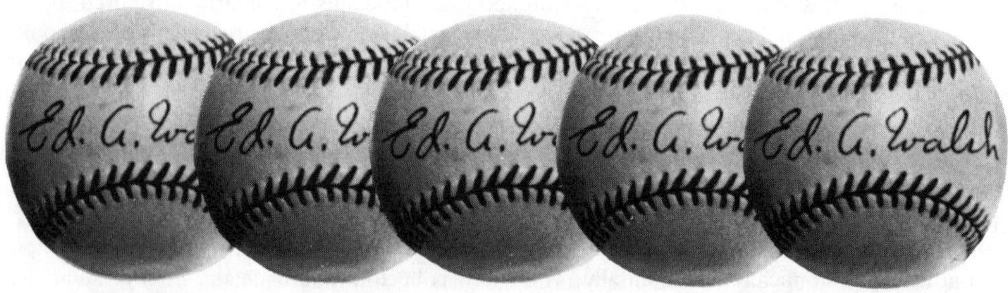

Balls signed by Ed Walsh can have a market value of $2,730.

With autographed sports memorabilia clearly a viable market, many major auction houses have entered the field in search of the finest collectibles. Although major firms, such as Sotheby's, are successful at flushing out items in the care of family and friends, they are equally as prodigious in escalating the cost of the collectibles. Although you may expect that this bit of irony would disappoint a collector, the contrary is true; most true collectors would opt for paying the additional cost, rather than continuing to search for years for a specific collectible. An additional trait of auction houses is their media draw. Auction results are often monitored like blue-chip stocks; their results are typically headline news in the next morning's paper.

With 1820 as the earliest birthdate of a Hall of Fame inductee, it is fair to assume that many collectibles are still possessed by family descendants. These items often find their way into collectors' hands through the many channels of the hobby, or become donations to the game's shrine in Cooperstown. The fact that the Hall of Fame does not purchase items gives collectors a competitive edge, too. Combine this with the growing awareness among major league ball players of memorabilia values and you have a future scenario that will naturally lead most baseball memorabilia into the hands of the wealthy collectors.

By the end of this decade the Hall of Fame may perhaps begin allocating funds for acquiring certain types of memorabilia. It is already clear to most advanced collectors and dealers that the quality merchandise surfacing in the market today is ending up in private collections. When and if institutions such as the Baseball Hall of Fame begin acquiring memorabilia it will be fair to assume that the historic or research value of a piece will be of utmost importance. This factor will naturally favor team, group or game baseballs, with less recognition given to single-signature balls.

Collectors are advised to exercise caution when purchasing from sources not specializing in, but offering for sale, autographed baseballs. Antique, stamp and coin dealers routinely sell sports memorabilia in conjunction with their major business. Before buying, be sure to qualify a seller's guarantee of authenticity, as well as return policy.

Autographed team baseballs, like most other forms of sports memorabilia, exhibit regional price variations. Therefore, a collector wanting a 1991 New York Yankees team baseball, although more likely to find the item in New York City, will undoubtedly pay a premium price in the tri-state area, compared to if he had purchased it in Arlington, Texas. Compared to team baseballs, single-signed baseballs show less regional price variation.

Value may also be impacted by popularity. Certain teams have a boundless and lasting impact on baseball fans. Collectors can expect to pay slightly higher prices for team baseballs for New York and Los Angeles teams. Also, collectors can expect to pay premium prices for team baseballs of some past popular franchises, such as the Brooklyn Dodgers or New York Giants.

The inclusion of a deceased player or manager on a ball will naturally increase the value of the item, particularily if the individual had a significant impact on the game. Popular players of the past, such as Billy Martin, Thurman Munson, Roger Maris, Roberto Clemente and Jackie Robinson, can have a profound impact on the value of an autographed team baseball, especially if they appear with other players with whom they were associated. Examples include Mickey Mantle and Roger Maris, or Jackie Robinson, Roy Campanella, Duke Snider and Pee Wee Reese.

****

TEAM BASEBALLS

A recent example of how the inclusion of key players affects value.

Item	Comments	Price Paid
1961 New York Yankees	24 signatures: includes Mickey Mantle, Roger Maris, Whitey Ford, Yogi Berra, Elston Howard, and all starters. Mint condition	$1,500

Autographed team baseballs, such as the one above signed by New York Yankee players, are not as popular as those signed by just one player.

1961 New York Yankees	18 signatures: Ford, Berra, Howard, and 15 others. No Mantle or Maris. Mint condition	$350

Note: The substantial price difference is not only attributed to the inclusion of both key players, but to the particular historical value associated with the baseball. Connotations associated with the ball include the "1961 World Champions," "The M & M Boys," and "61 in 61." Because Mantle and Maris personified the 1961 Yankees, and their contribution that year was of substantial historical significance to the game, most serious collectors would show little interest in a team ball without their signatures.

****

Just because a player's name does not appear on a team baseball, one can not conclude that subtracting the price of a single-signed baseball of this player will result in an accurate price for the ball. The pricing escalation of single-signature baseballs of deceased players, and the prolific signing habits of former and current stars, clearly negates the realism of this task. Great players who are clearly identified with one particular team — Ernie Banks with the Cubs; Ted Williams and Carl Yastrzemski with the Red Sox — should affect the value of a baseball. Although a Yastrzemski autograph is not particularly difficult to obtain, nor is it extremely valuable, the lack of it on a team baseball during the years he played could result in a 50 percent or more reduction in value. Many collectors believe if a team baseball does not include the signatures of all the club's starters, including normal pitching rotation and stars, then it should be re-classified as a group baseball.

Little is known about the signature habits of players deceased before World War II. Documentation regarding autograph collecting and player compliance with requests was scarce. This factor contributes greatly to the price increases exhibited by turn-of-the-century baseball autographs.

For example, single-signature baseballs of Jake Beckley, Willie Keeler, James Galvin and Tim Keefe each exceed $4,000.

Every collector should maintain realistic collecting goals, based on the subject or type of material being collected, and his budget. A budget is often the confines necessary for the collector to purchase wisely. Before purchasing an item, collectors should ponder the relevance of the acquisition, not only to their own collections, but to the hobby, too. Quality and value should play an equal role in determining whether to purchase a particular item.

Factors That Affect The Value Of Autographed Team Baseballs

There are six factors that can affect the value of an autographed team baseball — ball type; signature form, style and placement; medium or writing material; scarcity and demand; completeness (percentage of team); and condition.

Ball Type

Primarily for dating, authentication and aesthetics, collectors prefer to acquire autographs on "Official League" baseballs, or those balls manufactured specifically for use by the American or National League. The Official American League ball was produced by the A.J. Reach Co. and patented on April 6, 1909. The Official National League ball, manufactured by A.G. Spalding & Bros., was patented on Aug. 31, 1909. From the name of the league's president on the ball, collectors can approximate time period during which the baseball was signed. Collectors must bear in mind, however, that when a league president departs it is usually months before any official baseballs appear with the successor's signature on them.

Single-signed, team, or group signatures, appearing on baseballs not recognized by the major leagues, can reduce value by about 50 percent, depending upon the scarcity of the autograph in that form. Rawlings, the official league's manufacturer, has released exclusive commemorative baseballs for many major events. Since 1976, Rawlings has produced an exclusive baseball for use in the World Series. Each includes a Major League Baseball World Series logo, and the signature of the commissioner, which replaces those of the league presidents. Also, since 1979 the company has released a special baseball for use in the All-Star game. It includes the official logo used by the host city, and the commissioner's signature. During the 1991 season, the Chicago White Sox used a commemorative baseball for all the team's home games. This Official American League baseball only differs by the addition of a Comiskey Park inaugural logo, placed beneath the seam, directly underneath the signature of League President Bobby Brown. This is the first time in history, other than the World Series or All-Star game, that a commemorative ball was used in major league games. The ease of dating and aesthetic appeal of these commemorative baseballs will undoubtedly add to their long-term value.

"Game baseballs," or those balls that were actually used during a game, are scarce due to availability. They are difficult to authenticate. A few game baseballs do occasionally appear in the marketplace, and can command a significant price. For example, a ball used by Early Wynn during his 300th victory was recently offered for sale for $1,500. Game balls of greatest interest to collectors are those associated with a specific player or team reaching one of the game's milestones.

Signature Form, Style & Placement

The value of an autographed baseball can be influenced by the manner in which it was signed, and the signature's placement. Collectors often object to shortened or abbreviated signatures, such as "Reggie J." for Reggie Jackson, or "BB" for Bobby Bonilla. Many collectors even oppose extended signatures, such as "Edward Charles 'Whitey' Ford," claiming they are too gimmicky.

Legibility, as irritating as it can be to the collector, is considered part of the hobby. Each person's signature is unique, and thus exhibits various degrees of legibility. Tolerable to most collectors is the lack of character definition when it appears naturally, as in the signature of

Kenesaw Mountain Landis. Frustrating is when it comes in the form of a slipshod scroll placed hastily upon a baseball. Players' attendance at baseball card shows have only added to this enigma. With limited contractual signing time from star players, promoters encourage expedient responses to autograph requests. Players who realize that time is money have even gone so far as to modify their signatures for productivity purposes. At one show, Atlanta's two-sport star, Deion Sanders, was signing for a fee. The baseballs he signed were so illegible that I could not sell them, nor convince anyone that the scroll was indeed his signature.

Most collectors of single-signature balls prefer to have a player's autograph appear centered on the sweet spot, or the shortest distance between the two seams, opposite of the league president's signature on an Official League baseball. A single-signed autograph baseball, where the player's signature does not fall on the sweet spot, can impact value by as much as 30 percent.

This ball was signed in 1991 by Yankee star Joe DiMaggio.

Medium, or Writing Device

The writing device a player uses to sign a baseball can also affect its value. Official League baseballs, signed with a quality ink pen, are preferred over those signed with other devices. Most preferred are those durable or reservoir pens using ink least susceptible to deterioration. For example, a collector seeking a single-signed baseball of Joe DiMaggio in ballpoint pen may opt for a recent example instead of one signed in 1951. Earlier ballpoint pens, troublesome due to an ink that included a dye mixed with an oily base, produced signatures that faded considerably when exposed to light. Although hobby preference most often yields interest in earlier examples, a collector choosing to ignore the 1951 DiMaggio sample may have saved himself considerable frustration, and money, by choosing an autograph more tolerable to environmental factors.

Scarcity and Demand

Scarce or not, if there is no demand for a particular autographed baseball the price will remain low. However, if the supply is hearty and demand is strong, prices will still remain high. Nowhere is that better exemplified than with single-signature autographed baseballs of Babe Ruth. Ruth was always a willing and prolific signer, and despite the generous availability of single-signed baseballs from this man in the market today, the demand never seems to dissipate, despite the price. Perhaps a better example is that of Mickey Mantle, who routinely signs thousands of baseballs, yet the demand still has not been met. A Mantle single-signed baseball continues to show significant annual price increases and promises to be a lifelong collectible.

Autographed team baseballs, despite equivalent scarcity when compared to single-signature balls, remain subdued in popularity, perhaps due to the limited availablity of this collectible or the lack of a definitive resource to expedite identification, condition and value. Whatever the cause, autographed team baseballs remain undervalued in the sports memorabilia market.

A large contributor to the inflated prices of autographed baseballs has been the advent of the baseball card star show. With many past and present stars commanding exorbitant fees to sign for what seems to be a willfully-paying public, the day of the free autograph may come to pass. Although it's inexplicable by some accounts, it was Commissioner Fay Vincent who perhaps said it best when he once told me, "In the market, if people are willing to pay for a player's autograph, and the player is willing to accept payment, then I have no problem with that. What I do have a problem with is if the players at the ballpark refuse to sign for the fans. Fans are very important, and players shouldn't be reluctant to sign for them at the stadium, and I feel by and large the players are not reluctant to sign for them. If a retired player, however, feels he should charge for his signature and fans are willing to pay him for it, well, that's called the marketplace, and that's the way we allocate resources in this country. And I'm in no position to say that it isn't efficient, because it is."

The hobby is also not immune to trendsetters. Ever since Joe DiMaggio refused to sign non-flat items, other players have followed his lead. The predictable and unfortunate result was an enormous price escalation in autographed DiMaggio baseballs and bats, followed by an increased influx of forgeries. By restricting the materials they are signing, players believe they can command greater signing fees and maintain greater control over the distribution of their signatures. Unfortunately, the opposite scenario has occurred. Some major dealers believe there are more fake Joe DiMaggio autographed baseballs in the market than authentics. Many dealers even refuse to deal in autographed DiMaggio material. Although an autograph may be scarce in a particular format, the demand may be less than anticipated due to forgery concerns. Although an authentic DiMaggio baseball will forever be cherished by a serious collector, I do not recommend it as a primary investment.

Baseballs autographed by any recent inductees to the Baseball Hall of Fame will always be in immediate demand, until the supply is met. Additionally, upon a player's death there is often an immediate demand for his autograph. Collectors wishing to purchase an autographed baseball of a recently-deceased player can expect to pay two or three times more than what they would have had to pay prior to his death. In the case of an unpredictable circumstance claiming the player's life, demand can skyrocket, as exemplified by the tragic deaths of Roberto Clemente and Thurman Munson. Although Munson is not a member of the Baseball Hall of Fame, collectors can expect to pay well over $500 for a single-signed baseball from this Yankee great.

The hobby, as in any market, can periodically become flooded with material. This is usually a result of massive acquisitions of autographed material of a certain player, or by increased attendance by a player at baseball card shows. The result is often a temporary decrease in value until all the material has been absorbed into the hobby.

Completeness

Completeness, or the inclusion of certain signatures on team, group, or commemorative baseballs, can substantially impact value. For example, I purchased two 1991 New York Yankees Official League team baseballs. Both included the team's stars and starters, but the one for $79 had only 13 signatures. The other, which had 28 signatures, was $100. Since completeness is a concern to all collectors, I purchased the more expensive ball with 15 more signatures. The fortunate element of the transaction was the opportunity to choose between two baseballs that were truely "team" baseballs, because they included not only the names of all the starters and stars, but also the starting pitching rotation. Had the one baseball with only 13 signatures not included the autograph of Don Mattingly, it may have been worth only $50. Mattingly, the Yankee's captain, is not only the recognized superstar of the club, but is an elusive player to most autograph collectors. Having to acquire his signature to complete a team baseball could be a formidable, and costly, task.

A phenomenon I have witnessed, and one that concerns certain collectors, has been the building of team or group baseballs over an extended period of time. The obvious advantage is cost, but the one factor often forgotten is that a player's signature can vary with time. For example, a collector who completed a 1984 New York Yankees team baseball by obtaining Don Mattingly's signature in 1991 would confuse most who viewed it as a 1984 team baseball. Because Mattingly has varied his signature noticeably since 1984, if the ball were offered for sale it would raise immediate authenticity concerns. Additional confusion arises when collectors purchase older baseballs, such as a 1966 San Francisco Giants partial team baseball, and add new signatures to it. Altering a collectible in this fashion can dramatically reduce its value.

Condition

The factor with the greatest impact on value of an autographed baseball is condition. The better the condition, the greater the likelihood of obtaining full market value, especially if all other value factors are positive.

Most collectors assume that just because they obtain an older autographed baseball that it is naturally worth more. A quick glance into the next section of this book should nullify this misnomer. Although condition naturally affects value, it does not circumvent the effect of any of the five previously mentioned factors.

This 1920s' world championship team baseball is nearly worthless as an investment to serious collectors because it is only in fair condition.

Since autographed baseballs, like baseball cards, vary in condition, a grading standard becomes necessary. Buyers and sellers need a frame of reference to reach an informed agreement on a baseball's value, especially when the transaction is being conducted without the advantage of both parties viewing the item. An acknowledged grading standard is of utmost importance to any hobby and should be established with the collectors' best interest in mind. These condition definitions are provided for your reference. Since a grading guide has not been universally accepted by the hobby, collectors and dealers are not required to adhere to any condition standards, but certainly are invited to do so for convenience and reference purposes.

==

AUTOGRAPHED BASEBALL GRADING GUIDE

An autographed baseball can fall into, or between, six grading conditions. Unfortunately, for the collector, the grading scale is not linear. Therefore, choosing between the two conditions at the beginning and end of the scale presents the greatest challenge.

Condition	Description
Mint (MT)	A perfect baseball, no major surface flaws, and no stains. The ball is symmetrical, with all laces intact, and all printed ball markings are clear. There is no evidence of ink bleeding from the surface being printed, or from the signatures. All signatures are discernable, clear and unsmudged. Surface is cream or off-white, showing no sign of discoloration. Value expectation: Premium, or slightly over full book value.
Near Mint (NR MT)	At first glance, it appears to be mint condition. However, closer inspection reveals some minor flaws. The ball is symmetrical, with all laces intact, and all printed ball markings clear. Only slight evidence of ink bleeding, primarily in non-signature areas. All signatures are discernable, with the beginning signs of deterioration evidenced under a magnifying glass. There are no major stains, with the surface showing only natural discoloration. Value expectation: Full book value.
Excellent (EX)	The ball shows some minor flaws. Only 90 percent of all signatures are discernable; the other 10 percent require some interpretation or research to determine the player's identity. Normal ink deterioration is evidenced without the aid of magnification. No excessive ink bleeding. Surface shows natural discoloration and lack of original luster. Value expectation: 10 to 20 percent off full book value.
Very Good (VG)	The baseball shows obvious handling, with slight surface marks or stains. Only 75 percent of all signatures are discernable; half of the others require interpretation, while the rest are nearly impossible to recognize. Ink deterioration is evident, although not excessive. Surface shows natural, but not necessarily uniform, discoloration. Value expectation: 20 to 40 percent off full book value.
Good (G)	A well-handled autograph baseball, exhibiting surface marks that may impact some signatures' legibility. Only 50 percent of all signatures are discernable; the other half are nearly impossible to recognize due to deterioration. Surface discoloration is not uniform and may detract from the appeal of the baseball. Value expectation: 40 to 70 percent off full book value.
Fair (F)	The baseball shows excessive handling and abuse. If shellacked, the surface is chipping, resulting in permanent damage to the baseball. Surface

scars are evident and impact some signatures. The surface may even be defaced by additional markings. Only 25 to 30 percent of all signatures are discernable; the rest are hopeless. Surface discoloration is unappealing. Some major stains are evident.

Value expectation: 70 to 85 percent off full book value.

In addition to these grades, collectors will often encounter intermediate grades, such as VG to EX (Very Good to Excellent), or EX to MT (Excellent to Mint), all in an attempt to properly describe the autographed baseball. If the baseball is described as such it usually commands a price at a point midway between that of the two grades. Collectors should remember that no single source can provide a universally acceptable assessment of an autographed baseball. Naturally, it is expected that game-used memorabilia reflect wear. Therefore, using this grading guide to determine their value would be inappropriate.

Perhaps the greatest tragedy an autographed baseball collector faces is that ink fades, and there is no acceptable method of correcting it. A collector is warned to never attempt to retrace a signature, for fear it will be mistaken as a forgery. So many beautiful autographed baseballs have deteriorated to a point that makes them almost worthless, even when an attempt to preserve them is made. Additionally, collectors should never have players retrace their faded signatures on a ball. This may not only confuse a future prospective buyer, but even add to the deterioration that already exists.

In earlier years it was common to shellack a baseball to preserve it. Shellack, combined with various ink types, yields a variety of results, mostly disasterous. Preservation, especially when it includes the application of a chemical agent on to a collectible, should be left in the hands of the conservator, not the collector.

Auctions

Auctions can vary significantly in quality items being offered, assessed values and guarantees. As the hobby matures, the variance in value becomes less evident at the auction level, and somewhat more predictable. Premier auction houses, entering a legitimate market, have unearthed treasures that were unattainable to larger dealers. The attraction to the seller is the ability to receive top dollar for premium merchandise. Also, these auction houses bring a certain level of professionalism to the hobby that many dealers feel was long overdue. Full-color catalogs are published months in advance, providing the collector with all the necessary information he needs to properly assess, in his own mind, the items' values.

Sotheby's entrance into the hobby was firmly established in 1991 by its sale of the Copeland Collection, which totaled $ 4.6 million. Although little autographed material was sold, the prices commanded were eminent. For example, an autographed baseball from the 1939 Hall of Fame induction ceremonies, containing a dozen of the inductees' signatures, was sold for $20,900.

More and more, baseball autographs and memorabilia are being looked at as investments. The collector as an investor is a world unto its own, and not within the scope of this book, but certainly of interest to anyone who collects autographed baseballs. Some collectors, turned investors, have found themselves with loses, as investments in would-be superstars never paid off. A collector who buys for investment purposes must be familiar with every economic aspect associated with the marketplace. One such aspect is the impact a player's performance has on his memorabilia. This impact can be influenced by his life on, and off, the field; collectors of Pete Rose memorabilia undoubtedly understand this. Autographed baseball collectors can make money, but it requires insightful purchases and great patience.

As collectors, we control the marketplace. It is our willingness to pay $12,760 for a single-signed Cap Anson baseball that drives the market. If the market for certain autographed memorabilia is unreachable for the average collector, we have only ourselves to blame.

Authenticity, Identification and Signature Variation

The Pete Rose ball at right was signed in 1991; the other, in 1975.

Authenticity is a concern of everyone who collects valuable material. But the complexities involved in writing seem to add a greater degree of authenticity uncertainty for autograph collectors. Origin is the key factor in authentication; a collector must be able to verify the origin of an item in order to displace a majority of all authentication concerns. Whenever an item is questioned, it is particularly important for the buyer and seller to promptly and thoroughly examine all authentication factors of the piece to displace uncertainty. Unfortunately, for those involved in this task the process may be very tedious, time-consuming, and costly.

Dating

Most agree that determining the age of a particular item has the most profound impact on authenticity. Age determination is the starting point for most experts, so it should be the collector's first authentication task. Since most autographed baseballs are not dated, the process begins by identifying the item's printed marks. Official League baseballs are associated with particular time periods and are identified most often by the league president's signature on the ball. Because there are so many varieties of unofficial baseballs, their age will most likely be determined by the decipherment of the signatures on the ball.

Decipherment

The effectiveness of our language naturally depends on its ability to be written and read. This ability, however, can be hampered by many factors — unfamiliarity with the language; writing deformity due to haste or physical handicap; the characteristics of the item being signed, primarily attributable to its surface; and the deterioration characteristics of the item.

Major league baseball's boundless appeal has made it an international sport, with players from Canada, South America, Central America and the Caribbean. It is common for players who are unfamiliar with our language or penmanship to sign a baseball. For example, the signatures of Chico Carrasquel, Cesar Gutierrez and Pablo Torrealba can be a bit more difficult to decipher than an autograph of Charlie Gehringer. Also worth noting is that an individual's signature style can vary substantially during his lifetime. Players, such as Mickey Mantle and Joe DiMaggio, have even shown significant signature variations during their careers. Although it is unprobable that collectors will acquaint themselves with the signature styles of everyone who has played the game, it would prove helpful, particularly for dating purposes, to study the variations of some key players.

Writing deformity due to haste is a factor that every modern collector will face. The advent of the baseball card star show, and the economics surrounding the event, have only added to autograph expedience. During an autograph session, time is money. Thus, moderate legibility is acceptable. The hobby has reached such proportions — signature avoidance techniques are even being taught to players during spring training. One such technique of haste or expedience is the encouragement of players to never stop walking to respond to an autograph request. The reduced legibility of current player signatures will become an authentication nightmare to future collectors.

A player's signature may also be altered by some physical debility of the writer, as exemplified by the shaky writing attributable to old age. The signatures of Carl Hubbell, Luke Appling and Bill Terry all exhibited writing deformity due to old age.

The item being autographed can also add to the difficulty in signature decipherment. A player's signature on a team baseball may vary due to the ball's size and curved surface. Also, character recognition is greatly reduced on a baseball if the autograph was signed with a fibrous tip marker. These markers are far too large for use on team baseballs, and have unacceptable bleeding characteristics that will impede decipherment.

Autographs on baseballs, which would otherwise be easy to read, are frequently diminished in legibility by a variety of causes, such as faded ink, the surface characteristics of the item that was signed, and by the addition of or contact with a foreign substance. Magnification and varied light sources are perhaps of greatest assistance to the average collector. Ultraviolet illumination, infrared photography, laser lighting and a variety of chemical treatments are available, but generally out of the average collector's scope.

Qualification

Once a group of signatures has been identified on a team baseball, a quick reference to the Key Player Index in the back of this book should assist in identifying the ballclub and era. Cross-referencing this data with the team rosters provided as part of Section Two should help determine the exact year of the team baseball. Once an autographed baseball has been identified, its authenticity can be determined.

Forgery

Determining the authenticity of an autographed baseball can present a significant challenge. The rapid growth of the hobby, combined with the overall lack of accurate information, has fueled the influx of unauthentic material. Generally, the more valuable the item, the more likelihood it will be forged. Contrary opinions also exist among many collectors who believe that inexpensive items are often not thoroughly examined, and thus are easy targets for forgery. Whatever your viewpoint is, the advice remains the same: all collectors should have a comprehensive understanding of authenticity.

The following list should provide every collector with an initial understanding of how to spot forgeries. Although these factors are indicators, some are not in themselves conclusive proof of inauthenticity. However, others, such as an obvious use of an incorrect writing material, would immediately expose forgery.

Can you spot the fake Mickey Mantle signature? It's in the bottom row, second ball from the right.

AUTOGRAPHED BASEBALLS

COMMON SIGNS OF FORGERY

1. Incorrect baseball

Often, collectors have discovered forgeries simply by studying the material the signature adorns. During a baseball card show I discovered a single-signed baseball of Lloyd Waner. The signature was on an Official American League baseball, but Waner only played in the National League. This is not an unusual circumstance, but serious collectors prefer a player's signature on a proper league ball. What was equally perplexing was Bobby Brown's signature as American League president, a position he did not assume until a year-and-a-half after Waner's death.

2. Incorrect writing materials

The knowledge of writing instruments can only enhance an autographed baseball collector's chances of obtaining a genuine signature. Often, collectors overlook the type of writing device used on an autographed baseball, in favor of a more extensive investigation into the style or characteristics of an individual's signature. Ballpoint pen autographs of Christy Mathewson, Cap Anson and John McGraw have all entered the market, only to be promptly identified by serious collectors as forgeries because the writing device was not invented until after their deaths.

3. Off-scale writing

This characteristic is applicable more to single-signature baseballs than to team balls. Forgers often unconsciously reduce the size of their subject's signature. Occasionally, a forger may even inadvertently enlarge an element of the subject's writing, especially if he is trying to mimic an autograph that he is unfamiliar with on a particular type of material. Often a player's signature depicts his shifts in popularity. When Don Mattingly was an emerging rookie, his signature was much smaller and dramatically less flamboyant. As his popularity grew, so did the size of his signature.

4. Uncommon form

Any unusual variation of a subject's typical form of handwriting should elicit authenticity concerns from collectors. Signature breaks, character definitions, slant, and beginning and ending strokes should all be consistent with existing authentic examples. Variations do take place as part of the natural evolution of a player's signature, but dramatic, rather than subtle shifts, should evoke concern.

5. Tremulous writing

Tremulous writing is a characteristic of old age, illness, illiteracy, and forgery. Irregular pen pressure and a quivering line quality are indications of a slowly-drawn forgery. Typically, signatures are smooth and confident, with little pen pressure variation. Ascending and descending loops are excellent checkpoints for tremulous signature examination.

6. Tracing

Tracing is the most common form of forgery and generally very easy to recognize. Traced signatures are filled with unnatural characteristics, such as slowly-drawn lines that lack any natural variations or spontaneity. Also, indentations, erasures and pencil marks are usually noticeable under high magnification.

7. Stroke irregularity and retouching

Quick, carefree strokes of consistent pen pressure are indications of normal handwriting. On the contrary, forged signatures are often slowly drawn with too much emphasis placed on detail. Irregular "pen lifts," or areas that indicate that a writing device has ceased, paused, and then continued writing, also indicate a forgery. Retouching, although often a sign of forgery in other areas of autograph collecting, is far more common with autographed baseballs. I have witnessed nearly every living member of the Hall of Fame, at one time or another, casually retouch his signature. Although serious collectors frown on the thought, the hobby seems to accept the practice.

8. Writing applied to an old baseball

It is not uncommon for a forger to add a signature to an older baseball. If the forger is familiar with writing device origins, and dating Official League baseballs, his success rate is greatly improved. Some forgers even purchase inexpensive team baseballs with a few legitimate autographs, and add the prominent signatures necessary to entice a buyer. Complicating this issue is the fact that some collectors have also chosen to add new signatures to old baseballs as an acceptable method of collecting. Serious collectors, however, frown on the alteration of an autographed baseball in any fashion.

9. Additional factors

Occasionally, forgers will make a mistake by including a player who was not on the team's roster that year. Often, mistakes such as this are then passed off as the subsequent year's team baseball, or balls acquired during spring training.

****

A skilled forger using his freehand skills and possessing a strong knowledge of writing materials can achieve a high degree of perfection. Fortunately, however, autographed baseball experts agree that perfect forgeries are rare, if not impossible. Understanding the characteristics of forgery is the first step toward authentication. What to look for in a signature is the next step.

Bob Feller's autograph, signed with a Sharpie, bleeds into the baseball.

SIGNATURE COMPARISON CHARACTERISTICS

The two main writing characteristics used by most experts for signature comparison purposes are:

Line quality

Which includes:

[ ] Pen position (where a line or signature begins and ends)
[ ] Pen pressure (consistent or inconsistent; most noticeable in upward and downward strokes)
[ ] Writing speed, rhythm, or tremor (any slowly-drawn line indicators?)
[ ] Signature breaks (are the breaks between characters in a first or last name, if any, consistent with known examples?)

Form

Which includes:

[ ] Proportions (capitalization versus lower case)
[ ] Slant (right or left)
[ ] Beginning and ending strokes (location and flamboyance)
[ ] Character formation (particularly capitalization, and the letters e, a and o, the crossing of t's and the dotting of i's, and a character's descender)
[ ] Character spacing
[ ] Style (flamboyance)
[ ] Legibility

****

Authentic Fakes or Fraud?

Beginning autograph baseball collectors will sometime encounter the following confusing scenarios:

* Mistaken identity

Identical names can be a source of tremendous confusion. Collectors confronted with two distinctly different autographs of the same name may have a case of mistaken identity.

Here are just a few examples:

* Adams, Bob H.: 1946-59; Cinn. 1946-55, White Sox 1955, Balt. 1956, Cubs 1957-59.
* Adams, Bob M.: 1977; Det. 1977.
* Alomar, Sandy Sr.: 1964-78; Mil. 1964-65, Atl. 1966, Mets 1967, White Sox 1967-69, Cal. 1969-74, Yankees 1974-76, Texas 1977-78.
* Alomar, Sandy Jr.: 1988-present; S.D. 1988-89, Cleve. 1990-present.
* Averill, Earl Sr.: 1929-41; Cleve. 1929-39, Det. 1939-40, Bos. (N) 1941.
* Averill, Earl Jr.: 1956, 1958-63; Cleve. 1956, 1958, Cubs 1959-60, White Sox 1960, L.A. 1961-62, Phil. 1963.

* Ghost signatures

As baseball grew in popularity, so did the fame of its star players. Collectors should be forewarned that players such as Babe Ruth often condoned clubhouse personnel signing on their behalf. I met a former major league ball boy who admitted signing the home team manager's name to team baseballs.

* Printed signatures

Printed team baseballs have been sold at many major league ballpark souvenir stands for years. Stiff in appearance, and showing no natural writing characteristics, these facsimiles are easily recognized by collectors. The natural deterioration, or yellowing of older facsimile team baseballs, however, can make the identification task a bit more difficult. Ironically, the older team baseballs do have value, but are seldom acquired by serious collectors.

* Rubber-stamped signatures

Rubber-stamped signatures have been periodically used by certain players when responding to autograph requests. The task of stamping a baseball is not easy due to the ball's curved surface. Signatures often appear distorted. The unnatural appearance of these signatures also makes them easily recognizable to the collector.

* Secretarial signatures

In addition to clubhouse personnel, some former players and executives authorized their personal secretaries to sign their names. It's uncommon on a baseball, but this application most often appeared on correspondences. John Ward, Hugh Jennings and Kenesaw Landis are just a few of the Hall of Fame inductees who authorized this practice.

AUTOGRAPH VARIATIONS

Signature variations or deviations are common in the evolution of an individual's autograph. Our signatures are inconsistent, and often affected by circumstance. These variations can be related to a person's mood, health, age, setting, popularity, and writing materials.

Failure to identify an authentic autograph, due to variations in form, is a common problem faced by novice and experienced collectors. Pete Rose's stiff four-stroke signature of the mid-1960s is in great contrast to his flamboyant three-stroke, looped autograph of today. Although these anomalies add to the complex task of authentication, comprehensive study of these variations can actually prove to be tremendously helpful in dating an autographed baseball. Many experts can date Mickey Mantle autographed material just by viewing its form.

A strong understanding of signature variations is difficult due to a lack of chronological examples from a particular player. Unless a collector has access to a tremendous amount of material

Enos Slaughter signed these baseballs during an autograph session. Subtle variations include the "l" either being connected, or not, to the "a" in Slaughter, or the "S" connecting with the "l" or not.

surrounding a player's life, his familiarity with a subject is usually restricted to examples from a very specific time period. Many an expert collector has been fooled by early examples of the more difficult signatures to obtain from members of the Baseball Hall of Fame.

Unless an autograph deviation is associated with a particular major event or period of time, pinpointing its origin is usually very difficult. However, dramatic variations, such as those associated with a major illness or accident, as in the case of Roy Campanella or Walter Alston, are easily acknowledged.

Studying signature variations is a never-ending task, complicated by circumstance and cost. Serious collectors are advised to create a "clip file," or reference file, of examples cut from magazines or advertisements. Additional purchases of books or periodicals containing several examples of players' signatures are also recommended. Signature inconsistencies do occur over a subject's life, but it is the responsibility of the serious collector or dealer to determine if these variations, witnessed in autograph samples, are due to natural causes or to forgery. More often than not, style variations are dismissed as forgeries, allowing a better educated buyer an opportunity to purchase the collectible.

How To Use This Book

QUESTION: How do you identify this autographed team baseball?

Step One

Examine the baseball for recognizable (all-stars, minor stars) signatures. Prominent signatures will often appear on the ball's sweet spot or manager's spot. This is particularly true of older baseballs. In this example, the key names are Joe DiMaggio, Yogi Berra and Bobby Brown.

Step Two

Turn to the "Key Player Index" in the back of this book to determine the probable team and time period.

Berra, Yogi: 1946-63, 1965; Yankees 1946-63, Mets 1965.
Brown, Bobby: 1946-52, 1954; Yankees 1946-52, 1954.
DiMaggio, Joe: 1936-42, 1946-51; Yankees 1936-42, 1946-51.
Conclusion at this stage: The team is the Yankees
Time Period: 1946 to 1951

Step Three

In Section Two, using the chapter on Autographed Team Baseballs, turn to the year 1946. Beginning at this year, and continuing to 1951 if necessary, examine the team rosters and compare to the legible secondary signatures appearing on the ball.

Name	Year	Year	Year
	1946	1947	1948
Spec Shea	* No	Yes	Yes
Snuffy Stirnweiss	Yes	Yes	Yes
Aaron Robinson	Yes	Yes	** No
Johnny Lindell	Yes	Yes	Yes
George McQuinn	No	Yes	Yes

* Shea's first year on the Yankees was 1947.
** Robinson played with the White Sox in 1948.

Based on this analysis of secondary signatures, it is fair to conclude the ball is a 1947 New York Yankees autographed team baseball

DOMINANT MAJOR LEAGUE BASEBALL TEAMS

By Decade

Decade	National League	American League
1900 to 1909	Pittsburgh Pirates (01, 02, 03, 09)	Detroit Tigers (07, 08, 09)
1910 to 1919	New York Giants (11, 12, 13, 17)	Philadelphia A's (10, 11, 13, 14)
1920 to 1929	New York Giants (21, 22, 23, 24)	New York Yankees (21, 22, 23, 26, 27, 28)
1930 to 1939	St. Louis Cardinals (30, 31, 34)	New York Yankees (32, 36, 37, 38, 39)
	New York Giants (33, 37,)	
1940 to 1949	St. Louis Cardinals (42, 43, 44, 46)	New York Yankees (41, 42, 43, 47, 49)
1950 to 1959	Brooklyn Dodgers (52, 53, 55, 56)	New York Yankees (50, 51, 52, 53, 55, 56, 57, 58)
1960 to 1969	St. Louis Cardinals (64, 67, 68)	New York Yankees (60, 61, 62, 63, 64)
	Los Angeles Dodgers (63, 65, 66)	
1970 to 1979	Cincinnati Reds (70, 72, 75, 76)	Baltimore Orioles (70, 71, 79)
		Oakland A's (72, 73, 74)
		New York Yankees (76, 77, 78)
1980 to 1989	St. Louis Cardinals (82, 85, 87)	Kansas City Royals (80, 85)
		Oakland A's (88, 89)

TRAGIC DEATHS

The tragic death of a major league player on a team roster, particularly that of an all-star, can dramatically affect the value of an autographed team baseball. Here is a brief list of such occurrences:

Illness

Name	Age	Date	Cause
Pickles Dillhoefer	(27)	2/2/22	typhoid fever
Austin McHenry	(27)	11/27/22	brain tumor
Ross Youngs (HOF)	(30)	10/22/27	Bright's disease
Urban Shocker	(38)	9/9/28	heart disease
Hal Carlson	(38)	5/28/30	internal hemorrhage
Mickey Finn	(31)	7/7/33	duodenal ulcer
Ernie Bonham	(36)	9/15/49	appendicitis
Harry Agganis	(25)	6/27/55	massive pulmonary embolism
Jim Umbricht	(33)	4/8/64	cancer
Danny Thompson	(29)	12/10/76	leukemia

Violent deaths/suicides

Ed Morris	Prior to spring training in 1932
Don Wilson	1/5/75
Lyman Bostock	9/23/78

Transportation

Many players gave their lives for the United States during various wars and conflicts.

Airplane crash

Tommy Gastall	9/20/56
Charlie Peete	11/27/56
Nestor Chavez	3/16/69
Ken Hubbs	2/15/64
Roberto Clemente (HOF)	12/31/72
Thurman Munson	8/2/79

Ground accident

Tony Boeckel	2/16/24
Walt Lerian	10/22/29
Danny Frisella	1/1/77

New York Yankee catcher Thurman Munson signed this ball.

To understand the price variances in autographed team baseballs which include the signatures of deceased players, consult the chapter in this book on values.

From the brief list provided above, Clemente, Youngs, Munson and Hubbs have the greatest impact on value. The deaths of minor stars and average roster players have a limited effect on the value of an autographed team baseball, but are worth noting to accurately assess a price.

(HOF) = Member of the Baseball Hall of Fame.

****

Who signed this ball?
Oakland A's star Jose Canseco.

Below is my list of all-time favorite illegible signatures (particularly when they appear on a baseball) by decade.

ILLEGIBLE SIGNATURES

(1950 to 1990)

1950s

Roberto Clemente	Pirates
Gus Zernial	A's
Dick Brodowski	Indians
Julio Becquer	Senators
Luis Aparicio	White Sox
Chico Carrasquel	Indians
Luis Aloma	White Sox
Owen Friend	Browns
Willie Jones	Phillies

1960s

Mike Cuellar	Astros
Joe Nuxhall	Reds

1970s

Santo Alcala	Reds
Pablo Torrealba	Braves
Mark Fidrych	Tigers
Al Fitzmorris	Royals
Dave Concepcion	Reds
Angel Bravo	Reds
Deron Johnson	Phillies
Cesar Gutierrez	Tigers

1980s

Pepe Frias	Braves
Jesus Alou	Astros
Joaquin Andujar	Astros
Elias Sosa	Tigers
Frank Taveras	Expos
Carl Yastrzemski	Red Sox
Ivan DeJesus	Cubs
Luis Leal	Blue Jays
Victor Cruz	Pirates
Manny Trillo	Phillies
John Curtis	Padres
Enrique Romo	Pirates
Rennie Stennett	Giants
Tony Armas	A's
Darryl Strawberry	Mets
Jose Canseco	A's
Mark McGwire	A's
Andre Dawson	Expos
Deion Sanders	Braves

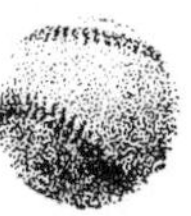

HIGHLY-SOUGHT TEAM BASEBALLS

Year	Team	Comments
1954	Cleveland Indians	4th in winning percentage (all time); 2nd in wins (all time); four Hall of Famers — Early Wynn, Bob Lemon, Bob Feller and Al Lopez
1927	New York Yankees	"Murderers' Row;" seven Hall of Famers — Lou Gehrig, Tony Lazzeri, Babe Ruth, Earle Combs, Waite Hoyt, Herb Pennock and Miller Huggins; highest slugging average (all time); Babe Ruth's 60 home run year
1961	New York Yankees	"M & M Boys;" three Hall of Famers — Whitey Ford, Yogi Berra and Mickey Mantle; most home runs (all time); Maris hit 61 home runs and was MVP
1969 and 1970	Baltimore Orioles	Three Hall of Famers — Frank Robinson, Jim Palmer and Brooks Robinson; most wins by a team in three consecutive seasons in the American League; in 1969 Mike Cuellar won the Cy Young Award; in 1970 Boog Powell won the MVP
1906, 1907, 1908	Chicago Cubs	Four Hall of Famers — Mordecai Brown, Joe Tinker, Johnny Evers and Frank Chance ("Tinker to Evers to Chance"); most wins by a team in three consecutive seasons (all time)
1975	Cincinnati Reds	"Big Red Machine;" two Hall of Famers — Joe Morgan and Johnny Bench, and five possible others — Sparky Anderson, Pete Rose, Tony Perez, George Foster and Dave Concepcion; highest number of wins recorded by a National League team since the Cubs of the 1900s
1986	New York Mets	Highest number of wins by a National League team since the "Big Red Machine;" stars include Keith Hernandez, Darryl Strawberry, Gary Carter and Dwight Gooden
1931	Philadelphia A's	Six Hall of Famers — Connie Mack, Jimmie Foxx, Al Simmons, Mickey Cochrane, Lefty Grove and Waite Hoyt; sixth in winning percentage (all time); Grove was the MVP
1990	Oakland A's	Highly sought due to award winners Bob Welch (A.L. Cy Young), Rickey Henderson (A.L. MVP), Willie McGee (N.L. batting title); Jose Canseco and Mark McGwire combination; Canseco, McGwire and Walt Weiss (Rookie of the Year award winners)

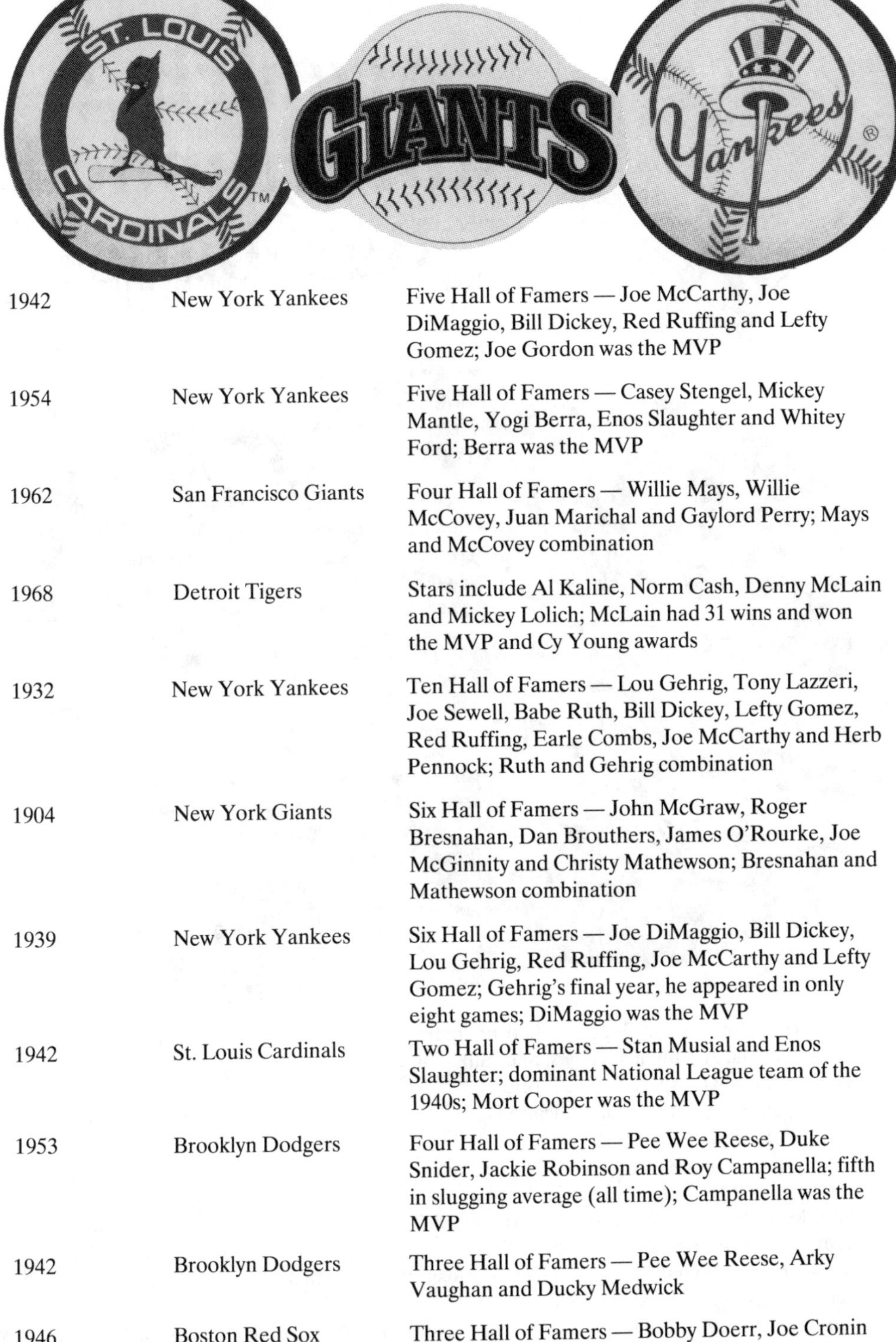

1942	New York Yankees	Five Hall of Famers — Joe McCarthy, Joe DiMaggio, Bill Dickey, Red Ruffing and Lefty Gomez; Joe Gordon was the MVP
1954	New York Yankees	Five Hall of Famers — Casey Stengel, Mickey Mantle, Yogi Berra, Enos Slaughter and Whitey Ford; Berra was the MVP
1962	San Francisco Giants	Four Hall of Famers — Willie Mays, Willie McCovey, Juan Marichal and Gaylord Perry; Mays and McCovey combination
1968	Detroit Tigers	Stars include Al Kaline, Norm Cash, Denny McLain and Mickey Lolich; McLain had 31 wins and won the MVP and Cy Young awards
1932	New York Yankees	Ten Hall of Famers — Lou Gehrig, Tony Lazzeri, Joe Sewell, Babe Ruth, Bill Dickey, Lefty Gomez, Red Ruffing, Earle Combs, Joe McCarthy and Herb Pennock; Ruth and Gehrig combination
1904	New York Giants	Six Hall of Famers — John McGraw, Roger Bresnahan, Dan Brouthers, James O'Rourke, Joe McGinnity and Christy Mathewson; Bresnahan and Mathewson combination
1939	New York Yankees	Six Hall of Famers — Joe DiMaggio, Bill Dickey, Lou Gehrig, Red Ruffing, Joe McCarthy and Lefty Gomez; Gehrig's final year, he appeared in only eight games; DiMaggio was the MVP
1942	St. Louis Cardinals	Two Hall of Famers — Stan Musial and Enos Slaughter; dominant National League team of the 1940s; Mort Cooper was the MVP
1953	Brooklyn Dodgers	Four Hall of Famers — Pee Wee Reese, Duke Snider, Jackie Robinson and Roy Campanella; fifth in slugging average (all time); Campanella was the MVP
1942	Brooklyn Dodgers	Three Hall of Famers — Pee Wee Reese, Arky Vaughan and Ducky Medwick
1946	Boston Red Sox	Three Hall of Famers — Bobby Doerr, Joe Cronin and Ted Williams; Williams was the MVP

Acquiring Autographed Baseballs

Once a collector has developed a field of interest, he can base his acquisition procedures around his personal and financial goals. Specialization will provide the framework for acquisition. For example, those who specialize in World Champion autographed team baseballs must realize their task requires a great deal of dedication and financing, especially when compared to a more general form of collecting.

The transition from collector to dealer is becoming more prevalent. Often, specialized collectors, who initially intended to collect for fun, have taken on the characteristics of a dealer, due to their knowledge base and understanding of value. If a collector is making this transition, it is important for him to also shift his acquisition goals. But a good collector does not necessarily make a good dealer. If you are tempted by this transition, understand its pitfalls.

Specialized collectors must also remember there is a fine balance between eccentric and commonplace collecting. Although you may be completely enthralled with collecting single-signature baseballs signed by United States senators, the hobby generally has little, if any, interest in your pursuit. Mindful of this infrequent choice of specialization, you will save yourself from the eventual disappointment encountered while searching for acquisition material. Also, when you want to sell your collection you will have a better understanding of the noticeable lack of interest in the marketplace.

Successful collectors and dealers must have a strong understanding of supply and demand. Supply refers to an item's scarcity (how many initially existed in that particular form), and rarity (how many actually survived or made it into the marketplace). Although scarcity and rarity are critical factors in assessing an item's value, the market, particularly for many highly-specialized collectibles, may not be cognizant of them. The unfortunate result is little interest or demand for some scarce collectibles. Purchasing unfamiliar items should be avoided until a collector has fully researched the item's demand.

The six major ways to acquire autographed baseballs are:

1. Personal correspondence with an individual
2. Direct requests to the individual or team
3. Purchasing at an auction
4. Purchasing from a dealer or promoter
5. Purchasing items from related sources (antique dealers, etc....)
6. Trading

Personal correspondence with an individual

Obtaining signatures via direct mail requests to the individual has an unpredictable success rate. In addition to requests being lost or misplaced, many simply go unanswered. The increased popularity of the hobby has overwhelmed major league baseball players, who routinely receive vast autograph requests through the mail, as well as invitations to attend many baseball card star shows.

Direct requests to the individual or team

Direct autograph requests to an individual is still the preferred method of acquisition. Although an environment can have its drawbacks, autographs obtained at the ballpark, an airport, a hotel, a restaurant or a baseball card show can at least confirm authenticity. Few are fortunate enough to have direct contact with a major league ballclub, or to know a player on a personal level. But those who do are usually successful in obtaining many choice collectibles. Fortunately for collectors, many of these items eventually enter into the marketplace. Many collectors have even been particularly successful in establishing personal relationships with players in areas often overlooked by many hobbyists, such as the minor leagues, or through sports agents and reporters. Also, nothing prohibits collectors from contacting a team and inquiring about available souvenirs, such as authentic team baseballs. Whatever source is most preferred, collectors are advised to establish access to direct requests.

Purchasing at an auction

Coincident with the hobby's maturity has been the increased participation in the market by many major auction houses. These auctions are a platform for the sale of key hobby collectibles typically unavailable through local dealers or at area baseball card shows. Although shrewd buyers can find bargains, the excitement of the event usually lends itself to overpriced items. However, there are two key benefits from major auctions — the gauging of market demand, and the unearthing or discovery of many major collectibles. Auction catalogs, most of which provide a detailed description of the items, are generally available for purchase weeks before the event. Serious collectors who can't attend these auctions are still advised to purchase these catalogs for the research value they offer. Mail auctions are also common and, depending upon the material being offered, can attract large participation from hobbyists. Before participating, collectors who wish to acquire material via an auction should be aware of all the terms and conditions of sale.

Purchasing from a dealer or promoter

Purchasing autographed baseballs from a dealer or promoter is the most common form of acquisition. Collectors who do this should acquaint themselves with each dealer's knowledge level of autographed material, purchasing ability, return policy and guarantee of authenticity. Dealers can be particularly helpful in finding difficult items for your collection. Collectors can also provide a dealer with a want list, which should indicate price range, condition and time frame of the desired acquisition. Also, collectors should request dealers' mailing lists for future catalogs or sale notifications. The importance of buying only from established and reputable dealers cannot be stressed enough; it reduces the likelihood of potential problems resulting from the purchase of forged or stolen merchandise.

Contacts with major promoters can be invaluable. After a baseball card star show, promoters often have an excess of autographed material. This material, autographed to help defer show costs, is often sold at a dramatically reduced price. Also, many major promoters hold private autograph sessions with major stars, and some even split sessions with larger collectors to reduce costs. Private autograph sessions, which bypass all the associated costs of a major baseball card show, are extremely cost-effective and a trend in the hobby.

Purchasing items from related sources

Some parallel hobby enthusiasts, such as stamp, coin, and antique dealers, do buy and sell autographed baseballs. Since this is not the vendors' primary area of expertise, their knowledge of autographed material differs. Be cautious when purchasing from these sources because the risk of acquiring an unauthentic autographed baseball is enhanced.

Trading

Fellow collectors can be a good source for acquiring autographed baseballs. Many established hobbyists have built a wonderful network of individuals to trade with across the country. This by far is the most rewarding form of acquisition, since you often receive items to fill your needs, while supplying items to fill another collector's wants. The hobby is filled with interesting people; trading is an excellent way to get to know some of them.

COLLECTING HINTS

* Be cautious of investing in autographed baseballs that do not have a book value associated with them.

* Quality is paramount. If investment is a concern, purchase only items in Mint, Near Mint, or Excellent condition.

* Establishing strong contacts with major dealers or promoters can lead to cost-effective purchases of quality merchandise.

* Weigh the advantages of acquiring autographed baseballs at star shows. The costs associated with these shows, not to mention the aggravation, is beginning to prohibit the logic behind them.

* Don't pay full retail for an autographed baseball at a card show. All dealers are aware that these events favor a buyer's market.

* Avoid the temptation of purchasing overpriced autographed baseballs through department store catalogs and satellite television shows.

* Be aware of unusual or gimmick autographed baseballs. The term "limited edition" has become ambiguous.

* Don't speculate on rumors; the hobby is filled with them.

* Invest in autographed group baseballs only if there is a common theme.

* Don't add new signatures to an old baseball, and never retrace over an old signature.

1920

Bill Wambsganss used this ball to complete an unassisted triple play in the 1920 World Series.

CY = **Cy Young Award winner** **ROY** = **Rookie of the Year** **MVP** = **MVP Award winner**

***** = **player was traded** **HOF** = **Hall of Famer**

1920 BOSTON (AL) - Gene Bailey *, Ed Barrow (MANAGER), Cliff Brady, Bullet Joe Bush, Hack Eibel, Gary Fortune, Eddie Foster, Harry Harper, Jim Hendryx, Hob Hiller, Harry Hooper, Waite Hoyt, Sad Sam Jones, Benn Karr, Stuffy McInnis, Mike McNally, Mike Menosky, Elmer Myers *, Herb Pennock, Allen Russell, Wally Schang, Everett Scott, Jigger Statz *, Ossie Vitt, Roxy Walters

LESS THAN 10 GAMES: Bert Chaplin, Mickey Devine, Hal Deviney, Hack Eibel, Oscar Grimes, Herb Hunter, George Orme, Ben Paschal, Paddy Smith

KEY SIGNATURES: Barrow, Hendryx, Hooper, Pennock, Hoyt.

VALUE: $975

1920 BOSTON (NL) - Gene Bailey *, Tony Boeckel, Lloyd Christenbury, Walt Cruise, Eddie Eayrs, Dana Fillingim, Hod Ford, Hank Gowdy, Bunny Hearn, Walter Holke, Les Mann, Rabbit Maranville, Hugh McQuillan, Mickey O'Neil, Joe Oeschger, Charlie Pick, Ray Powell, Dick Rudolph, Jack Scott, George Stallings (MANAGER), John Sullivan, Mule Watson *, Art Wilson

LESS THAN 10 GAMES: Oscar Dugey, Johnny Jones, Al Pierotti, Johnny Rawlings *, Red Torphy, Ira Townsend, Leo Townsend, Tom Whelan

KEY SIGNATURES: Maranville, Powell, Mann.

VALUE: $640

1920 BROOKLYN - Leon Cadore, Rowdy Elliott, Tommy Griffith, Burleigh Grimes, Jimmy Johnston, Pete Kilduff, Ed Konetchy, Ernie Krueger, Bill Lamar, Al Mamaux, Rube Marquard, Bill McCabe *, Otto Miller, Clarence Mitchell, George Mohart, Hy Myers, Bernie Neis, Ivy Olson, Jeff Pfeffer, Wilbert Robinson (MANAGER), Ray Schmandt, Sherry Smith, Chuck Ward, Zack Wheat

LESS THAN 10 GAMES: Doug Baird *, Wally Hood *, Johnny Miljus, Jack Sheehan, Red Sheridan, Zack Taylor

NOTES: 4 HOF'ers

KEY SIGNATURES: Robinson, Konetchy, Myers, Wheat, Grimes, Marquard.

VALUE: $1400

1920 CHICAGO (AL) - Eddie Cicotte, Eddie Collins, Shano Collins, Red Faber, Happy Felsch, Chick Gandil, Kid Gleason (MANAGER), Spencer Heath, Joe Jackson, Ted Jourdan, Dickie Kerr, Nemo Leibold, Byrd Lynn, Harvey McClellan, Fred McMullin, Eddie Murphy, George Payne, Swede Risberg, Ray Schalk, Amos Strunk *, Buck Weaver, Roy Wilkinson, Lefty Williams

LESS THAN 10 GAMES: Bibb Falk, Shovel Hodge, Bubber Jonnard, Joe Kiefer, Grover Lowdermilk

NOTES: Perhaps the most sought-after baseball of all time due to its historical significance (the exception being a 1919 Chicago White Sox ball). The value is uncertain.

KEY SIGNATURES: Collins, Risberg, Weaver, Leibold, Felsch, Jackson, Schalk, Faber, Williams, Kerr, Cicotte.

VALUE: Uncertain

1920 CINCINNATI - Nick Allen, Rube Bressler, Sam Crane, Jake Daubert, Pat Duncan, Hod Eller, Ray Fisher, Heinie Groh, Larry Kopf, Dolf Luque, Pat Moran (MANAGER), Greasy Neale, Bill Rariden, Morrie Rath, Jimmy Ring, Edd Roush, Dutch Ruether, Slim Sallee, Eddie Sicking *, Ivy Wingo

LESS THAN 10 GAMES: Lynn Brenton, Fritz Coumbe, George Lowe, Buddy Napier, Charlie See, Dazzy Swartz, Jack Theis

KEY SIGNATURES: Daubert, Roush.

VALUE: $560

1920 CLEVELAND - Jim Bagby, George Burns *, Ray Caldwell, Ray Chapman, Bob Clark, Stan Coveleski, Joe Evans, Tony Faeth, Larry Gardner, Jack Graney, Charlie Jamieson, Doc Johnston, Harry Lunte, Guy Morton, Elmer Myers, Dick Niehaus, Les Nunamaker, Steve O'Neill, Joe Sewell, Elmer Smith, Tris Speaker (MANAGER), Tris Speaker, George Uhle, Bill Wambsganss, Smokey Joe Wood

LESS THAN 10 GAMES: Joe Boehling, George Ellison, Duster Mails, Tim Murchison, Pinch Thomas

NOTES: World Champions! 3 HOF'ers; Chapman killed by pitch thrown by Carl Mays. (8/16/20)

KEY SIGNATURES: Wambsganss, Chapman, Gardner, Smith, Speaker, Jamieson, O'Neill, Sewell, Coveleski.

VALUE: $1650

1920 DETROIT - Eddie Ainsmith, Ernie Alten, Doc Ayres, Donie Bush, Ty Cobb, Hooks Dauss, Howard Ehmke, Bert Ellison, Ira Flagstead, Sammy Hale, Harry Heilmann, Clarence Huber, Hughie Jennings (MANAGER), Bob Jones, Dutch Leonard, Clyde Manion,

Frank Okrie, Red Oldham, Babe Pinelli, Chick Shorten, Oscar Stanage, Bobby Veach, Larry Woodall, Ralph Young

LESS THAN 10 GAMES: Harry Baumgartner, John Bogart, Bernie Boland, Dave Claire, Allen Conkwright, Jack Coombs, Red Cox, Ray Crumpler, Cy Fried, John Glaiser, Slim Love, Bill Morrisette, Lou Vedder, Mutt Wilson

KEY SIGNATURES: Jennings, Heilmann, Cobb, Veach.

VALUE: $2125

1920 NEW YORK (AL) - Ping Bodie, Rip Collins, Chick Fewster, Frank Gleich, Truck Hannah, Fred Hofmann, Miller Huggins (MANAGER), Duffy Lewis, Joe Lucey, Bob McGraw, Bob Meusel, George Mogridge, Roger Peckinpaugh, Wally Pipp, Del Pratt, Jack Quinn, Muddy Ruel, Babe Ruth, Bob Shawkey, Ernie Shore, Hank Thormahlen, Sammy Vick, Aaron Ward

LESS THAN 10 GAMES: Tom Connelly, Ray French, Carl Mays, Lefty O'Doul

KEY SIGNATURES: Huggins, Pratt, Ruth, Mays, Shawkey.

VALUE: $2700

1920 NEW YORK (NL) - Dave Bancroft *, Jesse Barnes, Rube Benton, George Burns, Phil Douglas, Larry Doyle, Art Fletcher *, Frankie Frisch, Mike Gonzalez, Roy Grimes, Bill Hubbell *, Benny Kauff, George Kelly, Lee King, Fred Lear, Al Lefevre, Lew McCarty *, John McGraw (MANAGER), Art Nehf, Eddie Sicking *, Earl Smith, Frank Snyder, Vern Spencer, Jigger Statz *, Fred Toney, Jesse Winters, Ross Youngs

LESS THAN 10 GAMES: Doug Baird *, Virgil Barnes, Eddie Brown, Claude Davenport, Alex Gaston, Pug Griffin, Tom Grubbs, Bob Kinsella, Pol Perritt, Rosy Ryan, Slim Sallee *, Curt Walker

NOTES: 5 HOF'ers.

KEY SIGNATURES: McGraw, Kelly, Bancroft, Frisch, Youngs, Toney, Nehf, Barnes.

VALUE: $2100

HOF = Hall of Famer

1920 PHILADELPHIA (AL) - Lyle Bigbee, George Burns *, Dick Burrus, Joe Dugan, Jimmy Dykes, Chick Galloway, Ivy Griffin, Slim Harriss, Bob Hasty, Charlie High, Paul Johnson, Dave Keefe, Walt Kinney, Connie Mack (MANAGER), Emmett McCann, Roy Moore, Glen Myatt, Rollie Naylor, Cy Perkins, Scott Perry, Eddie Rommel, Red Shannon *, Amos Strunk *, Lena Styles, Fred Thomas *, Frank Walker, Tilly Walker, Frank Welch, Ed Wingo *, Whitey Witt

LESS THAN 10 GAMES: Charlie Eckert, Fred Heimach, Bill Kelly, Dan Kerns, Bill Knowlton, Pat Martin, Bill Shanner, John Slappey, Johnny Walker

KEY SIGNATURES: Mack.

VALUE: $700

1920 PHILADELPHIA (NL) - Dave Bancroft *, Huck Betts, Red Causey, Gavvy Cravath, Johnny Enzmann, Art Fletcher *, Bert Gallia, Bill Hubbell *, Bevo LeBourveau, Fred Luderus, Lee Meadows, Irish Meusel, Dots Miller, Ralph Miller, Gene Paulette, Johnny Rawlings *, Eppa Rixey, George Smith, Casey Stengel, Walt Tragesser, Walt Walsh, Lefty Weinert, Mack Wheat, Cy Williams, Frank Withrow, Russ Wrighstone

LESS THAN 10 GAMES: Mike Cantwell, Gavvy Cravath (MANAGER), Jimmie Keenan

KEY SIGNATURES: Stengel, Williams, Meusel, Wheat, Rixey.

VALUE: $980

1920 PITTSBURGH - Babe Adams, Walter Barbare, Clyde Barnhart, Carson Bigbee, Max Carey, Hal Carlson, Buster Caton, Wilbur Cooper, George Cutshaw, Charlie Grimm, Bill Haeffner, Earl Hamilton, Bill Hinchman, Cliff Lee, Bill McKechnie, Fred Nicholson, Elmer Ponder, Walter Schmidt, Billy Southworth, Homery Summa, Cotton Tierney, Pie Traynor, Possum Whitted, John Wisner

LESS THAN 10 GAMES: Sheriff Blake, Nig Clarke, George Gibson (MANAGER), Whitey Glazner, Wally Hood *, Johnny Meador, Johnny Morrison, Mule Watson *, Jimmy Zinn

KEY SIGNATURES: Carey, McKechnie, Traynor, Cooper.

VALUE: $825

1920 ST. LOUIS (AL) - Jimmy Austin, Billy Bayne, Josh Billings, Jimmy Burke (MANAGER), Bill Burwell, Pat Collins, Dixie Davis, Joe DeBerry, Joe Gedeon, Wally Gerber, Johnnie Heving, Baby Doll Jacobson, Marty McManus, Earl Pruess, Hank Severeid, Urban Shocker, George Sisler, Earl Smith, Allen Sothoron, Frank Thompson, Jack Tobin, Elam Vangilder, Carl Weilman, Ken Williams

LESS THAN 10 GAMES: George Boehler, Bert Gallia, Lyman Lamb, Dud Lee, Lefty Leifield, Hod Leverette, Adrian Lynch, Billy Mullen, Ray Richmond, Roy Sanders, Jack Scheneberg, John Shovlin, Paul Speraw, Dutch Wetzel

NOTES: Sisler's .407 season.

KEY SIGNATURES: Sisler, Tobin, Jacobson, Williams, Shocker.

VALUE: $525

1920 ST. LOUIS (NL) - Vern Clemons, Pickles Dillhoefer, Bill Doak, Jack Fournier, Marv Goodwin, Jesse Haines, Cliff Heathcote, Rogers Hornsby, Elmer Jacobs, Hal Janvrin, Mike Knode, Doc Lavan, Jakie May, Austin McHenry, Lou North, Branch Rickey (MANAGER), Joe Schultz, Ferdie Schupp, Bill Sherdel, Burt Shotton, Jack Smith, Milt Stock

LESS THAN 10 GAMES: George Gilham, Bob Glenn, Tim Griesenbeck, Ed Hock, Hal Kime, Mike Kitcher, George Lyons, Lew McCarty *, Heinie Mueller, Bill Schindler, Walt Schulz, George Scott, Oscar Tuero

KEY SIGNATURES: Rickey, Fournier, Hornsby, Stock, Doak, Haines.

VALUE: $1400

1920 WASHINGTON - Jose Acosta, Frank Brower, Jack Calvo, Harry Courtney, Frank Ellerbe, Eric Erickson, Patsy Gharrity, Clark Griffith (MANAGER), Bucky Harris, Walter Johnson, Joe Judge, George McBride, Clyde Milan, Jim O'Neill, Frank O'Rourke, Val Picinich, Sam Rice, Braggo Roth, Al Schact, Howard Shanks, Red Shannon *, Jim Shaw, Bill Snyder, Ricardo Torres, Tom Zachary

LESS THAN 10 GAMES: Harry Biemiller, Gus Bono, Elmer Bowman, Leon Carlson, Jerry Conway, Joe Engel, Clarence Fisher, Joe Gleason, Bill Hollahan, Ed Johnson, Bobby LaMotte, Joe Leonard, Douc Prothro, Duke Shirey, Fred Thomas *

KEY SIGNATURES: Griffith, Judge, Harris, Rice, Milan, Johnson.

VALUE: $1650

1921

1921 New York Yankees World Series participants

* = **player was traded**

1921 BOSTON (AL) - Bullet Joe Bush, Hugh Duffy (MANAGER), Shano Collins, Eddie Foster, Tim Hendryx, Benn Karr, Nemo Leibold, Stuffy McInnis, Mike Menosky, Elmer Myers, Ernie Neitzke, Herb Pennock, Pinky Pittinger, Del Pratt, Muddy Ruel, Allen Russell, Everett Scott, Hank Thormahlen, Sammy Vick, Ossie Vitt, Roxy Walters

LESS THAN 10 GAMES: Bert Chaplin, Sam Dodge, Curt Fullerton, Hob Hiller, Sad Sam Jones, Jack Perrin, Allen Sothoron

KEY SIGNATURES: Duffy, McInnis, Pratt, Leibold, Menosky, Jones, Pennock.

VALUE: $680

1921 BOSTON (NL) - Walter Barbare, Tony Boeckel, Garland Braxton, Lloyd Christenbury, Walton Cruise, Dana Fillingim, Hod Ford, Frank Gibson, Hank Gowdy, Walter Holke, Hugh McQuillan, Fred Mitchell (MANAGER), Cy Morgan, Fred Nicholson, Al Nixon, Mickey O'Neil, Joe Oeschger, Ray Powell, Jack Scott, Billy Southworth, John Sullivan, Mule Watson

LESS THAN 10 GAMES: Johnny Cooney, Eddie Eayrs, Al Pierotti, Dick Rudolph, Ira Townsend, Leo Townsend

NOTES: Rudolph never played a game, but was on the team the entire year.

KEY SIGNATURES: Barbare, Boeckel, Southworth, Powell, Cruise, Oeschger.

VALUE: $500

1921 BROOKLYN - Leon Cadore, Tommy Griffith, Burleigh Grimes, Wally Hood, Hal Janvrin *, Jimmy Johnston, Pete Kilduff, Ed Konetchy *, Ernie Krueger, Al Mamaux, Johnny Miljus, Otto Miller, Clarence Mitchell, Hy Myers, Bernie Neis, Ivy Olson, Wilbert Robinson (MANAGER), Dutch Ruether, Ray Schmandt, Ferdie Schupp *, Sherry Smith, Zack Taylor, Chuck Ward, Zack Wheat

LESS THAN 10 GAMES: Sweetsbreads Bailey, Eddie Eayrs *, Ray Gordinier, Bill Lamar, George Mohart, Jeff Pfeffer *, Jack Sheehan

KEY SIGNATURES: Robinson, Schmandt, Johnston, Griffith, Wheat, Grimes.

VALUE: $1000

1921 CHICAGO (AL) - Bugs Bennett *, Babe Blackburn, Fred Bratchi, Eddie Collins, Lum Davenport, Red Faber, Bibb Falk, Hod Fenner, Shovel Hodge, Harry Hooper, Ernie Johnson, Dickie Kerr, George Lees, Harvey McClellan, Doug McWeeny, John Michaelson, Johnny Mostil, Eddie Mulligan, Dominick Mulrennan, Red Ostergard, Russ Pence, Jack Russell, Ray Schalk, Earl Sheely, Amos Strunk, Jack Wieneke, Roy Wilkinson, Yam Yaryan

LESS THAN 10 GAMES: Sarge Connally, Kid Gleason (MANAGER), Elmer Leifer, Eddie Murphy, Frank Pratt, Lee Thompson, Cy Twombly

NOTES: 4 HOF'ers.

KEY SIGNATURES: Sheely, Collins, Hooper, Strunk, Schalk, Faber.

HOF = Hall of Famer

VALUE: $920

1921 CHICAGO (NL) - Pete Alexander, Turner Barber, Virgil Cheeves, Tom Daly, Charlie Deal, Carter Elliott, Johnny Evers (MANAGER), Max Flack, Buck Freeman, Ray Grimes, Charlie Hollocher, Percy Jones, John Kelleher, Bill Killefer (MANAGER), George Maisel, Bill Marriott, Speed Martin, Bob O'Farrell, Elmer Ponder *, Dave Robertson *, John Sullivan *, Zeb Terry, Babe Twombly, Lefty Tyler, Hippo Vaughn, Hooks Warner, Lefty York

LESS THAN 10 GAMES: Sweetbreads Bailey *, Oscar Fuhr, Ollie Hanson, Claude Hendrix, Tony Kaufmann, Vic Keen, Joe Klugman, George Stueland, Red Thomas, Kettle Wirtz

NOTES: Hendrix was unofficially declared ineligible for life; Killefer was a player/manager during the season.

KEY SIGNATURES: Evers, Grimes, Flack, Maisel, Barber, Alexander.

VALUE: $1500

1921 CINCINNATI - Sammy Bohne, Lynn Brenton, Rube Bressler, Fritz Coumbe, Sam Crane, Jake Daubert, Pete Donohue, Pat Duncan, Hod Eller, Lew Fonseca, Bob Geary, Heinie Groh, Bubbles Hargrave, Larry Kopf, Dolf Luque, Cliff Markle, Rube Marquard, Pat Moran (MANAGER), Buddy Napier, Greasy Neale *, Dode Paskert, Eppa Rixey, Edd Roush, Charlie See, Denny Williams, Ivy Wingo

LESS THAN 10 GAMES: Alan Clarke, Astyanax Douglas, Ray Fisher, Kenny Hogan, Wally Kimmick, Clint Rogge

NOTES: Fisher was thrown out of the game for life.

KEY SIGNATURES: Daubert, Groh, Bressler, Roush, Duncan, Rixey, Marquard.

VALUE: $675

1921 CLEVELAND - Jim Bagby, George Burns, Ray Caldwell, Stan Coveleski, Joe Evans, Larry Gardner, Jack Graney, Charlie Jamieson, Doc Johnston, Duster Mails, Guy Morton, Les Nunamaker, Steve O'Neill, Ted Odenwald, Joe Sewell, Ginger Shinault, Elmer

Smith, Allen Sothoron *, Tris Speaker (MANAGER), Riggs Stephenson, Pinch Thomas, George Uhle, Bil Wambsganss, Smokey Joe Wood

LESS THAN 10 GAMES: Bob Clark, Lou Guisto, Bernie Henderson, Tex Jeanes, Jesse Petty, Luke Sewell, Art Wilson

NOTES: Speaker was a player/manager.

KEY SIGNATURES: Speaker, Sewell, Gardner, Jamieson, O'Neill, Coveleski.

VALUE: $900

1921 DETROIT - Eddie Ainsmith *, Johnny Bassler, Lu Blue, Donie Bush *, Ty Cobb (MANAGER), Bert Cole, Hooks Dauss, Howard Ehmke, Ira Flagstead, Harry Heilmann, Carl Holling, Bob Jones, Dutch Leonard, Clyde Manion, Herm Merritt, Jim Middleton, Red Oldham, Slicker Parks, Joe Sargent, Chick Shorten, Suds Sutherland, Bobby Veach, Larry Woodall, Ralph Young

LESS THAN 10 GAMES: Doc Ayres, Sammy Barnes, Danny Boone, George Cunningham, Sammy Hale, Clarence Huber, Pol Perritt, Lefty Stewart, Jackie Tavener, Jim Walsh

NOTES: Cobb was a player/manager.

KEY SIGNATURES: Cobb, Blue, Heilmann, Veach, Bassler, Jones.

VALUE: $1000

1921 NEW YORK (AL) - Frank Baker, Ping Bodie, Rip Collins, Al DeVormer, Alex Ferguson, Chick Fewster, Frank Gleich, Chicken Hawks, Fred Hofmann, Waite Hoyt, Miller Huggins (MANAGER), Carl Mays, Mike McNally, Bob Meusel, Elmer Miller, Johnny Mitchell, Roger Peckinpaugh, Bill Percy, Wally Pipp, Jack Quinn, Braggo Roth, Babe Ruth, Wally Schang, Bob Shawkey, Tom Sheehan, Aaron Ward

LESS THAN 10 GAMES: Tom Connelly, Harry Harper, Tom Rogers

NOTES: 4 HOF'ers.

KEY SIGNATURES: Huggins, Ward, Baker, Meusel, Ruth, Mays, Hoyt.

VALUE: $2700

HOF = Hall of Famer

1921 NEW YORK (NL) - Dave Bancroft, Jesse Barnes, Eddie Brown, George Burns, Bill Cunningham, Phil Douglas, Frankie Frisch, Alex Gaston, Mike Gonzalez, Claude Jonnard, George Kelly, Lee King *, John McGraw (MANAGER), Irish Meusel *, John Monroe *, Art Nehf, Bill Patterson, Goldie Rapp *, Johnny Rawlings *, Rosy Ryan, Slim Sallee, Earl Smith, Frank Snyder, Casey Stengel *, Fred Toney, Curt Walker *, Russ Youngs

LESS THAN 10 GAMES: Rube Benton, Howard Berry, Red Causey, Joe Connolly, Bud Heine, Butch Henline *, Benny Kauff, Wally Kopf, Jim Mahady, Pol Perritt, Hank Schreiber, Red Shea, Walt Zink

NOTES: World Champions! 6 HOF'ers; Benton was thrown out of league and Kauff was thrown out of game; Kauff's signature would be rare on this team baseball.

KEY SIGNATURES: McGraw, Kelly, Bancroft, Frisch, Youngs, Meusel, Snyder, Stengel, Nehf.

VALUE: $2400

1921 PHILADELPHIA (AL) - Bill Barrett, Frank Brazill, Frank Callaway, Zip Collins, Joe Dugan, Jimmy Dykes, Chick Galloway, Ivy Griffin, Slim Harriss, Bob Hasty, Paul Johnson, Dave Keefe, Connie Mack (MANAGER), Emmett McCann, Roy Moore,

Glenn Myatt, Rollie Naylor, Cy Perkins, Scott Perry, Eddie Rommel, Frank Walker, Johnny Walker, Tilly Walker, Frank Welch, Whitey Witt

LESS THAN 10 GAMES: Bill Bishop, Harvey Freeman, Dot Fulghum, Fred Heimach, Ben Mallonee, Ray Miner, Red Shannon, Lena Styles, Jim Sullivan, Arlas Taylor, Lefty Wolf, Elmer Yoter

KEY SIGNATURES: Mack, Witt, T. Walker.

VALUE: $620

1921 PHILADELPHIA (NL) - Stan Baumgartner, Huck Betts, Frank Bruggy, Wild Bill Donovan (MANAGER), Butch Henline *, Bill Hubbell, Jimmie Keenan, Lee King *, Ed Konetchy *, Cliff Lee, Bevo LeBourveau, Lee Meadows, Irish Meusel *, Dots Miller, Ralph Miller, John Monroe *, Greasy Neale *, Frank Parkinson, John Peters, Goldie Rapp *, Johnny Rawlings *, Lance Richbourg, Jimmy Ring, Duke Sedgwick, George Smith, Jimmy Smith, Casey Stengel, Curt Walker *, Mack Wheat, Kaiser Wilhelm (MANAGER), Cy Williams, Jesse Winters, Russ Wrightstone

LESS THAN 10 GAMES: Petie Behan, Red Causey *, Don Rader, Lefty Weinert, Kaiser Wilhelm

KEY SIGNATURES: Konetchy, Williams, Meusel, Bruggy, Stengel.

VALUE: $500

1921 PITTSBURGH - Babe Adams, Clyde Barnhart, Carson Bigbee, Tony Brottem *, Max Carey, Hal Carlson, Wilbur Cooper, George Cutshaw, Kiki Cuyler, George Gibson (MANAGER), Whitey Glazner, Johnny Gooch, Charlie Grimm, Earl Hamilton, Rabbit Maranville, Johnny Mokan, Johnny Morrison, Dave Robertson *, Ray Rohwer, Walter Schmidt, Bill Skiff, Cotton Tierney, Pie Traynor, Bill Warwick, Possum Whitted, Mike Wilson, Chief Yellowhorse, Jimmy Zinn

LESS THAN 10 GAMES: Lyle Bigbee, Bill Hughes, Phill Morrison, Elmer Ponder *, Drew Rader, Rip Wheeler

NOTES: 4 HOF'ers.

KEY SIGNATURES: Cuthsaw, Maranville, Carey, Bigbee, Traynor, Cuyler, Cooper.

HOF = Hall of Famer

VALUE: $1000

1921 ST. LOUIS (AL) - Jimmy Austin, Bill Bayne, Josh Billings, Bill Burwell, Pat Collins, Dixie Davis, Joe DeBerry, Frank Ellerbe *, Lee Fohl (MANAGER), Wally Gerber, Billy Gleason, Baby Doll Jacobson, Ray Kolp, Lyman Lamb, Dud Lee, Marty McManus, Emilio Palmero, Hank Severeid, Urban Shocker, George Sisler, Earl Smith *, Jack Tobin, Elam Vangilder, Dutch Wetzel, Ken Williams

LESS THAN 10 GAMES: Bugs Bennett *, George Boehler, Bernie Boland, Nick Cullop, Dutch Henry, Billy Mullen, Ray Richmond, Jim Riley, Allen Sothoron *, Luke Stuart

KEY SIGNATURES: Sisler, Tobin, Jacobson, Williams, Severeid, Shocker.

VALUE: $525

1921 ST. LOUIS (NL) - Eddie Ainsmith *, Bill Bailey, Vern Clemons, Pickles Dillhoefer, Bill Doak, Jack Fournier, Marv Goodwin, Jesse Haines, Cliff Heathcore, Rogers Hornsby, Hal Janvrin *, Doc Lavan, Les Mann, Austin McHenry, Heinie Mueller, Lou North, Bill Pertica, Jeff Pfeffer *, Branch Rickey (MANAGER), Tink Riviere, Joe Schultz, Bill Sherdel, Burt Shotton, Jack Smith, Milt Stock, Specs Toporcer, Roy Walker

LESS THAN 10 GAMES: Reuben Ewing, George Gilham, Herb Hunter, Walt Irwin,

Howie Jones, Mike Kircher, Jakie May, Lew McCarty, Charlie Niebergall, Ferdie Schupp *

NOTES: Dillhoefer died 2/22/22; McHenry died 11/27/22.

KEY SIGNATURES: Rickey, Fournier, Hornsby, Stock, Smith, Mann, McHenry, Clemons, Dillhoefer, Haines, Doak.

VALUE: $1350

1921 WASHINGTON - Jose Acosta, Frank Brower, Donie Bush *, Harry Courtney, Frank Ellerbe *, Eric Erickson, Patsy Gharrity, Goose Goslin, Bucky Harris, Walter Johnson, Joe Judge, Bobby LaMotte, Duffy Lewis, Clyde Milan, Bing Miller, George Mogridge, Frank O'Rourke, Val Picinich, Sam Rice, Al Schact, Howard Shanks, Jim Shaw, Earl Smith *, Tom Zachary

LESS THAN 10 GAMES: Red Bird, Tony Brottem *, George Foss, Nemo Gaines, George McBride (MANAGER), Vance McIlree, Ralph Miller, Tom Phillips, Ricardo Torres, Frank Woodward

NOTES: 4 HOF'ers.

KEY SIGNATURES: Judge, Harris, Shanks, Rice, Gharrity, Goslin, Johnson.

HOF = Hall of Famer

VALUE: $1250

1922

Rogers Hornsby won the Triple Crown in 1922.

1922 BOSTON (AL) - George Burns, Bert Chaplin, Rip Collins, Shano Collins, Hugh Duffy (MANAGER), Joe Dugan *, Alex Ferguson, Chick Fewster *, Eddie Foster *, Curt Fullerton, Joe Harris, Benn Karr, Nemo Leibold, Chick Maynard, Mike Menosky, Elmer Miller *, Johnny Mitchell *, Frank O'Rourke, Herb Pennock, Bill Piercy, Pinky Pittinger, Del Pratt, Jack Quinn, Muddy Ruel, Allen Russell, Elmer Smith *, Roxy Walters

LESS THAN 10 GAMES: Sam Dodge, Walt Lynch, Elmer Myers, Dick Reichle

KEY SIGNATURES: Duffy, Burns, Pratt, Harris, Pennock.

VALUE: $625

*** = player was traded**

1922 BOSTON (NL) - Walter Barbare, Tony Boeckel, Garland Braxton, Lloyd Christenbury, Walton Cruise, Dana Fillingim, Hod Ford, Frank Gibson, Hank Gowdy, Snake Henry, Walter Holke, Larry Kopf, Gene Lansing, Rube Marquard, Tim McNamara, Hugh McQuillan *, Frank Miller, Fred Mitchell (MANAGER), Fred Nicholson, Al Nixon, Mickey O'Neil, Joe Oeschger, Ray Powell, Bunny Roser, Billy Southworth, Mule Watson

LESS THAN 10 GAMES: Johnny Cooney, Gil Gallagher, Joe Genewich, Harry Hulihan, Joe Mathews, Cy Morgan, Dick Rudolph, Al Yeargin

KEY SIGNATURES: Marquard.

VALUE: $450

1922 BROOKLYN - Leon Cadore, Art Decatur, Hank DeBerry, Bert Griffith, Tommy Griffith, Burleigh Grimes, Andy High, Bernie Hungling, Hal Janvrin, Jimmy Johnston, Al Mamaux, Otto Miller, Clarence Mitchell, Hy Myers, Bernie Neis, Ivy Olson, Wilbert Robinson (MANAGER), Dutch Ruether, Ray Schmandt, Harry Shriver, Sherry Smith *, Dazzy Vance, Chuck Ward, Zack Wheat

LESS THAN 10 GAMES: Sam Crane, Ray Gordinier, Wally Hood, Jim Murray, Sam Post, Paul Schreiber, Zack Taylor, Possum Whitted

NOTES: 4 HOF'ers.

KEY SIGNATURES: Johnston, Robinson, Myers, Wheat, DeBerry, Ruether, Vance, Grimes, T. Griffith.

VALUE: $1250

HOF = Hall of Famer

1922 CHICAGO (AL) - Ted Blankenship, Eddie Collins, Harry Courtney *, Red Faber, Bibb Falk, Shovel Hodge, Harry Hooper, Ernie Johnson, Dickie Kerr, Dixie Leverett, Harvey McClellan, John Mostil, Eddie Mulligan, Charlie Robertson, Ray Schalk, Ferdie Schupp, Earl Sheely, Amos Strunk, Yam Yaryan

LESS THAN 10 GAMES: Jose Acosta, Homer Blankenship, Emmett Bowles, Hal Bubser, Ernie Cox, Lum Davenport, Larry Duff, Johnny Evers, Kid Gleason (MANAGER), Roy Graham, John Jenkins, Jimmie Long, Frank Mack, Dick McCabe, Doug McWeeny, Elmer Pence, Jack Russell, Augie Swentor, Roy Wilkinson

NOTES: 5 HOF'ers.

KEY SIGNATURES: Sheely, Collins, Hooper, Mostil, Schalk, Evers, Faber.

VALUE: $1350

1922 CHICAGO (NL) - Sparky Adams, Vic Aldridge, Pete Alexander, Turner Barber, Marty Callaghan, Virgil Cheeves, Max Flack *, Buck Freeman, Barney Friberg, Ray Grimes, Gabby Hartnett, Cliff Heathcote *, Charlie Hollocher, Percy Jones, Tony Kaufmann, John Kelleher, Bill Killefer (MANAGER), Marty Krug, George Maisel, Hack Miller, Bob O'Farrell, Tiny Osborne, Jigger Statz, George Stueland, Zeb Terry, Kettle Wirts

LESS THAN 10 GAMES: Harvey Cotter, Uel Eubanks, Howie Fitzgerald, Fred Fussel, Walt Golvin, George Grantham, Vic Keen, Joe Klugman, Speed Martin, Ed Morris, Butch Weis

KEY SIGNATURES: Grimes, Hollocher, Friberg, Miller, O'Farrell, Hartnett, Alexander.

VALUE: $1000

1922 CINCINNATI - Sammy Bohne, Rube Bressler, George Burns, Ike Caveney, Johnny Couch, Jake Daubert, Pete Donohue, Pat Duncan, Lew Fonesca, John Gillespie, Bubbles Hargrave, George Harper, Cactus Keck, Dolf Luque, Cliff Markle, Pat Moran (MAN-

AGER), Greasy Neale, Babe Pinelli, Eppa Rixey, Edd Roush, Karl Schnell, Ivy Wingo

LESS THAN 10 GAMES: Red Lutz, Jack Scott

KEY SIGNATURES: Daubert, Pinelli, Harper, Duncan, Hargrave, Roush, Rixey.

VALUE: $530

1922 CLEVELAND - Jim Bagby, Danny Boone, Joe Connolly, Stan Coveleski, Jim Joe Edwards, Joe Evans, Larry Gardner, Jack Graney, Lou Guisto, Charlie Jamieson, Dave Keefe, Jim Lindsey, Duster Mails, Stuffy McGinnis, Pat McNulty, Guy Morton, Les Nunamker, Steve O'Neill, Joe Sewell, Luke Sewell, Ginger Shinault, Tris Speaker (MANAGER), Riggs Stephenson, Homer Summa, George Uhle, Bill Wambsganss, Smokey Joe Wood

LESS THAN 10 GAMES: Phil Bedgood, Uke Clanton, Bill Doran, Logan Drake, George Edmondson, Doc Hamann, Jack Hammond *, Tex Jeanes, Ike Kahdot, Dewey Metivier, John Middleton, Ted Odenwald, Nellie Pott, Joe Rabbitt, Joe Shaute, Sherry Smith, Chick Sorrells, Allen Sothoron, George Winn

NOTES: Speaker was a player/coach.

KEY SIGNATURES: Speaker, McGinnis, Sewell, Uhle, Jamieson, O'Neill, Coveleski.

VALUE: $850

1922 DETROIT - Johnny Bassler, Lu Blue, Dan Clark, Ty Cobb (MANAGER), Bert Cole, George Cutshaw, Hooks Dauss, Howard Ehmke, Ira Flagstead, Bob Fotherfill, Fred Haney, Harry Heilmann, Syl Johnson, Bob Jones, Dutch Leonard, Clyde Manion, Red Oldham, Ole Olsen, Herman Pillette, Topper Rigney, Lil Stoner, Bobby Veach, Larry Woodall

LESS THAN 10 GAMES: Chick Gagnon, Carl Holling, Ken Holloway, Johnny Mohardt, Roy Moore *

NOTES: Cobb ".401" season; Cobb was a player/manager; Leonard retired.

KEY SIGNATURES: Cobb, Blue, Rigney, Heilmann, Veach, Bassler.

VALUE: $960

1922 NEW YORK (AL) - Frank Baker, Bullet Joe Bush, Al DeVormer, Joe Dugan *, Chick Fewster *, Fred Hofmann, Waite Hoyt, Miller Huggins (MANAGER), Sad Sam Jones, Carl Mays, Norm McMillan, Mike McNally, Bob Meusel, Elmer Miller *, George Murray, Wally Pipp, Babe Ruth, Wally Schang, Everett Scott, Bob Shawkey, Camp Skinner, Elmer Smith *, Aaron Ward, Whitey Witt

LESS THAN 10 GAMES: Clem Llewellyn, Johnny Mitchell *, Lefty O'Doul

NOTES: 4 HOF'ers; Ruth and Meusel were suspended during the year.

KEY SIGNATURES: Pipp, Meusel, Ruth, Schang, Baker, Bush, Shawkey, Hoyt, Huggins.

VALUE: $2550

HOF = Hall of Famer

1922 NEW YORK (NL) - Dave Bancroft, Jesse Barnes, Virgil Barnes, Red Causey, Bill Cunningham, Phil Douglas, Frankie Frisch, Alex Gaston, Heinie Groh, Claude Jonnard, George Kelly, Lee King *, John McGraw (MANAGER), Hugh McQuillan *, Irish Meusel, Art Nehf, Johnny Rawlings, Dave Robertson, Rosy Ryan, Jack Scott *, Red Shea, Ralph Shinners, Earl Smith, Frank Snyder, Casey Stengel, Fred Toney, Ross Youngs

LESS THAN 10 GAMES: Howard Berry, Clint Blume, Ike Boone, Mike Cvengros, Cozy Dolan, Mahlon Higbee, Carmen Hill, Travis Jackson, Fred Johnson, Waddy MacPhee, Freddie Maguire

NOTES: World Champions! 7 HOF'ers.

KEY SIGNATURES: McGraw, Kelly, Frisch, Bancroft, Youngs, Stengel, Meusel, Snyder, Jackson, Nehf.

VALUE: $2350

1922 PHILADELPHIA (AL) - Frank Bruggy, Frank Callaway, Jimmy Dykes, Charlie Eckert, Ollie Fuhrman, Chick Galloway, Slim Harriss, Bob Hasty, Joe Hauser, Fred Heimach, Doc Johnston, Connie Mack (MANAGER), Beauty McGowan, Bing Miller, Roy Moore *, Rollie Naylor, Curly Ogden, Eddie Rommel, Heinie Scheer, Jim Sullivan, Tilly Walker, Frank Welch, Rube Yarrison, Ralph Young

LESS THAN 10 GAMES: Johnny Berger, Frank Brazill, Gus Ketchum, Frank McCue, Harry O'Neill, Cy Perkins, Otto Rettig, Red Schillings

KEY SIGNATURES: Mack, Hauser, Galloway, Rommel, Miller.

VALUE: $600

1922 PHILADELPHIA (NL) - Art Fletcher, Butch Henline, Bill Hubbell, Lee King *, Cliff Lee, Roy Leslie, Bevo LeBourveau, Lee Meadows, Johnny Mokan *, Frank Parkinson, John Peters, Goldie Rapp, Jimmy Ring, John Singleton, George Smith, Jimmy Smith, Curt Walker, Lefty Weinert, Kaiser Wilhelm (MANAGER), Cy Williams, Jesse Winters, Frank Withrow, Russ Wrightstone

LESS THAN 10 GAMES: Stan Baumgartner, Petie Behan, Stan Benton, Huck Betts, Letron Pinto, Tom Sullivan

KEY SIGNATURES: Walker, Williams, Lee, Henline.

VALUE: $400

1922 PITTSBURGH - Babe Adams, Clyde Barnhart, Carson Bigbee, Max Carey, Hal Carlson, Wilbur Cooper, Jewel Ens, George Gibson (MANAGER), Whitey Glazner, Johnny Gooch, Charlie Grimm, Earl Hamilton, Rabbit Maranville, Jim Mattox, Johnny Mokan *, Johnny Morrison, Walter Mueller, Ray Rohwer, Reb Russell, Walter Schmidt, Cotton Tierney, Pie Traynor, Chief Yellowhorse

LESS THAN 10 GAMES: Myrl Brown, Kiki Cuyler, Jack Hammond *, Bonnie Hollingsworth, Bubber Jonnard, Grover Lovelace, Bill McKechnie (MANAGER), Tom McNamara, Art Merewether, Jake Miller, Stuffy Stewart, Rip Wheeler, Jimmy Zinn

NOTES: 5 HOF'ers.

KEY SIGNATURES: McKechnie, Tierney, Maranville, Traynor, Russell, Carey, Bigbee, Gooch, Cuyler, Cooper.

VALUE: $1200

HOF = Hall of Famer

1922 ST. LOUIS (AL) - Jimmy Austin, Bill Bayne, Herman Bronkie, Pat Collins, Dave Danforth, Dixie Davis, Cedric Durst, Frank Ellerbe, Lee Fohl (MANAGER), Eddie Foster *, Wally Gerber, Baby Doll Jacobson, Ray Kolp, Marty McManus, Hub Pruett, Gene Robertson, Hank Severeid, Urban Shocker, Chick Shorten, George Sisler, Jack Tobin, Elam Vangilder, Ken Williams, Rasty Wright

LESS THAN 10 GAMES: Josh Billings, Dutch Henry, Heinie Meine

NOTES: Sisler's .420 season.

KEY SIGNATURES: Sisler, McManus, Tobin, Jacobson, Williams, Severeid, Shocker.

VALUE: $525

1922 ST. LOUIS (NL) - Eddie Ainsmith, Bill Bailey, Clyde Barfoot, Ray Blades, Jim Bottomley, Vern Clemons, Pickles Dillhoefer, Bill Doak *, Max Flack, Jack Fournier, Del Gainer, Jesse Haines, Cliff Heathcote *, Rogers Hornsby, Doc Lavan, Les Mann, Harry McCurdy, Austin McHenry, Heinie Mueller, Lou North, Bill Pertica, Jeff Pfeffer, Branch Rickey (MANAGER), Joe Schultz, Bill Sherdel, Burt Shotton, Jack Smith, Milt Stock, Specs Toporcer, Roy Walker

LESS THAN 10 GAMES: Sid Benton, Eddie Dyer, Howard Freigau, Marv Goodwin, Jack Knight, Epp Sell, Johnny Stuart, Ernie Vick

NOTES: 4 HOF'ers; Hornsby, Triple Crown winner, hit .401.

KEY SIGNATURES: Rickey, Hornsby, Toporcer, Stock, Smith, Schultz, Bottomley, Haines.

VALUE: $1600

1922 WASHINGTON - Ossie Bluege, Jim Brillheart, Frank Brower, Donie Bush, Eric Erickson, Patsy Gharrity, Ed Goebel, Goose Goslin, Bucky Harris, Walter Johnson, Joe Judge, Pete Lapan, Bobby LaMotte, Clyde Milan (MANAGER), George Mogridge, Roger Peckinpaugh, Tom Phillips, Val Picinich, Sam Rice, Howard Shanks, Earl Smith, Chief Youngblood, Tom Zachary

LESS THAN 10 GAMES: Harry Courtney *, Joe Gleason, Slim McGrew, George McNamara, Ricardo Torres, Lucas Turk, Cy Warmouth, Frank Woodward

NOTES: 4 HOF'ers; Milan was a player/manager.

KEY SIGNATURES: Harris, Rice, Goslin, Johnson.

VALUE: $1100

*** = player was traded**

1923

1923 American League strikeout leader Walter Johnson

1923 BOSTON (AL) - George Burns, Frank Chance (MANAGER), Shano Collins, Al DeVormer, Howard Ehmke, Alex Ferguson, Chick Fewster, Ira Flagstead *, Curt Fullerton, Joe Harris, Les Howe, Nemo Leibold *, Norm McMillan, Mike Menosky, Johnny Mitchell, George Murray, Lefty O'Doul, Val Picinich, Bill Piercy, Pinky Pittinger, Jack Quinn, Dick Reichle, Howard Shanks, Roxy Walters

LESS THAN 10 GAMES: Dave Black, Clarence Blethen, Ike Boone, John Donohue, Frank Fuller, Camp Skinner, Carl Stimson

KEY SIGNATURES: Burns, Flagstead, Harris, Ehmke, Chance.

VALUE: $1100

1923 BOSTON (NL) - Bill Bagwell, Jesse Barnes *, Larry Benton, Tony Boeckel, Art Conlon, Johnny Cooney, Walt Cruise, Bob Emmerich, Gus Felix, Dana Fillingim, Rod Ford, Joe Genewich, Frank Gibson, Hank Gowdy *, Snake Henry, Al Hermann, Larry Kopf, Rube Marquard, Stuffy McInnis, Tim McNamara, Fred Mitchell (MANAGER), Al Nixon, Mickey O'Neil, Joe Oeschger, Ernie Padgett *, Ray Powell, Bob Smith, Earl Smith *, Billy Southworth, Mule Watson *

LESS THAN 10 GAMES: Joe Batchelder, Dee Cousineau, Frank Miller, Dick Rudolph

NOTES: Boeckel died 2/16/24.

KEY SIGNATURES: McInnis, Southworth, Powell, Marquard.

VALUE: $450

1923 BROOKLYN - Eddie Ainsmith *, Gene Bailey, Turner Barber, Moe Berg, Art Decatur, Hank DeBerry, Leo Dickerman, Jack Fournier, Ray French, Bert Griffith, Tommy Griffith, Burleigh Grimes, Charlie Hargreaves, Dutch Henry, Andy High, Jimmy Johnston, Bill McCarren, Bernie Neis, Ivy Olson, Wilbert Robinson (MANAGER), Dutch Ruether, Dutch Schliebner *, George Smith, Zack Taylor, Dazzy Vance, Zack Wheat

LESS THAN 10 GAMES: Leon Cadore *, Harry Harper, Bernie Hungling, Al Mamaux, Billy Mullen, Paul Schrieber, Harry Shriver, Stuffy Stewart

NOTES: 4 HOF'ers.

KEY SIGNATURES: Robinson, Fournier, Johnston, Wheat, Grimes, Vance.

HOF = Hall of Famer

VALUE: $1200

1923 CHICAGO (AL) - Maurice Archdeacon, Bill Barrett, Ted Blankenship, Eddie Collins, Buck Crouse, Mike Cvengros, Roy Elsh, Red Faber, Bibb Falk, Kid Gleason (MANAGER), Roy Graham, John Happenny, Harry Hooper, Ernie Johnson *, Willie Kamm, Dixie Leverett, Frank Mack, Harvey McClellan, Johnny Mostil, Charlie Robertson, Ray Schalk, Earl Sheely, Amos Strunk, Sloppy Thurston *

LESS THAN 10 GAMES: Homer Blankenship, Leon Cadore *, Paul Castner, Sarge Connally, Shine Cortazzo, Lum Davenport, Red Dorman, Slim Embry, Claral Gillenwater, Ted Lyons, Red Proctor, Lou Rosenberg, Roxy Snipes, Leo Taylor, Frank Woodward

NOTES: 5 HOF'ers.

KEY SIGNATURES: Collins, Hooper, Falk, Schalk, Faber, Lyons.

VALUE: $860

1923 CHICAGO (NL) - Sparky Adams, Vic Aldridge, Pete Alexander, Marty Callaghan, Virgil Cheeves, Nick Dumovich, Allen Elliott, Barney Friberg, Fred Fussell, George Grantham, Denver Grigsby, Ray Grimes, Gabby Hartnett, Cliff Heathcote, Charlie Hollocher, Tony Kaufmann, Vic Keen, John Kelleher, Bill Killefer (MANAGER), Hack Miller, Bob O'Farrell, Tiny Osborne, Jigger Statz, Otto Vogel, Butch Weis

LESS THAN 10 GAMES: Bob Barrett, Guy Bush, Phil Collins, Tony Murray, Ed Stauffer, George Stueland, Pete Turgeon, Rip Wheeler, Kettle Wirts

KEY SIGNATURES: Grimes, Friberg, Statz, Miller, O'Farrell, Hartnett, Alexander, Aldridge.

VALUE: $1000

1923 CINCINNATI - Rube Benton, Sammy Bohne, Rube Bressler, George Burns, Ike Caveney, Johnny Couch, Jake Daubert, Pete Donohue, Pat Duncan, Lew Fonseca, Boob Fowler, Bubbles Hargrave, George Harper, Bill Harris, Cactus Keck, Wally Kimmick, Dolf Luque, Herb McQuaid, Pat Moran (MANAGER), Babe Pinelli, Eppa Rixey, Edd Roush, Ivy Wingo

LESS THAN 10 GAMES: George Abrams, Haddie Gill, Ed Hock, Les Mann *, Eddie Pick, Gus Sanberg, Karl Schnell

KEY SIGNATURES: Roush, Duncan, Hargrave, Luque, Rixey.

VALUE: $500

1923 CLEVELAND - Danny Boone, Frank Brower, Joe Connolly, Stan Coveleski, Jim Joe Edwards, Larry Gardner, Lou Guisto, Charlie Jamieson, Ray Knode, Rube Lutzke, Dewey Metivier, Guy Morton, Glen Myatt, Steve O'Neill, Joe Sewell, Luke Sewell, Joe Shaute, Sherry Smith, Tris Speaker (MANAGER), Riggs Stephenson, Homer Summa, George Uhle, Bill Wambsganss

LESS THAN 10 GAMES: Phil Bedgood, Sumpter Clarke, Logan Drake, George Edmondson, Johnson Fry, Jackie Gallagher, Tom Gulley, Kenny Hogan, Emil Levsen, Wally Shaner, Jim Sullivan, George Winn

NOTES: Speaker was a player/manager.

KEY SIGNATURES: Speaker, Sewell, Summa, Jamieson, Uhle, Coveleski.

VALUE: $850

1923 DETROIT - Johnny Bassler, Lu Blue, Ty Cobb (MANAGER), Bert Cole, Rip Collins, George Cutshaw, Hooks Daus, Bob Fothergill, Ray Francis, Fred Haney, Harry Heilmann, Ken Holloway, Syl Johnson, Bob Jones, John Kerr, Clyde Manion, Heinie Manush, Ole Olsen, Herman Pillette, Del Pratt, Topper Rigney, Bobby Veach, Larry Woodall

LESS THAN 10 GAMES: Les Burke, Fred Carisch, Rufe Clarke, Ira Flagstead *, Roy Moore, Ed Wells, Earl Whitehill

NOTES: Heilmann's ".403" season; Leonard suspended from team; Cobb was a player/manager.

KEY SIGNATURES: Cobb, Rigney, Heilmann, Manush, Daus.

VALUE: $1100

1923 NEW YORK (AL) - Benny Bengough, Bullet Joe Bush, Joe Dugan, Lou Gehrig, Hinkey Haines, Harvey Hendrick, Fred Hofmann, Waite Hoyt, Miller Huggins (MANAGER), Ernie Johnson *, Sad Sam Jones, Carl Mays, Mike McNally, Bob Meusel, Herb Pennock, Wally Pipp, Babe Ruth, Wally Schang, Everett Scott, Bob Shawkey, Elmer Smith, Aaron Ward, Whitey Witt

LESS THAN 10 GAMES: Mike Gazella, George Pipgras, Oscar Roettger

NOTES: World Champions! 5 HOF'ers.

KEY SIGNATURES: Huggins, Pipp, Ruth, Witt, Meusel, Gehrig, Pennock, Hoyt.

VALUE: $3125

1923 NEW YORK (NL) - Dave Bancroft, Jesse Barnes, Virgil Barnes, Jack Bentley, Clint Blume, Bill Cunningham, Frankie Frisch, Alex Gaston, Hank Gowdy *, Heinie Groh, Travis Jackson, Claude Jonnard, George Kelly, Freddie Maguire, John McGraw (MANAGER), Hugh McQuillan, Irish Meusel, Art Nehf, Jimmy O'Connell, Rosy Ryan, Jack Scott, Ralph Shinners, Earl Smith *, Frank Snyder, Casey Stengel, Mule Watson, Ross Youngs

LESS THAN 10 GAMES: Dinty Gearin, Walter Huntzinger, Fred Johnson, Red Lucas, Moe Solomon, Bill Terry, Rube Walberg *, Hack Wilson

NOTES: 9 HOF'ers.

KEY SIGNATURES: McGraw, Kelly, Frisch, Bancroft, Youngs, Jackson, Stengel, Terry, Wilson, Ryan.

VALUE: $2625

1923 PHILADELPHIA (AL) - Frank Bruggy, Jimmy Dykes, Walt French, Chick Galloway, Sammy Hale, Slim Harriss, Bob Hasty, Joe Hauser, Fred Heimach, Connie Mack (MANAGER), Wid Matthews, Beauty McGowan, Bing Miller, Rollie Naylor, Curly Ogden, Cy Perkins, Harry Riconda, Eddie Rommel, Heinie Scheer, Rube Walberg *, Tilly Walker, Frank Welch

LESS THAN 10 GAMES: Denny Burns, Hank Hulvey, John Jones, Al Kellett, Ren Kelly, Walt Kinney, Roy Meeker, Harry O'Neill, Doc Ozmer, Chuck Rowland, Chuck Wolfe, Doc Wood

KEY SIGNATURES: Mack, Hauser.

VALUE: $575

1923 PHILADELPHIA (NL) - Petie Behan, Huck Betts, Jim Bishop, Johnny Couch *, Tod Dennehey, Art Fletcher (MANAGER), Whitey Glazner *, Ralph Head, Butch Henline, Walter Holke, Bill Hubbell, Freddy Leach, Cliff Lee, Carl Lord, Lenny Metz, Clarence Mitchell, Johnny Mokan, Mickey O'Brien, Frank Parkinson, Goldie Rapp, Jimmy Ring, Heinie Sand, Cotton Tierney *, Curt Walker, Lefty Weinert, Cy Williams, Jimmie Wilson, Jesse Winters, Andy Woehr, Russ Wrighstone

LESS THAN 10 GAMES: Joe Bennett, Art Gardiner, Jim Grant, Walter Holke, Broadway Jones, Lee Meadows *, Red Miller, Dixie Parker, Pat Ragan

KEY SIGNATURES: Holke, Tierney, Mokan, Henline.

VALUE: $385

1923 PITTSBURGH - Babe Adams, Spencer Adams, Jim Bagby, Clyde Barnhart, Carson Bigbee, Max Carey, Wilbur Cooper, Kiki Cuyler, Jewels Ens, Johnny Gooch, Charlie Grimm, Earl Hamilton, Earl Kunz, Rabbit Maranville, Jim Mattox, Bill McKechnie (MANAGER), Lee Meadows *, Johnny Morrison, Walter Mueller, Johnny Rawlings, Reb Russell, Walter Schmidt, Ray Steineder, Cotton Tierney *, Pie Traynor

LESS THAN 10 GAMES: Eppie Barnes, George Boehler, Hal Carlson, Whitey Glazner *, Frank Luce, Eddie Moore, Arnie Stone

NOTES: 5 HOF'ers.

KEY SIGNATURES: McKechnie, Grimm, Maranville, Traynor, Barnhart, Carey, Cuyler, Morrison.

VALUE: $1100

1923 ST. LOUIS (AL) - Jimmy Austin (MANAGER), Bill Bayne, Pat Collins, Dave Danforth, Dixie Davis, Cedric Durst, Frank Ellerbe, Homer Ezzell, Lee Fohl (MANAGER), Eddie Foster, Wally Gerber, Baby Doll Jacobson, Ray Kolp, Marty McManus, Hub Pruett, Gene Robertson, Charlie Root, Dutch Schleibner *, Hank Severeid, Urban Shocker, Chick Shorten, Syl Simon *, Jack Tobin, Elam Vangilder, Bill Whaley, Ken Williams, Rasty Wright

LESS THAN 10 GAMES: Jimmy Austin, Herschel Bennett, Josh Billings, Jumbo Jim Elliott, George Grant, Bill Mizeur, Harry Rice, Johnny Schulte, Sloppy Thurston *

NOTES: Shorten retired.

KEY SIGNATURES: McManus, Tobin, Jacobson, Williams, Severeid, Shocker.

VALUE: $450

1923 ST. LOUIS (NL) - Eddie Ainsmith *, Clyde Barfoot, Les Bell, Ray Blades, Jim Bottomley, Vern Clemons, Bill Doak, Eddie Dyer, Max Flack, Jake Flowers, Howard Freigau, Jesse Haines, Rogers Hornsby, Doc Lavan, Les Mann *, Harry McCurdy, Heinie Mueller, Hy Myers, Lou North, Jeff Pfeffer, Branch Rickey (MANAGER), Bill Sherdel, Bill Sherdel, Jack Smith, Milt Stock, Johnny Stuart, Fred Toney, Specs Toporcer

LESS THAN 10 GAMES: Taylor Douthit, Jimmy Hodgens, George Kopshaw, Austin McHenry, Charlie Niebergall, Bill Pertica, Joe Schultz, Epp Sell, Burt Shotton, Tige Stone, Joe Walker, Fred Wiginton

NOTES: 4 HOF'ers.

KEY SIGNATURES: Rickey, Bottomley, Hornsby, Myers, Smith, Haines.

VALUE: $1500

1923 WASHINGTON - Ossie Bluege, Jim Brillheart, Donie Bush (MANAGER), Pep Conroy, Joe Evans, Showboat Fisher, Patsy Gharrity, Goose Goslin, Pinky Hargrave, Bucky Harris, Bonnie Hollingsworth, Walter Johnson, Joe Judge, Nemo Leibold *, Firpo Marberry, George Mogridge, Jim O'Neill, Roger Peckinpaugh, Sam Rice, Muddy Ruel, Allen Russell, Rip Wade, Cy Warmoth, Tom Zachary, Paul Zahniser

LESS THAN 10 GAMES: Donie Bush, Skipper Friday, Pete Lapan, Slim McGrew, Monroe Mitchell, Bobby Murray, Squire Potter, Jake Propst, Doc Prothro, Jim Riley, Clay Roe, Fred Schemanske, Duke Sedgwick, Carr Smith, Ted Wingfield

NOTES: 4 HOF'ers.

KEY SIGNATURES: Judge, Harris, Rice, Leibold, Goslin, Ruel, Johnson.

VALUE: $1050

***** = **player was traded**

1924

National League pitcher A.C. "Dazzy" Vance

1924 BOSTON (AL) - Ike Boone, Danny Clark, Shano Collins, Joe Connolly, Howard Ehmke, Homer Ezzell, Alex Ferguson, Ira Flagstead, Lee Fohl (MANAGER), Oscar Fuhr, Curt Fullerton, Chappie Geygan, Joe Harris, Johnnie Heving, Dud Lee, George Murray, Steve O'Neill, Val Picinich, Bill Piercy, Jack Quinn, Buster Ross, Howard Shanks, Phil Todt, Bobby Veach, Bill Wambsganss, Denny Williams, Hoge Workman

LESS THAN 10 GAMES: Les Howe, Charley Jamerson, Al Kellett, Red Ruffing, Ted Wingfield *, Clarence Winters, John Woods

KEY SIGNATURES: Harris, Boone, Flagstead, Ruffing.

VALUE: $450

1924 BOSTON (NL) - Dave Bancroft (MANAGER), Dave Bancroft, Jess Barnes, Larry Benton, Johnny Cooney, Walt Cruise, Bill Cunningham, Gus Felix, Joe Genewich, Frank Gibson, Al Hermann, John Kelleher, Hunter Lane, Red Lucas, Les Mann, Stuffy McInnis, Tim McNamara, Mickey O'Neil, Ernie Padgett, Ray Powell, Marty Shay, Bob Smith, Earl Smith *, Ed Sperber, Casey Stengel, Dutch Stryker, Herb Thomas, Cotton Tierney, Frank Wilson, Al Yeargin

LESS THAN 10 GAMES: Joe Batchelder, Dee Cousineau, Dinty Gearin *, Kyle Graham, Ike Kamp, Wade Lefler *, Rube Marquard, Joe Muich, Lou North *, Eddie Phillips

NOTES: Bancroft was a player/manager.

KEY SIGNATURES: Stengel, Bancroft, Marquard.

VALUE: $700

1924 BROOKLYN - Gene Bailey, Eddie Brown, Art Decatur, Hank DeBerry, Bill Doak *, Rube Ehrhardt, Jack Fournier, Tommy Griffith, Burleigh Grimes, Charlie Hargreaves, Dutch Henry, Andy High, Jimmy Johnston, Joe Klugman, Dick Loftus, Johnny Mitchell, Bernie Neis, Tiny Osborne, Jim Roberts, Wilbert Robinson (MANAGER), Dutch Ruether, Milt Stock, Zack Taylor, Dazzy Vance, Zack Wheat

LESS THAN 10 GAMES: Leo Dickerman, Nelson Greene, Bonnie Hollingsworth, Fred Johnston, Binky Jones, Tom Long, Ivy Olson, Tex Wilson, Rube Yarrison

NOTES: 4 HOF'ers.

KEY SIGNATURES: Robinson, Fournier, High, Brown, Wheat, Grimes, Vance.

VALUE: $1200

1924 CHICAGO (AL) - Maurice Archdeacon, Bill Barrett, Ted Blankenship, Bud Clancy, Eddie Collins, Sarge Connally, Buck Crouse,. Mike Cvengros, Ike Davis, Roy Elsh, Johnny Evers (MANAGER), Red Faber, Bibb Falk, Ray French, Johnny Grabowski, Harry Hooper, Willie Kamm, Dixie Leverett, Ted Lyons, Leo Mangum, H. McClellan, Doug McWeeny, Ray Morehart, Johnny Mostil, Charlie Robertson, Ray Schalk, Earl Sheely, Sloppy Thurston

LESS THAN 10 GAMES: Bernie de Viveirios, Bob Barnes, Bill Black, Joe Burns, Wally Dashiell, Lum Davenport, John Dobb, Happy Foreman, Bob Lawrence, Frank Naleway, Webb Schultz, Milt Steengrafe, Amos Strunk *, Kettle Wirts

NOTES: 6 HOF'ers.

KEY SIGNATURES: Evers, Sheely, Collins, Hooper, Mostil, Falk, Schalk, Thurston, Lyons, Faber.

HOF = Hall of Famer

VALUE: $1425

1924 CHICAGO (NL) - Sparky Adams, Vic Aldridge, Pete Alexander, Bob Barrett, Sheriff Blake, Guy Bush, Harvey Cotter, Allen Elliott, Barney Friberg, George Grantham, Denver Grigsby, Ray Grimes, Gabby Hartnett, Cliff Heathcote, Charlie Hollocher, Elmer Jacobs, Tony Kaufmann, Vic Keen, Bill Killefer (MANAGER), Hack Miller, George Milstead, Bob O'Farrell, Jigger Statz, Otto Vogel, Butch Weis, Rip Wheeler

LESS THAN 10 GAMES: Herb Brett, John Churry, Howie Fitzgerald, Ted Kearns, Ralph Michaels, Tiny Osborne *, Ray Pierce

KEY SIGNATURES: Grantham, Heathcote, Hartnett, Alexander.

VALUE: $900

1924 CINCINNATI - Rube Benton, Sammy Bohne, Rube Bressler, George Burns, Ike Caveney, Hughie Critz, Jake Daubert, Pete Donohue, Pat Duncan, lew Fonesca, Boob Fowler, Bubbles Hargrave, George Harper *, Ed Hock, Dolf Luque, Jakie May, Carl Mays, Pat Moran, Babe Pinelli, Eppa Rixey, Ed Roush, Gus Sanberg, Tom Sheehan, Chick Shorten, Curt Walker *, Ivy Wingo

LESS THAN 10 GAMES: Jim Begley, Jack Blott, Pedro Dibut, Bill Harris, Jack Hendricks (MANAGER), Cliff Lee *, Greasy Neale, Eddie Pick

KEY SIGNATURES: Critz, Pinelli, Walker, Roush, Mays, Rixey.

VALUE: $450

1924 CLEVELAND - Frank Brower, George Burns, Watty Clark, Sumpter Clarke, Stan Coveleski, Frank Ellerbe *, Chick Fewster, Larry Gardner, Charlie Jamieson, Ray Knode, Rube Lutzke, Pat McNulty, Dewey Metivier, Glenn Myatt, Luther Roy, Joe Sewell, Luke Sewell, Joe Shaute, Sherry Smith, Tris Speaker (MANAGER), Riggs Stephenson, Homer Summa, George Uhle, Roxy Walters, Elmer Yoter

LESS THAN 10 GAMES: Frank Brower, Virgil Cheeves, Joe Dawson, Logan Drake, George Edmondson, Jim Joe Edwards, Bob Fitzke, Tom Gulley, Kenny Hogan, Bob Kuhn, Emil Levsen, Jim Lindsay, Bud Messenger, Jake Miller, Guy Morton, Freddie Spurgeon, Frank Wayenberg, Joe Wyatt, Carl Yowell

NOTES: Speaker was a player/manager.

KEY SIGNATURES: Speaker, Burns, Sewell, Jamieson, Myatt, Shaute, Coveleski.

VALUE: $800

1924 DETROIT - Johnny Bassler, Lu Blue, Les Burke, Ty Cobb (MANAGER), Bert Cole, Rip Collins, Hooks Dauss, Bob Fothergill, Fred Haney, Harry Heilmann, Ken Holloway, Syl Johnson, Bob Jones, John Kerr, Clyde Manion, Heinie Manush, Frank O'Rourke, Herman Pilette, Del Pratt, Topper Rigney, Lil Stoner, Ed Wells, Earl Whitehill, Al Wingo, Larry Woodall

LESS THAN 10 GAMES: Rufe Clarke, Charlie Gehringer, Ken Jones, Dutch Leonard, Willie Ludolph

NOTES: 4 HOF'ers; Cobb was a player/manager.

KEY SIGNATURES: Cobb, Blue, Pratt, Heilmann, Manush, Bassler, Gehringer.

VALUE: $1200

1924 NEW YORK (AL) - Benny Bengough, Bullet Joe Bush, Earle Combs, Joe Dugan, Milt Gaston, Harvey Hendrick, Fred Hofmann, Shags Horan, Wait Hoyt, Miller Huggins (MANAGER), Ernie Johnson, Sad Sam Jones, Al Mamaux, Mike McNally, Bob Meusel, Herb Pennock, Wally Pipp, Babe Ruth, Wally Schang, Everett Scott, Bob Shawkey, Aaron Ward, Whitey Witt

LESS THAN 10 GAMES: Martin Autry, Walter Beall, Lou Gehrig, Mack Hillis, Cliff Markle, Ben Paschal, George Pipgras, Oscar Roettger, Ben Shields

NOTES: 6 HOF'ers; Gehrig's signature rare due to limited appearances.

KEY SIGNATURES: Huggins, Dugan, Ruth, Meusel, Combs, Gehrig, Pennock, Hoyt.

VALUE: $3750

1924 NEW YORK (NL) - Eddie Ainsmith, Harry Baldwin, Virgil Barnes, Jack Bentley, Buddy Crump, Wayland Dean, Frankie Frisch, Hank Gowdy, Heinie Groh, Grover Hartley, Walter Huntzinger, Travis Jackson, Claude Jonnard, George Kelly, Fred Lindstrom, Ernie Maun, John McGraw (MANAGER), Hugh McQuillan, Irish Meusel, Art Nehf, Jimmy O'Connell, Rosy Ryan, Jack Scott, Frank Snyder, Billy Southworth, Bill Terry, Mule Watson, Hack Wilson, Ross Youngs

LESS THAN 10 GAMES: Leon Cadore, Dinty Gearin, Kent Greenfield, Joe Oeschger
NOTES: 8 HOF'ers; McGraw's last World Series.
KEY SIGNATURES: McGraw, Kelly, Frisch, Jackson, Youngs, Wilson, Snyder, Terry, Lindstrom, Bentley.

VALUE: $2300

1924 PHILADELPHIA (AL) - Stan Baumgartner, Max Bishop, Frank Bruggy, Denny Burns, John Chapman, Jimmy Dykes, Chick Galloway, Charlie Gibson, Sam Gray, Sammy Hale, Slim Harriss, Bob Hasty, Joe Hauser, Fred Heimach, Bill Lamar, Connie Mack (MANAGER), Roy Meeker, Bing Miller, Cy Perkins, Harry Riconda, Eddie Rommel, Al Simmons, Paul Strang, Amos Strunk *, Frank Welch
LESS THAN 10 GAMES: Joe Greene, Rollie Naylor, Curly Ogden *, Bill Pierson, Ed Sherling, Rube Walbert
KEY SIGNATURES: Miller, Simmons, Lamar.

VALUE: $700

1924 PHILADELPHIA (NL) - Huck Betts, Hal Carlson, Johnny Couch, Art Fletcher (MANAGER), Hod Ford, Whitey Glazner, George Harper *, Butch Henline, Fritz Henrich, Walter Holke, Bill Hubbell, Cliff Lee *, Bert Lewis, Lenny Metz, Clarence Mitchell, Johnny Mokan, Joe Oeschger *, Frank Parkinson, Jimmy Ring, Heinie Sand, Joe Schultz *, Curt Walker *, Lew Wendell, Cy Williams, Jimmie Wilson, Andy Woehr, Russ Wrightstone
LESS THAN 10 GAMES: Jim Bishop, Spoke Emery, Earl Hamilton, Freddy Leach, Lerton Pinto, Ray Steineder *, Lefty Weinert
KEY SIGNATURES: Holke, Wrightstone, Williams.

VALUE: $375

1924 PITTSBURGH - Clyde Barnhart, Carson Bigbee, Max Carey, Wilbur Cooper, Kiki Cuyler, Johnny Gooch, Charlie Grimm, Ray Kremer, Rabbit Maranville, Bill McKechnie (MANAGER), Lee Meadows, Eddie Moore, Johnny Morrison, Walter Mueller, Jeff Pfeffer *, Walter Schmidt, Earl Smith *, Arnie Stone, Pie Traynor, Glenn Wright, Emil Yde
LESS THAN 10 GAMES: Babe Adams, Eppie Barnes, Jewel Ens, Cliff Knox, Del Lundgren, Buckshot May, Johnny Rawlings, Fred Sale, Don Songer, Ray Steineder *
NOTES: 5 HOF'ers.
KEY SIGNATURES: McKechnie, Maranville, Traynor, Carey, Cuyler, Cooper.

HOF = Hall of Famer

VALUE: $1025

1924 ST. LOUIS (AL) - Bill Bayne, Herschel Bennett, Pat Collins, Dave Danforth, Eixie Davis, Frank Ellerbe *, Joe Evans, Wally Gerber, George Grant, Baby Doll Jacobson, Ray Kolp, George Lyons, Marty McManus, Norm McMillan, Hub Pruett, Tony Rego, Harry Rice, Gene Robertson, Hank Severeid, Urban Shocker, Syl Simon, George Sisler (MANAGER), Jack Tobin, Elam Vangilder, Ken Williams, Ernie Wingard
LESS THAN 10 GAMES: Ed Barnhart, Boom-Boom Beck, Pat Burke, Ellie Ellmore, Bill Lasley, Bill Mizeur, Ollie Voight
NOTES: Sisler was a player/manager.
KEY SIGNATURES: Sisler, McManus, Robertson, Jacobson, Williams, Severeid.

VALUE: $440

1924 ST. LOUIS (NL) - Hi Bell, Les Bell, Ray Blades, Jim Bottomley, Vern Clemons, Jimmy Cooney, Leo Dickerman *, Bill Doak *, Taylor Douthit, Eddie Dyer, Eddie Dyer, Max Flack, Jesse Fowler, Howard Freigau, Mike Gonzalez, Chick Hafey, Jesse Haines, Wattie Holm, Rogers Hornsby, Heinie Mueller, Hy Myers, Charlie Niebergall, Jeff Pfeffer *, Branch Rickey (MANAGER), Joe Schultz *, Bill Sherdel, Jack Smith, Allen Sothoron, Johnny Stuart, Tommy Thevenow, Specs Toporcer, Ernie Vick

LESS THAN 10 GAMES: Jack Berly, Joe Bratcher, Ed Clough, Pea Ridge Day, Art Delaney, Doc Lavan, Lou North *, Flint Rhem, Ray Shepardson, Vince Shields, Bob Vines

NOTES: 4 HOF'ers; Hornsby's ".424" season.

KEY SIGNATURES: Rickey, Bottomley, Hornsby, Blades, Hafey.

VALUE: $1400

1924 WASHINGTON - Ossie Bluege, Showboat Fisher, Goose Goslin, Pinky Hargrave, Bucky Harris (MANAGER), Bucky Harris, Walter Johnson, Joe Judge, Nemo Leibold, Firpo Marberry, Joe Martina, Wid Matthews, Earl McNeely, George Mogridge, Curly Ogden *, Roger Peckinpaugh, Doc Prothro, Sam Rice, Lance Richbourg, Muddy Ruel, Allen Russell, Mule Shirley, By Speece, Bennie Tate, Tommy Taylor, Tom Zachary, Paul Zahniser

LESS THAN 10 GAMES: Nick Altrock, Carl East, Chick Gagnon, Bert Griffith, Wade Lefler *, Slim McGrew, Ralph Miller, Carr Smith, Ted Wingfield *

NOTES: World Champions! 4 HOF'ers; Harris was a player/manager.

KEY SIGNATURES: Harris, Judge, Rice, Goslin, Johnson. **VALUE:** $1250

1925

Manager Bill McKechnie led the Pittsburgh Pirates to a World Championship in 1925.

*** = player was traded**

1925 BOSTON (AL) - George Bischoff *, Ike Boone, Roy Carlyle *, Bud Connolly, Howard Ehmke, Homer Ezzell, Ira Flagstead, Lee Fohl (MANAGER), Oscar Fuhr, Mike Herrara, Johnnie Heving, Tom Jenkins, Dud Lee, Val Picinich, Doc Prothro, Jack Quinn,

Billy Rogell, Si Rosenthal, Buster Ross, Jack Rothrock, Red Ruffing, Al Stokes, Phil Todt, Tex Vache, Bill Wambsganss, Herb Welch, Denny Williams, Ted Wingfield, Paul Zahniser

LESS THAN 10 GAMES: Bob Adams, Shano Collins, Alex Ferguson *, Ray Francis *, Curt Fullerton, Chappie Geygan, Turkey Gross, Joe Harris *, Rudy Kallio, Joe Kiefer, Joe Lucey, Hal Neubauer, Bobby Veach *

KEY SIGNATURES: Prothro, Boone, Carlyle, Ruffing.

VALUE: $400

1925 BOSTON (NL) - Dave Bancroft (MANAGER), Jesse Barnes, Larry Benton, Dick Burrus, Johnny Cooney, Gus Felix, Doc Gautreau *, Joe Genewich, Frank Gibson, Kyle Graham, Dave Harris, Andy High *, Ike Kamp, Hod Kibbie, Les Mann, Rube Marquard, Bill Marriott, Bernie Neis, Mickey O'Neil, Ernie Padgett, Rosy Ryan, Oscar Siemer, Bob Smith, Casey Stengel, Bill Vargus, Jim Welsh, Frank Wilson

LESS THAN 10 GAMES: Bill Anderson, Joe Batchelder, Dee Cousineau, Foster Edwards, Shanty Hogan, Abe Hood, Red Lucas, Tim McNamara, Joe Ogrodowski, Ed Sperber, Herb Thomas

NOTES: Bancroft was a player/manager.

KEY SIGNATURES: Bancroft, Burrus, Welsh, Felix, Stengel, Marquard.

VALUE: $690

1925 BROOKLYN - Eddie Brown, Lloyd Brown, Guy Cantrell, Chuch Corgan, Dick Cox, Hank DeBerry, Rube Ehrhardt, Hod Ford, Jack Fournier, Nelson Greene, Burleigh Grimes, Charlie Hargreaves, Andy High *, Bill Hubbell, Jimmy Johnston, Dick Loftus, Johnny Mitchell, Joe Oeschger, Tiny Osborne, Jesse Petty, Wilbert Robinson (MANAGER), Milt Stock, Zack Taylor, Cotton Tierney, Dazzy Vance, Zack Wheat

LESS THAN 10 GAMES: Bob Barrett *, Art Decatur *, Jimbo Jim Elliott, Tommy Griffith *, Roy Hutson, Bob McGraw, Jim Roberts, Andy Rush, Jerry Standaert, Hank Thormahlen

KEY SIGNATURES: Robinson, Fournier, Stock, Cox, Brown, Wheat, Taylor, Vance, Grimes.

VALUE: $1100

1925 CHICAGO (AL) - Maurice Archdeacon, Bill Barrett, Ted Blankenship, Eddie Collins (MANAGER), Sarge Connally, Buck Crouse, Mike Cvengros, Ike Davis, Roy Elsh, Red Faber, Bibb Falk, Johnny Grabowski, Spence Harris, Harry Hooper, Willie Kamm, John Kane, Dickie Kerr, Ted Lyons, Johnny Mostil, Charlie Robertson, Ray Schalk, Earl Sheely, Sloppy Thurston

LESS THAN 10 GAMES: Ken Ash, Chief Bender, George Bischoff *, Bud Clancy, Jim Joe Edwards *, Jake Freeze, Frank Mack, Jule Mallonee, Leo Mangum, Tink Riviere, Leo Tankersley

NOTES: 6 HOF'ers; Collins was a player/manager.

KEY SIGNATURES: Collins, Sheely, Hooper, Falk, Schalk, Lyons, Faber, Bender.

VALUE: $1100

1925 CHICAGO (NL) - Sparky Adams, Pete Alexander, Red Barrett *, Sheriff Blake, Mandy Brooks, Guy Bush, John Churry, Wilbur Cooper, Howard Freigau *, Barney Friberg *, George Gibson (MANAGER), Mike Gonzalez *, Tommy Griffith *, Denver Grigsby, Charlie Grimm, Gabby Hartnettt, Cliff Heathcote, Elmer Jacobs, Art Jahn, Percy Jones, Tony Kaufmann, Ted Kearns, Vic Keen, Mel Kerr, Bill Killefer (MANAGER), Rabbit Maranville (MANAGER), Ike McAuley, Ralph Michaels, Hack Miller, Bob O'Farrell *, Pinky Pittinger, Gale Staley, Jigger Statz, Chink Taylor, Butch Weis

LESS THAN 10 GAMES: Herb Brett, Jumbo Brown, Barney Friberg, Alex Metzler, George Milstead, Joe Munson, Bob Osborn, George Stueland

NOTES: Maranville was a player/manager.

KEY SIGNATURES: Maranville, Grimm, Freigau, Jahn, Hartnett, Alexander.

VALUE: $1000

1925 CINCINNATI - Rube Benton, Harry Biemiller, Sammy Bohne, Neal Brady, Rube Bressler, Ike Caveney, Hughie Critz, Pete Donohue, Chuck Dressen, Bubbles Hargrave, Jack Hendricks (MANAGER), Walter Holke *, Ernie Krueger, Dolf Luque, Jakie May, Carl Mays, Al Niehaus *, Babe Pinelli, Eppa Rixey, Edd Roush, Joe Schultz *, Tom Sheehan *, Elmer Smith, Curt Walker, Ivy Wingo, Billy Zitzmann

LESS THAN 10 GAMES: Frank Bruggy, Pedro Dibut, Astyanax Douglass, Boob Fowler, Marv Goodwin, Jimmy Hudgens, Ollie Klee, Hy Myers, Tom Sullivan

KEY SIGNATURES: Walker, Roush, Hargrave, Rixey.

VALUE: $435

1925 CLEVELAND - Garland Buckeye, George Burns, Bert Cole *, Jim Joe Edwards *, Fred Eichrodt, Chick Fewster, Harvey Hendrick, Johnny Hodapp, Charlie Jamieson, Benn Karr, Joe Klugmann, Ray Knode, Cliff Lee, Rube Lutzke, Frank McCrea, Pat McNulty, Jake Miller, Glenn Myatt, Joe Sewell, Luke Sewell, Joe Shaute, Sherry Smith, Tris Speaker (MANAGER), By Speece, Freddie Spurgeon, Riggs Stephenson, Homer Summa, Chick Tolson, George Uhle, Dutch Ussat, Carl Yowell

LESS THAN 10 GAMES: Jim Bedford, Ray Benge, Emil Levsen, Luther Roy, Roxy Walters

NOTES: Speaker was a player/manger.

KEY SIGNATURES: Speaker, Burns, Sewell, McNulty, Buckeye.

VALUE: $700

1925 DETROIT - John Bassler, Lu Blue, Les Burke, Ty Cobb (MANAGER), Bert Cole, Rip Collins, Hooks Dauss, Jess Doyle, Bob Fothergill, Fred Haney, Harry Heilmann, Ken Holloway, Bob Jones, Dutch Leonard, Heinie Manush, Johnny Neun, Frank O'Rourke, Topper Rigney, Lil Stoner, Jackie Tavener, Ed Wells, Earl Whitehill, Al Wingo, Larry Woodall

LESS THAN 10 GAMES: Ownie Carroll, Charlie Gehringer, Andy Harrington, Syl Johnson, Bill Moore, Oscar Stanage, Jack Warner

NOTES: 4 HOF'ers; Cobb was a player/manager.

KEY SIGNATURES: Cobb, Blue, Heilmann, Wingo, Manush, Gehringer.

VALUE: $1000

HOF = Hall of Famer

1925 NEW YORK (AL) - Benny Bengough, Earle Combs, Joe Dugan, Alex Ferguson *, Lou Gehrig, Waite Hoyt, Miller Huggins (MANAGER), Ernie Johnson, Hank Johnson, Sad Sam Jones, Frank Koenig, Bob Meusel, Steve O'Neill, Ben Paschal, Herb Pennock, Wally Pipp, Babe Ruth, Wally Schang, Everett Scott *, Howard Shanks, Bob Shawkey, Urban Shocker, Bobby Veach *, Pee Wee Wanninger, Aaron Ward, Whitey Witt

LESS THAN 10 GAMES: Walter Beall, Garland Braxton, Charlie Caldwell, Leo Durocher, Ray Francis *, Fred Hofmann, Roy Luebbe, Jim Marquis, Fred Merkle, Heinie Odom, Ben Shields

NOTES: 5 HOF'ers.

KEY SIGNATURES: Huggins, Gehrig, Ruth, Hoyt, Pennock, Durocher.

VALUE: $3475

1925 NEW YORK (NL) - Virgil Barnes, Jack Bentley, Wayland Dean, Mickey Devine, Doc Farrell, Freddie Fitzsimmons, Frankie Frisch, Hank Gowdy, Kent Greenfield, Heinie Groh, Grover Hartley, Walter Huntzinger, Travis Jackson, George Kelly, Pip Koehler, Fred Lindstrom, John McGraw (MANAGER), Hugh McQuillan, Irish Meusel, Art Nehf, Jack Scott, Frank Snyder, Billy Southworth, Bill Terry, Frank Walker, Hack Wilson, John Wisner, Ross Youngs

LESS THAN 10 GAMES: Harry Baldwin, Blackie Carter, Chick Davis, Hugh McMullen, Al Moore, Earl Webb

NOTES: 8 HOF'ers.

KEY SIGNATURES: McGraw, Terry, Kelly, Jackson, Lindstrom, Youngs, Meusel, Frisch, Wilson.

VALUE: $2250

1925 PHILADELPHIA (AL) - Bill Bagwell, Stan Baumgartner, Max Bishop, Mickey Cochrane, Jimmy Dykes, Walt French, Chick Galloway, Sam Gray, Lefty Grove, Sammy Hale, Slim Harriss, Joe Hauser, Red Holt, Bill Lamar, Connie Mack (MANAGER), Bing Miller, Cy Perkins, Jim Poole, Jack Quinn, Eddie Rommel, Al Simmons, Red Smith, Art Stokes, Rube Walberg, Frank Welch

LESS THAN 10 GAMES: Elbert Andrews, Charlie Berry, Charlie Engle, Jimmie Foxx, Doc Gautreau *, Tom Glass, Fred Heimach, Carl Husta, Jim Keesey, Lefty Willis

NOTES: 5 HOF'ers.

KEY SIGNATURES: Mack, Hale, Miller, Simmons, Lamar, Cochrane, Foxx, Rommel,Grove.

VALUE: $1700

1925 PHILADELPHIA (NL) - Huck Betts, George Burns, Hal Carlson, Johnny Couch, Art Decatur *, Art Fletcher (MANAGER), Lew Fonseca, Barney Friberg *, George Harper, Chicken Hawks, Butch Henline, Walter Holke *, Clarence Huber, Wally Kimmick, Jack Knight, Freddy Leach, Lenny Metz, Clarence Mitchell, Johnny Mokan, Skinny O'Neal, Ray Pierce, Jimmy Ring, Heinie Sand, Joe Schultz *, Dutch Ulrich, Lew Wendell, Cy Williams, Jimmie Wilson, Russ Wrightstone

LESS THAN 10 GAMES: Ray Crumpler, George Durning, Dana Fillingim, Barney Friberg *, Bill Hubbell, Benny Meyer, Bob Vines, Claude Willoughby

KEY SIGNATURES: Hawks, Williams, Harper.

VALUE: $350

1925 PITTSBURGH - Babe Adams, Vic Aldridge, Clyde Barnhart, Carson Bigbee, Max Carey, Kiki Cuyler, Johnny Gooch, George Grantham, Ray Kremer, Stuffy McInnis, Bill McKechnie (MANAGER), Lee Meadows, Eddie Moore, Johnny Morrison, Al Niehaus *, Red Oldham, Johnny Rawlings, Tom Sheehan *, Earl Smith, Roy Spencer, Fresco Thompson, Pie Traynor, Glenn Wright, Emil Yde

LESS THAN 10 GAMES: Bud Culloton, Jewel Ens, Mule Haas, Lou Koupal, Don Songer

NOTES: World Champions! 4 HOF'ers.

KEY SIGNATURES: McKechnie, Grantham, Wright, Traynor, Cuyler, Carey, Barnhart, Smith, Meadows.

VALUE: $900

1925 ST. LOUIS (AL) - Herschel Bennett, Bullet Joe Bush, Dave Danforth, Dixie Davis, Leo Dixon, Joe Evans, Chet Falk, Milt Gaston, Wally Gerber, Joe Giard, George Grant, Pinky Hargrave *, Baby Doll Jacobson, Bobby LaMotte, Marty McManus, Tony Rego, Harry Rice, Gene Robertson, Hank Severeid *, George Sisler (MANAGER), George Sisler, Ed Stauffer, Jack Tobin, Elam Vangilder, Ken Williams, Ernie Wingard

LESS THAN 10 GAMES: Johnny Austin, George Blaeholder, George Mogridge *, Brad Springer

NOTES: Sisler was a player/manager.

KEY SIGNATURES: Sisler, Rice, Jacobson, Williams.

VALUE: $435

1925 ST. LOUIS (NL) - Les Bell, Ray Blades, Jim Bottomley, Jimmy Cooney, Pea Ridge Day, Leo Dickerman, Taylor Douthit, Eddie Dyer, Max Flack, Mike Gonzalez *, Chick Hafey, Jesse Haines, Wattie Holm, Rogers Hornsby (MANAGER), Duster Mails, Heinie Mueller, Bob O'Farrell *, Art Reinhart, Flint Rhem, Branch Rickey (MANAGER), Walter Schmidt, Bill Sherdel, Ralph Shinners, Jack Smith, Allen Sothoron, Johnny Stuart, Tommy Thevenow, Specs Toporcer, Ernie Vick, Bill Warwick

LESS THAN 10 GAMES: Ed Clough, Howard Freigau, Wild Bill Hallahan, Hy Myers *, Gil Paulsen

NOTES: 5 HOF'ers; Hornsby, player/manager, was a Triple Crown winner and hit .403.

KEY SIGNATURES: Rickey, Bottomley, Hornsby, Hafey, Mueller, Blades, Haines.

VALUE: $1540

1925 WASHINGTON - Spencer Adams, Ossie Bluege, Stan Coveleski, Goose Goslin, Vean Gregg, Bucky Harris, Joe Harris *, Tex Jeanes, Walter Johnson, Joe Judge, Nemo Leibold, Firpo Marberry, Wid Matthews, Mike McNally, Earl McNeely, Curly Ogden, Roger Peckinpaugh, Sam Rice, Muddy Ruel, Dutch Ruether, Allen Russell, Everett Scott *, Hank Severeid *, Mule Shirley, Stuffy Stewart *, Bennie Tate, Bobby Veach *, Tom Zachary

LESS THAN 10 GAMES: Win Ballou, Roy Carlyle, Alex Ferguson *, Pinky Hargrave, Bucky Harris (MANAGER), Harry Kelley, Jim Lyle, Tubby McGee, George Mogridge *, Buddy Myer, Spence Pumpelly, Lefty Thomas

NOTES: 5 HOF'ers; Harris was a player/manager.

KEY SIGNATURES: Harris, Judge, Rice, Goslin, Johnson, Coveleski.

VALUE: $1250

1926

The New York Yankees used this ball while clinching the American League pennant in 1926.

1926 BOSTON (AL) - George Bischoff, Fred Bratchi, Roy Carlyle *, Howard Ehmke *, Howie Fitzgerald, Ira Flagstead, Lee Fohl (MANAGER), Alex Gaston, Fred Haney, Slim Harriss *, Fred Heimach *, Mike Herrera, Baby Doll Jacobson *, Tom Jenkins *, Joe Kiefer, Del Lundgren, Bill Regan, Topper Rigney, Si Rosenthal, Jack Rothrock, Red Ruffing, Jack Russell, Wally Shaner, Al Stokes, Jack Tobin *, Phil Todt, Tony Welzer, Hal Wiltse, Ted Wingfield, Paul Zahniser

LESS THAN 10 GAMES: Bill Clowers, Happy Foreman, Boob Fowler, Chappie Geygan, Sam Langford, Dud Lee, Danny MacFayden, Emmett McCann, Bill Moore, Buster Ross, Rudy Sommers

KEY SIGNATURES: Jacobson, Ruffing.

VALUE: $380

*** = player was traded**

1926 BOSTON (NL) - Dave Bancroft (MANAGER), Dave Bancroft, Larry Benton, Eddie Brown, Dick Burrus, Johnny Cooney, Doc Gautreau, Joe Genewich, Frank Gibson, Hal Goldsmith, Kyle Graham, Bunny Hearn, Andy High, Jimmy Johnston *, Les Mann, George Mogridge, Eddie Moore *, Bernie Neis, Oscar Siemer, Bob Smith, Jack Smith *, Eddie Taylor, Zack Taylor, Jim Welsh, Johnny Wertz, Frank Wilson

LESS THAN 10 GAMES: Foster Edwards, Shanty Hogan, Harry Riconda, Rosy Ryan, Bill Vargus, Sid Womack

NOTES: Bancroft was a player/manager.

KEY SIGNATURES: Bancroft, J. Smith, Brown.

VALUE: $400

1926 BROOKLYN - Jesse Barnes, George Boehler, Sammy Bohne *, Johnny Butler, Max Carey *, Moose Clabaugh, Dick Cox, Hank DeBerry, Rube Ehrhardt, Gus Felix, Chick Fewster, Jack Fournier, Burleigh Grimes, Charlie Hargreaves, Babe Herman, Merwin Jacobson, Rabbit Maranville, Bill Marriott, Bob McGraw, Doug McWeeny, Mickey O'Neil, Jesse Petty, Wilbert Robinson (MANAGER), Jerry Standaert, Dazzy Vance, Zack Wheat, Whitey Witt

LESS THAN 10 GAMES: Snooks Dowd, Ray Moss, Milt Stock, Dutch Stryker, Leon Williams

NOTES: 6 HOF'ers.

KEY SIGNATURES: Robinson, Herman, Wheat, Maranville, Carey, Grimes, Vance.

VALUE: $1350

1926 CHICAGO - Sparky Adams, Clyde Beck, Sheriff Blake, Mandy Brooks, Guy Bush, Jimmy Cooney, Howard Freigau, Mike Gonzalez, Charlie Grimm, Gabby Hartnett, Cliff Heathcote, Walter Huntzinger, Percy Jones, Tony Kaufmann, Joe Kelly, Joe McCarthy (MANAGER), George Milstead, Joe Munson, Bob Osborn, Bill Piercy, Charlie Root, Pete Scott, Red Shannon, Riggs Stephenson, Chuck Tolson, Hack Wilson

LESS THAN 10 GAMES: Pete Alexander *, John Churry, Wilbur Cooper *, Joe Graves, Ralph Michaels, Hank Schreiber, Johnny Welch

NOTES: 3 HOF'ers.

KEY SIGNATURES: McCarthy, Adams, Wilson, Stephenson, Hartnett, Alexander.

VALUE: $1100

1926 CHICAGO (AL) - Bill Barrett, Moe Berg, Ted Blankenship, Bud Clancy, Eddie Collins (MANAGER), Sarge Connally, Buck Crouse, Jim Joe Edwards, Red Faber, Bibb Falk, Johnny Grabowski, Tom Gulley, Spence Harris, Bill Hunnefield, Willie Kamm, Ted Lyons, Harry McCurdy, Ray Morehart, Johnny Mostil, Pid Purdy, Ray Schalk, Everett Scott *, Earl Sheely, Milt Steengrafe, Tommy Thomas, Sloppy Thurston

LESS THAN 10 GAMES: Les Cox, Dixie Leverett, Pryor McBee, Pat Veltman

NOTES: 4 HOF'ers; Collins was a player manager.

KEY SIGNATURES: Collins, Barrett, Mostil, Falk, Schalk, Lyons, Faber.

VALUE: $700

1926 CINCINNATI - Ethan Allen, Sammy Bohne *, Rube Bressler, Cuckoo Christensen, Hughie Critz, Pete Donohue, Chuck Dressen, Frank Emmer, Hod Ford, Bubbles Hargrave, Jimmy Hudgens, Red Lucas, Dolf Luque, Jackie May, Carl Mays, Val Picinich, Babe Pinelli, Wally Pipp, Eppa Rixey, Edd Roush, Curt Walker, Billy Zitzmann

LESS THAN 10 GAMES: Howard Carter, Pea Ridge Day, Jack Hendricks (MANAGER), Mul Holland, Rufe Meadows, Roy Meeker, Art Nehf *, Doc Prothro, Everett Scott *, Brad Springer, Clyde Sukeforth, Ivy Wingo

KEY SIGNATURES: Walker, Roush, Donohue, Rixey.

VALUE: $435

1926 CLEVELAND - Garland Buckeye, George Burns, Fred Eichrodt, Charlie Jamieson, Benn Karr, Ray Knode, Guy Lacy, Cliff Lee, Emil Levsen, Rube Lutzke, Pat McNulty, Jake Miller, Glenn Myatt, Ernie Padgett, Joe Sewell, Luke Sewell, Joe Shaute, Sherry Smith, Tris Speaker (MANAGER), Freddie Spurgeon, Homer Summa, George Uhle

LESS THAN 10 GAMES: Martin Autry, Ray Benge, Johnny Hodapp, Willis Hudlin, Norm Lehr, By Speece

NOTES: Speaker was a player/manager.

KEY SIGNATURES: Speaker, Burns, J. Sewell, Summa, Uhle.

VALUE: $700

1926 DETROIT - Clyde Barfoot, Johnny Bassler, Lu Blue, Les Burke, Ty Cobb (MANAGER), Rip Collins, Hooks Dauss, Bob Fothergill, Charlie Gehringer, Sam Gibson, Ray Hayworth, Harry Heilmann, Ken Holloway, Augie Johns, Clyde Manion, Heinie Manush, Billy Mullen, Johnny Neun, Frank O'Rourke, George Smith, Lil Stoner, Jackie Tavener, Jack Warner, Ed Wells, Earl Whitehill, Al Wingo, Larry Woodall

LESS THAN 10 GAMES: Wilbur Cooper, Jess Doyle, Rudy Kneisch

NOTES: 4 HOF'ers; Cobb was a player/manager.

KEY SIGNATURES: Cobb, Gehringer, Heilmann, Manush, Fothergill.

VALUE: $900

1926 NEW YORK (AL) - Spencer Adams, Walter Beall, Benny Bengough, Garland Braxton, Roy Carlyle *, Pat Collins, Earle Combs, Nick Cullop, Kiddo Davis, Joe Dugan, Mike Gazella, Lou Gehrig, Waite Hoyt, Miller Huggins (MANAGER), Sad Sam Jones, Mark Koenig, Tony Lazzeri, Herb McQuaid, Bob Meusel, Ben Paschal, Herb Pennock, Dutch Ruether *, Babe Ruth, Hank Severeid *, Bob Shawkey, Urban Shocker, Bill Skiff, Myles Thomas, Aaron Ward

LESS THAN 10 GAMES: Honey Barnes, Hank Johnson, Fred Merkle

NOTES: 7 HOF'ers.

KEY SIGNATURES: Huggins, Gehrig, Lazzeri, Ruth, Combs, Meusel, Pennock, Hoyt.

VALUE: $4000

1926 NEW YORK (NL) - Virgil Barnes, Andy Cohen, Chick Davies, Doc Farrell, Freddie Fitzsimmons, Paul Florence, Frankie Frisch, Kent Greenfield, Heinie Groh, Grover Hartley, Travis Jackson, Jimmy Johnston *, George Kelly, Fred Lindstrom, John McGraw (MANAGER), Hugh McMullen, Hugh McQuillan, Irish Meusel, Al Moore, Heinie Mueller *, Mel Ott, Jimmy Ring, Jack Scott, Frank Snyder, Billy Southworth *, Bill Terry, Ty Tyson, Ross Youngs

LESS THAN 10 GAMES: Jack Bentley *, Jim Boyle, Blackie Carter, Joe Connell, Pete Cote, Jack Cummings, Sam Hamby, Tim McNamara, Art Nehf *, Joe Poetz, Ned Porter, Scottie Slayback, Al Smith, Mike Smith, Fresco Thompson, John Wisner

NOTES: 8 HOF'ers; Youngs died 10/22/27.

KEY SIGNATURES: McGraw, Kelly, Frisch, Jackson, Lindstrom, Youngs, Terry, Ott.

VALUE: $2150

HOF = Hall of Famer

1926 PHILADELPHIA (AL) - Dave Barbee, Stan Baumgartner, Max Bishop, Mickey Cochrane, Jimmy Dykes, Howard Ehmke *, Charlie Engle, Jimmie Foxx, Walt French, Chick Galloway, Sam Gray, Lefty Grove, Sammy Hale, Slim Harriss *, Joe Hauser, Fred Heimach *, Bill Lamar, Connie Mack (MANAGER), Alex Metzler, Bing Miller *, Joe Pate, Cy Perkins, Jim Poole, Jack Quinn, Eddie Rommel, Frank Sigafoos, Al Simmons, Rube Walberg, Bill Wambsganss, Frank Welch, Lefty Willis

LESS THAN 10 GAMES: Tom Jenkins *.

NOTES: 5 HOF'ers.

KEY SIGNATURES: Mack, French, Simmons, Cochrane, Foxx.

VALUE: $1600

1926 PHILADELPHIA (NL) - Dick Attreau, Ed Baecht, Jack Bentley *, Hal Carlson, Ed Cotter, Wayland Dean, Art Fletcher (MANAGER), Barney Friberg, Ray Grimes, George Harper, Butch Henline, Clarence Huber, Bubber Jonnard, Wally Kimmick, Jack Knight, Freddy Leach, Ernie Maun, Clarence Mitchell, Johnny Mokan, Al Nixon, Ray Pierce, Bob Rice, Heinie Sand, Denny Sothern, Dutch Ulrich, Cy Williams, Claude Willoughby, Jimmie Wilson, Russ Wrightstone

LESS THAN 10 GAMES: Joe Buskey, Art Decatur, Lee Dunham, Chick Keating, Mike Kelly, Pete Rambo, George Stutz, Lefty Taber, Lew Wendell, Rusty Yarnell

KEY SIGNATURES: Williams, Leach, Mokan, Wilson.

VALUE: $340

1926 PITTSBURGH - Babe Adams, Vic Aldridge, Clyde Barnhart, Carson Bigbee, Fred Brickell, Bullet Joe Bush *, Max Carey *, Joe Cronin, Kiki Cuyler, Johnny Gooch, George Grantham, Ray Kremer, Stuffy McInnis, Bill McKechnie (MANAGER), Lee Meadows, Eddie Moore *, Johnny Morrison, Walter Mueller, Eddie Murphy, Red Oldham, Johnny Rawlings, Hal Rhyne, Earl Smith, Don Songer, Roy Spencer, Pie Traynor, Paul Waner, Glenn Wright, Emil Yde

LESS THAN 10 GAMES: Adam Comorosky, Bud Culloton, Carmen Hill, Lou Koupal, Roy Mahaffey, Chet Nichols, Tom Sheehan

NOTES: 6 HOF'ers.

KEY SIGNATURES: McKechnie, Grantham, Wright, Traynor, Waner, Carey, Cuyler, Smith, Cronin, Kremer, Meadows.

VALUE: $1000

1926 ST. LOUIS (AL) - Win Ballou, Herschel Bennett, Dixie Davis, Leo Dixon, Cedric Durst, Chet Falk, Milt Gaston, Wally Gerber, Joe Giard, Pinky Hargrave, Baby Doll Jacobson *, Claude Jonnard, Bobby LaMotte, Marty McManus, Oscar Melillo, Bing Miller *, Ernie Nevers, Harry Rice, Gene Robertson, Wally Shang, George Sisler (MANAGER), Elam Vangilder, Ken Williams, Ernie Wingard, Tom Zachary

LESS THAN 10 GAMES: Jimmy Austin, Stew Bolen, Charlie Robertson.

NOTES: Sisler was a player/manager.

KEY SIGNATURES: Sisler, Miller, Rice, Shang.

VALUE: $380

1926 ST. LOUIS (NL) - Grover Alexander *, Hi Bell, Les Bell, Ray Blades, Jim Bottomley, Taylor Douthit, Jake Flowers, Chick Hafey, Jesse Haines, Wild Bill Hallahan, Wattie Holm, Rogers Hornsby (MANAGER), Syl Johnson, Vic Keen, Heinie Mueller *, Bob O'Farrell, Art Reinhart, Flint Rhem, Bill Sherdel, Allen Sothoron, Billy Southworth *, Tommy Thevenow, Specs Toporcer, Ernie Vick

LESS THAN 10 GAMES: Ed Clough, Eddie Dyer, Walter Huntzinger *, Duster Mails, Jack Smith *, Bill Warwick

NOTES: World Champions! 5 HOF'ers.

KEY SIGNATURES: Hornsby, Bottomley, Bell, Southworth, Douthit, Blades, Hafey, Rhem, Haines, Alexander.

VALUE: $1825

1926 WASHINGTON - Ossie Bluege, Bullet Joe Bush, Stan Coveleski, General Crowder, Alex Ferguson, Goose Goslin, Bucky Harris (MANAGER), Bucky Harris, Joe Harris, Tex Jeanes, Walter Johnson, Joe Judge, Firpo Marberry, Earl McNeely, Bill Morrell, George Murray, Buddy Myer, Curly Ogden, Roger Peckinpaugh, Bobby Reeves, Sam Rice, Muddy Ruel, Dutch Ruether *, Hank Severeid *, Stuffy Stewart, Bennie Tate, Danny Taylor, Jack Tobin *

LESS THAN 10 GAMES: Russ Ennis, Bump Hadley, Dick Jones, Harry Kelley, Pat Loftus, Emilio Palmero, Lefty Thomas, Jimmie Uchrinscko

NOTES: 5 HOF'ers.

KEY SIGNATURES: Harris, Myer, Rice, McNeely, Goslin, Johnson, Coveleski.

VALUE: $1000

1927

Babe Ruth led the New York Yankees to the World Series by hitting 60 home runs in 1927.

*** = player was traded**

1927 BOSTON (AL) - Cleo Carlyle, Bill Carrigan (MANAGER), Ira Flagstead, Fred Haney *, Slim Harriss, Grover Hartley, Fred Hofmann, Baby Doll Jacobson *, Del Lundgren, Danny MacFayden, Bill Moore, Buddy Myer *, Bill Regan, Billy Rogell, Red Rollings, Jack Rothrock, Red Ruffing, Jack Russell, Wally Shaner, Arlie Tarbert, Jack Tobin, Phil Todt, Pee Wee Wanninger *, Frank Welch, Tony Welzer, Hal Wiltse, Ted Wingfield

LESS THAN 10 GAMES: Frank Bennett, Herb Bradley, Fred Bratchi, Frank Bushey, Bob Cremins, Elmer Eggert, John Freeman, Marty Karow, Topper Rigney *, Rudy Sommers, John Wilson

KEY SIGNATURES: Tobin, Ruffing.

VALUE: $375

1927 BOSTON (NL) - Dave Bancroft (MANAGER), Larry Benton *, Eddie Brown, Dick Burrus, Earl Clark, Johnny Cooney, Foster Edwards, Doc Farrell *, Jack Fournier, Doc Gautreau, Joe Genewich, Frank Gibson, Hal Goldsmith, Kent Greenfield *, Andy High, Shanty Hogan, Les Mann *, Dinny McNamara, Hugh McQuillan *, Art Mills, George Mogridge, Eddie Moore, Guy Morrison, Lance Richbourg, Charlie Robertson, Bob Smith, Jack Smith, Zack Taylor *, Herb Thomas *, Luke Urban, Jim Welsh, Johnny Wertz

LESS THAN 10 GAMES: Sid Graves, Bunny Hearn, Jack Knight, Dick Rudolph

NOTES: Bancroft was a player/manager.

KEY SIGNATURES: Bancroft, High, Richbourg, Brown.

VALUE: $375

1927 BROOKLYN - Jesse Barnes, Bob Barrett, John Butler, Max Carey, Watty Clark, Chuck Corgan, Hank DeBerry, Bill Doak, Rube Ehrhardt, Jumbo Jim Elliott, Gus Felix, Jake Flowers, Charlie Hargreaves, Harvey Hendrick, Butch Henline, Babe Herman, Merwin Jacobson, Doug McWeeney, Irish Meusel, Jay Partridge, Jesse Petty, Norman Plitt, Wilbert Robinson (MANAGER), Jigger Statz, Overton Tremper, Dazzy Vance

LESS THAN 10 GAMES: Guy Cantrell, Chick Fewster, Bill Mariott, Bob McGraw, Ray Moss, Oscar Roettger

KEY SIGNATURES: Robinson, Carey, Vance.

VALUE: $950

1927 CHICAGO (AL) - Charlie Barnabe, Bill Barrett, Jim Battle, Moe Berg, Lena Blackburne, Ted Blankenship, Ike Boone, Bud Clancy, Bert Cole, Sarge Connally, Buck Crouse, Fed Faber, Bibb Falk, Ray Flaskamper, Bill Hunnefield, Elmer Jacobs, Willie Kamm, Ted Lyons, Harry McCurdy, Alex Metzler, Randy Moore, Johnny Mostil, Bernie Neis *, Roger Peckinpaugh, Carl Reynolds, Ray Schalk (MANAGER), Earl Sheely, Tommy Thomas, Aaron Ward, Bobby Way, Kid Willson

LESS THAN 10 GAMES: Joe Brown, Frank Stewart

NOTES: Schalk was a player/manager.

KEY SIGNATURES: Schalk, Clancy, Metzler, Falk, Lyons, Faber.

VALUE: $400

1927 CHICAGO (NL) - Sparky Adams, Clyde Beck, Sheriff Blake, Jim Brillheart, Guy Bush, Hal Carlson *, Jimmy Cooney *, Woody English, Howard Freigau, Mike Gonzalez, Charlie Grimm, Gabby Hartnett, Cliff Heathcote, Percy Jones, Joe McCarthy (MANAGER), Bob Osborn, Eddie Pick, Charlie Root, Luther Roy, Pete Scott, Riggs Stephenson, Chuck Tolson, Earl Webb, Hack Wilson, Elmer Yoter

LESS THAN 10 GAMES: John Churry, Wayland Dean *, Hank Grampp, Fred Haney *, Tony Kaufmann *, Art Nehf *, Tommy Sewell, Lefty Weinert, Johnny Welch, Harry Wilke

KEY SIGNATURES: McCarthy, Grimm, Webb, Wilson, Stephenson, Hartnett, Root.

VALUE: $600

1927 CINCINNATI - Ethan Allen, Rube Bressler, Cuckoo Christenson, Hughie Critz, Pete Donohue, Chuck Dressen, Hod Ford, Bubbles Hargrave, Jack Hendricks (MANAGER), George Kelly, Ray Kolp, Red Lucas, Dolf Luque, Jakie May, Carl Mays, Art Nehf *, Val Picinich, Babe Pinelli, Wally Pipp, Pinky Pittinger, Pid Purdy, Eppa Rixey, Clyde Sukeforth, Curt Walker, Pee Wee Wanninger *, Billy Zitzmann

LESS THAN 10 GAMES: Pete Appleton, Jim Beckman, Jack White, Ray Wolf

KEY SIGNATURES: Hargrave, Kelly, Rixey.

VALUE: $360

1927 CLEVELAND - Martin Autry, Garland Buckeye, Johnny Burnett, George Burns, Nick Cullop *, Fred Eichrodt, Lew Fonseca, George Gerken, Johnny Gill, George Grant, Johnny Hodapp, Willis Hudlin, Baby Doll Jacobson *, Charlie Jamieson, Benn Karr, Sam Langford, Emil Levsen, Carl Lind, Rube Lutzke, Jack McCallister (MANAGER), Pat McNulty, Jake Miller, Glenn Myatt, Bernie Neis *, Ernie Padgett, Joe Sewell, Luke Sewell, Joe Shaute, Sherry Smith, Freddie Spurgeon, Homer Summa, George Uhle, Dutch Ussat

LESS THAN 10 GAMES: Jumbo Brown, Hap Collard, Nick Cullop *, Wes Ferrell, Hal McKain, Willie Underhill

KEY SIGNATURES: Burns, Fonseca, J. Sewell, Jamieson, Miller.

VALUE: $375

1927 DETROIT - Johnny Bassler, Haskell Billings, Lu Blue, Ownie Carroll, Rip Collins, Bob Fothergill, Charlie Gehringer, Sam Gibson, Don Hankins, Harry Heilmann, Ken Holloway, Heinie Manush, Marty McManus, George Moriarty (MANAGER), Johnny Neun, Art Ruble, Merv Shea, George Smith, Lil Stoner, Jackie Tavener, Bernie de Viveiros, Jack Warner, Earl Whitehill, Al Wingo, Larry Woodall

LESS THAN 10 GAMES: Jess Doyle, Augie Johns, Clyde Manion, Rufus Smith, Jim Walkup, Ed Wells

KEY SIGNATURES: Gehringer, Heilmann, Manush, Fothergill, Collins.

VALUE: $465

1927 NEW YORK (AL) - Benny Bengough, Pat Collins, Earle Combs, Joe Dugan, Cedric Durst, Mike Gazella, Lou Gehrig, Joe Giard, Johnny Grabowski, Waite Hoyt, Mark Koenig, Tony Lazzeri, Bob Meusel, Wilcy Moore, Ray Morehart, Ben Paschal, Herb Pennock, George Pipgras, Dutch Ruether, Babe Ruth, Bob Shawkey, Urban Shocker, Myles Thomas, Julie Wera

LESS THAN 10 GAMES: Walter Beall, Miller Huggins (MANAGER)

NOTES: World Champions! "Murderers' Row" - considered by some as the best team of all time; 7 HOF'ers; Ruth hit 60 home runs.

KEY SIGNATURES: Gehrig, Lazzeri, Ruth, Combs, Meusel, Hoyt, Moore, Pennock.

VALUE: $10000

HOF = Hall of Famer

1927 NEW YORK (NL) - Virgil Barnes, Larry Benton *, Bill Clarkson, Jack Cummings, Al DeVormer, Doc Farrell *, Freddie Fitzsimmons, Kent Greenfield *, Burleigh Grimes, Sam Hamby, George Harper, Dutch Henry, Rogers Hornsby, Travis Jackson, Tex Jeanes, Fred Lindstrom, Les Mann *, John McGraw (MANAGER), Hugh McQuillan *, Heinie Mueller, Mickey O'Neill *, Mel Ott, Andy Reese, Edd Roush, Don Songer *, Zack Taylor *, Bill Terry, Herb Thomas *, Ty Tyson, Ross Youngs

LESS THAN 10 GAMES: Jack Bentley, Hank Boney, Bullet Joe Bush *, Ben Cantwell, Virgil Cheeves, Jim Faulkner, Mul Holland, Art Johnson, Buck Jordan, Joe Klinger, Norman Plitt *, Ned Porter, Red Smith, Fay Thomas, Bill Walker

NOTES: 8 HOF'ers.

KEY SIGNATURES: McGraw, Terry, Hornsby, Jackson, Lindstrom, Harper, Roush, Grimes.

VALUE: $2250

1927 PHILADELPHIA (AL) - Max Bishop, Joe Boley, Dud Branom, Ty Cobb, Mickey Cochrane, Eddie Collins, Jimmy Dykes, Howard Ehmke, Jimmie Foxx, Walt French, Chick Galloway, Sam Gray, Lefty Grove, Sammy Hale, Baby Doll Jacobson *, Jing Johnson, Bill Lamar, Connie Mack (MANAGER), Joe Pate, Cy Perkins, Jim Poole, Ike Powers, Jack Quinn, Eddie Rommel, Al Simmons, Rube Walberg, Zack Wheat, Lefty Willis

LESS THAN 10 GAMES: Neal Baker, Charlie Bates, Guy Cantrell, Jimmy Dykes, Joe Mellana, Rusty Saunders, Buzz Wetzel, Carroll Yerkes

NOTES: 8 HOF'ers.

KEY SIGNATURES: Mack, Dykes, Hale, Cobb, Simmons, French, Cochrane, Collins, Wheat, Foxx, Grove.

VALUE: $2750

1927 PHILADELPHIA (NL) - Dick Attreau, Hal Carlson, Jimmy Cooney *, Art Decatur, Alex Ferguson, Barney Friberg, Bubber Jonnard, Freddy Leach, Stuffy McInnis (MANAGER), Clarence Mitchell, Johnny Mokan, Al Nixon, Harry O'Donnell, Hub Pruett, Heinie Sand, Jack Scott, Dick Spalding, Les Sweetland, Fresco Thompson, Dutch Ulrich, Cy Williams, Claude Willoughby, Jimmie Wilson, Russ Wrightstone

LESS THAN 10 GAMES: Ed Baecht, Henry Baldwin, Wayland Dean *, Bill Deitrick, Bill Hohman, Tony Kaufmann *, Stuffy McInnis, Russ Miller, Skinny O'Neal, Lefty Taber, Augie Walsh

KEY SIGNATURES: Wrightstone, Thompson, Leach.

VALUE: $315

1927 PITTSBURGH - Vic Aldridge, Clyde Barnhart, Fred Brickell, Donie Bush (MANAGER), Adam Comorosky, Joe Cronin, Kiki Cuyler, Mike Cvengros, Joe Dawson, Johnny Gooch, George Grantham, Heinie Groh, Joe Harris, Carmen Hill, Ray Kremer, Herman Layne, Lee Meadows, Johnny Miljus, Johnny Morrison, Hal Rhyne, Earl Smith, Roy Spencer, Pie Traynor, Lloyd Waner, Paul Waner, Glenn Wright

LESS THAN 10 GAMES: Dick Bartell, Bullet Joe Bush *, Roy Mahaffey, Chet Nichols, Red Peery, Eddie Sicking, Don Songer *, Emil Yde

NOTES: 5 HOF'ers.

KEY SIGNATURES: Harris, Grantham, Traynor, P. Waner, L. Waner, Barnhart, Cuyler, Groh, Cronin, Kremer.

VALUE: $775

1927 ST. LOUIS (AL) - Spencer Adams, Win Ballou, Herschel Bennett, General Crowder *, Leo Dixon, Milt Gaston, Wally Gerber, Dan Howley (MANAGER), Sad Sam Jones, Red Kress, Oscar Melillo, Bing Miller, Otto Miller, Ernie Nevers, Steve O'Neill, Frank O'Rourke, Harry Rice, Wally Schang, Fred Schulte, George Sisler, Lefty Stewart, Guy Sturdy, Elam Vangilder, Ken Williams, Ernie Wingard, Tom Zachary *

LESS THAN 10 GAMES: Boom-Boom Beck, George Blaeholder, Stew Bolen, Chet Falk, Jiggs Wright

KEY SIGNATURES: Sisler, Miller, Williams, Schang.

VALUE: $375

1927 ST. LOUIS (NL) - Pete Alexander, Hi Bell, Les Bell, Ray Blades, Jim Bottomley, Danny Clark, Taylor Douthit, Frankie Frisch, Chick Hafey, Jesse Haines, Wattie Holm, Vic Keen, Carlisle Littlejohn, Bob McGraw, Bob O'Farrell (MANAGER), Ernie Orsatti, Art Reinhart, Flint Rhem, Jimmy Ring, Heinie Schuble, Johnny Schulte, Bill Sherdel, Frank Snyder, Billy Southworth, Tommy Thevenow, Specs Toporcer

LESS THAN 10 GAMES: Eddie Dyer, Fred Frankhouse, Syl Johnson, Tony Kaufmann, Rabbit Maranville, Homer Peel, Wally Roettger, Bobby Schang

NOTES: 6 HOF'ers; O'Farrell was a player/manager.

KEY SIGNATURES: Bottomley, Frisch, Maranville, Haines, Alexander.

VALUE: $1350

1927 WASHINGTON - Ossie Bluege, Garland Braxton, Bobby Burke, General Crowder *, Nick Cullop *, Babe Ganzel, Grant Gillis, Goose Goslin, Bump Hadley, Bucky Harris (MANAGER), Jackie Hayes, Walter Johnson, Joe Judge, Hod Lisenbee, Firpo Marberry, Earl McNeely, Buddy Myer *, Bobby Reeves, Sam Rice, Topper Rigney *, Muddy Ruel, Tris Speaker, Stuffy Stewart, Bennie Tate, Sloppy Thurston, Ollie Tucker, Sammy West, Tom Zachary *

LESS THAN 10 GAMES: Lefty Atkinson, Red Barnes, Johnny Berger, Dick Coffman, Stan Coveleski, Buddy Dear, Paul Hopkins, Dick Jones, Ralph Judd, George Murray, Mickey O'Neil *, Eddie Onslow, Clay Van Alstyne

NOTES: 6 HOF'ers; Harris was a player/manager.

KEY SIGNATURES: Harris, Judge, Rice, Speaker, Goslin, Ruel, Lisenbee, Hadley, Johnson, Coveleski.

VALUE: $1400

1928

Hall of Famer Ty Cobb played his last game in 1928.

*** = player was traded**

1928 BOSTON (AL) - Charlie Berry, Herb Bradley, Bill Carrigan (MANAGER), Ira Flagstead, Wally Gerber *, Marty Griffin, Slim Harriss, Johnnie Heving, Fred Hofmann, George Loepp, Danny MacMayden, Ed Morris, Buddy Myer, Bill Regan, Billy Rogell, Red Rollings, Jack Rothrock, Red Ruffing, Red Ruggins, Jack Russell, Merle Settlemire, Pat Simmons, Carl Sumher, Doug Taitt, Phil Todt, Denny Williams, Ken Williams

LESS THAN 10 GAMES: Casper Asbjornson, Frank Bennett, Cliff Garrison, Paul Hinson, Freddie Moncewicz, John Shea, Steve Slayton, Doug Taitt, Arlie Tarbert, John Wilson, Hal Wiltse *

KEY SIGNATURES: Myer, Williams, Ruffing.

VALUE: $350

1928 BOSTON (NL) - Virgil Barnes *, Les Bell, Ed Brandt, Eddie Brown, Dick Burrus, Ben Cantwell *, Earl Clark, Bill Clarkson, Jimmy Cooney, Art Delaney, Foster Edwards, Doc Farrell, Charlie Fitzberger, Howard Freigau *, Doc Gautreau, Joe Genewich *, Kent Greenfield, Dave Harris, Rogers Hornsby (MANAGER), Eddie Moore, Heinie Mueller, Lance Richbourg, Charlie Robertson, George Sisler *, Jack Slattery (MANAGER), Bob Smith, Jack Smith, Al Spohrer *, Zack Taylor, Luke Urban, Johnny Wertz, Earl Williams

LESS THAN 10 GAMES: Ray Boggs, Bill Cronin, Hal Goldsmith, Bunny Hearn, Bonnie Hollingsworth, Dinny McNamera, Art Mills, Guy Morrison, Emilio Palmero, Clay Touchstone

NOTES: Hornsby was a player/manager.

KEY SIGNATURES: Hornsby, Sisler, Richbourg.

VALUE: $875

1928 BROOKLYN - Dave Bancroft, Del Bissonette, Rube Bressler, Max Carey, Watty Clark, Hank DeBerry, Bill Doak, Rube Ehrhardt, Jumbo Jim Elliott, Jake Flowers, Howard Freigau *, Wally Gilbert, Johnny Gooch *, Charlie Hargreaves *, Joe Harris *, Harvey Hendrick, Butch Henline, Babe Herman, Lou Koupal, Wilbert Robinson (MANAGER), Doug McWeeny, Ray Moss, Jay Partridge, Jesse Petty, Harry Riconda, Jigger Statz, Overton Tremper, Ty Tyson, Dazzy Vance

LESS THAN 10 GAMES: Al Lopez, Max West

NOTES: 5 HOF'ers.

KEY SIGNATURES: Robinson, Bissonette, Bancroft, Hendrick, Herman, Carey, Lopez, Vance.

VALUE: $1150

HOF = Hall of Famer

1928 CHICAGO (AL) - Grady Adkins, Bill Barrett, Moe Berg, Lena Blackburne (MANAGER), George Blackerby, Ted Blankenship, Bill Cissell, Bud Clancy, Sarge Connally, George Cox, Buck Crouse, Red Faber, Bibb Falk, Bill Hunnelfield, Willie Kamm, Ted Lyons, Harry McCurdy, Alex Metzler, Randy Moore, Johnny Mostil, Buck Redfern, Carl Reynolds, Ray Schalk (MANAGER), Art Shires, Karl Swanson, Tommy Thomas, Ed Walsh

LESS THAN 10 GAMES: Charlie Barnabe, Dan Dugan, John Goodell, Rudy Leopold, Johnny Mann, Bob Weiland, Al Williamson, Roy Wilson

NOTES: 4 HOF'ers; Schalk was a player/manager.

KEY SIGNATURES: Schalk, Kamm, Metzler, Lyons, Walsh, Faber.

VALUE: $600

1928 CHICAGO (NL) - Clyde Beck, Sheriff Blake, Guy Bush, Johnny Butler, Hal Carlson, Kiki Cuyler, Woody English, Mike Gonzalez, Charlie Grimm, Gabby Hartnett, Cliff Heathcote, Ed Holley, Percy Jones, Joe Kelly, Freddie Maguire, Pat Malone, Joe McCarthy (MANAGER), Norm McMillan, Art Nehf, Charlie Root, Riggs Stephenson, Earl Webb, Lefty Weinert, Hack Wilson

LESS THAN 10 GAMES: Ray Jacobs, Johnny Moore, Ben Tincup, Johnny Welch, Elmer Yoter

KEY SIGNATURES: McCarthy, Cuyler, Wilson, Stephenson, Hartnett.

VALUE: $560

1928 CINCINNATI - Ethan Allen, Pete Appleton, Marty Callaghan, Hughie Critz, Pete Donohue, Chuck Dressen, Jim Joe Edwards, Hod Ford, Bubbles Hargrave, Jack Hendricks (MANAGER), George Kelly, Ray Kolp, Red Lucas, Dolf Luque, Jakie May, Carl Mays, Val Picinich, Wally Pipp, Pinky Pittinger, Pid Purdy, Eppa Rixey, Joe Stripp, Clyde Sukeforth, Curt Walker, Billy Zitzmann

LESS THAN 10 GAMES: Ken Ash, Jim Beckman, Si Johnson, Harlan Pyle, Jack White

KEY SIGNATURES: Kelly, Allen, Rixey.

VALUE: $350

1928 CLEVELAND - Martin Autry, Bill Bayne, George Burns *, Bruce Caldwell, Red Dorman, Lew Fonseca, George Gerken, George Grant, Mel Harder, Luther Harvel, Johnny Hodapp, Willis Hudlin, Charlie Jamieson, Sam Langford, Emil Levsen, Carl Lind, Johnny Miljus *, Jake Miller, Ed Montague, Eddie Morgan, Glenn Myatt, Roger Peckinpaugh (MANAGER), Joe Sewell, Luke Sewell, Joe Shaute, Homer Summa, Ollie Tucker, George Uhle, Willie Underhill

LESS THAN 10 GAMES: Les Barnhart, Cecil Bolton, CLint Brown, Jumbo Brown, Garland Buckeye *, Johnny Burnett, Hap Collard, Wes Ferrell, Johnny Gill, Jonah Goldman, Jim Moore, Art Reinholz, Al Van Camp, Aaron Ward, Frank Wilson *

KEY SIGNATURES: Fonseca, Sewell, Hodapp, Jamieson.

VALUE: $350

1928 DETROIT - Haskell Billings, Ownie Carroll, Paul Easterling, Bob Fothergill, Chick Galloway, Charlie Gehringer, Sam Gibson, Pinky Hargrave, Harry Heilmann, Ken Holloway, Marty McManus, George Moriarty (MANAGER), Johnny Neun, Harry Rice, Merv Shea, George Smith, Vic Sorrell, John Stone, Lil Stoner, Bill Sweeney, Jackie Taverner, Elam Vangilder, Jack Warner, Earl Whitehill, Al Wingo, Larry Woodall

LESS THAN 10 GAMES: Phil Page, Charlie Sullivan

KEY SIGNATURES: Gehringer, Heilmann, Rice.

VALUE: $400

1928 NEW YORK (AL) - Benny Bengough, Cedric Burst, Archie Campbell, Pat Collins, Earl Combs, Stan Coveleski, Bill Dickey, Joe Dugan, Leo Durocher, Mike Gazella, Lou Gehrig, Johnny Grabowski, Fred Heimach, Waite Hoyt, Miller Huggins (MANAGER), Hank Johnson, Mark Koenig, Tony Lazzeri, Bob Meusel, Wilcy Moore, Ben Paschal, Herb Pennock, George Pipgras, Gene Robertson, Babe Ruth, Al Shealy, Myles Thomas

LESS THAN 10 GAMES: George Burns *, Rosy Ryan, Urban Shocker, Tom Zachary *

NOTES: World Champions! 9 HOF'ers; Shocker died 9/9/28.

KEY SIGNATURES: Huggins, Gehrig, Lazzeri, Koenig, Ruth, Combs, Dickey, Pipgras, Hoyt, Pennock, Coveleski.

VALUE: $4000

1928 NEW YORK (NL) - Vic Aldridge, Virgil Barnes *, Larry Benton, Tiny Chaplin, Andy Cohen, Jack Cummings, Jim Faulkner, Freddie Fitzsimmons, Chick Fullis, Joe Genewich *, George Harper *, Dutch Henry, Shanty Hogan, Carl Hubbell, Travis Jackson, Art Jahn *, Fred Lindstrom, Les Mann, John McGraw (MANAGER), Lefty O'Doul, Bob O'Farrell *, Mel Ott, Andy Reese, Edd Roush, Jack Scott, Bill Terry, Bill Walker, Jim Welsh, Russ Wrightstone *

LESS THAN 10 GAMES: Garland Buckeye *, Ben Cantwell *, Bill Clarkson *, Ray Foley, Bill Haeffner, Leo Mangum, Chet Nichols, Joe Price, Al Spohrer *, Pat Veltman

NOTES: 7 HOF'ers.

KEY SIGNATURES: McGraw, Terry, Jackson, Lindstrom, Ott, Welsh, O'Doul, Hogan, Roush, Benton, Fitzsimmons, Hubbell.

VALUE: $1400

1928 PHILADELPHIA (AL) - Max Bishop, Joe Boley, Bullet Joe Bush, Ty Cobb, Mickey Cochrane, Eddie Collins, Jimmy Dykes, George Earnshaw, Howard Ehmke, Jimmie Foxx, Walt French, Lefty Grove, Mule Haas, Sammy Hale, Joe Hassler, Joe Hauser, Connie Mack (MANAGER), Bing Miller, Ossie Orwoll, Cy Perkins, Jack Quinn, Eddie Rommel, Al Simmons, Tris Speaker, Rube Walberg

LESS THAN 10 GAMES: Art Daney, Jing Johnson, Ike Powers, Bill Shore, Carroll Yerkes

NOTES: 8 HOF'ers.

KEY SIGNATURES: Mack, Bishop, Hale, Cobb, Miller, Simmons, Cochrane, Foxx, Speaker, Collins, Grove, Quinn.

VALUE: $2500

1928 PHILADELPHIA (NL) - Ray Benge, Spud Davis *, Bill Deitrick, Alex Ferguson, Barney Friberg, Don Hurst, Art Jahn *, Bill Kelly, Chuck Klein, Freddy Leach, Walt Lerian, Harvey MacDonald, Bob McGraw, Russ Miller, John Milligan, Al Nixon, Hub Pruett, Jimmy Ring, Heinie Sand, Johnny Schulte, Burt Shotten (MANAGER), Denny Sothern, Les Sweetland, Fresco Thompson, Dutch Ulrich, Augie Walsh, Pinky Whitney, Cy Williams, Claude Willoughby, Jimmie Wilson *, Russ Wrightstone *

LESS THAN 10 GAMES: Ed Baecht, Earl Caldwell, June Green, Ed Lennon, Clarence Mitchell *, Marty Walker

KEY SIGNATURES: Whitney, Klein, Leach.

VALUE: $400

1928 PITTSBURGH - Sparky Adams, Clyde Barnhart, Dick Bartell, Erv Brame, Fred Brickell, Donie Bush (MANAGER), Adam Comorosky, Joe Dawson, Fred Fussell, Johnny Gooch *, George Grantham, Burleigh Grimes, Charlie Hargreaves *, Joe Harris *, Rolllie Hemsley, Carmen Hill, Mack Hillis, Ray Kremer, Johnny Miljus *, Eddie Mulligan, Pete Scott, Earl Smith *, Walt Tauscher, Pie Traynor, Lloyd Waner, Paul Waner, Glenn Wright

LESS THAN 10 GAMES: Glenn Spencer, Less Bartholomew, Homer Blankenship, Bill Burwell, Cobe Jones, Lee Meadows, John O'Connell, Elmer Tutwiler, Bill Windle

KEY SIGNATURES: Grantham, Wright, Traynor, P. Waner, L. Waner, Brickell, Grimes.

VALUE: $625

1928 ST. LOUIS (AL) - Boom-Boom Beck, Larry Bettencourt, George Blaeholder, Lu Blue, Otis Brannan, Dick Coffman, General Crowder, Sam Gray, Dan Howley (MANAGER), Red Kress, Clyde Manion, Heinie Manush, Beauty McGowen, Earl McNeely, Oscar Melillo, Billy Mullen, Steve O'Neill, Frank O'Rourke, Jack Ogden, Ollie Sax, Wally Schang, Fred Schulte, Lefty Stewart, Ed Strelecki, Guy Sturdy, Hal Wiltse *

LESS THAN 10 GAMES: Fred Bennett, Ike Danning, Wally Gerber *, Ernie Nevers, Frank Wilson *, Jiggs Wright

KEY SIGNATURES: Manush, Crowder.

VALUE: $375

1928 ST. LOUIS (NL) - Grover Alexander, Ray Blades, Jim Bottomley, Taylor Douthit, Fred Frankhouse, Frankie Frisch, Chick Hafey, Hal Haid, Jesse Haines, George Harper *, Andy High, Wattie Holm, Syl Johnson, Carlisle Littlejohn, Gus Mancuso, Rabbit Maranville, Pepper Martin, Bill McKechnie (MANAGER), Clarence Mitchell, Bob O'Farrell *, Ernie Orsatti, Art Reinhart, Flint Rhem, Wally Roettger, Bill Sherdel, Earl Smith *, Tommy Thevenow, Howie Williamson, Jimmie Wilson *

LESS THAN 10 GAMES: Spud Davis *, Tony Kaufmann, Specs Toporcer

NOTES: 7 HOF'ers.

KEY SIGNATURES: McKechnie, Bottomley, Frisch, Maranville, Hafey, Haines, Alexander.

VALUE: $1500

1928 WASHINGTON - Red Barnes, Ossie Bluege, Harley Boss, Garland Braxton, Lloyd Brown, Bobby Burke, Joe Cronin, Ed Crowley, Babe Ganzel, Milt Gaston, Grant Gilllis, Goose Goslin, Bump Hadley, Bucky Harris (MANAGER), Jackie Hayes, Sad Sam Jones, Joe Judge, Ed Kenna, Hod Lisenbee, Firpo Marberry, Bobby Reeves, Sam Rice, Muddy Ruel, George Sisler *, Dick Spaulding, Bennie Tate, Sammy West, Tom Zachary *

LESS THAN 10 GAMES: Pelham Ballenger, Al Bool, Hugh McMullen, Clay Van Alstyne, Jim Weaver

NOTES: 5 HOF'ers; Harris was a player/manager.

KEY SIGNATURES: Harris, Judge, Reeves, Rice, Barnes, Goslin, Cronin, Sisler, Jones.

VALUE: $600

1929

1929 Philadelphia Athletics

*** = player was traded**

1929 BOSTON (AL) - Casper Asbjornson, Bob Barrett, Bill Barrett *, Bill Bayne, Charlie Berry, Elliot Bigelow, Bill Carrigan (MANAGER), Ed Carroll, Joe Cicero, Ray Dobens, Ed Durham, Ira Flagstead *, Alex Gaston, Milt Gaston, Wally Gerber, Grant Gillis, Johnnie Heving, Danny MacFayden, Ed Morris, Bill Narleski, Bobby Reeves, Bill Regan,

Hal Rhyne, Jack Rothrock, Red Ruffing, Jack Russell, Russ Scarritt, Jerry Standaert, Doug Taitt *, Phil Todt, Ken Williams

LESS THAN 10 GAMES: Herb Bradley, Ed Connolly, Hod Lisenbee, Jack Ryan, Pat Simmons

KEY SIGNATURES: Rothrock, Ruffing.

VALUE: $275

1929 BOSTON (NL) - Red Barron, Les Bell, Buzz Boyle, Ed Brandt, Ben Cantwell, Earl Clark, Johnny Cooney, Bruce Cunningham, Art Delaney, Joe Dugan, Bill Dunlap, Judge Fuchs (MANAGER), Hank Gowdy, George Harper, Bunny Hearn, Bernie James, Percy Jones, Lou Legett, Dixie Leverett, Freddie Maguire, Rabbit Maranville, Heinie Mueller, Lance Richbourg, Socks Seibold, George Sisler, Bob Smith, Jack Smith, Al Spohrer, Zack Taylor *, Phil Voyles, Jim Welsh *

LESS THAN 10 GAMES: Bill Clarkson, Pat Collins, Bill Cronin, Jack Cummings, Johnny Evers, Doc Farrell *, Kent Greenfield *, Red Peery, Henry Peploski, Gene Robertson *, Clay Touchstone, Johnny Wertz, Al Weston

NOTES: The ball is worth $850 with the signature of Evers or $400 without his signature.

KEY SIGNATURES: Sisler, Maranville, Richbourg, Clark, Evers.

VALUE: $850

1929 BROOKLYN - Win Ballou, Dave Bancroft, Del Bissonette, Rube Bressler, Max Carey, Watty Clark, Nick Cullop, Hank DeBerry, Clise Dudley, Jake Flowers, Johnny Frederick, Wally Gilbert, Harvey Hendrick, Butch Henline, Babe Herman, Lou Koupal *, Doug McWeeny, Cy Moore, Eddie Moore, Johnny Morrison, Ray Moss, Val Picinich, Billy Rhiel, Wilbert Robinson (MANAGER), Dazzy Vance, Jack Warner, Glen Wright

LESS THAN 10 GAMES: Clarence Blethen, Joe Bradshaw, Jumbo Jim Elliott, Alex Ferguson *, Johnny Gooch *, Kent Greenfield *, Bobo Newsom, Jimmy Pattison, Luther Roy *, Max West

NOTES: 4 HOF'ers.

KEY SIGNATURES: Robinson, Bancroft, Gilbert, Herman, Frederick, Bressler, Carey, Vance.

VALUE: $975

1929 CHICAGO (AL) - Grady Adkins, Martin Autry, Moe Berg, Lena Blackburne (MANAGER), Bill Cissell, Bud Clancy, Sarge Connally, Buck Crouse, Dan Dugan, Red Faber, Dutch Hoffman, Bill Hunnefield, Willie Kamm, John Kerr, Ted Lyons, Hal McKain, Alex Metzler, Johnny Mostil, Buck Redfern, Carl Reynolds, Art Shires, Doug Taitt *, Tommy Thomas, Ed Walsh, Johnny Watwood, Bob Weiland

LESS THAN 10 GAMES: Bill Barrett *, Lena Blackburne, Ted Blankenship, Jerry Byrne, Dutch Henry *, Frank Sigafoos *, Karl Swanson

KEY SIGNATURES: Shires, Reynolds, Lyons, Faber.

VALUE: $330

1929 CHICAGO (NL) - Clyde Beck, Footsie Blair, Sheriff Blake, Guy Bush, Hal Carlson, Kiki Cuyler, Mike Cvengros, Woody English, Mike Gonzalez, Earl Grace, Charlie Grimm, Gabby Hartnett, Cliff Heathcote, Trader Horne, Rogers Hornsby, Claude Jonnard, Pat Malone, Joe McCarthy (MANAGER), Norm McMillan, Johnny Moore, Art Nehf, Charlie Root, Johnny Schulte, Riggs Stephenson, Zack Taylor *, Chuck Tolson, Hack Wilson

LESS THAN 10 GAMES: Tom Angley, Hank Grampp, Bob Osborne, Ken Penner, Danny Taylor

KEY SIGNATURES: McCarthy, Hornsby, Cuyler, Wilson, Hartnett, Malone.

VALUE: $1000

1929 CINCINNATI - Ethan Allen, Ken Ash, Hughie Critz, Leo Dixon, Pete Donohue, Chuck Dressen, Rube Ehrhardt, Hod Ford, Johnny Gooch *, Jack Hendricks (MANAGER), George Kelly, Ray Kolp, Red Lucas, Dolf Luque, Jakie May, Pinky Pittinger, Pid Purdy, Eppa Rixey, Wally Shaner, Joe Stripp, Clyde Sukeforth, Evar Swanson, Curt Walker, Ivy Wingo, Billy Zitzmann

LESS THAN 10 GAMES: Estel Crabtree, Benny Frey, Marv Gudat, Si Johnson, Dutch Kemner, Hugh McMullen, Paul Zahniser

KEY SIGNATURES: Kelly, Dressen, Swanson, Gooch, Rixey.

VALUE: $325

1929 CLEVELAND - Earl Averill, Johnny Burnett, Bibb Falk, Wes Ferrell, Lew Fonseca, Ray Gardner, George Grant, Mel Harder, Grover Hartley, Joe Hauser, Johnny Hodapp, Ken Holloway, Willis Hudlin, Charlie Jamieson, Carl Lind, Johnny Miljus, Jake Miller, Eddie Morgan, Glenn Myatt, Roger Peckinpaugh (MANAGER), Dick Porter, Joe Sewell, Luke Sewell, Joe Shaute, Milt Shoffner, Jackie Tavener, Jimmy Zinn

LESS THAN 10 GAMES: Clint Brown, Dan Jessee, Jim Moore.

KEY SIGNATURES: Fonseca, Hodapp, Sewell, Falk, Averill, Sewell, Ferrell.

VALUE: $400

1929 DETROIT - Bill Akers, Dale Alexander, Ownie Carroll, Bob Fothergill, Charlie Gehringer, Kyle Graham, Pinky Hargrave, Bucky Harris (MANAGER), Ray Hayworth, Harry Heilmann, Roy Johnson, Marty McManus, Phil Page, Eddie Phillips, Augie Prudhomme, Harry Rice, Nolen Richardson, Heinie Schuble, Merv Shea, Frank Sigafoos *, George Smith, Vic Sorrell, John Stone, Lil Stoner, George Uhle, Earl Whitehill, Yats Wuestling, Emil Yde

LESS THAN 10 GAMES: Frank Barnes, Haskell Billings, Bucky Harris, Art Herring, Chief Hogsett, Elam Vangilder, Larry Woodall, Whit Wyatt

KEY SIGNATURES: Harris, Alexander, Gehringer, Heilmann, Rice, Johnson.

HOF = Hall of Famer

VALUE: $400

1929 NEW YORK (AL) - Benny Bengough, Sammy Byrd, Earl Combs, Bill Dickey, Leo Durocher, Cedric Durst, Art Fletcher (MANAGER), Lou Gehrig, Johnny Grabowski, Fred Heimach, Waite Hoyt, Miller Huggins (MANAGER), Hank Johnson, Art Jorgens, Mark Koenig, Lyn Lary, Tony Lazzeri, Bob Meusel, Wilcy Moore, Ben Paschal, Herb Pennock, George Pipgras, Gordon Rhodes, Gene Robertson *, Babe Ruth, Roy Sherid, Ed Wells, Tom Zachary

LESS THAN 10 GAMES: George Burns *, Liz Funk, Bots Nekola, Myles Thomas *, Julie Wera

NOTES: 8 HOF'ers.

KEY SIGNATURES: Huggins, Gehrig, Lazzeri, Ruth, Combs, Dickey, Wells, Hoyt, Pennock.

VALUE: $3400

1929 NEW YORK (NL) - Larry Benton, Andy Cohen, Pat Crawford *, Doc Farrell, Freddie Fitzsimmons, Chick Fullis, Joe Genewich, Dutch Henry, Shanty Hogan, Carl Hubbell, Travis Jackson, Ralph Judd, Tony Kaufmann, Freddy Leach, Fred Lindstrom, Carl Mays, John McGraw (MANAGER), Bob O'Farrell, Mel Ott, Andy Reese, Edd Roush, Jack Scott, Bill Terry, Bill Walker, Jim Welsh *

LESS THAN 10 GAMES: Jack Cummings *, Buck Jordan, Sam Leslie, Ray Lucas, Doc Marshall, Roy Parmelee, Ray Schalk, Jim Tennant, Pat Veltman

NOTES: 7 HOF'ers.

KEY SIGNATURES: McGraw, Terry, Jackson, Lindstrom, Ott, Roush, Hubbell.

VALUE: $1325

1929 PHILADELPHIA (AL) - Max Bishop, Joe Boley, George Burns *, Mickey Cochrane, Jim Cronin, Jimmy Dykes, George Earnshaw, Howard Ehmke, Jimmie Foxx, Walt French, Lefty Grove, Mule Haas, Sammy Hale, Bevo LeBourveau, Connie Mack (MANAGER), Bing Miller, Ossie Orwoll, Cy Perkins, Jack Quinn, Eddie Rommel, Bill Shores, Al Simmons, Homer Summa, Rube Walberg, Carroll Yerkes

LESS THAN 10 GAMES: Bill Breckinridge, Eddie Collins, Doc Cramer, Joe Hassler, Cloy Mattox, Eric McNair, Rudy Miller, Bud Morse

NOTES: World Champions! 7 HOF'ers.

KEY SIGNATURES: Mack, Foxx, Miller, Haas, Simmons, Cochrane, Cronin, Collins, Earnshaw, Grove.

HOF = Hall of Famer

VALUE: $1000

1929 PHILADELPHIA (NL) - Ray Benge, Phil Collins, Sam Dailey, Spud Davis, Hal Elliott, Barney Friberg, June Green, Don Hurst, Chuck Klein, Lou Koupal *, Walt Lerian, Bob McGraw, Elmer Miller, Lefty O'Doul, Homer Peel, Luther Roy *, Burt Shotton (MANAGER), Tripp Sigman, Harry Smythe, Denny Sothern, George Susce, Les Sweetland, Tommy Thevenow, Fresco Thompson, Pinky Whitney, Cy Williams, Claude Willoughby

LESS THAN 10 GAMES: Alex Ferguson *, June Green, Jim Holloway, Terry Lyons, Elmer Miller, John Milligan, Joe O'Rourke.

NOTES: Lerian died 10/22/29.

KEY SIGNATURES: Hurst, Thompson, Thevenow, Whitney, Klein, Sothern, O'Doul.

VALUE: $375

1929 PITTSBURGH - Sparky Adams, Dick Bartell, Erv Brame, Fred Brickell, Donie Bush (MANAGER), Stu Clarke, Adam Comorosky, Jewel Ens (MANAGER), Ira Flagstead, Larry French, Fred Fussell, George Grantham, Burleigh Grimes, Charlie Hargreaves, Rollie Hemsley, Carmel Hill, Cobe Jones, Kay Kremer, Bob Linton, Heinie Meine, Jesse Petty, Earl Sheely, Steve Swetonic, Pie Traynor, Lloyd Waner, Paul Waner

LESS THAN 10 GAMES: Leon Chagnon, Joe Dawson, Ralph Erickson, Mel Ingram, Lee Meadows, Jim Mosolf, John O'Connell, Harry Riconda, Ben Sankey, Jim Stroner, Bill Windle

KEY SIGNATURES: Grantham, Bartell, Traynor, P. Waner, L. Wayner, Comorosky, Grimes.

VALUE: $620

1929 ST. LOUIS (AL) - Red Badgrow, George Blaeholder, Lu Blue, Otis Brannan, Dick Coffman, Rip Collins, General Crowder, Len Dondero, Rick Ferrell, Sam Gray, Dan Howley (MANAGER), Tom Jenkins, Chad Kimsey, Red Kress, Clyde Manion, Heinie Manush, Beauty McGowan, Earl McNeely, Oscar Mellilo, Frank O'Rourke, Jack Ogden, Ed Roetz, Wally Schang, Fred Schulte, Lefty Stewart

LESS THAN 10 GAMES: Jimmy Austin, Herb Cobb, Oscar Estrada, Paul Hopkins, Fred Stiely, Ed Strelecki

KEY SIGNATURES: Kress, Schulte, Manush, Ferrell.

VALUE: $400

1929 ST. LOUIS (NL) - Pete Alexander, Jim Bottomley, Johnny Butler, Eddie Delker, Taylor Douthit, Fred Frankhouse, Frankie Frisch, Charlie Gelbert, Chick Hafey, Hal Haid, Jesse Haines, Wild Bill Hallahan, Fred Haney, Andy High, Wattie Holm, Syl Johnson, Bubber Jonnard, Bill McKechnie (MANAGER), Clarence Mitchell, Ernie Orsatti, Wally Roettger, Carey Selph, Bill Sherdel, Earl Smith, Billy Southworth (MANAGER), Gabby Street (MANAGER), Jimmie Wilson

LESS THAN 10 GAMES: Hi Bell, Bill Doak, Hal Goldsmith, Al Grabowski, Carmen Hill *, Mul Holland, Jim Lindsey.

NOTES: 6 HOF'ers; Southworth was a player/manager.

KEY SIGNATURES: McKechnie, Bottomley, Frisch, Orsatti, Douthit, Hafey, Wilson, Johnson, Haines, Alexander.

HOF = Hall of Famer

VALUE: $1075

1929 WASHINGTON - Red Barnes, Ossie Bluege, Harley Boss, Garland Braxton, Lloyd Brown, Bobby Burke, Joe Cronin, Ira Flagstead *, Charlie Gooch, Goose Goslin, Bump Hadley, Jackie Hayes, Walter Johnson (MANAGER), Sad Sam Jones, Joe Judge, Ad Liska, Firpo Marberry, Buddy Myer, Sam Rice, Muddy Ruel, Roy Spencer, Stuffy Stewart, Bennie Tate, Myles Thomas *, Sammy West

LESS THAN 10 GAMES: Nick Altrock, Walter Beall, Archie Campbell, Patsy Gharrity, Spence Harris, Paul Hopkins *, Doc Land, Paul McCullough, Don Savidge, Ed Wineapple

NOTES: 4 HOF'ers.

KEY SIGNATURES: Johnson, Judge, Myer, Cronin, Rice, Goslin.

VALUE: $1450

1930

1930 Philadelphia Athletics

*** = player was traded**

1930 BOSTON (AL) - Charlie Berry, Frank Bushey, Joe Cicero, Ed Connolly, Ed Durham, Cedric Durst *, Milt Gaston, Johnnie Heving, Hod Lisenbee, Danny MacFayden, Otto Miller, Ed Morris, Bill Narleski, Tom Oliver, Bobby Reeves, Bill Regan, Hal Rhyne, Jack Rothrock, Jack Russell, Russ Scarritt, Charlie Small, George Smith, Bill Sweeney, Phil Todt, Heinie Wagner (MANAGER), Rabbit Warstler, Earl Webb

LESS THAN 10 GAMES: Bill Barrett *, Bill Bayne, Jim Galvin, Bob Kline, Frank Mulroney, Red Ruffing *, Ben Shields, Tom Winsett

KEY SIGNATURES: Webb and Ruffing.

VALUE: $270

1930 BOSTON (NL) - Wally Berger, Ed Brandt, Ben Cantwell, Buster Chatham, Earl Clark, Bill Cronin, Bruce Cunningham, Bill Dunlap, Fred Frankhouse *, Hank Gowdy, Burleigh Grimes *, Freddie Maguire, Rabbit Maranville, Bill McKechnie (MANAGER), Randy Moore, Johnny Neun, Billy Rhiel, Lance Richbourg, Gene Robertson, Red Rollings, Socks Seibold, Bill Sherdel *, George Sisler, Bob Smith, Al Spohrer, Jim Welsh, Tom Zachary *

LESS THAN 10 GAMES: Buzz Boyle, Bob Brown, Johnny Cooney, Bernie James, Ken Jones, Owen Kahm

NOTES: 4 HOF'ers.

KEY SIGNATURES: McKechnie, Sisler, Maranville, Grimes.

VALUE: $525

1930 BROOKLYN - Del Bissonette, Ike Boone, Rube Bressler, Watty Clark, Hank DeBerry, Clise Dudley, Jumbo Jim Elliott, Neal Finn, Jake Flowers, Johnny Frederick, Wally Gilbert, Harvey Hendrick, Babe Herman, Hal Lee, Al Lopez, Dolf Luque, Eddie

Moore, Johnny Morrison, Ray Moss, Ray Phelps, Val Picinich, Wilbert Robinson (MANAGER), Gordon Slade, Sloppy Thurston, Dazzy Vance, Jack Warner, Glenn Wright

LESS THAN 10 GAMES: Jim Faulkner, Fred Heimach, Cy Moore, Bobo Newsom

KEY SIGNATURES: Robinson, Bissonette, Wright, Herman, Frederick, Lopez, Vance.

VALUE: $850

1930 CHICAGO (AL) - Martin Autry, Red Barnes *, Moe Berg, Garland Braxton *, Donie Bush (MANAGER), Pat Caraway, Bill Cissell, Bud Clancy, Buck Crouse, Red Faber, Bob Fothergill *, Dave Harris *, Dutch Henry, Bill Hunnefield, Irv Jeffries, Smead Jolley, Willie Kamm, John Kerr, Ted Lyons, Hal McKain, Alex Metzler *, Jim Moore *, Greg Mulleavy, Carl Reynolds, Johnny Riddle, Blondy Ryan, Art Shires *, Ernie Smith, Bennie Tate *, Tommy Thomas, Ed Walsh, Johnny Watwood, Bob Weiland

LESS THAN 10 GAMES: Luke Appling, Ted Blankenship, Bruce Campbell, Butch Henline, Joe Klinger, Jim Moore, Biggs Wehde, Hugh Willingham

KEY SIGNATURES: Watwood, Jolley, Reynolds, Lyons, Appling, Faber.

VALUE: $300

1930 CHICAGO (NL) - Clyde Beck, Les Bell, Footsie Blair, Sheriff Blake, Guy Bush, Kiki Cuyler, Woody English, Doc Farrell *, Charlie Grimm, Gabby Hartnett, Cliff Heathcote, Rogers Hornsby (MANAGER), George Kelly *, Pat Malone, Joe McCarthy (MANAGER), Mal Moss, Lynn Nelson, Bob Osborn, Charlie Root, Al Shealy, Riggs Stephenson, Danny Taylor, Zack Taylor, Bud Teachout, Chuck Tolson, Hack Wilson

LESS THAN 10 GAMES: Hal Carlson, Bill McAfee, Jesse Petty *, Lon Warneke

NOTES: 7 HOF'ers; Hal Carlson died 5/28/30; Hornsby was a player/manager.

KEY SIGNATURES: McCarthy, Grimm, Cuyler, Wilson, Hartnett, Hornsby, Kelly.

VALUE: $1100

1930 CINCINNATI - Ethan Allen *, Ken Ash, Larry Benton *, Marty Callaghan, Archie Campbell, Pat Crawford *, Hughie Critz *, Tony Cuccinello, Chuck Dressen, Leo Durocher, Hod Ford, Benny Frey, Johnny Gooch, Harry Heilmann, Dan Howley (MANAGER), Si Johnson, George Kelly *, Ray Kolp, Red Lucas, Jakie May, Bob Meusel, Eppa Rixey, Joe Stripp, Clyde Sukeforth, Evar Swanson, Curt Walker

LESS THAN 10 GAMES: Ownie Carroll *, Nick Cullop, Pete Donohue *, Al Eckert, Doug McWeeny, Harry Riconda, Lena Styles, Biff Wysong

KEY SIGNATURES: Durocher, Cuccinello, Heilmann, Walker, Kelly, Rixey.

VALUE: $425

1930 CLEVELAND - Pete Appleton, Earl Averill, Belve Bean, Clint Brown, Johnny Burnett, Bib Falk, Wes Ferrell, Lew Fonseca, Ray Gardner, Jonah Goldman, Mel Harder, Grover Hartley, Johnny Hodapp, Ken Holloway *, Willis Hudlin, Charlie Jamieson, Carl Lind, Jake Miller, Ed Montague, Eddie Morgan, Glenn Myatt, Roger Peckinpaugh (MANAGER), Dick Porter, Bob Seeds, Joe Sewell, Luke Sewell, Milt Shoffner, Joe Sprinz, Joe Vosmik

LESS THAN 10 GAMES: Les Barnhart, George Detore, Sal Gliatto, Roxie Lawson, Joe Shaute, Ralph Winegarner

NOTES: Sewell brothers were on the same team.

KEY SIGNATURES: Morgan, Hodapp, J. Sewell, Porter, Averill, Jamieson, L. Sewell, Ferrell.

VALUE: $350

1930 DETROIT - Bill Akers, Dale Alexander, Guy Cantrell, Gene Desautels, Frank Doljack, Paul Easterling, Bob Fothergill *, Liz Funk, Charlie Gehringer, Pinky Hargrave *, Bucky Harris (MANAGER), Ray Hayworth, Art Herring, Chief Hogsett, Waite Hoyt *, Tom Hughs, Roy Johnson, Marty McManus, Phil Page, Tony Rensa *, Harry Rice *, Bill Rogell, Jimmy Shevlin, Vic Sorrell, John Stone, Charlie Sullivan, George Uhle, Earl Whitehill, Whit Wyatt

LESS THAN 10 GAMES: Tommy Bridges, Ownie Carroll *, Hank Greenberg, Mark Koenig *, Joe Samuels, Johnny Watson, Hughie Wise, Yats Wuestling

KEY SIGNATURES: Harris, Alexander, Gehringer, McManus, Stone, Hoyt, Greenerg.

VALUE: $365

1930 NEW YORK (AL) - Benny Bengough, Sammy Byrd, Ownie Carroll *, Ben Chapman, Earle Combs, Dusty Cooke, Bill Dickey, Cedric Durst, Lou Gehrig, Lefty Gomez, Bubbles Hargrave, Ken Holloway *, Hank Johnson, Art Jorgens, Mark Koenig *, Lyn Lary, Tony Lazzeri, Herb Pennock, George Pipgras, Jimmy Reese, Harry Rice *, Red Ruffing *, Babe Ruth, Bob Shawkey (MANAGER), Roy Sherid, Ed Wells, Yats Wuestling *, Tom Zachary *

LESS THAN 10 GAMES: Frank Barnes, Foster Edwards, Sam Gibson, Bill Henderson, Waite Hoyt *, Bill Karlon, Lou McEvoy, Gordon Rhodes, Bob Shawkey (MANAGER), Bill Werber

NOTES: 9 HOF'ers.

KEY SIGNATURES: Gehrig, Lazzeri, Chapman, Ruth, Hoyt, Combs, Ruffing, Gomez, Pennock, Dickey.

VALUE: $3400

1930 NEW YORK (NL) - Ethan Allen *, Dave Bancroft, Tiny Chaplin, Pat Crawford *, Hughie Critz *, Pete Donohue *, Freddie Fitzsimmons, Chick Fullis, Joe Genewich, Joe Heving, Shanty Hogan, Carl Hubbell, Travis Jackson, Freddy Leach, Fred Lindstrom, Doc Marshall, John McGraw (MANAGER), Clarence Mitchell *, Bob O'Farrell, Mel Ott, Roy Parmelee, Hub Pruett, Andy Reese, Wally Roettger, Ed Roush, Bill Terry, Bill Walker

LESS THAN 10 GAMES: Larry Benton *, Francis Healy, Ralph Judd, Sam Leslie, Ray Lucas, Joe Moore, Bill Morrell, Harry Rosenberg

NOTES: 8 HOF'ers; Terry's .401 season.

KEY SIGNATURES: McGraw, Terry, Jackson, Lindstrom, Ott, Leach, Hogan, Bancroft, Roush, Hubbell.

VALUE: $1450

1930 PHILADELPHIA (AL) - Max Bishop, Joe Boley, Mickey Cochrane, Doc Cramer, Jimmy Dykes, George Earnshaw, Jimmie Foxx, Lefty Grove, Mule Haas, Spence Harris, Pinky Higgins, Jim Keesey, Connie Mack (MANAGER), Roy Mahaffey, Eric McNair, Bing Miller, Jim Moore *, Cy Perkins, Jack Quinn, Eddie Rommel, Wally Schang, Bill Shores, Al Simmons, Homer Summa, Rube Walberg, Dib Williams

LESS THAN 10 GAMES: Eddie Collins, Howard Ehmke, Glenn Liebhardt, Al Mahon, Charlie Perkins

NOTES: World Champions! 6 HOF'ers.

KEY SIGNATURES: Mack, Foxx, Dykes, Miller, Simmons, Cochrane, Collins, Grove.

VALUE: $825

1930 PHILADELPHIA (NL) - Ray Benge, Fred Brickell *, Hap Collard, Phil Collins, Spud Davis, Hal Elliott, Barney Friberg, Snipe Hansen, Don Hurst, Chuck Klein, Lou Koupal, Harry McCurdy, Chet Nichols, Lefty O'Doul, Buz Phillips, Tony Rensa *, Monk Sherlock, Burt Shotton (MANAGER), Tripp Sigman, Harry Smythe, Denny Sothern *, By Speece, Les Sweetland, Tommy Thevenow, Fresco Thompson, Pinky Whitney, Cy Williams, Claude Willoughby

LESS THAN 10 GAMES: Grover Alexander, John Milligan, Jim Spotts

KEY SIGNATURES: Hurst, Whitney, O'Doul, Davis, Alexander, Klein.

VALUE: $860

1930 PITTSBURGH - Dick Bartell, Al Bool, Erv Brame, Fred Brickell *, Leon Chagnon, Adam Comorosky, Charlie Engle, Jewel Ens (MANAGER), Ira Flagstead, Larry French, George Grantham, Charlie Hargreaves, Rollie Hemsley, Ray Kremer, Heinie Meine, Jim Mosolf, Jesse Petty *, Ben Sankey, Denny Sothern, Glenn Spencer, Gus Suhr, Steve Swetonic, Pie Traynor, Lloyd Waner, Paul Waner

LESS THAN 10 GAMES: Andy Bednar, Stu Clarke, Gus Dugas, Ralph Erickson, Howie Groskloss, Percy Jones, Marty Lang, Lil Stoner, Bernie Walter, Spades Wood

KEY SIGNATURES: Grantham, Bartell, Traynor, P. Waner, L. Waner, Comorosky.

VALUE: $550

1930 ST. LOUIS (AL) - Red Badgro, George Blaeholder, Lu Blue, Dick Coffman, Rip Collins, General Crowder *, Rick Ferrell, Goose Goslin *, Sam Gray, Ted Gullic, Sammy Hale, Herm Holshouser, Bernie Hungling, Bill Killefer (MANAGER), Chad Kimsey, Red Kress, Clyde Manion, Heinie Manush *, Earl McNeely, Oscar Melillo, Alex Metzler *, Frank O'Rourke, Fred Schulte, Lefty Stewart, Rollie Stiles

LESS THAN 10 GAMES: Jack Burns, Jack Crouch, Joe Hassler, Tom Jenkins, Jim Levey, Fred Stiely, Lin Storti

KEY SIGNATURES: Kress, Goslin, Ferrell, Manush.

VALUE: $445

1930 ST. LOUIS (NL) - Sparky Adams, Hi Bell, Ray Blades, Jim Bottomley, Taylor Douthit, Doc Farrell *, Showboat Fisher, Frankie Frisch, Charlie Gelbert, Al Grabowski, Burleigh Grimes *, Chick Hafey, Hal Haid, Jesse Haines, Wild Bill Hallahan, Andy High, Syl Johnson, Jim Lindsey, Gus Mancuso, Ernie Orsatti, Homer Peel, George Puccinelli, Flint Rheim, Bill Sherdel *, Gabby Street (MANAGER), George Watkins, Jimmie Wilson

LESS THAN 10 GAMES: Dizzy Dean, Fred Frankhouse *, Carmen Hill, Tony Kaufmann, Pepper Martin, Clarence Mitchell *, Earl Smith

NOTES: 6 HOF'ers; all eight starters had batting averages over .300

KEY SIGNATURES: Street, Bottomley, Frisch, Gelbert, Adams, Watkins, Douthit, Hafey, Wilson, Grimes, Haines, Dean.

VALUE: $875

HOF = Hall of Famer

1930 WASHINGTON - Red Barnes *, Ossie Bluege, Garland Braxton *, Lloyd Brown, Bobby Burke, Joe Cronin, General Crowder *, Goose Goslin *, Bump Hadley, Pinky Hargrave *, Dave Harris *, Jackie Hayes, Walter Johnson (MANAGER), Sad Sam Jones, Joe Judge, Joe Kuhel, Ad Liska, George Loepp, Heinie Manush *, Firpo Marberry, Jim McLeod, Buddy Myer, Sam Rice, Muddy Ruel, Art Shires *, Roy Spencer, Bennis Tate *, Myles Thomas, Sammy West

LESS THAN 10 GAMES: Bill Barrett *, Harley Boss, Harry Child, Carl Fischer, Patsy Gharrity, Carlos Moore, Jake Powell, Ray Treadway

NOTES: 5 HOF'ers.

KEY SIGNATURES: Johnson, Judge, Myer, Cronin, Rice, Manush, Goslin, Marberry.

VALUE: $1700

*** = player was traded**

1931 National League MVP Frankie Frisch

1931 BOSTON (AL) - Charlie Berry, Jim Brillheart, Shano Collins (MANAGER), Ed Connolly, Pat Creeden, Ed Durham, Milt Gaston, Bob Kline, Hod Lisenbee, Johnny Lucas, Danny MacFayden, Ollie Marquardt, Bill Marshall, Marty McManus *, Bill McWilliams, Otto Miller, Wilcy Moore, Ed Morris, Tom Oliver, Marv Olson, Urban Pickering, Bobby Reeves, Hal Rhyne, J. Rothrock, Muddy Ruel *, Jack Russell, Gene Rye, John Smith, Howie Storie, Bill Sweeney, Al VanCamp, Rabbit Warstler, Earl Webb, Tom Winsett

LESS THAN 10 GAMES: Jud McLaughlin, Walter Murphy, Bobby Reeves, Russ Scarritt, George Stumpf

KEY SIGNATURES: Webb.

VALUE: $270

1931 BOSTON (NL) - Wally Berger, Al Bool, Ed Brandt, Ben Cantwell, Buster Chatham, Earl Clark, Bill Cronin, Bruce Cunningham, Bill Dreesen, Fred Frankhouse, Hal Hard, Bill Hunnefield *, Freddie Maguire, Rabbit Maranville, Bill McAlee, Bill McKechnie (MANAGER), Randy Moore, Ray Moss *, Johnny Neun, Lance Richbourg, Wes Schulmerich, Socks Seibold, Earl Sheely, Bill Sherdel, Al Spohrer, Billy Urbanski, Charlie Wilson, Red Worthington, Tom Zachary

LESS THAN 10 GAMES: Bob Brown, John Scalzi, Pat Veltman, Bucky Walters

KEY SIGNATURES: Maranville, Schulmerich, Berger, McKechnie.

VALUE: $400

1931 BROOKLYN - Del Bissonette, Rube Bressler, Watty Clark, Pea Ridge Day, Neal Finn, Jake Flowers *, Johnny Frederick, Wally Gilbert, Fred Heimach, Babe Herman, Ernie Lombardi, Al Lopez, Dolf Luque, Cy Moore, Lefty O'Doul, Ray Phelps, Val Picinich, Jack Quinn, Wilbert Robinson (MANAGER), Joe Shaute, Gordon Slade, Denny Sothern, Fresco Thompson, Sloppy Thurston, Dazzy Vance, Glenn Wright

LESS THAN 10 GAMES: Ike Boone, Alta Cohen, Phil Gallivan, Harvey Hendrick *, Earl Mattingly, Ray Moss *, Van Lingle Mungo, Bobby Reis, Max Rosenfeld, Jack Warner

NOTES: 4 HOF'ers.

KEY SIGNATURES: O'Doul, Lopez, Lombardi, Vance, Robinson.

VALUE: $1000

1931 CHICAGO (AL) - Luke Appling, Lu Blue, Grant Bowler, Garland Braxton *, Donie Bush (MANAGER), Pat Caraway, Bill Cissell, Fred Eichrodt, Red Faber, Lew Fonseca *, Bob Fothergill, Vic Frasier, Frank Grube, Butch Henline, Irv Jeffries, Smead Jolley, Willie Kamm *, John Kerr, Ted Lyons, Hal McKain, Jim Moore, Bill Norman, Carl Reynolds, Mel Simons, Billy Sullivan, Bennie Tate, Tommy Thomas, Johnny Watwood, Bob Weiland

LESS THAN 10 GAMES: Bruce Campbell, Lou Garland *, Hank Garrity, Biggs Wehde

KEY SIGNATURES: Blue, Appling, Faber, Lyons.

VALUE: $300

1931 CHICAGO (NL) - Jimmy Adair, Ed Baecht, Vince Barton, Les Bell, Footsie Blair, Sheriff Blake *, Guy Bush, Kiki Cuyler, Woody English, Charlie Grimm, Gabby Hartnett, Rollie Hemsley *, Billy Herman, Rogers Hornsby (MANAGER), Billy Jurges, Pat Malone, Jakie May, Johnny Moore, Charlie Root, Bob Smith, Riggs Stephenson, Les Sweetland, Danny Taylor, Bud Treachout, Lon Warneke, Hack Wilson

LESS THAN 10 GAMES: Earl Grace *, Mike Kreevich, Zack Taylor, John Welch

NOTES: 5 HOF'ers; Hornsby was a player/manager.

KEY SIGNATURES: Grimm, Hornsby, English, Cuyler, Wilson, Taylor, Hartnett, Herman.

VALUE: $875

1931 CINCINNATI - Casper Asbjornson, Clyde Beck, Larry Benton, Ownie Carroll, Estel Crabtree, Tony Cuccinello, Nick Cullop, Taylor Douthit *, Leo Durocher, Al Eckert, Hod Ford, Benny Frey, Cliff Heathcote, Harry Heilmann, Harvey Hendrick *, Dan Howley (MANAGER), Si Johnson, Ray Kolp, Red Lucas, Jack Ogden, Eppa Rixey, Wally Roettger *, Edd Roush, Frank Sigafoos, Ed Strelecki, Joe Stripp, Lena Styles, Clyde Sukeforth, Biff Wylong

LESS THAN 10 GAMES: Chuck Dressen, Ray Fitzgerald, Mickey Heath, Whitey Hilcher, Gene Moore

KEY SIGNATURES: Hendrick, Cuccinello, Stripp, Roush, Heilmann, Rixey.

VALUE: $400

1931 CLEVELAND - Earl Averill, Clint Brown, Johnny Burnett, Sarge Connally, Bruce Connatser, George Detore, Bibb Falk, Wes Ferrell, Lew Fonseca *, Jonah Goldman, Odell Hale, Mel Harder, Johnny Hodapp, Willis Hudlin, Bill Hunnefield *, Pete Jablonowski, Charlie Jamieson, Willie Kamm *, Roxie Lawson, Ed Montague, Eddie Morgan, Glenn Myatt, Roger Peckinpaugh (MANAGER), Dick Porter, Bob Seeds, Luke Sewell, Milt Shoffner, Fay Thomas, Joe Vosmik

LESS THAN 10 GAMES: Belve Bean, Moe Berg, Howard Craighead, Pete Donohue *, Oral Hildebrand, Jake Miller, Joe Sprinz

KEY SIGNATURES: Morgan, Porter, Averill.

VALUE: $300

1931 DETROIT - Bill Akers, Dale Alexander, Tommy Bridges, Lou Brower, Frank Dolijack, Charlie Gehringer, Johnny Grabowski, Bucky Harris (MANAGER), Ray Hayworth, Art Herring, Chief Hogsett, Waite Hoyt *, Roy Johnson, Mark Koenig, Marty McManus *, Marv Owen, George Quellich, Nolen Richardson, Billy Rogell, Muddy Ruel *, Wally Schang, Vic Sorrell, John Stone, Charlie Sullivan, George Uhle, Gee Walker, Hub Walker, Earl Whitehill

LESS THAN 10 GAMES: Orlin Collier, Gene Desautels, Joe Dugan, Bucky Harris, Ivey Shiver, Whit Wyatt

KEY SIGNATURES: Alexander, Gehringer, Rogell, Stone, Hoyt, Harris.

VALUE: $365

1931 NEW YORK (AL) - Sammy Byrd, Ben Chapman, Earle Combs, Dusty Cooke, Bill Dickey, Lou Gehrig, Lefty Gomez, Myril Hoag, Hank Johnson, Art Jorgens, Lyn Lary, Tony Lazzeri, Joe McCarthy (MANAGER), Herb Pennock, Cy Perkins, George Pipgras, Jimmy Reese, Gordon Rhodes, Red Ruffing, Babe Ruth, Joe Sewell, Roy Sherid, Jim Weaver, Lefty Weinert, Ed Wells

LESS THAN 10 GAMES: Ivy Andrews, Lou McEvoy, Red Rolfe, Dixie Walker

NOTES: 10 HOF'ers.

KEY SIGNATURES: Gehrig, Lazzeri, Sewell, Ruth, Combs, Chapman, Dickey, Ruffing, Gomez, Pennock, McCarthy.

VALUE: $3600

HOF = Hall of Famer

1931 NEW YORK (NL) - Ethan Allen, Jack Berly, Tiny Chaplin, Hugh Critz, Freddie Fitzsimmons, Chick Fullis, Joe Heving, Shanty Hogan, Carl Hubbell, Bill Hunnefield *, Travis Jackson, Freddy Leach, Sam Leslie, Fred Lindstrom, Doc Marshall, John McGraw (MANAGER), Clarence Mitchell, Bill Morrell, Bob O'Farrell, Mel Ott, Roy Parmelee, Bill Terry, Johnny Vergez, Bill Walker

LESS THAN 10 GAMES: Pete Donohue *, Gil English, Francis Healy, Ray Lucas, Jim Mooney, Jo-Jo Moore, Emil Planeta, Hal Schumacher

NOTES: 6 HOF'ers.

KEY SIGNATURES: Terry, Jackson, Lindstrom, Ott, Leach, Hogan, Walker, Hubbell, McGraw.

VALUE: $1200

1931 PHILADELPHIA (AL) - Max Bishop, Joe Boley, Mickey Cochrane, Doc Cramer, Jimmy Dykes, George Earnshaw, Jimmie Foxx, Lefty Grove, Mule Haas, Johnnie Heving, Waite Hoyt *, Connie Mack (MANAGER), Roy Mahaffey, Hank McDonald, Eric McNair, Bing Miller, Jim Moore, Joe Palmisano, Eddie Rommel, Al Simmons, Phil Todt, Rube Walberg, Dib Williams

LESS THAN 10 GAMES: Sol Carter, Lou Finney, Lew Krausse, Jim Peterson, Bill Shores

NOTES: 6 HOF'ers; Grove (MVP).

KEY SIGNATURES: Mack, Foxx, Simmons, Cochrane, Grove, Earnshaw, Hoyt.

VALUE: $780

1931 PHILADELPHIA (NL) - Buzz Arlett, Dick Bartell, Ray Benge, Sheriff Blake *, Stew Bolen, Fred Brickell, Phil Collins, Spud Davis, Clise Dudley, Hal Elliott, Jumbo Jim Elliott, Ed Failenstein, Barney Friberg, Don Hurst, Chuck Klein, Fred Koster, Hal Lee, Les Mallon, Harry McCurdy, Tony Rensa, Dutch Schesler, Burt Shotton (MANAGER), Bobby Stevens, Doug Taitt, Frank Watt, Pinky Whitney, Hugh Willingham

LESS THAN 10 GAMES: Bob Adams, Gene Connell, John Miligan, Chet Nichols, Ben Shields, Lil Stoner, Hal Wiltse

KEY SIGNATURES: Hurst, Mallon, Arlett, Klein, Davis.

VALUE: $375

1931 PITTSBURGH - Fred Bennett, Erv Brame, Adam Comorosky, Gus Dugas, Jewel Ens (MANAGER), Larry French, Earl Grace *, George Grant, George Grantham, Howie Groskloss, Woody Jensen, Ray Kremer, Heinie Meine, Jim Mosolf, Bob Osborn, Eddie Phillips, Tony Piet, Bill Regan, Ben Sankey, Glenn Spencer, Gus Suhr, Steve Swetonic, Tommy Thevenow, Pie Traynor, Lloyd Waner, Paul Waner, Spades Wood

LESS THAN 10 GAMES: Andy Bednar, Hal Finney, Bill Harris, Rollie Hemsley *, Pete McClanahan, Bill Steinecke, Claude Willoughby

KEY SIGNATURES: Grantham, Traynor, Waner, Waner.

VALUE: $525

1931 ST. LOUIS (AL) - Benny Bengough, Larry Bettencourt, George Blaeholder, Garland Braxton *, Jack Burns, Dick Coffman, Rip Collins, Rick Ferrell, Goose Goslin, Sam Gray, Ed Grimes, Wally Hebert, Tom Jenkins, Bill Killefer (MANAGER), Chad Kimsey, Red Kress, Jim Levey, Earl McNeely, Oscar Melillo, Fred Schulte, Buck Stanton, Lefty Stewart, Rollie Stiles, Lin Storti, Frank Waddey, Russ Young

LESS THAN 10 GAMES: Bob Cooney, Jack Crouch, Jess Doyle, Nap Kloza, Frank O'Rouke, Fred Stiely

KEY SIGNATURES: Melillo, Kress, Schulte, Goslin, Ferrell.

VALUE: $375

1931 ST. LOUIS (NL) - Sparky Adams, Joe Benes, Ray Blades, Jim Bottomley, Ripper Collins, Paul Derringer, Taylor Douthit *, Jake Flowers *, Frankie Frisch, Charlie Gelbert, Mike Gonzalez, Burleigh Grimes, Chick Hafey, Jesse Haines, Wild Bill Hallahan, Andy High, Syl Johnson, Tony Kaufmann, Jim Lindsey, Gus Mancuso, Pepper Martin, Ernie Orsatti, Flint Rhem, Wally Roettger *, Allyn Stout, Gabby Street (MANAGER), George Watkins, Jimmie Wilson

LESS THAN 10 GAMES: Ray Cunningham, Eddie Delker, Joel Hunt, Gabby Street

NOTES: World Champions! 5 HOF'ers; Frisch won the MVP Award.

KEY SIGNATURES: Bottomley, Frisch, Hafey, Hallahan, Grimes, Haines.

VALUE: $700

1931 WASHINGTON - Ossie Bluege, Cliff Bolton, Lloyd Brown, Bobby Burke, Joe Cronin, General Crowder, Carl Fischer, Bump Hadley, Pinky Hargrave, Dave Harris, Jackie Hayes, Walter Johnson (MANAGER), Sad Sam Jones, Joe Judge, Joe Kuhel, Heinie Manush, Firpo Marberry, Buddy Myer, Harry Rice, Sam Rice, Roy Spencer, Sammy West

LESS THAN 10 GAMES: Nick Altrock, Bill Andurss, Johnny Gill, Buck Jordan, Ad Liska, Walt Masters, Babe Phelps, Walt Tauscher, Monty Weaver

NOTES: 4 HOF'ers.

KEY SIGNATURES: Cronin, Rice, West, Manush, Crowder, Marberry, Johnson.

VALUE: $1500

1932

1932 American League MVP Jimmie Foxx

***** = **player was traded**

1932 BOSTON (AL) - Dale Alexander *, Ivy Andrews *, Pete Appleton *, Charlie Berry *, Larry Boerner, Shano Collins (MANAGER), Ed Connolly, Ed Durham, Roy Johnson *, Smead Jolley *, Bob Kline, Hod Lisenbee, Danny MacFayden *, Marty McManus (MANAGER), John Michaels, Wilcy Moore *, Ed Morris, Tom Oliver, Marv Olson, Urban Pickering, Johnny Reder, Gordon Rhodes *, Hal Rhyne, Jack Rothrock *, Jack Russell *, Andy Spognardi, George Stumpf, Bennie Tate *, Al Van Camp, Rabbit Warstler, Johnny Watwood *, Earl Webb *, Bob Weiland, Johnny Welch

LESS THAN 10 GAMES: Pete Donohue, Ed Gallagher, Regis Leheny, Johnny Lucas, Jud McLaughlin, Gordon McNaughton, Otto Miller, Hank Patterson, Howie Storie

NOTES: Morris died prior to spring training; McManus was named manager during the season.

KEY SIGNATURES: Alexander, Jolley, Morris.

VALUE: $285

1932 BOSTON (NL) - Bill Akers, Wally Berger, Huck Betts, Ed Brandt, Bob Brown, Ben Cantwell, Earl Clark, Bruce Cunningham, Hod Ford *, Fred Frankhouse, Pinky Hargrave, Dutch Holland, Buck Jordan, Fritz Knothe, Freddy Leach, Rabbit Maranville, Bill McKechnie (MANAGER), Randy Moore, Hub Pruett, Wes Schulmerich, Socks Seibold, Art Shires, Al Spohrer, Billy Urbanski, Bucky Walters, Red Worthington, Tom Zachary

LESS THAN 10 GAMES: Ox Eckhardt, Leo Margum, Johnny Schulte *, Bill Sherdel *

KEY SIGNATURES: Maranville, Berger, Worthington, McKechnie.

VALUE: $375

1932 BROOKLYN - Del Bissonette, Ike Boone, Max Carey (MANAGER), Bud Clancy, Watty Clark, Tony Cuccinello, Neal Finn, Johnny Frederick, Fred Heimach, George Kelly, Al Lopez, Cy Moore, Van Lingle Mungo, Lefty O'Doul, Ray Phelps, Val Picinich, Jack Quinn, Max Rosenfeld, Joe Shaute, Gordon Slade, Joe Stripp, Clyde Sukeforth, Danny Taylor *, Sloppy Thurston, Dazzy Vance, Hack Wilson, Glenn Wright

LESS THAN 10 GAMES: Bruce Caldwell, Alta Cohen, Waite Hoyt *, Art Jones, Ed Pipgras, Bobby Reis, Paul Richards, Dick Siebert, Fay Thomas, Fresco Thompson

NOTES: 6 HOF'ers.

KEY SIGNATURES: Kelly, Wright, Stripp, Wilson, Taylor, O'Doul, Lopez, Clark, Vance, Hoyt, Carey.

VALUE: $725

1932 CHICAGO (AL) - Hal Anderson, Luke Appling, Charlie Berry *, Lu Blue, Pat Caraway, Bill Chamberlain, Bill Cissell *, Pete Daglia, Charlie English, Red Faber, Lew Fonseca (MANAGER), Bob Fothergill, Vic Frasier, Liz Funk, Phil Gallivan, Milt Gaston, Paul Gregory, Frank Grube, Jackie Hayes, Johnny Hodapp *, Smead Jolley *, Sad Sam Jones, Red Kress *, Ted Lyons, Jim Moore, Bill Norman, Jack Rothrock *, Bob Seeds *, Carey Selph, Billy Sullivan, Evar Swanson, Tommy Thomas *, Johnny Watwood *

LESS THAN 10 GAMES: Les Bartholomew, Charlie Biggs, Grant Bowler, Bruce Campbell *, Art Evans, Clarence Fieber, Bump Hadley *, Chad Kimsey *, Fabian Kowalik, Hal McKain, Greg Mulleavy, Bob Poser, Mel Simons, Art Smith, Bennie Tate, Ed Walsh, Archie Wise

KEY SIGNATURES: Appling, Lyons, Faber.

NOTES: Fonseca was a player/manager.

VALUE: $400

1932 CHICAGO (NL) - Vince Barton, Guy Bush, Kiki Cuyler, Frank Demaree, Woody English, Burleigh Grimes, Charlie Grimm (MANAGER), Marv Gudat, Stan Hack, Gabby Harnett, Rollie Hemsley, Billy Herman, Rogers Hornsby (MANAGER), Rogers Hornsby, Billy Jurges, Mark Koenig, Pat Malone, Jakie May, Johnny Moore, Lance Richbourg, Charlie Root, Bob Smith, Riggs Stephenson, Zack Taylor, Bud Tinning, Lon Warneke

LESS THAN 10 GAMES: Ed Baecht, Leroy Hermann, Bobo Newsom, Harry Taylor, Danny Taylor *, Carroll Yerkes

NOTES: 5 HOF'ers; Grimm and Hornsby were player/managers.

KEY SIGNATURES: Grimm, Herman, Cuyler, Moore, Stephenson, Hartnett, Hornsby, Warneke, Grimes.

VALUE: $875

1932 CINCINNATI - Casper Asbjornson, Larry Benton, Ownie Carroll, Estel Crabtree, Taylor Douthit, Leo Durocher, Benny Frey *, Wally Gilbert, George Grantham, Chick Hafey, Mickey Heath, Harry Heilmann, Harvey Hendrick *, Babe Herman, Andy High, Whitey Hilcher, Dan Howley (MANAGER), Si Johnson, Ray Kolp, Ernie Lombardi, Red Lucas, Clyde Manion, Jo-Jo Morrissey, Jack Ogden, Eppa Rixey, Wally Roettger, Jimmy Shevlin

LESS THAN 10 GAMES: Otto Bluege, Cliff Heathcote *, Bipp Wysong

NOTES: 4 HOF'ers.

KEY SIGNATURES: Hendrick, Durocher, Herman, Lombardi, Hafey, Heilmann, Frey.

VALUE: $485

1932 CLEVELAND - Earl Averill, Joe Boley *, Clint Brown, Johnny Burnett, Bill Cissell *, Sarge Connally, Bruce Connatser, Wes Ferrell, Mel Harder, Oral Hildebrand, Willis Hudlin, Charlie Jamieson, Willie Kamm, Ed Montague, Eddie Morgan, Glenn Myatt, Roger Peckinpaugh (MANAGER), Dick Porter, Mike Powers, Frankie Pytlak, Jack Russell *, Luke Sewell, Joe Vosmik

LESS THAN 10 GAMES: Pete Appleton *, Boze Berger, Johnny Hodapp *, Leo Moon, Monte Pearson, Bob Seeds *, Ralph Winegarner

KEY SIGNATURES: Cissell, Porter, Averill, Vosmik.

VALUE: $300

1932 DETROIT - Dale Alexander *, Tommy Bridges, Harry Davis, Gene Desautels, Charlie Gehringer, Izzy Goldstein, Bucky Harris (MANAGER), Ray Hayworth, Art Herring, Chief Hogsett, Roy Johnson *, Bill Lawrence, Buck Marrow, Billy Rhiel, Nolen Richardson, Billy Rogell, Muddy Ruel, Heinie Schuble, Vic Sorrell, John Stone, George Uhle, Gee Walker, Earl Webb *, Jo-Jo White, Earl Whitehill, Whit Wyatt

LESS THAN 10 GAMES: Frank Doljack, Rip Sewell *, George Susce

KEY SIGNATURES: Gehringer, Walker, Harris.

VALUE: $365

1932 NEW YORK (AL) - Johnny Allen, Jumbo Brown, Sammy Byrd, Ben Chapman, Earle Combs, Frankie Crosetti, Bill Dickey, Doc Farrell, Lou Gehrig, Lefty Gomez, Myril Hoag, Art Jorgens, Lyn Lary, Tony Lazzeri, Danny MacFayden *, Joe McCarthy (MANAGER), Wilcy Moore *, Herb Pennock, George Pipgras, Red Ruffing, Babe Ruth, Jack Saltzgaver, Joe Sewell, Ed Wells

LESS THAN 10 GAMES: Ivy Andrews *, Dusty Cooke, Charlie Devens, Joe Glenn, Hank Johnson, Johnny Murphy, Eddie Phillips, Gordon Rhodes *, Roy Schalk

NOTES: World Champions! 11 HOF'ers; Possibly the best team in the history of the game.

KEY SIGNATURES: Gehrig, Lazzeri, Sewell, Ruth, Combs, Dickey, Ruffing, Gomez, Allen, Pennock, McCarthy.

VALUE: $5550

HOF = Hall of Famer

1932 NEW YORK (NL) - Ethan Allen, Hi Bell, Hughie Critz, Gil English, Freddie Fitzsimmons, Chick Fullis, Sam Gibson, Francis Healy, Shanty Hogan, Waite Hoyt *, Carl Hubbell, Travis Jackson, Len Koenecke, Sam Leslie, Fred Lindstrom, Dolf Luque, Doc Marshall, John McGraw (MANAGER), Jim Mooney, Eddie Moore, Jo-Jo Moore, Bob O'Farrell, Mel Ott, Hal Schumacher, Bill Terry (MANAGER), Johnny Vergez, Bill Walker

LESS THAN 10 GAMES: Art McLarney, Clarence Mitchell, Roy Parmelee, Jack Tobin, Pat Veltman

NOTES: 7 HOF'ers; Terry was a player/manager.

KEY SIGNATURES: Terry, Ott, Lindstrom, McGraw, Hogan, Jackson, Jo-Jo Moore, Hoyt, Hubbell.

VALUE: $1100

1932 PHILADELPHIA (AL) - Max Bishop, Joe Boley *, Sugar Cain, Mickey Cochrane, Ed Coleman, Doc Cramer, Jimmy Dykes, George Earnshaw, Jimmie Foxx, Tony Freitas, Lefty Grove, Mule Haas, Johnnie Heving, Lew Krause, Connie Mack (MANAGER), Ed Madjeski, Roy Mahaffey, Eric McNair, Bing Miller, Oscar Roettger, Eddie Rommel, Al Simmons, Rube Walberg, Dib Williams

LESS THAN 10 GAMES: Joe Bowman, Ed Cihocki, Jimmie DeShong, John Jones, Jim McKeithan, Al Reiss, Irv Stein

NOTES: Foxx (MVP); 5 HOF'ers.

KEY SIGNATURES: Cramer, Haas, Simmons, Cochrane, Grove, Mack.

VALUE: $625

1932 PHILADELPHIA (NL) - Dick Bartell, Ray Benge, Jack Berly, Rube Bressler *, Fred Brickell, Phil Collins, Kiddo Davis, Spud Davis, Eddie Delker *, Clise Dudley, Hal Elliott, Jumbo Jim Elliott, Barney Friberg, Reggie Grabowski, Snipe Hansen, Cliff Heathcote *, Ed Holley, Don Hurst, Chuck Klein, Hal Lee, Les Mallon, Harry McCurdy, Chet Nichols, Flint Rhem *, Russ Scarritt, Burt Shotton (MANAGER), Al Todd, Pinky Whitney

LESS THAN 10 GAMES: Bob Adams, Stew Bolen, Geroge Knothe, Ad Liska, Doug Taitt, Hugh Willingham

NOTES: Klein (MVP).

KEY SIGNATURES: Hurst, Bartell, Klein, Davis, Lee, Davis.

MVP = MVP Award winner

VALUE: $350

1932 PITTSBURGH - Dave Barbee, Erv Brame, Leon Chagnon, Adam Comorosky, Gus Dugas, Hal Finney, Larry French, George Gibson (MANAGER), Earl Grace, Howdie Groskloss, Bill Harris, Ray Kremer, Heinie Meine, Tom Padden, Tony Piet, Glenn Spencer, Gus Suhr, Steve Swetonic, Bill Swift, Tommy Thevenow, Pie Traynor, Arky Vaughn, Lloyd Waner, Paul Waner

LESS THAN 10 GAMES: Bill Brenzel, Bill Brubaker, George Gibson (MANAGER), Woody Jensen, Hal Smith

NOTES: 4 HOF'ers.

KEY SIGNATURES: Vaughn, Traynor, Waner, Waner.

VALUE: $600

1932 ST. LOUIS (AL) - Benny Bengough, Larry Bettencourt, George Blaeholder, Jack Burns, Bruce Campbell *, Bob Cooney, Rick Ferrell, Carl Fischer *, Showboat Fisher, Debs Garms, Goose Goslin, Sam Gray, Ed Grimes, Bump Hadley *, Wally Hebert, Tom Jenkins, Bill Killefer (MANAGER), Chad Kimsey *, Nap Kloza, Red Kress *, Jim Levey, Oscar Melillo, Art Scharein, Fred Schulte, Johnny Schulte *, Lefty Stewart, Lin Storti

LESS THAN 10 GAMES: Dick Coffman *, Jim McLaughlin, Lou Polli

KEY SIGNATURES: Burns, Scharein, Goslin, Ferrell.

VALUE: $365

1932 ST. LOUIS (NL) - Sparky Adams, Ray Blades, Jim Bottomley, Rube Bressler *, Tex Carleton, Ripper Collins, Ray Cunningham, Dizzy Dean, Eddie Delker *, Paul Derringer, Jake Flowers, Hod Ford *, Frankie Frisch, Charlie Gelbert, Mike Gonzalez, Jesse

Haines, Wild Bill Hallahan, Harvey Hendrick *, Wattie Holm, Joel Hunt, Syl Johnson, Jim Lindsey, Gus Mancuso, Pepper Martin, Joe Medwick, Ernie Orsatti, Ray Pepper, George Puccinelli, Jimmy Reese, Allyn Stout, Gabby Street (MANAGER), George Watkins, Charlie Wilson, Jimmie Wilson

LESS THAN 10 GAMES: Bill DeLancey, Benny Frey *, Flint Rhem *, Bill Sherdel *, Ray Starr, Bud Teachout, Dick Terwilliger, Skeeter Webb, Jim Winford

NOTES: 5 HOF'ers.

KEY SIGNATURES: Watkins, Martin, Orsatti, Frisch, Bottomley, Medwick, Dean, Haines.

VALUE: $560

1932 WASHINGTON - Moe Berg, Ossie Bluege, Lloyd Brown, Bobby Burke, Dick Coffman *, Joe Cronin, General Crowder, Carl Fischer *, Dave Harris, Walter Johnson (MANAGER), Joe Judge, John Kerr, Wes Kingdon, Joe Kuhel, Heinie Manush, Howie Maple, Firpo Marberry, Buddy Myer, Frank Ragland, Carl Reynolds, Sam Rice, Roy Spencer, Tommy Thomas *, Monte Weaver, Sammy West

LESS THAN 10 GAMES: Ed Edelen, Bob Friedrich, Bill McAfee, Jim McLeod, Danny Musser, Bud Thomas

KEY SIGNATURES: Cronin, Reynolds, Manush, Rice, Crowder, Johnson.

VALUE: $1500

1933

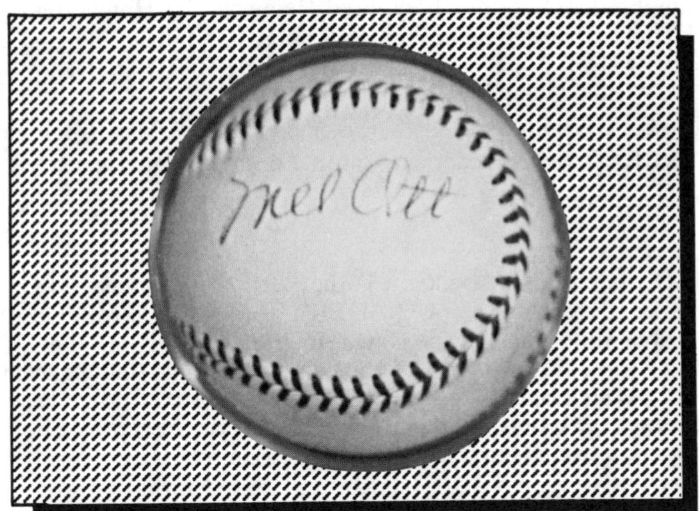

Mel Ott hit .389 in the 1933 World Series to lead the New York Giants to the championship.

*** = player was traded**

1933 BOSTON (AL) - Dale Alexander, Mel Almada, Ivy Andrews, Lloyd Brown *, Dusty Cookie, Rick Ferrell *, Bob Fothergill, Barney Friberg, Johnny Gooch, Johnny Hodapp, Hank Johnson, Roy Johnson, Smead Jolley, Joe Judge *, Bob Kline, Marty McManus

(MANAGER), Freddie Muller, Tom Oliver, George Pipgras *, Gordon Rhodes, Bob Seeds, Merv Shea *, George Stumpf, Bucky Walters, Rabbit Warstler, Johnny Watwood, Bob Weiland, Johnny Welch, Bill Werber *

LESS THAN 10 GAMES: Curt Fullerton, Lou Legett, Jud McLaughlin, Mike Meola, Greg Mulleavy, Marv Olson, Tom Winsett

NOTES: McManus was a player/manager.

KEY SIGNATURES: Hodapp, Johnson, Ferrell.

VALUE: $300

1933 BOSTON (NL) - Wally Berger, Huck Betts, Ed Brandt, Ben Cantwell, Fred Frankhouse, Dick Gyselman, Pinky Hargrave, Shanty Hogan, Dutch Holland, Buck Jordan, Fritz Knothe *, Hal Lee *, Leo Mangum, Rabbit Maranville, Bill McKechnie (MANAGER), Randy Moore, Joe Mowry, Wes Schulmerich *, Socks Seibold, Bob Smith *, Al Spohrer, Tommy Thompson, Billy Urbanski, Pinky Whitney *, Red Worthington, Tom Zachary

LESS THAN 10 GAMES: Bob Brown, Earl Clark, Ed Fallenstein, Hod Ford, Ray Starr *, Al Wright

KEY SIGNATURES: Maranville, Moore, Cantwell, McKechnie.

VALUE: $375

1933 BROOKLYN - Boom-Boom Beck, Ray Benge, Del Bissonette, Buzz Boyle, Max Carey (MANAGER), Ownie Carroll, Watty Clark *, Tony Cuccinello, Bert Delmas, Jake Flowers, Johnny Frederick, Lonny Frey, Fred Heimach, Joe Hutcheson, Jimmy Jordan, Joe Judge *, Dutch Leonard, Sam Leslie *, Al Lopez, Van Lingle Mungo, Lefty O'Doul *, Chick Outen, Rosy Ryan, Joe Shaute, Joe Stripp, Clyde Sukeforth, Danny Taylor, Sloppy Thurston, Hack Wilson, Glenn Wright

LESS THAN 10 GAMES: Lu Blue, Ray Lucas, Val Picinich *, Max Rosenfeld

KEY SIGNATURES: Wright, Frederick, Wilson, Lopez, Mungo, Carey.

VALUE: $575

1933 CHICAGO (AL) - Luke Appling, Charlie Berry, Milt Bocek, Ed Durham, Jimmy Dykes, Red Faber, Lew Fonseca (MANAGER), Vic Frasier *, Milt Gaston, Paul Gregory, Frank Grube, Mule Haas, Jackie Hayes, Joe Heving, Sad Sam Jones, Chad Kimsey, Red Kress, Ted Lyons, Jake Miller, Hal Rhyne, Al Simmons, Billy Sullivan, Evar Swanson, Earl Webb *, Whit Wyatt *

LESS THAN 10 GAMES: Charlie English, Liz Funk, Hal Haid, Ira Hutchinson, Mem Lovett, George Murray, John Stoneham, Les Tietje

NOTES: HOF'ers; Fonseca was a player/manager.

KEY SIGNATURES: Appling, Swanson, Simmons, Lyons, Faber.

VALUE: $450

HOF = Hall of Famer

1933 CHICAGO (NL) - Guy Bush, Dolph Camilli, Gilly Campbell, Kiki Cuyler, Frank Demaree, Taylor Douthit *, Woody English, Burleigh Grimes *, Charlie Grim (MANAGER), Stan Hack, Gabby Hartnett, Harvey Hendrick, Roy Henshaw, Babe Herman, Billy Herman, Billy Jurges, Mark Koenig, Pat Malone, Jim Mosolf, Lynn Nelson, Charlie Root, Riggs Stephenson, Zack Taylor, Rud Tinning, Lon Warneke

LESS THAN 10 GAMES: Leroy Herrmann, Babe Phelps, Beryl Richmond, Carroll Yerkes

NOTES: 4 HOF'ers; Grimm was a player/manager.

KEY SIGNATURES: Grimm, Stephenson, Hartnett, Cuyler, Bush, Grimes, Billy Herman.

VALUE: $500

HOF = Hall of Famer

1933 CINCINNATI - Sparky Adams *, Larry Benton, Otto Bluege, Jim Bottomley, Donie Bush (MANAGER), Paul Derringer *, Leo Durocher *, Benny Frey, George Grantham, Chick Hafey, Rollie Hemsley *, Andy High, Si Johnson, Ray Kolp, Ernie Lombardi, Red Lucas, Clyde Manion, Johnny Moore, Jo-Jo Morrissey, Jack Quinn, Harry Rice, Eppa Rixey, Tommy Robello, Wally Roettger, Bob Smith *, Allyn Stout *

LESS THAN 10 GAMES: Jack Crouch *, Taylor Douthit *, Eddie Hunter

NOTES: 4 HOF'ers.

KEY SIGNATURES: Bottomley, Hafey, Lombardi, Durocher, Rixey.

VALUE: $485

1933 CLEVELAND - Earl Averill, Belve Bean, Harley Boss, Clint Brown, John Burnett, Bill Cissell *, Sarge Connally, Wes Ferrell, Milt Galatzer, Odell Hale, Mel Harder, Oral Hildebrand, Willis Hudlin, Walter Johnson (MANAGER), Willie Kamm, Bill Knickerbocker, Eddie Morgan, Glenn Myatt, Johnny Oulliber, Monte Pearson, Roger Peckinpaugh (MANAGER), Dick Porter, Mike Powers, Frankie Pytlak, Roy Spencer, Hal Trosky, Joe Vosmik

LESS THAN 10 GAMES: Howard Craghead, Thornton Lee

KEY SIGNATURES: Averill, Johnson.

VALUE: $1000

1933 DETROIT - Eldon Auker, Del Baker (MANAGER), Tommy Bridges, Harry Davis, Gene Desautels, Frank Doljack, Carl Fischer, Pete Fox, Vic Frasier *, Charlie Gehringer, Hank Greenberg, Buck Harris (MANAGER), Ray Hayworth, Art Herring, Chief Hogsett, Firpo Marberry, Marv Owen, Johnny Pasek, Frank Reiber, Billy Rhiel, Billy Rogell, Schoolboy Rowe, Heinie Schuble, Vic Sorrell, John Stone, Gee Walker, Earl Webb *, Jo-Jo White, Whit Wyatt

LESS THAN 10 GAMES: Luke Hamlin, Roxie Lawson, Bots Nekola, George Uhle

KEY SIGNATURES: Greenberg, Gehringer, Harris.

VALUE: $425

1933 NEW YORK (AL) - Johnny Allen, Don Brennan, Jumbo Brown, Sammy Byrd, Ben Chapman, Earle Combs, Frankie Crosetti, Charlie Devens, Bill Dickey, Doc Farrell, Lou Gehrig, Lefty Gomez, Art Jorgens, Lyn Lary, Tony Lazzeri, Danny MacFayden, Joe McCarthy (MANAGER), Wilcy Moore, Herb Pennock, Red Ruffing, Babe Ruth, Joe Sewell, George Uhle *, Russ Van Atta, Dixie Walker

LESS THAN 10 GAMES: Pete Appleton, Joe Glenn, George Pipgras *, Tony Rensa, Bill Werber

NOTES: 10 HOF'ers.

KEY SIGNATURES: Gehrig, Lazzeri, Sewell, Ruth, Combs, Chapman, Dickey, Gomez, Allen, Ruffing, Pennock, McCarthy.

VALUE: $3475

1933 NEW YORK (NL) - Hi Bell, Watty Clark *, Hughie Critz, Kiddo Davis, Chuck Dressen, Freddie Fritzsimmons, Carl Hubbell, Travis Jackson, Bernie James, Sam Leslie *, Dolf Luque, Gus Mancuso, Jo-Jo Moore, Lefty O'Doul *, Mel Ott, Roy Parmelee, Homer Peel, Paul Richards, Blondy Ryan, Hal Schumacher, Glenn Spencer, Bill Terry (MANAGER), Bill Terry, Johnny Vergez

LESS THAN 10 GAMES: Harry Danning, Hank Leiber, Joe Maley, Jack Salveson, Bill Shores, Ray Starr *, George Uhle *, Phil Weintraub

NOTES: World Champions! 4 HOF'ers; Hubbell (MVP).

KEY SIGNATURES: Terry, Ott, Jackson, Hubbell.

MVP = MVP Award winner

VALUE: $650

1933 PHILADELPHIA (AL) - Dick Barrett, Max Bishop, Sugar Cain, Ed Cihocki, Mickey Cochrane, Ed Coleman, Bobby Coombs, Doc Cramer, George Earnshaw, Lou Finney, Jimmie Foxx, Tony Freitas, Lefty Grove, Pinky Higgins, Bob Johnson, Connie Mack (MANAGER), Ed Madjeski, Roy Mahaffey, Eric McNair, Bing Miller, Jim Peterson, Rube Walberg, Dib Williams

LESS THAN 10 GAMES: Gowell Claset, Bill Dietrich, Frankie Hayes, Johnny Marcum, Hank McDonald *, Tim McKeithan, Emile Roy, Hank Winston, Joe Zapustas

NOTES: 4 HOF'ers; Foxx won the MVP and was a Triple Crown winner.

KEY SIGNATURES: Foxx, Higgins, Cochrane, Grove, Mack.

VALUE: $490

1933 PHILADELPHIA (NL) - Dick Bartell, Jack Berly, Alta Cohen, Phil Collins, Spud Davis, Eddie Delker, Gus Dugas, Jumbo Jim Elliott, Neal Finn, Chick Fullis, Snipe Hansen, Mickey Haslin, Ed Holley, Don Hurst, Chuck Klein, Fritz Knothe *, Hal Lee *, Ad Liska, Harry McCurdy, Jim McLeod, Cy Moore, Frank Pearce, Frank Ragland, Flint Rhem, Wes Schulmerich *, Burt Shotton (MANAGER), Al Todd, Jack Warner, Pinky Whitney *

LESS THAN 10 GAMES: Fred Brickell, Charlie Butler, Reggie Grabowski, John Jackson, Clarence Pickrel, Hugh Willingham

NOTES: Klein was a Triple Crown winner; Finn died 7/7/33.

KEY SIGNATURES: Klein, Fullis, Schulmerich, Davis.

VALUE: $375

1933 PITTSBURGH - Leon Chagnon, Adam Comorosky, Hal Finney, Larry French, George Gibson (MANAGER), Earl Grace, Bill Harris, Waite Hoyt, Woody Jensen, Fred Lindstrom, Heinie Meine, Tom Padden, Val Picinich *, Tony Piet, Hal Smith, Gus Suhr, Steve Swetonic, Bill Swift, Tommy Thevenow, Pie Traynor, Arky Vaughan, Lloyd Waner, Paul Waner, Pep Young

LESS THAN 10 GAMES: Ralph Birkofer, Bill Brubaker, Clise Dudley, Ray Kremer, Red Nonnenkamp

NOTES: 6 HOF'ers.

KEY SIGNATURES: Piet, Vaughan, Traynor, Waner, Lindstrom, Waner, Hoyt.

VALUE: $700

1933 ST. LOUIS (AL) - George Blaeholder, Jack Burns, Bruce Campbell, Dick Coffman, Jack Crouch *, Rick Ferrell *, Debs Garms, Sam Gray, Ted Gullic, Bump Hadley, Wally Hebert, Rollie Hemsley *, Rogers Hornsby (MANAGER) *, Jack Knott, Bill Killefer (MANAGER), Jim Levey, Hank McDonald *, Oscar Melillo, Carl Reynolds, Muddy Ruel, Art Scharein, Merv Shea *, Allan Sothoron (MANAGER), Rollie Stiles, Lin Storti, Ed Wells, Sammy West

LESS THAN 10 GAMES: Garland Braxton, Lloyd Brown *.
NOTES: Hornsby was a player/manager.
KEY SIGNATURES: West, Ferrell, Hornsby.

VALUE: $550

1933 ST. LOUIS (NL) - Ethan Allen, Tex Carleton, Ripper Collins, Estel Crabtree, Pat Crawford, Dizzy Dean, Leo Durocher *, Frankie Frisch (MANAGER), Charlie Gelbert, Jesse Haines, Wild Bill Hallahan, Rogers Hornsby *, Syl Johnson, Bill Lewis, Pepper Martin, Joe Medwick, Jim Mooney, Gene Moore, Bob O'Farrell, Ernie Orsatti, Gordon Slade, Gabby Street (MANAGER), Dazzy Vance, Bill Walker, George Watkins, Burgess Whitehead, Jimmie Wilson

LESS THAN 10 GAMES: Sparky Adams *, Paul Derringer *, Burleigh Grimes *, Jim Lindsey, Ray Pepper, Joe Sprinz, Allyn Stout *, Charlie Wilson

NOTES: 8 HOF'ers.

KEY SIGNATURES: Collins, Frisch, Durocher, Martin, Medwick, Hornsby, Haines, Dean, Vance, Grimes.

VALUE: $1150

1933 WASHINGTON - Moe Berg, Ossie Bluege, Bob Boken, Cliff Bolton, Bobby Burke, Joe Cronin (MANAGER), General Crowder, Goose Goslin, Dave Harris, John Kerr, Joe Kuhel, Heinie Manush, Bil McAfee, Buddy Myer, Sam Rice, Jack Russell, Fred Schulte, Luke Sewell, Lefty Stewart, Tommy Thomas, Cecil Travis, Monte Weaver, Earl Whitehill

LESS THAN 10 GAMES: Nick Altrock, John Campbell, Ed Chapman, Ed Linke, Alex McColl, Ray Prim, Bud Thomas

NOTES: 4 HOF'ers; Cronin was a player/manager.

KEY SIGNATURES: Kuhel, Myer, Cronin, Goslin, Manush, Rice, Crowder, Whitehill.

VALUE: $550

HOF = Hall of Famer

1934

Hall of Famer Charlie Gehringer helped lead the Detroit Tigers to the World Series in 1934.

*** = player was traded**

1934 BOSTON (AL) - Mel Almada, Max Bishop, Bill Cissell, Dusty Cooke, Rick Ferrell, Wes Ferrell, Skinny Graham, Lefty Grove, Bucky Harris (MANAGER), Gordie Hinkle, Hank Johnson, Roy Johnson, Joe Judge, Lyn Lary *, Lou Legett, Eddie Morgan, Joe Mulligan, Fritz Ostermueller, Herb Pennock, Dick Porter *, Carl Reynolds, Gordon Rhodes, Moose Solters, Rube Walberg, Bucky Walters *, Bob Weiland *, Johnny Welch, Bill Werber

LESS THAN 10 GAMES: George Hockette, Don Kellett, Spike Merena, Freddie Muller, Al Niemiec, George Pipgras, Bob Seeds *

NOTES: 4 HOF'ers.

KEY SIGNATURES: Harris, Reynolds, Johnson, R. Ferrell, W. Ferrell, Grove, Pennock.

VALUE: $425

1934 BOSTON (NL) - Wally Berger, Huck Betts, Ed Brandt, Bob Brown, Ben Cantwell, Fred Frankhouse, Dick Gyselman, Shanty Hogan, Buck Jordan, Hal Lee, Les Mallon, Leo Mangum, Rabbit Maranville, Bill McKechnie (MANAGER), Marty McManus, Randy Moore, Joe Mowry, Dick Oliver, Clarence Pickrel, Flint Rhem *, Bob Smith, Al Spohrer, Tommy Thompson, Billy Urbanski, Pinky Whitney, Red Worthington *

LESS THAN 10 GAMES: Jumbo Jim Elliott *, Elbie Fletcher, Dan McGee, Johnnie Tyler, Tom Zachary *

KEY SIGNATURES: McKechnie, Jordan, Maranville, Frankhouse.

VALUE: $350

1934 BROOKLYN - Johnny Babich, Boom-Boom Beck, Ray Benge, Ray Berres, Buzz Boyle, Jim Bucher, Ownie Carroll, Glenn Chapman, Watty Clark *, Tony Cuccinello, Johnny Frederick, Lonny Frey, Art Herring, Jimmy Jordon, Len Koenecke, Dutch Leonard, Sam Leslie, Al Lopez, Ray Lucas, Johnny McCarthy, Van Lingle Mungo, Les Munns, Casey Stengel (MANAGER), Joe Stripp, Clyde Sukeforth, Danny Taylor, Nick Tremark, Hack Wilson *, Tom Zachary *

LESS THAN 10 GAMES: Bert Hogg, Wally Millies, Phil Page, Charlie Perkins, Harry Smythe *.

KEY SIGNATURES: Stengel, Leslie, Stripp, Boyle, Koenecke, Lopez, Mungo.

VALUE: $350

1934 CHICAGO (AL) - Luke Appling, Milt Bocek, Bob Boken *, Zeke Bonura, Frenchy Bordagaray, Joe Chamberlain, Jocko Conlan, Ed Durham, Jimmy Dykes (MANAGER), George Earnshaw, Lew Fonseca (MANAGER), Phil Gallivan, Milt Gaston, Mule Haas, Jackie Hayes, Joe Heving, Marty Hopkins *, Sad Sam Jones, Harry Kinzy, Ted Lyons, Ed Madjeski *, Mark Mauldin, Rip Radcliff, Muddy Ruel, Merv Shea, Al Simmons, Evar Swanson, Les Tietje, Frenchy Uhalt, Charlie Uhlir, Whit Wyatt

LESS THAN 10 GAMES: George Caithamer, Bill Fehring, Vern Kennedy, Hugo Klaerner, Red Kress *, Johnny Pasek, John Pomorski, Lee Stine, Monty Stratton

NOTES: 4 HOF'ers; Conlan's signature in this format is rare; Dykes was a player/manager.

KEY SIGNATURES: Appling, Simmons, Conlan.

VALUE: $470

HOF = Hall of Famer

1934 CHICAGO (NL) - Guy Bush, Dolph Camilli *, Kiki Cuyler, Woody English, Augie Galan, Charlie Grimm (MANAGER), Stan Hack, Gabby Hartnett, Babe Herman, Billy Herman, Don Hurst *, Roy Joiner, Billy Jurges, Chuck Klein, Bill Lee, Pat Malone, Bob O'Farrell *, Babe Phelps, Charlie Root, Tuck Stainback, Riggs Stephenson, Bennie Tate, Bud Tinning, Lon Warneke, Jim Weaver *

LESS THAN 10 GAMES: Phil Cavarretta, Lynn Nelson, Dick Ward, Chick Wiedemeyer

NOTES: 4 HOF'ers.

KEY SIGNATURES: Grimm, Billy Herman, Hack, Cuyler, Klein, Hartnett.

VALUE: $475

1934 CINCINNATI - Sparky Adams, Larry Benton, Link Blakely, Jim Bottomley, Don Brennan, Adam Comorosky, Paul Derringer, Chuck Dressen (MANAGER), Jake Flowers, Tony Freitas, Benny Frey, Chick Hafey, Si Johnson, Alex Kampouris, Ted Kleinhans *, Mark Koenig, Ray Kolp, Ernie Lombardi, Clyde Manion, Frankie McCormick, Johnny Moore *, Bob O'Farrell * (MANAGER), Tony Piet, Harlin Pool, Wes Schulmerich *, Jimmy Shevlin, Ivey Shiver, Burt Shotton (MANAGER), Gordon Slade, Allyn Stout

LESS THAN 10 GAMES: Junie Barnes, Sherman Edwards, Lee Grissom, Syl Johnson *, Jim Lindsey *, Bill Marshall, Harry McCurdy, Ted Petoskey, Beryl Richmond, Tommy Robello, Joe Shaute, Dazzy Vance *, Whitey Wistert

NOTES: O'Farrell was a player/manager.

KEY SIGNATURES: Bottomley, Hafey, Lombardi.

VALUE: $390

1934 CLEVELAND - Earl Averill, Belve Bean, Moe Berg *, Bill Brenzel, Clint Brown, Lloyd Brown, John Burnett, Milt Galatzer, Odell Hale, Mel Harder, Oral Hildebrand, Dutch Holland, Willie Hudlin, Walter Johnson (MANAGER), Willie Kamm, Bill Knickerbocker, Thornton Lee, Eddie Moore, Glenn Myatt, Monte Pearson, Dick Porter *, Frankie Pytlak, Sam Rice, Bob Seeds *, Hal Trosky, Joe Vosmik, Bob Weiland *, Ralph Winegarner

LESS THAN 10 GAMES: Kit Carson, Sarge Connally, Denny Galehouse, Bob Garbark, Bill Perrin, Roy Spencer

KEY SIGNATURES: Johnson, Trosky, Hale, Knickerbocker, Averill, Vosmik, Harder.

VALUE: $950

1934 DETROIT - Eldon Auker, Tommy Bridges, Flea Clifton, Mickey Cochrane (MANAGER), Mickey Cochrane, Frank Doljack, Carl Fischer, Pete Fox, Charlie Gehringer, Goose Goslin, Hank Greenberg, Luke Hamilin, Ray Hayworth, Chief Hogsett, Firpo Marberry, Marv Owen, Billy Rogell, Schoolboy Rowe, Heinie Schuble, Vic Sorrell, Gee Walker, Jo-Jo White

LESS THAN 10 GAMES: General Crowder *, Vic Frasier, Steve Larkin, Cy Perkins, Red Phillips, Frank Reiber, Icehouse Wilson, Rudy York

NOTES: 4 HOF'ers; Cochrane (MVP).

KEY SIGNATURES: Cochrane, Greenberg, Gehringer, Fox, Goslin, Cochrane, Rowe, Bridges.

VALUE: $610

MVP = MVP Award winner

1934 NEW YORK (AL) - Johnny Allen, Johnny Broaca, Sammy Byrd, Ben Chapman, Earle Combs, Frankie Crosetti, Jimmie DeShong, Bill Dickey, Lou Gehrig, Lefty Gomez, Burleigh Grimes *, Don Heffner, Myril Hoag, Art Jorgens, Tony Lazzeri, Danny MacFayden, Joe McCarthy (MANAGER), Johnny Murphy, Red Rolfe, Red Ruffing, Babe Ruth, Jack Saltzgaver, George Selkirk, George Uhle, Russ Van Atta, Dixie Walker

LESS THAN 10 GAMES: Charlie Devens, Lyn Lary *, Floyd Newkirk, Harry Smythe *, Vito Tamulis, Zack Taylor

NOTES: 9 HOF'ers; Gehrig was a Triple Crown winner.

KEY SIGNATURES: McCarthy, Gomez, Lazzeri, Dickey, Gehrig, Ruffing, Grimes, Ruth, Combs.

VALUE: $3250

1934 NEW YORK (NL) - Hi Bell, Joe Bowman, Hughie Critz, Harry Danning, Freddie Fitzsimmons, George Grantham, Carl Hubbell, Travis Jackson, Hank Leiber, Dolf Luque, Gus Mancuso, Jo-Jo Moore, Lefty O'Doul, Mel Ott, Roy Parmelee, Homer Peel, Paul Richards, Blondy Ryan, Jack Salveson, Hal Schumacher, Al Smith, Bill Terry (MANAGER), Johnny Vergez, George Watkins, Phil Weintraub

LESS THAN 10 GAMES: Slick Castleman, Watty Clark *, Fresco Thompson

NOTES: 4 HOF'ers; Terry was a player/manager.

KEY SIGNATURES: Terry, Jackson, Ott, Hubbell.

VALUE: $475

1934 PHILADELPHIA (AL) - Al Benton, Charlie Berry, Sugar Cain, Joe Cascarella, Ed Coleman, Doc Cramer, Bill Dietrich, Lou Finney, Mort Flohr, Jimmie Foxx, Frankie Hayes, Pinky Higgins, Bob Johnson, Bob Kline *, Connie Mack (MANAGER), Roy Mahaffey, Johnny Marcum, Harry Matuzak, Eric McNair, Bing Miller, Charlie Moss, Rabbit Warstler, Dib Williams

LESS THAN 10 GAMES: George Caster, Ed Lagger, Ed Madjeski *, Tim McKeithan, Jerry McQuaig, Roy Vaughn, Whitey Wilshere, Jack Wilson

KEY SIGNATURES: Mack, Foxx, Higgins, Cramer, Johnson.

VALUE: $385

1934 PHILADELPHIA (NL) - Ethan Allen, Dick Bartell, Dolph Camilli *, Lou Chiozza, Bud Clancy, Phil Collins, George Darrow, Curt Davis, Kiddo Davis *, Chick Fullis *, Reggie Grabowski, Snipe Hansen, Mickey Haslin, Harvey Hendrick, Andy High, Joe Holden, Ed Holley *, Marty Hopkins *, Don Hurst *, Irv Jeffries, Syl Johnson *, Cy Moore, Euel Moore, Johnny Moore *, Art Ruble, Wes Schulmerich *, Al Todd, Bucky Walters *, Jimmie Wilson (MANAGER)

LESS THAN 10 GAMES: Ed Boland, Jumbo Jim Elliott *, Fred Frink, Ted Kleinhans *, Bill Lohrman, Cy Malis, Prince Oana, Frank Pearce, Bucky Walters, Hack Wilson *

NOTES: Wilson was a player/manager.

KEY SIGNATURES: Chiozza, Bartell, J. Moore, Allen, Todd.

VALUE: $250

1934 PITTSBURGH - Ralph Birkofer, Leon Chagnon, Larry French, George Gibson (MANAGER), Earl Grace, Bill Harris, Waite Hoyt, Woody Jensen, Cookie Lavagetto, Fred Lindstrom, Red Lucas, Heinie Meine, Tom Padden, Wally Roettger, Hal Smith, Gus Suhr, Bill Swift, Tommy Thevenow, Pie Traynor (MANAGER), Arky Vaughan, Art Veltman, Lloyd Waner, Paul Waner, Pop Young

LESS THAN 10 GAMES: Cy Blanton, Bill Brubaker, Hal Finney, Burleigh Grimes *, Ed Holley *, Lloyd Johnson, Steamboat Struss

NOTES: 7 HOF'ers; Traynor was a player/manager.

KEY SIGNATURES: Traynor, Vaughan, P. Waner, L. Waner, Lindstrom, Hoyt, Grimes.

VALUE: $675

1934 ST. LOUIS (AL) - Ivy Andrews, Ollie Bejma, George Blaeholder, Jack Burns, Bruce Campbell, Earl Clark, Harlond Clift, Dick Coffman, Debs Garms, Sam Gray, Frank Grube, Bump Hadley, Rollie Hemsley, Rogers Hornsby (MANAGER), Jack Knott, Bill McAfee, Oscar Melillo, Bobo Newsom, Ray Pepper, George Puccinelli, Alan Strange, Ed Wells, Sammy West

LESS THAN 10 GAMES: Grover Hartley, Lefty Mills, Charley O'Leary, Art Scharein, Jim Walkup, Jim Weaver *

NOTES: Traynor was a player/manager.

KEY SIGNATURES: Hornsby, West, Hemsley.

VALUE: $510

1934 ST. LOUIS (NL) - Tex Carleton, Ripper Collins, Pat Crawford, Spud Davis, Kiddo Davis *, Dizzy Dean, Paul Dean, Bill DeLancey, Leo Durocher, Frankie Frisch (MANAGER), Chick Fullis *, Charley Gelbert, Jesse Haines, Wild Bill Hallahan, Francis Healy, Jim Lindsey *, Pepper Martin, Joe Medwick, Buster Mills, Jim Mooney, Ernie Orsatti, Jack Rothrock, Dazzy Vance *, Bill Walker, Burgess Whitehead

LESS THAN 10 GAMES: Burleigh Grimes *, Clarence Heise, Gene Moore, Flint Rhem *, Lew Riggs, Jim Winford, Red Worthington *

NOTES: World Champions! Dean (MVP); 6 HOF'ers; Frisch was a player/manager.

KEY SIGNATURES: Frisch, Collins, Durocher, Martin, Orsatti, Medwick, Davis, Dean, Haines, Grimes, Vance.

VALUE: $675

1934 WASHINGTON - Moe Berg *, Ossie Bluege, Bob Boken *, Cliff Bolton, Bobby Burke, Joe Cronin (MANAGER), General Crowder *, Gus Dugas, Johnny Gill, Dave Harris, John Kerr, Elmer Klumpp, Red Kress *, Joe Kuhel, Heinie Manush, Alex McColl, Buddy Myer, Eddie Phillips, Jack Russell, Fred Schulte, Luke Sewell, Fred Sington, Lefty Stewart, John Stone, Pete Susko, Tommy Thomas, Cecil Travis, Monte Weaver, Earl Whitehill

LESS THAN 10 GAMES: Orville Armbrust, Allen Benson, Sid Cohen, Reese Diggs, Marc Filley, Bob Kline *, Ed Linke, John Milligan, Jake Powell, Ray Prim

NOTES: Cronin was a player/manager.

KEY SIGNATURES: Cronin, Manush.

*** = player was traded**

VALUE: $325

1935

1935 National League MVP Leo "Gabby" Hartnett

1935 BOSTON (AL) - Mel Almada, Moe Berg, Max Bishop, Stew Bowers, Dusty Cooke, Joe Cronin (MANAGER), Babe Dahlgren, Rick Ferrell, Wes Ferrell, Lefty Grove, George Hockette, Hank Johnson, Roy Johnson, Oscar Melillo *, Bing Miller, Fritz Ostermueller, Carl Reynolds, Gordon Rhodes, Moose Solters *, Rube Walberg, Johnny Welch, Bill Werber, Dib Williams *, Jack Wilson

LESS THAN 10 GAMES: Joe Cascarella *, George Dickey, Doc Farrell, Skinny Graham, John Kroner, Lou Legett, George Pipgras, Walt Ripley, Hy Vandenberg

NOTES: Cronin was a player/manager.

KEY SIGNATURES: Cronin, Cooke, R. Johnson, R. Ferrell, W. Ferrell, Grove.

VALUE: $350

1935 CHICAGO (AL) - Luke Appling, Zeke Bonura, Jocko Conlan, Jimmy Dykes (MANAGER), Carl Fischer *, Mule Haas, Jackie Hayes, Joe Heving, Marty Hopkins, Sad Sam Jones, Vern Kennedy, Ted Lyons, Ray Phelps, Tony Piet *, Rip Radcliff, Jack Salveson *, Luke Sewell, Merv Shea, Al Simmons, Fred Tauby, Les Tietje, Joe Vance, George Washington, John Whitehead, Whit Wyatt

LESS THAN 10 GAMES: Talo Chelini *, George Earnshaw *, Frank Grube *, Bud Hafey *, Mike Kreevich, Lee Stine, Monty Stratton, Glenn Wright

NOTES: 4 HOF'ers; Conlan's signature in this format is rare; Dykes was a player/manager.

KEY SIGNATURES: Appling, Simmons, Conlan, Lyons, Stratton.

VALUE: $465

1935 BOSTON (NL) - Larry Benton, Wally Berger, Huck Betts, Ed Brandt, Bob Brown, Ben Cantwell, Joe Coscarart, Elbie Fletcher, Fred Frankhouse, Shanty Hogan, Buck Jordan, Hal Lee, Danny MacFayden *, Les Mallon, Rabbit Maranville, Bill McKechnie (MANAGER), Randy Moore, Joe Mowry, Ray Mueller, Flint Rhem, Babe Ruth, Bob Smith, Al Spohrer, Tommy Thompson, Johnnie Tyler, Billy Urbanski, Pinky Whitney

LESS THAN 10 GAMES: Al Blanche, Art Doll, Bill Lewis, Leo Mangum, Ed Moriarty

KEY SIGNATURES: McKechnie, Lee, Ruth, Maranville.

VALUE: $1250

1935 BROOKLYN - Johnny Babich, Tom Baker, Ray Benge, Frenchy Bordagaray, Buzz Boyle, Jim Bucher, Watty Clark, Johnny Cooney, Tony Cuccinello, George Earnshaw *, Lonny Frey, Jimmy Jordan, Len Koenecke, Dutch Leonard, Sam Leslie, Al Lopez, John McCarthy, Buster Mills, Van Lingle Mungo, Les Munns, Babe Phelps, Bobby Reis, Casey Stengel (MANAGER), Joe Stripp, Danny Taylor, Zack Taylor, Nick Tremark, Dazzy Vance, Tom Zachary

LESS THAN 10 GAMES: Bob Barr, Raoul Dedeaux, Harry Eisenstat, Harvey Green, Frank Lamanske, Bob Logan, Whitey Ock, Curly Onis, Vince Sherlock, Frank Skaff

NOTES: Koenecke died 9/17/35.

KEY SIGNATURES: Stengel, Leslie, Stripp, Lopez.

VALUE: $350

1935 CHICAGO (NL) - Tex Carleton, Hugh Casey, Phil Cavarretta, Kiki Cuyler *, Frank Demaree, Woody English, Larry French, Augie Galan, Charlie Grimm (MANAGER), Stan Hack, Gabby Hartnett, Roy Henshaw, Billy Herman, Billy Jurges, Chuck Klein, Fabian Kowalik, Bill Lee, Fred Lindstrom, Ken O'Dea, Charlie Root, Tuck Stainback, Walter Stephenson, Lon Warneke

LESS THAN 10 GAMES: Clay Bryant, Johnny Gill, Roy Joiner, Clyde Shoun

NOTES: 5 HOF'ers; Hartnett (MVP); Grimm was a player/manager.

KEY SIGNATURES: Grimm, Herman, Lee, Klein, Demaree, Galan, Hartnett, Cuyler, Lindstrom, Hack.

VALUE: $575

MVP = MVP Award winner

1935 CINCINNATI - Jim Bottomley, Don Brennan, Sammy Byrd, Gilly Campbell, Calvin Chapman, Adam Comorosky, Kiki Cuyler *, Paul Derringer, Chuck Dressen (MANAGER), Hank Erickson, Tony Freitas, Benny Frey, Val Goodman *, Chick Hafey, Babe Herman *, Leroy Herrmann, Al Hollingsworth, Si Johnson, Alex Kampouris, Ernie Lombardi, Billy Myers, Emmett Nelson, Harlin Pool, Lew Riggs, Gene Schott, Gordon Slade, Billy Sullivan

LESS THAN 10 GAMES: Lee Gamble, Lee Grissom, Whitey Hilcher, Danny MacFayden *, Ted Petoskey, Tony Piet, Les Scarsella

KEY SIGNATURES: Bottomley, Herman, Lombardi, Cuyler, Hafey, Derringer.

VALUE: $400

1935 CLEVELAND - Earl Averill, Boze Berger, Bill Brenzel, Clint Brown, Lloyd Brown, Bruce Campbell, Kit Carson, Milt Galatzer, Odell Hale, Mel Harder, Oral Hildebrand, Willis Hudlin, Roy Hughes, Walter Johnson (MANAGER), Bill Knickerbocker, Thorton Lee, Glenn Myatt *, Steve O'Neill (MANAGER), Monte Pearson, Eddie Phillips, Frankie Pytlak, Lefty Stewart *, Hal Trosky, Joe Vosmik, Ralph Winegarner, A.B. Wright

LESS THAN 10 GAMES: Belve Bean *, Denny Galehouse, Bob Garbark, Greek George, Willie Kamm

NOTES: The ball is worth $260 if O'Neill's signature is there instead of Johnson's.

KEY SIGNATURES: Johnson, Averill.

VALUE: $850

1935 DETROIT - Eldon Auker, Tommy Bridges, Flee Clifton, Mickey Cochrane (MANAGER), Mickey Cochrane, General Crowder, Pete Fox, Charlie Gehringer, Goose Goslin, Hank Greenberg, Ray Hayworth, Chief Hogsett, Chet Morgan, Marv Owen, Billy Rogell, Schoolboy Rowe, Hainie Schuble, Vic Sorrell, Joe Sullivan, Gee Walker, Jo-Jo White

LESS THAN 10 GAMES: Carl Fischer *, Clyde Hatter, Roxie Lawson, Firpo Marberry, Frank Reiber, Hugh Shelley, Hub Walker

NOTES: World Champions! 4 HOF'ers; Greenberg (MVP).

KEY SIGNATURES: Cochrane, Greenberg, Gehringer, Goslin.

VALUE: $575

MVP = MVP Award winner

1935 NEW YORK (AL) - Johnny Allen, Johnny Broaca, Jumbo Brown, Ben Chapman, Earle Combs, Frankie Crosetti, Jimmie DeShong, Bill Dickey, Lou Gehrig, Joe Glenn, Lefty Gomez, Don Heffner, Jesse Hill, Myril Hoag, Art Jorgens, Tony Lazzeri, Pat Malone, Joe McCarthy (MANAGER), Johnny Murphy, Nolen Richardsen, Red Rolfe, Red Ruffing, Blondy Ryan *, Jack Saltzgaver, George Selkirk, Vito Tamulis

LESS THAN 10 GAMES: Russ Van Atta *, Dixie Walker

NOTES: 7 HOF'ers.

KEY SIGNATURES: McCarthy, Gehrig, Lazzeri, Dickey, Combs, Ruffing, Gomez.

VALUE: $1700

1935 NEW YORK (NL) - Dick Bartell, Slick Castleman, Leon Chagnon, Hughie Critz, Al Cuccinello, Harry Danning, Kiddo Davis, Freddie Fitzsimmons, Frank Gabler, Carl Hubbell, Travis Jackson, Mark Koenig, Hank Leiber, Gus Mancuso, Jo-Jo Moore, Glenn Myatt *, Mel Ott, Roy Parmelee, Hal Schumacher, Al Smith, Allyn Stout, Bill Terry (MANAGER), Bill Terry, Phil Weintraub

LESS THAN 10 GAMES: Harry Gumbert, Dolf Luque, Joe Malay, Euel Moore *, Paul Richards *

NOTES: 4 HOF'ers.

KEY SIGNATURES: Terry, Jackson, Ott, Leiber, Hubbell.

VALUE: $450

1935 PHILADELPHIA (AL) - Al Benton, Charlie Berry, George Blaeholder *, George Caster, Ed Coleman *, Doc Cramer, Bill Dietrich, Carl Doyle, Lou Finney, Jimmie Foxx, Pinky Higgins, Alex Hooks, Bob Johnson, Dutch Lieber, Connie Mack (MANAGER), Roy Mahaffey, Johnny Marcum, Eric McNair, Wally Moses, Skeeter Newsome, Jack Peerson, Paul Richards *, Bernie Snyder, George Turbeville, Rabbit Warstler, Whitey Wilshere

LESS THAN 10 GAMES: Sugar Cain *, Joe Cascarella *, Bill Conroy, Vallie Eaves, Bill Ferrazzi, Herman Fink, Earl Huckleberry, Wedo Martini, Charlie Moss, Jack Owens, Bill Patton, Woody Upchurch, Al Veach, Dib Williams *

KEY SIGNATURES: Mack, Foxx, Moses, Cramer.

VALUE: $365

1935 PHILADELPHIA (NL) - Ethan Allen, Jim Bivin, Ed Boland, Joe Bowman, Dolph Camilli, Lou Chiozza, Curt Davis, Chile Gomez, Mickey Haslin, Syl Johnson, Orville Jorgens, Fred Lucas, Johnny Moore, Euel Moore *, Hugh Mulcahy, Pretzels Pezzullo, Ray Prim, Blondy Ryan *, Al Todd, Johnny Vergez, Bucky Walters, George Watkins, Jimmie Wilson (MANAGER)

LESS THAN 10 GAMES: Art Bramhall, Dino Chiozza, Phil Collins *, Snipe Hansen *, Joe Holden, Bubber Jonnard, Hal Kelleher, Frank Pearce, Tommy Thomas *

NOTES: Wilson was a player/manager.

KEY SIGNATURES: Moore, Allen.

VALUE: $215

1935 PITTSBURGH - Ralph Birkofer, Cy Blanton, Mace Brown, Guy Bush, Earl Grace, Bud Hafey *, Babe Herman *, Waite Hoyt, Woody Jensen, Cookie Lavagetto, Red Lucas, Tom Padden, Gus Suhr, Bill Swift, Tommy Thevenow, Pie Traynor (MANAGER), Arky Vaughan, Lloyd Waner, Paul Waner, Jim Weaver, Pep Young

LESS THAN 10 GAMES: Earl Browne, Bill Brubaker, Aubrey Epps, Wayne Osborne, Claude Passeau, Jack Salveson *, Hal Smith, Steve Swetonic

NOTES: 5 HOF'ers; Traynor was a player/manager.

KEY SIGNATURES: Traynor, Vaughan, P. Waner, L. Waner, Hoyt.

VALUE: $550

1935 ST. LOUIS (AL) - Ivy Andrews, Ollie Bejma, Beau Bell, John Burnett, Jack Burns, Sugar Cain *, Tom Carey, Harlond Clift, Dick Coffman, Ed Coleman *, Debs Garms, Snipe Hansen *, Tommy Heath, Rollie Hemsley, Rogers Hornsby (MANAGER), Jack Knott, Lyn Lary *, Mike Mazzera, Oscar Melillo *, Heinie Mueller, Ray Pepper, Moose Solters *, Alan Strange *, Fay Thomas, Russ Van Atta *, Jim Walkup, Bob Weiland, Sammy West

LESS THAN 10 GAMES: George Blaeholder *, Earl Caldwell, Frank Grube *, Bobo Newsom *, Bob Poser, Hal Warnock

NOTES: Hornsby was a player/manager.

KEY SIGNATURES: Hornsby, West, Solters, Andrews.

VALUE: $495

1935 ST. LOUIS (NL) - Ripper Collins, Phil Collins *, Spud Davis, Dizzy Dean, Paul Dean, Bill DeLancey, Leo Durocher, Frankie Frisch (MANAGER), Charlie Gelbert, Jesse Haines, Wild Bill Hallahan, Ray Harrell, Ed Heusser, Pepper Martin, Joe Medwick, Terry Moore, Bob O'Farrell, Ernie Orsatti, Jack Rothrock, Bill Walker, Burgess Whitehead, Charlie Wilson

LESS THAN 10 GAMES: Mays Copeland, Al Eckert, Lyle Judy, Tony Kaufmann, Lynn King, Nubs Kleinke, Bill McGee, Gene Moore, Sam Narron, Mike Ryba, Bud Tinning, Dick Ward, Jim Winford, Tom Winsett

NOTES: 4 HOF'ers; Frisch was a player/manager.

KEY SIGNATURES: Frisch, Collins, Durocher, Martin, Medwick, Haines, P. Dean, D. Dean.

VALUE: $450

1935 WASHINGTON - Belve Bean *, Ossie Bluege, Cliff Bolton, Bobby Burke, Henry Coppola, Bobby Estalella, Bump Hadley, Bucky Harris (MANAGER), Sammy Holbrook, Red Kress, Joe Kuhel, Lyn Lary *, Ed Linke, Heinie Manush, Dee Miles, Buddy Myer, Bobo Newsom *, Leon Pettit, Jake Powell, Jack Redmond, Jack Russell, Fred Schulte, Fred Sington, Chick Starr, John Stone, Alan Strange *, Cecil Travis, Earl Whitehill

LESS THAN 10 GAMES: Jim Hayes, Phil Hensiek, Dick Lanahan, Buddy Lewis, Red Marion, Al McLean, John Mihalic, Buck Rogers, Lefty Stewart *, Tommy Thomas *, Monte Weaver

KEY SIGNATURES: Harris, Myer, Travis, Powell, Manush, Bolton.

VALUE: $325

1936

1936 National League MVP Carl Hubbell

*** = player was traded**

1936 BOSTON (AL) - Mel Almada, Moe Berg, Joe Cascarella, Dusty Cooke, Doc Cramer, Joe Cronin (MANAGER), Babe Dahlgren, George Dickey, Rick Ferrell, Wes Ferrell, Jimmie Foxx, Fabian Gaffke, Lefty Grove, Jim Henry, John Kroner, Heinie Manush, Johnny Marcum, Eric McNair, Oscar Melillo, Bing Miller, Fritz Ostermueller, Jack Russell *, Rube Walberg, Bill Werber, Jack Wilson

LESS THAN 10 GAMES: Stew Bowers, Emerson Dickman, Mike Meola *, Ted Olson, Jennings Poindexter, Johnny Welch *

NOTES: 5 HOF'ers; Cronin was a player/manager.

KEY SIGNATURES: Cronin, Foxx, R. Ferrell, Manush, Grove.

VALUE: $500

1936 BOSTON (NL) - Ray Benge *, Wally Berger, Al Blanche, Guy Bush *, Ben Cantwell, Tiny Chaplin, Joe Coscarart, Tony Cuccinello, Mickey Haslin *, Buck Jordan, Johnny Lanning, Hal Lee, Bill Lewis, Al Lopez, Danny MacFayden, Bill McKechnie (MANAGER), Gene Moore, Ray Mueller, Bobby Reis, Bob Smith, Tommy Thompson, Billy Urbanski, Rabbit Warstler *, Roy Weir, Pinky Whitney *

LESS THAN 10 GAMES: Johnny Babich, Bob Brown, Art Doll, Gene Ford, Fabian Kowalik *, Swede Larsen, Irish McCloskey, Ed Moriarty, Amby Murray, Wayne Osborne, Andy Pilney, Hal Weafer

KEY SIGNATURES: McKechnie, Jordan, Cuccinello, Lopez.

VALUE: $285

1936 BROOKLYN - Tom Baker, Ray Berres, Frenchy Bordagaray, Ed Brandt, Jim Bucher, Max Butcher, Watty Clark, Johnny Cooney, George Earnshaw *, Ox Eckhardt, Fred Frankhouse, Lonny Frey, Sid Gautreaux, Ben Geraghty, Buddy Hassett, George Jeffcoat, Jimmy Jordan, Dutch Leonard, Fred Lindstrom, Randy Moore, Van Lingle Mungo, Babe Phelps, Jack Radtke, Casey Stengel (MANAGER), Joe Stripp, Danny Taylor, George Watkins *, Eddie Wilson, Tom Winsett, Hank Winston

LESS THAN 10 GAMES: Harry Eisenstat, Johnny Hudson, Dick Siebert, Nick Tremark, Tom Zachary *

KEY SIGNATURES: Stengel, Hassett, Stripp, Bordagaray, Lindstrom.

VALUE: $325

1936 CHICAGO (AL) - Luke Appling, Zeke Bonura, Clint Brown, Sugar Cain *, Italo Chelini, Bill Dietrich *, Jimmy Dykes (MANAGER), Red Evans, Frank Grube, Mule Haas, Jackie Hayes, Vern Kennedy, Mike Kreevich, Ted Lyons, Jo-Jo Morrissey, Ray Phelps, Tony Piet, Rip Radcliff, Larry Rosenthal, Luke Sewell, Merv Shea, Monty Stratton, George Stumpf, Dixie Walker *, George Washington, John Whitehead

LESS THAN 10 GAMES: Les Rock, Bill Shores, Les Tietje *, Whit Wyatt

NOTES: Dykes was a player/manager.

KEY SIGNATURES: Appling, Lyons, Stratton.

VALUE: $325

1936 CHICAGO (NL) - Ethan Allen *, Clay Bryant, Tex Carleton, Phil Cavarretta, Curt Davis *, Frank Demaree, Woody English, Larry French, Augie Galan, Johnny Gill, Charlie Grimm (MANAGER), Stan Hack, Gabby Hartnett, Roy Henshaw, Billy Herman, Billy Jurges, Chuck Klein *, Bill Lee, Gene Lillard, Ken O'Dea, Charlie Root, Tuck Stainback, Lon Warneke

LESS THAN 10 GAMES: Fabian Kowalik *, Clyde Shoun, Walter Stephenson

NOTES: Grimm was a player/manager.

KEY SIGNATURES: Grimm, Herman, Demaree, Hartnett, Klein, French.

VALUE: $375

1936 CINCINNATI - Don Brennan, Sammy Byrd, Gilly Campbell, Calvin Chapman, Kiki Cuyler, Peaches Davis, Paul Derringer, Chuck Dressen (MANAGER), Benny Frey, Ival Goodman, Chick Hafey, Wild Bill Hallahan *, Lee Handley, Babe Herman, Whitey Hilcher, Al Hollingsworth, Eddie Joost, Alex Kampouris, Ernie Lombardi, George McQuinn, Billy Myers, Lew Riggs, Les Scarsella, Gene Schott, Lee Stine, Tommy Thevenow, Hub Walker

LESS THAN 10 GAMES: Tony Freitas, Lee Grissom, Si Johnson *, Eddie Miller, Dee Moore, Whitey Moore, Jake Mooty, Emmett Nelson

KEY SIGNATURES: Scarsella, Cuyler, Lombardi, Hafey.

VALUE: $325

1936 CLEVELAND - Johnny Allen, Earl Averill, Joe Becker, Boza Berger, George Blaeholder, Lloyd Brown, Bruce Campbell, Bob Feller, Milt Galatzer, Denny Galehouse, Greek George, Jim Gleeson, Odell Hale, Mel Harder, Jeff Heath, Oral Hildebrand, Willis Hudlin, Roy Hughes, Bill Knickerbocker, Thornton Lee, Steve O'Neill (MANAGER), Frankie Pytlak, Billy Sullivan, Hal Trosky, George Uhle, Joe Vosmik, Roy Weatherly

LESS THAN 10 GAMES: Paul Kardow, Al Milnar, Ralph Winegarner, Bill Zuber

KEY SIGNATURES: Trosky, Hale, Weatherly, Averill, Sullivan, Allen.

VALUE: $260

1936 DETROIT - Eldon Auker, Tommy Bridges, Jack Burns *, Flea Clifton, Mickey Cochrane (MANAGER), Pete Fox, Charlie Gehringer, Goose Goslin, Hank Greenberg, Ray Hayworth, Chad Kimsey, Roxie Lawson, Glenn Myatt, Marv Owen, Salty Parker, Red Phillips, Frank Rieber, Billy Rogell, Schoolboy Rowe, Al Simmons, Vic Sorrell, Joe Sullivan, Birdie Tebbetts, Jake Wade, Gee Walker, Jo-Jo White

LESS THAN 10 GAMES: General Crowder, Gil English, Chief Hogsett *

NOTES: 5 HOF'ers; Cochrane was a player/manager.

KEY SIGNATURES: Cochrane, Gehringer, Simmons, Goslin, Greenberg.

VALUE: $470

1936 NEW YORK (AL) - Johnny Broaca, Jumbo Brown, Ben Chapman *, Frankie Crosetti, Bill Dickey, Joe DiMaggio, Lou Gehrig, Joe Glenn, Lefty Gomez, Bump Hadley, Don Heffner, Myril Hoag, Roy Johnson, Art Jorgens, Ted Kleinhans, Tony Lazzeri, Pat Malone, Joe McCarthy (MANAGER), Johnny Murphy, Monte Pearson, Jake Powell *, Red Rolfe, Red Ruffing, Jack Saltzgaver, Bob Seeds, George Selkirk

LESS THAN 10 GAMES: Steve Sundra, Dixie Walker *, Kemp Wicker

NOTES: World Champions! Gehrig (MVP); 7 HOF'ers.

KEY SIGNATURES: McCarthy, Gehrig, Lazzeri, DiMaggio, Dickey, Ruffing, Gomez.

VALUE: $1700

MVP = MVP Award winner

1936 NEW YORK (NL) - Dick Bartell, Slick Castleman, Dick Coffman, Harry Danning, Kiddo Davis, Freddie Fitzsimmons, Frank Gabler, Harry Gumbert, Carl Hubbell, Travis Jackson, Mark Koenig, Hank Leiber, Sam Leslie, Gus Mancuso, Eddie Mayo, Jo-Jo Moore, Mel Ott, Jimmy Ripple, Hal Schumacher, Al Smith, Roy Spencer, Bill Terry (MANAGER), Burgess Whitehead

LESS THAN 10 GAMES: Charlie English, Firpo Marberry *, Joe Martin, Johnny McCarthy, Jim Sheehan, Babe Young

NOTES: 4 HOF'ers; Hubbell (MVP); Terry was a player/manager.

KEY SIGNATURES: Terry, Jackson, Ott, Moore, Mancuso, Hubbell.

VALUE: $550

1936 PHILADELPHIA (AL) - Charlie Berry, Red Bullock, Chubby Dean, Bill Dietrich *, Herman Fink, Lou Finney, Stu Flythe, Randy Gumpert, Frankie Hayes, Pinky Higgins, Bob Johnson, Harry Kelley, Hod Lisenbee, Connie Mack (MANAGER), Emil Mailho, Wally Moses, Charlie Moss, Skeeter Newsome, Bill Nicholson, Al Niemiec, Rusty Peters, George Puccinelli, Gordon Rhodes, Buck Ross, George Turbeville, Rabbit Warstler *

LESS THAN 10 GAMES: Fred Archer, Bill Conroy, Dick Culler, Carl Doyle, Hank Johnson, Dutch Lieber, Hugh Luby, Harry Matuzak, Pete Naktenis, Jim Oglesby, Jack Peerson, Eddie Smith, Woody Upchurch, Whitey Wilshere

KEY SIGNATURES: Mack, Finney, Moses.

VALUE: $290

1936 PHILADELPHIA (NL) - Ethan Allen *, Morrie Arnovich, Bill Atwood, Walt Bashore, Ray Benge, Joe Bowman, Dolph Camilli, Lou Chiozza, Curt Davis *, Chile Gomez, Earl Grace, Mickey Haslin *, Syl Johnson, Orville Jorgens, Hal Kelleher, Chuck Klein *, Fabian Kowalik *, Euel Moore, Johnny Moore, Leo Norris, Claude Passeau, Charlie Sheerin, Pete Sivess, Stan Sperry, Ernie Sulik, Johnny Vergez *, Bucky Walters, George Watkins *, Pinky Whitney *, Jimmie Wilson (MANAGER)

LESS THAN 10 GAMES: Lefty Bertrand, Elmer Burkart, Gene Corbett, Herb Harris, Joe Holden, Hugh Mulcahy, Pretzels Pezzullo, Tom Zachary *

NOTES: Wilson was a player/manager.

KEY SIGNATURES: Camilli, Klein, Moore.

VALUE: $250

1936 PITTSBURGH - Ralph Birkofer, Cy Blanton, Mace Brown, Bill Brubaker, Guy Bush *, Hal Finney, Bud Hafey, Waite Hoyt, Woody Jensen, Cookie Lavagetto, Red Lucas, Tom Padden, Fred Schulte, Gus Suhr, Bill Swift, Jack Tising, Al Todd, Pie Traynor (MANAGER), Arky Vaughan, Lloyd Waner, Paul Waner, Jim Weaver, Pep Young

LESS THAN 10 GAMES: Russ Bauers, Earle Browne, Johnny Dickshot, Johnny Welch *

NOTES: 5 HOF'ers.

KEY SIGNATURES: Traynor, Suhr, Vaughan, P. Waner, L. Wayner, Hoyt.

VALUE: $525

1936 ST. LOUIS (AL) - Ivy Andrews, Ollie Bejma, Beau Bell, Jim Bottomley, Earl Caldwell, Tom Carey, Harlond Clift, Ed Coleman, Tony Giuliani, Rollie Hemsley, Chief Hogsett *, Rogers Hornsby (MANAGER), Harry Kimberlin, Jack Knott, Lyn Lary, Glenn Liebhardt, Roy Mahaffey, Ray Pepper, Moose Solters, Tommy Thomas, Les Tietje *, Russ Van Atta, Sammy West

LESS THAN 10 GAMES: Jack Burns *, Sugar Cain *, Sig Jakucki, Mike Meola *, Jim Walkup

NOTES: Hornsby was a player/manager.

KEY SIGNATURES: Hornsby, Bottomley, Clift, Bell.

VALUE: $540

1936 ST. LOUIS (NL) - Ripper Collins, Spud Davis, Dizzy Dean, Paul Dean, Bill DeLancey, Leo Durocher, George Earnshaw *, Frankie Frisch (MANAGER), Chick Fullis, Art Garibaldi, Charlie Gelbert, Don Gutteridge, Jesse Haines, Ed Heussel, Si Johnson *, Lynn King, Pepper Martin, Stu Martin, Joe Medwick, Johnny Mize, Terry Moore, Brusie Ogrodowski, Roy Parmelee, Flint Rhem, Mike Ryba, Bill Walker, Jim Winford

LESS THAN 10 GAMES: Walt Alston, Pat Ankenman, Bill Cox, Wild Bill Hallahan *, Bill McGee, Eddie Morgan, Les Munns, Cotton Pippen, Nels Potter, Heinie Schuble, Lou Scoffic, Johnny Vergez *

NOTES: 6 HOF'ers; Frisch was a player/manager.

KEY SIGNATURES: Frisch, Mize, Durocher, Martin, Alston, Dean, Haines.

VALUE: $525

1936 WASHINGTON - Pete Appleton, Ossie Bluege, Cliff Bolton, Joe Cascarella *, Ben Chapman *, Sid Cohen, Jimmie DeShong, Bobby Estalella, Bucky Harris (MANAGER), Jesse Hill, Shanty Hogan, Red Kress, Joe Kuhel, Buddy Lewis, Ed Linke, John Mihalic, Dee Miles, Wally Millies, Buddy Myer, Bobo Newsom, Jake Powell *, Carl Reynolds, Jack Russell *, Fred Sington, John Stone, Cecil Travis, Monte Weaver, Earl Whitehill

LESS THAN 10 GAMES: Joe Bokina, Ken Chase, Henry Coppola, Bill Dietrich *, Firpo Marberry *, Bill Phebus, Alex Sabo, Chick Starr

KEY SIGNATURES: Harris, Travis, Chapman, Stone.

VALUE: $270

*** = player was traded**

1937

1937 New York Yankees

1937 BOSTON (AL) - Mel Almada *, Moe Berg, Stew Bowers, Ben Chapman *, Doc Cramer, Joe Cronin (MANAGER), Dom Dallessandro, Gene Desautels, Bobby Doerr, Wes Ferrell, Rick Ferrell *, Jimmie Foxx *, Fabian Gaffke, Lefty Grove, Pinky Higgins, Johnny Marcum, Archie McKain, Eric McNair, Oscar Melillo, Buster Mills, Bobo Newsom *, Ted Olson, Fritz Ostermueller, Johnny Peacock, Rube Walberg, Jack Wilson

LESS THAN 10 GAMES: Bob Daughters, Joe Gonzales, Jim Henry, Tommy Thomas *

NOTES: 5 HOF'ers; Cronin was a player/manager.

KEY SIGNATURES: Foxx, Cronin, Higgins, Chapman, Cramer, Doerr, Ferrell, Grove.

VALUE: $500

1937 BOSTON (NL) - Wally Berger *, Guy Bush, Tony Cuccinello, Vince DiMaggio, Gil English *, Lou Fette, Elbie Fletcher, Frank Gabler *, Debs Garms, Ira Hutchinson, Roy Johnson *, Johnny Lanning, Al Lopez, Danny MacFayden, Eddie Mayo, Bill McKechnie (MANAGER), Gene Moore, Ray Mueller, Bobby Reis, Bob Smith, Tommy Thevenow, Jim Turner, Rabbit Warstler

LESS THAN 10 GAMES: Vic Frasier, Buck Jordan *, Frank McGowan, Bobby Reis, Johnny Riddle *, Milt Shoffner, Billy Urbanski, Link Wasem, Roy Weir

KEY SIGNATURES: Lopez, McKechnie.

VALUE: $285

1937 BROOKLYN - Ralph Birkofer, Gib Brack, Lindsay Brown, Jim Bucher, Max Butcher, Ben Cantwell *, Paul Chervinko, George Cisar, Johnny Cooney, Jake Daniel, Harry Eisenstat, Woody English, Freddie Fitzsimmons *, Fred Frankhouse, Sid Gautreaux, Burleigh Grimes (MANAGER), Bert Haas, Luke Hamlin, Buddy Hassett, Roy Henshaw, Waite Hoyt *, Johnny Hudson, George Jeffcoat, Cookie Lavagetto, Jim Lindsay, Tony Malinosky, Heinie Manush, Randy Moore *, Eddie Morgan, Van Lingle Mungo, Babe Phelps, Nick Polly, Goody Rosen, Roy Spencer, Joe Stripp, Eddie Wilson, Tom Winsett

LESS THAN 10 GAMES: Tom Baker *, Watty Clark, George Fallon, Elmer Klumpp, Buck Marrow, Art Parks, Jim Peterson

KEY SIGNATURES: Hassett, Manush, Phelps, Hoyt, Grimes.

VALUE: $420

1937 CHICAGO (AL) - Luke Appling, Boze Berger, Zeke Bonura, Clint Brown, Sugar Cain, Merv Connors, Bill Dietrich, Jimmy Dykes (MANAGER), Mule Haas, Jackie Hayes, Vern Kennedy, Mike Kreevich, Thornton Lee, Ted Lyons, Tony Piet, Rip Radcliff, Tony Rensa, Johnny Rigney, Larry Rosenthal, Luke Sewell, Merv Shea, Hank Steinbacher, Monte Stratton, Dixie Walker, John Whitehead

LESS THAN 10 GAMES: Italo Chelini, Bill Cox, George Gick

NOTES: Dykes was a player/manager.

KEY SIGNATURES: Appling, Stratton, Lyons.

VALUE: $325

1937 CHICAGO (NL) - John Bottarini, Clay Bryant, Tex Carleton, Phil Cavarreta, Ripper Collins, Curt Davis, Frank Demaree, Larry French, Lonny Frey, Augie Galan, Charlie Grimm (MANAGER), Stan Hack, Gabby Hartnett, Billy Herman, Billy Jurges, Bill Lee, Joe Marty, Ken O'Dea, Roy Parmelee, Charlie Root, Clyde Shoun, Tuck Stainback

LESS THAN 10 GAMES: Bob Garbark, Kirby Higbe, Newt Kimball, Bob Logan *, Dutch Meyer, Carl Reynolds

KEY SIGNATURES: Herman, Demaree, Hartnett, Carleton, Grimm.

VALUE: $325

1937 CINCINNATI - Don Brennan *, Gilly Campbell, Joe Cascarella *, Harry Craft, Kiki Cuyler, Peaches Davis, Spud Davis, Kiddo Davis *, Paul Derringer, Chuck Dressen (MANAGER), Double Joe Dwyer, Charlie English, Charlie Gelbert *, Ival Goodman, Lee Grissom, Chick Hafey, Wild Bill Hallahan, Al Hollingsworth, Buck Jordan *, Alex Kampouris, Ernie Lombardi, Frank McCormick, Eddie Miller, Whitey Moore, Jake Mooty, Billy Myers, Jimmy Outlaw, Lew Riggs, Les Scarsella, Gene Schott, Johnny Vander Meer, Hub Walker, Bobby Wallace (MANAGER), Phil Weinbtraub *

LESS THAN 10 GAMES: Red Barrett, Gus Brittain, Jumbo Brown *, Harry Chozen, Paul Gehrman, Eddie Joost, Pinky Jorgensen, Ted Kleinhans, Dutch Mele, Dee Moore, Arnie Moser

NOTES: 4 HOF'ers.

KEY SIGNATURES: Wallace, Hafey, Cuyler, Lombardi.

VALUE: $400

1937 CLEVELAND - Johnny Allen, Ivy Andrews *, Earl Averill, Joe Becker, Lloyd Brown, Bruce Campbell, Bob Feller, Denny Galehouse, Odell Hale, Mel Harder, Jeff Heath, Joe Heving, Willis Hudlin, Roy Hughes, John Kroner, Lyn Lary, Steve O'Neill (MANAGER), Frankie Pytlak, Moose Sotters, Billy Sullivan, Hal Trosky, Roy Weatherly, Earl Whitehill, Whit Wyatt

LESS THAN 10 GAMES: Hugh Alexander, Carl Fischer *, Ken Jungels, Ken Keltner, Blas Monaco, Bill Sodd

KEY SIGNATURES: Campbell, Sotters, Pytlak, Feller, Averill.

VALUE: $300

1937 DETROIT - Eldon Auker, Cliff Bolton, Tommy Bridges, Flee Clifton, Mickey Cochrane (MANAGER), Slick Coffman, Gil English *, Pete Fox, Charlie Gehringer, Charlie Gelbert *, George Gill, Goose Goslin, Hank Greenberg, Ray Hayworth, Babe Herman, Chet Laabs, Roxie Lawson, Marv Owen, Boots Poffenberger, Billy Rogell, Jack Russell, Birdie Tebbetts, Jake Wade, Gee Walker, Jo-Jo White, Rudy York

LESS THAN 10 GAMES: Clyde Hatter, Bob Logan *, Pat McLaughlin, Schoolboy Rowe, Vic Sorrell

NOTES: Gehringer (MVP); Cochrane was a player/manager; 4 HOF'ers.

KEY SIGNATURES: Greenberg, Gehringer, Goslin, Cochrane.

VALUE: $400

MVP = MVP Award winner

1937 NEW YORK (AL) - Ivy Andrews *, Spud Chandler, Frankie Crosetti, Bill Dickey, Joe DiMaggio, Lou Gehrig, Joe Glenn, Lefty Gomez, Bump Hadley, Don Heffner, Tommy Henrich, Myril Hoag, Roy Johnson *, Art Jorgens, Tony Lazzeri, Frank Makosky, Pat Malone, Joe McCarthy (MANAGER), Johnny Murphy, Monte Pearson, Jake Powell, Red Rolfe, Red Ruffing, Jack Saltzgaver, George Selkirk, Kemp Wicker

LESS THAN 10 GAMES: Johnny Broaca, Babe Dahlgren, Joe Vance

NOTES: 7 HOF'ers; Broaca jumped the team and thus can be a tough signature to find on a team baseball.

KEY SIGNATURES: Gehrig, Lazzeri, DiMaggio, Dickey, Gomez, Ruffing, McCarthy.

VALUE: $1700

HOF = Hall of Famer

1937 NEW YORK (NL) - Tom Baker *, Dick Bartell, Wally Berger *, Slick Castleman, Lou Chiozza, Dick Coffman, Harry Danning, Kiddo Davis *, Harry Gumbert, Mickey Haslin, Carl Hubbell, Hank Leiber, Sam Leslie, Gus Mancuso, Johnny McCarthy, Cliff Melton, Jo-Jo Moore, Mel Ott, Jimmy Ripple, Blondy Ryan, Hal Schumacher, Al Smith, Bill Terry (MANAGER), Burgess Whitehead

LESS THAN 10 GAMES: Don Brennan *, Jumbo Brown *, Ben Cantwell *, Freddie Fitzsimmons *, Frank Gabler *, Bill Lohrman, Ed Madjeski, Hy Vandenberg, Phil Weintraub *

KEY SIGNATURES: Bartell, Ott, Ripple, Moore, Hubbell, Melton, Terry.

VALUE: $500

1937 PHILADELPHIA (AL) - Wayne Ambler, Babe Barna, Earle Brucker, George Caster, Bill Cissell, Bill Conroy, Chubby Dean, Herman Fink, Lou Finney, Randy Gumpert, Gene Hasson, Frankie Hayes, Jesse Hill *, Warren Huston, Bob Johnson, Harry Kelley, Connie Mack (MANAGER), Wally Moses, Lynn Nelson, Skeeter Newsome, Ace Parker, Rusty Peters, Buck Ross, Jack Rothrock, Eddie Smith, Bud Thomas, George Turbeville, Bill Werber, Al Williams

LESS THAN 10 GAMES: Fred Archer, Chubby Dean, Bill Kalfass, Doyt Morris, Hal Wagner, Eddie Yount

KEY SIGNATURES: Moses, Johnson, Mack.

VALUE: $290

1937 PHILADELPHIA (NL) - Morrie Arnovich, Bill Atwood, Earl Brown, Dolph Camilli, Howie Gorman, Earl Grace, Syl Johnson, Orville Jorgens, Hal Kelleher, Chuck Klein, Wayne LaMaster, Hersh Martin, Johnny Moore, Hugh Mulcahy, Leo Norris, Claude Passeau, George Scharein, Walter Stephenson, Fred Tauby, Bucky Walters, Pinky Whitney, Jimmie Wilson (MANAGER), Del Young

LESS THAN 10 GAMES: Bob Allen, Bill Andrus, Elmer Burkart, Bobby Burke, Gene Corbett, Larry Crawford, Walt Masters, Leon Pettit, Pete Sivess

NOTES: Wilson was a player/manager.

KEY SIGNATURES: Camilli, Whitney, Klein.

VALUE: $250

1937 PITTSBURGH - Russ Bauers, Cy Blanton, Joe Bowman, Ed Brandt, Mace Brown, Bill Brubaker, Johnny Dickshot, Lee Handley, Waite Hoyt *, Woody Jensen, Red Lucas, Tom Padden, Fred Schulte, Gus Suhr, Bill Swift, Jim Tobin, Al Todd, Pie Traynor (MANAGER), Arky Vaughan, Lloyd Waner, Paul Waner, Jim Weaver, Pep Young

LESS THAN 10 GAMES: Ray Berres, Ken Heintzelman, Bill Schuster

NOTES: 5 HOF'ers; Traynor was a player/manager.

KEY SIGNATURES: Vaughan, Waner, Waner, Todd, Traynor, Hoyt.

VALUE: $525

1937 ST. LOUIS (AL) - Ethan Allen, Red Barkley, Beau Bell, Sheriff Blake *, Julio Bonneti, Jim Bottomley (MANAGER), Tom Carey, Harlond Clift, Harry Davis, Tony Giuliani, Tommy Heath, Rollie Hemsley, Oral Hildebrand, Chief Hogsett, Rogers Hornsby (MANAGER), Ben Huffman, Bill Knickerbocker, Jack Knott, Lou Koupal, Jerry Lipscomb, Eddie Silber, Tommy Thomas *, Bill Trotter, Russ Van Atta, Joe Vosmik, Jim Walkup, Sammy West

LESS THAN 10 GAMES: Ed Baecht, Emil Bildilli, Tom Cafego, Earl Caldwell, Sam Harshany, George Hennessey, Harry Kimberlin, Jerry Lipscomb, Mike Mazzera, Bill Miler, Lefty Mills, Bob Muncrief, Bill Strickland, Les Tietje

NOTES: Hornsby and Bottomley were player/managers.

KEY SIGNATURES: Clift, Bell, West, Vosmik, Hornsby, Bottomley.

VALUE: $525

1937 ST. LOUIS (NL) - Sheriff Blake *, Frenchy Bordagaray, Herb Bremer, Jimmy Brown, Dizzy Dean, Bill Delancy, Leo Durocher, Frankie Frisch (MANAGER), Don Gutteridge, Jesse Haines, Ray Harrell, Si Johnson, Pepper Martin, Stu Martin, Joe Medwick, Johnny Mize, Terry Moore, Brusie Ogrodowski, Mickey Owen, Don Padgett, Mike Ryba, Dick Siebert, Lon Warneke, Bob Weiland, Jim Winford

LESS THAN 10 GAMES: Nate Andrews, Johnnie Chambers, Paul Dean, Nubs Kleinke, Howie Krist, Bill McGee, Randy Moore *, Tom Sunkel, Abe White

NOTES: 5 HOF'ers; Frisch was a player/manager; Medwick won the MVP and was a Triple Crown winner.

KEY SIGNATURES: Mize, Durocher, Padgett, Medwick, Martin, Frisch, Dean, Haines.

VALUE: $455

*** = player was traded**

1938

Bill Dickey hit .400 in the 1938 World Series, leading the Yankees to victory.

1938 BOSTON (AL) - Jim Bagby, Moe Berg, Ben Chapman, Doc Cramer, Joe Cronin (MANAGER), Gene Desautels, Emerson Dickman, Bobby Doerr, Jimmie Foxx, Fabian Gaffke, Lefty Grove, Bill Harris, Joe Heving *, Pinky Higgins, Johnny Marcum, Archie McKain, Eric McNair, Dick Midkiff, Red Nonnenkamp, Fritz Ostermueller, Johnny Peacock, Lee Rogers *, Jim Tabor, Joe Vosmik, Charlie Wagner, Jack Wilson

LESS THAN 10 GAMES: Al Baker, Bill Humphrey, Bill LeFebvre, Ted Olson

NOTES: Foxx (MVP); Cronin was a player/manager.

KEY SIGNATURES: Foxx, Doerr, Cronin, Higgins, Chapman, Cramer, Vosmik, Grove.

VALUE: $480

MVP = MVP Award winner

1938 BOSTON (NL) - Johnny Cooney, Tony Cuccinello, Vince DiMaggio, Gil English, Dick Errickson, Lou Fette, Elbie Fletcher, Debs Garms, Jim Hitchcock, Ira Hutchinson, Johnny Lanning, Al Lopez, Danny MacFayden, Harl Maggert, Gene Moore, Ray Mueller, Bobby Reis, Johnny Riddle, Milt Shoffner, Casey Stengel (MANAGER), Joe Stripp *, Jim Turner, Rabbit Warstler, Max West

LESS THAN 10 GAMES: Mike Balas, Art Doll, Tom Earley, Frank Gabler *, Roy Johnson, Bob Kahle, Tom Kane, Art Kenney, Eddie Mayo, Ralph McLeod, Hiker Moran, Johnny Niggerling, Tommy Reis, Butch Sutcliffe, Joe Walsh, Roy Weir

KEY SIGNATURES: Stengel, Lopez, MacFayden.

VALUE: $285

1938 BROOKLYN - Gib Brack *, Max Butcher *, Dolph Camilli, Gilly Campbell, Paul Chervinko, Pete Coscarart, Kiki Cuyler, Leo Durocher, Woody English, Freddie Fitzsimmons, Fred Frankhouse, Burleigh Grimes (MANAGER), Bert Haas, Luke Hamlin, Buddy Hassett, Oris Hockett, Johnny Hudson, Ernie Koy, Cookie Lavagetto, Heinie Manush *, Buck Marrow, Van Lingle Mungo, Babe Phelps, Bill Posedel, Tot Pressnell, Packy Rogers, Lee Rogers *, Goody Rosen, Merv Shea, Fred Sington, Roy Spencer, Tuck Stainback *, Vito Tamulis *, Woody Williams, Tom Winsett

LESS THAN 10 GAMES: John Gaddy, Greek George, Ray Hayworth *, Waite Hoyt, Wayne LeMaster *, Sam Nahem, Dykes Potter, Ray Thomas, Jim Winford

NOTES: 4 HOF'ers.

KEY SIGNATURES: Grimes, Durocher, Phelps, Cuyler, Manush, Hoyt.

VALUE: $490

1938 CHICAGO (AL) - Luke Appling, Boze Berger, Merv Connors, Jimmy Dykes (MANAGER), Frank Gabler *, Jackie Hayes, Jack Knott *, Mike Kreevich, Joe Kuhel, Thornton Lee, Ted Lyons, George Meyer, Marv Owen, Rip Radcliff, Tony Rensa, Johnny Rigney, Larry Rosenthal, Norm Schlueter, Luke Sewell, Hank Steinbacher, Monty Stratton, Tommy Thompson, Gee Walker, John Whitehead

LESS THAN 10 GAMES: Harry Boyles, Clint Brown, Sugar Cain, Bill Cox *, Bill Dietrich, Gene Ford, John Gerlach, George Gick, Jesse Landrum, Joe Martin, Mike Tresh, Bob Uhle

NOTES: Dykes was a player/manager.

KEY SIGNATURES: Hayes, Appling, Steinbacher, Walker, Stratton.

VALUE: $325

1938 CHICAGO (NL) - Jim Asbell, Clay Bryant, Tex Carleton, Phil Cavarreta, Ripper Collins, Dizzy Dean, Frank Demaree, Larry French, Augie Galan, Bob Garbark, Charlie Grimm (MANAGER), Stan Hack, Gabby Hartnett (MANAGER), Billy Herman, Billy Jurges, Tony Lazzeri, Bill Lee, Bob Logan, Joe Marty, Ken O'Dea, Vance Page, Carl Reynolds, Charlie Root, Jack Russell, Coaker Triplett

LESS THAN 10 GAMES: Al Epperly, Kirby Higbe, Newt Kimball, Bobby Mattick, Steve Mesner

NOTES: 4 HOF'ers; Hartnett was a player/manager.

KEY SIGNATURES: Herman, Hack, Reynolds, Hartnett, Garbark, Lee, Grimm, Dean, Lazzeri.

VALUE: $470

1938 CINCINNATI - Wally Berger *, Joe Cascarella, Dusty Cooke, Harry Craft, Peaches Davis, Spud Davis *, Paul Derringer, Lonny Frey, Lee Gamble, Ival Goodman, Lee Grissom, Willard Hershberger, Alex Kampouris *, Don Lang, Ernie Lombardi, Frank McCormick, Bill McKechnie (MANAGER), Whitey Moore, Billy Myers, Nolen Richardson, Lew Riggs, Gene Schott, Justin Stein *, Johnny Vander Meer, Bucky Walters *, Jim Weaver *

LESS THAN 10 GAMES: Red Barrett, Ray Benge, Nino Bongiovanni, Kiddo Davis, Al Hollingsworth *, Buck Jordan *, Ted Kleinhans, Jimmy Outlaw, Dick West

NOTES: Lombardi (MVP).

KEY SIGNATURES: McKechnie, McCormick, Berger, Lombardi, Derringer, Vander Meer.

MVP = **MVP Award winner**

VALUE: $315

1938 CLEVELAND - Johnny Allen, Earl Averill, Bruce Campbell, Bob Feller, Denny Galehouse, Odell Hale, Mel Harder, Jeff Heath, Rollie Hemsley, Willis Hudlin, John Humphries, Ken Keltner, John Kroner, Lyn Lary, Al Milner, Frankie Pytlak, Moose Solters, Hal Trosky, Ossie Vitt (MANAGER), Roy Weatherly, Skeeter Webb, Earl Whitehill, Bill Zuber

LESS THAN 10 GAMES: Lou Boudreau, Oscar Grimes, Hank Helf, Joe Heving *, Tommy Irwin, Ken Jungels, Ray Mack, Lloyd Russell, Clay Smith, Charley Suche, Chuck Workman

KEY SIGNATURES: Trosky, Averill, Heath, Pytlak, Boudreau, Feller.

VALUE: $300

1938 DETROIT - Eldon Auker, Del Baker (MANAGER), Al Benton, Tommy Bridges, Mark Christman, Mickey Cochrane (MANAGER), Slick Coffman, Roy Cullenbine, Hary Eisenstat, Pete Fox, Charlie Gehringer, George Gill, Hank Greenberg, Vern Kennedy, Chet Laabs, Roxie Lawson, Chet Morgan, Tony Piet, Boots Poffenberger, Billy Rogell, Don Ross, Birdie Tebbetts, Jake Wade, Dixie Walker, Jo-Jo White, Rudy York

LESS THAN 10 GAMES: George Archie, Woody Davis, Bob Harris, Ray Hayworth *, Benny McKoy, Joe Rogalski, Schoolboy Rowe

KEY SIGNATURES: Cochrane, Greenberg, Gehringer, Walker, Bridges.

VALUE: $325

1938 NEW YORK (AL) - Ivy Andrews, Joe Beggs, Spud Chandler, Frankie Crosetti, Babe Dahlgren, Bill Dickey, Joe DiMaggio, Lou Gehrig, Joe Glenn, Lefty Gomez, Joe Gordon, Bump Hadley, Tommy Henrich, Myril Hoag, Bill Knickerbocker, Joe McCarthy (MANAGER), Johnny Murphy, Monte Pearson, Jake Powell, Red Rolfe, Red Ruffing, George Selkirk, Steve Sundra

LESS THAN 10 GAMES: Atley Donald, Wes Ferrell *, Art Jorgens, Lee Stine, Joe Vance, Kemp Wicker

NOTES: World Champions.

KEY SIGNATURES: McCarthy, Gehrig, DiMaggio, Dickey, Ruffing, Gomez.

VALUE: $1500

1938 NEW YORK (NL) - Dick Bartell, Wally Berger *, Jumbo Brown, Slick Castleman, Lou Chiozza, Bill Cissell, Dick Coffman, Harry Danning, Harry Gumbert, Mickey Haslin, Carl Hubbell, Alex Kampouris *, Hank Leiber, Sam Leslie, Bill Lohrman, Gus Mancuso, Johnny McCarthy, Cliff Melton, Jo-Jo Moore, George Myatt, Mel Ott, Jimmy Ripple, Blondy Ryan, Hal Schumacher, Bob Seeds, Bill Terry (MANAGER), Burgess Whitehead, Johnnie Wittig

LESS THAN 10 GAMES: Tom Baker, Oscar Georgy, Les Powers, Hy Vandenberg

KEY SIGNATURES: Terry, Ott, Moore, Danning, Hubbell.

VALUE: $425

1938 PHILADELPHIA (AL) - Wayne Ambler, Irv Bartling, Earle Brucker, George Caster, Sam Chapman, Chubby Dean, Nick Etten, Lou Finney, Mule Haas, Gene Hasson, Frankie Hayes, Bob Johnson, Dario Lodigiani, Connie Mack (MANAGER), Wally Moses, Lynn Nelson, Skeeter Newsome, Ace Parker, Nels Potter, Buck Ross, Dick Siebert *, Dave Smith, Eddie Smith, Stan Sperry, Bud Thomas, Hal Wagner, Bill Werber, Al Williams

LESS THAN 10 GAMES: Babe Barna, Charlie Berry, Ralph Buxton, Paul Easterling, Randy Gumpert, Harry Kelley *, Rusty Peters, Jim Reninger

KEY SIGNATURES: Mack, Moses, Johnson.

VALUE: $285

1938 PHILADELPHIA (NL) - Morrie Arnovich, Bill Atwood, Gib Brack *, Earl Browne, Max Butcher *, Cap Clark, Gene Corbett, Spud Davis *, Eddie Feinberg, Wild Bill Hallahan, Al Hollingsworth *, Syl Johnson, Buck Jordan *, Chuck Klein, Wayne LeMaster *, Hans Lobert (MANAGER), Hersh Martin, Emmett Mueller, Hugh Mulcahy, Claude Passeau, George Scharein, Pete Sivess, Al Smith, Tuck Stainback *, Justin Stein *, Ray Stoviak, Bucky Walters *, Phil Weintraub, Pinky Whitney, Jimmie Wilson (MANAGER), Del Young

LESS THAN 10 GAMES: Elmer Burkart, Howie Gorman, Ed Heusser, Hal Kelleher, Tom Lanning, Alex Pitko, Art Rebel, Tommy Reis

NOTES: Wilson was a player/manager.

KEY SIGNATURES: Weintraub.

VALUE: $245

1938 PITTSBURGH - Russ Bauers, Ray Berres, Cy Blanton, Joe Bowman, Ed Brandt, Mace Brown, Bill Brubaker, Johnny Dickshot, Lee Handley, Woody Jensen, Bob Klinger, Red Lucas, Heinie Manush *, Johnny Rizzo, Rip Sewell, Gus Suhr, Bill Swift, Tommy Thevenow, Jim Tobin, Al Todd, Pie Traynor (MANAGER), Arky Vaughan, Lloyd Waner, Paul Waner, Pep Young

LESS THAN 10 GAMES: Ken Heintzelman

NOTES: 5 HOF'ers.

KEY SIGNATURES: Traynor, Vaughan, Waner, Waner, Rizzo, Manush, Brown.

VALUE: $525

1938 ST. LOUIS (AL) - Ethan Allen, Mel Almada *, Beau Bell, Julio Bonetti, Harlond Clift, Ed Cole, Bill Cox *, Joe Grace, Sam Harshany, Tommy Heath, Don Heffner, Oral Hildebrand, Roy Hughes, Fred Johnson, Red Kress, Ed Linke, Mike Mazzera, Glenn McQuillan, George McQuinn, Buster Mills, Lefty Mills, Bobo Newsom, Gabby Street (MANAGER), Billy Sullivan, Les Tietje, Russ Van Atta, Jim Walkup, Sammy West *

LESS THAN 10 GAMES: Emil Bildilli, Sig Gryska, Harry Kimberlin, Jack Knott *, Glenn Liebhardt, Johnny Lucadello, Vito Tamulis *, Bill Trotter, Jim Weaver

KEY SIGNATURES: McQuinn, Kress, Almada.

VALUE: $250

1938 ST. LOUIS (NL) - Frenchy Bordagaray, Herb Bremer, Jimmy Brown, Jim Bucher, Curt Davis, Hal Epps, Frankie Frisch (MANAGER), Mike Gonzalez (MANAGER), Don Gutteridge, Ray Harrell, Roy Henshaw, Max Lanier, Max Macon, Pepper Martin, Stu Martin, Bill McGee, Joe Medwick, Johnny Mize, Terry Moore, Lynn Myers, Mickey Owen, Don Padgett, Clyde Shoun, Enos Slaughter, Joe Stripp *, Lon Warneke, Bob Weiland

LESS THAN 10 GAMES: Guy Bush, Mort Cooper, Creepy Crespi, Paul Dean, Si Johnson, Howie Krist, Preacher Roe, Mike Ryba, Dick Siebert *, Tuck Stainback *

NOTES: 4 HOF'ers.
KEY SIGNATURES: Frisch, Mize, Slaughter, Medwick, Martin.

VALUE: $420

1938 WASHINGTON - Mel Almada *, Pete Appleton, Ossie Bluege, Zeke Bonura, George Case, Ken Chase, Jimmie DeShong, Rick Ferrell, Wes Ferrell *, Tony Giuliani, Goose Goslin, Bucky Harris (MANAGER), Chief Hogsett, Harry Kelley *, Joe Krakauskas, Dutch Leonard, Buddy Lewis, Buddy Myer, Al Simmons, John Stone, Cecil Travis, Jimmy Wasdell, Monte Weaver, Sammy West *, Taffy Wright

LESS THAN 10 GAMES: Joe Kohlman, Mickey Livingston, Rene Monteagudo, Bill Phebus

KEY SIGNATURES: Harris, Myer, Travis, Case, Simmons, Ferrell, Goslin, Ferrell.

VALUE: $385

1939

Lou Gehrig's last year with the Yankees was 1939.

*** = player was traded**

1939 BOSTON (AL) - Eldon Auker, Jim Bagby, Moe Berg, Boze Berger, Tom Carey, Doc Cramer, Joe Cronin (MANAGER), Gene Desautels, Emerson Dickman, Bobby Doerr, Lou Finney *, Jimmie Foxx, Denny Galehouse, Lefty Grove, Joe Heving, Red Nonnenkamp, Fritz Ostermueller, Johnny Peacock, Woody Rich, Jim Tabor, Joe Vosmik, Jake Wade *, Ted Williams, Jack Wilson

LESS THAN 10 GAMES: Fabian Gaffke, Bill LeFebvre, Bill Sayles, Charlie Wagner, Monte Weaver

NOTES: 5 HOF'ers; Cronin was a player/manager.

KEY SIGNATURES: Cronin, Foxx, Doerr, Williams, Cramer, Grove.

VALUE: $525

1939 BOSTON (NL) - Stan Andrews, Red Barkley, Chet Clemens, Johnny Cooney, Tony Cuccinello, Tom Earley, Dick Errickson, Lou Fette, Elbie Fletcher *, Fred Frankhouse, Debs Garms, Buddy Hassett, John Hill, Ralph Hodgin, Otto Huber, Johnny Lanning, Al Lopez, Danny MacFayden, Hank Majeski, Phil Masi, Eddie Miller, Jimmy Outlaw, Bill Posedel, Chet Ross, Bama Rowell, Milt Shoffner *, Al Simmons *, Sibby Sisti, Casey Stengel (MANAGER), Joe Sullivan, Jim Turner, Rabbit Warstler, Max West, Whitey Wietelmann

LESS THAN 10 GAMES: George Barnicle, Joe Callahan, Hiker Moran, Bill Schuster, Al Veigel, Roy Weir

KEY SIGNATURES: Stengel, Hassett, Cuccinello, Lopez, Simmons.

VALUE: $360

1939 BROOKLYN - Mel Almada *, Dolph Camilli, Hugh Casey, Pete Coscarart, Lindsay Deal, Leo Durocher (MANAGER), Red Evans, Freddie Fitzsimmons, Luke Hamlin, Ray Hayworth *, Johnny Hudson, Ira Hutchinson, Ernie Koy, Lyn Lary *, Cookie Lavagetto, Tony Lazzeri *, Gene Moore, Van Lingle Mungo, Art Parks, Babe Phelps, Tot Pressnell, Jimmy Ripple *, Goody Rosen, Gene Schott, Fred Sington, Tuck Stainback, Vito Tamulis, Al Todd, Dixie Walker, Whit Wyatt

LESS THAN 10 GAMES: Bill Crouch, Carl Doyle, Chris Hartje, Oris Hockett, Al Hollingsworth *, George Jeffcoat, Boots Poffenberger

NOTES: Durocher was a player/manager.

KEY SIGNATURES: Durocher, Lazzeri.

VALUE: $460

1939 CHICAGO (AL) - Luke Appling, Ollie Bejma, Clint Brown, Bill Dietrich, Jimmie Dykes (MANAGER), Vic Fasier, Jackie Hayes, Jack Knott, Mike Kreevich, Joe Kuhel, Thornton Lee, Ted Lyons, Johnny Marcum *, Eric McNair, Marv Owen, Rip Radcliff, Tony Rensa, Johnny Rigney, Larry Rosenthal, Norm Schlueter, Ken Silvestri, Eddie Smith *, Hank Steinbacher, Mike Tresh, Gee Walker

LESS THAN 10 GAMES: Harry Boyles, Jess Dobernic, Vallie Eaves, John Gerlach, Art Herring, Bob Kennedy, Tommy Thompson *, John Whitehead *

NOTES: Dykes was a player/manager.

KEY SIGNATURES: Kuhel, Appling, McNair, Lyons.

VALUE: $270

1939 CHICAGO (NL) - Dick Bartell, Phil Cavarretta, Dizzy Dean, Larry French, Augie Galan, Bob Garbark, Jim Gleeson, Stan Hack, Gabby Hartnett (MANAGER), Billy Herman, Bill Lee, Hank Leiber, Gene Lillard, Gus Mancuso, Joe Marty *, Bobby Mattick, Steve Mesner, Bill Nicholson, Vance Page, Claude Passeau *, Carl Reynolds, Charlie Root, Jack Russell, Rip Russell, Earl Whitehill

LESS THAN 10 GAMES: Clay Bryant, Ray Harrell *, Kirby Higbe *, Vern Olsen

NOTES: Hartnett was a player/manager.

KEY SIGNATURES: Hartnett, Herman, Leiber, Galan, Hartnett, Dean.

VALUE: $300

1939 CINCINNATI - Wally Berger, Nino Bongiovanni, Frenchy Bordagary, Harry Craft, Peaches Davis, Paul Derringer, Lonny Frey, Lee Gamble, Ival Goodman, Lee Grissom, Willard Hershberger, Hank Johnson, Eddie Joost, Ernie Lombardi, Frank McCormick, Bill McKechnie (MANAGER), Whitey Moore, Billy Myers, Johnny Niggerling, Lew Riggs, Les Scarsella, Milt Shoffner *, Junior Thompson, Johnny Vander Meer, Bucky Walters, Bill Werber

LESS THAN 10 GAMES: Red Barrett, Vince DiMaggio, Milt Galatzer, Bud Hafey *, Art Jacobs, Wes Livengood, Pete Naktenis, Nolen Richardson, Elmer Riddle, Al Simmons *, Jim Weaver, Dick West, Jimmie Wilson

NOTES: Walters (MVP).

KEY SIGNATURES: McKechnie, McCormick, Goodman, Lombardi, Simmons, Walters, Derringer.

VALUE: $400

MVP = MVP Award winner

1939 CLEVELAND - Johnny Allen, Earl Averill *, Lou Boudreau, Johnny Broaca, Bruce Campbell, Ben Chapman, Joe Dobson, Harry Eisenstat *, Bob Feller, Oscar Grimes, Odell Hale, Mel Harder, Jeff Heath, Rollie Hemsley, Willis Hudlin, John Humphries, Ken Keltner, Ray Mack, Al Milnar, Frankie Pytlak, Luke Sewell, Jim Shilling *, Moose Solters, Hal Trosky, Ossie Vitt (MANAGER), Roy Weatherly, Skeeter Webb, Bill Zuber

LESS THAN 10 GAMES: Tom Drake, Lyn Lary *, Mike Naymick, Floyd Stromme, Lefty Sullivan

KEY SIGNATURES: Trosky, Hale, Keltner, Boudreau, Feller.

VALUE: $275

1939 DETROIT - Earl Averill *, Del Baker (MANAGER), Beau Bell *, Al Benton, Tommy Bridges, Slick Coffman, Frank Croucher, Roy Cullenbine, Harry Eisenstat *, Pete Fox, Charlie Gehringer, Hank Greenberg, Pinky Higgins, Fred Hutchinson, Red Kress, Barney McCosky, Johnny McCoy, Archie McKain, Bobo Newsom *, Billy Rogell, Schoolboy Rowe, Birdie Tebbetts, Bud Thomas *, Dizzy Trout, Dixie Walker *, Rudy York

LESS THAN 10 GAMES: Mark Christman *, Les Fleming, Floyd Giebell, George Gill *, Bob Harris *, Vern Kennedy *, Chet Laabs *, Roxie Lawson *, Red Lynn *, Hal Newhouser, Dixie Parsons, Cotton Pippen *, Merv Shea, Jim Walkup *

KEY SIGNATURES: Greenberg, Gehringer, McCosky, Averill, Bridges.

VALUE: $315

1939 NEW YORK (AL) - Spud Chandler, Frankie Crosetti, Babe Dahlgren, Bill Dickey, Joe DiMaggio, Atley Donald, Joe Gallagher *, Lefty Gomez, Joe Gordon, Bump Hadley, Tommy Henrich, Oral Hildebrand, Charlie Keller, Joe McCarthy (MANAGER), Johnny Murphy, Monte Pearson, Jake Powell, Red Rolfe, Buddy Rosar, Red Ruffing, Marius Russo, George Selkirk, Steve Sundra

LESS THAN 10 GAMES: Marv Breuer, Wes Ferrell, Lou Gehrig, Art Jorgens, Bill Knickerbocker

NOTES: World Champions for fourth straight year; team baseballs with with Gehrig's signature are rare; DiMaggio (MVP); a ball with Gehrig's signature is worth $1,500.

KEY SIGNATURES: McCarthy, Rolfe, Keller, DiMaggio, Selkirk, Dickey, Ruffing, Gehring, Gomez.

VALUE: $600

1939 NEW YORK (NL) - Zeke Bonura, Jumbo Brown, Slick Castleman, Lou Chiozza, Dick Coffman, Harry Danning, Frank Demaree, Johnny Dickshot, Al Glossop, Harry Gumbert, Tom Hafey, Carl Hubbell, Billy Jurges, Alex Kampouris, Tony Lazzeri *, Bill Lohrman, Red Lynn *, Johnny McCarthy, Cliff Melton, Jo-Jo Moore, George Myatt, Ken O'Dea, Mel Ott, Jimmy Ripple *, Manny Salvo, Skeeter Scalzi, Hal Schumacher, Bob Seeds, Bill Terry (MANAGER), Burgess Whitehead, Babe Young

LESS THAN 10 GAMES: Tom Gorman, Ray Hayworth *, Johnny McCarthy, Hy Vandenberg, Johnnie Wittig

KEY SIGNATURES: Terry, Bonura, Ott, Demaree, Danning, Lazzeri, Hubbell.

VALUE: $480

1939 PHILADELPHIA (AL) - Wayne Ambler, Bill Beckman, Al Brancato, Earle Brucker, George Caster, Fred Chapman, Sam Chapman, Eddie Collins, Chubby Dean, Nick Etten, Joe Gantenbein, Frankie Hayes, Bob Johnson, Bob Joyce, Dario Lodigiani, Connie Mack (MANAGER), Dee Miles, Wally Moses, Bill Nagel, Lynn Nelson, Skeeter Newsome, Roy Parmelee, Cotton Pippen *, Nels Potter, Bucky Ross, Dick Siebert, Eric Tipton

LESS THAN 10 GAMES: Lou Finney *, Bill Lillard, Walt Masters, Les McCrabb, Bob McNamara, Bill Nagel, Harry O'Neill, Sam Page, Jim Reninger, Jim Schelle, Dave Smith, Eddie Smith *, Bud Thomas *, Hal Wagner

KEY SIGNATURES: Mack, Moses, Johnson, Collins.

VALUE: $340

1939 PHILADELPHIA (NL) - Morrie Arnovich, Bud Bates, Boom-Boom Beck, Stan Benjamin, Jack Bolling, Gib Brack, Max Butcher *, Dave Coble, Spud Davis, Bud Hafey *, Ray Harrell *, Kirby Higbe *, Al Hollingsworth *, Roy Hughes *, Syl Johnson, Bill Kerksieck, Chuck Klein *, Charlie Letchas, Hersh Martin, Joe Marty *, Pinky May, Wally Millies, Emmett Mueller, Hugh Mulcahy, Ike Pearson, Jennings Poindexter, Les Powers, Doc Prothro (MANAGER), George Scharein, LeGrant Scott, Jim Shilling *, Gus Suhr *, Bennie Warren, Pinky Whitney, Del Young

LESS THAN 10 GAMES: Bill Atwood, Roy Bruner, Elmer Burkart, Eddie Feinberg, Len Gabrielson, Jim Henry, Bill Hoffman, Joe Kracher, Joe Marty *, Claude Passeau *, Gene Schott *, Al Smith, Cliff Watwood

KEY SIGNATURES: Suhr, Arnovich, Davis.

VALUE: $215

HOF = Hall of Famer

1939 PITTSBURGH - Russ Bauers, Fern Bell, Ray Berres, Cy Blanton, Joe Bowman, Mace Brown, Bill Brubaker, Max Butcher *, Bill Clemensen, Bob Elliott, Elbie Fletcher *, Frankie Gustine, Lee Handley, Ken Heintzelman, Woody Jensen, Jack Juelich, Chuck Klein *, Bob Klinger, Heinie Manush, Ray Mueller, Johnny Rizzo, Rip Sewell, Gus Suhr *, George Susce, Bill Swift, Jim Tobin, Pie Traynor (MANAGER), Maurice Van Robays, Arky Vaughan, Lloyd Waner, Paul Waner, Pep Young

LESS THAN 10 GAMES: Johnny Gee, Pep Rambert, Joe Schultz, Oad Swigart, Eddie Yount

NOTES: 5 HOF'ers.

KEY SIGNATURES: Traynor, Fletcher, Vaughan, P. Waner, L. Waner, Manush.

VALUE: $480

1939 ST. LOUIS (AL) - Mel Almada *, Beau Bell *, Johnny Bernadino, Mark Christman *, Harlond Clift, Joe Gallagher *, George Gill *, Joe Glenn, Joe Grace, Sig Gryska, Fred Haney (MANAGER), Bob Harris *, Sam Harshany, Don Heffner, Myril Hoag, Roy Hughes *, Vern Kennedy *, Harry Kimberlin, Jack Kramer, Red Kress *, Chet Laabs *, Roxie Lawson *, Johnny Marcum *, Mike Mazzera, George McQuinn, Lefty Mills, Moose Solters *, Hal Spindel, Billy Sullivan, Tommy Thompson *, Bill Trotter, John Whitehead *

LESS THAN 10 GAMES: Emil Bildilli, Ed Cole, Bill Cox, Roy Hanning, Myril Hoag, Fred Johnson, Johnny Lucadello, Bob Muncrief, Bob Neighbors, Bobo Newsom *, Ewald Pyle, Eddie Silber, Russ Van Atta, Jake Wade *, Jim Walkup *

KEY SIGNATURES: McQuinn, Laabs.

VALUE: $225

1939 ST. LOUIS (NL) - Nate Andrews, Ray Blades (MANAGER), Bob Bowman, Jimmy Brown, Mort Cooper, Creepy Crespi, Curt Davis, Paul Dean, Herman Franks, Don Gutteridge, Lynn King, Lyn Lary *, Pepper Martin, Stu Martin, Bill McGee, Joe Medwick, Johnny Mize, Terry Moore, Lynn Myers, Mickey Owen, Don Padgett, Clyde Shoun, Enos Slaughter, Tom Sunkel, Lon Warneke, Bob Weiland

LESS THAN 10 GAMES: Buster Adams, Frank Barrett, Herb Bremer, Murry Dickson, Johnny Echols, Johnny Hopp, Eddie Lake, Max Lanier, Terry Moore, Joe Orengo, Ken Raffensberger, Bob Repass

KEY SIGNATURES: Mize, Slaughter, Medwick, P. Martin.

VALUE: $395

1939 WASHINGTON - Pete Appleton, Tom Baker, Jimmy Bloodworth, Ossie Bluege, Alex Carrasquel, George Case, Ken Chase, Jake Early, Bobby Estalella, Rick Ferrell, Charlie Gelbert, Tony Giuliani, Bucky Harris (MANAGER), Joe Haynes, Harry Kelley, Joe Krakauskas, Dutch Leonard, Buddy Lewis, Walt Masterson, Buddy Myer, Bob Prichard, Hal Quick, Cecil Travis, Mickey Vernon, Jimmy Wasdell, Johnny Welaj, Sammy West, Taffy Wright

LESS THAN 10 GAMES: Morrie Aderholt, Dick Bass, Jimmie DeShong, Al Evans, Elmer Gedeon, Bill Holland, Bucky Jacobs, Ed Leip, Bobby Loane, Mike Palagyi, Alex Pitko, Bud Thomas *, Lou Thuman, Early Wynn

KEY SIGNATURES: Harris, Vernon, Lewis, Case, Wright, Ferrell, Leonard.

VALUE: $250

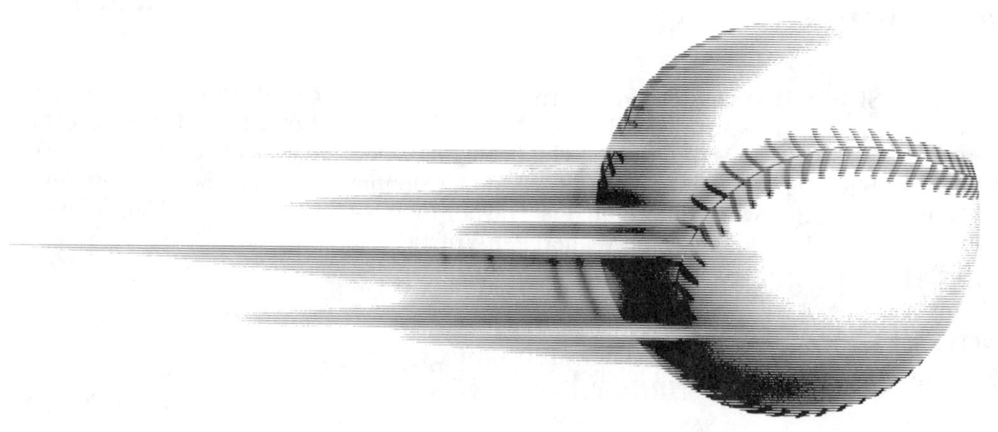

1940

1940 Cincinnati Reds

*** = player was traded**

1940 BOSTON (AL) - Jim Bagby, Tom Carey, Doc Cramer, Joe Cronin (MANAGER), Gene Desautels, Emerson Dickman, Dom DiMaggio, Bobby Doerr, Lou Finney, Bill Fleming, Jimmie Foxx, Denny Galehouse, Charlie Gelbert *, Joe Glenn, Lefty Grove, Mickey Harris, Herb Hash, Joe Heving, Earl Johnson, Tony Lupien, Fritz Ostermueller, Marv Owen, Johnny Peacock, Stan Spence, Jim Tabor, Charlie Wagner, Ted Williams, Jack Wilson

LESS THAN 10 GAMES: Bill Butland, Alex Mustaikis, Red Nonnenkamp, Woody Rich, Yank Terry, Ted Williams

NOTES: Cronin was a player/manager.

KEY SIGNATURES: Cronin, Foxx, Doerr, Williams, Wilson, Grove.

VALUE: $500

1940 BOSTON (NL) - Stan Andrews, George Barnicle, Ray Berres *, Siggy Broskie, Dick Coffman, Johnny Cooney, Tony Cuccinello *, Dick Errickson, Al Glossop *, Buddy Hassett, Al Javery, Bobby Loane, Al Lopez *, Hank Majeski, Phil Masi, Eddie Miller, Gene Moore *, Al Piechota, Bill Posedel, Mel Preibisch, Chet Ross, Bama Rowell, Manny Salvo, Les Scarsella, Sibby Sisti, Casey Stengel (MANAGER), Nick Strincevich, Joe Sullivan, Jim Tobin, Rabbit Warstler *, Max West, Whitey Wietelmann

LESS THAN 10 GAMES: Joe Callahan, Tom Earley, Lou Fette *, Buddy Gremp, Art Johnson, Frank LaManna, Don Manno, Bill Swift, Claude Wilborn, Ace Williams

KEY SIGNATURES: Stengel, Rowell, Cooney, Lopez.

VALUE: $300

1940 BROOKLYN - Dolph Camilli, Tex Carleton, Hugh Casey, Pete Coscarart, Roy Cullenbine *, Curt Davis *, Leo Durocher (MANAGER), Freddie Fitzsimmons, Herman Franks, Joe Gallagher *, Charlie Gilbert, Lee Grissom *, Luke Hamlin, Ed Head, Johnny Hudson, Newt Kimball *, Ernie Koy *, Cookie Lavagetto, Gus Mancuso, Joe Medwick *, Gene Moore *, Babe Phelps, Tot Pressnell, Pee Wee Reese, Pete Reiser, Don Ross, Vito Tamulis, Joe Vosmik, Dixie Walker, Jimmy Wasdell *, Whit Wyatt

LESS THAN 10 GAMES: Carl Doyle *, Wes Ferrell, Lou Fette *, Wes Flowers, Tony Giuliani, Max Macon, Van Lingle Mungo, Steve Rachunok, Jimmy Ripple *

NOTES: Durocher was a player/manager.

KEY SIGNATURES: Durocher, Reese, Medwick.

VALUE: $420

1940 CHICAGO (AL) - Pete Appleton, Luke Appling, Clint Brown, Bill Dietrich, Jimmy Dykes (MANAGER), Jackie Hayes, Bob Kennedy, Jack Knott, Don Kolloway, Mike Kreevich, Joe Kuhel, Thornton Lee, Ted Lyons, Eric McNair, Johnny Rigney, Larry Rosenthal, Ken Silvestri, Eddie Smith, Moose Solters, Mike Tresh, Tom Turner, Skeeter Webb, Taffy Wright

LESS THAN 10 GAMES: Vallie Eaves, Orval Grove, Jack Hallett, Dave Short, Ed Weiland

KEY SIGNATURES: Appling, Wright, Solters, Lyons.

VALUE: $260

1940 CHICAGO (NL) - Zeke Bonura *, Phil Cavarretta, Bob Collins, Dom Dallessandro, Dizzy Dean, Larry French, Augie Galan, Jim Gleeson, Stan Hack, Gabby Hartnett (MANAGER), Billy Herman, Bill Lee, Hank Leiber, Bobby Mattick, Jake Mooty, Bill Nicholson, Vern Olsen, Vance Page, Claude Passeau, Ken Raffensberger, Billy Rogell, Charlie Root, Rip Russell, Al Todd, Rabbit Warstler *

LESS THAN 10 GAMES: Julio Bonetti, Clay Bryant, Clyde McCullough, Bobby Sturgeon

NOTES: Hartnett was a player/manager.

KEY SIGNATURES: Hartnett, Herman, Dean.

VALUE: $265

1940 CINCINNATI - Morrie Arnovich *, Bill Baker, Joe Beggs, Harry Craft, Mike Dejan, Paul Derringer, Lonny Frey, Lew Gamble, Ival Goodman, Willard Hershberger, Johnny Hutchings, Eddie Joost, Ernie Lombardi, Frank McCormick, Mike McCormick, Bill McKechnie (MANAGER), Whitey Moore, Billy Myers, Elmer Riddle, Lew Riggs, Jimmy Ripple *, Johnny Rizzo *, Milt Shoffner, Junior Thompson, Jim Turner, Johnny Vander Meer, Bucky Walters, Bill Werber, Jimmie Wilson

LESS THAN 10 GAMES: Red Barrett, Wally Berger *, Vince DiMaggio *, Witt Guise, Dick West

NOTES: World Champions! F. McCormick won the MVP; Hershberger died 8/3/40.

KEY SIGNATURES: McKechnie, F. McCormick, Lombardi.

VALUE: $450

1940 CLEVELAND - Johnny Allen, Beau Bell, Lou Boudreau, Soup Campbell, Ben Chapman, Joe Dobson, Harry Eisenstat, Bob Feller, Oscar Grimes, Odell Hale, Mel Harder, Jeff Heath, Rollie Hemsley, John Humphries, Ken Keltner, Ray Mack, Al Milnar, Mike Naymick, Rusty Peters, Frankie Pytlak, Al Smith, Hal Trosky, Ossie Vitt (MANAGER), Roy Weatherly, Bill Zuber

LESS THAN 10 GAMES: Nate Andrews, Cal Dorsett, Hank Helf, Dixie Howell, Willis Hudlin *, Ken Jungels
KEY SIGNATURES: Boudreau, Weatherly, Feller, Smith.

VALUE: $250

1940 DETROIT - Earl Averill, Del Baker (MANAGER), Dick Bartell, Al Benton, Tommy Bridges, Bruce Campbell, Frank Croucher, Pete Fox, Charlie Gehringer, Johnny Gorsica, Hank Greenberg, Pinky Higgins, Fred Hutchinson, Red Kress, Barney McCosky, Archie McKain, Scat Metha, Dutch Meyer, Hal Newhouser, Bobo Newsom, Schoolboy Rowe, Tom Seats, Clay Smith, Tuck Stainback, Billy Sullivan, Birdie Tebbetts, Dizzy Trout, Rudy York
LESS THAN 10 GAMES: Dick Conger, Floyd Giebell, Pat Mullin, Lynn Nelson, Cotton Pippen, Frank Secory, Bud Thomas, Bob Uhle
NOTES: Greenberg (MVP).
KEY SIGNATURES: York, Gehringer, McCosky, Greenberg, Averill, Newsom.

VALUE: $420

1940 NEW YORK (AL) - Ernie Bonham, Marv Breuer, Spud Chandler, Mike Chartak, Frankie Crosetti, Babe Dahlgren, Bill Dickey, Joe DiMaggio, Atley Donald, Joe Gordon, Bump Hadley, Tommy Henrich, Oral Hildebrand, Charlie Keller, Bill Knickerbocker, Joe McCarthy (MANAGER), Buster Mills, Johnny Murphy, Monte Pearson, Jake Powell, Red Rolfe, Buddy Rosar, Red Ruffing, Marius Russo, George Selkirk, Steve Sundra
LESS THAN 10 GAMES: Lefty Gomez, Lee Grissom *
NOTES: 5 HOF'ers.
KEY SIGNATURES: McCarthy, DiMaggio, Dickey, Ruffing, Gomez.

VALUE: $525

1940 NEW YORK (NL) - Jumbo Brown, Tony Cuccinello *, Harry Danning, Paul Dean, Frank Demaree, Al Glossop *, Harry Gumbert, Carl Hubbell, Roy Joiner, Billy Jurges, Bill Lohrman, Red Lynn, Johnny McCarthy, Cliff Melton, Jo-Jo Moore, Ken O'Dea, Mel Ott, Johnny Rucker, Hal Schumacher, Bob Seeds, Glen Stewart, Bill Terry (MANAGER), Hy Vandenberg, Burgess Whitehead, Mickey Witek, Babe Young
LESS THAN 10 GAMES: Bob Carpenter, Willis Hudlin *, Buster Maynard, Red Tramback
KEY SIGNATURES: Terry, Ott, Demaree, Danning, Hubbell.

VALUE: $400

1940 PHILADELPHIA (AL) - Johnny Babich, Bill Beckmann, Herman Besse, Al Brancato, Earle Brucker, George Caster, Fred Chapman, Sam Chapman, Crash Davis, Chubby Dean, Sep Gantenbein, Frankie Hayes, Ed Heusser, Bob Johnson, Bill Lillard, Connie Mack (MANAGER), Benny McCoy, Dee Miles, Wally Moses, Nels Potter, Buck Ross, Al Rubeling, Dick Siebert, Al Simmons, Porter Vaughan, Hal Wagner
LESS THAN 10 GAMES: Buddy Hancken, Dario Lodigiani, Phil Marchildon, Les McCrabb, Pat McLaughlin, Carl Miles, Eric Tipton, Elmer Valo, Jack Wallaesa
KEY SIGNATURES: Mack, Moses, Hayes, Simmons.

VALUE: $325

1940 PHILADELPHIA (NL) - Morrie Arnovich *, Bill Atwood, Boom-Boom Beck, Wally Berger *, Cy Blanton, Bobby Bragan, Lloyd Brown, Charlie Frye, Kirby Higbe, Si Johnson, Syl Johnson, George Jumonville, Chuck Klein, Danny Litwhiler, Art Mahan,

Hal Marnie, Hersh Martin, Joe Marty, Pinky May, Mike Mazzera, Wally Millies, Al Monchak, Emmett Mueller, Hugh Mulcahy, Ike Pearson, Doc Prothro (MANAGER), Johnny Rizzo, Ham Schulte, Lefty Smoll, Neb Stewart, Gus Suhr, Bennie Warren, Del Young

LESS THAN 10 GAMES: Stan Benjamin, Roy Bruner, Sam File, Frank Hoerst, Ed Levy, Art Mahan, Paul Masterson, Johnny Podgajny, George Scharein, Maxie Wilson

VALUE: $200

1940 PITTSBURGH - Russ Bauers, Ray Berres *, Joe Bowman, Mace Brown, Bill Brubaker, Max Butcher, Spud Davis, Vince DiMaggio *, Bob Elliott, Ed Fernandes, Elbie Fletcher, Frankie Frisch (MANAGER), Debs Garms, Johnny Gee, Frankie Gustine, Lee Handley, Ken Heintzelman, Bob Klinger, Dick Lanahan, Johnny Lanning, Al Lopez *, Danny MacFayden, Joe Schultz, Rip Sewell, Maurice Van Robays, Arky Vaughan, Lloyd Waner, Paul Waner, Pep Young

LESS THAN 10 GAMES: Fern Bell, Dutch Dietz, Ray Harrell, Frank Kalin, Ed Leip, Ray Mueller, Pep Rambert, Johnny Rizzo *, Oad Swigart

NOTES: 5 HOF'ers; Final year at Pittsburgh for the Waner brothers.

KEY SIGNATURES: Frisch, Vaughan, P. Waner, L. Waner, Lopez.

VALUE: $395

1940 ST. LOUIS (AL) - Eldon Auker, Johnny Berardino, Emil Bildilli, Harlond Clift, Slick Coffman, Bill Cox, Roy Cullenbine *, Joe Gallagher *, Joe Grace, Fred Haney (MANAGER), Bob Harris, Don Heffner, Myril Hoag, Walt Judnich, Vern Kennedy, Jack Kramer, Chet Laabs, Lyn Lary, Roxie Lawson, Johnny Lucadello, George McQuinn, Lefty Mills, Johnny Niggeling, Rip Radcliff, Alan Strange, George Susce, Bob Swift, Bill Trotter, John Whitehead

LESS THAN 10 GAMES: Sam Harshany, Willis Hudlin *, Maury Newlin, Fuzz White

KEY SIGNATURES: Judnich, Radcliff.

VALUE: $225

1940 ST. LOUIS (NL) - Ray Blades (MANAGER), Bob Bowman, Jimmy Brown, Mort Cooper, Walker Cooper, Creepy Crespi, Curt Davis *, Bill DeLancey, Carl Doyle *, Hal Epps, Mike Gonzalez (MANAGER), Don Gutteridge, Johnny Hopp, Ira Hutchinson, Red Jones, Ernie Koy *, Eddie Lake, Max Lanier, Marty Marion, Pepper Martin, Stu Martin, Bill McGee, Joe Medwick *, Johnny Mize, Terry Moore, Joe Orengo, Mickey Owen, Don Padgett, Jack Russell, Clyde Shoun, Enos Slaughter, Billy Southworth (MANAGER), Lon Warneke

LESS THAN 10 GAMES: Harry Brecheen, Murry Dickson, Carden Gillenwater, Newt Kimball *, Gene Lillard, Harry Walker, Bob Weiland, Ernie White

KEY SIGNATURES: Mize, Slaughter, P. Martin, Medwick.

VALUE: $360

1940 WASHINGTON - Jimmy Bloodworth, Zeke Bonura *, Alex Carrasquel, George Case, Ken Chase, Jake Early, Al Evans, Rick Ferrell, Charlie Gelbert *, Bucky Harris (MANAGER), Joe Haynes, Sid Hudson, Joe Krakauskas, Dutch Leonard, Buddy Lewis, Walt Masterson, Rene Monteagudo, Buddy Myer, Jimmy Pofahl, Sherry Robertson, Jack Sanford, Cecil Travis, Gee Walker, Jimmy Wasdell *, Johnny Welaj, Sammy West

LESS THAN 10 GAMES: Morrie Aderholt, Red Anderson, Charlie Gelbert *, Dick Hahn, Al Hollingsworth, Willis Hudlin *, Bucky Jacobs, Jim Mallory, Lou Thuman, Gil Torres, Mickey Vernon

KEY SIGNATURES: Harris, Lewis, Ferrell, Vernon.

VALUE: $240

1941

Lon Warneke used this ball during his no-hitter in 1941.

*** = player was traded**

1941 BOSTON (AL) - Tom Carey, Joe Cronin (MANAGER), Dom DiMaggio, Joe Dobson, Bobby Doerr, Lou Finney, Al Flair, Bill Fleming, Pete Fox, Jimmie Foxx, Lefty Grove, Odell Hale *, Mickey Harris, Tex Hughson, Earl Johnson, Dick Newsome, Skeeter Newsome, Johnny Peacock, Nels Potter *, Frankie Pytlak, Mike Ryba, Stan Spence, Jim Tabor, Charlie Wagner, Ted Williams, Jack Wilson

LESS THAN 10 GAMES: Paul Campbell, Emerson Dickman, Herb Hash, Oscar Judd, Woody Rich

NOTES: 5 HOF'ers; Williams hit .406; Cronin was a player/manager.

KEY SIGNATURES: Cronin, Foxx, Doerr, DiMaggio, Williams, Grove.

VALUE: $550

HOF = Hall of Famer

1941 BOSTON (NL) - Ray Berres, Johnny Cooney, Babe Dahlgren *, Frank Demaree *, John Dudra, Tom Earley, Dick Errickson, Buddy Gremp, Buddy Hassett, Johnny Hutchings *, Al Javery, Art Johnson, Frank Lamanna, Hank Majeski, Don Manno, Phil Masi, Eddie Miller, Al Montgomery, Gene Moore, Bill Posedel, Mel Preibisch, Skippy Roberge, Chet Ross, Bama Rowell, Manny Salvo, Sibby Sisti, Casey Stengel (MANAGER), Joe Sullivan *, Jim Tobin, Lloyd Waner *, Paul Waner *, Max West, Whitey Wietelmann

LESS THAN 10 GAMES: Earl Averill, George Barnicle, Buster Bray, Eddie Carnett, Wes Ferrell, Al Piechota, Nick Strincevich *

KEY SIGNATURES: Cooney, Waner, Stengel.

VALUE: $300

1941 BROOKLYN - Johnny Allen *, Mace Brown *, Dolph Camilli, Alex Campouris, Hugh Casey, Pete Coscarart, Curt Davis, Leo Durocher (MANAGER), Tom Drake, Freddie Fitzsimmons, Herman Franks, Augie Galan *, Joe Gallagher, Tony Giuliani, Luke Hamlin, Billy Herman *, Kirby Higbe, Newt Kimball, Cookie Lavagetto, Joe Medwick, Mickey Owen, Babe Phelps, Pee Wee Reese, Pete Reiser, Lew Riggs, Vito Tamulis *, Joe Vosmik, Dixie Walker, Paul Waner *, Jimmy Wasdell, Kemp Wicker, Whit Wyatt

LESS THAN 10 GAMES: Ed Albosta, Bob Chipman, Larry French *, Lee Grissom *, Van Lingle Mungo, George Pfister, Bill Swift, Tommy Tatum

NOTES: Camilli (MVP); Durocher was a player/manager.

KEY SIGNATURES: Durocher, Camilli, Herman, Reese, Medwick, Waner.

MVP = MVP Award winner

VALUE: $465

1941 CHICAGO (AL) - Pete Appleton, Luke Appling, Ben Chapman *, George Dickey, Bill Dietrich, Jimmy Dykes (MANAGER), Jack Hallett, Myril Hoag *, John Humphries, Bob Kennedy, Bill Knickerbocker, Don Kolloway, Mike Kreevich, Joe Kuhel, Thornton Lee, Dario Lodigiani, Ted Lyons, Johnny Rigney, Larry Rosenthal *, Buck Ross *, Eddie Smith, Moose Solters, Mike Tresh, Tom Turner, Skeeter Webb, Taffy Wright

LESS THAN 10 GAMES: Stan Goletz, Orval Grove, Chet Hajduk, Joe Haynes, Jake Jones, Dave Philley, Dave Short

KEY SIGNATURES: Appling, Lyons.

VALUE: $275

1941 CHICAGO (NL) - Phil Cavarretta, Babe Dahlgren *, Dom Dallessandro, Vallie Eaves, Paul Erickson, Larry French *, Augie Galan *, Greek George *, Charlie Gilbert, Stan Hack, Billy Herman *, Johnny Hudson, Bill Lee, Hank Leiber, Clyde McCullough, Lennie Merullo, Jake Mooty, Billy Myers, Bill Nicholson, Lou Novikoff, Barney Olsen, Vern Olsen, Vance Page, Claude Passeau, Tot Pressnell, Ken Raffensberger, Charlie Root, Bob Scheffing, Lou Stringer, Bobby Sturgeon, Eddie Waitkus, Jimmie Wilson (MANAGER)

LESS THAN 10 GAMES: Dizzy Dean, Hank Gornicki *, Frank Jelincich, Emil Kush, Walt Lanfranconi, Russ Meers, Wimpy Quinn, Rip Russell, Johnny Schmitz, Al Todd

KEY SIGNATURES: Hack, Herman, Dean.

VALUE: $225

1941 CINCINNATI - Chuck Aleno, Bill Baker *, Joe Beggs, Harry Craft, Paul Derringer, Lonny Frey, Jim Gleeson, Ival Goodman, Eddie Joost, Ernie Koy *, Ernie Lombardi, Eddie Lukon, Bobby Mattick, Frank McCormick, Mike McCormick, Bill McKechnie (MANAGER), Whitey Moore, Elmer Riddle, Johnny Riddle, Jimmy Ripple, Junior Thompson, Jim Turner, Johnny Vander Meer, Bucky Walters, Lloyd Waner *, Bill Werber, Dick West

LESS THAN 10 GAMES: Johnny Hutchings *, Ray Lamanno, Bob Logan, Monte Pearson, Hank Sauer, Eddie Shokes, Ray Starr, Pep Young *, Benny Zientara

KEY SIGNATURES: McKechnie, Lombardi, Waner.

VALUE: $315

1941 CLEVELAND - Jim Bagby, Beau Bell, Lou Boudreau, Clint Brown, Soup Campbell, Jack Conway *, Gene Desautels, Hank Edwards, Harry Eisenstat, Bob Feller, Vern Freiberger, Oscar Grimes, Mel Harder, Jeff Heath, Jim Hegan, Rollie Hemsley, Joe Heving, Red Howell, Ken Keltner, Joe Krakauskas, Ray Mack, Al Milnar, Roger Peckinpaugh (MANAGER), Rusty Peters, Larry Rosenthal *, Al Smith, Hal Trosky, Gee Walker, Roy Weatherly

LESS THAN 10 GAMES: Nate Andrews, Chubby Dean *, Cal Dorsett, Red Embree, Les Fleming, Buck Frierson, Fabian Gaffke, Steve Gromek, Oris Hockett, Ken Jungels, Bob Lemon, George Susce, Chuck Workman

KEY SIGNATURES: Boudreau, Heath, Lemon, Feller.

VALUE: $230

1941 DETROIT - Del Baker (MANAGER), Al Benton, Tommy Bridges, Bruce Campbell, Frank Croucher, Murray Franklin, Charlie Gehringer, Floyd Giebell, Johnny Gorsica, Hank Greenberg, Ned Harris, Pinky Higgins, Barney McCosky, Archie McKain *, Eric McNair, Dutch Meyer, Pat Mullin, Hal Newhouser, Bobo Newsom, Boyd Perry, Rip Radcliff *, Schoolboy Rowe, Tuck Stainback, Billy Sullivan, Birdie Tebbetts, Bud Thomas, Dizzy Trout, Rudy York

LESS THAN 10 GAMES: Dick Bartell *, Earl Cook, Hoot Evers, Fred Hutchinson, Hal Manders, Les Mueller, Bob Patrick, Virgil Trucks, Dick Wakefiled, Hal White

KEY SIGNATURES: Gehringer, McCosky, Radcliff, Greenberg, Benton.

VALUE: $275

1941 NEW YORK (AL) - Ernie Bonham, Frenchy Bordagaray, Norm Branch, Marv Breuer, Spud Chandler, Frankie Crosetti, Bill Dickey, Joe DiMaggio, Atley Donald, Lefty Gomez, Joe Gordon, Tommy Henrich, Charlie Keller, Joe McCarthy (MANAGER), Johnny Murphy, Steve Peek, Jerry Priddy, Phil Rizzuto, Red Rolfe, Buddy Rosar, Red Ruffing, Marius Russo, George Selkirk, Ken Silvestri, Charley Stanceu, Johnny Sturm

LESS THAN 10 GAMES: Johnny Lindell, George Washburn

NOTES: World Champions! 4 HOF'ers; DiMaggio won the MVP award and had a 56-game hitting streak.

KEY SIGNATURES: McCarthy, Rizzuto, DiMaggio, Dickey, Gomez, Ruffing.

VALUE: $800

HOF = Hall of Famer

1941 NEW YORK (NL) - Ace Adams, Morrie Arnovich, Babe Barna, Dick Bartell *, Bob Bowman, Jumbo Brown, Bob Carpenter, Harry Danning, John Davis, Frank Demaree *, Odell Hale *, Gabby Hartnett, Carl Hubbell, Billy Jurges, Bill Lohrman, Johnny McCarthy, Bill McGee *, Cliff Melton, Jo-Jo Moore, Ken O'Dea, Joe Orengo, Mel Ott, Johnny Rucker, Hal Schumacher, Bill Terry (MANAGER), Burgess Whitehead, Mickey Witek, Johnnie Wittig, Babe Young

LESS THAN 10 GAMES: Jack Aragon, Rae Blaemire, Paul Dean, Hugh East, Harry Feldman, Rube Fischer, Sid Gordon, Harry Gumbert *, Bump Hadley *, Dave Koslo, Tom Sunkel

KEY SIGNATURES: Terry, Bartell, Ott, Hubbell.

VALUE: $400

1941 PHILADELPHIA (AL) - Johnny Babich, Bill Beckmann, Al Brancato, Fred Chapman, Sam Chapman, Eddie Collins, Crash Davis, Chubby Dean *, Tom Ferrick, Bump Hadley *, Lum Harris, Frankie Hayes, Bob Johnson, Jack Knott, Connie Mack (MANAGER), Phil Marchildon, Benny McCoy, Les McCrabb, Dee Miles, Wally Moses, Nels Potter *, Al Rubeling, Dick Siebert, Pete Suder, Elmer Valo, Hal Wagner

LESS THAN 10 GAMES: Herman Besse, Fred Caligiuri, Dick Fowler, Rankin Johnson, John Leovich, Felix Mackiewicz, Ray Poole, Don Richmond, Buck Ross *, Tex Shirley, Al Simmons, Eric Tipton, Pat Tobin, Porter Vaughn, Roger Wolff

KEY SIGNATURES: Mack, Siebert, Moses, Chapman, Collins, Simmons.

VALUE: $400

1941 PHILADELPHIA (NL) - Boom-Boom Beck, Stan Benjamin, Cy Blanton, Bobby Bragan, Roy Bruner, Paul Busby, Jim Carlin, Bill Crouch *, Nick Etten, Lee Grissom *, Bill Harman, Frank Hoerst, Tommy Hughes, Si Johnson, Chuck Klein, Danny Litwhiler, Mickey Livingston, Hal Marnie, Joe Marty, Pinky May, Rube Melton, Emmett Mueller, Danny Murtaugh, Bill Nagel, Ike Pearson, Johnny Podgajny, Doc Prothro (MANAGER), Johnny Rizzo, Bennie Warren

LESS THAN 10 GAMES: Dale Jones, George Jumonville, Gene Lambert, Paul Masterson, Wally Millies, Vito Tamulis *

KEY SIGNATURES: Litwhiler, Etten.

VALUE: $200

1941 PITTSBURGH - Alf Anderson, Bill Baker *, Joe Bowman, Max Butcher, Ripper Collins, Billy Cox, Spud Davis, Dutch Dietz, Vince DiMaggio, Bob Elliott, Elbie Fletcher, Frankie Frisch (MANAGER), Debs Garms, Frankie Gustine, Lee Handley, Ken Heintzelman, Bob Klinger, Johnny Lanning, Ed Leip, Al Lopez, Stu Martin, Rip Sewell, Vinnie Smith, Bud Stewart, Nick Strincevich *, Joe Sullivan *, Oad Swigert, Maurice Van Robays, Arky Vaughan, Lefty Wilkie

LESS THAN 10 GAMES: Russ Bauers, Bill Brandt, Mace Brown *, Bill Clemensen, Dick Conger, Johnny Gee, Dick Lanahan, Culley Rikard, Joe Schultz, Lloyd Waner *

KEY SIGNATURES: Frisch, Vaughan, Lopez, Waner.

VALUE: $315

1941 ST. LOUIS (AL) - Johnny Allen *, Eldon Auker, Johnny Berardino, George Caster, Harlond Clift, Roy Cullenbine, Bobby Estalella, Rick Ferrell *, Denny Galehouse, Joe Grace, Frank Grube, Fred Haney (MANAGER), Bob Harris, Don Heffner, Walt Judnich, Jack Kramer, Chet Laabs, Johnny Lucadello, George McQuinn, Bob Muncrief, Maury Newlin, Johnny Niggeling, Fritz Ostermueller, Rip Radcliff *, Luke Sewell (MANAGER), Alan Strange, Bob Swift, Bill Trotter

LESS THAN 10 GAMES: George Archie *, Emil Bildilli, Myril Hoag *, Hooks Iott, Vern Kennedy *, Archie McKain *, Glenn McQuillen, Vern Stephens, Chuck Stevens

KEY SIGNATURES: Ferrell.

VALUE: $240

1941 ST. LOUIS (NL) - Jimmy Brown, Mort Cooper, Walker Cooper, Estel Crabtree, Creepy Crespi, Bill Crouch *, Harry Gumbert *, Johnny Hopp, Ira Hutchinson, Ernie Koy *, Howie Krist, Eddie Lake, Max Lanier, Gus Mancuso, Marty Marion, Steve Mesner, Johnny Mize, Terry Moore, Stan Musial, Sam Nahem, Don Padgett, Clyde Shoun, Enos Slaughter, Billy Southworth (MANAGER), Coaker Triplett, Lon Warneke, Ernie White

LESS THAN 10 GAMES: Johnny Beazley, Erv Dusak, Hank Gornicki *, Johnny Grodszicki, Whitey Kurowski, Hersh Lyons, Charlie Marshall, Bill McGee *, Howie Pollet, Walter Sessi, Harry Walker, Pep Young *
KEY SIGNATURES: Mize, Brown, Slaughter, Hopp, Musial.

VALUE: $375

1941 WASHINGTON - Morrie Aderholt, Red Anderson, George Archie *, Jimmy Bloodworth, Cliff Bolton, Alex Carrasquel, George Case, Ben Chapman *, Ken Chase, Doc Cramer, Jake Early, Al Evans, Rick Ferrell *, Bucky Harris (MANAGER), Sid Hudson, Vern Kennedy *, Hilly Lane, Dutch Leonard, Charlie Letchas, Buddy Lewis, Walter Masterson, Buddy Myer, Roberto Ortiz, Jimmy Pofahl, Steve Sundra, Cecil Travis, Mickey Vernon, Johnny Welaj, Sammy West, Bill Zuber
LESS THAN 10 GAMES: Harry Dean, Danny MacFayden, Ronnie Miller, Dick Mulligan, Sherry Robertson, Jack Sanford, Early Wynn
KEY SIGNATURES: Harris, Vernon, Travis, Ferrell, Wynn.

VALUE: $280

1942

1942 New York Yankees

*** = player was traded**

1942 BOSTON (AL) - Mace Brown, Bill Butland, Paul Campbell, Ken Chase, Bill Conroy, Joe Cronin (MANAGER), Dom DiMaggio, Joe Dobson, Bobby Doerr, Lou Finney, Pete Fox, Jimmie Foxx *, Tex Hughson, Oscar Judd, Tony Lupien, Dick Newsome, Skeeter Newsome, Johnny Peacock, Johnny Pesky, Mike Ryba, Jim Tabor, Yank Terry, Charlie Wagner, Ted Williams

LESS THAN 10 GAMES: Tom Carey, Andy Gilbert

NOTES: Williams wins first of two career Triple Crowns; 4 HOF'ers; Cronin was a player/manager.

KEY SIGNATURES: Cronin, Doerr, Williams, Foxx.

VALUE: $475

1942 BOSTON (NL) - Johnny Cooney, Tony Cuccinello, Frank Demaree, Ducky Detweiler, Bill Donovan, Tom Earley, Dick Errickson *, Nanny Fernandez, Buddy Gremp, Tommy Holmes, Johnny Hutchings, Al Javery, Clyde Kluttz, Ernie Lombardi, Phil Masi, Eddie Miller, Skippy Roberge, Chet Ross, Johnny Sain, Manny Salvo, Sibby Sisti, Casey Stengel (MANAGER), Jim Tobin, Lou Tost, Lefty Wallace, Paul Waner, Max West, Whitey Wietelmann

LESS THAN 10 GAMES: George Diehl, Jim Hickey, Art Johnson, Frank Lamanna, Frank McElyea, Mike Sandlock, Warren Spahn

KEY SIGNATURES: Stengel, Lombardi, Sain, Spahn.

VALUE: $310

1942 BROOKLYN - Johnny Allen, Frenchy Bordagaray, Dolph Camilli, Hugh Casey, Babe Dahlgren *, Curt Davis, Leo Durocher (MANAGER), Larry French, Augie Galan, Ed Head, Billy Herman, Kirby Higbe, Alex Kampouris, Newt Kimball, Max Macon, Joe Medwick, Mickey Owen, Pee Wee Reese, Pete Reiser, Lew Riggs, Johnny Rizzo, Billy Sullivan, Arky Vaughan, Dixie Walker, Les Webber, Whit Wyatt

LESS THAN 10 GAMES: Bob Chipman, Cliff Dapper, Freddie Fitzsimmons, Chet Kehn, Bobo Newsom *, Stan Rojek, Schoolboy Rowe

NOTES: 4 HOF'ers.

KEY SIGNATURES: Durocher, Herman, Reese, Vaughan, Reiser, Medwick, Wyatt, French.

VALUE: $400

1942 CHICAGO (AL) - Luke Appling, George Dickey, Jimmy Dykes (MANAGER), Bill Dietrich, Jimmy Grant, Orval Grove, Joe Haynes, Val Heim, Myril Hoag, John Humphries, Bob Kennedy, Don Kolloway, Joe Kuhel, Thornton Lee, Dario Lodigiani, Ted Lyons, Wally Moses, Bill Mueller, Buck Ross, Bud Sketchley, Eddie Smith, Mike Tresh, Tom Turner, Jake Wade, Skeeter Webb, Leo Wells, Sammy West, Taffy Wright

LESS THAN 10 GAMES: Pete Appleton *, Jake Jones, Len Perme, Johnny Rigney, Thurman Tucker, Ed Weiland

KEY SIGNATURES: Appling, Lyons.

VALUE: $275

1942 CHICAGO (NL) - Hi Bithorn, Phil Cavarretta, Babe Dahlgren *, Dom Dallessandro, Paul Erickson, Dick Errickson *, Bill Fleming, Jimmie Foxx *, Charlie Gilbert, Stan Hack, Chico Hernandez, Bill Lee, Peanuts Lowrey, Clyde McCullough, Lennie Merullo, Jake Mooty, Bill Nicholson, Lou Novikoff, Vern Olsen, Claude Passeau, Tot Pressnell, Rip Russell, Bob Scheffing, Johnny Schmitz, Lou Stringer, Bobby Sturgeon, Lon Warneke *, Jimmie Wilson (MANAGER)

LESS THAN 10 GAMES: Joe Berry, Cy Block, Bob Bowman, Vallie Eaves, Marv Felderman, Jesse Flores, Paul Gillespie, Ed Hanyzewski, Emil Kush, Whitey Platt, Marv Rickert, Hank Wyse

KEY SIGNATURES: Cavarretta, Hack, Novikoff, Foxx.

VALUE: $280

1942 CINCINNATI - Joe Beggs, Harry Craft, Paul Derringer, Lonny Frey, Ival Goodman, Bert Haas, Rollie Hemsley *, Eddie Joost, Frankie Kelleher, Al Lakeman, Ray Lamanno, Max Marshall, Frank McCormick, Mike McCormick, Bill McKechnie (MANAGER), Damon Phillips, Elmer Riddle, Clyde Shoun *, Ray Starr, Junior Thompson, Eric Tipton, Johnny Vander Meer, Clyde Vollmer, Gee Walker, Bucky Walters, Dick West

LESS THAN 10 GAMES: Joe Abreu, Chuck Aleno, Ewell Blackwell, Jim Gleeson, Ernie Koy *, Bobby Mattick, Whitey Moore *, Hank Sauer, Frank Secory, Jim Turner *

KEY SIGNATURES: McKechnie, Vander Meer.

VALUE: $260

1942 CLEVELAND - Jim Bagby, Lou Boudreau (MANAGER), Chubby Dean, Otto Denning, Gene Desautels, Hank Edwards, Harry Eisenstat, Red Embree, Tom Ferrick, Les Fleming, Fabian Gaffke, Oscar Grimes, Steve Gromek, Mel Harder, Jeff Heath, Jim Hegan, Joe Heving, Oris Hockett, Ken Keltner, Vern Kennedy, Ray Mack, Buster Mills, Al Milnar, Rusty Peters, Al Smith, Hal Trosky, Roy Weatherly

LESS THAN 10 GAMES: Clint Brown, Paul Calvert, Pete Center, Joe Krakauskas, Bob Lemon, Ray Poat, Allie Reynolds, Eddie Robinson, Ted Sepkowski, George Susce

NOTES: Boudreau was a player/manager.

KEY SIGNATURES: Boudreau.

VALUE: $235

1942 DETROIT - Del Baker (MANAGER), Al Benton, Jimmy Bloodworth, Tommy Bridges, Doc Cramer, Murray Franklin, Charlie Gehringer, Johnny Gorsica, Ned Harris, Roy Henshaw, Pinky Higgins, Billy Hitchcock, Johnny Lipon, Hal Manders, Barney McCosky, Eric McNair *, Dutch Meyer, Hal Newhouser, Dixie Parsons, Rip Radcliff, Hank Riebe, Don Ross, Birdie Tebbetts, Dizzy Trout, Virgil Trucks, Hal White, Rudy York

LESS THAN 10 GAMES: Charley Fuchs, Bob Patrick, Schoolboy Rowe *, Al Unser, Jack Wilson *

KEY SIGNATURES: Gehringer, Trucks, Newhouser.

VALUE: $260

1942 NEW YORK (AL) - Ernie Bonham, Hank Borowy, Norm Branch, Marv Breuer, Spud Chandler, Frankie Crosetti, Roy Cullenbine *, Bill Dickey, Joe DiMaggio, Atley Donald, Lefty Gomez, Joe Gordon, Buddy Hassett, Rollie Hemsley *, Tommy Henrich, Ed Kearse, Charlie Keller, Ed Levy, Johnny Lindell, Joe McCarthy (MANAGER), Johnny Murphy, Jerry Priddy, Phil Rizzuto, Red Rolfe, Buddy Rosar, Red Ruffing, George Selkirk, Tuck Stainback

LESS THAN 10 GAMES: Mike Chartak *, Mel Queen, Marius Russo, Jim Turner *
NOTES: Gordon (MVP); 5 HOF'ers.
KEY SIGNATURES: McCarthy, Gordon, Rizzuto, DiMaggio, Dickey, Ruffing, Gomez.

VALUE: $750

1942 NEW YORK (NL) - Ace Adams, Babe Barna, Dick Bartell, Ray Berres, Bob Carpenter, Harry Danning, Harry Feldman, Carl Hubbell, Billy Jurges, Dave Koslo, Hank Leiber, Bill Lohrman *, Gus Mancuso *, Willard Marshall, Buster Maynard, Bill McGee, Cliff Melton, Johnny Mize, Mel Ott (MANAGER), Connie Ryan, Hal Schumacher, Tom Sunkel, Bill Werber, Mickey Witek, Babe Young
LESS THAN 10 GAMES: Hugh East, Charlie Fox, Sid Gordon, Hank Leiber, Howie Moss, Van Lingle Mungo, Bill Voiselle
NOTES: Ott was a player/manager.
KEY SIGNATURES: Ott, Mize, Hubbell.

VALUE: $400

1942 PHILADELPHIA (AL) - Herman Besse, Buddy Blair, Fred Caligiuri, Phil Carchildon, Jim Castiglia, Russ Christopher, Eddie Collins, Crash Davis, Larry Eschen, Dick Fowler, Lum Harris, Bob Harris *, Frankie Hayes *, Bob Johnson, Bill Knickerbocker, Jack Knott, Bruce Konopka, Mike Kreevich, Connie Mack (MANAGER), Felix Mackiewicz, Eric McNair *, Dee Miles, Ken Richardson, Tex Shirley, Dick Siebert, Pete Suder, Bob Swift *, Elmer Valo, Hal Wagner, Jack Wallaesa, Roger Wolff, George Yankowski
LESS THAN 10 GAMES: Tal Abernathy, Dick Adkins, Bill Beckmann *, Joe Coleman, Sam Lowry, Les McCrabb, Bob Savage
KEY SIGNATURES: Mack, Collins.

VALUE: $350

1942 PHILADELPHIA (NL) - Boom-Boom Beck, Stan Benjamin, Bobby Bragan, Bill Burich, Nick Etten, Ed Freed, Al Glossop, Frank Hoerst, Tommy Hughes, Si Johnson, Chuck Klein, Ernie Koy *, Danny Litwhiler, Mickey Livingston, Hans Lobert (MANAGER), Hal Marnie, Pinky May, Rube Melton, Ed Murphy, Danny Murtaugh, Sam Nahem, Earl Naylor, Ron Northey, Ike Pearson, Johnny Podgajny, Lloyd Waner, Bennie Warren
LESS THAN 10 GAMES: Cy Blanton, Benny Culp, Hilly Flitcraft, George Hennessey, Bert Hodge, Gene Lambert, Andy Lapihuska, Paul Masterson, Bill Peterman
KEY SIGNATURES: Waner.

VALUE: $240

1942 PITTSBURGH - Alf Anderson, Bill Baker, Johnny Barrett, Max Butcher, Frank Colman, Pete Coscarart, Dutch Dietz, Vince DiMaggio, Bob Elliott, Elbie Fletcher, Frankie Frisch (MANAGER), Johnny Gee, Hank Gornicki, Frankie Gustine, Luke Hamlin, Lee Handley, Ken Heintzelman, Bob Klinger, Johnny Lanning, Al Lopez, Stu Martin, Babe Phelps, Cully Rickard, Rip Sewell, Bud Stewart, Maurice Van Robeys, Jimmy Wasdell, Lefty Wilkie
LESS THAN 10 GAMES: Bill Brandt, Dick Conger, Huck Geary, Jack Hallett, Ken Jungels, Ed Leip, Jim Russell, Harry Shuman, Nick Strincevich, Johnny Wyrostek
KEY SIGNATURES: Frisch, Lopez.

VALUE: $250

1942 ST. LOUIS (AL) - Pete Appleton *, Eldon Auker, Johnny Berardino, Frank Biscan, George Caster, Mike Chartak *, Harlond Clift, Tony Criscola, Roy Cullenbine *, Stan Ferens, Rick Ferrell, Denny Galehouse, Don Gutteridge, Loy Hanning, Frankie Hayes *, Don Heffner, Al Hollingsworth, Walt Judnich, Chet Laabs, Glenn McQuillen, George McQuinn, Bob Muncrief, Johnny Niggeling, Fritz Ostermueller, Luke Sewell (MANAGER), Vern Stephens, Alan Strange, Steve Sundra *, Bob Swift *

LESS THAN 10 GAMES: Babe Dahlgren *, Bob Harris *, Ray Hayworth, Ewald Pyle, Bill Trotter *, John Whitehead

NOTES: Sewell was a player/manager.

KEY SIGNATURES: Ferrell.

VALUE: $245

1942 ST. LOUIS (NL) - Johnny Beazley, Buddy Blattner, Jimmy Brown, Mort Cooper, Walker Cooper, Estel Crabtree, Creepy Crespi, Murry Dickson, Erv Dusak, Harry Gumbert, Johnny Hopp, Howie Krist, Whitey Kurowski, Max Lanier, Marty Marion, Terry Moore, Stan Musial, Sam Narron, Ken O'Dea, Howie Pollet, Ray Sanders, Clyde Shoun *, Enos Slaughter, Billy Southworth (MANAGER), Coaker Triplett, Harry Walker, Lon Warneke *, Ernie White

LESS THAN 10 GAMES: Bill Beckmann *, Jeff Cross, Bill Lohrman *, Gus Mancuso *, Whitey Moore *

NOTES: World Champions! M. Cooper (MVP).

KEY SIGNATURES: Slaughter, Musial, W. Cooper, M. Cooper, Beazley.

VALUE: $450

MVP = MVP Award winner

1942 WASHINGTON - Bruce Campbell, Alex Carrasquel, George Case, Hardin Cathey, Mike Chartak *, Ellis Clary, Frank Croucher, Roy Cullenbine *, Jake Early, Bobby Estalella, Al Evans, Stan Galle, Chile Gomez, Bucky Harris (MANAGER), Sid Hudson, Walt Masterson, Bobo Newsom *, Roberto Ortiz, Jimmy Pofahl, Bob Repass, Ray Scarborough, Stan Spence, John Sullivan, Bill Trotter *, Mickey Vernon, Jack Wilson *, Early Wynn, Bill Zuber

LESS THAN 10 GAMES: Deway Adkins, Lou Bevil, Ray Hoffman, Bill Kennedy, Al Kvasnak, Dutch Leonard, Phil McCullough, Gene Moore, Steve Sundra *

KEY SIGNATURES: Harris, Vernon, Wynn.

VALUE: $250

1943

1943 A.L. batting champion Luke Appling

*** = player was traded**

1943 BOSTON (AL) - Babe Barna *, Mace Brown, Bill Conroy, Joe Cronin (MANAGER), Leon Culberson, Joe Dobson, Bobby Doerr, Danny Doyle, Pete Fox, Ford Garrison, Tex Hughson, Oscar Judd, Andy Karl *, Eddie Lake, Johnny Lazor, Lou Lucier, Tony Lupien, Tom McBride, Catfish Metkovich, Dee Miles, Dick Newsome, Skeeter Newsome, Emmett O'Neill, Roy Partee, Johnny Peacock, Mike Ryba, Al Simmons, Jim Tabor, Yank Terry, Pinky Woods

LESS THAN 10 GAMES: Ken Chase *

NOTES: Cronin was a player/manager.

KEY SIGNATURES: Cronin, Doerr.

VALUE: $260

1943 BOSTON (NL) - Nate Andrews, Red Barrett, Bill Brubaker, Joe Burns, Ben Cardoni, Tony Cuccinello *, Buck Etchison, Kerby Farrell, Heinie Heltzel, Tommy Holmes, Al Javery, Eddie Joost, Clyde Kluttz, Danny MacFayden, Phil Masi, Johnny McCarthy, Butch Nieman, Dave Odom, Hugh Poland *, Chet Ross, Connie Ryan, Manny Salvo *, Casey Stengel (MANAGER), Jim Tobin, Whitey Wietelmann, Chuck Workman

LESS THAN 10 GAMES: Connie Creedon, John Dagenhard, George Diehl, Bill Donovan, Sam Gentile, Ben Geraghty, George Jeffcoat, Carl Lindquist, Ray Martin, Allyn Stout, Roy Talcott, Lou Tost

KEY SIGNATURES: Stengel, McCarthy.

VALUE: $275

1943 BROOKLYN - Johnny Allen *, Pat Ankenman, Red Barkley, Frenchy Bordagaray, Bobby Bragan, Dolph Camilli, Johnny Cooney, Curt Davis, Leo Durocher (MANAGER), Augie Galan, Al Glossop, Ed Head, Billy Herman, Gene Hermanski, Kirby Higbe, Alex Kampouris *, Max Macon, Joe Medwick *, Rube Melton, Dee Moore *, Bobo Newsom *, Luis Olmo, Mickey Owen, Howie Schultz, Arky Vaughan, Dixie Walker, Paul Waner, Les Webber, Whit Wyatt

LESS THAN 10 GAMES: Rex Barney, Boyd Bartley, Al Campanis, Bob Chipman, Freddie Fitzsimmons, Carden Gillenwater, Hal Gregg, Bill Hart, Chris Haughey, Gil Hodges, Newt Kimball *, Bill Lohrman *, Joe Orengo *, Fritz Ostermueller *, Hal Peck, Bill Sayles *

NOTES: Durocher was a player/manager.

KEY SIGNATURES: Durocher, Herman, Vaughan, Bordagaray, Walker, Olmo, Waner, Hodges, Medwick, Wyatt.

VALUE: $400

1943 CHICAGO (AL) - Luke Appling, Vince Castino, Tony Cuccinello *, Dick Culler, Guy Curtright, Bill Dietrich, Jimmy Dykes (MANAGER), Jimmy Grant *, Orval Grove, Don Hanski, Joe Haynes, Ralph Hodgin, John Humphries, Don Kolloway, Joe Kuhel, Thornton Lee, Gordon Maltzberger, Wally Moses, Buck Ross, Eddie Smith, Moose Solters, Bill Swift, Mike Tresh, Thurman Tucker, Tom Turner, Jake Wade, Skeeter Webb

LESS THAN 10 GAMES: Frank Kalin, Cass Michaels, Floyd Speer

KEY SIGNATURES: Appling, Grove.

VALUE: $245

1943 CHICAGO (NL) - Dick Barrett *, Heinz Becker, Hi Bithorn, John Burrows *, Phil Cavarretta, Dom Dallessandro, Paul Derringer, Paul Erickson, Bill Fleming, Ival Goodman, Stan Hack, Ed Hanyzewski, Chico Hernandez, Don Johnson, Bill Lee *, Mickey Livingston *, Peanuts Lowrey, Stu Martin, Clyde McCullough, Lennie Merullo, Bill Nicholson, Lou Novikoff, John Ostrowski, Andy Pafko, Claude Passeau, Whitey Platt, Ray Prim, Ed Sauer, Bill Schuster, Eddie Stanky, Al Todd, Lon Warneke, Jimmie Wilson (MANAGER), Hank Wyse

LESS THAN 10 GAMES: Dale Alderson, Pete Eklo, Charlie Gilbert, Billy Holm, Mickey Kreitner, Jake Mooty, Walter Signer

KEY SIGNATURES: Cavarretta, Nicholson, Goodman.

VALUE: $245

1943 CINCINNATI - Joe Beggs, Dain Clay, Estel Crabtree, Tony DePhillips, Lonny Frey, Bert Haas, Ed Heusser, Al Lakeman, Max Marshall, Frank McCormick, Bill McKechnie (MANAGER), Steve Mesner, Eddie Miller, Ray Mueller, Elmer Riddle, Clyde Shoun, Ray Starr, Rocky Stone, Eric Tipton, Johnny Vander Meer, Gee Walker, Bucky Walters, Woody Williams

LESS THAN 10 GAMES: Chuck Aleno, Charlie Brewster *, Lonnie Goldstein, Frankie Kelleher, Bob Malloy, Mike McCormick, Jack Niemes, Dick West

KEY SIGNATURES: McKechnie, McCormick, Vander Meer.

VALUE: $260

1943 CLEVELAND - Jim Bagby, Lou Boudreau (MANAGER), Pete Center, Roy Cullenbine, Chubby Dean, Otto Denning, Gene Desautels, Hank Edwards, Jimmy Grant *, Mel Harder, Jeff Heath, Joe Heving, Oris Hockett, Ken Keltner, Vern Kennedy, Ray Mack, Al Milnar *, Mike Naymick, Rusty Peters, Ray Post, Allie Reynolds, Mickey Rocco, Buddy Rosar, Jack Salveson, Pat Serrey, Al Smith, Hal Trosky, Eddie Turchin

LESS THAN 10 GAMES: Paul Calvert, Frank Doljack, Steve Gromek, Eddie Klieman, Jim McDonnell, George Susce, Gene Woodling

NOTES: Boudreau was a player/manager.

KEY SIGNATURES: Boudreau, Smith.

VALUE: $235

1943 DETROIT - Jimmy Bloodworth, Tommy Bridges, Doc Cramer, Johnny Gorsica, Ned Harris, Roy Henshaw, Pinky Higgins, Joe Hoover, Charlie Metro, Hal Newhouser, Prince Oana, Steve O'Neill (MANAGER), Joe Orrell, Jimmy Outlaw, Stubby Overmire, Dixie Parsons, Rip Radcliff, Paul Richards, Don Ross, Dizzy Trout, Virgil Trucks, Al Unser, Dick Wakefield, Hal White, Joe Wood, Rudy York

LESS THAN 10 GAMES: Rufe Gentry, John McHale

KEY SIGNATURES: Cramer, Wakefield, Trout, Trucks.

VALUE: $245

1943 NEW YORK (AL) - Ernie Bonham, Hank Borowy, Tommy Bryne, Spud Chandler, Frankie Crosetti, Bill Dickey, Atley Donald, Nick Etten, Joe Gordon, Rollie Hemsley, Billy Johnson, Charlie Keller, Johnny Lindell, Joe McCarthy (MANAGER), Bud Metheny, Johnny Murphy, Marius Russo, Ken Sears, Tuck Stainback, Snuffy Stirnweiss, Jim Turner, Roy Weatherly, Butch Wensloff, Bill Zuber

LESS THAN 10 GAMES: Marv Breuer, Oscar Grimes, Aaron Robinson

NOTES: World Champions! Chandler (MVP).

KEY SIGNATURES: McCarthy, Dickey, Chandler.

MVP = MVP Award winner

VALUE: $475

1943 NEW YORK (NL) - Ace Adams, Johnny Allen *, Babe Barna *, Dick Bartell, Ray Berres, Ken Chase *, Hugh East, Harry Feldman, Rube Fischer, Sid Gordon, Carl Hubbell, Billy Jurges, Buddy Kerr, Bill Lohrman *, Ernie Lombardi, Gus Mancuso, Buster Maynard, Charlie Mead, Joe Medwick *, Cliff Melton, Van Lingle Mungo, Joe Orengo *, Mel Ott (MANAGER), Nap Reyes, Johnny Rucker, Bill Sayles *, Ken Trinkle, Mickey Witek, Johnnie Wittig

LESS THAN 10 GAMES: Vic Bradford, Bobby Coombs, Hugh Poland *, Frank Seward, Joe Stephenson, Tom Sunkel, Bill Voiselle

NOTES: Ott was a player/manager.

KEY SIGNATURES: Ott, Witek, Medwick, Lombardi, Adams.

VALUE: $400

1943 PHILADELPHIA (AL) - Orie Arntzen, Don Black, Bill Burgo, Russ Christopher, Lou Ciola, Bobby Estalella, Everett Fagan, Jesse Flores, Irv Hall, Lum Harris, Don Heffner *, Connie Mack (MANAGER), Eddie Mayo, Jimmy Ripple, Joe Rullo, Dick Siebert, Frank Skaff, George Staller, Pete Suder, Bob Swift, Jim Tyack, Elmer Valo, Hal Wagner, Johnny Welaj, Jo-Jo White, Roger Wolff

LESS THAN 10 GAMES: Tal Abernathy, Vern Benson, Herman Besse, Charlie Bowles, Norm Brown, Earl Brucker, John Burrows *, Ed Busch, Tom Clyde, Lew Flick, George Kell, Bruca Konopka, Bert Kucyznski, Sam Lowry, Felix Mackiewicz, Bud Mains, Tony Parisse, Carl Scheib, Woody Wheaton

KEY SIGNATURES: Mack, Kell.

VALUE: $260

1943 PHILADELPHIA (NL) - Freddie Fitzsimmons (MANAGER), Buster Adams *, Dick Barrett *, Charlie Brewster *, Paul Busby, Dick Conger, Benny Culp, Babe Dahlgren, Dutch Dietz *, Bob Finley, Charley Fuchs *, Al Gerheauser, Ray Hamrick, Bucky Harris (MANAGER), Si Johnson, Newt Kimball *, Chuck Klein, Tex Kraus, Bill ee *, Danny Litwhiler *, Mickey Livingston *, Dale Matthewson, Pinky May, Dee Moore *, Danny Murtaugh, Earl Naylor, Ron Northey, Tom Padden *, Johnny Podgajny *, Schoolboy Rowe, Andy Seminick, Glen Stewart, Coaker Triplett *, Jimmy Wasdell *

LESS THAN 10 GAMES: Boom-Boom Beck, Garton Del Savio, Deacon Donahue, George Eyrich, Andy Karl *, Andy Lapihuska, Rogers McKee, Ken Raffensberger, Manny Salvo *, Bill Webb

KEY SIGNATURES: Rowe, Barrett.

VALUE: $230

1943 PITTSBURGH - Bill Baker, Johnny Barrett, Bill Brandt, Max Butcher, Frank Colman, Pete Coscarart, Vince DiMaggio, Bob Elliott, Elbie Fletcher, Frankie Frisch (MANAGER), Huck Geary, Johnny Gee, Hank Gornicki, Frankie Gustine, Wally Hebert, Bob Klinger, Johnny Lanning, Al Lopez, Tommy O'Brien, Tony Ordenana, Johnny Podgajny *, Xavier Rescigno, Al Rubeling, Jim Russell, Rip Sewell, Harry Shuman, Maurice Van Robays, Johnny Wyrostek

LESS THAN 10 GAMES: Hank Camelli, Cookie Cuccurullo, Dutch Dietz *, Jack Hallett, Jimmy Wasdell *

KEY SIGNATURES: Frisch, Elliott, Lopez, Sewell.

VALUE: $250

1943 ST. LOUIS (AL) - Floyd Baker, Milt Byrnes, George Caster, Mike Chartak, Mark Christman, Ellis Clary *, Harlond Clift *, Tony Criscola, Rick Ferrell, Charley Fuchs *, Denny Galehouse, Don Gutteridge, Frankie Hayes, Don Heffner *, Al Hollingsworth, Mike Kreevich, Chet Laabs, Archie McKain, George McQuinn, Bob Muncrief, Bobo Newsom *, Johnny Niggeling *, Fritz Ostermueller *, Nels Potter, Joe Schultz, Luke Sewell (MANAGER), Vern Stephens, Steve Sundra, Al Zarilla

LESS THAN 10 GAMES: Paul Dean, Hal Epps, Jack Kramer, Al LaMacchia, Ox Miller *, Al Milnar *, Sid Peterson, Fred Sanford, Hank Schmulbach

KEY SIGNATURES: Ferrell, Dean.

VALUE: $245

1943 ST. LOUIS (NL) - Al Brazle, Harry Brecheen, Jimmy Brown, Mort Cooper, Walker Cooper, Frank Demaree, Murry Dickson, George Fallon, Debs Garms, Harry Gumbert, Johnny Hopp, Lou Klein, Howie Krist, Whitey Kurowski, Max Lanier, Danny Litwhiler *, Marty Marion, George Munger, Stan Musial, Sam Narron, Ken O'Dea, Howie Pollet, Ray Sanders, Billy Southworth (MANAGER), Harry Walker, Ernie White

LESS THAN 10 GAMES: Buster Adams *, Bud Byerly, Coaker Triplett *

NOTES: Musial (MVP).

KEY SIGNATURES: Musial, W. Cooper.

VALUE: $385

MVP = MVP Award winner

1943 WASHINGTON - Ossie Bluege (MANAGER), Milo Candini, Alex Carrasquel, George Case, Ellis Clary *, Jake Early, Tony Giuliani, Mickey Haefner, Bob Johnson, Alex Kampouris *, Dutch Leonard, Red Marion, Jim Mertz, Gene Moore, George Myatt, Jake Powell, Jerry Priddy, Ewald Pyle, Sherry Robertson, Ray Scarborough, Stan Spence, John Sullivan, Mickey Vernon, Early Wynn

LESS THAN 10 GAMES: Dewey Adkins, Red Barbary, Ed Butka, Len Carpenter, Harlond Clift *, Vern Curtis, Lefty Gomez, Bill LeFebvre, Ox Miller *, Bobo Newsom *, Johnny Niggeling *, Robert Ortiz, Tom Padden *, Red Roberts, Owen Scheetz

KEY SIGNATURES: Vernon, Wynn, Gomez.

VALUE: $275

1944

1944 New York Yankees

*** = player was traded**

1944 BOSTON (AL) - Frank Barrett, Joe Bowman, Jim Bucher, Rex Cecil, Bill Conroy, Joe Cronin (MANAGER), Leon Culberson, Bobby Doerr, Pete Fox, Ford Garrison *, Clem Hausmann, Tex Hughson, Bob Johnson, Eddie Lake, Johnny Lazor, Tom McBride, Catfish Metkovich, Skeeter Newsome, Emmett O'Neill, Roy Partee, Mike Ryba, Jim Tabor, Yank Terry, Hal Wagner *, Pinky Woods

LESS THAN 10 GAMES: Clem Dreisewerd, Vic Johnson, Oscar Judd, Eddie Lake, Lou Lucier, Stan Partenheimer, Johnny Peacock *, Joe Wood

NOTES: Cronin was a player/manager.

KEY SIGNATURES: Cronin, Doerr, Fox, Johnson, Hughson.

VALUE: $260

1944 BOSTON (NL) - Nate Andrews, Red Barrett, Ben Cardoni, Chet Clemens, Bob Coleman (MANAGER), Frank Drews, Buck Etchison, Ben Geraghty, Roland Gladu, Stew Hofferth, Tommy Holmes, Warren Huston, Johnny Hutchings, Ira Hutchinson, A Javery, Stan Klopp, Clyde Kluttz, Max Macon, Phil Masi, Butch Nieman, Damon Phillips, Chet Ross, Connie Ryan, Mike Sandlock, Steve Shemo, Jim Tobin, Whitey Wietelmann, Chuck Workman, Ab Wright

LESS THAN 10 GAMES: Pat Capri, Dick Culler, Jim Hickey, Carl Lindquist, Max Macon, Harry MacPherson, Gene Patton, Hugh Poland, Woody Rich, George Woodend

KEY SIGNATURES: Holmes.

VALUE: $230

1944 BROOKLYN - Morrie Aderholt, Pat Ankenman, Eddie Basinski, Jack Bolling, Frenchy Bordagaray, Bobby Bragan, Ralph Branca, Tommy Brown, Ben Chapman, Bob Chipman, Curt Davis, Leo Durocher (MANAGER), Red Durrett, Gil English, Augie Galan, Hal Gregg, Bill Hart, Art Herring, Clyde King, Barney Koch, Cal McLish, Rube Melton, Eddie Miksis, Luis Olmo, Mickey Owen, Goody Rosen, Howie Schultz, Eddie Stanky *, Tom Sunkel, Dixie Walker, Lloyd Waner *, Paul Waner *, Tommy Warren, Les Webber

LESS THAN 10 GAMES: Stan Andrews, Johnny Cooney, Claude Crocker, Fats Dantonio, Wes Flowers, Jack Franklin, Charley Fuchs, Ray Hayworth, Ed Head, Roy Jarvis, Bill Lohrman *, Gene Mauch, Charlie Osgood, Fritz Ostermueller, Lou Rochelli, Clancy Smyres, John Wells, Frank Wurm, Whit Wyatt, Chink Zachary

NOTES: Waner brothers appear on the same team for the final time.

KEY SIGNATURES: Durocher, Walker, Galan, P. Waner, L. Waner, Vaughan.

VALUE: $325

1944 CHICAGO (AL) - Eddie Carnett, Vince Castino, Grey Clarke, Tony Cuccinello, Guy Curtright, Johnny Dickshot, Bill Dietrich, Jimmy Dykes (MANAGER), Orval Grove, Joe Haynes, Myril Hoag *, Ralph Hodgin, John Humphries, Tom Jordan, Thornton Lee, Ed Lopat, Gordon Maltzberger, Cas Michaels, Wally Moses, Buck Ross, Roy Schalk, Mike Tresh, Hal Trosky, Thurman Tucker, Tom Turner *, Jake Wade, Skeeter Webb

LESS THAN 10 GAMES: Eddie Carnett, Don Hanski, Bill Metzig, Floyd Speer

KEY SIGNATURES: Schalk.

VALUE: $260

1944 CHICAGO (NL) - Dale Alderson, Phil Cavaretta, Bob Chipman, Dom Dallessandro, Paul Derringer, Roy Easterwood, Paul Erickson, Bill Fleming, Jimmie Foxx, Ival Goodman, Charlie Grimm (MANAGER), Stan Hack, Ed Hanyzewski, Billy Holm, Roy Hughes, Don Johnson, Roy Johnson (MANAGER), Mickey Krietner, Red Lynn, Lennie Mercullo, Bill Nicholson, Lou Novikoff, Andy Pafko, Claude Passeau, Ed Sauer, Bill Schuster, Frank Secory, Eddie Stanky *, Hy Vandenberg, Dewey Williams, Jimmie Wilson (MANAGER), Hank Wyse, Tony York

LESS THAN 10 GAMES: Charlie Brewster, John Burrows, Pete Elko, Charlie Gassaway, Paul Gillespie, Ben Mann, Hank Miklos, John Ostrowski, Joe Stephenson, Mack Stewart

KEY SIGNATURES: Grimm, Cavarretta, Dallessandro, Foxx.

VALUE: $260

1944 CINCINNATI - Tommy de la Cruz, Chuck Aleno, Arnold Carter, Dain Clay, Estel Crabtree, Tony Criscola, Buck Fausett, Harry Gumbert, Ed Heusser, Joe Just, Jim Konstanty, Max Marshall, Frank McCormick, Bill McKechnie (MANAGER), Steve Mesner, Eddie Miller, Ray Mueller, Clyde Shoun, Eric Tiptop, Gee Walker, Bucky Walters, Jo-Jo White *, Woody Williams

LESS THAN 10 GAMES: Jodie Beeler, Joe Beggs, Jake Eisenhardt, Bob Ferguson, Howie Fox, Bob Katz, Mike Kosman, Al Lakeman, Bill Lohrman *, Bob Malloy, Joe Nuxhall, Kent Peterson, Chucho Ramos, Lee Rice, Elmer Riddle, Johnny Riddle, Kermit Wahl

KEY SIGNATURES: McKechnie, McCormick, Tiptop, Walters.

VALUE: $260

1944 CLEVELAND - Jim Bagby, Steve Biras, Lou Boudreau (MANAGER), Paul Calvert, Roy Cullenbine, Jimmy Grant, Steve Gromek, Mel Harder, Jeff Heath, Joe Heving, Myril Hoag *, Oris Hockett, Ken Keltner, Vern Kennedy, Eddie Klieman, Hal Lein, Ray Mack, Jim McDonnell, Paul O'Dea, Rusty Peters, Ray Poat, Allie Reynolds, Mickey Rocco, Buddy Rosar, Norm Schlueter, Pat Seerey, Al Smith, George Susce

LESS THAN 10 GAMES: Bill Bonness, Jim Devlin, Red Embree, Earl Henry, Russ Lyon, Mike Naymick, Paul O'Dea, Hank Ruszkowski

NOTES: Boudreau was a player/manager.

KEY SIGNATURES: Boudreau.

VALUE: $235

1944 DETROIT - Boom-Boom Beck, Doc Cramer, Rufe Gentry, Johnny Gorsica, Pinky Higgins, Joe Hoover, Chuck Hostetler, Eddie Mayo, Charlie Metro *, Jake Mooty, Hal Newhouser, Steve O'Neill (MANAGER), Joe Orengo, Jimmy Outlaw, Stubby Overmire, Paul Richards, Don Ross, Bob Swift, Dizzy Trout, Al Unser, Dick Wakefield, Rudy York

LESS THAN 10 GAMES: Red Borom, Zeb Eaton, Bubba Floyd, Bob Gillespie, Don Heffner, Roy Henshaw, Chief Hogsett, John McHale, Hack Miller, Joe Orrell, Jack Sullivan

NOTES: Newhouser (MVP).

KEY SIGNATURES: Wakefield, Newhouser.

MVP = MVP Award winner

VALUE: $275

1944 NEW YORK (AL) - Ernie Bonham, Hank Borowy, Russ Derry, Atley Donald, Monk Dubiel, Nick Etten, Mike Garbark, Oscar Grimes, Rollie Hemsley, Johnny Johnson, Ed Levy, Johnny Lindell, Al Lyons, Hersh Martin, Joe McCarthy (MANAGER), Bud Metheny, Mike Milosevich, Joe Page, Mel Queen, Larry Rosenthal *, Steve Roser, Don Savage, Tuck Stainback, Snuffy Stirnweiss, Jim Turner, Bill Zuber

LESS THAN 10 GAMES: Bill Bevens, Spud Chandler, Bob Collins, Johnny Cooney *, Bill Drescher, Paul Waner *

NOTES: Waner's signature contributes significantly to the value, despite his limited appearances. With his signature, the ball is worth $320.

KEY SIGNATURES: McCarthy, Lindell, Martin, Waner.

VALUE: $265

1944 NEW YORK (NL) - Ace Adams, Johnny Allen, Ray Berres, Jack Brewer, Harry Feldman, Steve Filipowicz, Rube Fischer, Danny Gadella, Andy Hansen, George Hausmann, Billy Jurges, Buddy Kerr, Ernie Lombardi, Hugh Luby, Gus Mancuso, Charlie Mead, Joe Medwick, Cliff Melton, Roy Nichols, Mel Ott (MANAGER), Lou Polli, Ewald Pyle, Nap Reyes, Johnny Rucker, Frank Seward, Bruce Sloan, Red Treadway, Bill Voiselle, Phil Weintraub

LESS THAN 10 GAMES: Bob Barthelson, Ken Brondell, Johnny Gee *, Ken Miller, Walter Ockley, Frank Rosso

NOTES: Ott was a player/manager.

KEY SIGNATURES: Ott, Weintraub, Medwick, Lombardi, Voiselle.

VALUE: $400

1944 PHILADELPHIA (AL) - Joe Berry, Don Black, Bill Burgo, Joe Burns, Ed Busch, Russ Christopher, Hal Epps *, Bobby Estalella, Lew Flick, Jesse Flores, Bob Garbark, Ford Garrison *, Irv Hall, Luke Hamlin, Lum Harris, Frankie Hayes, George Kell, Connie Mack (MANAGER), Bill McGhee, Charlie Metro *, Bobo Newsom, Larry Rosenthal *, Joe Rullo, Carl Scheib, Dick Siebert, Woody Wheaton, Jo-Jo White *, Bobby Wilkins

LESS THAN 10 GAMES: Tal Abernathy, John McGillen, Bill Mills, Tony Parisse, Hal Peck, Jim Pruett, Al Simmons, Hal Wagner *

NOTES: The ball is worth $310 with Simmons' signature; $260 if it has Mack's signature.

KEY SIGNATURES: Mack, Simmons.

VALUE: $310

1944 PHILADELPHIA (NL) - Buster Adams, Dick Barrett, Ted Cieslak, Chet Covington, Bob Finley, Freddie Fitzsimmons (MANAGER), Al Gerheauser, Granny Hamner, Ray Hamrick, Heinie Heltzel, Andy Karl, Vern Kennedy *, Bill Lee, Charlie Letchas, Tony Lupien, Dale Matthewson, Moon Mullen, Barney Mussill, Ron Northey, Johnny Peacock *, Ken Raffensberger, Andy Seminick, Charley Shanz, Hary Shuman, Glen Stewart, Coaker Triplett, Jimmy Wasdell

LESS THAN 10 GAMES: Joe Antolik, Putsy Caballero, Benny Culp, Deacon Donahue, John Fick, Nick Goulish, Chuck Klein, Lou Lucier, Rogers McKee, Lee Riley, Charlie Ripple, Merv Shea, Turkey Tyson, Al Verdel

VALUE: $230

1944 PITTSBURGH - Johnny Barrett, Max Butcher, Hank Camelli, Frank Colman, Pete Coscarart, Cookie Cuccurullo, Babe Dahlgren, Spud Davis, Vince DiMaggio, Bob Elliott, Frankie Frisch (MANAGER), Frankie Gustine, Lee Handley, Al Lopez, Tommy O'Brien, Fritz Ostermueller *, Xavier Rescigno, Preacher Roe, Al Rubeling, Jim Russell, Rip Sewell, Ray Starr, Nick Strincevich, Hank Sweeney, Lloyd Waner *, Frankie Zak

LESS THAN 10 GAMES: Vic Barnhart, Johnny Gee, Len Gilmore, Al Gionfriddo, Bill Rodgers, Joe Vitelli, Roy Wise

KEY SIGNATURES: Russell, Lopez, Sewell, Frisch.

VALUE: $260

1944 ST. LOUIS (AL) - Floyd Baker, Milt Byrnes, George Caster, Mike Chartak, Mark Christman, Ellis Clary, Frank Demaree, Hal Epps *, Denny Galehouse, Don Gutteridge, Red Hayworth, Al Hollingsworth, Sig Jakucki, Jack Kramer, Mike Kreevich, Chet Laabs, Frank Mancuso, George McQuinn, Gene Moore, Bob Muncrief, Nels Potter, Luke Sewell (MANAGER), Tex Shirley, Vern Stephens, Tom Turner *, Lefty West, Al Zarilla, Sam Zoldak

LESS THAN 10 GAMES: Tom Hafey, Willis Hudlin, Babe Martin, Len Schulte, Joe Schultz, Steve Sundra

KEY SIGNATURES: Kreevich, Potter.

VALUE: $275

MVP = MVP Award winner

1944 ST. LOUIS (NL) - Augie Bergamo, Harry Brecheen, Mort Cooper, Walker Cooper, Blix Donnelly, George Fallon, Debs Garms, Johnny Hopp, Al Jurisich, Whitey Kurowski, Max Lanier, Danny Litwhiler, Marty Marion, Pepper Martin, George Munger, Stan Musial, Ken O'Dea, Ray Sanders, Freddy Schmidt, Billy Southworth (MANAGER), Emil Verban, Ted Wilks

LESS THAN 10 GAMES: John Antonelli, Bud Byerly, Harry Gumbert, Bob Keely, Mike Naymick, Bill Trotter

NOTES: World Champions! Marion (MVP).

KEY SIGNATURES: Marion, Musial, Hopp, W. Cooper, Martin, M. Cooper.

VALUE: $425

1944 WASHINGTON - Ossie Bluege (MANAGER), Ed Boland, Ed Butka, Milo Candini, Alex Carrasquel, George Case, Harlond Clift, Al Evans, Rick Ferrell, Mike Guerra, Mickey Haefner, Joe Kuhel, Hilly Layne, Dutch Leonard, Bill LeFebvre, George Myatt, Johnny Niggeling, Roberto Ortiz, Jake Powell, Stan Spence, John Sullivan, Gil Torres, Fred Vaughn, Joe Vosmik, Roger Wolff, Early Wynn

LESS THAN 10 GAMES: George Binks, Vern Curtis, Preston Gomez, Walt Holborow, Rene Monteagudo, Baby Ortiz, Luis Suarez, Jug Thesenga, Sandy Ullrich, Armando Valdes, Eddie Yost, Bill Zinser

KEY SIGNATURES: Spence, Ferrell, Wynn.

VALUE: $255

1945

Dick Fowler used this ball during his 1945 no-hitter.

*** = player was traded**

1945 BOSTON (AL) - Frank Barrett, Jim Bucher, Dolph Camilli, Otie Clark, Joe Cronin (MANAGER), Leon Culberson, Boo Ferriss, Pete Fox, Bob Garbark, Clem Hausmann, Randy Heflin, Billy Holm, Bob Johnson, Vic Johnson, Eddie Lake, Johnny Lazor, Ty LaForest, Tom McBride, Catfish Metkovich, Skeeter Newsome, Emmett O'Neill, Mike Ryba, Ben Steiner, Red Steiner *, Yank Terry, Jack Tobin, Fred Walters, Jim Wilson, Pinky Woods

LESS THAN 10 GAMES: Joe Bowman *, Rex Cecil, Lloyd Christopher *, Clem Dreisewerd, Lou Finney *, Oscar Judd *, Nick Polly, Frankie Pytlak

NOTES: Cronin was a player/manager.

KEY SIGNATURES: Cronin.

VALUE: $250

1945 BOSTON (NL) - Morrie Aderholt *, Nate Andrews, Del Bissonette (MANAGER), Bob Coleman (MANAGER), Mort Cooper *, Dick Culler, Frank Drews, Tom Earley, Carden Gillenwater, Don Hendrickson, Stew Hofferth, Tommy Holmes, Johnny Hutchings, Ira Hutchinson, Al Javery, Eddie Joost, Clyde Kluttz *, Bill Lee *, Bob Logan, Joe Mack, Phil Masi, Joe Medwick *, Tom Nelson, Butch Nieman, Bill Ramsey, Steve Shemo, Vince Shupe, Jim Tobin *, Mike Ulisney, Whitey Wietelmann, Chuck Workman, Ed Wright

LESS THAN 10 GAMES: Red Barrett *, Ben Cardoni, Charlie Cozart, Lou Fette, Joe Heving, Ewald Pyle *, Hal Schacker, Elmer Singleton, Lefty Wallace, Norm Wallen, Stan Wentzel, Bob Whitcher

KEY SIGNATURES: Holmes.

VALUE: $230

1945 BROOKLYN - Morrie Aderholt *, Stan Andrews *, Eddie Basinski, Frenchy Bordagaray, Ralph Branca, Tommy Brown, Cy Buker, Fats Dantonio, Curt Davis, Leo Durocher (MANAGER), Augie Galan, Hal Gregg, Bill Hart, Babe Herman, Art Herring, Clyde King, Vic Lombardi, Luis Olmo, Mickey Owen, Johnny Peacock *, Lee Pfund, Goody Rosen, Mike Sandlock, Howie Schultz, Tom Seats, Eddie Stanky, Ed Stevens, Clyde Sukeforth, Dixie Walker, Les Webber, Bill White

LESS THAN 10 GAMES: Ben Chapman, Claude Corbitt, Claude Crocker, John Douglas, Red Durrett, Ray Hathaway, Ray Hayworth, Don Lund, Nick Nitcholas, Erv Palica, Ernie Rudolph

NOTES: Durocher was a player/manager.

KEY SIGNATURES: Durocher, Galan, Walker, Rosen, Olmo.

VALUE: $225

1945 CHICAGO (AL) - Luke Appling, Floyd Baker, Earl Caldwell, Vince Castino, Tony Cuccinello, Guy Curtright, Johnny Dickshot, Bill Dietrich, Jimmy Dykes (MANAGER), Kerby Farrell, Orval Grove, Joe Haynes, Oris Hockett, John Humphries, Johnny Johnson, Thornton Lee, Ed Lopat, Cass Michaels, Wally Moses, Bill Mueller, Bill Nagel, Joe Orengo, Frank Papish, Danny Reynolds, Buck Russ, Roy Schalk, Mike Tresh, Hal Trosky

LESS THAN 10 GAMES: Clay Touchstone

KEY SIGNATURES: Appling.

VALUE: $240

HOF = Hall of Famer

1945 CHICAGO (NL) - Heinz Becker, Hank Borowy *, Phil Cavarretta, Bob Chipman, Paul Derringer, Paul Erickson, Paul Gillespie, Charlie Grimm (MANAGER), Stan Hack, Roy Hughes, Don Johnson, Mickey Livingston, Peanuts Lowrey, Lennie Merullo, Johhny Moore, Bill Nicholson, John Ostrowski, Reggie Otero, Andy Pafko, Claude Passeau, Ray Prim, Len Rice, Ed Sauer, Bill Schuster, Frank Secory, Mack Stewart, Hy Vandenberg, Dewey Williams, Hank Wyse

LESS THAN 10 GAMES: Cy Block, Lloyd Christopher *, Jorge Comellas, Ed Hanyzewski, George Hennessey, Walter Signer, Ray Starr *, Lon Warneke

NOTES: Cavarretta (MVP).

KEY SIGNATURES: Grimm, Cavarretta, Johnson, Hack, Wyse.

VALUE: $275

1945 CINCINNATI - Boom-Boom Beck, Joe Bowman, Arnold Carter, Dain Clay, Frank Dasso, Wally Flager *, Howie Fox, Earl Harrist, Ed Heusser, Joe Just, Vern Kennedy, Al Lakeman, Al Libke, Hod Lisenbee, Frank McCormick, Bill McKechnie (MANAGER), Steve Mesner, Eddie Miller, Mike Modak, Elmer Riddle, Johnny Riddle, Hank Sauer, Dick Sipek, Eric Tipton, Al Unser, Kermit Wahl, Gee Walker, Bucky Walters, Woody Williams

LESS THAN 10 GAMES: Mel Bosser, Guy Bush, Johnny Hetki, Al Libke, Eddie Lukon, Ray Mederios, Herm Wehmeier

KEY SIGNATURES: McKechnie.

VALUE: $260

1945 CLEVELAND - Jim Bagby, Stan Benjamin, Lou Boudreau (MANAGER), Eddie Carnett, Pete Center, Al Cihocki, Les Fleming, Steve Gromek, Mel Harder, Frankie Hayes *, Jeff Heath, Earl Henry, Myril Hoag, Eddie Klieman, Felix Mackiewicz, Jim McDonnell, Dutch Meyer, Paul O'Dea, Allie Reynolds, Mickey Rocco, Don Ross *, Hank Ruszkowski, Jack Salveson, Pat Searey, Al Smith, Red Steiner *, Elmer Weingartner, Ed Wheeler, Pop Williams

LESS THAN 10 GAMES: Paul Calvert, Eddie Carnett, Roy Cullenbine *, Gene Desautels, Red Embree, Bob Feller, Myril Hoag, Hal Klein, Paul O'Dea, Bob Rothel

NOTES: Boudreau was a player/manager.

KEY SIGNATURES: Boudreau, Feller.

VALUE: $235

1945 DETROIT (AL) - Al Benton, Red Borum, George Caster, Doc Cramer, Roy Cullenbine *, Zeb Eaton, Hank Greenberg, Joe Hoover, Chuck Hostetler, Art Houtteman, Bob Maier, Eddie Mayo, John McHale, Les Mueller, Hal Newhouser, Steve O'Neill (MANAGER), Joe Orrell, Jimmy Outlaw, Stubby Overmire, Paul Richards, Bob Swift, Jim Tobin, Dizzy Trout, Hub Walker, Skeeter Webb, Walter Wilson, Rudy York

LESS THAN 10 GAMES: Tommy Bridges, Russ Kerns, Pat McLaughlin, Carl McNabb, Ed Mierkowicz, Hack Miller, Prince Oana, Billy Pierce, Don Ross *, Virgil Trucks, Milt Welch

NOTES: World Champions! Newhouser (MVP).

KEY SIGNATURES: Greenberg, Newhouser.

VALUE: $325

1945 NEW YORK (AL) - Bill Bevens, Ernie Bonham, Hank Borowy *, Joe Buzas, Herb Crompton, Frankie Crosetti, Russ Derry, Bill Drescher, Monk Dubiel, Nick Etten, Mike Garbark, Al Gettel, Oscar Grimes, Ken Holcombe, Charlie Keller, Johnny Lindell, Hersh Martin, Joe McCarthy (MANAGER), Bud Metheny, Mike Milosevich, Joe Page, Aaron Robinson, Steve Roser, Red Ruffing, Don Savage, Tuck Stainback, Snuffy Stirnweiss, Jim Turner, Bill Zuber

LESS THAN 10 GAMES: Spud Chandler, Atley Donald, Paul Schreiber, Paul Waner

NOTES: Waner only appeared in one game.

KEY SIGNATURES: McCarthy, Waner, Ruffing.

VALUE: $265

1945 NEW YORK (NL) - Ace Adams, Ray Berres, Jack Brewer, Slim Emmerich, Harry Feldman, Steve Filipowicz, Rube Fischer, Al Gardella, Danny Gardella, Andy Hansen, Ray Harrell, George Hausmann, Johnny Hudson, Billy Jurgess, Buddy Kerr, Clyde Kluttz, Whitey Lockman, Ernie Lombardi, Sal Maglie, Jim Mallory *, Charlie Mead, Joe Medwick *, Van Lingle Mungo, Mel Ott (MANAGER), Nap Reyes, Johnny Rucker, Mike Schemer, Red Treadway, Bill Voiselle, Phil Weintraub, Adrian Zabala, Roy Zimmerman

LESS THAN 10 GAMES: Loren Bain, Bill DeKoning, Don Fisher, Johnny Gee, Roy Lee, John Phillips, Ewald Pyle *

KEY SIGNATURES: Ott, Lombardi, Mungo.

VALUE: $360

1945 PHILADELPHIA (AL) - Joe Berry, Don Black, Joe Burns, Ed Busch, Russ Christopher, Joe Cicero, Bobby Estalella, Jesse Flores, Charlie Gassaway, Greek George, Steve Gerkin, Irv Hall, Frankie Hayes *, George Kell, Ernie Kish, Lou Knerr, Connie Mack (MANAGER), Bill McGhee, Charlie Metro, Bobo Newsom, Hal Peck, Buddy Rosar, Larry Rosenthal, Dick Siebert, Mayo Smith, Bobby Wilkins

LESS THAN 10 GAMES: Joe Astroth, Charlie Bowles, Al Brancato, Sam Chapman, Bill Connelly, Woody Crowson, Larry Drake, Dick Fowler, Ford Garrison, Phil Marchildon, Jim Pruett, Carl Scheib

KEY SIGNATURES: Mack, Kell.

VALUE: $260

1945 PHILADELPHIA (NL) - Buster Adams *, Stan Andrews *, John Antonelli *, Dick Barrett, Ben Chapman * (MANAGER), Dick Coffman, Glenn Crawford *, Fred Daniels, Vance Dinges, Vince DiMaggio, Freddie Fitzsimmons (MANAGER), Wally Flager *, Jimmie Foxx, Nick Goulish, Garvin Hamner, Granny Hamner, Oscar Judd *, Andy Karl, Vern Kennedy, Tex Kraus, Bill Lee, Izzy Leon, Lou Lucier, Tony Lupien, Gus Mancuso, Dick Mauney, Rene Monteagudo, Bisty Mott, Johnny Peacock *, Nick Picciuto, Jake Powell *, Charley Schanz, Andy Seminick, Hal Spindel, Charlie Sproull, Coaker Triplett, Ed Walczak, Jimmy Wasdell, Whit Wyatt

LESS THAN 10 GAMES: Putsy Caballero, Mitch Chetkovich, Jimmie Foxx, Don Grate, Don Hasenmayer, Hugh Mulcahy, Ken Raffensberger, Charlie Ripple, Lefty Scott

KEY SIGNATURES: Wasdell, Foxx.

VALUE: $260

1945 PITTSBURGH - Vic Barnhart, Johnny Barrett, Boom-Boom Beck, Max Butcher, Frank Colman, Paet Coscarart, Cookie Cuccurullo, Babe Dahlgren, Spud Davis, Bob Elliott, Frankie Frisch (MANAGER), Ken Gables, Al Gerheauser, Al Gionfriddo, Frankie Gustine, Lee Handley, Al Lopez, Tommy O'Brien, Fritz Ostermueller, Xavier Rescigno, Preacher Roe, Jim Russell, Bill Salkeld, Jack Saltzgaver, Rip Sewell, Nick Strincevich, Lloyd Waner, Frankie Zak

LESS THAN 10 GAMES: Hank Camelli, Johnny Lanning, Bill Rodgers, Ray Starr, Joe Vitelli

KEY SIGNATURES: Frisch, Lopez, Waner.

VALUE: $285

1945 ST. LOUIS (AL) - Milt Byrnes, Mark Christman, Ellis Clary, Lou Finney *, Pete Gray, Don Gutteridge, Red Hayworth, Al Hollingsworth, Sig Jackucki, Jack Kramer, Mike Kreevich *, Chet Laabs, Frank Mancuso, Babe Martin, George McQuinn, Gene Moore, Bob Muncrief, Nels Potter, Len Schulte, Joe Schultz, Luke Sewell (MANAGER), Tex Shirley, Vern Stephens, Lefty West, Sam Zoldak

LESS THAN 10 GAMES: Pete Appleton, George Caster, Cliff Fannin, Earl Jones, Al LaMacchia, Ox Miller, Dee Sanders

KEY SIGNATURES: Muncrief.

VALUE: $235

1945 ST. LOUIS (NL) - Buster Adams *, Red Barrett, Dave Bartosch, Augie Bergamo, Harry Brecheen, Ken Burkhart, Bud Byerly, Jack Creel, George Dockins, Blix Donnelly, George Fallon, Glenn Gardner, Debs Garms, Johnny Hopp, Al Jurisich, Lou Klein, Whitey Kurowski, Jim Mallory *, Marty Marion, Ken O'Dea, Art Rebel, Del Rice, Ray Sanders, Red Schoendienst, Billy Southworth (MANAGER), Emil Verban, Ted Wilks, Pep Young

LESS THAN 10 GAMES: John Antonelli *, Mort Cooper, Walker Cooper, Glenn Crawford *, Bill Crouch, Gene Crumling, Bob Keely, Max Lanier, Art Lopatka, Stan Partenheimer

KEY SIGNATURES: Kurowski, Schoendienst, Barrett, Burkhart, Brecheen.

VALUE: $240

1945 WASHINGTON - George Binks, Ossie Bluege (MANAGER), Alex Carrasquel, George Case, Walt Chipple, Harlond Clift, Al Evans, Rick Ferrell, Mike Guerra, Mickey Haefner, Walt Holborow, Dick Kimble, Mike Kreevich *, Joe Kuhel, Hilly Layne, Dutch Leonard, Buddy Lewis, George Myatt, Johnny Niggeling, Marino Pieretti, Jake Powell *, Gil Torres, Cecil Travis, Sandy Ullrich, Fred Vaughn, Vince Ventura, Roger Wolff, Jose Zardon

LESS THAN 10 GAMES: Pete Appleton *, Joe Cleary, Walt Masterson, Howie McFarland, Armando Roche, Bert Shepard, Dick Stone

KEY SIGNATURES: Lewis, Ferrell, Wolff.

VALUE: $250

*** = player was traded**

1946

1946

1946 National League MVP Stan Musial

1946 BOSTON (AL) - Ernie Andres, Jim Bagby, Mace Brown, Paul Campbell, Joe Cronin (MANAGER), Leon Culberson, Dom DiMaggio, Joe Dobson, Bobby Doerr, Clem Dreisewerd, Boo Ferriss, Don Gutteridge, Mickey Harris, Pinky Higgins *, Tex Hughson, Earl Johnson, Bob Klinger, Johnny Lazor, Tom McBride, Ed McGah, Catfish Metkovich, Wally Moses *, Roy Partee, Eddie Pellagrini, Johnny Pesky, Rip Russell, Hal Wagner,

Ted Williams, Rudy York, Bill Zuber *

LESS THAN 10 GAMES: Bill Butland, Tom Carey, Mel Deutsch, Andy Gilbert, Randy Heflin, Frankie Pytlak, Mike Ryba, Ben Steiner, Charlie Wagner, Jim Wilson

NOTES: Williams (MVP).

KEY SIGNATURES: Cronin, Doerr, Pesky, DiMaggio, Williams, Ferriss.

VALUE: $400

1946 BOSTON (NL) - Frank Barrett, Johnny Barrett *, Mort Cooper, Dick Culler, Al Dark, Nanny Fernandez, Carden Gillenwater, Billy Herman *, Stew Hofferth, Tommy Holmes, Johnny Hopp, Si Johnson, Jim Konstanty, Bill Lee, Danny Litwhiler *, Phil Masi, Mike McCormick *, Tommy Neill, Ken O'Dea *, Don Padgett *, Bill Posedel, Skippy Roberge, Steve Roser, Bama Rowell, Connie Ryan, Johnny Sain, Ray Sanders, Elmer Singleton, Billy Southworth (MANAGER), Warren Spahn, Lefty Wallace, Ernie White, Whitey Wietelmann, Chuck Workman *, Ed Wright

LESS THAN 10 GAMES: Bob Brady, Ducky Detweiler, Dan Hendrickson, Johnny Hutchings, Al Javery, Johnny McCarthy, Dick Mulligan, Johnny Niggeling, Damon Phillips, Hugh Poland, Earl Reid, Sibby Sisti, Max West *, Ace Williams

KEY SIGNATURES: Holmes, Herman, Sain, Spahn.

VALUE: $265

1946 BROOKLYN - Ferrell Anderson, Rex Barney, Hank Behrman, Ralph Branca, Hugh Casey, Leo Durocher (MANAGER), Bruce Edwards, Carl Furillo, Augie Galan, Hal Gregg, Joe Hatten, Ed Head, Billy Herman *, Gene Hermanski, Art Herring, Kirby Higbe, Cookie Lavagetto, Vic Lombardi, Joe Medwick, Rube Melton, Eddie Miksis, Don Padgett *, Bob Ramazotti, Pee Wee Reese, Pete Reiser, Stan Rojek, Mike Sandlock, Howie Schultz, Eddie Stanky, Ed Stevens, Joe Tepsic, Dixie Walker, Les Webber, Dick Whitman

LESS THAN 10 GAMES: John Corriden, Curt Davis, Otis Davis, Jack Graham, Cal McLish, Paul Minner, Glen Moulder, Earl Naylor, Lew Riggs, Goody Rosen *, Jean Pierre Roy, Harry Taylor

KEY SIGNATURES: Durocher, Reese, Medwick, Higbe.

VALUE: $300

1946 CHICAGO (AL) - Luke Appling, Earl Caldwell, Guy Curtright, George Dickey, Bill Dietrich, Jimmy Dykes (MANAGER), Ed Fernandes, Orval Grove, Ralph Hamner, Frankie Hayes *, Joe Haynes, Ralph Hodgin, Al Hollingsworth *, Jake Jones, Tom Jordan *, Bob Kennedy, Don Kolloway, Joe Kuhel *, Dario Lodigiani, Ed Lopat, Ted Lyons (MANAGER), Gordon Maltzberger, Cass Michaels, Wally Moses *, Frank Papish, Dave Philley, Whitey Platt, Johnny Rigney, Eddie Smith, Mike Tresh, Hal Trosky, Thurman Tucker, Leo Wells, Frank Whitman, Taffy Wright

LESS THAN 10 GAMES: Floyd Baker, Thornton Lee, Emmett O'Neill *, Len Perme, Joe Smaza

KEY SIGNATURES: Lyons, Appling, Caldwell.

VALUE: $260

1946 CHICAGO (NL) - Russ Bauers, Hi Bithorn, Hank Borowy, Phil Cavarretta, Bob Chipman, Dom Dallessandro, Paul Erickson, Bill Fleming, Charlie Gilbert *, Al Glossop, Charlie Grimm (MANAGER), Stan Hack, Don Johnson, Billy Jurges, Emil Kush, Mickey Livingston, Peanuts Lowrey, Clyde McCullough, Lennie Merullo, Bill Nicholson, John Ostrowski, Andy Pafko, Claude Passeau, Ray Prim, Marv Rickert, Bob Scheffing, Johnny Schmitz, Frank Secory, Lou Stringer, Bobby Sturgeon, Eddie Waitkus, Hank Wyse

LESS THAN 10 GAMES: Red Adams, Heinz Becker *, Cy Block, Rabbit Garriott, Ed Hanyzewski, Doyle Lade, Clarence Maddern, Hal Manders, Russ Meers, Russ Meyer, Emmett O'Neill, Vern Olsen, Ted Pawelek, Hank Schenz, Dewey Williams

KEY SIGNATURES: Grimm, Waitkus.

VALUE: $225

1946 CINCINNATI - Bobby Adams, Joe Beggs, Ewell Blackwell, Dain Clay, Claude Corbitt, Lonny Frey, Harry Gumbert, Bert Haas, Grady Hatton, Johnny Hetki, Ed Heusser, Al Lakeman, Ray Lamanno, Clay Lambert, Al Libke, Eddie Lukon, Bob Malloy, Mike McCormick *, Bill McKechnie (MANAGER), Eddie Miller, Ray Mueller, Eddie Shokes, Clyde Shoun, Bob Usher, Johnny Vander Meer, Bucky Walters, Max West *, Benny Zientara

LESS THAN 10 GAMES: Nate Andrews, George Burpo, Frank Dasso, Howie Fox, Lonnie Goldstein, Garland Lawing *, Al Libke, Howie Moss *, Clyde Vollmer

KEY SIGNATURES: McKechnie, Walters.

VALUE: $260

1946 CLEVELAND - Heinz Becker *, Joe Berry *, Don Black, Lou Boudreau (MANAGER), George Case, Pete Center, Jack Conway, Hank Edwards, Red Embree, Bob Feller, Les Fleming, Charlie Gassaway, Steve Gromek, Mel Harder, Frankie Hayes *, Jim Hegan, Tom Jordan *, Ken Keltner, Joe Krakauskas, Bob Lemon, Sherm Lollar, Ray Mack, Felix Mackiewicz, Dutch Meyer, Dale Mitchell, Blas Monaco, Eddie Robinson, Mickey Rocco, Don Ross, Pat Seerey, Jimmy Wasdell *, Gene Woodling

LESS THAN 10 GAMES: Charlie Brewster, Tom Ferrick *, Ray Flanigan, Vic Johnson, Eddie Klieman, Bob Kuzava, Ralph McCabe, Buster Mills, Howie Moss *, Rusty Peters, Johnny Podgajny, Jackie Price, Allie Reynolds, Ted Sepkowski, Les Webber *, Ralph Weigel

NOTES: Boudreau was a player/manager.

KEY SIGNATURES: Boudreau, Edwards, Lemon, Feller.

VALUE: $265

1946 DETROIT - Al Benton, Jimmy Bloodworth, George Caster, Doc Cramer, Roy Cullenbine, Hoot Evers, Johnny Gorsica, Hank Greenberg, Pinky Higgins *, Fred Hutchinson, George Kell *, Eddie Lake, Johnny Lipon, Eddie Mayo, Barney McCosky *, Anse Moore, Pat Mullin, Hal Newhouser, Steve O'Neill (MANAGER), Jimmy Outlaw, Stubby Overmire, Paul Richards, Bob Swift, Birdie Tebbetts, Dizzy Trout, Virgil Trucks, Dick Wakefield, Skeeter Webb, Hal White

LESS THAN 10 GAMES: Tommy Bridges, Rufe Gentry, Ted Gray, Johnny Groth, Bob Harris, Billy Hitchcock *, Art Houtteman, Lou Kretlow, Hal Manders *

KEY SIGNATURES: Kell, Newhouser.

VALUE: $265

1946 NEW YORK (AL) - Bill Bevens, Ernie Bonham, Tommy Byrne, Spud Chandler, Frankie Crosetti, Bill Dickey (MANAGER), Joe DiMaggio, Nick Etten, Al Gettel, Joe Gordon, Oscar Grimes *, Randy Gumpert, Tommy Henrich, Billy Johnson, Charlie Keller, Johnny Lindell, Cuddles Marshall, Joe McCarthy (MANAGER), Johnny Murphy, Johnny Neun (MANAGER), Gus Niarhos, Joe Page, Mel Queen, Phil Rizzuto, Aaron Robinson, Ken Silvestri, Steve Souchock, Snuffy Stirnweiss, Jake Wade, Bill Wight

LESS THAN 10 GAMES: Yogi Berra, Eddie Bockman, Bobby Brown, Frank Colmen, Bill Drescher, Karl Drews, Frank Hiller, Herb Karpel, Al Lyons, Hank Majeski *, Bud Metheny, Vic Raschi, Steve Roser, Red Ruffing, Marius Russo, Charley Stanceau, Roy Weatherly, Bill Zuber

NOTES: $575 with Dickey and McCarthy; $500 with Neun; Dickey was a player/manager.

KEY SIGNATURES: McCarthy, Dickey, Rizzuto, DiMaggio, Dickey, Berra, Ruffing, Chandler.

VALUE: $575

1946 NEW YORK (NL) - Woody Abernathy, Buddy Blattner, Mike Budnick, Bob Carpenter, Walker Cooper, Vince DiMaggio *, Rube Fischer, Johnny Gee, Sid Gordon, Jack Graham *, Bob Joyce, Monte Kennedy, Buddy Kerr, Dave Koslo, Tex Kraus, Garland Lawing *, Ernie Lombardi, Willard Marshall, Johnny Mize, Mel Ott (MANAGER), Jess Pike, Bill Rigney, Goody Rosen *, Johnny Rucker, Hal Schumacher, Junior Thompson, Bobby Thomson, Ken Trinkle, Bill Voiselle, Bennie Warren, Mikey Witek, Babe Young

LESS THAN 10 GAMES: Ace Adams, Nate Andrews *, Morrie Arnovich, Dick Bartell, Jack Brewer, John Carden, Slim Emmerich, Harry Feldman, Jim Gladd, Mickey Grasso, Marv Grissom, Sheldon Jones, Clyde Kluttz *, Red Kress, Dick Lajeskie, Buster Maynard, Mike Schemer

NOTES: Ott was a player/manager.

KEY SIGNATURES: Ott, Mize, Lombardi.

VALUE: $425

1946 PHILADELPHIA (AL) - John Caulfield, Sam Chapman, Russ Christopher, Russ Derry, Gene Desautels, Everett Fagan, Jesse Flores, Dick Fowler, Lee Griffeth, Oscar Grimes *, Irv Hall, Gene Handley, Lum Harris, George Kell *, Lou Knerr, Bruce Konopka, Connie Mack (MANAGER), Hank Majeski *, Phil Marchildon, Barney McCosky *, George McQuinn, Bobo Newsom, Hal Peck, Don Richmond, Buddy Rosar, Bob Savage, Tuck Stainback, Pete Suder, Elmer Valo, Jack Wallaesa

LESS THAN 10 GAMES: George Armstrong, Joe Astroth, Vern Benson, Joe Berry, Herman Besse, Norm Brown, Joe Coleman, Pat Cooper, Ford Garrison, Jack Knott, Bill McCahan, Porter Vaughan

KEY SIGNATURES: Mack, Valo, McCosky, Kell.

VALUE: $265

1946 PHILADELPHIA (NL) - Ben Chapman (MANAGER), Vance Dinges, Blix Donnelly *, Del Ennis, Charlie Gilbert *, Rollie Hemsley, Frank Hoerst, Roy Hughes, Tommy Hughes, John Humphries, Oscar Judd, Al Jurisich, Andy Karl, Dick Mauney, Frank McCormick, Dee Moore, Hugh Mulcahy, Dick Mulligan *, Skeeter Newsome, Ron Northey, Lou Novikoff, John O'Neil, Ken Raffensberger, Schoolboy Rowe, Charley Schanz, Andy Seminick, Charley Stanceu *, Jim Tabor, Emil Verban *, Jimmy Wasdell *, Johnny Wyrostek

LESS THAN 10 GAMES: Bill Burich, Glenn Crawford, Vince DiMaggio, Don Grate, Granny Hamner, Ron Hasenmayer, Eli Hodkey, Si Johnson *, Dick Koecher, Charlie Letchas, Art Lopatka, Al Milnar *, Danny Murtaugh, Ike Pearson, Lou Possehl, Ken Richardson, Charlie Ripple, Hal Spindel

NOTES: Chapman played in one game.

KEY SIGNATURES: Ennis, Rowe.

VALUE: $245

1946 PITTSBURGH - Ed Albosta, Ed Bahr, Bill Baker, Johnny Barrett *, Jimmy Brown, Hank Camelli, Frank Colman *, Billy Cox, Spud Davis (MANAGER), Bob Elliott, Elbie Fletcher, Frankie Frisch (MANAGER), Ken Gables, Al Gerheauser, Al Gionfriddo, Frankie Gustine, Jack Hallett, Lee Handley, Ken Heintzelman, Ralph Kiner, Johnny Lanning, Al Lopez, Fritz Ostermueller, Preacher Roe, Jim Russell, Bill Salkeld, Rip Sewell, Nick Strincevich, Maurice Van Robays, Burgess Whitehead, Chuck Workman *, Frankie Zak

LESS THAN 10 GAMES: Alf Anderson, Vic Barnhart, Bill Clemensen, Pete Coscarat, Hank Gornicki, Ben Guintini, Jim Hopper, Lee Howard, Roy Jarvis, Vinnie Smith, Al Tate, Junior Walsh, Lefty Wilkie

KEY SIGNATURES: Frisch, Kiner, Lopez.

VALUE: $265

1946 ST. LOUIS (AL) - Johnny Berardino, Frank Biscan, Mark Christman, Babe Dahlgren, Bob Dillinger, Cliff Fannin, Stan Ferens, Tom Ferrick, Lou Finney, Denny Galehouse, Joe Grace *, Jeff Heath *, Hank Helf, Walt Judnich, Elllis Kinder, Jack Kramer, Chet Laabs, Paul Lehner, Johnny Lucadello, Frank Mancuso, Glenn McQuillen, Ox Miller, Les Moss, Bob Muncrief, Nels Potter, Joe Schultz, Luke Sewell (MANAGER), Tex Shirley, Vern Stephens, Chuck Stevens, Zack Taylor (MANAGER), Jerry Witte, Al Zarilla, Sam Zoldak

LESS THAN 10 GAMES: George Archie, George Bradley, Al Hollingsworth, Chet Johnson, Al LaMacchia, Babe Martin, Al Milnar, Fred Sanford, Len Schulte, Ken Sears, Ray Shure, Steve Sundra

KEY SIGNATURES: Stephens.

VALUE: $235

1946 ST. LOUIS (NL) - Buster Adams, Red Barrett, Johnny Beazley, Al Brazle, Harry Brecheen, Ken Burkhart, Jeff Cross, Murray Dickson, Blix Donnelly *, Erv Dusak, Eddie Dyer (MANAGER), Bill Endicott, Joe Garagiola, Nippy Jones, Lou Klein, Clyde Kluttz *, Howie Krist, Whitey Kurowski, Marty Marion, Terry Moore, George Munger, Stan Musial, Ken O'Dea *, Howie Pollet, Del Rice, Freddy Schmidt, Red Schoendienst, Walter Sessi, Dick Sisler, Enos Slaughter, Harry Walker, Ted Wilks

LESS THAN 10 GAMES: Johnny Grodzicki, Max Lanier, Danny Litwhiler *, Freddie Martin, Emil Verban *, Del Wilber

NOTES: World Champions! Musial (MVP).

KEY SIGNATURES: Musial, Schoendienst, Kurowski, Slaughter, Walker, Garagiola, Pollet.

MVP = MVP Award winner

VALUE: $475

1946 WASHINGTON - George Binks, Ossie Bluege (MANAGER), Gil Coan, Vern Curtis, Jake Early, Al Evans, Joe Grace *, Mike Guerra, Mickey Haefner, Jeff Heath *, Billy Hitchcock *, Sid Hudson, Bill Kennedy, Joe Kuhel *, Dutch Leonard, Buddy Lewis, Walt Masterson, George Myatt, Bobo Newsom *, Marino Pieretti, Jerry Priddy, Sherry Robertson, Jack Sanford, Ray Scarborough, Stan Spence, Gil Torres, Cecil Travis, Mickey Vernon, Roger Wolff, Early Wynn

LESS THAN 10 GAMES: Milo Candini, Ray Goolsby, Al LaMacchia, Johnny Niggeling, Jake Wade, Maxie Wilson, Eddie Yost

KEY SIGNATURES: Vernon, Grace, Leonard, Wynn.

VALUE: $235

1947

1947 New York Yankees

***** = **player was traded**

1947 BOSTON (AL) - Merrill Combs, Joe Cronin (MANAGER), Leon Culberson, Sam Dente, Dom DiMaggio, Joe Dobson, Bobby Doerr, Harry Dorish, Boo Ferriss, Denny Galehouse, Billy Goodman, Don Gutteridge, Mickey Harris, Tex Hughson, Earl Johnson, Jake Jones *, Bob Klinger, Sam Mele, Wally Moses, Johnny Murphy, Mel Parnell, Roy Partee, Eddie Pellegrini, Johnny Pesky, Rip Russell, Birdie Tebbetts *, Hal Wagner *, Ted Williams, Rudy York *, Bill Zuber

LESS THAN 10 GAMES: Doyle Aulds, Matt Batts, Bill Butland, Cot Deal, Tommy Fine, Frankie Hayes, Tom McBride *, Ed McGah, Strick Shofner, Eddie Smith, Chuck Stobbs, Al Widmar

NOTES: Williams won the Triple Crown.

KEY SIGNATURES: Cronin, Doerr, Pesky, Williams, Dobson.

VALUE: $275

1947 BOSTON (NL) - Red Barrett, Hank Camelli, Mort Cooper *, Dick Culler, Bob Elliott, Glenn Elliott, Nanny Fernandez, Tommy Holmes, Johnny Hopp, Si Johnson, Andy Karl, Walt Lanfranconi, Danny Litwhiler, Phil Masi, Frank McCormick *, Danny Murtaugh, Tommy Neill, Bama Rowell, Connie Ryan, Johnny Sain, Clyde Shoun *, Sibbi Sisti, Billy Southworth (MANAGER), Warren Spahn, Earl Torgeson, Bill Voiselle *, Ed Wright

LESS THAN 10 GAMES: Johnny Beazley, Bob Brady, Johnny Lanning, Max Macon, Ray Martin, Mike McCormick, Dick Mulligan, Danny Murtaugh, Ernie White

NOTES: Elliott (MVP).

KEY SIGNATURES: Elliott, Holmes, Spahn, Sain.

VALUE: $260

1947 BROOKLYN - Rex Barney, Hank Behrman *, Bobby Bragan, Ralph Branca, Tommy Brown, Hugh Casey, Ed Chandler, Bruce Edwards, Carl Furillo, Al Gionfriddo *, Hal Gregg, Joe Hatten, Gene Hermanski, Gil Hodges, Spider Jorgensen, Clyde King, Cookie Lavagetto, Vic Lombardi, Don Lund, Eddie Miksis, Marv Rackley, Pee Wee Reese, Pete Reiser, Jackie Robinson, Stan Rojek, Burt Shotton (MANAGER), Duke Snider, Eddie Stanky, Clyde Sukeforth (MANAGER), Harry Taylor, Arky Vaughan, Dixie Walker

LESS THAN 10 GAMES: Dan Bankhead, Jack Banta, George Dockins, Phil Haugstad, Kirby Higbe *, Rube Melton, Erv Palica, Willie Ramsdell, Howie Schultz *, Ed Stevens, Tommy Tatum *, Johnny Van Cuyk, Dick Whitman

NOTES: Robinson won the Rookie of the Year award.

KEY SIGNATURES: Robinson, Reese, Vaughan, Snider, Hodges, Branca, Hatten.

VALUE: $700

1947 CHICAGO (AL) - Luke Appling, Floyd Baker, Earl Caldwell, George Dickey, Pete Gebrian, Bob Gillespie, Orval Grove, Earl Harrist, Joe Haynes, Ralph Hodgin, Jake Jones *, Bob Kennedy, Don Kolloway, Thornton Lee, Ed Lopat, Ted Lyons (MANAGER), Gordon Maltzberger, Cass Michaels, Frank Papish, Dave Philley, Johnny Rigney, Eddie Smith, Joe Stephenson, Mike Tresh, Thurman Tucker, Jack Wallaesa, Taffy Wright, Rudy York *

LESS THAN 10 GAMES: Hi Bithorn, Lloyd Christopher, Joe Kuhel, Red Ruffing

KEY SIGNATURES: Lyons, Appling, Wright.

VALUE: $255

1947 CHICAGO (NL) - Cliff Aberson, Hank Borowy, Phil Cavarretta, Bob Chipman, Dom Dallessandro, Paul Erickson, Lonny Frey *, Charlie Grimm (MANAGER), Stan Hack, Don Johnson, Billy Jurges, Emil Kush, Doyle Lade, Bill Lee, Mickey Livingston *, Peanuts Lowrey, Ray Mack *, Clyde McCullough, Russ Meers, Lennie Merullo, Russ Meyer, Bill Nicholson, Andy Pafko, Claude Passeau, Marv Rickert, Bob Scheffing, Johnny Schmitz, Bobby Sturgeon, Eddie Waitkus, Hank Wyse

LESS THAN 10 GAMES: Bob Carpenter, Ralph Hamner, Sal Madrid, Ox Miller, Hank Schenz, Freddy Schmidt, Dewey Williams

KEY SIGNATURES: Grimm, Pafko, Cavarretta.

VALUE: $225

1947 CINCINNATI - Bobby Adams, Frankie Baumholtz, Joe Beggs, Ewell Blackwell, Eddie Erautt, Augie Galan, Harry Gumbert, Bert Haas, Grady Hatton, Johnny Hetki, Charlie Kress, Ray Lemanno, Bud Lively, Eddie Lukon, Eddie Miller, Ray Mueller, Johnny Neun (MANAGER), Kent Peterson, Hugh Poland *, Ken Raffensberger, Elmer Riddle, Clyde Shoun, Tommy Tatum *, Johnny Vander Meer, Clyde Vollmer, Kermit Wahl, Bucky Walters, Babe Young *, Benny Zientara

LESS THAN 10 GAMES: Ted Kluszewski, Al Lakeman *, Clay Lambert, Bob Malloy, Harry Perkowski, Ken Polivka, Mike Schultz, Virgil Stallcup, Bob Usher, Herm Wehmeier

KEY SIGNATURES: Galan, Kluszewski, Blackwell.

VALUE: $225

1947 CLEVELAND - Don Black, Eddie Bockman, Lou Boudreau (MANAGER), Jack Conway, Larry Doby, Hank Edwards, Red Embree, Bob Feller, Les Fleming, Al Gettel, Joe Gordon, Steve Gromek, Mel Harder, Jim Hegan, Ken Keltner, Eddie Klieman, Bob Lemon, Al Lopez, Catfish Metkovich, Dale Mitchell, Hal Peck, Eddie Robinson, Hank Ruszkowski, Pat Seerey, Bryan Stephens, Les Willis

LESS THAN 10 GAMES: Gene Bearden, Heinz Becker, Cal Dorsett, Joe Frazier, Ernie Groth, Bob Kuzava, Lymie Linde, Felix Mackiewicz *, Al Rosen, Ted Sepkowski *, Jimmy Wasdell, Roger Wolff

NOTES: Boudreau was a player/manager.

KEY SIGNATURES: Boudreau, Mitchell, Feller, Lemon.

VALUE: $265

1947 DETROIT - Al Benton, Doc Cramer, Roy Cullenbine, Hoot Evers, Johnny Gorsica, Art Houtteman, Fred Hutchinson, George Kell, Eddie Lake, Eddie Mayo, John McHale, Ed Mierkowicz, Pat Mullin, Hal Newhouser, Steve O'Neill (MANAGER), Jimmy Outlaw, Stubby Overmire, Bob Swift, Birdie Tebbetts *, Dizzy Trout, Virgil Trucks, Hal Wagner *, Dick Wakefield, Skeeter Webb, Vic Wertz, Hal White

LESS THAN 10 GAMES: Rufe Gentry, Johnny Groth, Hank Riebe, Ben Steiner

KEY SIGNATURES: Kell.

VALUE: $265

1947 NEW YORK (AL) - Yogi Berra, Bill Bevens, Bobby Brown, Spud Chandler, Allie Clark, Frank Colman, Joe DiMaggio, Karl Drews, Lonny Frey *, Randy Gumpert, Bucky Harris (MANAGER), Tommy Henrich, Ralph Houk, Billy Johnson, Don Johnson, Charlie Keller, Johnny Lindell, Sherm Lollar, Johnny Lucadello, George McQuinn, Bobo Newsom, Joe Page, Jack Phillips, Vic Raschi, Allie Reynolds, Phil Rizzuto, Aaron Robinson, Spec Shea, Snuffy Stirnweiss, Butch Wensloff

LESS THAN 10 GAMES: Rugger Ardizoia, Tommy Byrne, Frankie Crosetti, Al Lyons, Ray Mack, Mel Queen, Ted Sepkowski *, Ken Silvestri, Dick Starr, Bill Wight

NOTES: World Champions! DiMaggio (MVP).

KEY SIGNATURES: McQuinn, Rizzuto, DiMaggio, Berra, Reynolds, Shea.

VALUE: $750

1947 NEW YORK (NL) - Ace Adams, Bill Ayers, Joe Beggs, Buddy Blattner, Walker Cooper, Harry Feldman, Danny Gardella, Lloyd Gearhart, Sid Gordon, Andy Hansen, Clint Hartung, George Hausmann, Hooks Iott, Larry Jansen, Sheldon Jones, Monte Kennedy, Buddy Kerr, Dave Koslo, Joe Lafata, Whitey Lockman, Lucky Lohrke, Ernie Lombardi, Sal Maglie, Willard Marshall, Johnny Mize, Mel Ott (MANAGER), Nap Reyes, Bobby Rhawn, Bill Rigney, Junior Thompson, Bobby Thomson, Ken Trinkle, Bill Voiselle, Bennie Warren, Mickey Witek, Babe Young, Sal Yvers, Adrian Zabala

LESS THAN 10 GAMES: Woody Abernathy, Hub Andrews, Mike Budnick, Bob Carpenter, Mort Cooper, Mickey Livingston, Mel Ott, Mario Picone, Ray Poat, Wes Westrum, Fuzz White

KEY SIGNATURES: Ott, Mize, Cooper, Jansen.

VALUE: $400

1947 PHILADELPHIA (AL) - Dick Adams, George Binks, Sam Chapman, Russ Christopher, Joe Coleman, Pat Cooper, Bill Dietrich, Ferris Fain, Jesse Flores, Dick Fowler, Mike Guerra, Gene Handley, Eddie Joost, Austin Knickerbocker, Chet Laabs, Connie Mack (MANAGER), Hank Majeski, Phil Marchildon, Bill McCahan, Barney McCosky, Ray Poole, Don Richmond, Buddy Rosar, Mickey Rutner, Bob Savage, Carl Scheib, Pete Suder, Elmer Valo

LESS THAN 10 GAMES: Lou Brissie, Nellie Fox, Herman Franks, Tom Kirk

KEY SIGNATURES: Mack, Valo, Fox, Marchildon.

VALUE: $265

1947 PHILADELPHIA (NL) - Buster Adams, Jack Albright, Ben Chapman (MANAGER), Blix Donnelly, Del Ennis, Nick Etten, Charlie Gilbert, Lee Handley, Ken Heintzelman *, Tommy Hughes, Willie Jones, Oscar Judd, Al Jurisich, Al Lakeman *, Ralph LaPointe, Dutch Leonard, Frank McCormick *, Skeeter Newsome, Ron Northey *, Don Padgett, Ken Raffensberger *, Schoolboy Rowe, Charley Schanz, Freddy Schmidt *, Howie Schultz *, Andy Seminick, Jim Tabor, Emil Verban, Harry Walker *, Johnny Wyrostek

LESS THAN 10 GAMES: Putsy Caballero, Lou Finney, Granny Hamner, Rollie Hemsley, Frank Hoerst, Dick Koecher, Jesse Levan, Dick Mauney, Hugh Poland *, Lou Possehl, Curt Simmons, Homer Spragins

KEY SIGNATURES: Walker, Leonard, Rowe.

VALUE: $250

1947 PITTSBURGH - Jim Bagby, Ed Bahr, Eddie Basinski, Hank Behrman, Jimmy Bloodworth, Ernie Bonham, Bill Burwell (MANAGER), Pete Castiglione, Billy Cox, Elbie Fletcher, Hank Greenberg, Frankie Gustine, Billy Herman (MANAGER), Art Herring, Kirby Higbe, Dixie Howell, Roy Jarvis, Ralph Kiner, Clyde Kluttz, Al Lyons, Gene Mauch, Fritz Ostermueller, Mel Queen, Culley Rikard, Preacher Roe, Jim Russell, Bill Salkeld, Rip Sewell, Elmer Singleton, Nick Strincevich, Billy Sullivan, Wally Westlake, Whitey Wietelmann, Roger Wolff, Gene Woodling

LESS THAN 10 GAMES: Ken Gables, Al Gionfriddo *, Ken Heintzelman, Lee Howard, Cal McLish, Hugh Mulcahy, Steve Nagy, Lou Tost

NOTES: Herman was a player/manager.

KEY SIGNATURES: Herman, Greenberg, Kiner.

VALUE: $260

1947 ST. LOUIS (AL) - Johnny Berardino, Walter Brown, Willard Brown, Ray Coleman, Bob Dillinger, Jake Early, Cliff Fannin, Jeff Heath, Billy Hitchcock, Walt Judnich, Ellis Kinder, Jack Kramer, Paul Lehner, Les Moss, Glen Moulder, Bob Muncrief, Rusty Peters, Nels Potter, Muddy Ruel (MANAGER), Fred Sanford, Joe Schultz, Vern Stephens, Hank Thompson, Jerry Witte, Al Zarilla, Sam Zoldak

LESS THAN 10 GAMES: Perry Currin, Dizzy Dean, Denny Galehouse *, Hooks Iott *, Glenn McQuillen, Bud Swartz

NOTES: Dean's final year.

KEY SIGNATURES: Dean.

VALUE: $270

1947 ST. LOUIS (NL) - Al Brazle, Harry Brecheen, Ken Burkhart, Bernie Creger, Jeff Cross, Murry Dickson, Chuck Diering, Erv Dusak, Eddie Dyer (MANAGER), Joe Garagiola, Johnny Grodzicki, Jim Hearn, Nippy Jones, Whitey Kurowski, Marty Marion, Joe Medwick, Terry Moore, George Munger, Stan Musial, Ron Northey *, Howie Pollet, Del Rice, Red Schoendienst, Dick Sisler, Enos Slaughter, Gerry Staley, Harry Walker *, Del Wilber, Ted Wilks

LESS THAN 10 GAMES: Ken Johnson, Freddy Schmidt *

KEY SIGNATURES: Musial, Schoendienst, Garagiola, Medwick, Munger.

VALUE: $325

1947 WASHINGTON - Ossie Bluege (MANAGER), Milo Candini, Scott Cary, George Case, Mark Christman, Gil Coan, Al Evans, Rick Ferrell, Tom Ferrick, Joe Grace, Mickey Haefner, Sid Hudson, Buddy Lewis, Frank Mancuso, Walt Masterson, Tom McBride *, George Myatt, Bobo Newsom, Marino Pieretti, Jerry Priddy, Sherry Robertson, Ray Scarborough, Stan Spence, John Sullivan, Cecil Travis, Mickey Vernon, Early Wynn, Eddie Yost

LESS THAN 10 GAMES: Buzz Dozier, Cal Ermer, Lum Harris, Bill Kennedy, Lou Knerr, Ed Lyons, Felix Mackiewicz *, Hal Toenes, Earl Wooten

KEY SIGNATURES: Vernon, Wynn.

VALUE: $235

1948

1948 New York Yankees

*** = player was traded**

1948 BOSTON (AL) - Matt Batts, Dom DiMaggio, Joe Dobson, Bobby Doerr, Boo Ferriss, Denny Galehouse, Billy Goodman, Mickey Harris, Billy Hitchcock, Tex Hughson, Earl Johnson, Jake Jones, Ellis Kinder, Jack Kramer, Joe McCarthy (MANAGER), Sam Mele, Wally Moses, Mel Parnell, Johnny Pesky, Stan Spence, Vern Stephens, Birdie Tebbetts, Ted Williams

LESS THAN 10 GAMES: Earl Caldwell, Cot Deal, Harry Dorish, Babe Martin, Windy McCall, Mickey McDermott, John Ostrowski, Mike Palm, Neill Sheridan, Chuck Stobbs, Lou Stringer, Tom Wright

KEY SIGNATURES: McCarthy, Doerr, Pesky, Williams.

VALUE: $265

1948 BOSTON (NL) - Red Barrett, Vern Bickford, Clint Conatser, Al Dark, Bob Elliott, Jeff Heath, Bobby Hogue, Tommy Holmes, Danny Litwhiler *, Al Lyons, Phil Masi, Frank McCormick, Mike McCormick, Nels Potter *, Jim Prendergast, Jim Russell, Connie Ryan, Johnny Sain, Bill Salkeld, Ray Sanders, Clyde Shoun, Sibby Sisti, Billy Southworth (MANAGER), Warren Spahn, Eddie Stanky, Bobby Sturgeon, Earl Torgeson, Bill Voiselle, Ernie White

LESS THAN 10 GAMES: Johnny Antonelli, Johnny Beazley, Paul Burris, Glenn Elliott, Ray Martin, Marv Rickert *, Ed Wright

NOTES: Dark won the Rookie of the Year award.

KEY SIGNATURES: Dark, Sain, Spahn.

VALUE: $325

1948 BROOKLYN - Rex Barney, Hank Behrman, Ralph Branca, Tommy Brown, Roy Campanella, Hugh Casey, Billy Cox, Leo Durocher (MANAGER), Bruce Edwards, Carl Erskine, Carl Furillo, Joe Hatten, Gene Hermanski, Gil Hodges, Spider Jorgensen, Don Lund *, Gene Mauch *, Eddie Miksis, Paul Minner, Erv Palica, Marv Rackley, Willie Ramsdell, Pee Wee Reese, Pete Reiser, Jackie Robinson, Preacher Roe, Burt Shotton (MANAGER), George Shuba, Duke Snider, Harry Taylor, Arky Vaughan, Preston Ward, Dick Whitman

LESS THAN 10 GAMES: Jack Banta, Bobby Bragan, Johnny Hall, Phil Haugstad, Clyde King, Bob Ramazzotti, Elmer Sexauer, Dwain Sloat, Johnny Van Cuyk

KEY SIGNATURES: Durocher, Hodges, Robinson, Reese, Furillo, Campanella, Roe, Vaughan, Snider, Branca, Erskine.

VALUE: $700

1948 CHICAGO (AL) - Luke Appling, Floyd Baker, Earl Caldwell, Jim Delsing, Al Gettel *, Bob Gillespie, Orval Grove, Randy Gumpert *, Earl Harrist, Joe Haynes, Ralph Hodgin, Howie Judson, Bob Kennedy *, Don Kolloway, Tony Lupien, Ted Lyons (MANAGER), Cass Michaels, Glen Moulder, Frank Papish, Ike Pearson, Dave Philley, Marino Pieretti *, Aaron Robinson, Pat Seerey *, Mike Tresh, Jack Wallaesa, Ralph Weigel, Bill Wight, Taffy Wright

LESS THAN 10 GAMES: Herb Adams, Fred Bradley, Jim Goodwin, Marv Rotblatt, Jerry Scala, Frank Whitman

KEY SIGNATURES: Lyons, Appling.

VALUE: $255

1948 CHICAGO (NL) - Cliff Aberson, Hank Borowy, Phil Cavarretta, Cliff Chambers, Bob Chipman, Jeff Cross *, Dick Culler, Jess Dobernic, Charlie Grimm (MANAGER), Ralph Hamner, Hal Jeffcoat, Emil Kush, Doyle Lade, Peanuts Lowrey, Clarence Maddern, Gene Mauch *, Dutch McCall, Clyde McCullough, Russ Meyer, Bill Nicholson, Andy Pafko, Bob Rush, Bob Scheffing, Hank Schenz, Johnny Schmitz, Roy Smalley, Emil Verban *, Eddie Waitkus, Rube Walker

LESS THAN 10 GAMES: Don Carlsen, Paul Erickson *, Warren Hacker, Tony Jacobs, Don Johnson, Dummy Lynch, Carmen Mauro, Carl Sawatski, Ben Wade

KEY SIGNATURES: Grimm.

VALUE: $225

1948 CINCINNATI - Bobby Adams, Frankie Baumholtz, Jim Blackburn, Ewell Blackwell, Ken Burkhart *, Claude Corbitt, Walker Cress, Howie Fox, Augie Galan, Harry Gumbert, Grady Hatton, Tommy Hughes, Ted Kluszewski, Ray Lamanno, Danny Litwhiler *, Bud Lively, Ray Mueller, Johnny Neun (MANAGER), Kent Peterson, Ken Raffensberger, Hank Sauer, Howie Schultz *, Virgil Stallcup, Johnny Vander Meer, Bucky Walters (MANAGER), Herm Wehmeier, Dewey Williams, Johnny Wyrostek, Babe Young *, Benny Zientara

LESS THAN 10 GAMES: Eddie Erautt, Steve Filipowicz, Johnny Hetki, Ken Holcombe, Hugh Poland, Marv Rickert *, Clyde Vollmer *

NOTES: Walters was a player/manager.

KEY SIGNATURES: Kluszewski.

VALUE: $225

1948 CLEVELAND - Gene Bearden, Johnny Berardino, Don Black, Lou Boudreau (MANAGER), Russ Christopher, Allie Clark, Larry Doby, Hank Edwards, Bob Feller, Joe Gordon, Steve Gromek, Jim Hegan, Walt Judnich, Ken Keltner, Bob Kennedy *, Eddie Klieman, Bob Lemon, Dale Mitchell, Bob Muncrief, Satchel Paige, Hal Peck, Eddie Robinson, Pat Seerey *, Joe Tipton, Thurman Tucker, Sam Zoldak

LESS THAN 10 GAMES: Ray Boone, Mike Garcia, Al Gettel, Ernie Groth, Bill Kennedy, Lyman Linde, Ray Murray, Al Rosen, Les Webber, Butch Wensloff

NOTES: World Champions! Boudreau (MVP); 4 HOF'ers; Boudreau was a player/manager.

KEY SIGNATURES: Boudreau, Mitchell, Bearden, Lemon, Feller, Paige.

VALUE: $450

MVP = MVP Award winner

1948 DETROIT - Al Benton, Neil Berry, Paul Campbell, Hoot Evers, Joe Ginsberg, Ted Gray, Art Houtteman, Fred Hutchinson, George Kell, Eddie Lake, Johnny Lipon, Eddie Mayo, Pat Mullin, Hal Newhouser, Steve O'Neill (MANAGER), Jimmy Outlaw, Stubby Overmire, Billy Pierce, Hank Riebe, Bob Swift, Dizzy Trout, Virgil Trucks, George Vico, Hal Wagner *, Dick Wakefield, Vic Wertz, Hal White

LESS THAN 10 GAMES: Johnny Bero, Doc Cramer, Rufe Gentry, Johnny Groth, Lou Kretlow, John McHale, Ed Mierkowicz

KEY SIGNATURES: Kell, Cramer, Newhouser, Trucks.

VALUE: $265

1948 NEW YORK (AL) - Hank Bauer, Yogi Berra, Bobby Brown, Tommy Byrne, Frankie Crosetti, Joe DiMaggio, Karl Drews *, Red Embree, Randy Gumpert *, Bucky Harris (MANAGER), Tommy Henrich, Frank Hiller, Ralph Houk, Billy Johnson, Charlie Keller, Johnny Lindell, Sherm Lollar, Ed Lopat, Cliff Mapes, George McQuinn, Gus Niarhos, Joe Page, Bob Porterfield, Vic Raschi, Allie Reynolds, Phil Rizzuto, Spec Shea, Steve Souchock, Snuffy Stirnweiss

LESS THAN 10 GAMES: Joe Collins, Lonny Frey *, Cuddles Marshall, Jack Phillips, Charlie Silvera, Dick Starr, Bud Stewart *

KEY SIGNATURES: Rizzuto, DiMaggio, Berra, Raschi.

VALUE: $525

1948 NEW YORK (NL) - Jack Conway, Walker Cooper, Leo Durocher (MANAGER), Lonny Frey *, Sid Gordon, Andy Hansen, Clint Hartung, Larry Jansen, Sheldon Jones, Monte Kennedy, Buddy Kerr, Alex Konikowski, Dave Koslo, Les Layton, Thornton Lee,

Mickey Livingston, Whitey Lockman, Lucky Lohrke, Willard Marshall, Johnny McCarthy, Pete Milne, Johnny Mize, Don Mueller, Bobo Newsom, Mel Ott (MANAGER), Ray Poat, Bobby Rhawn, Bill Rigney, Bobby Thomson, Ken Trinkle, Wes Westrum, Sal Yvars

LESS THAN 10 GAMES: Hub Andrews, Hal Bamberger, Joe Beggs, Buddy Blattner, Clem Dreisewerd, Paul Erickson, Jack Hallett, Jack Harshman, Joe Lafata, Lou Lombardo, Mickey McGowan, Red Webb

NOTES: The ball is worth $400 if it has Ott's signature, or $375 if it has Durocher's signature.

KEY SIGNATURES: Ott, Durocher, Mize.

VALUE: $400

1948 PHILADELPHIA (AL) - George Binks *, Lou Brissie, Sam Chapman, Joe Coleman, Ray Coleman *, Billy DeMars, Ferris Fain, Dick Fowler, Herman Franks, Mike Guerra, Charlie Harris, Eddie Joost, Alex Kellner, Connie Mack (MANAGER), Hank Majeski, Phil Marchildon, Bill McCahan, Barney McCosky, Buddy Rosar, Bob Savage, Carl Scheib, Pete Suder, Elmer Valo, Skeeter Webb, Don White, Rudy York

LESS THAN 10 GAMES: Earle Brucker, Bill Dietrich, Nellie Fox, Walt Holborow, Nels Potter, Bob Wellman

KEY SIGNATURES: Mack, Fox.

VALUE: $265

1948 PHILADELPHIA (NL) - Richie Ashburn, Charlie Bicknell, Johnny Blatnik, Putsy Caballero, Ben Chapman (MANAGER), Dusty Cooke (MANAGER), Blix Donnelly, Monk Dubiel, Del Ennis, Bert Haas, Granny Hamner, Ken Heintzelman, Ed Heusser, Willie Jones, Al Lakeman, Dutch Leonard, Jackie Mayo, Eddie Miller, Sam Nahem, Don Padgett, Robin Roberts, Schoolboy Rowe, Bama Rowell, Eddie Sawyer (MANAGER), Andy Seminick, Curt Simmons, Dick Sisler, Emil Verban *, Harry Walker

LESS THAN 10 GAMES: Paul Erickson, Lou Grasmick, Oscar Judd, Dick Koecher, Jim Konstanty, Al Lakeman, Stan Lopata, Al Porto, Lou Possehl, Howie Schultz *, Nick Strincevich, Jocko Thompson, Hal Wagner *

KEY SIGNATURES: Sisler, Ashburn, Leonard, Rowe, Roberts.

VALUE: $250

1948 PITTSBURGH - Monty Basgall, Ted Beard, Eddie Bockman, Ernie Bonham, Bob Chesnes, Ed Fitz Gerald, Hal Gregg, Frankie Gustine, Kirby Higbe, Johnny Hopp, Ralph Kiner, Clyde Kluttz, Vic Lombardi, Woody Main, Billy Meyer (MANAGER), Danny Murtaugh, Fritz Ostermueller, Mel Queen, Elmer Riddle, Johnny Riddle, Stan Rojek, Rip Sewell, Elmer Singleton, Ed Stevens, Dixie Walker, Max West, Wally Westlake, Grady Wilson

LESS THAN 10 GAMES: Pete Castiglione, Don Gutteridge, Cal McLish, Nick Strincevich, Earl Turner, Junior Walsh

KEY SIGNATURES: Kiner.

VALUE: $230

1948 ST. LOUIS (AL) - Andy Anderson, Hank Arft, George Binks *, Frank Biscan, Ray Coleman *, Sam Dente, Bob Dillinger, Clem Dreisewerd, Karl Drews, Cliff Fannin, Ned Garver, Al Gerheauser, Bill Kennedy, Dick Kokos, Pete Layden, Paul Lehner, Don Lund *, Les Moss, Joe Ostrowski, Roy Partee, Eddie Pellagrini, Whitey Platt, Jerry Priddy, Fred Sanford, Joe Schultz, Blackie Schwamb, Ray Shore, Bryan Stephens, Chuck Stevens, Zack Taylor (MANAGER), Al Widmar, Ken Wood, Al Zarilla, Sam Zoldak

LESS THAN 10 GAMES: Tom Jordan, Jerry McCarthy, Nels Potter, Jim Wilson

VALUE: $235

1948 ST. LOUIS (NL) - Bill Baker, Al Brazle, Harry Brecheen, Ken Burkhart, Murry Dickson, Erv Dusak, Eddie Dyer (MANAGER), Joe Garagiola, Jim Hearn, Ken Johnson, Nippy Jones, Whitey Kurowski, Don Lang, Ralph LaPointe, Marty Marion, Joe Medwick, Larry Miggins, Terry Moore, George Munger, Stan Musial, Ron Northey, Al Papai, Howie Pollet, Del Rice, Red Schoendienst, Enos Slaughter, Gerry Staley, Del Wilber, Ted Wilks, Babe Young *

LESS THAN 10 GAMES: Clarence Beers, Johnny Bucha, Jeff Cross, Chuck Diering, Erv Dusak, Eddie Kazak, Hal Rice, Ray Yochim, Bobby Young

NOTES: Medwick's final year; 4 HOF'ers; Musial (MVP).

KEY SIGNATURES: Schoendienst, Slaughter, Musial, Garagiola, Medwick.

VALUE: $325

1948 WASHINGTON - Milo Candini, Mark Christman, Gil Coan, Leon Culberson, Jake Early, Al Evans, Tom Ferrick, Angel Fleitas, Carden Gillenwater, Mickey Haefner, Earl Harrist *, Sid Hudson, Al Kozar, Joe Kuhel (MANAGER), Walt Masterson, Tom McBride, Sammy Meeks, Len Okrie, Sherry Robertson, Ray Scarborough, Bud Stewart *, John Sullivan, Forrest Thompson, Mickey Vernon, Dick Welteroth, Earl Wooten, Early Wynn, Eddie Yost

LESS THAN 10 GAMES: Jim Clark, Cal Cooper, Jay Difani, Larry Drake, Ramon Garcia, Marino Pieretti *, Clyde Vollmer *, Dick Weik, Earl Wooten

KEY SIGNATURES: Vernon, Wynn.

*** = player was traded**

VALUE: $235

1949

1949 National League MVP Jackie Robinson

1949 BOSTON (AL) - Matt Batts, Merrill Combs, Dom DiMaggio, Joe Dobson, Bobby Doerr, Walt Dropo, Billy Goodman, Billy Hitchcock, Tex Hughson, Earl Johnson, Ellis Kinder, Jack Kramer, Walt Masterson *, Joe McCarthy (MANAGER), Mickey McDermott, Sam Mele *, Tommy O'Brien, Mel Parnell, Johnny Pesky, Vern Stephens, Chuck Stobbs, Lou Stringer, Birdie Tebbetts, Ted Williams, Al Zarilla *

LESS THAN 10 GAMES: Harry Dorish, Boo Ferriss, Denny Galehouse, Mickey Harris, Babe Martin, Windy McCall, Frank Quinn, Jack Robinson, Stan Spence *, Johnnie Wittig, Tom Wright

NOTES: Williams (MVP); 3 HOF'ers.

KEY SIGNATURES: McCarthy, Doerr, Williams, Parnell.

VALUE: $265

1949 BOSTON (NL) - Johny Antonelli, Red Barrett, Vern Bickford, Clint Conatser, Del Crandall, Al Dark, Bob Elliott, Glenn Elliott, Elbie Fletcher, Bob Hall, Jeff Heath, Bobby Hogue, Tommy Holmes, Mickey Livingston *, Phil Masi *, Nels Potter, Pete Reiser, Marv Rickert, Jim Russell, Connie Ryan, Johnny Sain, Bill Salkeld, Ed Sauer *, Sibby Sisti, Billy Southworth (MANAGER), Warren Spahn, Eddie Stanky, Earl Torgeson, Bill Voiselle

LESS THAN 10 GAMES: Johnny Beazley, Steve Kuczek, Al Lakeman, Ray Sanders, Clyde Shoun, Don Thompson

KEY SIGNATURES: Spahn, Sain.

VALUE: $250

1949 BROOKLYN - Jack Banta, Rex Barney, Ralph Branca, Tommy Brown, Roy Campanella, Billy Cox, Bruce Edwards, Carl Erskine, Carl Furillo, Joe Hatten, Gene Hermanski, Gil Hodges, Spider Jorgensen, Mike McCormick, Eddie Miksis, Paul Minner, Don Newcombe, Luis Olmo, Erv Palica, Marv Rackley *, Pee Wee Reese, Jackie Robinson, Preacher Roe, Burt Shotton (MANAGER), Duke Snider, Dick Whitman

LESS THAN 10 GAMES: Cal Abrams, Chuck Connors, Johnny Hopp *, Morrie Martin, Pat McGlothin, Bud Podbielan, Bob Ramazzoti *, George Shuba, Johnny Van Cuyk

NOTES: Newcombe (ROY); Robinson (MVP); 4 HOF'ers.

KEY SIGNATURES: Hodges, Robinson, Reese, Furillo, Roe, Newcombe, Campanella,Snider, Connors.

VALUE: $750

ROY = Rookie of the Year

1949 CHICAGO (AL) - Herb Adams, Luke Appling, Floyd Baker, Billy Bowers, Al Gettel, Gordon Goldsberry, Randy Gumpert, Mickey Haefner, Fred Hancock, Bill Higdon, Howie Judson, Eddie Klieman, Charlie Kress *, Rocky Krsnich, Bob Kuzava, Dick Lane, Eddie Malone, Catfish Metkovich, Cass Michaels, Jack Onslow (MANAGER), John Ostrowski, Dave Philley, Billy Pierce, Marino Pieretti, Earl Rapp *, Bobby Rhawn *, Jerry Scala, Clyde Shoun *, Steve Souchock, Max Surkont, Joe Tipton, Don Wheeler, Bill Wight, George Yankowski, Gus Zernial

LESS THAN 10 GAMES: Jim Baumer, Fred Bradley, Jack Bruner, Bob Cain, Alex Carrasquel, Bill Evans, Ernie Groth, Orval Grove, Don Kolloway *, Pat Seerey

KEY SIGNATURES: Appling.

VALUE: $250

1949 CHICAGO (NL) - Dewey Adkins, Frankie Baumholtz *, Smoky Burgess, Phil Cavarretta, Bob Chipman, Monk Dubiel, Hank Edwards *, Frankie Frisch (MANAGER), Charlie Grimm (MANAGER), Frankie Gustine, Warren Hacker, Hal Jeffcoat, Emil Kush, Doyle Lade, Dutch Leonard, Peanuts Lowrey *, Clarence Maddern, Gene Mauch, Bob Muncrief *, Rube Novotney, Mickey Owen, Andy Pafko, Bob Ramazzotti *, Herm Reich *, Bob Rush, Hank Sauer *, Bob Scheffing, Johnny Schmitz, Bill Serena, Roy Smalley, Wayne Terwilliger, Emil Verban, Rube Walker, Harry Walker *

LESS THAN 10 GAMES: Cliff Aberson, Mort Cooper, Jess Dobernic *, Ralph Hamner, Jim Kirby, Cal McLish, Hank Schenz, Dwain Sloat

KEY SIGNATURES: Grimm, Frisch, Burgess.

VALUE: $250

1949 CINCINNATI - Bobby Adams, Frankie Baumholtz *, Ewell Blackwell, Jimmy Bloodworth, Ken Burkhart, Walker Cooper *, Claude Corbitt, Jess Dobernic, Eddie Erautt, Frank Fanovich, Howie Fox, Harry Gumbert, Grady Hatton, Dixie Howell, Ted Kluszewski, Charlie Kress *, Danny Litwhiler, Bud Lively, Peanuts Lowrey *, Sammy Meeks, Lloyd Merriman, Ray Mueller *, Kent Peterson, Johnny Pramesa, Ken Raffensberger, Hank Sauer *, Luke Sewell (MANAGER), Virgil Stallcup, Johnny Vander Meer, Harry Walker *, Bucky Walters (MANAGERS), Herm Wehmeier, Johnny Wyrostek

LESS THAN 10 GAMES: Walker Cress, Harry Perkowski, Wally Post

KEY SIGNATURES: Kluszewski.

VALUE: $225

1949 CLEVELAND - Bobby Avila, Gene Bearden, Al Benton, Johnny Berardino, Ray Boone, Lou Boudreau (MANAGER), Russ Christopher, Allie Clark, Larry Doby, Luke Easter, Bob Feller, Mike Garcia, Joe Gordon, Steve Gromek, Jim Hegan, Ken Keltner, Bob Kennedy, Bob Lemon, Dale Mitchell, Stachel Paige, Frank Papish, Hal Peck, Al Rosen, Mike Tresh, Thurman Tucker, Mickey Vernon, Early Wynn, Sam Zoldak

LESS THAN 10 GAMES: Hank Edwards, Freddie Marsh, Minnie Minoso, Milt Nielsen, Herm Reich

NOTES: 4 HOF'ers.

KEY SIGNATURES: Boudreau, Vernon, Mitchell, Lemon, Feller, Wynn.

VALUE: $250

1949 DETROIT - Neil Berry, Paul Campbell, Hoot Evers, Ted Gray, Marv Grissom, Johnny Groth, Art Houtteman, Fred Hutchinson, George Kell, Don Kolloway *, Lou Kretlow, Eddie Lake, Johnny Lipon, Pat Mullin, Hal Newhouser, Stubby Overmire, Hank Riebe, Aaron Robinson, Red Rolfe (MANAGER), Marlin Stuart, Bob Swift, Dizzy Trout, Virgil Trucks, George Vico, Dick Wakefield, Vic Wertz

LESS THAN 10 GAMES: Don Lund, Bob Mavis, Jimmy Outlaw, Earl Rapp *, Saul Rogovin, Hal White

KEY SIGNATURES: Kell, Wertz, Evers, Trucks.

VALUE: $265

1949 NEW YORK (AL) - Hank Bauer, Yogi Berra, Bobby Brown, Ralph Buxton, Tommy Byrne, Jerry Coleman, Joe DiMaggio, Tommy Henrich, Billy Johnson, Charlie Keller, Dick Kryhoski, Johnny Lindell, Ed Lopat, Cliff Mapes, Cuddles Marshall, Johnny Mize *, Gus Niarhos, Joe Page, Jack Phillips *, Duane Pillette, Bob Porterfield, Vic Raschi, Allie Reynolds, Phil Rizzuto, Fred Sanford, Spec Shea, Charlie Silvera, Casey Stengel (MANAGER), Snuffy Stirnweiss, Gene Woodling

LESS THAN 10 GAMES: Hugh Casey, Joe Collins, Jim Delsing, Frank Hiller, Wally Hood, Ralph Houk, Fenton Mole, Mickey Whitek

NOTES: The beginning of Stengel's Yankee dynasty, when he won fivestraight World Championships; 4 HOF'ers.

KEY SIGNATURES: Stengel, Rizzuto, Berra, DiMaggio, Mize, Raschi, Reynolds.

VALUE: $800

1949 NEW YORK (NL) - Hank Behrman, Walker Cooper *, Leo Durocher (MANAGER), Augie Galan *, Sid Gordon, Bert Haas *, Andy Hansen, Clint Hartung, George Hausmann, Kirby Higbe, Bobby Hofman, Monte Irvin, Larry Jansen, Sheldon Jones, Monte Kennedy, Buddy Kerr, Dave Koslo, Joe Lafata, Mickey Livingston *, Whitey Lockman, Lucky Lohrke, Willard Marshall, Pete Milne, Johnny Mize *, Don Mueller, Ray Mueller *, Bobby Rhawn *, Bill Rigney, Hank Thompson, Bobby Thomson, Red Webb, Wes Westrum, Davey Williams, Adrian Zabala

LESS THAN 10 GAMES: Roger Bowman, Dick Culler, Herman Franks, Ray Post, Rudy Rufer, Andy Tomasic, Sal Yvars

KEY SIGNATURES: Durocher, Mize, Marshall, Thomson, Irvin.

VALUE: $325

1949 PHILADELPHIA (AL) - Joe Astroth, Hank Biasetti, Lou Brissie, Sam Chapman, Joe Coleman, Tod Davis, Ferris Fain, Dick Fowler, Nellie Fox, Augie Galan *, Mike Guerra, Charlie Harris, Eddie Joost, Alex Kellner, Connie Mack (MANAGER), Hank Majeski, Wally Moses, Buddy Rosar, Carl Scheib, Bobby Shantz, Pete Suder, Elmer Valo, Don White, Taffy Wright

LESS THAN 10 GAMES: Bobby Estalella, Clem Housmann, Phil Marchildon, Bill McCahan, Jim Wilson

KEY SIGNATURES: Mack, Fox.

VALUE: $265

1949 PHILADELPHIA (NL) - Richie Ashburn, Charlie Bicknell, Buddy Blattner, Hank Borowy, Putsy Cabellero, Blix Donnelly, Del Ennis, Mike Goliat, Granny Hamner, Ken Heintzelman, Stan Hollmig, Willie Jones, Jim Konstanty, Stan Lopata, Jackie Mayo, Russ Meyer, Eddie Miller, Bill Nicholson, Robin Roberts, Schoolboy Rowe, Eddie Sawyer (MANAGER), Andy Seminick, Curt Simmons, Dick Sisler, Ken Trinkle, Eddie Waitkus

LESS THAN 10 GAMES: Johnny Blatnik, Bill Glynn, Bert Haas *, Bob Miller, Ed Sanicki, Ken Silvestri, Jocko Thompson, Hal Wagner

KEY SIGNATURES: Sisler, Meyer, Roberts.

VALUE: $260

1949 PITTSBURGH - Monty Basgall, Ted Beard, Eddie Bockman, Ernie Bonham, Hugh Casey *, Pete Castiglione, Cliff Chambers, Bob Chesnes, Murry Dickson, Ed Fitz Gerald, Les Fleming, Harry Gumbert *, Johnny Hopp *, Walt Judnich, Ralph Kiner, Vic Lombardi, Phil Masi *, Clyde McCullough, Billy Meyer (MANAGER), Bob Muncrief *, Danny Murtaugh, Jack Phillips *, Ray Poat *, Marv Rackley *, Dino Restelli, Elmer Riddle, Stan Rojek, Tom Saffell, Rip Sewell, Ed Stevens, Dixie Walker, Bill Werle, Wally Westlake

LESS THAN 10 GAMES: Jack Cassini, Hal Gregg, Kirby Higbe, Bobby Rhawn, Junior Walsh

NOTES: Bonham died Sept. 15, 1949.

KEY SIGNATURES: Hopp, Kiner.

VALUE: $240

1949 ST. LOUIS (AL) - Andy Anderson, Bob Dillinger, Karl Drews, George Elder, Red Embree, Cliff Fannin, Tom Ferrick, Ned Garver, Jack Graham, Bill Kennedy, Dick Kokos, Paul Lehner, Sherm Lollar, Les Moss, Joe Ostrowski, Al Papai, Eddie Pellagrini,

Whitey Plattt, Jerry Priddy, Ray Shore, Roy Sievers, Stan Spence *, Dick Starr, John Sullivan, Zack Taylor (MANAGER), Al Zarilla *

LESS THAN 10 GAMES: Ed Albrecht, Hank Arft, Jim Bilbrey, Owen Friend, Bob Malloy, Irv Medlinger, Al Naples, Frankie Pack, Ribs Raney, Bob Savage, Ralph Winegarner, Ken Wood

NOTES: Sievers (ROY).

KEY SIGNATURES: Dillinger, Sievers.

VALUE: $235

ROY = Rookie of the Year

1949 ST. LOUIS (NL) - Bill Baker, Al Brazle, Harry Brecheen, Chuck Diering, Eddie Dyer (MANAGER), Joe Garagiola, Tommy Glaviano, Jim Hearn, Solly Hemus, Ken Johnson, Nippy Jones, Eddie Kazak, Lou Klein, Whitey Kurowski, Max Lanier, Marty Marion, Freddie Martin, George Munger, Stan Musial, Rocky Nelson, Ron Northey, Howie Pollet, Bill Reeder, Del Rice, Hal Rice, Ed Sauer *, Red Schoendienst, Enos Slaughter, Gerry Staley, Ted Wilks

LESS THAN 10 GAMES: Steve Bilko, Cloyd Boyer, Russ Derry, Erv Dusak, Bill Howerton, Kurt Krieger, Del Wilber, Ray Yochim

KEY SIGNATURES: Schoendienst, Musial, Slaughter, Garagiola, Pollet.

VALUE: $275

1949 WASHINGTON - Paul Calvert, Mark Christman, Gil Coan, Sam Dente, Jake Early, Al Evans, Al Gettel *, Julio Gonzales, Mickey Haefner, Mickey Harris, Joe Haynes, Lloyd Hittle, Sid Hudson, Al Kozar, Joe Kuhel (MANAGER), Buddy Lewis, Sam Mele *, Roberto Oritz, Sherry Roberston, Eddie Robinson, Ray Scarborough, John Simmons, Bud Stewart, Clyde Vollmer, Ralph Weigel, Dick Weik, Dick Welteroth, Eddie Yost

LESS THAN 10 GAMES: Milo Candini, Jay Difani, Buzz Dozier, Hal Keller, Eddie Klieman, Walt Masterson, Jim Pearce, Herm Reich *, Dizzy Sutherland, Forrest Thompson

VALUE: $225

1950

1950 Philadelphia Phillies

* = player was traded

1950 BOSTON (AL) - Matt Batts, Merrill Combs *, Dom DiMaggio, Joe Dobson, Bobby Doerr, Walt Dropo, Billy Goodman, Earl Johnson, Ken Keltner, Ellis Kinder, Dick Littlefield, Walt Masterson, Joe McCarthy (MANAGER), Mickey McDermott, Willard Nixon, Steve O'Neill (MANAGER), Al Papai *, Mel Parnell, Johnny Pesky, Buddy Rosar, Charley Schanz, Vern Stephens, Chuck Stobbs, Lou Stringer, Birdie Tebbetts, Clyde Vollmer *, Ted Williams, Tom Wright, Al Zarilla

LESS THAN 10 GAMES: Jim Atkins, Boo Ferriss, Bob Gillespie, Fred Hatfield, Phil Marchildon, Charlie Maxwell, Jim McDonald, Gordy Mueller, Tommy O'Brien *, Jimmy Piersall, Frank Quinn, Bob Scherbarth, Jim Suchecki, Harry Taylor

NOTES: Dropo (ROY).

KEY SIGNATURES: McCarthy, Dropo, Doerr, Pesky, Williams.

VALUE: $265

1950 BOSTON (NL) - Bob Addis, Johnny Antonelli, Vern Bickford, Paul Burris, Bob Chipman, Walker Cooper *, Del Crandall, Dick Donovan, Bob Elliott, Sid Gordon, Bob Hall, Roy Hartsfield, Bobby Hogue, Tommy Holmes, Sam Jethroe, Ernie Johnson, Buddy Kerr, Willard Marshall, Gene Mauch, Luis Olmo, Pete Reiser, Norm Roy, Connie Ryan *, Johnny Sain, Sibby Sisti, Billy Southworth (MANAGER), Warren Spahn, Earl Torgeson

LESS THAN 10 GAMES: Dave Cole, Mickey Haefner, Walt Linden, Dick Manville, Max Surkont, Emil Verban *, Murray Wall, Bucky Walters

NOTES: Jethroe (ROY).

KEY SIGNATURES: Jethroe, Spahn, Sain.

VALUE: $225

1950 BROOKLYN - Cal Abrams, Dan Bankhead, Jack Banta, Rex Barney, Ralph Branca, Tommy Brown, Roy Campanella, Billy Cox, Bruce Edwards, Carl Erskine, Carl Furillo, Joe Hatten, Gene Hermanski, Gil Hodges, Billy Loes, Eddie Miksis, Bobby Morgan, Don Newcombe, Erv Palica, Bud Podbielan, Pee Wee Reese, Jackie Robinson, Preacher Roe, Jim Russell, Burt Shotton (MANAGER), George Shuba, Duke Snider, Chris Van Cuyk

LESS THAN 10 GAMES: Wayne Belardi, Al Epperly, Spider Jorgensen *, Clem Labine, Joe Landrum, Steve Lembo, Mal Mallette, Pat McGlothin, Willie Ramsdell *, Jim Romano

KEY SIGNATURES: Hodges, Robinson, Reese, Furillo, Roe, Campanella, Newcombe, Snider.

VALUE: $700

1950 CHICAGO (AL) - Herb Adams, Luis Aloma, Luke Appling, Floyd Baker, Jim Busby, Bob Cain, Chico Carrasquel, Red Corriden (MANAGER), Joe Erautt, Nellie Fox, Gordon Goldsberry, Randy Gumpert, Mickey Haefner *, Ken Holcombe, Howie Judson, Lou Kretlow *, Hank Majeski, Eddie Malone, Phil Masi, Mike McCormick *, Cass Michaels *, Gus Niarhos *, Jack Onslow (MANAGER), John Ostrowski *, Dave Philley, Billy Pierce, Marv Rickert *, Eddie Robinson *, Jerry Scala, Ray Scarborough *, Bill Wight, Gus Zernial

LESS THAN 10 GAMES: Jack Bruner *, Bill Connelly *, Charlie Cuellar, Gus Keriazakos, Joe Kirrene, Al Kozar *, Charlie Kress, Bob Kuzava *, Ed McGhee, John Perkovich, Marv Rotblatt, Bill Salkeld, Dick Wakefield *, Bill Wilson

NOTES: Appling's final year.

KEY SIGNATURES: Fox, Appling.

VALUE: $250

1950 CHICAGO (NL) - Bob Borkowski, Phil Cavarretta, Monk Dubiel, Hank Edwards, Frankie Frisch (MANAGER), Frank Hiller, Randy Jackson, Hal Jeffcoat, Johnny Klippstein, Doyle Lade, Dutch Leonard, Carmen Mauro, Paul Minner, Ron Northey *, Mickey Owen, Andy Pafko, Bob Ramazzotti, Bob Rush, Hank Sauer, Carl Sawatski, Bob Scheffing *, Johnny Schmitz, Bill Serena, Roy Smalley, Wayne Terwilliger, Johnny Vander Meer, Emil Verban *, Bill Voiselle, Rube Walker, Preston Ward

LESS THAN 10 GAMES: Harry Chiti, Warren Hacker, Andy Varga

KEY SIGNATURES: Frisch, Pafko.

VALUE: $250

1950 CINCINNATI - Bobby Adams, Joe Adcock, Ewell Blackwell, Walker Cooper *, Eddie Erautt, Howie Fox, Grady Hatton, Johnny Hetki, Dixie Howell, Ted Kluszewski, Danny Litwhiler, Peanuts Lowery *, Sammy Meeks, Lloyd Merriman, Ron Northey *, Harry Perkowski, Johnny Pramesa, Ken Raffensberger, Willie Ramsdell *, Connie Ryan *, Bob Scheffing *, Luke Sewell (MANAGER), Frank Smith, Virgil Stallcup, Bob Usher, Herm Wehmeier, Johnny Wyrostek

LESS THAN 10 GAMES: Jim Avrea, Jimmy Bloodworth *, Jim Bolger, Bud Byerly, Hobie Landrith, Kent Peterson, Marv Rackley, Ted Tappe

KEY SIGNATURES: Kluszewski, Adcock.

VALUE: $225

1950 CLEVELAND - Bobby Avila, Gene Bearden *, Al Benton, Ray Boone, Lou Boudreau (MANAGER), Allie Clark, Larry Doby, Luke Easter, Bob Feller, Jesse Flores, Mike Garcia, Joe Gordon, Steve Gromek, Jim Hegan, Bob Kennedy, Bob Lemon, Jim Lemon, Dale Mitchell, Ray Murray, Marino Pieretti, Al Rosen, Dick Rozek, Thurman Tucker, Mickey Vernon *, Dick Weik *, Early Wynn, Sam Zoldak

LESS THAN 10 GAMES: Al Aber, Johnny Berardino *, Herb Conyers

NOTES: Boudreau was a player/manager.

KEY SIGNATURES: Boudreau, Rosen, Doby, Mitchell, Lemon, Wynn, Feller.

VALUE: $250

1950 DETROIT - Neil Berry, Hank Borowy *, Paul Calvert, Hoot Evers, Joe Ginsberg, Ted Gray, Johnny Groth, Art Houtteman, Fred Hutchinson, George Kell, Charlie Keller, Don Kolloway, Dick Kryhoski, Eddie Lake, Johnny Lipon, Pat Mullin, Hal Newhouser, Jerry Priddy, Aaron Robinson, Saul Rogovin, Red Rolfe (MANAGER), Marlin Stuart, Bob Swift, Dizzy Trout, Vic Wertz, Hal White

LESS THAN 10 GAMES: Paul Campbell, Bill Connelly *, Ray Herbert, Frank House, Virgil Trucks

KEY SIGNATURES: Kell, Wertz, Groth, Evers.

VALUE: $240

1950 NEW YORK (AL) - Hank Bauer, Yogi Berra, Bobby Brown, Tommy Byrne, Jerry Coleman, Joe Collins, Jim Delsing *, Joe DiMaggio, Tom Ferrick *, Whitey Ford, Tommy Henrich, Johnny Hopp *, Jackie Jensen, Billy Johnson, Ed Lopat, Cliff Mapes, Billy Martin, Johnny Mize, Joe Ostrowski *, Joe Page, Vic Raschi, Allie Reynolds, Phil Rizzuto, Fred Sanford, Charlie Silvera, Casey Stengel (MANAGER), Gene Woodling

LESS THAN 10 GAMES: Lew Burdette, Ralph Houk, Don Johnson, Johnny Lindell *, Dave Madison, Ernie Nevel, Gus Niarhos *, Duane Pillette, Bob Porterfield, Snuffy Stirnweiss *, Dick Wakefield, Hank Workman

NOTES: World Champions! Rizzuto (MVP).

KEY SIGNATURES: Stengel, Martin, Rizzuto, Bauer, DiMaggio, Woodling, Berra, Mize, Ford.

VALUE: $860

1950 NEW YORK (NL) - Sammy Calderone, Al Dark, Leo Durocher (MANAGER), Tookie Gilbert, Andy Hansen, Clint Hartung, Jim Hearn, Kirby Higbe, Monte Irvin, Larry Jansen, Sheldon Jones, Spider Jorgensen *, Monte Kennedy, Dave Koslo, Jack Kramer, Whitey Lockman, Lucky Lohrke, Sal Maglie, Jack Maguire, Don Mueller, Bill Rigney, Rudy Rufer, George Spencer, Eddie Stanky, Hank Thompson, Bobby Thomson, Roy Weatherly, Wes Westrum

LESS THAN 10 GAMES: Marv Blaylock, Jack Harshman, Mike McCormick *, Pete Milne, Ray Mueller *, Nap Reyes, Sal Yvars

KEY SIGNATURES: Dark, Irvin, Jansen, Maglie.

VALUE: $375

1950 PHILADELPHIA (AL) - Joe Astroth, Lou Brissie, Sam Chapman, Joe Coleman, Bob Dillinger *, Ferris Fain, Dick Fowler, Mike Guerra, Billy Hitchcock, Bob Hooper, Eddie Joost, Alex Kellner, Paul Lehner, Connie Mack (MANAGER), Barney McCosky, Wally Moses, Carl Scheib, Bobby Shantz, Pete Suder, Joe Tipton, Elmer Valo, Kermit Wahl, Bob Wellman, Hank Wyse

LESS THAN 10 GAMES: Moe Burtschy, Harry Byrd, Ben Guintini, Eddie Klieman, Johnny Kucab, Gene Markland, Les McCrabb, Joe Murray, Roberto Ortiz *, Bob Rinker

NOTES: Mack's final year as manager.

KEY SIGNATURES: Mack, Dillinger, Lehner.

VALUE: $260

1950 PHILADELPHIA (NL) - Richie Ashburn, Jimmy Bloodworth *, Putsy Caballero, Milo Candini, Bubba Church, Blix Donnelly, Del Ennis, Mike Goliat, Granny Hamner, Ken Heintzelman, Stan Hollmig, Ken Johnson *, Willie Jones, Jim Konstanty, Stan Lopata, Jackie Mayo, Russ Meyer, Bob Miller, Bill Nicholson, Robin Roberts, Eddie Sawyer (MANAGER), Andy Seminick, Ken Silvestri, Curt Simmons, Dick Sisler, Eddie Waitkus, Dick Whitman

LESS THAN 10 GAMES: Johnny Blatnik *, Hank Borowy, John Brittin, Steve Ridzik, Paul Stuffel, Jocko Thompson

NOTES: "Whiz Kids;" Konstanty (MVP).

KEY SIGNATURES: Ennis, Ashburn, Roberts, Simmons, Konstanty.

VALUE: $360

MVP = MVP Award winner

1950 PITTSBURGH - Ted Beard, Gus Bell, Johnny Berardino *, Hank Borowy *, Pete Castiglione, Cliff Chambers, Dale Coogan, Murry Dickson, Bob Dillinger *, Nanny Fernandez, Johnny Hopp *, Ralph Kiner, Vern Law, Vic Lombardi, Bill Macdonald, Woody Main, Clyde McCullough, Billy Meyer (MANAGER), Ray Mueller *, Danny Murtaugh, Danny O'Connell, Jack Phillips, Bill Pierro, Mel Queen, Marv Rickert *, Stan Rojek, Tom Saffell, Hank Schenz, Ed Stevens, George Strickland, Earl Turner, Junior Walsh, Bill Werle, Wally Westlake

LESS THAN 10 GAMES: Frank Barrett, Bob Chesnes, Ed Fitz Gerald, Hal Gregg, Harry Gumbert, Windy McCall, Frank Papish, Jack Phillips

KEY SIGNATURES: Hopp, Kiner.

VALUE: $240

1950 ST. LOUIS (AL) - Hank Arft, Jack Bruner *, Ray Coleman, Jim Delsing *, Billy DeMars, Harry Dorish, Cliff Fannin, Tom Ferrick *, Tommy Fine, Owen Friend, Ned Garver, Don Johnson *, Dick Kokos, Don Lenhardt, Sherm Lollar, Cuddles Marshall, Les Moss, Stubby Overmire, Duane Pillette *, Roy Sievers, Bill Sommers, Dick Starr, Snuffy Stirnweiss *, Zack Taylor (MANAGER), Leo Thomas, Tom Upton, Al Widmar, Ken Wood

LESS THAN 10 GAMES: Ed Albrecht, Russ Bauers, Frankie Gustine, Bill Kennedy, Lou Kretlow *, Joe Ostrowski *, Ribs Raney, Sid Schacht, Lou Sleater

VALUE: $230

1950 ST. LOUIS (NL) - Steve Bilko, Cloyd Boyer, Al Brazle, Harry Brecheen, Johnny Bucha, Chuck Diering, Erv Dusak, Joe Garagiola, Tommy Glaviano, Solly Hemus, Bill Howerton, Nippy Jones, Eddie Kazak, Max Lanier, Johnny Lindell *, Peanuts Lowery *, Marty Marion, Freddie Martin, Eddie Miller, George Munger, Stan Musial, Rocky Nelson, Al Papai, Howie Pollett, Del Rice, Hal Rice, Red Schoendienst, Enos Slaughter, Gerry Staley, Harry Walker, Ted Wilks

LESS THAN 10 GAMES: Johnny Blatnik *, Don Bollweg, Cot Deal, Eddie Dyer (MANAGER), Danny Gardella, Jim Hearn, Ken Johnson, Ed Mickelson, Ed Mierkowicz, Tom Poholsky

KEY SIGNATURES: Musial, Schoendienst, Garagiola.

VALUE: $250

1950 WASHINGTON - Gene Bearden, Gil Coan, Merrill Combs *, Sandy Consuegra, Sam Dente, Al Evans, Mickey Gresso, Bucky Harris (MANAGER), Mickey Harris, Joe Haynes, Lloyd Hittle, Sid Hudson, Hal Keller, Al Kozar *, Bob Kuzava, Connie Marrero, Sam Mele, Cass Michaels *, Irv Noren, Len Okria, Roberto Ortiz, John Ostrowski *, Jim Pearce, Sherry Robertson, Eddie Robinson *, Al Sima, Elmer Singleton, Bud Stewart, Mickey Vernon *, Dick Weik, Eddie Yost

LESS THAN 10 GAMES: George Genovese, Rogelio Martinez, Julio Moreno, Steve Nagy, Tommy O'Brien *, Carlos Pascual, Bob Ross, Ray Scarborough, Fred Taylor, Clyde Vollmer *, Dick Welteroth

KEY SIGNATURES: Vernon.

VALUE: $225

1951

1951 American League MVP Yogi Berra

*** = player was traded**

1951 BOSTON (AL) - Matt Batts *, Lou Boudreau, Dom DiMaggio, Bobby Doerr, Walt Dropo, Al Evans, Billy Goodman, Mike Guerra *, Fred Hatfield, Leo Kiely, Ellis Kinder, Walt Masterson, Charlie Maxwell, Mickey McDermott, Les Moss *, Willard Nixon, Steve O'Neill (MANAGER), Mel Parnell, Johnny Pesky, Aaron Robinson *, Buddy Rosar, Ray Scarborough, Vern Stephens, Chuck Stobbs, Harry Taylor, Clyde Vollmer, Sammy White, Bill Wight, Ted Williams

LESS THAN 10 GAMES: Bob DiPietro, Bill Evans, Ben Flowers, Paul Hinrichs, Harley Hisner, Mel Hoderlein, Karl Olson, Al Richter, Tom Wright, Norm Zauchin

KEY SIGNATURES: Doerr, Pesky, Boudreau.

VALUE: $265

1951 BOSTON (NL) - Bob Addis, Vern Bickford, Bob Chipman, Dave Cole, Walker Cooper, Bob Elliott, George Estock, Sid Gordon, Roy Hartsfield, Tommy Holmes (MANAGER), Sam Jethroe, Buddy Kerr, Johnny Logan, Luis Marquez, Willard Marshall, Gene Mauch, Ray Mueller, Chet Nichols, Luis Olmo, Phil Paine, Johnny Sain *, Sibby Sisti, Billy Southworth (MANAGER), Warren Spahn, Ebba St. Claire, Max Surkont, Earl Torgeson, Jim Wilson

LESS THAN 10 GAMES: Lew Burdette, Blix Donnelly, Dick Donovan, Bobby Hogue *, Sid Schacht *, Bob Thorpe

NOTES: Holmes was a player/manager.

KEY SIGNATURES: Spahn, Sain.

VALUE: $225

1951 BROOKLYN - Cal Abrams, Ralph Branca, Rocky Bridges, Tommy Brown *, Roy Campanella, Billy Cox, Chuck Dressen (MANAGER), Bruce Edwards *, Hank Edwards *, Carl Erskine, Carl Furillo, Joe Hatten *, Phil Haugstad, Gene Hermanski *, Gil Hodges, Clyde King, Clem Labine, Eddie Miksis *, Don Newcombe, Andy Pafko *, Erv Palica, Bud Podbielan, Pee Wee Reese, Jackie Robinson, Preacher Roe, Jim Russell, Johnny Schmitz *, Duke Snider, Wayne Terwilliger *, Don Thompson, Rube Walker *, Dick Williams

LESS THAN 10 GAMES: Dan Bankhead, Wayne Belardi, Mickey Livingston, Earl Mossor, Chris Van Cuyk

NOTES: Campanella (MVP).

KEY SIGNATURES: Hodges, Robinson, Reese, Snider, Campanella, Roe, Newcombe.

VALUE: $700

MVP = MVP Award winner

1951 CHICAGO (AL) - Luis Aloma, Floyd Baker, Bob Boyd, Jim Busby, Chico Carrasquel, Ray Coleman *, Joe DeMaestri, Bob Dillinger, Joe Dobson, Harry Dorish, Joe Erautt, Nellie Fox, Gordon Goldsberry, Randy Gumpert, Bert Haas, Ken Holcombe, Howie Judson, Lou Kretlow, Paul Lehner *, Don Lenhardt *, Hank Majeski *, Phil Masi, Minnie Minoso *, Gus Niarhos, Billy Pierce, Paul Richards (MANAGER), Eddie Robinson, Saul Rogovin *, Marv Rotblatt, Bud Sheely, Bud Stewart, Al Zarilla, Gus Zernial *

LESS THAN 10 GAMES: Hal Brown, Bob Cain *, Ross Grimsley, Sam Hairston, Dick Littlefield, Bob Mahoney *, Rocky Nelson *, Dave Philley *, Red Wilson

KEY SIGNATURES: Fox, Minoso.

VALUE: $240

1951 CHICAGO (NL) - Frankie Baumholtz, Bob Borkowski, Smoky Burgess, Phil Cavarretta (MANAGER), Chuck Connors, Jack Cusick, Monk Dubiel, Bruce Edwards *, Dee Fondy, Frankie Frisch (MANAGER), Joe Hatten *, Gene Hermanski *, Frank Hiller, Randy Jackson, Hal Jeffcoat, Bob Kelly, Johnny Klippstein, Dutch Leonard, Turk Lown, Carmen Mauro, Cal McLish, Eddie Miksis *, Paul Minner, Mickey Owen, Andy Pafko *, Bob Ramazzotti, Fred Richards, Bob Rush, Hank Sauer, Bob Schultz, Bill Serena, Roy Smalley, Wayne Terwilliger *, Rube Walker *

LESS THAN 10 GAMES: Harry Chiti, Warren Hacker, Johnny Schmitz *, Andy Varga

NOTES: Cavarretta was a player/manager.

KEY SIGNATURES: Frisch, Connors, Burgess.

VALUE: $260

1951 CINCINNATI - Bobby Adams, Joe Adcock, Ewell Blackwell, Bud Byerly, Hank Edwards *, Eddie Erautt, Howie Fox, Grady Hatton, Dixie Howell, Ted Kluszewski, Danny Litwhiler, Barney McCosky *, Roy McMillan, Sammy Meeks, Lloyd Merriman, Harry Perkowski, Wally Post, Johnny Pramesa, Ken Rafffensberger, Willie Ramsdell, Connie Ryan, Bob Scheffing *, Luke Sewell (MANAGER), Frank Smith, Virgil Stallcup, Bob Usher, Herm Wehmeier, Johnny Wyrostek

LESS THAN 10 GAMES: Jim Blackburn, Ed Blake, Jim Bolger, Hobie Landrith, Kent Peterson, Ted Tappe

KEY SIGNATURES: Kluszewski, Adcock.

VALUE: $225

1951 CLEVELAND - Bobby Avila, Ray Boone, Lou Brissie *, Bob Chakales, Sam Chapman *, Merrill Combs, Larry Doby, Luke Easter, Bob Feller, Mike Garcia, Steve Gromek, Jim Hegan, Bob Kennedy, Paul Lehner *, Bob Lemon, Al Lopez (MANAGER), Clarence Maddern, Berney McCosky *, Minnie Minoso *, Dale Mitchell, Milt Nielsen, Al Rosen, Harry Simpson, Snuffy Stirnweiss, Birdie Tebbetts, Early Wynn, George Zuverink

LESS THAN 10 GAMES: Allie Clark *, Red Fahr, Doug Hansen, Charlie Harris, Sam Jones, Lou Klein *, Ray Murray *, Hal Naragon, Dick Rozek, Thurman Tucker, Johnny Vander Meer

KEY SIGNATURES: Lopez, Avila, Feller, Wynn, Lemon.

VALUE: $250

1951 DETROIT - Gene Bearden *, Neil Berry, Hank Borowy, Bob Cain *, Hoot Evers, Joe Ginsberg, Ted Gray, Johnny Groth, Frank House, Fred Hutchinson, George Kell, Charlie Keller, Don Kolloway, Dick Kryhoski, Johnny Lipon, Pat Mullin, Hal Newhouser, Jerry Priddy, Aaron Robinson *, Saul Rogovin *, Red Rolfe (MANAGER), Steve Souchock, Marlin Stuart, Bob Swift, Dizzy Trout, Virgil Trucks, Vic Wertz, Hal White

LESS THAN 10 GAMES: Paul Calvert, Doc Daugherty, Al Federoff, Ray Herbert, Earl Johnson, Dick Marlowe, Wayne McLeland, Russ Sullivan

KEY SIGNATURES: Kell, Trucks.

VALUE: $230

ROY = **Rookie of the Year**

1951 NEW YORK (AL) - Hank Bauer, Yogi Berra, Bobby Brown, Bob Cerv, Jerry Coleman, Joe Collins, Joe DiMaggio, Johnny Hopp, Jackie Jensen, Billy Johnson *, Jack Kramer *, Bob Kuzava *, Ed Lopat, Mickey Mantle, Cliff Mapes *, Billy Martin, Gil McDougald, Johnny Mize, Tom Morgan, Joe Ostrowski, Stubby Overmire *, Vic Raschi, Allie Reynolds, Phil Rizzuto, Fred Sanford *, Art Schallock, Spec Shea, Charlie Silvera, Casey Stengel (MANAGER), Gene Woodling

LESS THAN 10 GAMES: Jim Brideweser, Tommy Byrne *, Clint Courtney, Tom Ferrick *, Bobby Hogue *, Ralph Houk, Bob Muncrief, Ernie Nevel, Bob Porterfield *, Johnny Sain *, Bob Wiesler, Archie Wilson

NOTES: World Champions! Berra (MVP); McDougald (ROY); DiMaggio's final year.

KEY SIGNATURES: Stengel, Mize, Rizzuto, Brown, DiMaggio, Mantle, McDougald, Berra, Martin.

VALUE: $900

1951 NEW YORK (NL) - Sammy Calderone, Al Corwin, Al Dark, Leo Durocher (MANAGER), Al Gettel, Clint Hartung, Jim Hearn, Monte Irvin, Larry Jansen, Sheldon Jones, Spider Jorgensen, Monte Kennedy, Dave Koslo, Whitey Lockman, Lucky Lohrke, Sal Maglie, Jack Maguire, Willie Mays, Don Mueller, Ray Noble, Earl Rapp, Bill Rigney, Hank Schenz, George Spencer, Eddie Stanky, Hank Thompson, Bobby Thomson, Wes Westrum, Davey Williams, Artie Wilson, Sal Yvars

LESS THAN 10 GAMES: George Bamberger, Roger Bowman, Red Hardy, Alex Konikowski, Jack Kramer

NOTES: Mays (ROY).

KEY SIGNATURES: Durocher, Dark, Mays, Irvin, Maglie.

VALUE: $475

ROY = **Rookie of the Year**

1951 PHILADELPHIA (AL) - Joe Astroth, Sam Chapman *, Allie Clark *, Joe Coleman, Tod Davis, Jimmy Dykes (MANAGER), Ferris Fain, Dick Fowler, Billy Hitchcock, Bob Hooper, Eddie Joost, Alex Kellner, Lou Klein *, Johnny Kucab, Lou Limmer, Hank Majeski *, Morrie Martin, Barney McCosky *, Wally Moses, Ray Murray *, Dave Philley *, Carl Scheib, Bobb Shantz, Pete Suder, Joe Tipton, Elmer Valo, Kermit Wahl *, Gus Zernial *, Sam Zoldak

LESS THAN 10 GAMES: Lou Brissie, Moe Burtschy, Charlie Harris, Paul Lehner *, Eddie Samcoff, Hank Wyse

KEY SIGNATURES: Fain, Shantz.

VALUE: $230

1951 PHILADELPHIA (NL) - Richie Ashburn, Jimmy Bloodworth, Tommy Brown *, Putsy Caballero, Milo Candini, Bubba Church, Mel Clark, Leo Cristante, Del Ennis, Mike Goliet *, Granny Hamner, Andy Hansen, Ken Heintzelman, Ken Johnson, Willie Jones, Jim Konstanty, Russ Meyer, Bob Miller, Bill Nicholson, Eddie Pellagrini, Robin Roberts, Ed Sanicki, Eddie Sawyer (MANAGER), Andy Seminick, Dick Sisler, Jocko Thompson, Eddie Waitkus, Dick Whitman, Del Wilber, Dick Young

LESS THAN 10 GAMES: John Brittin, Karl Drews, Stan Hollmig, Niles Jordan, Stan Lopata, Jackie Mayo, Lou Possehl, Ken Silvestri

KEY SIGNATURES: Ashburn, Roberts.

VALUE: $225

1951 PITTSBURGH - Monty Basgall, Ted Beard, Gus Bell, Pete Castiglione, Cliff Chambers, Dick Cole *, Murry Dickson, Bob Dillinger *, Erv Dusak, Ed Fitz Gerald, Bob Friend, Joe Garagiola *, Bill Howerton *, Ralph Kiner, Bill Koski, Vern Law, Paul LaPalme, Dale Long *, Clyde McCullough, Jack Merson, Catfish Metkovich, Billy Meyer (MANAGER), Danny Murtaugh, Rocky Nelson *, Jack Phillips, Howie Pollet, Mel Queen, Pete Reiser, Dino Restelli, Tom Saffell, Hank Schenz *, Dick Smith, George Strickland, Frank Thomas, Junior Walsh, Bill Werle, Wally Westlake *, Ted Wilks

LESS THAN 10 GAMES: Don Carlsen, Con Dempsey, Erv Dusak *, Harry Fisher, Jack Maguire *, Joe Muir, Paul Pettit, Stan Rojek *, Len Yochim

KEY SIGNATURES: Kiner, Garagiola.

VALUE: $240

1951 ST. LOUIS (AL) - Hank Arft, Matt Batts *, Johnny Berardino, Johnny Bero, Tommy Byrne *, Ray Coleman *, Jim Delsing, Ned Garver, Bobby Hogue *, Bill Jennings, Bill Kennedy, Paul Lehner *, Don Lenhardt *, Sherm Lollar, Dale Long *, Joe

Lutz, Jack Maguire *, Bob Mahoney *, Cliff Mapes *, Freddie Marsh, Jim McDonald, Les Moss *, Bob Nieman, Satchel Paige, Duane Pillette, Earl Rapp *, Frank Saucier, Roy Sievers, Lou Sleater, Dick Starr *, Jim Suchecki, Bennie Taylor, Bud Thomas, Tom Upton, Al Widmar, Ken Wood, Bobby Young

LESS THAN 10 GAMES: Billy DeMars, Jim Dyck, Cliff Fannin, Eddie Gaedel, Mike Goliat *, Tito Herrera, Don Johnson *, Clyde Kluttz *, Duke Markell, Irv Medlinger, Stubby Overmire *, Fred Sanford *, Sid Schacht *, Zack Taylor (MANAGER), Bob Turley, Kermit Wahl *

NOTES: Gaedel was a promotional stunt used by Bill Veeck.

KEY SIGNATURES: Paige, Gaedel.

VALUE: $280

1951 ST. LOUIS (NL) - Dick Bakelmann, Vern Benson, Steve Bilko, Cloyd Boyer, Al Brazle, Harry Brecheen, Cliff Chambers *, Dick Cole *, Jack Crimian, Chuck Diering, Erv Dusak *, Joe Garagiola *, Tommy Glaviano, Solly Hemus, Bill Howerton *, Billy Johnson *, Nippy Jones, Eddie Kazak, Max Lanier, Peanuts Lowery, Marty Marion (MANAGER), George Munger, Stan Musial, Tom Polholsky, Joe Presko, Del Rice, Hal Rice, Don Richmond, Stan Rojek *, Bill Sarni, Bob Scheffing *, Red Schoendienst, Enos Slaughter, Gerry Staley, Wally Westlake *, Ted Wilks *

LESS THAN 10 GAMES: Don Bollweg, Larry Ciaffone, Jackie Collum, Erv Dusak *, Bob Habenicht, Kurt Krieger, Dan Lewandowski, Rocky Nelson *, Howie Pollet *, Jay Van Noy, Harry Walker

KEY SIGNATURES: Schoendienst, Slaughter, Musial, Garagiola.

VALUE: $250

1951 WASHINGTON - Gil Coan, Sandy Consuegra, Sam Dente, Tom Ferrick *, Mickey Grasso, Mike Guerra *, Bucky Harris (MANAGER), Mickey Harris, Joe Haynes, Sid Hudson, Don Johnson *, Clyde Kluttz *, Connie Marrero, Mike McCormick, Sam Mele, Cass Michaels, Julio Moreno, Irv Noren, Dan Porter, Bob Porterfield *, Sherry Robertson, Bob Ross, Pete Runnels, Al Sima, Dick Starr *, Gene Verble, Mickey Vernon, Eddie Yost

LESS THAN 10 GAMES: Gene Bearden *, Alton Brown, Frank Campos, Roy Hawes, Bob Kuzava *, Willie Miranda, Len Okrie, Frank Sacka, Fred Sanford *, Fred Taylor, Hank Wyse *

KEY SIGNATURES: Vernon.

VALUE: $200

1952

1952 New York Yankees

***** = **player was traded**

1952 BOSTON (AL) - Al Benton, Milt Bolling, Lou Boudreau (MANAGER), Ralph Brickner, Dick Brodowski, Ike Delock, Dom DiMaggio, Walt Dropo *, Hoot Evers *, Dick Gernert, Billy Goodman, Randy Gumpert *, Fred Hatfield *, Bill Henry, Sid Hudson *, George Kell *, Ellis Kinder, Don Lenhardt *, Ted Lepcio, Johnny Lipon *, Mickey McDermott, Gus Niarhos, Willard Nixon, Mel Parnell, Johnny Pesky *, Jimmy Piersall, Ray Scarborough *, George Schmees *, Gene Stephens, Vern Stephens, Faye Throneberry, Dizzy Trout *, Clyde Vollmer, Sammy White, Bill Wight *, Del Wilber *, Archie Wilson *, Ken Wood *, Al Zarilla *

LESS THAN 10 GAMES: Jim Atkins, Hal Bevan *, Hersh Freeman, Paul Lehner, Walt Masterson *, Charlie Maxwell, Len Okrie, Harry Taylor, Ted Williams

NOTES: Boudreau was a player/manager.

KEY SIGNATURES: Boudreau, Goodman, Kell, Williams.

VALUE: $240

1952 BOSTON (NL) - Vern Bickford, Lew Burdette, Paul Burris, Bob Chipman, Buzz Clarkson, Dave Cole, Walker Cooper, George Crowe, Jack Cusick, Jack Daniels, Jack Dittmer, Sid Gordon, Charlie Grimm (MANAGER), Roy Hartsfield, Tommy Holmes (MANAGER), Virgil Jester, Sam Jethroe, Ernie Johnson, Sheldon Jones, Johnny Logan, Willard Marshall *, Eddie Mathews, Bill Reed, Sibby Sisti, Warren Spahn, Ebba St. Claire, Max Surkont, Bob Thorpe, Earl Torgeson, Pete Whisenant, Jim Wilson

LESS THAN 10 GAMES: Gene Conley, Dick Donovan, Dick Hoover, Billy Klaus, Bert Thiel

NOTES: Final Boston Braves team.

KEY SIGNATURES: Grimm, Mathews, Spahn.

VALUE: $250

1952 BROOKLYN - Cal Abrams *, Sandy Amoros, Joe Black, Ralph Branca, Rocky Bridges, Roy Campanella, Billy Cox, Chuck Dressen (MANAGER), Carl Erskine, Carl Furillo, Gil Hodges, Tommy Holmes *, Clyde King, Clem Labine, Billy Loes, Ray Moore, Bobby Morgan, Rocky Nelson, Andy Pafko, Pee Wee Reese, Jackie Robinson, Preacher Roe, Johnny Rutherford, Johnny Schmitz, George Shuba, Duke Snider, Chris Van Cuyk, Ben Wade, Rube Walker, Dick Williams

LESS THAN 10 GAMES: Jim Hughes, Joe Landrum, Ken Lehman, Steve Lembo, Ron Negray, Bud Podbielan

NOTES: Black (ROY).

KEY SIGNATURES: Hodges, Robinson, Reese, Furillo, Snider, Campanella, Black, Erskine.

VALUE: $750

ROY = Rookie of the Year

1952 CHICAGO (AL) - Luis Aloma, Hal Brown, Jim Busby *, Chico Carrasquel, Ray Coleman *, Sam Dente, Joe Dobson, Harry Dorish, Nellie Fox, Marv Grissom, Darrell Johnson *, Howie Judson, Billy Kennedy, Lou Kretlow, Rocky Krsnich, Sherm Lollar, Phil Masi, Sam Mele *, Minnie Minoso, Willie Miranda *, Don Nicholas *, Billy Pierce, Paul Richards (MANAGER), Jim Rivera *, Eddie Robinson, Hector Rodriquez, Saul Rogovin, Bud Sheely, Bud Stewart, Chuck Stobbs, Leo Thomas *, Tom Wright *, Al Zarilla *

LESS THAN 10 GAMES: Hank Edwards *, Sammy Esposito, Ken Holcombe, Hal Hudson, Ken Landenberger, Al Widmar, Red Wilson, Ted Wilson *

KEY SIGNATURES: Fox, Minoso.

VALUE: $250

1952 CHICAGO (NL) - Bob Addis, Toby Atwell, Frankie Baumholtz, Tommy Brown *, Phil Cavarretta (MANAGER), Harry Chiti, Bruce Edwards, Dee Fondy, Warren Hacker, Joe Hatten, Gene Hermanski, Randy Jackson, Hal Jeffcoat, Bob Kelly, Johnny Klippstein, Dutch Leonard, Turk Lown, Dick Manville, Eddie Miksis, Paul Minner, Johnny Pramesa, Bob Ramazzotti, Willie Ramsdell, Bob Rush, Hank Sauer, Bob Schultz, Bill Serena, Roy Smalley

LESS THAN 10 GAMES: Leon Brinkopf, Monk Dubiel, Vern Fear, Bud Hardin, Cal Howe, Ron Northey, Bob Usher

NOTES: Sauer (MVP); Cavarretta was a player/manager.

KEY SIGNATURES: Fondy, Baumholtz, Sauer, Hacker.

VALUE: $220

MVP = MVP Award winner

1952 CINCINNATI - Cal Abrams *, Bobby Adams, Joe Adcock, Ewell Blackwell *, Bob Borkowski, Earle Brucker (MANAGER), Bud Byerly, Bubba Church *, Hank Edwards *, Jim Greengrass, Grady Hatton, Frank Hiller, Rogers Hornsby (MANAGER), Dixie Howell, Eddie Kazak *, Ted Kluszewski, Hobie Landrith, Willard Marshall *, Roy McMillan, Joe Nuxhall, Eddie Pellagrini, Harry Perkowski, Bud Podbielan *, Wally Post, Ken Raffensberger, Joe Rossi, Andy Seminick, Luke Sewell (MANAGER), Dick Sisler *, Frank Smith, Johnny Temple, Herm Wehmeier, Wally Westlake *, Johnny Wyrostek *

LESS THAN 10 GAMES: Ed Blake, Phil Haugstad, Niles Jordan, Johnny Schmitz *, Virgil Stallcup *

KEY SIGNATURES: Hornsby, Kluszewski, Adcock.

VALUE: $320

1952 CLEVELAND - Bobby Avila, Johnny Berardino *, Ray Boone, Lou Brissie, Merrill Combs, Larry Doby, Luke Easter, Bob Feller, Jim Fridley, Mike Garcia, Bill Glynn, Steve Gromek, Mickey Harris, Jim Hegan, Sam Jones, Bob Kennedy, Bob Lemon, Al Lopez (MANAGER), Hank Majeski *, Barney McCosky, Dale Mitchell, Dave Pope, Pete Reiser, Al Rosen, Dick Rozek, Harry Simpson, George Strickland *, Birdie Tebbetts, Joe Tipton *, Wally Westlake *, Early Wynn

LESS THAN 10 GAMES: Bill Abernathie, Bob Chakales, Snuffy Stirnweiss, Quincy Trouppe, Ted Wilks *, George Zuverink

KEY SIGNATURES: Avila, Rosen, Mitchell, Wynn, Garcia, Lemon, Feller.

VALUE: $255

1952 DETROIT - Matt Batts, Neil Berry, Jim Delsing *, Walt Dropo *, Al Federoff, Joe Ginsberg, Ted Gray, Johnny Groth, Fred Hatfield *, Billy Hoeft, Johnny Hopp *, Art Houtteman, Fred Hutchinson (MANAGER), George Kell *, Don Kolloway, Harvey Kuenn, Don Lenhardt *, George Lerchen, Johnny Lipon *, Dick Littlefield, Don Lund, Dave Madison *, Cliff Mapes, Pat Mullin, Hal Newhouser, Johnny Pesky *, Jerry Priddy, Red Rolfe (MANAGER), Steve Souchock, Marlin Stuart *, Russ Sullivan, Bob Swift, Dizzy Trout, Virgil Trucks, Vic Wertz *, Hal White, Bill Wight *

LESS THAN 10 GAMES: Bill Black, Hoot Evers *, Alex Garbowski, Ned Garver *, Ken Johnson, Carl Linhart, Dick Marlowe, Wayne McLeland, Bennie Taylor, Bill Tuttle

NOTES: Hutchinson was a player/manager.

KEY SIGNATURES: Kell, Kuenn.

VALUE: $225

1952 NEW YORK (AL) - Loren Babe, Hank Bauer, Yogi Berra, Jim Brideweser, Bobby Brown, Andy Carey, Bob Cerv, Jerry Coleman, Joe Collins, Tom Gorman, Bobby Hogue *, Johnny Hopp *, Bob Kuzava, Ed Lopat, Mickey Mantle, Billy Martin, Jim McDonald, Gil McDougald, Bill Miller, Johnny Mize, Tom Morgan, Irv Noren *, Joe Ostrowski, Vic Raschi, Allie Reynolds, Phil Rizzuto, Johnny Sain, Kal Segrist, Charlie Silvera, Casey Stengel (MANAGER), Gene Woodling

LESS THAN 10 GAMES: Ewell Blackwell, Ralph Houk, Jackie Jensen *, Charlie Keller, Ray Scarborough *, Harry Schaeffer, Art Schallock, Johnny Schmitz *, Archie Wilson *

NOTES: World Champions!

KEY SIGNATURES: Stengel, Martin, Reynolds, Mantle, Berra, Raschi, Woodling, Brown, Mize, Rizzuto.

VALUE: $650

1952 NEW YORK (NL) - Bill Connelly, Al Corwin, Al Dark, Chuck Diering, Leo Durocher (MANAGER), Bob Elliott, Hal Gregg, Clint Hartung, Jim Hearn, Bobby Hofman, Bill Howerton *, Monte Irvin, Larry Jansen, Monte Kennedy, Dave Koslo, Max Lanier, Whitey Lockman, Sal Maglie, Willie Mays, Don Mueller, Dusty Rhodes, Bill Rigney, George Spencer, Hank Thompson, Bobby Thomson, Wes Westrum, Hoyt Wilhelm, Davey Williams, George Wilson *, Sal Yvars

LESS THAN 10 GAMES: George Bamberger, Roger Bowman, Jack Harshman, Ray Katt, Ray Noble, Mario Picone, Daryl Spencer, Dick Wakefield

KEY SIGNATURES: Durocher, Dark, Irvin, Maglie, Wilhelm.

VALUE: $350

1952 PHILADELPHIA (AL) - Joe Astroth, Harry Byrd, Allie Clark, Jimmy Dykes (MANAGER), Ferris Fain, Dick Fowler, Billy Hitchcock, Bob Hooper, Eddie Joost, Skeeter Kell, Alex Kellner, Johnny Kucab, Hank Majeski *, Cass Michaels *, Ray Murray, Bobo

Newsome *, Dave Philley, Sherry Robertson *, Carl Scheib, Bobby Shantz, Pete Suder, Kite Thomas, Joe Tipton *, Elmer Valo, Ed Wright, Gus Zernial, Sam Zoldak

LESS THAN 10 GAMES: Hal Bevan *, Charlie Bishop, Marion Fricano, Tom Hamilton, Tex Hoyle, Walt Kellner, Jack Littrell, Morrie Martin, Len Matarazzo

NOTES: Shantz (MVP); Byrd (ROY).

KEY SIGNATURES: Fain, Shantz.

VALUE: $225

MVP = MVP Award winner ROY = Rookie of the Year

1952 PHILADELPHIA (NL) - Richie Ashburn, Tommy Brown *, Smoky Burgess, Putsy Caballero, Mel Clark, Karl Drews, Del Ennis, Howie Fox, Granny Hamner, Andy Hansen, Ken Heintzelman, Willie Jones, Jim Konstanty, Lucky Lohrke, Stan Lopata, Jackie Mayo, Russ Meyer, Bill Nicholson, Steve O'Neill (MANAGER), Steve Ridzik, Robin Roberts, Connie Ryan, Eddie Sawyer (MANAGER), Curt Simmons, Eddie Waitkus, Johnny Wyrostek *

LESS THAN 10 GAMES: Bubba Church, Nippy Jones, Bob Miller, Kent Peterson, Lou Possehl, Paul Stuffel, Del Wilber *, Dick Young

KEY SIGNATURES: Ashburn, Roberts.

VALUE: $225

1952 PITTSBURGH - Tony Bartirome, Ted Beard, Gus Bell, Johnny Berardino *, Pete Castiglione, Brandy Davis, Bobby Del Greco, Murry Dickson, Erv Dusak, Ed Fitz Gerald, Bob Friend, Joe Garagiola, Dick Groat, Dick Hall, Cal Hogue, Bill Howerton *, Ralph Kiner, Ron Kline, Clem Koshorek, Paul LaPalme, Woody Main, Jim Mangan, Clyde McCullough, Jack Merson, Catfish Metkovich, Bill Meyer (MANAGER), Joe Muir, Ron Necciai, Howie Pollet, Sonny Senerchia, Dick Smith, George Strickland *, Lee Walls, Jim Waugh, Ted Wilks *

LESS THAN 10 GAMES: Bill Bell, Don Carlsen, Jim Dunn, Harry Fisher, George Munger *, Jack Phillips, Mel Queen, Jim Suchecki, Frank Thomas, Bill Werle *, Ed Wolfe

KEY SIGNATURES: Groat, Kiner, Garagiola.

VALUE: $250

1952 ST. LOUIS (AL) - Hank Arft, Gene Bearden, Tommy Byrne, Bob Cain, Ray Coleman *, Clint Courtney, Jim Delsing *, Joe DeMaestri, Jim Dyck, Cliff Fannin, Ned Garver *, Gordon Goldsberry, Earl Harrist, Ken Holcombe *, Rogers Hornsby (MANAGER), Darrell Johnson *, Dick Kryhoski, Don Lenhardt *, Dave Madison *, Marty Marion (MANAGER), Freddie Marsh *, Cass Michaels *, Les Moss, Bob Nieman, Stubby Overmire, Satchel Paige, Duane Pillette, Jay Porter, Earl Rapp *, Jim Rivera *, George Schmees *, Roy Sievers, Leo Thomas *, Vic Wertz *, Tom Wright *, Bobby Young, Al Zarilla *

LESS THAN 10 GAMES: Rufus Crawford, Mike Goliat, Johnny Hetki, Bobby Hogue *, Hal Hudson *, Dick Littlefield *, Bob Mahoney, Willie Miranda *, Stan Rojek, Lou Sleater *, Marlin Stuart *, Pete Taylor

NOTES: Marion was a player/manager.

KEY SIGNATURES: Hornsby, Paige.

VALUE: $350

1952 ST. LOUIS (NL) - Vern Benson, Steve Bilko, Dick Bokelman, Cloyd Boyer, Al Brazle, Harry Brecheen, Cliff Chambers, Mike Clark, Les Fusselman, Tommy Glaviano, Solly Hemus, Billy Johnson, Peanuts Lowery, Larry Miggins, Stu Miller, Vinegar Bend

Mizell, Stan Musial, Joe Presko, Del Rice, Hal Rice, Willard Schmidt, Red Schoendienst, Dick Sisler *, Enos Slaughter, Gerry Staley, Virgil Stallcup *, Eddie Stanky (MANAGER), Bill Werle *, Wally Westlake *, Eddie Yuhas

LESS THAN 10 GAMES: Jackie Collum, Hack Crimian, Herb Gorman, Harvey Haddix, Fred Hahn, Neal Hertweck, Eddie Kazak *, Gene Mauch, George Munger *, Bill Sarni, Bobby Tiefenauer

NOTES: Stanky was a player/manager.

KEY SIGNATURES: Schoendienst, Slaughter, Musial.

VALUE: $250

1952 WASHINGTON - Floyd Baker, George Bradshaw, Jim Busby *, Frank Campos, Gil Coan, Sandy Consuegra, Tom Ferrick, Mickey Grasso, Randy Gumpert *, Bucky Harris (MANAGER), Joe Haynes, Mel Hoderlein, Jackie Jensen *, Don Johnson, Hal Keller, Clyde Kluttz, Connie Marrero, Walt Masterson *, Cass Michaels *, Julio Moreno, Bobo Newsom *, Irv Noren *, Bob Porterfield, Earl Rapp *, Pete Runnels, Spec Shea, Lou Sleater *, Jerry Snyder, Fred Taylor, Mickey Vernon, Archie Wilson *, Ken Wood *, Eddie Yost

LESS THAN 10 GAMES: Mike Fornieles, Harley Grossman, Mickey Harris *, Sid Hudson *, Freddie Marsh *, Sam Mele *, Sherry Robertson *, Raul Sanchez, Bunky Stewart, Tom Upton, Buck Varner

KEY SIGNATURES: Vernon.

VALUE: $200

1953

1953 Brooklyn Dodgers

*** = player was traded**

1953 BOSTON - Floyd Baker *, Milt Bolling, Lou Boudreau (MANAGER), Hal Brown, Billy Consolo, Ike Delock, Hoot Evers, Ben Flowers, Hersh Freeman, Dick Gernert, Billy Goodman, Marv Grissom *, Bill Henry, Sid Hudson, George Kell, Bill Kennedy, Ellis Kinder, Ted Lepcio, Johnny Lipon *, Mickey McDermott, Gus Niarhos, Willard Nixon,

Karl Olson, Mel Parnell, Jimmy Piersall, Gene Stephens, Frank Sullivan, Tommy Umphlett, Sammy White, Del Wilber, Ted Williams, Al Zarilla

LESS THAN 10 GAMES: Dom DiMaggio, Ken Holcombe, Jack Merson, Al Richter, Clyde Vollmer *, Bill Werle

KEY SIGNATURES: Boudreau, Goodman, Kell, Williams, Parnell.

VALUE: $240

1953 BROOKLYN - Bill Antonello, Wayne Belardi, Joe Black, Roy Campanella, Billy Cox, Chuck Dressen (MANAGER), Carl Erskine, Carl Furillo, Jim Gilliam, Gil Hodges, Jim Hughes, Clem Labine, Billy Loes, Russ Meyer, Bob Milliken, Bobby Morgan, Johnny Podres, Pee Wee Reese, Jackie Robinson, Preacher Roe, George Shuba, Duke Snider, Don Thompson, Ben Wade, Rube Walker, Dick Williams

LESS THAN 10 GAMES: Ralph Branca *, Dixie Howell, Carmen Mauro *, Glenn Mickens, Ray Moore, Erv Palica, Dick Teed

NOTES: Campanella (MVP); Gilliam (ROY).

KEY SIGNATURES: Hodges, Meyer, Reese, Furillo, Snider, Robinson, Campanella,Erskine, Gilliam.

VALUE: $800

MVP = MVP Award winner

1953 CHICAGO (AL) - Luis Aloma, Gene Bearden, Bob Boyd, Tommy Byrne *, Chico Carrasquel, Sandy Consuegra *, Joe Dobson, Harry Dorish, Bob Elliott *, Ferris Fain, Mike Fornieles, Nellie Fox, Connie Johnson, Bob Keegan, Rocky Krsnich, Sherm Lollar, Freddie Marsh, Sam Mele, Minnie Minoso, Billy Pierce, Paul Richards (MANAGER), Jim Rivera, Saul Rogovin, Connie Ryan *, Bud Sheely, Vern Stephens *, Bud Stewart, Virgil Trucks *, Red Wilson, Tom Wright

LESS THAN 10 GAMES: Neil Berry *, Tommy Byrne *, Allie Clark *, Sam Dente, Earl Harrist *, Hal Hudson, Lou Kretlow *, Bill Wilson

KEY SIGNATURES: Fox, Minoso, Trucks.

VALUE: $275

1953 CHICAGO (NL) - Bob Addis *, Toby Atwell *, Ernie Banks, Frankie Baumholtz, Tommy Brown, Phil Cavarretta (MANAGER), Bubba Church *, Don Elston, Dee Fondy, Joe Garagiola *, Warren Hacker, Gene Hermanski *, Randy Jackson, Hal Jeffcoat, Sheldon Jones, Bob Kelly *, Ralph Kiner *, Johnny Klippstein, Dutch Leonard, Turk Lown, Clyde McCullough, Catfish Metkovich *, Eddie Miksis, Paul Minner, Howie Pollet *, Bob Ramazotti, Bob Rush, Hank Sauer, Carl Sawatski, Bill Serena, Duke Simpson, Roy Smalley, Preston Ward *, Jim Willis

LESS THAN 10 GAMES: Fred Baczewski *, Gene Baker, Bill Moisan, Paul Schramka, Bob Schultz *, Dale Talbot

NOTES: Cavarretta was a player/manager.

KEY SIGNATURES: Fondy, Baumholtz, Kiner, Garagiola, Banks.

VALUE: $250

1953 CINCINNATI - Bobby Adams, Fred Baczewski *, Frank Baldwin, Gus Bell, Bob Borkowski, Rocky Bridges, Bubba Church *, Jackie Collum *, Jim Greengrass, Grady Hatton, Rogers Hornsby (MANAGER), Howie Judson, Bob Kelly *, Clyde King, Ted

Kluszewski, Hobie Landrith, George Lerchen, Bob Marquis, Willard Marshall, Roy McMillan, Buster Mills (MANAGER), Ernie Nevel, Joe Nuxhall, Harry Perkowski, Bud Podbielan, Wally Post, Ken Raffensberger, Andy Seminick, Frank Smith, Johnny Temple, Herm Wehmeier

LESS THAN 10 GAMES: Ed Bailey, Ed Blake, Eddie Erautt *, Hank Foiles *, Barney Martin, Joe Szekely

KEY SIGNATURES: Hornsby, Kluszewski, Bell.

VALUE: $320

1953 CLEVELAND - Bobby Avila, Ray Boone *, Lou Brissie, Larry Doby, Luke Easter, Bob Feller, Owen Friend *, Mike Garcia, Joe Ginsberg *, Bill Glynn, Jim Hegan, Bob Hooper, Dave Hoskins, Art Houtteman *, Bob Kennedy, Bob Lemon, Jim Lemon, Al Lopez (MANAGER), Hank Majeski, Barney McCosky, Dale Mitchell, Al Rosen, Harry Simpson, Al Smith, George Strickland, Joe Tipton, Wally Westlake, Bill Wight *, Ted Wilks, Early Wynn

LESS THAN 10 GAMES: Al Aber *, Dick Aylward, Bob Chakales, Hank Foiles *, Steve Gromek *, Dick Tomanek

NOTES: Rosen (MVP).

KEY SIGNATURES: Lopez, Rosen, Westlake, Mitchell, Lemon, Wynn, Feller.

VALUE: $295

1953 DETROIT - Al Aber *, Matt Batts, Ray Boone *, Ralph Branca *, Johnny Bucha, Frank Carswell, Jim Delsing, Walt Dropo, Hal Erickson, Owen Friend *, Ned Garver, Joe Ginsberg *, Ted Gray, Steve Gromek *, Fred Hatfield, Ray Herbert, Billy Hitchcock, Billy Hoeft, Art Houtteman *, Fred Hutchinson (MANAGER), Al Kaline, Harvey Kuenn, Don Lund, Dave Madison, Dick Marlowe, Bob Miller, Pat Mullin, Bob Nieman, Johnny Pesky, Jerry Priddy, Ray Scarborough *, Steve Souchock, Russ Sullivan, Dick Weik, Bill Wight *

LESS THAN 10 GAMES: John Baumgartner, Reno Bertoia, Paul Foytack, George Freese, Earl Harrist *, Milt Jordan, Hal Newhouser, Bob Swift

NOTES: Kuenn (ROY); Hutchinson was a player/manager.

KEY SIGNATURES: Kuenn, Boone, Kaline.

VALUE: $225

ROY = Rookie of the Year

1953 WASHINGTON - Jim Busby, Tommy Byrne *, Frank Campos, Gil Coan, Yo-Yo Davalillo, Sonny Dixon, Ed Fitz Gerald *, Mickey Grasso, Bucky Harris (MANAGER), Mel Holderlein, Jackie Jensen, Jerry Lane, Connie Marrero, Walt Masterson, Carmen Mauro *, Julio Moreno, Bob Porterfield, Pete Runnels, Johnny Schmitz, Spec Shea, Al Sima, Jerry Snyder, Chuck Stobbs, Wayne Terwilliger, Kite Thomas *, Gene Verble, Mickey Vernon, Clyde Vollmer *, Ken Wood, Eddie Yost

LESS THAN 10 GAMES: Floyd Baker *, Bruce Barmes, Sandy Consuegra *, Bob Oldis, Jim Pearce, Les Peden, Tony Roig, Frank Sacka, Bunky Stewart, Dean Stone

KEY SIGNATURES: Vernon, Busby, Porterfield.

VALUE: $200

1954

1954 Cincinnati Reds

*** = player was traded**

1954 BALTIMORE - Cal Abrams *, Mike Blyzka, Jim Brideweser, Bob Chakales *, Gil Coan, Joe Coleman, Clint Courtney, Chuck Diering, Joe Durham, Jimmy Dykes (MANAGER), Howie Fox, Jim Fridley, Chico Garcia, Billy Hunter, Frank Kellert, Bob Kennedy *, Dick Kokos, Lou Kretlow, Dick Kryhoski, Don Larsen, Don Lenhardt *, Sam Mele *, Les Moss, Ray Murray, Duane Pillette, Vern Stephens, Marlin Stuart *, Bob Turley, Eddie Waitkus, Vic Wertz *, Bobby Young

LESS THAN 10 GAMES: Neil Berry, Vern Bickford, Ryne Duren, Jay Heard, Dave Koslo *, Bob Kuzava *, Dick Littlefield *, Billy O'Dell

VALUE: $180

1954 BOSTON - Harry Agganis, Floyd Baker *, Milt Bolling, Lou Boudreau (MANAGER), Tom Brewer, Hal Brown, Tex Clevenger, Billy Consolo, Dick Gernert, Billy Goodman, Grady Hatton *, Bill Henry, Tom Herrin, Sid Hudson, Tom Hurd, Jackie Jensen, George Kell *, Russ Kemmerer, Leo Kiely, Ellis Kinder, Don Lenhardt *, Ted Lepcio, Charlie Maxwell, Sam Mele *, Willard Nixon, Karl Olson, Mickey Owen, Mel Parnell, Jimmy Piersall, Frank Sullivan, Bill Werle, Sammy White, Del Wilber, Ted Williams

LESS THAN 10 GAMES: Joe Dobson, Hoot Evers *, Guy Morton

KEY SIGNATURES: Boudreau, Jensen, Williams.

VALUE: $230

1954 BROOKLYN - Walt Alston (MANAGER), Sandy Amoros, Wayne Belardi *, Roy Campanella, Billy Cox, Carl Erskine, Carl Furillo, Jim Gilliam, Don Hoak, Gil Hodges, Jim Hughes, Charlie Kress *, Clem Labine, Billy Loes, Russ Meyer, Bob Milliken, Walt Moryn, Don Newcombe, Erv Palcia, Johnny Podres, Pee Wee Reese, Jackie Robinson, Preacher Roe, George Shuba, Duke Snider, Don Thompson, Tim Thompson, Ben Wade *, Rube Walker, Dick Williams, Pete Wojey, Don Zimmer

LESS THAN 10 GAMES: Joe Black, Bob Darnell, Tom Lasorda, Karl Spooner

KEY SIGNATURES: Alston, Hodges, Gilliam, Reese, Furillo, Lasorda, Robinson, Campanella, Erskine, Newcombe, Snider.

VALUE: $600

1954 CHICAGO (AL) - Matt Batts *, Bob Boyd, Chico Carrasquel, Phil Cavarretta, Sandy Consuegra, Harry Dorish, Ferris Fain, Mike Fornieles, Nellie Fox, Johnny Groth, Jack Harshman, Grady Hatton *, Ron Jackson, Don Johnson, Bob Keegan, George Kell *, Sherm Lollar, Marty Marion (MANAGER), Freddie Marsh, Willard Marshall, Morrie Martin *, Ed McGlee *, Cass Michaels, Minnie Minoso, Billy Pierce, Paul Richards (MANAGER), Jim Rivera, Carl Sawatski, Bud Stewart, Virgil Trucks, Bill Wilson *

LESS THAN 10 GAMES: Bob Cain, Tom Flanigan, Stan Jok *, Joe Kirrene, Don Nicholas, Al Sima *, Dick Strahs, Vito Valentinetti, Red Wilson *

KEY SIGNATURES: Fox, Kell, Trucks, Minoso.

VALUE: $260

1954 CHICAGO (NL) - Gene Baker, Ernie Banks, Frankie Baumholtz, Steve Bilko *, Jim Brosnan, Dave Cole, Walker Cooper *, Jim Davis, Jim Fanning, Dee Fondy, Joe Garagiola *, Stan Hack (MANAGER), Warren Hacker, Randy Jackson, Hal Jeffcoat, Ralph Kiner, Johnny Klippstein, Turk Lown, Luis Marquez *, Clyde McCullough, Eddie Miksis, Paul Minner, Vern Morgan, Howie Pollet, Hal Rice *, Don Robertson, Bob Rush, Hank Sauer, Bill Serena, Dale Talbot, El Tappe, Bill Tremel, Jim Willis

LESS THAN 10 GAMES: Bubba Church, Bruce Edwards, Charis Kitsos, Al Lary, John Pyecha, Bob Zick

KEY SIGNATURES: Banks, Kiner, Garagiola.

VALUE: $250

1954 CINCINNATI - Bobby Adams, Fred Baczewski, Ed Bailey, Gus Bell, Bob Borkowski, Rocky Bridges, Jackie Collum, Karl Drews, Nino Escalera, Art Fowler, Jim Greengrass, Chuck Harmon, Howie Judson, Ted Kluszewski, Hobie Landrith, Roy McMillan, Lloyd Merriman, Joe Nuxhall, Harry Perkowski, Bud Podbielan, Wally Post, Moe Savransky, Andy Seminick, Frank Smith, Birdie Tebbetts (MANAGER), Johnny Temple, Corky Valentine, Herm Wehmeier

LESS THAN 10 GAMES: Jim Bolger, Grady Hatton *, Jerry Lane, Johnny Lipon, Dick Murphy, Jim Pearce, Mario Picone, Ken Raffensberger, Cliff Ross, Connie Ryan, George Zuverink

KEY SIGNATURES: Kluszewski, Temple.

VALUE: $220

1954 CLEVELAND - Bobby Avila, Sam Dente, Larry Doby, Bob Feller, Mike Garcia, Billy Glynn, Jim Hegan, Bob Hooper, Dave Hoskins, Art Houtteman, Bob Lemon, Al Lopez (MANAGER), Hank Majeski, Dale Mitchell, Don Mossi, Hal Naragon, Ray Narleski, Hal Newhouser, Dave Philley, Dave Pope, Rudy Regelado, Al Rosen, Al Smith, George Strickland, Vic Wertz *, Wally Westlake, Early Wynn

LESS THAN 10 GAMES: Bob Chakales, Jim Dyck, Luke Easter, Joe Ginsberg, Mickey Grasso, Bob Kennedy *, Rocky Nelson, Jose Santiago, Dick Tomanek

NOTES: Despite Hall of Famers Lopez, Wynn, Lemon and Feller, it is very undervalued, considering winning percentage and personnel.

KEY SIGNATURES: Lopez, Avila, Lemon, Wynn, Feller.

VALUE: $375

1954 DETROIT - Al Aber, Matt Batts *, Wayne Belardi *, Reno Bertoia, Frank Bolling, Ray Boone, Ralph Branca *, Jim Delsing, Walt Dropo, Hoot Evers *, Ned Garver, Ted Gray, Steve Gromek, Fred Hatfield, Ray Herbert, Billy Hoeft, Frank House, Fred Hutchinson (MANAGER), Al Kaline, Charlie King, Charlie Kress *, Harvey Kuenn, Al Lakeman, Don Lund, Dick Marlowe, Bob Miller, Bob Nieman, Johnny Pesky *, Steve Souchock, Bill Tuttle, Red Wilson *, George Zuverink *

LESS THAN 10 GAMES: George Bullard, Dick Donovan, Frank Lary, Walt Streuli, Dick Weik

KEY SIGNATURES: Kuenn, Kaline.

VALUE: $225

1954 MILWAUKEE - Hank Aaron, Joe Adcock, Bill Bruton, Bob Buhl, Lew Burdette, Sammy Calderone, Gene Conley, Del Crandall, Ray Crone, Jack Dittmer, Charlie Grimm (MANAGER), Joey Jay, Ernie Johnson, Dave Jolly, Dave Koslo *, Johnny Logan, Eddie Mathews, Catfish Metkovich, Chet Nichols, Danny O'Connell, Andy Pafko, Phil Paine, Jim Pendleton, Roy Smalley, Warren Spahn, Bobby Thomson, Charlie White, Jim Wilson

LESS THAN 10 GAMES: Charlie Gorin, Billy Queen, Mel Roach, Sibby Sisti

KEY SIGNATURES: Grimm, Adcock, Mathews, Aaron, Spahn, Burdette.

VALUE: $300

1954 NEW YORK (AL) - Hank Bauer, Yogi Berra, Bobby Brown, Harry Byrd, Andy Carey, Bob Cerv, Jerry Coleman, Joe Collins, Whitey Ford, Tom Gorman, Bob Grim, Bob Kuzeva *, Frank Leja, Ed Lopat, Mickey Mantle, Jim McDonald, Gil McDougald, Willie Miranda, Tom Morgan, Irv Noren, Allie Reynolds, Phil Rizzuto, Eddie Robinson, Johnny Sain, Charlie Silvera, Bill Skowron, Enos Slaughter, Casey Stengel (MANAGER), Marlin Stuart *, Gene Woodling

LESS THAN 10 GAMES: Lou Berberet, Ralph Branca *, Tommy Byrne, Woodie Held, Ralph Houk, Jim Konstanty *, Bill Miller, Art Schallock, Gus Triandos, Bob Wiesler

NOTES: Berra (MVP); Grim (ROY).

KEY SIGNATURES: Stengel, Rizzuto, Mantle, Berra, Slaughter, Grim, Ford.

VALUE: $575

1954 NEW YORK (NL) - Johnny Antonelli, Foster Castleman, Al Corwin, Al Dark, Leo Durocher (MANAGER), Hoot Evers *, Billy Gardner, Ruben Gomez, Marv Grissom, Jim Hearn, Bobby Hofman, Monte Irvin, Larry Jansen, Ray Katt, Alex Konikowski, Don Liddle, Whitey Lockman, Sal Maglie, Willie Mays, Windy McCall, Don Mueller, Dusty Rhodes, Ron Samford, Ebba St. Claire, Bill Taylor, Hank Thompson, Wes Westrum, Hoyt Wilhelm, Davey Williams, Al Worthington

LESS THAN 10 GAMES: Joey Amalfitano, Joe Garagiola *, Harvey Gentry, Paul Giel, Bob Lennon, Ray Monzant, Mario Picone *, Eric Rodin, George Spencer

NOTES: World Champions! Mays (MVP).

KEY SIGNATURES: Durocher, Mays, Irvin, Antonelli, Maglie, Wilhelm.

VALUE: $500

1954 PHILADELPHIA - Richie Ashburn, Floyd Baker *, Smoky Burgess, Mel Clark, Murry Dickson, Del Ennis, Bob Greenwood, Granny Hamner, Willie Jones, Ted Kazanski, Thornton Kipper, Jim Konstanty *, Stan Lopata, Bob Micalotta, Bob Miller, Terry Moore (MANAGER), Bobby Morgan, Ron Mrozinski, Steve O'Neill (MANAGER), Steve Ridzik, Robin Roberts, Danny Schell, Curt Simmons, Earl Torgeson, Herm Wehmeier *, Johnny Wyrostek
LESS THAN 10 GAMES: Jim Command, Karl Drews *, Stan Jok *, Johnny Lindell, Gus Niarhos, Stan Palys, Paul Penson, Tom Qualters
KEY SIGNATURES: Ashburn, Burgess, Roberts.

VALUE: $210

1954 PHILADELPHIA (AL) - Joe Astroth, Charlie Bishop, Don Bollweg, Moe Burtschy, Joe DeMaestri, Art Ditmar, Sonny Dixon *, Jim Finigan, Marion Fricano, John Gray, Spook Jacobs, Alex Kellner, Lou Limmer, Morrie Martin *, Ed McGhee *, Arnie Portocarrero, Vic Power, Bill Renna, Jim Robertson, Dutch Romberger, Billy Shantz, Al Sima *, Pete Suder, Joe Taylor, Bob Trice, Elmer Valo, Bill Wilson *, Gus Zernial
LESS THAN 10 GAMES: Eddie Joost (MANAGER), Jack Littrell, Bill Oster, Hal Raether, Dick Rozek, Carl Scheib *, Bobby Shantz, Bill Upton, Ozzie Van Brabent, Lee Wheat
NOTES: Philadelphia Athletics final team! Joost was a player/manager.
KEY SIGNATURES: Finigan.

VALUE: $200

1954 PITTSBURGH - Cal Abrams *, Gair Allie, Toby Atwell, Dick Cole, Walker Cooper *, Bob Friend, Sid Gordon, Dick Hall, Fred Haney (MANAGER), Gail Henley, Johnny Hetki, Vic Janowicz, Vern Law, Paul LaPalme, Dick Littlefield *, Jerry Lynch, Jim Mangan, Luis Marquez *, George O'Donnell, Eddie Pellagrini, Laurin Pepper, Bob Purkey, Hal Rice *, Curt Roberts, Jack Shepard, Bob Skinner, Dick Smith, Max Surkont, Jake Theis, Frank Thomas, Preston Ward, Len Yochim
LESS THAN 10 GAMES: Bill Hall, Cal Hogue, Sam Jethroe, Nellie King, Nick Koback, Joe Page
KEY SIGNATURES: Gordon.

VALUE: $200

1954 ST. LOUIS - Tom Alston, Ralph Beard, Al Brazle, Tom Burgess, Joe Cunningham, Cot Deal, Joe Frazier, Alex Grammas, Harvey Haddix, Solly Hemus, Ray Jablonski, Gordon Jones, Brooks Lawrence, Royce Lint, Peanuts Lowery, Stu Miller, Wally Moon, Stan Musial, Tom Poholsky, Joe Presko, Vic Raschi, Rip Repulski, Del Rice, Bill Sarni, Red Schoendienst, Dick Schofield, Gerry Staley, Eddie Stanky (MANAGER), Ben Wade *, Sal Yvars
LESS THAN 10 GAMES: Steve Bilko *, Pete Castiglione, Willie Greason, Memo Luna, Carl Scheib *, Hal White, Mel Wright
NOTES: Moon (ROY).
KEY SIGNATURES: Schoendienst, Musial, Moon.

VALUE: $225

1954 WASHINGTON - Jim Busby, Sonny Dixon *, Ed Fitz Gerald, Bucky Harris (MANAGER), Mel Hoderlein, Gus Keriazakos, Jim Lemon, Connie Marrero, Mickey McDermott, Bob Oldis, Camilo Pascual, Johnny Pesky *, Bob Porterfield, Pete Runnels, Johnny Schmitz, Spec Shea, Roy Sievers, Jerry Snyder, Bunky Stewart, Chuck Stobbs, Dean Stone, Wayne Terwilliger, Joe Tipton, Tommy Umphlett, Mickey Vernon, Clyde Vollmer, Tom Wright, Eddie Yost

LESS THAN 10 GAMES: Roy Dietzel, Harmon Killebrew, Steve Korcheck, Jesse Levan, Carlos Paula

KEY SIGNATURES: Vernon, Killebrew.

VALUE: $190

1955

1955 New York Yankees

*** = player was traded**

1955 BALTIMORE - Cal Abrams, Hal Brown *, Harry Byrd *, Wayne Causey, Gil Coan *, Billy Cox, Chuck Diering, Harry Dorish *, Jim Dyck, Hoot Evers *, Tommy Gastall, Bob Hale, Don Johnson, Bob Kennedy *, Lou Kretlow, Don Leppert, Ed Lopat *, Hank Majeski *, Freddie Marsh, Jim McDonald, Willie Miranda, Ray Moore, Les Moss *, Bob Nelson, Erv Palica, Dave Philley *, Dave Pope *, Jim Pyburn, Paul Richards (MANAGER), Saul Rogovin *, Art Schallock *, Hal Smith, Gus Triandos, Eddie Waitkus *, Bill Wight *, Jim Wilson, Gene Woodling *, Bobby Young *, George Zuverink *

LESS THAN 10 GAMES: Bob Alexander, Joe Coleman *, Angie Dagres, Don Ferrarese, Ted Gray *, Bob Harrison, Bob Kuzava *, Charlie Locke, Roger Marquis, Charlie Maxwell *, Bill Miller, Duane Pillette, Brooks Robinson, Kal Segrist, Vern Stephens *, Wally Westlake

KEY SIGNATURES: Robinson.

VALUE: $190

1955 BOSTON - Harry Agganis, Tom Brewer, Dick Brodowski, Pete Daley, Ike Delock, Owen Friend *, Billy Goodman, Grady Hatton, Bill Henry, Pinky Higgins (MANAGER), Tom Hurd, Jackie Jensen, Eddie Joost, Leo Kiely, Ellis Kinder, Billy Klaus, Ted Lepcio, Sam Mele *, Willard Nixon, Karl Olson, Mel Parnell, Jimmy Piersall, Gene Stephens, Frank Sullivan, George Susce, Faye Throneberry, Sammy White, Ted Williams, Norm Zauchin

LESS THAN 10 GAMES: Frank Baumann, Milt Bolling, Hal Brown *, Billy Consolo, Hersh Freeman *, Dick Gernert, Russ Kemmerer, Frank Malzone, Jim Pagliaroni, Bob Smith, Haywood Sullivan, Joe Trimble

KEY SIGNATURES: Goodman, Jensen, Piersall, Williams.

VALUE: $230

1955 BROOKLYN - Walt Alston (MANAGER), Sandy Amoros, Don Bessent, Roy Campanella, Roger Craig, Carl Erskine, Carl Furillo, Jim Gilliam, Don Hoak, Gil Hodges, Dixie Howell, Jim Hughes, Frank Kellert, Sandy Koufax, Clem Labine, Billy Loes, Russ Meyer, Walt Moryn, Don Newcombe, Johnny Podres, Pee Wee Reese, Jackie Robinson, Ed Roebuck, George Shuba, Duke Snider, Karl Spooner, Rube Walker, Don Zimmer

LESS THAN 10 GAMES: Joe Black *, Bob Borkowski *, Bert Hamric, Tom Lasorda, Chuck Templeton

NOTES: World Champions (Brooklyn's only one); Campanella (MVP).

KEY SIGNATURES: Hodges, Gilliam, Reese, Labine, Furillo, Snider, Campanella, Newcombe, Robinson, Erskine, Koufax.

VALUE: $1200

MVP = MVP Award winner

1955 CHICAGO (AL) - Bobby Adams *, Jim Brideweser, Jim Busby *, Harry Byrd *, Chico Carrasquel, Gil Coan *, Sandy Consuegra, Clint Courtney *, Dick Donovan, Harry Dorish *, Walt Dropo, Mike Fornieles, Nellie Fox, Johnny Groth *, Jack Harshman, Dixie Howell, Ron Jackson, Connie Johnson, Bob Keegan, George Kell, Bob Kennedy *, Sherm Lollar, Marty Marion (MANAGER), Willard Marshall, Morrie Martin, Ed McGhee, Minnie Minoso, Les Moss *, Bob Nieman, Ron Northey, Billy Pierce, Jim Rivera, Vern Stephens *, Virgil Trucks

LESS THAN 10 GAMES: Earl Battey, Phil Cavaretta, Bob Chakales *, Sammy Esposito, Ted Gray *, Stan Jok, Lloyd Merriman *, Al Papai, Buddy Peterson, Bob Powell, Ed White

KEY SIGNATURES: Fox, Kell, Donovan, Trucks.

VALUE: $250

1955 CHICAGO (NL) - John Andre, Gene Baker, Ernie Banks, Frankie Baumholtz, Jim Bolger, Harry Chiti, Walker Cooper, Jim Davis, Jim Fanning, Dee Fondy, Stan Hack (MANAGER), Warren Hacker, Dave Hillman, Randy Jackson, Hal Jeffcoat, Sam Jones, Don Kaiser, Jim King, Clyde McCullough, Lloyd Merriman *, Eddie Miksis, Paul Minner, Harry Parkowski, Howie Pollet, Bob Rush, Hank Sauer, Bob Speake, Ted Tappe, Bill Tremel

LESS THAN 10 GAMES: Vicente Amor, Bubba Church, Hy Cohen, Owen Friend *, Al Lary, Vern Morgan, El Tappe, Bob Thorpe, Gale Wade

KEY SIGNATURES: Banks.

VALUE: $200

1955 CINCINNATI - Bobby Adams *, Ed Bailey, Matt Batts, Gus Bell, Joe Black *, Bob Borkowski *, Rocky Bridges, Joe Brovia, Smokey Burgess *, Jackie Collum, Art Fowler, Hersh Freeman, Jim Greengrass *, Don Gross, Chuck Harmon, Ray Jablonski, Johnny Klippstein, Ted Kluszewski, Hobie Landrith, Roy McMillan, Sam Mele *, Rudy Minarcin, Joe Nuxhall, Stan Palys *, Bud Podbielan, Wally Post, Steve Ridzik *, Al Silvera, Milt Smith, Gerry Staley, Birdie Tebbetts (MANAGER), Johnny Temple, Bob Thurman, Corky Valentine,

LESS THAN 10 GAMES: Fred Baczewski, Maury Fisher, Glen Gorbous *, Bob Hazle, Bob Hooper, Jerry Lane, Jim Pearce, Andy Seminick *

KEY SIGNATURES: Kluszewski, Burgess.

VALUE: $225

1955 CLEVELAND - Joe Altobelli, Bobby Avila, Sam Dente, Larry Doby, Hoot Evers *, Ferris Fain *, Bob Feller, Hank Foiles, Mike Garcia, Billy Harrell, Jim Hegan, Art Houtteman, Ralph Kiner, Bob Lemon, Stu Locklin, Al Lopez (MANAGER), Sal Maglie *, Hank Majeski *, Dale Mitchell, Don Mossi, Hal Naragon, Ray Narleski, Dave Philley *, Dave Pope *, Rudy Regalado, Al Rosen, Jose Santiago, Herb Score, Al Smith, George Strickland, Vic Wertz, Wally Westlake *, Bill Wight *, Gene Woodling *, Early Wynn, Bobby Young *,

LESS THAN 10 GAMES: Hank Aquirre, Rocky Colavito, Bud Daley, Ted Gray *, Kenny Kuhn, Hal Newhouser, Stan Pawloski, Harry Simpson *

NOTES: Score (ROY).

KEY SIGNATURES: Lopez, Smith, Kiner, Colavito, Lemon, Wynn, Score, Feller.

VALUE: $300

1955 DETROIT - Al Aber, Reno Bertoia, Babe Birrer, Ray Boone, Jim Bunning, Joe Coleman *, Leo Cristante, Jim Delsing, Ferris Fain *, Paul Foytack, Ned Garver, Steve Gromek, Bucky Harris (MANAGER), Fred Hatfield, Billy Hoeft, Frank House, Al Kaline, Harvey Kuenn, Frank Lary, Duke Maas, Harry Malmberg, Charlie Maxwell *, Bubba Phillips, Jack Phillips, Jay Porter, Jim Small, Earl Torgeson *, Bill Tuttle, Red Wilson, George Zuverink *

LESS THAN 10 GAMES: Wayne Belardi, Bill Black, Van Fletcher, Ben Flowers *, Bill Froats, Charlie King, Dick Marlowe, Bob Miller, Ron Samford, Bob Schultz, Steve Souchock, Walt Streuli

KEY SIGNATURES: Kuenn, Kaline, Bunning.

VALUE: $225

1955 KANSAS CITY - Joe Astroth, Ewell Blackwell, Don Bollweg, Lou Boudreau (MANAGER), Clete Boyer, Cloyd Boyer, Art Ceccarelli, Joe DeMaestri, Art Ditmar, Sonny Dixon, Jim Finigan, Marion Fricano, Tom Gorman, Bill Harrington, Ray Herbert, Spook Jacobs, Alex Kellner, Dick Kryhoski, Jack Littrell, Hector Lopez, A. Portocarrero, Vic Power, Vic Raschi, Bill Renna, Johnny Sain, Jerry Schypinski, Billy Shantz, Bobby Shantz, Harry Simpson, Enox Slaughter, Lou Sleater, Bob Spicer, Bill Stewart, Pete Suder, Bob Trice, Elmer Valo, Ozzie Van Brabant, Lee Wheat, Bill Wilson, Bill Wilson, Gus Zernial

LESS THAN 10 GAMES: Hal Bevan, Charlie Bishop, Moe Burtschy, Glen Cox, Walt Craddock, Alex George, John Gray, Gus Keriazakos, John Kume, Eric MacKenzie, Don Plarski, Jim Robertson, Tom Saffell *

NOTES: Kansas City's first year!

KEY SIGNATURES: Boudreau, Slaughter.

VALUE: $210

1955 MILWAUKEE - Hank Aaron, Joe Adcock, Bill Bruton, Bob Buhl, Lew Burdette, Gene Conley, Del Crandall, Ray Crone, George Crowe, Jack Dittmer, Charlie Grimm (MANAGER), Joey Jay, Ernie Johnson, Dave Jolly, Johnny Logan, Eddie Mathews, Chet Nichols, Danny O'Connell, Andy Pafko, Phil Paine, Del Rice *, Humberto Robinson, Warren Spahn, Chuck Tanner, Bennie Taylor, Bobby Thomson, Roberto Vargas, Charlie White

LESS THAN 10 GAMES: John Edelman, Charlie Gorin, Dave Koslo, Jim Pendleton, Bob Roselli

KEY SIGNATURES: Mathews, Aaron, Adcock, Spahn, Burdette.

VALUE: $325

1955 NEW YORK (AL) - Hank Bauer, Yogi Berra, Tommy Byrne, Andy Carey, Tommy Carroll, Bob Cerv, Jerry Coleman, Rip Coleman, Joe Collins, Whitey Ford, Bob Grim, Elston Howard, Billy Hunter, Jim Konstanty, Johnny Kucks, Don Larsen, Ed Lopat *, Mickey Mantle, Billy Martin, Gill McDougald, Tom Morgan, Irv Noren, Bobby Richardson, Phil Rizzuto, Eddie Robinson, Charlie Silvera, Bill Skowron, Enos Slaughter *, Casey Stengel (MANAGER), Tom Sturdivant, Bob Turley, Bob Wiesler

LESS THAN 10 GAMES: Lou Berberet, Johnny Blanchard, Ted Gray *, Frank Leja, Johnny Sain *, Art Schallock *, Gerry Staley *, Dick Tettelbach, Marv Throneberry

NOTES: Berra (MVP).

KEY SIGNATURES: Stengel, Mantle, Slaughter, Howard, Martin, Berra, Rizzuto, Ford, Larsen.

VALUE: $725

MVP = MVP Award winner

1955 NEW YORK (NL) - Joey Amalfitano, Johnny Antonelli, Foster Castleman, Al Corwin, Al Dark, Leo Durocher (MANAGER), Billy Gardner, Paul Giel, Ruben Gomez, Sid Gordon *, Marv Grissom, Gail Harris, Jim Hearn, Bobby Hofman, Monte Irvin, Ray Katt, Don Liddle, Whitey Lockman, Sal Maglie *, Willie Mays, Windy McCall, Ray Monzant, Don Mueller, Dusty Rhodes, Bill Taylor, Wayne Terwilliger, Hank Thompson, Wes Westrum, Hoyt Wilhelm, Davey Williams

LESS THAN 10 GAMES: Pete Burnside, Gil Coan *, Mickey Grasso, George Spencer

KEY SIGNATURES: Durocher, Mays, Irvin, Antonelli.

VALUE: $325

1955 PHILADELPHIA - Richie Ashburn, Marv Blaylock, Mel Clark, Murry Dickson, Del Ennis, Glen Gorbous *, Jim Greengrass *, Granny Hamner, Willie Jones, Thornton Kipper, Bob Kuzava *, Stan Lopata, Lynn Lovenguth, Peanuts Lowery, Jack Meyer, Bob Miller, Bobby Morgan, Ron Mrozinski, Ron Negray, Stan Palys *, Robin Roberts, Saul Rogovin *, Andy Seminick *, Curt Simmons, Roy Smalley, Mayo Smith (MANAGER), Earl Torgeson *, Eddie Waitkus *, Herm Wehmeier

LESS THAN 10 GAMES: Floyd Baker, Bob Bowman, Smoky Burgess *, Dave Cole, Jim Command, John Easton, Bob Greenwood, Ted Kazanski, Bob Micelotta, Gus Niarhos, Jim Owens, Steve Ridzik *, Danny Schell, Jack Spring, Fred Van Dusen, Jim Westlake

KEY SIGNATURES: Ashburn, Roberts.

VALUE: $200

1955 PITTSBURGH - Toby Atwell, Roberto Clemente, Dick Cole, Lino Donoso, Roy Face, Gene Freese, George Freese, Bob Friend, Sid Gordon *, Dick Groat, Dick Hall, Fred Haney (MANAGER), Nellie King, Ron Kline, Vern Law, Dick Littlefield, Dale Long, Jerry Lynch, Roman Mejias, Felipe Montemayor, Eddie O'Brien, Johnny O'Brien, Laurin Pepper, Hardy Peterson, Bob Purkey, Tom Saffell *, Jack Shepard, Max Surkont, Frank Thomas, Ben Wade, Preston Ward

LESS THAN 10 GAMES: Bill Bell, Roger Bowman, Al Grunwald, Nick Kobeck, Paul Martin, Johnny Powers, Curt Roberts, Dick Smith, Earl Smith, Red Swanson, Jake Theis, Fred Waters

KEY SIGNATURES: Groat, Clemente, Friend.

VALUE: $600

1955 ST. LOUIS - Tom Alston, Luis Arroyo, Ken Boyer, Nels Burbrink, Harry Elliott, Joe Frazier, Alex Grammas, Harvey Haddix, Solly Hemus, Larry Jackson, Gordon Jones, Brooks Lawrence, Paul LaPalme, Johnny Mackinson, Herb Moford, Wally Moon, Stan Musial, Tom Poholsky, Rip Repulski, Del Rice *, Bill Sarni, Willard Schmidt, Red Schoendienst, Dick Schofield, Barney Schultz, Frank Smith, Ed Stanky (MANAGER), Bobby Stephenson, Bobby Tiefenauer, Bill Virdon, Harry Walker (MANAGER), Pete Whisenant, Floyd Wooldridge, Mel Wright

LESS THAN 10 GAMES: Don Blasingame, Ben Flowers *, Al Gettel, Tony Jacobs, Lindy McDaniel, Dick Rand, Vic Raschi *

NOTES: Virdon (ROY); Walker was a player/manager.

KEY SIGNATURES: Musial, Schoendienst, Boyer, Virdon, Haddix.

VALUE: $225

ROY = Rookie of the Year

1955 WASHINGTON - Ted Abernathy, Julio Becquer, Jim Busby *, Bob Chakales *, Clint Courtney *, Juan Delis, Chuck Dressen (MANAGER), Bruce Edwards, Ed Fitz Gerald, Johnny Groth *, Harmon Killebrew, Bobby Kline, Steve Korcheck, Jim Lemon, Jesse Levan, Mickey McDermott, Ernie Oravetz, Camilo Pascual, Carlos Paula, Bob Porterfield, Pedro Ramos, Tony Roig, Pete Runnels, Johnny Schmitz, Jerry Schoonmaker, Spec Shea, Roy Sievers, Jerry Snyder, Chuck Stobbs, Dean Stone, Tommy Umphlett, Joe Valdivielso, Mickey Vernon, Tom Wright, Eddie Yost

LESS THAN 10 GAMES: Webbo Clarke, Bill Currie, Vince Gonzales, Dick Hyde, Bobby Kline, Bob Oldis, Bunky Stewart

KEY SIGNATURES: Vernon, Killebrew.

VALUE: $175

1956

1956 New York Yankees

*** = player was traded**

1956 BALTIMORE - Bobby Adams, Bob Boyd, Hal Brown, Wayne Causey, Chuck Diering, Harry Dorish *, Jim Dyck *, Hoot Evers *, Don Ferrarese, Mike Fornieles, Tito Francona, Joe Frazier *, Billy Gardner, Tommy Gastall, Joe Ginsberg *, Bob Hale, Grady Hatton *, Connie Johnson, George Kell *, Billy Loes *, Freddie Marsh, Willie Miranda, Ray Moore, Bob Nelson, Bob Nieman *, Erv Palica, Dave Philley *, Dave Pope *, Jim Pyburn, Brooks Robinson, Hal Smith *, Gus Triandos, Bill Wight, Dick Williams *, George Zuverink

LESS THAN 10 GAMES: Charlie Beamon, Fred Besana, Babe Birrer, Sandy Conquegra *, Bob Harrison, Mel Held, Morrie Martin *, Ron Moeller, Billy O'Dell, Paul Richards (MANAGER), Johnny Schmitz *, Gordie Sundin, George Werley, Jim Wilson

NOTES: Gastall died 9/20/56.

KEY SIGNATURES: Kell, Gastall, Robinson.

VALUE: $200

1956 BOSTON - Milt Bolling, Tom Brewer, Don Buddin, Billy Consolo, Pete Daley, Ike Delock, Harry Dorish, Dick Gernert, Billy Goodman, Pinky Higgins (MANAGER), Tom Hurd, Jackie Jensen, Leo Kiely, Billy Klaus, Ted Lepcio, Frank Malzone, Willard Nixon, Mel Parnell, Jimmy Piersall, Bob Porterfield, Dave Sisler, Gene Stephens, Frank Sullivan, George Susce, Faye Throneberry, Mickey Vernon, Sammy White, Ted Williams, Norm Zauchin

LESS THAN 10 GAMES: Frank Baumann, Grady Hatton *, Marty Keough, Gene Mauch, Rudy Minarcin, Johnny Schmitz

KEY SIGNATURES: Vernon, Jensen, Williams.

VALUE: $230

1956 BROOKLYN - Walter Alston (MANAGER), Sandy Amoros, Don Bessent, Roy Campanella, Gino Cimoli, Roger Craig, Don Drysdale, Carl Erskine, Chico Fernandez, Carl Furillo, Jim Gilliam, Gil Hodges, Randy Jackson, Sandy Koufax, Clem Labine, Ken Lehman, Sal Maglie *, Dale Mitchell *, Charlie Neal, Rocky Nelson *, Don Newcombe, Pee Wee Reese, Jackie Robinson, Ed Roebuck, Duke Snider, Rube Walker, Don Zimmer

LESS THAN 10 GAMES: Bob Aspromonte, Ralph Branca, Bob Darnell, Don Demeter, Dixie Howell, Jim Hughes, Billy Loes, Chuck Templeton, Dick Williams *

NOTES: Newcombe was the first-ever winner of the Cy Young Award and also won the MVP.

KEY SIGNATURES: Hodges, Gilliam, Reese, Furillo, Snider, Campanella, Koufax, Newcombe, Erskine, Drysdale, Robinson.

VALUE: $750

1956 CHICAGO (AL) - Luis Aparacio, Jim Brideweser *, Sandy Consuegra *, Jim Delsing *, Larry Doby, Dick Donovan, Walt Dropo, Sammy Esposito, Nellie Fox, Jack Harshman, Fred Hatfield *, Dixie Howell, Ron Jackson, Bob Keegan, George Kell *, Ellis Kinder *, Paul LaPalme *, Sherm Lollar, Marty Marion (MANAGER), Morrie Martin *, Minnie Minoso, Les Moss, Bob Nieman *, Ron Northey, Dave Philley *, Bubba Phillips, Billy Pierce, Howie Pollet *, Jim Rivera, Gerry Staley *, Jim Wilson *

LESS THAN 10 GAMES: Cal Abrams, Earl Battey, Harry Byrd, Jerry Dahlke, Jim Derrington, Bill Fischer, Mike Fornieles *, Connie Johnson *, Bob Kennedy *, Dick Marlowe *, Jim McDonald

NOTES: Aparicio (ROY).

KEY SIGNATURES: Fox, Aparicio, Kell.

VALUE: $250

ROY = Rookie of the Year

1956 CHICAGO (NL) - Gene Baker, Ernie Banks, Jim Brosnan, Harry Chiti, Jim Davis, Solly Drake, Dee Fondy, Stan Hack (MANAGER), Warren Hacker, Don Hoak, Jim Hughes *, Monte Irvin, Sam Jones, Don Kaiser, Frank Kellert, Jerry Kindall, Jim King, Hobie Landrith, Turk Lown, Clyde McCullough, Russ Meyer *, Eddie Miksis, Paul Minner, Walt Moryn, Bob Rush, Vito Valentinetti, Gale Wade, Pete Whisenant, Ed Winceniak

LESS THAN 10 GAMES: Johnny Briggs, Moe Drabowski, Jim Fanning, Owen Friend, Dave Hillman, Richie Myers, George Piktuzis, El Tappe, Bill Tremel

KEY SIGNATURES: Banks, Irvin.

VALUE: $200

1956 CINCINNATI - Tom Acker, Ed Bailey, Gus Bell, Joe Black, Rocky Bridges, Smoky Burgess, George Crowe, Jim Dyck *, Art Fowler, Joe Frazier *, Hersh Freeman, Alex Grammas *, Don Gross, Chuck Harmon *, Ray Jablonski, Hal Jeffcoat, Johnny Klippstein, Ted Kluzewski, Brooks Lawrence, Paul LaPalme *, Roy McMillan, Joe Nuxhall, Stan Palys, Wally Post, Frank Robinson, Johnny Temple, Bob Thurman

LESS THAN 10 GAMES: Bobby Balcena, Matt Batts, Bruce Edwards, Curt Flood, Larry Jansen, Bill Kennedy, Russ Meyer *, John Oldham, Pat Scantlebury, Art Schult, Al Silvera, Frank Smith, Birdie Tebbetts (MANAGER)

NOTES: Robinson (ROY).

KEY SIGNATURES: Kluszewski, Robinson.

VALUE: $275

1956 CLEVELAND - Hank Aguirre, Earl Averill, Bobby Avila, Jim Busby, Joe Caffie, Chico Carrasquel, Rocky Colavito, Bud Daley, Bob Feller, Mike Garcia, Jim Hegan, Art Houtteman, Kenny Kuhn, Bob Lemon, Al Lopez (MANAGER), Cal McLish, Sam Mele, Dale Mitchell *, Don Mossi, Hal Naragon, Ray Narleski, Dave Pope *, Rudy Regalado, Al Rosen, Herb Score, Al Smith, George Strickland, Preston Ward *, Vic Wertz, Gene Woodling, Early Wynn

LESS THAN 10 GAMES: Hoot Evers *, Hank Foiles *, Stu Locklin, Sal Maglie *, Bobby Young

KEY SIGNATURES: Lopez, Colavito, Lemon, Wynn, Score, Feller.

VALUE: $275

1956 DETROIT - Al Aber, Wayne Belardi, Reno Bertoia, Frank Bolling, Ray Boone, Jim Brideweser *, Jim Bunning, Jim Delsing *, Paul Foytack, Steve Gromek, Bucky Harris (MANAGER), Buddy Hicks, Billy Hoeft, Frank House, Al Kaline, Bob Kennedy *, Harvey Kuenn, Frank Lary, Duke Maas, Walt Masterson, Charlie Maxwell, Bob Miller, Jack Phillips, Jay Porter, Jim Small, Earl Torgeson, Virgil Trucks, Bill Tuttle, Red Wilson

LESS THAN 10 GAMES: Bill Black, Jim Brady, Ned Garver, Fred Hatfield *, Gene Host, Charlie King, Charlie Lau, Dick Marlowe *, Walt Streuli, Pete Wojey, Hal Woodeshick

KEY SIGNATURES: Kuenn, Kaline, Bunning.

VALUE: $225

1956 KANSAS CITY - Mike Baxes, Lou Boudreau (MANAGER), Clete Boyer, Wally Burnette, Moe Burtschy, Jack Crimian, Joe DeMaestri, Art Ditmar, Jim Finigan, Joe Ginsberg *, Tom Gorman, Johnny Groth, Bill Harrington, Troy Herriage, Spook Jacobs *, Alex Kellner, Lou Kretlow, Tom Lasorda, Hector Lopez, Jack McMahan *, Al Pilarcik, Jim Pisoni, Rance Pless, Vic Power, Bill Renna, Eddie Robinson *, Bobby Shantz, Harry Simpson, Lou Skizas *, Enos Slaughter *, Hal Smith *, Tim Thompson, Gus Zernial

LESS THAN 10 GAMES: Joe Astroth, Bill Bradford, George Brunet, Art Ceccarelli, Glenn Cox, Walt Craddock, Carl Duser, Dave Melton, Arnie Portocarrero, Jose Santiago, Bob Spicer, Elmer Valo *

KEY SIGNATURES: Boudreau, Slaughter, Lasorda.

VALUE: $225

1956 MILWAUKEE - Hank Aaron, Joe Adcock, Toby Atwell *, Bill Bruton, Bob Buhl, Lew Burdette, Gene Conley, Wes Covington, Del Crandall, Ray Crone, Jack Dittmer, Charlie Grimm (MANAGER), Fred Haney (MANAGER), Ernie Johnson, Dave Jolly, Johnny Logan, Felix Mantilla, Eddie Mathews, Red Murff, Danny O'Connell, Andy Pafko, Jim Pendleton, Taylor Phillips, Del Rice, Lou Sleater, Warren Spahn, Chuck Tanner, Bobby Thomson, Frank Torre, Bob Trowbridge

LESS THAN 10 GAMES: Earl Hersh, Chet Nichols, Phil Paine, Humberto Robinson, Bob Roselli

KEY SIGNATURES: Grimm, Adcock, Mathews, Aaron, Spahn, Burdette.

VALUE: $330

1956 NEW YORK (AL) - Hank Bauer, Yogi Berra, Tommy Byrne, Andy Carey, Tommy Carroll, Bob Cerv, Jerry Coleman, Rip Coleman, Joe Collins, Whitey Ford, Bob Grim, Elston Howard, Billy Hunter, Johnny Kucks, Don Larsen, Jerry Lumpe, Mickey Mantle, Billy Martin, Mickey McDermott, Gil McDougald, Tom Morgan, Irv Noren, Phil Rizzuto, Eddie Robinson *, Norm Siebern, Bill Skowron, Enos Slaughter *, Casey Stengel (MANAGER), Tom Sturdivant, Bob Turley, Ted Wilson *

LESS THAN 10 GAMES: Jim Coates, Sonny Dixon, Jim Konstanty *, Bobby Richardson, Charlie Silvera, Lou Skizas *, Gerry Staley *, Ralph Terry
NOTES: World Champions! Mantle won the Triple Crown and MVP.
KEY SIGNATURES: Stengel, Martin, Mantle, Howard, Rizzuto, Slaughter, Berra, Bauer, Ford.

VALUE: $800

1956 NEW YORK (NL) - John Antonelli, Jackie Brandt *, Ed Bressoud, Foster Castleman, Al Dark *, Ruben Gomez, Marv Grissom, Gail Harris, Jim Hearn, Bobby Hofman, Ray Katt *, Bob Lennon, Don Liddle, Dick Littlefield *, Whitey Lockman *, Jim Mangan, Joe Margoneri, Willie Mays, Windy McCall, Don Mueller, Dusty Rhodes, Steve Ridzik, Bill Sarni *, Red Schoendienst *, Daryl Spencer, Wayne Terwilliger, Hank Thompson, Wes Westrum, Bill White, Hoyt Wilhelm, George Wilson *, Al Worthington
LESS THAN 10 GAMES: Gil Coan, Jim Constable, Mike McCormick, Ray Monzant, Bill Rigney (MANAGER), Max Surkont *, Bill Taylor, Ozzie Virgil, Roy Wright
KEY SIGNATURES: White, Schoendienst, Mays, Antonelli.

VALUE: $275

1956 PHILADELPHIA - Richie Ashburn, Frank Baumholtz, Marv Blaylock, Mack Burk, Del Ennis, Ben Flowers *, Glen Gorbous, Jim Greengrass, Harvey Haddix *, Granny Hamner, Solly Hemus *, Willie Jones, Ted Kazanski, Joe Lonnett, Stan Lopata, Jack Meyer, Bob Miller, Stu Miller *, Ron Negray, Jim Owens, Duane Pillette, Robin Roberts, Saul Rogovin, Andy Saminick, Curt Simmons, Roy Smalley, Elmer Valo *
LESS THAN 10 GAMES: Ed Bouchee, Bob Bowman, Murry Dickson *, Dick Farrell, Angelo LiPetri, Bobby Morgan *, Bob Ross, Jack Sanford, Mayo Smith (MANAGER), Herm Wehmeier *, Wally Westlake *
KEY SIGNATURES: Ashburn, Roberts.

VALUE: $180

1956 PITTSBURGH - Luis Arroyo, Toby Atwell *, Bobby Bragan (MANAGER), Roberto Clemente, Dick Cole, Bobby Del Greco *, Roy Face, Hank Foiles *, Gene Freese, Bob Friend, Dick Groat, Dick Hall, Spook Jacobs *, Nellie King, Ron Kline, Danny Kravitz, Vern Law, Dale Long, Jerry Lynch, Bill Mazeroski, Jack McMahan *, George Munger, Cholly Naranjo, Johnny O'Brien, Laurin Pepper, Howie Pollet *, Johnny Powers, Curt Roberts, Jack Shepard, Bob Skinner, Frank Thomas, Bill Virdon *, Lee Walls, Preston Ward *, Fred Waters
LESS THAN 10 GAMES: Lino Donoso, Bob Garber, Bill Hall, Dick Littlefield *, Eddie O'Brien, Johnny O'Brien, Bob Purkey, Max Surkont, Red Swanson
KEY SIGNATURES: Mazeroski, Groat, Clemente, Virdon.

VALUE: $640

1956 ST. LOUIS - Don Blasingame, Bob Blaylock, Ken Boyer, Jackie Brandt *, Jackie Collum, Walker Cooper, Al Dark *, Bobby Del Greco *, Murry Dickson *, Joe Frazier *, Chuck Harmon *, Grady Hatton *, Fred Hutchinson (MANAGER), Larry Jackson, Ray Katt *, Ellis Kinder *, Jim Konstanty *, Don Liddle *, Whitey Lockman *, Lindy McDaniel, Vinegar Bend Mizell, Wally Moon, Bobby Morgan *, Stan Musial, Rocky Nelson *, Charlie Peete, Tom Poholsky, Rip Repulski, Bill Sarni *, Hank Sauer, Willard Schmidt, Red Schoendienst *, Dick Schofield, Hal Smith, Bill Virdon *, Herm Wehmeier *

LESS THAN 10 GAMES: Tom Alston, Joe Cunningham, Ben Flowers *, Alex Grammas *, Harvey Haddix *, Solly Hemus *, Gordon Jones, Paul LaPalme *, Dick Littlefield *, Stu Miller *, Max Surkont *

NOTES: Peete died Nov. 27, 1956.

KEY SIGNATURES: Musial, Boyer, Schoendienst, Peete.

VALUE: $240

1956 WASHINGTON - Lou Berberet, Bud Byerly, Bob Chakales, Tex Clevenger, Clint Courtney, Chuck Dressen (MANAGER), Ed Fitz Gerald, Hal Griggs, Connie Grob, Whitey Herzog, Harmon Killebrew, Jim Lemon, Lyle Luttrell, Karl Olson, Ernie Oravetz, Camilo Pascual, Carlos Paula, Herb Plews, Pedro Ramos, Tony Roig, Pete Runnels, Roy Sievers, Jerry Snyder, Bunky Stewart, Chuck Stobbs, Dean Stone, Dick Tettelbach, Joss Valdivielso, Bob Wiesler, Eddie Yost

LESS THAN 10 GAMES: Ted Abernathy, Dick Brodowski, Evelio Hernandez, Tom Wright

KEY SIGNATURES: Killebrew.

VALUE: $180

1957

1957 N.L. Cy Young Award winner Warren Spahn

*** = player was traded**

1957 BALTIMORE - Bob Boyd, Jim Brideweser, Hal Brown, Jim Busby *, Wayne Causey, Art Ceccarelli, Joe Durham, Mike Fornieles *, Tito Francona, Billy Gardner, Joe Ginsberg, Billy Goodman *, Lenny Green, Bob Hale, Connie Johnson, George Kell, Ken Lehman *, Billy Loes, Willie Miranda, Ray Moore, Bob Nelson, Bob Nieman, Billy O'Dell, Al Pilarcik, Carl Powis, Jim Pyburn, Paul Richards (MANAGER), Brooks Robinson, Gus Triandos, Jerry Walker, Bill Wight, Dick Williams *, Frank Zupo, George Zuverink

LESS THAN 10 GAMES: Charlie Beamon, Sandy Consuegra *, Don Ferrarese, Art Houtteman *, Eddie Miksis *, Milt Pappas, Tom Patton, Buddy Peterson, Eddie Robinson *, Dizzy Trout

KEY SIGNATURES: Kell, Robinson.

VALUE: $190

1957 BOSTON - Ken Aspromonte, Tom Brewer, Bob Chakales *, Billy Consolo, Pete Daley, Ike Delock, Mike Fornieles *, Dick Gernert, Billy Goodman *, Pinky Higgins (MANAGER), Jackie Jensen, Billy Klaus, Ted Lepcio, Frank Malzone, Gene Mauch, Rudy Minarcin, Willard Nixon, Jimmy Piersall, Bob Porterfield, Dave Sisler, Gene Stephens, Dean Stone *, Frank Sullivan, George Susce, Mickey Vernon, Murray Wall, Sammy White, Ted Williams, Norm Zauchin

LESS THAN 10 GAMES: Frank Baumann, Milt Bolling *, Russ Kemmerer *, Marty Keough, Russ Meyer, Jack Spring, Haywood Sullivan, Faye Throneberry *

KEY SIGNATURES: Jensen, Williams, Vernon.

VALUE: $225

1957 BROOKLYN - Walt Alston (MANAGER), Sandy Amoros, Don Bessent, Roy Campanella, Gino Cimoli, Roger Craig, Don Drysdale, Carl Erskine, Carl Furillo, Jim Gilliam, Gil Hodges, Randy Jackson, Bob Kennedy *, Sandy Koufax, Clem Labine, Sal Maglie *, Danny McDevitt, Charlie Neal, Don Newcombe, Johnny Podres, Pee Wee Reese, Ed Roebuck, Johnny Roseboro, Duke Snider, Elmer Valo, Rube Walker, Don Zimmer

LESS THAN 10 GAMES: Jackie Collum *, Don Elston *, Jim Gentile, Bill Harris, Fred Kipp, Ken Lehman *, Rod Miller, Joe Pignatano, Rene Valdes

NOTES: Campanella's final season.

KEY SIGNATURES: Hodges, Gilliam, Reese, Furillo, Snider, Campanella, Koufax, Drysdale.

VALUE: $500

1957 CHICAGO (AL) - Luis Aparicio, Earl Battey, Ted Beard, Jim Derrington, Larry Doby, Dick Donovan, Walt Dropo, Sammy Esposito, Bill Fischer, Nellie Fox, Jack Harshman, Fred Hatfield, Dixie Howell, Ron Jackson, Bob Keegan, Jim Landis, Paul LaPalme, Sherm Lollar, Jim McDonald, Minnie Minoso, Les Moss, Ron Northey *, Dave Philley *, Bubba Phillips, Billy Pierce, Jim Rivera, Gerry Staley, Earl Torgeson *, Jim Wilson

LESS THAN 10 GAMES: Jim Hughes, Bob Kennedy *, Ellis Kinder, Barry Latman, Al Lopez (MANAGER), Stover McIlwain, Bob Powell, Don Rudolph

KEY SIGNATURES: Lopez, Fox, Aparicio.

VALUE: $250

1957 CHICAGO (NL) - Bobby Adams, Gene Baker *, Ernie Banks, Jim Bolger, Jim Brosnan, Bobby Del Greco *, Moe Drabowsky, Dick Drott, Don Elston *, Frank Ernaga, Jim Fanning, Dee Fondy *, Eddie Haas, Dave Hillman, Don Kaiser, Jerry Kindall, Dick Littlefield, Jack Littrell, Dale Long *, Turk Lown, Bobby Morgan *, Walt Moryn, Cal Neeman, Tom Poholsky, Bob Rush, Bob Scheffing (MANAGER), Charlie Silvera, Bob Speaks, Chuck Tanner *, Lee Walls *, Bob Will, Ed Winceniak, Casey Wise

LESS THAN 10 GAMES: Bob Anderson, Johnny Briggs, Jackie Collum *, Johnny Goryl, Glen Hobbie, Bob Lennon, Gordon Massa, Ed Mayer, Ed Mickelson, Elmer Singleton, Vito Valentinetti *, Jim Woods
KEY SIGNATURES: Banks.

VALUE: $200

1957 CINCINNATI - Tom Acker, Ed Bailey, Gus Bell, Smoky Burgess, George Crowe, Art Fowler, Hersh Freeman, Alex Grammas, Don Gross, Warren Hacker *, Bobby Henrich, Don Hoak, Hal Jeffcoat, Johnny Klippstein, Ted Kluszewski, Brooks Lawrence, Jerry Lynch, Roy McMillan, Joe Nuxhall, Wally Post, Frank Robinson, Raul Sanchez, Art Schult *, Joe Taylor, Birdie Tebbetts (MANAGER), Johnny Temple, Bob Thurman, Pete Whisenant
LESS THAN 10 GAMES: Vicente Amor, Rocky Bridges *, Dutch Dotterer, Bobby Durnbaugh, Curt Flood, Jay Hook, Bill Kennedy, Claude Osteen, Don Pavletich, Bud Podbielan, Charlie Rabe, Dave Skaugstad
KEY SIGNATURES: Robinson, Kluszewski.

VALUE: $275

1957 CLEVELAND - Hank Aguirre, Joe Altobelli, Bobby Avila, Dick Brown, Jim Busby *, Joe Caffie, Chico Carrasquel, Rocky Colavito, Bud Daley, Mike Garcia, Billy Harrell, Jim Hegan, Kenny Kuhn, Bob Lemon, Roger Maris, Cal McLish, Don Mossi, Hal Naragon, Ray Narleski, Russ Nixon, Stan Pitula, Larry Raines, Eddie Robinson *, Al Smith, George Strickland, Dick Tomanek, Bob Usher *, Vito Valentinetti *, Preston Ward, Vic Wertz, Dick Williams *, Gene Woodling, Early Wynn
LESS THAN 10 GAMES: Bob Alexander, Kerby Farrell (MANAGER), John Gray, Art Houtteman *, Herb Score, Hoyt Wilhelm *
KEY SIGNATURES: Colavito, Maris, Wynn, Wilhelm.

VALUE: $225

1957 DETROIT - Al Aber *, Reno Bertoia, Frank Bolling, Ray Boone, Steve Boros, Jim Bunning, Harry Byrd, Jack Dittmer, Jim Finigan, Paul Foytack, Steve Gromek, Johnny Groth *, Billy Hoeft, Frank House, Al Kaline, Harvey Kuenn, Frank Lary, Don Lee, Duke Maas, Charlie Maxwell, Bobo Osborne, Dave Philley *, Jay Porter, Eddie Robinson *, Ron Samford, Lou Sleator, Jim Small, Jack Tighe (MANAGER), Earl Torgeson *, Bill Tuttle, Red Wilson
LESS THAN 10 GAMES: Mel Clark, Jack Crimian, Chuck Daniel, Karl Olson *, Jack Phillips, Joe Presko, Bob Shaw, Jim Stump, Bill Taylor *, George Thomas, John Tsitouris, Pete Wojey, Tom Yewcic
KEY SIGNATURES: Kuenn, Kaline, Bunning.

VALUE: $225

1957 KANSAS CITY - Lou Boudreau (MANAGER), Clete Boyer, Wally Burnette, Bob Cerv, Rip Coleman, Glenn Cox, Harry Craft (MANAGER), Joe DeMaestri, Ryne Duren, Ned Garver, Tom Gorman, Milt Graff, Johnny Groth *, Woodie Held *, Gene Host, Billy Hunter, Alex Kellner, Hector Lopez, Billy Martin *, Bob Martyn, Mickey McDermott, Tom Morgan, Irv Noren *, Jim Pisoni, Arnie Portocarrero, Vic Power, Harry Simpson *, Lou Skizas, Hal Smith, Ralph Terry *, Tim Thompson, Virgil Trucks, Jack Urban, Gus Zernial

LESS THAN 10 GAMES: Al Aber *, Ed Blake, George Brunet, Dave Hill, Hal Raether, Harry Taylor

KEY SIGNATURES: Martin.

VALUE: $225

1957 MILWAUKEE - Hank Aaron, Joe Adcock, Bill Bruton, Bob Buhl, Lew Burdette, Dick Cole, Gene Conley, Wes Covington, Del Crandall, Ray Crone *, John DeMerit, Fred Haney (MANAGER), Bob Hazle, Ernie Johnson, Dave Jolly, Nippy Jones, Johnny Logan, Bobby Malkmus, Felix Mantilla, Eddie Mathews, Don McMahon, Red Murff, Danny O'Connell *, Andy Pafko, Taylor Phillips, Juan Pizarro, Del Rice, Carl Sawatski, Red Schoendienst *, Warren Spahn, Chuck Tanner *, Bobby Thomson *, Frank Torre, Bob Trowbridge

LESS THAN 10 GAMES: Harry Hanebrink, Joey Jay, Phil Paine, Mel Roach, Ray Shearer, Hawk Taylor

NOTES: World Champions! Spahn (Cy Young); Aaron (MVP).

KEY SIGNATURES: Schoendienst, Mathews, Aaron, Adcock, Spahn.

VALUE: $450

1957 NEW YORK (AL) - Hank Bauer, Yogi Berra, Tommy Byrne, Andy Carey, Al Cicotte, Jerry Coleman, Joe Collins, Art Ditmar, Whitey Ford, Bob Grim, Elston Howard, Darrell Johnson, Tony Kubek, Johnny Kucks, Don Larsen, Jerry Lumpe, Mickey Mantle, Billy Martin *, Gil McDougald, Bobby Richardson, Bobby Shantz, Harry Simpson *, Bill Skowron, Enos Slaughter, Casey Stengel (MANAGER), Tom Sturdivant, Bob Turley

LESS THAN 10 GAMES: Zeke Bella, Bobby Del Greco *, Woodie Held *, Sal Maglie *, Ralph Terry *

NOTES: Mantle (MVP); Kubek (ROY).

KEY SIGNATURES: Stengel, Slaughter, Berra, Howard, Sturdivant, Ford.

ROY = Rookie of the Year

VALUE: $575

1957 NEW YORK (NL) - Johnny Antonelli, Curt Barclay, Ed Bressoud, Pete Burnside, Foster Castleman, Jim Constable, Ray Crone *, Jim Davis *, Ruben Gomez, Marv Grissom, Gail Harris, Ray Jablonski, Grodon Jones, Ray Katt, Whitey Lockman, Joe Margoneri, Willie Mays, Mike McCormick, Stu Miller, Ray Monzant, Don Mueller, Danny O'Connell *, Dusty Rhodes, Steve Ridzik, Bill Rigney (MANAGER), Andre Rodgers, Hank Sauer, Red Schoendienst *, Daryl Spencer, Bill Taylor *, Valmy Thomas, Bobby Thomson *, Ozzie Virgil, Wes Westrum, Al Worthington

LESS THAN 10 GAMES: Sandy Consuegra *, Bobby Hofman, Windy McCall, Max Surkont

NOTES: Giants final year in New York.

KEY SIGNATURES: Mays, Schoendienst, McCormick, White.

VALUE: $275

1957 PHILADELPHIA - Harry Anderson, Richie Ashburn, Marv Blaylock, Ed Bouchee, Bob Bowman, Don Cardwell, Dick Farrell, Chico Fernandez, Warren Hacker *, Harvey Haddix, Granny Hamner, Chuck Harmon *, Jim Hearn, Solly Hemus, Willie Jones, Ted Kazanski, Joe Lonnett, Stan Lopata, Jack Meyer, Bob Miller, Seth Morehead, Ron Northey *, Rip Repulski, Robin Roberts, Jack Sanford, Curt Simmons, Roy Smalley, Mayo Smith (MANAGER)

LESS THAN 10 GAMES: Frankie Baumholtz, Glen Gorbous, John Kennedy, Don Landrum, Bobby Morgan *, Tom Qualters, Saul Rogovin, Andy Seminick
NOTES: Sanford (ROY).
KEY SIGNATURES: Ashburn, Sanford, Roberts.

VALUE: $175

1957 PITTSBURGH - Luis Arroyo, Gene Baker *, Bobby Bragan (MANAGER), Roberto Clemente, Whammy Douglas, Roy Face, Hank Foiles, Dee Fondy *, Gene Freese, Bob Friend, Dick Groat, Nellie King, Ron Kline, Danny Kravitz, Vern Law, Bill Mazeroski, Roman Mejias, Danny Murtaugh (MANAGER), Johnny O'Brien, Jim Pendleton, Hardy Peterson, Johnny Powers, Buddy Pritchard, Bob Purkey, Dick Rand, Bob Skinner, Paul Smith, Bob Smith *, Red Swanson, Frank Thomas, Bill Virdon
LESS THAN 10 GAMES: Chuck Churn, Bennie Daniels, Dick Hall, Ken Hamlin, Bob Kuzava *, Dale Long *, Eddie O'Brien, Laurin Pepper, Joe Trimble, Lee Walls *, George Witt
KEY SIGNATURES: Mazeroski, Groat, Clemente, Friend.

VALUE: $640

1957 ST. LOUIS - Don Blasingame, Ken Boyer, Walker Cooper, Joe Cunningham, Al Dark, Jim Davis *, Murry Dickson, Del Ennis, Fred Hutchinson (MANAGER), Larry Jackson, Sam Jones, Eddie Kasko, Jim King, Hobie Landrith, Lindy McDaniel, Von McDaniel, Lloyd Merritt, Eddie Miksis *, Vinegar Bend Mizell, Wally Moon, Billy Muffett, Stan Musial, Irv Noren *, Willard Schmidt, Dick Schofield, Bobby Gene Smith, Hal Smith, Herm Wehmeier, Hoyt Wilhelm *
LESS THAN 10 GAMES: Tom Alston, Frank Barnes, Tom Cheney, Gene Green, Chuck Harmon *, Bob Kuzava *, Don Lassetter, Lynn Lovenguth, Morrie Martin, Bob Miller, Bob Smith *
KEY SIGNATURES: Musial, Boyer, Wilhelm.

VALUE: $240

1957 WASHINGTON - Ted Abernathy, Julio Becquer, Lou Berberet, Milt Bolling *, Rocky Bridges *, Bud Byerly, Neil Chrisley, Tex Clevenger, Clint Courtney, Chuck Dressen (MANAGER), Ed Fitz Gerald, Evelio Hernandez, Whitey Herzog, Dick Hyde, Russ Kemmerer *, Jim Lemon, Lyle Luttrell, Camilo Pascual, Herb Plews, Pedro Ramos, Pete Runnels, Jerry Schoonmaker, Art Schult *, Roy Sievers, Jerry Snyder, Chuck Stobbs, Faye Throneberry *, Bob Usher *, Eddie Yost
LESS THAN 10 GAMES: Joe Black, Dick Brodowski, Bob Chakales *, Hal Griggs, Jim Heise *, Harmon Killebrew, Ralph Lumenti, Don Minnick, Karl Olson *, Garland Shifflett, Dean Stone, Dick Tettelbach, Bob Wiesler
KEY SIGNATURES: Killebrew.

VALUE: $175

1958

1958 Milwaukee Braves

*** = player was traded**

1958 BALTIMORE - Jerry Adair, Charlie Beamon, Bob Boyd, Hal Brown, Jim Busby, Foster Castleman, Billy Gardner, Joe Ginsberg, Lenny Green, Bob Hale, Ron Hansen, Jack Harshman, Connie Johnson, Ken Lehman, Billy Loes, Jim Marshall *, Willie Miranda, Bob Nieman, Billy O'Dell, Chuck Oertel, Milt Pappas, Al Pilarcik, Arnie Portocarrero, Paul Richards (MANAGER), Brooks Robinson, Willie Tasby, Joe Taylor *, Gus Triandos, Dick Williams, Gene Woodling, George Zuverink

LESS THAN 10 GAMES: Leo Burke, Bert Hamric, Eddie Miksis *, Ron Moeller, Lou Sleater *, Jerry Walker, Hoyt Wilhelm *, Frank Zupo

KEY SIGNATURES: Robinson, Wilhelm.

VALUE: $190

1958 BOSTON - Frank Baumann, Lou Berberet *, Ted Bowsfield, Tom Brewer, Don Buddin, Bud Byerly *, Billy Consolo, Pete Daley, Ike Delock, Mike Fornieles, Dick Gernert, Pinky Higgins (MANAGER), Jackie Jensen, Marty Keough, Leo Kiely, Billy Klaus, Ted Lepcio, Frank Malzone, Bill Monbouquette, Willard Nixon, Jimmy Piersall, Bill Renna, Pete Runnels, Dave Sisler, Riverboat Smith, Gene Stephens, Frank Sullivan, Haywood Sullivan, Murray Wall, Sammy White, Ted Williams

LESS THAN 10 GAMES: Ken Aspromonte *, Jerry Casale, Bob Porterfield *, Al Schroll, George Susce *, Duane Wilson

NOTES: Jensen (MVP).

KEY SIGNATURES: Runnels, Williams.

VALUE: $225

1958 CHICAGO (AL) - Luis Aparicio, Earl Battey, Ted Beard, Ray Boone *, Johnny Callison, Norm Cash, Dick Donovan, Walt Dropo *, Sammy Esposito, Bill Fischer *, Nellie Fox, Tito Francona *, Billy Goodman, Ron Jackson, Bob Keegan, Jim Landis, Barry Latman, Sherm Lollar, Al Lopez (MANAGER), Turk Lown *, Ray Moore, Don Mueller, Bubba Phillips, Billy Pierce, Tom Qualters *, Jim Rivera, Bob Shaw *, Al Smith, Gerry Staley, Earl Torgeson, Jim Wilson, Early Wynn

LESS THAN 10 GAMES: Dixie Howell, Charlie Lindstrom, Jim McAnany, Jim McDonald, Stover McIlwain, Les Moss, Johnny Romano, Don Rudolph, Hal Trosky

KEY SIGNATURES: Fox, Aparicio, Cash, Wynn.

VALUE: $250

1958 CHICAGO (NL) - Bobby Adams, Bob Anderson, Ernie Banks, Jim Bolger, Johnny Briggs, Al Dark *, Moe Drabowsky, Dick Drott, Don Elston, Gene Fodge, Johnny Goryl, Bill Henry, Dave Hillman, Glen Hobbie, Lou Jackson, Dale Long, Jim Marshall *, Gordon Massa, Ed Mayer, Walt Moryn, Cal Neeman, Dolan Nichols, Taylor Phillips, Bob Scheffing (MANAGER), Paul Smith *, Marcelino Solis, Chuck Tanner, El Tappe, Sammy Taylor, Tony Taylor, Moe Thacker, Bobby Thomson, Lee Walls

LESS THAN 10 GAMES: Jim Brosnan *, John Buzhardt, Dick Ellsworth, Frank Ernaga, Hersh Freeman *, Bill Gabler, Dick Johnson, Jerry Kindall, Charlie King, Turk Lown *, Bobby Morgan, Freddy Rodriguez, Elmer Singleton, Bob Will

NOTES: Banks (MVP).

KEY SIGNATURES: Banks.

VALUE: $200

MVP = MVP Award winner

1958 CINCINNATI - Tom Acker, Ed Bailey, Gus Bell, Steve Bilko *, Smoky Burgess, George Crowe, Dutch Dotterer, Walt Dropo *, Jimmy Dykes (MANAGER), Dee Fondy, Alex Grammas, Harvey Haddix, Don Hoak, Hal Jeffcoat, Alex Kellner *, Johnny Klippstein *, Brooks Lawrence, Turk Lown *, Jerry Lynch, Roy McMillan, Eddie Miksis *, Dan Morejon, Don Newcombe *, Joe Nuxhall, Vada Pinson, Bob Purkey, Frank Robinson, Willard Schmidt, Birdie Tebbetts (MANAGER), Johnny Temple, Bob Thurman, Pete Whisenant

LESS THAN 10 GAMES: Chuck Coles, Hersh Freeman *, Jim Fridley, Fred Hatfield *, Gene Hayden, Bobby Henrich, Jay Hook, Bob Kelly *, Jim O'Toole, Orlando Pena, Charlie Rabe, Ted Wieand, Bill Wight *

KEY SIGNATURES: Robinson, Pinson.

VALUE: $275

1958 CLEVELAND - Earl Averill, Bobby Avila, Gary Bell, Bobby Bragan (MANAGER), Dick Brown, Chico Carrasquel *, Rocky Colavito, Larry Doby, Don Ferrarese, Joe Gordon (MANAGER), Rod Graber, Mudcat Grant, Carroll Hardy, Billy Harrell, Woodie Held *, Billy Hunter *, Randy Jackson *, Bob Kelly *, Bob Lemon, Roger Maris *, Morrie Martin *, Cal McLish, Minnie Minoso, Billy Moran, Don Mossi, Ray Narleski, Russ Nixon, Jay Porter, Vic Power *, Herb Score, Dick Tomanek *, Mickey Vernon, Preston Ward *, Vic Wertz, Hoyt Wilhelm *, Hal Woodeshick

LESS THAN 10 GAMES: Dick Brodowski, Chuck Churn, Rocky Colavito, Jim Constable *, Mike Garcia, Gary Geiger, Gary Geiger, Fred Hatfield *, Hal Naragon, Larry Raines, Steve Ridzik

KEY SIGNATURES: Vernon, Colavito, Maris, Wilhelm, Lemon.

VALUE: $225

1958 DETROIT - Hank Aguirre, Reno Bertoia, Frank Bolling, Milt Bolling, Ray Boone *, Jim Bunning, Al Cicotte *, Bill Fischer *, Paul Foytack, Tito Francona *, Johnny Groth, Gail Harris, Bob Hazle *, Jim Hegan *, Billy Hoeft, Al Kaline, Harvey Kuenn, Frank Lary, Charlie Lau, Billy Martin, Charlie Maxwell, Herb Moford, Tom Morgan, Bill Norman (MANAGER), Bob Shaw *, Lou Skizas, George Susce *, Jack Tighe (MANAGER), Vito Valentinetti *, Coot Veal, Ozzie Virgil, Red Wilson, Gus Zernial

LESS THAN 10 GAMES: George Alusik, Steve Boros, Jack Feller, Don Lee, Mickey McDermott, Bobo Osborne, Joe Presko, Lou Sleater *, George Spencer, Bill Taylor, George Thomas, Tim Thompson, Herm Wehmeier *

KEY SIGNATURES: Martin, Kaline, Kuenn, Bunning.

VALUE: $225

1958 KANSAS CITY - Harry Craft (MANAGER), Mike Baxes, Wally Burnette, Chico Carrasquel *, Bob Cerv, Harry Chiti, Walt Craddock, Bud Daley, Joe DeMaestri, Murry Dickson *, Ned Garver, Tom Gorman, Bob Grim *, Woodie Held *, Ray Herbert, Whitey Herzog *, Frank House, Billy Hunter *, Hector Lopez, Duke Maas *, Roger Maris *, Bob Martyn, Vic Power *, Harry Simpson *, Hal Smith, Ralph Terry, Dick Tomanek *, Virgil Trucks *, Bill Tuttle, Jack Urban, Preston Ward *

LESS THAN 10 GAMES: Glen Cox, Bob Davis, Carl Duser, Milt Graff, Kent Hadley, Ken Johnson, Alex Kellner *, Lou Klimchock, Dave Melton, Howie Reed, Jim Small, John Tsitouris

KEY SIGNATURES: Maris.

VALUE: $225

1958 LOS ANGELES - Walt Alston (MANAGER), Don Bessent, Steve Bilko *, Babe Birrer, Gino Cimoli, Don Demeter, Don Drysdale, Carl Erskine, Ron Fairly, Carl Furillo, Jim Gentile, Jim Gilliam, Dick Gray, Gil Hodges, Randy Jackson *, Fred Kipp, Johnny Klippstein *, Sandy Koufax, Clem Labine, Norm Larker, Bob Lillis, Danny McDevitt, Charlie Neal, Don Newcombe *, Joe Pignatano, Johnny Podres, Pee Wee Reese, Ed Roebuck, Johnny Roseboro, Duke Snider, Elmer Valo, Rube Walker, Stan Williams, Don Zimmer

LESS THAN 10 GAMES: Jackie Collum, Roger Craig, Bob Giallombardo, Frank Howard, Ralph Mauriello, Don Miles, Ron Negray, Earl Robinson, Larry Sherry, Bob Wilson

KEY SIGNATURES: Alston, Hodges, Furillo, Snider, Reese, Drysdale, Koufax, Howard.

VALUE: $350

1958 MILWAUKEE - Hank Aaron, Joe Adcock, Bill Bruton, Bob Buhl, Lew Burdette, Gene Conley, Wes Covington, Del Crandall, John DeMerit, Harry Hanebrink, Fred Haney (MANAGER), Bob Hazle *, Joey Jay, Ernie Johnson, Joe Koppe, Johnny Logan, Felix Mantilla, Eddie Mathews, Don McMahon, Andy Pafko, Juan Pizarro, Del Rice, Mel Roach, Humberto Robinson, Bob Rush, Carl Sawatski *, Red Schoendienst, Warren Spahn, Frank Torre, Bob Trowbridge, Carl Willey, Casey Wise

LESS THAN 10 GAMES: Eddie Haas, Dick Littlefield, Bob Roselli, Hawk Taylor

KEY SIGNATURES: Schoendienst, Mathews, Aaron, Spahn, Burdette.

VALUE: $360

1958 NEW YORK - Hank Bauer, Yogi Berra, Andy Carey, Bobby Del Greco, Art Ditmar, Ryne Duren, Whitey Ford, Bob Grim *, Elston Howard, Tony Kubek, Johnny Kucks, Don Larsen, Jerry Lumpe, Duke Maas *, Mickey Mantle, Gil McDougald, Zack Monroe, Bobby Richardson, Bobby Shantz, Norm Siebern, Harry Simpson *, Bill Skowron, Enos Slaughter, Casey Stengel (MANAGER), Tom Sturdivant, Marv Throneberry, Virgil Trucks *, Bob Turley

LESS THAN 10 GAMES: Fritzie Brickell, Murry Dickson *, Johnny James, Darrell Johnson, Sal Maglie *

NOTES: World Champions! Turley (Cy Young).

KEY SIGNATURES: Kubek, Mantle, Berra, Howard, Slaughter, Turley, Ford, Larsen.

VALUE: $600

1958 PHILADELPHIA - Harry Anderson, Richie Ashburn, Ed Bouchee, Bob Bowman, Don Cardwell, Chuck Essegian, Dick Farrell, Chico Fernandez, John Gray, Granny Hamner, Jim Hearn, Jim Hegan *, Solly Hemus, Pancho Herrera, Willie Jones, Ted Kazanski, Joe Lonnett, Stan Lopata, Jack Meyer, Bob Miller, Seth Morehead, Dave Philley, Wally Post, Rip Repulski, Robin Roberts, Jack Sanford, Carl Sawatski *, Eddie Sawyer (MANAGER), Ray Semproch, Curt Simmons, Mayo Smith (MANAGER), Bobby Young

LESS THAN 10 GAMES: John Anderson, Mack Burk, Jimmie Coker, Bob Conley, Don Erickson, Warren Hacker, Angelo LiPetri, Hank Mason, Jim Owens, Tom Qualters *, Roy Smalley

KEY SIGNATURES: Ashburn, Roberts.

VALUE: $150

1958 PITTSBURGH - Gene Baker, Ron Blackburn, Harry Bright, Roberto Clemente, Roy Face, Hank Foiles, Gene Freese *, Bob Friend, Dick Groat, Don Gross, Bill Hall, Ron Kline, Ted Kluszewski, Danny Kravitz, Vern Law, Bill Mazeroski, Roman Mejias, Danny Murtaugh (MANAGER), Bob Porterfield *, Johnny Powers, Curt Raydon, Dick Schofield *, Bob Skinner, Bob Smith, R.C. Stevens, Dick Stuart, Frank Thomas, Bill Virdon, George Witt

LESS THAN 10 GAMES: Bennie Daniels, Eddie O'Brien, Johnny O'Brien *, Jim Pendleton, George Perez, Hardy Peterson, Paul Smith, Don Williams

KEY SIGNATURES: Kluszewski, Mazeroski, Groat, Clemente, Friend.

VALUE: $675

1958 SAN FRANCISCO - Felipe Alou, Johnny Antonelli, Jackie Brandt, Ed Bressoud, Orlando Cepeda, Ray Crone, Jim Davenport, Jim Finigan, Paul Giel, Ruben Gomez, Marv Grissom, Ray Jablonski, Don Johnson, Gordon Jones, Jim King, Willie Kirkland, Whitey Lockman, Willie Mays, Mike McCormick, Stu Miller, Ray Monzant, Danny O'Connell, Bill Rigney (MANAGER), Andre Rodgers, Hank Sauer, Bob Schmidt, Bob Speake, Daryl Spencer, Don Taussig, Valmy Thomas, Leon Wagner, Bill White, Al Worthington

LESS THAN 10 GAMES: Curt Barclay, Pete Burnside, Jim Constable *, John Fitzgerald, Joe Shipley, Nick Testa, Dom Zanni

NOTES: Cepeda (ROY).

KEY SIGNATURES: Cepeda, Mays, White, McCormick.

VALUE: $280

1958 ST. LOUIS - Ruben Amaro, Don Blasingame, Ken Boyer, Jim Brosnan *, Nels Chittum, Joe Cunningham, Al Dark *, Del Ennis, Curt Flood, Gene Freese *, Gene Green, Stan Hack (MANAGER), Fred Hutchinson (MANAGER), Larry Jackson, Sam Jones, Eddie Kasko, Ray Katt, Hobie Landrith, Bob Mabe, Sal Maglie *, Morrie Martin

*, Lindy McDaniel, Vinegar Bend Mizell, Wally Moon, Billy Muffet, Stan Musial, Irv Noren, Johnny O'Brien *, Phil Paine, Dick Schofield *, Bobby Gene Smith, Hal Smith Chuck Stobbs *, Lee Tate, Joe Taylor *, Benny Valenzuela, Bill Wight *

LESS THAN 10 GAMES: Frank Barnes, Ellis Burton, Phil Clark, Tom Flanigan, Von McDaniel, Bill Smith, Herm Wehmeier *

KEY SIGNATURES: Musial, Boyer.

ROY = Rookie of the Year **VALUE:** $200

1958 WASHINGTON - Bob Allison, Ossie Alvarez, Ken Aspromonte *, Julio Becquer Rocky Bridges, Bud Byerly *, Neil Chrisley, Tex Clevenger, Jim Constable *, Clint Courtney, Ed Fitz Gerald, Hal Griggs, Dick Hyde, Russ Kemmerer, Harmon Killebrew, Steve Korcheck, Cookie Lavagetto (MANAGER), Jim Lemon, Bobby Malkmus, Camilo Pascual, Albie Pearson, Herb Plews, Pedro Ramos, John Romonosky, Roy Sievers, Chuck Stobbs *, Faye Throneberry, Vito Valentinetti *, Eddie Yost, Norm Zauchin

LESS THAN 10 GAMES: Joe Albanese, Lou Berberet *, Al Cicotte, Bill Fischer * Whitey Herzog *, Ralph Lumenti, Johnny Schaive, Jerry Snyder, Jack Spring, Bob Wiesler

NOTES: Pearson (ROY).

KEY SIGNATURES: Pearson, Killebrew.

*** = player was traded** **VALUE:** $175

1959

1959 New York Yankees

1959 BALTIMORE - Jerry Adair, Bobby Avila *, Bob Boyd, Hal Brown, Leo Burke, Chico Carrasquel, Walt Dropo *, Jim Finigan, Jack Fisher, Billy Gardner, Joe Ginsberg, Lenny Green *, Bob Hale, Jack Harshman *, Billy Hoeft *, Ernie Johnson, Billy Klaus,

Whitey Lockman *, Billy Loes, Willie Miranda, Bob Nieman, Billy O'Dell, Milt Pappas, Albie Pearson *, Al Pilarcik, Arnie Portocarrero, Paul Richards (MANAGER), Brooks Robinson, Barry Shetrone, Willie Tasby, Joe Taylor *, Gus Triandos, Fred Valentine, Jerry Walker, Hoyt Wilhelm, Gene Woodling

LESS THAN 10 GAMES: George Bamberger, Rip Coleman *, Ron Hansen, Bob Saverine, Wes Stock, George Zuverink

KEY SIGNATURES: Robinson, Wilhelm.

VALUE: $200

1959 BOSTON - Bobby Avila *, Frank Baumann, Tom Brewer, Don Buddin, Jim Busby, Jerry Casale, Nels Chittum, Billy Consolo *, Pete Daley, Ike Delock, Mike Fornieles, Gary Geiger, Dick Gernert, Pumpsie Green, Pinky Higgins (MANAGER), Jackie Jensen, Billy Jurges (MANAGER), Marty Keough, Leo Kiely, Jim Mahoney, Frank Malzone, Bill Monbouquette, Herb Plews *, Bill Renna, Pete Runnels, Al Schroll *, Gene Stephens, Frank Sullivan, Murray Wall *, Vic Wertz, Sammy White, Ted Williams, Rudy York (MANAGER)

LESS THAN 10 GAMES: Ted Bowsfield, Don Gile, Jack Harshman *, Billy Hoeft *, Ted Lepcio *, Jerry Mallett, Herb Moford, Dave Sisler *, Haywood Sullivan, Ted Wills, Earl Wilson

KEY SIGNATURES: Runnels, Williams.

VALUE: $225

1959 CHICAGO (AL) - Luis Aparicio, Rudy Arias, Earl Battey, Johnny Callison, Norm Cash, Larry Doby *, Dick Donovan, Del Ennis *, Sammy Esposito, Nellie Fox, Billy Goodman, Ron Jackson, Ted Kluszewski *, Jim Landis, Barry Latman, Sherm Lollar, Al Lopez (MANAGER), Turk Lown, Jim McAnany, Ken McBride, Ray Moore, Bubba Phillips, Billy Pierce, Jim Rivera, Johnny Romano, Bob Shaw, Harry Simpson *, Al Smith, Gerry Staley, Earl Torgeson, Early Wynn

LESS THAN 10 GAMES: Ray Boone *, Cam Carreon, Joe Hicks, J.C. Martin, Don Mueller, Gary Peters, Claude Raymond, Don Rudolph *, Lou Skizas, Joe Stanka

NOTES: Fox (MVP); Wynn (Cy Young).

KEY SIGNATURES: Lopez, Fox, Aparicio, Cash, Kluszewski, Wynn.

VALUE: $425

1959 CHICAGO (NL) - George Altman, Bob Anderson, Earl Averill, Ernie Banks, John Buzhardt, Art Ceccarelli, Al Dark, Moe Drabowsky, Don Eaddy, Don Elston, Johnny Goryl, Bill Henry, Dave Hillman, Glen Hobbie, Randy Jackson *, Dale Long, Jim Marshall, Seth Morehead *, Walt Moryn, Cal Neeman, Irv Noren *, Bob Scheffing (MANAGER), Art Schult, Elmer Singleton, Sammy Taylor, Tony Taylor, Bobby Thomson, Lee Walls, Billy Williams

LESS THAN 10 GAMES: Bobby Adams, Ed Donnelly, Dick Drott, Lou Jackson, Ben Johnson, Charlie King *, Morrie Martin, Taylor Phillips *, Bob Porterfield *, Joe Schaffernoth, Riverboat Smith *

NOTES: Banks (MVP).

KEY SIGNATURES: Banks, Williams.

VALUE: $200

1959 CINCINNATI - Tom Acker, Luis Arroyo, Ed Bailey, Gus Bell, Jim Brosnan *, Dutch Dotterer, Walt Dropo *, Bobby Henrich, Jay Hook, Fred Hutchinson (MANAGER), Hal Jeffcoat *, Willie Jones *, Eddie Kasko, Brooks Lawrence, Whitey Lockman

*, Jerry Lynch, Bob Mabe, Roy McMillan, Don Newcombe, Joe Nuxhall, Jim O'Toole, Orlando Pena, Jim Pendleton, Vada Pinson, Johnny Powers, Bob Purkey, Frank Robinson, Willard Schmidt, Mayo Smith (MANAGER), Johnny Temple, Frank Thomas, Pete Whisenant

LESS THAN 10 GAMES: Jim Bailey, Cliff Cook, Mike Cuellar, Del Ennis *, Buddy Gilbert, Claude Osteen, Don Pavletich, Don Rudolph *, Bob Thurman

KEY SIGNATURES: Robinson, Pinson.

VALUE: $275

1959 CLEVELAND - Jim Baxes *, Gary Bell, Dick Brodowski, Dick Brown, Al Cicotte, Rocky Colavito, Don Dillard, Don Ferrarese, Ed Fitz Gerald *, Tito Francona, Mike Garcia, Joe Gordon (MANAGER), Mudcat Grant, Granny Hamner *, Carroll Hardy, Jack Harshman *, Woodie Held, Willie Jones *, Gene Leek, Bobby Locke, Billy Martin, Cal McLish, Minnie Minoso, Billy Moran, Hal Naragon *, Russ Nixon, Jim Perry, Jimmy Piersall, Vic Power, Herb Score, Riverboat Smith *, George Strickland, Chuck Tanner, Elmer Valo, Ray Webster

LESS THAN 10 GAMES: Jim Bolger *, Johnny Briggs, Gordy Coleman, Randy Jackson *, Bud Podbielan, Humberto Robinson *, Jake Striker

KEY SIGNATURES: Martin, Colavito, Perry, Score.

VALUE: $200

1959 DETROIT - Lou Berberet, Frank Bolling, Rocky Bridges, Jim Bunning, Pete Burnside, Neil Christley, Jerry Davie, Steve Demeter, Larry Doby *, Jimmy Dykes (MANAGER), Paul Foytack, Johnny Groth, Gail Harris, Al Kaline, Harvey Kuenn, Frank Lary, Ted Lepcio *, Charlie Maxwell, Tom Morgan, Don Mossi, Ray Narleski, Bill Norman (MANAGER), Bobo Osborne, Barney Schultz, Dave Sisler *, Coot Veal, Red Wilson, Eddie Yost, Gus Zernial

LESS THAN 10 GAMES: Hank Aguirre, Ossie Alvarez, Bob Bruce, Billy Hoeft *, Charlie Lau, Jim Proctor, Ron Shoop, Bob Smith *, Jim Stump, George Susce

KEY SIGNATURES: Kuenn, Kaline, Bunning.

VALUE: $175

1959 KANSAS CITY - Zeke Bella, Ray Boone *, Tommy Carroll, Bob Cerv, Harry Chiti, Rip Coleman *, Harry Craft (MANAGER), Bud Daley, Joe DeMaestri, Murry Dickson, Ned Garver, Tom Gorman, Bob Grim, Kent Hadley, Ray Herbert, Whitey Herzog, Frank House, Ray Jablonski *, Lou Klimchock, Johnny Kucks *, Hector Lopez *, Jerry Lumpe *, Roger Maris, Russ Meyer, Joe Morgan *, Hal Smith, Russ Snyder, Tom Sturdivant *, Wayne Terwilliger, Dick Tomanek, John Tsitouris, Bill Tuttle, Preston Ward, Dick Williams

LESS THAN 10 GAMES: George Brunet, Mark Freeman *, Al Grumwald, Ken Johnson, Evans Killeen, Marty Kutyna, Bob Martyn, Howie Reed, Harry Simpson *, Ralph Terry *

KEY SIGNATURES: Maris.

VALUE: $225

1959 LOS ANGELES - Walt Alston (MANAGER), Jim Baxes *, Chuck Churn, Roger Craig, Don Demeter, Don Drysdale, Carl Erskine, Chuck Essegian *, Ron Fairly, Art

Fowler, Carl Furillo, Jim Gilliam, Dick Gray *, Gil Hodges, Johnny Klippstein, Sandy Koufax, Clem Labine, Norm Larker, Bob Lillis, Danny McDevitt, Wally Moon, Charlie Neal, Joe Pignatano, Johnny Podres, Rip Repulski, Johnny Roseboro, Larry Sherry, Duke Snider, Gene Snyder, Stan Williams, Maury Wills, Don Zimmer

LESS THAN 10 GAMES: Sandy Amoros, Tommy Davis, Solly Drake *, Bill Harris, Frank Howard, Fred Kipp, Norm Sherry

NOTES: World Champions!

KEY SIGNATURES: Alston, Hodges, Gilliam, Snider, Koufax, Furillo, Drysdale, Howard, Wills.

VALUE: $400

1959 MILWAUKEE - Hank Aaron, Joe Adcock, Bobby Avila *, Ray Boone *, Bill Bruton, Bob Buhl, Lew Burdette, Chuck Cottier, Wes Covington, Del Crandall, John DeMerit, Bob Giggie, Fred Haney (MANAGER), Joey Jay, Johnny Logan, Stan Lopata, Felix Mantilla, Eddie Mathews, Lee Maye, Don McMahon, Joe Morgan *, Johnny O'Brien, Andy Pafko, Juan Pizarro, Del Rice, Mel Roach, Bob Rush, Enos Slaughter *, Warren Spahn, Frank Torre, Bob Trowbridge, Mickey Vernon, Carl Willey, Casey Wise

LESS THAN 10 GAMES: Bob Hartman, Jim Pisoni *, Red Schoendienst, Al Spangler

KEY SIGNATURES: Adcock, Mathews, Aaron, Vernon, Slaughter, Schoendienst, Spahn.

VALUE: $300

1959 NEW YORK - Hank Bauer, Yogi Berra, Johnny Blanchard, Gary Blaylock *, Clete Boyer, Fritzie Brickell, Jim Bronstad, Andy Carey, Jim Coates, Art Ditmar, Ryne Duren, Whitey Ford, Eli Grba, Elston Howard, Tony Kubek, Don Larsen, Hector Lopez *, Jerry Lumpe *, Duke Maas, Mickey Mantle, Gil McDougald, Jim Pisoni *, Bobby Richardson, Bobby Shantz, Norm Siebern, Bill Skowron, Enos Slaughter *, Casey Stengel (MANAGER), Ralph Terry *, Marv Throneberry, Bob Turley

LESS THAN 10 GAMES: Mark Freeman *, John Gabler, Ken Hunt, Johnny Kucks *, Zack Monroe, Tom Sturdivant *, Gordon Windhorn

KEY SIGNATURES: Stengel, Kubek, Mantle, Berra, Howard, Slaughter, Ford, Larsen.

VALUE: $485

1959 PHILADELPHIA - Harry Anderson, Sparky Anderson, Richie Ashburn, Jim Bolger *, Ed Bouchee, Bob Bowman, Don Cardwell, Gene Conley, Solly Drake *, Dick Farrell, Chico Fernandez, Gene Freese, Ruben Gomez, Granny Hamner *, Harry Hanebrink, Jim Hegan *, Willie Jones *, Joe Koppe, Joe Lonnett, Jack Meyer, Jim Owens, Dave Philley, Taylor Phillips *, Wally Post, Robin Roberts, Humberto Robinson *, Carl Sawatski, Eddie Sawyer (MANAGER), Ray Semproch, Valmy Thomas

LESS THAN 10 GAMES: John Easton, Jim Hearn, Ed Keegan, Seth Morehead *, Freddy Rodriguez, Al Schroll, Chris Short, Curt Simmons

KEY SIGNATURES: Sparky Anderson, Ashburn, Roberts.

VALUE: $150

1959 PITTSBURGH - Ron Blackburn, Harry Bright, Smoky Burgess, Joe Christopher, Roberto Clemente, Bennie Daniels, Roy Face, Hank Foiles, Bob Friend, Freddie Green, Dick Groat, Don Gross, Harvey Haddix, Don Hoak, Ron Kline, Ted Kluszewski *, Danny Kravitz, Vern Law, Bill Mazeroski, Roman Mejias, Danny Murtaugh (MANAGER),

Rocky Nelson, Bob Porterfield *, Dick Schofield, Bob Skinner, Bob Smith *, Dick Stuart, Bill Virdon, George Witt

LESS THAN 10 GAMES: Paul Giel, Dick Hall, Ken Hamlin, Al Jackson, Hardy Peterson, Harry Simpson *, R.C. Stevens, Jim Umbricht, Don Williams

KEY SIGNATURES: Stuart, Mazeroski, Groat, Clemente, Kluszewski, Friend.

VALUE: $675

1959 SAN FRANCISCO - Felipe Alou, Johnny Antonelli, Jackie Brandt, Ed Bressoud, Bud Byerly, Orlando Cepeda, Jim Davenport, Eddie Fisher, Jim Hegan *, Gordon Jones, Sam Jones, Willie Kirkland, Hobie Landrith, Willie Mays, Mike McCormick, Willie McCovey, Stu Miller, Danny O'Connell, Jose Pagan, Dusty Rhodes, Bill Rigney (MANAGER), Andre Rodgers, Jack Sanford, Hank Sauer, Bob Schmidt, Joe Shipley, Bob Speake, Daryl Spencer, Leon Wagner, Al Worthington

LESS THAN 10 GAMES: Curt Barclay, Roger McCardell, Billy Muffett, Marshall Renfroe, Dom Zanni

NOTES: McCovey (ROY).

KEY SIGNATURES: Cepeda, Mays, McCovey, McCormick.

VALUE: $300

ROY = Rookie of the Year

1959 ST. LOUIS - Don Blasingame, Gary Blaylock *, Ken Boyer, Marshall Bridges, Ernie Broglio, Jim Brosnan *, Duke Carmel, Tom Cheney, Gino Cimoli, George Crowe, Joe Cunningham, Bob Duliba, Chuck Essegian *, Curt Flood, Bob Gibson, Alex Grammas, Dick Gray *, Gene Green, Solly Hemus (MANAGER), Ray Jablonski *, Larry Jackson, Hal Jeffcoat *, Ray Katt, Alex Kellner, Lindy McDaniel, Bob Miller, Vinegar Bend Mizell, Stan Musial, Howie Nunn, Gene Oliver, Jay Porter *, Dick Ricketts, Wally Shannon, Bobby Gene Smith, Hal Smith, Dean Stone, Lee Tate, Bill White

LESS THAN 10 GAMES: Bob Blaylock, Phil Clark, Joe Durham, Marv Grissom, Tom Hughes, Charlie King *, Tim McCarver, Irv Noren *, Charlie O'Rourke, Bill Smith, Jack Urban

NOTES: Hemus was a player/manager.

KEY SIGNATURES: Musial, Boyer, White, McDaniel, Gibson.

VALUE: $200

1959 WASHINGTON - Bob Allison, Ken Aspromonte, Julio Becquer, Reno Bertoia, Tex Clevenger, Billy Consolo *, Clint Courtney, Dan Dobbek, Bill Fischer, Ed Fitz Gerald *, Lenny Green *, Hal Griggs, Dick Hyde, Russ Kemmerer, Harmon Killebrew, Steve Korcheck, Cookie Lavagetto (MANAGER), Jim Lemon, Hal Naragon *, Camilo Pascual, Albie Pearson *, Herb Plews *, Jay Porter *, Pedro Ramos, John Romonosky, Ron Samford, Johnny Schaive, Roy Sievers, Chuck Stobbs, Faye Throneberry, Josie Valdivielso, Zoilo Versalles, Hal Woodeschick, Norm Zauchin,

LESS THAN 10 GAMES: Jim Kaat, Jack Kralick, Ralph Lumenti, Bobby Malkmus, Tom McAvoy, Vito Valentinetti, Murray Wall *

NOTES: Allison (ROY).

KEY SIGNATURES: Killebrew, Allison, Kaat.

VALUE: $175

1960

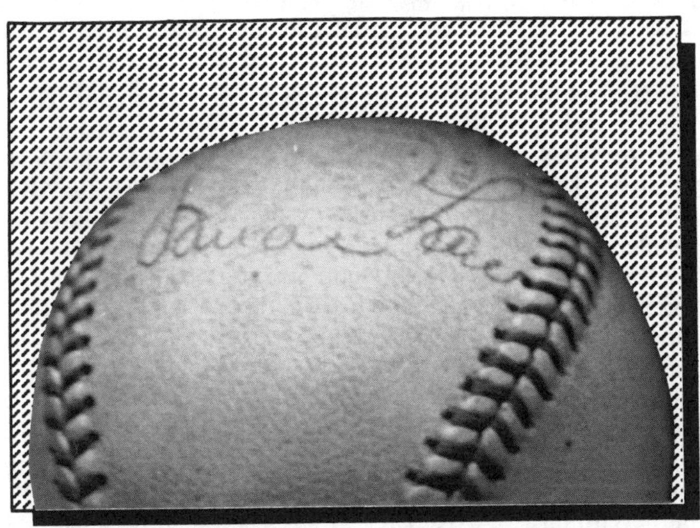

Pittsburgh's Vern Law used this ball to beat the Yankees in the opening game of 1960.

*** = player was traded**

1960 BALTIMORE - Steve Barber, Bob Boyd, Jackie Brandt, Marv Breeding, Hal Brown, Clint Courtney, Walt Dropo, Chuck Estrada, Jack Fisher, Jim Gentile, Joe Ginsberg *, Ron Hansen, Billy Hoeft, Gordon Jones, Billy Klaus, Dave Nicholson, Milt Pappas, Albie Pearson, Dave Philley *, Al Pilarcik, Arnie Portocarrero, Johnny Powers *, Paul Richards (MANAGER), Brooks Robinson, Gene Stephens *, Wes Stock, Willie Tasby *, Valmy Thomas, Gus Triandos, Jerry Walker, Hoyt Wilhelm, Gene Woodling

LESS THAN 10 GAMES: Jerry Adair, John Anderson, Ray Barker, Jim Busby *, Rip Coleman, Gene Green, Bob Mabe, Del Rice *, Barry Shetrone, Bobby Thomson *

NOTES: Hansen (ROY).

KEY SIGNATURES: Hansen, Robinson, Wilhelm.

VALUE: $200

ROY = Rookie of the Year

1960 BOSTON - Ray Boone *, Tom Borland, Ted Bowsfield *, Tom Brewer, Don Buddin, Jim Busby *, Jerry Casale, Lu Clinton, Marlan Coughtry, Ike Delock, Mike Fornieles, Gary Geiger, Don Gile, Pumpsie Green, Carroll Hardy *, Pinky Higgins (MANAGER), Dave Hillman, Ron Jackson, Billy Jurges (MANAGER), Marty Keough *, Frank Malzone, Bill Monbouquette, Billy Muffet, Russ Nixon *, Jim Pagliaroni, Rip Repulski *, Pete Runnels, Eddie Sadowski, Gene Stephens *, Tom Sturdivant, Frank Sullivan, Haywood Sullivan, Willie Tasby *, Bobby Thomson *, Vic Wertz, Ted Williams, Ted Wills, Earl Wilson

LESS THAN 10 GAMES: Nels Chittum, Arnie Earley, Chet Nichols, Tracy Stallard, Ray Webster, Al Worthington *

NOTES: Jensen retired.

KEY SIGNATURES: Runnels, Williams.

VALUE: $225

1960 CHICAGO (AL) - Luis Aparicio, Earl Averill *, Frank Baumann, Dick Brown, Dick Donovan, Sammy Esposito, Nellie Fox, Gene Freese, Mike Garcia, Joe Ginsberg *, Billy Goodman, Joe Hicks, Russ Kemmerer *, Ted Kluszewski, Jim Landis, Sherm Lollar, Al Lopez (MANAGER), Turk Lown, Minnie Minoso, Ray Moore *, Billy Pierce, Jim Rivera, Floyd Robinson, Herb Score, Bob Shaw, Roy Sievers, Al Smith, Gerry Staley, Earl Torgeson, Early Wynn

LESS THAN 10 GAMES: Cam Carreon, Don Ferrarese, Stan Johnson, J.C. Martin, Jim McAnany, Ken McBride, Gary Peters, Bob Rush *, Jake Striker, Al Worthington *

KEY SIGNATURES: Lopez, Fox, Aparicio, Kluszewski, Wynn, Score.

VALUE: $200

1960 CHICAGO (NL) - George Altman, Bob Anderson, Richie Ashburn, Earl Averill *, Ernie Banks, Ed Bouchee *, Lou Boudreau (MANAGER), Don Cardwell *, Moe Drabowsky, Sammy Drake, Dick Drott, Dick Ellsworth, Don Elston, Mark Freeman, Dick Gernert *, Charlie Grimm (MANAGER), Grady Hatton, Jim Hegan, Al Heist, Glen Hobbie, Ben Johnson, Lou Johnson, Jerry Kindall, Seth Morehead, Walt Moryn *, Danny Murphy, Irv Noren *, Del Rice *, Ron Santo, Joe Schaffernoth, Art Schult, El Tappe, Sammy Taylor, Tony Taylor *, Moe Thacker, Frank Thomas, Bob Will, Billy Williams, Don Zimmer

LESS THAN 10 GAMES: Dick Bertell, Jim Brewer, Dick Burwell, Art Ceccarelli, John Goetz, Nelson Mathews, Jim McKnight, Cal Neeman *, Al Schroll, Mel Wright

KEY SIGNATURES: Grimm, Boudreau, Banks, Santo, Ashburn, Williams.

VALUE: $200

1960 CINCINNATI - Harry Anderson *, Joe Azcue, Ed Bailey, Gus Bell, Marshall Bridges *, Jim Brosnan, Leo Cardenas, Elio Chacon, Gordy Coleman, Cliff Cook, Dutch Dotterer, Joe Gaines, Tony Gonzalez *, Bob Grim *, Bill Henry, Jay Hook, Frank House, Fred Hutchinson (MANAGER), Willie Jones, Eddie Kasko, Whitey Lockman, Jerry Lynch, Jim Maloney, Billy Martin, Cal McLish, Roy McMillan, Don Newcombe *, Joe Nuxhall, Jim O'Toole, Claude Osteen, Vada Pinson, Wally Post *, Bob Purkey, Frank Robinson, Lee Walls *

LESS THAN 10 GAMES: Rogelio Alvarez, Brooks Lawrence, Orlando Pena, Duane Richards, Raul Sanchez, Pete Whisenant *, Ted Wieand

KEY SIGNATURES: Robinson, Martin, Pinson.

VALUE: $300

1960 CLEVELAND - Mike de la Hoz, Ken Aspromonte *, Gary Bell, Walt Bond, Ted Bowsfield *, Rocky Bridges *, Johnny Briggs *, Jimmy Dykes (MANAGER), Hank Foiles *, Tito Francona, Joe Gordon (MANAGER), Mudcat Grant, Bob Hale, Carroll Hardy *, Jack Harshman, Wynn Hawkins, Woodie Held, Marty Keough *, Johnny Klippstein, Harvey Kuenn, Barry Latman, Bobby Locke, Joe Morgan *, Don Newcombe *, Russ Nixon *, Jim Perry, Bubba Phillips, Jimmy Piersall, Vic Power, Johnny Romano, Dick Stigman, George Strickland, Chuck Tanner, Johnny Temple, Jo-Jo White (MANAGER), Red Wilson *

LESS THAN 10 GAMES: Ty Cline, Steve Demeter, Don Dillard, Frank Funk, Bob Grim *, Mike Lee, Carl Mathias, Johnny Powers *, Carl Thomas, Bobby Tiefenauer, Pete Whisenant *

KEY SIGNATURES: Aspromonte, Kuenn, Piersall, Perry.

VALUE: $125

1960 DETROIT - Hank Aguirre, Sandy Amoros *, Lou Berberet, Steve Bilko, Frank Bolling, Rocky Bridges *, Bob Bruce, Jim Bunning, Pete Burnside, Norm Cash, Harry Chiti *, Neil Chrisley, Rocky Colavito, Jimmy Dykes (MANAGER), Chico Fernandez, Bill Fischer *, Hank Foiles *, Paul Foytack, Dick Gernert *, Joe Gordon (MANAGER), Johnny Groth, Billy Hitchcock (MANAGER), Al Kaline, Clem Labine *, Frank Lary, Charlie Maxwell, Tom Morgan *, Don Mossi, Phil Regan, Ray Semproch, Dave Sisler, Coot Veal, Ozzie Virgil, Red Wilson *, Casey Wise, Eddie Yost

LESS THAN 10 GAMES: Gail Harris, Em Lindbeck, Dick McAuliffe, George Spencer

KEY SIGNATURES: Cash, Colavito, Kaline, Bunning.

VALUE: $175

1960 KANSAS CITY - Hank Bauer, Andy Carey *, Bob Cerv *, Harry Chiti *, Bud Daley, Pete Daley, Bob Davis, Jim Delsing, Bob Elliott (MANAGER), Ned Garver, Bob Giggie *, Dick Hall, Ken Hamlin, Ray Herbert, Whitey Herzog, Ray Jablonski, Bob Johnson, Ken Johnson, Leo Kiely, Lou Klimchock, Danny Kravitz *, Johnny Kucks, Marty Kutyna, Don Larsen, Jerry Lumpe, Leo Posada, Norm Siebern, Russ Snyder, Marv Throneberry, Bob Trowbridge, John Tsitouris, Bill Tuttle, Dick Williams

LESS THAN 10 GAMES: Ray Blemker, Chet Boak, Johnny Briggs *, George Brunet *, Hank Foiles *, Jim McManus, Howie Reed, Wayne Terwilliger, Dave Wickersham

VALUE: $125

1960 LOS ANGELES - Walt Alston (MANAGER), Bob Aspromonte, Roger Craig, Tommy Davis, Willie Davis, Don Demeter, Don Drysdale, Chuck Essegian, Ron Fairly, Jim Gilliam, Gil Hodges, Frank Howard, Sandy Koufax, Clem Labine *, Norm Larker, Bob Lillis, Danny McDevitt, Wally Moon, Charlie Neal, Irv Noren *, Ed Palmquist, Joe Pignatano, Johnny Podres, Ed Roebuck, Johnny Roseboro, Larry Sherry, Norm Sherry, Charley Smith, Duke Snider, Stan Williams, Maury Wills

LESS THAN 10 GAMES: Sandy Amoros *, Doug Camilli, Carl Furillo, Jim Golden, Phil Ortega, Ed Rakow, Rip Repulski *

NOTES: Howard (ROY).

KEY SIGNATURES: Alston, Wills, Howard, Davis, Snider, Hodges, Davis, Koufax, Drysdale, Gilliam.

VALUE: $325

ROY = **Rookie of the Year**

1960 MILWAUKEE - Hank Aaron, Joe Adcock, George Brunet *, Bill Bruton, Bob Buhl, Lew Burdette, Chuck Cottier, Wes Covington, Del Crandall, Al Dark *, Chuck Dressen (MANAGER), Eddie Haas, Joey Jay, Charlie Lau, Johnny Logan, Felix Mantilla, Eddie Mathews, Lee Maye, Don McMahon, Ron Piche, Juan Pizarro, Mel Roach, Bob Rush *, Red Schoendienst, Warren Spahn, Al Spangler, Frank Torre, Carl Willey

LESS THAN 10 GAMES: Ray Boone *, Terry Fox, Len Gabrielson, Bob Giggie *, Mike Krsnich, Stan Lopata, Ken MacKenzie, Don Nottebart, Joe Torre

KEY SIGNATURES: Adcock, Mathews, Aaron, Schoendienst, Spahn, Burdette, Torre.

VALUE: $260

1960 NEW YORK - Luis Arroyo, Yogi Berra, Johnny Blanchard, Clete Boyer, Bob Cerv *, Jim Coates, Joe DeMaestri, Art Ditmar, Ryne Duren, Whitey Ford, John Gabler, Eli Grba, Kent Hadley, Elston Howard, Ken Hunt, Johnny James, Tony Kubek, Dale Long *, Hector Lopez, Duke Maas, Mickey Mantle, Roger Maris, Gil McDougald, Jim Pisoni, Bobby Richardson, Bobby Shantz, Bill Short, Bill Skowron, Bill Stafford, Casey Stengel (MANAGER), Ralph Terry, Bob Turley

LESS THAN 10 GAMES: Andy Carey, Jesse Gonder, Deron Johnson, Fred Kipp, Billy Shantz, Hal Stowe, Elmer Valo *

NOTES: Stengel's final year with Yankees; Maris (MVP).

KEY SIGNATURES: Stengel, Kubek, Maris, Mantle, Howard, Berra, Ford.

VALUE: $625

1960 PHILADELPHIA - Ruben Amaro, Harry Anderson *, Ed Bouchee *, John Buzhardt, Johnny Callison, Don Cardwell *, Andy Cohen (MANAGER), Jimmie Coker, Gene Conley, Tony Curry, Clay Dalrymple, Al Dark *, Bobby Del Greco, Dick Farrell, Ruben Gomez, Tony Gonzalez *, Dallas Green, Pancho Herrara, Joe Koppe, Ted Lepcio, Art Mahaffey, Bobby Malkmus, Gene Mauch (MANAGER), Joe Morgan *, Cal Neeman *, Jim Owens, Dave Philley *, Taylor Phillips, Wally Post *, Robin Roberts, Humberto Robinson, Eddie Sawyer (MANAGER), Chris Short, Bobby Gene Smith, Tony Taylor *, Lee Walls *, Ken Walters, Jim Woods

LESS THAN 10 GAMES: Hank Mason, Jack Meyer, Al Neiger, Curt Simmons *, Bobby Wine

KEY SIGNATURES: Roberts.

VALUE: $125

1960 PITTSBURGH - Gene Baker, Smoky Burgess, Tom Cheney, Joe Christopher, Gino Cimoli, Roberto Clemente, Bennie Daniels, Roy Face, Bob Friend, Joe Gibbon, Paul Giel, Freddie Green, Dick Groat, Harvey Haddix, Don Hoak, Clem Labine *, Vern Law, Bill Mazeroski, Vinegar Bend Mizell *, Danny Murtaugh (MANAGER), Rocky Nelson, Bob Oldis, Dick Schofield, Bob Skinner, Hal Smith, Dick Stuart, Jim Umbricht, Bill Virdon, George Witt

LESS THAN 10 GAMES: Dick Barone, Harry Bright, Earl Francis, Don Gross, Danny Kravitz *, Roman Mejias, Diomedes Olivo, R.C. Stevens, Mickey Vernon

NOTES: Law (Cy Young); Groat (MVP).

KEY SIGNATURES: Stuart, Mazeroski, Clemente, Law, Vernon.

VALUE: $1000

1960 SAN FRANCISCO - Felipe Alou, Matty Alou, Joey Amalfitano, Johnny Antonelli, Don Blasingame, Ed Bressoud, Bud Byerly, Orlando Cepeda, Jim Davenport, Sam Jones, Sherman Jones, Willie Kirkland, Hobie Landrith, Billy Loes, Dale Long *, Georges Maranda, Juan Marichal, Jim Marshall, Willie Mays, Mike McCormick, Willie McCovey, Stu Miller, Billy O'Dell, Jose Pagan, Dave Philley *, Bill Rigney (MANAGER), Andre Rodgers, Jack Sanford, Bob Schmidt, Tom Sheehan (MANAGER), Joe Shipley

LESS THAN 10 GAMES: Don Choate, Eddie Fisher, Ray Monzant, Neil Wilson

KEY SIGNATURES: McCovey, Mays, Cepeda, McCormick, Marichal.

VALUE: $300

1960 ST. LOUIS - Ken Boyer, Marshall Bridges *, Ernie Broglio, Ellis Burton, George Crowe, Joe Cunningham, Bob Duliba, Curt Flood, Bob Gibson, John Glenn, Alex Gramnas, Bob Grim *, Solly Hemus (MANAGER), Larry Jackson, Charlie James, Julian Javier, Ron Kline, Don Landrum, Tim McCarver, Lindy McDaniel, Bob Miller, Walt Moryn *, Stan Musial, Bob Nieman, Ray Sadecki, Carl Sawatski, Wally Shannon, Curt Simmons *, Hal Smith, Daryl Spencer, Leon Wagner, Bill White

LESS THAN 10 GAMES: Frank Barnes, Ed Bauta, Rocky Bridges *, Cal Browning, Chris Cannizzaro, Duke Carmel, Doug Clemens, Julio Gotay, Dick Gray, Darrell Johnson, Gary Kolb, Vinegar Bend Mizell *, Mel Nelson, Ed Olivares, Del Rice *, Bob Sadowski

KEY SIGNATURES: White, Boyer, Musial, McCarver, Gibson.

VALUE: $285

1960 WASHINGTON - Bob Allison, Ken Aspromonte *, Earl Battey, Julio Becquer, Reno Bertoia, Tex Clevenger, Billy Consolo, Dan Dobbek, Bill Fischer *, Billy Gardner, Lenny Green, Rudy Hernandez, Jim Kaat, Harmon Killebrew, Jack Kralick, Cookie Lavagetto (MANAGER), Don Lee, Jim Lemon, Don Mincher, Ray Moore *, Tom Morgan *, Hal Naragon, Camilo Pascual, Pedro Ramos, Chuck Stobbs, Faye Throneberry, Jose Valdivielso, Elmer Valo *, Zoilo Versalles, Pete Whisenant *, Hal Woodeshick

LESS THAN 10 GAMES: Ted Abernathy, Julio Becquer, Dick Hyde, Lamar Jacobs, Russ Kemmerer *, Hector Maestri, Ted Sadowski, Johnny Schaive

KEY SIGNATURES: Killebrew, Versalles, Kaat.

VALUE: $175

*** = player was traded**

1961

1961 Los Angeles Dodgers

1961 BALTIMORE - Jerry Adair, Steve Barber, Jackie Brandt, Marv Breeding, Hal Brown, Jim Busby, Clint Courtney *, Walt Dropo, Chuck Essegian, Chuck Estrada, Jack Fisher, Hank Foiles, Jim Gentile, Dick Hall, Ron Hansen, Lum Harris (MANAGER), Whitey Herzog, Billy Hoeft, Dick Hyde, Charlie Lau *, Milt Pappas, Dave Philley, Boog Powell, Paul Richards (MANAGER), Brooks Robinson, Earl Robinson, Russ Snyder, Gene Stephens *, Wes Stock, Marv Throneberry *, Gus Triandos, Hoyt Wilhelm, Dick Williams

LESS THAN 10 GAMES: Gordon Jones, Jim Lehew, John Papa, Barry Shetrone, Frank Zupo

KEY SIGNATURES: Robinson, Powell, Wilhelm.

VALUE: $180

1961 BOSTON - Tom Brewer, Don Buddin, Galen Cisco, Lu Clinton, Gene Conley, Ike Delock, Arnie Earley, Mike Fornieles, Gary Geiger, Joe Ginsberg *, Pumpsie Green, Carroll Hardy, Billy Harrell, Pinky Higgins (MANAGER), Dave Hillman, Jackie Jensen, Frank Malzone, Bill Monbouquette, Billy Muffet, Chet Nichols, Russ Nixon, Jim Pagliaroni, Rip Repulski, Pete Runnels, Chuck Schilling, Don Schwall, Tracy Stallard, Vic Wertz *, Ted Wills, Carl Yastrzemski

LESS THAN 10 GAMES: Tom Borland, Don Gile, Wilbur Wood

NOTES: Schwall (ROY).

KEY SIGNATURES: Jensen, Yastrzemski.

VALUE: $200

ROY = Rookie of the Year

1961 CHICAGO (AL) - Luis Aparicio, Frank Baumann, Andy Carey *, Cam Carreon, Wes Covington *, Sammy Esposito, Nellie Fox, Billy Goodman, Warren Hacker, Ray Herbert *, Mike Hershberger, Russ Kemmerer, Jim Landis, Don Larsen *, Sherm Lollar, Al Lopez (MANAGER), Turk Lown, J.C. Martin, Cal McLish, Minnie Minoso, Billy Pierce, Al Pilarcik *, Juan Pizarro, Floyd Robinson, Bob Roselli, Bob Shaw *, Roy Sievers, Al Smith, Gerry Staley *, Earl Torgeson *, Early Wynn

LESS THAN 10 GAMES: Alan Brice, Mike DeGerick, Joe Ginsberg *, Joe Horlen, Ted Lepcio *, Dean Look, Gary Peters, Jim Rivera *, Herb Score

KEY SIGNATURES: Lopez, Fox, Aparicio, Pierce, Wynn.

VALUE: $185

1961 CHICAGO (NL) - George Altman, Bob Anderson, Richie Ashburn, Ernie Banks, Cuno Barragan, Dick Bertell, Ed Bouchee, Jim Brewer, Don Cardwell, Harry Craft (MANAGER), Jack Curtis, Sammy Drake, Dick Drott, Dick Ellsworth, Don Elston, Al Heist, Vedie Himsl (MANAGER), Glen Hobbie, Ken Hubbs, Jerry Kindall, Lou Klein (MANAGER), Jim McAnany, Mel Roach *, Andre Rodgers, Ron Santo, Joe Schaffernoth *, Barney Schultz, El Tappe (MANAGER), Sammy Taylor, Moe Thacker, Frank Thomas *, Bob Will, Billy Williams, Mel Wright, Don Zimmer

LESS THAN 10 GAMES: Lou Brock, Dick Burwell, George Freese, Nelson Mathews, Moe Morhardt, Danny Murphy

NOTES: Williams (ROY).

KEY SIGNATURES: Banks, Santo, Ashburn, Hubbs, Brock, Williams.

VALUE: $220

1961 CINCINNATI - Ed Bailey *, Jim Baumer, Gus Bell, Don Blasingame *, Marshall Bridges, Jim Brosnan, Leo Cardenas, Elio Chacon, Gordy Coleman, Cliff Cook, Johnny Edwards, Gene Freese, Dick Gernert *, Bill Henry, Jay Hook, Ken Hunt, Fred Hutchinson (MANAGER), Joey Jay, Darrell Johnson *, Ken Johnson *, Sherman Jones, Eddie Kasko, Jerry Lynch, Jim Maloney, Howie Nunn, Jim O'Toole, Vada Pinson, Wally Post, Bob Purkey, Frank Robinson, Bob Schmidt *, Pete Whisenant *, Jerry Zimmerman

LESS THAN 10 GAMES: Harry Anderson, Hal Bevan, Joe Gaines, Willie Jones, Claude

)steen *

IOTES: Robinson (MVP).

.EY SIGNATURES: Robinson, Pinson, Jay.

VALUE: $400

961 CLEVELAND - Mike de la Hoz, Bob Allen, Johnny Antonelli *, Ken Aspromonte *, ìary Bell, Walt Bond, Ty Cline, Bill Dailey, Don Dillard, Jimmy Dykes (MANAGER), 'huck Essegian *, Tito Francona, Frank Funk, Mudcat Grant, Bob Hale *, Mel Harder MANAGER), Wynn Hawkins, Woodie Held, Hal Jones, Willie Kirkland, Jack Kubzyn, Barry Latman, Bobby Locke, Bob Nieman *, Jim Perry, Bubba Phillips, Jimmy iersall, Vic Power, Johnny Romano, Joe Schaffernoth *, Dick Stigman, Johnny Temple, 'almy Thomas

ESS THAN 10 GAMES: Steve Hamilton, Russ Heman *, Al Luplow, Sam McDowell,)e Morgan

.EY SIGNATURES: Piersall, McDowell.

VALUE: $115

961 DETROIT - Hank Aguirre, George Alusik, Reno Bertoia *, Steve Boros, Dick rown, Bob Bruce, Bill Bruton, Jim Bunning, Norm Cash, Rocky Colavito, Chuck Cottier , Jim Donohue *, Chico Fernandez, Bill Fischer *, Terry Fox, Paul Foytack, Frank louse, Al Kaline, Ron Kline *, Frank Lary, Charlie Maxwell, Dick McAuliffe, Manny lontejo, Bubba Morton, Don Mossi, Bobo Osborne, Phil Regan, Mike Roarke, Bob cheffing (MANAGER), Gerry Staley *, George Thomas *, Ozzie Virgil *, Jake Wood, lal Woodeshick *

ESS THAN 10 GAMES: Jerry Casale *, Harry Chiti, Bill Freehan, Dick Gernert *, Fred ìladding, Joe Grzenda, Howie Koplitz, Ron Nischwitz, Vic Wertz *

EY SIGNATURES: Cash, Kaline, Colavito, Bunning, Freehan.

VALUE: $170

961 KANSAS CITY - Jim Archer, Norm Bass, Hank Bauer (MANAGER), Reno Bertoia , Bob Boyd *, Andy Carey *, Wayne Causey, Frank Cipriani, Wes Covington *, Bud)aley *, Bobby Del Greco *, Art Ditmar *, Bill Fischer *, Joe Gordon (MANAGER), Jay lankins, Ray Herbert *, Dick Howser, Stan Johnson, Deron Johnson *, Lou Klimchock, .ew Krausse, Bill Kunkel, Jerry Lumpe, Gordon MacKenzie, Joe Nuxhall, Joe Pignatano, l Pilarcik *, Leo Posada, Bobby Prescott, Ed Rakow, Jim Rivera *, Bob Shaw *, Norm iebern, Gerry Staley *, Gene Stephens *, Haywood Sullivan, Marv Throneberry *, Bill 'uttle *, Ozzie Virgil *, Jerry Walker, Dave Wickersham

.ESS THAN 10 GAMES: Billy Bryan, Clint Courtney *, Chuck Essegian *, Paul Giel *, 'en Johnson *, Ed Keegan, Bill Kirk, Don Larsen *, Mickey McDermott *, Dan Pfister, 'harlie Shoemaker, John Wyatt

VALUE: $125

1961 LOS ANGELES (AL) - Ken Aspromonte *, Earl Averill, Julio Becquer *, Steve 3ilko, Ted Bowsfield, Fritzie Brickell, Rocky Bridges, Leo Burke, Jerry Casale *, Bob 'erv *, Tex Clevenger *, Jim Donohue *, Ryne Duren *, Art Fowler, Jim Fregosi, Ned 3arver, Eli Grba, Ken Hamlin, Ken Hunt, Johnny James *, Ron Kline *, Ted Kluszewski, 'oe Koppe *, Gene Leek, Ken McBride, Ron Moeller, Billy Moran, Tom Morgan, Albie 'earson, Del Rice, Bill Rigney (MANAGER), Bob Rodgers, Eddie Sadowski, Tom Satriano, Jack Spring, George Thomas *, Lee Thomas *, Faye Thronberry, Leon Wagner, 'ddie Yost

LESS THAN 10 GAMES: Danny Ardell, Dean Chance, Russ Heman *, Lou Johnson, Ray Semproch, Bob Sprout, Chuck Tanner

NOTES: Team's first year.

VALUE: $250

1961 LOS ANGELES (NL) - Walt Alston (MANAGER), Bob Aspromonte, Doug Camilli, Roger Craig, Tommy Davis, Willie Davis, Don Demeter *, Don Drysdale, Ron Fairly, Dick Farrell *, Jim Gilliam, Jim Golden, Gil Hodges, Frank Howard, Sandy Koufax, Norm Larker, Wally Moon, Charlie Neal, Ron Perranoski, Johnny Podres, Johnny Roseboro, Larry Sherry, Norm Sherry, Duke Snider, Daryl Spencer *, Carl Warwick *, Stan Williams, Maury Wills, Gordie Windhorn

LESS THAN 10 GAMES: Tim Harkness, Bob Lillis *, Phil Ortega, Ed Palmquist *, Ed Roebuck, Charley Smith *

KEY SIGNATURES: Alston, Wills, T. Davis, W. Davis, Howard, Snider, Drysdale, Koufax.

VALUE: $300

1961 MILWAUKEE - Hank Aaron, Joe Adcock, Frank Bolling, Bob Boyd *, Bob Buhl, Lew Burdette, Neil Chrisley, Gino Cimoli *, Tony Cloninger, Del Crandell, John DeMerit, Moe Drabowsky, Chuck Dressen (MANAGER), Bob Hendley, Mack Jones, Charlie Lau *, Johnny Logan *, Felix Mantilla, Eddie Mathews, Lee Maye, Don McMahon, Roy McMillan, Seth Morehead, Don Nottebart, Ron Piche, Claude Raymond, Mel Roach *, Warren Spahn, Al Spangler, Hawk Taylor, Birdie Tebbetts (MANAGER), Frank Thomas *, Joe Torre, Sammy White, Carl Willey

LESS THAN 10 GAMES: Johnny Antonelli *, George Brunet, Wes Covington *, Ken MacKenzie, Billy Martin *, Chi Chi Olivo, Phil Roof

KEY SIGNATURES: Adcock, Mathews, Aaron, Torre, Spahn, Martin.

VALUE: $225

1961 MINNESOTA - Bob Allison, Joe Altobelli, Earl Battey, Julio Becquer *, Reno Bertoia, Billy Consolo, Dan Dobbek, Billy Gardner *, Paul Giel *, Lenny Green, Ron Henry, Jim Kaat, Harmon Killebrew, Jack Kralick, Cookie Lavagetto (MANAGER), Don Lee, Jim Lemon, Ted Lepcio *, Billy Martin *, Danny McDevitt *, Sam Mele (MANAGER), Don Mincher, Ray Moore, Hal Naragon, Camilo Pascual, Bill Pleis, Pedro Ramos, Rich Rollins, Ted Sadowski, Al Schroll, Jim Snyder, Chuck Stobbs, Bill Tuttle *, Jose Valdivielso, Elmer Valo *, Zoilo Versalles

LESS THAN 10 GAMES: Jerry Arrigo, Julio Becquer *, Fred Bruckbauer, Berto Cueto, Gary Dotter, Lamar Jacobs, Ed Palmquist *, Lee Stange, Pete Whisennant *

KEY SIGNATURES: Lavagetto, Killebrew, Martin, Versalles, Kaat.

VALUE: $250

1961 NEW YORK - Luis Arroyo, Yogi Berra, Johnny Blanchard, Clete Boyer, Bob Cerv *, Tex Clevenger *, Jim Coates, Bud Daley *, Joe DeMaestri, Art Ditmar *, Whitey Ford, Billy Gardner *, Jesse Gonder, Bob Hale *, Ralph Houk (MANAGER), Elston Howard, Deron Johnson *, Tony Kubek, Hector Lopez, Mickey Mantle, Roger Maris, Jack Reed, Hal Reniff, Bobby Richardson, Rollie Sheldon, Bill Skowron, Bill Stafford, Ralph Terry, Earl Torgeson *, Tom Tresh, Bob Turley

LESS THAN 10 GAMES: Al Downing, Ryne Duren *, Johnny James *, Duke Maas, Danny McDevitt *, Lee Thomas *

NOTES: World Champions! Maris won the MVP and set the single-seasonhome run record; "M&M" Boys (Mantle/Maris); Ford (Cy Young)

KEY SIGNATURES: Kubek, Maris, Mantle, Berra, Howard, Tresh, Ford.

VALUE: $1100

1961 PHILADELPHIA - Ruben Amaro, Jack Baldschun, John Buzhardt, Johnny Callison, Jimmie Coker, Choo Choo Coleman, Wes Covington *, Tony Curry, Clay Dalrymple, Bobby Del Greco *, Don Demeter *, Don Ferrarese, Tony Gonzalez, Dallas Green, Pancho Herrera, Darrell Johnson *, Al Kenders, Ken Lehman, Art Mahaffey, Bobby Malkmus, Gene Mauch (MANAGER), Cal Neeman, Jim Owens, Robin Roberts, Bob Sadowski, Chris Short, Bobby Gene Smith, Charley Smith *, Frank Sullivan, Tony Taylor, Elmer Valo *, Lee Walls, Ken Walters, George Williams, Jim Woods

LESS THAN 10 GAMES: Paul Brown, Dick Farrell *, Joe Koppe *, Jack Meyer

VALUE: $120

1961 PITTSBURGH - Smoky Burgess, Joe Christopher, Gino Cimoli *, Roberto Clemente, Roy Face, Earl Francis, Bob Friend, Joe Gibbon, Freddie Green, Dick Groat, Harvey Haddix, Don Hoak, Clem Labine, Vern Law, Don Leppert, Johnny Logan *, Bill Mazeroski, Al McBean, Roman Mejias, Vinegar Bend Mizell, Walt Moryn *, Danny Murtaugh (MANAGER), Rocky Nelson, Bob Oldis, Dick Schofield, Bobby Shantz, Bob Skinner, Hal Smith, Dick Stuart, Tom Sturdivant *, Bill Virdon

LESS THAN 10 GAMES: Gene Baker, Tom Cheney *, Donn Clendenon, Larry Foss, Al Jackson, Jim Umbricht, George Witt

KEY SIGNATURES: Stuart, Mazeroski, Clemente, Clendenon, Friend.

VALUE: $675

1961 SAN FRANCISCO - Felipe Alou, Matty Alou, Joey Amalfitano, Ed Bailey *, Don Blasingame *, Bobby Bolin, Ernie Bowman, Ed Bressoud, Orlando Cepeda, Al Dark (MANAGER), Jim Davenport, Jim Duffalo, Bob Farley, Eddie Fisher, Tom Haller, Chuck Hiller, Sam Jones, Harvey Kuenn, Hobie Landrith, Dick LeMay, Billy Loes, Juan Marichal, Jim Marshall, Willie Mays, Mike McCormick, Willie McCovey, Stu Miller, Billy O'Dell, John Orsino, Jose Pagan, Jack Sanford

LESS THAN 10 GAMES: Bob Schmidt, Dom Zanni

KEY SIGNATURES: McCovey, Mays, Cepeda, Marichal, McCormick.

VALUE: $290

1961 ST. LOUIS - Craig Anderson, Ed Bauta, Ken Boyer, Ernie Broglio, Jerry Buchek, Al Cicotte, George Crowe, Joe Cunningham, Curt Flood, Bob Gibson, Julio Gotay, Alex Grammas, Solly Hemus (MANAGER), Larry Jackson, Charlie James, Julian Javier, Johnny Keane (MANAGER), Don Landrum, Bob Lillis *, Tim McCarver, Lindy McDaniel, Mickey McDermott *, Bob Miller, Walt Moryn *, Stan Musial, Ed Olivares, Gene Oliver, Ray Sadecki, Carl Sawatski, Jimmie Schaffer, Red Schoendienst, Curt Simmons, Hal Smith, Daryl Spencer *, Don Taussig, Carl Warwick *, Bill White

LESS THAN 10 GAMES: Chris Cannizzaro, Doug Clemens, Bob Nieman *, Bobby Tiefenauer, Ray Washburn

KEY SIGNATURES: White, Boyer, Musial, Schoendienst, McCarver, Gibson.

VALUE: $275

1961 WASHINGTON - Harry Bright, Pete Burnside, Tom Cheney *, Chuck Cottier *, Pete Daley, Bennie Daniels, Dick Donovan, John Gabler, Mike Garcia, Gene Green, Joe Hicks, Chuck Hinton, Ed Hobaugh, Bob Johnson, Marty Keough, Jim King, Billy Klaus, Johnny Klipstein, Marty Kutyna, Dale Long, Jim Mahoney, Joe McClain, Danny O'Connell, Ken Retzer, Dave Sisler, R.C. Stevens, Tom Sturdivant *, Willie Tasby, Coot Veal, Mickey Vernon (MANAGER), Gene Woodling, Bud Zipfel

LESS THAN 10 GAMES: Chet Boak, Carl Bouldin, Eddie Brinkman, Dutch Dotterer, Roy Heiser, Rudy Hernandez, Hector Maestri, Carl Mathias, Claude Osteen *, Ron Stillwell, Hal Woodeshick *

KEY SIGNATURES: Vernon.

VALUE: $160

1962

1962 San Francisco Giants

*** = player was traded**

1962 BALTIMORE - Jerry Adair, Steve Barber, Jackie Brandt, Marv Breeding, Hal Brown *, Chuck Estrada, Jack Fisher, Jim Gentile, Dick Hall, Ron Hansen, Whitey Herzog, Billy Hitchcock (MANAGER), Billy Hoeft, Hobie Landrith *, Charlie Lau, Dick Luebke, Dave Nicholson, Milt Pappas, Boog Powell, Robin Roberts, Brooks Robinson, Earl Robinson, Barry Shetrone, Russ Snyder, Wes Stock, Johnny Temple *, Gus Triandos, Ozzie Virgil, Hoyt Wilhelm, Dick Williams

LESS THAN 10 GAMES: Andy Etchebarren, Darrell Johnson *, Jim Lehew, Mickey McGuire, Dave McNally, John Miller, John Papa, Art Quirk, Bob Saverine, Bill Short, Nate Smith, Marv Throneberry *, Pete Ward

KEY SIGNATURES: Robinson, Powell, Roberts, Wilhelm.

VALUE: $200

1962 BOSTON - Ed Bressoud, Galen Cisco *, Lu Clinton, Gene Conley, Ike Delock, Arnie Earley, Mike Fornieles, Billy Gardner *, Gary Geiger, Don Gile, Pumpsie Green, Carroll Hardy, Pinky Higgins (MANAGER), Hal Kolstad, Frank Malzone, Bill Monbouquette, Chet Nichols, Russ Nixon, Jim Pagliaroni, Dave Philley, Dick Radatz, Pete Runnels, Chuck Schilling, Don Schwall, Bob Tillman, Earl Wilson, Carl Yastrzemski

LESS THAN 10 GAMES: Bill MacLeod, Billy Muffett, Merlin Nippert, Pete Smith, Tracy Stallard, Ted Wills *, Wilbur Wood

KEY SIGNATURES: Yastrzemski.

VALUE: $200

1962 CHICAGO (AL) - Luis Aparicio, Frank Baumann, John Buzhardt, Cam Carreon, Ramon Conde, Joe Cunningham, Dave DeBusschere, Sammy Esposito, Bob Farley *, Eddie Fisher, Nellie Fox, Ray Herbert, Mike Hershberger, Joe Horlen, Deacon Jones, Mike Joyce, Russ Kemmerer *, Jim Landis, Sherm Lollar, Al Lopez (MANAGER), Turk Lown, J.C. Martin, Charlie Maxwell *, Juan Pizarro, Floyd Robinson, Bob Roselli, Bob Sadowski, Al Smith, Charley Smith, Dean Stone *, Early Wynn, Dom Zanni

LESS THAN 10 GAMES: Ken Berry, Mike Degerick, Dick Kenworthy, Frank Kreutzer, Brian McCall, Gary Peters, Herb Score, Verle Tiefenthaler, Al Weis

KEY SIGNATURES: Lopez, Fox, Wynn, Peters, DeBusschere.

VALUE: $175

1962 CHICAGO (NL) - George Altman, Bob Anderson, Tony Balsamo, Ernie Banks, Cuno Barragan, Dick Bertell, Lou Brock, Bob Buhl *, Don Cardwell, Dick Ellsworth, Don Elston, Jug Gerard, Alex Grammas *, Glen Hobbie, Ken Hubbs, Lou Klein (MANAGER), Cal Koonce, Don Landrum *, Al Lary, Nelson Mathews, Jim McKnight, Charlie Metro (MANAGER), Moe Morhardt, Danny Murphy, Billy Ott, Andre Rodgers, Ron Santo, Barney Schultz, Bobby Gene Smith *, Morrie Steevens, El Tappe (MANAGER), Moe Thacker, Elder White, Bob Will, Billy Williams

LESS THAN 10 GAMES: Jim Brewer, Freddie Burdette, Jack Curtis *, George Gerberman, Jim McAnany, Don Prince, Daryl Robertson, Sammy Taylor *, Paul Toth *, Jack Warner

NOTES: Hubbs (ROY).

KEY SIGNATURES: Banks, Hubbs, Santo, Brock, Williams.

VALUE: $215

ROY = Rookie of the Year

1962 CINCINNATI - Rogelio Alvarez, Don Blasingame, Jim Brosnan, Leo Cardenas, Gordy Coleman, Moe Drabowsky *, Johnny Edwards, Hank Foiles, Gene Freese, Joe Gaines, Bill Henry, Fred Hutchinson (MANAGER), Joey Jay, Eddie Kasko, Marty Keough, Johnny Klippstein, Jerry Lynch, Jim Maloney, Joe Nuxhall *, Jim O'Toole, Don Pavletich, Vada Pinson, Wally Post, Bob Purkey, Frank Robinson, Cookie Rojas, Dave Sisler, Ted Wills *, Don Zimmer *

LESS THAN 10 GAMES: Cliff Cook *, Sammy Ellis, Jesse Gonder, Tommy Harper, Dave Hillman *, Darrell Johnson *, Bob Miller *, Howie Nunn, John Tsitouris

KEY SIGNATURES: Robinson, Pinson.

VALUE: $220

1962 CLEVELAND - Mike de la Hoz, Bob Allen, Max Alvis, Ken Aspromonte *, Gary Bell, Walt Bond, Ty Cline, Bill Dailey, Don Dillard, Dick Donovan, Doc Edwards, Chuck Essegian, Tito Francona, Frank Funk, Ruben Gomez *, Mudcat Grant, Gene Green, Woodie Held, Jerry Kindall, Willie Kirkland, Jack Kubiszyn, Barry Latman, Al Luplow, Jim Mahoney, Sam McDowell, Mel McGaha (MANAGER), Bob Nieman *, Jim Perry, Bubba Phillips, Pedro Ramos, John Romano, Willie Tasby *

LESS THAN 10 GAMES: Tommie Agee, Jackie Collum *, Marlan Coughtry *, Bob Hartman, Wynn Hawkins, Hal Jones, Don Rudolph *, Ron Taylor, Dave Tyriver, Floyd Weaver

KEY SIGNATURES: McDowell.

VALUE: $115

1962 DETROIT - Hank Aguirre, Steve Boros, Dick Brown, Bill Bruton, Don Buddin *, Jim Bunning, Jerry Casale, Norm Cash, Rocky Colavito, Bob Farley *, Chico Fernandez, Terry Fox, Paul Foytack, Purnal Goldy, Sam Jones, Al Kaline, Ron Kline, Howie Koplitz, Frank Kostro, Frank Lary, Charlie Maxwell *, Dick McAuliffe, Bubba Morton, Don Mossi, Ron Nischwitz, Bobo Osborne, Phil Regan, Mike Roarke, Bob Scheffing (MANAGER), Vic Wertz, Jake Wood

LESS THAN 10 GAMES: George Alusik *, Reno Bertoia, Bill Faul, Tom Fletcher, Doug Gallagher, Fred Gladding, Bob Humphreys

KEY SIGNATURES: Cash, Kaline, Colavito, Bunning.

VALUE: $150

1962 HOUSTON - Joey Amalfitano, Bob Aspromonte, Pidge Browne, Bob Bruce, George Brunet, Don Buddin *, Jim Busby, Jim Campbell, Bob Cerv *, Al Cicotte, Harry Craft (MANAGER), Dick Farrell, Ernie Fazio, Dick Gernert, Dave Giusti, Jim Golden, Billy Goodman, J.C. Hartman, Al Heist, Ken Johnson, Russ Kemmerer *, Norm Larker, Bob Lillis, Don McMahon *, Roman Mejias, Jim Pendleton, Merritt Ranew, Dave Roberts, Hal Smith, Al Spangler, Dean Stone *, Don Taussig, Johnny Temple *, Bobby Tiefenauer, Jim Umbricht, Carl Warwick *, Johnny Weekly, George Witt *, Hal Woodeshick

LESS THAN 10 GAMES: John Anderson *, Ron Davis, Dick Drott, Bobby Shantz *, George Williams

NOTES: Team's first year!

KEY SIGNATURES: Aspromonte.

VALUE: $260

1962 KANSAS CITY - George Alusik *, Jim Archer, Joe Azcue, Norm Bass, Hank Bauer (MANAGER), Billy Bryan, Wayne Causey, Ed Charles, Gino Cimoli, Billy Consolo *, Bobby Del Greco, Moe Drabowsky *, Bill Fischer, Bob Grim, Dick Howser, Manny Jiminez, Deron Johnson, Gordon Jones, Jerry Lumpe, Danny McDevitt, Orlando Pena, Dan Pfister, Leo Posada, Ed Rakow, Diego Segui, Norm Siebern, Haywood Sullivan, Jose Tartabull, Jerry Walker, Dave Wickersham, Gordie Windhorn *, John Wojcik, John Wyatt

LESS THAN 10 GAMES: Marlan Coughtry *, Art Ditmar, Bob Giggie, Granny Hamner, Bill Kern, Bill Kunkel, Hector Martinez, Fred Norman, Dan Osinski *, Charlie Shoemaker, Gene Stephens, Rupe Toppin, Don Williams

VALUE: $115

1962 LOS ANGELES (AL) - Earl Averill, Bo Belinsky, Steve Bilko, Bob Botz, Ted Bowsfield, Tom Burgess, Leo Burke, Dean Chance, Billy Consolo *, Marlan Coughtry *, Jim Donohue *, Ryne Duren, Art Fowler, Jim Fregosi, Eli Grba, Ken Hunt, Joe Koppe, Don Lee *, Ken McBride, Billy Moran, Tom Morgan, Dan Osinski *, Albie Pearson, Bill Rigney (MANAGER), Bob Rodgers, Eddie Sadowski, Tom Satriano, Jack Spring, George Thomas, Lee Thomas, Felix Torres, Leon Wagner, Gordie Windhorn *, Eddie Yost

LESS THAN 10 GAMES: Bobby Darwin, Ed Kirkpatrick, Gene Leek, Frank Leja, Julio Navarro, Fred Newman, Joe Nuxhall *, Dick Simpson, Chuck Tanner, George Witt *

KEY SIGNATURES: Lee Thomas, Fregosi.

VALUE: $175

1962 LOS ANGELES (NL) - Walt Alston (MANAGER), Larry Burright, Doug Camilli, Andy Carey, Tommy Davis, Willie Davis, Don Drysdale, Ron Fairly, Jim Gilliam, Tim Harkness, Frank Howard, Sandy Koufax, Joe Moeller, Wally Moon, Phil Ortega, Ron Perranoski, Johnny Podres, Pete Richert, Ed Roebuck, Johnny Roseboro, Larry Sherry, Norm Sherry, Duke Snider, Daryl Spencer, Dick Tracewski, Lee Walls, Stan Williams, Maury Wills

LESS THAN 10 GAMES: Willard Hunter *, Ken McMullen, Jack Smith

NOTES: Drysdale (Cy Young); Wills (MVP).

KEY SIGNATURES: Alston, Gilliam, Wills, Howard, W. Davis, T. Davis, Snider, Drysdale, Koufax.

VALUE: $300

MVP = MVP Award winner

1962 MILWAUKEE - Hank Aaron, Tommie Aaron, Joe Adcock, Ken Aspromonte *, Howie Bedell, Gus Bell *, Frank Bolling, Lew Burdette, Tony Cloninger, Del Crandall, Jack Curtis *, Hank Fischer, Bob Hendley, Lou Johnson, Mack Jones, Mike Krsnich, Denny Lemaster, Eddie Mathews, Lee Maye, Roy McMillan, Denis Menke, Don Nottebart, Ron Piche, Claude Raymond, Amado Samuel, Bob Shaw, Warren Spahn, Hawk Taylor, Birdie Tebbetts (MANAGER), Joe Torre, Bob Uecker, Carl Willey

LESS THAN 10 GAMES: Ethan Blackaby, Bob Buhl *, Cecil Butler, Jim Constable, Lou Klimchock, Don McMahon *

KEY SIGNATURES: Adcock, Mathews, Aaron, Uecker, Spahn.

VALUE: $190

1962 MINNESOTA - Bernie Allen, Bob Allison, George Banks, Earl Battey, Joe Bonikowski, Johnny Goryl, Lenny Green, Jim Kaat, Harmon Killebrew, Jack Kralick, Jim Lemon, Georges Maranda, Marty Martinez, Sam Mele (MANAGER), Don Mincher, Ray Moore, Hal Naragon, Camilo Pascual, Bill Pleis, Vic Power, Rich Rollins, Ted Sadowski, Jim Snyder, Lee Stange, Dick Stigman, Frank Sullivan *, Bill Tuttle, Zoilo Versalles, Jerry Zimmerman

LESS THAN 10 GAMES: Jerry Arrigo, Jackie Collum *, Jim Donohue *, Ruben Gomez *, Don Lee *, Jim Manning, Tony Oliva, Jim Roland

KEY SIGNATURES: Versalles, Killebrew, Oliva, Kaat.

VALUE: $220

1962 NEW YORK (AL) - Luis Arroyo, Yogi Berra, Johnny Blanchard, Jim Bouton, Clete Boyer, Marshall Bridges, Bob Cerv *, Tex Clevenger, Jim Coates, Bud Daley, Whitey Ford, Ralph Houk (MANAGER), Elston Howard, Tony Kubek, Phil Linz, Dale Long *, Hector Lopez, Mickey Mantle, Roger Maris, Joe Pepitone, Jack Reed, Bobby Richardson, Rollie Sheldon, Bill Skowron, Bill Stafford, Ralph Terry, Tom Tresh, Bob Turley

LESS THAN 10 GAMES: Hal Brown *, Jack Cullen, Al Downing, Billy Gardner *, Jake Gibbs, Hal Reniff

NOTES: World Champions! Mantle (MVP), Tresh (ROY).

KEY SIGNATURES: Tresh, Maris, Mantle, Howard, Berra, Kubek, Terry, Ford.

VALUE: $575

ROY = Rookie of the Year

1962 NEW YORK (NL) - Craig Anderson, Richie Ashburn, Gus Bell *, Ed Bouchee, Chris Cannizzaro, Elio Chacon, Harry Chiti, Joe Christopher, Choo Choo Coleman, Cliff Cook *, Roger Craig, Ray Daviault, John DeMerit, Sammy Drake, Rick Herrscher, Jim Hickman, Dave Hillman, Gil Hodges, Jay Hook, Willard Hunter *, Al Jackson, Rod Kanehl, Hobie Landrith *, Ken MacKenzie, Felix Mantilla, Jim Marshall *, Bob Miller *, Vinegar Bend Mizell *, Bob Moorhead, Charlie Neal, Joe Pignatano *, Casey Stengel (MANAGER), Sammy Taylor *, Frank Thomas, Marv Throneberry *, Gene Woodling *, Don Zimmer *

LESS THAN 10 GAMES: Galen Cisco *, Larry Foss, Joe Ginsberg, Sherman Jones, Ed Kranepool, Clem Labine, Herb Moford, Bobby Gene Smith *

NOTES: Team's first year!

KEY SIGNATURES: Stengel, Hodges, Kranepool.

VALUE: $375

1962 PHILADELPHIA - Ruben Amaro, Jack Baldschun, Dennis Bennett, Paul Brown, Johnny Callison, Wes Covington, Clay Dalrymple, Jacke Davis, Don Demeter, Tony Gonzalez, Dallas Green, Jack Hamilton, John Herrnstein, Billy Klaus, Art Mahaffey, Gene Mauch (MANAGER), Carl McLish, Bob Oldis, Jim Owens, Mel Roach, Ted Savage, Chris Short, Roy Sievers, Bill Smith, Frank Sullivan *, Tony Taylor, Frank Torre, Sammy White, Bobby Wine

LESS THAN 10 GAMES: John Boozer, Jimmie Coker, Billy Consolo *, Don Ferrarese *, Ed Keegan, Bobby Locke *, Bobby Malkmus

VALUE: $115

1962 PITTSBURGH - Bob Bailey, Smoky Burgess, Roberto Clemente, Donn Clendenon, Roy Face, Earl Francis, Bob Friend, Joe Gibbon, Howie Goss, Dick Groat, Harvey Haddix, Don Hoak, Jack Lamabe, Vern Law, Don Leppert, Johnny Logan, Jim Marshall *, Bill Mazeroski, Al McBean, Danny Murtaugh (MANAGER), Cal Neeman, Diomedes Olivo, Dick Schofield, Bob Skinner, Willie Stargell, Dick Stuart, Tom Sturdivant, Bob Veale, Bill Virdon

LESS THAN 10 GAMES: Tom Butters, Larry Elliot, Orlando McFarlane, Vinegar Bend Mizell *, Elmo Plaskett, Bob Priddy, Tommie Sisk, Coot Veal

KEY SIGNATURES: Mazeroski, Groat, Clemente, Clendenon, Stargell.

VALUE: $625

1962 SAN FRANCISCO - Felipe Alou, Matty Alou, Ed Bailey, Carl Boles, Bobby Bolin, Ernie Bowman, Orlando Cepeda, Al Dark (MANAGER), Jim Davenport, Jim Duffalo, Tom Haller, Chuck Hiller, Harvey Kuenn, Don Larsen, Juan Marichal, Willie Mays, Mike McCormick, Willie McCovey, Stu Miller, Manny Mota, Bob Nieman *, Billy O'Dell, John Orsino, Jose Pagan, Gaylord Perry, Billy Pierce, Jack Sanford

LESS THAN 10 GAMES: Bob Garibaldi, Dick LeMay, Cap Peterson, Dick Phillips, Joe Pignatano *

KEY SIGNATURES: Cepeda, Mays, McCovey, Marichal, McCormick, Perry.

VALUE: $460

1962 ST. LOUIS - Ed Bauta, Ken Boyer, Ernie Broglio, Doug Clemens, Bob Duliba, Don Ferrarese *, Curt Flood, Bob Gibson, Julio Gotay, Alex Grammas *, Larry Jackson, Charlie James, Julian Javier, Johnny Keane (MANAGER), Gary Kolb, Don Landrum *, Dal Maxvill, Lindy McDaniel, Minnie Minoso, Stan Musial, Gene Oliver, Ray Sadecki, Carl Sawatski, Jimmie Schaffer, Red Schoendienst, Mike Shannon, Bobby Shantz *, Curt Simmons, Bobby Gene Smith *, Carl Warwick *, Ray Washburn, Bill White, Fred Whitfield

LESS THAN 10 GAMES: John Anderson *, Harvey Branch, Bob Burda, Bobby Locke *, Paul Toth *

KEY SIGNATURES: White, Boyer, Musial, Schoendienst, Gibson.

VALUE: $275

1962 WASHINGTON - Harry Bright, Eddie Brinkman, Pete Burnside, Tom Cheney, Chuck Cottier, Bennie Daniels, Steve Hamilton, Ken Hamlin, Jim Hannan, Joe Hicks, Chuck Hinton, Ed Hobaugh, Bob Johnson, John Kennedy, Jim King, Marty Kutyna, Don Lock, Dale Long *, Joe McClain, Danny O'Connell, Claude Osteen, Jimmy Piersall, Ken Retzer, Ray Ripplemeyer, Don Rudolph *, Johnny Schaive, Bob Schmidt, Dave Stenhouse, Willie Tasby *, Mickey Vernon (MANAGER), Gene Woodling, Bud Zipfel

LESS THAN 10 GAMES: Bob Baird, Carl Bouldin, Freddie Green, Jack Jenkins, Ron Stilwell

KEY SIGNATURES: Vernon.

VALUE: $160

1963

1963 N.L. Rookie of the Year Pete Rose

*** = player was traded**

1963 BALTIMORE - Jerry Adair, Luis Aparicio, Steve Barber, Sam Bowens, Jackie Brandt, Dick Brown, George Brunet *, Joe Gaines, Jim Gentile, Dick Hall, Billy Hitchcock (MANAGER), Bob Johnson, Hobie Landrith *, Charlie Lau *, Mike McCormick, Dave McNally, Stu Miller, John Orsino, Milt Pappas, Boog Powell, Robin Roberts, Brooks Robinson, Bob Saverine, Al Smith, Russ Snyder, Herm Starrette, Wes Stock, Dean Stone, Fred Valentine

LESS THAN 10 GAMES: Wally Bunker, Pete Burnside *, Ike Delock *, Chuck Estrada, John Miller, Buster Narum

KEY SIGNATURES: Aparicio, Robinson, Powell, Roberts.

VALUE: $200

1963 BOSTON - Ed Bressoud, Lu Clinton, Arnie Earley, Billy Gardner, Gary Geiger, Jim Gosger, Bob Heffner, Jack Lamabe, Frank Malzone, Felix Mantilla, Roman Mejias, Bill Monbouquette, Dave Morehead, Chet Nichols, Russ Nixon, Johnny Pesky (MANAGER), Dick Radatz, Chuck Schilling, Dick Stuart, Bob Tillman, Bob Turley *, Dick Williams, Earl Wilson, Wilbur Wood, Carl Yastrzemski

LESS THAN 10 GAMES: Gene Conley, Ike Delock *, Mike Fornieles *, Hal Kolstad, Rico Petrocelli, Pete Smith, Jerry Stephenson

KEY SIGNATURES: Yastrzemski.

VALUE: $210

1963 CHICAGO (AL) - Frank Baumann, Jim Brosnan *, Don Buford, John Buzhardt, Cam Carreon, Joe Cunningham, Dave DeBusschere, Eddie Fisher, Nellie Fox, Ron Hansen, Ray Herbert, Mike Hershberger, Joe Horlen, Deacon Jones, Jim Landis, Jim Lemon *, Sherm Lollar, Al Lopez (MANAGER), J.C. Martin, Charlie Maxwell, Brian McCall, Tommy McCraw, Dave Nicholson, Gary Peters, Juan Pizarro, Floyd Robinson, Pete Ward, Al Weis, Hoyt Wilhelm

LESS THAN 10 GAMES: Fritz Ackley, Ken Berry, Sammy Esposito *, Bruce Howard, Mike Joyce, Frank Kreutzer, Taylor Phillips, Joe Shipley, Charley Smith, Gene Stephens, Fred Talbot, Dom Zanni *

NOTES: Peters (ROY).

KEY SIGNATURES: Lopez, Fox, Peters, Wilhelm, DeBusschere.

VALUE: $145

ROY = Rookie of the Year

1963 CHICAGO (NL) - Ken Aspromonte, Tom Baker, Ernie Banks, Dick Bertell, John Boccabella, Steve Boros, Jim Brewer, Lou Brock, Bob Buhl, Leo Burke *, Ellis Burton *, Billy Cowan, Dick Ellsworth, Don Elston, Alex Grammas, Glen Hobbie, Ken Hubbs, Larry Jackson, Bob Kennedy (MANAGER), Cal Koonce, Don Landrum, Nelson Mathews, Lindy McDaniel, Merritt Ranew, Andre Rodgers, Ron Santo, Jimmie Schaffer, Barney Schultz *, Jimmy Stewart, Paul Toth, Bob Will, Billy Williams

LESS THAN 10 GAMES: Cuno Barragan, Freddie Burdette, Dick LeMay, Phil Murdock, Jack Warner

KEY SIGNATURES: Banks, Hubbs, Santo, Brock, Williams.

VALUE: $200

1963 CINCINNATI - Don Blasingame *, Leo Cardenas, Gordy Coleman, Johnny Edwards, Gene Freese, Jesse Gonder *, Gene Green, Tommy Harper, Billy Henry, Fred Hutchinson (MANAGER), Joey Jay, Eddie Kasko, Marty Keough, Jerry Lynch *, Jim Maloney, Charlie Neal *, Joe Nuxhall, Jim O'Toole, Jim Owens, Don Pavletich, Vada Pinson, Bob Purkey, Frank Robinson, Pete Rose, Bob Skinner *, Daryl Spencer *, Sammy Taylor *, John Tsitouris, Ken Walters, Al Worthington, Dom Zanni *

LESS THAN 10 GAMES: Harry Bright *, Jim Brosnan *, Jim Coates *, Hank Foiles *, Wally Post *

NOTES: Rose (ROY).

KEY SIGNATURES: Rose, Harper, Pinson, Robinson.

VALUE: $220

1963 CLEVELAND - Mike de la Hoz, Ted Abernathy, Joe Adcock, Tommie Agee, Bob Allen, Max Alvis, Joe Azcue *, Gary Bell, Larry Brown, Ellis Burton *, Bob Chance, Vic Davalillo, Dick Donovan, Doc Edwards *, Tito Francona, Mudcat Grant, Gene Green *, Woodie Held, Dick Howser *, Jerry Kindall, Willie Kirkland, Jack Kralick *, Barry Latman, Jim Lawrence, Al Luplow, Tony Martinez, Sam McDowell, Ron Nischwitz, Pedro Ramos, Johnny Romano, Willie Tasby, Birdie Tebbetts (MANAGER), Jerry Walker, Fred Whitfield, Early Wynn

LESS THAN 10 GAMES: Jack Curtis, Tommy John, Bob Lipski, Cal Neeman *, Jim Perry *, Gordon Seyfried, Sammy Taylor *

KEY SIGNATURES: Adcock, McDowell, John.

VALUE: $115

1963 DETROIT - Hank Aguirre, Bob Anderson, Gates Brown, Bill Bruton, Jim Bunning, Norm Cash, Rocky Colavito, Chuck Dressen (MANAGER), Dick Egan, Bill Faul, Chico Fernandez *, Terry Fox, Bill Freehan, Fred Gladding, Whitey Herzog, Willie Horton, Al Kaline, Frank Kostro *, Frank Lary, Mickey Lolich, Dick McAuliffe, Don Mossi, Bubba Phillips, Phil Regan, Mike Roarke, Bob Scheffing (MANAGER), George Smith, Willie Smith, Tom Sturdivant *, George Thomas *, Gus Triandos, Coot Veal, Don Wert, Jake Wood

LESS THAN 10 GAMES: Bob Dustal, Larry Foster, Paul Foytack *, Purnal Goldy, Alan Koch, Denny McLain, Bubba Morton *, John Sullivan, Vic Wertz *

KEY SIGNATURES: Cash, Kaline, Colavito, Lolich, McLain.

VALUE: $150

1963 HOUSTON - Bob Aspromonte, John Bateman, Hal Brown, Bob Bruce, Jim Campbell, Harry Craft (MANAGER), Brock Davis, Jim Dickson, Dick Drott, Dick Farrell, Ernie Fazio, Howie Goss, Caroll Hardy, J.C. Hartman, Ken Johnson, Russ Kemmerer, Bob Lillis, Don McMahon, Don Nottebart, Pete Runnels, Hal Smith, Al Spangler, Rusty Staub, Johnny Temple, Jim Umbricht, Carl Warwick, Johnny Weekly, Hal Woodeshick, Jim Wynn, Chris Zachary

LESS THAN 10 GAMES: Dave Adlesh, George Brunet *, Randy Cardinal, Danny Coombs, Jay Dahl, Jim Golden, Jerry Grote, Joe Hoerner, Sonny Jackson, Joe Morgan, Ivan Murrell, John Paciorek, Aaron Pointer, Glenn Vaughan, Mike White, Larry Yellen

NOTES: Umbricht died 4/6/64.

KEY SIGNATURES: Staub, Aspromonte, Morgan, Umbricht.

VALUE: $190

1963 KANSAS CITY - George Alusik, Ted Bowsfield, Billy Bryan, Wayne Causey, Ed Charles, Gino Cimoli, Bobby Del Greco, Moe Drabowsky, Doc Edwards *, Sammy Esposito *, Chuck Essegian, Bill Fischer, Dick Green, Tom Hankins, Ken Harrelson, Dick Howser *, Manny Jiminez, Tony La Russa, Charlie Lau *, Ed Lopat (MANAGER), Pete Lovrich, Jerry Lumpe, Orlando Pena, Ed Rakow, Diego Segui, Norm Siebern, Tom Sturdivant *, Haywood Sullivan, Jose Tartabull, Dave Wickersham, Dale Willis, John Wojcik, John Wyatt

LESS THAN 10 GAMES: Joe Azcue *, Norm Bass, Bill Landis, Hector Martinez, Aurelio Monteagudo, Fred Norman, John O'Donoghue, Dan Pfister, Tommie Reynolds, Jose Santiago, Dave Thies

VALUE: $110

1963 LOS ANGELES (AL) - Bo Belinsky, Dean Chance, Charlie Dees, Hank Foiles *, Art Fowler, Paul Foytack *, Jim Fregosi, Eli Grba, Ken Hunt *, Ed Kirkpatrick, Joe Koppe, Frank Kostro *, Don Lee, Ken McBridge, Billy Moran, Tom Morgan, Julio Navarro, Mel Nelson, Fred Newman, Dan Osinski, Albie Pearson, Bob Perry, Jimmy Piersall *, Bill Rigney (MANAGER), Bob Rodgers, Bob Sadowski, Eddie Sadowski, Tom Satriano, Jack Spring, Lee Thomas, George Thomas *, Felix Torres, Bob Turley *, Leon Wagner

LESS THAN 10 GAMES: Bob Duliba, Aubrey Gatewood, Mike Lee, Ron Moeller *

KEY SIGNATURES: Fregosi, Chance.

VALUE: $100

1963 LOS ANGELES (NL) - Walt Alston (MANAGER), Marv Breeding *, Dick Calmus, Doug Camilli, Tommy Davis, Willie Davis, Don Drysdale, Ron Fairly, Al Ferrara, Jim Gilliam, Frank Howard, Sandy Koufax, Ken McMullen, Bob Miller, Wally Moon, Nate Oliver, Ron Perranoski, Johnny Podres, Pete Richert, Ed Roebuck *, Johnny Roseboro, Ken Rowe, Larry Sherry, Bill Skowron, Dick Tracewski, Lee Walls, Maury Wills, Don Zimmer *

LESS THAN 10 GAMES: Roy Gleason, Derrell Griffith, Dick Nen, Phil Ortega, Dick Scott, Jack Smith, Daryl Spencer *, Nick Willhite

NOTES: World Champions! Koufax (Cy Young and MVP).

KEY SIGNATURES: Alston, Gilliam, Wills, Howard, W. Davis, T. Davis, Koufax, Drysdale.

VALUE: $400

1963 MILWAUKEE - Hank Aaron, Tommie Aaron, Frank Bolling, Bobby Bragan (MANAGER), Ty Cline, Tony Cloninger, Del Crandall, Don Dillard, Hank Fischer, Frank Funk, Len Gabrielson, Bob Hendley, Mack Jones, Lou Klimchock *, Norm Larker *, Denny Lemaster, Eddie Mathews, Lee Maye, Roy McMillan, Denis Menke, Bubba Morton *, Gene Oliver *, Ron Piche, Claude Raymond, Bob Sadowski, Amado Samuel, Don Schneider, Bob Shaw, Warren Spahn, Hawk Taylor, Bobby Tiefenauer, Joe Torre, Bob Uecker, Woody Woodward

LESS THAN 10 GAMES: Gus Bell, Wade Blasingame, Lew Burdette, Rico Carty

KEY SIGNATURES: Mathews, Aaron, Torre, Uecker, Spahn.

VALUE: $180

1963 MINNESOTA - Bernie Allen, Bob Allison, George Banks, Earl Battey, Bill Daily, Mike Fornieles *, Johnny Goryl, Lenny Green, Jimmie Hall, Jim Kaat, Harmon Killebrew, Fred Lasher, Sam Mele (MANAGER), Don Mincher, Ray Moore, Camilo Pascual, Jim Perry *, Bill Pleis, Wally Post *, Vic Power, Paul Ratliff, Garry Roggenburk, Jim Roland, Rich Rollins, Lee Stange, Dick Stigman, Frank Sullivan, Bill Tuttle, Zoilo Versalles, Vic Wertz *, Jerry Zimmerman

LESS THAN 10 GAMES: Jerry Arrigo, Julio Becquer, Gary Dotter, Jack Kralick *, Jim Lemon *, Tony Oliva, Dwight Siebler, Jay Ward, Don Williams

KEY SIGNATURES: Versalles, Killebrew, Oliva, Kaat.

VALUE: $210

1963 NEW YORK (AL) - Yogi Berra, Johnny Blanchard, Jim Bouton, Clete Boyer, Marshall Bridges, Harry Bright *, Al Downing, Whitey Ford, Pedro Gonzalez, Steve Hamilton *, Ralph Houk (MANAGER), Elston Howard, Tony Kubek, Bill Kunkel, Phil Linz, Dale Long, Hector Lopez, Mickey Mantle, Roger Maris, Joe Pepitone, Jack Reed, Hal Reniff, Bobby Richardson, Bill Stafford, Ralph Terry, Tom Tresh, Stan Williams

LESS THAN 10 GAMES: Luis Arroyo, Bud Daley, Jake Gibbs, Tom Metcalf

NOTES: Howard (MVP).

KEY SIGNATURES: Maris, Howard, Mantle, Berra, Ford.

VALUE: $475

1963 NEW YORK (NL) - Larry Bearnarth, Larry Burright, Chris Cannizzaro, Duke Carmel *, Joe Christopher, Galen Cisco, Choo Choo Coleman, Cliff Cook, Roger Craig, Chico Fernandez *, Jesse Gonder *, Pumpsie Green, Tim Harkness, Jim Hickman, Joe Hicks, Gil Hodges, Jay Hook, Ron Hunt, Al Jackson, Rod Kanehl, Ed Kranepool, Ken

MacKenzie *, Al Moran, Charlie Neal *, Jimmy Piersall *, Grover Powell, Don Rowe, Ted Schreiber, Norm Sherry, Dick Smith, Duke Snider, Tracy Stallard, Casey Stengel (MANAGER), Sammy Taylor *, Frank Thomas, Marv Throneberry, Carl Willey

LESS THAN 10 GAMES: Craig Anderson, Ed Bauta *, Steve Dillon, Cleon Jones

KEY SIGNATURES: Stengel, Snider, Kranepool, Hodges.

VALUE: $300

1963 PHILADELPHIA - Dick Allen, Ruben Amaro, Earl Averill, Jack Baldschun, Dennis Bennett, John Boozer, Johnny Callison, Wes Covington, Ray Culp, Clay Dalrymple, Don Demeter, Ryne Duren, Cal Emery, Tony Gonzalez, Wayne Graham, Dallas Green, Jack Hamilton, John Herrnstein, Don Hoak, Billy Klaus, Johnny Klippstein, Jim Lemon *, Art Mahaffey, Gene Mauch (MANAGER), Cal McLish, Bob Oldis, Cookie Rojas, Chris Short, Roy Sievers, Tony Taylor, Frank Torre, Bobby Wine

LESS THAN 10 GAMES: Paul Brown, Mike Harrington, Bobby Locke, Marcelino Lopez

KEY SIGNATURES: Allen.

VALUE: $110

1963 PITTSBURGH - Gene Alley, Bob Bailey, Ron Brand, Smoky Burgess, Don Cardwell, Roberto Clemente, Donn Clendenon, Roy Face, Earl Francis, Bob Friend, Joe Gibbon, Harvey Haddix, Vern Law, Johnny Logan, Jerry Lynch *, Bill Mazeroski, Al McBean, Manny Mota, Danny Murtaugh (MANAGER), Jim Pagliaroni, Elmo Plaskett, Ted Savage, Dick Schofield, Don Schwall, Tommie Sisk, Bob Skinner *, Willie Stargell, Bob Veale, Bill Virdon

LESS THAN 10 GAMES: Tom Butters, Larry Elliot, Julio Gotay, Tom Parsons, Tom Sturdivant *

KEY SIGNATURES: Clendenon, Mazeroski, Clemente, Stargell, Mota.

VALUE: $600

1963 SAN FRANCISCO - Felipe Alou, Jesus Alou, Matty Alou, Joey Amalfitano, Ed Bailey, Bobby Bolin, Ernie Bowman, Orlando Cepeda, Al Dark (MANAGER), Jim Davenport, Jim Duffalo, Jack Fisher, Tom Haller, Chuck Hiller, Billy Hoeft, Harvey Kuenn, Norm Larker *, Don Larsen, Juan Marichal, Willie Mays, Willie McCovey, Billy O'Dell, Jose Pagan, Gaylord Perry, Cap Peterson, Billy Pierce, Jack Sanford, Al Stanek

LESS THAN 10 GAMES: Jose Cardenal, Jimmie Coker, Jim Constable, Bob Garibaldi, Jim Ray Hart, Ron Herbel, Frank Linzy, John Pregenzer

KEY SIGNATURES: Cepeda, Mays, McCovey, Marichal, Larsen, Perry.

VALUE: $275

1963 ST. LOUIS - George Altman, Ed Bauta *, Ken Boyer, Ernie Broglio, Lew Burdette *, Leo Burke *, Duke Carmel *, Harry Fanok, Curt Flood, Phil Gagliano, Bob Gibson, Dick Groat, Charlie James, Julian Javier, Sam Jones, Johnny Keane (MANAGER), Gary Kolb, Dal Maxvill, Tim McCarver, Stan Musial, Gene Oliver *, Diomedes Olivo, Ray Sadecki, Carl Sawatski, Barney Schultz *, Mike Shannon, Bobby Shantz, Curt Simmons, Ron Taylor, Ray Washburn, Bill White

LESS THAN 10 GAMES: Jim Beauchamp, Clyde Bloomfield, Jerry Buchek, Doug Clemens, Jack Damaska, Bob Humphreys, Jeoff Long, Ken MacKenzie *, Dave Ricketts, Red Schoendienst, Moe Thacker, Corky Withrow

KEY SIGNATURES: Groat, Boyer, McCarver, Musial, Gibson.

VALUE: $300

1963 WASHINGTON - Don Blasingame *, Carl Bouldin, Marv Breeding *, Eddie Brinkman, Jim Bronstad, Tom Brown, Pete Burnside *, Tom Cheney, Jim Coates *, Chuck Cottier, Bennie Daniels, Jim Duckworth, Jim Hannan, Chuck Hinton, Gil Hodges (MANAGER) *, John Kennedy, Jim King, Ron Kline, Hobie Landrith *, Don Leppert, Don Lock, Minnie Minoso, Cal Neeman *, Bobo Osborne, Claude Osteen, Dick Phillips, Jimmy Piersall *, Ken Retzer, Steve Ridzik, Ed Roebuck *, Don Rudolph, Dave Stenhouse, Mickey Vernon (MANAGER), Don Zimmer *

LESS THAN 10 GAMES: Bob Baird, Steve Hamilton *, Ed Hobaugh, Ken Hunt *, Jack Jenkins, Lou Klimchock *, Ron Moeller *, Art Quirk, Johnny Schaive, Bob Schmidt, Barry Shetrone

KEY SIGNATURES: Vernon, Hodges.

VALUE: $130

1964

1964 American League MVP Brooks Robinson

*** = player was traded**

1964 BALTIMORE - Jerry Adair, Luis Aparicio, Steve Barber, Hank Bauer (MANAGER), Sam Bowens, Jackie Brandt, Dick Brown, Wally Bunker, Gino Cimoli *, Chuck Estrada, Joe Gaines *, Lenny Green *, Harvey Haddix, Dick Hall, Bob Johnson, Willie Kirkland *, Charlie Lau *, Dave McNally, Stu Miller, John Orsino, Milt Pappas, Boog Powell, Robin Roberts, Brooks Robinson, Earl Robinson, Bob Saverine, Norm Siebern, Russ Snyder, Wes Stock *, Dave Vineyard

LESS THAN 10 GAMES: Frank Bertaina, Paul Blair, Lou Jackson, Sam Jones, Mike McCormick, Lou Piniella, Ken Rowe, Herm Starrette

NOTES: B. Robinson (MVP).

KEY SIGNATURES: Aparicio, Robinson, Powell, Piniella, Roberts.

VALUE: $200

1964 BOSTON - Ed Bressoud, Pete Charton, Lu Clinton *, Tony Conigliaro, Ed Connolly, Arnie Earley, Bob Heffner, Billy Herman (MANAGER), Tony Horton, Dalton Jones, Jack Lamabe, Frank Malzone, Felix Mantilla, Roman Mejias, Bill Monbouquette, Dave Morehead, Russ Nixon, Johnny Pesky (MANAGER), Dick Radatz, Jay Ritchie, Chuck Schilling, Al Smith *, Bill Spanswick, Dick Stuart, Lee Thomas *, Bob Tillman, Dick Williams, Earl Wilson, Carl Yastrzemski

LESS THAN 10 GAMES: Gary Geiger, Dave Gray, Bob Guindon, Mike Ryan, Wilbur Wood *

KEY SIGNATURES: Herman, Yastrzemski.

VALUE: $220

1964 CHICAGO (AL) - Frank Baumann, Ken Berry, Don Buford, John Buzhardt, Cam Carreon, Joe Cunningham *, Eddie Fisher, Ron Hansen, Ray Herbert, Mike Hershberger, Joe Horlen, Frank Kreutzer *, Jim Landis, Jeoff Long *, Al Lopez (MANAGER), J.C. Martin, Tommy McCraw, Jerry McNertney, Minnie Minoso, Don Mossi, Dave Nicholson, Gary Peters, Juan Pizarro, Floyd Robinson, Bill Skowron *, Gene Stephens, Fred Talbot, Pete Ward, Al Weis, Hoyt Wilhelm

LESS THAN 10 GAMES: Fritz Ackley, Smoky Burgess *, Jim Hicks, Bruce Howard, Dick Kenworthy, Charlie Maxwell, Charley Smith *, Marv Staehle

KEY SIGNATURES: Lopez, Wilhelm.

VALUE: $130

1964 CHICAGO (NL) - Joey Amalfitano, Ernie Banks, Dick Bertell, Lou Brock *, Ernie Broglio *, Bob Buhl, Freddie Burdette, Lew Burdette *, Leo Burke, Ellis Burton, Ron Campbell, Doug Clemens *, Billy Cowan, Dick Ellsworth, Don Elston, Len Gabrielson *, Lee Gregory, Larry Jackson, Bob Kennedy (MANAGER), Don Landrum, Lindy McDaniel, Billy Ott, Merritt Ranew *, Andre Rodgers, Vic Roznovsky, Ron Santo, Jimmie Schaffer, Wayne Schurr, Bobby Shantz *, Sterling Slaughter, Jimmy Stewart, Billy Williams

LESS THAN 10 GAMES: John Boccabella, John Flavin, Glen Hobbie *, Paul Jaeckel, Don Kessinger, Cal Koonce, Fred Norman, Paul Popovich, Dick Scott, Jack Spring *, Paul Toth, Jack Warner

KEY SIGNATURES: Banks, Santo, Williams, Brock, Kessinger.

VALUE: $175

1964 CINCINNATI - Steve Boros, Leo Cardenas, Jimmie Coker, Gordy Coleman, Ryne Duren *, Johnny Edwards, Sammy Ellis, Tommy Harper, Bill Henry, Fred Hutchinson (MANAGER), Joey Jay, Deron Johnson, Marty Keough, Bobby Klaus *, Jim Maloney, Billy McCool, Joe Nuxhall, Jim O'Toole, Don Pavletich, Tony Perez, Vada Pinson, Bob Purkey, Mel Queen, Frank Robinson, Pete Rose, Chico Ruiz, Dick Sisler (MANAGER), Bob Skinner *, Hal Smith, Johnny Temple, John Tsitouris

LESS THAN 10 GAMES: Jim Dickson, Tommy Helms, Chet Nichols, Al Worthington *

KEY SIGNATURES: Rose, Robinson, Pinson, Perez.

VALUE: $200

1964 CLEVELAND - Ted Abernathy, Tommie Agee, Max Alvis, Joe Azcue, Gary Bell, Larry Brown, Bob Chance, Vic Davalillo, Paul Dicken, Dick Donovan, Tito Francona, Mudcat Grant *, Woodie Held, Dick Howser, Tommy John, Jerry Kindall *, Jack Kralick, Al Luplow, Sam McDowell, Dom McMahon, Billy Moran *, Pedro Ramos *, Johnny Romano, Chico Salmon, Sonny Siebert, Al Smith *, Lee Stange *, Birdie Tebbetts (MANAGER), Luis Tiant, Leon Wagner, Fred Whitfield

LESS THAN 10 GAMES: George Banks *, Vern Fuller, Tom Kelley, Tony Martinez, Wally Post, Gordon Seyfried, Duke Sims, Jerry Walker

KEY SIGNATURES: McDowell, Tiant, John.

VALUE: $115

1964 DETROIT - Hank Aguirre, Gates Brown, Bill Bruton, Norm Cash, Don Demeter, Chuck Dressen (MANAGER), Dick Egan, Terry Fox, Bill Freehan, Fred Gladding, Willie Horton, Al Kaline, Mickey Lolich, Jerry Lumpe, Dick McAuliffe, Denny McLain, Julio Navarro *, Bubba Phillips, Ed Rakow, Phil Regan, Mike Roarke, Larry Sherry, Joe Sparma, George Thomas, Don Wert, Dave Wickersham, Jake Wood

LESS THAN 10 GAMES: Bill Faul, Fritz Fisher, Jack Hamilton, Alan Koch *, Frank Lary *, Jim Northrup, Bill Roman, Johnny Seale, George Smith, Mickey Stanley, John Sullivan

KEY SIGNATURES: Cash, Kaline, Freehan, Lolich, McLain.

VALUE: $160

1964 HOUSTON - Bob Aspromonte, John Bateman, Jim Beauchamp, Walt Bond, Hal Brown, Bob Bruce, Harry Craft (MANAGER), Dick Farrell, Nellie Fox, Joe Gaines *, Jerry Grote, Carroll Hardy, Lum Harris (MANAGER), Ken Johnson, Gordon Jones, Eddie Kasko, Don Larsen *, Bob Lillis, Joe Morgan, Ivan Murrell, Don Nottebart, Jim Owens, Claude Raymond, Dave Roberts, Pete Runnels, Al Spangler, Rusty Staub, Mike White, Walt Williams, Hal Woodeshick, Jim Wynn, Larry Yellen

LESS THAN 10 GAMES: Dave Adlesh, Don Bradley, Danny Coombs, Brock Davis, Larry Dierker, Dave Giusti, Steve Hertz, Joe Hoerner, John Hoffman, Sonny Jackson, Johnny Weekly, Chris Zachary

KEY SIGNATURES: Fox, Aspromonte, Staub, Morgan.

VALUE: $110

1964 KANSAS CITY - George Alusik, Ted Bowsfield, Billy Bryan, Bert Campaneris, Wayne Causey, Ed Charles, Rocky Colavito, Moe Drabowsky, Dave Duncan, Doc Edwards, Jim Gentile, Dick Green, Joe Grzenda, Vernm Handrahan, Ken Harrelson, Manny Jiminez, Rick Joseph, Charlie Lau *, Ed Lopat (MANAGER), Nelson Mathews, Mel McGaha (MANAGER), Aurelio Monteagudo, John O'Donoghue, Orlando Pena, Dan Pfister, Tommie Reynolds, Ken Sanders, Jose Santiago, Diego Segui, Charlie Shoemaker, Larry Stahl, Wes Stock *, Jose Tartabull, George Williams, John Wyatt

LESS THAN 10 GAMES: Jack Aker, Gino Camoli *, Lew Krausse, Bob Meyer *, Blue Moon Odom, Tom Sturdivant *, John Wojcik

KEY SIGNATURES: Colavito, Campaneris, Odom.

VALUE: $110

1964 LOS ANGELES (AL) - Joe Adcock, Bo Belinsky, George Brunet, Dean Chance, Lu Clinton *, Charlie Dees, Bob Duliba, Jim Fregosi, Aubrey Gatewood, Lenny Green *, Bill Kelso, Ed Kirkpatrick, Bobby Knoop, Joe Koppe, Barry Latman, Bob Lee, Don Lee, Ken McBride, Billy Moran *, Fred Newman, Dan Osinski, Albie Pearson, Bob Perry, Jimmy Piersall, Vic Power *, Rick Reichardt, Bill Rigney (MANAGER), Bob Rodgers, Tom Satriano, Paul Schaal, Dick Simpson, Willie Smith, Lee Thomas *, Felix Torres

LESS THAN 10 GAMES: Hank Foiles, Art Fowler, Paul Foytack, Jack Hiatt, Bob Meyer *, Julio Navarro *, Jack Spring *, Ed Sukla

NOTES: Chance (Cy Young).

KEY SIGNATURES: Adcock, Fregosi, Chance.

VALUE: $100

1964 LOS ANGELES (NL) - Walt Alston (MANAGER), Jim Brewer, Doug Camilli, Willie Crawford, Tommy Davis, Willie Davis, Don Drysdale, Ron Fairly, Jim Gilliam, Derrell Griffith, Frank Howard, Sandy Koufax, Ken McMullen, Bob Miller, Larry Miller, Joe Moeller, Wally Moon, Nate Oliver, Phil Ortega, Wes Parker, Ron Perranoski, Howie Reed, Johnny Roseboro, Bart Shirley, Jeff Torborg, Dick Tracewski, Lee Walls, Johnny Werhas, Nick Willhite, Maury Wills

LESS THAN 10 GAMES: Johnny Podres, John Purdin, Pete Richert, Bill Singer

KEY SIGNATURES: Alston, Wills, Howard, W. Davis, T. Davis, Koufax, Drysdale.

VALUE: $300

1964 MILWAUKEE - Mike de la Hoz, Hank Aaron, Sandy Alomar, Felipe Alou, Ed Bailey, Wade Blasingmae, Frank Bolling, Bobby Bragan (MANAGER), Clay Carroll, Rico Carty, Ty Cline, Tony Cloninger, Hank Fischer, Len Gabrielson *, Billy Hoeft, Lou Klimchock, Gary Kolb, Denny Lemaster, Eddie Mathews, Lee Maye, Denis Menke, Phil Niekro, Gene Oliver, Chi Chi Olivo, Bob Sadowski, Dan Schneider, Jack Smith, Warren Spahn, Bobby Tiefenauer, Joe Torre, Woody Woodward

LESS THAN 10 GAMES: Gus Bell, Ethan Blackaby, John Braun, Cecil Butler, Dave Eilers, Dick Kelley, Frank Lary *, Roy McMillan *, Merritt Ranew *, Phil Roof, Bill Southworth, Arnie Umbach

KEY SIGNATURES: Mathews, Aaron, Carty, Torre, Spahn, Niekro.

VALUE: $200

ROY = Rookie of the Year

1964 MINNESOTA - Bernie Allen, Bob Allison, Jerry Arrigo, Earl Battey, Bill Bethea, Bill Dailey, Johnny Goryl, Mudcat Grant *, Lenny Green *, Jimmie Hall, Ron Henry, Jim Kaat, Harmon Killebrew, Jerry Kindall *, Johnny Klippstein *, Frank Kostro, Joe McCabe, Sam Mele (MANAGER), Don Mincher, Tony Oliva, Camilo Pascual, Jim Perry, Bill Pleis, Vic Power *, Rich Reese, Jim Roland, Rich Rollins, Garland Shiffert, Jim Snyder, Lee Stange *, Dick Stigman, Zoilo Versalles, Jay Ward, Al Worthington *, Jerry Zimmerman,

LESS THAN 10 GAMES: George Banks *, Clyde Bloomfield, Dave Boswell, Gary Dotter, Bill Fischer, Jerry Fosnow, Chuck Nieson, Joe Nossek, Dwight Siebler, Bill Whitby

NOTES: Oliva (ROY).

KEY SIGNATURES: Versalles, Oliva, Killebrew, Kaat.

VALUE: $225

1964 NEW YORK (AL) - Yogi Berra (MANAGER), Johnny Blanchard, Jim Bouton, Clete Boyer, Bud Daley, Al Downing, Whitey Ford, Pedro Gonzalez, Steve Hamilton, Elston Howard, Tony Kubek, Phil Linz, Hector Lopez, Mickey Mantle, Roger Maris, Pete Mikkelsen, Archie Moore, Joe Pepitone, Pedro Ramos *, Hal Reniff, Roger Repoz, Bobby Richardson, Rollie Sheldon, Bill Stafford, Mel Stottlemyre, Ralph Terry, Tom Tresh, Stan Williams

LESS THAN 10 GAMES: Harry Bright, Jake Gibbs, Mike Hegan, Elvio Jiminez, Bob Meyer *

KEY SIGNATURES: Berra, Maris, Mantle, Howard, Ford, Stottlemyre.

VALUE: $400

1964 NEW YORK (NL) - George Altman, Larry Bearnarth, Chris Cannizzaro, Joe Christopher, Galen Cisco, Larry Elliott, Jack Fisher, Jesse Gonder, Wayne Graham, Tim Harkness, Jim Hickman, Ron Hunt, Willard Hunter, Al Jackson, Rod Kanehl, Bobby Klaus *, Ed Kranepool, Frank Lary *, Ron Locke, Roy McMillan *, Al Moran, Tom Parsons, Dennis Ribant, Amado Samuel, Dick Smith, Charley Smith *, Tracy Stallard, Casey Stengel (MANAGER), Johnny Stephenson, Tom Sturdivant *, Darrell Sutherland, Hawk Taylor, Frank Thomas *, Bill Wakefield, Carl Willey

LESS THAN 10 GAMES: Craig Anderson, Ed Bauta, Larry Burright, Steve Dillon, Jerry Hinsley, Jay Hook, Gary Kroll *

KEY SIGNATURES: Stengel, Kranepool.

VALUE: $250

1964 PHILADELPHIA - Dick Allen, Ruben Amaro, Jack Baldschun, Dennis Bennett, John Boozer, Johnny Briggs, Jim Bunning, Johnny Callison, Danny Cater, Wes Covington, Ray Culp, Clay Dalrymple, Tony Gonzalez, Dallas Green, John Herrnstein, Alex Johnson, Johnny Klippstein *, Art Mahaffey, Gene Mauch (MANAGER), Adolfo Phillips, Vic Power *, Ed Roebuck *, Cookie Rojas, Bobby Shantz *, Costen Shockley, Chris Short, Roy Sievers *, Tony Taylor, Frank Thomas *, Gus Triandos, Bobby Wine, Rick Wise

LESS THAN 10 GAMES: Dave Bennett, Pat Corrales, Ryne Duren *, Don Hoak, Gary Kroll *, Bobby Locke, Cal McLish, Morrie Steevens

NOTES: Allen (ROY).

KEY SIGNATURES: Allen, Bunning.

VALUE: $110

ROY = Rookie of the Year

1964 PITTSBURGH - Gene Alley, Bob Bailey, Steve Blass, Frank Bork, Smoky Burgess *, Tom Butters, Roberto Clemente, Donn Clendenon, Roy Face, Gene Freese, Bob Friend, Joe Gibbon, Rex Johnston, Vern Law, Jerry Lynch, Jerry May, Bill Mazeroski, Al McBean, Orlando McFarlane, Manny Mota, Danny Murtaugh (MANAGER), Jim Pagliaroni, Bob Priddy, Dick Schofield, Don Schwall, Tommie Sisk, Willie Stargell, Bob Veale, Bill Virdon, Dave Wissman

LESS THAN 10 GAMES: Don Cardwell, Earl Francis, John Gelnar, Julio Gotay, Freddie Green, Wilbur Wood *

KEY SIGNATURES: Clendenon, Mazeroski, Clemente, Mota.

VALUE: $525

1964 SAN FRANCISCO - Jesus Alou, Matty Alou, Bobby Bolin, Jose Cardenal, Orlando Cepeda, Del Crandall, Al Dark (MANAGER), Jim Davenport, Jim Duffalo, Gil Garrido Tom Haller, Jim Ray Hart, Bob Hendley, Ron Herbel, Chuck Hiller, Harvey Kuenn, Ha Lanier, Ken MacKenzie, Juan Marichal, Willie Mays, Willie McCovey, Billy O'Dell, Jose Pagan, Gaylord Perry, Cap Peterson, Billy Pierce, John Pregenzer, Jack Sanford, Bob Shaw, Duke Snider

LESS THAN 10 GAMES: Dick Estelle, Randy Hundley, Don Larsen *, Masanori Murakami

KEY SIGNATURES: Cepeda, Mays, McCovey, Snider, Marichal, Perry, Larsen.

VALUE: $250

1964 ST. LOUIS - Ken Boyer, Lou Brock *, Ernie Broglio *, Jerry Buchek, Doug Clemens *, Roger Craig, Mike Cuellar, Curt Flood, Phil Gagliano, Bob Gibson, Dick Groat, Glen Hobbie *, Bob Humphreys, Charlie James, Julian Javier, Johnny Keane (MANAGER), Johnny Lewis, Jeoff Long *, Dal Maxvill, Tim McCarver, Gordie Richardson, Ray Sadecki, Barney Schultz, Mike Shannon, Bobby Shantz *, Curt Simmons, Bob Skinner *, Ed Spiezio, Ron Taylor, Bob Uecker, Carl Warwick, Ray Washburn, Bill White

LESS THAN 10 GAMES: Dave Bakenhaster, Lew Burdette *, Dave Dowling, Harry Fanok, Joe Morgan, Jack Spring *

NOTES: World Champions! Boyer (MVP).

KEY SIGNATURES: White, Boyer, Brock, McCarver, Uecker, Gibson.

VALUE: $460

1964 WASHINGTON - Don Blasingame, Marshall Bridges, Eddie Brinkman, Mike Brumley, Tom Cheney, Chuck Cottier, Joe Cunningham *, Bennie Daniels, Jim Duckworth, Jim Hannan, Chuck Hinton, Gil Hodges (MANAGER), Ken Hunt, John Kennedy, Jim King, Willie Kirkland *, Ron Kline, Alan Koch *, Frank Kreutzer *, Don Leppert, Don Lock, Buster Narum, Claude Osteen, Dick Phillips, Ken Retzer, Steve Ridzik, Don Rudolph, Roy Sievers *, Bill Skowron *, Dave Stenhouse, Fred Valentine, Don Zimmer

LESS THAN 10 GAMES: Carl Bouldin, Jim Bronstad, Pete Craig, Howie Koplitz, Don Loun, Ed Roebuck *

KEY SIGNATURES: Hodges.

VALUE: $130

1965

1965 New York Mets

= player was traded

965 BALTIMORE - Jerry Adair, Luis Aparicio, Steve Barber, Hank Bauer (MAN-GER), Mark Belanger, Paul Blair, Curt Blefary, Sam Bowens, Jackie Brandt, Dick rown, Wally Bunker, Harvey Haddix, Dick Hall, Bob Johnson, Dave Johnson, Don arsen *, Charlie Lau, Dave McNally, John Miller, Stu Miller, John Orsino, Jim Palmer, ilt Pappas, Boog Powell, Robin Roberts *, Brooks Robinson, Norm Siebern, Russ nyder

ESS THAN 10 GAMES: Ed Barnowski, Frank Bertaina, Andy Etchebarren, Darold nowles, Ken Rowe, Herm Starrette, Carl Warwick *

OTES: Blefary (ROY).

EY SIGNATURES: Powell, Aparicio, Robinson, Blefary, Palmer, Roberts.

VALUE: $230

OY = Rookie of the Year

965 BOSTON - Dennis Bennett, Ed Bressoud, Tony Conigliaro, Bob Duliba, Arnie Ear-y, Gary Geiger, Jim Gosger, Lenny Green, Bob Heffner, Billy Herman (MANAGER), ony Horton, Dalton Jones, Jack Lamabe *, Jim Lonborg, Frank Malzone, Felix Man-lla, Bill Monbouquette, Dave Morehead, Jerry Moses, Russ Nixon, Rico Petrocelli, Dick adatz, Jay Ritchie, Mike Ryan, Chuck Schilling, Jerry Stephenson, Lee Thomas, Bob illman, Earl Wilson, Carl Yastrzemski

ESS THAN 10 GAMES: Rudy Schlesinger

EY SIGNATURES: Herman, Yastrzemski.

VALUE: $230

1965 CALIFORNIA - Joe Adcock, George Brunet, Jose Cardenal, Dean Chance, Lu Clinton *, Jim Coates, Charlie Dees, Tom Egan, Jim Fregosi, Aubrey Gatewood, Julio Gotay, Ed Kirkpatrick, Bobby Knopp, Joe Koppe, Barry Latman, Bob Lee, Don Lee *, Marcelino Lopez, Rudy May, Fred Newman, Albie Pearson, Ron Piche, Jimmy Piersall, Vic Power, Merritt Ranew, Rick Reichardt, Bill Rigney (MANAGER), Bob Rodgers, Tom Satriano, Paul Schaal, Costen Shockley, Bobby Gene Smith, Willie Smith, Al Spangler *, Ed Sukla

LESS THAN 10 GAMES: Gino Cimoli, Jackie Hernandez, Ken McBride, Jim McGlothin, Phil Roof *, Jack Sanford *, Dick Simpson, Dick Wantz

KEY SIGNATURES: Fregosi.

VALUE: $100

1965 CHICAGO (AL) - Tommie Agee, Ken Berry, Greg Bollo, Don Buford, Smoky Burgess, John Buzhardt, Danny Cater, Eddie Fisher, Gene Freese *, Ron Hansen, Jim Hicks, Joe Horlen, Bruce Howard, Tommy John, Frank Lary *, Bob Locker, Al Lopez (MANAGER), J.C. Martin, Tommy McCraw, Dave Nicholson, Gary Peters, Juan Pizarro, Floyd Robinson, Johnny Romano, Jimmie Schaffer *, Bill Skowron, Bill Voss, Pete Ward, Al Weis, Hoyt Wilhelm, Ted Wills

LESS THAN 10 GAMES: Bill Heath, Duane Josephson, Dick Kenworthy, Marv Staehle

KEY SIGNATURES: Lopez, John, Wilhelm.

VALUE: $125

1965 CHICAGO (NL) - Ted Abernathy, George Altman, Joey Amalfitano, Ed Bailey *, Ernie Banks, Glenn Beckert, Dick Bertell *, John Boccabella, Harry Bright, Ernie Broglio, Byron Browne, Bob Buhl, Leo Burke, Ellis Burton, Ron Campbell, Doug Clemens, Dick Ellsworth, Bill Faul, Len Gabrielson *, Chuck Hartenstein, Bob Hendley *, Billy Hoeft, Bob Humphreys, Larry Jackson, Bob Kennedy (MANAGER), Don Kessinger, Lou Klein (MANAGER), Cal Koonce, Chris Krug, Harvey Kuenn *, Don Landrum, Lindy McDaniel, Roberto Pena, Vic Roznovsky, Ron Santo, Jimmy Stewart, Jack Warner, Billy Williams, Don Young

LESS THAN 10 GAMES: Frank Baumann, Lew Burdette *, Ken Holtzman

KEY SIGNATURES: Banks, Santo, Williams.

VALUE: $130

1965 CINCINNATI - Jerry Arrigo, Leo Cardenas, Jimmie Coker, Gordy Coleman, Roger Craig, Ted Davidson, Jim Duffalo *, Johnny Edwards, Sammy Ellis, Tommy Harper, Tommy Helms, Charlie James, Joey Jay, Deron Johnson, Marty Keough, Bobby Locke, Jim Maloney, Billy McCool, Joe Nuxhall, Jim O'Toole, Don Pavletich, Tony Perez, Vada Pinson, Frank Robinson, Pete Rose, Chico Ruiz, Art Shamsky, Dick Sisler (MANAGER), John Tsitouris

LESS THAN 10 GAMES: Steve Boros, Bill Henry *, Lee May, Darrell Osteen, Mel Queen, Dom Zanni

KEY SIGNATURES: Rose, Robinson, Pinson, Perez.

VALUE: $180

1965 CLEVELAND - Max Alvis, Joe Azcue, Ray Barker *, Gary Bell, Larry Brown, Cam Carreon, Lu Clinton *, Rocky Colavito, Vic Davalillo, Bill Davis, Dick Donovan, Pedro Gonzalez *, Steve Hargan, Chuck Hinton, Dick Howser, Jack Kralick, Al Luplow, Sam

McDowell, Don McMahon, Billy Moran, Phil Roof *, Chico Salmon, Sonny Siebert, Duke Sims, Jack Spring, Lee Stange, Birdie Tebbetts (MANAGER), Ralph Terry, Luis Tiant, Bobby Tiefenauer *, Leon Wagner, Floyd Weaver, Fred Whitfield

LESS THAN 10 GAMES: George Banks, Ralph Gagliano, Mike Hedlund, Tom Kelley, Tony Martinez, Richie Scheinblum, Stan Williams

KEY SIGNATURES: Colavito, McDowell, Tiant.

VALUE: $115

1965 DETROIT - Hank Aguirre, Gates Brown, Norm Cash, Don Demeter, Chuck Dressen (MANAGER), Terry Fox, Bill Freehan, Fred Gladding, Willie Horton, Al Kaline, Mickey Lolich, Jerry Lumpe, Dick McAuliffe, Denny McLain, Jackie Moore, Julio Navarro, Ron Nischwitz, Jim Northrup, Ray Oyler, Orlando Pena *, Phil Regan, Bill Roman, Larry Sherry, George Smith, Joe Sparma, Mickey Stanley, John Sullivan, George Thomas, Don Wert, Dave Wickersham, Jake Wood

LESS THAN 10 GAMES: Jack Hamilton, John Hiller, Vern Holtgrave, Leo Marentette, Ed Rakow, Wayne Redmond, Johnny Seale

KEY SIGNATURES: Cash, Kaline, Freehan, McLain, Lolich.

VALUE: $160

1965 HOUSTON - Dave Adlesh, Bob Aspromonte, John Bateman, Jim Beauchamp *, Walt Bond, Ron Brand, Bob Bruce, Danny Coombs, Mike Cuellar, Larry Dierker, Dick Farrell, Nellie Fox, Joe Gaines, Jim Gentile *, Dave Giusti, Lum Harris (MANAGER), Chuck Harrison, Sonny Jackson, Eddie Kasko, Bob Lillis, Ken MacKenzie, Lee Maye *, Norm Miller, Joe Morgan, Don Nottebart, Jim Owens, Claude Raymond, Robin Roberts *, Al Spangler *, Rusty Staub, Ron Taylor *, Frank Thomas *, Gus Triandos *, Hal Woodeshick *, Jim Wynn

LESS THAN 10 GAMES: Don Arlich, John Hoffman, Ken Johnson *, Gordon Jones, Jack Lamabe *, Don Lee *, Jim Mahoney, Gene Ratliff, Jim Ray, Carroll Sembera, Bruce Von Hoff, Mike White, Chris Zachary

KEY SIGNATURES: Morgan, Staub, Fox, Roberts.

VALUE: $120

1965 KANSAS CITY - Jack Aker, Johnny Blanchard *, Billy Bryan, Don Buschhorn, Bert Campaneris, Wayne Causey, Ed Charles, Jim Dickson, Moe Drabowsky, Jim Gentile *, Dick Green, Ken Harrelson, Mike Hershberger, Jess Hickman, Catfish Hunter, Rene Lachemann, Jim Landis, Skip Lockwood, Nelson Mathews, Mel McGaha (MANAGER), Don Mossi, John O'Donoghue, Orlando Pena *, Tommie Reynolds, Santiago Rosario, Diego Segui, Rollie Sheldon *, Larry Stahl, Wes Stock, Haywood Sullivan (MANAGER), Fred Talbot, Jose Tartabull, John Wyatt

LESS THAN 10 GAMES: Lu Clinton *, Doc Edwards *, Tom Harrison, Dick Joyce, Lew Krausse, Paul Lindblad, Aurelio Monteagudo *, Blue Moon Odom, Satchel Paige, John Sanders, Jose Santiago, Randy Schwartz, Ron Tompkins

KEY SIGNATURES: Campaneris, Hunter, Paige, Odom.

VALUE: $120

1965 LOS ANGELES - Walt Alston (MANAGER), Jim Brewer, Willie Crawford, Tommy Davis, Willie Davis, Don Drysdale, Ron Fairly, Al Ferrara, Jim Gilliam, Derrell Griffith, Lou Johnson, John Kennedy, Sandy Koufax, Jim Lefebvre, Don LeJohn, Bob Miller, Wally Moon, Claude Osteen, Wes Parker, Ron Perranoski, Johnny Podres, John

Purdin, Howie Reed, Johnny Roseboro, Dick Smith, Jeff Torborg, Dick Tracewski, Nick Willhite *, Maury Wills

LESS THAN 10 GAMES: Mike Kekich, Nate Oliver, Bill Singer, Hec Valle, Johnny Werhas

NOTES: Koufax (Cy Young); Lefebvre (ROY).

KEY SIGNATURES: Alston, Lefebvre, Wills, W. Davis, Koufax, Drysdale.

VALUE: $400

1965 MILWAUKEE - Mike de la Hoz, Hank Aaron, Sandy Alomar, Felipe Alou, Johnny Blanchard *, Wade Blasingame, Frank Bolling, Bobby Bragan (MANAGER), Clay Carroll, Rico Carty, Ty Cline, Tony Cloninger, Billy Cowan *, Don Dillard, Hank Fischer, Jesse Gonder *, Ken Johnson *, Mack Jones, Dick Kelley, Lou Klimchock, Gary Kolb *, Denny Lemaster, Eddie Mathews, Lee Maye *, Denis Menke, Phil Niekro, Billy O'Dell, Gene Oliver, Dan Osinski, Bob Sadowski, Frank Thomas *, Joe Torre, Woody Woodward

LESS THAN 10 GAMES: Tommie Aaron, Jim Beauchamp *, Dave Eilers *, Chi Chi Olivo, Bobby Tiefenauer *

KEY SIGNATURES: Mathews, Aaron, Torre, Niekro.

VALUE: $200

1965 MINNESOTA - Bernie Allen, Bob Allison, Earl Battey, Dave Boswell, Jerry Fosnow, Mudcat Grant, Jimmie Hall, Jim Kaat, Harmon Killebrew, Jerry Kindall, Johnny Klippstein, Andy Kosco, Frank Kostro, Sam Mele (MANAGER), Jim Merritt, Don Mincher, Mel Nelson, Joe Nossek, Tony Oliva, Camilo Pascual, Jim Perry, Bill Pleis, Frank Quilici, Rich Reese, Garry Roggenburk, Rich Rollins, John Sevcik, Dick Stigman, Cesar Tovar, Ted Uhlaender, Sandy Valdespino, Zoilo Versalles, Al Worthington, Jerry Zimmerman

LESS THAN 10 GAMES: Pete Cimino, Dwight Siebler

NOTES: Versalles (MVP).

KEY SIGNATURES: Versalles, Oliva, Killebrew, Kaat.

VALUE: $295

1965 NEW YORK (AL) - Ray Barker *, Johnny Blanchard *, Gil Blanco, Jim Bouton, Clete Boyer, Horace Clarke, Jack Cullen, Al Downing, Doc Edwards *, Whitey Ford, Jake Gibbs, Steve Hamilton, Elston Howard, Johnny Keane (MANAGER), Tony Kubek, Phil Linz, Art Lopez, Hector Lopez, Mickey Mantle, Roger Maris, Pete Mikkelsen, Ross Moschitto, Bobby Murcer, Joe Pepitone, Pedro Ramos, Hal Reniff, Roger Repoz, Bobby Richardson, Bob Schmidt, Bill Stafford, Mel Stottlemyre, Bobby Tiefenauer *, Tom Tresh, Roy White

LESS THAN 10 GAMES: Rick Beck, Jim Brenneman, Duke Carmel, Pedro Gonzalez *, Mike Jurewicz, Archie Moore, Rollie Sheldon *

KEY SIGNATURES: Mantle, Howard, Maris, Murcer, Stottlemyre, Ford.

VALUE: $370

1965 NEW YORK (NL) - Larry Bearnarth, Jim Bethke, Chris Cannizzaro, Joe Christopher, Galen Cisco, Kevin Collins, Billy Cowan *, Dave Eilers *, Jack Fisher, Jesse Gonder *, Greg Goossen, Bud Harrelson, Jim Hickman, Chuck Hiller *, Ron Hunt, Al Jackson, Cleon Jones, Bobby Klaus, Gary Kolb *, Ed Kranepool, Gary Kroll, Frank Lary *, Johnny Lewis, Tug McGraw, Roy McMillan, Larry Miller, Danny Napoleon, Tom Parsons, Denis Ribant, Gordie Richardson, Jimmie Schaffer *, Charley Smith, Warren Spahn *, ;asey Stengel (MANAGER), Johnny Stephenson, Darrell Sutherland, Ron Swoboda, Iawk Taylor, Wes Westrum (MANAGER), Carl Willey

,ESS THAN 10 GAMES: Yogi Berra, Rob Gardner, Bob Moorhead, Dennis Musgraves,)ick Selma

EY SIGNATURES: Stengel, Kranepool, Swoboda, Berra, Spahn.

VALUE: $300

965 PHILADELPHIA - Dick Allen, Ruben Amaro, Jack Baldschun, Bo Belinsky, Johnny riggs, Jim Bunning, Lew Burdette *, Johnny Callison, Pat Corrales, Wes Covington, Ray ;ulp, Clay Dalrymple, Tony Gonzalez, Ray Herbert, John Herrnstein, Alex Johnson, Art Aahaffey, Gene Mauch (MANAGER), Adolfo Phillips, Ed Roebuck, Cookie Rojas, ;hris Short, Bill Sorrell, Dick Stuart, Tony Taylor, Frank Thomas *, Gus Triandos *, ;ary Wagner, Bobby Wine

,ESS THAN 10 GAMES: Bobby Del Greco, Ryne Duren *, Grant Jackson, Ferguson enkins, Morrie Steevens

EY SIGNATURES: Allen, Bunning, Jenkins.

VALUE: $110

965 PITTSBURGH - Gene Alley, Bob Bailey, Don Cardwell, Frank Carpin, Roberto ;lemente, Donn Clendenon, Del Crandall, Roy Face, Gene Freese *, Bob Friend, Joe ;ibbon, Vern Law, Jerry Lynch, Bill Mazeroski, Al McBean, Manny Mota, Jim Paglia-oni, Andre Rodgers, Don Schwall, Tommie Sisk, Willie Stargell, Bob Veale, Bill Virdon,)zzie Virgil, Harry Walker (MANAGER), Wilbur Wood

,ESS THAN 10 GAMES: Tom Butters, Jerry May, Bob Oliver, Jose Pagan, Dick chofield, Hal Smith, George Spriggs, Luke Walker

EY SIGNATURES: Mazeroski, Clemente, Stargell.

VALUE: $510

965 SAN FRANCISCO - Jesus Alou, Matty Alou, Ed Bailey *, Dick Bertell *, Bobby 3olin, Bob Burda, Orlando Cepeda, Jim Davenport, Herman Franks (MANAGER), Tito uentes, Len Gabrielson *, Tom Haller, Jim Ray Hart, Ken Henderson, Bill Henry *, on Herbel, Jack Hiatt, Harvey Kuenn *, Hal Lanier, Frank Linzy, Juan Marichal, Willie Aays, Willie McCovey, Masanori Murakami, Jose Pagan *, Gaylord Perry, Cap Peterson, ack Sanford *, Dick Schofield *, Bob Schroder, Bob Shaw, Warren Spahn *

,ESS THAN 10 GAMES: Bob Barton, Ollie Brown, Jim Duffalo *, Dick Estelle, Bill Iands, Bob Hendley *, Chuck Hiller *, Randy Hundley, Bob Priddy

NOTES: Mays (MVP).

EY SIGNATURES: McCovey, Mays, Cepeda, Marichal, Perry, Spahn.

VALUE: $220

AVP = MVP Award winner

1965 ST. LOUIS - Ken Boyer, Nelson Briles, Lou Brock, Jerry Buchek, Steve Carlton,)on Dennis, Curt Flood, Tito Francona, Phil Gagliano, Bob Gibson, Dick Groat, Julian avier, George Kernek, Dal Maxvill, Tim McCarver, Bob Purkey, Dave Ricketts, Ray adecki, Ted Savage, Red Schoendienst (MANAGER), Barney Schultz, Mike Shannon, ;urt Simmons, Bob Skinner, Ed Spiezio, Tracy Stallard, Ron Taylor *, Bobby Tolan, Bob Jecker, Carl Warwick *, Ray Washburn, Bill White, Hal Woodeshick *

LESS THAN 10 GAMES: Dennis Aust, Earl Francis, Larry Jaster

KEY SIGNATURES: Schoendienst, White, Boyer, Brock, McCarver, Uecker, Gibson, Carlton.

VALUE: $250

1965 WASHINGTON - Don Blasingame, Marshall Bridges, Eddie Brinkman, Mike Brumley, Doug Camilli, Bob Chance, Joe Cunningham, Bennie Daniels, Jim Duckworth, Ryne Duren *, Jim French, Ken Hamlin, Woodie Held, Gil Hodges (MANAGER), Frank Howard, Jim King, Willie Kirkland, Ron Kline, Howie Koplitz, Frank Kreutzer, Don Lock, Joe McCabe, Mike McCormick, Ken McMullen, Buster Narum, Dick Nen, Phil Ortega, Pete Richert, Steve Ridzik, Roy Sievers, Fred Valentine, Don Zimmer

LESS THAN 10 GAMES: Brant Alyea, Paul Casanova, Joe Coleman, Chuck Cottier, Pete Craig, Dallas Green, Jim Hannan, Barry Moore, Nick Willhite *

KEY SIGNATURES: Hodges, Howard, McCormick.

*** = player was traded**

VALUE: $150

Cleveland Indians' pitcher Sonny Siebert used this ball during his 1966 no-hitter.

1966 ATLANTA - Mike de la Hoz, Hank Aaron, Ted Abernathy *, Sandy Alomar, Felipe Alou, Lee Bales, Wade Blasingame, Frank Bolling, Bobby Bragan (MANAGER), Clay Carroll, Rico Carty, Ty Cline *, Tony Cloninger, Hank Fischer *, Gary Geiger, John Herrnstein *, Billy Hitchcock (MANAGER), Pat Jarvis, Ken Johnson, Mack Jones, Dick Kelley, Marty Keough *, Denny Lemaster, Eddie Mathews, Denis Menke, Felix Millan, Phil Niekro, Billy O'Dell *, Gene Oliver, Chi Chi Olivo, Jay Ritchie, Dan Schneider, Don Schwall *, Lee Thomas *, Joe Torre, Arnie Umbach, Woody Woodward

LESS THAN 10 GAMES: Adrian Garrett, Herb Hippauf, Joey Jay *, George Kopacz, Ron Reed, Bill Robinson, Eddie Sadowski, Cecil Upshaw, Charlie Vaughan

NOTES: Braves' first year in Atlanta.

KEY SIGNATURES: Mathews, Aaron, Torre, Niekro.

VALUE: $190

966 BALTIMORE - Jerry Adair *, Luis Aparicio, Steve Barber, Hank Bauer (MANAGER), Frank Bertaina, Paul Blair, Curt Blefary, Sam Bowens, Gene Brabender, Wally Bunker, Moe Drabowsky, Andy Etchebarren, Eddie Fisher *, Dick Hall, Larry Haney, Woodie Held, Bob Johnson, Dave Johnson, Charlie Lau, Dave McNally, John Miller, Stu Miller, Jim Palmer, Boog Powell, Brooks Robinson, Frank Robinson, Vic Roznovsky, Russ Snyder, Eddie Watt

LESS THAN 10 GAMES: Ed Barnowski, Mark Belanger, Cam Carreon, Mike Epstein, Tom Phoebus, Bill Shurt *

NOTES: Frank Robinson won the Triple Crown and MVP Award.

KEY SIGNATURES: Aparicio, B. Robinson, F. Robinson, Palmer.

VALUE: $385

966 BOSTON - Dennis Bennett, Darrell Brandon, Joe Christopher, Tony Conigliaro, Don Demeter, Joe Foy, Jim Gosger *, Lenny Green, Billy Herman (MANAGER), Dalton Jones, Eddie Kasko, Jim Lonborg, Don McMahon *, Dave Morehead, Dan Osinski, Rico Petrocelli, Dick Radatz *, Pete Runnels (MANAGER), Mike Ryan, Bob Sadowski, Ken Sanders *, Jose Santiago, George Scott, Rollie Sheldon *, George Smith, Lee Stange , Jerry Stephenson, Dick Stigman, Jose Tartabull *, George Thomas, Bob Tillman, Earl Wilson *, John Wyatt *, Carl Yastrzemski

LESS THAN 10 GAMES: Mike Andrews, Hank Fischer *, Guido Grilli *, Tony Horton, Pete Magrini, Garry Roggenburk *, Bill Short *, Reggie Smith

KEY SIGNATURES: Herman, Yastrzemski, Lonborg.

VALUE: $260

966 CALIFORNIA - Joe Adcock, George Brunet, Lew Burdette, Jose Cardenal, Dean Chance, Dick Egan, Jim Fregosi, Jackie Hernandez, Jay Johnstone, Ed Kirkpatrick, Bobby Knoop, Bob Lee, Marcelino Lopez, Frank Malzone, Jim McGlothin, Bubba Morton, Fred Newman, Jimmy Piersall, Howie Reed *, Rick Reichardt, Bill Rigney (MANAGER), Bob Rodgers, Minnie Rojas, Jack Sanford, Tom Satriano, Paul Schaal, Norm Siebern, Willie Smith, Ed Sukla, Chuck Vinson, Jackie Warner, Clyde Wright

LESS THAN 10 GAMES: Ed Bailey, Jim Coates, Tom Egan, Bill Kelso, Ramon Lopez, Willie Montanez, Albie Pearson, Jorge Rubio, Al Spangler

KEY SIGNATURES: Fregosi.

VALUE: $100

ROY = Rookie of the Year

966 CHICAGO (AL) - Jerry Adair *, Tommie Agee, Ken Berry, Buddy Bradford, Don Buford, Smoky Burgess, John Buzhardt, Danny Cater *, Wayne Causey *, Lee Elia, Eddie Fisher *, Gene Freese *, Ron Hansen, Jim Hicks, Dennis Higgins, Joe Horlen, Bruce Howard, Tommy John, Duane Josephson, Jack Lamabe, Bob Locker, J.C. Martin, Tommy McCraw, Jerry McNertney, Gary Peters, Juan Pizarro, Floyd Robinson, Johnny Romano, Bill Skowron, Eddie Stanky (MANAGER), Ed Stroud, Pete Ward, Al Weis, Hoyt Wilhelm

LESS THAN 10 GAMES: Greg Bollo, Deacon Jones, Dick Kenworthy, Fred Klages, Marv Staehle, Bill Voss

NOTES: Agee (ROY).

KEY SIGNATURES: Agee, John, Wilhelm.

VALUE: $125

1966 CHICAGO (NL) - Ted Abernathy *, George Altman, Joey Amalfitano, Ernie Banks, Glenn Beckert, John Boccabella, Ernie Broglio, Byron Browne, Don Bryant, Ron Campbell, Billy Connors, Leo Durocher (MANAGER), Arnie Earley, Dick Ellsworth, Bill Faul, Bill Hands, Bob Hendley, Billy Hoeft *, Ken Holtzman, Randy Hundley, Ferguson Jenkins *, Marty Keough *, Don Kessinger, Cal Koonce, Chris Krug, Don Lee *, Adolfo Phillips *, Robin Roberts *, Ron Santo, Curt Simmons *, Jimmy Stewart, Lee Thomas *, Carl Warwick, Billy Williams

LESS THAN 10 GAMES: Bob Buhl *, Len Church, Ty Cline *, Wes Covington *, Dave Dowling, Chuck Estrada, Chuck Hartenstein, John Hernstein *, Larry Jackson *, Harvey Kuenn *, Fred Norman, Rich Nye, Roberto Pena, Paul Popovich, Bob Raudman, Frank Thomas

KEY SIGNATURES: Banks, Santo, Jenkins, Roberts.

VALUE: $150

1966 CINCINNATI - Jack Baldschun, Dave Bristol (MANAGER), Leo Cardenas, Jimmie Coker, Gordy Coleman, Ted Davidson, Johnny Edwards, Sammy Ellis, Hank Fischer *, Tommy Harper, Don Heffner (MANAGER), Tommy Helms, Joey Jay *, Deron Johnson, Jim Maloney, Lee May, Billy McCool, Don Nottebart, Joe Nuxhall, Jim O'Toole, Darrell Osteen, Milt Pappas, Don Pavletich, Tony Perez, Vada Pinson, Mel Queen, Pete Rose, Chico Ruiz, Art Shamsky, Dick Simpson

LESS THAN 10 GAMES: Jerry Arrigo *, Mel Queen, John Tsitouris, Dom Zanni

NOTES: Helms (ROY).

KEY SIGNATURES: Perez, Rose, Helms, Harper, Pinson.

VALUE: $180

ROY = Rookie of the Year

1966 CLEVELAND - Bob Allen, Max Alvis, Joe Azcue, Gary Bell, Buddy Booker, Larry Brown, Rocky Colavito, Del Crandall, Tony Curry, Vic Davalillo, Bill Davis, Vern Fuller, Jim Gentile *, Pedro Gonzalez, Steve Hargan, Chuck Hinton, Dick Howser, Tom Kelly, Jack Kralick, Jim Landis, Tony Martinez, Sam McDowell, Don McMahon *, John O'Donoghue, Dick Radatz *, Chico Salmon, Sonny Siebert, Duke Sims, George Strickland (MANAGER), Birdie Tebbetts (MANAGER), Luis Tiant, Jose Vidal, Leon Wagner, Fred Whitfield

LESS THAN 10 GAMES: George Banks, George Culver, Paul Dicken, Bob Heffner, Lee Stange *

KEY SIGNATURES: Colavito, Tiant, McDowell.

VALUE: $115

1966 DETROIT - Hank Aguirre, Gates Brown, Norm Cash, Don Demeter *, Chuck Dressen (MANAGER), Bill Freehan, Fred Gladding, Willie Horton, Al Kaline, Mickey Lolich, Jerry Lumpe, Dick McAuliffe, Orlando McFarlane, Denny McLain, Bill Monbouquette, Jim Northrup, Ray Oyler, Orlando Pena, Johnny Podres *, Larry Sherry, Frank Skaff (MANAGER), Joe Sparma, Mickey Stanley, Bob Swift (MANAGER), Dick Tracewski, Don Wert, Dave Wickersham, Earl Wilson *, Jake Wood

LESS THAN 10 GAMES: Arlo Brunsberg, Terry Fox *, Bill Graham, John Hiller, George Korince, Julio Navarro, Don Pepper

KEY SIGNATURES: Cash, Kaline, Freehan, McLain, Lolich.

VALUE: $160

966 HOUSTON - Bob Aspromonte, John Bateman, Ron Brand, Bob Bruce, Frank 'arpin, Nate Colbert, Mike Cuellar, Brock Davis, Ron Davis, Larry Dierker, Dick Far-ell, Gene Freese *, Joe Gaines, Jim Gentile *, Dave Giusti, Chuck Harrison, Grady Iatton (MANAGER), Bill Heath, Sonny Jackson, Gary Kroll, Barry Latman, Bob Lillis, elix Mantilla, Lee Maye, Norm Miller, Joe Morgan, Dave Nicholson, Jim Owens, Aaron 'ointer, Claude Raymond, Robin Roberts *, Carroll Sembera, Greg Sims, Rusty Staub, on Taylor, Jim Wynn, Chris Zachary

ESS THAN 10 GAMES: Dave Adlesh, Don Arlich, Danny Coombs, Julio Gotay, Don ee *, Aurelio Monteagudo, Jim Ray, Bob Watson, Don Wilson

EY SIGNATURES: Morgan, Staub, Roberts.

VALUE: $120

966 KANSAS CITY - Jack Aker, Sal Bando, Gil Blanco, Don Blasingame *, Billy Bryan , Bert Campaneris, Danny Cater *, Wayne Causey *, Ed Charles, Ossie Chavarria, Al)ark (MANAGER), Jim Dickson, Chuck Dobson, John Donaldson, Ernie Fazio, Jim Josger *, Dick Green, Guido Grilli *, Jose Grzenda, Vern Handrahan, Ken Harrelson *, Aike Hershberger, Catfish Hunter, Manny Jiminez, Lew Krausse, Paul Lindblad, Rick Aonday, Jim Nash, Joe Nossek *, Blue Moon Odom, Roger Repoz *, Phil Roof, Ken anders *, Randy Schwartz, Rollie Sheldon *, Larry Stahl, Wes Stock, Ron Stone, Ken uarez, Fred Talbot *, Tim Talton, Jose Tartabull *, Ralph Terry *, John Wyatt *

ESS THAN 10 GAMES: Jim Duckworth *, Bill Edgerton, Jess Hickman, Rene Lache-nann, Aurelio Monteagudo *, Bill Stafford

EY SIGNATURES: Campaneris, Hunter, Odom.

VALUE: $120

1966 LOS ANGELES - Walt Alston (MANAGER), Jim Barbieri, Jim Brewer, Wes Cov-ngton *, Tommy Davis, Willie Davis, Don Drysdale, Ron Fairly, Al Ferrara, Jim Gilliam,)errell Griffith, Lou Johnson, John Kennedy, Sandy Koufax, Jim Lefebvre, Bob Miller, oe Moeller, Nate Oliver, Claude Osteen, Wes Parker, Ron Perranoski, Phil Regan, ohnny Roseboro, Dick Schofield *, Bart Shirley, Dick Stuart *, Don Sutton, Jeff Tor-org, Maury Wills

LESS THAN 10 GAMES: Jim Campanis, Willie Crawford, Tommy Hutton, Johnny Po-dres *, Howie Reed *, Bill Singer, Nick Willhite

NOTES: Koufax (Cy Young).

KEY SIGNATURES: Wills, W. Davis, T. Davis, Koufax, Drysdale, Sutton.

VALUE: $365

1966 MINNESOTA - Bernie Allen, Bob Allison, Earl Battey, Dave Boswell, Pete Cimino, Mudcat Grant, Jimmie Hall, Jim Kaat, Harmon Killebrew, Johnny Klippstein, Andy Kosco, Sam Mele (MANAGER), Jim Merritt, Don Mincher, Russ Nixon, Tony Oliva, Camilo Pascual, Jim Perry, Rich Reese, Garry Roggenburk *, Rich Rollins, Dwight Siebler, Cesar Tovar, Ted Uhlaender, Sandy Valdespino, Zoilo Versalles, Al Worthing-ton, Jerry Zimmerman

LESS THAN 10 GAMES: Ron Clark, Ron Keller, George Mitterwald, Joe Nossek *, Jim Ollom, Bill Pleis, Jim Roland

KEY SIGNATURES: Killebrew, Oliva, Kaat.

VALUE: $200

1966 NEW YORK (AL) - Ruben Amaro, Ray Barker, Jim Bouton, Clete Boyer, Bill Bryan *, Horace Clarke, Lu Clinton, Al Downing, Mike Ferraro, Whitey Ford, Bob Friend * Jake Gibbs, Steve Hamilton, Mike Hegan, Ralph Houk (MANAGER), Elston Howard Johnny Keane (MANAGER), Hector Lopez, Mickey Mantle, Roger Maris, Bobby Murcer, Joe Pepitone, Fritz Peterson, Pedro Ramos, Hal Reniff, Roger Repoz *, Bobby Richardson, Dick Schofield *, Mel Stottlemyre, Fred Talbot *, Tom Tresh, Steve Whitaker, Roy White, Dooley Womack,

LESS THAN 10 GAMES: Stan Bahnsen, Jack Cullen, Bill Henry, John Miller

KEY SIGNATURES: Maris, Mantle, Howard, Stottlemyre, Ford.

VALUE: $340

1966 NEW YORK (NL) - Jerry Arrigo *, Larry Bearnarth, Ken Boyer, Ed Bressoud, Dave Eilers, Larry Elliot, Jack Fisher, Bob Friend *, Rob Gardner, Greg Goossen, Jerry Grote, Jack Hamilton, Bud Harrelson, Bill Hepler, Jim Hickman, Chuck Hiller, Ron Hunt, Cleon Jones, Ed Kranepool, Johnny Lewis, Al Luplow, Tug McGraw, Roy McMillan, Billy Murphy, Danny Napoleon, Dennis Ribant, Gordie Richardson, Dick Selma, Bob Shaw *, Johnny Stephenson, Dick Stuart *, Darrell Sutherland, Ron Swoboda, Hawk Taylor, Ralph Terry *, Wes Westrum (MANAGER)

LESS THAN 10 GAMES: Choo Choo Coleman, Shaun Fitzmaurice, Dallas Green, Lou Klimchock, Larry Miller, Dick Rusteck, Nolan Ryan

KEY SIGNATURES: Kranepool, Boyer, Swoboda, Ryan.

VALUE: $280

1966 PHILADELPHIA - Dick Allen, Jackie Brandt, Johnny Briggs, Bob Buhl *, Jim Bunning, Johnny Callison, Doug Clemens, Roger Craig, Ray Culp, Clay Dalrymple, Terry Fox *, Tony Gonzalez, Dick Groat, Ray Herbert, Larry Jackson *, Darold Knowles, Harvey Kuenn *, Phil Linz, Gene Mauch (MANAGER), John Morris, Cookie Rojas, Chris Short, Tony Taylor, Bob Uecker, Joe Verbanic, Bill White, Bobby Wine, Rick Wise

LESS THAN 10 GAMES: Bo Belinsky, John Boozer, John Herrnstein *, Grant Jackson, Ferguson Jenkins *, Adolfo Phillips *, Steve Ridzik, Ed Roebuck, Jimmie Schaffer, Gary Sutherland, Gary Wagner

KEY SIGNATURES: White, Allen, Uecker, Bunning, Jenkins.

VALUE: $110

MVP = MVP Award winner

1966 PITTSBURGH - Gene Alley, Matty Alou, Bob Bailey, Steve Blass, Don Cardwell, Roberto Clemente, Donn Clendenon, Roy Face, Woody Fryman, Jesse Gonder, Vern Law, Jerry Lynch, Jerry May, Bill Mazeroski, Al McBean, Gene Michael, Pete Mikkelsen, Manny Mota, Billy O'Dell *, Jose Pagan, Jim Pagliaroni, Bob Purkey, Dave Roberts, Andre Rodgers, Don Schwall *, Tommie Sisk, Willie Stargell, Bob Veale, Harry Walker (MANAGER), Luke Walker

LESS THAN 10 GAMES: Don Bosch, Jim Shellenback, George Spriggs

NOTES: Clemente (MVP).

KEY SIGNATURES: Clendenon, Mazeroski, Clemente, Stargell, Mota.

VALUE: $500

966 SAN FRANCISCO - Jesus Alou, Bob Barton, Bobby Bolin, Ollie Brown, Bob Burda, rlando Cepeda *, Jim Davenport, Dick Dietz, Herman Franks (MANAGER), Tito uentes, Len Gabrielson, Joe Gibbon, Tom Haller, Jim Ray Hart, Ken Henderson, Bill enry, Ron Herbel, Jack Hiatt, Frank Johnson, Don Landrum, Hal Lanier, Frank Linzy, ıan Marichal, Don Mason, Willie Mays, Willie McCovey, Lindy McDaniel, Gaylord erry, Cap Peterson, Bob Priddy, Ray Sadecki *, Dick Schofield *, Bob Schroder, Bob haw *, Ozzie Virgil

ESS THAN 10 GAMES: Bob Garibaldi, Billy Hoeft *, Rich Robertson

EY SIGNATURES: McCovey, Mays, Cepeda, Marichal, Perry.

VALUE: $200

966 ST. LOUIS - Nelson Briles, Lou Brock, Jerry Buchek, Orlando Cepeda *, Pat Corles, Don Dennis, Curt Flood, Tito Francona, Phil Gagliano, Bob Gibson, Joe Hoerner, l Jackson, Larry Jaster, Julian Javier, Alex Johnson, George Kernek, Art Mahaffey, Dal laxvill, Tim McCarver, Ron Piche, Ted Savage, Red Schoendienst (MANAGER), Mike hannon, Curt Simmons *, Bob Skinner, Charley Smith, Ed Spiezio, Tracy Stallard, obby Tolan, Ray Washburn, Jim Williams, Hal Woodeshick

ESS THAN 10 GAMES: Dennis Aust, Steve Carlton, Jim Cosman, Dick Hughes, Ray adecki *, Ron Willis

EY SIGNATURES: Schoendienst, Cepeda, Brock, McCarver, Gibson, Carlton.

VALUE: $250

966 WASHINGTON - Don Blasingame *, Dick Bosman, Eddie Brinkman, Doug amilli, Paul Casanova, Bob Chance, Casey Cox, Tim Cullen, Jim French, Ken Hamlin, m Hannan, Ken Harrelson *, Gil Hodges (MANAGER), Frank Howard, Bob lumphreys, Jim King, Willie Kirkland, Ron Kline, Dick Lines, Don Lock, Mike lcCormick, Ken McMullen, Barry Moore, Dick Nen, John Orsino, Phil Ortega, Dick hillips, Pete Richert, Bob Saverine, Diego Segui, Fred Valentine

ESS THAN 10 GAMES: Hank Allen, Dave Baldwin, Mike Brumley, Tom Cheney, Al loster, Joe Coleman, Pete Craig, Joe Cunningham, Jim Duckworth *, Howie Koplitz, rank Kreutzer, Buster Narum

EY SIGNATURES: Hodges, Howard.

VALUE: $145

1967

1967 Cleveland Indians

*** = player was traded**

1967 ATLANTA - Mike de la Hoz, Hank Aaron, Felipe Alou, Clete Boyer, Bob Bruce, Clay Carroll, Rico Carty, Ty Cline *, Tony Cloninger, Tito Francona *, Gary Geiger, Angel Hermoso, Ramon Hernandez, Billy Hitchock (MANAGER), Pat Jarvis, Ken Johnson, Mack Jones, Dick Kelley, Charlie Lau *, Denny Lemaster, Marty Martinez, Denis Menke, Felix Millan, Phil Niekro, Gene Oliver *, Ed Rakow, Claude Raymond *, Jay Ritchie, Ken Silvestri (MANAGER), Joe Torre, Bob Uecker *, Cecil Upshaw, Woody Woodward

LESS THAN 10 GAMES: Jim Beauchamp, Wade Blasingame *, Jim Britton, Glen Clark, Cito Gaston, Mike Lum, Dave Nicholson, Ron Reed, Don Schwall, George Stone

KEY SIGNATURES: Aaron, Carty, Uecker, Niekro.

VALUE: $180

1967 BALTIMORE (AL) - Luis Aparicio, Steve Barber *, Hank Bauer (MANAGER), Mark Belanger, Paul Blair, Curt Blefary, Sam Bowens, Gene Brabender, Wally Bunker, Bill Dillman, Moe Drabowsky, Andy Etchebaren, Eddie Fisher, Larry Haney, Jim Hardin, Woodie Held *, Dave Johnson, Charlie Lau *, Dave May, Dave McNally, Stu Miller, Curt Motton, Tom Phoebus, Boog Powell, Pete Richert *, Brooks Robinson, Frank Robinson, Vic Roznovosky, Russ Snyder, Eddie Watt

LESS THAN 10 GAMES: Mike Adamson, Frank Bertaina *, John Buzhardt *, Mike Epstein *, Tom Fisher, Paul Gilliford, Bob Johnson *, Dave Leonhard, Marcelino Lopez *, Mickey McGuire, John Miller, Jim Palmer

KEY SIGNATURES: Powell, Aparicio, B. Robinson, F. Robinson, Palmer.

VALUE: $225

1967 BOSTON (AL) - Jery Adair *, Mike Andrews, Gary Bell *, Dennis Bennett *, Darrell Brandon, Galen Cisco, Tony Conigliaro, Don Demeter *, Joe Foy, Russ Gibson, Ken Harrelson *, Tony Horton *, Elston Howard *, Dalton Jones, Bill Landis, Jim Lonborg, Sparky Lyle, Don McMahon *, Dan Osinski, Rico Petrocelli, Mike Ryan, Jose Santiago, George Scott, Norm Siebern *, Reggie Smith, Lee Stange, Jose Tartabull, George Thomas, Bob Tillman *, Gary Waslewski, Dick Williams (MANAGER), John Wyatt, Carl Yastzremski

LESS THAN 10 GAMES: Ken Brett, Hank Fischer, Jim Landis *, Dave Morehead, Ken Poulsen, Billy Rohr, Jerry Stephenson

NOTES: Yastrzemski won the Triple Crown and MVP Award; Lonborg (CyYoung).

KEY SIGNATURES: Yastrzemski, Howard, Lonborg, Lyle.

VALUE: $385

1967 CALIFORNIA (AL) - George Brunet, Lew Burdette, Jose Cardenal, Pete Cimino, Rickey Clark, Jim Coates, Jim Fregosi, Len Gabrielson *, Jimmie Hall, Jack Hamilton *, Woddie Held *, Jim Hibbs, Jay Johnstone, Bill Kelso, Bobby Knoop, Orlando McFarlane, Jim McGlothlin, Don Mincher, Bubba Morton, Rick Reichardt, Roger Repoz *, Bill Rigney (MANAGER), Bob Rodgers, Aurelio Rodriguez, Minnie Rojas, Jack Sanford *, Tom Satriano, Paul Schaal, Curt Simmons *, Bill Skowron *, Hawk Taylor *, Ken Turner, Don Wallace, Jim Weaver, Johnny Werhas *, Clyde Wright

LESS THAN 10 GAMES: Tom Egan, Ed Kirkpatrick, Bobby Locke, Marcelino Lopez *, Fred Newman, Jimmy Piersall, Jorge Rubio, Larry Stubing, Nick Willhite *

KEY SIGNATURES: Fregosi.

VALUE: $100

1967 CHICAGO (AL) - Jerry Adair *, Tommie Agee, Sandy Alomar *, Ken Berry, Ken Boyer *, Buddy Bradford, Don Buford, Smoky Burgess, John Buzhardt *, Wayne Causey, Rocky Colavito *, Ron Hansen, Joe Horlen, Bruce Howard, Tommy John, Steve Jones, Duane Josephson, Dick Kenworthy, Jim King *, Fred Klages, Bob Locker, J.C. Martin, Tommy McCraw, Don McMahon *, Jery McNertney, Jim O'Toole, Gary Peters, Marv Staehle, Eddie Stanky (MANAGER), Jimmy Stewart *, Ed Stroud *, Bill Voss, Pete Ward, Al Weis, Hoyt Wilhelm, Walt Williams, Wilbur Wood

LESS THAN 10 GAMES: Cisco Carlos, Ed Herrmann, Dennis Higgins, Jack Lamabe *, Aurelio Monteagudo, Rich Morales, Cotton Nash, Roger Nelson, Bill Skowron *

KEY SIGNATURES: Colavito, Boyer, John, Wilhelm.

VALUE: $125

1967 CHICAGO (NL) - George Altman, Ernie Banks, Glenn Beckert, John Boccabella, Joe Campbell, Ray Culp, Leo Durocher (MANAGER), Rob Gardner, Norm Gigon, Bill Hands, Chuck Hartenstein, Ken Holtzman, Randy Hundley, Ferguson Jenkins, Clarence Jones, Don Kessinger, Cal Koonce *, Joe Niekro, Rich Nye, Adolfo Phillips, Paul Popovich, Dick Radatz *, Ron Santo, Ted Savage *, Curt Simmons *, Al Spangler, Johnny Stephenson, Bill Stoneman, Lee Thomas, Billy Williams

LESS THAN 10 GAMES: Joey Amalfitano, Dick Bertell, Byron Browne, Dick Calmus, Jim Ellis, Bob Hendley *, Rick James, Don Larsen, Pete Mikkelsen *, Fred Norman, Bob Raudman, Bob Shaw *, Jimmy Stewart *, John Upham

KEY SIGNATURES: Durocher, Banks, Santo, Williams, Jenkins.

VALUE: $150

1967 CINCINNATI - Ted Abernathy, Jerry Arrigo, Johnny Bench, Dave Bristol (MANAGER), Leo Cardenas, Jimmie Coker, Johnny Edwards, Sammy Ellis, Tommy Harper, Tommy Helms, Deron Johnson, Bob Lee *, Jim Maloney, Lee May, Billy McCool, Gary Nolan, Don Nottebart, Milt Pappas, Don Pavletich, Tony Perez, Vada Pinson, Mel Queen, Floyd Robinson, Pete Rose, Chico Ruiz, Art Shamsky, Dick Simpson, Jake Wood *

LESS THAN 10 GAMES: Jack Baldschun, Len Boehmer, Gordy Coleman, Ted Davidson, Darrell Osteen, John Tsitouris

KEY SIGNATURES: Pinson, Rose, Bench.

VALUE: $180

1967 CLEVELAND (AL) - Joe Adcock (MANAGER), Bob Allen, Max Alvis, Joe Azcue, Steve Bailey, Larry Brown, Rocky Colavito *, Ed Connolly, George Culver, Vic Davalillo, Don Demeter *, Vern Fuller, Gus Gil, Pedro Gonzalez, Steve Hargan, Chuck Hinton, Tony Horton *, Jim King *, Lee Maye, Sam McDowell, John O'Donoghue, Orlando Pena *, Chico Salmon, Richie Scheinblum, Sonny Siebert, Duke Sims, Willie Smith, Luis Tiant, Jose Vidal, Leon Wagner, Fred Whitfield, Stan Williams

LESS THAN 10 GAMES: Gary Bell *, Ray Fosse, Tom Kelley, Jack Kralick, Gordon Lund, Dick Radatz *, Bobby Tiefenauer

KEY SIGNATURES: Adcock, McDowell, Tiant.

VALUE: $110

1967 DETROIT (AL) - Hank Aguirre, Gates Brown, Norm Cash, Pat Dobson, Bill Freehan, Fred Gladding, Lenny Green, Bill Heath *, John Hiller, Willie Horton, Al Kaline, Jim Landis *, Fred Lasher, Mickey Lolich, Jerry Lumpe, Mike Marshall, Eddie Mathews *, Dick McAuliffe, Denny McLain, Jim Northrup, Ray Oyler, Johnny Podres, Jim Price, Larry Sherry *, Mayo Smith (MANAGER), Joe Sparma, Mickey Stanley, Dick Tracewski, Don Wert, Dave Wickersham, Earl Wilson, Jake Wood *

LESS THAN 10 GAMES: Dave Campbell, Wayne Comer, Johnny Klippstein, George Korince, Tom Matchick *, Bill Monbouquette *, Orlando Pena *

KEY SIGNATURES: Cash, Kaline, Freehan, Mathews, McLain, Lolich.

VALUE: $175

1967 HOUSTON - Dave Adlesh, Bob Aspromonte, Lee Bales, John Bateman, Bo Belinsky, Wade Blasingame *, Ron Brand, Jackie Brandt *, Mike Cuellar, Ron Davis, Larry Dierker, Tom Dukes, Dave Eilers, Dave Giusti, Julio Gotay, Chuck Harrison, Grady Hatton (MANAGER), Sonny Jackson, Hal King, Jim Landis *, Barry Latman, Bob Lillis, Eddie Mathews *, Norm Miller, Joe Morgan, Ivan Murrell, Aaron Pointer, Doug Rader, Claude Raymond *, Dan Schneider, Carroll Sembera, Larry Sherry *, Rusty Staub, Don Wilson, Jim Wynn

LESS THAN 10 GAMES: John Buzhardt *, Danny Coombs, Arnie Earley, Dick Farrell *, Alonzo Harris, Bill Heath *, Jose Herrara, Pat House, Jim Owens, Howie Reed, Bruce Von Hoff, Bob Watson, Chris Zachary

KEY SIGNATURES: Mathews, Morgan, Staub.

VALUE: $120

1967 KANSAS CITY (AL) - Jack Aker, Luke Appling (MANAGER), Sal Bando, Bert Campaneris, Danny Cater, Ed Charles *, Ossie Chavarria, Al Dark (MANAGER), Chuck Dobson, John Donaldson, Dave Duncan, Jim Gosger, Dick Green, Ken Harrelson

*, Mike Hershberger, Catfish Hunter, Reggie Jackson, Lew Krausse, Ted Kubiak, Allan Lewis, Paul Lindblad, Rick Monday, Jim Nash, Joe Nossek, Blue Moon Odom, Tony Pierce, Roger Repoz *, Roberto Rodriguez, Phil Roof, Joe Rudi, Jack Sanford *, Diego Segui, Bill Stafford, Ken Suarez, Tim Talton, Ramon Webster

LESS THAN 10 GAMES: Hoss Bowlin, Bob Duliba, Bill Edgerton, George Lauzerique, Wes Stock

KEY SIGNATURES: Appling, Jackson, Hunter, Odom.

VALUE: $170

1967 LOS ANGELES - Luis Alcaraz, Walt Alston (MANAGER), Bob Bailey, Jim Brewer, Jim Campanis, Willie Davis, Tommy Dean, Don Drysdale, Dick Egan, Ron Fairly, Al Ferrara, Len Gabrielson *, Jim Hickman, Ron Hunt, Lou Johnson, Jim Lefebvre, Gene Michael, Bob Miller, Nate Oliver, Claude Osteen, Wes Parker, Ron Perranoski, Phil Regan, Johnny Roseboro, Dick Schofield, Bill Singer, Don Sutton, Jeff Torborg

LESS THAN 10 GAMES: Bruce Brubaker, Willie Crawford, John Duffie, Alan Foster, Jim Hickman, Bob Lee *, Joe Moeller, Johnny Werhas *

KEY SIGNATURES: Alston, Davis, Drysdale, Sutton.

VALUE: $240

1967 MINNESOTA (AL) - Bob Allison, Earl Battey, Dave Boswell, Rod Carew, Dean Chance, Ron Clark, Cal Ermer (MANAGER), Mudcat Grant, Carroll Hardy, Jackie Hernandez, Hank Izquierdo, Jim Kaat, Harmon Killebrew, Ron Kline, Frank Kostro, Sam Mele (MANAGER), Jim Merritt, Graig Nettles, Russ Nixon, Tony Oliva, Jim Ollom, Jim Perry, Frank Quilici, Rich Reese, Jim Roland, Rich Rollins, Cesar Tovar, Ted Uhlaender, Sandy Valdespino, Zoilo Versalles, Al Worthington, Jerry Zimmerman

LESS THAN 10 GAMES: Walt Bond, Pat Kelly, Andy Kosco, Mel Nelson, Dwight Siebler

NOTES: Carew (ROY).

KEY SIGNATURES: Killebrew, Carew, Oliva, Kaat.

VALUE: $200

ROY = Rookie of the Year

1967 NEW YORK (AL) - Ruben Amaro, Steve Barber *, Ray Barker, Jim Bouton, Billy Bryan, Horace Clarke, Al Downing, Jake Gibbs, Steve Hamilton, Mike Hegan, Ralph Houk (MANAGER), Elston Howard *, Dick Howser, John Kennedy, Jerry Kenney, Mickey Mantle, Bill Monbouquette *, Ross Moschito, Joe Pepitone, Fritz Peterson, Hal Reniff *, Bill Robinson, Charley Smith, Mel Stottlemyre, Fred Talbot, Bob Tillman *, Thad Tillotson, Tom Tresh, Joe Verbanic, Steve Whitaker, Roy White, Dooley Womack

LESS THAN 10 GAMES: Lu Clinton, Frank Fernandez, Whitey Ford, Cecil Perkins, Dale Roberts, Charlie Sands, Tom Shopay, Frank Tepedino

KEY SIGNATURES: Mantle, Howard, Stottlemyre, Ford.

VALUE: $285

1967 NEW YORK (NL) - Sandy Alomar *, Don Bosch, Ken Boswell, Ken Boyer *, Jerry Buchek, Don Cardwell, Ed Charles *, Tommy Davis, Bill Denehy, Jack Fisher, Danny Frisella, Greg Goossen, Jerry Grote, Joe Grzenda, Jack Hamilton *, Bud Harrelson, Bob Heise, Bob Hendley *, Chuck Hiller *, Bob Johnson *, Cleon Jones, Cal Koonce *, Ed Kranepool, Jack Lamabe *, Johnny Lewis, Phil Linz *, Al Luplow *, Joe Moock, Amos Otis, Salty Parker (MANAGER), Hal Reniff *, Tommie Reynolds, Tom Seaver, Dick

Selma, Don Shaw, Bob Shaw *, Larry Stahl, John Sullivan, Ron Swoboda, Ron Taylor, Hawk Taylor *, Wes Westrum (MANAGER)

LESS THAN 10 GAMES: Dennis Bennett *, Kevin Collins, Bill Connors, Chuck Estrada, Bill Graham, Jerry Hinsley, Jerry Koosman, Tug McGraw, Les Rohr, Al Schmelz, Bart Shirley, Ralph Terry, Nick Willhite *, Billy Wynne

NOTES: Seaver (ROY).

KEY SIGNATURES: Kranepool, Harrelson, Swoboda, Seaver, Koosman.

VALUE: $400

ROY = Rookie of the Year

1967 PHILADELPHIA - Dick Allen, John Boozer, Jackie Brandt *, Johnny Briggs, Jim Bunning, Johnny Callison, Doug Clemens, Billy Cowan, Caly Dalrymple, Dick Ellsworth, Dick Farrell *, Tito Francona *, Tony Gonzalez, Dick Groat *, Dick Hall, Chuck Hiller *, Grant Jackson, Larry Jackson, Rick Joseph, Phil Linz *, Don Lock, Gene Mauch (MANAGER), Gene Oliver *, Cookie Rojas, Chris Short, Gary Sutherland, Tony Taylor, Bob Uecker *, Bill White, Bobby Wine, Rick Wise

LESS THAN 10 GAMES: Bob Buhl, Ruben Gomez, Dallas Green, Terry Harmon, Larry Loughlin, Pedro Ramos, Jimmie Schaffer, Dick Thoenen, Gary Wagner

KEY SIGNATURES: White, Allen, Uecker, Groat, Bunning.

VALUE: $110

1967 PITTSBURGH - Gene Alley, Matty Alou, Steve Blass, Roberto Clemente, Donn Clendenon, Roy Face, Woody Fryman, Jesse Gonder, Manny Jimenez, Vern Law, Al Luplow *, Jerry May, Bill Mazeroski, Al McBean, Pete Mikkelsen *, Manny Mota, Danny Murtaugh (MANAGER), Bill O'Dell, Jose Pagan, Jim Pagliaroni, Juan Pizarro, Dennis Ribant, Andre Rodgers, Manny Sanguillen, Tommie Sisk, George Spriggs, Willie Stargell, Bob Veale, Harry Walker (MANAGER), Maury Wills

LESS THAN 10 GAMES: Bruce Dal Canton, John Gelnar, Bob Moose, Bob Robertson, Jim Shellenback, Bill Short

KEY SIGNATURES: Mazeroski, Wills, Clemente, Stargell.

VALUE: $500

1967 SAN FRANCISCO (NL) - Jesus Alou, Bobby Bolin, Ollie Brown, Ty Cline *, Jim Davenport, Dick Dietz, Bobby Etheridge, Herman Franks (MANAGER), Tito Fuentes, Joe Gibbon, Dick Groat *, Cesar Gutierrez, Tom Haller, Jim Ray Hart, Ken Henderson, Bill Henry, Ron Herbel, Jack Hiatt, Hal Lanier, Frank Linzy, Juan Marichal, Willie Mays, Mike McCormick, Willie McCovey, Lindy McDaniel, Gaylord Perry, Ray Sadecki, Bob Schroder, Norm Siebern *, Bill Sorrell

LESS THAN 10 GAMES: Bob Barton, Ron Bryant, Nestor Chavez, Frank Johnson, Dave Marshall, Don Mason, Rich Robertson

NOTES: McCormick (Cy Young).

KEY SIGNATURES: McCovey, Mays, McCormick, Perry, Marichal.

VALUE: $200

1967 ST. LOUIS - Ed Bressoud, Nelson Briles, Lou Brock, Steve Carlton, Orlando Cepeda, Curt Flood, Phil Gagliano, Bob Gibson, Joe Hoerner, Dick Hughes, Al Jackson, Larry Jaster, Julian Javier, Alex Johnson, Jack Lamabe *, Roger Maris, Dal Maxvill, Tom McCarver, Dave Ricketts, Johnny Romano, Red Schoendienst (MANAGER), Mike Shannon, Ed Spiezio, Bobby Tolan, Ray Washburn, Ron Willis, Hal Woodeshick

LESS THAN 10 GAMES: Jim Cosman, Steve Huntz, Ted Savage *, Mike Torrez, Jim Williams

NOTES: Cepeda (MVP).

KEY SIGNATURES: Schoendienst, Cepeda, Maris, Brock, McCarver, Carlton, Gibson.

VALUE: $360

1967 WASHINGTON (AL) - Bernie Allen, Hank Allen, Dave Baldwin, Frank Bertaina *, Eddie Brinkman, Doug Camilli, Paul Casanova, Bob Chance, Frank Coggins, Joe Coleman, Casey Cox, Tim Cullen, Mike Epstein *, Ken Harrelson *, Gil Hodges (MANAGER), Frank Howard, Bob Humphreys, Jim King *, Darold Knowles, Dick Lines, Ken McMullen, Barry Moore, Dick Nen, Phil Ortega, Camilo Pascual, Cap Peterson, Bob Priddy, Pete Richert *, Bob Saverine, Ed Stroud *, Fred Valentine

LESS THAN 10 GAMES: Dick Bosman, Jim French, Jim Hannan, Buster Narum, Dick Nold, John Orsino

KEY SIGNATURES: Hodges, Howard.

VALUE: $145

* = **player was traded**

1968

1968 N.L. Cy Young/MVP winner Bob Gibson

1968 ATLANTA - Hank Aaron, Tommie Aaron, Felipe Alou, Clete Boyer, Jim Britton, Clay Carroll *, Rico Carty, Wayne Causey *, Tito Francona, Ralph Garr, Gil Garrido, Lum Harris (MANAGER), Sonny Jackson, Pat Jarvis, Deron Johnson, Ken Johnson, Bob Johnson *, Dick Kelley, Mike Lum, Marty Martinez, Felix Millan, Phil Niekro, Mike Page, Milt Pappas *, Claude Raymond, Ron Reed, George Stone, Bob Tillman, Joe Torre, Cecil Upshaw, Sandy Valdespino, Woody Woodward *

LESS THAN 10 GAMES: Dusty Baker, Tony Cloninger *, Ted Davidson *, Skip Guinn, Walt Hriniak, Rick Kester, Stu Miller, Al Santorini

KEY SIGNATURES: Aaron, Torre, Niekro.

VALUE: $180

1968 BALTIMORE - Hank Bauer (MANAGER), Mark Belanger, Paul Blair, Curt Blefary, Gene Brabender, Don Buford, Wally Bunker, Moe Drabowsky, Andy Etchebarren, Chico Fernandez, Larry Haney, Jim Hardin, Ellie Hendricks, Bruce Howard *, Dave Johnson, Dave Leonhard, Dave May, Dave McNally, John Morris, Curt Motton, Roger Nelson, John O'Donoghue, Tom Phoebus, Boog Powell, Merv Rettenmund, Pete Richert, Brooks Robinson, Frank Robinson, Fred Valentine *, Eddie Watt, Earl Weaver (MANAGER)

LESS THAN 10 GAMES: Mike Adamson, Fred Beene, Mike Fiore, Bobby Floyd

KEY SIGNATURES: Weaver, Powell, B. Robinson, F. Robinson.

VALUE: $225

1968 BOSTON - Jerry Adair, Luis Alvarado, Mike Andrews, Gary Bell, Ray Culp, Dick Ellsworth, Joe Foy, Russ Gibson, Ken Harrelson, Elston Howard, Dalton Jones, Joe Lahoud, Bill Landis, Jim Lonborg, Sparky Lyle, Dave Morehead, Russ Nixon, Gene Oliver *, Rico Petrocelli, Juan Pizarro *, Floyd Robinson *, Jose Santiago, George Scott, Norm Siebern, Reggie Smith, Lee Stange, Jerry Stephenson, Jose Tartabull, George Thomas, Gary Waslewski, Dick Williams (MANAGER), Carl Yastrezmski

LESS THAN 10 GAMES: Darrell Brandon, Jerry Moses, Garry Roggenburk, Fred Wenz, John Wyatt *

KEY SIGNATURES: Yastrzemski, Howard, Lyle.

VALUE: $150

1968 CALIFORNIA - Dennis Bennett, George Brunet, Tom Burgmeier, Rickey Clark, Chuck Cottier, Vic Davalillo *, Tom Egan, Sammy Ellis, Jim Fregosi, Jimmie Hall *, Jack Hamilton, Bill Harrelson, Woodie Held *, Chuck Hinton, Jay Johnstone, Ed Kirkpatrick, Bobby Knoop, Winston Llenas, Bobby Locke, Orlando McFarlane, Jim McGlothlin, Andy Messersmith, Don Mincher, Bubba Morton, Tom Murphy, Marty Pattin, Rick Reichardt, Roger Repoz, Bill Rigney (MANAGER), Bob Rodgers, Aurelio Rodriguez, Minnie Rojas, Tom Satriano, Paul Schaal, Jim Spencer, Jarvis Tatum, Bobby Trevino, Jim Weaver, Clyde Wright

LESS THAN 10 GAMES: Wayne Causey *, Pete Cimino, Bob Heffner, Steve Kealey, Larry Sherry

KEY SIGNATURES: Fregosi.

VALUE: $100

1968 CHICAGO (AL) - Sandy Alomar, Luis Aparicio, Ken Berry, Ken Boyer *, Buddy Bradford, Cisco Carlos, Wayne Causey *, Tim Cullen *, Tommy Davis, Jack Fisher, Ron Hansen *, Woodie Held *, Gail Hopkins, Joe Horlen, Tommy John, Duane Josephson, Dick Kenworthy, Bob Locker, Al Lopez (MANAGER), Carlos May, Tommy McCraw, Don McMahon *, Jerry McNertney, Bill Melton, Rich Morales, Les Moss (MANAGER), Gary Peters, Bob Priddy, Dennis Ribant *, Russ Snyder *, Eddie Stanky (MANAGER), Bill Voss, Leon Wagner *, Pete Ward, Hoyt Wilhelm, Walt Williams, Wilbur Wood

LESS THAN 10 GAMES: Buddy Booker, Danny Lazar, Jerry Nyman, Fred Rath, Billy Wynne

KEY SIGNATURES: Lopez, Aparicio, John.

VALUE: $125

1968 CHICAGO (NL) - Jose Arcia, Ernie Banks, Glenn Beckert, Leo Durocher (MANAGER), Lee Elia, Bill Hands, Chuck Hartenstein, Jim Hickman, Ken Holtzman, Randy Hundley, Ferguson Jenkins, Lou Johnson *, Don Kessinger, Jack Lamabe, Dick Nen, Joe Niekro, Rich Nye, Adolfo Phillips, Bill Plummer, Phil Regan *, Gary Ross, Ron Santo, Willie Smith *, Al Spangler, Bill Stoneman, John Upham, Billy Williams

LESS THAN 10 GAMES: Randy Bobb, John Boccabella, Jophery Brown, Darcy Fast, John Felske, Ramon Hernandez, Clarence Jones, Vic LaRosa, Jimmy McMath, Pete Mikkelson *, Gene Oliver *, Frank Reberger, Archie Reynolds, Ted Savage *, Willie Smith *, Johnny Stephenson, Bobby Tiefenauer

KEY SIGNATURES: Durocher, Banks, Santo, Williams, Jenkins.

VALUE: $150

1968 CINCINNATI - Ted Abernathy, Jerry Arrigo, Jim Beauchamp, Johnny Bench, Dave Bristol (MANAGER), Leo Cardenas, Clay Carroll *, Tony Cloninger *, Pat Corrales, George Culver, Ted Davidson *, Tommy Helms, Alex Johnson, Bob Johnson *, Mack Jones, Bill Kelso, Bob Lee, Jim Maloney, Lee May, Billy McCool, Dan McGinn, Hal McRae, Gary Nolan, Milt Pappas *, Don Pavletich, Tony Perez, Vada Pinson, Jay Ritchie, Pete Rose, Chico Ruiz, Fred Whitfield, Woody Woodward *

LESS THAN 10 GAMES: Mel Queen, Jimmie Schaffer, John Tsitouris

NOTES: Bench (ROY).

KEY SIGNATURES: Perez, Rose, Pinson, Bench.

VALUE: $200

ROY = Rookie of the Year

1968 CLEVELAND - Max Alvis, Joe Azcue, Larry Brown, Jose Cardenal, Al Dark (MANAGER), Vic Davalillo *, Eddie Fisher, Vern Fuller, Jimmie Hall *, Steve Hargan, Tommy Harper, Billy Harris, Tony Horton, Lou Johnson *, Lou Klimchock, Hal Kurtz, Lee Maye, Sam McDowell, Dave Nelson, Mike Paul, Horacio Pina, Billy Rohr, Vincente Romo *, Chico Salmon, Richie Scheinblum, Sonny Siebert, Duke Sims, Willie Smith *, Russ Snyder *, Ken Suarez, Luis Tiant, Jose Vidal, Leon Wagner *, Stan Williams

LESS THAN 10 GAMES: Steve Bailey, Ray Fosse, Rob Gardner, Tommy Gramly, Mike Hedlund, Eddie Leon, Russ Nagelson, Lou Piniella, Willie Smith *, Darrell Sutherland

KEY SIGNATURES: Tiant, McDowell.

VALUE: $100

1968 DETROIT - Gates Brown, Norm Cash, Wayne Comer, Pat Dobson, Bill Freehan, John Hiller, Willie Horton, Al Kaline, Fred Lasher, Mickey Lolich, Tom Matchick, Eddie Mathews, Dick McAuliffe, Denny McLain, Don McMahon *, Jim Northrup, Ray Oyler, Daryl Patterson, Jim Price, Dennis Ribant *, Mayo Smith (MANAGER), Joe Sparma, Mickey Stanley, Dick Tracewski, Jon Warden, Don Wert, Earl Wilson, John Wyatt *

LESS THAN 10 GAMES: Les Cain, Dave Campbell, Bob Christian, Roy Face *, Lenny Green, Jim Rooker

NOTES: World Champions! McLain won the MVP and Cy Young awards.

KEY SIGNATURES: Cash, Freehan, Kaline, McLain, Lolich.

VALUE: $290

1968 HOUSTON - Dave Adlesh, Bob Aspromonte, John Bateman, Wade Blasingame, Ron Brand, Byron Browne, John Buzhardt, Nate Colbert, Danny Coombs, Mike Cuellar, Ron Davis *, Larry Dierker, Tom Dukes, Dave Giusti, Julio Gotay, Grady Hatton (MANAGER), Joe Herrara, Pat House, Hal King, Denny Lemaster, Leon McFadden, Denis Menke, Norm Miller, Joe Morgan, Ivan Murrell, Doug Rader, Jim Ray, Steve Shea, Dick Simpson *, Rusty Staub, Lee Thomas, Hector Torres, Harry Walker (MANAGER), Bob Watson, Don Wilson, Jim Wynn

LESS THAN 10 GAMES: Hal Gilson *, Fred Gladding, John Mayberry, Danny Walton

KEY SIGNATURES: Staub, Morgan.

VALUE: $100

1968 LOS ANGELES - Hank Aguirre, Luis Alcaraz, Walt Alston (MANAGER), Bob Bailey, Jack Billingham, Ken Boyer *, Jim Brewer, Rocky Colavito *, Willie Crawford, Willie Davis, Don Drysdale, Jim Fairey, Ron Fairly, Len Gabrielson, Mudcat Grant, Tom Haller, Cleo James, Mike Kekich, Jim Lefebvre, Claude Osteen, Wes Parker, Paul Popovich, John Purdin, Ted Savage *, Bart Shirley, Bill Singer, Bill Sudakis, Don Sutton, Jeff Torborg, Zoilo Versalles

LESS THAN 10 GAMES: Jim Campanis, Al Ferrara, Alan Foster, Joe Moeller, Phil Regan *, Vicente Romo *

KEY SIGNATURES: Alston, Davis, Drysdale, Sutton.

VALUE: $210

1968 MINNESOTA - Bob Allison, Dave Boswell, Rod Carew, Dean Chance, Ron Clark, Cal Ermer (MANAGER), Jackie Hernandez, Jim Holt, Jim Kaat, Pat Kelly, Harmon Killebrew, Frank Kostro, Bruce Look, Jim Merritt, Bob Miller, George Mitterwald, Graig Nettles, Tony Oliva, Ron Perranoski, Jim Perry, Frank Quilici, Rich Reese, Rick Renick, Jim Roland, Rich Rollins, Johnny Roseboro, Cesar Tovar, Ted Uhlaender, Al Worthington, Jerry Zimmerman

LESS THAN 10 GAMES: Tom Hall, Ron Keller, Danny Morris, Buzz Stephen

KEY SIGNATURES: Carew, Oliva, Killebrew, Kaat.

VALUE: $200

1968 NEW YORK (AL) - Ruben Amaro, Stan Bahnsen, Steve Barber, Jim Bouton, Horace Clarke, Rocky Colavito *, Bobby Cox, Al Downing, Frank Fernandez, Mike Ferraro, Jake Gibbs, Steve Hamilton, Ralph Houk (MANAGER), Dick Howser, Andy Kosco, Mickey Mantle, Lindy McDaniel *, Gene Michael, Bill Monbouquette *, Joe Pepitone, Fritz Peterson, Bill Robinson, Charley Smith, Mel Stottlemyre, Fred Talbot, Tom Tresh, Joe Verbanic, Steve Whitaker, Roy White, Dooley Womack

LESS THAN 10 GAMES: John Cumberland, Gene Michael, Ellie Rodriguez, Tony Solaita, Thad Tillotson, John Wyatt *

NOTES: Bahnsen (ROY); Mantle's final season.

VALUE: $235

ROY = Rookie of the Year

1968 NEW YORK (NL) - Tommie Agee, Don Bosch, Ken Boswell, Jerry Buchek, Don Cardwell, Ed Charles, Kevin Collins, Danny Frisella, Greg Goossen, Jerry Grote, Bud Harrelson, Gil Hodges (MANAGER), Al Jackson, Cleon Jones, Cal Koonce, Jerry Koosman, Ed Kranepool, Phil Linz, J.C. Martin, Jim McAndrew, Nolan Ryan, Tom Seaver, Dick Selma, Art Shamsky, Bill Short, Larry Stahl, Ron Swoboda, Ron Taylor, Al Weis

LESS THAN 10 GAMES: Billy Connors, Duffy Dyer, Bob Heise, Mike Jorgensen, Les Rohr, Don Shaw

KEY SIGNATURES: Hodges, Kranepool, Harrelson, Swoboda, Koosman, Seaver, Ryan.

VALUE: $475

1968 OAKLAND - Jack Aker, Sal Bando, Warren Bogle, Bert Campaneris, Danny Cater, Chuck Dobson, John Donaldson, Dave Duncan, Jim Gosger, Dick Green, Mike Hershberger, Catfish Hunter, Reggie Jackson, Bob Kennedy (MANAGER), Joe Keough, Lew Krausse, Ted Kubiak, Rene Lachemann, Allan Lewis, Paul Lindblad, Rick Monday, Jim Nash, Blue Moon Odom, Jim Pagliaroni, Tony Pierce, Floyd Robinson *, Phil Roof, Joe Rudi, Diego Segui, Ed Sprague, Ramon Webster

LESS THAN 10 GAMES: Rollie Fingers, George Lauzerique, Tony LaRussa, Ken Sanders

KEY SIGNATURES: Bando, Jackson, Odom, Hunter, Fingers.

VALUE: $170

1968 PHILADELPHIA - Dick Allen, John Boozer, Johnny Briggs, Johnny Callison, Doug Clemens, Clay Dalrymple, Dick Farrell, Woody Fryman, Tony Gonzalez, Dick Hall, Grant Jackson, Larry Jackson, Jeff James, Jerry Johnson, Rick Joseph, Don Lock, Gene Mauch (MANAGER), George Myatt (MANAGER), Roberto Pena, Cookie Rojas, Mike Ryan, Chris Short, Bob Skinner (MANAGER), John Sullivan, Gary Sutherland, Tony Taylor, Gary Wagner, Bill White, Bobby Wine, Rick Wise

LESS THAN 10 GAMES: Howie Bedell, Paul Brown, Larry Colton, Larry Hisle, Don Money

KEY SIGNATURES: White, Allen.

VALUE: $100

1968 PITTSBURGH - Gene Alley, Matty Alou, Steve Blass, Jim Bunning, Chris Cannizzaro, Roberto Clemente, Donn Clendenon, Dock Ellis, Roy Face *, Bill Henry *, Chuck Hiller, Manny Jiminez, Ron Kline, Gary Kolb, Jerry May, Bill Mazeroski, Al McBean, Bob Moose, Manny Mota, Jose Pagan, Freddie Patek, Juan Pizarro *, Larry Shepard (MANAGER), Tommie Sisk, Willie Stargell, Carl Taylor, Bob Veale, Luke Walker, Dave Wickersham, Maury Wills

LESS THAN 10 GAMES: Bruce Dal Canton, Richie Hebner, Al Oliver, Bill Virdon

KEY SIGNATURES: Mazeroski, Wills, Clemente, Stargell, Oliver, Bunning.

VALUE: $500

1968 SAN FRANCISCO - Jesus Alou, Bob Barton, Bob Bolin, Bobby Bonds, Ollie Brown, Ty Cline, Jim Davenport, Dick Dietz, Herman Franks (MANAGER), Joe Gibbon, Jim Ray Hart, Ron Herbel, Jack Hiatt, Ron Hunt, Frank Johnson, Hal Lanier, Frank Linzy, Juan Marichal, Dave Marshall, Don Mason, Willie Mays, Mike McCormick, Willie McCovey, Lindy McDaniel *, Nate Oliver, Gaylord Perry, Ray Sadecki, Bob Schroder

LESS THAN 10 GAMES: Ken Henderson, Bill Henry *, Bill Monbouquette *, Rich Robertson

KEY SIGNATURES: McCovey, Bonds, Mays, Marichal, Perry, McCormick.

VALUE: $200

1968 ST. LOUIS - Nelson Briles, Lou Brock, Steve Carlton, Orlando Cepeda, Ron Davis *, Johnny Edwards, Curt Flood, Phil Gagliano, Bob Gibson, Hal Gilson *, Wayne Granger, Joe Hoerner, Dick Hughes, Larry Jaster, Julian Javier, Roger Maris, Dal Maxvill, Tim McCarver, Mel Nelson, Dave Ricketts, Red Schoendienst (MANAGER), Dick Schofield, Mike Shannon, Dick Simpson *, Ed Spiezio, Bobby Tolan, Ray Washburn, Ron Willis

LESS THAN 10 GAMES: Joe Hague, Pete Mikkelsen *, Ted Simmons, Mike Torrez, Floyd Wicker

NOTES: Gibson won the MVP and Cy Young awards.

KEY SIGNATURES: Schoendienst, Cepeda, Maris, Brock, Simmons, Gibson, Carlton, McCarver.

VALUE: $260

1968 WASHINGTON - Bernie Allen, Hank Allen, Brant Alyea, Dave Baldwin, Frank Bertaina, Dick Billings, Dick Bosman, Sam Bowens, Eddie Brinkman, Billy Bryan, Paul

Casanova, Frank Coggins, Joe Coleman, Tim Cullen *, Mike Epstein, Jim French, Jim Hannan, Ron Hansen *, Bill Haywood, Denny Higgins, Gary Holman, Frank Howard, Bruce Howard *, Bob Humphreys, Darold Knowles, Jim Lemon (MANAGER), Ken McMullen, Barry Moore, Phil Ortega, Camilo Pascual, Cap Peterson, Ed Stroud, Del Unser, Fred Valentine *

LESS THAN 10 GAMES: Casey Cox, Bill Denehy, Steve Jones, Gene Martin, Jim Miles, Jerry Schoen

KEY SIGNATURES: Howard.

VALUE: $110

1969

1969 Atlanta Braves

* = player was traded

1969 ATLANTA - Hank Aaron, Tommie Aaron, Felipe Alou, Bob Aspromonte, Clete Boyer, Jim Britton, Rico Carty, Orlando Cepeda, Bob Didier, Paul Doyle, Darrell Evans, Tito Francona *, Ralph Garr, Gil Garrido, Tony Gonzalez *, Lum Harris (MANAGER), Sonny Jackson, Pat Jarvis, Mike Lum, Felix Millan, Gary Neibauer, Phil Niekro, Milt Pappas, Claude Raymond *, Ron Reed, George Stone, Bob Tillman, Cecil Upshaw

LESS THAN 10 GAMES: Dusty Baker, Jim Breazeale, Oscar Brown, Garry Hill, Walt Hriniak *, Ken Johnson *, Rick Kester, Larry Maxie, Mike McQueen, Bob Priddy *, Charlie Vaughan, Hoyt Wilhelm *

NOTES: The Aaron brothers were on the same team.

KEY SIGNATURES: Cepeda, Aaron, Evans, Niekro, Wilhelm.

VALUE: $200

1969 BALTIMORE - Mark Belanger, Paul Blair, Don Buford, Mike Cuellar, Clay Dalrymple, Andy Etchebarren, Bobby Floyd, Dick Hall, Jim Hardin, Ellie Hendricks, Dave Johnson, Dave Leonhard, Marcelino Lopez, Dave May, Dave McNally, Curt Motton, Jim Palmer, Tom Phoebus, Boog Powell, Merv Rettenmund, Pete Richert, Brooks Robinson, Frank Robinson, Chico Salmon, Al Severinsen, Eddie Watt, Earl Weaver (MANAGER)

LESS THAN 10 GAMES: Mike Adamson, Fred Beene, Frank Bertaina *, Terry Crowley

NOTES: Cuellar (Cy Young).

KEY SIGNATURES: Weaver, Powell, B. Robinson, F. Robinson, Cueller, Palmer.

VALUE: $275

1969 BOSTON - Mike Andrews, Joe Azcue *, Billy Conigliaro, Tony Conigliaro, Ray Culp, Russ Gibson, Ray Jarvis, Dalton Jones, Ron Kline *, Joe Lahoud, Bill Landis, Bill Lee, Don Lock *, Jim Lonborg, Sparky Lyle, Jerry Moses, Mike Nagy, Syd O'Brien, Rico Petrocelli, Eddie Popowski (MANAGER), Vincente Romo *, Jose Santiago, Tom Satriano *, Dick Schofield, George Scott, Sonny Siebert *, Reggie Smith, Lee Stange, George Thomas, Dick Williams (MANAGER), Carl Yastrzemski

LESS THAN 10 GAMES: Luis Alvarado, Ken Brett, Dick Ellsworth *, Carlton Fisk, Mike Garman, Ken Harrelson *, Tony Muser, Juan Pizarro *, Gerry Roggenburk *, Gary Wagner *, Fred Wenz

KEY SIGNATURES: Yastrzemski, Lyle.

VALUE: $145

1969 CALIFORNIA - Sandy Alomar *, Ruben Amaro, Joe Azcue *, Pedro Borbon, Randy Brown, George Brunet *, Billy Cowan *, Vic Davalillo *, Tom Egan, Eddie Fisher, Jim Fregosi, Vern Geishert, Jim Hicks *, Lou Johnson, Jay Johnstone, Steve Kealey, Bobby Knoop *, Winston Llenas, Rudy May, Jim McGlothlin, Andy Messersmith, Bubba Morton, Tom Murphy, Marty Perez, Lefty Phillips (MANAGER), Bob Priddy *, Rick Reichardt, Roger Repoz, Bill Rigney (MANAGER), Bob Rodgers, Aurelio Rodriguez, Tom Satriano *, Jim Spencer, Dick Stuart, Jarvis Tatum, Ken Tatum, Bill Voss, Hoyt Wilhelm *, Clyde Wright

LESS THAN 10 GAMES: Lloyd Allen, Tom Bradley, Bob Chance, Rickey Clark, Chuck Cottier, Phil Ortega, Greg Washburn, Wally Wolf

KEY SIGNATURES: Fregosi, Wilhelm.

VALUE: $100

1969 CHICAGO (AL) - Sandy Alomar *, Luis Aparicio, Gary Bell *, Ken Berry, Buddy Bradford, Angel Bravo, Chuck Brinkman, Cisco Carlos *, Bob Christian, Paul Edmondson, Don Gutteridge (MANAGER), Ron Hansen, Woody Held, Ed Herrmann, Gail Hopkins, Joe Horlen, Tommy John, Duane Josephson, Bobby Knoop *, Danny Lazar *, Bob Locker *, Al Lopez (MANAGER), Carlos May, Tommy McCraw, Bill Melton, Rich Morales, Danny Murphy, Jerry Nyman, Jose Ortiz, Dan Osinski, Don Pavletich, Gary Peters, Don Secrist, Bob Spence, Pete Ward, Walt Williams, Wilbur Wood, Billy Wynne

LESS THAN 10 GAMES: Doug Adams, Sammy Ellis, Jack Hamilton *, Bart Johnson, Denny O'Toole, Bob Priddy *, Fred Rath

KEY SIGNATURES: Lopez, Aparicio, John.

VALUE: $125

1969 CHICAGO (NL) - Ted Abernathy, Hank Aguirre, Ernie Banks, Glenn Beckert, Rick Bladt, Randy Bobb *, Leo Durocher (MANAGER), Oscar Gamble, Jimmie Hall *, Bill Hands, Bill Heath, Jim Hickman, Ken Holtzman, Randy Hundley, Ferguson Jenkins,

Don Kessinger, Don Nottebart *, Rich Nye, Gene Oliver, Nate Oliver *, Adolpho Phillips *, Paul Popovich *, Jim Qualls, Phil Regan, Ken Rudolph, Ron Santo, Dick Selma *, Willie Smith, Al Spangler, Billy Williams, Don Young

LESS THAN 10 GAMES: Jim Colborn, Joe Decker, Alec Distaso, John Hairston, Manny Jiminez, Ken Johnson *, Dave Lemonds, Joe Niekro *, Archie Reynolds, Gary Ross *, Charley Smith

KEY SIGNATURES: Durocher, Banks, Santo, Williams, Jenkins.

VALUE: $150

1969 CINCINNATI - Jerry Arrigo, Jim Beauchamp, Johnny Bench, Dave Bristol (MANAGER), Clay Carroll, Darrel Chaney, Tony Cloninger, Pat Corrales, George Culver, Jack Fisher, Wayne Granger, Tommy Helms, Al Jackson *, Alex Johnson, Jim Maloney, Lee May, Jim Merritt, Gary Nolan, Tony Perez, Pedro Ramos *, Pete Rose, Chico Ruiz, Ted Savage, Jimmy Stewart, Bobby Tolan, Fred Whitfield, Woody Woodward

LESS THAN 10 GAMES: Mike de la Hoz, Danny Breeden, Bernie Carbo, Clyde Mashore, John Noreiga, Camilo Pascual *, Jose Pena, Mel Queen, Dennis Ribant *, Bill Short

KEY SIGNATURES: Perez, Rose, Bench.

VALUE: $200

1969 CLEVELAND - Max Alvis, Frank Baker, Larry Brown, Larry Burchart, Lou Camilli, Jose Cardenal, Al Dark (MANAGER), Dick Ellsworth *, Ray Fosse, Vern Fuller, Jack Hamilton *, Steve Hargan, Ken Harrelson *, Jack Heidemann, Chuck Hinton, Tony Horton, Lou Klimchock, Gary Kroll, Ron Law, Eddie Leon, Lee Maye *, Sam McDowell, Rusty Nagelson, Dave Nelson, Mike Paul, Cap Peterson, Horacio Pina, Juan Pizarro *, Richie Scheinblum, Duke Sims, Russ Snyder, Ken Suarez, Luis Tiant, Zoilo Versalles *, Stan Williams

LESS THAN 10 GAMES: Joe Azcue *, Gary Boyd, Jimmie Hall *, Phil Hennigan, Vincente Romo *, Sonny Siebert *

KEY SIGNATURES: McDowell, Tiant.

VALUE: $100

1969 DETROIT - Gates Brown, Ike Brown, Dave Campbell, Norm Cash, Pat Dobson, Bill Freehan, Cesar Gutierrez *, John Hiller, Willie Horton, Al Kaline, Mike Kilkenny, Fred Lasher, Mickey Lolich, Tom Matchick, Dick McAuliffe, Denny McLain, Don McMahon *, Jim Northrup, Daryl Patterson, Jim Price, Dick Radatz *, Mayo Smith (MANAGER), Joe Sparma, Mickey Stanley, Tom Timmerman, Dick Tracewski, Tom Tresh *, Jon Warden, Don Wert, Earl Wilson, Ron Woods *

LESS THAN 10 GAMES: Norm McRae, Wayne Redmond, Bob Reed, Fred Scherman, Gary Taylor

NOTES: McLain (Cy Young).

KEY SIGNATURES: Cash, Kaline, Freehan, McLain, Lolich.

VALUE: $150

1969 HOUSTON - Jesus Alou, Jack Billingham, Wade Blasingame, Curt Blefary, Jim Bouton *, Don Bryant, Tommy Davis *, Larry Dierker, Johnny Edwards, Gary Geiger, Cesar Geronimo, Fred Gladding, Julio Gotay, Tom Griffin, Skip Guinn, Denny Lemaster, Marty Martinez, Leon McFadden, Denis Menke, Norm Miller, Joe Morgan, Doug Rader, Jim Ray, Hector Torres, Sandy Valdespino *, Harry Walker (MANAGER), Bob Watson, Don Wilson, Dooley Womack *, Jim Wynn

LESS THAN 10 GAMES: Danny Coombs, Bill Henry, Keith Lampard, John Mayberry, Dan Schneider, Scipio Spinks, Bob Watkins, Ron Willis *

KEY SIGNATURES: Morgan.

VALUE: $100

1969 KANSAS CITY - Jerry Adair, Luis Alcaraz, Wally Bunker, Tom Burgmeier, Bill Butler, Jim Campanis, Galen Cisco, Moe Drabowsky, Dick Drago, Mike Fiore, Joe Foy, Joe Gordon (MANAGER), Chuck Harrison, Mike Hedlund, Jackie Hernandez, Steve Jones, Pat Kelly, Joe Keough, Ed Kirkpatrick, Buck Martinez, Dave Morehead, Roger Nelson, Scott Northey, Don O'Riley, Bob Oliver, Dennis Paepke, Lou Piniella, Fred Rico, Juan Rios, Ellie Rodriguez, Jim Rooker, Paul Schaal, George Spriggs, Hawk Taylor, Dave Wickersham

LESS THAN 10 GAMES: Jerry Cram, Al Fitzmorris, Billy Harris, Fran Healy, Chris Zachary

NOTES: Team's first year as the Royals! Piniella (ROY).

KEY SIGNATURES: Piniella.

VALUE: $300

1969 LOS ANGELES - Walt Alston (MANAGER), Ken Boyer, Jim Brewer, Willie Crawford, Willie Davis, Don Drysdale, Ron Fairly *, Alan Foster, Len Gabrielson, Billy Grabarkewitz, Tom Haller, Tommy Hutton, Von Joshua, Andy Kosco, Jim Lefebvre, Al McBean *, Pete Mikkelsen, John Miller, Joe Moeller, Manny Mota *, Claude Osteen, Wes Parker, Paul Popovich *, Bill Russell, Bill Singer, Ted Sizemore, Bill Sudakis, Don Sutton, Jeff Torborg, Maury Wills *

LESS THAN 10 GAMES: Bill Buckner, Jim Bunning *, Bobby Darwin, Steve Garvey, Jack Jenkins, Ray Lamb, John Purdin, Bob Stinson, Bobby Valentine

NOTES: Sizemore (ROY).

KEY SIGNATURES: Alston, Sizemore, Wills, Davis, Drysdale, Bunning, Buckner, Garvey.

VALUE: $200

*** = player was traded**

1969 MINNESOTA - Bob Allison, Dave Boswell, Leo Cardenas, Rod Carew, Dean Chance, Jerry Crider, Joe Grzenda, Tom Hall, Herman Hill, Jim Holt, Jim Kaat, Harmon Killebrew, Chuck Manuel, Billy Martin (MANAGER), Bob Miller, George Mitterwald, Graig Nettles, Tony Oliva, Ron Perranoski, Jim Perry, Frank Quilici, Rich Reese, Rick Renick, Johnny Roseboro, Tom Tischinski, Cesar Tovar, Ted Uhlaender, Dick Woodson, Al Worthington

LESS THAN 10 GAMES: Darrell Brandon *, Ron Clark *, Rick Dempsey, Frank Kostro, Danny Morris, Cotton Nash, Charley Walters, Bill Zepp

NOTES: Killebrew (MVP).

KEY SIGNATURES: Carew, Killebrew, Oliva, Nettles, Kaat.

VALUE: $220

1969 MONTREAL - Bob Bailey, John Bateman, John Boccabella, Don Bosch, Ron Brand, Donn Clendenon *, Ty Cline, Kevin Collins *, Roy Face, Jim Fairey, Ron Fairly *, Mudcat Grant *, Angel Hermoso, Joe Herrara, Larry Jaster, Mack Jones, Coco Laboy, Gene Mauch (MANAGER), Dan McGinn, Manny Mota *, Adolfo Phillips *, Dick Radatz *, Claude Raymond *, Howie Reed, Steve Renko, Jerry Robertson, Carroll Sembera, Don Shaw, Rusty Staub, Bill Stoneman, Gary Sutherland, Gary Waslewski *, Mike Wegener, Floyd Wicker, Maury Wills *, Bobby Wine

LESS THAN 10 GAMES: Don Hahn, Gerry Jestadt, Leo Marentette, Carl Morton, Bob Reynolds, Steve Shea, Marv Staehle

NOTES: Team's first year!

KEY SIGNATURES: Staub.

VALUE: $225

1969 NEW YORK (AL) - Jack Aker *, Stan Bahnsen, Len Boehmer, Bill Burbach, Horace Clarke, Billy Cowan *, Bobby Cox, Al Downing, Johnny Ellis, Frank Fernandez, Jake Gibbs, Jimmie Hall *, Steve Hamilton, Ralph Houk (MANAGER), Ken Johnson *, Mike Kekich, Jerry Kenney, Jim Lyttle, Lindy McDaniel, Gene Michael, Thurman Munson, Bobby Murcer, Joe Pepitone, Fritz Peterson, Bill Robinson, Tom Shopay, Mel Stottlemyre, Frank Tepedino, Tom Tresh *, Roy White, Ron Woods *

LESS THAN 10 GAMES: Ron Blomberg, John Cumberland, Ron Klimkowski, Dave McDonald, Don Nottebart *, Nate Oliver *, Dick Simpson *, Fred Talbot *

KEY SIGNATURES: Murcer, Munson, Stottlemyre.

VALUE: $225

1969 NEW YORK (NL) - Tommie Agee, Ken Boswell, Don Cardwell, Ed Charles, Donn Clendenon *, Kevin Collins *, Jack DiLauro, Duffy Dyer, Wayne Garrett, Rod Gaspar, Gary Gentry, Jim Gosger *, Jerry Grote, Bud Harrelson, Bob Heise, Gil Hodges (MANAGER), Cleon Jones, Cal Koonce, Jerry Koosman, Ed Kranepool, J.C. Martin, Jim McAndrew, Tug McGraw, Amos Otis, Bobby Pfeil, Nolan Ryan, Tom Seaver, Art Shamsky, Ron Swoboda, Ron Taylor, Al Weis

LESS THAN 10 GAMES: Danny Frisella, Jesse Hudson, Al Jackson *, Bob Johnson, Les Rohr

NOTES: World Champions! Seaver (Cy Young).

KEY SIGNATURES: Harrelson, Swoboda, Seaver, Koosman, Ryan.

VALUE: $525

1969 OAKLAND - Sal Bando, Hank Bauer (MANAGER), Vida Blue, Bobby Brooks, Bert Campaneris, Danny Cater, Chuck Dobson, John Donaldson *, Dave Duncan, Rollie Fingers, Tito Francona *, Dick Green, Larry Haney *, Mike Hershberger, Catfish Hunter, Reggie Jackson, Bob Johnson *, Lew Krausse, Ted Kubiak, Marcel Lachemann, George Lauzerique, Allan Lewis, Paul Lindblad, John McNamara (MANAGER), Rick Monday, Jim Nash, Joe Nossek *, Blue Moon Odom, Jim Pagliaroni *, Tommie Reynolds, Jim Roland, Phil Roof, Joe Rudi, Ed Sprague, Fred Talbot *, Jose Tartabull, Gene Tenace, Ramon Webster

LESS THAN 10 GAMES: Tony LaRussa, Bill McNulty, Juan Pizarro *, John Wyatt

KEY SIGNATURES: Bando, Jackson, Odom, Hunter, Fingers, Blue.

VALUE: $180

1969 PHILADELPHIA - Dick Allen, Rich Barry, John Boozer, Johnny Briggs, Johnny Callison, Billy Champion, Dick Farrell, Woody Fryman, Terry Harmon, Larry Hisle, Grant Jackson, Deron Johnson, Jerry Johnson, Rick Joseph, Don Money, George Myatt (MANAGER), Lowell Palmer, Al Raffo, Scott Reid, Cookie Rojas, Vic Roznovsky, Mike Ryan, Bob Skinner (MANAGER), Gene Stone, Ron Stone, Tony Taylor, Dave Watkins, Billy Wilson, Rick Wise

LESS THAN 10 GAMES: Jeff James, Barry Lersch, Don Lock *, Lou Peraza, Leroy Reams, Chris Short, Gary Wagner *

KEY SIGNATURES: Allen.

VALUE: $110

1969 PITTSBURGH - Gene Alley, Matty Alou, Steve Blass, Jim Bunning *, Dave Cash, Roberto Clemente, Bruce Dal Canton, Ron Davis, Dock Ellis, Joe Gibbon *, Alex Grammas (MANAGER), Chuck Hartenstein, Richie Hebner, John Jeter, Ron Kline *, Gary Kolb, Lou Marone, Jose Martinez, Jerry May, Bill Mazeroski, Bob Moose, Al Oliver, Jose Pagan, Freddie Patek, Bob Robertson, Manny Sanguillen, Larry Shephard (MANAGER), Willie Stargell, Carl Taylor, Bob Veale, Luke Walker

LESS THAN 10 GAMES: Bo Belinsky, Frank Brosseau, Gene Garber, Angel Mangual, Pedro Ramos *, Jim Shellenback *

KEY SIGNATURES: Oliver, Mazeroski, Clemente, Stargell, Bunning.

VALUE: $475

1969 SAN DIEGO - Jose Arcia, Jack Baldschun, Ollie Brown, Chris Cannizzaro, Nate Colbert, Bill Davis, Jerry DaVanon *, Tommy Dean, Tom Dukes, Al Ferrara, Cito Gaston, Preston Gomez (MANAGER), Tony Gonzalez *, Walt Hriniak *, Dick Kelley, Van Kelly, Clay Kirby, Francisco Libran, Billy McCool, Jerry Morales, Ivan Murrell, Joe Niekro *, Roberto Pena, Johnny Podres, Frank Reberger, Dave Roberts, Gary Ross *, Sonny Ruberto, Al Santorini, John Sipin, Tommie Sisk, Ron Slocum, Ed Spiezio, Larry Stahl, Jim Williams,

LESS THAN 10 GAMES: Steve Arlin, Mike Corkins, Leon Everitt, Fred Kendall, Chris Krug, Al McBean *, Rafael Robles, Dick Selma *

NOTES: Team's first year!

VALUE: $250

1969 SAN FRANCISCO - Bob Barton, Bob Bolin, Bobby Bonds, Ron Bryant, Bob Burda, Jim Davenport, Dick Dietz, Bobby Etheridge, Tito Fuentes, Joe Gibbon *, Cesar Gutierrez *, Jim Ray Hart, Ken Henderson, Ron Herbel, Jack Hiatt, Ron Hunt, Clyde King (MANAGER), Hal Lanier, Frank Linzy, Juan Marichal, Dave Marshall, Don Mason, Willie Mays, Mike McCormick, Willie McCovey, Don McMahon *, Gaylord Perry, Rich Robertson, Ray Sadecki, Johnny Stephenson, Leon Wagner

LESS THAN 10 GAMES: Mike Davison, George Foster, Bob Garibaldi, John Harrell, Frank Johnson, Ron Kline *, Ozzie Virgil

NOTES: McCovey (MVP).

KEY SIGNATURES: McCovey, Bonds, Mays, Marichal, Perry.

VALUE: $200

1969 SEATTLE - Jack Aker *, Steve Barber, Gary Bell *, Jim Bouton *, Gene Brabender, George Brunet *, Ron Clark *, Wayne Comer, Tommy Davis *, John Donaldson *, Mike Ferraro, John Gelnar, Gus Gil, Greg Goossen, Jim Gosger *, Larry Haney *, Tommy Harper, Mike Hegan, Steve Hovley, John Kennedy, Bob Locker *, Gordon Lund, Mike Marshall, Jerry McNertney, Don Mincher, John Morris, John O'Donoghue, Ray Oyler, Jim Pagliaroni *, Marty Patin, Merrit Ranew, Rich Rollins, Joe Schultz (MANAGER), Diego Segui, Dick Simpson *, Fred Stanley, Fred Talbot *, Sandy Valdespino *, Jose Vidal, Danny Walton, Steve Whitaker

LESS THAN 10 GAMES: Dick Baney, Dick Bates, Darrell Brandon *, Bill Edgerton, Mickey Fuentes, Skip Lockwood, Bob Meyer, Garry Roggenburk *, Jerry Stephenson, Gary Timberlake, Federico Velazquez, Billy Williams, Dooley Womack *

NOTES: Team's first and only year as the Pilots.

KEY SIGNATURES: Harper.

VALUE: $400

1969 ST. LOUIS - Nelson Briles, Lou Brock, Byron Browne, Steve Carlton, Vic Davalillo *, Boots Day, Jerry DaVanon *, Curt Flood, Phil Gagliano, Bob Gibson, Mudcat Grant *, Dave Guisti, Joe Hague, Jim Hicks *, Joe Hoerner, Steve Huntz, Julian Javier, Bob Johnson *, Dal Maxvill, Tim McCarver, Vada Pinson, Dave Ricketts, Red Schoendienst (MANAGER), Mike Shannon, Chuck Taylor, Joe Torre, Mike Torrez, Ray Washburn, Gary Waslewski *, Bill White, Ron Willis *

LESS THAN 10 GAMES: Sal Campisi, Reggie Cleveland, Tom Coulter, Vic Davallio *, Jim Ellis, Santiago Guzman, Tom Hilgendorf, Leron Lee, Mel Nelson, Joe Nossek *, Jerry Reuss, Dennis Ribant *, Ted Simmons

KEY SIGNATURES: Pinson, Torre, Simmons, Gibson, Carlton, Schoendienst, Brock, McCarver.

VALUE: $175

1969 WASHINGTON - Bernie Allen, Hank Allen, Brant Alyea, Dave Baldwin, Frank Bertaina *, Dick Billings, Dick Bosman, Sam Bowens, Eddie Brinkman, Paul Casanova, Joe Coleman, Casey Cox, Tim Cullen, Mike Epstein, Jim French, Jim Hannan, Denny Higgins, Gary Holman, Frank Howard, Bob Humphreys, Darold Knowles, Lee Maye *, Ken McMullen, Barry Moore, Camilo Pascual *, Jim Shellenback *, Dick Smith, Ed Stroud, Del Unser, Zoilo Versalles *, Ted Williams (MANAGER)

LESS THAN 10 GAMES: Doug Camilli, Cisco Carlos *, Jan Dukes, Toby Harrah, Frank Kreutzer, Jim Miles

KEY SIGNATURES: Williams, Howard.

VALUE: $160

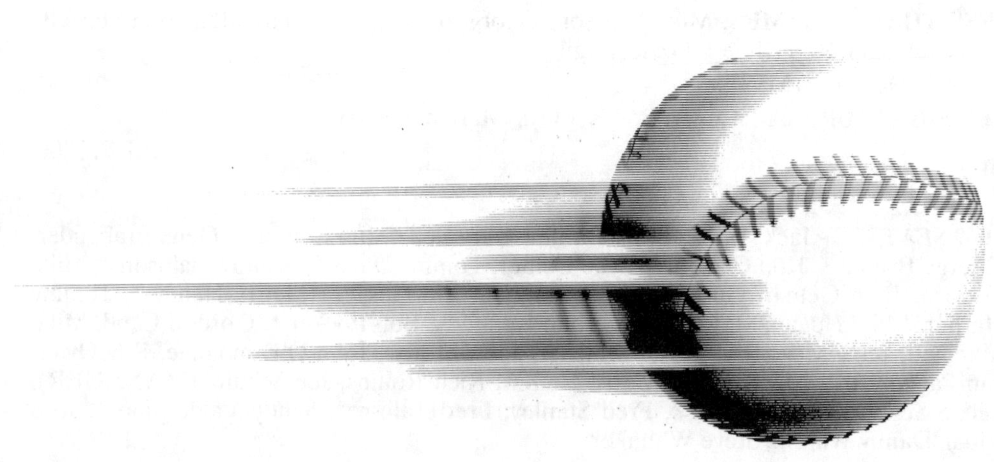

1970

1970 National League MVP Johnny Bench

*** = player was traded**

1970 ATLANTA - Hank Aaron, Tommie Aaron, Bob Aspromonte, Clete Boyer, Oscar Brown, Don Cardwell *, Rico Carty, Orlando Cepeda, Bob Didier, Darrell Evans, Ralph Garr, Gil Garrido, Tony Gonzalez *, Jimmie Hall *, Lum Harris (MANAGER), Sonny Jackson, Pat Jarvis, Larry Jaster, Rick Kester, Hal King, Mike Lum, Mike McQueen, Felix Millan, Jim Nash, Julio Navarro, Phil Niekro, Milt Pappas *, Bob Priddy, Ron Reed, George Stone, Bob Tillman, Hoyt Wilhelm *, Earl Williams

LESS THAN 10 GAMES: Dusty Baker, Steve Barber *, Jim Britton, Aubrey Gatewood, Ron Kline, Gary Neibauer

NOTES: The Aaron brothers were on the same team.

KEY SIGNATURES: Cepeda, Aaron, Evans, Niekro, Wilhelm.

VALUE: $150

1970 BALTIMORE - Mark Belanger, Paul Blair, Don Buford, Terry Crowley, Mike Cuellar, Clay Dalrymple, Moe Drabowsky *, Andy Etchebarren, Bobby Grich, Dick Hall, Jim Hardin, Ellie Hendricks, Dave Johnson, Dave Leonhard, Marcelino Lopez, Dave May *, Dave McNally, Curt Motton, Jim Palmer, Tom Phoebus, Boog Powell, Merv Rettenmund, Pete Richert, Brooks Robinson, Frank Robinson, Chico Salmon, Eddie Watt, Earl Weaver (MANAGER)

LESS THAN 10 GAMES: Don Baylor, Fred Beene, Bobby Floyd *, Roger Freed, Johnny Oates

NOTES: World Champions! Powell was the MVP winner.

KEY SIGNATURES: Weaver, Powell, B. Robinson, F. Robinson, Palmer.

VALUE: $325

1970 BOSTON - Luis Alvarado, Mike Andrews, Ken Brett, Billy Conigliaro, Tony Conigliaro, Ray Culp, Mike Derrick, Mike Fiore *, Chuck Hartenstein *, Ray Jarvis, Eddie Kasko (MANAGER), John Kennedy *, Cal Koonce *, Joe Lahoud, Bill Lee, Sparky Lyle, Bob Montgomery, Jerry Moses, Mike Nagy, Don Pavletich, Gary Peters, Rico Petrocelli, Ed Phillips, Vicente Romo, Tom Satriano, Dick Schofield, George Scott, Sonny Siebert, Reggie Smith, Lee Stange *, George Thomas, Gary Wagner, Carl Yastrzemski

LESS THAN 10 GAMES: Bob Bolin *, John Curtis, Carmen Fanzone, Jim Lonborg, Tom Matchick *, Dick Mills, Roger Moret, Jose Santiago

KEY SIGNATURES: Yastrzemski, Lyle.

VALUE: $145

1970 CALIFORNIA - Sandy Alomar, Joe Azcue, Tom Bradley, Billy Cowan, Paul Doyle *, Tom Egan, Eddie Fisher, Jim Fregosi, Greg Garrett, Tony Gonzalez *, Doug Griffin, Alex Johnson, Jay Johnstone, Steve Kealey, Dave LaRoche, Rudy May, Ken McMullen *, Andy Messersmith, Tom Murphy, Ray Oyler, Lefty Phillips (MANAGER), Mel Queen, Rich Reichardt *, Roger Repoz, Tommie Reynolds, Mickey Rivers, Aurelio Rodriguez *, Chico Ruiz, Tom Silverio, Jim Spencer, Jarvis Tatum, Ken Tatum, Bill Voss, Clyde Wright

LESS THAN 10 GAMES: Lloyd Allen, Randy Brown, Terry Cox, Jim Hicks, Marty Perez, Harvey Shank, Wally Wolf

KEY SIGNATURES: Fregosi.

VALUE: $95

1970 CHICAGO (AL) - Jimmy Adair (MANAGER), Luis Aparicio, Ken Berry, Ossie Blanco, Buddy Bradford *, Bob Christian, Jerry Crider, Don Guttgeridge (MANAGER), Ed Herrman, Gail Hopkins, Joe Horlen, Jerry Janeski, Tommy John, Bart Johnson, Duane Josephson, Bobby Knoop, Jim Magnuson, John Matias, Carlos May, Tommy McCraw, Rich McKinney, Bill Melton, Bob Miller *, Barry Moore *, Rich Morales, Danny Murphy, Syd O'Brien, Jose Ortiz, Tommie Sisk, Bob Spence, Lee Stange *, Chuck Tanner (MANAGER), Floyd Weaver, Walt Williams, Wilbur Wood, Billy Wynne

LESS THAN 10 GAMES: Jerry Arrigo, Chuck Brinkman, Don Eddy, Steve Hamilton *, Art Kusnyer, Lee Maye *, Rich Moloney, Denny O'Toole, Gene Rounsaville, Don Secrist

KEY SIGNATURES: Aparicio, John.

VALUE: $115

1970 CHICAGO (NL) - Ted Abernathy *, Hank Aguirre, Ernie Banks, Glenn Beckert, Johnny Callison, Jim Colborn, Brock Davis, Tommy Davis *, Boots Day *, Joe Decker, Leo Durocher (MANAGER), Phil Gagliano *, Larry Gura, Jimmie Hall *, Bill Hands, Jack Hiatt *, Jim Hickman, Ken Holtzman, Randy Hundley, Cleo James, Ferguson Jenkins, Don Kessinger, J.C. Martin, Milt Pappas *, Joe Pepitone *, Juan Pizarro, Paul Popovich, Phil Regan, Roberto Rodriquez *, Ken Rudolph, Ron Santo, Willie Smith, Al Spangler, Billy Williams

LESS THAN 10 GAMES: Steve Barber *, Jim Cosman, Jimmy Dunegan, Adrian Garrett, Terry Hughes, Roger Metzger, Bob Miller *, Archie Reynolds, Roe Skidmore, Hoyt Wilhelm *

KEY SIGNATURES: Durocher, Banks, Santo, Williams, Jenkins, Wilhelm.

VALUE: $150

1970 CINCINNATI - Sparky Anderson (MANAGER), Johnny Bench, Pedro Borbon, Angel Bravo, Bernie Carbo, Clay Carroll, Darrel Chaney, Ty Cline *, Tony Cloninger, Dave Concepcion, Pat Corrales, Wayne Granger, Don Gullett, Tommy Helms, Lee May, Jim McGlothlin, Hal McRae, Jim Merritt, Gary Nolan, Tony Perez, Pete Rose, Wayne Simpson, Jimmy Stewart, Bobby Tolan, Ray Washburn, Woody Woodward

LESS THAN 10 GAMES: Mel Behney, Bo Belinsky, Frank Duffy, Jim Maloney, John Noriega, Bill Plummer, Jay Ward, Milt Wilcox

NOTES: Bench (MVP).

KEY SIGNATURES: Anderson, Concepcion, Perez, Rose, Bench.

VALUE: $240

MVP = MVP Award winner

1970 CLEVELAND - Rick Austin, Buddy Bradford *, Larry Brown, Lou Camilli, Dean Chance *, Vince Colbert, Al Dark (MANAGER), Steve Dunning, Dick Ellsworth *, Ted Ford, Ray Fosse, Roy Foster, Vern Fuller, Rich Hand, Steve Hargan, Ken Harrelson, Jack Heidemann, Phil Hennigan, Denny Higgins, Chuck Hinton, Tony Horton, Lou Klimchock, Fred Lasher *, Eddie Leon, John Lowenstein, Sam McDowell, Bob Miller *, Steve Mingori, Barry Moore *, Russ Nagelson *, Graig Nettles, Mike Paul, Vada Pinson, Rich Rollins *, Duke Sims, Ted Uhlaender

LESS THAN 10 GAMES: Jim Rittwage

KEY SIGNATURES: Nettles, Pinson, McDowell.

VALUE: $100

1970 DETROIT - Gates Brown, Ike Brown, Les Cain, Norm Cash, Kevin Collins, Bill Freehan, Cesar Gutierrez, John Hiller, Willie Horton, Dalton Jones, Al Kaline, Mike Kilkenny, Gene Lamont, Fred Lasher *, Mickey Lolich, Elliott Maddox, Dick McAuliffe, Denny McLain, Norm McRae, Rusty Nagelson *, Joe Niekro, Jim Northrup, Daryl Patterson, Jim Price, Bob Reed, Jerry Robertson, Fred Scherman, Mayo Smith (MANAGER), Mickey Stanley, Ken Szotkiewicz, Tom Timmerman, Don Wert, Earl Wilson *

LESS THAN 10 GAMES: Tim Hosley, Lerrin LaGrow, Dennis Saunders

KEY SIGNATURES: Cash, Klaine, Freehan, Lolich.

VALUE: $130

1970 HOUSTON - Jesus Alou, Jim Beauchamp *, Jack Billingham, Wade Blasingame, Jim Bouton, Don Bryant, Cesar Cedeno, Ron Cook, George Culver *, Tommy Davis *, Larry Dierker, Jack DiLauro, Johnny Edwards, Cesar Geronimo, Fred Gladding, Tom Griffin, Larry Howard, Keith Lampard, Denny Lemaster, Marty Martinez, John Mayberry, Denis Menke, Norm Miller, Joe Morgan, Joe Pepitone *, Doug Rader, Jim Ray, Hector Torres, Harry Walker (MANAGER), Bob Watson, Don Wilson, Jim Wynn

LESS THAN 10 GAMES: Ken Forsch, Gary Geiger, Buddy Harris, Mike Marshall *, Leon McFadden, Dan Osinski, Scipio Spinks

KEY SIGNATURES: Morgan.

VALUE: $95

1970 KANSAS CITY - Ted Abernathy *, Luis Alcaraz, Wally Bunker, Tom Burgmeier, Bill Butler, Jim Campanis, Moe Drabowsky *, Dick Drago, Mike Fiore *, Al Fitzmorris, Bobby Floyd *, Jackie Hernandez, Bob Johnson, Pat Kelly, Joe Keough, Ed Kirkpatrick, Bob Lemon (MANAGER), Tom Matchick *, Charlie Metro (MANAGER), Aurelio Monteagudo, Dave Morehead, Bob Oliver, Amos Otis, Lou Piniella, Ellie Rodriguez, Cookie Rojas *, Jim Rooker, Paul Schaal, Rich Severson, Bill Sorrell, George Spriggs, Hawk Taylor, Ken Wright

LESS THAN 10 GAMES: Jerry Adair, Mike Hedlund, Buck Martinez, Roger Nelson, Don O'Riley, Paul Splittorff, Jim York
NOTES: Team's second year!
KEY SIGNATURES: Lemon, Piniella.

VALUE: $150

1970 LOS ANGELES - Walt Alston (MANAGER), Jim Brewer, Bill Buckner, Willie Crawford, Willie Davis, Alan Foster, Len Gabrielson, Steve Garvey, Billy Grabarkewitz, Tom Haller, Von Joshua, Andy Kosco, Ray Lamb, Jim Lefebvre, Pete Mikkelsen, Joe Moeller, Manny Mota, Fred Norman *, Claude Osteen, Tom Paciorek, Wes Parker, Camilo Pascual, Jose Pena, Bill Russell, Bill Singer, Ted Sizemore, Bill Sudakis, Don Sutton, Jeff Torborg, Sandy Vance, Maury Wills
LESS THAN 10 GAMES: Joe Ferguson, Charlie Hough, Al McBean *, Gary Moore, Jerry Stephenson, Bob Stinson, Mike Strahler
KEY SIGNATURES: Alston, Wills, Garvey, Buckner, Sutton.

VALUE: $200

1970 MILWAUKEE - Hank Allen *, Max Alvis, Dave Baldwin, Bob Bolin *, Gene Brabender, Dave Bristol (MANAGER), Bob Burda *, Wayne Comer *, Al Downing *, Dick Ellsworth *, Tito Francona *, John Gelnar, Gus Gil, Greg Goossen *, Tommy Harper, Mike Hegan, Mike Hershberger, Steve Hovley *, Bob Humphreys *, John Kennedy *, Pete Koegel, Lew Krausse, Ted Kubiak, George Lauzerique, Bob Locker *, Skip Lockwood, Dave May *, Jerry McNertney, John Morris, John O'Donoghue *, Marty Pattin, Roberto Pena *, Rich Rollins *, Phil Roof, Ken Sanders, Ted Savage, Bernie Smith, Russ Snyder, Danny Walton, Floyd Wicker
LESS THAN 10 GAMES: Bruce Brubaker, Bob Meyer, Ray Peters, Fred Stanley, Wayne Twitchell, Sandy Valdespino
NOTES: Team's first year! (formerly the Seattle Pilots).
KEY SIGNATURES: Harper.

VALUE: $95

1970 MINNESOTA - Bob Allison, Brant Alyea, Steve Barber, Bert Blyleven, Dave Boswell, Leo Cardenas, Rod Carew, Tom Hall, Herm Hill, Jim Holt, Jim Kaat, Harmon Killebrew, Chuck Manuel, Minnie Mendoza, George Mitterwald, Jim Nettles, Tony Oliva, Ron Perranoski, Jim Perry, Frank Quilici, Paul Ratliff, Rich Reese, Rick Renick, Bill Rigney (MANAGER), Danny Thompson, Luis Tiant, Tom Tischinski, Cesar Tovar, Stan Williams, Dick Woodson, Bill Zepp
LESS THAN 10 GAMES: Steve Brye, Rick Dempsey, Pete Hamm, Hal Haydel, Cotton Nash
NOTES: Perry won the Cy Young Award.
KEY SIGNATURES: Killebrew, Oliva, Carew, Perry, Kaat, Tiant.

VALUE: $175

1970 MONTREAL - Bob Bailey, John Bateman, John Boccabella, Ron Brand, Boots Day *, Bill Dillman, Jim Fairey, Ron Fairly, Jim Gosger, Don Hahn, Angel Hermoso, Jose Herrara, Jack Hiatt *, Mack Jones, Coco Laboy, Mike Marshall *, Clyde Mashore, Gene Mauch (MANAGER), Dan McGinn, Carl Morton, Adolfo Phillips, Claude Raymond, Howie Reed, Steve Renko, Marv Staehle, Rusty Staub, Bill Stoneman, John Strohmayer, Gary Sutherland, Mike Wegener, Bobby Wine

LESS THAN 10 GAMES: Ty Cline *, Ken Johnson, Baylor Moore, Rich Nye *, John O'Donoghue *, Jim Qualls, Carroll Sembera, Joe Sparma, Gary Waslewski *, Fred Whitfield

NOTES: Morton won the Rookie of the Year Award.

KEY SIGNATURES: Staub, Morton.

VALUE: $130

1970 NEW YORK (AL) - Jack Aker, Stan Bahnsen, Frank Baker, Curt Blefary, Danny Cater, Horace Clarke, John Cumberland *, Johnny Ellis, Jake Gibbs, Steve Hamilton *, Ron Hansen, Ralph Houk (MANAGER), Mike Kekich, Jerry Kenney, Ron Klimkowski, Steve Kline, Jim Lyttle, Lindy McDaniel, Gene Michael, Thurman Munson, Bobby Murcer, Fritz Peterson, Mel Stottlemyre, Frank Tepedino, Pete Ward, Gary Waslewski *, Roy White, Ron Woods

LESS THAN 10 GAMES: Bill Burbach, Loyd Colson, Rob Gardner, Gary Jones, Mike McCormick *, Bobby Mitchell, Joe Verbanic

NOTES: Munson won the Rookie of the Year Award.

KEY SIGNATURES: Murcer, Munson, Stottlemyre.

VALUE: $225

1970 NEW YORK (NL) - Tommie Agee, Ken Boswell, Don Cardwell *, Donn Clendenon, Duffy Dyer, Rich Folkers, Joe Foy, Danny Frisella, Wayne Garrett, Rod Gaspar, Gary Gentry, Jerry Grote, Bud Harrelson, Ron Herbel *, Gil Hodges (MANAGER), Cleon Jones, Mike Jorgenson, Cal Koonce *, Jerry Koosman, Ed Kranepool, Dave Marshall, Jim McAndrew, Tug McGraw, Nolan Ryan, Ray Sadecki, Tom Seaver, Art Shamsky, Ken Singleton, Ron Swoboda, Ron Taylor, Al Weis

LESS THAN 10 GAMES: Dean Chance *, Tim Foli, Teddy Martinez, Leroy Stanton

KEY SIGNATURES: Hodges, Koosman, Harrelson, Swoboda, Kranepool, Seaver, Ryan, Clendenon.

VALUE: $310

1970 OAKLAND - Felipe Alou, Sal Bando, Bert Campaneris, Tommy Davis *, Chuck Dobson, John Donaldson, Al Downing *, Jim Driscoll, Dave Duncan, Frank Fernandez, Rollie Fingers, Tito Francona *, Mudcat Grant *, Dick Green, Steve Hovley *, Catfish Hunter, Reggie Jackson, Bob Johnson, Marcel Lachemann, Tony LaRussa, Allan Lewis, Paul Lindblad, Bob Locker *, John McNamara (MANAGER), Don Mincher, Rick Monday, Blue Moon Odom, Roberto Pena *, Jim Roland, Joe Rudi, Diego Segui, Jose Tartabull, Gene Tenace

LESS THAN 10 GAMES: Vida Blue, Bobby Brooks, Larry Haney, Darrell Osteen, Roberto Rodriquez *, Fred Talbot, Dooley Womack

KEY SIGNATURES: Bando, Jackson, Hunter, Fingers.

VALUE: $185

1970 PHILADELPHIA - Del Bates, Larry Bowa, Johnny Briggs, Byron Browne, Jim Bunning, Mike Compton, Denny Doyle, Doc Edwards, Woody Fryman, Oscar Gamble, Terry Harmon, Larry Hisle, Joe Hoerner, Jim Hutto, Grant Jackson, Deron Johnson, Rick Joseph, Barry Lersch, Joe Lis, Frank Lucchesi (MANAGER), Tim McCarver, Don Money, Willie Montanez, Lowell Palmer, Sam Parrilla, Scott Reid, Mike Ryan, Dick Selma, Chris Short, Ron Stone, Tony Taylor, Fred Wenz, Billy Wilson, Rick Wise

LESS THAN 10 GAMES: Billy Champion, Mike Jackson, Bill Laxton, Greg Luzinski, Ke Reynolds, John Vukovich

KEY SIGNATURES: Bowa, McCarver, Bunning, Luzinski.

VALUE: $12

1970 PITTSBURGH - Gene Alley, Matty Alou, Steve Blass, George Brunet *, Dave Cash Roberto Clemente, Gene Clines, Bruce Dal Canton, Doc Ellis, Gene Garber, Joe Gibbon, Dave Giusti, Chuck Hartenstein *, Richie Hebner, Johnnie Jeter, George Kopacz John Lamb, Jose Martinez, Jerry May, Milt May, Bill Mazeroski, Bob Moose, Dann Murtaugh (MANAGER), Jim Nelson, Al Oliver, Jose Pagan, Freddie Patek, Orlando Pena, Dave Ricketts, Bob Robertson, Manny Sanguillen, Willie Stargell, Bob Veale Luke Walker

LESS THAN 10 GAMES: Ed Acosta, Fred Cambria, Dick Colpaert, Mudcat Grant *, Lo Marone, Al McBean *

KEY SIGNATURES: Mazeroski, Clemente, Stargell, Oliver.

VALUE: $55

1970 SAN DIEGO - Jose Arcia, Jack Baldschun, Bob Barton, Ollie Brown, Dav Campbell, Chris Cannizzaro, Nate Colbert, Danny Coombs, Mike Corkins, Tomm Dean, Pat Dobson, Tom Dukes, Al Ferrara, Cito Gaston, Preston Gomez (MANAGER) Ron Herbel *, Steve Huntz, Van Kelly, Clay Kirby, Jerry Morales, Ivan Murrell, Dave Roberts, Dave Robinson, Rafael Robles, Roberto Rodriquez *, Gary Ross, Al Santorini Ed Spiezio, Larry Stahl, Ron Stocum, Ramon Webster, Ron Willis *, Earl Wilson

LESS THAN 10 GAMES: Steve Arlin, Paul Doyle *, Fred Kendall, Jerry Nyman, Jin Williams

VALUE: $12

1970 SAN FRANCISCO - Bobby Bonds, Ron Bryant, Bob Burda *, Don Carrithers, Jim Davenport, Mike Davison, Dick Dietz, Charlie Fox (MANAGER), Tito Fuentes, Alan Gallagher, Russ Gibson, Jim Ray Hart, Bob Heise, Ken Henderson, Ron Hunt, Frank Johnson, Jerry Johnson *, Clyde King (MANAGER), Hal Lanier, Frank Linzy *, Juan Marichal, Don Mason, Willie Mays, Mike McCormick *, Willie McCovey, Don McMahon, Gaylord Perry, Skip Pitlock, Frank Reberger, Rich Robertson, Johnny Stephenson Bob Taylor, Steve Whitaker

LESS THAN 10 GAMES: John Cumberland *, Bill Faul, George Foster, Ed Goodson Jim Johnson, Miguel Puente, Bernie Williams

KEY SIGNATURES: McCovey, Bonds, Mays, Foster, Perry, Marichal.

VALUE: $20

1970 ST. LOUIS - Ted Abernathy *, Dick Allen, Jim Beauchamp *, Nelson Briles, Lou Brock, Jim Campbell, Sal Campisi, Jose Cardenal, Steve Carlton, Bob Chlupsa, Reggie Cleveland, Ed Crosby, Jose Cruz, George Culver *, Vic Davalillo, Jerry DaVanon, Phi Gagliano *, Bob Gibson, Joe Hague, Tom Hilgendorf, Al Hrabosky, Julian Javier, Jim Kennedy, Leron Lee, Frank Linzy *, Dal Maxvill, Billy McCool, Luis Melendez, Joe Nossek, Milt Ramirez, Jerry Reuss, Cookie Rojas *, Red Schoendienst (MANAGER), Mike Shannon, Ted Simmons, Carl Taylor, Chuck Taylor, Joe Torre, Mike Torrez

LESS THAN 10 GAMES: Frank Bertaina, Santiago Guzman, Chuck Hartenstein *, Jerry Johnson *, Fred Norman *, Rich Nye *, Harry Parker, Bart Zeller

NOTES: Gibson won the Cy Young Award.

KEY SIGNATURES: Allen, Torre, Brock, Simmons, Gibson, Carlton.

VALUE: $160

1970 WASHINGTON - Bernie Allen, Hank Allen *, Dick Billings, Dick Bosman, Eddie Brinkman, Jackie Brown, George Brunet *, Jeff Burroughs, Paul Casanova, Joe Coleman, Wayne Comer *, Casey Cox, Tim Cullen, Mike Epstein, Jim French, Greg Goossen *, Tommy Grieve, Joe Grzenda, Jim Hannan, Frank Howard, Darold Knowles, Lee Maye *, Ken McMullen *, Dave Nelson, Horacio Pina, Rick Reichardt *, Aurelio Rodriguez *, Johnny Roseboro, Jim Shellenback, Ed Stroud, Dick Such, Del Unser, Ted Williams (MANAGER)

LESS THAN 10 GAMES: Larry Biittner, Cisco Carlos, Jan Dukes, Bill Gogolewski, Bob Humphreys *, Dick Nen, Pedro Ramos, Denny Riddleberger

KEY SIGNATURES: Williams, Howard.

VALUE: $160

*** = player was traded**

1971

1971 N.L. Cy Young Award winner Ferguson Jenkins

1971 ATLANTA - Hank Aaron, Tommie Aaron, Dusty Baker, Steve Barber, Clete Boyer, Jim Breazeale, Oscar Brown, Orlando Cepeda, Bob Didier, Darrell Evans, Ralph Garr, Gil Garrido, Lum Harris (MANAGER), Ron Herbel, Tom House, Sonny Jackson, Pat Jarvis, Tom Kelley, Hal King, Mike Lum, Mike McQueen, Felix Millan, Jim Nash, Phil Niekro, Marty Perez, Bob Priddy, Ron Reed, Marv Staehle, George Stone, Cecil Upshaw, Zoilo Versalles, Earl Williams

LESS THAN 10 GAMES: Leo Foster, Tony LaRussa *, Gary Neibauer, Hoyt Wilhelm *
NOTES: Aaron brothers were on the same team; Williams (ROY).
KEY SIGNATURES: Aaron, Evans, Williams, Cepeda, Niekro, Wilhelm.

VALUE: $150

1971 BALTIMORE - Mark Belanger, Paul Blair, Dave Boswell *, Don Buford, Terry Crowley, Mike Cuellar, Clay Dalrymple, Jerry DaVanon, Pat Dobson, Tom Dukes, Andy Etchebarren, Dick Hall, Ellie Hendricks, Grant Jackson, Dave Johnson, Dave Leonhard, Dave McNally, Curt Motton, Jim Palmer, Boog Powell, Merv Rettenmund, Pete Richert, Brooks Robinson, Frank Robinson, Chico Salmon, Tom Shopay, Eddie Watt, Earl Weaver (MANAGER)
LESS THAN 10 GAMES: Don Baylor, Bobby Grich, Jim Hardin *, Orlando Pena
KEY SIGNATURES: Weaver, Powell, B. Robinson, F. Robinson, Palmer.

VALUE: $250

1971 BOSTON - Luis Aparicio, Juan Beniquez, Bob Bolin, Ken Brett, Billy Conigliaro, Cecil Cooper, Ray Culp, Mike Fiore, Carlton Fisk, Phil Gagliano, Doug Griffin, Ray Jarvis, Duane Josephson, Eddie Kasko (MANAGER), John Kennedy, Cal Koonce, Joe Lahoud, Bill Lee, Jim Lonborg, Sparky Lyle, Rick Miller, Bob Montgomery, Roger Moret, Mike Nagy, Ben Oglivie, Don Pavletich, Gary Peters, Rico Petrocelli, George Scott, Sonny Siebert, Reggie Smith, Ken Tatum, Luis Tiant, Carl Yastrzemski
LESS THAN 10 GAMES: John Curtis, Mike Garman, Buddy Hunter, George Thomas *
KEY SIGNATURES: Aparicio, Fisk, Lyle, Tiant.

VALUE: $160

1971 CALIFORNIA - Lloyd Allen, Sandy Alomar, Ken Berry, Bruce Christensen, Rickey Clark, Tony Conigliaro, Billy Cowan, Eddie Fisher, Jim Fregosi, Tony Gonzalez, Alex Johnson, Dave LaRoche, Jim Maloney, Rudy May, Ken McMullen, Andy Messersmith, Jerry Moses, Tom Murphy, Syd O'Brien, Lefty Philips (MANAGER), Mel Queen, Roger Repoz, Archie Reynolds, Tommie Reynolds, Mickey Rivers, Chico Ruiz, Jim Spencer, Johnny Stephenson, Jeff Torborg, Clyde Wright
LESS THAN 10 GAMES: Andy Hassler, Art Kusnyer, Fred Lasher, Rudy Meoli, Billy Parker, Tommy Silverio, Billy Wynne
KEY SIGNATURES: Fregosi.

VALUE: $95

1971 CHICAGO (AL) - Luis Alvarado, Mike Andrews, Tom Bradley, Chuck Brinkman, Don Eddy, Tom Egan, Terry Forster, Ed Herrmann, Mike Hershberger, Rich Hinton, Joe Horlen, Steve Huntz, Tommy John, Bart Johnson, Jay Johnstone, Steve Kealey, Pat Kelly, Jim Magnuson, Carlos May, Rich McKinney, Bill Melton, Rich Morales, Tony Muser, Rick Reichardt, Lee Richard, Vicente Romo, Bob Spence, Ed Stroud, Chuck Tanner (MANAGER), Walt Williams, Wilbur Wood
LESS THAN 10 GAMES: Ken Hottman, Pat Jacquez, Ron Lolich, Lee Maye, Denny O'Toole, Stan Perzanowski
KEY SIGNATURES: John.

VALUE: $100

1971 CHICAGO (NL) - Ernie Banks, Glenn Beckert, Bill Bonham, Pat Bourque, Danny Breeden, Hal Breeden, Johnny Callison, Chris Cannizzaro *, Jim Colborn, Brock Davis, Joe Decker, Leo Durocher (MANAGER), Carmen Fanzone, Frank Fernandez *, Bill Hands, Jim Hickman, Gene Hiser, Ken Holtzman, Cleo James, Ferguson Jenkins, Don Kessinger, J.C. Martin, Ray Newman, Jose Ortiz, Milt Pappas, Joe Pepitone, Juan Pizarro, Paul Popovich, Phil Regan, Ken Rudolph, Ron Santo, Earl Stephenson, Ron Thompkins, Hector Torres, Ramon Webster *, Billy Williams

LESS THAN 10 GAMES: Larry Gura, Burt Hooton, Randy Hundley, Gary Jestadt *, Bob Miller *, Billy North, Al Spangler

NOTES: Jenkins (CY).

KEY SIGNATURES: Santo, Williams, Banks, Jenkins.

VALUE: $125

CY = **Cy Young Award winner**

1971 CINCINNATI - Sparky Anderson (MANAGER), Johnny Bench, Buddy Bradford *, Bernie Carbo, Clay Carroll, Darrel Chaney, Ty Cline, Tony Cloninger, Dave Concepcion, Pat Corrales, Frank Duffy *, Al Ferrara *, George Foster *, Joe Gibbon, Wayne Granger, Ross Grimsley, Don Gullett, Tommy Helms, Lee May, Jim McGlothlin, Hal McRae, Jim Merritt, Gary Nolan, Tony Perez, Bill Plummer, Pete Rose, Wayne Simpson, Willie Smith, Jimmy Stewart, Milt Wilcox, Woody Woodward

LESS THAN 10 GAMES: Steve Blateric, Pedro Borbon, Angel Bravo *, Greg Garrett, Ed Sprague, Bobby Tolan

KEY SIGNATURES: Concepcion, Perez, Rose, Foster, Bench.

VALUE: $225

1971 CLEVELAND - Rick Austin, Frank Baker, Mark Ballinger, Kurt Bevacqua, Buddy Bradford *, Larry Brown *, Lou Camilli, Chris Chambliss, Jim Clark, Vince Colbert, Al Dark (MANAGER), Steve Dunning, Ed Farmer, Ted Ford, Ray Fosse, Alan Foster, Roy Foster, Rich Hand, Steve Hargan, Ken Harrelson, Jack Heidemann, Phil Henningan, Chuck Hinton, Gomer Hodge, Ray Lamb, Eddie Leon, Johnny Lipon (MANAGER), John Lowenstein, Chuck Machemehl, Sam McDowell, Steve Mingori, Graig Nettles, Mike Paul, Vada Pinson, Fred Stanley, Ken Suarez, Ted Uhlaender

LESS THAN 10 GAMES: Bob Kaiser, Camilo Pascual

NOTES: Chambliss (ROY).

KEY SIGNATURES: Chambliss, Nettles, Pinson, McDowell.

VALUE: $100

ROY = **Rookie of the Year**

1971 DETROIT - Eddie Brinkman, Gates Brown, Ike Brown, Les Cain, Norm Cash, Dean Chance, Joe Coleman, Kevin Collins, Bill Denehy, Bill Freehan, Cesar Gutierrez, Willie Horton, Dalton Jones, Al Kaline, Mike Kilkenny, Mickey Lolich, Billy Martin (MANAGER), Dick McAuliffe, Joe Niekro, Jim Northrup, Daryl Patterson *, Ron Perranoski *, Jim Price, Aurelio Rodriguez, Fred Scherman, Mickey Stanley, Tony Taylor *, Tom Timmerman, Bill Zepp

LESS THAN 10 GAMES: Dave Boswell *, Jim Foor, Bill Gilbreth, Jim Hannan *, Tim Hosley, Gene Lamont, Marvin Lane, Chuck Seelbach, Jack Whillock, John Young

KEY SIGNATURES: Martin, Cash, Kaline, Freehan, Lolich.

VALUE: $160

1971 HOUSTON - Jesus Alou, Jack Billingham, Wade Blasingame, Ray Busse, Cesar Cedeno, Rich Chiles, George Culver, Larry Dierker, Johnny Edwards, Ken Forsch, Cesar Geronimo, Fred Gladding, Tom Griffin, Buddy Harris, Jack Hiatt, Larry Howard, Denny Lemaster, Marty Martinez, John Mayberry, Denis Menke, Roger Metzger, Norm Miller Joe Morgan, Doug Rader, Jim Ray, Harry Walker (MANAGER), Bob Watson, Don Wilson, Jim Wynn

LESS THAN 10 GAMES: Ron Cook, Bill Greif, Skip Guinn, J.R. Richard, Jay Schlueter Scipio Spinks, Derrell Thomas, Larry Yount

KEY SIGNATURES: Morgan.

VALUE: $90

1971 KANSAS CITY - Ted Abernathy, Tom Burgmeier, Bill Butler, Lance Clemons, Bruce Dal Canton, Dick Drago, Al Fitzmorris, Bobby Floyd, Chuck Harrison, Mike Hedlund, Gail Hopkins, Joe Keough, Ed Kirkpatrick, Bobby Knoop, Bob Lemon (MANAGER), Buck Martinez, Jerry May, Roger Nelson, Bob Oliver, Amos Otis, Dennis Paepke, Freddie Patek, Lou Piniella, Cookie Rojas, Jim Rooker, Ted Savage *, Paul Schaal, Rich Severson, Paul Splittorff, Carl Taylor *, Sandy Valdespino, Ken Wright, Jim York

LESS THAN 10 GAMES: Wally Bunker, Mike McCormick, Monty Montgomery

KEY SIGNATURES: Lemon, Piniella.

VALUE: $100

1971 LOS ANGELES - Doyle Alexander, Dick Allen, Walt Alston (MANAGER), Jim Brewer, Bill Buckner, Willie Crawford, Willie Davis, Al Downing, Joe Ferguson, Steve Garvey, Billy Grabarkewitz, Tom Haller, Jim Lefebvre, Pete Mikkelsen, Joe Moeller, Manny Mota, Bob O'Brien, Claude Osteen, Wes Parker, Jose Pena, Bill Russell, Duke Sims, Bill Singer, Bill Sudakis, Don Sutton, Bob Valentine, Sandy Vance, Maury Wills

LESS THAN 10 GAMES: Ron Cey, Bobby Darwin, Charlie Hough, Von Joshua, Tom Paciorek, Mike Strahler, Hoyt Wilhelm *

KEY SIGNATURES: Alston, Wills, Garvey, Buckner, Sutton, Wilhelm.

VALUE: $200

1971 MILWAUKEE - Rick Auerbach, Johnny Briggs *, Dave Bristol (MANAGER), Jose Cardenal *, Rob Ellis, Dick Ellsworth, Gus Gil, Jim Hannan *, Tommy Harper, Mike Hegan *, Bob Heise *, Andy Kosco, Lew Krausse, Ted Kubiak *, Skip Lockwood, Marcelino Lopez, Tom Matchick, Dave May, Bobby Mitchell, John Morris, Bill Parsons, Marty Pattin, Roberto Pena, Darrel Porter, Paul Ratliff *, Ellie Rodriguez, Phil Roof *, Ken Sanders, Ted Savage *, Dick Schofield *, Jim Slaton, Bernie Smith, Frank Tepedino *, Ron Theobald, Bill Voss, Danny Walton *, Floyd Weaver, Al Yates

LESS THAN 10 GAMES: Larry Bearnarth, Jerry Bell, John Gelnar, Pete Koegel *, Bob Reynolds *, Floyd Wicker *

KEY SIGNATURES: Harper.

VALUE: $95

1971 MINNESOTA - Brant Alyea, Bert Blyleven, Steve Braun, Steve Brye, Leo Cardenas, Rod Carew, Ray Corbin, Bob Gebhard, Tom Hall, Pete Hamm, Hal Haydel, Jim Holt, Jim Kaat, Harmon Killebrew, Steve Luebber, Chuck Manuel, George Mitterwald, Jim Nettles, Tony Oliva, Ron Perranoski *, Jim Perry, Paul Powell, Paul Ratliff *, Rich Reese,

Rick Renick, Bill Rigney (MANAGER), Phil Roof *, Eric Soderholm, Jim Strickland, George Thomas *, Danny Thompson, Tom Tischinski, Cesar Tovar, Stan Williams *

LESS THAN 10 GAMES: Steve Barber, Sal Campisi, Rick Dempsey

KEY SIGNATURES: Killebrew, Carew, Oliva, Blyleven, Kaat.

VALUE: $130

1971 MONTREAL - Bob Bailey, John Bateman, John Boccabella, Ron Brand, Jim Britton, Boots Day, Jim Fairey, Ron Fairly, Jim Gosger, Rich Hacker, Ron Hunt, Mack Jones, Coco Laboy, Mike Marshall, Clyde Mashore, Gene Mauch (MANAGER), Ernie McAnally, Dave McDonald, Dan McGinn, Carl Morton, John O'Donoghue, Claude Raymond, Howie Reed, Steve Renko, Rusty Staub, Bill Stoneman, John Strohmayer, Gary Sutherland, Stan Swanson, Ron Swoboda *, Bobby Wine, Ron Woods *

LESS THAN 10 GAMES: Terry Humphrey, Mike Torrez *

NOTES: Staub.

VALUE: $90

1971 NEW YORK (AL) - Jack Aker, Felipe Alou *, Stan Bahnsen, Frank Baker, Curt Blefary *, Ron Blomberg, Danny Cater, Horace Clarke, Alan Closter, Johnny Ellis, Jake Gibbs, Roger Hambright, Ron Hansen, Jim Hardin *, Ralph Houk (MANAGER), Gary Jones, Mike Kekich, Jerry Kenney, Steve Kline, Jim Lyttle, Lindy McDaniel, Gene Michael, Thurman Munson, Bobby Murcer, Fritz Peterson, Mel Stottlemyre, Ron Swoboda *, Gary Waslewski, Roy White, Ron Woods *

LESS THAN 10 GAMES: Len Boehmer, Bill Burbach, Rob Gardner *, Terry Ley, Frank Tepedino *, Rusty Torres, Danny Walton *

KEY SIGNATURES: Murcer, Munson, Stottlemyre.

VALUE: $225

1971 NEW YORK (NL) - Tommie Agee, Bob Aspromonte, Ken Boswell, Donn Clendenon, Duffy Dyer, Tim Foli, Danny Frisella, Wayne Garrett, Gary Gentry, Jerry Grote, Don Hahn, Bud Harrelson, Gil Hodges (MANAGER), Cleon Jones, Mike Jorgensen, Jerry Koosman, Ed Kranepool, Dave Marshall, Ted Martinez, Jim McAndrew, Tug McGraw, Nolan Ryan, Ray Sadecki, Tom Seaver, Art Shamsky, Ken Singleton, Ron Taylor, Al Weis, Charlie Williams

LESS THAN 10 GAMES: Buzz Capra, Francisco Estrada, Jon Matlack, John Milner, Don Rose, Leroy Stanton

KEY SIGNATURES: Hodges, Kranepool, Harrelson, Seaver, Ryan, Koosman.

VALUE: $275

1971 OAKLAND - Dwain Anderson, Sal Bando, Curt Blefary *, Vida Blue, Larry Brown *, Bert Campaneris, Tommy Davis, Chuck Dobson, Dave Duncan, Mike Epstein *, Rollie Fingers, Adrian Garrett, Mudcat Grant *, Dick Green, Mike Hegan *, George Hendrick, Steve Hovley, Catfish Hunter, Reggie Jackson, Ron Klimkowski, Darold Knowles *, Tony LaRussa *, Bob Locker, Angel Mangual, Don Mincher *, Rick Monday, Blue Moon Odom, Jim Roland, Joe Rudi, Diego Segui, Gene Tenace, Dick Williams (MANAGER)

LESS THAN 10 GAMES: Felipe Alou *, Ron Clark, Frank Fernandez *, Rob Gardner *, Marcel Lachemann, Paul Lindblad *, Jim Panther, Daryl Patterson *, Ramon Webster *

NOTES: Blue (CY) & (MVP).

KEY SIGNATURES: Bando, Jackson, Hunter, Blue, Fingers.

VALUE: $225

1971 PHILADELPHIA - Mike Anderson, Larry Bowa, Darrell Brandon, Johnny Briggs *, Byron Browne, Jim Bunning, Billy Champion, Denny Doyle, Roger Freed, Woody Fryman, Oscar Gamble, Terry Harmon, Larry Hisle, Joe Hoerner, Deron Johnson, Pete Koegel *, Barry Lersch, Joe Lis, Frank Lucchesi (MANAGER), Greg Luzinski, Tim McCarver, Don Money, Willie Montanez, Bobby Pfeil, Ken Reynolds, Mike Ryan, Dick Selma, Chris Short, Ron Stone, Tony Taylor *, John Vukovich, Billy Wilson, Rick Wise

LESS THAN 10 GAMES: Manny Muniz, Lowell Palmer, Wayne Twitchell

KEY SIGNATURES: Bowa, McCarver, Luzinski, Bunning.

VALUE: $130

1971 PITTSBURGH - Gene Alley, Steve Blass, Nelson Briles, Dave Cash, Roberto Clemente, Gene Clines, Vic Davalillo, Dock Ellis, Dave Giusti, Mudcat Grant *, Richie Hebner, Jackie Hernandez, Ramon Hernandez, Bob Johnson, Bruce Kison, Milt May, Bill Mazeroski, Bob Miller *, Bob Moose, Danny Murtaugh (MANAGER), Jim Nelson, Al Oliver, Jose Pagan, Bob Robertson, Charlie Sands, Manny Sanguillen, Willie Stargell, Rennie Stennett, Bob Veale, Luke Walker

LESS THAN 10 GAMES: Frank Brosseau, John Lamb, Rimp Lanier, Frank Taveras, Carl Taylor *, Richie Zisk

NOTES: World Champions!

KEY SIGNATURES: Clemente, Oliver, Stargell, Mazeroski.

VALUE: $650

1971 SAN DIEGO - Steve Arlin, Bob Barton, Angel Bravo *, Ollie Brown, Dave Campbell, Chris Cannizzaro *, Nate Colbert, Danny Coombs, Tommy Dean, Al Ferrara *, Rod Gaspar, Cito Gaston, Preston Gomez (MANAGER), Enzo Hernandez, Garry Jestadt *, Johnnie Jeter, Dick Kelley, Fred Kendall, Clay Kirby, Bill Laxton, Leron Lee *, Don Mason, Bob Miller *, Jerry Morales, Ivan Murrell, Fred Norman *, Tom Phoebus, Dave Roberts, Gary Ross, Al Santorini *, Al Severinsen, Ed Spiezio, Larry Stahl, Ramon Webster *

LESS THAN 10 GAMES: Ed Acosta, Mike Caldwell, Mike Corkins, Jay Franklin, Mike Ivie, Dave Robinson, Ron Slocum

VALUE: $90

1971 SAN FRANCISCO - Jim Barr, Bobby Bonds, Ron Bryant, Don Carrithers, John Cumberland, Dick Dietz, Frank Duffy *, George Foster *, Charlie Fox (MANAGER), Tito Fuentes, Alan Gallagher, Russ Gibson, Ed Goodson, Steve Hamilton, Jim Ray Hart, Fran Healy, Bob Heise *, Ken Henderson, Frank Johnson, Jerry Johnson, Dave Kingman, Hal Lanier, Juan Marichal, Willie Mays, Willie McCovey, Don McMahon, Gaylord Perry, Frank Reberger, Rich Robertson, Jimmy Rosario, Chris Speier, Steve Stone, Bernie Williams

LESS THAN 10 GAMES: Chris Arnold, Jim Howarth, Dave Rader, Floyd Wicker *, Jim Willoughby

KEY SIGNATURES: McCovey, Bonds, Mays, Kingman, Foster, Marichal, Perry.

VALUE: $200

1971 ST. LOUIS - Matty Alou, Jim Beauchamp, Lou Brock, Bob Burda, Jose Cardenal *, Steve Carlton, Reggie Cleveland, Jose Cruz, Moe Drabowsky, Bob Gibson, Joe Hague, Julian Javier, Ted Kubiak *, Leron Lee *, Frank Linzy, Dal Maxvill, Jerry McNertney, Luis Melendez, Daryl Patterson *, Jerry Reuss, Al Santorini *, Red Schoendienst (MANAGER), Dick Schofield *, Don Shaw, Ted Simmons, Ted Sizemore, Bob Stinson, Chuck Taylor, Joe Torre, Stan Williams *, Chris Zachary

LESS THAN 10 GAMES: Rudy Arroyo, George Brunet, Bob Chlupsa, Santiago Guzman, Denny Higgins, Al Hrabosky, Mike Jackson, Fred Norman *, Harry Parker, Milt Ramirez, Bob Reynolds *, Jorge Roque, Mike Torrez *

NOTES: Torre (MVP).

KEY SIGNATURES: Schoendienst, Torre, Brock, Simmons, Carlton, Gibson.

VALUE: $150

1971 WASHINGTON - Bernie Allen, Larry Biittner, Dick Billings, Dick Bosman, Pete Broberg, Jackie Brown, Jeff Burroughs, Paul Casanova, Casey Cox, Tim Cullen, Mike Esptein *, Frank Fernandez *, Joe Foy, Jim French, Bill Gogolewski, Joe Grzenda, Toby Harrah, Frank Howard, Jerry Janeski, Darold Knowles *, Paul Lindblad *, Elliott Maddox, Tommy McCraw, Denny McLain, Don Mincher *, Dave Nelson, Horacio Pina, Tom Ragland, Lenny Randle, Denny Riddleberger, Richie Scheinblum, Jim Shellenback, Mike Thompson, Del Unser, Don Wert, Ted Williams (MANAGER)

LESS THAN 10 GAMES: Bill Fahey, Curt Flood, Jim Mason, Dick Stelmaszek

NOTES: Senators' last year.

KEY SIGNATURES: Williams, Harrah, Howard, McLain.

VALUE: $200

*** = player was traded**

1972

1972 A.L. Cy Young Award winner Gaylord Perry

1972 ATLANTA - Hank Aaron, Dusty Baker, Larvell Blanks, Jim Breazeale, Oscar Brown, Rico Carty, Paul Casanova, Orlando Cepeda *, Bob Didier, Darrell Evans, Ralph Garr, Gil Garrido, Rod Gilbreath, Jim Hardin, Lum Harris (MANAGER), Joe Hoerner *, Sonny Jackson, Pat Jarvis, Tom Kelley, Mike Lum, Eddie Mathews (MANAGER), Denny McLain *, Mike McQueen, Felix Millan, Jim Nash *, Phil Niekro, Marty Perez, Ron Reed, Ron Schueler, George Stone, Cecil Upshaw, Earl Williams

LESS THAN 10 GAMES: Steve Barber *, Jimmy Freeman, Tom House, Larry Jaster, Gary Neibauer *, Rowland Office

KEY SIGNATURES: Mathews, Aaron, Evans, Cepeda, Niekro.

VALUE: $150

1972 BALTIMORE - Doyle Alexander, Don Baylor, Mark Belanger, Paul Blair, Don Buford, Rich Coggins, Terry Crowley, Mike Cuellar, Tommy Davis *, Pat Dobson, Andy Etchebarren, Bobby Grich, Roric Harrison, Ellie Hendricks *, Grant Jackson, Dave Johnson, Dave Leonhard, Dave McNally, Johnny Oates, Jim Palmer, Boog Powell, Merv Rettenmund, Brooks Robinson, Chico Salmon, Mickey Scott, Tom Shopay, Eddie Watt, Earl Weaver (MANAGER)

LESS THAN 10 GAMES: Al Bumbry, Enos Cabell, Tom Matchick, Bob Reynolds, Sergio Robles

KEY SIGNATURES: Weaver, Powell, Robinson.

VALUE: $135

1972 BOSTON - Luis Aparicio, Juan Beniquez, Bob Bolin, Bob Burda, Danny Cater, Ray Culp, John Curtis, Dwight Evans, Carlton Fisk, Phil Gagliano, Doug Griffin, Tommy Harper, Duane Josephson, Eddie Kasko (MANAGER), John Kennedy, Andy Kosco *, Lew Krausse, Bill Lee, Lynn McGlothen, Rick Miller, Bob Montgomery, Don Newhauser, Ben Oglivie, Marty Pattin, Gary Peters, Rico Petrocelli, Sonny Siebert, Reggie Smith, Ken Tatum, Luis Tiant, Carl Yastrzemski

LESS THAN 10 GAMES: Cecil Cooper, Vic Correll, Bob Gallagher, Mike Garman, Roger Moret, Mike Nagy, Bob Veale *, Stan Williams

NOTES: Fisk (ROY).

KEY SIGNATURES: Aparicio, Yastrzemski, Fisk, Tiant.

VALUE: $160

ROY = Rookie of the Year

1972 CALIFORNIA - Lloyd Allen, Sandy Alomar, Steve Barber *, Ken Berry, Leo Cardenas, Rickey Clark, Chris Coletta, Eddie Fisher *, Jack Hiatt *, Doug Howard, Andy Kosco *, Art Kusnyer, Winston Llenas, Rudy May, Ken McMullen, Andy Messersmith, Curt Motton *, Syd O'Brien *, Bob Oliver *, Billy Parker, Vada Pinson, Mel Queen, Del Rice (MANAGER), Mickey Rivers, Don Rose, Nolan Ryan, Dave Sells, Tommy Silverio, Jim Spencer, Leroy Stanton, Johnny Stephenson, Jeff Torborg, Clyde Wright

LESS THAN 10 GAMES: Joe Azcue *, Billy Cowan, Paul Doyle, Tom Dukes, Alan Foster, Dick Lange, Tom Murphy *, Roger Repoz

KEY SIGNATURES: Pinson, Ryan.

VALUE: $100

1972 CHICAGO (AL) - Cy Acosta, Dick Allen, Luis Alvarado, Mike Andrews, Stan Bahnsen, Buddy Bradford, Tom Bradley, Chuck Brinkman, Tom Egan, Terry Forster, Goose Gossage, Ed Herrmann, Jay Johnstone, Steve Kealey, Pat Kelly, Dave Lemonds, Jim Lyttle, Carlos May, Bill Melton, Rich Morales, Tony Muser, Jorge Orta, Phil Regan

*, Lee Richard, Rick Riechardt, Vicente Romo, Ed Spiezio *, Chuck Tanner (MANAGER), Walt Williams, Wilbur Wood

LESS THAN 10 GAMES: Hank Allen, Moe Drabowsky *, Eddie Fisher *, Ken Frailing, Jim Geddes, Rudy Hernandez, Bart Johnson, Dan Neumeier, Denny O'Toole, Jim Qualls, Hugh Yancy

NOTES: Allen (MVP).

KEY SIGNATURES: Allen, Gossage.

VALUE: $100

MVP = MVP Award winner

1972 CHICAGO (NL) - Glenn Beckert, Bill Bonham, Pat Bourque, Jose Cardenal, Leo Durocher (MANAGER), Carmen Fanzone, Frank Fernandez, Steve Hamilton, Bill Hands, Ellie Hendricks *, Jim Hickman, Gene Hiser, Burt Hooton, Randy Hundley, Ferguson Jenkins, Don Kessinger, Whitey Lockman (MANAGER), J.C. Martin, Dan McGinn, Rick Monday, Billy North, Milt Pappas, Joe Pepitone, Tom Phoebus *, Juan Pizarro, Paul Popovich, Rick Reuschel, Ken Rudolph, Ron Santo, Jim Tyrone, Billy Williams

LESS THAN 10 GAMES: Jack Aker *, Frank Coggins, Clint Compton, Tommy Davis *, Joe Decker, Larry Gura, Pete LaCock, Al Montreuil, Phil Regan *, Dave Rosello, Art Shamsky *, Chris Ward

KEY SIGNATURES: Durocher, Santo, Williams, Jenkins.

VALUE: $115

1972 CINCINNATI - , Sparky Anderson (MANAGER), Johnny Bench, Jack Billingham, Pedro Borbon, Bernie Carbo *, Clay Carroll, Darrel Chaney, Dave Concepcion, George Foster, Cesar Geronimo, Ross Grimsley, Don Gullett, Joe Hague *, Tom Hall, Julian Javier, Jim McGlothlin, Hal McRae, Denis Menke, Joe Morgan, Gary Nolan, Tony Perez, Bill Plummer, Pete Rose, Wayne Simpson, Ed Sprague, Bobby Tolan, Ted Uhlaender

LESS THAN 10 GAMES: Pat Corrales *, Joe Gibbon *, Jim Merritt, Sonny Ruberto, Dave Tomlin

NOTES: Bench (MVP).

KEY SIGNATURES: Anderson, Perez, Morgan, Concepcion, Rose, Bench, Foster.

VALUE: $300

1972 CLEVELAND - Ken Aspromonte (MANAGER), Buddy Bell, Kurt Bevacqua, Jack Brohamer, Lou Camilli, Chris Chambliss, Vince Colbert, Frank Duffy, Steve Dunning, Ed Farmer, Ray Fosse, Roy Foster, Steve Hargan, Jack Heidemann, Phil Hennigan, Tom Hilgendorf, Alex Johnson, Mike Kilkenny *, Ray Lamb, Eddie Leon, Ron Lolich, John Lowenstein, Tommy McCraw, Steve Mingori, Jerry Moses, Graig Nettles, Gaylord Perry, Adolfo Phillips, Denny Riddleberger, Dick Tidrow, Del Unser, Milt Wilcox

LESS THAN 10 GAMES: Bill Butler, Larry Johnson, Marcelino Lopez, Lowell Palmer *, Fred Stanley *

NOTES: Perry (CY).

KEY SIGNATURES: Nettles, Bell, Perry.

VALUE: $100

CY = Cy Young Award winner

1972 DETROIT - Eddie Brinkman, Gates Brown, Ike Brown, Norm Cash, Joe Coleman, Wayne Comer, Bill Freehan, Woody Fryman *, Tom Haller, John Hiller, Willie Horton, Frank Howard *, Paul Jata, Al Kaline, John Knox, Lerrin LaGrow, Mickey Lolich, Billy Martin (MANAGER), Dick McAuliffe, Joe Niekro, Jim Northrup, Ron Perranoski *, Aurelio Rodriguez, Fred Scherman, Chuck Seelbach, Duke Sims *, Bill Slayback, Mickey Stanley, Tony Taylor, Tom Timmerman, Chris Zachary

LESS THAN 10 GAMES: Ike Blessitt, Les Cain, Jim Foor, John Gamble, Bill Gilbreth, Fred Holdsworth, Dalton Jones *, Mike Kilkenny *, Gene Lamont, Marvin Lane, Don Leshnock, Phil Meeler, Joe Staton, Bob Strampe

KEY SIGNATURES: Cash, Northrup, Freehan, Kaline, Lolich.

VALUE: $175

1972 HOUSTON - Jesus Alou, Wade Blasingame *, Cesar Cedeno, George Culver, Larry Dierker, Leo Durocher (MANAGER), Johnny Edwards, Bob Fenwick, Ken Forsch, Fred Gladding, Tom Griffin, Tommy Helms, Jack Hiatt *, Larry Howard, Lee May, Roger Metzger, Norm Miller, Doug Rader, Jim Ray, Jerry Reuss, Dave Roberts, Jimmy Stewart, Bob Stinson, Harry Walker (MANAGER), Bob Watson, Don Wilson, Jim Wynn, Jim York

LESS THAN 10 GAMES: Rich Chiles, Mike Cosgrove, Joe Gibbon *, Cliff Johnson, J.R. Richard, Gary Sutherland

KEY SIGNATURES: Durocher.

VALUE: $90

1972 KANSAS CITY - Ted Abernathy, Norm Angelini, Tom Burgmeier, Bruce Del Canton, Dick Drago, Al Fitzmorris, Bobby Floyd, Mike Hedlund, Gail Hopkins, Steve Hovley, Joe Keough, Ed Kirkpatrick, Bobby Knoop, Bob Lemon (MANAGER), Jerry May, John Mayberry, Tom Murphy *, Roger Nelson, Bob Oliver *, Amos Otis, Freddie Patek, Lou Piniella, Cookie Rojas, Jim Rooker, Paul Schaal, Richie Scheinblum, Paul Splittorff, Carl Taylor, Ken Wright

LESS THAN 10 GAMES: Steve Busby, Ron Hansen, Mike Jackson, Monte Montgomery, Dennis Paepke, Jim Wohlford

KEY SIGNATURES: Piniella.

VALUE: $100

1972 LOS ANGELES - Walt Alston (MANAGER), Jim Brewer, Bill Buckner, Chris Cannizzaro, Ron Cey, Willie Crawford, Willie Davis, Dick Dietz, Al Downing, Steve Garvey, Billy Grabarkewitz, Tommy John, Lee Lacy, Jim Lefebvre, Davey Lopes, Pete Mikkelsen, Manny Mota, Claude Osteen, Tom Paciorek, Wes Parker, Pete Richert, Frank Robinson, Bill Russell, Duke Sims *, Bill Singer, Mike Strahler, Don Sutton, Bobby Valentine, Hoyt Wilhelm, Maury Wills, Steve Yeager

LESS THAN 10 GAMES: Joe Ferguson, Charlie Hough, Terry McDermott, Jose Pena, Ron Perranoski *, Doug Rau

KEY SIGNATURES: Alston, Garvey, Robinson, Davis, Sutton, John, Wilhelm.

VALUE: $200

1972 MILWAUKEE - Rick Auerbach, Joe Azcue *, Jerry Bell, Ken Brett, Johnny Briggs, Dave Bristol (MANAGER), Ollie Brown *, Ron Clark *, Jim Colborn, Billy Conigliaro, Del Crandall (MANAGER), Brock Davis, John Felske, Mike Ferraro, Bob Heise, Joe

Lahoud, Frank Linzy, Skip Lockwood, Jim Lonborg, Dave May, Roy McMillan (MANAGER), Syd O'Brien *, Bill Parsons, Darrell Porter, Paul Ratliff, Tommie Reynolds, Ellie Rodriguez, Gary Ryerson, Ken Sanders, George Scott, Earl Stephenson, Ron Theobald, Bill Voss *

LESS THAN 10 GAMES: Curt Motton *, Ray Newman, Archie Reynolds, Jim Slaton, Chuck Taylor *

VALUE: $95

1972 MINNESOTA - Bert Blyleven, Glenn Borgmann, Steve Braun, Steve Brye, Rod Carew, Ray Corbin, Bobby Darwin, Rick Dempsey, Bob Gebhard, Dave Goltz, Wayne Granger, Jim Holt, Jim Kaat, Harmon Killebrew, Dave LaRoche, Chuck Manuel, George Mitterwald, Dan Monzon, Jim Nettles, Tom Norton, Tony Oliva, Jim Perry, Frank Quilici (MANAGER), Rich Reese, Rick Renick, Bill Rigney (MANAGER), Phil Roof, Eric Soderholm, Jim Strickland, Danny Thompson, Cesar Tovar, Dick Woodson

LESS THAN 10 GAMES: Mike Adams, Bucky Guth, Steve Luebber

KEY SIGNATURES: Killebrew, Carew, Oliva, Blyleven, Kaat.

VALUE: $130

1972 MONTREAL - Bob Bailey, John Bateman *, John Boccabella, Hal Breeden, Boots Day, Jim Fairey, Ron Fairly, Tim Foli, Joe Gilbert, Terry Humphrey, Ron Hunt, Mike Jorgensen, Coco Laboy, Denny Lemaster, Mike Marshall, Clyde Mashore, Gene Mauch (MANAGER), Ernie McAnally, Tim McCarver *, Balor Moore, Carl Morton, Steve Renko, Ken Singleton, Bill Stoneman, John Strohmayer, Hector Torres, Mike Torrez, Tom Walker, Bobby Wine, Ron Woods

LESS THAN 10 GAMES: Pepe Mangual

KEY SIGNATURES: Singleton, McCarver.

VALUE: $85

1972 NEW YORK (AL) - Bernie Allen, Felipe Alou, Fred Beene, Wade Blasingame *, Ron Blomberg, Johnny Callison, Horace Clarke, Johnny Ellis, Rob Gardner, Ralph Houk (MANAGER), Mike Kekich, Jerry Kenney, Ron Klimkowski, Steve Kline, Hal Lanier, Sparky Lyle, Lindy McDaniel, Rich McKinney, Gene Michael, Thurman Munson, Bobby Murcer, Fritz Peterson, Jim Roland *, Celerino Sanchez, Charlie Spikes, Mel Stottlemyre, Ron Swoboda, Rusty Torres, Roy White

LESS THAN 10 GAMES: Jack Aker *, Steve Blateric, Alan Closter, Casey Cox *, Larry Gowell, Rich Hinton *, Doc Medich, Frank Tepedino

KEY SIGNATURES: Murcer, Munson, Stottlemyre.

VALUE: $225

1972 NEW YORK (NL) - Tommie Agee, Lute Barnes, Jim Beauchamp, Yogi Berra (MANAGER), Ken Boswell, Buzz Capra, Duffy Dyer, Jim Fregosi, Danny Frisella, Wayne Garrett, Gary Gentry, Jerry Grote, Don Hahn, Bud Harrelson, Gil Hodges (MANAGER), Cleon Jones, Jerry Koosman, Ed Kranepool, Dave Marshall, Ted Martinez, Jon Matlack, Willie Mays *, Jim McAndrew, Tug McGraw, John Milner, Bob Rauch, Ray Sadecki, Dave Schneck, Tom Seaver, Rusty Staub, Brent Strom, Bill Sudakis, Chuck Taylor *

LESS THAN 10 GAMES: Tommy Moore, Joe Nolan, Hank Webb

NOTES: Matlack (ROY).

KEY SIGNATURES: Hodges, Berra, Kranepool, Harrelson, Mays, Staub, Seaver, Matlack, Koosman.

VALUE: $250

ROY = Rookie of the Year

1972 OAKLAND - Matty Alou *, Brant Alyea *, Sal Bando, Vida Blue, Bobby Brooks, Larry Brown, Ollie Brown *, Bert Campaneris, Ron Clark *, Tim Cullen, Dave Duncan, Mike Epstein, Rollie Fingers, Adrian Garrett, Dick Green, Dave Hamilton, Mike Hegan, George Hendrick, Ken Holtzman, Joe Horlen, Catfish Hunter, Reggie Jackson, Darold Knowles, Ted Kubiak *, Allen Lewis, Bob Locker, Angel Mangual, Gonzalo Marquez, Marty Martinez *, Dal Maxvill *, Don Mincher *, Blue Moon Odom, Joe Rudi, Gene Tenace, Bill Voss *, Dick Williams (MANAGER)

LESS THAN 10 GAMES: Dwain Anderson *, Curt Blefary *, Orlando Cepeda *, Larry Haney, Mike Kilkenny *, Denny McLain *, Bill McNulty, Jim Roland *, Diego Segui *, Art Shamsky *, Don Shaw *, Gary Waslewski

NOTES: World Champions!

KEY SIGNATURES: Bando, Jackson, Cepeda, Hunter, Fingers, Blue.

VALUE: $340

1972 PHILADELPHIA - Mike Anderson, John Bateman *, Bob Boone, Larry Bowa, Darrell Brandon, Byron Browne, Steve Carlton, Billy Champion, Denny Doyle, Roger Freed, Woody Fryman *, Oscar Gamble, Terry Harmon, Joe Hoerner *, Tommy Hutton, Deron Johnson, Pete Koegel, Barry Lersch, Joe Lis, Frank Lucchesi (MANAGER), Greg Luzinski, Tim McCarver *, Don Money, Willie Montanez, Paul Owens (MANAGER), Ken Reynolds, Bill Robinson, Mike Ryan, Mac Scarce, Mike Schmidt, Dick Selma, Chris Short, Ron Stone, Wayne Twitchell, Billy Wilson

LESS THAN 10 GAMES: Dave Downs, Jim Nash *, Gary Neibauer *, Craig Robinson, Bob Terlecki

NOTES: Carlton (CY).

KEY SIGNATURES: Bowa, Luzinski, McCarver, Boone, Schmidt, Carlton.

VALUE: $130

CY = Cy Young Award winner

1972 PITTSBURGH - Gene Alley, Steve Blass, Nelson Briles, Dave Cash, Roberto Clemente, Gene Clines, Vic Davalillo, Dock Ellis, Dave Giusti, Richie Hebner, Jackie Hernandez, Ramon Hernandez, Bob Johnson, Bruce Kison, Milt May, Bill Mazeroski, Bob Miller, Bob Moose, Al Oliver, Jose Pagan, Bob Robertson, Manny Sanguillen, Willie Stargell, Rennie Stennett, Bill Virdon (MANAGER), Luke Walker

LESS THAN 10 GAMES: Gene Garber, Chuck Goggin, Fernando Gonzalez, Jim McKee, Charlie Sands, Frank Taveras, Bob Veale *, Richie Zisk

NOTES: Clemente's final season; he died 12/31/72.

KEY SIGNATURES: Stargell, Clemente, Oliver, Mazeroski.

VALUE: $600

1972 SAN DIEGO - Ed Acosta, Steve Arlin, Bob Barton, Curt Blefary *, Ollie Brown *, Mike Caldwell, Dave Campbell, Nate Colbert, Mike Corkins, Pat Corrales *, Randy Elliott, Cito Gaston, Joe Goddard, Preston Gomez (MANAGER), Bill Greif, Enzo Hernandez, Dave Hilton, Garry Jestadt, Johnnie Jeter, Fred Kendall, Clay Kirby, Leron Lee, Jerry Morales, Fred Norman, Dave Roberts, Rafael Robles, Gary Ross, Mark Schaeffer,

Al Severinsen, Ed Spiezio *, Larry Stahl, Fred Stanley *, Derrell Thomas, Don Zimmer (MANAGER),
LESS THAN 10 GAMES: Mike Fiore, Jay Franklin, Ralph Garcia, Johnny Grubb, Mike Kilkenny *, Don Mason, Ivan Murrell, Tom Phoebus *, Steve Simpson, Ron Taylor

VALUE: $90

1972 SAN FRANCISCO - Chris Arnold, Jim Barr, Damie Blanco, Bobby Bonds, Ron Bryant, Don Carrithers, Charlie Fox (MANAGER), Tito Fuentes, Alan Gallagher, Russ Gibson, Ed Goodson, Jim Ray Hart, Fran Healy, Ken Henderson, Jim Howarth, Jerry Johnson, Dave Kingman, Garry Maddox, Juan Marichal, Gary Matthews, Willie Mays *, Willie McCovey, Sam McDowell, Don McMahon, Randy Moffitt, Dave Rader, Frank Reberger, Chris Speier, Steve Stone, Gary Thomasson, Bernie Williams, Jim Willoughby
LESS THAN 10 GAMES: John Cumberland *, John Morris, Jimmy Rosario, Elias Sosa, Charlie Williams
KEY SIGNATURES: McCovey, Bonds, Mays, Marichal.

VALUE: $150

1972 ST. LOUIS - Matty Alou *, Dwain Anderson *, Ray Bare, Lou Brock, Bernie Carbo *, Donn Cledenon, Reggie Cleveland, Tony Cloninger, Ed Crosby, Jose Cruz, Moe Drabowsky *, Don Durham, Mike Fiore *, Bob Gibson, Joe Grzenda, Joe Hague *, Denny Higgins, Charlie Hudson, Skip Jutze, Mick Kelleher, Dal Maxvill *, Jerry McNertney, Luis Melendez, Lowell Palmer *, Ken Reitz, Jorge Roque, Al Santorini, Red Schoendienst (MANAGER), Diego Segui *, Ted Simmons, Ted Sizemore, Scipio Spinks, Bill Stein, Joe Torre, Mike Tyson, Bill Voss *, Rick Wise
LESS THAN 10 GAMES: Ron Allen, Brant Alyea *, Jim Bibby, Lance Clemons, John Cumberland *, Rich Folkers, Santiago Guzman, Al Hrabosky, Marty Martinez *, Tim Plodinec, Don Shaw *
KEY SIGNATURES: Schoendienst, Torre, Brock, Simmons, Gibson.

VALUE: $125

1972 TEXAS - Larry Biittner, Dick Billings, Dick Bosman, Pete Broberg, Casey Cox *, Bill Fahey, Ted Ford, Bill Gogolewski, Tommy Grieve, Rich Hand, Toby Harrah, Vic Harris, Frank Howard *, Dalton Jones *, Hal King, Ted Kubiak *, Paul Lindblad, Joe Lovitto, Elliott Maddox, Marty Martinez *, Jim Mason, Don Mincher *, Dave Nelson, Jim Panther, Mike Paul, Horacio Pina, Tom Ragland, Lenny Randle, Jim Shellenback, Don Stanhouse, Ken Suarez, Ted Williams (MANAGER)
LESS THAN 10 GAMES: Jeff Burroughs, Jim Driscoll, Jan Dukes, Rich Hinton *, Jerry Janeski, Steve Lawson, Jim Roland *
NOTES: Rangers' first year.
KEY SIGNATURES: Williams, Howard, Harrah.

VALUE: $175

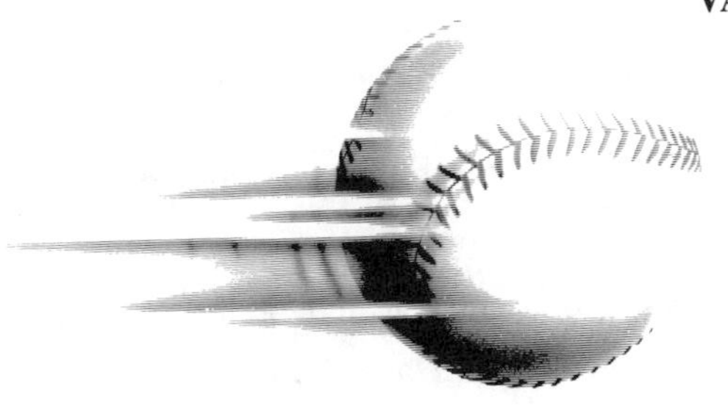

1973

1973 Oakland A's

*** = player was traded**

1973 ATLANTA - Hank Aaron, Dusty Baker, Larvell Blanks, Oscar Brown, Paul Casanova, Adrian Devine, Dick Dietz, Pat Dobson *, Darrell Evans, Jimmy Freeman, Danny Frisella, Ralph Garr, Gary Gentry, Rod Gilbreath, Chuck Goggin *, Roric Harrison, Joe Hoerner *, Tom House, Sonny Jackson, Dave Johnson, Max Leon, Mike Lum, Eddie Mathews (MANAGER), Carl Morton, Gary Niebauer, Joe Niekro, Phil Niekro, Johnny Oates, Jim Panther, Marty Perez, Ron Reed, Ron Schueler, Frank Tepedino, Freddy Velazquez

LESS THAN 10 GAMES: Dave Cheadle, Alan Closter, Wenty Ford, Leo Foster, Larry Howard *, Tom Kelley, Norm Miller *, Joe Pepitone *, Jack Pierce, Cecil Upshaw *

NOTES: The Niekro brothers were on the same team.

KEY SIGNATURES: Mathews, Aaron, P. Niekro, J. Niekro.

VALUE: $150

1973 BALTIMORE - Doyle Alexander, Frank Baker, Don Baylor, Mark Belanger, Paul Blair, Larry Brown, Al Bumbry, Enos Cabell, Rich Coggins, Terry Crowley, Mike Cuellar, Tommy Davis, Doug DeCinces, Andy Etchebarren, Bobby Grich, Ellie Hendricks, Grant Jackson, Jesse Jefferson, Dave McNally, Jim Palmer, Orlando Pena *, Boog Powell, Merv Rettenmund, Bob Reynolds, Brooks Robinson, Eddie Watt, Earl Weaver (MANAGER), Earl Williams

LESS THAN 10 GAMES: Jim Fuller, Wayne Garland, Don Hood, Curt Motton, Sergio Robles, Mickey Scott *

NOTES: Palmer (CY); Bumbry (ROY).

KEY SIGNATURES: Weaver, Powell, Robinson, Bumbry, Palmer.

VALUE: $260

1973 BOSTON - Luis Aparicio, Bob Bolin, Danny Cater, Orlando Cepeda, Cecil Cooper, Ray Culp, John Curtis, Dwight Evans, Carlton Fisk, Mike Garman, Doug Griffin, Mike Guerrero, Tommy Harper, Buddy Hunter, Duane Josephson, Eddie Kasko (MANAGER), John Kennedy, Bill Lee, Rick Miller, Bob Montgomery, Roger Moret, Ben Oglivie, Marty Pattin, Rico Petrocelli, Dick Pole, Craig Skok, Reggie Smith, Luis Tiant, Bob Veale, Carl Yastrzemski

LESS THAN 10 GAMES: Lynn McGlothen, Don Newhauser, Sonny Siebert *, Ken Tatum

KEY SIGNATURES: Yastrzemski, Aparicio, Fisk, Cepeda, Evans, Tiant.

VALUE: $175

1973 CALIFORNIA - Sandy Alomar, Steve Barber, Ken Berry, Dave Chalk, Jerry DaVanon, Mike Epstein *, Alan Gallagher *, Billy Grabarkewitz *, Rich Hand *, Doug Howard *, Art Kusnyer, Dick Lange, Winston Llenas, Rudy May, Tommy McCraw, Rudy Meoli, Aurelio Monteagudo, Bob Oliver, Billy Parker, Vada Pinson, Mickey Rivers, Frank Robinson, Nolan Ryan, Charlie Sands, Richie Scheinblum *, Dave Sells, Bill Singer, Jim Spencer *, Lee Stanton, Dick Stelmaszek *, Johnny Stephenson, Jeff Torborg, Bobby Valentine, Terry Wilshusen, Bobby Winkles (MANAGER), Clyde Wright

LESS THAN 10 GAMES: Lloyd Allen *, Bobby Brooks, Andy Hassler, Ron Perranoski, Frank Tanana

KEY SIGNATURES: Pinson, Robinson, Ryan.

VALUE: $115

1973 CHICAGO (AL) - Cy Acosta, Dick Allen, Hank Allen, Luis Alvarado, Mike Andrews *, Stan Bahnsen, Buddy Bradford, Chuck Brinkman, Bucky Dent, Brian Downing, Sam Ewing, Eddie Fisher *, Terry Forster, Ken Frailing, Goose Gossage, Jerry Hairston, Ken Henderson, Ed Herrmann, Johnnie Jeter, Bart Johnson, Pat Kelly, Dave Lemonds, Eddie Leon, Carlos May, Bill Melton, Tony Muser, Jorge Orta, Rick Reichardt *, Bill Sharp, Steve Stone, Chuck Tanner (MANAGER), Wilbur Wood

LESS THAN 10 GAMES: Dave Baldwin, Jim Geddes, Jim Kaat *, Steve Kealey, Joe Keough, Jim McGlothlin *, Rich Morales *, Denny O'Toole, Pete Varney

KEY SIGNATURES: Kaat, Gossage.

VALUE: $100

1973 CHICAGO (NL) - Jack Aker, Matt Alexander, Glenn Beckert, Bill Bonham, Pat Bourque *, Ray Burris, Jose Cardenal, Rico Carty *, Carmen Fanzone, Adrian Garrett, Larry Gura, Jim Hickman, Gene Hiser, Burt Hooton, Randy Hundley, Cleo James, Ferguson Jenkins, Don Kessinger, Pete LaCock, Dave LaRoche, Bob Locker, Whitey Lockman (MANAGER), Gonzalo Marquez *, Rick Monday, Milt Pappas, Mike Paul *, Joe Pepitone *, Paul Popovich, Rick Reuschel, Dave Rosello, Ken Rudolph, Ron Santo, Andy Thornton, Billy Williams

LESS THAN 10 GAMES: Tony LaRussa, Tom Lundstedt, Juan Pizarro *

KEY SIGNATURES: Kessinger, Williams, Jenkins.

VALUE: $85

1973 CINCINNATI - Sparky Anderson (MANAGER), Ed Armbrister, Dick Baney, Johnny Bench, Jack Billingham, Pedro Borbon, Clay Carroll, Darrel Chaney, Dave Concepcion, Ed Crosby *, Dan Driessen, George Foster, Phil Gagliano, Cesar Geronimo, Ken Griffey, Ross Grimsley, Don Gullett, Joe Hague, Tom Hall, Hal King, Andy Kosco, Gene Locklear *, Denis Menke, Joe Morgan, Roger Nelson, Fred Norman *, Tony Perez, Bill Plummer, Pete Rose, Richie Scheinblum *, Ed Sprague *, Larry Stahl, Bobby Tolan, Dave Tomlin

LESS THAN 10 GAMES: Bob Barton, Jim McGlothin, Gary Nolan

NOTES: Rose (MVP).

KEY SIGNATURES: Anderson, Perez, Concepcion, Rose, Bench, Foster.

VALUE: $275

MVP = MVP Award winner

1973 CLEVELAND - Alan Ashby, Ken Aspromonte (MANAGER), Buddy Bell, Dick Bosman *, Jack Brohamer, Leo Cardenas, Chris Chambliss, Frank Duffy, Dave Duncan, Johnny Ellis, Ed Farmer *, Ted Ford, Oscar Gamble, George Hendrick, Tom Hilgendorf, Jerry Johnson, Mike Kekich *, Ray Lamb, Ron Lolich, John Lowenstein, Gaylord Perry, Tom Ragland, Ken Sanders *, Tommy Smith, Charlie Spikes, Brent Strom, Dick Tidrow, Tom Timmerman *, Rusty Torres, Milt Wilcox, Walt Williams

LESS THAN 10 GAMES: Steve Dunning, Mike Jackson *, Jerry Kenney, Mike Kilkenny, Steve Mingori *

KEY SIGNATURES: Perry.

VALUE: $100

1973 DETROIT - Eddie Brinkman, Gates Brown, Ike Brown, Norm Cash, Ron Cash, Joe Coleman, Ed Farmer *, Bill Freehan, Woody Fryman, John Hiller, Willie Horton, Frank Howard, Al Kaline, John Knox, Lerrin LaGrow, Mickey Lolich, Billy Martin (MANAGER), Dick McAuliffe, Bob Miller *, Jim Northrup, Jim Perry, Rich Reese *, Aurelio Rodriquez, Fred Scherman, Joe Schultz (MANAGER), Chuck Seelbach, Dick Sharon, Duke Sims *, Mickey Stanley, Mike Strahler, Tony Taylor, Tom Timmerman *, Tom Veryzer

LESS THAN 10 GAMES: Bob Didier, John Gamble, Fred Holdsworth, Gary Ignasiak, Marvin Lane, Dave Lemanczyk, Bill Slayback, Joe Staton

KEY SIGNATURES: Martin, Cash, Northrup, Freehan, Kaline, Lolich, Perry.

VALUE: $150

1973 HOUSTON - Tommy Agee *, Jesus Alou *, Rafael Batista, Ray Busse *, Cesar Cedeno, Mike Cosgrove, Jim Crawford, Larry Dierker, Leo Durocher (MANAGER), Johnny Edwards, Ken Forsch, Bob Gallagher, Fred Gladding, Tom Griffin, Greg Gross, Tommy Helms, Larry Howard *, Skip Jutze, Lee May, Roger Metzger, Juan Pizarro *, Doug Rader, Jim Ray, Jerry Reuss, J.R. Richard, Dave Roberts, Jimmy Stewart, Gary Sutherland, Hector Torres, Cecil Upshaw *, Bob Watson, Don Wilson, Jim Wynn, Jim York

LESS THAN 10 GAMES: Dave Campbell *, Mike Easler, Cliff Johnson, Doug Konieczny, Norm Miller *, Otis Thornton

KEY SIGNATURES: Richard.

VALUE: $85

1973 KANSAS CITY - Kurt Bevacqua, Doug Bird, George Brett, Steve Busby, Bruce Dal Canton, Dick Drago, Al Fitzmorris, Bobby Floyd, Gene Garber, Fran Healy, Joe Hoerner

*, Gail Hopkins, Steve Hovley, Ed Kirkpatrick, Buck Martinez, Jerry May *, John Mayberry, Jack McKeon (MANAGER), Hal McRae, Steve Mingori *, Amos Otis, Freddie Patek, Lou Piniella, Tom Poquette, Rick Reichardt *, Cookie Rojas, Paul Schaal, Wayne Simpson, Paul Splittorff, Carl Taylor, Frank White, Jim Wohlford, Ken Wright

LESS THAN 10 GAMES: Norm Angelini, Tom Burgmeier, Mike Jackson *, Mark Littell, Keith Marshall, Frank Ortenzio, Barry Raziano

KEY SIGNATURES: Piniella, Brett.

VALUE: $115

1973 LOS ANGELES - Walt Alston (MANAGER), Jim Brewer, Bill Buckner, Chris Cannizzaro, Ron Cey, Willie Crawford, George Culver *, Willie Davis, Al Downing, Jim Fairey, Joe Ferguson, Steve Garvey, Charlie Hough, Tommy John, Von Joshua, Lee Lacy, Davey Lopes, Ken McMullen, Andy Messersmith, Manny Mota, Claude Osteen, Tom Paciorek, Doug Rau, Pete Richert, Jerry Royster, Bill Russell, Don Sutton, Steve Yeager

LESS THAN 10 GAMES: Jesus Alvarez, Greg Heydeman, Paul Powell, Greg Shanahan, Eddie Solomon, Geoff Zahn

KEY SIGNATURES: Alston, Buckner, Cey, Davis, Garvey, Sutton, John.

VALUE: $150

1973 MILWAUKEE - Jerry Bell, Johnny Briggs, Ollie Brown, Billy Champion, Jim Colborn, Bob Coluccio, Del Crandall (MANAGER), John Felske, Pedro Garcia, Rob Gardner *, Bob Heise, Wilbur Howard, Tim Johnson, Joe Lahoud, Frank Linzy, Skip Lockwood, Dave May, Bobby Mitchell, Don Money, Ray Newman, Bill Parsons, Darrell Porter, Eduardo Rodriguez, Ellie Rodriguez, George Scott, Chris Short, Jim Slaton, Gorman Thomas, Carlos Velazquez, John Vukovich

LESS THAN 10 GAMES: Rick Auerbach, Kevin Kobel, Charlie Moore, Ken Reynolds, Gary Ryerson, Ed Sprague *

KEY SIGNATURES: Thomas.

VALUE: $100

1973 MINNESOTA - Mike Adams, Vic Albury, Eddie Bane, Bert Blyleven, Glenn Borgmann, Steve Braun, Steve Brye, Bill Campbell, Rod Carew, Ray Corbin, Bobby Darwin, Joe Decker, Dan Fife, Dave Goltz, Bill Hands, Larry Hisle, Jim Holt, Jim Kaat *, Harmon Killebrew, Craig Kusick, Joe Lis, George Mitterwald, Dan Monzon, Tony Oliva, Frank Quilici (MANAGER), Rich Reese *, Phil Roof, Ken Sanders *, Eric Soderholm, Jerry Terrell, Danny Thompson, Danny Walton, Dick Woodson

LESS THAN 10 GAMES: Jim Strickland

KEY SIGNATURES: Carew, Oliva, Killebrew, Blyleven, Kaat.

VALUE: $130

1973 MONTREAL - Bernie Allen *, Felipe Alou *, Bob Bailey, John Boccabella, Hal Breeden, Boots Day, Ron Fairly, Tim Foli, Pepe Frias, Joe Gilbert, Terry Humphrey, Ron Hunt, Pat Jarvis, Mike Jorgensen, Coco Laboy, Larry Lintz, Jim Lyttle, Pepe Mangual, Mike Marshall, Clyde Mashore, Gene Mauch (MANAGER), Ernie McAnally, Balor Moore, Steve Renko, Steve Rogers, Tony Scott, Mickey Scott *, Ken Singleton, Bob Stinson, Bill Stoneman, John Strohmayer *, Mike Torrez, Tom Walker, Ron Woods

LESS THAN 10 GAMES: Curt Brown, Craig Caskey, Jim Cox, Barry Foote, John Montague, Jose Morales *, Jorge Roque, Chuck Taylor
KEY SIGNATURES: Singleton.

VALUE: $85

1973 NEW YORK (AL) - Bernie Allen *, Felipe Alou *, Matty Alou *, Fred Beene, Ron Blomberg, Johnny Callison, Horace Clarke, Pat Dobson *, Jim Ray Hart *, Mike Hegan *, Ralph Houk (MANAGER), Steve Kline, Hal Lanier, Sparky Lyle, Lindy McDaniel, Sam McDowell *, Doc Medich, Gene Michael, Jerry Moses, Thurman Munson, Bobby Murcer, Graig Nettles, Fritz Peterson, Celerino Sanchez, Fred Stanley, Mel Stottlemyre, Ron Swoboda, Otto Velez, Roy White
LESS THAN 10 GAMES: Tom Buskey, Casey Cox, Rick Dempsey, Wayne Granger *, Mike Kekich *, Jim Magnuson, Dave Pagan, Duke Sims *
KEY SIGNATURES: Nettles, Murcer, Munson, Stottlemyre, McDowell, Lyle.

VALUE: $235

1973 NEW YORK (NL) - Jim Beauchamp, Yogi Berra (MANAGER), Ken Boswell, Buzz Capra, Duffy Dyer, Jim Fregosi *, Wayne Garrett, Jim Gosger, Jerry Grote, Don Hahn, Bud Harrelson, Phil Hennigan, Ron Hodges, Cleon Jones, Jerry Koosman, Ed Kranepool, Ted Martinez, Jon Matlack, Willie Mays, Jim McAndrew, Tug McGraw, Felix Millan, John Milner, Harry Parker, Ray Sadecki, Tom Seaver, Rusty Staub, George Stone, George Theodore
LESS THAN 10 GAMES: Bob Apodaca, Lute Barnes, Rich Chiles, Greg Harts, Jerry May *, Bob Miller *, Tommy Moore, Brian Ostrosser, Dave Schneck, John Strohmayer *, Craig Swan, Hank Webb
NOTES: Seaver (CY).
KEY SIGNATURES: Berra, Harrelson, Staub, Jones, Kranepool, Seaver, Koosman.

VALUE: $250

CY = Cy Young Award winner

1973 OAKLAND - Jesus Alou *, Mike Andrews *, Sal Bando, Vida Blue, Pat Bourque *, Bert Campaneris, Billy Conigliaro, Vic Davalillo *, Rollie Fingers, Ray Fosse, Dick Green, Dave Hamilton, Mike Hegan *, Ken Holtzman, Tim Hosley, Catfish Hunter, Reggie Jackson, Deron Johnson *, Jay Johnstone, Darold Knowles, Ted Kubiak, Allen Lewis, Paul Lindblad, Angel Mangual, Gonzalo Marquez *, Dal Maxvill *, Rich McKinney, Billy North, Blue Moon Odom, Horacio Pina, Joe Rudi, Gene Tenace, Manny Trillo, Dick Williams (MANAGER)
LESS THAN 10 GAMES: Glenn Abbott, Rico Carty *, Chuck Dobson, Rob Gardner *, Phil Garner, Larry Haney *, Jose Morales *
NOTES: World Champions! Jackson (MVP).
KEY SIGNATURES: Bando, Jackson, Hunter, Blue, Fingers.

VALUE: $350

MVP = MVP Award winner

1973 PHILADELPHIA - Mike Anderson, Bob Boone, Larry Bowa, Darrell Brandon, Ken Brett, Steve Carlton, Larry Christenson, George Culver *, Ron Diorio, Denny Doyle, Billy Grabarkewitz *, Terry Harmon, Tommy Hutton, Deron Johnson *, Barry Lersch, Jim Lonborg, Greg Luzinski, Willie Montanez, Danny Ozark (MANAGER), Jose Pagan, Bill Robinson, Craig Robinson, Mike Rogodzinski, Dick Ruthven, Mike Ryan, Mac

Scarce, Mike Schmidt, Cesar Tovar, Wayne Twitchell, Del Unser, Mike Wallace, Billy Wilson

LESS THAN 10 GAMES: Larry Cox, Jim Essian, Dick Selma, Dave Wallace

KEY SIGNATURES: Bowa, Schmidt, Luzinski, Boone, Carlton.

VALUE: $125

1973 PITTSBURGH - Gene Alley, Dave Augustine, Steve Blass, Nelson Briles, Dave Cash, Gene Clines, Vic Davalillo *, Tom Dettore, Dock Ellis, Dave Giusti, Fernando Gonzalez, Richie Hebner, Jackie Hernandez, Ramon Hernandez, Bob Johnson, John Lamb, Dal Maxvil *, Milt May, Jim McKee, Bob Moose, John Morlan, Danny Murtaugh (MANAGER), Al Oliver, Dave Parker, Bob Robertson, Jim Rooker, Manny Sanguillen, Willie Stargell, Rennie Stennett, Bill Virdon (MANAGER), Luke Walker, Richie Zisk

LESS THAN 10 GAMES: Jim Campanis, Jim Foor, Chuck Goggin *, Bruce Kison, Jerry McNertney, Chris Zachary

KEY SIGNATURES: Oliver, Stargell, Parker.

VALUE: $135

1973 SAN DIEGO - Dwain Anderson *, Steve Arlin, Mike Caldwell, Dave Campbell *, Nate Colbert, Mike Corkins, Pat Corrales, Cito Gaston, Bill Greif, Johnny Grubb, Enzo Hernandez, Dave Hilton, Randy Jones, Fred Kendall, Clay Kirby, Leron Lee, Gene Locklear *, Dave Marshall, Bob Miller *, Jerry Morales, Rich Morales *, Ivan Murrell, Fred Norman *, Dave Roberts, Vicente Romo, Gary Ross, Frank Snook, Derrel Thomas, Rich Troedson, Dave Winfield, Don Zimmer (MANAGER)

LESS THAN 10 GAMES: Bob Davis, Don Mason

KEY SIGNATURES: Winfield.

VALUE: $95

1973 SAN FRANCISCO - Chris Arnold, Jim Barr, Damie Blanco, Bobby Bonds, Tom Bradley, Ron Bryant, Don Carrithers, Charlie Fox (MANAGER), Tito Fuentes, Ed Goodson, Jim Howarth, Dave Kingman, Garry Maddox, Juan Marichal, Gary Matthews, Willie McCovey, Sam McDowell *, Don McMahon, Bruce Miller, Randy Moffitt, Steve Ontiveros, Mike Phillips, Dave Rader, Mike Sadek, Elias Sosa, Chris Speier, Gary Thomasson, Charlie Williams, Jim Willoughby

LESS THAN 10 GAMES: John D'Acquisto, Alan Gallagher *, Jim Ray Hart *, Dave Kingman, John Morris

NOTES: Matthews (ROY).

KEY SIGNATURES: McCovey, Bonds, Matthews, Marichal.

VALUE: $125

ROY = Rookie of the Year

1973 ST. LOUIS - Tommy Agee *, Matty Alou *, John Andrews, Lou Brock, Ray Busse *, Dave Campbell *, Bernie Carbo, Reggie Cleveland, Ed Crosby *, Hector Cruz, Jose Cruz, Jim Dwyer, Rich Folkers, Alan Foster, Bob Gibson, Wayne Granger *, Tom Heintzelman, Al Hrabosky, Terry Hughes, Mike Kelleher, Bake McBride, Tim McCarver, Luis Melandez, Tom Murphy, Orlando Pena *, Ken Reitz, Red Schoendienst (MANAGER), Diego Segui, Ted Simmons, Ted Sizemore, Bill Stein, Joe Torre, Mike Tyson, Rick Wise

LESS THAN 10 GAMES: Dwain Anderson *, Jim Bibby *, Tommy Cruz, Bob Fenwick, Eddie Fisher *, Larry Haney, Marc Hill, Lew Krausse, Mike Nagy, Al Santorini, Scipio Spinks, Ed Sprague *, Mike Thompson

KEY SIGNATURES: Schoendienst, Torre, Brock, Simmons, McCarver, Gibson.

VALUE: $120

1973 TEXAS - Lloyd Allen *, Jim Bibby *, Larry Biittner, Dick Billings, Pete Broberg, Jackie Brown, Jeff Burroughs, Rico Carty *, David Clyde, Steve Dunning *, Don Durham, Mike Epstein *, Steve Foucault, Jim Fregosi *, Bill Gogolewski, Tommy Grieve, Toby Harrah, Vic Harris, Whitey Herzog (MANAGER), Charlie Hudson, Alex Johnson, Joe Lovitto, Pete Mackanin, Elliott Maddox, Bill Madlock, Billy Martin (MANAGER), Jim Mason, Jim Merritt, Dave Nelson, Mike Paul *, Lenny Randle, Sonny Siebert *, Jim Spencer *, Don Stanhouse, Ken Suarez, Bill Sudakis, Del Wilber (MANAGER)

LESS THAN 10 GAMES: Dick Bosman *, Don Castle, Rich Hand *, Rick Henninger, Jim Kremmel, Jim Shellenback, Dick Stelmaszek *, Rick Waits

NOTES: Martin, Harrah, Burroughs, Madlock.

VALUE: $120

*** = player was traded**

1974

1974 A.L. Cy Young Award winner Catfish Hunter

1974 ATLANTA - Hank Aaron, Jack Aker *, Dusty Baker, Buzz Capra, Paul Casanova, Vic Correll, Darrell Evans, Leo Foster, Danny Frisella, Ralph Garr, Roric Harrison, Tom House, Dave Johnson, Clyde King (MANAGER), Lew Krausse, Max Leon, Mike Lum, Eddie Mathews (MANAGER), Norm Miller, Carl Morton, Ivan Murrell, Joe Niekro, Phil Niekro, Johnny Oates, Rowland Office, Marty Perez, Ron Reed, Craig Robinson, Frank Tepedino

LESS THAN 10 GAMES: Mike Beard, Larvell Blanks, Jamie Easterly, John Fuller, Gary Gentry, Rod Gilbreath, Sonny Jackson, Jack Pierce, Mike Thompson *

KEY SIGNATURES: Mathews, Evans, Aaron, P. Niekro.

VALUE: $150

1974 BALTIMORE - Doyle Alexander, Frank Baker, Don Baylor, Mark Belanger, Paul Blair, Al Bumbry, Enos Cabell, Rich Coggins, Mike Cuellar, Tommy Davis, Andy Etchebarren, Jim Fuller, Wayne Garland, Bobby Grich, Ross Grimsley, Ellie Hendricks, Don Hood, Grant Jackson, Jesse Jefferson, Dave Johnson, Dave McNally, Jim Palmer, Boog Powell, Mike Reinbach, Bob Reynolds, Brooks Robinson, Earl Weaver (MANAGER), Earl Williams

LESS THAN 10 GAMES: Doug DeCinces, Curt Motton, Tim Nordbrook, Jim Northrup *, Bob Oliver *

KEY SIGNATURES: Weaver, Powell, Robinson, Palmer.

VALUE: $260

1974 BOSTON - Juan Beniquez, Tim Blackwell, Rick Burleson, Bernie Carbo, Danny Cater, Reggie Cleveland, Cecil Cooper, Dick Drago, Dwight Evans, Carlton Fisk, Doug Griffin, Mike Guerrero, Tommy Harper, Terry Hughes, Darrell Johnson (MANAGER), Deron Johnson *, John Kennedy, Bill Lee, Fred Lynn, Juan Marichal, Dick McAuliffe, Tim McCarver *, Rick Miller, Bob Montgomery, Roger Moret, Rico Petrocelli, Dick Pole, Jim Rice, Diego Segui, Luis Tiant, Bob Veale, Carl Yastrzemski

LESS THAN 10 GAMES: Steve Barr, Lance Clemons, Bob Didier, Chuck Goggin, Don Newhauser, Rick Wise

KEY SIGNATURES: Yastrzemski, Evans, Fisk, Cooper, Rice, Lynn, McCarver, Marichal.

VALUE: $175

1974 CALIFORNIA - Sandy Alomar *, John Balaz, Bruce Bochte, Dave Chalk, John Cumberland, John Doherty, Denny Doyle, Tom Egan, Mike Epstein, Ed Figueroa, Andy Hassler, Bob Heise *, Whitey Herzog (MANAGER), Doug Howard, Joe Lahoud, Dick Lange, Winston Llenas, Skip Lockwood, Rudy May *, Tommy McCraw *, Rudy Meoli, Morris Nettles, Bob Oliver *, Horacio Pina *, Luis Quintana, Orlando Ramirez, Barry Raziano, Mickey Rivers, Frank Robinson *, Ellie Rodriquez, Nolan Ryan, Charlie Sands, Paul Schaal *, Richie Scheinblum, Dave Sells, Dick Selma *, Bill Singer, Lee Stanton, Bill Stoneman, Frank Tanana, Bobby Valentine, Dick Williams (MANAGER), Bobby Winkles (MANAGER)

LESS THAN 10 GAMES: Chuck Dobson, Bill Gilbreth, Don Kirkwood, Orlando Pena *, Ken Sanders *

KEY SIGNATURES: Robinson, Ryan.

VALUE: $115

1974 CHICAGO (AL) - Cy Acosta, Dick Allen, Stan Bahnsen, Buddy Bradford, Bucky Dent, Brian Downing, Terry Forster, Goose Gossage, Jerry Hairston, Ken Henderson, Ed Herrmann, Bart Johnson, Lamar Johnson, Jim Kaat, Pat Kelly, Eddie Leon, Carlos May, Bill Melton, Bill Moran, Tony Muser, Jorge Orta, Skip Pitlock, Lee Richard, Ron Santo, Bill Sharp, Bill Stein, Chuck Tanner (MANAGER), Wilbur Wood

LESS THAN 10 GAMES: Lloyd Allen *, Luis Alvarado *, Francisco Barrios, Chuck Brinkman *, Wayne Granger, Joe Henderson, Jack Kucek, Nyls Nyman, Jim Otten, Stan Perzanowski, Ken Tatum, Pete Varney, Hugh Yancy

KEY SIGNATURES: Allen, Kaat, Gossage.

VALUE: $100

1974 CHICAGO (NL) - Matt Alexander, Bill Bonham, Ray Burris, Jose Cardenal, Tom Dettore, Ron Dunn, Carmen Fanzone, Ken Frailing, Adrian Garrett, Billy Grabarkewitz *, Vic Harris, Gene Hiser, Burt Hooton, Herb Hutson, Don Kessinger, Jim Kremmel, Pete LaCock, Dave LaRoche, Whitey Lockman (MANAGER), Tom Lundstedt, Bill Madlock, Jim Marshall (MANAGER), George Mitterwald, Rick Monday, Jerry Morales, Horacio Pina, Rick Reuschel, Dave Rosello, Rob Sperring, Dick Stelmaszek, Steve Stone, Steve Swisher, Andre Thornton, Jim Todd, Jim Tyrone, Chris Ward, Billy Williams, Oscar Zamora

LESS THAN 10 GAMES: Gonzalo Marquez, Mike Paul

KEY SIGNATURES: Kessinger, Madlock.

VALUE: $85

1974 CINCINNATI - Sparky Anderson (MANAGER), Dick Baney, Johnny Bench, Jack Billingham, Pedro Borbon, Clay Carroll, Tom Carroll, Darrell Chaney, Dave Concepcion, Terry Crowley, Dan Driessen, George Foster, Phil Gagliano, Cesar Geronimo, Ken Griffey, Don Gullett, Tom Hall, Junior Kennedy, Hal King, Clay Kirby, Ray Knight, Andy Kosco, Will McEnaney, Mike McQueen, Joe Morgan, Roger Nelson, Fred Norman, Tony Perez, Bill Plummer, Merv Rettenmund, Pete Rose

LESS THAN 10 GAMES: Ed Armbrister, Pat Darcy, Rawly Eastwick, Roger Freed, Pat Osburn

KEY SIGNATURES: Anderson, Perez, Morgan, Concepcion, Foster, Rose, Bench.

VALUE: $275

1974 CLEVELAND - Luis Alvarado *, Steve Arlin *, Ken Aspromonte (MANAGER), Fred Beene *, Buddy Bell, Ossie Blanco, Dick Bosman, Jack Brohamer, Tom Buskey *, Rico Carty, Chris Chambliss *, Ed Crosby, Frank Duffy, Dave Duncan, Bruce Ellingsen, Johnny Ellis, Oscar Gamble, George Hendrick, Angel Hermoso, Tom Hilgendorf, Bob Johnson, Steve Kline *, Duane Kuiper, Leron Lee, Joe Lis *, John Lowenstein, Tommy McCraw *, Gaylord Perry, Jim Perry, Fritz Peterson *, Frank Robinson *, Tommy Smith, Charlie Spikes, Rusty Torres, Milt Wilcox

LESS THAN 10 GAMES: Dwain Anderson, Alan Ashby, Bill Gogolewski, Jack Heidemann *, John Jeter, Larry Johnson, Jim Kern, Ken Sanders *, Dick Tidrow *, Tom Timmerman, Cecil Upshaw *

NOTES: The Perry brothers, who both won Cy Young Awards, were on the same team.

KEY SIGNATURES: G. Perry, J. Perry.

VALUE: $125

1974 DETROIT - Eddie Brinkman, Gates Brown, Norm Cash, Ron Cash, Joe Coleman, Bill Freehan, Woody Fryman, Willie Horton, Ralph Houk (MANAGER), Al Kaline, John Knox, Gene Lamont, Marvin Lane, Lerrin LaGrow, Dave Lemanczyk, Ron LeFlore, Mickey Lolich, Dan Meyer, John Miller, Jerry Moses, Jim Nettles, Jim Northrup

*, Ben Ogilvie, Jim Ray, Leon Roberts, Aurelio Rodriguez, Vern Ruhle, Reggie Sanders, Dick Sharon, Bill Slayback, Mickey Stanley, Gary Sutherland, Tom Veryzer, Luke Walker, John Wockenfuss

LESS THAN 10 GAMES: Ike Brown, Fred Holdsworth, Chuck Seelbach

KEY SIGNATURES: Freehan, Horton, Kaline, Lolich.

VALUE: $115

1974 HOUSTON - Ollie Brown *, Ray Busse, Dave Campbell, Cesar Cedeno, Mike Cosgrove, Ramon De los Santos, Larry Dierker, Mike Easler, Johnny Edwards, Ken Forsch, Bob Gallagher, Preston Gomez (MANAGER), Tom Griffin, Greg Gross, Tommy Helms, Wilbur Howard, Cliff Johnson, Jerry Johnson, Mike Kelleher, Lee May, Milt May, Denis Menke, Roger Metzger, Larry Milbourne, Claude Osteen *, Doug Rader, J.R. Richard, Dave Roberts, Fred Scherman, Bob Watson, Don Wilson, Jim York

LESS THAN 10 GAMES: Skip Jutze, Doug Konieczny, Mike Nagy, Paul Siebert

NOTES: Wilson died 1/5/75.

KEY SIGNATURES: Wilson, Richard.

VALUE: $85

1974 KANSAS CITY - Kurt Bevacqua *, Doug Bird, George Brett, Nelson Briles, Steve Busby, Orlando Cepeda, Al Cowens, Bruce Dal Canton, Al Fitzmorris, Bobby Floyd, Gene Garber *, Fran Healy, Joe Hoerner, Buck Martinez, John Mayberry, Lindy McDaniel, Jack McKeon (MANAGER), Hal McRae, Steve Mingori, Amos Otis, Freddie Patek, Marty Pattin, Vada Pinson, Cookie Rojas, Richie Scheinblum *, Tony Solaita, Paul Splitorff, Frank White, Jim Wohlford

LESS THAN 10 GAMES: Fernando Gonzalez *, Dennis Leonard, Aurelio Lopez, Dennis Paepke, Rick Reichardt, Paul Schaal *

KEY SIGNATURES: Brett, Pinson.

VALUE: $110

MVP = MVP Award winner

1974 LOS ANGELES - Walt Alston (MANAGER), Rick Auerbach, Jim Brewer, Bill Buckner, Ron Cey, Willie Crawford, Al Downing, Joe Ferguson, Steve Garvey, Gail Hopkins, Charlie Hough, Tommy John, Von Joshua, Lee Lacy, Davey Lopes, Mike Marshall, Ken McMullen, Andy Messersmith, Manny Mota, Tom Paciorek, Doug Rau, Bill Russell, Don Sutton, Jim Wynn, Steve Yeager, Geoff Zahn

LESS THAN 10 GAMES: Jesus Alvarez, Ivan DeJesus, John Hale, Rex Hudson, Chuck Manuel, Kevin Pasley, Rick Rhoden, Jerry Royster, Greg Shanahan, Eddie Solomon

NOTES: Mike Marshall (CY); Garvey (MVP).

KEY SIGNATURES: Alston, Garvey, Cey, Buckner, Sutton, Marshall, John.

VALUE: $250

CY = Cy Young Award winner

1974 MILWAUKEE - Ken Berry, Johnny Briggs, Billy Champion, Jim Colborn, Bob Coluccio, Del Crandall (MANAGER), Rob Ellis, Pedro Garcia, Bob Hansen, Mike Hegan *, Tim Johnson, Deron Johnson *, Kevin Kobel, Sixto Lezcano, Dave May, Bobby Mitchell, Don Money, Charlie Moore, Tom Murphy, Darrell Porter, Eduardo Rodriguez, George Scott, Jim Slaton, Ed Sprague, Gorman Thomas, Bill Travers, John Vukovich, Clyde Wright, Robin Yount

LESS THAN 10 GAMES: Felipe Alou, Larry Anderson, Jerry Bell, Bill Castro, Jack Lind, Roger Miller, Dick Selma *, Bobby Sheldon
KEY SIGNATURES: Yount.

VALUE: $100

1974 MINNESOTA - Vic Albury, Bert Blyleven, Glenn Borgmann, Pat Bourque *, Steve Braun, Steve Brye, Tom Burgmeier, Bill Butler, Bill Campbell, Rod Carew, Ray Corbin, Bobby Darwin, Joe Decker, Sergio Ferrer, Dave Goltz, Luis Gomez, Bill Hands *, Larry Hisle, Jim Holt *, Randy Hundley, Harmon Killebrew, Craig Kusick, Tony Oliva, Frank Quilici (MANAGER), Phil Roof, Eric Soderholm, Jerry Terrell, Danny Thompson
LESS THAN 10 GAMES: Dan Fife, Jim Hughes, Tom Johnson, Joe Lis *, Dick Woodson *

KEY SIGNATURES: Carew, Oliva, Killebrew, Blyleven.

VALUE: $125

1974 MONTREAL - Bob Bailey, Larry Biittner, Dennis Blair, Hal Breeden, Don Carrithers, Jim Cox, Willie Davis, Boots Day, Don DeMola, Ron Fairly, Tim Foli, Barry Foote, Pepe Frias, Terry Humphrey, Ron Hunt *, Mike Jorgensen, Larry Lintz, Pepe Mangual, Gene Mauch (MANAGER), Ernie McAnally, John Montague, Jose Morales, Dale Murray, Jim Northrup *, Larry Parrish, Steve Renko, Steve Rogers, Tony Scott, Ken Singleton, Bob Stinson, Chuck Taylor, Mike Torrez, Tom Walker, Ron Woods
LESS THAN 10 GAMES: Gary Carter, Warren Cromartie, Terry Enyart, Bob Gebhard, Jim Lyttle, Balor Moore, Pat Scanlon, Jerry White
KEY SIGNATURES: Singleton, Davis, Carter.

VALUE: $85

1974 NEW YORK (AL) - Sandy Alomar *, Ron Blomberg, Chris Chambliss *, Horace Clarke *, Rick Demspey, Pat Dobson, Fernando Gonzalez *, Jim Ray Hart, Mike Hegan *, Sparky Lyle, Elliott Maddox, Jim Mason, Rudy May *, Sam McDowell, Doc Medich, Gene Michael, Thurman Munson, Bobby Murcer, Craig Nettles, Dave Pagan, Lou Piniella, Fred Stanley, Mel Stottlemyre, Bill Sudakis, Dick Tidrow *, Cecil Upshaw *, Otto Velez, Bill Virdon (MANAGER), Mike Wallace *, Roy White, Walt Williams
LESS THAN 10 GAMES: Fred Beene *, Tom Buskey *, Jim Deidel, Larry Gura, Alex Johnson *, Steve Kline *, Tippy Martinez, Larry Murray, Fritz Peterson *, Rick Sawyer, Duke Sims *, Terry Whitfield, Dick Woodson, Ken Wright
KEY SIGNATURES: Nettles, Murcer, Munson, Lyle, McDowell.

VALUE: $235

1974 NEW YORK (NL) - Jack Aker *, Bob Apodaca, Benny Ayala, Yogi Berra (MANAGER), Ken Boswell, Jerry Cram, Duffy Dyer, Wayne Garrett, Jim Gosger, Jerry Grote, Don Hahn, Bud Harrelson, Ron Hodges, Cleon Jones, Jerry Koosman, Ed Kranepool, Ted Martinez, Jon Matlack, Tug McGraw, Felix Millan, Bob Miller, John Milner, Harry Parker, Brock Pemberton, Ray Sadecki, Dave Schneck, Tom Seaver, Rusty Staub, George Stone, George Theodore

LESS THAN 10 GAMES: Bruce Boisclair, Nino Espinosa, Ike Hampton, Rich Puig, Randy Sterling, John Strohmayer, Craig Swan, Hank Webb

KEY SIGNATURES: Harrelson, Staub, Jones, Kranepool, Koosman, Seaver.

VALUE: $160

1974 OAKLAND - Glenn Abbott, Jesus Alou, Sal Bando, Vida Blue, Pat Bourque *, Bert Campaneris, Al Dark (MANAGER), John Donaldson, Rollie Fingers, Ray Fosse, Phil Garner, Dick Green, Dave Hamilton, Larry Haney, Jim Holt *, Ken Holtzman, Tim Hosley, Catfish Hunter, Reggie Jackson, Deron Johnson *, Darold Knowles, Ted Kubiak, Paul Lindblad, Angel Mangual, Dal Maxvill *, Billy North, Blue Moon Odom, Gaylen Pitts, Joe Rudi, Gene Tenace, Manny Trillo, Claudell Washington, Herb Washington

LESS THAN 10 GAMES: Vic Davalillo, Leon Hooten, Rich McKinney, Bill Parsons, Champ Summers

NOTES: World Champions! Hunter (CY)

KEY SIGNATURES: Bando, Jackson, Hunter, Blue, Fingers.

VALUE: $340

CY = Cy Young Award winner

1974 PHILADELPHIA - Mike Anderson, Alan Bannister, Bob Boone, Larry Bowa, Ollie Brown, Steve Carlton, Dave Cash, Larry Cox, George Culver, Jim Essian, Ed Farmer, Gene Garber *, Billy Grabarkewitz *, Terry Harmon, Jesus Hernaiz, Tommy Hutton, Jay Johnstone, Frank Linzy, Jim Lonborg, Greg Luzinski, Jerry Martin, Willie Montanez, Danny Ozark (MANAGER), Pete Richert *, Bill Robinson, Dick Ruthven, Mac Scarce, Mike Schmidt, Ron Schueler, Tony Taylor, Wayne Twitchell, Del Unser, Eddie Watt

LESS THAN 10 GAMES: Larry Christenson, Ron Diorio, Mike Rogodzinski, John Stearns, Erskine Thomason, Tom Underwood, Dave Wallace, Mike Wallace *

KEY SIGNATURES: Bowa, Schmidt, Luzinski, Boone.

VALUE: $125

1974 PITTSBURGH - Dave Augustine, Kurt Bevacqua *, Ken Brett, Gene Clines, Larry Demery, Miguel Dilone, Dock Ellis, Dave Giusti, Richie Hebner, Ramon Hernandez, Art Howe, Ed Kirkpatrick, Bruce Kison, Mario Mendoza, John Morlan, Danny Murtaugh (MANAGER), Al Oliver, Dave Parker, Daryl Patterson, Paul Popovich, Jerry Reuss, Bob Robertson, Jim Rooker, Manny Sanguillen, Willie Stargell, Rennie Stennett, Frank Taveras, Richie Zisk

LESS THAN 10 GAMES: Steve Blass, Chuck Brinkman *, Juan Jiminez, Ken Macha, Dal Maxvill *, Jim Minshall, Bob Moose, Ed Ott, Juan Pizarro, Mike Ryan, Jim Sadowski, Kent Tekulve

KEY SIGNATURES: Oliver, Stargell, Parker, Tekulve.

VALUE: $175

1974 SAN DIEGO - Bill Almon, Matty Alou, Steve Arlin *, Bob Barton, Glenn Beckert, Chris Cannizzaro, Horace Clarke *, Nate Colbert, Mike Corkins, Randy Elliott, Dave Freisleben, Rod Gaspar, Cito Gaston, Rusty Gerhardt, Bill Greif, Johnny Grubb, Larry Hardy, Enzo Hernandez, Dave Hilton, Mike Ivie, Mike Johnson, Randy Jones, Fred Kendall, Bill Laxton, Gene Locklear, Jim McAndrew, Willie McCovey, Joe McIntosh, John McNamara (MANAGER), Rich Morales, Lowell Palmer, Dave Roberts, Vicente Romo, John Scott, Dan Spillner, Derrel Thomas, Bobby Tolan, Dave Tomlin, Rich Troedson, Jerry Turner, Bernie Williams, Dave Winfield

LESS THAN 10 GAMES: Ralph Garcia, Gary Ross
KEY SIGNATURES: McCovey, Winfield.

VALUE: $100

1974 SAN FRANCISCO - Chris Arnold, Steve Barber, Jim Barr, John Boccabella, Bobby Bonds, Tom Bradley, Ron Bryant, Mike Caldwell, John D'Acquisto, Charlie Fox (MANAGER), Tito Fuentes, Ed Goodson, Ed Halicki, Dave Kingman, Gary Lavelle, Garry Maddox, Gary Matthews, Butch Metzger, Bruce Miller, Randy Moffitt, John Morris, Steve Ontiveros, Mike Phillips, Dave Rader, Ken Rudolph, Elias Sosa, Chris Speier, Gary Thomasson, Wes Westrum (MANAGER), Charlie Williams, Jim Willoughby
LESS THAN 10 GAMES: Damie Blanco, Jim Howarth, Don McMahon, John Montefusco, Glenn Redmon, Don Rose
KEY SIGNATURES: Kingman, Bonds.

VALUE: $85

1974 ST LOUIS - Luis Alvarado *, Ray Bare, Lou Brock, Jose Cruz, John Curtis, Jerry DaVanon, Jim Dwyer, Rich Folkers, Bob Forsch, Alan Foster, Mike Garman, Bob Gibson, Danny Godby, Jack Heidemann *, Tom Heintzelman, Keith Hernandez, Larry Herndon, Jim Hickman, Marc Hill, Al Hrabosky, Bake McBride, Tim McCarver *, Lynn McGlothen, Luis Melendez, Orlando Pena *, Ken Reitz, Pete Richert *, Red Schoendienst (MANAGER), Sonny Siebert, Ted Simmons, Ted Sizemore, Reggie Smith, Mike Thompson, Joe Torre, Mike Tyson
LESS THAN 10 GAMES: Dick Billings *, John Denny, Bob Heise *, Ron Hunt *, Barry Lersch, Jerry Mumphrey, Claude Osteen *, Stan Papi, Richie Scheinblum *
NOTES: McBride (ROY).
KEY SIGNATURES: Torre, McBride, Brock, Simmons, McCarver, Gibson.

VALUE: $115

ROY = Rookie of the Year

1974 TEXAS - Lloyd Allen *, Jim Bibby, Pete Broberg, Jackie Brown, Larry Brown, Jeff Burroughs, Leo Cardenas, David Clyde, Steve Foucault, Jim Fregosi, Tommy Grieve, Steve Hargan, Mike Hargrove, Toby Harrah, Roy Howell, Ferguson Jenkins, Alex Johnson *, Joe Lovitto, Billy Martin (MANAGER), Jim Merritt, Dave Nelson, Lenny Randle, Jim Shellenback, Duke Sims *, Jim Spencer, Don Stanhouse, Jim Sundberg, Stan Thomas, Cesar Tovar
LESS THAN 10 GAMES: Dick Billings *, Mike Cubbage, Steve Dunning, Bill Fahey, Bill Hands *, Bobby Jones, Pete Mackanin, Tom Robson, Jeff Terpko
NOTES: Hargrove (ROY); Burroughs (MVP).
KEY SIGNATURES: Martin, Hargrove, Harrah, Burroughs, Jenkins.

VALUE: $120

1975

1975 Cincinnati Reds

1975 ATLANTA - Dusty Baker, Bob Beall, Mike Beard, Rob Belloir, Larvell Blanks, Buzz Capra, Vic Correll, Bruce Dal Canton *, Jamie Easterly, Darrell Evans, Ralph Garr, Cito Gaston, Rod Gilbreath, Ed Goodson *, Roric Harrison *, Tom House, Clyde King (MANAGER), Max Leon, Mike Lum, Dave May, Carl Morton, Phil Niekro, Blue Moon Odom *, Rowland Office, Marty Perez, Biff Pocoroba, Ron Reed *, Craig Robinson *, Connie Ryan (MANAGER), Ray Sadecki *, Elias Sosa, Mike Thompson, Earl Williams

LESS THAN 10 GAMES: Adrian Devine, Gary Gentry, Preston Hanna, Dave Johnson, Frank LaCorte, Joe Nolan, Johnny Oates *, Frank Tepedino, Pablo Torrealba

KEY SIGNATURES: Evans, Niekro.

VALUE: $85

1975 BALTIMORE - Doyle Alexander, Don Baylor, Mark Belanger, Paul Blair, Al Bumbry, Mike Cuellar, Tommy Davis, Doug DeCinces, Dave Duncan, Wayne Garland, Bobby Grich, Ross Grimsley, Ellie Hendricks, Grant Jackson, Lee May, Dyar Miller, Paul Mitchell, Tony Muser *, Tim Nordbrook, Jim Northrup, Jim Palmer, Brooks Robinson, Tom Shopay, Ken Singleton, Royle Stillman, Mike Torrez, Earl Weaver (MANAGER)

LESS THAN 10 GAMES: Bob Bailor, Andy Etchebarren *, Mike Flanagan, Larry Harlow, Jim Hutto, Jesse Jefferson *, Dave Johnson, Bob Reynolds *

NOTES: Palmer (CY).

KEY SIGNATURES: Weaver, Robinson, Palmer.

VALUE: $130

CY = Cy Young Award winner

1975 BOSTON - Juan Beniquez, Tim Blackwell, Rick Burleson, Jim Burton, Bernie Carbo, Reggie Cleveland, Tony Conigliaro, Cecil Cooper, Denny Doyle *, Dick Drago, Dwight Evans, Carlton Fisk, Doug Griffin, Bob Heise, Darrell Johnson (MANAGER), Bill Lee, Fred Lynn, Tim McCarver *, Rick Miller, Bob Montgomery, Roger Moret, Rico

Petrocelli, Dick Pole, Jim Rice, Diego Segui, Luis Tiant, Jim Willoughby, Rick Wise, Carl Yastrzemski

LESS THAN 10 GAMES: Kim Andrew, Steve Barr, Steve Dillard, Butch Hobson, Buddy Hunter, Deron Johnson *, Rick Kreuger, Dick McAuliffe, Andy Merchant

NOTES: Lynn (ROY), Lynn (MVP).

KEY SIGNATURES: Yastrzemski, Evans, Lynn, Rice, Fisk, Cooper, Conigliaro, McCarver, Tiant.

VALUE: $275

ROY = **Rookie of the Year**

1975 CALIFORNIA - John Balaz, Bruce Bochte, Jim Brewer *, Dan Briggs, Dave Chalk, Dave Collins, Paul Dade, John Doherty, Tom Egan, Andy Etchebarren *, Ed Figueroa, Adrian Garrett *, Ike Hampton, Tommy Harper *, Andy Hassler, Chuck Hockenbery, Ron Jackson, Don Kirkwood, Joe Lahoud, Dick Lange, Winston Llenas, Rudy Meoli, Mike Miley, Morris Nettles, Orlando Ramirez, Jerry Remy, Mickey Rivers, Ellie Rodriguez, Nolan Ryan, Mickey Scott, Bill Singer, Billy Smith, Lee Stanton, Frank Tanana, Bobby Valentine *, Dick Williams (MANAGER)

LESS THAN 10 GAMES: Bob Allietta, Steve Blateric, Chuck Dobson, Denny Doyle *, Danny Goodwin, Charles Hudson, Sid Monge, Joe Pactwa, Horacio Pina, Luis Quintana, Gary Ross, Dave Sells *, Bill Sudakis *

KEY SIGNATURES: Ryan.

VALUE: $100

1975 CHICAGO (AL) - Stan Bahnsen *, Buddy Bradford *, Bob Coluccio *, Bucky Dent, Brian Downing, Terry Forster, Bill Gogolewski, Goose Gossage, Jerry Hairston, Dave Hamilton *, Ken Henderson, Rich Hinton, Jesse Jefferson *, Deron Johnson *, Jim Kaat, Pat Kelly, Carlos May, Bill Melton, Tony Muser *, Nyls Nyman, Jorge Orta, Danny Osborn, Claude Osteen, Lee Richard, Bill Sharp *, Mike Squires, Bill Stein, Chiuck Tanner (MANAGER), Cecil Upshaw, Pete Varney, Wilbur Wood

LESS THAN 10 GAMES: Lloyd Allen, Lamar Johnson, Chris Knapp, Ken Kravec, Jack Kucek, Chet Lemon, Jerry Moses *, Jim Otten, Skip Pitlock, Tim Stoddard, Pete Vuckovich

KEY SIGNATURES: Kaat, Gossage.

VALUE: $90

1975 CHICAGO (NL) - Bill Bonham, Ray Burris, Jose Cardenal, Tom Dettore, Ron Dunn, Ken Frailing, Adrian Garrett *, Vic Harris, Gene Hiser, Tim Hosley, Don Kessinger, Darold Knowles, Pete LaCock, Bob Locker, Bill Madlock, Jim Marshall (MANAGER), George Mitterwald, Rick Monday, Jerry Morales, Paul Reuschel, Rick Reuschel, Dave Rosello, Rob Sperring, Steve Stone, Champ Summers, Steve Swisher, Andy Thornton, Manny Trillo, Jim Tyrone, Joe Wallis, Milt Wilcox, Geoff Zahn *, Oscar Zamora

LESS THAN 10 GAMES: Ken Crosby, Burt Hooton *, Donnie Moore, Willie Prall, Buddy Schultz, Eddie Solomon, Eddie Watt

KEY SIGNATURES: Madlock.

VALUE: $85

1975 CINCINNATI - Sparky Anderson (MANAGER), Ed Armbrister, Johnny Bench, Jack Billingham, Pedro Borbon, Clay Carroll, Tom Carroll, Darrel Chaney, Dave Conepcion, Terry Crowley, Pat Darcy, Dan Driessen, Rawly Eastwick, Doug Flynn, George Foster, Cesar Geronimo, Ken Griffey, Don Gullett, Clay Kirby, Will McEnaney, Joe Morgan, Gary Nolan, Fred Norman, Tony Perez, Bill Plummer, Merv Rettenmund, Pete Rose, John Vukovich

LESS THAN 10 GAMES: Tom Hall, Don Werner

NOTES: World Champions! Morgan (MVP).

KEY SIGNATURES: Anderson, Perez, Morgan, Concepcion, Rose, Foster, Bench.

VALUE: $400

MVP = MVP Award winner

1975 CLEVELAND - Alan Ashby, Fred Beene, Buddy Bell, Ken Berry, Jim Bibby *, Jack Brohamer, Jackie Brown *, Tom Buskey, Rico Carty, Ed Crosby, Frank Duffy, Dennis Eckersley, Johnny Ellis, Oscar Gamble, Roric Harrison *, George Hendrick, Don Hood, Jim Kern, Duane Kuiper, Dave LaRoche, Leron Lee *, Johnny Lowenstein, Rick Manning, Tommy McCraw, Gaylord Perry *, Fritz Peterson, Boog Powell, Eric Raich, Frank Robinson (MANAGER), Bill Sadakis *, Charlie Spikes, Rick Waits

LESS THAN 10 GAMES: Larry Andersen, Dick Bosman *, Rick Cerone, Joe Lis, Blue Moon Odom *, Jim Perry *, Bob Reynolds *, Tommy Smith, Jim Strickland

NOTES: Robinson became the first black manager in Major League history.

KEY SIGNATURES: Robinson.

VALUE: $130

1975 DETROIT - Fernando Arroyo, Billy Baldwin, Ray Bare, Gates Brown, Nate Colbert *, Joe Coleman, Bill Freehan, John Hiller, Willie Horton, Ralph Houk (MANAGER), Terry Humphrey, Art James, John Knox, Lerrin LaGrow, Dave Lemanczyk, Ron LeFlore, Mickey Lolich, Dan Meyer, Gene Michael, Ben Oglivie, Gene Pentz, Jack Pierce, Bob Reynolds *, Leon Roberts, Aurelio Rodriguez, Vern Ruhle, Mickey Stanley, Gary Sutherland, Tom Veryzer, Tom Walker, John Wockenfuss

LESS THAN 10 GAMES: Ike Brookens, Ed Glynn, Steve Grilli, Gene Lamont, Tom Makowski, Jerry Manuel, Bob Molinaro, Chuck Scrivener

KEY SIGNATURES: Freehan, Horton, Lolich.

VALUE: $95

1975 HOUSTON - Rob Andrews, Rafael Batista, Ken Boswell, Enos Cabell, Cesar Cedeno, Mike Cosgrove, Jim Crawford, Jose Cruz, Jerry DaVanon, Larry Dierker, Ken Forsch, Art Gardner, Preston Gomez (MANAGER), Wayne Granger, Tom Griffin, Greg Gross, Tommy Helms, Wilbur Howard, Cliff Johnson, Skip Jutze, Doug Konieczny, Milt May, Roger Metzger, Larry Milbourne, Joe Niekro, Doug Rader, J.R. Richard, Dave Roberts, Fred Scherman *, Jose Sosa, Bill Virdon (MANAGER), Bob Watson, Jim York

LESS THAN 10 GAMES: Jesus De La Rosa, Mike Easler, Paul Siebert, Mike Stanton

KEY SIGNATURES: Richard.

VALUE: $80

1975 KANSAS CITY - Doug Bird, George Brett, Nelson Briles, Steve Busby, Al Cowens, Al Fitzmorris, Fran Healy, Whitey Herzog (MANAGER), Harmon Killebrew, Dennis Leonard, Buck Martinez, John Mayberry, Bob McClure, Lindy McDaniel, Jack McKeon (MANAGER), Hal McRae, Steve Mingori, Amos Otis, Freddie Patek, Marty Pattin, Vada Pinson, Jamie Quirk, Cookie Rojas, Rodney Scott, Tony Solaita, Paul Splittorff, Bob Stinson, Frank White, Jim Wohlford

LESS THAN 10 GAMES: Bruce Dal Canton *, Mark Littell, Gary Martz, Ray Sadecki *, George Throop

KEY SIGNATURES: Brett, Killebrew.

VALUE: $110

1975 LOS ANGELES - Walt Alston (MANAGER), Rick Auerbach, Jim Brewer *, Bill Buckner, Ron Cey, Willie Crawford, Henry Cruz, Ivan DeJesus, Al Downing, Joe Ferguson, Steve Garvey, John Hale, Burt Hooton *, Charlie Hough, Lee Lacy, Leron Lee *, Davey Lopes, Chuck Manuel, Mike Marshall, Ken McMullen, Andy Messersmith, Manny Mota, Tom Paciorek, Doug Rau, Rick Rhoden, Jerry Royster, Bill Russell, Don Sutton, Jim Wynn, Steve Yeager

LESS THAN 10 GAMES: Jesus Alvarez, Dennis Lewallyn, Juan Marichal, Paul Powell, Dave Sells *, Joe Simpson, Stan Wall, Geoff Zahn *

KEY SIGNATURES: Alston, Garvey, Cey, Buckner, Sutton.

VALUE: $130

1975 MILWAUKEE - Hank Aaron, Rick Austin, Kurt Bevacqua, Tommy Bianco, Johnny Briggs *, Pete Broberg, Bill Castro, Billy Champion, Jim Colborn, Bob Coluccio *, Del Crandall (MANAGER), Bobby Darwin *, Pedro Garcia, Tom Hausman, Mike Hegan, Tim Johnson, Harvey Kuenn (MANAGER), Sixto Lezcano, Bobby Mitchell, Don Money, Charlie Moore, Tom Murphy, Darrell Porter, Eduardo Rodriguez, George Scott, Bill Sharp *, Bobby Sheldon, Jim Slaton, Ed Sprague, Gorman Thomas, Bill Travers, Robin Yount

LESS THAN 10 GAMES: Larry Anderson, Jerry Augustine, Lafayette Currence, Rob Ellis, Jack Lind, Pat Osburn

KEY SIGNATURES: Yount, Aaron.

VALUE: $125

1975 MINNESOTA - Vic Albury, Bert Blyleven, Glenn Borgmann, Lyman Bostock, Steve Braun, Johnny Briggs *, Steve Brye, Tom Burgmeier, Bill Butler, Bill Campbell, Rod Carew, Ray Corbin, Bobby Darwin *, Dan Ford, Dave Goltz, Luis Gomez, Larry Hisle, Jim Hughes, Tom Johnson, Tom Kelly, Craig Kusick, Dave McKay, Tony Oliva, Frank Quilici (MANAGER), Phil Roof, Eric Soderholm, Jerry Terrell, Danny Thompson, Danny Walton, Mark Wiley

LESS THAN 10 GAMES: Eddie Bane, Joe Decker, Sergio Ferrer, Tom Lundstedt, Mike Pazik, Mike Poepping

KEY SIGNATURES: Carew, Bostock, Oliva, Blyleven.

VALUE: $110

1975 MONTREAL - Bob Bailey, Larry Biittner, Dennis Blair, Hal Breeden, Don Carrithers, Gary Carter, Rich Coggins *, Nate Colbert *, Jim Cox, Don DeMola, Jim Dwyer *, Tim Foli, Barry Foote, Pepe Frias, Woody Fryman, Mike Jorgensen, Larry Lintz *, Jim Lyttle, Pete Mackanin, Pepe Mangual, Gene Mauch (MANAGER), Dave McNally, John Montague *, Jose Morales, Dale Murray, Larry Parrish, Steve Renko, Steve Rogers, Pat Scanlon, Fred Scherman *, Tony Scott, Chuck Taylor, Ellis Valentine, Dan Warthen, Jerry White

LESS THAN 10 GAMES: Larry Johnson, Chip Lang, Bombo Rivera, Don Stanhouse
KEY SIGNATURES: Carter.

VALUE: $85

1975 NEW YORK (AL) - Sandy Alomar, Rick Bladt, Ron Blomberg, Bobby Bonds, Eddie Brinkman *, Chris Chambliss, Rich Coggins *, Rick Dempsey, Pat Dobson, Ron Guidry, Larry Gura, Ed Herrmann, Catfish Hunter, Alex Johnson, Sparky Lyle, Elliott Maddox, Billy Martin (MANAGER), Tippy Martinez, Jim Mason, Rudy May, Doc Medich, Thurman Munson, Graig Nettles, Bob Oliver, Dave Pagan, Lou Piniella, Fred Stanley, Dick Tidrow, Bill Virdon (MANAGER), Roy White, Terry Whitfield, Walt Williams

LESS THAN 10 GAMES: Dave Bergman, Kerry Dineen, Eddie Leon, Larry Murray, Rick Sawyer, Otto Velez, Mike Wallace *

KEY SIGNATURES: Martin, Nettles, Bonds, Munson, Piniella, Hunter, Lyle, Guidry.

VALUE: $240

1975 NEW YORK (NL) - Jesus Alou, Bob Apodaca, Rick Baldwin, Yogi Berra (MANAGER), Gene Clines, Wayne Garrett, Jerry Grote, Tom Hall *, Bud Harrelson, Jack Heidemann, Cleon Jones, Dave Kingman, Jerry Koosman, Ed Kranepool, Skip Lockwood, Jon Matlack, Roy McMillan (MANAGER), Felix Millan, John Milner, Harry Parker *, Mike Phillips *, Ken Sanders, Tom Seaver, Roy Staiger, Rusty Staub, John Stearns, George Stone, Craig Swan, Randy Tate, Joe Torre, Del Unser, Mike Vail, Hank Webb

LESS THAN 10 GAMES: Jerry Cram, Nino Espinosa, Bob Gallagher, Ron Hodges, Brock Pemberton, Mac Scarce

NOTES: Seaver (CY).

KEY SIGNATURES: Kranepool, Staub, Kingman, Grote, Seaver, Koosman.

VALUE: $150

CY = Cy Young Award winner

1975 OAKLAND - Glenn Abbott, Matt Alexander, Stan Bahnsen *, Sal Bando, Vida Blue, Dick Bosman *, Bert Campaneris, Al Dark (MANAGER), Rollie Fingers, Ray Fosse, Phil Garner, Dave Hamilton, Larry Haney, Tommy Harper *, Jim Holt, Ken Holtzman, Don Hopkins, Reggie Jackson, Ted Kubiak *, Paul Lindblad, Angel Mangual, Ted Martinez *, Dal Maxvill, Billy North, Jim Perry *, Gaylen Pitts, Joe Rudi, Sonny Siebert *, Gene Tenace, Jim Todd, Cesar Tovar *, Claudell Washington, Herb Washington, Billy Williams

LESS THAN 10 GAMES: Charlie Chant, Billy Grabarkewitz, Rich McKinney, Craig Mitchell, Mike Norris, Blue Moon Odom *, Charlie Sands, Tom Sandt, Denny Walling

KEY SIGNATURES: Bando, Jackson, Williams, Blue, Fingers, Odom.

VALUE: $175

1975 PHILADELPHIA - Dick Allen *, Mike Anderson, Alan Bannister, Bob Boone, Larry Bowa, Ollie Brown, Steve Carlton, Dave Cash, Larry Christenson, Larry Cox, Gene Garber, Terry Harmon, Tom Hilgendorf, Joe Hoerner, Tommy Hutton, Jay Johnstone, Jim Lonborg, Greg Luzinski, Garry Maddox *, Jerry Martin, Tim McCarver *, Tug McGraw, Willie Montanez *, Johnny Oates *, Danny Ozark (MANAGER), Mike Rogodzinski, Dick Ruthven, Mike Schmidt, Ron Schueler, Tony Taylor, Wayne Twitchell, Tom Underwood

LESS THAN 10 GAMES: Cy Acosta, Ron Clark, Jim Essian, Larry Fritz, Don Hahn *, Randy Lerch, John Montague *, Wayne Simpson

KEY SIGNATURES: Allen, Schmidt, Luzinski, Boone, McCarver, Carlton.

VALUE: $125

1975 PITTSBURGH - Ken Brett, John Candelaria, Larry Demery, Miguel Dilone, Duffy Dyer, Dock Ellis, Dave Giusti, Richie Hebner, Ramon Hernandez, Art Howe, Ed Kirkpatrick, Bruce Kison, Sam McDowell, Mario Mendoza, Bob Moose, Danny Murtaugh (MANAGER), Al Oliver, Dave Parker, Paul Popovich, Willie Randolph, Jerry Reuss, Craig Reynolds, Bob Robertson, Bill Robinson, Jim Rooker, Manny Sanguillen, Willie Stargell, Rennie Stennett, Frank Taveras, Kent Tekulve, Richie Zisk

LESS THAN 10 GAMES: Odell Jones, Jim Minshall, Omar Moreno, Ed Ott

KEY SIGNATURES: Stargell, Parker, Oliver, Candelaria, Tekulve.

VALUE: $175

1975 SAN DIEGO - Bob Davis, Rich Folkers, Alan Foster, Dave Freisleben, Danny Frisella, Tito Fuentes, Bill Greif, Johnny Grubb, Don Hahn *, Enzo Hernandez, Randy Hundley, Steve Huntz, Mike Ivie, Jerry Johnson, Randy Jones, Fred Kendall, Ted Kubiak *, Gene Locklear, Willie McCovey, Joe McIntosh, John McNamara (MANAGER), Jerry Moses *, Dave Roberts, John Scott, Dick Sharon, Dan Spillner, Brent Strom, Bobby Tolan, Dave Tomlin, Hector Torres, Jerry Turner, Dave Winfield

LESS THAN 10 GAMES: Bill Almon, Glenn Beckert, Larry Hardy, Dave Hilton, Butch Metzger, Sonny Siebert, Bobby Valentine *

KEY SIGNATURES: McCovey, Winfield.

VALUE: $95

1975 SAN FRANCISCO - Glenn Adams, Chris Arnold, Jim Barr, Tom Bradley, Jake Brown, Mike Caldwell, John D'Acquisto, Pete Falcone, Ed Goodson *, Ed Halicki, Dave Heaverlo, Marc Hill, Von Joshua, Gary Lavelle, Johnnie LeMaster, Garry Maddox *, Gary Matthews, Bruce Miller, Randy Moffitt, Willie Montanez *, John Montefusco, Bobby Murcer, Steve Ontiveros, Mike Phillips *, Dave Rader, Craig Robinson *, Mike Sadek, Chris Speier, Darrel Thomas, Gary Thomasson, Wes Westrum (MANAGER), Charlie Williams

LESS THAN 10 GAMES: Gary Alexander, Jack Clark, Rob Dressler, Greg Minton, Horace Speed, Tommy Toms

NOTES: Montefusco (ROY).

KEY SIGNATURES: Murcer, Clark.

VALUE: $90

ROY = **Rookie of the Year**

1975 ST LOUIS - Buddy Bradford *, Eddie Brinkman *, Lou Brock, Danny Cater, Hector Cruz, John Curtis, Willie Davis *, John Denny, Jim Dwyer *, Ron Fairly, Bob Forsch, Mike Garman, Bob Gibson, Mike Guerrero, Keith Hernandez, Doug Howard, Al Hrabosky, Larry Lintz, Teddy Martinez *, Bake McBride, Lynn McGlothen, Luis Melendez, Tommy Moore *, Jerry Mumphrey, Harry Parker *, Harry Rasmussen, Ron Reed *, Ken Reitz, Ken Reynolds, Ken Rudolph, Red Schoendienst (MANAGER), Ted Simmons, Ted Sizemore, Reggie Smith, Elias Sosa *, Greg Terlecky, Mike Tyson

LESS THAN 10 GAMES: Mike Barlow, Dick Billings, Ron Bryant, Don Hahn *, Mick Kelleher, Ryan Kurosaki, Ray Sadecki *, Mike Wallace *

KEY SIGNATURES: Schoendienst, Brock, Simmons, Hernandez, Gibson.

VALUE: $110

1975 TEXAS - Jim Bibby *, Jackie Brown *, Jeff Burroughs, Leo Cardenas, Mike Cubbage, Willie Davis *, Bill Fahey, Steve Foucault, Jim Fregosi, Tommy Grieve, Bill Hands, Mike Hargrove, Toby Harrah, Roy Howell, Ferguson Jenkins, Mike Kekich, Joe Lovitto, Frank Lucchesi (MANAGER), Billy Martin (MANAGER), Dave Moates, Tommy Moore *, Dave Nelson, Gaylord Perry *, Stan Perzanowski, Ron Pruitt, Lenny Randle, Tom Robson, Roy Smalley, Jim Spencer, Jim Sundberg, Stan Thomas, Cesar Tovar *, Jim Umbarger, Clyde Wright,

LESS THAN 10 GAMES: Mike Bacsik, Eddie Brinkman *, David Clyde, Jim Gideon, Bobby Jones, Jim Merritt

KEY SIGNATURES: Martin, Harrah, Jenkins, Perry.

VALUE: $120

1976

1976 National League MVP Joe Morgan

*** = player was traded**

1976 ATLANTA - Brian Asselstine, Mike Beard, Rob Belloir, Dave Bristol (MANAGER), Darrel Chaney, Vic Correll, Bruce Dal Canton, Adrian Devine, Darrell Evans *, Cito Gaston, Rod Gilbreath, Ken Henderson, Lee Lacy *, Frank LaCorte, Max Leon, Mike Marshall *, Dave May, Andy Messersmith, Willie Montanez *, Junior Moore,

Roger Moret, Carl Morton, Dale Murphy, Phil Niekro, Rowland Office, Tom Paciorek, Marty Perez *, Biff Pocoroba, Jerry Royster, Dick Ruthven, Elias Sosa *, Pablo Torrealba, Earl Williams *, Jim Wynn

LESS THAN 10 GAMES: Al Autry, Rick Camp, Buzz Capra, Terry Crowley *, Jamie Easterly, Mike Eden, Preston Hanna, Craig Robinson *, Pat Rockett, Pete Varney *

KEY SIGNATURES: Murphy, Niekro.

VALUE: $80

1976 BALTIMORE - Doyle Alexander *, Mark Belanger, Paul Blair, Al Bumbry, Terry Crowley *, Mike Cuellar, Rich Dauer, Rick Dempsey *, Doug DeCinces, Dave Duncan, Mike Flanagan, Kiko Garcia, Wayne Garland, Bobby Grich, Ross Grimsley, Tommy Harper, Ellie Hendricks *, Fred Holdsworth, Ken Holtzman *, Reggie Jackson, Grant Jackson *, Tippy Martinez *, Lee May, Rudy May *, Dyar Miller, Andres Mora, Tony Muser, Tim Nordbrook *, Dave Pagan *, Jim Palmer, Brooks Robinson, Tom Shopay, Ken Singleton, Royle Stillman, Earl Weaver (MANAGER)

LESS THAN 10 GAMES: Bob Bailor, Dennis Martinez, Scott McGregor

NOTES: Palmer (CY).

KEY SIGNATURES: Weaver, Jackson, Robinson, Palmer.

VALUE: $130

CY = Cy Young Award winner

1976 BOSTON - Jack Baker, Rick Burleson, Bernie Carbo *, Reggie Cleveland, Cecil Cooper, Bobby Darwin *, Steve Dillard, Denny Doyle, Dwight Evans, Carlton Fisk, Doug Griffin, Bob Heise, Butch Hobson, Tom House, Ferguson Jenkins, Darrell Johnson (MANAGER), Deron Johnson, Rick Jones, Bill Lee, Fred Lynn, Rick Miller, Bob Montgomery, Tom Murphy *, Rico Petrocelli, Dick Pole, Jim Rice, Luis Tiant, Jim Willoughby, Rick Wise, Carl Yastrzemski, Don Zimmer (MANAGER)

LESS THAN 10 GAMES: Rick Kreuger, Andy Merchant, Ernie Whitt

KEY SIGNATURES: Yastrzemski, Evans, Lynn, Rice, Fisk, Cooper, Tiant, Jenkins.

VALUE: $135

1976 CALIFORNIA - Jesus Alvarez, Bruce Bochte, Bobby Bonds, Jim Brewer, Dan Briggs, Dave Chalk, Dave Collins, Paul Dade, Tommy Davis *, Dick Drago, Mike Easler, Andy Etchebarren, Adrian Garrett, Mike Guerrero, Paul Hartzell, Andy Hassler *, Ed Herrmann *, Terry Humphrey, Ron Jackson, Bobby Jones, Don Kirkwood, Joe Lahoud *, Bill Melton, Sid Monge, Orlando Ramirez, Jerry Remy, Gary Ross, Nolan Ryan, Mickey Scott, Norm Sherry (MANAGER), Billy Smith, Tony Solaita *, Lee Stanton, Frank Tanana, Rusty Torres, John Verhoeven, Dick Williams (MANAGER)

LESS THAN 10 GAMES: Steve Dunning *, Ike Hampton, Carlos Lopez, Mike Miley, Tim Nordbrook *, Mike Overy, Gary Wheelock

KEY SIGNATURES: Ryan.

VALUE: $100

1976 CHICAGO (AL) - Alan Bannister, Francisco Barrios, Kevin Bell, Buddy Bradford, Ken Brett *, Jack Brohamer, Clay Carroll, Rich Coggins *, Bucky Dent, Brian Downing, Jim Essian, Sam Ewing, Terry Forster, Ralph Garr, Goose Gossage, Dave Hamilton, Jerry Hariston, Jesse Jefferson, Bart Johnson, Lamar Johnson, Pat Kelly, Chris Knapp, Chet Lemon, Carlos May *, Wayne Nordhagen, Jorge Orta, Paul Richards (MANAGER), Jim Spencer, Bill Stein, Pete Varney *, Pete Vuckovich

LESS THAN 10 GAMES: George Enright, Cleon Jones, Ken Kravec, Jack Kucek, Minnie Minoso, Larry Monroe, Nyls Nyman, Blue Moon Odom, Jim Otten, Phil Roof *, Wilbur Wood, Hugh Yancy

KEY SIGNATURES: Gossage.

VALUE: $75

1976 CHICAGO (NL) - Mike Adams, Larry Biittner *, Bill Bonham, Ray Burris, Jose Cardenal, Joe Coleman *, Mike Garman, Randy Hundley, Mick Kelleher, Darold Knowles, Pete LaCock, Bill Madlock, Jim Marshall (MANAGER), George Mitterwald, Rick Monday, Jerry Morales, Steve Renko *, Paul Reuschel, Rick Reuschel, Dave Rosello, Buddy Schultz, Rob Sperring, Steve Stone, Champ Summers, Bruce Sutter, Steve Swisher, Jerry Tabb, Andy Thornton *, Manny Trillo, Wayne Tyrone, Joe Wallis, Oscar Zamora

LESS THAN 10 GAMES: Ken Crosby, Tom Dettore, Ken Frailing, Ramon Hernandez *, Tim Hosley *, Mike Krukow, Ed Putman, Geoff Zahn

KEY SIGNATURES: Madlock.

VALUE: $75

1976 CINCINNATI - Santo Alcala, Sparky Anderson (MANAGER), Ed Armbrister, Bob Bailey, Johnny Bench, Jack Billingham, Pedro Borbon, Dave Concepcion, Pat Darcy, Dan Driessen, Rawly Eastwick, Doug Flynn, George Foster, Cesar Geronimo, Ken Griffey, Don Gullett, Rich Hinton, Mike Lum, Will McEnaney, Joe Morgan, Gary Nolan, Fred Norman, Tony Perez, Bill Plummer, Pete Rose, Manny Sarmiento, Joel Youngblood, Pat Zachry

LESS THAN 10 GAMES: Joe Henderson, Don Werner

NOTES: World Champions! Morgan (MVP); Zachry (ROY).

KEY SIGNATURES: Anderson, Perez, Morgan, Concepcion, Rose, Griffey, Foster, Bench, Zachry.

VALUE: $325

ROY = **Rookie of the Year**

1976 CLEVELAND - Alan Ashby, Buddy Bell, Jim Bibby, Larvell Blanks, Jackie Brown, Tom Buskey, Rico Carty, Pat Dobson, Frank Duffy, Dennis Eckersley, Ray Fosse, Orlando Gonzalez, George Hendrick, Don Hood, Doug Howard, Jim Kern, Duane Kuiper, Dave LaRoche, Joe Lis, John Lowenstein, Rick Manning, Boog Powell, Ron Pruitt, Frank Robinson (MANAGER), Tommy Smith, Charlie Spikes, Stan Thomas, Rick Waits

LESS THAN 10 GAMES: Rick Cerone, Ed Crosby, Alfredo Griffin, Harry Parker, Fritz Peterson *, Eric Raich

NOTES: Robinson was a player/manager.

KEY SIGNATURES: Robinson, Powell, Bell.

VALUE: $85

1976 DETROIT - Ray Bare, Joe Coleman *, Jim Crawford, Mark Fidrych, Bill Freehan, Pedro Garcia *, Steve Grilli, John Hiller, Willie Horton, Ralph Houk (MANAGER), Art James, Alex Johnson, Bruce Kimm, Marv Lane, Bill Laxton, Dave Lemanczyk, Ron LeFlore, Phil Mankowski, Jerry Manuel, Dan Meyer, Ben Oglivie, Dave Roberts, Aurelio Rodriguez, Vern Ruhle, Chuck Scrivener, Mickey Stanley, Rusty Staub, Gary Sutherland *, Jason Thompson, Tom Veryzer, Mark Wagner, John Wockenfuss

LESS THAN 10 GAMES: Ed Glynn, Frank MacCormack, Milt May
NOTES: Fidrych (ROY).
KEY SIGNATURES: Staub, Freehan, Horton, Fidrych.

VALUE: $95

ROY = Rookie of the Year

1976 HOUSTON - Rob Andrews, Joaquin Andujar, Mike Barlow, Ken Boswell, Enos Cabell, Cesar Cedeno, Mike Cosgrove, Jose Cruz, Jerry DaVanon, Larry Dierker, Ken Forsch, Tom Griffin *, Greg Gross, Larry Hardy, Ed Herrmann *, Wilbur Howard, Art Howe, Cliff Johnson, Skip Jutze, Dan Larson, Joe McIntosh, Bo McLaughlin, Roger Metzger, Larry Milbourne, Joe Niekro, Gene Pentz, J.R. Richard, Leon Roberts, Gil Rondon, Joe Sambito, Paul Siebert, Alex Taveras, Bill Virdon (MANAGER), Bob Watson
LESS THAN 10 GAMES: Rich Chiles, Al Javier, Mark Lemongello, Jose Sosa
KEY SIGNATURES: Richard.

VALUE: $75

1976 KANSAS CITY - Doug Bird, George Brett, Tom Bruno, Steve Busby, Al Cowens, Al Fitzmorris, Larry Gura, Tom Hall *, Andy Hassler *, Whitey Herzog (MANAGER), Ruppert Jones, Dennis Leonard, Mark Littell, Buck Martinez, John Mayberry, Hal McRae, Steve Mingori, Dave Nelson, Amos Otis, Freddie Patek, Marty Pattin, Tom Poquette, Jamie Quirk, Cookie Rojas, Tony Solaita *, Paul Splittorff, Bob Stinson, John Wathan, Frank White, Willie Wilson, Jim Wohlford
LESS THAN 10 GAMES: Jerry Cram, Tommy Davis *, Fran Healy *, Bob McClure, Roger Nelson, Ray Sadecki *, Ken Sanders *
KEY SIGNATURES: Brett.

VALUE: $150

1976 LOS ANGELES - Walt Alston (MANAGER), Rick Auerbach, Dusty Baker, Bill Buckner, Glenn Burke, Ron Cey, Henry Cruz, Ivan DeJesus, Al Downing, Joe Ferguson *, Steve Garvey, Ed Goodson, John Hale, Burt Hooton, Charlie Hough, Tommy John, Lee Lacy *, Leron Lee, Davey Lopes, Jim Lyttle *, Mike Marshall *, Manny Mota, Kevin Pasley, Doug Rau, Rick Rhoden, Ellie Rodriguez, Bill Russell, Joe Simpson, Ted Sizemore, Reggie Smith *, Elias Sosa *, Don Sutton, Stan Wall, Steve Yeager
LESS THAN 10 GAMES: Dennis Lewallyn, Sergio Robles, Rick Sutcliffe, Danny Walton
KEY SIGNATURES: Alston, Garvey, Cey, Buckner, Sutton, John.

VALUE: $130

1976 MILWAUKEE - Hank Aaron, Jerry Augustine, Kurt Bevacqua, Steve Bowling, Pete Broberg, Bernie Carbo *, Bill Castro, Billy Champion, Jim Colborn, Bobby Darwin *, Danny Frisella *, Jim Gantner, Pete Garcia *, Alex Grammas (MANAGER), Bob Hansen, Mike Hegan, Jack Heidemann *, Tim Johnson, Von Joshua *, Art Kusnyer, Sixto Lezcano, Don Money, Charlie Moore, Tom Murphy *, Darrell Porter, Eduardo Rodriguez, Jimmy Rosario, Ray Sadecki *, George Scott, Bill Sharp, Jim Slaton, Gary Sutherland *, Danny Thomas, Gorman Thomas, Bill Travers, Robin Yount

LESS THAN 10 GAMES: Rick Austin, Gary Beare, Moose Haas, Tom Hausman, Kevin Kobel, Ed Sprague

NOTES: Frisella died 1/1/77.

KEY SIGNATURES: Yount, Aaron, Frisella.

VALUE: $125

1976 MINNESOTA - Vic Albury, Eddie Bane, Bert Blyleven *, Glenn Borgmann, Lyman Bostock, Steve Braun, Steve Brye, Tom Burgmeier, Bill Campbell, Rod Carew, Mike Cubbage *, Joe Decker, Dan Ford, Dave Goltz, Luis Gomez, Larry Hisle, Jim Hughes, Tom Johnson, Craig Kusick, Steve Luebber, Gene Mauch (MANAGER), Dave McKay, Tony Oliva, Bob Randall, Pete Redfern, Phil Roof *, Bill Singer *, Roy Smalley *, Jerry Terrell, Danny Thompson *, Butch Wynegar

LESS THAN 10 GAMES: Mike Pazik

KEY SIGNATURES: Carew, Bostock, Oliva, Blyleven.

VALUE: $90

1976 MONTREAL - Larry Biittner *, Don Carrithers, Gary Carter, Nate Colbert *, Jim Cox, Warren Cromartie, Andre Dawson, Steve Dunning *, Jim Dwyer *, Tim Foli, Barry Foote, Charlie Fox (MANAGER), Pepe Frias, Woody Fryman, Wayne Garrett *, Wayne Granger, Mike Jorgensen, Joe Kerrigan, Clay Kirby, Karl Kuehl (MANAGER), Chip Lang, Jim Lyttle *, Pete Mackanin, Pepe Mangual *, Jose Morales, Dale Murray, Larry Parrish, Bombo Rivera, Gary Roenicke, Steve Rogers, Pat Scanlon, Fred Scherman, Don Stanhouse, Chuck Taylor, Andy Thornton *, Del Unser *, Ellis Valentine, Dan Warthen, Jerry White, Earl Williams *

LESS THAN 10 GAMES: Bill Atkinson, Dennis Blair, Roger Freed, Gerald Hannahs, Larry Johnson, Joe Keener, Larry Landreth, Steve Renko *, Rodney Scott

KEY SIGNATURES: Carter, Dawson.

VALUE: $90

1976 NEW YORK (AL) - Doyle Alexander *, Sandy Alomar, Juan Bernhardt, Chris Chambliss, Rick Dempsey *, Dock Ellis, Ed Figueroa, Oscar Gamble, Fran Healy *, Ellie Hendricks *, Ken Holtzman *, Catfish Hunter, Grant Jackson *, Sparky Lyle, Elliott Maddox, Billy Martin (MANAGER), Tippy Martinez *, Jim Mason, Carlos May *, Rudy May *, Thurman Munson, Graig Nettles, Lou Piniella, Willie Randolph, Mickey Rivers, Fred Stanley, Dick Tidrow, Cesar Tovar *, Otto Velez, Roy White

LESS THAN 10 GAMES: Ron Blomberg, Ken Brett *, Rich Coggins *, Kerry Dineen, Ron Guidry, Mickey Klutts, Gene Locklear *, Larry Murray, Dave Pagan *, Terry Whitfield, Jim York

NOTES: Munson (MVP).

KEY SIGNATURES: Martin, Nettles, Munson, Hunter, Lyle.

VALUE: $270

MVP = MVP Award winner

1976 NEW YORK (NL) - Bob Apodaca, Rick Baldwin, Bruce Boisclair, Leon Brown, Jim Dwyer, Nino Espinosa, Leo Foster, Joe Frazier (MANAGER), Wayne Garrett *, Jerry Grote, Bud Harrelson, Ron Hodges, Dave Kingman, Jerry Koosman, Ed Kranepool, Skip Lockwood, Mickey Lolich, Pepe Mangual *, Jon Matlack, Leo Mazzilli, Felix Millan,

John Milner, Bobby Myrick, Mike Phillips, Ken Sanders *, Tom Seaver, Roy Staiger, John Stearns, Craig Swan, Joe Torre, Del Unser *, Mike Vail
LESS THAN 10 GAMES: Benny Ayala, Bobby Baldwin, Tom Hall *, Jack Heidemann *, Jay Kleven, Hank Webb
KEY SIGNATURES: Kranepool, Harrelson, Kingman, Torre, Koosman, Seaver, Lolich.

VALUE: $145

1976 OAKLAND - Glenn Abbott, Matt Alexander, Stan Bahnsen, Sal Bando, Don Baylor, Vida Blue, Dick Bosman, Bert Campaneris, Ron Fairly *, Rollie Fingers, Phil Garner, Wayne Gross, Larry Haney, Tim Hosley *, Paul Lindblad, Larry Lintz, Willie McCovey *, Ken McMullen, Paul Mitchell, Jeff Newman, Mike Norris, Billy North, Joe Rudi, Tommy Sandt, Chuck Tanner (MANAGER), Gene Tenace, Jim Todd, Mike Torrez, Cesar Tovar *, Claudell Washington, Billy Williams
LESS THAN 10 GAMES: Chris Batton, Nate Colbert *, Jim Holt, Don Hopkins, Angel Mangual, Craig Mitchell, Denny Walling, Gary Woods
KEY SIGNATURES: Williams, Blue, Fingers.

VALUE: $95

1976 PHILADELPHIA - Dick Allen, Bob Boone, Rick Bosetti, Larry Bowa, Ollie Brown, Steve Carlton, Dave Cash, Larry Christenson, Gene Garber, Terry Harmon, Tommy Hutton, Jay Johnstone, Jim Kaat, Jim Lonborg, Greg Luzinski, Garry Maddox, Jerry Martin, Tim McCarver, Tug McGraw, Johnny Oates, Danny Ozark (MANAGER), Ron Reed, Mike Schmidt, Ron Schueler, Tony Taylor, Bobby Tolan, Wayne Twitchell, Tom Underwood
LESS THAN 10 GAMES: Fred Andrews, Tim Blackwell, Randy Lerch, Bill Nahorodny, John Vukovich
KEY SIGNATURES: Allen, Bowa, Schmidt, Luzinski, Boone, McCarver, Carlton, Kaat.

VALUE: $150

1976 PITTSBURGH - John Candelaria, Larry Demery, Miguel Dilone, Duffy Dyer, Dave Giusti, Richie Hebner, Tommy Helms, Ramon Hernandez *, Ed Kirkpatrick, Bruce Kison, Rick Langford, Doc Medich, Mario Mendoza, Bob Moose, Omar Moreno, Danny Murtaugh (MANAGER), Al Oliver, Dave Parker, Jerry Reuss, Bob Robertson, Bill Robinson, Jim Rooker, Manny Sanguillen, Willie Stargell, Rennie Stennett, Frank Taveras, Kent Tekulve, Richie Zisk
LESS THAN 10 GAMES: Tony Armas, Doug Bair, Ed Ott, Craig Reynolds
KEY SIGNATURES: Stargell, Parker, Oliver, Candelaria, Tekulve.

VALUE: $145

1976 SAN DIEGO - Bill Almon, Mike Champion, Bob Davis, Willie Davis, Mike Dupree, Rich Folkers, Alan Foster, Dave Freisleben, Tito Fuentes, Tom Griffin *, Johnny Grubb, Enzo Hernandez, Mike Ivie, Jerry Johnson, Randy Jones, Fred Kendall, Ted Kubiak, Gene Locklear *, Willie McCovey *, John McNamara (MANAGER), Luis Melendez *, Butch Metzger, Doug Rader, Merv Rettenmund, Ken Reynolds, Rick Sawyer, Dan Spillner, Brent Strom, Dave Tomlin, Hector Torres, Jerry Turner, Bobby Valentine, Dave Winfield

LESS THAN 10 GAMES: Tucker Ashford, Bill Greif *, Bob Owchinko, Dave Wehrmeister

NOTES: Metzger (ROY); Jones (CY).

KEY SIGNATURES: Winfield, McCovey, Jones, Metzger.

ROY = Rookie of the Year

VALUE: $110

1976 SAN FRANCISCO - Glenn Adams, Gary Alexander, Chris Arnold, Jim Barr, Mike Caldwell, Jack Clark, John D'Acquisto, Rob Dressler, Darrell Evans *, Ed Halicki, Dave Heaverlo, Larry Herndon, Marc Hill, Von Joshua *, Gary Lavelle, Johnnie LeMaster, Gary Matthews, Bruce Miller, Greg Minton, Randy Moffitt, Willie Montanez *, John Montefusco, Bobby Murcer, Steve Ontiveros, Marty Perez *, Dave Rader, Ken Reitz, Bill Rigney (MANAGER), Craig Robinson *, Mike Sadek, Chris Speier, Derrel Thomas, Gary Thomasson, Charlie Williams

LESS THAN 10 GAMES: Bob Knepper, Frank Ricelli, Tommy Toms

KEY SIGNATURES: Evans, Murcer, Clark.

VALUE: $85

1976 ST. LOUIS - Luis Alvarado, Mike Anderson, Lou Brock, Charlie Chant, Willie Crawford, Hector Cruz, John Curtis, John Denny, Ron Fairly *, Pete Falcone, Joe Ferguson *, Bob Forsch, Danny Frisella *, Bill Greif *, Vic Harris, Keith Hernandez, Al Hrabosky, Don Kessinger, Bake McBride, Lynn McGlothen, Sammy Mejias, Luis Melendez *, Jerry Mumphrey, Mike Proly, Harry Rasmussen, Lee Richard, Ken Rudolph, Red Schoendienst (MANAGER), Ted Simmons, Reggie Smith *, Eddie Solomon, John Tamargo, Garry Templeton, Mike Tyson, Tom Walker, Mike Wallace

LESS THAN 10 GAMES: Doug Capilla, Doug Clarey, Lerrin LaGrow, Mike Potter, Steve Waterbury

KEY SIGNATURES: Schoendienst, Hernandez, Brock, Simmons.

VALUE: $110

1976 TEXAS - Mike Bacsik, Steve Barr, Juan Beniquez, Bert Blyleven *, Tommy Boggs, Nelson Briles, Jeff Burroughs, Gene Clines, Mike Cubbage *, Johnny Ellis, Bill Fahey, Steve Foucault, Jim Fregosi, Tommy Grieve, Steve Hargan, Mike Hargrove, Toby Harrah, Joe Hoerner, Roy Howell, Joe Lahoud *, Frank Lucchesi (MANAGER), Dave Moates, Ken Pape, Gaylord Perry, Lenny Randle, Bill Singer *, Roy Smalley *, Jim Sundberg, Jeff Terpko, Danny Thompson *, Jim Umbarger

LESS THAN 10 GAMES: Doug Ault, Len Barker, Stan Perzanowski, Fritz Peterson *, Greg Pryor, Craig Skok

NOTES: Thompson died 12/10/76.

KEY SIGNATURES: Harrah, Thompson, Perry, Blyleven.

VALUE: $90

1977

1977 American League Rod Carew

*** = player was traded**

1977 ATLANTA - Brian Asseltine, Vern Benson (MANAGER), Barry Bonnell, Dave Bristol (MANAGER), Dave Bristol (MANAGER), Jeff Burroughs, Rick Camp, Dave Campbell, Buzz Capra, Darrel Chaney, Don Collins, Vic Correll, Mike Davey, Jamie Easterly, Cito Gaston, Rod Gilbreath, Preston Hanna, Steve Hargan *, Bob Johnson, Steve Kline, Frank LaCorte, Max Leon, Gary Matthews, Andy Messersmith, Willie Montanez, Junior Moore, Dale Murphy, Phil Niekro, Joe Nolan, Rowland Office, Tom Paciorek, Biff Pocoroba, Craig Robinson, Pat Rockett, Jerry Royster, Dick Ruthven, Eddie Solomon, Duane Theiss, Ted Turner (MANAGER)

LESS THAN 10 GAMES: Mike Beard, Rob Belloir, Larry Bradford, Mickey Mahler, Mike Marshall *, Joey McLaughlin, Larry Whisenton

KEY SIGNATURES: Niekro.

VALUE: $75

1977 BALTIMORE - Mark Belanger, Al Bumbry, Terry Crowley, Rich Dauer, Rick Dempsey, Doug DeCinces, Mike Dimmel, Dick Drago *, Mike Flanagan, Kiko Garcia, Ross Grimsley, Larry Harlow, Fred Holdsworth *, Pat Kelly, Elliott Maddox, Dennis Martinez, Tippy Martinez, Lee May, Rudy May, Scott McGregor, Dyar Miller *, Andres Mora, Eddie Murray, Tony Muser, Jim Palmer, Brooks Robinson, Ken Rudolph *, Tom Shopay, Ken Singleton, Dave Skaggs, Billy Smith, Earl Weaver (MANAGER)

LESS THAN 10 GAMES: Nelson Briles *, Tony Chevez, Dave Criscione, Ed Farmer, Randy Miller, Mike Parrott, Earl Stephenson

NOTES: Murray (ROY); Brooks Robinson retired.

KEY SIGNATURES: Weaver, Murray, Robinson, Palmer.

VALUE: $125

ROY = Rookie of the Year

1977 BOSTON - Don Aase, Rick Burleson, Bill Campbell, Bernie Carbo, Reggie Cleveland, Dave Coleman, Ted Cox, Steve Dillard, Denny Doyle, Dwight Evans, Carlton Fisk, Tommy Helms *, Ramon Hernandez *, Butch Hobson, Ferguson Jenkins, Bill Lee, Fred Lynn, Rick Miller, Bob Montgomery, Tom Murphy *, Mike Paxton, Jim Rice, George Scott, Bob Stanley, Luis Tiant, Jim Willoughby, Rick Wise, Carl Yastrzemski, Don Zimmer (MANAGER)

LESS THAN 10 GAMES: Ramon Aviles, Bob Bailey *, Jack Baker, Sam Bowen, Jim Burton, Bobby Darwin *, Bo Diaz, Doug Griffin, Tom House *, Rick Kreuger

KEY SIGNATURES: Evans, Lynn, Yastrzemski, Fisk, Rice, Tiant, Jenkins.

VALUE: $135

1977 CALIFORNIA - Willie Aikens, Mike Barlow, Don Baylor, Bruce Bochte *, Bobby Bonds, Thad Bosley, Ken Brett *, Dan Briggs, Dave Chalk, Dick Drago *, Andy Etchebarren, Gil Flores, Dave Garcia (MANAGER), Danny Goodwin, Bobby Grich, Mike Guerrero, Ike Hampton, Paul Hartzell, Terry Humphrey, Ron Jackson, Bobby Jones, Dave Kingman *, Don Kirkwood *, Ken Landreaux, Dave LaRoche *, Carlos May *, Dyar Miller *, Rance Mulliniks, Orlando Ramirez, Jerry Remy, Gary Ross, Joe Rudi, Nolan Ryan, Mickey Scott, Norm Sherry (MANAGER), Wayne Simpson, Tony Solaita, Frank Tanana, Rusty Torres

LESS THAN 10 GAMES: John Caneira, Mike Cuellar, Fred Kuhaulua, Sid Monge *, Balor Moore, Gary Nolan *, John Verhoeven *, Tom Walker *

KEY SIGNATURES: Grich, Bonds, Ryan.

VALUE: $100

1977 CHICAGO (AL) - Alan Bannister, Francisco Barrios, Ken Brett *, Jack Brohamer, Bob Coluccio, Henry Cruz, Brian Downing, Jim Essian, Oscar Gamble, Ralph Garr, Jerry Hairston *, Dave Hamilton, Bart Johnson, Lamar Johnson, Don Kessinger *, Don Kirkwood *, Chris Knapp, Ken Kravec, Lerrin LaGrow, Bob Lemon (MANAGER), Chet Lemon, Silvio Martinez, Tim Nordbrook *, Wayne Nordhagen, Jorge Orta, Eric Soderholm, Jim Spencer, Royle Stillman, Steve Stone, Wilbur Wood, Richie Zisk

LESS THAN 10 GAMES: Larry Anderson, Kevin Bell, Clay Carroll *, Tommy Cruz, Bruce Dal Canton, John Flannery, Dave Frost, Jack Kucek, Bob Molinaro *, Bill Nahorodny, Nyls Nyman, Steve Renko *, Mike Squires, John Verhoeven *, Randy Wiles

KEY SIGNATURES: B. Lemon.

VALUE: $75

1977 CHICAGO (NL) - Larry Biittner, Bill Bonham, Pete Broberg, Bill Buckner, Ray Burris, Jose Cardenal, Gene Clines, Bobby Darwin *, Ivan DeJesus, Herman Franks (MANAGER), Dave Giusti *, Greg Gross, Willie Hernandez, Mick Kelleher, Mike Krukow, Dennis Lamp, George Mitterwald, Donnie Moore, Jerry Morales, Bobby Murcer, Steve Ontiveros, Steve Renko *, Paul Reuschel, Rick Reuschel, Dave Roberts *, Dave Rosello, Bruce Sutter, Steve Swisher, Jim Todd, Manny Trillo, Joe Wallis

LESS THAN 10 GAMES: Mike Adams, Mike Gordon, Ramon Hernandez *, Randy Hundley, Mike Sember

KEY SIGNATURES: Buckner, Trillo, Murcer, R. Reuschel.

VALUE: $75

1977 CINCINNATI - Sparky Anderson (MANAGER), Ed Armbrister, Rick Auerbach, Bob Bailey *, Johnny Bench, Jack Billingham, Pedro Borbon, Mike Caldwell *, Doug Capilla *, Dave Concepcion, Dan Driessen, Rawly Eastwick *, Doug Flynn *, George Foster, Woody Fryman, Cesar Geronimo, Ken Griffey, Tom Hume, Ray Knight, Mike Lum, Joe Morgan, Paul Moskau, Dale Murray, Fred Norman, Bill Plummer, Pete Rose, Manny Sarmiento, Tom Seaver *, Mario Soto, Champ Summers, Don Werner, Pat Zachry *

LESS THAN 10 GAMES: Santo Alcala *, Dan Dumoulin, Joe Henderson, Joe Hoerner, Gary Nolan *, Angel Torres

NOTES: Foster (MVP).

KEY SIGNATURES: Anderson, Morgan, Concepcion, Rose, Griffey, Foster, Bench, Seaver.

VALUE: $145

MVP = **MVP Award winner**

1977 CLEVELAND - Larry Anderson, Buddy Bell, Jim Bibby, Larvell Blanks, Bruce Bochte *, Tom Buskey, Rico Carty, Paul Dade, Pat Dobson, Frank Duffy, Dennis Eckersley, Al Fitzmorris, Ray Fosse *, Wayne Garland, Alfredo Griffin, Johnny Grubb, Don Hood, Fred Kendall, Jim Kern, Duane Kuiper, Dave LaRoche *, John Lowenstein, Rick Manning, Bill Melton, Sid Monge *, Jim Norris, Ron Pruitt, Frank Robinson (MANAGER), Charlie Spikes, Andy Thornton, Jeff Torborg (MANAGER), Rick Waits

LESS THAN 10 GAMES: Card Camper, Bill Laxton *, Dave Oliver

KEY SIGNATURES: Robinson, Bell, Eckersley.

VALUE: $85

1977 DETROIT - Bob Adams, Fernando Arroyo, Tim Corcoran, Jim Crawford, Mark Fidrych, Steve Foucault, Tito Fuentes, Steve Grilli, John Hiller, Ralph Houk (MANAGER), Steve Kemp, Bruce Kimm, Ron LeFlore, Phil Mankowski, Milt May, Ben Oglivie, Lance Parrish, Dave Roberts *, Auerlio Rodriguez, Dave Rozema, Vern Ruhle, Chuck Scrivener, Mickey Stanley, Rusty Staub, Bob Sykes, Bruce Taylor, Jason Thompson, Alan Trammell, Tom Veryzer, Mark Wagner, Lou Whitaker, Milt Wilcox, John Wockenfuss

LESS THAN 10 GAMES: Luis Alvarado *, Ray Bare, Ed Glynn, Willie Horton *, Bob Molinaro *, Jack Morris

KEY SIGNATURES: Staub, Trammell, Whitaker, Morris.

VALUE: $125

1977 HOUSTON - Joaquin Andujar, Floyd Bannister, Ken Boswell, Enos Cabell, Cesar Cedeno, Willie Crawford *, Jose Cruz, Joe Ferguson, Mike Fischlin, Ken Forsch, Jim Fuller, Art Gardner, Julio Gonzalez, Ed Herrmann, Wilbur Howard, Art Howe, Cliff Johnson *, Dan Larson, Mark Lemongello, Bo McLaughlin, Roger Metzger, Joe Niekro, Gene Pentz, Terry Puhl, J.R. Richard, Leon Roberts, Joe Sambito, Rob Sperring, Bill Virdon (MANAGER), Danny Walton, Bob Watson

LESS THAN 10 GAMES: Craig Cacek, Joe Cannon, Tom Dixon, Doug Konieczny, Luis Pujols, Roy Thomas, Dennis Walling

KEY SIGNATURES: Richard.

VALUE: $75

1977 KANSAS CITY - Doug Bird, George Brett, Jim Colborn, Al Cowens, Larry Gura, Andy Hassler, Bob Heise, Whitey Herzog (MANAGER), Joe Lahoud, Pete LaCock, Dennis Leonard, Mark Littell, Buck Martinez, John Mayberry, Hal McRae, Steve Mingori, Dave Nelson, Amos Otis, Freddie Patek, Marty Pattin, Tom Poquette, Darrell Porter, Cookie Rojas, Paul Splittorff, U.L. Washington, John Wathan, Frank White, Willie Wilson, Joe Zdeb

LESS THAN 10 GAMES: Tom Hall, Clint Hurdle, Gary Lance, Randy McGilberry, George Throop

KEY SIGNATURES: Brett.

VALUE: $150

1977 LOS ANGELES - Dusty Baker, Glenn Burke, Ron Cey, Vic Davalillo, Al Downing, Mike Garman, Steve Garvey, Ed Goodson, Jerry Grote *, John Hale, Burt Hooton, Charlie Hough, Tommy John, Lee Lacy, Rafael Landestoy, Tom Lasorda (MANAGER), Jeff Leonard, Dave Lopes, Ted Martinez, Rick Monday, Manny Mota, Johnny Oates, Boog Powell, Doug Rau, Lance Rautzhan, Rick Rhoden, Bill Russell, Joe Simpson, Reggie Smith, Elias Sosa, Don Sutton, Stan Wall, Ron Washington, Steve Yeager

LESS THAN 10 GAMES: Bobby Castillo, Dennis Lewallyn, Kevin Pasley *, Hank Webb

KEY SIGNATURES: Lasorda, Garvey, Cey, Mota, John, Sutton.

VALUE: $215

1977 MILWAUKEE - Jerry Augustine, Sal Bando, Gary Beare, Steve Brye, Mike Caldwell *, Bill Castro, Cecil Cooper, Dick Davis, Jim Gantner, Alex Grammas (MANAGER), Moose Haas, Larry Haney, Mike Hegan, Sam Hinds, Tim Johnson, Von Joshua, Ed Kirkpatrick *, Sixto Lezcano, Bob McClure, Ken McMullen, Don Money, Charlie Moore, Jamie Quirk, Eduardo Rodriguez, Ed Romero, Lenn Sakata, Bobby Sheldon, Jim Slaton, Lary Sorensen, Danny Thomas, Bill Travers, Jim Wohlford, Jim Wynn *, Robin Yount

LESS THAN 10 GAMES: Barry Cort, Rich Folkers, Jack Heidemann

KEY SIGNATURES: Cooper, Yount.

VALUE: $95

1977 MINNESOTA - Glenn Adams, Glenn Borgmann, Lyman Bostock, Terry Bulling, Tom Burgmeier, Rod Carew, Rich Chiles, Mike Cubbage, Dan Ford, Dave Goltz, Luis Gomez, Bob Gorinski, Larry Hisle, Jeff Holly, Dave Johnson, Tom Johnson, Craig Kusick, Gene Mauch (MANAGER), Willie Norwood, Sam Perlozzo, Bob Randall, Pete Redfern, Ron Schueler, Roy Smalley, Jerry Terrell, Paul Thormodsgard, Rob Wilfong, Butch Wynegar, Geoff Zahn

LESS THAN 10 GAMES: Randy Bass, Bill Butler, Don Carrithers, Jim Hughes, Mike Pazik, Gary Serum, Jim Shellenback, Larry Wolfe

NOTES: Carew (MVP).

KEY SIGNATURES: Carew, Bostock.

VALUE: $85

1977 MONTREAL - Santo Alcala *, Bill Atkinson, Stan Bahnsen *, Tim Blackwell *, Jackie Brown, Gary Carter, Dave Cash, Warren Cromartie, Andre Dawson, Tim Foli *, Barry Foote *, Pepe Frias, Wayne Garrett, Fred Holdsworth *, Mike Jorgensen *, Joe

Kerrigan, Pete Mackanin, Will McEnaney, Sammy Mejias, Jose Morales, Stan Papi, Larry Parrish, Tony Perez, Steve Rogers, Chris Speier *, Don Stanhouse, Jeff Terpko, Wayne Twitchell *, Del Unser, Ellis Valentine, Tom Walker *, Dan Warthen *, Jerry White, Dick Williams (MANAGER)

LESS THAN 10 GAMES: Hal Dues, Gerald Hannahs, Larry Landreth, Dan Schatzeder

NOTES: Dawson (ROY).

KEY SIGNATURES: Perez, Dawson, Carter.

VALUE: $100

ROY = Rookie of the Year

1977 NEW YORK (AL) - Dell Alston, Paul Blair, Chris Chambliss, Ken Clay, Bucky Dent, Ed Figueroa, Ron Guidry, Don Gullett, Fran Healy, Ellie Hendricks, Ken Holtzman, Catfish Hunter, Reggie Jackson, Cliff Johnson *, Sparky Lyle, Billy Martin (MANAGER), Carlos May *, Thurman Munson, Graig Nettles, Gil Patterson, Lou Piniella, Willie Randolph, Mickey Rivers, Fred Stanley, Dick Tidrow, Mike Torrez *, Roy White, Jim Wynn *, George Zeber

LESS THAN 10 GAMES: Dave Bergman, Dock Ellis *, Dave Kingman *, Mickey Klutts, Gene Locklear, Larry McCall, Marty Perez *, Stan Thomas *

NOTES: World Champions! Lyle (CY).

KEY SIGNATURES: Martin, Nettles, Jackson, Munson, Piniella, Guidry, Lyle, Hunter.

VALUE: $325

CY = Cy Young Award winner

1977 NEW YORK (NL) - Bob Apodaca, Rick Baldwin, Bruce Boisclair, Nino Espinosa, Doug Flynn *, Leo Foster, Joe Frazier (MANAGER), Jerry Grote *, Bud Harrelson, Steve Henderson, Ron Hodges, Dave Kingman *, Jerry Koosman, Ed Kranepool, Skip Lockwood, Jon Matlack, Lee Mazzilli, Felix Millan, John Milner, Bobby Myrick, Mike Phillips *, Lenny Randle *, Tom Seaver *, Paul Siebert *, Roy Staiger, John Stearns, Craig Swan, Jackson Todd, Joe Torre (MANAGER), Mike Vail, Bobby Valentine *, Joel Youngblood *, Pat Zachry *

LESS THAN 10 GAMES: Luis Alvarado *, Roy Lee Jackson, Pepe Mangual, Doc Medich *, Dan Norman, Johnny Pacella, Luis Rosado, Ray Sadecki

NOTES: Torre played and managed during the year.

KEY SIGNATURES: Harrelson, Kranepool, Kingman, Grote, Koosman, Seaver.

VALUE: $125

1977 OAKLAND - Matt Alexander, Dick Allen, Tony Armas, Stan Bahnsen *, Doug Bair, Vida Blue, Joe Coleman, Willie Crawford *, Steve Dunning *, Dave Giusti *, Wayne Gross, Tim Hosley, Mike Jorgensen *, Matt Keough *, Bob Lacey, Rick Langford, Larry Lintz, Sheldon Mallory, Jack McKeon (MANAGER), Rich McKinney, Doc Medich *, Larry Murray, Jeff Newman, Jeff Newman, Mike Norris, Billy North, Mitchell Page, Marty Perez *, Rob Picciolo, Manny Sanguillen, Rodney Scott, Jerry Tabb, Pablo Torrealba, Jim Tyrone, Jim Umbarger *, Earl Williams, Mark Williams *, Bobby Winkles (MANAGER)

LESS THAN 10 GAMES: Dock Ellis *, Steve McCatty, Craig Mitchell, Paul Mitchell *, Mike Torrez *

KEY SIGNATURES: Allen, Armas, Blue.

VALUE: $75

1977 PHILADELPHIA - Fred Andrews, Bob Boone, Larry Bowa, Ollie Brown, Warren Brusstar, Steve Carlton, Larry Christenson, Barry Foote *, Gene Garber, Terry Harmon, Richie Hebner, Tommy Hutton, Dane Iorg *, Dave Johnson, Jay Johnstone, Jim Kaat, Randy Lerch, Jim Lonborg, Greg Luzinski, Garry Maddox, Jerry Martin, Bake McBride *, Tim McCarver, Tug McGraw, Danny Ozark (MANAGER), Ron Reed, Mike Schmidt, Ted Sizemore, Bobby Tolan *, Wayne Twitchell *, Tom Underwood *

LESS THAN 10 GAMES: Tim Blackwell *, Mike Buskey, Jim Morrison, Manny Seoane, John Vukovich, Dan Warthen *

NOTES: Carlton (CY).

KEY SIGNATURES: Bowa, Schmidt, Luzinski, Boone, McCarver, Carlton, Kaat.

VALUE: $150

CY = Cy Young Award winner

1977 PITTSBURGH - Dale Berra, John Candelaria, Larry Demery, Miguel Dilone, Duffy Dyer, Mike Easler, Terry Forster, Jim Fregosi *, Phil Garner, Fernandez Gonzalez, Goose Gossage, Jerry Hairston *, Tommy Helms *, Grant Jackson, Odell Jones, Ed Kirkpatrick *, Bruce Kison, Ken Macha, Mario Mendoza, Omar Moreno, Al Oliver, Ed Ott, Dave Parker, Jerry Reuss, Bill Robinson, Jim Rooker, Willie Stargell, Rennie Stennett, Chuck Tanner (MANAGER), Frank Taveras, Kent Tekulve, Bobby Tolan *

LESS THAN 10 GAMES: Mike Edwards, Al Holland, Tim Jones, Dave Pagan *, Ed Whitson

KEY SIGNATURES: Stargell, Parker, Oliver, Gossage, Tekulve.

VALUE: $145

1977 SAN DIEGO - Bill Almon, Tucker Ashford, Vic Bernal, Mike Champion, John D'Acquisto, Al Dark (MANAGER), Bob Davis, Rollie Fingers, Dave Freisleben, Tom Griffin, George Hendrick, Mike Ivie, Randy Jones, Dave Kingman *, John McNamara (MANAGER), Butch Metzger *, Bob Owchinko, Doug Rader *, Merv Rettenmund, Gene Richards, Dave Roberts, Rick Sawyer, Pat Scanlon, Bob Shirley, Dan Spillner, Gary Sutherland, Gene Tenace, Dave Tomlin, Jerry Turner, Bobby Valentine *, Dave Wehrmeister, Dave Winfield

LESS THAN 10 GAMES: Brian Greer, Enzo Hernandez, Luis Melendez, Paul Siebert *, Brent Strom

KEY SIGNATURES: Winfield, Kingman, Fingers.

VALUE: $110

1977 SAN FRANCISCO - Gary Alexander, Joe Altobelli (MANAGER), Rob Andrews, Jim Barr, Jack Clark, Terry Cornutt, John Curtis, Randy Elliott, Darrell Evans, Tim Foli *, Ed Halicki, Vic Harris, Dave Heaverlo, Larry Herndon, Marc Hill, Skip James, Bob Knepper, Gary Lavelle, Johnnie LeMaster, Bill Madlock, Willie McCovey, Lynn McGlothen, Randy Moffitt, John Montefusco, Ken Rudolph *, Mike Sadek, Derrel Thomas, Gary Thomasson, Terry Whitfield, Charlie Williams

LESS THAN 10 GAMES: Tom Heintzelman, Greg Minton, Chris Speier *, Tommy Toms

KEY SIGNATURES: McCovey, Madlock, Clark.

VALUE: $110

1977 SEATTLE - Glenn Abbott, Jose Baez, Juan Bernhardt, Steve Braun, Dave Collins, Larry Cox, Julio Cruz, Luis Delgado, Ray Fosse *, Bob Galasso, Rick Honeycutt, Tom

House *, Darrell Johnson (MANAGER), Rick Jones, Ruppert Jones, Skip Jutze, Mike Kekich, Bill Laxton *, Joe Lis, Carlos Lopez, Dan Meyer, Larry Milbourne, John Montague, Tommy Moore, Dave Pagan *, Dick Pole, Craig Reynolds, Enrique Romo, Diego Segui, Jimmy Sexton, Tommy Smith, Lee Stanton, Bill Stein, Bob Stinson, Stan Thomas *, Gary Wheelock

LESS THAN 10 GAMES: Steve Burke, Greg Erardi, Frank MacCormack, Byron McLaughlin, Tommy McMillan, Doc Medich *, Paul Mitchell *, Kevin Pasley *

NOTES: Team's first year.

VALUE: $150

1977 ST. LOUIS - Mike Anderson, Rick Bosetti, Lou Brock, Clay Carroll *, Hector Cruz, John Denny, Larry Dierker, Jim Dwyer, Rawly Eastwick *, Pete Falcone, Bob Forsch, Roger Freed, Keith Hernandez, Al Hrabosky, Dane Iorg *, Don Kessinger *, Bake McBride *, Butch Metzger *, Jerry Mumphrey, Mike Phillips *, Dave Rader, Vern Rapp (MANAGER), Eric Rasmussen, Ken Reitz, Buddy Schultz, Tony Scott, Ted Simmons, Johnny Sutton, Garry Templeton, Mike Tyson, Tom Underwood *, John Urrea, Joel Youngblood *

LESS THAN 10 GAMES: Benny Ayala, Doug Capilla *, John D'Acquisto *, Jerry DaVanon, Taylor Duncan, Ken Oberkfell, Mike Potter, John Tamargo

KEY SIGNATURES: Hernandez, Brock, Simmons.

VALUE: $100

1977 TEXAS - Doyle Alexander, Sandy Alomar, Len Barker, Lew Beasley, Juan Beniquez, Kurt Bevacqua, Bert Blyleven, Nelson Briles *, Bert Campaneris, Adrian Devine, Johnny Ellis, Dock Ellis *, Bill Fahey, Jim Fregosi *, Tommy Grieve, Mike Hargrove, Toby Harrah, Ken Henderson, Willie Horton *, Billy Hunter (MANAGER), Ed Kirkpatrick *, Darold Knowles, Paul Lindblad, Frank Lucchesi (MANAGER), Mike Marshall *, Jim Mason *, Dave May, Eddie Miller, Roger Moret, Gaylord Perry, Pat Putnam, Lenny Randle *, Connie Ryan (MANAGER), Keith Smith, Eddie Stanky (MANAGER), Jim Sundberg, Claudell Washington, Bump Wills

LESS THAN 10 GAMES: Mike Bacsik, Tommy Boggs, Bobby Cuellar, Gary Gray, Steve Hargan *, Roy Howell *, John Poloni, Jim Umbarger *, Mike Wallace

KEY SIGNATURES: Perry, Blyleven.

VALUE: $85

1977 TORONTO - Alan Ashby, Doug Ault, Bob Bailor, Steve Bowling, Tom Bruno, Jeff Byrd, Rick Cerone, Jim Clancy, Dennis DeBarr, Sam Ewing, Ron Fairly, Pedro Garcia, Jerry Garvin, Chuck Hartenstein, Roy Hartsfield (MANAGER), Roy Howell *, Jesse Jefferson, Jerry Johnson, Dave Lemanczyk, Jim Mason *, Dave McKay, Tom Murphy *, Tim Nordbrook *, Doug Rader *, Phil Roof, John Scott, Bill Singer, Steve Staggs, Hector Torres, Otto Velez, Pete Vuckovich, Ernie Whitt, Mike Willis, Al Woods, Gary Woods

LESS THAN 10 GAMES: Mike Darr, Steve Hargan *

NOTES: Team's first year.

VALUE: $175

1978

1978 New York Yankees

***** = **player was traded**

1978 ATLANTA - Brian Asselstine, Bob Beall, Bruce Benedict, Tommy Boggs, Barry Bonnell, Jeff Burroughs, Rick Camp, Dave Campbell, Darrel Chaney, Bobby Cox (MANAGER), Adrian Devine, Jamie Easterly, Gene Garber *, Cito Gaston *, Rod Gilbreath, Preston Hanna, Bob Horner, Glenn Hubbard, Mickey Mahler, Gary Matthews, Larry McWilliams, Dale Murphy, Phil Niekro, Joe Nolan, Rowland Office, Biff Pocoroba, Pat Rockett, Jerry Royster, Chico Ruiz, Dick Ruthven *, Craig Skok, Buddy Solomon

LESS THAN 10 GAMES: Rob Belloir, Jim Bouton, Mike Davey, Frank LaCorte, Max Leon, Jerry Maddox, Eddie Miller, Tom Paciorek *, Hank Small, Duane Theiss, Larry Whisenton

NOTES: Horner (ROY).

KEY SIGNATURES: Murphy, Horner, Niekro.

VALUE: $90

ROY = **Rookie of the Year**

1978 BALTIMORE - Mike Anderson, Mark Belanger, Nelson Briles, Al Bumbry, Terry Crowley, Rich Dauer, Rick Dempsey, Doug DeCinces, Mike Flanagan, John Flinn, Kiko Garcia, Larry Harlow, Ellie Hendricks, Pat Kelly, Joe Kerrigan, Carlos Lopez, Dennis Martinez, Tippy Martinez, Lee May, Scott McGregor, Andres Mora, Eddie Murray, Jim Palmer, Gary Roenicke, Ken Singleton, Dave Skaggs, Billy Smith, Don Stanhouse, Earl Weaver (MANAGER)

LESS THAN 10 GAMES: Mike Dimmel, Dave Ford, Larry Harlow, Ellie Hendricks, Earl Stephenson, Sammy Stewart, Tim Stoddard

KEY SIGNATURES: Weaver, Murray, Palmer.

VALUE: $135

1978 BOSTON - Bob Bailey, Jack Brohamer, Tom Burgmeier, Rick Burleson, Bill Campbell, Bernie Carbo *, Dick Drago, Frank Duffy, Dennis Eckersley, Dwight Evans, Carlton Fisk, Garry Hancock, Andy Hassler *, Butch Hobson, Fred Kendall, Bill Lee, Fred Lynn, Bob Montgomery, Jerry Remy, Jim Rice, Allen Ripley, George Scott, Bob Stanley, Luis Tiant, Mike Torrez, Jim Wright, Carl Yastrzemski, Don Zimmer (MANAGER)

LESS THAN 10 GAMES: Sam Bowen, Reggie Cleveland *, John LaRose, Bobby Sprowl

NOTES: Rice (MVP).

KEY SIGNATURES: Evans, Lynn, Yastrzemski, Fisk, Rice, Eckersley.

VALUE: $120

MVP = MVP Award winner

1978 CALIFORNIA - Don Aase, Jim Anderson, Don Baylor, Lyman Bostock, Ken Brett, Dave Chalk, Brian Downing, Ron Fairly, Dave Forst, Jim Fregosi (MANAGER), Dave Garcia (MANAGER), Danny Goodwin, Bobby Grich, Tom Griffin, Ike Hampton, Paul Hartzell, Terry Humphrey, Ron Jackson, Chris Knapp, Ken Landreaux, Carney Lansford, Dave LaRoche, Dave Machemer, Dyar Miller, Rick Miller, Rance Mulliniks, Merv Rettenmund, Joe Rudi, Nolan Ryan, Tony Solaita, Frank Tanana

LESS THAN 10 GAMES: Mike Barlow, John Caneira, Al Fitzmorris *

NOTES: Bostock died 9/23/78.

KEY SIGNATURES: Bostock, Ryan.

VALUE: $100

1978 CHICAGO (AL) - Alan Bannister, Francisco Barrios, Kevin Bell, Ron Blomberg, Bobby Bonds *, Thad Bosley, Jim Breazeale, Harry Chappas, Mike Colbern, Henry Cruz, Larry Doby (MANAGER), Mike Eden, Marv Foley, Ralph Garr, Rich Hinton, Lamar Johnson, Don Kessinger, Ken Kravec, Jack Kucek, Lerrin LaGrow, Bob Lemon (MANAGER), Chet Lemon, Bob Molinaro, Junior Moore, Bill Nahorodny, Wayne Nordhagen, Jorge Orta, Mike Proly, Greg Pryor, Ron Schueler, Eric Soderholm, Tom Spencer, Mike Squires, Steve Stone, Pablo Torrealba, Rusty Torres, Claudell Washington *, Jim Willoughby, Wilbur Wood

LESS THAN 10 GAMES: Ross Baumgarten, Britt Burns, Joe Gates, Larry Johnson, Steve Trout, Rich Wortham

KEY SIGNATURES: Bob Lemon.

VALUE: $75

1978 CHICAGO (NL) - Larry Biittner, Tim Blackwell, Bill Buckner, Ray Burris, Gene Clines, Larry Cox, Hector Cruz *, Ivan DeJesus, Herman Franks (MANAGER), Woody Fryman *, Dave Geisel, Greg Gross, Willie Hernandez, Ken Holtzman *, Dave Johnson *, Mick Kelleher, Dave Kingman, Mike Krukow, Denns Lamp, Lynn McGlothen *, Rudy Meoli, Donnie Moore, Bobby Murcer, Steve Ontiveros, Ed Putman, Dave Rader, Rick Reuschel, Paul Reuschel *, Dave Roberts, Rodney Scott, Bruce Sutter, Scott Thompson, Manny Trillo, Mike Vail *, Joe Wallis *, Jerry White *

LESS THAN 10 GAMES: Mike Gordon, Karl Pagel, Mike Sember, Manny Seoane

KEY SIGNATURES: Murcer, Kingman.

VALUE: $75

1978 CINCINNATI - Sparky Anderson (MANAGER), Rick Auerbach, Doug Bair, Johnny Bench, Bill Bonham, Pedro Borbon, Dave Collins, Dave Concepcion, Vic Correll, Dan Driessen, George Foster, Cesar Geronimo, Ken Griffey, Ken Henderson *, Tom Hume, Junior Kennedy, Ray Knight, Mike LaCoss, Mike Lum, Joe Morgan, Paul Moskau, Dale Murray *, Fred Norman, Pete Rose, Manny Sarmiento, Tom Seaver, Champ Summers, Dave Tomlin, Don Werner

LESS THAN 10 GAMES: Doug Capilla, Art DeFreites, Dan Dumoulin, Mike Grace, Ron Oester, Mario Soto, Harry Spillman

KEY SIGNATURES: Anderson, Morgan, Concepcion, Rose, Foster, Bench, Seaver.

VALUE: $145

1978 CLEVELAND - Gary Alexander *, Buddy Bell, Larvell Blanks, Dan Briggs, Wayne Cage, Bernie Carbo *, David Clyde, Ted Cox, Paul Dade, Bo Diaz, Dave Freisleben *, Johnny Grubb *, Ron Hassey, Don Hood, Willie Horton *, Jim Kern, Dennis Kinney *, Duane Kuiper, Rick Manning, Sid Monge, Jim Norris, Mike Paxton, Ron Pruitt, Paul Reuschel *, Horace Speed, Dan Spillner *, Andy Thornton, Jeff Torborg (MANAGER), Mike Vail *, Tom Veryzer, Rick Waits, Rick Wise

LESS THAN 10 GAMES: Al Fitzmorris *, Wayne Garland, Alfredo Griffin, Rick Kreuger, Larry Lintz

KEY SIGNATURES: Bell.

VALUE: $75

1978 DETROIT - Steve Baker, Jack Billingham, Tim Corcoran, Jim Crawford, Steve Dillard, Steve Foucault *, Ed Glynn, John Hiller, Ralph Houk (MANAGER), Steve Kemp, Ron LeFlore, Phil Mankowski, Milt May, Jack Morris, Lance Parrish, Aurelio Rodriguez, Dave Rozema, Jim Slaton, Charlie Spikes, Mickey Stanley, Rusty Staub, Bob Sykes, Jason Thompson, Alan Trammell, Mark Wagner, Lou Whitaker, Milt Wilcox, John Wockenfuss, Kip Young

LESS THAN 10 GAMES: Fernando Arroyo, Sheldon Burnside, Mark Fidrych, Dave Stegman, Bruce Taylor, Dave Tobik

NOTES: Whitaker (ROY).

KEY SIGNATURES: Whitaker, Trammell, Staub, Morris.

VALUE: $125

ROY = Rookie of the Year

1978 HOUSTON - Jesus Alou, Joaquin Andujar, Reggie Baldwin, Floyd Bannister, Dave Bergman, Bruce Bochy, Enos Cabell, Cesar Cedeno, Jose Cruz, Tom Dixon, Keith Drumright, Joe Ferguson *, Mike Fischlin, Ken Forsch, Julio Gonzalez, Ed Herrmann *, Wilbur Howard, Art Howe, Rafael Landestoy, Mark Lemongello, Bo McLaughlin, Roger Metzger *, Joe Niekro, Jim O'Bradovich, Gene Pentz, Terry Puhl, Luis Pujols, J.R. Richard, Vern Ruhle, Joe Sambito, Jimmy Sexton, Bill Virdon (MANAGER), Denny Walling, Bob Watson, Rick Williams, Oscar Zamora

LESS THAN 10 GAMES: Joe Cannon, Jeff Leonard, Frank Riccelli, Dan Warthen

KEY SIGNATURES: Richard.

VALUE: $75

1978 KANSAS CITY - Doug Bird, Steve Braun *, George Brett, Al Cowens, Rich Gale, Larry Gura, Andy Hassler *, Whitey Herzog (MANAGER), Al Hrabosky, Clint Hurdle, Joe Lahoud, Pete LaCock, Dennis Leonard, Randy McGilberry, Hal McRae, Steve Mingori, Amos Otis, Freddie Patek, Marty Pattin, Tom Poquette, Darrell Porter, Jamie Quirk, Paul Splittorff, Jerry Terrell, U.L. Washington, John Wathan, Frank White, Willie Wilson, Joe Zdeb

LESS THAN 10 GAMES: Randy Bass, Steve Busby, Jim Colborn *, Dave Cripe, Steve Foucault *, Jim Gaudet, Art Kusnyer, Bill Paschall, Luis Silverio, George Throop

KEY SIGNATURES: Brett.

VALUE: $150

1978 LOS ANGELES - Dusty Baker, Glenn Burke *, Bobby Castillo, Ron Cey, Vic Davalillo, Joe Ferguson *, Terry Forster, Mike Garman *, Steve Garvey, Jerry Grote, Burt Hooton, Charlie Hough, Tommy John, Lee Lacy, Tom Lasorda (MANAGER), Rudy Law, Davey Lopes, Ted Martinez, Rick Monday, Manny Mota, Billy North *, Johnny Oates, Doug Rau, Lance Rautzhan, Rick Rhoden, Bill Russell, Joe Simpson, Reggie Smith, Don Sutton, Bob Welch, Steve Yeager

LESS THAN 10 GAMES: Pedro Guerrero, Brad Gulden, Gerald Hannahs, Enzo Hernandez, Dennis Lewallyn, Dave Stewart, Rick Stucliffe, Myron White

KEY SIGNATURES: Lasorda, Garvey, Cey, Guerrero, John, Sutton.

VALUE: $215

1978 MILWAUKEE - Jerry Augustine, George Bamberger (MANAGER), Sal Bando, Mike Caldwell, Bill Castro, Cecil Cooper, Dick Davis, Jim Gantner, Larry Hisle, Sixto Lezcano, Buck Martinez, Dave May *, Bob McClure, Paul Molitor, Don Money, Charlie Moore, Tony Muser, Ben Oglivie, Andy Replogle, Eduardo Rodriguez, Lenn Sakata, Lary Sorensen, Randy Stein, Gorman Thomas, Bill Travers, Jim Wohlford, Robin Yount

LESS THAN 10 GAMES: Mark Bomback, Andy Etchebarren, Ed Farmer, Moose Haas, Larry Haney, Tim Johnson *, Willie Mueller, Tim Nordbrook *, Jeff Yurak

KEY SIGNATURES: Molitor, Yount.

VALUE: $100

1978 MINNESOTA - Glenn Adams, Glenn Borgmann, Rod Carew, Rich Chiles, Mike Cubbage, Dave Edwards, Roger Erickson, Dan Ford, Dave Goltz, Jeff Holly, Darrell Jackson, Tom Johnson, Craig Kusick, Mike Marshall, Gene Mauch (MANAGER), Jose Morales, Willie Norwood, Stan Perzanowski, Hosken Powell, Bob Randall, Bombo Rivera, Mac Scarce, Gary Serum, Roy Smalley, Johnny Sutton, Greg Thayer, Paul Thormodsgard, Rob Wilfong, Larry Wolfe, Butch Wynegar, Geoff Zahn

LESS THAN 10 GAMES: Roric Harrison, Dave Johnson, Pete Redfern

KEY SIGNATURES: Carew.

VALUE: $85

1978 MONTREAL - Bill Atkinson, Stan Bahnsen, Gary Carter, Dave Cash, Warren Cromartie, Andre Dawson, Hal Dues, Pepe Frias, Woody Fryman *, Mike Garman *, Wayne

Garrett *, Ross Grimsley, Ed Herrmann *, Tommy Hutton *, Darold Knowles, Rudy May, Sammy Mejias, Stan Papi, Larry Parrish, Tony Perez, Gerry Pirtle, Steve Rogers, Scott Sanderson, Dan Schatzeder, Chris Speier, Wayne Twitchell, Del Unser, Ellis Valentine, Jerry White *, Dick Williams (MANAGER)

LESS THAN 10 GAMES: Jerry Fry, Fred Holdsworth, Bobby James, Randy Miller, David Palmer, Bobby Ramos, Bob Reece

KEY SIGNATURES: Perez, Dawson, Carter.

VALUE: $100

1978 NEW YORK (AL) - Jim Beattie, Paul Blair, Chris Chambliss, Ken Clay, Bucky Dent, Brian Doyle, Ed Figueroa, Damaso Garcia, Goose Gossage, Ron Guidry, Mike Heath, Dick Howser (MANAGER), Catfish Hunter, Reggie Jackson, Cliff Johnson, Jay Johnstone *, Bob Lemon (MANAGER), Sparky Lyle, Billy Martin (MANAGER), Thurman Munson, Graig Nettles, Lou Piniella, Willie Randolph, Mickey Rivers, Jim Spencer, Fred Stanley, Gary Thomasson *, Dick Tidrow, Roy White

LESS THAN 10 GAMES: Dell Alston *, Ron Davis, Rawly Eastwick *, Don Gullett, Fran Healy, Ken Holtzman *, Bob Kammeyer, Mickey Klutts *, Paul Lindblad *, Larry McCall, Andy Messersmith, Dave Rajsich, Domingo Ramos, Denny Sherrill, George Zeber

NOTES: World Champions! Guidry (CY).

KEY SIGNATURES: Martin, Jackson, Lyle, Munson, Guidry, Hunter, Gossage, Lemon, Piniella.

VALUE: $325

CY = Cy Young Award winner

1978 NEW YORK (NL) - Dwight Bernard, Bruce Boisclair, Mike Bruhert, Mardie Cornejo, Nino Espinosa, Sergio Ferrer, Gil Flores, Doug Flynn, Tim Foli, Tommy Grieve, Tom Hausman, Steve Henderson, Ron Hodges, Kevin Kobel, Jerry Koosman, Ed Kranepool, Skip Lockwood, Elliott Maddox, Lee Mazzilli, Butch Metzger, Willie Montanez, Dale Murray *, Bobby Myrick, Dan Norman, Lenny Randle, Paul Siebert, John Stearns, Craig Swan, Joe Torre (MANAGER), Bobby Valentine, Joel Youngblood, Pat Zachry

LESS THAN 10 GAMES: Butch Benton, Juan Berenguer, Ken Henderson *, Roy Lee Jackson, Alex Trevino

KEY SIGNATURES: Kranepool, Koosman.

VALUE: $90

1978 OAKLAND - Mike Adams, Gary Alexander *, Dell Alston *, Tony Armas, Pete Broberg, Glenn Burke *, Rico Carty *, Joe Coleman *, Miguel Dilone, Taylor Duncan, Mike Edwards, Jim Essian, Tito Fuentes, Wayne Gross, Mike Guerrero, Dave Heaverlo, Willie Horton *, Tim Hosley, John Henry Johnson, Matt Keough, Bob Lacey, Rick Langford, Jack McKeon (MANAGER), Dwayne Murphy, Larry Murray, Jeff Newman, Mike Norris, Billy North *, Mitchell Page, Marty Perez, Rob Picciolo, Steve Renko, Dave Revering, Bruce Robinson, Elias Sosa, Steve Staggs, Jerry Tabb, Gary Thomasson *, Joe Wallis *, Bobby Winkles (MANAGER), Alan Wirth, Darrell Woodard

LESS THAN 10 GAMES: Mark Budaska, Tim Conroy, Mickey Klutts, Steve McCatty, Scott Meyer, Craig Minetto, Mike Morgan

KEY SIGNATURES: Armas.

VALUE: $75

1978 PHILADELPHIA - Bob Boone, Larry Bowa, Warren Brusstar, Jose Cardenal, Steve Carlton, Larry Christenson, Rawly Eastwick *, Barry Foote, Gene Garber *, Orlando Gonzalez, Bud Harrelson, Richie Hebner, Dave Johnson *, Jay Johnstone *, Jim Kaat, Randy Lerch, Jim Lonborg, Greg Luzinski, Garry Maddox, Jerry Martin, Bake McBride, Tim McCarver, Tug McGraw, Jim Morrison, Danny Ozark (MANAGER), Ron Reed, Dick Ruthven *, Mike Schmidt, Ted Sizemore, Lonnie Smith

LESS THAN 10 GAMES: Danny Boitano, Todd Cruz, Kerry Dineen, Dan Larson, Pete Mackanin, Keith Moreland, Horacio Pina, Kevin Saucier

KEY SIGNATURES: Schmidt, Luzinski, Boone, Carlton, Kaat.

VALUE: $150

1978 PITTSBURGH - Dale Berra, Jim Bibby, Bert Blyleven, Steve Brye, John Candelaria, Duffy Dyer, Jim Fregosi, Phil Garner, Dave Hamilton *, Grant Jackson, Bruce Kison, Ken Macha, Mario Mendoza, John Milner, Omar Moreno, Ed Ott, Dave Parker, Jerry Reuss, Bill Robinson, Don Robinson, Jim Rooker, Manny Sanguillen, Willie Stargell, Rennie Stennett, Chuck Tanner (MANAGER), Frank Taveras, Kent Tekulve, Ed Whitson

LESS THAN 10 GAMES: Matt Alexander, Dorian Boyland, Clay Carroll, Cito Gaston *, Fernando Gonzalez *, Odell Jones, Al Lois, Dave May *, Will McEnaney, Steve Nicosia

NOTES: Parker (MVP).

KEY SIGNATURES: Stargell, Parker, Blyleven, Candelaria, Tekulve.

VALUE: $145

MVP = MVP Award winner

1978 SAN DIEGO - Bill Almon, Tucker Ashford, Chuck Baker, Jim Beswick, Mike Champion, Roger Craig (MANAGER), John D'Acquisto, Bob Davis, Barry Evans, Rollie Fingers, Dave Freisleben *, Oscar Gamble, Fernando Gonzalez *, George Hendrick *, Randy Jones, Mark Lee, Mickey Lolich, Bob Owchinko, Broderick Perkins, Gaylord Perry, Eric Rasmussen *, Don Reynolds, Gene Richards, Dave Roberts, Bob Shirley, Ozzie Smith, Dan Spillner *, Rick Sweet, Gene Tenace, Derrel Thomas, Jerry Turner, Jim Wilhelm, Dave Winfield

LESS THAN 10 GAMES: Tony Castillo, Juan Eichelberger, Dennis Kinney *, Steve Mura, Dave Wehrmeister, Mark Wiley *

NOTES: Perry (CY).

KEY SIGNATURES: Smith, Winfield, Perry, Fingers.

VALUE: $130

CY = Cy Young Award winner

1978 SAN FRANCISCO - Joe Altobelli (MANAGER), Rob Andrews, Jim Barr, Vida Blue, Jack Clark, Hector Cruz *, John Curtis, Jim Dwyer *, Darrell Evans, Ed Halicki, Vic Harris, Tom Heintzelman, Larry Herndon, Marc Hill, Mike Ivie, Skip James, Bob Knepper, Gary Lavelle, Johnny LeMaster, Bill Madlock, Willie McCovey, Roger Metzger *, Greg Minton, Randy Moffitt, John Montefusco, Mike Sadek, John Tamargo *, Terry Whitfield, Charlie Williams

LESS THAN 10 GAMES: Terry Cornutt, Art Gardner, Dennis Littlejohn, Lynn McGlothen *, Phil Natsu, Ed Plank

KEY SIGNATURES: McCovey, Clark, Blue.

VALUE: $110

1978 SEATTLE - Glenn Abbott, Jose Baez, Charlie Beamon, Juan Bernhardt, Bruce Bochte, Steve Braun *, Steve Burke, Jim Colburn *, Julio Cruz, John Hale, Rick Honeycutt, Tom House, Darrell Johnson (MANAGER), Ruppert Jones, Byron McLaughlin, Dan Meyer, Larry Milbourne, Paul Mitchell, John Montague, Tom Paciorek *, Mike Parrott, Kevin Pasley, Bill Plummer, Dick Pole, Shane Rawley, Craig Reynolds, Leon Roberts, Bob Robertson, Enrique Romo, Lee Stanton, Bill Stein, Bob Stinson, Jim Todd

LESS THAN 10 GAMES: Tom Brown, Rick Jones

VALUE: $75

1978 ST. LOUIS - Ken Boyer (MANAGER), Lou Brock, Tom Bruno, John Denny, Jim Dwyer *, Pete Falcone, Bob Forsch, George Frazier, Roger Freed, Wayne Garrett *, Dave Hamilton *, George Hendrick *, Keith Hernandez, Dane Iorg, Terry Kennedy, Jack Krol (MANAGER), Mark Littell, Aurelio Lopez, Silvio Martinez, Jerry Morales, Jerry Mumphrey, Ken Oberkfell, Mike Phillips, Mike Ramsey, Vern Rapp (MANAGER), Eric Rasmussen *, Ken Reitz, Tony Scott, Buddy Shultz, Ted Simmons, Gary Sutherland, Steve Swisher, Garry Templeton, Roy Thomas, Mike Tyson, John Urrea, Pete Vuckovich

LESS THAN 10 GAMES: Bob Coluccio, Rob Dressler, Jim Lentine, Dan O'Brien, John Tamargo *

KEY SIGNATURES: Boyer, Hernandez, Brock, Simmons.

VALUE: $100

1978 TEXAS - Doyle Alexander, Sandy Alomar, Len Barker, Juan Beniquez, Kurt Bevacqua, Bobby Bonds *, Bert Campaneris, Reggie Cleveland *, Steve Comer, Pat Corrales (MANAGER), Dock Ellis, Johnny Ellis, Gary Gray, Johnny Grubb *, Mike Hargrove, Toby Harrah, Billy Hunter (MANAGER), Ferguson Jenkins, Mike Jorgensen, Paul Lindbald *, John Lowenstein, Jim Mason, Jon Matlack, Doc Medich, Paul Mirabella, Nelson Norman, Al Oliver, Pat Putnam, Jim Sundberg, Bobby Thompson, Jim Umbarger, Claudell Washington *, Bump Wills, Richie Zisk

LESS THAN 10 GAMES: Danny Darwin, Greg Mahlberg, Roger Moret, Billy Sample, LaRue Washington

KEY SIGNATURES: Harrah, Oliver, Jenkins.

VALUE: $80

1978 TORONTO - Alan Ashby, Doug Ault, Bob Bailor, Rick Bosetti, Rico Carty *, Rick Cerone, Jim Clancy, Joe Coleman *, Victor Cruz, Sam Ewing, Jerry Garvin, Luis Gomez, Roy Hartsfield (MANAGER), Willie Horton *, Roy Howell, Tommy Hutton *, Garth Iorg, Jesse Jefferson, Tim Johnson *, Don Kirkwood, Dave Lemanczyk, John Mayberry, Dave McKay, Balor Moore, Tom Murphy, Tom Underwood, Willie Upshaw, Otto Velez, Mike Willis, Al Woods

LESS THAN 10 GAMES: Butch Alberts, Tom Buskey, Brian Milner, Tim Nordbrook *, Dave Wallace, Ernie Whitt, Mark Wiley *, Gary Woods

VALUE: $140

1979

1979 Cincinnati Reds

1979 ATLANTA - Bob Beall, Bruce Benedict, Barry Bonnell, Larry Bradford, Tony Brizzolara, Jeff Burroughs, Darrel Chaney, Bobby Cox (MANAGER), Adrian Devine, Pepe Frias, Gene Garber, Bob Horner, Glenn Hubbard, Mike Lum, Mickey Mahler, Rick Mahler, Gary Matthews, Rick Matula, Joey McLaughlin, Bo McLaughlin *, Larry McWilliams, Eddie Miller, Dale Murphy, Phil Niekro, Joe Nolan, Rowland Office, Biff Pocoroba, Jerry Royster, Craig Skok, Buddy Solomon, Charlie Spikes, Jim Wessinger, Larry Whisenton

LESS THAN 10 GAMES: Brian Asselstine, Tommy Boggs, Jamie Easterly, Preston Hanna, Frank LaCorte *, Mike Macha

KEY SIGNATURES: Murphy, Horner, Niekro.

VALUE: $90

1979 BALTIMORE - Benny Ayala, Mark Belanger, Al Bumbry, Mark Corey, Terry Crowley, Rich Dauer, Rick Dempsey, Doug DeCinces, Mike Flanagan, Kiko Garcia, Larry Harlow *, Pat Kelly, Wayne Krenchicki, John Lowenstein, Dennis Martinez, Tippy Martinez, Lee May, Scott McGregor, Eddie Murray, Jim Palmer, Gary Roenicke, Ken Singleton, Dave Skaggs, Billy Smith, Don Stanhouse, Sammy Stewart, Tim Stoddard, Steve Stone, Earl Weaver (MANAGER)

LESS THAN 10 GAMES: Tom Chism, John Flinn, Dave Ford, Ellie Hendricks, Bob Molinaro, Jeff Rineer

NOTES: Flanagan (CY).

KEY SIGNATURES: Weaver, Murray, Flanagan, Palmer.

VALUE: $200

CY = Cy Young Award winner

1979 BOSTON - Gary Allenson, Jack Brohamer, Tom Burgmeier, Rick Burleson, Bill Campbell, Dick Drago, Jim Dwyer, Dennis Eckersley, Dwight Evans, Joel Finch, Carlton Fisk, Butch Hobson, Fred Lynn, Bob Montgomery, Mike O'Berry, Stan Papi, Tom Poquette *, Chuck Rainey, Jerry Remy, Steve Renko, Jim Rice, Allen Ripley, George Scott *, Ted Sizemore *, Bob Stanley, Mike Torrez, Bob Watson, Larry Wolfe, Jim Wright, Carl Yastrzemski, Don Zimmer (MANAGER)

LESS THAN 10 GAMES: Frank Duffy, Andy Hassler, Win Remmerswaal, John Tudor

KEY SIGNATURES: Lynn, Rice, Fisk, Yastrzemski, Eckersley.

VALUE: $120

1979 CALIFORNIA - Don Aase, Willie Aikens, Jim Anderson, Mike Barlow, Jim Barr, Don Baylor, Ralph Botting, Bert Campaneris *, Rod Carew, Bobby Clark, Mark Clear, Willie Davis, Tom Donohue, Brian Downing, Dan Ford, Jim Fregosi (MANAGER), Dave Frost, Bobby Grich, Larry Harlow *, Chris Knapp, Carney Lansford, Dave LaRoche, Rick Miller, Dyar Miller *, John Montague *, Rance Mulliniks, Orlando Ramirez, Merv Rettenmund, Joe Rudi, Nolan Ryan, Frank Tanana, Dickie Thon

LESS THAN 10 GAMES: Steve Eddy, Bob Ferris, Ralph Garr *, Ike Hampton, Brian Harper, John Harris, Terry Humphrey, Dave Schuler

NOTES: Baylor (MVP).

KEY SIGNATURES: Carew, Lansford, Baylor, Ryan.

VALUE: $145

MVP = MVP Award winner

1979 CHICAGO (AL) - Alan Bannister, Francisco Barrios, Ross Baumgarten, Kevin Bell, Thad Bosley, Harry Chappas, Mike Colbern, Ed Farmer *, Marv Foley, Ralph Garr *, Joe Gates, Rich Hinton *, Guy Hoffman, Fred Howard, Lamar Johnson, Don Kessinger (MANAGER), Ken Kravec, Rusty Kurtz *, Lerrin LaGrow *, Tony LaRussa (MANAGER), Chet Lemon, Milt May *, Junior Moore, Jim Morrison, Bill Nahorodny, Wayne Nordhagen, Jorge Orta, Mike Proly, Greg Pryor, Dewey Robinson, Randy Scarbery, Eric Soderholm *, Mike Squires, Rusty Torres, Steve Trout, Claudell Washington, Rich Wortham

LESS THAN 10 GAMES: Britt Burns, Rich Dotson, Mark Esser, LaMarr Hoyt, Jack Kucek *, Wayne Nordhagen, Gil Rondon, Ron Schueler, Pablo Torrealba

VALUE: $75

1979 CHICAGO (NL) - Joey Amalfitano (MANAGER), Larry Biittner, Tim Blackwell, Bill Buckner, Ray Burris *, Doug Capilla *, Bill Caudill, Gene Clines, Ivan DeJesus, Steve Dillard, Miguel Dilone *, Barry Foote, Herman Franks (MANAGER), Ken Henderson *, Willie Hernandez, Ken Holtzman, Mick Kelleher, Dave Kingman, Mike Krukow, Dennis Lamp, Steve Macko, Jerry Martin, Lynn McGlothen, Sammy Mejias *, Donnie Moore, Bobby Murcer *, Steve Ontiveros, Rick Reuschel, Ted Sizemore *, Bruce Sutter, Scot Thompson, Dick Tidrow *, Mike Vail

LESS THAN 10 GAMES: Steve Davis, Dave Geisel, Bruce Kimm, Karl Pagel, George Riley, Kurt Seibert

NOTES: Sutter (CY).

KEY SIGNATURES: Buckner, Kingman, Sutter.

VALUE: $75

CY = Cy Young Award winner

1979 CINCINNATI - Rick Auerbach, Doug Bair, Johnny Bench, Paul Blair *, Bill

Bonham, Pedro Borbon *, Dave Collins, Dave Concepcion, Vic Correll, Hector Cruz *, Art DeFreitas, Dan Driessen, George Foster, Cesar Geronimo, Ken Griffey, Ken Henderson *, Tom Hume, Junior Kennedy, Ray Knight, Mike LaCoss, John McNamara (MANAGER), Joe Morgan, Paul Moskau, Fred Norman, Frank Pastore, Manny Sarmiento, Tom Seaver, Mario Soto, Harry Spilman, Champ Summers *, Dave Tomlin

LESS THAN 10 GAMES: Doug Capilla *, Charlie Leibrandt, Sammy Mejias *, Ron Oester, Rafael Santo Domingo

KEY SIGNATURES: Morgan, Concepcion, Griffey, Foster, Bench, Seaver.

VALUE: $110

1979 CLEVELAND - Gary Alexander, Dell Alston, Len Barker, Bobby Bonds, Wayne Cage, Ted Cox, Victor Cruz, Paul Dade *, Bo Diaz, Dave Garcia (MANAGER), Wayne Garland, Mike Hargrove *, Toby Harrah, Ron Hassey, Don Hood *, Cliff Johnson *, Duane Kuiper, Rick Manning, Sid Monge, Jim Norris, Mike Paxton, Ron Pruitt, Paul Reuschel, Dave Rosello, Horace Speed, Dan Spillner, Andy Thornton, Jeff Torborg (MANAGER), Tom Veryzer, Rick Waits, Eric Wilkins, Rick Wise

LESS THAN 10 GAMES: Larry Andersen, David Clyde, Sandy Wihtol

KEY SIGNATURES: Harrah.

VALUE: $75

1979 DETROIT - Sparky Anderson (MANAGER), Steve Baker, Jack Billingham, Tom Brookens, Sheldon Burnside, Mike Chris, Tim Corcoran, Kirk Gibson, Al Greene, John Hiller, Lynn Jones, Steve Kemp, Ron LeFlore, Aurelio Lopez, Dave Machemer, Phil Mankowski, Jerry Morales, Jack Morris, Les Moss (MANAGER), Lance Parrish, Rickey Peters, Dan Petry, Ed Putman, Bruce Robbins, Aurelio Rodriguez, Dave Rozema, Rusty Staub *, Dave Stegman, Champ Summers *, Bruce Taylor, Jason Thompson, Dave Tobik, Alan Trammell, Pat Underwood, Mark Wagner, Lou Whitaker, Milt Wilcox, John Wockenfuss, Kip Young

LESS THAN 10 GAMES: Fernando Arroyo, Mark Fidrych, Dan Gonzales, Milt May *

KEY SIGNATURES: Anderson, Whitaker, Trammell, Staub, Morris.

VALUE: $125

1979 HOUSTON - Jesus Alou, Joaquin Andujar, Alan Ashby, Reggie Baldwin, Dave Bergman, Bruce Bochy, Enos Cabell, Cesar Cedeno, Jose Cruz, Tom Dixon, Ken Forsch, Julio Gonzalez, Danny Heep, Art Howe, Pete Ladd, Rafael Landestoy, Frank LaCorte *, Jeff Leonard, Bo McLaughlin *, Joe Niekro, Randy Niemann, Terry Puhl, Luis Pujols, Craig Reynolds, Frank Riccelli, J.R. Richard, Bert Roberge, Vern Ruhle, Joe Sambito, Jimmy Sexton, George Throop *, Bill Virdon (MANAGER), Denny Walling, Bob Watson *, Rick Williams

LESS THAN 10 GAMES: Alan Knicely, Mike Mendoza, Gordy Pladson, Bobby Sprowl, Tom Wiedenbauer, Gary Wilson

KEY SIGNATURES: Richard.

VALUE: $90

1979 KANSAS CITY - Steve Braun, George Brett, Steve Busby, Craig Chamberlain, Al Cowens, Todd Cruz, Rich Gale, Larry Gura, Whitey Herzog (MANAGER), Al Hrabosky, Clint Hurdle, Pete LaCock, Dennis Leonard, Renie Martin, Hal McRae, Steve Mingori, Jim Nettles, Amos Otis, Freddie Patek, Marty Pattin, Tom Poquette *, Darrell

Porter, Jamie Quirk, Dan Quisenberry, Eduardo Rodriguez, George Scott *, Paul Splittorff, Jerry Terrell, U.L. Washington, John Wathan, Frank White, Willie Wilson, Joe Zdeb

LESS THAN 10 GAMES: German Barranca, Gary Christenson, Craig Eaton, Jim Gaudet, Bill Paschall, Jerry Terrell, George Throop *

KEY SIGNATURES: Brett, Quisenberry.

VALUE: $125

1979 LOS ANGELES - Dusty Baker, Joe Beckwith, Ken Brett *, Bobby Castillo, Ron Cey, Vic Davalillo, Joe Ferguson, Terry Forster, Steve Garvey, Pedro Guerrero, Mickey Hatcher, Burt Hooton, Charlie Hough, Von Joshua, Tom Lasorda (MANAGER), Lerrin LaGrow *, Davey Lopes, Ted Martinez, Andy Messersmith, Rick Monday, Manny Mota, Johnny Oates, Dave Patterson, Doug Rau, Lance Rautzhan *, Jerry Reuss, Bill Russell, Reggie Smith, Rick Sutcliffe, Don Sutton, Derrel Thomas, Gary Thomasson, Bob Welch, Steve Yeager

LESS THAN 10 GAMES: Gerald Hannahs, Dennis Lewallyn

NOTES: Sutcliffe (ROY).

KEY SIGNATURES: Lasorda, Garvey, Cey, Guerrero, Sutcliffe, Sutton.

VALUE: $125

1979 MILWAUKEE - Jerry Augustine, George Bamberger (MANAGER), Sal Bando, Mike Caldwell, Bill Castro, Reggie Cleveland, Cecil Cooper, Dick Davis, Ray Fosse, Bob Galasso, Jim Gantner, Moose Haas, Larry Hisle, Sixto Lezcano, Buck Martinez, Bob McClure, Paul Mitchell *, Paul Molitor, Don Money, Charlie Moore, Ben Oglivie, Jim Slaton, Lary Sorensen, Gorman Thomas, Bill Travers, Jim Wohlford, Robin Yount

LESS THAN 10 GAMES: Danny Boitano, Jim Gantner, Tim Nordbrook, Lance Rautzhan *, Andy Replogle, Lenn Sakata

KEY SIGNATURES: Molitor, Yount.

VALUE: $100

1979 MINNESOTA - Glenn Adams, Mike Bacsik, Glenn Borgmann, John Castino, Mike Cubbage, Dave Edwards, Roger Erickson, Dave Goltz, Danny Goodwin, Paul Hartzell, Darrell Jackson, Ron Jackson, Jerry Koosman, Craig Kusick *, Ken Landreaux, Mike Marshall, Gene Mauch (MANAGER), Jose Morales, Willie Norwood, Hosken Powell, Bob Randall, Pete Redfern, Bombo Rivera, Gary Serum, Roy Smalley, Rick Sofield, Rob Wilforg, Butch Wynegar, Geoff Zahn

LESS THAN 10 GAMES: Ken Brett *, Terry Felton, Dan Graham, Jeff Holly, Kevin Stanfield, Paul Thormodsgard, Jesus Vega, Gary Ward

NOTES: Castino (ROY).

KEY SIGNATURES: Castino, Koosman.

VALUE: $75

ROY = Rookie of the Year

1979 MONTREAL - Bill Atkinson, Stan Bahnsen, Tony Bernazard, Gary Carter, Dave Cash, Warren Cromartie, Andre Dawson, Duffy Dyer, Woody Fryman, Ross Grimsley,

Tommy Hutton, Bill Lee, Ken Macha, Jim Mason, Rudy May, David Palmer, Larry Parrish, Tony Perez, Steve Rogers, Scott Sanderson, Dan Schatzeder, Rodney Scott, Tony Solaita *, Elias Sosa, Chris Speier, Rusty Staub *, John Tamargo *, Ellis Valentine, Jerry White, Dick Williams (MANAGER)

LESS THAN 10 GAMES: Randy Bass, Bill Gullickson, Bob James, Dale Murray *, Tim Raines

KEY SIGNATURES: Perez, Dawson, Carter, Staub, Raines.

VALUE: $125

1979 NEW YORK (AL) - Jim Beattie, Juan Beniquez, Bobby Brown *, Ray Burris *, Chris Chambliss, Ron Davis, Bucky Dent, Brian Doyle, Ed Figueroa, Oscar Gamble *, Damaso Garcia, Goose Gossage, Mike Griffin, Ron Guidry, Brad Gulden, Don Hood *, Catfish Hunter, Reggie Jackson, Tommy John, Cliff Johnson *, Jay Johnstone *, Darryl Jones, Jim Kaat *, Bob Lemon (MANAGER), Billy Martin (MANAGER), Paul Mirabella, Thurman Munson, Bobby Murcer *, Jerry Narron, Graig Nettles, Lou Piniella, Lenny Randle, Willie Randolph, Mickey Rivers *, George Scott *, Jim Spencer, Fred Stanley, Luis Tiant, Dick Tidrow *, Roy White

LESS THAN 10 GAMES: Rick Anderson, Paul Blair *, Ken Clay, Bob Kammeyer, Dave Righetti, Bruce Robinson, Roger Slagle, Roy Staiger, Dennis Werth

NOTES: Mundson died 8/2/79.

KEY SIGNATURES: Martin, Nettles, Jackson, Munson, Murcer, John, Guidry, Tiant, Gossage, Kaat, Hunter.

VALUE: $210

1979 NEW YORK (NL) - Neil Allen, Dwight Bernard, Bruce Boisclair, Jose Cardenal *, Kelvin Chapman, Dock Ellis *, Pete Falcone, Sergio Ferrer, Gil Flores, Doug Flynn, Ed Glynn, Andy Hassler *, Tom Hausman, Richie Hebner, Steve Henderson, Ron Hodges, Kevin Kobel, Ed Kranepool, Skip Lockwood, Elliott Maddox, Lee Mazzilli, Willie Montanez *, Dan Norman, Jesse Orosco, Jeff Reardon, Mike Scott, John Stearns, Craig Swan, Frank Taveras *, Joe Torre (MANAGER), Alex Trevino, Wayne Twitchell, Joel Youngblood

LESS THAN 10 GAMES: Juan Berenguer, Ray Burris *, Tim Foli *, Roy Lee Jackson, Dale Murray, Johnny Pacella, Pat Zachry

KEY SIGNATURES: Kranepool.

VALUE: $90

1979 OAKLAND - Tony Armas, Derek Bryant, Glenn Burke, Dave Chalk *, Miguel Dilone *, Mike Edwards, Jim Essian, Wayne Gross, Mike Guerrero, Dave Hamilton, Mike Heath, Dave Heaverlo, Rickey Henderson, John Henry Johnson *, Matt Keough, Brian Kingman, Mickey Klutts *, Bob Lacey, Rick Langford, Jim Marshall (MANAGER), Steve McCatty, Craig Minetto, Mike Morgan, Dwayne Murphy, Larry Murray, Jeff Newman, Mike Norris, Mitchell Page, Rob Picciolo, Milt Ramirez, Dave Revering, Jim Todd, Joe Wallis

LESS THAN 10 GAMES: Alan Wirth
KEY SIGNATURES: Armas, Henderson.

VALUE: $90

1979 PHILADELPHIA - Mike Anderson, Ramon Aviles, Doug Bird, Bob Boone, Larry Bowa, Warren Brusstar, Jose Cardenal *, Steve Carlton, Larry Christenson, Rawly Eastwick, Nino Espinosa, Dallas Green (MANAGER), Greg Gross, Bud Harrelson, Randy Lerch, Greg Luzinski, Pete Mackanin, Garry Maddox, Bake McBride, Tim McCarver, Tug McGraw, Rudy Meoli, Keith Moreland, Dickie Noles, Danny Ozark (MANAGER), John Poff, Dave Rader, Ron Reed, Pete Rose, Dick Ruthven, Kevin Saucier, Mike Schmidt, Lonnie Smith, Manny Trillo, Del Unser, John Vukovich
LESS THAN 10 GAMES: Jim Kaat *, Jack Kucek *, Dan Larson, Jim Lonborg
KEY SIGNATURES: Rose, Trillo, Bowa, Schmidt, Luzinski, Boone, Carlton, Kaat.

VALUE: $140

1979 PITTSBURGH - Matt Alexander, Dale Berra, Jim Bibby, Bert Blyleven, John Candelaria, Joe Coleman *, Mike Easler, Tim Foli *, Phil Garner, Grant Jackson, Bruce Kison, Lee Lacy, Al Lois, Bill Madlock *, John Milner, Omar Moreno, Steve Nicosia, Ed Ott, Dave Parker, Dave Roberts *, Bill Robinson, Don Robinson, Enrique Romo, Jim Rooker, Manny Sanguillen, Willie Stargell, Rennie Stennett, Chuck Tanner (MANAGER), Frank Taveras *, Kent Tekulve, Ed Whitson *
LESS THAN 10 GAMES: Dorian Boyland, Dock Ellis *, Gary Hargis, Rick Rhoden
NOTES: World Champions! Stargell (MVP).
KEY SIGNATURES: Stargell, Madlock, Parker, Candelaria, Blyleven, Tekulve.

VALUE: $300

MVP = MVP Award winner

1979 SAN DIEGO - Bill Almon, Kurt Bevacqua, Dan Briggs, Roger Craig (MANAGER), John D'Acquisto, Paul Dade *, Barry Evans, Bill Fahey, Rollie Fingers, Tim Flannery, Fernando Gonzalez, Mike Hargrove *, Jay Johnstone *, Randy Jones, Fred Kendall, Dennis Kinney, Mark Lee, Mickey Lolich, Steve Mura, Bob Owchinko, Broderick Perkins, Gaylord Perry, Eric Rasmussen, Don Reynolds, Gene Richards, Bob Shirley, Ozzie Smith, Gene Tenace, Bobby Tolan, Jerry Turner, Jim Wilhelm, Dave Winfield
LESS THAN 10 GAMES: Juan Eichelberger, Brian Greer, Sam Perlozzo, Tom Tellmann
KEY SIGNATURES: Smith, Winfield, Perry, Fingers, Lolich.

VALUE: $130

1979 SAN FRANCISCO - Joe Altobelli (MANAGER), Rob Andrews, Vida Blue, Pedro Borbon *, Dave Bristol (MANAGER), Jack Clark, Hector Cruz *, John Curtis, Darrell Evans, Tom Griffin, Ed Halicki, Larry Herndon, Marc Hill, Mike Ivie, Greg Johnston, Bob Knepper, Gary Lavelle, Johnny LeMaster, Dennis Littlejohn, Bill Madlock *, Willie McCovey, Roger Metzger, Greg Minton, Randy Moffitt, John Montefusco, Phil Natsu, Billy North, Dave Roberts *, Mike Sadek, Joe Strain, John Tamargo *, Max Venable, Terry Whitfield, Ed Whitson *
LESS THAN 10 GAMES: Joe Coleman *, Al Holland, Bob Kearney, Ed Plank
KEY SIGNATURES: McCovey, Clark, Madlock, Blue.

VALUE: $110

1979 SEATTLE - Glenn Abbott, Floyd Bannister, Charlie Beamon, Bruce Bochte, Larry Cox, Rodney Craig, Julio Cruz, Rob Dressler, John Hale, Rich Hinton *, Rick Honeycutt, Willie Horton, Darrell Johnson (MANAGER), Odell Jones, Ruppert Jones, Byron McLaughlin, Mario Mendoza, Dan Meyer, Larry Milbourne, Paul Mitchell *, John Montague *, Tom Paciorek, Mike Parrott, Shane Rawley, Leon Roberts, Joe Simpson, Bill Stein, Randy Stein, Bob Stinson, Bobby Valentine

LESS THAN 10 GAMES: Juan Bernhardt, Roy Branch, Joe Decker, Jim Lewis, Wayne Twitchell *, Rafael Vasquez

VALUE: $75

1979 ST. LOUIS - Ken Boyer (MANAGER), Lou Brock, Tom Bruno, Bernie Carbo, John Denny, Bob Forsch, George Frazier, Roger Freed, John Fulgham, George Hendrick, Keith Hernandez, Tommy Herr, Dane Iorg, Terry Kennedy, Darold Knowles, Jim Lentine, Mark Littell, Silvio Martinez, Will McEnaney, Jerry Mumphrey, Ken Oberkfell, Mike Phillips, Ken Reitz, Buddy Schultz, Tony Scott, Ted Simmons, Steve Swisher, Bob Sykes, Garry Templeton, Roy Thomas, Mike Tyson, Pete Vuckovich

LESS THAN 10 GAMES: Mike Dimmel, Tommy Grieve, Dan O'Brien, Kim Seaman, Keith Smith, John Urrea

NOTES: Hernandez (MVP).

KEY SIGNATURES: Boyer, Hernandez, Brock, Simmons.

VALUE: $100

MVP = MVP Award winner

1979 TEXAS - Doyle Alexander, Buddy Bell, Larvell Blanks, Steve Comer, Pat Corrales (MANAGER), Danny Darwin, Johnny Ellis, Doc Ellis *, Ed Farmer *, Oscar Gamble *, Gary Gray, Johnny Grubb, Ferguson Jenkins, John Henry Johnson *, Mike Jorgensen, Jim Kern, Sparky Lyle, Jon Matlack, Doc Medich, Willie Montanez *, Nelson Norman, Al Oliver, Pat Putnam, Dave Raisich, Mickey Rivers *, Dave Roberts, Billy Sample, Eric Soderholm *, Jim Sundberg, LaRue Washington, Bump Wills, Richie Zisk

LESS THAN 10 GAMES: Brian Allard, Bob Babcock, Bert Campaneris *, Dave Chalk *, Jerry Gleaton, Gary Holle, Greg Mahlberg, Larry McCall

KEY SIGNATURES: Bell, Oliver, Jenkins, Lyle.

VALUE: $80

1979 TORONTO - Danny Ainge, Bob Bailor, Rick Bosetti, Tom Buskey, Joe Cannon, Rico Carty, Rick Cerone, Jim Clancy, Bob Davis, Dave Freisleben, Luis Gomez, Alfredo Griffin, Roy Hartsfield (MANAGER), Roy Howell, Phil Huffman, Jesse Jefferson, Tim Johnson, Craig Kusick *, Dave Lemanczyk, Mark Lemongello, John Mayberry, Dave McKay, Dyar Miller *, Balor Moore, Tom Murphy, Bob Robertson, Tony Solaita *, Dave Stieb, Jackson Todd, Tom Underwood, Otto Velez, Ted Wilborn, Mike Willis, Al Woods

LESS THAN 10 GAMES: Bobby Brown *, Butch Edge, Jerry Garvin, Steve Grilli, Pedro Hernandez, Craig Kusick, Steve Luebber

NOTES: Griffin (ROY).

KEY SIGNATURES: Griffin, Stieb.

VALUE: $75

ROY = Rookie of the Year

1980

1980 Kansas City Royals

1980 ATLANTA - Doyle Alexander, Brian Asselstine, Bruce Benedict, Larvell Blanks, Tommy Boggs, Larry Bradford, Jeff Burroughs, Rick Camp, Chris Chamblisss, Gary Cooper, Bobby Cox (MANAGER), Gene Garber, Luis Gomez, Preston Hanna, Terry Harper, Bob Horner, Al Hrabosky, Glenn Hubbard, Mike Lum, Gary Matthews, Rick Matula, Larry McWilliams, Eddie Miller, Dale Murphy, Bill Nahorodny, Phil Niekro, Joe Nolan *, Biff Pocoroba, Rafael Ramirez, Jerry Royster, Chico Ruiz, Charlie Spikes

LESS THAN 10 GAMES: Rick Mahler

KEY SIGNATURES: Horner, Murphy, Niekro.

VALUE: $90

1980 BALTIMORE - Benny Ayala, Mark Belanger, Al Bumbry, Mark Corey, Terry Crowley, Rich Dauer, Rick Dempsey, Doug DeCinces, Mike Flanagan, Dave Ford, Kiko Garcia, Dan Graham, Pat Kelly, Wayne Krenchicki, John Lowenstein, Dennis Martinez, Tippy Martinez, Lee May, Scott McGregor, Eddie Murray, Jim Palmer, Gary Roenicke, Lenn Sakata, Ken Singleton, Sammy Stewart, Tim Stoddard, Steve Stone, Earl Weaver (MANAGER)

LESS THAN 10 GAMES: Mike Boddicker, Bob Bonner, Paul Hartzell, Drungo Hazewood, Joe Kerigan, Floyd Rayford, Dave Skaggs

NOTES: Stone (CY).

KEY SIGNATURES: Weaver, Murray, Stone, Palmer.

VALUE: $125

CY = Cy Young Award winner

1980 BOSTON - Gary Allenson, Jack Brohamer *, Tom Burgmeier, Rick Burleson, Bill Campbell, Dick Drago, Jim Dwyer, Dennis Eckersley, Dwight Evans, Carlton Fisk, Garry Hancock, Butch Hobson, Glenn Hoffman, Bruce Hurst, Skip Lockwood, Fred Lynn, Keith MacWhorter, Reid Nichols, Tony Perez, Johnny Pesky (MANAGER), Dave Rader, Chuck Rainey, Win Remmerswaal, Jerry Remy, Steve Renko, Jim Rice, Bob Stanley, Dave Stapleton, Mike Torrez, John Tudor, Chico Walker, Larry Wolfe, Carl Yastrzemski, Don Zimmer (MANAGER)

LESS THAN 10 GAMES: Luis Aponte, Jack Billingham *, Sam Bowen, Steve Crawford, Rich Gedman, Bob Ojeda, Stan Papi *, Ted Sizemore, Julio Valdez

KEY SIGNATURES: Perez, Evans, Lynn, Rice, Fisk, Yastrzemski, Eckersley.

VALUE: $150

1980 CALIFORNIA - Don Aase, Jim Barr, Don Baylor, Bert Campaneris, Rod Carew, Bobby Clark, Mark Clear, Stan Cliburn, Al Cowens *, Todd Cruz *, Tom Donohue, Brian Downing, Dan Ford, Jim Fregosi (MANAGER), Dave Frost, Ralph Garr, Bobby Grich, Ed Halicki *, Larry Harlow, John Harris, Andy Hassler *, Bruce Kison, Chris Knapp, Gil Kubski, Carney Lansford, Dave LaRoche, Dave Lemanczyk *, Freddie Martinez, Rick Miller, John Montague, Freddie Patek, Joe Rudi, Dave Skaggs *, Frank Tanana, Jason Thompson *, Dickie Thon, Dan Whitmer

LESS THAN 10 GAMES: Ralph Botting, Jim Dorsey, Bob Ferris, Merv Rettenmund, Dave Schuler

KEY SIGNATURES: Carew, Lansford.

VALUE: $75

1980 CHICAGO (AL) - Harold Baines, Alan Bannister *, Ross Baumgarten, Kevin Bell, Glenn Borgmann, Thad Bosley, Britt Burns, Harry Chappas, Todd Cruz *, Rich Dotson, Ed Farmer, Marv Foley, Guy Hoffman, LaMarr Hoyt, Lamar Johnson, Randy Johnson, Bruce Kimm, Ken Kravec, Rusty Kuntz, Tony LaRussa (MANAGER), Chet Lemon, Bob Molinero, Junior Moore, Jim Morrison, Fran Mullins, Wayne Nordhagen, Mike Proly, Ron Pruitt *, Greg Pryor, Dewey Robinson, Randy Scarbery, Rick Seilheimer, Mike Squires, Leo Sutherland, Steve Trout, Claudell Washington *, Rich Wortham

LESS THAN 10 GAMES: Francisco Barrios, Nardi Contreras, Minnie Minoso

KEY SIGNATURES: Baines.

VALUE: $75

1980 CHICAGO (NL) - Joey Amalfitano (MANAGER), Larry Bittner, Tim Blackwell, Bill Buckner, Doug Capilla, Bill Caudill, Ivan DeJesus, Steve Dillard, Jesus Figueroa, Barry Foote, Preston Gomez (MANAGER), Ken Henderson, Willie Hernandez, Cliff Johnson *, Mike Kelleher, Dave Kingman, Mike Krukow, Dennis Lamp, Carlos Lezcano, Jerry Martin, Lynn McGlothen, Mike O'Berry, Steve Ontiveros, Lenny Randle, Rick Reuschel, George Riley, Lee Smith, Bruce Sutter, Scot Thompson, Dick Tidrow, Jim Tracy, Mike Tyson, Mike Vail

LESS THAN 10 GAMES: Bill Hayes, Steve Macko, Randy Martz

KEY SIGNATURES: Buckner, Kingman.

VALUE: $75

1980 CINCINNATI - Rick Auerbach *, Doug Bair, Johnny Bench, Dave Collins, Dave

Concepcion, Hector Cruz, Dan Driessen, George Foster, Cesar Geronimo, Ken Griffey, Paul Householder, Tom Hume, Junior Kennedy, Ray Knight, Mike LaCoss, Charlie Leibrandt, John McNamara (MANAGER), Sammy Mejias, Paul Moskau, Joe Nolan *, Ron Oester, Frank Pastore, Joe Price, Tom Seaver, Mario Soto, Harry Spilman, Dave Tomlin, Don Werner

LESS THAN 10 GAMES: Bruce Berenyi, Bill Bonham, Sheldon Burnside, Geoff Combe, Vic Correll, Jay Howell, Eddie Milner

KEY SIGNATURES: Concepcion, Griffey, Foster, Bench, Seaver.

VALUE: $90

1980 CLEVELAND - Gary Alexander, Del Alston, Alan Bannister *, Len Barker, Jack Brohamer *, Joe Charboneau, Victor Cruz, John Denny, Bo Diaz, Miguel Dilone, Jerry Dybzinski, Dave Garcia (MANAGER), Wayne Garland, Gary Grey, Ross Grimsley *, Mike Hargrove, Toby Harrah, Ron Hassey, Cliff Johnson *, Duane Kuiper, Rick Manning, Sid Monge, Jorge Orta, Bob Owchinko, Ron Pruitt *, Dave Rosello, Dan Spillner, Mike Stanton, Tom Veryzer, Rick Waits, Sandy Wihtol

LESS THAN 10 GAMES: Don Collins, Andres Moran, Mike Paxton

NOTES: Charboneau (ROY)

KEY SIGNATURES: Harrah, Charboneau.

VALUE: $80

ROY = Rookie of the Year

1980 DETROIT - Sparky Anderson (MANAGER), Tom Brookens, Tim Corcoran, Al Cowens *, Duffy Dyer, Kirk Gibson, Richie Hebner, John Hiller, Lynn Jones, Steve Kemp, Jim Lentine *, Aurelio Lopez, Jack Morris, Stan Papi *, Lance Parrish, Rickey Peters, Dan Petry, Bruce Robbins, Dave Rozema, Dan Schatzeder, Dave Stegman, Champ Summers, Jason Thompson *, Dave Tobik, Alan Trammell, Pat Underwood, Mark Wagner, Roger Weaver, Lou Whitaker, Milt Wilcox, John Wockenfuss

LESS THAN 10 GAMES: Jack Billingham *, Mark Fidrych, Dan Gonzales, Jerry Ujdur

KEY SIGNATURES: Anderson, Whitaker, Trammell, Gibson, Morris.

VALUE: $125

1980 HOUSTON - Joaquin Andujar, Alan Ashby, Dave Bergman, Bruce Bochy, Enos Cabell, Cesar Cedeno, Jose Cruz, Ken Forsch, Julio Gonzalez, Danny Heep, Art Howe, Rafael Landestoy, Frank LaCorte, Jeff Leonard, Joe Morgan, Randy Neimann, Joe Niekro, Gordy Pladson, Terry Puhl, Luis Pujols, Craig Reynolds, J.R. Richard, Bert Roberge, Vern Ruhle, Nolan Ryan, Joe Sambito, Dave Smith, Bill Virdon (MANAGER), Denny Walling, Gary Woods

LESS THAN 10 GAMES: Mike Fischlin, Alan Knicely, Scott Loucks, Bobby Sprowl

NOTES: Richard suffered a stroke during the season.

KEY SIGNATURES: Morgan, Ryan.

VALUE: $145

1980 KANSAS CITY - Willie Aikens, Steve Braun *, George Brett, Steve Busby, Jose Cardenal *, Dave Chalk, Gary Christenson, Onix Concepcion, Bobby Detherage, Rawly Eastwick, Jim Frey (MANAGER), Rich Gale, Larry Gura, Clint Hurdle, Pete LaCock, Dennis Leonard, Renie Martin, Hal McRae, Rance Mulliniks, Amos Otis, Marty Pattin,

Darrell Porter, Jamie Quirk, Dan Quisenberry, Paul Splittorff, Jerry Terrell, Rusty Torres, Jeff Twitty, U.L. Washington, John Wathan, Frank White, Willie Wilson

LESS THAN 10 GAMES: German Barranca, Ken Brett, Manny Castillo, Craig Chamberlain, Mike Jones, Ken Phelps, Jerry Terrell

NOTES: Brett (MVP).

KEY SIGNATURES: Brett, Quisenberry.

VALUE: $215

MVP = MVP Award winner

1980 LOS ANGELES - Dusty Baker, Joe Beckwith, Bobby Castillo, Ron Cey, Joe Ferguson, Pepe Frias *, Steve Garvey, Dave Goltz, Pedro Guerrero, Mickey Hatcher, Burt Hooton, Charlie Hough *, Steve Howe, Jay Johnstone, Rudy Law, Tom LaSorda (MANAGER), Davey Lopes, Rick Monday, Jack Perconte, Doug Rau, Jerry Reuss, Bill Russell, Mike Scioscia, Reggie Smith, Don Stanhouse, Rick Sutcliffe, Don Sutton, Derrel Thomas, Gary Thomasson, Bob Welch, Steve Yeager

LESS THAN 10 GAMES: Vic Davalillo, Terry Forster, Bobby Mitchell, Manny Mota, Fernando Valenzuela, Gary Weiss

NOTES: Howe (ROY).

KEY SIGNATURES: Lasorda, Garvey, Guerrero, Welch, Sutton, Howe, Valenzuela.

VALUE: $125

ROY = Rookie of the Year

1980 MILWAUKEE - Jerry Augustine, George Bamberger (MANAGER), Sal Bando, Danny Boitano, Mark Brouhard, Mike Caldwell, Bill Castro, Reggie Cleveland, Cecil Cooper, Dick Davis, John Flinn, Jim Gantner, Moose Haas, Vic Harris, Larry Hisle, Sixto Lezcano, Buck Martinez, Bob McClure, Paul Mitchell, Paul Molitor, Don Money, Charlie Moore, Ben Oglivie, John Poff, Bob Rodgers (MANAGER), Ed Romero, Lary Sorensen, Gorman Thomas, Bill Travers, Ned Yost, Robin Yount

LESS THAN 10 GAMES: Fred Holdsworth, Buster Keeton, Dave LaPoint, Jim Slaton

KEY SIGNATURES: Molitor, Yount.

VALUE: $100

1980 MINNESOTA - Glenn Adams, Fernando Arroyo, Mike Bacsik, Sal Butera, John Castino, Doug Corbett, Mike Cubbage, Dave Edwards, Roger Erickson, Danny Goodwin, Johnny Goryl (MANAGER), Darrell Jackson, Ron Jackson, Greg Johnston, Mike Kinnunen, Jerry Koosman, Ken Landreaux, Pete Mackanin, Mike Marshall, Gene Mauch (MANAGER), Jose Morales, Willie Norwood, Hosken Powell, Pete Redfern, Bombo Rivera, Roy Smalley, Rick Sofield, Jesus Vega, John Verhoeven, Gary Ward, Rob Wilfong, Al Williams, Butch Wynegar, Geoff Zahn

LESS THAN 10 GAMES: Lenny Faedo, Terry Felton, Bob Randall, Bob Veselic

KEY SIGNATURES: Koosman.

VALUE: $75

1980 MONTREAL - Bill Almon *, Stan Bahnsen, Tony Bernazard, Gary Carter, Warren Cromartie, John D'Acquisto *, Andre Dawson, Woodie Fryman, Ross Grimsley *, Bill Gullickson, Tommy Hutton, Charlie Lea, Bill Lee, Ron LeFlore, Ken Macha, Brad Mills, Willie Montanez *, Dale Murray, Fred Norman, Rowland Office, David Palmer, Larry

Parrish, Bob Pate, Tim Raines, Bobby Ramos, Steve Rogers, Scott Sanderson, Rodney Scott, Elias Sosa, Chris Speier, John Tamargo, Ellis Valentine, Jerry White, Dick Williams (MANAGER)

LESS THAN 10 GAMES: Hal Dues, Tommy Hutton, Jerry Manuel, Steve Ratzer, Tim Wallach

KEY SIGNATURES: Dawson, Carter, Raines.

VALUE: $125

1980 NEW YORK (AL) - Doug Bird, Paul Blair, Brian Boyle, Bobby Brown, Rick Cerone, Ron Davis, Bucky Dent, Ed Figueroa *, Oscar Gamble, Goose Gossage, Mike Griffin, Ron Guidry, Dick Howser (MANAGER), Reggie Jackson, Tommy John, Ruppert Jones, Joe Lefebvre, Tim Lollar, Rudy May, Bobby Murcer, Graig Nettles, Johnny Oates, Gaylord Perry *, Lou Piniella, Willie Randolph, Aurelio Rodriguez, Eric Soderholm, Jim Spencer, Fred Stanley, Luis Tiant, Tom Underwood, Bob Watson, Dennis Werth

LESS THAN 10 GAMES: Marshall Brant, Brad Gulden, Roger Holt, Jim Kaat *, Bruce Robinson, Denny Sherrill, Ted Wilborn

KEY SIGNATURES: Nettles, Jackson, Piniella, Murcer, Guidry, Tiant, Gossage, John, Perry, Kaat.

VALUE: $200

1980 NEW YORK (NL) - Neil Allen, Bill Almon *, Wally Backman, Butch Benton, Mark Bomback, Hubie Brooks, Ray Burris, Jose Cardenal *, Pete Falcone, Doug Flynn, Ed Glynn, Tom Hausman, Steve Henderson, Ron Hodges, Roy Lee Jackson, Mike Jorgensen, Kevin Kobel, Elliott Maddox, Lee Mazzilli, Dyar Miller, Jerry Morales, Jose Moreno, Dan Norman, Johnny Pacella, Mario Ramirez, Jeff Reardon, John Stearns, Craig Swan, Frank Taveras, Joe Torre (MANAGER), Alex Trevino, Claudell Washington *, Mookie Wilson, Joel Youngblood, Pat Zachry

LESS THAN 10 GAMES: Juan Berenguer, Scott Holman, Ed Lynch, Phil Mankowski, Luis Rosado, Mike Scott

KEY SIGNATURES: Wilson.

VALUE: $90

1980 OAKLAND - Tony Armas, Dave Beard, Jeff Cox, Mike Davis, Mike Edwards, Randy Elliott, Jim Essian, Orlando Gonzalez, Wayne Gross, Mike Guerrero, Dave Hamilton, Mike Heath, Rickey Henderson, Jeff Jones, Matt Keough, Brian Kingman, Mickey Klutts, Bob Lacey, Rick Langford, Billy Martin (MANAGER), Steve McCatty, Dave McKay, Dwayne Murphy, Jeff Newman, Mike Norris, Mitchell Page, Rob Picciolo, Dave Revering

LESS THAN 10 GAMES: Rich Bordi, Ernie Camacho, Ray Cosey, Rick Lysander, Craig Minetto, Mark Souza, Alan Wirth

KEY SIGNATURES: Martin, Henderson.

VALUE: $175

1980 PHILADELPHIA - Luis Aguayo, Ramon Aviles, Bob Boone, Larry Bowa, Warren Brusstar, Marrty Bystrom, Steve Carlton, Larry Christenson, Nino Espinosa, Dallas Green (MANAGER), Greg Gross, Dan Larson, Lerrin LaGrow, Randy Lerch, Jay Loviglio, Greg Luzinski, Garry Maddox, Bake McBride, Tug McGraw, Keith Moreland,

Dickie Noles, Ron Reed, Pete Rose, Dick Ruthven, Kevin Saucier, Mike Schmidt, Lonnie Smith, Manny Trillo, Del Unser, John Vuckovich, George Vukovich, Bob Walk

LESS THAN 10 GAMES: Mark Davis, Bob Dernier, Orlando Isales, Sparky Lyle *, Tim McCarver, Don McCormack, Scott Munninghoff, Ossie Virgil

NOTES: World Champions! Carlton (CY), Schmidt (MVP).

KEY SIGNATURES: Rose, Bowa, Schmidt, Luzinski, Boone, Carlton, Lyle.

VALUE: $315

CY = Cy Young Award winner

1980 PITTSBURGH - Matt Alexander, Bob Beall, Dale Berra, Kurt Bevacqua *, Jim Bibby, Bert Blyleven, John Candelaria, Mike Easler, Tim Foli, Phil Garner, Grant Jackson, Lee Lacy, Vance Law, Bill Madlock, John Milner, Omar Moreno, Steve Nicosia, Ed Ott, Dave Parker, Rick Rhoden, Bill Robinson, Don Robinson, Enrique Romo, Manny Sanguillen, Rod Scurry, Eddie Solomon, Willie Stargell, Chuck Tanner (MANAGER), Kent Tekulve

LESS THAN 10 GAMES: Bernie Carbo *, Andy Hassler, Jesse Jefferson *, Mark Lee, Mickey Mahler, Tony Pena, Pascual Perez, Dave Roberts, Jim Rooker

KEY SIGNATURES: Stargell, Madlock, Parker, Candelaria, Tekulve, Blyleven.

VALUE: $125

1980 SAN DIEGO - Mike Armstrong, Randy Bass, Kurt Bevacqua *, Dave Cash, Jerry Coleman (MANAGER), John Curtis, John D'Acquisto *, Paul Dade, Juan Eichelberger, Barry Evans, Bill Fahey, Rollie Fingers, Tim Flannery, Randy Jones, Von Joshua, Fred Kendall, Dennis Kinney, Gary Lucas, Willie Montanez *, Jerry Mumphrey, Steve Mura, Broderick Perkins, Eric Rasmussen, Gene Richards, Aurelio Rodriguez, Luis Salazar, Bob Shirley, Ozzie Smith, Craig Stimac, Gene Tenace, Jerry Turner, Dave Winfield, Rick Wise

LESS THAN 10 GAMES: Chuck Baker, Dennis Blair, George Stablein, Tom Tellmann

KEY SIGNATURES: Smith, Winfield, Fingers.

VALUE: $100

1980 SAN FRANCISCO - Vida Blue, Chris Bourjos, Dave Bristol (MANAGER), Jack Clark, Darrell Evans, Tom Griffin, Ed Halicki *, Alan Hargesheimer, Larry Herndon, Marc Hill, Al Holland, Mike Ivie, Bob Knepper, Gary Lavelle, Johnnie LeMaster, Dennis Littlejohn, Milt May, Willie McCovey, Roger Metzger, Greg Minton, Randy Moffitt, John Montefusco, Rich Murray, Billy North, Joe Pettini, Allen Ripley, Mike Rowland, Mike Sadek, Rennie Stennett, Joe Strain, Guy Sularz, Max Venable, Terry Whitfield, Ed Whitson, Jim Wohlford

LESS THAN 10 GAMES: Bill Bordley, Fred Braining, Phil Natsu, Jeff Stember

KEY SIGNATURES: Clark, McCovey, Blue.

VALUE: $100

1980 SEATTLE - Glenn Abbott, Kim Allen, Jim Anderson, Floyd Bannister, Jim Beattle, Juan Beniquez, Bruce Bochte, Larry Cox, Ted Cox, Rodney Craig, Julio Cruz, Rob Dressler, Dave Edler, Dave Heaverlo, Marc Hill *, Rick Honeycutt, Willie Horton, Darrel Johnson (MANAGER), Byron McLaughlin, Mario Mendoza, Dan Meyer, Larry Milbourne, Jerry Narron, Tom Paciorek, Mike Parrott, Shane Rawley, Leon Roberts, Dave

Roberts *, Joe Simpson, Bill Stein, Bob Stinson, Reggie Walton, Maury Wills (MANAGER)

LESS THAN 10 GAMES: Rick Anderson, Manny Sarmiento, Gary Wheelock

VALUE: $75

1980 ST. LOUIS - Red Schoendienst (MANAGER), Bobby Bonds, Ken Boyer (MANAGER), Bernie Carbo *, Leon Durham, Bob Forsch, George Frazier, John Fulgham, George Hendrick, Keith Hernandez, Tommy Herr, Whitey Herzog (MANAGER), Don Hood, Dane Iorg, Jim Kaat *, Terry Kennedy, Jack Krol (MANAGER), Tito Landrum, Mark Littell, John Littlefield, Silvio Martinez, Donnie Moore, Ken Oberkfell, Jim Otten, Mike Phillips, Mike Ramsey, Ken Reitz, Tony Scott, Kim Seaman, Ted Simmons, Keith Smith, Steve Swisher, Bob Sykes, Garry Templeton, Roy Thomas, John Urrea, Pete Vuckovich

LESS THAN 10 GAMES: Pedro Borbon, Joe DeSa, Darold Knowles, Jim Lantine *, Jeff Little, John Martin, Al Olmsted, Andy Rincon, Ty Walker

KEY SIGNATURES: Schoendienst, Hernandez, Simmons, Kaat.

VALUE: $100

1980 TEXAS - Tucker Ashford, Rick Auerbach *, Bob Babcock, Buddy Bell, John Butcher, Steve Comer, Pat Corrales (MANAGER), Danny Darwin, Odie Davis, Adrian Devine, Johnny Ellis, Pepe Frias *, Johnny Grubb, Bud Harrelson, Charlie Hough *, Ferguson Jenkins, John Henry Johnson, Jim Kern, Sparky Lyle *, Jon Matlack, Doc Medich, Nelson Norman, Jim Norris, Al Oliver, Gaylord Perry *, Pat Putnam, Dave Rajsich, Mike Richardt, Mickey Rivers, Dave Roberts, Billy Sample, Rusty Staub, Jim Sundberg, Bump Wills, Richie Zisk

LESS THAN 10 GAMES: Brian Allard, Ken Clay, Ed Figueroa *, Jerry Gleaton, Mike Hart, Don Kainer, Dennis Lewallyn, Danny Walton

KEY SIGNATURES: Bell, Oliver, Staub, Jenkins, Perry, Lyle.

VALUE: $80

1980 TORONTO - Danny Ainge, Doug Ault, Bob Bailor, Mike Barlow, Barry Bonnell, Rick Bosetti, Steve Braun *, Tom Buskey, Joe Cannon, Jim Clancy, Bob Davis, Damaso Garcia, Jerry Garvin, Alfredo Griffin, Paul Hodgson, Roy Howell, Garth Iorg, Jesse Jefferson *, Jack Kucek, Luis Leal, Bobby Mattick (MANAGER), John Mayberry, Joey McLaughlin, Paul Mirabella, Balor Moore, Lloyd Moseby, Ken Schrom, Dave Stieb, Jackson Todd, Willie Upshaw, Otto Velez, Ernie Whitt, Mike Willis, Al Woods

LESS THAN 10 GAMES: Pat Kelly, Dave Lemanczyk *, Mike Macha, Domingo Ramos

KEY SIGNATURES: Stieb.

VALUE: $75

1981

Rickey Henderson stole 56 bases to lead the American League during the strike season of 1981.

1981 ATLANTA - Brian Asselstine, Steve Bedrosian, Bruce Benedict, Tommy Boggs, Larry Bradford, Brett Butler, Rick Camp, Chris Chambliss, Bobby Cox (MANAGER), Gene Garber, Luis Gomez, Preston Hanna, Terry Harper, Bob Horner, Al Hrabosky, Glenn Hubbard, Brook Jacoby, Rufino Linares, Rick Mahler, Eddie Miller, John Montefusco, Dale Murphy, Bill Nahorodny, Phil Niekro, Larry Owen, Gaylord Perry, Biff Pocoroba, Bob Porter, Rafael Ramirez, Jerry Royster, Matt Sinatro, Bob Walk, Claudell Washington

LESS THAN 10 GAMES: Jose Alvarez, Luis Gomez, Albert Hall, Mike Lum *, Rick Matula, Larry McWilliams, Paul Runge, Ken Smith, Larry Whisenton

NOTES: Two 300-win pitchers on the same team.

KEY SIGNATURES: Murphy, Butler, Perry, Niekro.

VALUE: $125

1981 BALTIMORE - Benny Ayala, Mark Belanger, Al Bumbry, Terry Crowley, Rich Dauer, Rick Dempsey, Doug DeCinces, Jim Dwyer, Mike Flanagan, Dave Ford, Dan Graham, Wayne Krenchicki, John Lowenstein, Dennis Martinez, Tippy Martinez, Scott McGregor, Jose Morales, Eddie Murray, Jim Palmer, Cal Ripken, Gary Roenicke, Lenn Sakata, Jeff Schneider, Ken Singleton, Sammy Stewart, Tim Stoddard, Steve Stone, Earl Weaver (MANAGER)

LESS THAN 10 GAMES: Mike Boddicker, Bob Bonner, Mark Corey, Steve Luebber, Willie Royster, John Shelby, Dallas Williams

KEY SIGNATURES: Weaver, Murray, Ripken, Palmer.

VALUE: $125

1981 BOSTON - Gary Allenson, Tom Burgmeier, Bill Campbell, Mark Clear, Steve Crawford, Dennis Eckersley, Dwight Evans, Rich Gedman, Garry Hancock, Glenn Hoffman, Ralph Houk (MANAGER), Carney Lansford, Rick Miller, Reid Nichols, Tony Perez, Chuck Rainey, Jerry Remy, Jim Rice, Joe Rudi, Dave Schmidt, Bob Stanley, Dave Stapleton, Frank Tanana, Mike Torrez, John Tudor, Julio Valdez, Carl Yastrzemski

LESS THAN 10 GAMES: Luis Aponte, Bruce Hurst, John Lickert, Bob Ojeda, Tom Poquette *, Chico Walker

KEY SIGNATURES: Lansford, Rice, Yastrzemski, Eckersley.

VALUE: $125

1981 CALIFORNIA - Don Aase, Don Baylor, Juan Beniquez, Tom Brunansky, Rick Burleson, Bert Campaneris, Rod Carew, Bobby Clark, Brian Downing, Joe Ferguson *, Dan Ford, Ken Forsch, Jim Fregosi (MANAGER), Dave Frost, Bobby Grich, Larry Harlow, John Harris, Andy Hassler, Butch Hobson, Jesse Jefferson, Bruce Kison, Fred Lynn, Gene Mauch (MANAGER), Ed Ott, Freddie Patek, Steve Renko, Luis Sanchez, Daryl Sconiers, Mike Witt, Geoff Zahn

LESS THAN 10 GAMES: John D'Acquisto, Bob Davis, Brian Harper, Steve Lubratich, Mickey Mahler, Freddie Martinez, Angel Moreno, Doug Rau, Bill Travers

KEY SIGNATURES: Carew, Lynn.

VALUE: $75

1981 CHICAGO (AL) - Bill Almon, Harold Baines, Ross Baumgarten, Tony Bernazard, Britt Burns, Rich Dotson, Jim Essian, Ed Farmer, Carlton Fisk, Kevin Hickey, Mark Hill, LaMarr Hoyt, Lamar Johnson, Rusty Kuntz, Dennis Lamp, Tony LaRussa (MANAGER), Chet Lemon, Ron LeFlore, Jay Loviglio, Greg Luzinski, Lynn McGlothen *, Bob Molinaro, Jim Morrison, Wayne Nordhagen, Greg Pryor, Mike Squires, Leo Sutherland, Steve Trout

LESS THAN 10 GAMES: Juan Agosto, Francisco Barrios, Jerry Hairston, Jerry Koosman *, Reggie Patterson, Dewey Robinson, Jerry Turner *

KEY SIGNATURES: Baines, Fisk, Luzinski, Hoyt.

VALUE: $90

1981 CHICAGO (NL) - Joey Amalfitano (MANAGER), Doug Bird *, Tim Blackwell, Bobby Bonds, Bill Buckner, Doug Capilla, Bill Caudill, Hector Cruz, Jody Davis, Ivan DeJesus, Steve Dillard, Leon Durham, Rawly Eastwick, Scott Fletcher, Dave Geisel, Mike Griffin *, Steve Henderson, Willie Hernandez, Jay Howell, Ken Kravec, Mike Krukow, Mike Lum *, Randy Martz, Lynn McGlothen *, Jerry Morales, Ken Reitz, Rick Reuschel *, Lee Smith, Joe Strain, Pat Tabler, Scott Thompson, Dick Tidrow, Jim Tracy, Mike Tyson, Ty Waller

LESS THAN 10 GAMES: Barry Foote *, Mel Hall, Bill Hayes, Gary Krug, Carlos Lezcano

KEY SIGNATURES: Buckner.

VALUE: $75

1981 CINCINNATI - Doug Bair *, Johnny Bench, Bruce Berenyi, Larry Biittner, Scott Brown, Dave Collins, Geoff Combe, Dave Concepcion, Dan Driessen, George Foster,

Ken Griffey, Paul Householder, Tom Hume, Junior Kennedy, Ray Knight, Rafael Landestoy *, Mike LaCoss, John McNamara (MANAGER), Sammy Mejias, Paul Moskau, Joe Nolan, Mike O'Berry, Ron Oester, Frank Pastore, Joe Price, Tom Seaver, Mario Soto, Harry Spilman *, Mike Vail

LESS THAN 10 GAMES: German Barranca, Joe Edelen *, Neil Fiala *, Charlie Leibrandt, Eddie Milner

KEY SIGNATURES: Concepcion, Griffey, Foster, Bench, Seaver.

VALUE: $90

1981 CLEVELAND - Chris Bando, Alan Bannister, Len Barker, Bert Blyleven, Joe Charboneau, John Denny, Bo Diaz, Miguel Dilone, Jerry Dybzinski, Mike Fischlin, Dave Garcia (MANAGER), Wayne Garland, Mike Hargrove, Toby Harrah, Ron Hassey, Von Hayes, Pat Kelly, Duane Kuiper, Bob Lacey *, Larry Littleton, Rick Manning, Sid Monge, Jorge Orta, Karl Pagel, Dave Rosello, Dan Spillner, Mike Stanton, Andre Thornton, Tom Veryzer, Rick Waits

LESS THAN 10 GAMES: Tom Brennan, Ed Glynn, Dennis Lewallyn, Ron Pruitt

KEY SIGNATURES: Harrah, Blyleven.

VALUE: $75

1981 DETROIT - Sparky Anderson (MANAGER), Tom Brookens, Darrell Brown, George Cappuzzello, Al Cowens, Bill Fahey, Kirk Gibson, Richie Hebner, Ron Jackson *, Lynn Jones, Mick Kelleher, Steve Kemp, Rick Leach, Aurelio Lopez, Jack Morris, Stan Papi, Lance Parrish, Rickey Peters, Dan Petry, Dave Rozema, Kevin Saucier, Dan Schatzeder, Champ Summers, Dave Tobik, Alan Trammell, Lou Whitaker, Milt Wilcox, John Wockenfuss

LESS THAN 10 GAMES: Howard Bailey, Marty Castillo, Duffy Dyer, Dennis Kinney, Larry Rothschild, Dave Rucker, Jerry Ujdur

KEY SIGNATURES: Anderson, Whitaker, Trammell, Gibson, Morris.

VALUE: $125

1981 HOUSTON - Alan Ashby, Cesar Cedeno, Jose Cruz, Kiko Garcia, Phil Garner *, Danny Heep, Art Howe, Mike Ivie *, Bob Knepper, Rafael Landestoy *, Frank LaCorte, Scott Loucks, Joe Niekro, Joe Pittman, Terry Puhl, Luis Pujols, Craig Reynolds, Dave Roberts, Vern Ruhle, Nolan Ryan, Joe Sambito, Tony Scott *, Dave Smith, Harry Spilman *, Bobby Sprowl, Don Sutton, Dickie Thon, Bill Virdon (MANAGER), Denny Walling, Gary Woods

LESS THAN 10 GAMES: Joaquin Andujar, Dave Bergman *, Alan Knicely, Jeff Leonard *, Bert Pena, Gordy Pladson, Billy Smith, Tim Tolman

KEY SIGNATURES: Ryan, Sutton.

VALUE: $90

1981 KANSAS CITY - Willie Aikens, George Brett, Ken Brett, Dave Chalk, Jim Frey (MANAGER), Rich Gale, Danny Garcia, Cesar Geronimo, Jerry Grote *, Larry Gura, Atlee Hammaker, Dick Howser (MANAGER), Clint Hurdle, Mike Jones, Dennis Leonard, Renie Martin, Lee May, Hal McRae, Darryl Motley, Rance Mulliniks, Amos Otis, Ken Phelps, Jamie Quirk, Dan Quisenberry, Paul Splittorff, U.L. Washington, John Wathan, Frank White, Willie Wilson, Jim Wright

LESS THAN 10 GAMES: Juan Berenguer *, Onix Concepcion, Tim Ireland, Greg Keatley, Bill Paschall, Jeff Schattinger, Pat Sheridan
KEY SIGNATURES: Brett, Quisenberry.

VALUE: $80

1981 LOS ANGELES - Dusty Baker, Bobby Castillo, Ron Cey, Joe Ferguson *, Pepe Frias, Steve Garvey, Dave Goltz, Pedro Guererro, Burt Hooton, Steve Howe, Jay Johnstone, Ken Landreaux, Tom Lasorda (MANAGER), Davey Lopes, Candy Maldonado, Mike Marshall, Bobby Mitchell, Rick Monday, Tom Niedenfuer, Alejandro Pena, Jerry Reuss, Ron Roenicke, Bill Russell, Steve Sax, Mike Scioscia, Reggie Smith, Dave Stewart, Rick Sutcliffe, Derrel Thomas, Fernando Valenzuela, Gary Weiss, Bob Welch, Steve Yeager
LESS THAN 10 GAMES: Mark Bradley, Terry Forster, Jerry Grote, Jack Perconte, Ted Power
NOTES: World Champions! Valenzuela (ROY) & (MVP).
KEY SIGNATURES: Garvey, Cey, Guerrero, Sax, Valenzuela, Stewart.

VALUE: $295

ROY = Rookie of the Year

1981 MILWAUKEE - Jerry Augustine, Sal Bando, Thad Bosley, Mark Brouhard, Mike Caldwell, Reggie Cleveland, Cecil Cooper, Jamie Easterly, Marshall Edwards, Rollie Fingers, Jim Gantner, Moose Haas, Larry Hisle, Roy Howell, Buster Keeton, Randy Lerch, Paul Molitor, Don Money, Charlie Moore, Ben Oglivie, Bob Rodgers (MANAGER), Ed Romero, Ted Simmons, Jim Slaton, Gorman Thomas, Pete Vuckovich, Ned Yost, Robin Yount
LESS THAN 10 GAMES: Dwight Bernard, Frank DiPino, Bob McClure, Donnie Moore, Willie Mueller, Chuck Porter
NOTES: Fingers (CY) & (MVP).
KEY SIGNATURES: Yount, Molitor, Fingers.

VALUE: $125

CY = Cy Young Award winner

1981 MINNESOTA - Glenn Adams, Fernando Arroyo, Chuck Baker, Sal Butera, John Castino, Don Cooper, Doug Corbett, Tim Corcoran, Dave Engle, Roger Erickson, Lenny Faedo, Billy Gardner (MANAGER), Danny Goodwin, Johnny Goryl (MANAGER), Mickey Hatcher, Brad Havens, Kent Hrbek, Darrell Jackson, Ron Jackson *, Jerry Koosman *, Tim Laudner, Pete MacKanin, Jack O'Connor, Hosken Powell, Pete Redfern, Roy Smalley, Ray Smith, Rick Sofield, John Verhoeven, Gary Ward, Ron Washington, Rob Wilfong, Al Williams, Butch Wynegar
LESS THAN 10 GAMES: Terry Felton, Mark Funderburk, Gary Gaetti, Jack Hobbs, Greg Johnston, Bob Veselic

VALUE: $75

1981 MONTREAL - Stan Bahnsen, Ray Burris, Gary Carter, Warren Cromartie, Andre Dawson, Jim Fanning (MANAGER), Terry Francona, Woodie Fryman, Bill Gullickson, Tommy Hutton, Grant Jackson, Tony Johnson, Wallace Johnson, Charlie Lea, Bill Lee, Jerry Manuel, Brad Mills, John Milner *, Willie Montanez *, Rowland Office, Larry Parrish, Mike Phillips *, Tim Raines, Bobby Ramos, Jeff Reardon *, Steve Rogers, Scott Sanderson, Rodney Scott, Bryn Smith, Chris Speier, Ellis Valentine *, Tim Wallach, Jerry White, Tom Wieghaus, Dick Williams (MANAGER)

LESS THAN 10 GAMES: Dan Briggs, Rick Engle, Mike Gates, Tom Gorman, Dave Hostetler, Bob Pate, Steve Ratzer, Pat Rooney, Chris Smith, Elias Sosa

KEY SIGNATURES: Dawson, Raines, Carter.

VALUE: $145

1981 NEW YORK - Neil Allen, Wally Backman, Bob Ballor, Danny Boitano, Hubie Brooks, Mike Cubbage, Pete Falcone, Doug Flynn, Ron Gardenhire, Greg Harris, Tom Hausman, Ron Hodges, Mike Howard, Randy Jones, Mike Jorgensen, Dave Kingman, Terry Leach, Ed Lynch, Mike Marshall, Lee Mazzilli, Dyar Miller, Jeff Reardon *, Mike Scott, Ray Searage, Rusty Staub, John Stearns, Frank Taveras, Joe Torre (MANAGER), Alex Trevino, Ellis Valentine *, Mookie Wilson, Joel Youngblood, Pat Zachry

LESS THAN 10 GAMES: Brian Giles, Tim Leary, Jesse Orosco, Charlie Puleo, Dave Roberts, Criag Swan

KEY SIGNATURES: Kingman, Staub.

VALUE: $95

1981 NEW YORK (AL) - Doug Bird *, Bobby Brown, Bill Castro, Rick Cerone, Ron Davis, Bucky Dent, Barry Foote *, George Frazier, Oscar Gamble, Goose Gossage, Ron Guidry, Reggie Jackson, Tommy John, Dave LaRoche, Bob Lemon (MANAGER), Rudy May, Gene Michael (MANAGER), Larry Milbourne, Jerry Mumphrey, Bobby Murcer, Graig Nettles, Lou Piniella, Willie Randolph, Rick Reuschel *, Dave Revering *, Dave Righetti, Aurelio Rodriguez, Jim Spencer *, Bob Watson, Dennis Werth, Dave Winfield

LESS THAN 10 GAMES: Tucker Ashford, Steve Balboni, Mike Griffin *, Andy McGaffigan, Gene Nelson, Johnny Oates, Mike Patterson, Andre Robertson, Tom Underwood *, Dave Wehmeister

NOTES: Righetti (ROY).

KEY SIGNATURES: Nettles, Jackson, Winfield, Murcer, Piniella, Guidry, John,Gossage.

VALUE: $250

ROY = Rookie of the Year

1981 OAKLAND - Tony Armas, Shooty Babitt, Mike Davis, Brian Doyle, Keith Drumright, Wayne Gross, Mike Heath, Rickey Henderson, Tim Hosley, Cliff Johnson, Jeff Jones, Matt Keough, Brian Kingman, Mickey Klutts, Rick Langford, Billy Martin (MANAGER), Steve McCatty, Dave McKay, Byron McLaughlin, Kelvin Moore, Dwayne Murphy, Jeff Newman, Mike Norris, Bob Owchinko, Mitchell Page, Mike Patterson *, Rob Picciolo, Dave Revering *, Jim Spencer *, Fred Stanley, Tom Underwood *

LESS THAN 10 GAMES: Dave Beard, Rich Bordi, Rick Bosetti *, Mark Budaska, Jeff Cox, Ed Figueroa, Dave Heaverlo, Bob Kearney, Craig Minetto, Jim Nettles, Jimmy Sexton

KEY SIGNATURES: Martin, Henderson.

VALUE: $175

1981 PHILADELPHIA - Luis Aguayo, Ramon Aviles, Bob Boone, Larry Bowa, Warren Brusstar, Steve Carlton, Larry Christenson, Dick Davis, Bob Dernier, Nino Espinosa *, Dallas Green (MANAGER), Greg Gross, Sparky Lyle, Garry Maddox, Gary Mathews, Len Matuszek, Bake McBride, Tug McGraw, Keith Moreland, Dickie Noles, Mike Proly, Ron Reed, Pete Rose, Dick Ruthven, Ryne Sandberg, Mike Schmidt, Lonnie Smith, Manny Trillo, Del Unser, George Vuckovich, John Vuckovich

LESS THAN 10 GAMES - Marty Bystrom, Mark Davis, Dan Larson, Don McCormack, Jerry Reed, Ozzie Virgil

NOTES: Schmidt (MVP).

KEY SIGNATURES: Rose, Bowa, Schmidt, Boone, Sandberg, Carlton, Lyle.

VALUE: $125

MVP = MVP Award winner

1981 PITTSBURGH - Gary Alexander, Matt Alexander, Dale Berra, Kurt Bevacqua, Jim Bibby, Dorian Boyland, Victor Cruz, Mike Easler, Tim Foli, Phil Garner *, Grant Jackson *, Odell Jones, Lee Lacy, Vance Law, Mark Lee, Bill Madlock, John Milner *, Willie Montanez *, Omar Moreno, Steve Nicosia, Dave Parker, Tony Pena, Pascual Perez, Johnny Ray, Rick Rhoden, Bill Robinson, Don Robinson, Enrique Romo, Rod Scurry, Eddie Solomon, Willie Stargell, Chuck Tanner (MANAGER), Kent Tekulve, Jason Thompson

LESS THAN 10 GAMES: Ernie Camacho, John Candelaria, Bob Long, Luis Tiant

KEY SIGNATURES: Parker, Stargell, Madlock.

VALUE: $90

1981 SAN DIEGO - Randy Bass, Juan Bonilla, Dan Boone, John Curtis, Dave Edwards, Juan Eichelberger, Barry Evans, Tim Flannery, Doug Gwosdz, Frank Howard (MANAGER), Ruppert Jones, Terry Kennedy, Joe Lefebvre, John Littlefield, Tim Lollar, Gary Lucas, Jose Moreno, Steve Mura, Broderick Perkins, Mike Phillips *, Mario Ramirez, Gene Richards, Luis Salazar, Eric Show, Ozzie Smith, Steve Swisher, Jerry Turner *, John Urrea, Chris Welsh, Alan Wiggins, Rick Wise

LESS THAN 10 GAMES: Mike Armstrong, Steve Fireovid, Fred Kuhualua, Craig Stimac

KEY SIGNATURES: Smith, Kennedy.

VALUE: $90

1981 SAN FRANCISCO - Doyle Alexander, Dave Bergman *, Vida Blue, Bill Bordley, Fred Breining, Bob Brenly, Enos Cabell, Jack Clark, Darrell Evans, Tom Griffin, Larry Herndon, Al Holland, Gary Lavelle, Jeff Leonard *, Johnnie LeMaster, Jerry Martin, Milt May, Greg Minton, Joe Morgan, Billy North, Joe Pettini, Allen Ripley, Frank Robinson (MANAGER), Mike Sadek, Billy Smith, Rennie Stennett, Bob Tufts, Max Venable, Ed Whitson, Jim Wohlford

LESS THAN 10 GAMES: Chili Davis, Alan Hargesheimer, Mike Ivie *, Randy Moffitt, Jeff Ransom, Mike Rowland, Guy Sularz

KEY SIGNATURES: Morgan, Clark, Blue.

VALUE: $80

1981 SEATTLE - Glenn Abbott, Brian Allard, Kim Allen, Larry Andersen, Jim Anderson, Rick Auerbach, Floyd Bannister, Jim Beattie, Bruce Bochte, Terry Bulling, Jeff Burroughs, Bryan Clark, Ken Clay, Julio Cruz, Dick Drago, Dave Edler, Dan Firova, Bob Galasso, Jerry Gleaton, Gary Gray, Dave Henderson, Rene Lachemann (MANAGER), Jim Maler, Vance McHenry, Dan Meyer, Jerry Narron, Tom Paciorek, Mike Parrott, Casey Parsons, Lenny Randle, Shane Rawley, Paul Serna, Joe Simpson, Reggie Walton, Maury Willis (MANAGER), Richie Zisk

LESS THAN 10 GAMES: Bud Black, Brad Gulden, Randy Stein, Bob Stoddard

KEY SIGNATURES: Henderson.

VALUE: $7

1981 ST. LOUIS - Joaquin Andujar, Doug Bair, Steve Braun, Glenn Brunner, Luis DeLeon, Luis DeLeon, Joe Edelen, Neil Fiala, Bob Forsch, John Fulgham, Julio Gonzalez, David Green, George Hendrick, Keith Hernandez, Tommy Herr, Whitey Herzog (MANAGER), Dane Iorg, Jim Kaat, Tito Landrum, Dave LaPoint, Sixto Lezcano, Mark Littell, John Mann, Silvo Martinez, Ken Oberkfell, Jim Otten, Darrell Porter, Mike Ramsey, Andy Rincon, Gene Roof, Orlando Sanchez, Tony Scott, Bob Shirley, Lary Sorensen, Bruce Sutter, Bob Sykes, Garry Templeton, Gene Tenace

KEY SIGNATURES: Hernandez, Kaat.

VALUE: $110

1981 TEXAS - Bob Babcock, Buddy Bell, Steve Comer, Danny Darwin, Dan Duran, Johnny Ellis, Johnny Grubb, Rick Honeycutt, Charlie Hough, Ferguson Jenkins, John Henry Johnson, Jim Kern, Jon Matlack, Doc Medich, Mario Mendoza, Al Oliver, Tom Poquette *, Pat Putnam, Mickey Rivers, Leon Roberts, Billy Sample, Dave Schmidt, Bill Stein, Jim Sundberg, Wayne Tolleson, Mark Wagner, Bump Wills, Don Zimmer (MANAGER)

LESS THAN 10 GAMES: John Butcher, Larry Cox, Bobby Johnson, Bobby Jones, Bob Lacey *, Rick Lis, Mark Mercer, Nelson Norman, Don Werner, Len Whitehouse

KEY SIGNATURES: Bell, Oliver, Jenkins.

VALUE: $80

1981 TORONTO - Danny Ainge, Jesse Barfield, Mike Barlow, George Bell, Juan Berenguer *, Mark Bomback, Barry Bonnell, Rick Bosetti *, Jim Clancy, Ted Cox, Damaso Garcia, Jerry Garvin, Alfredo Griffin, Garth Iorg, Roy Lee Jackson, Luis Leal, Ken Macha, Fred Manrique, Buck Martinez, Bobby Mattick (MANAGER), John Mayberry, Joey McLaughlin, Lloyd Moseby, Dale Murray, Dave Stieb, Jackson Todd, Willie Upshaw, Otto Velez, Greg Wells, Ernie Whitt, Mike Willis, Al Woods

LESS THAN 10 GAMES: Charlie Beamon, Nino Espinosa *, Paul Mirabella, Dan Whitmer

KEY SIGNATURES: Bell, Barfield, Stieb.

VALUE: $75

1982

1982 Milwaukee Brewers

1982 ATLANTA - Steve Bedrosian, Bruce Benedict, Tommy Boggs, Brett Butler, Rick Camp, Chris Chambliss, Joe Cowley, Ken Dayley, Carlos Diaz *, Gene Garber, Preston Hanna *, Terry Harper, Bob Horner, Al Hrabosky, Glenn Hubbard, Randy Johnson, Rufino Linares, Rick Mahler, Larry McWilliams *, Donnie Moore, Dale Murphy, Phil Niekro, Pascual Perez, Biff Pocoroba, Bob Porter, Rafael Ramirez, Jerry Royster, Matt Sinatro, Ken Smith, Joe Torre (MANAGER), Bob Walk, Claudell Washington, Bob Watson *, Larry Whisenton

LESS THAN 10 GAMES: Jose Alvarez, Albert Hall, Tom Hausman *, Larry Owen, Paul Runge, Paul Zuvella

NOTES: Murphy (MVP).

KEY SIGNATURES: Murphy, Butler, Niekro.

VALUE: $145

MVP = MVP Award winner

1982 BALTIMORE - Benny Ayala, Bob Bonner, Al Bumbry, Terry Crowley, Rich Dauer, Storm Davis, Rick Dempsey, Jim Dwyer, Mike Flanagan, Dan Ford, Ross Grimsley, Glenn Gulliver, John Lowenstein, Dennis Martinez, Tippy Martinez, Scott McGregor, Eddie Murray, Joe Nolan, Jim Palmer, Floyd Rayford, Cal Ripken, Gary Roenicke, Lenn Sakata, John Shelby, Ken Singleton, Don Stanhouse, Sammy Stewart, Tim Stoddard, Earl Weaver (MANAGER)

LESS THAN 10 GAMES: Mike Boddicker, John Flinn, Leo Hernandez, Jose Morales *, Don Welchel, Mike Young

NOTES: Ripken (ROY).

KEY SIGNATURES: Weaver, Murray, Ripken, Palmer.

VALUE: $130

ROY = Rookie of the Year

1982 BOSTON - Gary Allenson, Luis Aponte, Wade Boggs, Tom Burgmeier, Mark Clear, Dennis Eckersley, Dwight Evans, Rich Gedman, Garry Hancock, Glenn Hoffman, Ralph Houk (MANAGER), Bruce Hurst, Ed Jurak, Carney Lansford, Rick Miller, Reid Nichols, Bob Ojeda, Tony Perez, Chuck Rainey, Jerry Remy, Jim Rice, Bob Stanley, Dave Stapleton, Mike Torrez, John Tudor, Julio Valdez, Carl Yastrzemski

LESS THAN 10 GAMES: Marty Barrett, Oil Can Boyd, Mike Brown, Steve Crawford, Brian Denman, Roger LaFrancois, Marc Sullivan

KEY SIGNATURES: Lansford, Rice, Yastrzemski, Boggs, Perez, Eckersley.

VALUE: $125

1982 CALIFORNIA - Don Aase, Don Baylor, Juan Beniguez, Bob Boone, Rick Burleson, Rod Carew, Bobby Clark, Doug Corbett *, Doug DeCinces, Brian Downing, Joe Ferguson, Tim Foli, Ken Forsch, Dave Goltz *, Bobby Grich, Andy Hassler, Reggie Jackson, Ron Jackson, Mick Kelleher *, Bruce Kison, Fred Lynn, Gene Mauch (MANAGER), Angel Moreno, Jose Moreno, Gary Pettis, Steve Renko, Luis Sanchez, Daryl Sconiers, Rick Steirer, Rob Wilfong *, Mike Witt, Geoff Zahn

LESS THAN 10 GAMES: Rick Adams, Stan Bahnsen *, John Curtis *, Tommy John *, Mickey Mahler, Luis Tiant

KEY SIGNATURES: Carew, Jackson, Lynn, Boone, John, Tiant.

VALUE: $150

1982 CHICAGO (AL) - Bill Almon, Harold Baines, Salome Barojas, Tony Bernazard, Warren Brusstar *, Britt Burns, Steve Dillard, Rich Dotson, Chico Escarrega, Carlton Fisk, Marv Foley, Lorenzo Gray, Jerry Hairston, Kevin Hickey, Marc Hill, LaMarr Hoyt, Steve Kemp, Jim Kern *, Ron Kittle, Jerry Koosman, Rusty Kuntz, Dennis Lamp, Rudy Law, Vance Law, Tony LaRussa (MANAGER), Ron LeFlore, Jay Loviglio, Greg Luzinski, Sparky Lyle *, Jim Morrison *, Chris Nyman, Tom Paciorek, Aurelio Rodriguez, Mike Squires, Steve Trout, Greg Walker

LESS THAN 10 GAMES: Juan Agosto, Rich Barnes, Jim Siwy, Eddie Solomon *

KEY SIGNATURES: Baines, Fisk, Luzinski, Hoyt, Lyle.

VALUE: $90

1982 CHICAGO (NL) - Doug Bird, Larry Bowa, Dan Briggs, Bill Buckner, Bill Campbell, Heity Cruz, Jody Davis, Leon Durham, Lee Elia (MANAGER), Scott Fletcher, Mel Hall, Steve Henderson, Willie Hernandez, Freguson Jenkins, Jay Johnstone *, Junior Kennedy, Ken Kravec, Dan Larson, Randy Martz, Bob Molinaro *, Jerry Morales, Keith Moreland, Dickie Noles, Mike Proly, Allen Ripley, Ryne Sandberg, Lee Smith, Pat Tabler, Scot Thompson, Dick Tidrow, Ty Waller, Bump Wills, Gary Woods

LESS THAN 10 GAMES: Butch Benton, Larry Cox, Tom Filer, Herman Segelke, Randy Stein

KEY SIGNATURES: Buckner, Sandberg, Jenkins, Hernandez.

VALUE: $100

1982 CINCINNATI - German Barranca, Johnny Bench, Bruce Berenyi, Larry Biittner, Cesar Cedeno, Dave Concepcion, Dan Driessen, Greg Harris, Ben Hayes, Paul Householder, Tom Hume, Clint Hurdle, Jim Kern *, Wayne Krenchicki, Rafael Landestoy,

Tom Lawless, Brad Lesley, Charlie Liebrandt, John McNamara (MANAGER), Eddie Milner, Russ Nixon (MANAGER), Mike O'Berry, Ron Oester, Frank Pastore, Joe Price, Gary Redus, Tom Seaver, Bob Shirley, Mario Soto, Alex Trevino, Mike Vail, Dave Van Gorder, Duane Walker

LESS THAN 10 GAMES: Joe Edelen, Bill Scherrer

KEY SIGNATURES: Concepcion, Bench, Seaver.

VALUE: $85

1982 CLEVELAND - Bud Anderson, Chris Bando, Alan Bannister, Len Barker, Tom Brennan, Carmen Castillo, Joe Charboneau, Rodney Craig, John Denny *, Miguel Dilone, Jerry Dybzinski, Mike Fischlin, Dave Garcia (MANAGER), Ed Glynn, Mike Hargrove, Toby Harrah, Ron Hassey, Von Hayes, Rick Manning, Bake McBride, Larry Milbourne *, Bill Nahorodny, Karl Pagel, Jack Perconte, Kevin Rhomberg, Lary Sorensen, Dan Spillner, Rick Sutcliffe, Andre Thornton, Rick Waits, Ed Whitson

LESS THAN 10 GAMES: Bert Blyleven, John Bohnet, Neal Heaton, Dennis Lewallyn, Jerry Reed *, Sandy Wihtol

KEY SIGNATURES: Harrah, Blyleven.

VALUE: $75

1982 DETROIT - Sparky Anderson (MANAGER), Tom Brookens, Enos Cabell, Mark DeJohn, Bill Fahey, Kirk Gibson, Richie Hebner *, Larry Herndon, Mike Ivie *, Bob James *, Howard Johnson, Lynn Jones, Mike Laga, Rick Leach, Chet Lemon, Aurelio Lopez, Eddie Miller, Jack Morris, Lance Parrish, Larry Pashnick, Dan Petry, Dave Rozema, Dave Rucker, Kevin Saucier, Elias Sosa, Dave Tobik, Alan Trammell, Jerry Turner, Jerry Ujdur, Pat Underwood, Lou Whitaker, Milt Wilcox, Glenn Wilson, John Wockenfuss

LESS THAN 10 GAMES: Howard Bailey, Juan Berenguer, Marty Castillo, Dave Gumpert, Mick Kelleher *, Larry Rothschild

KEY SIGNATURES: Anderson, Whitaker, Trammell, Gibson, Johnson, Morris.

VALUE: $125

1982 HOUSTON - Alan Ashby, Kevin Bass *, Dan Boone *, George Cappuzzello, Jose Cruz, Bill Doran, Kiko Garcia, Phil Garner, Danny Heep, Art Howe, Bob Knepper, Alan Knicely, Ray Knight, Frank LaCorte, Mike LaCoss, Bob Lillis (MANAGER), Scott Loucks, Randy Moffitt, Joe Niekro, Joe Pittman *, Terry Puhl, Luis Pujois, Craig Reynolds, Bert Roberge, Vern Ruhle, Nolan Ryan, Tony Scott, Dave Smith, Harry Spilman, Don Sutton *, Dickie Thon, Tim Tolman, Bill Virdon (MANAGER), Denny Walling

LESS THAN 10 GAMES: Frank DiPino, Mike Ivie *, Gordy Pladson, Larry Ray, Mark Ross, Joe Sambito

KEY SIGNATURES: Ryan, Sutton.

VALUE: $90

1982 KANSAS CITY - Willie Aikens, Mike Armstrong, Bud Black, Vida Blue, George Brett, Bill Castro, Onix Concepcion, Dave Frost, Cesar Geronimo, Larry Gura, Steve Hammond, Don Hood, Dick Howser (MANAGER), Grant Jackson *, Dennis Leonard, Jerry Martin, Lee May, Hal McRae, Amos Otis, Tom Poquette, Greg Pryor, Jamie Quirk, Dan Quisenberry, Don Slaught, Paul Splittorff, Bob Tufts, U.L. Washington, John Wathan, Dennis Werth, Frank White, Willie Wilson

LESS THAN 10 GAMES: Buddy Biancalana, Dick Botelho, Keith Creel, Kelly Heath, Tim Ireland, Ron Johnson, Bombo Rivera, Mark Ryal, Jim Wright

KEY SIGNATURES: Brett, Quisenberry.

VALUE: $80

1982 LOS ANGELES - Dusty Baker, Joe Beckwith, Mark Belanger, Greg Brock, Ron Cey, Terry Forster, Steve Garvey, Pedro Guerrero, Burt Hooton, Steve Howe, Jay Johnstone *, Ken Landreaux, Tom Lasorda (MANAGER), Mike Marshall, Rick Monday, Jose Morales *, Tom Niedenfuer, Jorge Orta, Alejandro Pena, Ted Power, Jerry Reuss, Ron Roenicke, Vicente Romo, Bill Russell, Steve Sax, Mike Scioscia, Steve Shirley, Dave Stewart, Alex Taveras, Derrel Thomas, Fernando Valenzuela, Bob Welch, Ricky Wright, Steve Yeager

LESS THAN 10 GAMES: Mark Bradley, Don Crow, Dave Goltz *, Candy Maldonado, Manny Mota, Dave Sax

NOTES: Sax (ROY).

KEY SIGNATURES: Garvey, Sax, Guerrero, Valenzuela, Stewart.

VALUE: $125

ROY = Rookie of the Year

1982 MILWAUKEE - Jerry Augustine, Kevin Bass *, Dwight Bernard, Mark Brouhard, Mike Caldwell, Cecil Cooper, Jamie Easterly, Marshall Edwards, Rollie Fingers, Jim Gantner, Moose Haas, Roy Howell, Harvey Kuenn (MANAGER), Pete Ladd, Randy Lerch, Bob McClure, Doc Medich *, Paul Molitor, Don Money, Charlie Moore, Ben Oglivie, Rob Picciolo *, Bob Rodgers (MANAGER), Ed Romero, Ted Simmons, Jim Slaton, Gorman Thomas, Pete Vuckovich, Ned Yost, Robin Yount

LESS THAN 10 GAMES: Larry Hisle, Doug Jones, Chuck Porter, Bob Skube, Don Sutton *

NOTES: Yount (MVP); Vuckovich (CY).

KEY SIGNATURES: Yount, Molitor, Vuckovich, Fingers, Sutton.

VALUE: $200

CY = Cy Young Award winner

1982 MINNESOTA - Paul Boris, Tom Brunansky, Randy Bush, Sal Butera, Bobby Castillo, John Castino, Doug Corbett *, Ron Davis, Jim Eisenrich, Dave Engle, Lenny Faedo, Terry Felton, Gary Gaetti, Billy Gardner (MANAGER), Mickey Hatcher, Brad Havens, Kent Hrbek, Darrell Jackson, Randy Johnson, Tim Laudner, Jeff Little, Larry Milbourne *, Bobby Mitchell, Jack O'Connor, John Pacella *, Pete Redfern, Jesus Vega, Frank Viola, Gary Ward, Ron Washington, Greg Wells, Rob Wilfong *, Al Williams, Butch Wynegar *

LESS THAN 10 GAMES: Fernando Arroyo *, Don Cooper, Roger Erickson *, Pete Filson, Roy Smalley *, Ray Smith

KEY SIGNATURES: Hrbek, Brunansky, Viola.

VALUE: $75

1982 MONTREAL - Tim Blackwell, Ray Burris, Gary Carter, Warren Cromartie, Andre Dawson, Jim Fanning (MANAGER), Doug Flynn *, Terry Francona, Woody Fryman, Mike Gates, Bill Gullickson, Roy Johnson, Wallace Johnson, Charlie Lea, Bryan Little, Brad Mills, John Milner *, Dan Norman, Al Oliver, David Palmer, Ken Phelps, Mike

Phillips, Tim Raines, Jeff Reardon, Steve Rogers, Scott Sanderson, Dan Schatzeder *, Rodney Scott *, Bryn Smith, Chris Speier, Frank Taveras, Tim Wallach, Jerry White, Joel Youngblood *

LESS THAN 10 GAMES: Tom Gorman *, Brad Gulden, Bob James *, Bill Lee, Randy Lerch, Roland Office, Chris Smith, Mike Stenhouse, Dave Tomlin

KEY SIGNATURES: Oliver, Dawson, Raines, Carter, Reardon.

VALUE: $90

1982 NEW YORK (AL) - Doyle Alexander, Steve Balboni, Rick Cerone, Dave Collins, Bucky Dent *, Roger Erickson *, Barry Evans, Barry Foote, George Frazier, Oscar Gamble, Goose Gossage, Ken Griffey, Ron Guidry, Butch Hobson, Tommy John *, Clyde King (MANAGER), Dave LaRoche, Bob Lemon (MANAGER), Rudy May, John Mayberry *, Lee Mazzilli *, Gene Michael (MANAGER), Larry Milbourne *, Mike Morgan, Jerry Mumphrey, Bobby Murcer, Graig Nettles, Mike Patterson, Lou Piniella, Willie Randolph, Shane Rawley, Dave Revering *, Dave Righetti, Andre Robertson, Rodney Scott *, Roy Smalley *, Dave Winfield, Butch Wynegar *

LESS THAN 10 GAMES: Juan Espino, Jay Howell, Curt Kaufman, Jim Lewis, Don Mattingly, Lynn McGlothen, John Pacella *, Bobby Ramos, Eddie Rodriguez, Dave Stegman, Bob Watson *, Stefan Wever

KEY SIGNATURES: Lemon, Nettles, Winfield, Piniella, Murcer, Mattingly, John, Guidry, Gossage.

VALUE: $150

1982 NEW YORK (NL) - Neil Allen, Wally Backman, Bob Bailor, George Bamberger (MANAGER), Bruce Bochy, Hubie Brooks, Pete Falcone, George Foster, Ron Gardenhire, Brian Giles, Tom Hausman *, Ron Hodges, Mike Howard, Randy Jones, Mike Jorgensen, Dave Kingman, Terry Leach, Ed Lynch, Phil Mankowski, Jesse Orosco, Charlie Puleo, Gary Rajsich, Mike Scott, Rusty Staub, John Stearns, Craig Swan, Rusty Tillman, Ellis Valentine, Tom Veryzer, Mookie Wilson, Joel Youngblood *, Pat Zachry

LESS THAN 10 GAMES: Carlos Diaz *, Brent Gaff, Tom Gorman *, Scott Holman, Rick Ownbey, Ronn Reynolds, Doug Sisk, Rick Sweet *, Walt Terrell

KEY SIGNATURES: Kingman, Foster.

VALUE: $100

1982 OAKLAND - Tony Armas, Fernando Arroyo *, Dave Beard, Jeff Burroughs, John D'Acquisto, Mike Davis, Danny Goodwin, Wayne Gross, Preston Hanna *, Mike Heath, Rickey Henderson, Cliff Johnson, Jeff Jones, Bob Kearney, Matt Keough, Brian Kingman, Mickey Klutts, Rick Langford, Davey Lopes, Billy Martin (MANAGER), Dave Mckay, Steve McCatty, Bo McLaughlin, Dan Meyer, Kelvin Moore, Dwayne Murphy, Jeff Newman, Mike Norris, Bob Owchinko, Mitchell Page, Tony Phillips, Rob Picciolo *, Joe Rudi, Jimmy Sexton, Jim Spencer, Fred Stanley, Tom Underwood

LESS THAN 10 GAMES: Steve Baker, Kevin Bell, Rick Bosetti, Darrell Brown, Chris Codiroli, Tim Conroy, Dennis Kinney

KEY SIGNATURES: Martin, Henderson.

VALUE: $150

1982 PHILADELPHIA - Luis Aguayo, Porfirio Altamirano, Warren Brusstar *, Marty

Bystrom, Steve Carlton, Larry Christenson, Pat Corrales (MANAGER), Dick Davis *, Bob Dernier, Ivan DeJesus, Bo Diaz, Ed Farmer, Julio Franco, Greg Gross, Mike Krukow, Sparky Lyle *, Garry Maddox, Gary Matthews, Len Matuszek, Tug McGraw, Bob Molinaro *, Sid Monge, Willie Montanez *, Ron Reed, Dave Roberts, Bill Robinson *, Pete Rose, Dick Ruthven, Mike Schmidt, Manny Trillo, Del Unser, Ozzie Virgil, George Vukovich

LESS THAN 10 GAMES: Stan Bahnsen *, Jay Baller, John Denny *, Jerry Reed *, Alex Sanchez

NOTES: Carlton (CY).

KEY SIGNATURES: Rose, Schmidt, Carlton, Lyle.

VALUE: $125

CY = **Cy Young Award winner**

1982 PITTSBURGH - Ross Baumgarten, Dale Berra, John Candelaria, Dick Davis *, Mike Easler, Doug Frobel, Cecilio Guante, Brian Harper, Richie Hebner *, Lee Lacy, Bill Madlock, Larry McWilliams *, John Milner *, Willie Montanez *, Omar Moreno, Jim Morrison *, Paul Moskau, Steve Nicosia, Randy Niemann, Dave Parker, Tony Pena, Johnny Ray, Rick Rhoden, Don Robinson, Bill Robinson *, Enrique Romo, Manny Sarmiento, Rod Scurry, Jimmy Smith, Eddie Solomon *, Willie Stargell, Chuck Tanner (MANAGER), Kent Tekulve, Jason Thompson, Reggie Walton

LESS THAN 10 GAMES: Rafael Belliard, Tom Griffin, Grant Jackson *, Wayne Nordhagen *, Nelson Norman, Junior Ortiz, Ken Reitz, Lee Tunnell, Hedi Vargas

KEY SIGNATURES: Madlock, Parker, Stargell, Candelaria, Tekulve.

VALUE: $90

1982 SAN DIEGO - Randy Bass *, Kurt Bevacqua, Juan Bonilla, Dan Boone *, Floyd Chiffer, John Curtis *, Luis DeLeon, Dave Dravecky, Dave Edwards, Juan Eichelberger, Tim Flannery, Tony Gwynn, Andy Hawkins, Ruppert Jones, Terry Kennedy, Rick Lancellotti, Jody Lansford, Joe Lefebvre, Sixto Lezcano, Tim Lollar, Gary Lucas, John Montefusco, Broderick Perkins, Joe Pittman *, Mario Ramirez, Gene Richards, Luis Salazar, Eric Show, Steve Swisher, Garry Templeton, Chris Welsh, Alan Wiggins, Dick Williams (MANAGER)

LESS THAN 10 GAMES: Mike Griffin, Doug Gwosdz, George Hinshaw, Jerry Manuel, Ron Tingley, Rick Wise

KEY SIGNATURES: Kennedy, Gwynn.

VALUE: $90

1982 SAN FRANCISCO - Jim Barr, Jose Barrios, Dave Bergman, Fred Breining, Bob Brenly, Jack Clark, Chili Davis, Darrell Evans, Alan Fowlkes, Rich Gale, Atlee Hammaker, Al Holland, Duane Kuiper, Bill Laskey, Gary Lavelle, Jeff Leonard, Johnnie LeMaster, Renie Martin, Milt May, Greg Minton, Joe Morgan, Tom O'Malley, Joe Pettini, Jeff Ransom, Frank Robinson (MANAGER), Dan Schatzeder *, Reggie Smith, Guy Sularz, Champ Summers, Max Venable, Jim Wohlford

LESS THAN 10 GAMES: Mike Chris, Mark Dempsey, Scott Garrelts, Andy McGaffigan, Ron Pruitt, John Rabb, Brad Wellman

KEY SIGNATURES: Robinson, Morgan, Clark, Leonard.

VALUE: $75

1982 SEATTLE - Larry Andersen, Floyd Bannister, Jim Beattie, Bruce Bochte, Thad Bosley, Bobby Brown, Terry Bulling, Manny Castillo, Bill Caudill, Bryan Clark, Al Cowens, Julio Cruz, Todd Cruz, Dave Edler, Jim Essian, Gary Gray, Dave Henderson, Rene Lachemann (MANAGER), Jim Maler, Mike Moore, John Moses, Ron Musselman, Gene Nelson, Gaylord Perry, Lenny Randle, Dave Revering *, Paul Serna, Joe Simpson, Mike Stanton, Steve Stroughter, Rick Sweet *, Ed Vande Berg, Richie Zisk

LESS THAN 10 GAMES: Rich Bordi, Dan Firova, Jerry Don Gleaton, Vance McHenry, Orlando Mercado, Edwin Nunez, Domingo Ramos, Bob Stoddard

KEY SIGNATURES: Perry.

VALUE: $75

1982 ST. LOUIS - Joaquin Andujar, Doug Bair, Steve Braun, Glenn Brummer, Bob Forsch, Julio Gonzalez, David Green, George Hendrick, Keith Hernandez, Tommy Herr, Whitey Herzog (MANAGER), Dane Iorg, Jim Kaat, Jeff Keener, Jeff Lahti, Tito Landrum, Dave LaPoint, Mark Littell, John Martin, Willie McGee, Steve Mura, Ken Oberkfell, Kelly Paris, Darrell Porter, Mike Ramsey, Andy Rincon, Gene Roof, Orlando Sanchez, Lonnie Smith, Ozzie Smith, John Stuper, Bruce Sutter, Gene Tenace

LESS THAN 10 GAMES: Eric Rasmussen

NOTES: World Champions!

KEY SIGNATURES: Hernandez, Smith, McGee.

VALUE: $325

1982 TEXAS - Randy Bass *, Buddy Bell, Terry Bogener, Danny Boitano, John Butcher, Nick Capra, Steve Comer, Danny Darwin, Bucky Dent *, Doug Flynn *, Johnny Grubb, Rick Honeycutt, Dave Hostetler, Charlie Hough, Bobby Johnson, Lamar Johnson, Darrell Johnson (MANAGER), Jon Matlack, Lee Mazzilli *, Doc Medich *, Mario Mendoza, Paul Mirabella, Pete O'Brien, Larry Parrish, Pat Putnam, Mike Richardt, Mickey Rivers, Leon Roberts *, Billy Sample, Dave Schmidt, Bill Stein, Jim Sundberg, Frank Tanana, Wayne Tolleson, Mark Wagner, Don Werner, George Wright, Don Zimmer (MANAGER)

LESS THAN 10 GAMES: Jim Farr, Tom Henke, Mike Mason, Mike Smithson

KEY SIGNATURES: Bell.

VALUE: $75

1982 TORONTO - Glenn Adams, Jesse Barfield, Mark Bomback, Barry Bonnell, Jim Clancy, Bobby Cox (MANAGER), Dick Davis *, Damaso Garcia, Jerry Garvin, Dave Geisel, Jim Gott, Alfredo Griffin, Garth Iorg, Roy Lee Jackson, Tony Johnson, Luis Leal, Buck Martinez, John Mayberry *, Joey McLaughlin, Lloyd Moseby, Rance Mulliniks, Dale Murray, Wayne Nordhagen *, Geno Petralli, Hosken Powell, Dave Revering *, Leon Roberts *, Steve Senteney, Dave Stieb, Willie Upshaw, Otto Velez, Ernie Whitt, Al Woods

LESS THAN 10 GAMES: Dave Baker, Dick Davis *, Mark Eichhorn, Pedro Hernandez, Ken Schrom

KEY SIGNATURES: Barfield, Stieb.

VALUE: $75

1983

1983 New York Mets

1983 ATLANTA - Steve Bedrosian, Rick Behenna *, Bruce Benedict, Tony Brizzolara, Brett Butler, Rick Camp, Chris Chambliss, Ken Dayley, Pete Falcone, Terry Forster, Gene Garber, Albert Hall, Terry Harper, Bob Horner, Glenn Hubbard, Randy Johnson, Mike Jorgensen *, Brad Komminsk, Rick Mahler, Craig McMurtry, Donnie Moore, Dale Murphy, Phil Niekro, Larry Owen, Pascual Perez, Gerald Perry, Biff Pocoroba, Rafael Ramirez, Jerry Royster, Ken Smith, Joe Torre (MANAGER), Claudell Washington, Bob Watson

LESS THAN 10 GAMES: Len Barker *, Tommy Boggs, Jeff Dedmon, Brook Jacoby, Paul Runge, Matt Sinatro, Bob Walk, Paul Zuvella

NOTES: Murphy (MVP).

KEY SIGNATURES: Murphy, Butler, Niekro.

VALUE: $75

MVP = MVP Award winner

1983 BALTIMORE - Joe Altobelli (MANAGER), Benny Ayala, Mike Boddicker, Al Bumbry, Todd Cruz *, Rich Dauer, Storm Davis, Rick Dempsey, Jim Dwyer, Mike Flanagan, Dan Ford, Glenn Gulliver, Leo Hernandez, Tito Landrum *, John Lowenstein, Dennis Martinez, Tippy Martinez, Scott McGregor, Dan Morogiello, Eddie Murray, Joe Nolan, Jim Palmer, Allan Ramirez, Gary Reonicke, Cal Ripken, Aurelio Rodriguez *, Lenn Sakata, John Shelby, Ken Singleton, Sammy Stewart, Tim Stoddard, Don Welchel, Mike Young

LESS THAN 10 GAMES: Bob Bonner, Dave Huppert, Paul Mirabella, John Stefero, Bill Swaggerty

NOTES: World Champions! Ripken (MVP)

KEY SIGNATURES: Murray, Ripken, Palmer.

VALUE: $300

*** = player was traded**

1983 BOSTON - Gary Allenson, Luis Aponte, Tony Armas, Marty Barrett, Doug Bird, Wade Boggs, Oil Can Boyd, Mike Brown, Mark Clear, Dennis Eckersley, Dwight Evans, Rich Gedman, Glenn Hoffman, Ralph Houk (MANAGER), Bruce Hurst, John Henry Johnson, Ed Jurak, Rick Miller, Jeff Newman, Reid Nichols, Bob Ojeda, Jerry Remy, Jim Rice, Bob Stanley, Dave Stapleton, John Tudor, Julio Valez, Carl Yastrzemski

LESS THAN 10 GAMES: Lee Graham, Jackie Gutierrez, Al Nipper, Chico Walker

KEY SIGNATURES: Boggs, Rice, Yastrzemski, Eckersley.

VALUE: $125

1983 CALIFORNIA - Don Aase, Rick Adams, Juan Beniguez, Bob Boone, Curt Brown, Mike Brown, Steve Brown, Rick Burleson, Rod Carew, Bobby Clark, Doug Corbett, John Curtis, Doug DeCinces, Brian Downing, Joe Ferguson, Tim Foli, Ken Forsch, Dave Goltz, Bobby Grich, Andy Hassler, Reggie Jackson, Ron Jackson, Tommy John, Bruce Kison, Steve Lubratich, Fred Lynn, Byron McLaughlin, John McNamara (MANAGER), Jerry Narron, Mike O'Berry, Ed Ott, Gary Pettis, Luis Sanchez, Dick Schofield, Daryl Sconiers, Rick Steirer, Bill Travers, Ellis Valentine, Rob Wilfong, Mike Witt, Geoff Zahn

LESS THAN 10 GAMES: Bob Lacey

KEY SIGNATURES: Carew, Lynn, Boone, Jackson, John.

VALUE: $100

1983 CHICAGO (AL) - Juan Agosto, Harold Baines, Floyd Bannister, Salome Barojas, Tony Bernazard *, Britt Burns, Julio Cruz *, Rich Dotson, Jerry Dybzinski, Carlton Fisk, Scott Fletcher, Lorenzo Gray, Jerry Hairston, Kevin Hickey, Marc Hill, Guy Hoffman, LaMarr Hoyt, Ron Kittle, Jerry Koosman, Rusty Kuntz *, Dennis Lamp, Rudy Law, Vance Law, Tony LaRussa (MANAGER), Greg Luzinski, Chris Nyman, Tom Paciorek, Aurelio Rodriguez *, Mike Squires, Dave Stegman, Dick Tidrow, Greg Walker

LESS THAN 10 GAMES: Miguel Dilone *, Tim Hulett, Al Jones, Jim Kern, Randy Martz, Steve Mura, Casey Parsons, Joel Skinner

NOTES: Hoyt (CY), Kittle (ROY).

KEY SIGNATURES: Baines, Kittle, Fisk, Hoyt.

VALUE: $150

CY = Cy Young Award winner

1983 CHICAGO (NL) - Rich Bordi, Thad Bosley, Larry Bowa, Warren Brusstar, Bill Buckner, Bill Campbell, Joe Carter, Ron Cey, Jody Davis, Leon Durham, Lee Elia (MANAGER), Charlie Fox (MANAGER), Tom Grant, Mel Hall, Willie Hernandez *, Ferguson Jenkins, Bill Johnson, Jay Johnstone, Junior Kennedy, Steve Lake, Craig Lefferts, Carmelo Martinez, Jerry Morales, Keith Moreland, Dickie Noles, Wayne Nordhagen, Dave Owen, Mike Proly, Chuck Rainey, Dan Rohn, Dick Ruthven *, Ryne Sandberg, Lee Smith, Scot Thompson, Steve Trout, Tom Veryzer, Gary Woods

LESS THAN 10 GAMES: Fritz Connally, Mike Diaz, Alan Hargesheimer, Jay Loviglio, Paul Moskau, Reggie Patterson, Rick Reuschel *, Don Schulze

KEY SIGNATURES: Buckner, Sandberg, Jenkins, Hernandez.

VALUE: $125

1983 CINCINNATI - Skeeter Barnes, Johnny Bench, Bruce Berenyi, Dann Bilardello, Cesar Cedeno, Steve Christmas *, Dave Concepcion, Dan Driessen, Nick Esasky, Tom Foley, Rich Gale, Ben Hayes, Paul Householder, Tom Hume, Jeff Jones, Alan Knicely, Wayne Krenchicki *, Eddie Milner, Russ Nixon (MANAGER), Ron Oester, Kelly Paris, Frank Pastore, Ted Power, Joe Price, Charlie Puleo, Gary Redus, Jeff Russell, Bill Scherrer, Mario Soto, Alex Trevino, Duane Walker, Dallas Williams

LESS THAN 10 GAMES: Keefe Cato, Greg Harris, Rafael Landestoy *, Brad Lesley

KEY SIGNATURES: Concepcion, Bench.

VALUE: $75

1983 CLEVELAND - Bud Anderson, Chris Bando, Alan Bannister, Len Barker *, Bert Blyleven, Tom Brennan, Carmen Castillo, Pat Corrales (MANAGER), Miguel Dilone *, Jamie Easterly *, Juan Eichelberger, Jim Essian, Mike Ferraro (MANAGER), Mike Fischlin, Julio Franco, Ed Glynn, Mike Hargrove, Toby Harrah, Ron Hassey, Neal Heaton, Mike Jeffcoat, Rick Manning, Bake McBride, Jack Perconte, Broderick Perkins, Kevin Rhomberg, Lary Sorensen, Dan Spillner, Rick Sutcliffe, Pat Tabler, Gorman Thomas *, Andre Thornton, Manny Trillo *, George Vukovich

LESS THAN 10 GAMES: Rich Barnes, Rick Behenna *, Ernie Camacho, Wil Culmer, Karl Pagel, Jerry Reed, Otto Velez, Rick Waits *

KEY SIGNATURES: Franco, Harrah, Blyleven.

VALUE: $75

1983 DETROIT - Sparky Anderson (MANAGER), Howard Bailey, Doug Bair *, Juan Berenguer, Tom Brookens, Enos Cabell, Marty Castillo, Bill Fahey, Kirk Gibson, Julio Gonzalez, Johnny Grubb, Dave Gumpert, Larry Herndon, Mike Ivie, Howard Johnson, Lynn Jones, Wayne Krenchicki *, Mike Laga, Rick Leach, Chet Lemon, Aurelio Lopez, John Martin *, Jack Morris, Lance Parrish, Larry Pashnick, Dan Petry, Dave Rozema, Alan Trammell, Jerry Ujdur, Lou Whitaker, Milt Wilcox, Glenn Wilson, John Wockenfuss

LESS THAN 10 GAMES: Glenn Abbott *, Sal Butera, Bob James *, Bob Molinaro *, Bill Nahorodny, Dave Rucker *, Pat Underwood

KEY SIGNATURES: Anderson, Whitaker, Trammell, Johnson, Morris.

VALUE: $125

1983 HOUSTON - Alan Ashby, Kevin Bass, George Bjorkman, Jose Cruz, Bill Dawley, Frank DiPino, Bill Doran, Phil Garner, Bob Knepper, Ray Knight, Frank LaCorte, Mike LaCoss, Bob Lillis (MANAGER), Mike Madden, John Mizerock, Omar Moreno *, Jerry Mumphrey *, Joe Niekro, Terry Puhl, Luis Pujols, Craig Reynolds, Vern Ruhle, Nolan Ryan, Mike Scott, Tony Scott, Dave Smith, Harry Spilman, Dickie Thon, Tim Tolman, Denny Walling

LESS THAN 10 GAMES: Jeff Heathcock, Scott Loucks, Bert Pena, Julio Solano

KEY SIGNATURES: Ryan.

VALUE: $90

1983 KANSAS CITY - Willie Aikens, Mike Armstrong, Bud Black, Vida Blue, George Brett, Bill Castro, Onix Concepcion, Keith Creel, Butch Davis, Cesar Geronimo, Larry

Gura, Don Hood, Dick Howser (MANAGER), Mark Huismann, Dennis Leonard, Jerry Martin, Hal McRae, Darryl Motley, Amos Otis, Gaylord Perry *, Greg Pryor, Dan Quisenberry, Eric Rasmussen *, Steve Renko, Leon Roberts, Pat Sheridan, Joe Simpson, Don Slaught, Paul Splittorff, U.L. Washington, John Wathan, Frank White, Willie Wilson

LESS THAN 10 GAMES: Buddy Biancalana, Danny Jackson, Ron Johnson, Cliff Pastericky, Bob Tufts, Frnak Wills

KEY SIGNATURES: Brett, Quisenberry, Perry.

VALUE: $100

1983 LOS ANGELES - Dave Anderson, Dusty Baker, Joe Beckwith, Sid Bream, Greg Brock, Cecil Espy, Jack Fimple, Pedro Guerrero, Burt Hooton, Steve Howe, Rafael Landestoy *, Ken Landreaux, Tom Lasorda (MANAGER), Candy Maldonado, Mike Marshall, Rick Monday, Jose Morales, Tom Niedenfuer, Alejandro Pena, Jerry Reuss, Gil Reyes, R.J. Reynolds, German Rivera, Ron Roenicke *, Bill Russell, Steve Sax, Mike Scioscia, Dave Stewart *, Alex Taveras, Derrell Thomas, Fernando Valenzuela, Bob Welch, Steve Yeager, Pat Zachry,

LESS THAN 10 GAMES: Sid Fernandez, Orel Hershiser, Rick Honeycutt *, Rich Rodas, Dave Sax, Larry White, Ricky Wright *

KEY SIGNATURES: Sax, Guerrero, Valenzuela, Welch, Stewart, Hershiser.

VALUE: $145

1983 MILWAUKEE - Jerry Augustine, Mark Brouhard, Mike Caldwell, Tom Candiotti, Cecil Cooper, Jamie Easterly *, Marshall Edwards, Jim Gantner, Bob Gibson, Moose Haas, Roy Howell, Dion James, Harvey Kuenn (MANAGER), Pete Ladd, Rick Manning *, Bob McClure, Paul Molitor, Don Money, Charlie Moore, Ben Oglivie, Rob Picciolo, Chuck Porter, Randy Ready, Ed Romero, Bill Schroeder, Ted Simmons, Bob Skube, Jim Slaton, Don Sutton, Tom Tellmann, Gorman Thomas *, Ned Yost, Robin Yount

LESS THAN 10 GAMES: Andy Beene, Jaime Cocanower, Pete Vuckovich, Rick Waits *

KEY SIGNATURES: Yount, Molitor, Simmons.

VALUE: $90

1983 MINNESOTA - Darrell Brown, Tom Brunansky, Randy Bush, Bobby Castillo, John Castino, Ron Davis, Dave Engle, Lenny Faedo, Pete Filson, Gary Gaetti, Greg Gagne, Billy Gardner (MANAGER), Mickey Hatcher, Brad Havens, Kent Hrbek, Houston Jiminez, Rusty Kuntz *, Tim Laudner, Rick Lysander, Bobby Mitchell, Jack O'Connor, Bryan Oelkers, Ken Schrom, Ray Smith, Tim Teufel, Scott Ullger, Frank Viola, Mike Walters, Gary Ward, Ron Washington, Len Whitehouse, Al Williams

LESS THAN 10 GAMES: Jim Eisenreich, Jim Lewis, Jay Pettibone, Tack Wilson

KEY SIGNATURES: Hrbek, Brunansky, Viola.

VALUE: $75

1983 MONTREAL - Ray Burris, Gary Carter, Warren Cromartie, Terry Crowley, Andre Dawson, Doug Flynn, Terry Francona, Bill Gullickson, Bob James *, Charlie Lea, Randy Lerch *, Bryan Little, Brad Mills, Al Oliver, Tim Raines, Bobby Ramos, Jeff Reardon, Steve Rogers, Angel Salazar, Scott Sanderson, Dan Schatzeder, Bryn Smith, Chris Speier, Mike Stenhouse, Manny Trillo *, Mike Vail *, Bill Virdon (MANAGER), Tim Wallach, Chris Welsh *, Jerry White, Jim Wohlford

LESS THAN 10 GAMES: Greg Bargar, Tim Blackwell, Tom Dixon, Woody Fryman, Mike Fuentes, Dick Grapenthin, Wallace Johnson *, Mike Phillips, Gene Roof *, Razor Shines, Tom Wieghaus

KEY SIGNATURES: Oliver, Dawson, Raines, Carter.

VALUE: $90

1983 NEW YORK (AL) - Doyle Alexander *, Steve Balboni, Don Baylor, Bert Campaneris, Rick Cerone, Brian Dayett, Ray Fontenot, George Frazier, Oscar Gamble, Goose Gossage, Ken Griffey, Ron Guidry, Jay Howell, Steve Kemp, Matt Keough *, Billy Martin (MANAGER), Don Mattingly, Rudy May, Bobby Meacham, Larry Milourne *, Omar Moreno *, Jerry Mumphrey, Dale Murray, Graig Nettles, Otis Nixon, Lou Piniella, Willie Randolph, Shane Rawley, Rick Reuschel *, Dave Righetti, Andre Roberston, Bob Shirley, Roy Smalley, Dave Winfield, Butch Wynegar

LESS THAN 10 GAMES: Roger Erickson, Juan Espino, Curt Kaufman, Dave LaRoche, John Montefusco *, Bobby Murcer, Rowland Office

KEY SIGNATURES: Martin, Nettles, Winfield, Piniella, Murcer, Guidry, Gossage.

VALUE: $200

1983 NEW YORK (NL) - Neil Allen *, Tucker Ashford, Wally Backman, Bob Bailor, George Bamberger (MANAGER), Mark Bradley, Hubie Brooks, Carlos Diaz, George Foster, Ron Gardenhire, Brian Giles, Tom Gorman, Danny Heep, Keith Hernandez *, Ron Hodges, Scott Holman, Frank Howard (MANAGER), Clint Hurdle, Mike Jorgensen *, Dave Kingman, Ed Lynch, Jose Oquendo, Jesse Orosco, Junior Ortiz *, Rick Ownbey, Gary Rajsich, Ronn Reynolds, Tom Seaver, Doug Sisk, Rusty Staub, Darryl Strawberry, Craig Swan, Walt Terrell, Mike Torrez, Mookie Wilson

LESS THAN 10 GAMES: Mike Bishop, Ron Darling, Mike Fitzgerald, Brent Gaff, Mike Howard, Tim Leary, John Stearns

NOTES: Strawberry (ROY).

KEY SIGNATURES: Strawberry, Foster, Staub, Kingman, Seaver.

VALUE: $125

ROY = Rookie of the Year

1983 OAKLAND - Bill Almon, Keith Atherton, Steve Baker *, Dave Beard, Steve Boros (MANAGER), Tom Burgmeier, Jeff Burroughs, Darryl Cias, Chris Codiroli, Tim Conroy, Mike Davis, Wayne Gross, Garry Hancock, Mike Heath, Gorman Heimueller, Rickey Henderson, Donnie Hill, Jeff Jones, Bob Kearney, Matt Keough *, Bill Krueger, Carney Lansford, Davey Lopes, Steve McCatty, Rusty McNealy, Dan Meyer, Kelvin Moore, Dwayne Murphy, Mike Norris, Mitchell Page, Rickey Peters, Tony Phillips, Luis Quinones, Tom Underwood, Mike Warren

LESS THAN 10 GAMES: Bert Bradley, Marshall Brant, Ben Callahan, Ed Farmer *, Dave Hudgens, Rick Langford, Mark Smith, Rich Wortham, Curt Young

KEY SIGNATURES: Lansford, Henderson.

VALUE: $75

1983 PHILADELPHIA - Porfirio Altamirano, Larry Andersen, Marty Bystrom, Steve Carlton, Pat Corrales (MANAGER), John Denny, Bob Dernier, Ivan DeJesus, Bo Diaz, Ed Farmer *, Kiko Garcia, Greg Gross, Kevin Gross, Von Hayes, Willie Hernandez *, Al

Holland, Charlie Hudson, Steve Jeltz, Joe Lefebvre *, Sixto Lezcano *, Garry Maddox, Gary Matthews, Len Matuszek, Tug McGraw, Larry Milbourne *, Bob Molinaro *, Sid Monge *, Joe Morgan, Paul Owens (MANAGER), Tony Perez, Ron Reed, Bill Robinson, Pete Rose, Juan Samuel, Mike Schmidt, Ozzie Virgil

LESS THAN 10 GAMES: Luis Aguayo, Don Carman, Larry Christenson, Steve Comer, Tim Corcoran, Darren Daulton, Tony Ghelfi, Dick Ruthven *, Alex Sanchez, Jeff Stone

NOTES: Denny (CY).

KEY SIGNATURES: Rose, Morgan, Schmidt, Perez, Denny, Hernandez.

VALUE: $250

CY = Cy Young Award winner

1983 PITTSBURGH - Dale Berra, Jim Bibby, John Candelaria, Jose DeLeon, Mike Easler, Doug Frobel, Cecilio Guante, Brian Harper, Richie Hebner, Lee Lacy, Bill Madlock, Lee Mazzilli, Larry McWilliams, Jim Morrison, Steve Nicosia *, Dave Parker, Tony Pena, Johnny Ray, Rick Rhoden, Manny Sarmiento, Rod Scurry, Chuck Tanner (MANAGER), Kent Tekulve, Gene Tenace, Jason Thompson, Lee Tunnell, Marvell Wynne

LESS THAN 10 GAMES: Rafael Belliard, Miguel Dilone *, Milt May *, Randy Niemann, Joe Orsulak, Junior Ortiz *, Bob Owchinko, Alfonso Pulido, Don Robinson, Dave Tomlin, Jim Winn, Ron Wotus

KEY SIGNATURES: Madlock, Parker, Candelaria, Tekulve.

VALUE: $75

1983 SAN DIEGO - Kurt Bevacqua, Bruce Bochy, Juan Bonilla, Bobby Brown, Floyd Chiffer, Luis DeLeon, Dave Dravecky, Tim Flannery, Steve Garvey, Doug Gwosdz, Tony Gwynn, Andy Hawkins, Ruppert Jones, Terry Kennedy, Jody Lansford, Joe Lefebvre *, Sixto Lezcano *, Tim Lollar, Gary Lucas, Kevin McReynolds, Sid Monge *, John Montefusco *, Mario Ramirez, Gene Richards, Luis Salazar, Eric Show, Elias Sosa, Garry Templeton, Mark Thurmond, Jerry Turner, Ed Whitson, Alan Wiggins, Dick Williams (MANAGER)

LESS THAN 10 GAMES: Greg Booker, Mike Couchee, Jerry Davis, Marty Decker, Steve Fireovid, George Hinshaw, Dennis Rasmussen, Eddie Rodriguez, Chris Welsh *

KEY SIGNATURES: Garvey, Gwynn.

VALUE: $125

1983 SAN FRANCISCO - Jim Barr, Dave Bergman, Fred Breining, Bob Brenly, Mark Calvert, Jack Clark, Chili Davis, Mark Davis, Darrell Evans, Dan Gladden, Atlee Hammaker, Mike Krukow, Duane Kuiper, Bill Laskey, Gary Lavelle, Jeff Leonard, Johnnie LeMaster, Renie Martin, Milt May *, Andy McGaffigan, Greg Minton, Steve Nicosia *, Tom O'Malley, Joe Pettini, John Rabb, Frank Robinson (MANAGER), Chris Smith, Guy Sularz, Champ Summers, Mike Vail *, Max Venable, Brad Weilman, Joel Youngblood

LESS THAN 10 GAMES: Mike Chris, Scott Garrelts, Wallace Johnson *, Brian Kingman, Pat Larkin, Randy Lerch *, Rich Murray, Ron Pruitt, Jeff Ransom

KEY SIGNATURES: Robinson.

VALUE: $75

1983 SEATTLE - Glenn Abbott *, Jamie Allen, Rod Allen, Jim Beattie, Tony Bernazard *, Phil Bradley, Manny Castillo, Bill Caudill, Al Chambers, Bryan Clark, Darnell Coles,

Al Cowens, Del Crandall (MANAGER), Julio Cruz *, Todd Cruz *, Dave Edler, Dave Henderson, Steve Henderson, Rene Lachemann (MANAGER), Jim Maier, Orlando Mercado, Mike Moore, John Moses, Gene Nelson, Jamie Nelson, Ricky Nelson, Edwin Nunez, Spike Owen, Gaylord Perry *, Ken Phelps, Pat Putnam, Domingo Ramos, Harold Reynolds, Ron Roenicke *, Mike Stanton, Bob Stoddard, Rick Sweet, Roy Thomas, Ed Vande Berg, Matt Young, Richie Zisk

LESS THAN 10 GAMES: Karl Best, Terry Bulling, Bobby Castillo

KEY SIGNATURES: Perry.

VALUE: $75

1983 ST. LOUIS - Jim Adduci, Neil Allen *, Joaquin Andujar, Doug Bair *, Steve Braun, Glenn Brummer, Danny Cox, Jeff Doyle, Bob Forsch, David Green, George Hendrick, Keith Hernandez *, Tommy Herr, Whitey Herzog (MANAGER), Dane Iorg, Jim Kaat, Jeff Lahti, Dave LaPoint, Billy Lyons, John Martin *, Willie McGee, Ken Oberkfell, Darrell Porter, Jamie Quirk, Mike Ramsey, Floyd Raylord, Dave Rucker *, Rafael Santana, Lonnie Smith, Ozzie Smith, John Stuper, Bruce Sutter, Andy Van Slyke, Dave Von Ohlen

LESS THAN 10 GAMES: Steve Baker *, Ralph Citarella, Kevin Hagen, Jeff Keener, Tito Landrum *, Eric Rasmussen *, Gene Roof *, Orlando Sanchez, Jimmy Sexton

KEY SIGNATURES: Smith, McGee, Hernandez.

VALUE: $125

1983 TEXAS - Jim Anderson, Buddy Bell, Larry Biittner, John Butcher, Victor Cruz, Danny Darwin, Bucky Dent, Tommy Dunbar, Rick Honeycutt *, Dave Hostetler, Charlie Hough, Bobby Johnson, Bobby Jones, Odell Jones, Jon Matlack, Pete O'Brien, Larry Parrish, Doug Radar (MANAGER), Mike Richardt, Mickey Rivers, Billy Sample, Dave Schmidt, Mike Smithson, Bill Stein, Jim Sundberg, Frank Tanana, Dave Tobik, Wayne Tolleson, Curt Wilkerson, George Wright

LESS THAN 10 GAMES: Nick Capra, Tom Henke, Al Lachowicz, Mike Mason, Donnie Scott, Dave Stewart *, Mark Wagner, Ricky Wright *

KEY SIGNATURES: Bell, Stewart.

VALUE: $75

*** = player was traded**

1983 TORONTO - Jim Acker, Doyle Alexander *, Jesse Barfield, George Bell, Barry Bonnell, Jim Clancy, Stan Clarke, Dave Collins, Bobby Cox (MANAGER), Tony Fernandez, Damaso Garcia, Dave Geisel, Jim Gott, Alfredo Griffin, Garth Iorg, Roy Lee Jackson, Cliff Johnson, Mickey Klutts, Luis Leal, Buck Martinez, Joey McLaughlin, Randy Moffitt, Mike Morgan, Lloyd Moseby, Rance Mulliniks, Jorge Orta, Hosken Powell, Dave Stieb, Willie Upshaw, Mitch Webster, Ernie Whitt

LESS THAN 10 GAMES: Don Cooper, Geno Petralli, Matt Williams

KEY SIGNATURES: Bell, Fernandez, Stieb.

VALUE: $75

1984

1984 Detroit Tigers

* = player was traded

1984 ATLANTA - Len Barker, Steve Bedrosian, Bruce Benedict, Tony Brizzolara, Rick Camp, Chris Chambliss, Jeff Dedmon, Pete Falcone, Terry Forster, Gene Garber, Albert Hall, Terry Harper, Bob Horner, Glenn Hubbard, Randy Johnson, Mike Jorgensen *, Brad Komminsk, Rufino Linares, Rick Mahler, Craig McMurtry, Donnie Moore, Dale Murphy, Ken Oberkfell *, Pascual Perez, Gerald Perry, Rafael Ramirez, Jerry Royster, Paul Runge, Milt Thompson, Joe Torre (MANAGER), Alex Trevino *, Claudell Washington, Bob Watson, Paul Zuvella

LESS THAN 10 GAMES: Ken Dayley *, Mike Payne, Biff Pocoroba, Matt Sinatro, Zane Smith

KEY SIGNATURES: Murphy.

VALUE: $75

1984 BALTIMORE - Joe Altobelli (MANAGER), Benny Ayala, Mike Boddicker, Al Bumbry, Todd Cruz, Rich Dauer, Storm Davis, Rick Dempsey, Jim Dwyer, Mike Flanagan, Dan Ford, Wayne Gross, Ron Jackson *, John Lowenstein, Dennis Martinez, Tippy Martinez, Scott McGregor, Eddie Murray, Joe Nolan, Floyd Rayford, Cal Ripken, Vic Rodriguez, Gary Roenicke, Lenn Sakata, Orlando Sanchez *, John Shelby, Ken Singleton, Sammy Stewart, Bill Swaggerty, Jim Traber, Tom Underwood, Mike Young

LESS THAN 10 GAMES: Mark Brown, Todd Cruz, Ken Dixon, John Pacella, Jim Palmer, Larry Sheets, Nate Snell

KEY SIGNATURES: Murray, Ripken, Palmer.

VALUE: $125

1984 BOSTON - Gary Allenson, Tony Armas, Marty Barrett, Wade Boggs, Oil Can Boyd, Mike Brown, Bill Buckner *, Mark Clear, Roger Clemens, Steve Crawford, Mike Easler,

Dennis Eckersley *, Dwight Evans, Rich Gale, Rich Gedman, Jackie Gutierrez, Glenn Hoffman, Ralph Houk (MANAGER), Bruce Hurst, John Henry Johnson, Ed Jurak, Rick Miller, Charlie Mitchell, Jeff Newman, Reid Nichols, Al Nipper, Bob Ojeda, Jerry Remy, Jim Rice, Bob Stanley, Dave Stapleton

LESS THAN 10 GAMES: Jim Dorsey, Marc Sullivan, Chico Walker

KEY SIGNATURES: Buckner, Boggs, Rice, Clemens.

VALUE: $90

1984 CALIFORNIA - Don Aase, Juan Beniquez, Bob Boone, Mike Brown, Rod Carew, Doug Corbett, John Curtis, Doug Decinces, Brian Downing, Bobby Grich, Reggie Jackson, Ron Jackson *, Tommy John, Curt Kaufman, Bruce Kison, Frank LaCorte, Fred Lynn, John McNamara (MANAGER), Darrell Miller, Jerry Narron, Gary Pettis, Rob Picciolo, Ron Romanick, Luis Sanchez, Dick Schofield, Darryl Sconiers, Jim Slaton, Derrel Thomas *, Ellis Valentine, Rob Wilfong, Mike Witt, Geoff Zahn

LESS THAN 10 GAMES: Steve Brown, Rick Burleson, Stew Cliburn, Ken Forsch, D.W. Smith, Rick Steirer, Craig Swan *

KEY SIGNATURES: Carew, Lynn, Boone, Jackson, John.

VALUE: $100

1984 CHICAGO (AL) - Juan Agosto, Harold Baines, Floyd Bannister, Salome Barojas *, Daryl Boston, Britt Burns, Steve Christmas, Julio Cruz, Rich Dotson, Jerry Dybzinski, Carlton Fisk, Scott Fletcher, Jerry Gleaton, Jerry Hairston, Marc Hill, LaMarr Hoyt, Al Jones, Ron Kittle, Rudy Law, Vance Law, Tony LaRussa (MANAGER), Greg Luzinski, Gene Nelson, Tom O'Malley *, Tom Paciorek, Ron Reed, Bert Roberge, Tom Seaver, Joel Skinner, Roy Smalley *, Dan Spillner *, Mike Squires, Dave Stegman, Greg Walker

LESS THAN 10 GAMES: Tom Brennan, Bob Fallon, Tim Hulett, Randy Niemann, Casey Parsons, Jamie Quirk *, Jim Siwy, Mike Squires

KEY SIGNATURES: Baines, Fisk, Seaver.

VALUE: $75

1984 CHICAGO (NL) - Rich Bordi, Thad Bosley, Larry Bowa, Warren Brusstar, Bill Buckner *, Ron Cey, Henry Cotto, Jody Davis, Bob Dernier, Leon Durham, Dennis Eckersley *, George Frazier *, Jim Frey (MANAGER), Mel Hall *, Ron Hassey, Richie Hebner, Jay Johnstone, Steve Lake, Davey Lopes *, Gary Matthews, Keith Moreland, Dickie Noles *, Dave Owen, Reggie Patterson, Chuck Rainey *, Rick Reuschel, Dan Rohn, Dick Ruthven, Ryne Sandberg, Scott Sanderson, Lee Smith, Tim Stoddard, Rick Sutcliffe *, Steve Trout, Tom Veryzer, Gary Woods

LESS THAN 10 GAMES: Porfirio Altamirano, Billy Hatcher, Bill Johnson, Ron Meredith, Don Schulze *

NOTES: Sutcliffe (CY); Sandberg (MVP).

KEY SIGNATURES: Sandberg, Sutcliffe, Eckersley.

VALUE: $145

CY = Cy Young Award winner

1984 CINCINNATI - Skeeter Barnes, Bruce Berenyi *, Dann Bilardello, Cesar Cedeno, Dave Concepcion, Eric Davis, Dan Driessen *, Nick Esasky, Tom Foley, John Franco, Brad Gulden, Paul Householder *, Tom Hume, Alan Knicely, Wayne Krenchicki, Tom Lawless *, Brad Lesley, Eddie Milner, Ron Oester, Bob Owchinko, Dave Parker, Frank

Pastore, Tony Perez, Ted Power, Joe Price, Vern Rapp (MANAGER), Gary Redus, Ron Robinson, Pete Rose (MANAGER)*, Jeff Russell, Bill Scherrer *, Mario Soto, Jay Tibbs, Dave Van Gorder, Duane Walker

LESS THAN 10 GAMES: Tom Browning, Keefe Cato, Andy McGaffigan *, Charlie Puleo, Wade Rowden, Mike Smith, Freddie Toliver, Alex Trevino *, Carl Willis *

NOTES: Rose was traded to the Reds during the season and was a player/manager during the year.

KEY SIGNATURES: Rose, Concepcion, Parker, Perez, Davis.

VALUE: $90

1984 CLEVELAND - Luis Aponte, Chris Bando, Tony Bernazard, Bert Blyleven, Brett Butler, Ernie Camacho, Joe Carter, Carmen Castillo, Steve Comer, Pat Corrales (MANAGER), Jamie Easterly, Steve Farr, Mike Fischlin, Julio Franco, George Frazier *, Mel Hall *, Mike Hargrove, Ron Hassey *, Neal Heaton, Brook Jacoby, Mike Jeffcoat, Otis Nixon, Junior Noboa, Broderick Perkins, Kevin Rhomberg, Don Schulze *, Roy Smith, Dan Spillner *, Rick Sutcliffe *, Pat Tabler, Andre Thornton, George Vuckovich, Tom Waddell, Jerry Willard

LESS THAN 10 GAMES: Jeff Barkley, Rick Behenna, Jeff Moronko, Jamie Quirk *, Jose Roman, Ramon Romero, Jerry Ujdur

KEY SIGNATURES: Franco, Blyleven.

VALUE: $75

1984 DETROIT - Glenn Abbott, Rod Allen, Sparky Anderson (MANAGER), Doug Bair, Doug Baker, Juan Berenguer, Dave Bergman, Tom Brookens, Marty Castillo, Scott Earl, Darrell Evans, Barbaro Garbey, Kirk Gibson, Johnny Grubb, Willie Hernandez, Larry Herndon, Howard Johnson, Ruppert Jones, Rusty Kuntz, Chet Lemon, Aurelio Lopez, Dwight Lowry, Sid Monge *, Jack Morris, Lance Parrish, Dan Petry, Dave Rozema, Bill Scherrer *, Alan Trammell, Lou Whitaker, Milt Wilcox, Carl Willis *

LESS THAN 10 GAMES: Mike Laga, Roger Mason, Randy O'Neal, Nelson Simmons

NOTES: World Champions! Hernandez (CY) & (MVP).

KEY SIGNATURES: Anderson, Whitaker, Trammell, Johnson, Gibson, Morris, Hernandez.

VALUE: $325

CY = Cy Young Award winner

1984 HOUSTON - Alan Ashby, Mark Bailey, Alan Bannister *, Kevin Bass, Enos Cabell, Jose Cruz, Glenn Davis, Bill Dawley, Frank DiPino, Bill Doran, Phil Garner, Bob Knepper, Ray Knight *, Mike LaCoss, Bob Lillis (MANAGER), Scott Loucks, Mike Madden, John Mizerock, Jerry Mumphrey, Joe Niekro, Jim Pankovits, Bert Pena, Terry Puhl, Craig Reynolds, Mike Richardt *, Vern Ruhle, Nolan Ryan, Joe Sambito, Mike Scott, Tony Scott *, Dave Smith, Julio Solano, Harry Spilman, Denny Walling

LESS THAN 10 GAMES: Jeff Calhoun, Mark Ross, Dickie Thon, Tim Tolman, Tom Wieghaus

KEY SIGNATURES: Davis, Ryan.

VALUE: $90

1984 KANSAS CITY - Steve Balboni, Joe Beckwith, Buddy Biancalana, Bud Black, George Brett, Onix Concepcion, Butch Davis, Bucky Dent, Mark Gubicza, Larry Gura,

Dick Howser (MANAGER), Mark Huismann, Dane Iorg *, Danny Jackson, Lynn Jones Mike Jones, Charlie Leibrandt, Hal McRae, Darryl Motley, Jorge Orta, Greg Pryor, Da Quisenberry, Leon Roberts, Bret Saberhagen, Orlando Sanchez *, Pat Sheridan, Do Slaught, Paul Splittorff, U.L. Washington, John Wathan, Frank White, Frank Wills, Willie Wilson

LESS THAN 10 GAMES: Tucker Ashford, Dave Leeper, Luis Pujols, Leon Roberts, Jim Scranton

KEY SIGNATURES: Brett, Saberhagen.

VALUE: $12

1984 LOS ANGELES - Ed Amelung, Dave Anderson, Bob Bailor, Sid Bream, Tom Brewer, Greg Brock, Carlos Diaz, Jack Fimple, Pedro Guerrero, Orel Hershiser, Rick Honeycutt, Burt Hooton, Ken Howell, Rafael Landestoy, Ken Landreaux, Tom Lasorda (MANAGER), Candy Maldonado, Mike Marshall, Rick Monday, Jose Morales, Tom Niedenfuer, Alejandro Pena, Jerry Reuss, R.J. Reynolds, German Rivera, Bill Russell Steve Sax, Mike Scioscia, Franklin Stubbs, Mike Vail, Fernando Valenzuela, Bob Welch Terry Whitfield, Steve Yeager, Pat Zachry

LESS THAN 10 GAMES: Lemmie Miller, Gil Reyes, Rich Rodas, Larry White

KEY SIGNATURES: Sax, Guerrero, Valenzuela, Hershiser.

VALUE: $12

1984 MILWAUKEE - Mark Brouhard, Mike Caldwell, Bobby Clark, Jaime Cocanower Cecil Cooper, Rollie Fingers, Jim Gantner, Bob Gibson, Moose Haas, Roy Howell, Dion James, Rene Lachemann (MANAGER), Pete Ladd, Jack Lazorko, Doug Loman, Willie Lozado, Rick Manning, Bob McClure, Paul Molitor, Charlie Moore, Ben Oglivie, Chuck Porter, Randy Ready, Ed Romero, Bill Schroeder, Ray Searage, Ted Simmons, Jim Sundberg, Don Sutton, Tom Tellmann, Pete Vuckovich, Rick Waits, Robin Yount

LESS THAN 10 GAMES: Jerry Augustine, Andy Beene, Tom Candiotti, Paul Hartzell Jim Kern *

KEY SIGNATURES: Yount, Sutton.

VALUE: $9(

1984 MINNESOTA - Darrell Brown, Tom Brunansky, Randy Bush, John Butcher, Bobby Castillo, John Castino, Andre David, Ron Davis, Jim Eisenreich, Dave Engle, Lenny Faedo, Pete Filson, Gary Gaetti, Billy Gardner (MANAGER), Mike Hart, Mickey Hatcher, Ed Hodge, Kent Hrbek, Houston Jimenez, Tim Laudner, Rick Lysander, Dave Meier, Larry Pashnick, Kirby Puckett, Pat Putnam *, Jeff Reed, Ken Schrom, Mike Smithson, Chris Speier *, Tim Teufel, Frank Viola, Mike Walters, Ron Washington, Len Whitehouse, Al Williams

LESS THAN 10 GAMES: Keith Comstock, Alvaro Espinoza, Greg Gagne, Jack O'Connor, Curt Wardle

KEY SIGNATURES: Hrbek, Puckett, Viola.

VALUE: $9(

1984 MONTREAL - Gary Carter, Andre Dawson, Miguel Dilone, Dan Driessen *, Jim Fanning (MANAGER), Doug Flynn, Terry Francona, Rene Gonzales, Dick Grapenthin Bill Gullickson, Greg Harris *, Joe Hesketh, Bob James, Roy Johnson, Wallace Johnson Tom Lawless *, Charlie Lea, Bryan Little, Gary Lucas, Andy McGaffigan *, David

Palmer, Tim Raines, Bobby Ramos, Mike Ramsey *, Jeff Reardon, Steve Rogers, Pete Rose *, Angel Salazar, Dan Schatzeder, Tony Scott *, Razor Shines, Bryn Smith, Chris Speier *, Mike Stenhouse, Derrel Thomas *, Max Venable, Bill Virdon (MANAGER), Tim Wallach, Jim Wohlford

LESS THAN 10 GAMES: Greg Bargar, Fred Breining, Sal Butera, Mike Fuentes, Ron Johnson, Randy St. Claire

KEY SIGNATURES: Dawson, Raines, Carter, Rose.

VALUE: $90

1984 NEW YORK (AL) - Mike Armstrong, Don Baylor, Yogi Berra (MANAGER), Curt Brown, Rick Cerone, Clay Christiansen, Joe Cowley, Brian Dayett, Tim Foli, Ray Fontenot, Oscar Gamble, Ken Griffey, Ron Guidry, Toby Harrah, Jay Howell, Steve Kemp, Vic Mata, Don Mattingly, Bobby Meacham, John Montefusco, Omar Moreno, Dale Murray, Phil Niekro, Mike O'Berry, Mike Pagliarulo, Lou Piniella, Willie Randolph, Dennis Rasmussen, Shane Rawley *, Dave Righetti, Jose Rijo, Andre Robertson, Bob Shirley, Roy Smalley *, Dave Winfield, Butch Wynegar

LESS THAN 10 GAMES: Scott Bradley, Marty Bystrom *, Jim Deshaies, Rex Hudler, Stan Javier, Keith Smith

KEY SIGNATURES: Berra, Mattingly, Winfield, Piniella, Niekro, Guidry.

VALUE: $150

1984 NEW YORK (NL) - Wally Backman, Bruce Berenyi *, Hubie Brooks, Kelvin Chapman, Ron Darling, Sid Fernandez, Mike Fitzgerald, George Foster, Brent Gaff, Ron Gardenhire, Wes Gardner, John Gibbons, Dwight Gooden, Tom Gorman, Danny Heep, Keith Hernandez, Ron Hodges, Dave Johnson (MANAGER), Ross Jones, Ray Knight *, Tim Leary, Ed Lynch, Jerry Martin, Jose Oquendo, Jesse Orosco, Junior Ortiz, Rafael Santana, Doug Sisk, Rusty Staub, Darryl Strawberry, Craig Swan *, Walt Terrell, Dick Tidrow, Mookie Wilson, Herm Winningham

LESS THAN 10 GAMES: Billy Beane, John Christensen, Kevin Mitchell, Calvin Schiraldi, John Stearns, Mike Torrez *

NOTES: Gooden (ROY).

KEY SIGNATURES: Hernandez, Strawberry, Foster, Gooden.

VALUE: $125

ROY = Rookie of the Year

1984 OAKLAND - Bill Almon, Keith Atherton, Bruce Bochte, Steve Boros (MANAGER), Tom Burgmeier, Ray Burns, Jeff Burroughs, Bill Caudill, Chris Codiroli, Tim Conroy, Mike Davis, Jim Essian, Garry Hancock, Mike Heath, Rickey Henderson, Donnie Hill, Jeff Jones, Steve Kiefer, Dave Kingman, Bill Krueger, Carney Lansford, Davey Lopes *, Steve McCatty, Dan Meyer, Jackie Moore (MANAGER), Joe Morgan, Dwayne Murphy, Tony Phillips, Chuck Rainey *, Lary Sorensen, Mickey Tettleton, Mike Torrez *, Mark Wagner, Mike Warren, Curt Young

LESS THAN 10 GAMES: Jeff Bettendorf, Gorman Heimueller, Rick Langford, Dave Leiper, Mark Wagner

KEY SIGNATURES: Morgan, Lansford, Henderson.

VALUE: $90

1984 PHILADELPHIA - Luis Aguayo, Larry Andersen, Marty Bystrom *, Bill Campbell, Steve Carlton, Don Carman, Tim Corcoran, John Denny, Ivan DeJesus, Bo Diaz, Kiko

Garcia, Greg Gross, Kevin Gross, Von Hayes, Al Holland, Charlie Hudson, Steve Jeltz, Jerry Koosman, Joe Lefebvre, Sixto Lezcano, Garry Maddox, Len Matuszek, Tug McGraw, Francisco Melendez, Al Oliver *, Paul Owens (MANAGER), Shane Rawley *, John Russell, Juan Samuel, Mike Schmidt, Rick Schu, Jeff Stone, Ozzie Virgil, Glenn Wilson, John Wockenfuss

LESS THAN 10 GAMES: Steve Fireovid, Jim Kern *, Mike Lavalliere, Renie Martin *, Dave Wehrmeister

KEY SIGNATURES: Schmidt, Carlton.

VALUE: $125

1984 PITTSBURGH - Rafael Belliard, Dale Berra, John Candelaria, Jose DeLeon, Benny Distefano, Doug Frobel, Denny Gonzalez, Cecilio Guante, Brian Harper, Lee Lacy, Bill Madlock, Milt May, Lee Mazzilli, Larry McWilliams, Jim Morrison, Joe Orsulak, Amos Otis, Mitchell Page, Tony Pena, Johnny Ray, Rick Rhoden, Don Robinson, Rod Scurry, Chuck Tanner (MANAGER), Kent Tekulve, Jason Thompson, John Tudor, Lee Tunnell, Hedi Vargas, Ron Wotus, Marvell Wynne

LESS THAN 10 GAMES: Mike Bielecki, Chris Green, Ray Krawczyk, Alfonso Pulido, Bob Walk, Jim Winn, Jeff Zaske

KEY SIGNATURES: Madlock, Candelaria, Tekulve.

VALUE: $75

1984 SAN DIEGO - Kurt Bevacqua, Bruce Bochy, Greg Booker, Bobby Brown, Floyd Chiffer, Luis DeLeon, Dave Dravecky, Tim Flannery, Steve Garvey, Goose Gossage, Tony Gwynn, Greg Harris *, Andy Hawkins, Terry Kennedy, Craig Lefferts, Tim Lollar, Carmelo Martinez, Kevin McReynolds, Eddie Miller, Sid Monge *, Graig Nettles, Mario Ramirez, Ron Roenicke, Luis Salazar, Eric Show, Champ Summers, Garry Templeton, Mark Thurmond, Ed Whitson, Alan Wiggins, Dick Williams (MANAGER)

LESS THAN 10 GAMES: Doug Gwosdz

KEY SIGNATURES: Garvey, Nettles, Gwynn, Gossage.

VALUE: $225

1984 SAN FRANCISCO - Dusty Baker, Bob Brenly, Chris Brown, Mark Calvert, Jack Clark, Jeff Cornell, Chili Davis, Mark Davis, Rob Deer, Scott Garrelts, Dan Gladden, Randy Gomez, Mark Grant, Mike Krukow, Duane Kuiper, Bob Lacey, Bill Laskey, Gary Lavelle, Johnnie Le Master, Jeff Leonard, Randy Lerch, Renie Martin *, Greg Minton, Fran Mullins, Steve Nicosia, Tom O'Malley *, Al Oliver *, Danny Ozark (MANAGER), Joe Pittman, John Rabb, Gene Richards, Frank Robinson (MANAGER), Jeff Robinson, Alex Sanchez, Scot Thompson, Manny Trillo, Brad Wellman, Frank Williams, Joel Youngblood

LESS THAN 10 GAMES: Atlee Hammaker, George Riley

KEY SIGNATURES: Oliver, Leonard, Clark.

VALUE: $75

1984 SEATTLE - Salome Barojas *, Dave Beard, Jim Beattie, Barry Bonnell, Phil Bradley, Ivan Calderon, Al Chambers, Darnell Coles, Chuck Cottier (MANAGER), Al Cowens, Del Crandall (MANAGER), Alvin Davis, Dave Geisel, Dave Henderson, Steve Henderson, Bob Kearney, Mark Langston, Orlando Mercado, Larry Milbourne, Paul Mirabella, Mike Moore, John Moses, Bill Nahorodny, Edwin Nunez, Spike Owen, Jack

Perconte, Ken Phelps, Jim Presley, Pat Putnam *, Domingo Ramos, Harold Reynolds, Mike Stanton, Bob Stoddard, Danny Tartabull, Gorman Thomas, Roy Thomas, Dave Valle, Ed Vande Berg, Matt Young

LESS THAN 10 GAMES: Karl Best, Lee Guetterman, Ricky Nelson

NOTES: Davis (ROY).

KEY SIGNATURES: Davis, Tartabull, Langston.

VALUE: $75

ROY = Rookie of the Year

1984 ST. LOUIS - Neil Allen, Joaquin Andujar, Steve Braun, Glenn Brummer, Ralph Citarella, Danny Cox, Bob Forsch, David Green, George Hendrick, Tommy Herr, Whitey Herzog (MANAGER), Ricky Horton, Paul Householder *, Art Howe, Dane Iorg *, Mike Jorgensen, Kurt Kepshire, Jeff Lahti, Tito Landrum, Dave LaPoint, Billy Lyons, Willie McGee, Tom Nieto, Ken Oberkfell *, Terry Pendleton, Darrell Porter, Mike Ramsey *, Dave Rucker, Mark Salas, Lonnie Smith, Ozzie Smith, Chris Speier *, John Stuper, Bruce Sutter, Andy Van Slyke, Dave Von Ohlen

LESS THAN 10 GAMES: Ken Dayley *, Jose Gonzalez, Kevin Hagen, Andy Hassler, Rick Ownbey, Gary Rajsich

KEY SIGNATURES: O. Smith, McGee.

VALUE: $125

1984 TEXAS - Jim Anderson, Alan Bannister *, Buddy Bell, Danny Darwin, Tommy Dunbar, Marv Foley, Tom Henke, Dave Hostetler, Charlie Hough, Bobby Jones, Odell Jones, Jeff Kunkel, Mike Mason, Joey McLaughlin *, Dickie Noles *, Pete O'Brien, Larry Parrish, Doug Rader (MANAGER), Mickey Rivers, Billy Sample, Dave Schmidt, Donnie Scott, Bill Stein, Dave Stewart, Frank Tanana, Dave Tobik, Wayne Tolleson, Gary Ward, Curt Wilkerson, George Wright, Ned Yost

LESS THAN 10 GAMES: Jim Bibby, Kevin Buckley, Dwayne Henry, Mike Richardt *, Ricky Wright

KEY SIGNATURES: Stewart.

VALUE: $75

1984 TORONTO - Jim Acker, Willie Aikens, Doyle Alexander, Jesse Barfield, George Bell, Jim Clancy, Bryan Clark, Dave Collins, Bobby Cox (MANAGER), Tony Fernandez, Damaso Garcia, Jim Gott, Alfredo Griffin, Kelly Gruber, Garth Iorg, Roy Lee Jackson, Cliff Johnson, Jimmy Key, Dennis Lamp, Rick Leach, Luis Leal, Fred Manrique, Buck Martinez, Lloyd Moseby, Rance Mulliniks, Ron Musselman, Ron Shepherd, Dave Stieb, Willie Upshaw, Mitch Webster, Ernie Whitt

LESS THAN 10 GAMES: Toby Hernandez, Rick Leach, Joey McLaughlin *, Geno Petralli

KEY SIGNATURES: Bell, Fernandez, Stieb.

VALUE: $100

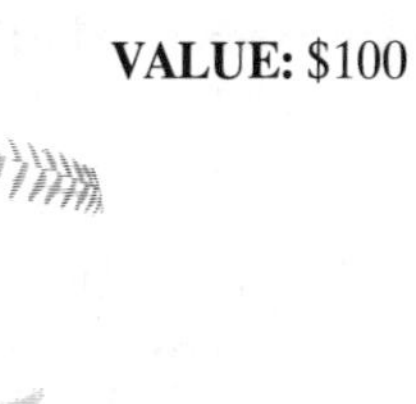

1985

1985 American League MVP Don Mattingly

* = player was traded

1985 ATLANTA - Len Barker, Steve Bedrosian, Bruce Benedict, Rick Camp, Rick Cerone, Chris Chambliss, Jeff Dedmon, Terry Forster, Gene Garber, Eddie Haas (MANAGER), Albert Hall, Terry Harper, Bob Horner, Glenn Hubbard, Joe Johnson, Brad Komminsk, Rick Mahler, Craig McMurtry, Dale Murphy, Ken Oberkfell, Larry Owen, Pascual Perez, Gerald Perry, Rafael Ramirez, Paul Runge, Steve Shields, Zane Smith, Bruce Sutter, Andres Thomas, Milt Thompson, Claudell Washington, Bobby Wine (MANAGER), Paul Zuvella

LESS THAN 10 GAMES: John Rabb, Dave Schuler

KEY SIGNATURES: Murphy.

VALUE: $75

1985 BALTIMORE - Don Aase, Joe Altobelli (MANAGER), Mike Boddicker, Fritz Connally, Rich Dauer, Storm Davis, Rick Dempsey, Ken Dixon, Jim Dwyer, Mike Flanagan, Dan Ford, Wayne Gross, Leo Hernandez, Lee Lacy, John Lowenstein, Fred Lynn, Dennis Martinez, Tippy Martinez, Scott McGregor, Eddie Murray, Joe Nolan, Al Pardo, Floyd Rayford, Cal Ripken, Cal Ripken Sr. (MANAGER), Gary Roenicke, Lenn Sakata, Larry Sheets, John Shelby, Nate Snell, Sammy Stewart, Earl Weaver (MANAGER), Alan Wiggins *, Mike Young

LESS THAN 10 GAMES: Eric Bell, John Habyan, Brad Havens, Phil Huffman, Tom O'Malley, Kelly Paris, Bill Swaggerty

KEY SIGNATURES: Weaver, Murray, Ripken, Lynn.

VALUE: $75

1985 BOSTON - Tony Armas, Marty Barrett, Wade Boggs, Oil Can Boyd, Bill Buckner, Mark Clear, Roger Clemens, Steve Crawford, Mike Easler, Dwight Evans, Rich Gedman, Mike Greenwell, Jackie Gutierrez, Glenn Hoffman, Bruce Hurst, Ed Jurak, Bruce Kison, Tim Lollar *, Steve Lyons, John McNamara (MANAGER), Rick Miller, Reid Nichols *, Al Nipper, Bob Ojeda, Jerry Remy, Jim Rice, Kevin Romine, Dave Sax, Bob Stanley, Dave Stapleton, Marc Sullivan, Mike Trujillo

LESS THAN 10 GAMES: Mike Brown, Jim Dorsey, Tom McCarthy, Charlie Mitchell, Jeff Sellers, Rob Woodward

KEY SIGNATURES: Boggs, Rice, Clemens.

VALUE: $75

1985 CALIFORNIA - Juan Beniquez, Bob Boone, Mike Brown *, Rick Burleson, John Candelaria *, Rod Carew, Pat Clements *, Stew Cliburn, Doug Corbett, Doug DeCinces, Brian Downing, Craig Gerber, Bobby Grich, George Hendrick *, Al Holland *, Jack Howell, Reggie Jackson, Tommy John *, Ruppert Jones, Rufino Linares, Urbano Lugo, Gene Mauch (MANAGER), Kirk McCaskill, Darrell Miller, Donnie Moore, Jerry Narron, Gary Pettis, Ron Romanick, Luis Sanchez, Dick Schofield, Daryl Sconiers, Jim Slaton, Devon White, Rob Wilfong, Mike Witt

LESS THAN 10 GAMES: Alan Fowlkes, Pat Keedy, Bob Kipper *, Tony Mack, Gus Polidor, D.W. Smith, Don Sutton *, Geoff Zahn

KEY SIGNATURES: Carew, Jackson, Boone, Sutton, John.

VALUE: $100

1985 CHICAGO (AL) - Juan Agosto, Harold Baines, Floyd Bannister, Daryl Boston, Britt Burns, Julio Cruz, Joel Davis, Joe DeSa, Carlton Fisk, Scott Fletcher, Oscar Gamble, Jerry Gleaton, Ozzie Guillen, Jerry Hairston, Marc Hill, Tim Hulett, Bob James, Ron Kittle, Rudy Law, Tony LaRussa (MANAGER), Bryan Little, Tim Lollar *, Gene Nelson, Reid Nichols *, Tom Paciorek *, Mark Ryal, Luis Salazar, Tom Seaver, Joel Skinner, Dan Spillner, Mike Stanton *, Greg Walker, Dave Wehrmeister

LESS THAN 10 GAMES: John Cangelosi, Ed Correa, Rich Dotson, Bob Fallon, Steve Fireovid, Mark Gilbert, Al Jones, Bill Long, Mike Squires, Bruce Tanner

NOTES: Guillen (ROY).

KEY SIGNATURES: Guillen, Baines, Fisk, Seaver.

VALUE: $75

ROY = Rookie of the Year

1985 CHICAGO (NL) - Jay Baller, Thad Bosley, Derek Botelho, Larry Bowa *, Warren Brusstar, Ron Cey, Jody Davis, Brian Dayett, Bob Dernier, Shawon Dunston, Leon Durham, Dennis Eckersley, Steve Engel, Ray Fontenot, George Frazier, Jim Frey (MANAGER), Billy Hatcher, Richie Hebner, Steve Lake, Davey Lopes, Gary Matthews, Ron Meridith, Keith Moreland, Dave Owen, Dick Ruthven, Ryne Sandberg, Scott Sanderson, Lee Smith, Lary Sorensen, Chris Speier, Rick Sutcliffe, Steve Trout, Chico Walker, Gary Woods

LESS THAN 10 GAMES: Johnny Abrego, Dave Beard, Dave Gumpert, Larry Gura *, Darrin Jackson, Reggie Patterson, Jon Perlman

KEY SIGNATURES: Sandberg, Eckersley.

VALUE: $75

1985 CINCINNATI - Buddy Bell *, Dann Bilardello, Tom Browning, Bob Buchanan, Cesar Cedeno *, Dave Concepcion, Eric Davis, Bo Diaz *, Nick Esasky, Tom Foley *, John Franco, Tom Hume, Alan Knicely *, Wayne Krenchicki, Andy McGaffigan, Eddie Milner, Ron Oester, Dave Parker, Frank Pastore, Tony Perez, Ted Power, Joe Price, Gary Redus, Ron Robinson, Pete Rose (MANAGER), Pete Rose, Tom Runnells, Mario Soto, John Stuper, Jay Tibbs, Dave Van Gorder, Max Venable, Duane Walker *, Carl Willis

LESS THAN 10 GAMES: Rob Murphy, Paul O'Neil, Wade Rowdon, Mike Smith

KEY SIGNATURES: Rose, Concepcion, Parker, Perez, Davis.

VALUE: $90

1985 CLEVELAND - Benny Ayala, Chris Bando, Jeff Barkley, Butch Benton, Tony Bernazard, Bert Blyleven *, Brett Butler, Joe Carter, Carmen Castillo, Bryan Clark, Pat Corrales (MANAGER), Keith Creel, Jamie Easterly, Mike Fischlin, Julio Franco, Mel Hall, Mike Hargrove, Neal Heaton, Brook Jacoby, Johnny LeMaster *, Otis Nixon, Jerry Reed, Ramon Romero, Vern Ruhle, Don Schulze, Roy Smith, Pat Tabler, Rich Thompson, Andre Thornton, Dave Von Ohlen, George Vuckovich, Tom Waddell, Curt Wardle *, Jerry Willard

LESS THAN 10 GAMES: Rick Behenna, Ernie Camacho, Mike Jeffcoat *, Jose Roman, Jim Wilson

KEY SIGNATURES: Franco, Carter, Blyleven.

VALUE: $70

1985 DETROIT - Sparky Anderson (MANAGER), Doug Bair *, Doug Baker, Juan Berenguer, Dave Bergman, Tom Brookens, Chuck Cary, Marty Castillo, Darrell Evans, Doug Flynn *, Barbaro Garbey, Kirk Gibson, Johnny Grubb, Willie Hernandez, Larry Herndon, Chet Lemon, Aurelio Lopez, Bob Melvin, Jack Morris, Randy O'Neal, Lance Parrish, Dan Petry, Chris Pittaro, Alex Sanchez, Bill Scherrer, Nelson Simmons, Frank Tanana *, Walt Terrell, Alan Trammell, Jim Weaver, Lou Whitaker

LESS THAN 10 GAMES: Rusty Kuntz, Mike Laga, Scotti Madison, Mickey Mahler *, Bob Stoddard, Milt Wilcox

KEY SIGNATURES: Anderson, Whitaker, Trammell, Gibson, Morris.

VALUE: $90

1985 HOUSTON - Alan Ashby, Mark Bailey, Kevin Bass, Eric Bullock, Enos Cabell *, Jeff Calhoun, Jose Cruz, Glenn Davis, Bill Dawley, Frank DiPino, Bill Doran, Ty Gainey, Phil Garner, Jeff Heathcock, Chris Jones, Charlie Kerfeld, Bob Knepper, Bob Lillis (MANAGER), Mike Madden, Ron Mathis, John Mizerock, Jerry Mumphrey, Joe Niekro *, Jim Pankovits, Bert Pena, Terry Puhl, Craig Reynolds, German Rivera, Nolan Ryan, Mike Scott, Dave Smith, Julio Solano, Harry Spilman, Dickie Thon, Tim Tolman, Denny Walling

LESS THAN 10 GAMES: Jim Deshaies, Mark Knudson, Mark Ross

KEY SIGNATURES: Davis, Ryan.

VALUE: $90

1985 KANSAS CITY - Steve Balboni, Joe Beckwith, Buddy Biancalana, Bud Black, George Brett, Onix Concepcion, Steve Farr, Mark Gubicza, Dick Howser (MANAGER),

Dane Iorg, Danny Jackson, Lynn Jones, Mike Jones, Mike LaCoss, Dave Leeper, Charlie Leibrandt, Hal McRae, Omar Moreno *, Darryl Motley, Jorge Orta, Greg Pryor, Jamie Quirk, Dan Quisenberry, Bret Saberhagen, Pat Sheridan, Lonnie Smith *, Jim Sundberg, John Wathan, Frank White, Willie Wilson

LESS THAN 10 GAMES: Tony Ferriera, Larry Gura *, Bob Hegman, Mark Huismann, Dennis Leonard, Jim Scranton

NOTES: World Champions! Saberhagen (CY).

KEY SIGNATURES: Brett, Saberhagen.

VALUE: $295

CY = Cy Young Award winner

1985 LOS ANGELES - Dave Anderson, Bob Bailor, Sid Bream *, Tom Brennan, Greg Brock, Enos Cabell *, Bobby Castillo, Carlos Diaz, Mariano Duncan, Jose Gonzalez, Pedro Guerrero, Orel Hershiser, Rick Honeycutt, Steve Howe *, Ken Howell, Jay Johnstone, Ken Landreaux, Tom Lasorda (MANAGER), Bill Madlock *, Candy Maldonado, Mike Marshall, Len Matuszek *, Tom Niedenfuer, Al Oliver *, Dennis Powell, Jerry Reuss, R.J. Reynolds *, Bill Russell, Steve Sax, Mike Scioscia, Fernando Valenzuela, Bob Welch, Terry Whitfield, Reggie Williams, Steve Yeager

LESS THAN 10 GAMES: Ralph Bryant, Brian Holton, Stu Pederson, Alejandro Pena, Mike Ramsey, Gil Reyes, Franklin Stubbs

KEY SIGNATURES: Sax, Oliver, Hershiser, Valenzuela.

VALUE: $145

1985 MILWAUKEE - George Bamberger (MANAGER), Mark Brouhard, Ray Burris, Bobby Clark, Jaime Cocanower, Cecil Cooper, Danny Darwin, Mike Felder, Rollie Fingers, Jim Gantner, Bob Gibson, Brain Giles, Moose Haas, Teddy Higuera, Paul Householder, Dave Huppert, Dion James, Pete Ladd, Doug Loman, Rick Manning, Bob McClure, Paul Molitor, Charlie Moore, Ben Oglivie, Carlos Ponce, Randy Ready, Ernest Riles, Billy Jo Robidoux, Ed Romero, Bill Schroeder, Ray Searage, Ted Simmons, Pete Vuckovich, Rick Waits, Robin Yount

LESS THAN 10 GAMES: Jim Kern, Tim Leary, Brad Lesley, Chuck Porter, Bill Wegman

KEY SIGNATURES: Yount, Fingers.

VALUE: $75

1985 MINNESOTA - Bert Blyleven *, Tom Brunansky, Randy Bush, John Butcher, John Castino, Ron Davis, Dave Engle, Alvaro Espinoza, Frank Eufemia, Pete Filson, Mark Funderburk, Gary Gaetti, Greg Gagne, Billy Gardner (MANAGER), Mickey Hatcher, Steve Howe *, Kent Hrbek, Tim Laudner, Steve Lombardozzi, Rick Lysander, Dave Meier, Ray Miller (MANAGER), Kirby Puckett, Mark Salas, Ken Schrom, Roy Smalley, Mike Smithson, Mike Stenhouse, Tim Teufel, Frank Viola, Curt Wardle *, Ron Washington

LESS THAN 10 GAMES: Mark Brown, Dennis Burtt, Tom Klawitter, Mark Portugal, Jeff Reed, Len Whitehouse, Rich Yett

KEY SIGNATURES: Hrbek, Puckett, Viola, Blyleven.

VALUE: $90

1985 MONTREAL - Skeeter Barnes, Hubie Brooks, Tim Burke, Sal Butera, Andre Dawson, Miguel Dilone *, Dan Driessen *, Mike Fitzgerald, Terry Francona, Doug Frobel *, Andres Galarraga, Bill Gullickson, Joe Hesketh, Bill Laskey *, Vance Law, Gary Lucas, Al Newman, Steve Nicosia *, Mike O'Berry, Jack O'Connor, David Palmer, Tim Raines, Jeff Reardon, Bert Roberge, Bob Rodgers (MANAGER), Dan Schatzeder, Razor Shines, Bryn Smith, Randy St. Claire, Scot Thompson *, Tim Wallach, U.L. Washington, Mitch Webster *, Herm Winningham, Jim Wohlford, Floyd Youmans

LESS THAN 10 GAMES: Sal Butera, John Dopson, Doug Flynn *, Ed Glynn, Dick Grapenthin, Roy Johnson, Mickey Mahler *, Fred Manrique, Steve Rogers, Ned Yost

KEY SIGNATURES: Dawson, Raines.

VALUE: $75

1985 NEW YORK (AL) - Neil Allen *, Don Baylor, Dale Berra, Yogi Berra (MANAGER), Rich Bordi, Scott Bradley, Henry Cotto, Joe Cowley, Brian Fisher, Ken Griffey, Ron Guidry, Ron Hassey, Rickey Henderson, Rex Hudler, Billy Martin (MANAGER), Don Mattingly, Bobby Meacham, Omar Moreno *, Phil Niekro, Mike Pagliarulo, Dan Pasqua, Willie Randolph, Dennis Rasmussen, Dave Righetti, Andre Roberston, Billy Sample, Bob Shirley, Ed Whitson, Dave Winfield, Butch Wynegar

LESS THAN 10 GAMES: Mike Armstrong, Juan Bonilla, Marty Bystrom, Don Cooper, Juan Espino, Vic Mata, John Montefusco, Dale Murray *, Joe Nierko *, Rod Scurry *, Keith Smith

NOTES: Mattingly (MVP).

KEY SIGNATURES: Berra, Martin, Mattingly, Winfield, Henderson, Guidry, Niekro.

VALUE: $150

MVP = MVP Award winner

1985 NEW YORK (NL) - Rick Aguilera, Wally Backman, Terry Blocker, Larry Bowa *, Gary Carter, Kelvin Chapman, John Christensen, Ron Darling, Len Dykstra, Sid Fernandez, George Foster, Ron Gardenhire, Dwight Gooden, Tom Gorman, Danny Heep, Keith Hernandez, Clint Hurdle, Dave Johnson (MANAGER), Howard Johnson, Ray Knight, Terry Leach, Ed Lynch, Roger McDowell, Jesse Orosco, Tom Paciorek *, Ronn Reynolds, Rafael Santana, Doug Sisk, Rusty Staub, Darryl Strawberry, Mookie Wilson

LESS THAN 10 GAMES: Billy Beane, Bruce Berenyi, Wes Gardner, Bill Latham, Randy Meyers, Randy Niemann, Joe Sambito, Calvin Schiraldi

NOTES: Gooden (CY).

KEY SIGNATURES: Hernandez, Johnson, Strawberry, Foster, Carter, Gooden.

VALUE: $135

CY = Cy Young Award winner

1985 OAKLAND - Keith Atherton, Dusty Baker, Tim Birtsas, Bruce Bochte, Jose Canseco, Chris Codiroli, Dave Collins, Tim Conroy, Mike Davis, Mike Gallego, Alfredo Griffin, Mike Heath, Steve Henderson, Donnie Hill, Jay Howell, Tommy John *, Jeff Kaiser, Steve Kiefer, Dave Kingman, Bill Krueger, Rick Langford, Carney Lansford, Steve McCatty, Dan Meyer, Jackie Moore (MANAGER), Steve Mura, Dwayne Murphy, Charlie O'Brien, Steve Ontiveros, Tony Phillips, Rob Picciolo, Jose Rijo, Don Sutton *, Tom Tellmann, Mickey Tettleton, Mike Warren, Curt Young

KEY SIGNATURES: Lansford, Kingman, Sutton.

VALUE: $75

1985 PHILADELPHIA - Luis Aguayo, Larry Andersen, Steve Carlton, Don Carman, Rocky Childress, Tim Corcoran, Darren Daulton, John Denny, Bo Diaz *, John Felske (MANAGER), Jom Foley *, Greg Gross, Kevin Gross, Von Hayes, Charlie Hudson, Steve Jeltz, Jerry Koosman, Garry Maddox, Shane Rawley, Dave Rucker, John Russell, Juan Samuel, Mike Schmidt, Rick Schu, Dave Shipanoff, Jeff Stone, Kent Tekulve *, Derrel Thomas, Freddie Toliver, Ozzie Virgil, Glenn Wilson, John Wockenfuss

LESS THAN 10 GAMES: Kiko Garcia, Al Holland *, Alan Knicely *, Dave Stewart *, Rick Surhoff *, Pat Zachry

KEY SIGNATURES: Schmidt, Carlton.

VALUE: $75

1985 PITTSBURGH - Bill Almon, Rafael Belliard, Mike Bielecki, Sid Bream *, Mike Brown *, John Candelaria *, Pat Clements *, Jose DeLeon, Tim Foli, Doug Frobel *, Denny Gonzalez, Cecilio Guante, George Hendrick *, Al Holland *, Steve Kemp, Sammy Khalifa, Sixto Lezcano, Johnnie LeMaster *, Bill Madlock *, Lee Mazzilli, Larry McWilliams, Jim Morrison, Joe Orsulak, Junior Ortiz, Tony Pena, Johnny Ray, Rick Reuschel, R.J. Reynolds *, Rick Rhoden, Don Robinson, Rod Scurry *, Chuck Tanner (MANAGER), Jason Thompson, Lee Tunnell, Jim Winn, Marvell Wynne

LESS THAN 10 GAMES: Trench Davis, Jerry Dybzinski, Bob Kipper *, Ray Krawczyk, Scott Loucks, Kent Tekulve *, Dave Tomlin, Bob Walk

KEY SIGNATURES: Madlock.

VALUE: $75

1985 SAN DIEGO - Kurt Bevacqua, Bruce Bochy, Greg Booker, Bobby Brown, Al Bumbry, Jerry Davis, Luis DeLeon, Miguel Dilone *, Dave Dravecky, Tim Flannery, Steve Garvey, Goose Gossage, Tony Gwynn, Andy Hawkins, LaMarr Hoyt, Roy Lee Jackson, Terry Kennedy, Craig Lefferts, Carmelo Martinez, Lance McCullers, Kevin McReynolds, Graig Nettles, Mario Ramirez, Jerry Royster, Eric Show, Tim Stoddard, Garry Templeton, Mark Thurmond, Gene Walter, Alan Wiggins *, Dick Williams (MANAGER), Ed Wojna

LESS THAN 10 GAMES: Bob Patterson, Eddie Rodriguez

KEY SIGNATURES: Garvey, Nettles, Gwynn, Gossage.

VALUE: $90

1985 SAN FRANCISCO - Rick Adams, Vida Blue, Bob Brenly, Chris Brown, Roger Craig (MANAGER), Jim Davenport (MANAGER), Chili Davis, Mark Davis, Rob Deer, Dan Driessen *, Scott Garrelts, Dan Gladden, Jim Gott, David Green, Atlee Hammaker, Mike Jeffcoat *, Mike Krukow, Bill Laskey *, Dave LaPoint, Jeff Leonard, Johnnie LeMaster, Greg Minton, Bobby Moore, Matt Nokes, Gary Rajsich, Ron Roenicke, Scot Thompson *, Alex Trevino, Manny Trillo, Jose Uribe, Brad Wellman, Frank Williams, Mike Woodward, Joel Youngblood,

LESS THAN 10 GAMES: Duane Kuiper, Roger Mason, Jeff Robinson, Colin Ward

KEY SIGNATURES: Leonard.

VALUE: $75

1985 SEATTLE - Salome Barojas, Jim Beattie, Karl Best, Barry Bonnell, Phil Bradley, Ivan Calderon, Darnell Coles, Chuck Cottier (MANAGER), Al Cowens, Alvin Davis, Dave Geisel, Dave Henderson, Bob Kearney, Mark Langston, Jack Lazorko, Bob Long, Mike Moore, John Moses, Edwin Nunez, Spike Owen, Jack Perconte, Ken Phelps, Jim Presley, Domingo Ramos, Harold Reynolds, Donnie Scott, Brian Snyder, Mike Stanton *, Bill Swift, Danny Tartabull, Gorman Thomas, Roy Thomas, Dave Valle, Ed Vande Berg, Frank Wills, Matt Young

LESS THAN 10 GAMES: Al Chambers, Jim Lewis, Paul Mirabella, Mike Morgan, Ricky Nelson, Dave Tobik, Bill Wilkinson

KEY SIGNATURES: Tartabull, Langston.

VALUE: $75

1985 ST. LOUIS - Neil Allen *, Joaquin Andujar, Joe Boever, Steve Braun, Bill Campbell, Cesar Cedeno *, Jack Clark, Vince Coleman, Danny Cox, Ken Dayley, Ivan DeJesus, Curt Ford, Bob Forsch, Brian Harper, Tommy Herr, Whitey Herzog (MANAGER), Ricky Horton, Randy Hunt, Mike Jorgensen, Kurt Kepshire, Jeff Lahti, Tito Landrum, Tom Lawless, Mike LaValliere, Willie McGee, Tom Nieto, Terry Pendleton, Darrell Porter, Ozzie Smith, Lonnie Smith *, John Tudor, Andy Van Slyke, Todd Worrell

LESS THAN 10 GAMES: Doug Bair *, Andy Hassler, Art Howe, Matt Keough, Pat Perry

NOTES: Coleman (ROY), McGee (MVP).

KEY SIGNATURES: Clark, McGee, Coleman.

VALUE: $200

ROY = Rookie of the Year

1985 TEXAS - Alan Bannister, Buddy Bell *, Glenn Brummer, Steve Buchele, Tommy Dunbar, Toby Harrah, Greg Harris, Dwayne Henry, Burt Hooton, Charlie Hough, Cliff Johnson *, Bobby Jones, Mike Mason, Oddibe McDowell, Dickie Noles, Pete O'Brien, Larry Parrish, Geno Petralli, Doug Rader (MANAGER), Dave Rozema, Jeff Russell, Dave Schmidt, Don Slaught, Bill Stein, Dave Stewart *, Frank Tanana *, Wayne Tolleson, Ellis Valentine, Bobby Valentine (MANAGER), Duane Walker *, Gary Ward, Chris Welsh, Curt Wilkerson, George Wright

LESS THAN 10 GAMES: Tommy Boggs, Nick Capra, Glen Cook, Jose Guzman, Jeff Kunkel, Dale Murray *, Luis Pujols, Bob Sebra, Rick Surhoff *, Matt Williams, Ricky Wright

KEY SIGNATURES: Harrah.

VALUE: $75

1985 TORONTO - Jim Acker, Willie Aikens, Doyle Alexander, Gary Allenson, Jesse Barfield, George Bell, Jeff Burroughs, Bill Caudill, Jim Clancy, Bobby Cox (MANAGER), Tony Fernandez, Cecil Fielder, Tom Filer, Damaso Garcia, Tom Henke, Garth Iorg, Cliff Johnson *, Jimmy Key, Dennis Lamp, Gary Lavelle, Rick Leach, Luis Leal, Manny Lee, Buck Martinez, Len Matuszek *, Lloyd Moseby, Rance Mulliniks, Ron Musselman, Al Oliver *, Ron Shepherd, Dave Stieb, Lou Thornton, Willie Upshaw, Ernie Whitt

LESS THAN 10 GAMES: John Cerutti, Stan Clarke, Steve Davis, Kelly Gruber, Jeff Hearron, Steve Nicosia, Mitch Webster *

KEY SIGNATURES: Fernandez, Bell, Fielder, Stieb.

VALUE: $125

1986

1986 Los Angeles Dodgers

*** = player was traded**

1986 ATLANTA - Jim Acker *, Doyle Alexander *, Paul Assenmacher, Bruce Benedict, Chris Chambliss, Jeff Dedmon, Gene Garber, Ken Griffey *, Albert Hall, Terry Harper, Bob Horner, Glenn Hubbard, Joe Johnson *, Rick Mahler, Craig McMurtry, Omar Moreno, Dale Murphy, Ken Oberkfell, Ed Olwine, David Palmer, Gerald Perry, Rafael Ramirez, Billy Sample, Ted Simmons, Zane Smith, Cliff Speck, Bruce Sutter, Chuck Tanner (MANAGER), Andrew Thomas, Ozzie Virgil, Duane Ward *, Claudell Washington *

LESS THAN 10 GAMES: Brad Komminsk, Darryl Motley *, Charlie Puleo, Paul Runge, Steve Shields

KEY SIGNATURES: Murphy.

VALUE: $60

1986 BALTIMORE - Don Aase, Tony Arnold, Juan Beniquez, Mike Boddicker, Juan Bonilla, Rich Bordi, Storm Davis, Rick Dempsey, Ken Dixon, Jim Dwyer, Mike Flanagan, Ken Gerhart, Jackie Gutierrez, Brad Havens, Rex Hudler, Odell Jones, Ricky Jones, Lee Lacy, Fred Lynn, Tippy Martinez, Scott McGregor, Eddie Murray, Tom O'Malley, Al Pardo, Floyd Rayford, Cal Ripken, Larry Sheets, John Shelby, Nate Snell, John Stefero, Jim Traber, Earl Weaver (MANAGER), Alan Wiggins, Mike Young

LESS THAN 10 GAMES: Eric Bell, Tom Dodd, John Habyan, Mike Kinnunen, Dennis Martinez *, Carl Nichols, Kelly Paris, Bill Swaggerty

KEY SIGNATURES: Weaver, Murray, Ripken, Lynn.

VALUE: $60

1986 BOSTON - Tony Armas, Marty Barrett, Don Baylor, Wade Boggs, Oil Can Boyd,

Mike Brown *, Bill Buckner, Roger Clemens, Steve Crawford, Dwight Evans, Rich Gedman, Mike Greenwell, Dave Henderson *, Glenn Hoffman, Bruce Hurst, Tim Lollar, Steve Lyons *, John McNamara (MANAGER), Al Nipper, Spike Owen *, Rey Quinones *, Jim Rice, Ed Romero, Kevin Romine, Joe Sambito, Calvin Schiraldi, Tom Seaver *, Jeff Sellers, Bob Stanley, Dave Stapleton, Mike Stenhouse, Sammy Stewart, Marc Sullivan, LaSchelle Tarver

LESS THAN 10 GAMES: Pat Dodson, Wes Gardner, Dave Sax, Mike Trujillo *, Rob Woodward

NOTES: Clemens (CY) & (MVP).

KEY SIGNATURES: Boggs, Rice, Clemens, Seaver.

VALUE: $200

CY = Cy Young Award winner

1986 CALIFORNIA - Rob Boone, T.R. Bryden, Rick Burleson, John Candelaria, Doug Corbett, Doug DeCinces, Brian Downing, Chuck Finley, Terry Forster, Bobby Grich, George Hendrick, Jack Howell, Reggie Jackson, Ruppert Jones, Wally Joyner, Gary Lucas, Gene Mauch (MANAGER), Kirk McCaskill, Darrell Miller, Donnie Moore, Jerry Narron, Gary Pettis, Ron Romanick, Vern Ruhle, Mark Ryal, Dick Schofield, Jim Slaton *, Don Sutton, Devon White, Rob Wilfong, Mike Witt

LESS THAN 10 GAMES: Ray Chadwick, Mike Cook, Todd Fischer, Ken Forsch, Willie Fraser, Urbano Lugo, Mark McLemore, Gus Polidor

KEY SIGNATURES: Joyner, Boone, Jackson, Sutton.

VALUE: $70

1986 CHICAGO (AL) - Neil Allen, Harold Baines, Floyd Bannister, Bobby Bonilla *, Daryl Boston, Scott Bradley *, Ivan Calderon *, John Cangelosi, Dave Cochrane, Joe Cowley, Rodney Craig, Julio Cruz, Joel Davis, Bill Dawley, Jose DeLeon *, Rich Dotson, Carlton Fisk, George Foster *, Jim Fregosi (MANAGER), Brian Giles, Ozzie Guillen, Jerry Hairston, Ron Hassey *, Marc Hill, Tim Hulett, Bob James, Ron Karkovice, Ron Kittle *, Tony LaRussa (MANAGER), Bryan Little *, Steve Lyons *, Joel McKeon, Russ Morman, Gene Nelson, Reid Nichols, Jack Perconte, Doug Rader (MANAGER), Dave Schmidt, Ray Searage *, Tom Seaver *, Joel Skinner *, Bobby Thigpen, Wayne Tolleson *, Greg Walker, Kenny Williams

LESS THAN 10 GAMES: Juan Agosto *, Steve Carlton *, Bryan Clark, Pete Filson *, Luis Salazar

NOTES: Two 300-win pitchers (Carlton/Seaver) on the same team.

KEY SIGNATURES: Baines, Fisk, Carlton, Seaver.

VALUE: $75

1986 CHICAGO (NL) - Jay Baller, Thad Bosley, Ron Cey, Jody Davis, Ron Davis *, Brian Dayett, Bob Dernier, Frank DiPino *, Shawon Dunston, Leon Durham, Dennis Eckersley, Ray Fontenot *, Terry Francona, George Frazier *, Jim Frey (MANAGER), Dave Gumpert, Guy Hoffman, Matt Keough *, Steve Lake *, Davey Lopes *, Ed Lynch *, Dave Martinez, Gary Matthews, Gene Michael (MANAGER), Keith Moreland, Jamie Moyer, Jerry Mumphrey, Rafael Palmeiro, Ryne Sandberg, Scott Sanderson, Lee Smith, Chris Speier, Rick Sutcliffe, Manny Trillo, Steve Trout, John Vuckovich (MANAGER), Chico Walker

LESS THAN 10 GAMES: Steve Christmas, Drew Hall, Greg Maddux, Mike Martin, Dick Ruthven

KEY SIGNATURES: Sandberg, Palmeiro, Eckersley.

VALUE: $60

1986 CINCINNATI - Buddy Bell, Tom Browning, Sal Butera, Dave Concepcion, Kal Daniels, Eric Davis, John Denny, Bo Diaz, Nick Esasky, John Franco, Bill Gullickson, Tracy Jones, Bill Landrum, Barry Larkin, Eddie Milner, Rob Murphy, Ron Oester, Dave Parker, Tony Perez, Ted Power, Joe Price, Ron Robinson, Pete Rose (MANAGER), Pete Rose, Wade Rowdon, Tom Runnells, Mario Soto, Kurt Stillwell, Scott Terry, Max Venable, Chris Welsh, Carl Willis

LESS THAN 10 GAMES: Paul O'Neill, Mike Smith, Dave Van Gorder

KEY SIGNATURES: Parker, Davis, Concepcion, Perez, Rose.

VALUE: $75

1986 CLEVELAND - Andy Allanson, Scott Bailes, Chris Bando, Tony Bernazard, John Butcher *, Brett Butler, Ernie Camacho, Tom Candiotti, Joe Carter, Carmen Castillo, Dave Clark, Pat Corrales (MANAGER), Jamie Easterly, Julio Franco, Mel Hall, Neal Heaton *, Brook Jacoby, Doug Jones, Jim Kern, Fran Mullins, Phil Niekro, Otis Nixon, Dickie Noles, Bryan Oelkers, Ken Schrom, Don Schulze, Cory Snyder, Pat Tabler, Andre Thornton, Frank Wills, Rich Yett

LESS THAN 10 GAMES: Jay Bell, Reggie Ritter, Dan Rohn, Jose Roman, Greg Swindell, Eddie Williams

KEY SIGNATURES: Franco, Carter, Niekro.

VALUE: $60

1986 DETROIT - Sparky Anderson (MANAGER), Doug Baker, Dave Bergman, Tom Brookens, Bill Campbell, Chuck Cary, Darnell Coles, Dave Collins, Dave Engle, Darrell Evans, Bruce Fields, Kirk Gibson, Johnny Grubb, Brian Harper, Mike Heath *, Willie Hernandez, Larry Herndon, Eric King, Mike Laga *, Dave LaPoint *, Chet Lemon, Dwight Lowry, Jack Morris, Randy O'Neal, Lance Parrish, Dan Petry, Bill Scherrer, Pat Sheridan, Jim Slaton *, Harry Spilman *, Frank Tanana, Walt Terrell, Mark Thurmond *, Tim Tolman, Alan Trammell, Lou Whitaker

LESS THAN 10 GAMES: Bryan Kelly, Jack Lazorko, Scott Madison, Matt Nokes, John Pacella

KEY SIGNATURES: Anderson, Whitaker, Trammell, Gibson, Morris.

VALUE: $100

1986 HOUSTON - Larry Andersen *, Alan Ashby, Mark Bailey, Kevin Bass, Jeff Calhoun, Jose Cruz, Danny Darwin *, Glenn Davis, Jim Deshaies, Frank DiPino *, Bill Doran, Dan Driessen *, Ty Gainey, Phil Garner, Billy Hatcher, Matt Keough *, Charlie Kerfeld, Bob Knepper, Hal Lanier (MANAGER), Davey Lopes *, Aurelio Lopez, Mike Madden, John Mizerock, Jim Pankovits, Bert Pena, Terry Puhl, Craig Reynolds, Nolan Ryan, Mike Scott, Dave Smith, Julio Solano, Dickie Thon, Tony Walker, Denny Walling

LESS THAN 10 GAMES: Eric Bullock, Tom Funk, Manny Hernandez, Mark Knudson *, Louie Meadows, Rafael Montalvo, Craig Reynolds, Robbie Wine

NOTES: Scott (CY).

KEY SIGNATURES: Davis, Scott, Ryan.

VALUE: $125

CY = Cy Young Award winner

1986 KANSAS CITY - Steve Balboni, Scott Bankhead, Buddy Biancalana, Bud Black, George Brett, Mike Brewer, David Cone, Steve Farr, Mike Ferraro (MANAGER), Mark Gubicza, Dick Howser (MANAGER), Mark Huismann *, Bo Jackson, Danny Jackson, Rondin Johnson, Lynn Jones, Mike Kingery, Rudy Law, Charlie Leibrandt, Dennis Leonard, Hal McRae, Darryl Motley *, Jorge Orta, Bill Pecota, Greg Pryor, Jamie Quirk, Dan Quisenberry, Bret Saberhagen, Angel Salazar, Kevin Seitzer, Lonnie Smith, Jim Sundberg, Frank White, Willie Wilson

LESS THAN 10 GAMES: Terry Bell, Alan Hargesheimer, Steve Shields *, Dwight Taylor

NOTES: Howser died 6/17/87.

KEY SIGNATURES: Howser, Brett, Jackson, Saberhagen.

VALUE: $75

1986 LOS ANGELES - Dave Anderson, Joe Beckwith, Greg Brock, Ralph Bryant, Enos Cabell, Cesar Cedeno, Carlos Diaz, Mariano Duncan, Jack Fimple, Balvino Galvez, Jose Gonzalez, Pedro Guerrero, Jeff Hamilton, Orel Hershiser, Brian Holton, Rick Honeycutt, Ken Howell, Ken Landreaux, Tom Lasorda (MANAGER), Bill Madlock, Mike Marshall, Len Matuszek, Tom Niedenfuer, Alejandro Pena, Dennis Powell, Jerry Reuss, Bill Russell, Steve Sax, Mike Scioscia, Larry See, Craig Shipley, Franklin Stubbs, Alex Trevino, Fernando Valenzuela, Ed Vande Berg, Bob Welch, Terry Whitfield, Reggie Williams

LESS THAN 10 GAMES: Ed Amelund

KEY SIGNATURES: Guerrero, Valenzuela, Hershiser.

VALUE: $85

1986 MILWAUKEE - George Bamberger (MANAGER), Chris Bosio, Glenn Braggs, Juan Castillo, Rick Cerone, Mark Clear, Bryan Clutterbuck, Jaime Cocanower, Cecil Cooper, Danny Darwin *, Rob Deer, Mike Felder, Jim Gantner, Bob Gibson, Teddy Higuera, Paul Householder, John Henry Johnson, Tim Leary, Rick Manning, Bob McClure *, Paul Molitor, Charlie Moore, Juan Nieves, Ben Oglivie, Dan Plesac, Randy Ready *, Erniest Riles, Billy Joe Robidoux, Bill Schroeder, Ray Searage *, Dale Sveum, Gorman Thomas *, Tom Trebelhorn (MANAGER), Bill Wegman, Robin Yount

LESS THAN 10 GAMES: Jim Adduci, Mike Birkbeck, Edgar Diaz, Steve Kiefer, Mark Knudson *, Pete Vuckovich

KEY SIGNATURES: Yount.

VALUE: $60

1986 MINNESOTA - Juan Agosto *, Allan Anderson, Keith Atherton *, Billy Beane, Bert Blyleven, Tom Brunansky, Randy Bush, John Butcher *, Mark Davidson, Ron Davis *, Alvaro Espinoza, Ray Fontenot *, Goerge Frazier *, Gary Gaetti, Greg Gagne, Mickey Hatcher, Neal Heaton *, Kent Hrbek, Roy Lee Jackson, Tom Kelly (MANAGER), Tim Laudner, Steve Lombardozzi, Ray Miller (MANAGER), Frank Pastore, Chris Pittaro, Mark Portugal, Kirby Puckett, Jeff Reed, Mark Salas, Roy Smalley, Mike Smithson, Frank Viola, Ron Washington, Al Woods

LESS THAN 10 GAMES: Dennis Burtt, Andre David, Pete Filson *, Bill Latham, Alex Sanchez, Roy Smith

KEY SIGNATURES: Hrbek, Puckett, Blyleven, Viola.

VALUE: $100

1986 MONTREAL - Dann Bilardello, Hubie Brooks, Tim Burke, Casey Candaele, Andre Dawson, Mike Fitzgerald, Tom Foley *, Andres Galarraga, Rene Gonzales, Joe Hesketh, Randy Hunt, Wallace Johnson, Wayne Krenchicki, Vance Law, Dennis Martinez *, Bob

McClure *, Andy McGaffigan, Al Newman, Tom Nieto, Jeff Parrett, Tim Raines, Jeff Reardon, Luis Rivera, Bert Roberge, Bob Rodgers (MANAGER), Dan Schatzeder *, Bob Sebra, Bryn Smith, Randy St. Claire, Jason Thompson, Jay Tibbs, Tim Wallach, Mitch Webster, Herm Winningham, Jim Wohlford, George Wright *, Floyd Youmans

LESS THAN 10 GAMES: Curt Brown, Billy Moore, Bob Owchinko, George Riley, Wil Tejada, Dave Tomlin, Sergio Valdez

KEY SIGNATURES: Dawson, Raines.

VALUE: $60

1986 NEW YORK (AL) - Dale Berra, Henry Cotto, Doug Drabek, Mike Easler, Juan Espino, Mike Fischlin, Brian Fisher, Ken Griffey *, Ron Guidry, Ron Hassey *, Rickey Henderson, Al Holland, Tommy John, Ron Kittle *, Bryan Little *, Phil Lombardi, Don Mattingly, Bobby Meacham, Joe Niekro, Mike Pagliarulo, Dan Pasqua, Lou Piniella (MANAGER), Willie Randolph, Dennis Rasmussen, Dave Righetti, Gary Roenicke, Rod Scurry, Bob Shirley, Joel Skinner *, Tim Stoddard *, Bob Tewksbury, Wayne Tolleson *, Claudell Washington *, Ed Whitson *, Dave Winfield, Butch Wynegar, Paul Zuvella

LESS THAN 10 GAMES: Mike Armstrong, Brad Arnsberg, Ivan DeJesus, Leo Hernandez, John Montefusco, Scott Nielsen, Alfonso Pulido

KEY SIGNATURES: Mattingly, Winfield, Henderson, Guidry, John.

VALUE: $100

1986 NEW YORK (NL) - Rick Aguilera, Rick Anderson, Wally Backman, Bruce Berenyi, Gary Carter, Ron Darling, Len Dykstra, Kevin Elster, Sid Fernandez, George Foster *, Dwight Gooden, Ed Hearn, Danny Heep, Keith Hernandez, Stan Jefferson, Dave Johnson (MANAGER), Howard Johnson, Ray Knight, Lee Mazzilli *, Roger McDowell, Kevin Mitchell, Randy Niemann, Bob Ojeda, Jesse Orosco, Rafael Santana, Doug Sisk, Darryl Strawberry, Tim Teufel, Mookie Wilson

LESS THAN 10 GAMES: Tim Corcoran, John Gibbons, Terry Leach, Ed Lynch *, Barry Lyons, Dave Magadan, Randy Meyers, John Mitchell

NOTES: World Champions!

KEY SIGNATURES: Hernandez, Strawberry, Carter, Mitchell, Foster, Gooden.

VALUE: $295

1986 OAKLAND - Joaquin Andujar, Keith Atherton *, Doug Bair, Dusty Baker, Bill Bathe, Bruce Bochte, Jose Canseco, Chris Codiroli, Mike Davis, Mike Gallego, Alfredo Griffin, Moose Haas, Steve Henderson, Donnie Hill, Jay Howell, Stan Javier, Dave Kingman, Bill Krueger, Rick Langford, Carney Lansford, Tony LaRussa (MANAGER), Dave Leiper, Mark McGwire, Bill Mooneyham, Jackie Moore (MANAGER), Dwayne Murphy, Jeff Newman (MANAGER), Steve Ontiveros, Rickey Peters, Tony Phillips, Eric Plunk, Jose Rijo, Lenn Sakata, Dave Stewart *, Mickey Tettleton, Rusty Tillman, Dave Von Ohlen, Jerry Willard, Curt Young

LESS THAN 10 GAMES: Darrel Akerfelds, Fernando Arroyo, Tim Birtsas, Tom Dozier, Wayne Gross, Rob Nelson, Rick Rodriguez, Terry Steinbach

NOTES: Canseco (ROY).

KEY SIGNATURES: Canseco, McGwire, Stewart.

VALUE: $100

ROY = Rookie of the Year

1986 PHILADELPHIA - Luis Aguayo, Steve Bedrosian, Steve Carlton *, Don Carman, Darren Daulton, John Felske (MANAGER), Tom Foley *, Greg Gross, Kevin Gross, Von Hayes, Charlie Hudson, Tom Hume, Chris James, Steve Jeltz, Joe Lefebvre, Greg Legg, Mike Maddux, Shane Rawley, Gary Redus, Ronn Reynolds, Ron Roenicke, Dave Rucker, Bruce Ruffin, John Russell, Juan Samuel, Dan Schatzeder *, Mike Schmidt, Rick Schu, Jeff Stone, Kent Tekulve, Milt Thompson, Glenn Wilson

LESS THAN 10 GAMES: Larry Andersen *, Jeff Bittiger, Rocky Childress, Marvin Freeman, Tom Gorman, Greg Gross, Mike Jackson, Randy Lerch, Garry Maddox, Francisco Melendez, Dave Stewart *, Freddie Toliver

NOTES: Schmidt (MVP).

KEY SIGNATURES: Schmidt, Carlton.

VALUE: $70

MVP = MVP Award winner

1986 PITTSBURGH - Bill Almon, Rafael Belliard, Mike Bielecki, Barry Bonds, Bobby Bonilla *, Sid Bream, Mike Brown, Pat Clements, Trench Davis, Mike Diaz, Benny Distefano, Cecilio Guante, Barry Jones, Steve Kemp, Sammy Khalifa, Bob Kipper, Ray Krawczyk, Jim Leyland (MANAGER), Lee Mazzilli *, Larry McWilliams, Jim Morrison, Joe Orsulak, Junior Ortiz, Bob Patterson, Hipolito Pena, Tony Pena, Johnny Ray, Rich Renteria, Rick Reuschel, R.J. Reynolds, Rick Rhoden, Don Robinson, John Smiley, Bob Walk, U.L. Washington, Jim Winn

LESS THAN 10 GAMES: Jose DeLeon *, Stan Fansler, Ruben Rodriguez, Rich Sauveur

KEY SIGNATURES: Bonds, Bonilla.

VALUE: $60

1986 SAN DIEGO - Randy Asadoor, Bruce Bochy, Steve Boros (MANAGER), Dave Dravecky, Tim Flannery, Steve Garvey, Goose Gossage, Gary Green, Tony Gwynn, Alex Hawkins, LaMarr Hoyt, Dane Iorg, Terry Kennedy, John Kruk, Dave LaPoint *, Craig Lefferts, Carmelo Martinez, Lance McCullers, Kevin McReynolds, Graig Nettles, Tim Pyznarski, Bip Roberts, Jerry Royster, Benito Santiago, Eric Show, Bob Stoddard, Tim Stoddard *, Garry Templeton, Mark Thurmond, Gene Walter, Ed Whitson *, Marvell Wynne

LESS THAN 10 GAMES: Greg Booker, Ray Hayward, Jimmy Jones, Mark Parent, Randy Ready *, Ed Vosberg, Mark Wasinger, Ed Wojna

KEY SIGNATURES: Garvey, Gwynn, Gossage.

VALUE: $60

1986 SAN FRANCISCO - Mike Aldrete, Juan Berenguer, Vida Blue, Bob Brenly, Chris Brown, Will Clark, Roger Craig (MANAGER), Chili Davis, Mark Davis, Kelly Downs, Dan Driessen *, Scott Garrelts, Dan Gladden, Brad Gulden, Chuck Hensley, Mike Krukow, Randy Kutcher, Rick Lancellotti, Bill Laskey, Mike LaCoss, Jeff Leonard, Candy Maldonado, Roger Mason, Bob Melvin, Greg Minton, Terry Mulholland, Phil Ouellette, Luis Quinones, Jeff Robinson, Harry Spilman *, Robby Thompson, Jose Uribe, Brad Wellman, Frank Williams, Mike Woodard, Joel Youngblood

LESS THAN 10 GAMES: Randy Bockus, Steve Carlton *, Jim Gott, Mark Grant, Chris Jones

KEY SIGNATURES: Clark, Carlton.

VALUE: $60

1986 SEATTLE - Karl Best, Barry Bonnell, Phil Bradley, Scott Bradley *, Mickey Brantley, Ivan Calderon *, Chuck Cottier (MANAGER), Al Cowens, Alvin Davis, Steve Fireovid, Lee Guetterman, Dave Henderson *, Dave Hengel, Mark Huismann *, Ross Jones, Bob Kearney, Pete Ladd, Mark Langston, Marty Martinez (MANAGER), Mike Moore, Mike Morgan, John Moses, Edwin Nunez, Spike Owen *, Ken Phelps, Jim Presley, Rey Quinones *, Domingo Ramos, Jerry Reed, Harold Reynolds, Bill Swift, Danny Tartabull, Gorman Thomas *, Mike Trujillo *, Dave Valle, Milt Wilcox, Dick Williams (MANAGER), Steve Yeager, Matt Young

LESS THAN 10 GAMES: Jim Beattie, Mike Brown *, Paul Mirabella, Ricky Nelson

KEY SIGNATURES: Tartabull, Langston.

VALUE: $60

1986 ST. LOUIS - Greg Bargar, Joe Boever, Ray Burris, Jack Clark, Vince Coleman, Tim Conroy, Danny Cox, Ken Dayley, Curt Ford, Bob Forsch, Mike Heath *, Tommy Herr, Whitey Herzog (MANAGER), Ricky Horton, Clint Hurdle, Alan Knicely, Mike Laga *, Steve Lake *, Tito Landrum, Tom Lawless, Mike LaValliere, Jim Lindeman, Fred Manrique, Greg Mathews, Willie McGree, John Morris, Jose Oquendo, Rick Ownbey, Terry Pendleton, Pat Perry, Ozzie Smith, Ray Soff, John Tudor, Andy Van Slyke, Jerry White, Todd Worrell

LESS THAN 10 GAMES: Bill Earley, Kurt Kepshire, Jeff Lahti

NOTES: Worrell (ROY).

KEY SIGNATURES: Smith, McGee.

VALUE: $60

ROY = Rookie of the Year

1986 TEXAS - Bob Brower, Jerry Browne, Steve Buechele, Ed Correa, Scott Fletcher, Jose Guzman, Toby Harrah, Greg Harris, Dwayne Henry, Charlie Hough, Pete Incaviglia, Bobby Jones, Mickey Mahler *, Mike Mason, Oddibe McDowell, Orlando Mercado, Dale Mohorcic, Pete O'Brien, Tom Paciorek, Larry Parrish, Geno Petralli, Darrell Porter, Jeff Russell, Ruben Sierra, Don Slaught, Mike Stanley, Bobby Valentine (MANAGER), Gary Ward, Curt Wilkerson, Mitch Williams, Bobby Witt, Ricky Wright, George Wright *

LESS THAN 10 GAMES: Kevin Brown, Jeff Kunkel, Mike Loynd, Ron Meridith, Dave Rozema

KEY SIGNATURES: Sierra.

VALUE: $60

1986 TORONTO - Jim Acker *, Doyle Alexander *, Jesse Barfield, George Bell, Bill Caudill, John Cerutti, Jim Clancy, Stan Clarke, Mark Eichhorn, Tony Fernandez, Cecil Fielder, Damaso Garcia, Don Gordon, Kelly Gruber, Jeff Hearron, Tom Henke, Garth Iorg, Cliff Johnson, Joe Johnson *, Jimmy Key, Dennis Lamp, Rick Leach, Manny Lee, Buck Martinez, Lloyd Moseby, Rance Mulliniks, Ron Shepherd, Dave Stieb, Willie Upshaw, Ernie Whitt, Jimy Williams (MANAGER)

LESS THAN 10 GAMES: Luis Aquino, Steve Davis, Mickey Mahler *, Fred McGriff, Jeff Musselman, Duane Ward *

KEY SIGNATURES: Fernandez, Bell, Stieb.

VALUE: $60

1987

1987 Detroit Tigers

*** = player was traded**

1987 ATLANTA - Jim Acker, Doyle Alexander *, Paul Assenmacher, Bruce Benedict, Jeff Blauser, Joe Boever, Chuck Cary, Jeff Dedmon, Ron Gant, Gene Garber *, Ken Griffey, Albert Hall, Glenn Hubbard, Dion James, Rick Mahler, Dale Murphy, Graig Nettles, Randy O'Neal *, Ken Oberkfell, Ed Olwine, David Palmer, Gerald Perry, Charlie Puleo, Rafael Ramirez, Gary Roenicke, Paul Runge, Ted Simmons, Zane Smith, Chuck Tanner (MANAGER), Andres Thomas, Ozzie Virgil
LESS THAN 10 GAMES: Terry Bell, Marty Clary, Kevin Coffman, Trench Davis, Mike Fischlin, Tom Glavine, Larry McWilliams, Darryl Motley, Phil Niekro *, Pete Smith, Steve Ziem
KEY SIGNATURES: Murphy, Niekro.

VALUE: $60

1987 BALTIMORE - Tony Arnold, Jeff Ballard, Eric Bell, Mike Boddicker, Rick Burleson, Doug Corbett, Luis DeLeon, Ken Dixon, Jim Dwyer, Mike Flanagan *, Ken Gerhart, Rene Gonzales, Mike Griffin, John Habyan, Mike Hart, Terry Kennedy, Mike Kinnunen, Ray Knight, Lee Lacy, Fred Lynn, Scott McGregor, Eddie Murray, Carl Nichols, Tom Niedenfuer *, Jack O'Connor, Floyd Rayford, Billy Ripken, Cal Ripken, Cal Ripken Sr. (MANAGER), Dave Schmidt, Larry Sheets, John Shelby, Nelson Simmons, Pete Stanicek, Dave Van Gorder, Ron Washington, Alan Wiggins, Mark Williamson, Mike Young
LESS THAN 10 GAMES: Don Aase, Jackie Gutierrez, Jose Mesa
KEY SIGNATURES: Murray, Ripken, Lynn.

VALUE: $60

1987 BOSTON - Marty Barrett, Don Baylor, Todd Benzinger, Wade Boggs, Tom Bolton, Bill Buckner *, Ellis Burks, Roger Clemens, Steve Crawford, Pat Dodson, Dwight Evans, Wes Gardner, Rich Gedman, Mike Greenwell, Dave Henderson *, Glenn Hoffman *, Sam Horn, Bruce Hurst, John Marzano, John McNamara (MANAGER), Al Nipper, Spike Owen, Jim Rice, Ed Romero, Joe Sambito, Calvin Schiraldi, Jeff Sellers, Denny Sheaffer, Bob Stanley, Marc Sullivan

LESS THAN 10 GAMES: Oil Can Boyd, John Leister, Jody Reed, Kevin Romine, Dave Sax, Rob Woodward

NOTES: Clemens (CY).

KEY SIGNATURES: Boggs, Rice, Clemens.

VALUE: $60

CY = Cy Young Award winner

1987 CALIFORNIA - Tony Armas, Bob Boone, Bill Buckner *, DeWayne Buice, John Candelaria *, Mike Cook, Doug DeCinces *, Brian Downing, Jim Eppard *, Jack Fimple, Chuck Finley, Willie Fraser, George Hendrick, Jack Howell, Ruppert Jones, Wally Joyner, Jack Lazorko, Gary Lucas, Gene Mauch (MANAGER), Kirk McCaskill, Mark McLemore, Darrell Miller, Greg Minton *, Gary Pettis, Gus Polidor, Johnny Ray *, Jerry Reuss *, Mark Ryal, Dick Schofield, Don Sutton, Devon White, Mike Witt, Butch Wynegar

LESS THAN 10 GAMES: Miguel Garcia *, Bryan Harvey, Urbano Lugo, Tack Wilson

KEY SIGNATURES: Joyner, Boone, Buckner, Sutton.

VALUE: $65

1987 CHICAGO - Jay Baller, Damon Berryhill, Mike Brumley, Jody Davis, Ron Davis *, Andre Dawson, Brian Dayett, Bob Dernier, Frank DiPino, Shawon Dunston, Leon Durham, Drew Hall, Les Lancaster, Frank Lucchesi (MANAGER), Ed Lynch, Greg Maddux, Dave Martinez, Mike Mason *, Gary Matthews *, Gene Michael (MANAGER), Keith Moreland, Jamie Moyer, Jerry Mumphrey, Paul Noce, Dickie Noles *, Rafael Palmeiro, Luis Quinones, Wade Rowdon, Ryne Sandberg, Scott Sanderson, Lee Smith, Jim Sundberg, Rick Sutcliffe, Manny Trillo, Steve Trout *, Chico Walker

LESS THAN 10 GAMES: Darrin Jackson, Bob Tewksbury *

NOTES: Dawson (MVP).

KEY SIGNATURES: Sandberg, Dawson, Palmeiro.

VALUE: $60

MVP = MVP Award winner

1987 CHICAGO (NL) - Neil Allen *, Harold Baines, Floyd Bannister, Daryl Boston, Ivan Calderon, Bryan Clark, Joel Davis, Jose DeLeon, Rich Dotson, Carlton Fisk, Jim Fregosi (MANAGER), Ozzie Guillen, Jerry Hairston, Ron Hassey, Donnie Hill, Tim Hulett, Bob James, Ron Karkovice, Pat Keedy, Dave LaPoint *, Bill Long, Steve Lyons, Fred Manrique, Joel McKeon, Scott Nielson, Gary Redus, Jerry Royster *, Ray Searage, Bobby Thigpen, Greg Walker, Kenny Williams, Jim Winn

LESS THAN 10 GAMES: Ralph Citarella, Bill Lindsey, Jack McDowell, John Pawlowski, Adam Peterson

KEY SIGNATURES: Fisk, Baines.

VALUE: $60

1987 CINCINNATI - Buddy Bell, Tom Browning, Dave Collins, Dave Concepcion, Kal Daniels, Eric Davis, Bo Diaz, Nick Esasky, John Franco, Terry Francona, Leo Garcia, Bill Gullickson *, Guy Hoffman, Tom Hume *, Tracy Jones, Bill Landrum, Barry Larkin, Lloyd McClendon, Terry McGriff, Jeff Montgomery, Rob Murphy, Paul O'Neill, Ron Oester, Pat Pacillo, Dave Parker, Pat Perry *, Ted Power, Ron Robinson, Pete Rose (MANAGER), Bill Scherrer, Kurt Stillwell, Jeff Treadway, Frank Williams

LESS THAN 10 GAMES: Sal Butera *, Paul O'Neill, Dennis Rasmussen *, Jerry Reuss *, Mario Soto, Max Venable

KEY SIGNATURES: Rose, Parker, Davis, Concepcion.

VALUE: $70

1987 CLEVELAND - Darrel Akerfelds, Andy Allanson, Mike Armstrong, Scott Bailes, Chris Bando, Jay Bell, Tony Bernazard *, Brett Butler, Ernie Camacho, Tom Candiotti, Steve Carlton *, Joe Carter, Carmen Castillo, Dave Clark, Pat Corrales (MANAGER), Rick Dempsey, Jamie Easterly, Doc Edwards (MANAGER), John Farrell, Julio Franco, Doug Frobel, Dave Gallagher, Don Gordon *, Mel Hall, Tommy Hinzo, Mark Huismann *, Brook Jacoby, Doug Jones, Phil Niekro *, Otis Nixon, Junior Noboa, Casey Parsons, Reggie Ritter, Ken Schrom, Cory Snyder, Sammy Stewart, Greg Swindell, Pat Tabler, Andre Thornton, Ed Vane Berg, Eddie Williams, Rick Yett

LESS THAN 10 GAMES: Brian Dorsett, Jeff Kaiser, Tom Waddell, Frank Willis

NOTES: Two 300-win (Niekro/Carlton) pitchers on the same team.

KEY SIGNATURES: Carter, Franco, Niekro, Carlton.

VALUE: $75

1987 DETROIT - Doyle Alexander *, Sparky Anderson (MANAGER), Billy Bean, Dave Bergman, Tom Brookens, Darnell Coles *, Darrell Evans, Kirk Gibson, Johnny Grubb, Terry Harper *, Mike Heath, Mike Henneman, Willie Hernandez, Larry Herndon, Eric King, Chet Lemon, Dwight Lowry, Scott Lusader, Bill Madlock *, Orlando Mercado *, Jack Morris, Jim Morrison *, Matt Nokes, Dan Petry, Jeff Robinson, Pat Sheridan, Nate Snell, Frank Tanana, Walt Terrell, Mark Thurmond, Alan Trammell, Jim Wallewander, Lou Whitaker

LESS THAN 10 GAMES: Doug Baker, Bryan Kelly, Morris Madden, Dickie Noles *, Tim Tolman

KEY SIGNATURES: Anderson, Whitaker, Trammell, Gibson, Morris.

VALUE: $160

1987 HOUSTON - Troy Afenir, Juan Agosto, Larry Andersen, Alan Ashby, Mark Bailey, Kevin Bass, Dale Berra, Buddy Biancalana *, Ken Caminiti, Rocky Childress, Jose Cruz, Danny Darwin, Glenn Davis, Jim Deshaies, Bill Doran, Ty Gainey, Phil Garner *, Billy Hatcher, Jeff Heathcock, Paul Householder, Chuck Jackson, Charlie Kerfeld, Bob Knepper, Hal Lanier (MANAGER), Davey Lopes, Aurelio Lopez, Dave Meads, Jim Pankovits, Bert Pena, Terry Puhl, Craig Reynolds, Ronn Reynolds, Nolan Ryan, Mike Scott, Dave Smith, Julio Solano, Dickie Thon, Ty Waller, Denny Walling, Robbie Wine, Gerald Young

LESS THAN 10 GAMES: Manny Hernandez, Rob Mallicoat, Ron Mathis

KEY SIGNATURES: Davis, Ryan.

VALUE: $70

1987 KANSAS CITY - Steve Balboni, Juan Beniquez *, Buddy Biancalana *, Bud Black, Thad Bosley, George Brett, John Davis, Jim Eisenreich, Steve Farr, Gene Garber *, Billy Gardner (MANAGER), Jerry Don Gleaton, Mark Gubicza, Bo Jackson, Danny Jackson, Ross Jones, Charlie Leibrandt, Hal McRae, Jorge Orta, Larry Owen, Bill Pecota, Jamie Quirk, Dan Quisenberry, Bret Saberhagen, Angel Salazar, Kevin Seitzer, Lonnie Smith, Bob Stoddard, Danny Tartabull, Gary Thurman, John Wathan (MANAGER), Frank White, Willie Wilson

LESS THAN 10 GAMES: Rick Anderson, Dave Gumpert, Ed Hearn, Mike Macfarlane, Scotti Madison, Melido Perez, Bob Shirley *

KEY SIGNATURES: Brett, Tartabull, Jackson, Saberhagen.

VALUE: $75

1987 LOS ANGELES - Dave Anderson, Tim Belcher, Ralph Bryant, Tim Crews, Mike Devereaux, Mariano Duncan, Phil Garner *, Jose Gonzalez, Pedro Guerrero, Chris Gwynn, Jeff Hamilton, Mickey Hatcher, Brad Havens, Danny Heep, Orel Hershiser, Shawn Hillegas, Glenn Hoffman *, Brian Holton, Rick Honeycutt *, Ken Howell, Ken Landreaux, Tito Landrum *, Tom Lasorda (MANAGER), Tim Leary, Bill Madlock *, Mike Marshall, Len Matuszek, Tom Niedenfuer *, Alejandro Pena, Mike Ramsey, Steve Sax, Mike Scioscia, Mike Sharperson *, John Shelby *, Craig Shipley, Franklin Stubbs, Alex Trevino, Fernando Valenzuela, Bob Welch, Reggie Williams, Tracy Woodson, Matt Young

LESS THAN 10 GAMES: Ron Davis *, Bill Krueger *, Orlando Mercado *, Jerry Reuss *, Gil Reyes, Jack Savage, Brad Wellman

KEY SIGNATURES: Lasorda, Sax, Guerrero, Hershiser, Valenzuela.

VALUE: $100

1987 MILWAUKEE - Jay Aldrich, Len Barker, Mike Birkbeck, Chris Bosio, Glenn Braggs, Greg Brock, Ray Burris, Juan Castillo, Mark Clear, Cecil Cooper, Chuck Crim, Rob Deer, Mike Felder, Jim Gantner, Teddy Higuera, John Henry Johnson, Steve Kiefer, Mark Knudson, Rick Manning, Paul Mirabella, Paul Molitor, Juan Nieves, Charlie O'Brien, Jim Paciorek, Dan Plesac, Ernest Riles, Billy Jo Robidoux, Bill Schroeder, B.J. Surhoff, Dale Sveum, Tom Trebelhorn (MANAGER), Bill Wegman, Robin Yount

LESS THAN 10 GAMES: Mark Ciardi, Brad Komminsk, Alex Madrid, Steve Stanicek, Dave Stapleton

KEY SIGNATURES: Yount.

VALUE: $60

1987 MINNESOTA - Keith Atherton, Don Baylor *, Billy Beane, Juan Berenguer, Bert Blyleven, Tom Brunansky, Randy Bush, Sal Butera *, Mark Davidson, George Frazier, Gary Gaetti, Greg Gagne, Dan Gladden, Kent Hrbek, Tom Kelly (MANAGER), Joe Klink, Gene Larkin, Tim Laudner, Steve Lombardozzi, Al Newman, Joe Niekro *, Tom Nieto, Chris Pittaro, Mark Portugal, Kirby Puckett, Jeff Reardon, Mark Salas *, Dan Schatzeder *, Roy Smalley, Mike Smithson, Les Straker, Frank Viola

LESS THAN 10 GAMES: Allan Anderson, Jeff Bittiger, Steve Carlton *, Randy Niemann, Roy Smith

NOTES: World Champions!

KEY SIGNATURES: Hrbek, Puckett, Viola, Blyleven, Carlton.

VALUE: $295

1987 MONTREAL - Hubie Brooks, Tim Burke, Casey Candaele, Jack Daugherty, Dave Engle, Mike Fitzgerald, Tom Foley, Andres Galarraga, Neal Heaton, Joe Hesketh, Wallace Johnson, Vance Law, Dennis Martinez, Bob McClure, Andy McGaffigan, Reid Nichols, Jeff Parrett, Pasquel Perez, Alonzo Powell, Tim Raines, Jeff Reed, Luis Rivera, Buck Rodgers (MANAGER), Bob Sebra, Bryn Smith, Lary Sorenson, Randy St. Claire, John Stefero, Jay Tibbs, Tim Wallach, Mitch Webster, Herm Winningham, Floyd Youmans

LESS THAN 10 GAMES: Curt Brown, Bill Campbell, Jeff Fischer, Ubaldo Heredia, Vance Law, Charlie Lea, Nelson Norman, Tom Romano, Nelson Santovenia, Razor Shines

KEY SIGNATURES: Raines.

VALUE: $60

1987 NEW YORK (AL) - Juan Bonilla, Rich Bordi, Rick Cerone, Pat Clements, Henry Cotto, Mike Easler *, Cecilio Guante, Ron Guidry, Rickey Henderson, Charlie Hudson, Tommy John, Roberto Kelly, Ron Kittle, Al Leiter, Don Mattingly, Bobby Meacham, Mike Pagliarulo, Dan Pasqua, Lou Piniella (MANAGER), Willie Randolph, Dennis Rassmussen *, Rick Rhoden, Dave Righetti, Jerry Royster *, Lenn Sakata, Mark Salas *, Bob Shirley *, Joel Skinner, Tim Stoddard, Wayne Tolleson, Steve Trout *, Gary Ward, Claudell Washington, Dave Winfield, Paul Zuvella

LESS THAN 10 GAMES: Neil Allen *, Brad Arnsberg, Jay Buhner, Orestes Destrade, Pete Filson, Bill Fulton, Bill Gullickson *, Al Holland, Keith Hughes *, Phil Lombardi, Jeff Moronko, Joe Niekro *, Bob Tewksbury *, Randy Velarde

KEY SIGNATURES: Mattingly, Henderson, Winfield, John, Guidry.

VALUE: $100

1987 NEW YORK (NL) - Rick Aguilera, Bill Almon *, Wally Backman, Gary Carter, David Cone, Ron Darling, Len Dykstra, Sid Fernandez, Dwight Gooden, Keith Hernandez, Jeff Innis, Dave Johnson (MANAGER), Howard Johnson, Terry Leach, Barry Lyons, Dave Magadan, Lee Mazzilli, Roger McDowell, Kevin McReynolds, Keith Miller, John Mitchell, Randy Myers, Bob Ojeda, Jesse Orosco, Rafael Santana, Doug Sisk, Darryl Strawberry, Tim Teufel, Gene Waller, Mookie Wilson

LESS THAN 10 GAMES: John Candelaria *, Mark Carreon, Tom Edens, Kevin Elster, Bob Gibson, Clint Hurdle, Gregg Jefferies, Randy Milligan, Al Pedrique *, Don Schulze

KEY SIGNATURES: Hernandez, Johnson, Strawberry, Carter, Gooden.

VALUE: $135

1987 OAKLAND - Joaquin Andujar, Tony Bernazard *, Greg Cadaret, Jose Canseco, Ron Cey, Mike Davis, Dennis Eckersley, Mike Gallego, Alfredo Griffin, Brian Harper, Steve Henderson, Jay Howell, Reggie Jackson, Stan Javier, Dennis Lamp, Carney Lansford, Tony LaRussa (MANAGER), Dave Leiper *, Johnnie LeMaster, Mark McGwire, Dwayne Murphy, Gene Nelson, Steve Ontiveros, Tony Phillips, Eric Plunk, Luis Polonia, Jose Rijo, Rick Rodriguez, Terry Steinbach, Dave Stewart, Mickey Tettleton, Walt Weiss, Curt Young

LESS THAN 10 GAMES: Bill Caudill, Chris Codiroli, Storm Davis *, Moose Haas, Rick Honeycutt *, Bill Krueger *, Gary Lavelle *, Rob Nelson *, Dave Otto, Alex Sanchez, Matt Sinatro, Dave Von Ohlen, Jerry Willard

NOTES: McGwire (ROY).

KEY SIGNATURES: McGwire, Canseco, Jackson, Stewart, Eckersley.

VALUE: $125

ROY = Rookie of the Year

1987 PHILADELPHIA - Luis Aguayo, Doug Bair, Steve Bedrosian, Jeff Calhoun, Don Carman, Darren Daulton, Ken Dowell, Mike Easler *, Lee Elia (MANAGER), John Felske (MANAGER), Todd Frohwirth, Greg Gross, Kevin Gross, Von Hayes, Keith Hughes *, Tom Hume *, Mike Jackson, Chris James, Greg Jelks, Steve Jeltz, Lance Parrish, Shane Rawley, Wally Ritchie, Ron Roenicke, Bruce Ruffin, John Russell, Juan Samuel, Dan Schatzeder *, Mike Schmidt, Rick Schu, Jeff Stone, Kent Tekulve, Milt Thompson, Freddie Toliver, Glenn Wilson

LESS THAN 10 GAMES: Joe Cowley, Ken Jackson, Greg Legg, Mike Maddux, Tom Newell, Glenn Wilson

NOTES: Bedrosian (CY).

KEY SIGNATURES: Schmidt.

VALUE: $60

CY = Cy Young Award winner

1987 PITTSBURGH - Bill Almon *, Rafael Belliard, Barry Bonds, Bobby Bonilla, Sid Bream, John Cangelosi, Darnell Coles *, Mike Diaz, Doug Drabek, Mike Dunne, Logan Easley, Felix Fermin, Brian Fisher, Brett Gideon, Jim Gott *, Tommy Gregg, Terry Harper *, Barry Jones, Bob Kipper, Mike LaValliere, Jim Leyland (MANAGER), Jose Lind, Jim Morrison *, Junior Ortiz, Bob Patterson, Al Pedrique *, Hipolito Pena, Johnny Ray *, Rick Reuschel *, R.J. Reynolds, Don Robinson *, Jeff Robinson *, Mickey Sasser *, John Smiley, Dorn Taylor, Andy Van Slyke, Bob Walk, U.L. Washington

LESS THAN 10 GAMES: Mike Bielecki, Onix Concepcion, Butch Davis, Tim Drummond, Miguel Garcia *, Denny Gonzalez, Houston Jimenez, Dave Johnson, Sammy Khalifa, Vicente Palacios, Tom Prince, Mark Ross

KEY SIGNATURES: Bonilla, Van Slyke, Bonds.

VALUE: $60

1987 SAN DIEGO - Shawn Abner, Bruce Bochy, Greg Booker, Larry Bowa (MANAGER), Chris Brown *, Randy Byers, Keith Comstock *, Joey Cora, Mark Davis *, Storm Davis *, Dave Dravecky *, Tim Flannery, Steve Garvey, Goose Gossage, Mark Grant *, Tony Gwynn, Andy Hawkins, Stan Jefferson, Jimmy Jones, John Kruk, Craig Lefferts *, Dave Leiper *, Shane Mack, Carmelo Martinez, Lance McCullers, Kevin Mitchell *, Rob Nelson *, Eric Nolte, Mark Parent, Randy Ready, Luis Salazar, Benito Santiago, Eric Show, James Steels, Garry Templeton, Ed Whitson, Marvell Wynne

LESS THAN 10 GAMES: Tom Gorman, Ray Hayward, Ed Wojna

NOTES: Santiago (ROY).

KEY SIGNATURES: Gwynn, Garvey, Gossage.

VALUE: $60

ROY = Rookie of the Year

1987 SAN FRANCISCO - Mike Aldrete, Randy Bockus, Bob Brenly, Chris Brown *, Will Clark, Keith Comstock *, Roger Craig (MANAGER), Chili Davis, Mark Davis *, Kelly Downs, Dave Dravecky *, Scott Garrelts, Jim Gott *, Mark Grant *, Atlee Hammaker, Dave Henderson *, Mike Krukow, Randy Kutcher, Mike LaCoss, Craig Lefferts *, Jeff Leonard, Candy Maldonado, Francisco Melendez, Bob Melvin, Eddie Milner, Greg Minton *, Kevin Mitchell *, Jon Perlman, Joe Price, Dan Robinson *, Jeff Robinson *, Chris Speier, Harry Spilman, Robby Thompson, Jose Uribe, Mark Wasinger, Matt Williams, Mike Woodard, Joel Youngblood

LESS THAN 10 GAMES: John Burkett, Ivan DeJesus, Kirt Manwaring, Roger Mason, Jessie Reid, Rick Reuschel *, Mackey Sasser *, Rob Wilfong

KEY SIGNATURES: Clark, Mitchell, Williams.

VALUE: $125

1987 SEATTLE - Scott Bankhead, Phil Bradley, Scott Bradley, Mickey Brantley, John Christensen, Stan Clarke, Alvin Davis, Mario Diaz, Lee Guetterman, Dave Hengel, Bob Kearney, Mike Kingery, Mark Langston, Ed Martinez, Gary Matthews *, Mike Moore, Mike Morgan, John Moses, Donell Nixon, Edwin Nunez, Ken Phelps, Dennis Powell, Jim Presley, Rey Quinones, Domingo Ramos, Jerry Reed, Rich Renteria, Harold Reynolds, Steve Shields, Mike Trujillo, Dave Valle, Bill Wilkinson, Dick Williams (MANAGER)

LESS THAN 10 GAMES: Mike Brown, Mike Campbell, Mike Huismann *, Rich Monteleone, Jerry Narron, Clay Parker, Brick Smith, Roy Thomas, Jim Weaver

KEY SIGNATURES: Langston.

VALUE: $60

1987 ST. LOUIS - Rod Booker, Jack Clark, Vince Coleman, Tim Conroy, Danny Cox, Bill Dawley, Ken Dayley, Dan Driessen, Curt Ford, Bob Forsch, David Green, Tommy Herr, Whitey Herzog (MANAGER), Ricky Horton, Lance Johnson, Mike Laga, Steve Lake, Tito Landrum *, Tom Lawless, Jim Lindeman, Joe Magrane, Greg Mathews, Willie McGee, John Morris, Jose Oquendo, Tom Pagnozzi, Tony Pena, Terry Pendleton, Pat Perry *, Steve Peters, Ozzie Smith, Ray Soff, Scott Terry, John Tudor, Lee Tunnell, Todd Worrell

LESS THAN 10 GAMES: Skeeter Barnes, Doug DeCinces *, Dave LaPoint *, Randy O'Neal *

KEY SIGNATURES: Smith, McGee.

VALUE: $200

1987 TEXAS - Bob Brower, Jerry Browne, Steve Buechele, Ed Correa, Cecil Espy, Scott Fletcher, Jose Guzman, Greg Harris, Charlie Hough, Steve Howe, Pete Incaviglia, Paul Kilgus, Jeff Kunkel, Mike Loynd, Oddibe McDowell, Dave Meier, Ron Meridith, Dale Mohorcic, Pete O'Brien, Tom O'Malley, Tom Paciorek, Larry Parrish, Geno Petralli, Darrell Porter, Jeff Russell, Ruben Sierra, Don Slaught, Mike Stanley, Bobby Valentine (MANAGER), Curt Wilkerson, Mitch Williams, Bobby Witt

LESS THAN 10 GAMES: Scott Anderson, Keith Creel, Dwayne Henry, Mike Jeffcoat, Bob Malloy, Mike Mason *, Gary Mielke, Greg Tabor

KEY SIGNATURES: Sierra.

VALUE: $60

1987 TORONTO - Jesse Barfield, George Bell, Juan Beniquez *, John Cerutti, Jim Clancy, Jeff DeWillis, Rob Ducey, Mark Eichhorn, Tony Fernandez, Cecil Fielder, Kelly Gruber, Tom Henke, Garth Iorg, Joe Johnson, Jimmy Key, Gary Lavelle *, Rick Leach, Manny Lee, Nelson Liriano, Fred McGriff, Charlie Moore, Lloyd Moseby, Rance Mulliniks, Jeff Musselman, Jose Nunez, Mike Sharperson *, Dave Stieb, Lou Thornton, Willie Upshaw, Duane Ward, David Wells, Ernie Whitt, Jimy Williams (MANAGER)

LESS THAN 10 GAMES: Mike Flanagan *, Don Gordon *, Alexis Infante, Greg Myers, Phil Niekro *, Matt Stark

NOTES: Bell (MVP).

KEY SIGNATURES: Fernandez, Bell, McGriff, Stieb, Niekro.

VALUE: $65

MVP = MVP Award winner

1988

1988 San Diego Padres

*** = player was traded**

1988 ATLANTA - Jim Acker, Jose Alvarez, Paul Assenmacher, Bruce Benedict, Jeff Blauser, Terry Blocker, Joe Boever, Kevin Coffman, Juan Eichelberger, Ron Gant, Damaso Garcia, Tom Glavine, Tommy Gregg *, Ken Griffey *, Albert Hall, Dion James, German Jimenez, Mark Lemke, Rick Mahler, Jim Morrison *, Dale Murphy, Russ Nixon (MANAGER), Ken Oberkfell, Ed Olwine, Gerald Perry, Charlie Puleo, Gary Roenicke, Jerry Royster, Paul Runge, Ted Simmons, Lonnie Smith, Pete Smith, Zane Smith, John Smoltz, Bruce Sutter, Chuck Tanner (MANAGER), Andres Thomas, Ozzie Virgil

LESS THAN 10 GAMES: Kevin Blankenship *, Chuck Cary, Jody Davis *, Gary Eave, Jim Morrison *

KEY SIGNATURES: Murphy.

VALUE: $60

1988 BALTIMORE - Don Aase, Brady Anderson *, Jeff Ballard, Jose Bautista, Mike Boddicker *, Butch Davis, Jim Dwyer *, Ken Gerhart, Rene Gonzales, Keith Hughes, Terry Kennedy, Tito Landrum, Fred Lynn *, Mike Morgan, Eddie Murray, Carl Nichols, Tom Niedenfuer, Gregg Olson, Joe Orsulak, Oswald Peraza, Billy Ripken, Cal Ripken, Cal Ripken, Sr. (MANAGER), Frank Robinson (MANAGER), Wade Rowdon, Dave Schmidt, Rick Schu, Larry Sheets, Doug Sisk, Pete Stanicek, Jeff Stone, Mickey Tettleton, Mark Thurmond, Jay Tibbs, Jim Traber, Mark Williamson, Craig Worthington

LESS THAN 10 GAMES: Gordon Dillard, John Habyan, Pete Harnisch, Scott McGregor, Bob Milacki, Dickie Noles, Bill Scherrer *, Curt Schilling

KEY SIGNATURES: Robinson, Murray, Ripken, Lynn.

VALUE: $60

1988 BOSTON - Brady Anderson *, Marty Barrett, Todd Benzinger, Mike Boddicker *, Wade Boggs, Tom Bolton, Oil Can Boyd, Ellis Burks, Rick Cerone, Roger Clemens, Pat Dodson, Dwight Evans, Wes Gardner, Rich Gedman, Mike Greenwell, Sam Horn, Bruce Hurst, Randy Kutcher, Dennis Lamp, John Marzano, John McNamara (MANAGER), Spike Owen, Larry Parrish *, Jody Reed, Jim Rice, Ed Romero, Kevin Romine, Jeff Sellers, Lee Smith, Mike Smithson, Bob Stanley

LESS THAN 10 GAMES: Zach Crouch, Steve Curry, Steve Ellsworth, Carlos Quintana, Mike Rochford, John Trautwein, Rob Woodward

KEY SIGNATURES: Boggs, Rice, Clemens.

VALUE: $125

1988 CALIFORNIA - Tony Armas, Dante Bichette, Bob Boone, Thad Bosley *, Mike Brown, Bill Buckner *, DeWayne Buice, Terry Clark, Stew Cliburn, Sherman Corbett, Chili Davis, Brian Downing, Jim Eppard, Chuck Finley, Willie Fraser, Bryan Harvey, George Hendrick, Jack Howell, Wally Joyner, Ray Krawczyk, Jack Lazorko, Kirk McCaskill, Mark McLemore, Darrell Miller, Greg Minton, Donnie Moore, Junior Noboa, Dan Petry, Gus Polidor, Domingo Ramos *, Johnny Ray, Cookie Rojas (MANAGER), Dick Schofield, Moose Stubing (MANAGER), Chico Walker, Devon White, Mike Witt, Butch Wynegar

LESS THAN 10 GAMES: Mike Cook, Doug Davis, Frank DiMichele, Brian Dorsett, Vance Lovelace, Urbano Lugo, Rich Monteleone, Joe Redfield

KEY SIGNATURES: Joyner, Boone, Buckner.

VALUE: $60

1988 CHICAGO (AL) - Harold Baines, Jeff Bittiger, Daryl Boston, Ivan Calderon, John Davis, Mike Diaz *, Carlton Fisk, Jim Fregosi (MANAGER), Dave Gallagher, Ozzie Guillen, Donnie Hill, Ricky Horton *, Lance Johnson, Barry Jones *, Ron Karkovice, Dave LaPoint *, Bill Long, Steve Lyons, Fred Manrique, Carlos Martinez, Jack McDowell, Russ Morman, Donn Pall, Kelly Paris, Dan Pasqua, Melido Perez, Gary Redus *, Jerry Reuss, Steve Rosenberg, Mark Salas, Bobby Thigpen, Greg Walker, Kenny Williams, Mike Woodard

LESS THAN 10 GAMES: Joel Davis, Jerry Hairston, Shawn Hillegas *, Ravelo Manzanillo, Tom McCarthy, Ken Patterson, John Pawlowski, Adam Peterson, Sap Randall, Jose Segura, Carl Willis

KEY SIGNATURES: Fisk, Baines.

VALUE: $60

1988 CHICAGO (NL) - Damon Berryhill, Mike Bielecki, Mike Capel, Doug Dascenzo, Jody Davis *, Andre Dawson, Frank DiPino, Shawon Dunston, Leon Durham *, Goose Gossage, Mark Grace, Darrin Jackson, Les Lancaster, Vance Law, Greg Maddux, Dave Martinez *, Jamie Moyer, Jerry Mumphrey, Al Nipper, Rafael Palmeiro, Pat Perry *, Jeff Pico, Rolando Roomes, Angel Salazar, Ryne Sandberg, Scott Sanderson, Calvin Schiraldi, Jim Sundberg *, Rick Sutcliffe, Manny Trillo, Gary Varsho, Mitch Webster *, Don Zimmer (MANAGER)

LESS THAN 10 GAMES: Kevin Blankenship *, Drew Hall, Mike Harkey, Bill Landrum, Dave Meier, Bob Tewksbury, Rick Wrona

KEY SIGNATURES: Grace, Sandberg, Dawson, Palmeiro, Gossage.

VALUE: $65

1988 CINCINNATI - Jack Armstrong, Buddy Bell *, Tim Birtsas, Tom Borwning, Marty Brown, Norm Charlton, Dave Collins, Dave Concepcion, Kal Daniels, Eric Davis, Bo Diaz, Rob Dibble, Leon Durham *, Nick Esasky, John Franco, Leo Garcia, Ken Griffey *, Lenny Harris, Danny Jackson, Tracy Jones *, Barry Larkin, Lloyd McClendon, Terry McGriff, Eddie Milner, Rob Murphy, Paul O'Neill, Ron Oester, Pat Perry *, Luis Quinones, Dennis Rasmussen *, Jeff Reed *, Jose Rijo, Ron Robinson *, Ron Roenicke, Pete Rose (MANAGER), Chris Sabo, Van Snider, Mario Soto *, Randy St. Claire *, Jeff Treadway, Frank Williams, Herm Winningham *

LESS THAN 10 GAMES: Keith Brown, Jeff Gray, Pat Pacillo, Candy Sierra *

KEY SIGNATURES: Sabo (ROY).

VALUE: $70

ROY = Rookie of the Year

1988 CLEVELAND - Andy Allanson, Scott Bailes, Chris Bando *, Jay Bell, Bud Black *, Tom Candiotti, Joe Carter, Carmen Castillo, Dave Clark, Chris Codiroil, Jeff Dedmon, Doc Edwards (MANAGER), John Farrell, Julio Franco, Terry Francona, Don Gordon, Mel Hall, Brad Havens *, Brook Jacoby, Doug Jones, Ron Kittle, Bill Laskey, Luis Medina, Rod Nichols, Jon Perlman, Domingo Ramos *, Rick Rodriguez, Dan Schatzeder *, Cory Snyder, Greg Swindell, Pat Tabler *, Willie Upshaw, Ron Washington, Eddie Williams, Reggie Williams, Rich Yett, Paul Zuvella

LESS THAN 10 GAMES: Rod Allen, Dan Firova, Houston Jimenez, Scott Jordan, Jeff Kaiser, Tom Lampkin, Ron Tingley, Mike Walker

KEY SIGNATURES: Franco, Carter.

VALUE: $60

1988 DETROIT - Doyle Alexander, Sparky Anderson (MANAGER), Billy Bean, Dave Bergman, Tom Brookens, Darrell Evans, Paul Gibson, Mike Heath, Don Heinkel, Mike Henneman, Willie Hernandez, Larry Herndon, Eric King, Ray Knight, Chet Lemon, Tony Lovullo, Scott Lusader, Fred Lynn *, Jack Morris, Jim Morrison *, Dwayne Murphy, Matt Nokes, Gary Pettis, Jeff Robinson, Luis Salazar, Pat Sheridan, Frank Tanana, Walt Terrell, Alan Trammell, Jim Walewander, Lou Whitaker

LESS THAN 10 GAMES: Billy Beane, Ivan DeJesus, Mark Huismann, Ted Power *, Steve Sercy, Mike Trujillo

KEY SIGNATURES: Whitaker, Trammell, Lynn, Morris.

VALUE: $60

1988 HOUSTON - Juan Agosto, Larry Andersen, Joaquin Andujar, Alan Ashby, Kevin Bass, Buddy Bell *, Craig Biggio, Ernie Camacho, Ken Caminiti, Casey Candaele *, Rocky Childress, Danny Darwin, Glenn Davis, Jim Deshaies, Bill Doran, John Fishel, Billy Hatcher, Jeff Heathcock, Steve Henderson, Chuck Jackson, Bob Knepper, Hal Lanier (MANAGER), Louie Meadows, Dave Meads, Jim Pankovits, Terry Puhl, Rafael Ramirez, Craig Reynolds, Nolan Ryan, Mike Scott, Dave Smith, Alex Trevino, Denny Walling *, Gerald Young

LESS THAN 10 GAMES: Mark Bailey, Cameron Drew, Bob Forsch *, Brian Meyer, Craig Smajstrla, Harry Spilman *

KEY SIGNATURES: Davis, Ryan.

VALUE: $70

1988 KANSAS CITY - Luis de los Santos, Steve Balboni *, Floyd Bannister, Bud Black *, Thad Bosley *, George Brett, Bill Buckner *, Nick Capra, Jim Eisenreich, Steve Farr, Gene Garber, Jerry Don Gleaton, Mark Gubicza, Bo Jackson, Charlie Liebrandt, Mike Macfarlane, Scotti Madison, Jeff Montgomery, Larry Owen, Bill Pecota, Ted Power *, Jamie Quirk, Dan Quisenberry *, Bret Saberhagen, Israel Sanchez, Kevin Seitzer, Kurt Stillwell, Pat Tabler *, Danny Tartabull, Gary Thurman, John Wathan (MANAGER), Brad Wellman, Frank White, Willie Wilson

LESS THAN 10 GAMES: Rick Anderson, Luis Aquino, Jose DeJesus, Tom Gordon, Ed Hearn, Mark Lee, Dave Owen, Rey Palacios

KEY SIGNATURES: Brett, Tartabull, Jackson, Buckner, Saberhagen.

VALUE: $75

1988 LOS ANGELES - Dave Anderson, Tim Belcher, Tim Crews, Mike Davis, Rick Dempsey, Mike Devereaux, Kirk Gibson, Jose Gonzalez, Alfredo Griffin, Pedro Guerrero *, Chris Gwynn, Jeff Hamilton, Mickey Hatcher, Danny Heep, Orel Hershiser, Shawn Hillegas *, Brian Holton, Ricky Horton *, Jay Howell, Tom Lasorda (MANAGER), Tim Leary, Mike Marshall, Jesse Orosco, Alejandro Pena, Steve Sax, Mike Scioscia, Mike Sharperson, John Shelby, Franklin Stubbs, Don Sutton, Fernando Valenzuela, Tracy Woodson

LESS THAN 10 GAMES: William Brennan, Brad Havens *, Danny Heep, Ken Howell, Bill Krueger, Ramon Martinez, Gil Reyes, John Tudor *

NOTES: World Champions! Hershiser (CY); Gibson (MVP).

KEY SIGNATURES: Sax, Gibson, Hershiser, Valenzuela.

VALUE: $295

1988 MILWAUKEE - Jim Adduci, Don August, Mike Birkbeck, Chris Bosio, Glenn Braggs, Greg Brock, Juan Castillo, Mark Clear, Chuck Crim, Rob Deer, Mike Felder, Tom Filer, Jim Gantner, Darryl Hamilton, Teddy Higuera, Odell Jones, Jeff Leonard *, Joey Meyer, Paul Mirabella, Paul Molitor, Juan Nieves, Charlie O'Brien, Dan Plesac, Ernest Riles *, Billy Jo Robidoux, Bill Schroeder, Gary Sheffield, B.J. Surhoff, Dale Sveum, Tom Trebelhorn (MANAGER), Bill Wegman, Robin Yount

LESS THAN 10 GAMES: Steve Kiefer, Mark Knudson, Dave Stapleton, Mike Young *

KEY SIGNATURES: Yount.

VALUE: $60

1988 MINNESOTA - Allan Anderson, Keith Atherton, Doug Baker, Juan Berenguer, Karl Best, Bert Blyleven, Tom Brunansky *, Eric Bullock, Randy Bush, John Christensen, Mark Davidson, Jim Dwyer *, Gary Gaetti, Greg Gagne, Dan Gladden, German Gonzalez, Brian Harper, Tommy Herr *, Kent Hrbek, Tom Kelly (MANAGER), Gene Larkin, Tim Laudner, Charlie Lea, Steve Lombardozzi, Dwight Lowry *, John Moses, Al Newman, Tom Nieto, Mark Portugal, Kirby Puckett, Jeff Reardon, Dan Schatzeder *, Les Straker, Freddie Toliver, Kelvin Torve, Frank Viola

LESS THAN 10 GAMES: Steve Carlton, Dan Gladden, Tippy Martinez, Mike Mason, Joe Niekro, Roy Smith, Jim Winn

NOTES: Viola (CY).

KEY SIGNATURES: Hrbek, Puckett, Viola, Blyleven, Carlton.

VALUE: $60

CY = Cy Young Award winner

1988 MONTREAL - Hubie Brooks, Tim Burke, Casey Candaele *, John Dopson, Dave Engle, Mike Fitzgerald, Tom Foley, Andres Galarraga, Neal Heaton, Joe Hesketh, Brian Holman, Rex Hudler, Jeff Huson, Wallace Johnson, Tracy Jones *, Dennis Martinez, Dave Martinez *, Bob McClure *, Andy McGaffigan, Graig Nettles, Otis Nixon, Tom O'Malley, Johnny Paredes, Jeff Parrett, Pascual Perez, Tim Raines, Jeff Reed *, Luis Rivera, Buck Rodgers (MANAGER), Nelson Santovenia, Bryn Smith, Tim Wallach, Mitch Webster *, Herm Winningham *, Floyd Youmans

LESS THAN 10 GAMES: Tim Barrett, Randy Johnson, Rick Sauveur, Mike Smith, Randy St. Claire *, Wil Tejada

KEY SIGNATURES: Raines.

VALUE: $60

1988 NEW YORK (AL) - Luis Aguayo *, Neil Allen, Jay Buhner *, John Candelaria, Jack Clark, Jose Cruz, Rich Dotson, Bob Geren, Cecilio Guante *, Lee Guetterman, Ron Guidry, Rickey Henderson, Charlie Hudson, Tommy John, Roberto Kelly, Al Leiter, Billy Martin (MANAGER), Don Mattingly, Bobby Meacham, Dale Mohorcic *, Hal Morris, Mike Pagliarulo, Hipolito Pena, Ken Phelps *, Lou Piniella (MANAGER), Willie Randolph, Rick Rhoden, Dave Righetti, Rafael Santana, Steve Shields, Joel Skinner, Don Slaught, Tim Stoddard, Wayne Tolleson, Randy Velarde, Gary Ward, Claudell Washington, Dave Winfield

LESS THAN 10 GAMES: Chris Chambliss, Pat Clements, Dave Eiland, Alvaro Espinoza, Scott Nielsen

NOTES: Last time Martin managed Yankees.

KEY SIGNATURES: Martin, Mattingly, Winfield, Henderson, John, Guidry.

1988 NEW YORK (NL) - Rick Aguilera, Wally Backman, Gary Carter, David Cone, Ron Darling, Len Dykstra, Kevin Elster, Sid Fernandez, Dwight Gooden, Keith Hernandez, Jeff Innis, Gregg Jefferies, Dave Johnson (MANAGER), Howard Johnson, Terry Leach, Barry Lyons, Dave Magadan, Lee Mazzilli, Bob McClure *, Roger McDowell, Kevin McReynolds, Randy Meyers, Keith Miller, Edwin Nunez *, Bob Ojeda, Mackey Sasser, Darryl Strawberry, Tim Teufel, Gene Walter *, Mookie Wilson

LESS THAN 10 GAMES: Mark Carreon, John Mitchell, David West

KEY SIGNATURES: Hernandez, Johnson, Strawberry, Carter, Gooden.

VALUE: $125

1988 OAKLAND - Don Baylor, Lance Blankenship, Todd Burns, Greg Cadaret, Jose Canseco, Jim Corsi, Storm Davis, Dennis Eckersley, Mike Gallego, Ron Hassey, Dave Henderson, Rick Honeycutt, Glenn Hubbard, Stan Javier, Doug Jennings, Carney Lansford, Tony LaRussa (MANAGER), Mark McGwire, Orlando Mercado, Gene Nelson, Steve Ontiveros, Dave Parker, Tony Phillips, Eric Plunk, Luis Polonia, Matt Sinatro, Terry Steinbach, Dave Stewart, Walt Weiss, Bob Welch, Curt Young

LESS THAN 10 GAMES: Rich Bordi, Felix Jose, Ed Jurak, Dave Otto, Jeff Shaver

NOTES: Canseco (MVP); Weiss (ROY).

KEY SIGNATURES: McGwire, Lansford, Canseco, Parker, Stewart, Welch, Eckersley.

VALUE: $200

ROY = Rookie of the Year

1988 PHILADELPHIA - Luis Aguayo *, Bill Almon, Tommy Barrett, Steve Bedrosian, Phil Bradley, Don Carman, Danny Clay, Darren Daulton, Bob Dernier, Lee Elia (MANAGER), Marvin Freeman, Todd Frohwirth, Greg Gross, Kevin Gross, Jackie Gutierrez, Greg Harris, Von Hayes, Chris James, Steve Jeltz, Ron Jones, Ricky Jordan, Mike Maddux, Keith Miller, David Palmer, Lance Parrish, Shane Rawley, Wally Ritchie, Bruce Ruffin, John Russell, Juan Samuel, Mike Schmidt, Kent Tekulve, Milt Thompson, Shane Turner, John Vuckovich (MANAGER), Mike Young *

LESS THAN 10 GAMES: Salome Barojas, Jeff Calhoun, Bill Dawley, Alex Madrid, Brad Moore, Al Pardo, Bill Scherrer *, Bob Sebra, Scott Service

KEY SIGNATURES: Schmidt.

VALUE: $60

1988 PITTSBURGH - Rafael Belliard, Barry Bonds, Bobby Bonilla, Sid Bream, John Cangelosi, Darnell Coles *, Orestes Destrade, Mike Diaz *, Benny Distefano, Doug Drabek, Mike Dunne, Felix Fermin, Brian Fisher, Denny Gonzalez, Jim Gott, Tommy Gregg *, Barry Jones *, Bob Kipper, Mike La Valliere, Jim Leyland (MANAGER), Jose Lind, Scott Medvin, Randy Milligan, Ken Oberkfell *, Junior Ortiz, Al Pedrique, Tom Prince, Gary Redus *, R.J. Reynolds, Jeff Robinson, Dave Rucker, John Smiley, Andy Van Slyke, Bob Walk, Glenn Wilson *

LESS THAN 10 GAMES: Miguel Garcia, Dave Hostetler, Randy Kramer, Dave LaPoint *, Morris Madden, Vicente Palacios, Rick Reed, Ruben Rodriguez

KEY SIGNATURES: Bonilla, Van Slyke, Bonds, Drabek.

VALUE: $60

1988 SAN DIEGO - Shawn Abner, Roberto Alomar, Greg Booker, Larry Bowa (MANAGER), Chris Brown, Randy Byers, Mark Davis, Tim Flannery, Mark Grant, Tony Gwynn, Andy Hawkins, Stan Jefferson, Jimmy Jones, John Kruk, Dave Leiper, Shane Mack, Carmelo Martinez, Lance McCullers, Jack McKeon (MANAGER), Keith Moreland, Mark Parent, Dennis Rasmussen *, Randy Ready, Benito Santiago, Eric Show, Candy Sierra *, Garry Templeton, Dickie Thon, Ed Whitson, Marvell Wynne

LESS THAN 10 GAMES: Sandy Alomar, Jerald Clark, Keith Comstock, Greg Harris, Rob Nelson, Eric Nolte, Bip Roberts

KEY SIGNATURES: Gwynn.

VALUE: $60

1988 SAN FRANCISCO - Mike Aldrete, Randy Bockus, Bob Brenly, Brett Butler, Will Clark, Roger Craig (MANAGER), Kelly Downs, Phil Garner, Scott Garrelts, Atlee Hammaker, Charlie Hayes, Mike Krukow, Mike LaCoss, Craig Lefferts, Jeff Leonard *, Candy Maldonado, Kirt Manwaring, Francisco Melendez, Bob Melvin, Kevin Mitchell, Donell Nixon, Joe Price, Rick Reuschel, Ernest Riles *, Don Robinson, Roger Samuels, Lary Sorensen, Chris Speier, Harry Spilman *, Robby Thompson, Jose Uribe, Matt Williams, Joel Youngblood,

LESS THAN 10 GAMES: Jeff Brantley, Dennis Cook, Ron Davis, Dave Dravecky, Angel Escobar, Terry Mulholland, Tony Perezchica, Jessie Reid, Rusty Tillman, Mark Wasinger, Trevor Wilson

KEY SIGNATURES: Clark, Mitchell, Williams.

VALUE: $70

1988 SEATTLE - Steve Balboni *, Scott Bankhead, Scott Bradley, Mickey Brantley, Greg Briley, Jay Buhner *, Mike Campbell, Darnell Coles, Henry Cotto, Alvin Davis, Mario Diaz, Bruce Fields, Dave Hengel, Mike Jackson, Mike Kingery, Mark Langston, Ed Martinez, Mike Moore, Edwin Nunez *, Ken Phelps, Dennis Powell, Jim Presley, Rey Quinones, Jerry Reed, Rich Renteria, Harold Reynolds, Mike Schooler, Rod Scurry, Jimmy Snyder (MANAGER), Julio Solano, Bill Swift, Steve Trout, Dave Valle, Gene Walter *, Bill Wilkinson, Dick Williams (MANAGER), Glenn Wilson *

LESS THAN 10 GAMES: Erik Hanson, Bill McGuire, John Rabb, Brick Smith, Terry Taylor

KEY SIGNATURES: Langston.

VALUE: $60

1988 ST. LOUIS - Luis Alicea, Rod Booker, Tom Brunansky *, Vince Coleman, John Costello, Danny Cox, Ken Dayley, Jose DeLeon, Mike Fitzgerald, Curt Ford, Bob Forsch *, Pedro Guerrero *, Tommy Herr *, Whitey Herzog (MANAGER), Bob Horner, Tim Jones, Mike Laga, Steve Lake, Tom Lawless, Jim Lindeman, Joe Magrane, Greg Mathews, Willie McGee, Larry McWilliams, John Morris, Randy O'Neal, Jose Oquendo, Tom Pagnozzi, Tony Pena, Terry Pendleton, Steve Peters, Dan Quisenberry *, Ozzie Smith, Scott Terry, John Tudor *, Duane Walker, Denny Walling *, Todd Worrell

LESS THAN 10 GAMES: Gibson Alba, Scott Arnold, Chris Carpenter, Ken Hill

KEY SIGNATURES: Smith, McGee, Guerrero.

VALUE: $60

1988 TEXAS - Bob Brower, Jerry Browne, Steve Buechele, Jose Cecena, Cecil Espy, Scott Fletcher, Barbaro Garbey, Jose Guzman, Ray Hayward, Dwayne Henry, Guy Hoffman, Charlie Hough, Pete Incaviglia, Steve Kemp, Paul Kilgus, Chad Kreuter, Jeff Kunkel, Oddibe McDowell, Craig McMurty, Dale Mohorcic *, Pete O'Brien, Larry Parrish *, Geno Petralli, Kevin Reimer, Jeff Russell, Larry See, Ruben Sierra, Mike Stanley, James Steels, Jim Sunberg *, Bobby Valentine (MANAGER), Ed Vande Berg, Curt Wilkerson, Mitch Williams, Bobby Witt

LESS THAN 10 GAMES: Kevin Brown, Tony Fossas, Cecilio Guante *, Mike Jeffcoat, Jeff Kunkel, Scott May, DeWayne Vaughn, Steve Wilson

KEY SIGNATURES: Sierra.

VALUE: $60

1988 TORONTO - Doug Bair, Jesse Barfield, George Bell, Juan Beniquez, Pat Borders, Sal Butera, Sil Campusano, Tony Castillo, John Cerutti, Jim Clancy, Rob Ducey, Mark Eichhorn, Tony Fernandez, Cecil Fielder, Mike Flanagan, Kelly Gruber, Tom Henke, Alex Infante, Jimmy Key, Rick Leach, Manny Lee, Nelson Liriano, Fred McGriff, Lloyd Moseby, Rance Mulliniks, Jeff Musselman, Jose Nunez, Dave Stieb, Todd Stottlemyre, Lou Thornton, Duane Ward, David Wells, Ernie Whitt, Jimy Williams (MANAGER), Frank Wills

LESS THAN 10 GAMES: Mark Ross

KEY SIGNATURES: McGriff, Fernandez, Bell, Stieb.

VALUE: $60

1989

1989 St.Louis Cardinals

*** = player was traded**

1989 ATLANTA - Jim Acker *, Jose Alvarez, Paul Assenmacher *, Bruce Benedict, Geronimo Berroa, Jeff Blauser, Terry Blocker, Joe Boever, Tony Castillo *, Marty Clary, Jody Davis, Drew Denson, Mark Eichhorn, Darrell Evans, Ron Gant, Tom Glavine, Tommy Gregg, Dwayne Henry, Dion James *, Dave Justice, Mark Lemke, Derek Lilliquist, Oddibe McDowell *, John Mizerock, Dale Murphy, Russ Nixon (MANAGER), Gerald Perry, Charlie Puleo, John Russell, Lonnie Smith, Pete Smith, Zane Smith *, John Smoltz, Mike Stanton, Andres Thomas, Jeff Treadway, Sergio Valdez, Jeff Wetherby, Ed Whited

LESS THAN 10 GAMES: Jay Aldrich *, Terry Blocker, Francisco Cabrera *, Gary Eave, Tommy Greene, Kelly Mann, Kent Mercker, Rusty Richards, Ed Romero *, John Russell

KEY SIGNATURES: Murphy.

VALUE: $50

1989 BALTIMORE - Brady Anderson, Jeff Ballard, Jose Bautista, Phil Bradley, Mike Devereaux, Steve Finley, Rene Gonzales, Pete Harnisch, Kevin Hickey, Brian Holton, Tim Hulett, Stan Jefferson *, Dave Johnson, Bob Melvin, Bob Milacki, Randy Milligan, Keith Moreland *, Gregg Olson, Joe Orsulak, Jamie Quirk *, Billy Ripken, Cal Ripken, Frank Robinson (MANAGER), Dave Schmidt, Larry Sheets, Mike Smith, Mickey Tettleton, Mark Thurmond, Jay Tibbs, Jim Traber, Mark Williamson, Craig Worthington

LESS THAN 10 GAMES: Juan Bell, Butch Davis, Chris Hoiles, Mark Huismann, Ben McDonald, Francisco Melendez, Curt Schilling, Rich Schu *, Mickey Weston

KEY SIGNATURES: Robinson, Ripken.

VALUE: $60

1989 BOSTON - Marty Barrett, Mike Boddicker, Wade Boggs, Oil Can Boyd, Ellis Burks, Rick Cerone, Roger Clemens, John Dopson, Nick Esasky, Dwight Evans, Wes Gardner, Rich Gedman, Mike Greenwell, Greg Harris *, Danny Heep, Eric Hetzel, Sam Horn, Randy Kutcher, Dennis Lamp, Joe Morgan (MANAGER), Rob Murphy, Joe Price *, Carlos Quintana, Jody Reed, Jim Rice, Luis Rivera, Ed Romero *, Kevin Romine, Lee Smith, Mike Smithson, Bob Stanley, Jeff Stone

LESS THAN 10 GAMES: Tom Bolton, John Marzano, Mike Rochford, Dana Williams

KEY SIGNATURES: Boggs, Clemens.

VALUE: $60

1989 CALIFORNIA - Jim Abbott, Kent Anderson, Tony Armas, Dante Bichette, Bert Blyleven, Chili Davis, Brian Downing, Jim Eppard, Chuck Finley, Willie Fraser, Bryan Harvey, Glenn Hoffman, Jack Howell, Wally Joyner, Kirk McCaskill, Bob McClure, Mark McLemore, Greg Minton, Rich Monteleone, John Orton, Lance Parrish, Dan Petry, Doug Rader (MANAGER), Johnny Ray, Bobby Rose, Dick Schofield, Bill Schroeder, Max Venable, Claudell Washington, Devon White, Mike Witt

LESS THAN 10 GAMES: Brian Brady, Terry Clark, Sherman Corbett, Gary Disarcina, Mike Fetters, Vance Lovelace, Ron Tingley

KEY SIGNATURES: Joyner, Blyleven.

VALUE: $50

1989 CHICAGO (AL) - Harold Baines *, Daryl Boston, Ivan Calderon, Rich Dotson *, Carlton Fisk, Scott Fletcher *, Dave Gallagher, Ozzie Guillen, Greg Hibbard, Shawn Hillegas, Lance Johnson, Barry Jones, Ron Karkovice, Eric King, Ron Kittle, Bill Long, Steve Lyons, Fred Manrique *, Carlos Martinez, Tom McCarthy, Matt Merullo, Russ Morman, Donn Pall, Dan Pasqua, Ken Patterson, Melido Perez, Jerry Reuss *, Billy Jo Robidoux, Steve Rosenberg, Jeff Schaefer, Sammy Sosa *, Bobby Thigpen, Jeff Torborg (MANAGER), Robin Ventura, Greg Walker, Eddie Williams

LESS THAN 10 GAMES: Jeff Bittiger, John Davis, Wayne Edwards, Jerry Hairston, Jack Hardy, Adam Peterson, Jose Segura

KEY SIGNATURES: Fisk, Baines.

VALUE: $60

1989 CHICAGO (NL) - Paul Assenmacher *, Damon Berryhill, Mike Bielecki, Doug Dascenzo, Andre Dawson, Shawon Dunston, Joe Girardi, Mark Grace, Darrin Jackson *, Paul Kilgus, Les Lancaster, Vance Law, Greg Maddux, Lloyd McClendon, Pat Perry, Jeff Pico, Domingo Ramos, Luis Salazar *, Ryne Sandberg, Scott Sanderson, Calvin Schiraldi *, Dwight Smith, Phil Stephenson, Rick Sutcliffe, Gary Varsho, Jerome Walton, Mitch Webster, Curt Wilkerson, Dean Wilkins, Mitch Williams, Steve Wilson, Rick Wrona *, Marvell Wynne *, Don Zimmer (MANAGER)

LESS THAN 10 GAMES: Kevin Blankenship, Joe Kraemer, Greg Smith

NOTES: Walton (ROY).

KEY SIGNATURES: Grace, Sandberg, Dawson.

VALUE: $125

ROY = Rookie of the Year

1989 CINCINNATI - Todd Benzinger, Tim Birtsas, Marty Brown, Tom Browning, Norm Charlton, Dave Collins, Kal Daniels *, Eric Davis, Bo Diaz, Rob Dibble, Mariano Duncan *, John Franco, Ken Griffey, Lenny Harris *, Tommy Helms (MANAGER), Danny Jackson, Barry Larkin, Tim Leary *, Scotti Madison, Rick Mahler, Paul O'Neill, Ron Oester, Joe Oliver, Luis Quinones, Jeff Reed, Jeff Richardson, Jose Rijo, Ron Robinson, Mike Roesler, Rolando Roomes, Pete Rose (MANAGER), Chris Sabo, Scott Scudder, Bob Sebra *, Kent Tekulve, Manny Trillo, Herm Winningham, Joel Youngblood

LESS THAN 10 GAMES: Jack Armstrong, Skeeter Barnes, Mike Griffin, Terry McGriff, Rosario Rodriguez, Van Snider

KEY SIGNATURES: Davis.

VALUE: $60

1989 CLEVELAND - Luis Aguayo, Andy Allanson, Beau Allred, Keith Atherton, Scott Bailes, Joey Belle, Bud Black, Jerry Browne, Tom Candiotti, Joe Carter, Dave Clark, Steve Davis, Doc Edwards (MANAGER), John Farrell, Felix Fermin, John Hart (MANAGER), Dave Hengel, Tommy Hinzo, Brook Jacoby, Dion James *, Doug Jones, Brad Komminsk, Oddibe McDowell *, Luis Medina, Rod Nichols, Pete O'Brien, Steve Olin, Jesse Orosco, Mark Salas, Joel Skinner, Cory Snyder, Tim Stoddard, Greg Swindell, Rich Yett, Mike Young, Paul Zuvella

LESS THAN 10 GAMES: Neil Allen, Pete Dalena, Denny Gonzalez, Brad Havens *, Mark Higgins, Jeff Kaiser, Pat Keedy, Tom Magrann, Rudy Seanez, Danny Sheaffer, Joe Skalski, Kevin Wickander, Ed Wojna

KEY SIGNATURES: Carter.

VALUE: $50

1989 DETROIT - Doyle Alexander, Sparky Anderson (MANAGER), Dave Bergman, Chris Brown, Mike Brumley, Paul Gibson, Brad Havens *, Mike Heath, Mike Henneman, Willie Hernandez, Charlie Hudson, Tracy Jones *, Chet Lemon, Torey Lovullo, Scott Lusader, Fred Lynn, Keith Moreland *, Jack Morris, Matt Nokes, Edwin Nunez, Al Pedrique, Gary Pettis, Rob Ritchie, Kevin Ritz, Jeff Robinson, Rick Schu *, Mike Schwabe, Pat Sheridan *, Matt Sinatro, Doug Strange, Frank Tanana, Alan Trammell, Gary Ward *, Lou Whitaker, Frank Williams, Kenny Williams

LESS THAN 10 GAMES: Billy Bean *, Dave Beard, Randy Bockus, Jeff Datz, Brian DuBois, Shawn Holman, Randy Nosek, David Palmer, Ramon Pena, Steve Searcy, Mike Trujillo

KEY SIGNATURES: Anderson, Trammell, Lynn, Morris.

VALUE: $60

1989 HOUSTON - Juan Agosto, Larry Andersen, Eric Anthony, Alan Ashby, Kevin Bass, Craig Biggio, Ken Caminiti, Jim Clancy, Danny Darwin, Mark Davidson, Glenn Davis, Jim Deshaies, Bill Doran, Bob Forsch, Greg Gross, Billy Hatcher *, Art Howe (MANAGER), Bob Knepper *, Steve Lombardozzi, Louie Meadows, Dave Meads, Brian Meyer, Mark Portugal, Terry Puhl, Rafael Ramirez, Craig Reynolds, Rick Rhoden, Dan Schatzeder, Mike Scott, Dave Smith, Harry Spilman, Alex Trevino, Glenn Wilson *, Eric Yelding, Gerald Young

LESS THAN 10 GAMES: Jose Cano, Greg Gross, Roger Mason, Carl Nichols, Craig Reynolds, Ron Washington

KEY SIGNATURES: Davis.

VALUE: $50

1989 KANSAS CITY - Luis de los Santos, Luis Aquino, Floyd Bannister, Bob Boone, George Brett, Bill Buckner, Steve Crawford, Jim Eisenreich, Steve Farr, Jerry Don Gleason, Tom Gordon, Mark Gubicza, Bo Jackson, Terry Leach *, Charlie Leibrandt, Rick Luecken, Mike Macfarlane, Jeff Montgomery, Rex Palacios, Bill Pecota, Bret Saberhagen, Kevin Seitzer, Kurt Stillwell, Pat Tabler, Danny Tartabull, Gary Thurman, John Wathan (MANAGER), Brad Wellman, Frank White, Willie Wilson, Matt Winters

LESS THAN 10 GAMES: Kevin Appier, Bob Buchanan, Stan Clarke, Jose DeJesus, Larry McWilliams *, Jeff Schulz

NOTES: Saberhagen (CY).

KEY SIGNATURES: Brett, Jackson, Boone, Tartabull, Saberhagen.

VALUE: $75

CY = Cy Young Award winner

1989 LOS ANGELES - Dave Anderson, Billy Bean *, Tim Belcher, Tim Crews, Kal Daniels *, Mike Davis, Rick Dempsey, Mariano Duncan *, Kirk Gibson, Jose Gonzalez, Alfredo Griffin, Chris Gwynn, Jeff Hamilton, Lenny Harris *, Mickey Hatcher, Orel Hershiser, Ricky Horton *, Jay Howell, Mike Huff, Tom Lasorda (MANAGER), Tim Leary , Mike Marshall, Ramon Martinez, Mike Morgan, Eddie Murray, Alejandro Pena, Willie Randolph, Mike Scioscia, Ray Searage, Mike Sharperson, John Shelby, Franklin Stubbs, Fernando Valenzuela, John Wetteland

LESS THAN 10 GAMES: Jeff Fischer, Darrin Fletcher, Jeff Hamilton, Mike Hartley, Mickey Hatcher, Mike Munoz, John Tudor, Jose Vizcaino, Tracy Woodson

KEY SIGNATURES: Lasorda, Murray, Randolph, Gibson, Hershiser, Valenzuela.

VALUE: $100

1989 MILWAUKEE - Jay Aldrich *, Don August, Chris Bosio, Glenn Braggs, Greg Brock, George Canale, Bryan Clutterbuck, Chuck Crim, Rob Deer, Dave Engle, Mike Felder, Tom Filer, Tony Fossas, Terry Francona, Jim Gantner, Teddy Higuera, Mark Knudson, Bill Krueger, Joey Meyer, Paul Mirabella, Paul Molitor, Jaime Navarro, Charlie O'Brien, Dan Plesac, Gus Polidor, Ed Romero *, Gary Sheffield, Bill Spiers, B.J. Surhoff, Tom Trebelhorn (MANAGER), Greg Vaughn, Bill Wegman, Robin Yount

LESS THAN 10 GAMES: Billy Bates, Mike Birkbeck, Juan Castillo, LaVel Freeman, Ray Krawczyk, Jeff Peterek, Jerry Reuss *, Randy Veres

NOTES: Yount (MVP).

KEY SIGNATURES: Yount.

VALUE: $60

MVP = MVP Award winner

1989 MINNESOTA - Rick Aguilera *, Allan Anderson, Wally Backman, Doug Baker, Juan Berenguer, Randy Bush, Carmen Castillo, Mike Cook, Jim Dwyer *, Mike Dyer, Gary Gaetti, Greg Gagne, Dan Gladden, German Gonzalez, Mark Guthrie, Chip Hale, Brian Harper, Kent Hrbek, Terry Jorgensen, Tom Kelly (MANAGER), Gene Larkin,

Tim Laudner, Orlando Mercado, John Moses, Al Newman, Francisco Oliveras, Kirby Puckett, Shane Rawley, Jeff Reardon, Steve Shields, Roy Smith, Paul Sorrento, Randy St. Claire, Lee Tunnell, Frank Viola *, Gary Wayne, Lenny Webster, David West *

LESS THAN 10 GAMES: Greg Booker *, Tim Drummond, Dan Gladden, John Moses, Greg Olson, Vic Rodriguez, Kevin Tapani *, Freddie Toliver *

KEY SIGNATURES: Hrbek, Puckett, Viola.

VALUE: $60

1989 MONTREAL - Mike Aldrete, Hubie Brooks, Tim Burke, John Candelaria *, Jim Dwyer *, Mike Fitzgerald, Tom Foley, Steve Frey, Andres Galarraga, Damaso Garcia, Marquis Grissom, Kevin Gross, Gene Harris *, Joe Hesketh, Brian Holman *, Rex Hudler, Jeff Huson, Wallace Johnson, Mark Langston *, Dave Martinez, Dennis Martinez, Andy McGaffigan, Otis Nixon, Junior Noboa, Spike Owen, Pascual Perez, Marty Pevey, Tim Raines, Buck Rodgers (MANAGER), Nelson Santovenia, Bryn Smith, Zane Smith *, Rich Thompson, Larry Walker, Tim Wallach

LESS THAN 10 GAMES: Tom Foley, Mark Gardner, Brett Gideon, Randy Johnson *, Urbano Lugo, Gil Reyes, Tim Wallach

KEY SIGNATURES: Raines.

VALUE: $60

1989 NEW YORK (AL) - Steve Balboni, Jesse Barfield *, Mike Blowers, Tom Brookens, Bob Brower, Greg Cadaret *, John Candelaria *, Chuck Cary, Bucky Dent (MANAGER), Rich Dotson *, Alvaro Espinoza, Bob Geren, Goose Gossage *, Dallas Green (MANAGER), Lee Guetterman, Mel Hall, Andy Hawkins, Rickey Henderson *, Stan Jefferson *, Tommy John, Jimmy Jones, Roberto Kelly, Marcus Lawton, Dave LaPoint, Don Mattingly, Lance McCullers, Dale Mohorcic, Hal Morris, Mike Pagliarulo *, Clay Parker, Ken Phelps *, Eric Plunk *, Luis Polonia *, Jamie Quirk *, Dave Righetti, Deion Sanders, Steve Sax, Don Slaught, Walt Terrell *, Wayne Tolleson, Randy Velarde

LESS THAN 10 GAMES: Bobby Davidson, Brian Dorsett, Dave Eiland, Steve Kiefer, Al Leiter *, Hensley Meulens, Kevin Mmahat, Scott Nielsen, Don Schulze *, Gary Ward *

KEY SIGNATURES: Mattingly, Sax, Winfield, Gossage.

VALUE: $100

1989 NEW YORK (NL) - Don Aase, Rick Aguilera *, Mark Carreon, Gary Carter, David Cone, Ron Darling, Len Dykstra *, Kevin Elster, Sid Fernandez, Dwight Gooden, Keith Hernandez, Jeff Innis, Gregg Jefferies, Dave Johnson (MANAGER), Howard Johnson, Terry Leach *, Phil Lombardi, Barry Lyons, Julio Machado, Dave Magadan, Lee Mazzilli *, Roger McDowell *, Kevin McReynolds, Keith Miller, Jeff Musselman *, Randy Myers, Bob Ojeda, Juan Samuel *, Mackey Sasser, Darryl Strawberry, Tim Teufel, Lou Thornton, Frank Viola *, David West *, Mookie Wilson *

LESS THAN 10 GAMES: Blaine Beatty, Manny Hernandez, Jeff McKnight, John Mitchell, Tom O'Malley, Craig Shipley, Kevin Tapani *, Wally Whitehurst

KEY SIGNATURES: Johnson, Strawberry, Hernandez, Carter, Gooden.

VALUE: $100

1989 OAKLAND - Billy Beane, Lance Blankeship, Todd Burns, Greg Cadaret *, Jose Canseco, Jim Corsi, Storm Davis, Dennis Eckersley, Mike Gallego, Ron Hassey, Dave Henderson, Rickey Henderson *, Rick Honeycutt, Glenn Hubbard, Stan Javier, Felix Jose, Carney Lansford, Tony LaRussa (MANAGER), Mark McGwire, Mike Moore, Gene Nelson, Dave Parker, Ken Phelps *, Tony Phillips, Eric Plunk *, Luis Polonia *, Terry Steinbach, Dave Stewart, Walt Weiss, Bob Welch, Curt Young, Matt Young

LESS THAN 10 GAMES: Larry Arndt, Chris Bando, Bill Dawley, Scott Hemond, Dan Howitt, Doug Jennings, Dave Otto, Jamie Quirk *, Dick Scott, Brian Snyder

KEY SIGNATURES: LaRussa, McGwire, Canseco, D. Henderson, R. Henderson, Parker, Stewart, Eckersly.

VALUE: $295

1989 PHILADELPHIA - Jim Adduci, Tommy Barrett, Steve Bedrosian *, Don Carman, Pat Combs, Dennis Cook *, Darren Daulton, Bob Dernier, Len Dykstra *, Curt Ford, Todd Frohwirth, Greg Harris *, Von Hayes, Charlie Hayes *, Tommy Herr, Ken Howell, Chris James *, Steve Jeltz, Ron Jones, Ricky Jordan, John Kruk *, Steve Lake, Nick Leyva (MANAGER), Mike Maddux, Roger McDowell *, Chuck McElroy, Larry McWilliams *, Dwayne Murphy, Tom Nieto, Randy O'Neal, Jeff Parrett, Randy Ready *, Bruce Ruffin, Mark Ryal, Juan Samuel *, Mike Schmidt, Dickie Thon, Floyd Youmans

LESS THAN 10 GAMES: Eric Bullock, Gordon Dillard, Marvin Freeman, Jason Grimsley, Alex Madrid, Keith Miller, Terry Mulholland *, Steve Ontiveros, Al Pardo, Bob Sebra *, Steve Stanicek

NOTES: Schmidt retired.

KEY SIGNATURES: Dykstra, Schmidt.

VALUE: $50

1989 PITTSBURGH - Doug Bair, Jay Bell, Rafael Belliard, Dann Bilardello, Barry Bonds, Bobby Bonilla, Sid Bream, John Cangelosi, Benny Distefano, Doug Drabek, Logan Easley, Miguel Garcia, Albert Hall, Billy Hatcher *, Neal Heaton, Jeff King, Bob Kipper, Randy Kramer, Bill Landrum, Mike LaValliere, Jim Leyland (MANAGER), Jose Lind, Ken Oberkfell *, Junior Ortiz, Bob Patterson, Tom Prince, Rey Quinones *, Gary Redus, Rick Reed, R.J. Reynolds, Jeff Robinson, John Smiley, Mike Smith, Andy Van Slyke, Bob Walk, Glenn Wilson *

LESS THAN 10 GAMES: Stan Belinda, Steve Carter, Mike Dunne *, Brian Fisher, Jim Gott, Scott Little, Morris Madden, Scott Medvin, Roger Samuels, Dorn Taylor

KEY SIGNATURES: Bonilla, Van Slyke, Bonds.

VALUE: $60

1989 SAN DIEGO - Shawn Abner, Roberto Alomar, Andy Benes, Greg Booker *, Jack Clark, Jerald Clark, Pat Clements, Joey Cora, Mark Davis, Tim Flannery, Mark Grant, Gary Green, Tony Gwynn, Greg Harris, Bruce Hurst, Darrin Jackson *, Chris James *, John Kruk *, Dave Leiper, Carmelo Martinez, Jack McKeon (MANAGER), Rob Nelson, Mike Pagliarulo *, Mark Parent, Dennis Rasmussen, Randy Ready *, Bip Roberts, Luis Salazar *, Benito Santiago, Eric Show, Phil Stephenson *, Garry Templeton, Walt Terrell *, Ed Whitson, Marvell Wynne *

LESS THAN 10 GAMES: Sandy Alomar, Dan Murphy, Eric Nolte, Calvin Schiraldi *, Don Schulze *, Freddie Toliver *

NOTES: Davis (CY).

KEY SIGNATURES: Clark, Gwynn.

VALUE: $60

CY = Cy Young Award winner

1989 SAN FRANCISCO - Bill Bathe, Steve Bedrosian *, Mike Benjamin, Jeff Brantley, Bob Brenly *, Brett Butler, Ernie Camacho, Will Clark, Roger Craig (MANAGER), Kelly Downs, Scott Garrelts, Goose Gossage *, Atlee Hammaker, Tracy Jones *, Ed Jurak, Terry Kennedy, Bob Knepper *, Mike Laga, Mike LaCoss, Craig Lefferts, Greg Litton, Candy Maldonado, Kirt Manwaring, Randy McCament, Kevin Mitchell, Donell Nixon, Ken Oberkfell *, Rick Reuschel, Ernest Riles, Don Robinson, Pat Sheridan *, Chris Speier, James Steels, Robby Thompson, Jose Uribe, Jim Weaver, Matt Williams, Trevor Wilson

LESS THAN 10 GAMES: Dennis Cook *, Dave Dravecky, Charlie Hayes *, Mike Krukow, Terry Mulholland, Joe Price *, Russ Swan, Stu Tate

NOTES: Mitchell (MVP).

KEY SIGNATURES: Clark, Williams, Mitchell, Gossage.

VALUE: $200

MVP = MVP Award winner

1989 SEATTLE - Scott Bankhead, Scott Bradley, Mickey Brantley, Greg Briley, Jay Buhner, Mike Campbell *, Dave Cochrane, Darnell Coles, Keith Comstock, Henry Cotto, Alvin Davis, Mario Diaz, Mike Dunne *, Ken Griffey Jr., Erik Hanson, Gene Harris, Brian Holman *, Mike Jackson, Randy Johnson *, Mike Kingery, Mark Langston *, Jim Lefebvre (MANAGER), Jeff Leonard, Ed Martinez, Bill McGuire, Tom Niedenfuer, Dennis Powell, Jim Presley, Jerry Reed, Harold Reynolds, Mike Schooler, Julio Solano, Bill Swift, Steve Trout, Dave Valle, Omar Vizquel, Clint Zavaras

LESS THAN 10 GAMES: Luis DeLeon, Bruce Fields, Rey Quinones *, Jim Wilson

KEY SIGNATURES: Griffey Jr.

VALUE: $60

1989 ST. LOUIS - Rod Booker, Tom Brunansky, Cris Carpenter, Vince Coleman, John Costello, Ken Dayley, Jose DeLeon, Frank DiPino, Leon Durham, Pedro Guerrero, Whitey Herzog (MANAGER), Ken Hill, Ricky Horton *, Tim Jones, Jim Lindeman, Joe Magrane, Willie McGee, John Morris, Jose Oquendo, Tom Pagnozzi, Tony Pena, Terry Pendleton, Ted Power, Dan Quisenberry, Ozzie Smith, Scott Terry, Milt Thompson, Denny Walling, Todd Worrell, Todd Zeile

LESS THAN 10 GAMES: Don Heinkel, Matt Kinzer, Bob Tewksbury, Craig Wilson

KEY SIGNATURES: Guerrero, Smith, McGee.

VALUE: $60

1989 TEXAS - Brad Arnsberg, Harold Baines *, Buddy Bell, Thad Bosley, Kevin Brown, Steve Buechele, Scott Coolbaugh, Jack Daugherty, Cecil Espy, Scott Fletcher *, Julio Franco, Juan Gonzalez, Cecilio Guante, Drew Hall, Charlie Hough, Pete Incaviglia, Mike

Jeffcoat, Chad Kreuter, Jeff Kunkel, Rick Leach, Fred Manrique *, Craig McMurtry, Gary Mielke, Jamie Moyer, Rafael Palmeiro, Dean Palmer, Geno Petralli, Kenny Rogers, Jeff Russell, Nolan Ryan, Ruben Sierra, Sammy Sosa *, Mike Stanley, Jeff Stone *, Jim Sundberg, Bobby Valentine (MANAGER), Bobby Witt

LESS THAN 10 GAMES: Darrel Akerfelds, Wilson Alvarez, John Barfield, Jeff Kunkel, Kevin Reimer, Paul Wilmet

KEY SIGNATURES: Palmeiro, Franco, Sierra, Baines, Ryan.

VALUE: $75

1989 TORONTO - Jim Acker *, Jesse Barfield *, George Bell, Pat Borders, Bob Brenly *, Tony Castillo *, John Cerutti, Rob Ducey, Junior Felix, Tony Fernandez, Mike Flanagan, Kelly Gruber, Tom Henke, Glenallen Hill, Alex Infante, Jimmy Key, Tom Lawless, Manny Lee, Nelson Liriano, Lee Mazzilli *, Fred McGriff, Lloyd Moseby, Rance Mulliniks, Greg Myers, Dave Stieb, Todd Stottlemyre, Duane Ward, David Wells, Ernie Whitt, Jimy Williams (MANAGER), Frank Wills, Mookie Wilson *

LESS THAN 10 GAMES: Kevin Batiste, DeWayne Buice, Francisco Cabrera *, Steve Cummings, Mauro Gozzo, Xavier Hernandez, Al Leiter *, Jeff Musselman *, Jose Nunez, John Olerud, Alex Sanchez, Ozzie Virgil

KEY SIGNATURES: McGriff, Fernandez, Stieb.

VALUE: $125

1990

1990

*** = player was traded**

1990 ATLANTA - Steve Avery, Mike Bell, Jeff Blauser, Joe Boever *, Francisco Cabrera, Tony Castillo, Marty Clary, Bobby Cox (MANAGER), Jody Davis, Nick Esasky, Ron Gant, Tom Glavine, Mark Grant *, Tommy Gregg, Dwayne Henry, Joe Hesketh *, Alex Infante, Dave Justice, Charley Kerfeld *, Jimmy Kremers, Charlie Leibrandt, Mark Lemke, Derek Lilliquist *, Rick Luecken *, Kelly Mann, Oddibe McDowell, Kent Mercker, Dale Murphy *, Russ Nixon (MANAGER), Greg Olson, Jeff Parrett *, Jim Presley, Lonnie Smith, Pete Smith, John Smoltz, Andres Thomas, Jeff Treadway, Jim Vatcher *, Ernie Whitt

LESS THAN 10 GAMES: Geronimo Berroa, Marvin Freeman *, Tommy Greene *, Paul Marak, Rusty Richards, Victor Rosario, Doug Sisk, Mike Stanton, Sergio Valdez *

NOTES: Justice (ROY).

KEY SIGNATURES: Justice, Murphy.

VALUE: $50

ROY = Rookie of the Year

1990 BALTIMORE - Brady Anderson, Jeff Ballard, Jose Bautista, Phil Bradley *, Mike Deveraux, Brian DuBois *, Steve Finley, Dave Gallagher *, Leo Gomez, Rene Gonzales, Pete Harnisch, Kevin Hickey, Chris Hoiles, Brian Holton, Sam Horn, Tim Hulett, Stan Jefferson *, Dave Johnson, Ron Kittle *, Brad Komminsk *, Ben McDonald, Jeff McKnight, Bob Melvin, Bob Milacki, Randy Milligan, John Mitchell, Gregg Olson, Joe Orsulak, Joe Price, Billy Ripken, Cal Ripken, Frank Robinson (MANAGER), Curt Schilling, David Segui, Mickey Tettleton, Jay Tibbs *, Greg Walker *, Mark Williamson, Craig Worthington

LESS THAN 10 GAMES: Jay Aldrich, Juan Bell, Dan Boone, Marty Brown, Jose Mesa, Donell Nixon, Mike Smith, Dorn Taylor, Anthony Telford, Mickey Weston

KEY SIGNATURES: F. Robinson, C. Ripken Jr.

VALUE: $60

1990 BOSTON - Larry Andersen *, Marty Barrett, Mike Boddicker, Wade Boggs, Tom Bolton, Tom Brunansky *, Bill Buckner, Ellis Burks, Roger Clemens, Dwight Evans, Wes Gardner, Rich Gedman *, Jeff Gray, Mike Greenwell, Greg Harris, Danny Heep, Joe Hesketh *, Daryl Irvine, Dana Kiecker, Randy Kutcher, Dennis Lamp, Mike Marshall *, John Marzano, Joe Morgan (MANAGER), Rob Murphy, Tim Naehring, Tony Pena, Phil Plantier, Carlos Quintana, Jeff Reardon, Jody Reed, Jerry Reed *, Luis Rivera, Billy Jo Robidoux, Kevin Romine, Lee Smith *, Jeff Stone

LESS THAN 10 GAMES: Scott Cooper, John Dopson, Eric Hetzel, Rick Lancellotti, John Leister, Jim Panovits, Mike Rochford

KEY SIGNATURES: Boggs, Clemens.

VALUE: $110

1990 CALIFORNIA - Jim Abbott, Kent Anderson, Scott Bailes, Dante Bichette, Bert Blyleven, Pete Coachman, Chili Davis, Gary Disarcina, Brian Downing, Mark Eichhorn, Mike Fetters, Chuck Finley, William Fraser, Bryan Harvey, Donnie Hill, Jack Howell, Wally Joyner, Mark Langston, Kirk McCaskill, Bob McClure, Mark McLemore *, Greg Minton, John Orton, Lance Parrish, Luis Polonia *, Doug Rader (MANAGER), Johnny Ray, Dick Schofield, Bill Schroeder, Rick Schu, Lee Stevens, Max Venable, Claudell Washington *, Devon White, Dave Winfield *, Mike Witt *, Cliff Young

LESS THAN 10 GAMES: Mark Clear, Sherman Corbett, Joe Grahe, Donnie Hill, Scott Lewis, Jeff Richardson, Bobby Rose, Ron Tingley

KEY SIGNATURES: Joyner, Winfield, Blyleven.

VALUE: $50

1990 CHICAGO (AL) - Phil Bradley *, Ivan Calderon, Wayne Edwards, Alex Fernandez, Carlton Fisk, Scott Fletcher, Dave Gallagher *, Craig Grebeck, Ozzie Guillen, Greg Hibbard, Lance Johnson, Barry Jones, Ron Karkovice, Eric King, Ron Kittle *, Steve Lyons, Carlos Martinez, Rodney McCray, Jack McDowell, Donn Pall, Dan Pasqua, Ken Patterson, Melido Perez, Adam Peterson, Scott Radinsky, Sammy Sosa, Bobby Thigpen, Frank Thomas, Jeff Torborg (MANAGER), Robin Ventura

LESS THAN 10 GAMES: Daryl Boston *, Shawn Hillegas, Jerry Kutzler, Bill Long *, Steve Lyons, Steve Rosenberg, Matt Stark, Greg Walker *, Jerry Willard

KEY SIGNATURES: Fisk.

VALUE: $60

1990 CHICAGO (NL) - Paul Assenmacher, Damon Berryhill, Mike Bielecki, Shawn Boskie, Dave Clark, Doug Dascenzo, Andre Dawson, Shawon Dunston, Joe Girardi, Mark Grace, Mike Harkey, Joe Kraemer, Randy Kramer *, Les Lancaster, Bill Long *, Greg Maddux, Derrick May, Lloyd McClendon *, Jose Nunez, Dave Pavlas, Jeff Pico, Domingo Ramos, Luis Salazar, Ryne Sandberg, Dwight Smith, Greg Smith, Gary Varsho, Hector Villanueva, Jerome Walton, Curt Wilkerson, Mitch Williams, Steve Wilson, Rick Wrona, Marvell Wynne, Don Zimmer (MANAGER)

LESS THAN 10 GAMES: Kevin Blankenship, Kevin Coffman, Doug Dascenzo, Lance Dickson, Rick Sutcliffe, Dean Wilkins

KEY SIGNATURES: Dawson, Grace, Sandberg.

VALUE: $70

1990 CINCINNATI - Jack Armstrong, Todd Benzinger, Tim Birtsas, Glenn Braggs *, Tom Browning, Norm Charlton, Eric Davis, Rob Dibble, Bill Doran *, Mariano Duncan, Ken Griffey *, Billy Hatcher, Danny Jackson, Barry Larkin, Tim Layana, Terry Lee, Rick Mahler, Hal Morris, Randy Myers, Paul O'Neill, Ron Oester, Joe Oliver, Lou Piniella (MANAGER), Luis Quinones, Jeff Reed, Jose Rijo, Rolando Roomes *, Chris Sabo, Scott Scudder, Herm Winningham

LESS THAN 10 GAMES: Billy Bates *, Keith Brown, Kip Gross, Chris Hammond, Terry McGriff *, Gino Minutelli, Paul Noce, Ron Robinson *, Rosario Rodriguez, Glenn Sutko, Alex Trevino *

NOTES: World Champions!

KEY SIGNATURES: Larkin, Davis, Piniella.

VALUE: $250

1990 CLEVELAND - Sandy Alomar, Carlos Baerga, Bud Black *, Tom Brookens, Jerry Browne, Tom Candiotti, Alex Cole, John Farrell, Felix Fermin, Cecilio Guante, Keith Hernandez, Brook Jacoby, Chris James, Dion James, Stan Jefferson *, Doug Jones, Candy Maldonado, Jeff Manto, John McNamara (MANAGER), Steve Olin, Jesse Orosco, Ken Phelps *, Rudy Seanez, Jeff Shaw, Joel Skinner, Cory Snyder, Greg Swindell, Efrain Valdez, Sergio Valdez *, Mike Walker, Colby Ward, Turner Ward, Mitch Webster, Kevin Wickander

LESS THAN 10 GAMES: Beau Allred, Kevin Bearse, Joey Belle, Mauro Gozzo, Jeff Kaiser, Mark McLamore *, Charles Nagy, Rod Nichols, Al Nipper, Rafael Santana, Steve Springer

NOTES: S. Alomar (ROY).

KEY SIGNATURES: Hernandez.

VALUE: $50

ROY = Rookie of the Year

1990 DETROIT - Sparky Anderson (MANAGER), Dave Bergman, Darnell Coles *, Milt Cuyler, Brian DuBois *, Cecil Fielder, Travis Fryman, Paul Gibson, Jerry Don Gleaton, Mike Heath, Mike Henneman, Tracy Jones *, Chet Lemon, Jim Lindeman, Urbano Lugo, Scott Lusader, Jack Morris, Lloyd Moseby, Matt Nokes *, Edwin Nunez, Clay Parker *, Dan Petry, Tony Phillips, Jeff Robinson, Ed Romero, Mark Salas, Steve Searcy, Larry Sheets, John Shelby *, Frank Tanana, Walt Terrell *, Alan Trammell, Gary Ward, Lou Whitaker, Kenny Williams *

LESS THAN 10 GAMES: Scott Aldred, Matt Kinzer, Lance McCullers *, Randy Nosek, Johnny Paredes *, Kevin Ritz, Rich Rowland, Mike Schwabe, Steve Wapnick

NOTES: Fielder became first major leaguer to hit more than 50 homers in a season since 1977.

KEY SIGNATURES: Anderson, Fielder, Morris, Trammell, Whitaker.

VALUE: $60

1990 HOUSTON - Juan Agosto, Larry Andersen *, Eric Anthony, Craig Biggio, Ken Caminiti, Casey Candaele, Jim Clancy, Danny Darwin, Mark Davidson, Glenn Davis, Jim Deshaies, Bill Doran *, Rich Gedman *, Luis Gonzalez, Bill Gullickson, Xavier Hernandez, Art Howe (MANAGER), Louie Meadows *, Brian Meyer, Carl Nichols, Ken Oberkfell, Javier Ortiz, Al Osuna, Mark Portugal, Terry Puhl, Rafael Ramirez, Dave Rhode, Tuffy Rhodes, Dan Schatzeder *, Mike Scott, Mike Simms, Dave Smith, Franklin Stubbs, Alex Trevino *, Glenn Wilson, Eric Yelding, Gerald Young

LESS THAN 10 GAMES: Jeff Baldwin, Andujar Cedeno, Terry Clark, Brian Fisher, Randy Harris, Charley Kerfeld *, Steve Lombardozzi, Terry McGriff *

KEY SIGNATURES: Davis.

VALUE: $50

1990 KANSAS CITY - Kevin Appier, Luis Aquino, Bob Boone, George Brett, Steve Crawford, Mark Davis, Storm Davis, Jim Eisenreich, Steve Farr, Tom Gordon, Mark Gubicza, Bo Jackson, Steve Jeltz, Mike Macfarlane, Andy McGaffigan *, Brian McRae, Larry McWilliams, Jeff Montgomery, Russ Morman, Ray Palacios, Bill Pecota, Gerald Perry, Bret Saberhagen, Israel Sanchez, Jeff Schulz, Kevin Seitzer, Terry Shumpert, Kurt Stillwell, Mel Stottlemyre, Pat Tabler *, Danny Tartabull, Gary Thurman, John Wathan (MANAGER), Frank White, Willie Wilson

LESS THAN 10 GAMES: Jay Baller, Sean Berry, Jim Campbell, Chris Codiroli, Jeff Conine, Rich Dotson, Luis Encarnacion, Pete Filson, Carlos Maldonado, Brent Mayne, Daryl Smith, Hector Wagner

NOTES: George Brett became the only player in history to win a batting title in three different decades!

KEY SIGNATURES: Brett, Tartabull, Jackson, Saberhagen.

VALUE: $75

1990 LOS ANGELES - Don Aase, Tim Belcher, Hubie Brooks, Tim Crews, Kal Daniels, Rick Dempsy, Kirk Gibson, Jose Gonzales, Jim Gott, Alfredo Griffin, Chris Gwynn, Lenny Harris, Mike Hartley, Mickey Hatcher, Carlos Hernandez, Darren Holmes, Jay Howell, Stan Javier *, Tom Lasorda (MANAGER), Mike Maddux, Ramon Martinez, Mike Morgan, Eddie Murray, Jim Neidlinger, Jose Offerman, Pat Perry, Jim Poole, Willie Randolph *, Juan Samuel, Mike Scioscia, Ray Searage, Mike Sharperson, John Shelby, Fernando Valenzuela, Jose Vizcaino, Dave Walsh, John Wetteland

LESS THAN 10 GAMES: Dennis Cook *, Darrin Fletcher *, Jeff Hamilton, Dave Hansen, Orel Hershiser, Luis Lopez, Barry Lyons *, Mike Munoz, Brian Traxler, Terry Wells

KEY SIGNATURES: Lasorda, Murray, Gibson, Valenzuela.

VALUE: $100

1990 MILWAUKEE - Billy Bates *, Chris Bosio, Glenn Braggs *, Greg Brock, George Canale, Chuck Crim, Rob Deer, Edgar Diaz, Tom Edens, Mike Felder, Tony Fossas, Jim Gantner, Darryl Hamilton, Teddy Higuera, Mark Knudson, Bill Krueger, Mark Lee, Julio Machado *, Paul Mirabella, Paul Molitor, Jaime Navarro, Charlie O'Brien *, Dave Parker, Dan Plesac, Gus Polidor, Ron Robinson *, Bob Sebra, Gary Sheffield, Bill Spiers, B.J. Surhoff, Dave Sveum, Tom Trebelhorn (MANAGER), Greg Vaughn, Randy Veres, Robin Yount

LESS THAN 10 GAMES: Don August, Kevin Brown *, Mike Capel, Narciso Elvira, Tom Filer, Terry Francona, Tim McIntosh, Dennis Powell *, Bill Wegman

KEY SIGNATURES: Yount, Molitor, Parker.

VALUE: $60

1990 MINNESOTA - Rick Aguilera, Allan Anderson, Juan Berenguer, Randy Bush, John Candelaria *, Carmen Castillo, Tim Drummond, Jim Dwyer, Scott Erickson, Gary Gaetti,

Greg Gagne, Dan Gladden, Mark Guthrie, Brian Harper, Kent Hrbek, Tom Kelly (MANAGER), Gene Larkin, Terry Leach, Scott Leius, Nelson Liriano *, Shane Mack, Fred Manrique, John Moses, Pedro Munoz, Al Newman, Junior Ortiz, Kirby Puckett, Jack Savage, Roy Smith, Paul Sorrento, Kevin Tapani, Gary Wayne, David West

LESS THAN 10 GAMES: Paul Abbott, Doug Baker, Larry Casian, Rich Garces, Chip Hale, John Moses, Lenny Webster, Rich Yett

KEY SIGNATURES: Hrbek, Puckett.

VALUE: $60

1990 MONTREAL - Mike Aldrete, Moises Alou *, Oil Can Boyd, Tim Burke, Delino DeShields, Mike Fitzgerald, Tom Foley, Steve Frey, Andres Galarraga, Mark Gardner, Jerry Goff, Marquis Grissom, Kevin Gross, Drew Hall, Wallace Johnson, Dave Martinez, Dennis Martinez, Dale Mohorcic, Chris Nabholz, Otis Nixon, Junior Noboa, Spike Owen, Tim Raines, Buck Rodgers (MANAGER), Mel Rojas, Rolando Roomes *, Scott Ruskin *, Bill Sampen, Nelson Santovenia, Dave Schmidt, Zane Smith *, Larry Walker, Tim Wallach

LESS THAN 10 GAMES: Scott Anderson, Brian Barnes, Eric Bullock, John Costello *, Howard Farmer, Brett Gideon, Joe Hesketh *, Rex Hudler *, Bob Malloy, Orlando Mercado *, Johnny Paredes *, Rich Thompson

KEY SIGNATURES: Raines.

VALUE: $60

1990 NEW YORK (AL) - Oscar Azocar, Steve Balboni, Jesse Barfield, Mike Blowers, Greg Cadaret, Chuck Cary, Rick Cerone, Bucky Dent (MANAGER), Brian Dorsett, Alvaro Espinoza, Bob Geren, Lee Guetterman, Mel Hall, Andy Hawkins, Jimmy Jones, Roberto Kelly, Dave LaPoint, Tim Leary, Jim Leyritz, Kevin Maas, Don Mattingly, Lance McCullers *, Stump Merrill (MANAGER), Hensley Meulens, Alan Mills, Matt Nokes *, Eric Plunk, Luis Polonia *, Dave Righetti, Jeff Robinson, Deion Sanders, Steve Sax, Wayne Tolleson, Randy Velarde, Claudell Washington *, Dave Winfield *, Mike Witt *

LESS THAN 10 GAMES: Steve Adkins, Dave Eiland, John Habyan, Mark Leiter, Rich Monteleone, Clay Parker *, Pascual Perez, Jim Walewander

KEY SIGNATURES: Mattingly.

VALUE: $100

1990 NEW YORK (NL) - Daryl Boston *, Mark Carreon, David Cone, Ron Darling, Mario Diaz, Kevin Elster, Sid Fernandez, John Franco, Dwight Gooden, Bud Harrelson (MANAGER), Tommy Herr *, Todd Hundley, Jeff Innis, Gregg Jefferies, Dave Johnson (MANAGER), Howard Johnson, Barry Lyons *, Julio Machado *, Dave Magadan, Mike Marshall *, Kevin McReynolds, Orlando Mercado *, Keith Miller, Jeff Musselman, Charlie O'Brien *, Tom O'Malley, Bob Ojeda, Alejandro Pena, Darren Reed, Mackey Sasser, Darryl Strawberry, Pat Tabler *, Tim Teufel, Kelvin Torve, Frank Viola, Wally Whitehurst

LESS THAN 10 GAMES: Kevin Baez, Kevin Brown *, Chuck Carr, Keith Hughs, Chris Jelic, Dave Liddell, Dan Schatzeder *, Lou Thornton, Alex Trevino *, Julio Valera

KEY SIGNATURES: Strawberry, Johnson, Viola, Gooden.

VALUE: $100

1990 OAKLAND - Troy Afenir, Harold Baines *, Lance Blankenship, Mike Bordick, Todd Burns, Jose Canseco, Jim Corsi, Dennis Eckersley, Mike Gallego, Reggie Harris, Ron Hassey, Dave Henderson, Rickey Henderson, Rick Honeycutt, Steve Howard, Dann Howitt, Stan Javier *, Doug Jennings, Felix Jose *, Joe Klink, Carney Lansford, Tony LaRussa (MANAGER), Darren Lewis, Willie McGee *, Mark McGwire, Mike Moore, Gene Nelson, Mike Norris, Ken Phelps *, Jamie Quirk, Willie Randolph *, Scott Sanderson, Terry Steinbach, Dave Stewart, Walt Weiss, Bob Welch, Curt Young

LESS THAN 10 GAMES: Joe Bitker *, Ozzie Canseco, Steve Chitren, Scott Hemond, Dave Otto

NOTES: Highly sought baseball due to award and title winners: Welch (A.L. CY), R. Henderson (MVP), McGee (N.L. batting title).

KEY SIGNATURES: McGwire, Randolph, Canseco, R. Henderson, D. Henderson, Baines, McGee, Welch, Stewart, Eckersley.

VALUE: $200

CY = Cy Young Award winner

1990 PHILADELPHIA - Darrel Akerfelds, Joe Boever *, Rod Booker, Sil Campusano, Don Carman, Wes Chamberlain, Pat Combs, Dennis Cook, Darren Daulton, Jose DeJesus, Len Dykstra, Curt Ford, Marvin Freeman *, Tommy Greene *, Jason Grimsley, Charlie Hayes, Von Hayes, Tommy Herr *, Dave Hollins, Ken Howell, Ron Jones, Ricky Jordan, John Kruk, Steve Lake, Nick Leyva (MANAGER), Carmelo Martinez *, Roger McDowell, Chuck McElroy, Louie Meadows *, Mickey Morandini, Terry Mulholland *, Dale Murphy *, Tom Nieto, Jeff Parrett *, Randy Ready, Bruce Ruffin, Dickie Thon, Jim Vatcher *, Floyd Youmans

LESS THAN 10 GAMES: Darrin Fletcher *, Todd Frohwirth, Chuck Malone, Brad Moore, Dickie Noles, Steve Ontiveros

KEY SIGNATURES: Dykstra, Murphy.

VALUE: $50

1990 PITTSBURGH - Wally Backman, Doug Bair, Stan Belinda, Jay Bell, Rafael Belliard, Dann Bilardello, Barry Bonds, Bobby Bonilla, Sid Bream, John Cangelosi, Doug Drabek, Neal Heaton, Jeff King, Bob Kipper, Randy Kramer *, Bill Landrum, Mike LaValliere, Jim Leyland (MANAGER), Jose Lind, Carmelo Martinez *, Orlando Merced, Bob Patterson, Ted Power, Gary Redus, Rick Reed, R.J. Reynolds, Scott Ruskin *, Don Slaught, John Smiley, Zane Smith *, Walt Terrell *, Randy Tomlin, Andy Van Slyke, Bob Walk

LESS THAN 10 GAMES: Moises Alou, Steve Carter, Carlos Garcia, Mark Huismann, Lloyd McClendon *, Vicente Palacios, Tom Prince, Jerry Reuss, Mike Roesler, Mark Rose, Mark Ryal, Jay Tibbs *, Mike York

NOTES: Bonds (MVP), Drabek (CY).

KEY SIGNATURES: Bonds, Bonilla, Van Slyke, Drabek.

VALUE: $100

CY = Cy Young Award winner

1990 SAN DIEGO - Shawn Abner, Roberto Alomar, Andy Benes, Joe Carter, Jack Clark, Jerald Clark, Joey Cora, Mike Dunne, Paul Faries, Mark Grant *, Tony Gwynn, Greg Harris, Thomas Howard, Bruce Hurst, Darrin Jackson, Tom Lampkin, Craig Lefferts, Derek Lilliquist *, Fred Lynn, Jack McKeon (MANAGER), Mike Pagliarulo, Mark Parent, Dennis Rasmussen, Greg Riddoch (MANAGER), Bip Roberts, Rich Rodriguez, Benito Santiago, Calvin Schiraldi, Eric Show, Phil Stephenson, Garry Templeton, Ed Whitson, Eddie Williams

LESS THAN 10 GAMES: Pat Clements, John Davis, Atlee Hammaker *, Rob Nelson, Ronn Reynolds, Rafael Valdez

KEY SIGNATURES: Gwynn, Carter, Clark.

VALUE: $60

1990 SAN FRANCISCO - Dave Anderson, Kevin Bass, Bill Bathe, Steve Bedrosian, Mike Benjamin, Jeff Brantley, John Burkett, Brett Butler, Gary Carter, Will Clark, Roger Craig (MANAGER), Steve Decker, Mark Dewey, Kelly Downs, Scott Garrelts, Atlee Hammaker *, Terry Kennedy, Mike Kingery, Bob Knepper, Mike Laga, Mike LaCoss, Rick Leach, Mark Leonard, Greg Litton, Kevin Mitchell, Randy O'Neal, Francisco Oliveras, Rick Parker, Rick Reuschel, Ernest Riles, Don Robinson, Robby Thompson, Mark Thurmond, Jose Uribe, Ed Vosburg, Matt Williams, Trevor Wilson

LESS THAN 10 GAMES: Mark Bailey, Greg Booker, Ernie Camacho *, Eric Gunderson, Brad Komminsk *, Kirt Manwaring, Randy McCament, Paul McClellan, Andy McGaffigan *, Rafael Novoa, Tony Perezchica, Dan Quisenberry, Rick Rodriguez, Andres Santana, Russ Swan *

KEY SIGNATURES: Clark, Mitchell, Williams.

VALUE: $70

1990 SEATTLE - Scott Bradley, Greg Briley, Mike Brumley, Jay Buhner, Bryan Clark, Dave Cochrane, Darnell Coles *, Keith Comstock, Henry Cotto, Alvin Davis, Brian Giles, Ken Griffey Jr., Ken Griffey Sr. *, Erik Hanson, Gene Harris, Brian Holman, Mike Jackson, Randy Johnson, Tracy Jones *, Brent Knackert, Jim Lefebvre (MANAGER), Jeff Leonard, Ed Martinez, Tino Martinez, Pete O'Brien, Harold Reynolds, Jeff Schaefer, Mike Schooler, Matt Sinatro, Russ Swan *, Bill Swift, Dave Valle, Omar Vizquel, Matt Young, Clint Zavaras

LESS THAN 10 GAMES: Scott Bankhead, Dave Burba, Rich DeLucia, Gary Eave, Mike Gardiner, Vance Lovelace, Scott Medvin, Jose Melendez, Dennis Powell *, Jerry Reed *

NOTES: First time a father and son played for the same team.

KEY SIGNATURES: Ken Griffey Jr., Ken Griffey Sr.

VALUE: $70

1990 ST. LOUIS - Red Schoendienst (MANAGER), Rod Brewer, Tom Brunansky *, Vince Coleman, Dave Collins, Ken Dayley, Jose DeLeon, Frank DiPino, Bernard Gilkey, Pedro Guerrero, Whitey Herzog (MANAGER), Ken Hill, Ricky Horton, Rex Hudler *, Tim Jones, Felix Jose *, Ray Lankford, Joe Magrane, Greg Mathews, Willie McGee *, John Morris, Tom Niedenfuer, Jose Oquendo, Tom Pagnozzi, Geronimo Pena, Terry Pendleton, Mike Perez, Bryn Smith, Ozzie Smith, Lee Smith *, Scott Terry, Bob Tewksbury, Milt Thompson, Joe Torre (MANAGER), John Tudor, Denny Walling, Craig Wilson, Todd Worrell, Todd Zeile

LESS THAN 10 GAMES: Ernie Camacho *, Chris Carpenter, Stan Clarke, John Costello *, Howard Hilton, Tim Jones, Omar Olivares, Tim Sherrill, Ray Stephens

KEY SIGNATURES: Guerrero, Smith, McGee.

VALUE: $60

1990 TEXAS - Brad Arnsberg, Harold Baines *, John Barfield, Kevin Belcher, Thad Bosley, Kevin Brown, Steve Buechele, Scott Coolbaugh, Jack Daugherty, Cecil Espy, Julio Franco, Juan Gonzalez, Gary Green, Charlie Hough, Jeff Huson, Pete Incaviglia, Mike

Jeffcoat, Chad Kreuter, Jeff Kunkel, Craig McMurtry, Gary Mielke, Jamie Moyer, Rafael Palmeiro, Geno Petralli, Gary Pettis, Kevin Reimer, Kenny Rogers, Jeff Russell, John Russell, Nolan Ryan, Ruben Sierra, Mike Stanley, Bobby Valentine (MANAGER), Bobby Witt

LESS THAN 10 GAMES: Gerald Alexander, Joe Bitker *, Scott Chiamparino, Bill Haselman, John Hoover, Ramon Manon

KEY SIGNATURES: Palmeiro, Franco, Sierra, Ryan.

VALUE: $75

1990 TORONTO - Jim Acker, George Bell, Willie Blair, Pat Borders, John Candelaria *, John Cerutti, Rob Ducey, Junior Felix, Tony Fernandez, Cito Gaston (MANAGER), Kelly Gruber, Tom Henke, Glenallen Hill, Jimmy Key, Paul Kilgus, Tom Lawless, Manny Lee, Nelson Liriano *, Fred McGriff, Rance Mulliniks, Greg Myers, John Olerud, Luis Sojo, Dave Stieb, Todd Stottlemyre, Duane Ward, David Wells, Mark Whiten, Kenny Williams *, Frank Wills, Mookie Wilson

LESS THAN 10 GAMES: Bud Black *, Steve Cummings, Carlos Diaz, Jim Eppard, Mike Flanagan, Tom Gilles, Al Leiter, Rick Luecken *, Rob MacDonald, Tom Quinlan, Ozzie Virgil

KEY SIGNATURES: McGriff, Stieb, Fernandez.

VALUE: $60

1991

*** = player was traded**

1991 ATLANTA - Steve Avery, Mike Bell, Rafael Belliard, Juan Berenguer, Jeff Blauser, Sid Bream, Francisco Cabrera, Tony Castillo *, Jim Clancy *, Bobby Cox (MANAGER), Marvin Freeman, Ron Gant, Tom Glavine, Tommy Gregg, Mike Heath, Danny Heep *, Brian Hunter, Dave Justice, Charlie Leibrandt, Mark Lemke, Rick Mahler *, Kent Mercker, Keith Mitchell, Otis Nixon, Greg Olson, Jeff Parrett, Alejandro Pena *, Terry Pendleton, Dan Petry *, Deion Sanders, Doug Sisk, Lonnie Smith, Pete Smith, John Smoltz, Randy St. Claire, Mike Stanton, Jeff Treadway, Jerry Willard, Mark Wohlers

LESS THAN 10 GAMES: Damon Berryhill, Mike Bielecki, Armando Reynoso, Rico Rossy

KEY SIGNATURES: Glavine (CY) and Pendleton (MVP).

VALUE: $175

CY = Cy Young Award winner

1991 BALTIMORE - Brady Anderson, Jeff Ballard, Juan Bell, Glenn Davis, Mike Devereaux, Dwight Evans, Mike Flanagan, Todd Frohwirth, Leo Gomez, Kevin Hickey, Chris Hoiles, Sam Horn, Tim Hulett, Dave Johnson, Paul Kilgus, Chito Martinez, Ben McDonald, Jeff McKnight, Bob Melvin, Luis Mercedes, Jose Mesa, Bob Milacki, Randy Milligan, Mike Mussina, Johnny Oates (MANAGER), Gregg Olson, Joe Orsulak, Jim Poole, Billy Ripken, Cal Ripken, Frank Robinson (MANAGER), Jeff Robinson, David Segui, Roy Smith, Shane Turner, Ernie Whitt, Mark Williamson, Craig Worthington

LESS THAN 10 GAMES: Jose Bautista, Francisco De la Rosa, Stacy Jones, Karl Rhodes, Jeff Tackett, Anthony Telford

KEY SIGNATURES: F. Robinson, C. Ripken (MVP).

VALUE: $55

1991 BOSTON - Wade Boggs, Tom Bolton, Mike Brumley, Tom Brunansky, Ellis Burks, Jack Clark, Roger Clemens, Scott Cooper, Danny Darwin, Tony Fossas, Mike Gardiner, Jeff Gray, Mike Greenwell, Greg Harris, Joe Hesketh, Wayne Housie, Dana Kiecker, Dennis Lamp, Steve Lyons, Mike Marshall *, John Marzano, Joe Morgan (MANAGER), Kevin Morton, Tim Naehring, Tony Pena, Dan Petry *, Phil Plantier, Carlos Quintana, Jeff Reardon, Jody Reed, Luis Rivera, Kevin Romine, Maurice Vaughn, Matt Young, Bob Zupcic

LESS THAN 10 GAMES: John Dopson, Daryl Irvine, Randy Kutcher, Josias Manzanillo, Jeff Plympton, Eric Wedge

KEY SIGNATURES: Boggs, Clemens (CY).

VALUE: $75

CY = Cy Young Award winner

1991 CALIFORNIA - Jim Abbott, Shawn Abner *, Ruben Amaro, Scott Bailes, Floyd Bannister, Chris Beasley, Gary Disarcina, Mark Eichhorn, Junior Felix, Mike Fetters, Chuck Finley, Gary Gaetti, Dave Gallagher, Joe Grahe, Bryan Harvey, Donnie Hill, Jack Howell *, Wally Joyner, Mark Langston, Scott Lewis, Kirk McCaskill, Bob McClure *, John Orton, Dave Parker *, Lance Parrish, Luis Polonia, Doug Rader (MANAGER), Jeff Robinson, Buck Rodgers (MANAGER), Bobby Rose, Dick Schofield, Luis Sojo, Lee Stevens, Ron Tingley, Max Venable, Dave Winfield, Cliff Young

LESS THAN 10 GAMES: Kyle Abbott, Chris Cron, Mark Davis, Kevin Flora, Barry Lyons, Mike Marshall *, Fernando Valenzuela

KEY SIGNATURES: Joyner, Winfield.

VALUE: $40

1991 CHICAGO (AL) - Wilson Alvarez, Joey Cora, Brian Drahman, Wayne Edwards, Alex Fernandez, Carlton Fisk, Scott Fletcher, Ramon Garcia, Graig Grebeck, Ozzie Guillen, Greg Hibbard, Charlie Hough, Mike Huff *, Bo Jackson, Lance Johnson, Ron Karkovice, Ron Kittle, Rodney McCray, Jack McDowell, Matt Merullo, Warren Newson, Donn Pall, Dan Pasqua, Ken Patterson, Melido Perez, Scott Radinsky, Tim Raines, Cory Snyder *, Sammy Sosa, Bobby Thigpen, Frank Thomas, Jeff Torborg (MANAGER), Robin Ventura, Don Wakamatsu,

LESS THAN 10 GAMES: Esteban Beltre, Jeff Carter, Tom Drees, Danny Heep *, Roberto Hernandez, Steve Wapnick *

KEY SIGNATURES: Fisk, Thomas.

VALUE: $75

1991 CHICAGO (NL) - Paul Assenmacher, George Bell, Damon Berryhill *, Mike Bielecki *, Shawn Boskie, Frank Castillo, Doug Dascenzo, Andre Dawson, Shawon Dunston, Jim Essian (MANAGER), Joe Girardi, Mark Grace, Danny Jackson, Les Lancaster, Ced Landrum, Greg Maddux, Derrick May, Chuck McElroy, Luis Salazar, Rey Sanchez, Ryne Sandberg, Bob Scanlan, Gary Scott, Heathcliff Slocumb, Dave Smith, Dwight Smith, Rick Sutcliffe, Hector Villanueva, Jose Vizcaino, Chico Walker, Jerome Walton, Rick Wilkins, Don Zimmer (MANAGER)

LESS THAN 10 GAMES: Mike Harkey, S. May, Erik Pappas, Dave Pavlas, Yorkas Perez *, Laddie Renfroe, Doug Strange

KEY SIGNATURES: Sandberg, Dawson.

VALUE: $70

1991 CINCINNATI - Jack Armstrong, Freddie Benavides, Todd Benzinger *, Glenn Braggs, Keith Brown, Tom Browning, Don Carman, Norm Charlton, Eric Davis, Rob Dibble, Bill Doran, Mariano Duncan, Steve Foster, Kip Gross, Chris Hammond, Billy Hatcher, Milt Hill, Reggie Jefferson, Stan Jefferson, Chris Jones, Barry Larkin, Tim Layana, Carmelo Martinez *, Gino Minutelli, Hal Morris, Randy Myers, Paul O'Neill, Joe Oliver, Lou Piniella (MANAGER), Ted Power, Luis Quinones, Jeff Reed, Jose Rijo, Chris Sabo, Donnie Scott, Scott Scudder, Glenn Sutko, Herm Winningham

LESS THAN 10 GAMES: Reggie Jefferson, Terry Lee, Reggie Sanders, Mo Sanford

KEY SIGNATURES: Larkin, Davis, Piniella.

VALUE: $75

1991 CLEVELAND - Mike Aldrete *, Beau Allred, Sandy Alomar, Carlos Baerga, Eric Bell, Joey Belle, Dennis Boucher, Jerry Browne, Tom Candiotti *, Alex Cole, Jose Escobar, Felix Fermin, Jose Gonzalez, Mike Hargrove (MANAGER), Glenallen Hill, Shawn Hillegas, Mike Huff *, Brook Jacoby *, Dion James, Stan Jefferson, Doug Jones, Eric King, Wayne Kirby, Mark Lewis, Luis Lopez, Jeff Manto, Carlos Martinez, John McNamara (MANAGER), Charles Nagy, Rod Nichols, Steve Olin, Jesse Orosco, Dave Otto, Tony Perezchica, Jeff Shaw, Joel Skinner, Greg Swindell, Eddie Taubensee, Jim Thome, Turner Ward *, Mitch Webster *, Mark Whiten

LESS THAN 10 GAMES: Willie Blair, Bruce Egloff, Mauro Gozzo, Garland Kiser, Tom Kramer, Ever Magallanes, Luis Medina, Jeff Mutis, Rudy Seanez, Efrain Valdez, Sergio Valdez, Mike Walker, Mike York *

KEY SIGNATURES: Swindell.

VALUE: $40

1991 DETROIT - Scott Aldred, Andy Allanson, Sparky Anderson (MANAGER), Skeeter Barnes, Dave Bergman, John Cerutti, Milt Cuyler, Luis De los Santos, Rob Deer, Cecil Fielder, Travis Fryman, Dan Gakeler, Paul Gibson, Jerry Don Gleaton, Bill Gullickson, David Haas, Mike Henneman, Pete Incaviglia, Jeff Kaiser, Mark Leiter, Scott Livingstone, Rusty Meacham, Lloyd Moseby, John Moses, Johnny Paredes, Dan Petry *, Tony Phillips, Kevin Ritz, Mark Salas, Steve Searcy, John Shelby, Frank Tanana, Walt Terrell, Mickey Tettleton, Alan Trammell, Lou Whitaker

LESS THAN 10 GAMES: Tony Bernazard, Mike Dalton, Shawn Hare, John Kiely, Mike Munoz, Rich Rowland

KEY SIGNATURES: Anderson, Whitaker, Trammell, Fielder.

VALUE: $45

1991 HOUSTON - Eric Anthony, Jeff Bagwell, Craig Biggio, Ryan Bowen, Ken Caminiti, Casey Candaele, Mike Capel, Andujar Cedeno, Jim Clancy *, Jim Corsi, Mark Davidson, Jim Deshaies, Tony Eusebio, Steve Finley, Luis Gonzalez, Pete Harnisch, Butch Henry, Xavier Hernandez, Art Howe (MANAGER), Jimmy Jones, Darryl Kile, Kenny Lofton, Rob Mallicoat, Mark McLemore, Andy Mota, Carl Nichols, Ken Oberkfell, Javier Ortiz, Al Osuna, Mark Portugal, Rafael Ramirez, Karl Rhodes, Dave Rohde, Curt Schilling, Calvin Schiraldi *, Scott Servais, Mike Simms, Jose Toletino, Eric Yelding, Gerald Young

LESS THAN 10 GAMES: Gary Cooper, Chris Gardner, Jeff Juden, Mike Scott, Dean Wilkins, Brian Williams

KEY SIGNATURES: Bagwell (ROY), Harnisch.

VALUE: $60

1991 KANSAS CITY - Kevin Appier, Luis Aquino, Todd Benzinger *, Sean Berry, Mike Boddicker, George Brett, David Clark, Steve Crawford, Warren Cromartie, Mark Davis, Storm Davis, Jim Eisenreich, Kirk Gibson, Tom Gordon, Mark Gubicza, David Howard, Joel Johnston, Nelson Liriano, Mike Macfarlane, Mike Magnante, Carmelo Martinez *, Brent Mayne, Brian McRae, Hal McRae (MANAGER), Jeff Montgomery, Kerwin Moore, Russ Morman, Jorge Pedre, Terry Puhl, Harvey Pulliam, Bret Saberhagen, Kevin Seitzer, Terry Shumpert, Tim Spehr, Kurt Stillwell, Danny Tartabull, Gary Thurman, John Wathan (MANAGER)

LESS THAN 10 GAMES: Victor Cole, Archie Corbin, Wes Gardner, Carlos Maldonado, Andy McGaffigan, Bill Pecota, Dan Schatzeder *, Hector Wagner, Paul Zuvella

KEY SIGNATURES: Brett, Saberhagen, Tartabull.

VALUE: $45

1991 LOS ANGELES - Tim Belcher, Brett Butler, John Candelaria, Gary Carter, Braulio Castillo *, Dennis Cook, Tim Crews, Kal Daniels, Jose Gonzalez *, Tom Goodwin, Jim Gott, Alfredo Griffin, Kevin Gross, Chris Gwynn, Jeff Hamilton, Dave Hansen, Lenny Harris, Mike Hartley *, Carlos Hernandez, Orel Hershiser, Jay Howell, Stan Javier, Eric Karros, Tom Lasorda (MANAGER), Ramon Martinez, Roger McDowell, Mike Morgan, Eddie Murray, Jose Offerman, Bob Ojeda, Juan Samuel, Mike Scioscia, Mike Sharperson, Darryl Strawberry, Mitch Webster, Steve Wilson

LESS THAN 10 GAMES: Mike Christopher, Butch Davis, Barry Lyons, Greg Smith, John Wetteland

KEY SIGNATURES: Lasorda, Murray, Strawberry.

VALUE: $80

1991 MILWAUKEE - Don August, Dante Bichette, Chris Bosio, Greg Brock, Kevin Brown, George Canale, Chuck Crim, Rick Dempsey, Cal Eldred, Jim Gantner, Darryl Hamilton, Doug Henry, Darren Holmes, Mark Knudson, Mark Lee, Julio Machado, Candy Maldonado *, Paul Molitor, Jaime Navarro, Edwin Nunez, Jim Olander, Dan Plesac, Willie Randolph, Gary Sheffield, Billy Spiers, Franklin Stubbs, B.J. Surhoff, Dale Sveum, Tom Trebelhorn (MANAGER), Greg Vaughn, Bill Wegman, Robin Yount

LESS THAN 10 GAMES: Jim Austin, Matias Carrillo, Chris George, Teddy Higuera, Jim Hunter, Mike Ignasiak, Tim McIntosh, Ron Robinson

KEY SIGNATURES: Yount, Molitor.

VALUE: $40

1991 MINNESOTA - Paul Abbott, Rick Aguilera, Allan Anderson, Steve Bedrosian, Jarvis Brown, Randy Bush, Chili Davis, Scott Erickson, Greg Gagne, Danny Gladden, Mark Guthrie, Brian Harper, Kent Hrbek, Tom Kelly (MANAGER), Chuck Knoblauch, Gene Larkin, Terry Leach, Scott Leius, Shane Mack, Jack Morris, Pedro Munoz, Al Newman, Junior Ortiz, Mike Pagliarulo, Kirby Puckett, Paul Sorrento, Kevin Tapani, Lenny Webster, Dave West, Carl Willis

LESS THAN 10 GAMES: Willie Banks, Larry Casian, Carmen Castillo, Tom Edens, Dennis Neagle, Gary Wayne

NOTES: World Champions!

KEY SIGNATURES: Knoblauch (ROY), Morris, Puckett, Hrbek.

VALUE: $200

ROY = Rookie of the Year

1991 MONTREAL - Bret Barberie, Brian Barnes, Dennis Boyd, Eric Bullock, Tim Burke *, Ivan Calderon, Ron Darling, Ron Darling *, Delino DeShields, Jeff Fassero, Mike Fitzgerald, Tom Foley, Steve Frey, Andres Galarraga, Mark Gardner, Marquis Grissom, Chris Haney, Ron Hassey, Barry Jones, Rick Mahler *, Dave Martinez, Denny Martinez, Chris Nabholz, Otis Nixon *, Junior Noboa, Spike Owen, Doug Piatt, Gilberto Reyes, Buck Rodgers (MANAGER), Mel Rojas, Tom Runnells (MANAGER), Scott Ruskin, Bill Sampen, Nelson Santovenia, John VanderWal, Larry Walker, Tim Wallach, Kenny Williams

LESS THAN 10 GAMES: Bill Long, Nicko Riesgo, Dave Schmidt, Dave Wainhouse

KEY SIGNATURES: Calderon.

VALUE: $40

1991 NEW YORK (AL) - Jesse Barfield, Mike Blowers *, Greg Cadaret, Chuck Cary, Dave Eiland, Alvaro Espinoza, Steve Farr, Bob Geren, Lee Guetterman, John Habyan, Mel Hall, Steve Howe, Mike Humphreys, Jeff Johnson, Pat Kelly, Roberto Kelly, Tim Leary, Jim Leyritz, Torey Lovullo, Scott Lusader, Kevin Maas, Don Mattingly, Stump Merrill (MANAGER), Hensley Meulens, Rich Monteleone, Matt Nokes, Pascual Perez, Eric Plunk, John Ramos, Carlos Rodriguez, Scott Sanderson, Steve Sax, Pat Sheridan, Bucky Showalter (MANAGER), Wade Taylor, Randy Velarde, Bernie Williams

LESS THAN 10 GAMES: Darrin Chapin, Scott Kamieniecki, Alan Mills, Mike Witt

KEY SIGNATURES: Mattingly.

VALUE: $75

1991 NEW YORK (NL) - Daryl Boston, Hubie Brooks, Tim Burke, Chuck Carr, Mike Carreon, Tony Castillo, Rick Cerone, Vince Coleman, David Cone, Mike Cubbage (MANAGER), Ron Darling *, Chris Donnels, Kevin Elster, John Franco, Jeff Gardner, Dwight Gooden, Bud Harrelson (MANAGER), Todd Hundley, Jeff Innis, Gregg Jefferies, Howard Johnson, Dave Magadan, Terry McDaniel, Kevin McReynolds, Keith Miller, Charlie O'Brien, Alejandro Pena *, Mackey Sasser, Dan Schatzeder *, Pete Schourek, Doug Simons, Garry Templeton, Tim Teufel *, Kelvin Torve, Frank Viola, Wally Whitehurst, Anthony Young

LESS THAN 10 GAMES: Blaine Beatty, Terry Bross, Sid Fernandez, Rich Sauveur, Julio Valera

KEY SIGNATURES: Johnson, Gooden, Viola.

VALUE: $75

1991 OAKLAND - Dana Allison, Harold Baines, Lance Blankenship, Mike Bordick, John Briscoe, Scott Brosius, Kevin Campbell, Jose Canseco, Steve Chitren, Ron Darling *, Dennis Eckersley, Mike Gallego, Andy Hawkins, Scott Hemond, Dave Henderson, Rickey Henderson, Rick Honeycutt, Dann Howitt, Brook Jacoby *, Joe Klink, Brad Komminsk, Vance Law, Tony LaRussa (MANAGER), Mark McGwire, Mike Moore, Gene Nelson, Jaime Quirk, Ernie Riles, Eric Show, Joe Slusarski, Terry Steinbach, Dave Stewart, Bruce Walton, Walt Weiss, Bob Welch, Willie Wilson, Ron Witmeyer, Curt Young

LESS THAN 10 GAMES: Troy Afenir, Todd Burns, Kirk Dressendorfer, Johnny Guzman, Reggie Harris, Doug Jennings, Carney Lansford, Fred Manrique, Todd Van Poppel

KEY SIGNATURES: R. Henderson, Stewart, Eckersley, Canseco.

VALUE: $100

1991 PHILADELPHIA - Darrel Akerfelds, Wally Backman, Kim Batiste, Joe Boever, Rod Booker, Sil Campusano, Braulio Castillo, Wes Chamberlain, Pat Combs, Danny Cox, Darren Daulton, Jose DeJesus, Len Dykstra, Darrin Fletcher, Jim Fregosi (MANAGER), Tommy Greene, Jason Grimsley, Mike Hartley, Charlie Hayes, Von Hayes, Dave Hollins, Ron Jones, Ricky Jordan, John Kruk, Steve Lake, Nick Leyva (MANAGER), Jim Lindeman, Roger McDowell *, Mickey Morandini, John Morris, Terry Mulholland, Dale Murphy, Randy Ready, Wally Ritchie, Bruce Ruffin, Rick Schu, Steve Searcy, Dickie Thon, Mitch Williams

LESS THAN 10 GAMES: Andy Ashby, Cliff Brantley, Amalio Carreno, Dave LaPoint, Doug Lindsey, Tim Mauser

KEY SIGNATURES: Dykstra, Murphy.

VALUE: $40

1991 PITTSBURGH - Stan Belinda, Jay Bell, Barry Bonds, Bobby Bonilla, Steve Buechele, Scott Bullett, Doug Drabek, Cecil Espy, Carlos Garcia, Jose Gonzalez, Neal Heaton, Jeff King, Bob Kipper, Bill Landrum, Mike LaValliere, Jose Lind, Carmelo Martinez *, Roger Mason, Lloyd McClendon, Orlando Merced, Vicente Palacios, Bob Patterson, Tom Prince, Joe Redfield, Gary Redus, Rosario Rodriguez, Don Slaught, John Smiley, Zane Smith, Randy Tomlin, Andy Van Slyke, Gary Varsho, Bob Walk, Mitch Webster *, John Wehner, Curtis Wilkerson

LESS THAN 10 GAMES: Jeffrey Banister, Hector Fajardo, Mark Huismann, Kurt Miller, Rick Reed, Richard Richardson, Jeff Schulz

KEY SIGNATURES: Bonds, Bonilla.

VALUE: $100

1991 SAN DIEGO - Shawn Abner *, Mike Aldrete, Larry Andersen, Oscar Azocar, Marty Barrett, Andy Benes, Dann Bilardello, Ricky Bones, Jerald Clark, Pat Clements, Scott Coolbaugh, John Costello, Brian Dorsett, Paul Faries, Tony Fernandez, Wes Gardner, Tony Gwynn, Greg Harris, Thomas Howard, Jack Howell *, Bruce Hurst, Darrin Jackson, Tom Lampkin, Craig Lefferts, Jim Lewis, Mike Maddux, Fred McGriff, Jose Melendez, Jose Mota, Adam Peterson, Jim Presley, Dennis Rasmussen, Greg Riddoch (MANAGER), Bip Roberts, Rich Rodriguez, Steve Rosenberg, Benito Santiago, Craig Shipley, Phil Stephenson, Tim Teufel *, Jim Vatcher, Kevin Ward, Eddie Whitson

LESS THAN 10 GAMES: Atlee Hammaker, Jeremy Hernandez, Darrin Jackson, Derek Lilliquist, Eric Nolte, Tim Scott

KEY SIGNATURES: Gwynn, McGriff, Fernandez.

VALUE: $40

1991 SAN FRANCISCO - Dave Anderson, Kevin Bass, Rod Beck, Mike Benjamin, Bud Black, Jeff Brantley, John Burkett, Will Clark, Darnell Coles, Roger Craig (MANAGER), Steve Decker, Kelly Downs, Mike Felder, Tommy Herr, Bryan Hickerson, Terry Kennedy, Mike Kingery, Mike LaCoss, Mark Leonard, Darren Lewis, Greg Litton, Kirt Manwaring, Paul McClellan, Willie McGee, Kevin Mitchell, Francisco Oliveras, Rick Parker, Tony Perezchica *, Dave Righetti, Don Robinson, Jose Segura, Robby Thompson, Jose Uribe, Matt Williams, Trevor Wilson, Ted Wood

LESS THAN 10 GAMES: Royce Clayton, Scott Garrelts, Eric Gunderson, Gil Heredia, Mike Remlinger, Rick Reuschel

KEY SIGNATURES: Mitchell, Clark.

VALUE: $50

1991 SEATTLE - Rich Amaral, Scott Bankhead, Scott Bradley, Greg Briley, Jay Buhner, Dave Burba, Dave Cochrane, Henry Cotto, Alvin Davis, Rich DeLucia, Ken Griffey Jr., Ken Griffey Sr., Erik Hanson, Brian Holman, Mike Jackson, Randy Johnson, Calvin Jones, Tracy Jones, Bill Krueger, Jim LeFebvre (MANAGER), Edgar Martinez, Tino Martinez, Rob Murphy, Pete O'Brien, Alonzo Powell, Harold Reynolds, Jeff Schaefer, Mike Schooler, Russ Swan, Bill Swift, Dave Valle, Omar Vizquel

LESS THAN 10 GAMES: Keith Comstock, Dave Fleming, Gene Harris, Chris Howard, Patrick Lennon, Pat Rice, Matt Sinatro

KEY SIGNATURES: Griffey Jr., Griffey Sr.

VALUE: $60

1991 ST. LOUIS - Juan Agosto, Luis Alicea, Rod Brewer, Cris Carpenter, Rheal Cormier, Jose DeLeon, Willie Fraser *, Rich Gedman, Bernard Gilkey, Pedro Guerrero, Ken Hill, Rex Hudler, Tim Jones, Felix Jose, Ray Lankford, Bob McClure *, Omar Olivares, Jose Oquendo, Tom Pagnozzi, Geronimo Pena, Mike Perez, Gerald Perry, Tim Sherrill, Bryn Smith, Lee Smith, Ozzie Smith, Scott Terry, Bob Tewksbury, Milt Thompson, Joe Torre (MANAGER), Craig Wilson, Todd Zeile

LESS THAN 10 GAMES: Mark Clark, Mark Grater, Jamie Moyer, Stan Royer, Ray Stephens

KEY SIGNATURES: O. Smith, L. Smith.

VALUE: $40

1991 TEXAS - Gerald Alexander, Brad Arnsberg, John Barfield, Jeff Bitker, Brian Bohanon, Oil Can Boyd *, Kevin Brown, Steve Buechele *, Nick Capra, Scott Chiamparino, Jack Daugherty, Mario Diaz, Brian Downing, Hector Fajardo *, Monty Fariss, Julio Franco, Juan Gonzalez, Goose Gossage, Gary Green, Jose Guzman, Donald Harris, Jose Hernandez, Jeff Huson, Mike Jeffcoat, Chad Kreuter, Barry Manuel, Terry Mathews, Rob Maurer, Eric Nolte, Rafael Palmeiro, Dean Palmer, Mark Parent, Mark Petkovsek, Geno Petralli, Gary Pettis, Kevin Reimer, Ivan Rodriguez, Kenny Rogers, Wayne Rosenthal, Jeff Russell, John Russell, Nolan Ryan, Calvin Schiraldi *, Tony Scruggs, Ruben Sierra, Mike Stanley, Bobby Valentine (MANAGER), Denny Walling, Bobby Witt

KEY SIGNATURES: Franco, Ryan, Sierra, Palmeiro.

VALUE: $75

1991 TORONTO - Jim Acker, Roberto Alomar, Derek Bell, Pat Borders, Dennis Boucher *, Tom Candiotti, Joe Carter, Ken Dayley, Rob Ducey, Willie Fraser, Cito Gaston (MANAGER), Ray Giannelli, Rene Gonzales, Kelly Gruber, Juan Guzman, Tom Henke, Pat Hentgen, Glenallen Hill *, Vince Horsman, Jimmy Key, Randy Knorr, Manny Lee, Al Leiter, Bob MacDonald, Candy Maldonado, Rance Mulliniks, Greg Myers, John Olreud, Dave Parker, Cory Snyder, Ed Sprague, Dave Stieb, Todd Stottlemyre, Pat Tabler, Mike Timlin, Efrain Valdez *, Steve Wapnick *, Duane Ward, Turner Ward, Dave Weathers, David Wells, Mickey Weston, Devon White, Mark Whiten *, Ken Williams, Frank Wills, Mookie Wilson, Eddie Zosky

KEY SIGNATURES: Carter, Alomar, Stieb.

VALUE: $100

Autographed All-Star Baseballs

The All-Star game, as we know it today, began when Arch Ward, the sports editor of the Chicago Tribune, persuaded league owners on his proposal for a game between stars from the American and National leagues. The first game was played in Chicago during the city's Century of Progress Exposition in 1933.

Players for the first two games were selected by the fans and the All-Star managers who, except for the first game, have been the pilots of the previous year's pennant winners. From 1935 through

1946 the managers were allowed to select their own teams. The fans chose the starters from 1947 to 1957, while the managers picked their pitchers and all other players. A ballot-stuffing incident in 1957 shifted the selection to major league players, coaches and managers. By 1970, however, the selection of starting lineups was returned to the fans.

Since 1979, Rawlings, the manufacturer of Official League baseballs, has produced a special baseball for use in the All-Star game. These baseballs include the official logo used by the host city, along with the commissioner's signature.

Considering the uniqueness involved with this event, most dealers agree that autographed All-Star team baseballs are undervalued. Collectors are recommended to acquire team balls signed on Official All-Star baseballs.

HOF = Hall of Famer

A team ball for the 1933 American League All-Stars is worth $8,000.

1933 AMERICAN LEAGUE ALL-STAR TEAM - Earl Averill, Ben Chapman, Eddie Collins (COACH), Joe Cronin, General Crowder, Bill Dickey, Jimmy Dykes, Rick Ferrell, Wes Ferrell, Art Fletcher (COACH), Jimmie Foxx, Lou Gehrig, Charlie Gehringer, Lefty Gomez, Lefty Grove, Oral Hildebrand, Tony Lazzeri, Connie Mack (MANAGER), Babe Ruth, Al Simmons, Sammy West

NOTES: 14 HOF'ers - debut team.

KEY SIGNATURES: Mack, Collins, Gehrig, Ruth.

VALUE: $8000

1933 NATIONAL LEAGUE ALL-STAR TEAM - Dick Bartell, Wally Berger, Max Carey (COACH), Tony Cuccinello, Woody English, Frankie Frisch, Chick Hafey, Bill Hallahan, Gabby Hartnett, Carl Hubbell, Chuck Klein, Pepper Martin, John McGraw (MANAGER), Bill McKechnie (COACH), Lefty O'Doul, Hal Schumacher, Bill Terry, Pie Traynor, Paul Waner, Lon Warneke, Jimmie Wilson

NOTES: 11 HOF'ers - debut team.

KEY SIGNATURES: McGraw, Traynor, Waner, Frisch.

VALUE: $2800

1934 AMERICAN LEAGUE ALL-STAR TEAM - Earl Averill, Tommy Bridges, Ben Chapman, Mickey Cochrane, Joe Cronin (MANAGER), Bill Dickey, Jimmy Dykes, Rick Ferrell, Jimmie Foxx, Lou Gehrig, Charlie Gehringer, Lefty Gomez, Mel Harder, Pinky Higgins, Walter Johnson (COACH), Heinie Manush, Red Ruffing, Jack Russell, Babe Ruth, Al Schacht (COACH), Al Simmons, Sammy West

NOTES: 14 HOF'ers.

KEY SIGNATURES: Gehrig, Ruth, Foxx.

VALUE: $7000

1934 NATIONAL LEAGUE ALL-STAR TEAM - Wally Berger, Kiki Cuyler, Dizzy Dean, Fred Frankhouse, Frankie Frisch, Gabby Hartnett, Billy Herman, Carl Hubbell, Travis Jackson, Chuck Klein, Al Lopez, Pepper Martin, Bill McKechnie (COACH), Joe Medwick, Van Mungo, Mel Ott, Casey Stengel (COACH), Bill Terry (MANAGER), Pie Traynor, Arky Vaughan, Paul Waner, Lon Warneke

PLAYERS WHO WERE REPLACED: Joe Moore

NOTES: 17 HOF'ers.

KEY SIGNATURES: Ott, Traynor, Vaughan, Waner.

VALUE: $2500

1935 AMERICAN LEAGUE ALL-STAR TEAM - Del Baker (COACH), Ossie Bluege, Tommy Bridges, Ben Chapman, Mickey Cochrane (MANAGER), Doc Cramer, Joe Cronin, Rick Ferrell, Jimmie Foxx, Lou Gehrig, Charlie Gehringer, Lefty Gomez, Lefty Grove, Mel Harder, Rollie Hemsley, Rogers Hornsby (COACH), Bob Johnson, Buddy Myer, Schoolboy Rowe, Al Simmons, Joe Vosmik, Sammy West

PLAYERS WHO WERE REPLACED: Earl Averill

NOTES: 11 HOF'ers; Cochrane was a player/manager.

KEY SIGNATURES: Foxx, Gehrig, Hornsby.

VALUE: $5000

1935 NATIONAL LEAGUE ALL-STAR TEAM - Wally Berger, Ripper Collins, Dizzy Dean, Paul Derringer, Chuck Dressen (COACH), Frankie Frisch (MANAGER), Charlie Grimm (COACH), Gabby Hartnett, Billy Herman, Carl Hubbell, Gus Mancuso, Pepper Martin, Joe Medwick, Joe Moore, Mel Ott, Hal Schumacher, Bill Terry, Arky Vaughan, Bill Walker, Paul Waner, Burgess Whitehead, Jimmie Wilson

NOTES: 10 HOF'ers.

KEY SIGNATURES: Frisch, Ott, Vaughan.

VALUE: $1700

1936 AMERICAN LEAGUE ALL-STAR TEAM - Luke Appling, Earl Averill, Ben Chapman, Joseph Cronin (COACH), Frankie Crosetti, Bill Dickey, Joe DiMaggio, Rick Ferrell, Arthur Fletcher (COACH), Jimmie Foxx, Lou Gehrig, Charlie Gehringer, Lefty Gomez, Goose Goslin, Lefty Grove, Mel Harder, Rollie Hemsley, Pinky Higgins, Vern Kennedy, Joseph McCarthy (MANAGER), Monte Pearson, Rip Radcliff, Schoolboy Rowe, George Selkirk

PLAYERS WHO WERE REPLACED: Tommy Bridges

NOTES: 13 HOF'ers.

KEY SIGNATURES: Foxx, Gehrig, DiMaggio.

VALUE: $6000

1936 NATIONAL LEAGUE ALL-STAR TEAM - Wally Berger, Rip Collins, Curt Davis, Dizzy Dean, Frank Demaree, Leo Durocher, Augie Galan, Charlie Grimm (MANAGER), Gabby Hartnett, Billy Herman, Carl Hubbell, Ernie Lombardi, Stu Martin, Bill McKechnie (COACH), Joe Medwick, Joe Moore, Van Mungo, Mel Ott, Lew Riggs, Gus Suhr, Pie Traynor (COACH), Arky Vaughan, Lon Warneke, Pinky Whitney

NOTES: 10 HOF'ers.

KEY SIGNATURES: Ott, Vaughan, Traynor.

VALUE: $1500

A team ball for the 1937 American League All-Stars is worth $5,000.

1937 AMERICAN LEAGUE ALL-STAR TEAM - Earl Averill, Del Baker (COACH), Roy Bell, Tommy Bridges, Harlond Clift, Doc Cramer, Joe Cronin, Bill Dickey, Joe DiMaggio, Rick Ferrell, Wes Ferrell, Art Fletcher (COACH), Jimmie Foxx, Lou Gehrig, Charlie Gehringer, Lefty Gomez, Hank Greenberg, Lefty Grove, Mel Harder, Joe McCarthy (MANAGER), Wally Moses, John Murphy, Buddy Myer, Red Rolfe, Luke Sewell, Sammy West

PLAYERS WHO WERE REPLACED: Monty Stratton, Gee Walker

NOTES: 12 HOF'ers.

KEY SIGNATURES: Foxx, DiMaggio, Gehrig.

VALUE: $5000

1937 NATIONAL LEAGUE ALL-STAR TEAM - Dick Bartell, Cy Blanton, Rip Collins, Dizzy Dean, Frank Demaree, Chuck Dressen (COACH), Frankie Frisch (COACH), Lee Grissom, Jessie Haines (COACH), Gabby Hartnett, Billy Herman, Carl Hubbell, Billy Jurges, Ernie Lombardi, Gus Mancuso, Pepper Martin, Joe Medwick, Johnny Mize, Gene Moore, Joe Moore, Van Mungo, Mel Ott, Bill Terry (MANAGER), Arky Vaughan, Bucky Walters, Paul Waner, Burgess Whitehead

NOTES: 13 HOF'ers.

KEY SIGNATURES: Frisch, Ott, Vaughan.

VALUE: $1800

1938 AMERICAN LEAGUE ALL-STAR TEAM - John Allen, Earl Averill, Del Baker (COACH), Doc Cramer, Joe Cronin, Bill Dickey, Joe DiMaggio, Bob Feller, Rick Ferrell, Art Fletcher (COACH), Jimmie Foxx, Lou Gehrig, Charlie Gehringer, Lefty Gomez, Lefty Grove, Bob Johnson, Vern Kennedy, Mike Kreevich, Buddy Lewis, Joe McCarthy (MANAGER), Johnny Murphy, Bobo Newsom, Red Rolfe, Red Ruffing, Cecil Travis, Rudy York

PLAYERS WHO WERE REPLACED: Hank Greenberg

NOTES: 14 HOF'ers.

KEY SIGNATURES: Foxx, DiMaggio, Gehrig.

VALUE: $5500

1938 NATIONAL LEAGUE ALL-STAR TEAM - Mace Brown, Tony Cuccinello, Harry Danning, Paul Derringer, Leo Durocher, Frank Frisch (COACH), Ival Goodman, Stan Hack, Gabby Hartnett, Billy Herman, Carl Hubbell, Cookie Lavagetto, Bill Lee, Hank Leiber, Ernie Lombardi, Herschel Martin, Frank McCormick, William McKechnie (COACH), Joe Medwick, Joe Moore, Mel Ott, William Terry (MANAGER), Jim Turner, Johnny Vander Meer, Arky Vaughan, Lloyd Waner

PLAYERS WHO WERE REPLACED: Babe Phelps

NOTES: 11 HOF'ers.

KEY SIGNATURES: Ott, Vaughan, Frisch.

VALUE: $1500

1939 AMERICAN LEAGUE ALL-STAR TEAM - Luke Appling, Lena Blackburne (COACH), Tommy Bridges, George Case, Doc Cramer, Joe Cronin, Frankie Crosetti, Bill Dickey, Joe DiMaggio, Bob Feller, Art Fletcher (COACH), Jimmie Foxx, Lou Gehrig, Lefty Gomez, Joe Gordon, Hank Greenberg, Lefty Grove, Frankie Hayes, Rollie Hemsley, Myril Hoag, Bob Johnson, Ted Lyons, Joe McCarthy (MANAGER), George McQuinn, John Murphy, Bobo Newsom, Red Rolfe, Red Ruffing, George Selkirk

NOTES: 13 HOF'ers; Gehrig was an honorary member.

KEY SIGNATURES: Foxx, DiMaggio, Gehrig.

VALUE: $5000

1939 NATIONAL LEAGUE ALL-STAR TEAM - Morrie Arnovich, Dolf Camilli, Red Corriden (COACH), Harry Danning, Curt Davis, Paul Derringer, Lou Fette, Lonny Frey, Ival Goodman, Stan Hack, Gabby Hartnett (MANAGER), Billy Herman, Bill Jurges, Cookie Lavagetto, Bill Lee, Ernie Lombardi, Frank McCormick, Joe Medwick, Johnny Mize, Terry Moore, Mel Ott, Babe Phelps, Bill Terry (COACH), Johnny Vander Meer,

Arky Vaughan, Bucky Walters, Lon Warneke, Whit Wyatt
NOTES: 8 HOF'ers.
KEY SIGNATURES: Ott, Vaughan.

VALUE: $1000

1940 AMERICAN LEAGUE ALL-STAR TEAM - Luke Appling, Del Baker (COACH), Lou Boudreau, Tommy Bridges, Doc Cramer, Joe Cronin (MANAGER), Tom Daly (COACH), Bill Dickey, Joe DiMaggio, Bob Feller, Lou Finney, Jimmie Foxx, Joe Gordon, Hank Greenberg, Frankie Hayes, Rollie Hemsley, Robert Johnson, Charlie Keller, Ken Keltner, Dutch Leonard, Ray Mack, George McQuinn, Al Milnar, Bobo Newsom, Monte Pearson, Red Ruffing, Cecil Travis, Ted Williams
PLAYERS WHO WERE REPLACED: Red Rolfe
NOTES: 10 HOF'ers.
KEY SIGNATURES: Foxx, Williams, DiMaggio.

VALUE: $650

1940 NATIONAL LEAGUE ALL-STAR TEAM - Pete Coscarart, Harry Danning, Paul Derringer, Leo Durocher, Larry French, Billy Herman, Kirby Higbe, Carl Hubbell, Cookie Lavagetto, Ernie Lombardi, Pinky May, Frank McCormick, Bill McKechnie (MANAGER), Joe Medwick, Eddie Miller, Johnny Mize, Joe Moore, Terry Moore, Hugh Mulcahy, William Nicholson, Mel Ott, Babe Phelps, Doc Prothro (COACH), Casey Stengel (COACH), Arky Vaughan, Bucky Walters, Max West, Whit Wyatt
PLAYERS WHO WERE REPLACED: Bill Jurges, Hank Leiber
NOTES: 9 HOF'ers.
KEY SIGNATURES: Ott, Vaughan.

VALUE: $900

1941 AMERICAN LEAGUE ALL-STAR TEAM - Luke Appling, Del Baker (MANAGER), Al Benton, Lou Boudreau, Joe Cronin, Roy Cullenbine, Bill Dickey, Dom DiMaggio, Joe DiMaggio, Bobby Doerr, Bob Feller, Art Fletcher (COACH), Jimmie Foxx, Joe Gordon, Frankie Hayes, Jeff Heath, Sid Hudson, Charlie Keller, Ken Keltner, Thornton Lee, Red Ruffing, Marius Russo, Merv Shea (COACH), Eddie Smith, Birdie Tebbetts, Cecil Travis, Ted Williams, Rudy York
NOTES: 10 HOF'ers.
KEY SIGNATURES: Foxx, Williams, Joe DiMaggio.

VALUE: $700

1941 NATIONAL LEAGUE ALL-STAR TEAM - Cy Blanton, Harry Danning, Paul Derringer, Leo Durocher (COACH), Bob Elliott, Lonny Frey, Stan Hack, Billy Herman, Carl Hubbell, Cookie Lavagetto, Al Lopez, Frank McCormick, Bill McKechnie (MANAGER), Joe Medwick, Eddie Miller, Johnny Mize, Terry Moore, Bill Nicholson, Mel Ott, Mickey Owen, Claude Passeau, Pete Reiser, Enos Slaughter, Arky Vaughan, Bucky Walters, Lon Warneke, Jimmie Wilson (COACH), Whit Wyatt
PLAYERS WHO WERE REPLACED: Dolf Camilli, Hank Leiber
NOTES: 9 HOF'ers.
KEY SIGNATURES: Ott, Vaughan.

VALUE: $800

1942 AMERICAN LEAGUE ALL-STAR TEAM - Jim Bagby, Al Benton, Ernie Bonham, Lou Boudreau, Spud Chandler, Bill Dickey, Dom DiMaggio, Joe DiMaggio, Bobby Doerr, Art Fletcher (COACH), Joe Gordon, Bucky Harris (COACH), Thommy Henrich, Sid Hudson, Tex Hughson, Bob Johnson, Ken Keltner, Joe McCarthy (MANAGER), George McQuinn, Hal Newhouser, Phil Rizzuto, Buddy Rosar, Red Ruffing, Eddie Smith, Stan Spence, Birdie Tebbetts, Harold Wagner, Ted Williams, Rudy York

NOTES: 8 HOF'ers.

KEY SIGNATURES: Williams, Joe DiMaggio

VALUE: $600

1942 NATIONAL LEAGUE ALL-STAR TEAM - Jimmy Brown, Mort Cooper, Walker Cooper, Leo Durocher (MANAGER), Bob Elliott, Frankie Frisch (COACH), Billy Herman, Carl Hubbell, Danny Litwhiler, Ernie Lombardi, Willard Marshall, Frank McCormick, Bill McKechnie (COACH), Joe Medwick, Cliff Melton, Eddie Miller, Johnny Mize, Terry Moore, Mel Ott, Mickey Owen, Claude Passeau, Pee Wee Reese, Pete Reiser, Enos Slaughter, Ray Starr, Johnny Vander Meer, Arky Vaughan, Bucky Walters, Whit Wyatt

PLAYERS WHO WERE REPLACED: Paul Derringer

NOTES: 11 HOF'ers.

KEY SIGNATURES: McKechnie, Frisch, Ott, Vaughan.

VALUE: $850

1943 AMERICAN LEAGUE ALL-STAR TEAM - Luke Appling, Jim Bagby, Russell Blackburne (COACH), Ernie Bonham, Lou Boudreau, George Case, Spud Chandler, Bill Dickey, Bobby Doerr, Jake Early, Arthur Fletcher (COACH), Joe Gordon, Jeff Heath, Tex Hughson, Bob Johnson, Oscar Judd, Ken Keltner, Chet Laabs, Dutch Leonard, Johnny Lindell, Joe McCarthy (MANAGER), Hal Newhouser, Buddy Rosar, Dick Siebert, Al Smith, Vern Stephens, Dick Wakefield, Rudy York

PLAYERS WHO WERE REPLACED: Charlie Keller

NOTES: 5 HOF'ers.

KEY SIGNATURES: McCarthy.

VALUE: $500

1943 NATIONAL LEAGUE ALL-STAR TEAM - Ace Adams, Mort Cooper, Walker Cooper, Babe Dahlgren, Vince DiMaggio, Elbie Fletcher, Lonny Frey, Frank Frisch (COACH), Augie Galan, Mike Gonzalez (COACH), Stan Hack, Billy Herman, Al Javery, Whitey Kurowski, Max Lanier, Ernie Lombardi, Marty Marion, Eddie Miller, Stan Musial, Bill Nicholson, Mel Ott, Mickey Owen, Claude Passeau, Rip Sewell, William Southworth (MANAGER), Johnny Vander Meer, Dixie Walker, Harry Walker

PLAYERS WHO WERE REPLACED: Frank McCormick, Howie Pollett

NOTES: 5 HOF'ers.

KEY SIGNATURES: Frisch, Ott, Musial.

VALUE: $600

1944 AMERICAN LEAGUE ALL-STAR TEAM - Hank Borowy, Lou Boudreau, Joe Cronin (COACH), Roy Cullenbine, Bobby Doerr, Rick Ferrell, Art Fletcher (COACH), Pete Fox, Orval Grove, Frankie Hayes, Rollie Hemsley, Pinky Higgins, Oris Hockett, Tex Hughson, Bob Johnson, Ken Keltner, Dutch Leonard, Joe McCarthy (MANAGER),

George McQuinn, Bob Muncrief, Hal Newhouser, Bobo Newsom, Joe Page, Stan Spence, Vern Stephens, Dizzy Trout, Thurman Tucker, Rudy York

PLAYERS WHO WERE REPLACED: George Case

NOTES: 5 HOF'ers.

KEY SIGNATURES: McCarthy, Cronin.

VALUE: $500

1944 NATIONAL LEAGUE ALL-STAR TEAM - Nate Andrews, Phil Cavarretta, Walker Cooper, Vince DiMaggio, Bob Elliott, Fred Fitzsimmons (COACH), Augie Galan, Mike Gonzalez (COACH), Al Javery, Don Johnson, Whitey Kurowski, Marty Marion, Frank McCormick, Joe Medwick, Ray Mueller, Stan Musial, Bill Nicholson, Mel Ott, Mickey Owen, Ken Raffensberger, Connie Ryan, Rip Sewell, Billy Southworth (MANAGER), Jim Tobin, Bill Voiselle, Honus Wagner (COACH), Dixie Walker, Bucky Walters, Frank Zak

PLAYERS WHO WERE REPLACED: Max Lanier, Eddie Miller, George Munger

NOTES: 4 HOF'ers.

KEY SIGNATURES: Wagner, Ott, Musial.

VALUE: $600

1945 (THERE WAS NO ALL-STAR GAME)

1946 AMERICAN LEAGUE ALL-STAR TEAM - Luke Appling, Spud Chandler, Sam Chapman, Bill Dickey, Dom DiMaggio, Joe DiMaggio, Bobby Doerr, Bob Feller, Boo Ferriss, Joe Gordon, Mickey Harris, Frankie Hayes, Charlie Keller, Ken Keltner, Jack Kramer, Art Mills (COACH), Hal Newhouser, Steve O'Neill (MANAGER), Johnny Pesky, Buddy Rosar, Luke Sewell (COACH), Stan Spence, Vern Stephens, George Stirnweiss, Mickey Vernon, Hal Wagner, Ted Williams, Rudy York

NOTES: 6 HOF'ers.

KEY SIGNATURES: Williams, Joe DiMaggio.

VALUE: $550

A team ball for the 1946 National League All-Stars is worth $600.

1946 NATIONAL LEAGUE ALL-STAR TEAM - Ewell Blackwell, Phil Cavarretta, Mort Cooper, Walker Cooper, Del Ennis, Charlie Grimm (MANAGER), Frankie Gustine, Kirby Higbe, Johnny Hopp, Whitey Kurowski, Ray Lamanno, Peanuts Lowrey, Marty Marion, Phil Masi, Frank McCormick, Bill McKechnie (COACH), Johnny Mize, Stan Musial, Claude Passeau, Howie Pollett, Pete Reiser, Johnny Schmitz, Red Schoendienst, Rip Sewell, Enos Slaughter, Billy Southworth (COACH), Emil Verban, Dixie Walker

PLAYERS WHO WERE REPLACED: Eddie Miller, Pee Wee Reese

NOTES: 6 HOF'ers.

KEY SIGNATURES: Musial.

VALUE: $600

1947 AMERICAN LEAGUE ALL-STAR TEAM - Luke Appling, Del Baker (COACH), Lou Boudreau, Spud Chandler, Joe Cronin (MANAGER), Joe DiMaggio, Bobby Doerr, Joe Gordon, Jim Hegan, Tommy Henrich, Billy Johnson, George Kell, John Kramer, Buddy Lewis, Walt Masterson, George McQuinn, Pat Mullin, Hal Newhouser, Steve O'Neill (COACH), Joe Page, Aaron Robinson, Buddy Rosar, Spec Shea, Stan Spence, Dizzy Trout, Ted Williams, Early Wynn, Rudy York

PLAYERS WHO WERE REPLACED: Bob Feller, Charlie Keller

NOTES: 9 HOF'ers.

KEY SIGNATURES: Williams, DiMaggio.

VALUE: $575

1947 NATIONAL LEAGUE ALL-STAR TEAM - Ewell Blackwell, Ralph Branca, Harry Brecheen, Phil Cavarretta, Ben Chapman (COACH), Walker Cooper, Edwin Dyer (MANAGER), Bruce Edwards, Frankie Gustine, Bert Haas, Whitey Kurowski, Marty Marion, Willard Marshall, Phil Masi, Johnny Mize, George Munger, Stan Musial, Mel Ott (COACH), Andy Pafko, Pee Wee Reese, Schoolboy Rowe, Johnny Sain, Enos Slaughter, Warren Spahn, Eddie Stanky, Emil Verban, Dixie Walker, Harry Walker

PLAYERS WHO WERE REPLACED: Bob Elliott, Eddie Miller

NOTES: 6 HOF'ers.

KEY SIGNATURES: Ott, Musial.

VALUE: $650

1948 AMERICAN LEAGUE ALL-STAR TEAM - Yogi Berra, Lou Boudreau, Joe Coleman, John Corriden (COACH), Joe DiMaggio, Joe Dobson, Bobby Doerr, Charlie Dressen (COACH), Hoot Evers, Joe Gordon, Bucky Harris (MANAGER), Joe Haynes, Tommy Henrich, George Kell, Ken Keltner, Bob Lemon, Walt Masterson, George McQuinn, Pat Mullin, Hal Newhouser, Joe Page, Vic Raschi, Buddy Rosar, Vernon Stephens, Birdie Tebbetts, Mickey Vernon, Ted Williams, Al Zarilla

PLAYERS WHO WERE REPLACED: Bob Feller

NOTES: 8 HOF'ers.

KEY SIGNATURES: Williams, DiMaggio.

VALUE: $575

1948 NATIONAL LEAGUE ALL-STAR TEAM - Richie Ashburn, Ewell Blackwell, Ralph Branca, Harry Brecheen, Walker Cooper, Leo Durocher (MANAGER), Eddie Dyer (COACH), Bob Elliott, Sid Gordon, Frankie Gustine, Tommy Holmes, Buddy Kerr,

Ralph Kiner, Phil Masi, Clyde McCullough, Johnny Mize, Stan Musial, Mel Ott (COACH), Andy Pafko, Pee Wee Reese, Elmer Riddle, Bill Rigney, Johnny Sain, Johnny Schmitz, Red Schoendienst, Enos Slaughter, Bobby Thomson, Eddie Waitkus

PLAYERS WHO WERE REPLACED: Marty Marion, Eddie Stanky

NOTES: 7 HOF'ers.

KEY SIGNATURES: Ott, Musial.

VALUE: $650

1949 AMERICAN LEAGUE ALL-STAR TEAM - Yogi Berra, Lou Boudreau (MANAGER), Lou Brissie, Bob Dillinger, Dom DiMaggio, Joe DiMaggio, Larry Doby, Billy Goodman, Joe Gordon, Jim Hegan, Tommy Henrich, Eddie Joost, George Kell, Alex Kellner, Bob Lemon, Bill McKechnie (COACH), Cass Michaels, Dale Mitchell, Mel Parnell, Vic Raschi, Allie Reynolds, Eddie Robinson, Muddy Ruel (COACH), Vern Stephens, Birdie Tebbetts, Virgil Trucks, Vic Wertz, Ted Williams

NOTES: 7 HOF'ers.

KEY SIGNATURES: Williams, DiMaggio.

VALUE: $575

1949 NATIONAL LEAGUE ALL-STAR TEAM - Vern Bickford, Ewell Blackwell, Ralph Branca, Roy Campanella, Walker Cooper, Sid Gordon, Gil Hodges, Eddie Kazak, Ralph Kiner, Marty Marion, Willard Marshall, Johnny Mize, George Munger, Stan Musial, Don Newcombe, Andy Pafko, Howie Pollett, Pee Wee Reese, Jackie Robinson, Preacher Roe, Red Schoendienst, Andy Seminick, Burt Shotton (COACH), Enos Slaughter, Billy Southworth (MANAGER), Warren Spahn, Bobby Thomson, Eddie Waitkus, Bucky Walters (COACH)

NOTES: 9 HOF'ers; Waitkus was an honorary member.

KEY SIGNATURES: Campanella, Robinson, Musial.

VALUE: $675

1950 AMERICAN LEAGUE ALL-STAR TEAM - Yogi Berra, Tommy Byrne, Jerry Coleman, Frankie Crosetti (COACH), Bill Dickey (COACH), Dom DiMaggio, Joe DiMaggio, Larry Doby, Bobby Doerr, Walt Dropo, Hoot Evers, Ferris Fain, Bob Feller, Ted Gray, Jim Hegan, Tommy Henrich, Art Houtteman, George Kell, Bob Lemon, Sherm Lollar, Cass Michaels, Vic Raschi, Allie Reynolds, Phil Rizzuto, Ray Scarborough, Casey Stengel (MANAGER), Vern Stephens, Ted Williams

NOTES: 9 HOF'ers.

KEY SIGNATURES: Williams, Joe DiMaggio.

VALUE: $600

1950 NATIONAL LEAGUE ALL-STAR TEAM - Ewell Blackwell, Roy Campanella, Walker Cooper, Gil Hodges, Larry Jansen, Willie Jones, Ralph Kiner, Jim Konstanty, Marty Marion, Stan Musial, Don Newcombe, Andy Pafko, Jake Pitler (COACH), Pee Wee Reese, Robin Roberts, Jackie Robinson, Preacher Roe, Bob Rush, Hank Sauer, Red Schoendienst, Burt Shotten (MANAGER), Dick Sisler, Enos Slaughter, Duke Snider, Warren Spahn, Eddie Stanky, Milt Stock (COACH), Johnny Wyrostek

NOTES: 10 HOF'ers.

KEY SIGNATURES: Campanella, Robinson, Musial.

VALUE: $675

1951 AMERICAN LEAGUE ALL-STAR TEAM - Yogi Berra, Jim Busby, Chico Carrasquel, Bill Dickey (COACH), Dom DiMaggio, Joe DiMaggio, Larry Doby, Bobby Doerr, Ferris Fain, Nellie Fox, Ned Garver, Randy Gumpert, Jim Hegan, Tommy Henrich (COACH), Fred Hutchinson, George Kell, Bob Lemon, Ed Lopat, Connie Marrero, Minnie Minoso, Mel Parnell, Phil Rizzuto, Eddie Robinson, Bobby Shantz, Casey Stengel (MANAGER), Vern Stephens, Vic Wertz, Ted Williams

NOTES: 8 HOF'ers.

KEY SIGNATURES: Williams, Joe DiMaggio.

VALUE: $600

1951 NATIONAL LEAGUE ALL-STAR TEAM - Richie Ashburn, Benny Bengough (COACH), Ewell Blackwell, Roy Campanella, Dusty Cooke (COACH), Al Dark, Bruce Edwards, Bob Elliott, Del Ennis, Gil Hodges, Larry Jansen, Willie Jones, Ralph Kiner, Dutch Leonard, Sal Maglie, Stan Musial, Don Newcombe, Ralph Perkins (COACH), Pee Wee Reese, Robin Roberts, Jackie Robinson, Preacher Roe, Eddie Sawyer (MANAGER), Red Schoendienst, Enos Slaughter, Duke Snider, Warren Spahn, Wally Weslake, Johnny Wyrostek

NOTES: 10 HOF'ers.

KEY SIGNATURES: Campanella, Robinson, Musial.

VALUE: $675

1952 AMERICAN LEAGUE ALL-STAR TEAM - Bobby Avila, Hank Bauer, Yogi Berra, Tony Cuccinello (COACH), Dom DiMaggio, Larry Doby, Ferris Fain, Nellie Fox, Mike Garcia, Jim Hegan, Jackie Jensen, Eddie Joost, Bob Lemon, Al Lopez (COACH), Mickey Mantle, Gil McDougald, Minnie Minoso, Dale Mitchell, Satchel Paige, Vic Raschi, Allie Reynolds, Phil Rizzuto, Eddie Robinson, Al Rosen, Bobby Shantz, Casey Stengel (MANAGER), Vic Wertz, Eddie Yost

PLAYERS WHO WERE REPLACED: George Kell

NOTES: 7 HOF'ers.

KEY SIGNATURES: Mantle, Paige.

VALUE: $990

1952 NATIONAL LEAGUE ALL-STAR TEAM - Toby Atwell, Roy Campanella, Al Dark, Leo Durocher (MANAGER), Carl Furillo, Granny Hamner, Grady Hatton, Jim Hearn, Gil Hodges, Monte Irvin, Ralph Kiner, Whitey Lockman, Sal Maglie, Stan Musial, Pee Wee Reese, Robin Roberts, Jackie Robinson, Bob Rush, Hank Sauer, Red Schoendienst, Frank Shellenback (COACH), Curt Simmons, Enos Slaughter, Duke Snider, Warren Spahn, Gerry Staley, Eddie Stanky (COACH), Bobby Thomson, Wes Westrum

PLAYERS WHO WERE REPLACED: Preacher Roe

NOTES: 11 HOF'ers.

KEY SIGNATURES: Campanella, Robinson, Musial.

VALUE: $675

1953 AMERICAN LEAGUE ALL-STAR TEAM - Hank Bauer, Yogi Berra, Lou Boudreau (COACH), Chico Carrasquel, Larry Doby, Ferris Fain, Nellie Fox, Mike Garcia, Billy Goodman, Billy Hunter, George Kell, Harvey Kuenn, Bob Lemon, Mickey Mantle, Minnie Minoso, Johnny Mize, Satchel Paige, Billy Pierce, Allie Reynolds, Phil Rizzuto,

Eddie Robinson, Al Rosen, Johnny Sain, Casey Stengel (MANAGER), Jim Turner (COACH), Mickey Vernon, Sammy White, Ted Williams, Gus Zernial

NOTES: 9 HOF'ers; includes Williams, who was an honorary member.

KEY SIGNATURES: Mantle, Williams, Paige.

VALUE: $600

1953 NATIONAL LEAGUE ALL-STAR TEAM - Richie Ashburn, Gus Bell, Roy Campanella, Murry Dickson, Chuck Dressen (MANAGER), Carl Furillo, Harvey Haddix, Granny Hamner, Billy Herman (COACH), Gil Hodges, Ralph Kiner, Ted Kluszewski, Cookie Lavagetto (COACH), Eddie Mathews, Clyde McCullough, Stan Musial, Jake Pitler (COACH), Pee Wee Reese, Robin Roberts, Jackie Robinson, Red Schoendienst, Curt Simmons, Enos Slaughter, Duke Snider, Warren Spahn, Gerry Staley, Wes Westrum, Hoyt Wilhelm, David Williams

PLAYERS WHO WERE REPLACED: Del Crandall, Del Rice

NOTES: 13 HOF'ers.

KEY SIGNATURES: Campanella, Robinson, Musial.

VALUE: $675

1954 AMERICAN LEAGUE ALL-STAR TEAM - Bob Avila, Hank Bauer, Yogi Berra, Ray Boone, Chico Carrasquel, Sandy Consuegra, Larry Doby, Jim Finigan, Whitey Ford, Nelson Fox, Fred Hutchinson (COACH), Bob Keegan, Harvey Kuenn, Bob Lemon, Sherm Lollar, Mickey Mantle, Marty Marion (COACH), Orestes Minoso, Irv Noren, Jim Piersall, Bob Porterfield, Al Rosen, Casey Stengel (MANAGER), Dean Stone, Virgil Trucks, Bob Turley, Mickey Vernon, Ted Williams

PLAYERS WHO WERE REPLACED: Ferris Fain, Mike Garcia, George Kell, Allie Reynolds

NOTES: 7 HOF'ers.

KEY SIGNATURES: Williams, Mantle.

VALUE: $550

A team ball for the 1954 National League All-Stars is worth $675.

954 NATIONAL LEAGUE ALL-STAR TEAM - Walter Alston (MANAGER), Johnny .ntonelli, Gus Bell, Smoky Burgess, Roy Campanella, Gene Conley, Del Crandall, Al)ark, Leo Durocher (COACH), Carl Erskine, Charlie Grimm (COACH), Marv Gris-)m, Granny Hamner, Gil Hodges, Ray Jablonski, Randy Jackson, Ted Kluszewski, Wil- e Mays, Don Mueller, Stan Musial, Pee Wee Reese, Robin Roberts, Jackie Robinson, .ed Schoendienst, Duke Snider, Warren Spahn, Frank Thomas, Jim Wilson

LAYERS WHO WERE REPLACED: Harvey Haddix

IOTES: 10 HOF'ers.

EY SIGNATURES: Campanella, Robinson, Musial.

VALUE: $675

955 AMERICAN LEAGUE ALL-STAR TEAM - Bobby Avila, Yogi Berra, Chico Car- asquel, Tony Cuccinello (COACH), Larry Doby, Dick Donovan, Jim Finigan, Whitey 'ord, Nellie Fox, Don Gutteridge (COACH), Billy Hoeft, Jackie Jensen, Al Kaline, Har- ey Kuenn, Sherm Lollar, Al Lopez (MANAGER), Mickey Mantle, Billy Pierce, Vic 'ower, Al Rosen, Herb Score, Al Smith, Frank Sullivan, Bob Turley, Mickey Vernon, 'ed Williams, Jim Wilson, Early Wynn

IOTES: 7 HOF'ers.

EY SIGNATURES: Williams, Mantle.

VALUE: $500

A team ball for the 1955 National League All-Stars is worth $475.

955 NATIONAL LEAGUE ALL-STAR TEAM - Hank Aaron, Luis Arroyo, Gene Baker, rnie Banks, Smoky Burgess, Gene Conley, Del Crandall, Leo Durocher (MANAGER),)el Ennis, Harvey Haddix, Fred Haney (COACH), Gil Hodges, Randy Jackson, Sam ones, Ted Kluszewski, Johnny Logan, Stan Lopata, Eddie Mathews, Willie Mays, Don Aueller, Stan Musial, Don Newcombe, Joe Nuxhall, Robin Roberts, Red Schoendienst, Aayo Smith (COACH), Duke Snider, Frank Thomas

'LAYERS WHO WERE REPLACED: Roy Campanella

IOTES: 9 HOF'ers.

EY SIGNATURES: Musial.

VALUE: $475

1956 AMERICAN LEAGUE ALL-STAR TEAM - Yogi Berra, Ray Boone, Tom Brewer Chuck Dressen (COACH), Whitey Ford, Nellie Fox, Al Kaline, George Kell, Johnny Kucks, Harvey Kuenn, Sherm Lollar, Mickey Mantle, Billy Martin, Charlie Maxwell, Gil McDougald, Billy Pierce, Jimmy Piersall, Vic Power, Herb Score, Roy Sievers, Harry Simpson, Casey Stengel (MANAGER), Frank Sullivan, Jim Turner (COACH), Mickey Vernon, Ted Williams, Jim Wilson, Early Wynn

PLAYERS WHO WERE REPLACED: Ray Narleski

NOTES: 8 HOF'ers.

KEY SIGNATURES: Williams, Mantle - "Yogi, Billy, Whitey & Mickey."

VALUE: $550

1956 NATIONAL LEAGUE ALL-STAR TEAM - Hank Aaron, Walter Alston (MANAGER), Johnny Antonelli, Ed Bailey, Ernie Banks, Gus Bell, Ken Boyer, Roy Campanella, Bob Friend, Jim Gilliam, Fred Hutchinson (COACH), Ted Kluszewski, Clem Labine, Brooks Lawrence, Dale Long, Stan Lopata, Eddie Mathews, Willie Mays, Roy McMillan, Stan Musial, Joe Nuxhall, Rip Repulski, Robin Roberts, Frank Robinson, Edwin Snider, Warren Spahn, Birdie Tebbetts (COACH), Johnny Temple

PLAYERS WHO WERE REPLACED: Del Crandall

NOTES: 11 HOF'ers.

KEY SIGNATURES: Campanella, Musial.

VALUE: $600

1957 AMERICAN LEAGUE ALL-STAR TEAM - Yogi Berra, Jim Bunning, Frankie Crosetti (COACH), Joe DeMaestri, Nellie Fox, Bob Grim, Elston Howard, Al Kaline, George Kell, Harvey Kuenn, Billy Loes, Frank Malzone, Mickey Mantle, Charlie Maxwell, Gil McDougald, Minnie Minoso, Don Mossi, Bill Pierce, Bobby Richardson, Bobby Shantz, Roy Sievers, Bill Skowron, Casey Stengel (MANAGER), Gus Triandos, Jim Turner (COACH), Vic Wertz, Ted Williams, Early Wynn

NOTES: 7 HOF'ers.

KEY SIGNATURES: Williams, Mantle.

VALUE: $475

1957 NATIONAL LEAGUE ALL-STAR TEAM - Hank Aaron, Walter Alson (MANAGER), Johnny Antonelli, Ed Bailey, Ernie Banks, Gus Bell, Bobby Bragan (COACH), Lew Burdette, Gino Cimoli, Hank Foiles, Don Hoak, Gil Hodges, Larry Jackson, Clem Labine, Johnny Logan, Eddie Mathews, Willie Mays, Roy McMillan, Wally Moon, Stan Musial, Frank Robinson, Jack Sanford, Bob Scheffing (COACH), Red Schoendienst, Curt Simmons, Hal Smith, Warren Spahn, Johnny Temple

NOTES: 9 HOF'ers.

KEY SIGNATURES: Musial.

VALUE: $475

1958 AMERICAN LEAGUE ALL-STAR TEAM - Luis Aparicio, Yogi Berra, Rocky Bridges, Bob Cerv, Ryne Duren, Whitey Ford, Nellie Fox, Lum Harris (COACH), Elston Howard, Jackie Jensen, Al Kaline, Tony Kubek, Harvey Kuenn, Sherm Lollar, Frank Malzone, Mickey Mantle, Gil McDougald, Ray Narleski, Billy O'Dell, Billy Pierce, Bill

kowron, Casey Stengel (MANAGER), Gus Triandos, Bob Turley, Jim Turner COACH), Mickey Vernon, Ted Williams, Early Wynn
OTES: 8 HOF'ers.
EY SIGNATURES: Williams, Mantle - "Yogi, Whitey & Mickey."

VALUE: $475

958 NATIONAL LEAGUE ALL-STAR TEAM - Hank Aaron, Johnny Antonelli, Richie shburn, Ernie Banks, Don Blasingame, Del Crandall, George Crowe, Dick Farrell, Bob riend, Fred Haney (MANAGER), Larry Jackson, Johnny Logan, Eddie Mathews, Wile Mays, Bill Mazeroski, Don McMahon, Walt Moryn, Stan Musial, Johnny Podres, Bob urkey, Bill Rigney (COACH), Johnny Roseboro, Bob Schmidt, Bob Skinner, Mayo mith (COACH), Warren Spahn, Frank Thomas, Lee Walls
OTES: 6 HOF'ers.
EY SIGNATURES: Musial.

VALUE: $450

959 AMERICAN LEAGUE ALL-STAR TEAM - Luis Aparicio, Yogi Berra, Jim Buning, Rocky Colavito, Harry Craft (COACH), Tony Cuccinello (COACH), Buddy Daley, yne Duren, Whitey Ford, Nellie Fox, Al Kaline, Harmon Killebrew, Harvey Kuenn, herm Lollar, Frank Malzone, Mickey Mantle, Gil McDougald, Minnie Minoso, Billy ierce, Vic Power, Pete Runnels, Roy Sievers, Bill Skowron, Casey Stengel (MANGER), Gus Triandos, Hoyt Wilhelm, Ted Williams, Early Wynn
OTES: 10 HOF'ers.

VALUE: $500

959 AMERICAN LEAGUE 2ND GAME ALL-STARS - Bobby Allison, Luis Aparicio, ogi Berra, Rocky Colavito, Frank Crosetti (COACH), Buddy Daley, Ryne Duren, Nele Fox, Elston Howard, Al Kaline, Harmon Killebrew, Tony Kubek, Harry Lavagetto COACH), Sherm Lollar, Frank Malzone, Mickey Mantle, Roger Maris, Cal McLish, linnie Minoso, William O'Dell, Vic Power, Pedro Ramos, Bobby Richardson, Pete Runels, Roy Sievers, Casey Stengel (MANAGER), Gus Triandos, Jerry Walker, Hoyt Wilelm, Ted Williams, Eugene Woodling, Early Wynn
LAYERS WHO WERE REPLACED: Camilo Pascual
OTES: 10 HOF'ers.
EY SIGNATURES: Mantle, Maris, Williams.

VALUE: $575

959 NATIONAL LEAGUE ALL-STAR TEAM - Hank Aaron, John Antonelli, Ernie anks, Ken Boyer, Lew Burdette, Smoky Burgess, Orlando Cepeda, Gene Conley, Del randall, Joe Cunningham, Don Drysdale, Don Elston, Roy Face, Dick Groat, Fred laney (MANAGER), Eddie Mathews, Willie Mays, Bill Mazeroski, Wally Moon, Dan lurtaugh (COACH), Stan Musial, Vada Pinson, Frank Robinson, Eddie Sawyer COACH), Hal Smith, Warren Spahn, John Temple, Bill White
LAYERS WHO WERE REPLACED: Wilmer Mizell
OTES: 9 HOF'ers.
EY SIGNATURES: Musial.

VALUE: $475

1959 NATIONAL LEAGUE 2ND GAME ALL-STARS - , Hank Aaron, John Antonelli Ernie Banks, Ken Boyer, Lew Burdette, Smoky Burgess, Orlando Cepeda, Gene Conley Del Crandell, Joe Cunningham, Don Drysdale, Don Elston, Roy Face, John Fitzpatrick (COACH), Jim Gilliam, Dick Groat, Fred Haney (MANAGER), Billy Herman (COACH), Sam Jones, Johnny Logan, Eddie Mathews, Willie Mays, Bill Mazeroski Wally Moon, Stan Musial, Charles Neal, Vada Pinson, Frank Robinson, Hal Smith, Warren Spahn, Johnny Temple

PLAYERS WHO WERE REPLACED: Wilmer Mizell

NOTES: 8 HOF'ers.

KEY SIGNATURES: Musial.

VALUE: $47

1960 AMERICAN LEAGUE ALL-STAR TEAM - Luis Aparicio, Gary Bell, Yogi Berra Jim Coates, Tony Cuccinello (COACH), Buddy Daley, Chuck Estrada, Whitey Ford Nellie Fox, Jim Gentile, Don Gutteridge (COACH), Ron Hansen, Elston Howard, A Kaline, Harvey Kuenn, Frank Lary, Jim Lemon, Sherm Lollar, Al Lopez (MANAGER) Frank Malzone, Mickey Mantle, Roger Maris, Minnie Minoso, Bill Monbouquette Camilo Pascual, Vic Power, Brooks Robinson, Pete Runnels, Bill Skowron, Al Smith Gerald Staley, Dick Stigman, Ted Williams, Early Wynn

NOTES: 9 HOF'ers; There were no roster changes for the second all-star game played in the 1960 season.

KEY SIGNATURES: Mantle, Maris.

VALUE: $57

1960 NATIONAL LEAGUE ALL-STAR TEAM - Hank Aaron, Joe Adcock, Walter Alston (MANAGER), Ed Bailey, Ernie Banks, Ken Boyer, Bob Buhl, Smoky Burgess Orlando Cepeda, Roberto Clemente, Del Crandall, Roy Face, Bob Friend, Dick Groat Solly Hemus (COACH), Bill Henry, Fred Hutchinson (COACH), Lawrence Jackson Norm Larker, Vern Law, Eddie Mathews, Willie Mays, Bill Mazeroski, Mike McCormick, Lindy McDaniel, Stan Musial, Charles Neal, Vada Pinson, Johnny Podres Bob Skinner, Tony Taylor, William White, Stan Williams

NOTES: 7 HOF'ers; There were no roster changes for the second all-star game played in 1960.

KEY SIGNATURES: Clemente.

VALUE: $52

1961 AMERICAN LEAGUE ALL-STAR TEAM - Yogi Berra, John Brandt, Jim Bunning Norm Cash, Rocky Colavito, Frank Crosetti (COACH), Dick Donovan, Ryne Duren Whitey Ford, Miguel Fornieles, Nellie Fox, Jim Gentile, Elston Howard, Dick Howser Al Kaline, Harmon Killebrew, Tony Kubek, Frank Lary, Mickey Mantle, Roger Maris Jim Perry, Billy Pierce, Paul Richards (MANAGER), Brooks Robinson, John Romano John Temple, James Vernon (COACH), Hoyt Wilhelm

NOTES: 7 HOF'ers.

KEY SIGNATURES: Mantle, Maris.

VALUE: $60

1961 AMERICAN LEAGUE 2ND GAME ALL-STARS - James Adair (COACH), Luis Aparicio, Luis Arroyo, Yogi Berra, John Brandt, Jim Bunning, Norm Cash, Rocky Colavito, Dick Donovan, Whitey Ford, Nellie Fox, Tito Francona, Jim Gentile, Mike Hig ins (COACH), Elston Howard, Dick Howser, Al Kaline, Harmon Killebrew, Tony Kubek, Barry Latman, Mickey Mantle, Roger Maris, Ken McBride, Camilo Pascual, Paul Richards (MANAGER), Brooks Robinson, John Romano, Don Schwall, Roy Sievers, Bill Skowron, Johnny Temple, Hoyt Wilhelm

NOTES: 8 HOF'ers.

KEY SIGNATURES: Mantle, Maris.

VALUE: $600

A team ball for the 1961 American League All-Stars is worth $600. Players signing this ball, from the first 1961 game, include Al Kaline, Jim Gentile, Elston Howard, Ryne Duren, Yogi Berra and Frank Lary.

1961 NATIONAL LEAGUE ALL-STAR TEAM - Henry Aaron, George Altman, Frank Bolling, Ken Boyer, Forrest (Smokey) Burgess, Orlando Cepeda, Roberto Clemente, Al Dark (COACH), Roy Face, Joe Jay, Ed Kasko, Sandy Koufax, Art Mahaffey, Ed Mathews, Gene Mauch (COACH), Willie Mays, Mike McCormick, Stu Miller, Dan Murtaugh (MANAGER), Stan Musial, Bob Purkey, Frank Robinson, John Roseboro, Warren Spahn, Dick Stuart, Bill White, Maury Wills, Don Zimmer

NOTES: 10 HOF'ers.

KEY SIGNATURES: Clemente.

VALUE: $525

1961 NATIONAL LEAGUE 2ND GAME ALL-STARS - Henry Aaron, George Altman, Edgar Bailey, Ernie Banks, Frank Bolling, Ken Boyer, Forrest (Smokey) Burgess, Orlando Cepeda, Roberto Clemente, Chuck Dressen (COACH), Don Drysdale, Roy Face, Joe Jay, Ed Kasko, Sandy Koufax, Art Mahaffey, Ed Mathews, Willie Mays, Mike McCormick, Stu Miller, Dan Murtaugh (MANAGER), Stan Musial, Bob Purkey, Frank Robinson, John Roseboro, Warren Spahn, Dick Stuart, Elvin Tappe (COACH), Bill White, Maury Wills, Don Zimmer

NOTES: 10 HOF'ers.

KEY SIGNATURES: Clemente.

VALUE: $525

1962 AMERICAN LEAGUE ALL-STAR TEAM - Hank Aguirre, Luis Aparicio, Earl Battey, Jim Bunning, Rocco Colavito, Dick Donovan, Jim Gentile, Billy Hitchcock (COACH), Ralph Houk (MANAGER), Elston Howard, Jim Landis, Mickey Mantle, Roger Maris, Bill Monbouquette, Billy Moran, Milt Pappas, Camilo Pascual, Bobby Richardson, Brooks Robinson, Richard Rollins, Johyn Romano, Norm Siebern, David Stenhouse, Ralph Terry, LeRoy Thomas, Tom Tresh, Mickey Vernon (COACH), Leon Wagner, Hoyt Wilhelm

NOTES: 5 HOF'ers.

KEY SIGNATURES: Mantle, Maris.

VALUE: $500

1962 AMERICAN LEAGUE 2ND GAME ALL-STARS - Hank Aguirre, Luis Aparicio, Earl Battey, Hank Bauer (COACH), Yogi Berra, Jim Bunning, Rocky Colavito, Dick Donovan, Jim Gentile, Ray Herbert, Ralph Houk (MANAGER), Elston Howard, Jim Kaat, Al Kaline, Mickey Mantle, Roger Maris, Billy Moran, Camilo Pascual, Bobby Richardson, Bill Rigney (COACH), Brooks Robinson, Rich Rollins, John Romano, Pete Runnels, Norm Siebern, David Stenhouse, Ralph Terry, LeRoy Thomas, Tom Tresh, Leon Wagner, Hoyt Wilhelm

PLAYERS WHO WERE REPLACED: Ken McBride

KEY SIGNATURES: Mantle, Maris.

VALUE: $500

1962 NATIONAL LEAGUE ALL-STAR TEAM - Felipe Alou, Richie Ashburn, Ernie Banks, Frank Bolling, Ken Boyer, John Callison, Orlando Cepeda, Roberto Clemente, Del Crandall, Jim Davenport, Tommy Davis, Don Drysdale, Dick Farrell, Bob Gibson, Dick Groat, Fred Hutchinson (MANAGER), John Keane (COACH), Sandy Koufax, Juan Marichal, Willie Mays, Bill Mazeroski, Stan Musial, Bob Purkey, John Roseboro, Robert Shaw, Warren Spahn, Casey Stengel (COACH), Maury Wills

PLAYERS WHO WERE REPLACED: Hank Aaron

NOTES: 14 HOF'ers.

KEY SIGNATURES: Clemente.

VALUE: $525

1962 NATIONAL LEAGUE 2ND GAME ALL-STARS - Hank Aaron, George Altman, Richie Ashburn, Ernie Banks, Frank Bolling, Ken Boyer, Johny Callison, Orlando Cepeda, Roberto Clemente, Harry Craft (COACH), Del Crandall, Jim Davenport, Tommy Davis, Dick Farrell, Bob Gibson, Dick Groat, Fred Hutchinson (MANAGER), Art Mahaffey, Juan Marichal, Eddie Mathews, Willie Mays, Bill Mazeroski, Stan Musial, Johnny Podres, Bob Purkey, Frank Robinson, Johnny Roseboro, Birdie Tebbetts (COACH), Billy Williams, Maury Wills

NOTES: 11 HOF'ers.

KEY SIGNATURES: Clemente.

VALUE: $525

1963 AMERICAN LEAGUE ALL-STAR TEAM - Bob Allison, Luis Aparicio, Earl Battey Jim Bouton, Jim Bunning, Nellie Fox, Jim Grant, Ralph Houk (MANAGER), Elston Howard, Al Kaline, Harmon Killebrew, Don Leppert, Frank Malzone, Ken McBride Sam Mele (COACH), Bill Monbouquette, Albie Pearson, Joe Pepitone, Johnny Pesky

COACH), Juan Pizarro, Dick Radatz, Bobby Richardson, Brooks Robinson, Norm iebern, Tom Tresh, Zoilo Versalles, Leon Wagner, Carl Yastrzemski

'LAYERS WHO WERE REPLACED: Steve Barber, Mickey Mantle

IOTES: 6 HOF'ers.

VALUE: $350

963 NATIONAL LEAGUE ALL-STAR TEAM - Hank Aaron, Ed Bailey, Ken Boyer,)rlando Cepeda, Roberto Clemente, Ray Culp, Al Dark (MANAGER), Tommy Davis,)on Drysdale, Johnny Edwards, Dick Groat, Larry Jackson, Julian Javier, Bob Kennedy COACH), Sandy Koufax, Juan Marichal, Gene Mauch (COACH), Willie Mays, Willie 1cCovey, Stan Musial, Jim O'Toole, Ron Santo, Duke Snider, Warren Spahn, Joe Torre, ill White, Maury Wills, Hal Woodeshick

'LAYERS WHO WERE REPLACED: Bill Mazeroski

IOTES: 10 HOF'ers; Musial's final year.

VALUE: $450

964 AMERICAN LEAGUE ALL-STAR TEAM - Bobby Allison, Ed Bressoud, Dean hance, Rocky Colavito, Tony Cuccinello (COACH), Whitey Ford, Bill Freehan, Jim regosi, Jimmie Hall, Chuck Hinton, Gil Hodges (COACH), Elston Howard, Harmon illebrew, John Kralick, Al Lopez (MANAGER), Jerry Lumpe, Frank Malzone, Mickey Iantle, Tony Oliva, Camilo Pascual, Joe Pepitone, Gary Peters, Juan Pizarro, Dick Raatz, Bobby Richardson, Brooks Robinson, Norm Siebern, John Wyatt

LAYERS WHO WERE REPLACED: Luis Aparicio, Al Kaline

OTES: 7 HOF'ers.

EY SIGNATURES: Mantle.

VALUE: $400

964 NATIONAL LEAGUE ALL-STAR TEAM - Hank Aaron, Walter Alston (MANGER), Ken Boyer, Jim Bunning, Smoky Burgess, Johnny Callison, Chico Cardenas, rlando Cepeda, Roberto Clemente, Don Drysdale, Johnny Edwards, Dick Ellsworth, ick Farrell, Curt Flood, Dick Groat, Ron Hunt, Fred Hutchinson (COACH), Sandy oufax, Juan Marichal, Willie Mays, Bill Mazeroski, Ron Santo, Chris Short, Willie argell, Casey Stengel (COACH), Joe Torre, Bill White, Billy Williams

OTES: 10 HOF'ers.

EY SIGNATURES: Clemente.

VALUE: $500

965 AMERICAN LEAGUE ALL-STAR TEAM - Max Alvis, Earl Battey, Rocky Colavito, ic Davalillo, Eddie Fisher, Bill Freehan, Jim Grant, Don Gutteridge (COACH), Jimmie all, Willie Horton, Elston Howard, Al Kaline, Harmon Killebrew, Bob Lee, Al Lopez IANAGER), Felix Mantilla, Dick McAuliffe, Sam McDowell, Sam Mele (COACH), hn O'Donoghue, Tony Oliva, Milt Pappas, Joe Pepitone, Bobby Richardson, Pete ichert, Brooks Robinson, Mel Stottlemyre, Zoilo Versalles

LAYERS WHO WERE REPLACED: Mickey Mantle, Bill Skowron, Carl Yastrzemski

OTES: 6 HOF'ers.

VALUE: $350

1965 NATIONAL LEAGUE ALL-STAR TEAM - Hank Aaron, Richie Allen, Ernie Banks, Bobby Bragan (COACH), Johnny Callison, Leo Cardenas, Roberto Clemente, Don Drysdale, Johnny Edwards, Sam Ellis, Dick Farrell, Bob Gibson, Sandy Koufax, Ed Kranepool, Jim Maloney, Juan Marichal, Gene Mauch (MANAGER), Willie Mays, Frank Robinson, Cookie Rojas, Pete Rose, Ron Santo, Dick Sisler (COACH), Willie Stargell, Joe Torre, Bob Veale, Billy Williams, Maury Wills

NOTES: 11 HOF'ers.

KEY SIGNATURES: Clemente.

VALUE: $55[illegible]

1966 AMERICAN LEAGUE ALL-STAR TEAM - Tommie Agee, Steve Barber, Earl Battey, Hank Bauer (COACH), Gary Bell, Norm Cash, Rocky Colavito, Andy Etchebarren, Bill Freehan, Jim Fregosi, Jim Hunter, Jim Kaat, Al Kaline, Harmon Killebrew, Bobby Knoop, Dick McAuliffe, Denny McLain, Sam Mele (MANAGER), Tony Oliva, Bobby Richardson, Pete Richert, Brooks Robinson, Frank Robinson, George Scott, Sonny Siebert, Mel Stottlemyre, Birdie Tebbetts (COACH), Carl Yastrzemski

PLAYERS WHO WERE REPLACED: Sam McDowell

NOTES: 6 HOF'ers.

VALUE: $45[illegible]

1966 NATIONAL LEAGUE ALL-STAR TEAM - Hank Aaron, Richie Allen, Felipe Alou, Walter Alston (MANAGER), Jim Bunning, Leo Cardenas, Roberto Clemente, Curt Flood, Herman Franks (COACH), Tom Haller, Jim Ray Hart, Ron Hunt, Sandy Koufax, Jim Lefebvre, Juan Marichal, Willie Mays, Tim McCarver, Billy McCool, Willie McCovey, Gaylord Perry, Claude Raymond, Phil Regan, Ron Santo, Willie Stargell, Joe Torre, Bob Veale, Harry Walker (COACH), Maury Wills

PLAYERS WHO WERE REPLACED: Bob Gibson, Joe Morgan

NOTES: 11 HOF'ers.

KEY SIGNATURES: Clemente.

VALUE: $50[illegible]

1967 AMERICAN LEAGUE ALL-STAR TEAM - Tommie Agee, Max Alvis, Hank Bauer (MANAGER), Ken Berry, Rod Carew, Paul Casanova, Dean Chance, Tony Conigliaro, Al Downing, Andy Etchebarren, Bill Freehan, Jim Fregosi, Steve Hargan, Joel Horlen, Jim Hunter, Harmon Killebrew, Jim Lonborg, Mickey Mantle, Dick McAuliffe, Jim McGlothlin, Don Mincher, Tony Oliva, Gary Peters, Rico Petrocelli, Bill Rigney (COACH), Brooks Robinson, Eddie Stanky (COACH), Carl Yastrzemski

PLAYERS WHO WERE REPLACED: Al Kaline, Frank Robinson

NOTES: 8 HOF'ers.

KEY SIGNATURES: Mantle.

VALUE: $45[illegible]

1967 NATIONAL LEAGUE ALL-STAR TEAM - Hank Aaron, Richie Allen, Gene Alley, Walter Alston (MANAGER), Ernie Banks, Lou Brock, Orlando Cepeda, Roberto Clemente, Mike Cuellar, Don Drysdale, Herman Franks (COACH), Bob Gibson, Tom Haller, Tommy Helms, Fergie Jenkins, Juan Marichal, Willie Mays, Bill Mazeroski, Tim McCarver, Claude Osteen, Tony Perez, Pete Rose, Tom Seaver, Chris Short, Rusty Staub, Joe Torre, Harry Walker (COACH), Jim Wynn

PLAYERS WHO WERE REPLACED: Denny Lemaster
NOTES: 10 HOF'ers.
KEY SIGNATURES: Clemente.

VALUE: $500

1968 AMERICAN LEAGUE ALL-STAR TEAM - Jose Azcue, Gary Bell, Bert Campaneris, Rod Carew, Cal Ermer (COACH), Bill Freehan, Jim Fregosi, Ken Harrelson, Willie Horton, Frank Howard, Tommy John, Dave Johnson, Duane Josephson, Harmon Killebrew, Mickey Mantle, Sam McDowell, Denny McLain, Rick Monday, Blue Moon Odom, Tony Oliva, Boog Powell, Brooks Robinson, Mayo Smith (COACH), Mel Stottlemyre, Luis Tiant, Don Wert, Dick Williams (MANAGER), Carl Yastrzemski
PLAYERS WHO WERE REPLACED: Jose Santiago
NOTES: 5 HOF'ers.
KEY SIGNATURES: Mantle.

VALUE: $425

A team ball for the 1968 American League All-Stars is worth $425.

1968 NATIONAL LEAGUE ALL-STAR TEAM - Hank Aaron, Felipe Alou, Matty Alou, Johnny Bench, Dave Bristol (COACH), Chico Cardenas, Steve Carlton, Don Drysdale, Curt Flood, Herman Franks (COACH), Woodie Fryman, Bob Gibson, Jerry Grote, Tom Haller, Tommy Helms, Julian Javier, Don Kessinger, Jerry Koosman, Juan Marichal, Willie Mays, Willie McCovey, Tony Perez, Ron Reed, Ron Santo, Red Schoendienst (MANAGER), Tom Seaver, Rusty Staub, Billy Williams
PLAYERS WHO WERE REPLACED: Gene Alley, Pete Rose
NOTES: 10 HOF'ers.

VALUE: $425

1969 AMERICAN LEAGUE ALL-STAR TEAM - Mike Andrews, Sal Bando, Paul Blair, Rod Carew, Ray Culp, Al Dark (COACH), Bill Freehan, Jim Fregosi, Frank Howard, Reggie Jackson, Harmon Killebrew, Darold Knowles, Mickey Lolich, Carlos May, Sam McDowell, Denny McLain, Dave McNally, Don Mincher, Blue Moon Odom, Rico Petrocelli, Boog Powell, Brooks Robinson, Frank Robinson, Elly Rodriguez, Johnny Roseboro, Mayo Smith (MANAGER), Reggie Smith, Mel Stottlemyre, Earl Weaver (COACH), Roy White, Ted Williams (COACH), Carl Yastrzemski

PLAYERS WHO WERE REPLACED: Mike Hegan, Dave Johnson, Tony Oliva

NOTES: 6 HOF'ers.

KEY SIGNATURES: Williams.

VALUE: $425

1969 NATIONAL LEAGUE ALL-STAR TEAM - Hank Aaron, Matty Alou, Ernie Banks, Glenn Beckert, Johnny Bench, Dave Bristol (COACH), Chris Cannizzaro, Steve Carlton, Roberto Clemente, Larry Dierker, Leo Durocher (COACH), Bob Gibson, Randy Hundley, Grant Jackson, Cleon Jones, Don Kessinger, Jerry Koosman, Juan Marichal, Lee May, Willie Mays, Willie McCovey, Denis Menke, Felix Millan, Phil Niekro, Tony Perez, Pete Rose, Ron Santo, Red Schoendienst (MANAGER), Tom Seaver, Bill Singer, Rusty Staub

NOTES: 10 HOF'ers.

KEY SIGNATURES: Clemente.

VALUE: $475

1970 AMERICAN LEAGUE ALL-STAR TEAM - Sandy Alomar, Luis Aparicio, Mike Cuellar, Ray Fosse, Bill Freehan, Jim Fregosi, Tommy Harper, Willie Horton, Ralph Houk (COACH), Frank Howard, Jim Hunter, Alex Johnson, Dave Johnson, Harmon Killebrew, Sam McDowell, Dave McNally, Gerry Moses, Tony Oliva, Amos Otis, Jim Palmer, Jim Perry, Fritz Peterson, Lefty Phillips (COACH), Boog Powell, Brooks Robinson, Frank Robinson, Mel Stottlemyre, Earl Weaver (MANAGER), Roy White, Clyde Wright, Carl Yastrzemski

PLAYERS WHO WERE REPLACED: Rod Carew

VALUE: $400

1970 NATIONAL LEAGUE ALL-STAR TEAM - Hank Aaron, Richie Allen, Glenn Beckert, Johnny Bench, Rico Carty, Roberto Clemente, Dick Dietz, Leo Durocher (COACH), Clarence Gaston, Bob Gibson, Billy Grabarkewitz, Bud Harrelson, Lum Harris (COACH), Jim Hickman, Gil Hodges (MANAGER), Joe Hoerner, Don Kessinger, Willie Mays, Willie McCovey, Denis Menke, Jim Merritt, Joe Morgan, Claude Osteen, Tony Perez, Gaylord Perry, Pete Rose, Tom Seaver, Wayne Simpson, Rusty Staub, Joe Torre, Hoyt Wilhelm

PLAYERS WHO WERE REPLACED: Felix Millan

KEY SIGNATURES: Hodges, Clemente.

VALUE: $475

1971 AMERICAN LEAGUE ALL-STAR TEAM - Luis Aparicio, Vida Blue, Don Buford, Leo Cardenas, Rod Carew, Norm Cash, Mike Cuellar, Dave Duncan, Bill Freehan, Frank Howard, Billy Hunter (COACH), Reggie Jackson, Al Kaline, Harmon Killebrew, Mickey Lolich, Billy Martin (COACH), Bill Melton, Andy Messersmith, Thurman Munson, Bobby Murcer, Amos Otis, Jim Palmer, Marty Pattin, Jim Perry, Brooks Robinson, Frank

Robinson, Cookie Rojas, Sonny Siebert, Earl Weaver (MANAGER), Wilbur Wood, Carl Yastrzemski

PLAYERS WHO WERE REPLACED: Ray Fosse, Sam McDowell, Tony Oliva, Boog Powell

KEY SIGNATURES: Munson, Martin.

VALUE: $450

A team ball for the 1971 American League All-Stars is worth $450.

1971 NATIONAL LEAGUE ALL-STAR TEAM - Hank Aaron, Walter Alston (COACH), Sparky Anderson (MANAGER), Glenn Beckert, Johnny Bench, Bobby Bonds, Lou Brock, Steve Carlton, Clay Carroll, Roberto Clemente, Nate Colbert, Willie Davis, Dock Ellis, Preston Gomez (COACH), Bud Harrelson, Fergie Jenkins, Don Kessinger, Juan Marichal, Lee May, Willie Mays, Willie McCovey, Felix Millan, Danny Murtaugh (COACH), Pete Rose, Manny Sanguillen, Ron Santo, Tom Seaver, Willie Stargell, Rusty Staub, Joe Torre, Don Wilson, Rick Wise

PLAYERS WHO WERE REPLACED: Larry Dierker

KEY SIGNATURES: Clemente.

VALUE: $475

1972 AMERICAN LEAGUE ALL-STAR TEAM - Richie Allen, Sal Bando, Bert Campaneris, Rod Carew, Norm Cash, Pat Dobson, Carlton Fisk, Bill Freehan, Bobby Grich, Ken Holtzman, Jim Hunter, Reggie Jackson, Bob Lemon (COACH), Mickey Lolich, Carlos May, Dave McNally, Bobby Murcer, Jim Palmer, Gaylord Perry, Lou Piniella, Brooks Robinson, Elly Rodriguez, Cookie Rojas, Joe Rudi, Nolan Ryan, Richie Scheinblum, Reggie Smith, Earl Weaver (MANAGER), Dick Williams (COACH), Wilbur Wood, Carl Yastrzemski

PLAYERS WHO WERE REPLACED: Luis Aparicio, Joe Coleman, Toby Harrah, Amos Otis, Freddie Patek

VALUE: $375

1972 NATIONAL LEAGUE ALL-STAR TEAM - Hank Aaron, Glenn Beckert, Johnny Bench, Steve Blass, Lou Brock, Steve Carlton, Clay Carroll, Cesar Cedeno, Roberto Clemente, Nate Colbert, Charlie Fox (COACH), Bob Gibson, Fergie Jenkins, Don Kessinger, Lee May, Willie Mays, Tug McGraw, Joe Morgan, Danny Murtaugh (MANAGER), Al Oliver, Manny Sanguillen, Ron Santo, Red Schoendienst (COACH), Tom Seaver, Ted Simmons, Chris Speier, Willie Stargell, Bill Stoneman, Don Sutton, Joe Torre, Billy Williams

PLAYERS WHO WERE REPLACED: Gary Nolan

KEY SIGNATURES: Clemente.

VALUE: $500

1973 AMERICAN LEAGUE ALL-STAR TEAM - Sal Bando, Buddy Bell, Paul Blair, Bert Blyleven, Eddie Brinkman, Bert Campaneris, Rod Carew, Jim Colborn, Rollie Fingers, Carlton Fisk, Bill Freehan, Whitey Herzog (COACH), Ken Holtzman, Willie Horton, Jim Hunter, Reggie Jackson, Pat Kelly, Bill Lee, Sparky Lyle, Dave May, John Mayberry, Thurman Munson, Bobby Murcer, Dave Nelson, Amos Otis, Brooks Robinsin, Cookie Rojas, Nolan Ryan, Bill Singer, Jim Spencer, Chuck Tanner (COACH), Dick Williams (MANAGER)

PLAYERS WHO WERE REPLACED: Richie Allen, Carl Yastrzemski

KEY SIGNATURES: Munson.

VALUE: $400

1973 NATIONAL LEAGUE ALL-STAR TEAM - Hank Aaron, Sparky Anderson (MANAGER), Johnny Bench, Jack Billingham, Bobby Bonds, Jim Brewer, Cesar Cedeno, Nate Colbert, Willie Davis, Darrell Evans, Ron Fairly, Dave Giusti, Dave Johnson, Gene Mauch (COACH), Willie Mays, Joe Morgan, Manny Mota, Claude Osteen, Pete Rose, Bill Russell, Ron Santo, Tom Seaver, Ted Simmons, Chris Speier, Willie Stargell, Don Sutton, Joe Torre, Wayne Twitchell, Bill Virdon (COACH), Bob Watson, Billy Williams, Rick Wise

PLAYERS WHO WERE REPLACED: Dave Concepcion

VALUE: $375

1974 AMERICAN LEAGUE ALL-STAR TEAM - Richie Allen, Jeff Burroughs, Steve Busby, Bert Campaneris, Rod Carew, Dave Chalk, Mike Cuellar, Rollie Fingers, Bob Grich, George Hendrick, Whitey Herzog (COACH), John Hiller, Jim Hunter, Reggie Jackson, Al Kaline, John Mayberry, Jack McKeon (COACH), Don Money, Thurman Munson, Bobby Murcer, Gaylord Perry, Darrell Porter, Brooks Robinson, Frank Robinson, Cookie Rojas, Joe Rudi, Jim Sundberg, Luis Tiant, Earl Weaver (COACH), Dick Williams (MANAGER), Wilbur Wood, Carl Yastrzemski

PLAYERS WHO WERE REPLACED: Sal Bando, Carlton Fisk, Ed Herrmann

NOTES: Weaver was an honorary manager.

VALUE: $400

1974 NATIONAL LEAGUE ALL-STAR TEAM - Hank Aaron, Sparky Anderson (COACH), Johnny Bench, Yogi Berra (MANAGER), Larry Bowa, Ken Brett, Lou Brock, Buzz Capra, Steve Carlton, Dave Cash, Cesar Cedeno, Ron Cey, Ralph Garr, Steve Garvey, Jerry Grote, Johnny Grubb, Don Kessinger, Mike Marshall, Jon Matlack, Lynn McGlothen, Andy Messersmith, Joe Morgan, Tony Perez, Steve Rogers, Pete Rose,

Mike Schmidt, Red Schoendienst (COACH), Ted Simmons, Reggie Smith, Chris Speier, Jim Wynn

VALUE: $400

1975 AMERICAN LEAGUE ALL-STAR TEAM - Hank Aaron, Vida Blue, Bobby Bonds, Steve Busby, Bert Campaneris, Rod Carew, Dave Chalk, Del Crandall (COACH), Al Dark (MANAGER), Bucky Dent, Rollie Fingers, Bill Freehan, Rich Gossage, Mike Hargrove, Toby Harrah, George Hendrick, Jim Hunter, Reggie Jackson, Jim Kaat, Fred Lynn, Billy Martin (COACH), Hal McRae, Thurman Munson, Graig Nettles, Jim Palmer, Joe Rudi, Nolan Ryan, George Scott, Gene Tenace, Claudell Washington, Carl Yastrzemski

PLAYERS WHO WERE REPLACED: Jorge Orta

KEY SIGNATURES: Munson, Martin.

VALUE: $400

1975 NATIONAL LEAGUE ALL-STAR TEAM - Walter Alston (MANAGER), Johnny Bench, Larry Bowa, Lou Brock, Gary Carter, Dave Cash, Ron Cey, Dave Concepcion, Steve Garvey, Randy Jones, Greg Luzinski, Bill Madlock, Mike Marshall, Jon Matlack, Tug McGraw, Andy Messersmith, Joe Morgan, Bobby Murcer, Danny Murtaugh (COACH), Phil Niekro, Al Oliver, Tony Perez, Jerry Reuss, Pete Rose, Manny Sanguillen, Red Schoendienst (COACH), Tom Seaver, Reggie Smith, Don Sutton, Bob Watson, Jim Wynn

VALUE: $350

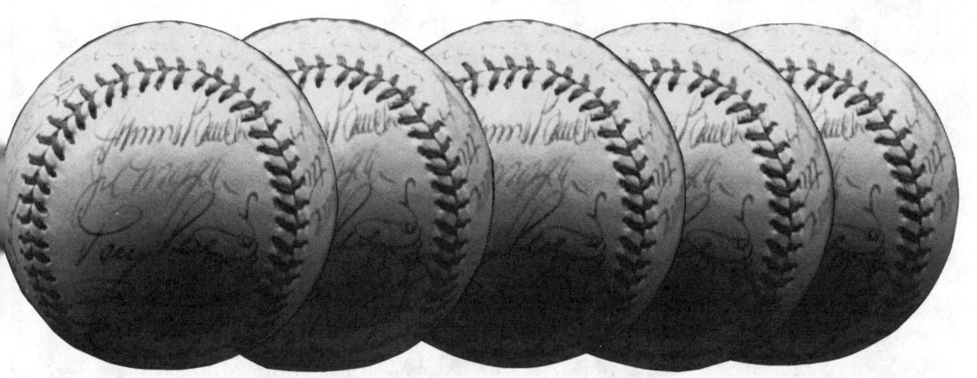

A team ball for the 1975 National League All-Stars is worth $350.

1976 AMERICAN LEAGUE ALL-STAR TEAM - Mark Belanger, George Brett, Rod Carew, Chris Chambliss, Mark Fidrych, Rollie Fingers, Carlton Fisk, Phil Garner, Rich Gossage, Bobby Grich, Toby Harrah, Jim Hunter, Darrell Johnson (MANAGER), Dave LaRoche, Ron LeFlore, Sparky Lyle, Fred Lynn, Gene Mauch (COACH), Hal McRae, Don Money, Thurman Munson, Amos Otis, Fred Patek, Mickey Rivers, Frank Robinson (COACH), Rusty Staub, Frank Tanana, Luis Tiant, Bill Travers, Butch Wynegar, Carl Yastrzemski

PLAYERS WHO WERE REPLACED: Willie Randolph

KEY SIGNATURES: Munson.

VALUE: $400

1977 AMERICAN LEAGUE ALL-STAR TEAM - George Brett, Rick Burleson, Bert Campaneris, Bill Campbell, Rod Carew, Dennis Eckersley, Ron Fairly, Carlton Fisk, Alex Grammas (COACH), Wayne Gross, Larry Hisle, Reggie Jackson, Ruppert Jones, Jim Kern, Dave LaRoche, Bob Lemon (COACH), Sparky Lyle, Fred Lynn, Billy Martin (MANAGER), Thurman Munson, Graig Nettles, Jim Palmer, Willie Randolph, Jim Rice, George Scott, Ken Singleton, Jim Slaton, Jason Thompson, Butch Wynegar, Carl Yastrzemski, Rich Zisk

PLAYERS WHO WERE REPLACED: Vida Blue, Mark Fidrych, Don Money, Nolan Ryan, Frank Tanana

NOTES: Demand centers around "Martin, Munson, and Jackson" combination.

KEY SIGNATURES: Munson, Martin.

VALUE: $425

A team ball for the 1977 National League All-Stars is worth $325.

1977 NATIONAL LEAGUE ALL-STAR TEAM - Sparky Anderson (MANAGER), Joaquin Andujar, Johnny Bench, John Candelaria, Steve Carlton, Ron Cey, Dave Concepcion, George Foster, Steve Garvey, Rich Gossage, Ken Griffey, Tommy Lasorda (COACH), Gary Lavelle, Greg Luzinski, Willie Montanez, Julio (Jerry) Morales, Joe Morgan, Danny Ozark (COACH), Dave Parker, Pete Rose, Rick Rueschel, Mike Schmidt, Tom Seaver, Ted Simmons, Reggie Smith, John Stearns, Don Sutton, Garry Templeton, Manny Trillo, Ellis Valentine, Dave Winfield

PLAYERS WHO WERE REPLACED: Bruce Sutter

VALUE: $325

1978 AMERICAN LEAGUE ALL-STAR TEAM - George Brett, Rod Carew, Dwight Evans, Carlton Fisk, Mike Flanagan, Rich Gossage, Ron Guidry, Whitey Herzog (COACH), Larry Hisle, Roy Howell, Matt Keough, Jim Kern, Chet Lemon, Fred Lynn, Billy Martin (MANAGER), Don Money, Eddie Murray, Jim Palmer, Freddie Patek, Darrell Porter, Jerry Remy, Craig Reynolds, Jim Rice, Lary Sorensen, Jim Sundberg, Frank Tanana, Jason Thompson, Frank White, Don Zimmer (COACH), Richie Zisk

PLAYERS WHO WERE REPLACED: Rick Burleson, Reggie Jackson, Thurman Munson, Graig Nettles, Carl Yastrzemski

KEY SIGNATURES: Martin.

VALUE: $375

1978 NATIONAL LEAGUE ALL-STAR TEAM - Vida Blue, Bob Boone, Larry Bowa, Jeff Burroughs, Ron Cey, Jack Clark, Dave Concepcion, Rollie Fingers, George Foster, Steve Garvey, Ross Grimsley, Tommy John, Tommy Lasorda (MANAGER), Davey Lopes, Greg Luzinski, Rick Monday, Joe Morgan, Phil Niekro, Danny Ozark (COACH), Biff Pocoroba, Terry Puhl, Steve Rogers, Pete Rose, Tom Seaver, Ted Simmons, Reggie Smith, Willie Stargell, Bruce Sutter, Chuck Tanner (COACH), Dave Winfield, Pat Zachry

PLAYERS WHO WERE REPLACED: Johnny Bench

VALUE: $325

1979 AMERICAN LEAGUE ALL-STAR TEAM - Don Baylor, Bruce Bochte, George Brett, Rick Burleson, Mark Clear, Cecil Cooper, Pat Corrales (COACH), Brian Downing, Bob Grich, Ron Guidry, Roy Hartsfield (COACH), Reggie Jackson, Tom John, Darrell Johnson (COACH), Steve Kemp, Jim Kern, Dave Lemanczyk, Bob Lemon (MANAGER), Chet Lemon, Fred Lynn, Sid Monge, Graig Nettles, Jeff Newman, Darrell Porter, Jim Rice, Nolan Ryan, Ken Singleton, Roy Smalley, Don Stanhouse, Bob Stanley, Frank White, Carl Yastrzemski

PLAYERS WHO WERE REPLACED: Rod Carew

VALUE: $350

1979 NATIONAL LEAGUE ALL-STAR TEAM - Joaquin Andujar, Bob Boone, Larry Bowa, Lou Brock, Steve Carlton, Gary Carter, Ron Cey, Jack Clark, George Foster, Steve Garvey, Keith Hernandez, Tommy Lasorda (MANAGER), Mike LaCoss, Davey Lopes, Gary Matthews, Lee Mazzilli, Joe Morgan, Joe Niekro, Danny Ozark (COACH), Dave Parker, Larry Parrish, Gaylord Perry, Craig Reynolds, Steve Rogers, Pete Rose, Joe Sambito, Mike Schmidt, John Stearns, Bruce Sutter, Chuck Tanner (COACH), Dave Winfield

PLAYERS WHO WERE REPLACED: Johnny Bench, Dave Concepcion, Dave Kingman, Ted Simmons, Garry Templeton

VALUE: $300

1980 AMERICAN LEAGUE ALL-STAR TEAM - Buddy Bell, Al Bumbry, Tom Burgmeier, Rod Carew, Cecil Cooper, Bucky Dent, Ed Farmer, Carlton Fisk, Jim Frey (COACH), Rich Gossage, Bob Grich, Larry Gura, Rickey Henderson, Rick Honeycutt, Reggie Jackson, Tommy John, Ken Landreaux, Fred Lynn, Graig Nettles, Ben Oglivie, Al Oliver, Jorge Orta, Lance Parrish, Darrell Porter, Willie Randolph, Frank Robinson (COACH), Dave Stieb, Steve Stone, Alan Trammell, Earl Weaver (MANAGER), Robin Yount

PLAYERS WHO WERE REPLACED: George Brett, Paul Molitor, Jim Rice

VALUE: $350

1980 NATIONAL LEAGUE ALL-STAR TEAM - Johnny Bench, Jim Bibby, Steve Carlton, Gary Carter, Dave Concepcion, Jose Cruz, Phil Garner, Steve Garvey, Ken Griffey, George Hendrick, Keith Hernandez, Dave Kingman, Ray Knight, Dave Lopes, John McNamara (COACH), Dale Murphy, Dave Parker, Ken Reitz, Jerry Reuss, J.R. Richard, Pete Rose, Bill Russell, Reggie Smith, John Stearns, Bruce Sutter, Chuck Tanner (MANAGER), Kent Tekulve, Bill Virdon (COACH), Bob Welch, Ed Whitson, Dave Winfield

PLAYERS WHO WERE REPLACED: Vida Blue, Mike Schmidt

VALUE: $300

1981 AMERICAN LEAGUE ALL-STAR TEAM - Tony Armas, Len Barker, Buddy Bell, George Brett, Rick Burleson, Britt Burns, Rod Carew, Doug Corbett, Ron Davis, Bucky Dent, Bo Diaz, Dwight Evans, Rollie Fingers, Carlton Fisk, Ken Forsch, Jim Frey (MANAGER), Dave Garcia (COACH), Reggie Jackson, Fred Lynn, Scott McGregor, Jack Morris, Eddie Murray, Mike Norris, Al Oliver, Tom Paciorek, Willie Randolph, Ted Simmons, Ken Singleton, Dave Stieb, Gorman Thomas, Frank White, Dave Winfield, Don Zimmer (COACH)

PLAYERS WHO WERE REPLACED: Rich Gossage

VALUE: $350

1981 NATIONAL LEAGUE ALL-STAR TEAM - Dusty Baker, Bruce Benedict, Vida Blue, Bill Buckner, Steve Carlton, Gary Carter, Dave Concepcion, Andre Dawson, Mike Easler, George Foster, Phil Garner, Steve Garvey, Dallas Green (MANAGER), Pedro Guerrero, Burt Hooton, Terry Kennedy, Bob Knepper, Davey Lopes, Bill Madlock, Dave Parker, Tim Raines, Pete Rose, Dick Ruthven, Nolan Ryan, Mike Schmidt, Tom Seaver, Ozzie Smith, Bruce Sutter, Manny Trillo, Fernando Valenzuela, Bill Virdon (COACH), Dick Williams (COACH), Joel Youngblood

VALUE: $350

1982 AMERICAN LEAGUE ALL-STAR TEAM - Sparky Anderson (COACH), Floyd Bannister, Buddy Bell, George Brett, Jim Clancy, Mark Clear, Cecil Cooper, Dennis Eckersley, Rollie Fingers, Carlton Fisk, Rich Gossage, Bobby Grich, Ron Guidry, Toby Harrah, Rickey Henderson, Dick Howser (COACH), Kent Hrbek, Reggie Jackson, Fred Lynn, Billy Martin (MANAGER), Hal McRae, Eddie Murray, Ben Oglivie, Lance Parrish, Dan Quisenberry, Andre Thornton, Frank White, Willie Wilson, Dave Winfield, Carl Yastrzemski, Robin Yount

VALUE: $375

1982 NATIONAL LEAGUE ALL-STAR TEAM - Dusty Baker, Steve Carlton, Gary Carter, Dave Concepcion, Andre Dawson, Leon Durham, Jim Fanning (COACH), Bob Horner, Steve Howe, Tom Hume, Ruppert Jones, Ray Knight, Tommy Lasorda (MANAGER), John McNamara (COACH), Greg Minton, Dale Murphy, Phil Niekro, Al Oliver, Tony Pena, Tim Raines, Steve Rogers, Pete Rose, Steve Sax, Mike Schmidt, Lonnie Smith, Ozzie Smith, Mario Soto, John Stearns, Chuck Tanner (COACH), Jason Thompson, Manny Trillo, Fernando Valenzuela

VALUE: $315

1983 AMERICAN LEAGUE ALL-STAR TEAM - Joe Altobelli (COACH), Bob Boone, George Brett, Rod Carew, Cecil Cooper, Doug DeCinces, Billy Gardner (COACH), Rickey Henderson, Rick Honeycutt, Ron Kittle, Harvey Kuenn (MANAGER), Aurelio Lopez, Fred Lynn, Tippy Martinez, Eddie Murray, Ben Oglivie, Lance Parrish, Dan Quisenberry, Jim Rice, Cal Ripken, Ted Simmons, Bob Stanley, Dave Stieb, Rick Sutcliffe, Manny Trillo, Gary Ward, Lou Whitaker, Willie Wilson, Dave Winfield, Carl Yastrzemski, Matt Young, Robin Yount

PLAYERS WHO WERE REPLACED: Ron Guidry, Reggie Jackson

VALUE: $300

1983 NATIONAL LEAGUE ALL-STAR TEAM - Johnny Bench, Bruce Benedict, Gary Carter, Pat Corrales (COACH), Bill Dawley, Andre Dawson, Dave Dravecky, Leon Durham, Darrell Evans, Pedro Guerrero, Atlee Hammaker, George Hendrick, Whitey Herzog (MANAGER), Glenn Hubbard, Terry Kennedy, Tommy Lasorda (COACH), Gary Lavelle, Bill Madlock, Willie McGee, Dale Murphy, Al Oliver, Jesse Orosco, Pascual Perez, Tim Raines, Steve Rogers, Steve Sax, Mike Schmidt, Lee Smith, Ozzie Smith, Mario Soto, Dickie Thon, Fernando Valenzuela

VALUE: $300

1984 AMERICAN LEAGUE ALL-STAR TEAM - Joe Altobelli (MANAGER), Sparky Anderson (COACH), Tony Armas, Buddy Bell, Mike Boddicker, George Brett, Rod Carew, Bill Caudill, Alvin Davis, Rich Dotson, Dave Engle, Damaso Garcia, Alfredo Griffin, Rickey Henderson, Willie Hernandez, Reggie Jackson, Tony LaRussa (COACH), Chet Lemon, Don Mattingly, Jack Morris, Eddie Murray, Phil Niekro, Lance Parrish, Dan Quisenberry, Jim Rice, Cal Ripken, Dave Stieb, Jim Sundberg, Andre Thornton, Lou Whitaker, Dave Winfield

PLAYERS WHO WERE REPLACED: Alan Trammell

VALUE: $300

1984 NATIONAL LEAGUE ALL-STAR TEAM - Bob Brenly, Gary Carter, Chili Davis, Jody Davis, Steve Garvey, Dwight Gooden, Rich Gossage, Tony Gwynn, Keith Hernandez, Al Holland, Tom Lasorda (COACH), Charlie Lea, Mike Marshall, Jerry Mumphrey, Dale Murphy, Jesse Orosco, Paul Owens (MANAGER), Tony Pena, Tim Raines, Rafael Ramirez, Juan Samuel, Ryne Sandberg, Mike Schmidt, Ozzie Smith, Mario Soto, Darryl Strawberry, Bruce Sutter, Chuck Tanner (COACH), Joe Torre (COACH), Fernando Valenzuela, Tim Wallach, Claudell Washington

PLAYERS WHO WERE REPLACED: Joaquin Andujar

VALUE: $300

1985 AMERICAN LEAGUE ALL-STAR TEAM - Sparky Anderson (MANAGER), Harold Baines, Bert Blyleven, Wade Boggs, Phil Bradley, George Brett, Tom Brunansky, Cecil Cooper, Bobby Cox (COACH), Carlton Fisk, Damaso Garcia, Rich Gedman, Rickey Henderson, Willie Hernandez, Jay Howell, Dick Howser (COACH), Jimmy Key, Don Mattingly, Paul Molitor, Donnie Moore, Jack Morris, Eddie Murray, Dan Petry, Jim Rice, Cal Ripken, Dave Stieb, Alan Trammell, Gary Ward, Lou Whitaker, Dave Winfield, Ernie Witt

PLAYERS WHO WERE REPLACED: Lance Parrish

VALUE: $300

1985 NATIONAL LEAGUE ALL-STAR TEAM - Jack Clark, Jose Cruz, Ron Darling, Jim Frey (COACH), Scott Garrelts, Steve Garvey, Dwight Gooden, Rich Gossage, Tony Gwynn, Tom Herr, LaMarr Hoyt, Terry Kennedy, Bob Lillis (COACH), Willie McGee, Dale Murphy, Graig Nettles, Dave Parker, Tony Pena, Tim Raines, Jeff Reardon, Pete Rose, Nolan Ryan, Ryne Sandberg, Ozzie Smith, Darryl Strawberry, Garry Templeton, Fernando Valenzuela, Ozzie Virgil, Tim Wallach, Dick Williams (MANAGER), Glenn Wilson
PLAYERS WHO WERE REPLACED: Joaquin Andujar, Gary Carter, Pedro Guerrero

VALUE: $325

1986 AMERICAN LEAGUE ALL-STAR TEAM - Don Aase, Harold Baines, Jesse Barfield, Wade Boggs, George Brett, Jose Canseco, Roger Clemens, Pat Corrales (COACH), Tony Fernandez, Rich Gedman, Rickey Henderson, Willie Hernandez, Teddy Higuera, Charlie Hough, Dick Howser (MANAGER), Wally Joyner, Don Mattingly, John McNamara (COACH), Lloyd Moseby, Eddie Murray, Lance Parrish, Jim Presley, Kirby Puckett, Jim Rice, Dave Righetti, Cal Ripken, Ken Schrom, Lou Whitaker, Frank White, Dave Winfield, Mike Witt

VALUE: $300

1986 NATIONAL LEAGUE ALL-STAR TEAM - Kevin Bass, Hubie Brooks, Chris Brown, Gary Carter, Chili Davis, Glenn Davis, Jody Davis, Sid Fernandez, John Franco, Dwight Gooden, Tony Gwynn, Keith Hernandez, Whitey Herzog (MANAGER), Davey Johnson (COACH), Mike Krukow, Tommy Lasorda (COACH), Dale Murphy, Dave Parker, Tony Pena, Tim Raines, Shane Rawley, Jeff Reardon, Rick Rhoden, Ryne Sandberg, Steve Sax, Mike Schmidt, Mike Scott, Dave Smith, Ozzie Smith, Darryl Strawberry, Fernando Valenzuela

VALUE: $300

1987 AMERICAN LEAGUE ALL-STAR TEAM - Harold Baines, George Bell, Wade Boggs, George Brett, Dwight Evans, Tony Fernandez, Jim Fregosi (COACH), Rickey Henderson, Tom Henke, Jay Howell, Bruce Hurst, Terry Kennedy, Mark Langston, Tony LaRussa (COACH), Don Mattingly, Mark McGwire, John McNamara (MANAGER), Jack Morris, Matt Nokes, Larry Parrish, Dan Plesac, Kirby Puckett, Willie Randolph, Dave Righetti, Cal Ripken, Bret Saberhagen, Pat Tabler, Alan Trammell, Lou Whitaker, Dave Winfield, Mike Witt

VALUE: $300

1987 NATIONAL LEAGUE ALL-STAR TEAM - Steve Bedrosian, Hubie Brooks, Gary Carter, Jack Clark, Roger Craig (COACH), Eric Davis, Andre Dawson, Bo Diaz, Sid Fernandez, John Franco, Pedro Guerrero, Tony Gwynn, Keith Hernandez, Orel Hershiser, Davey Johnson (MANAGER), Hal Lanier (COACH), Jeffrey Leonard, Willie McGee, Dale Murphy, Tim Raines, Rick Reuschel, Juan Samuel, Ryne Sandberg, Mike Schmidt, Mike Scott, Lee Smith, Ozzie Smith, Darryl Strawberry, Rick Sutcliffe, Ozzie Virgil, Tim Wallach

VALUE: $300

1988 AMERICAN LEAGUE ALL-STAR TEAM - Doyle Alexander, Wade Boggs, George Brett, Jose Canseco, Roger Clemens, Dennis Eckersley, Gary Gaetti, Mike Greenwell, Mark Gubicza, Ozzie Guillen, Rickey Henderson, Doug Jones, Tom Kelly (MAN-

AGER), Carney Lansford, Tim Laudner, Don Mattingly, Mark McGwire, Paul Molitor, Dan Plesac, Kirby Puckett, Johnny Ray, Jeff Reardon, Harold Reynolds, Cal Ripken, Jeff Russell, Terry Steinbach, Dave Stieb, Kurt Stillwell, Alan Trammell, Tom Trebelhorn (COACH), Bobby Valentine (COACH), Frank Viola, Dave Winfield

VALUE: $275

1988 NATIONAL LEAGUE ALL-STAR TEAM - Bobby Bonilla, Gary Carter, Will Clark, Vince Coleman, David Cone, Roger Craig (COACH), Mark Davis, Andre Dawson, Shawon Dunston, Andres Galarraga, Dwight Gooden, Kevin Gross, Orel Hershiser, Whitey Herzog (MANAGER), Danny Jackson, Bob Knepper, Barry Larkin, Vance Law, Greg Maddux, Willie McGee, Rafael Palmeiro, Lance Parrish, Gerald Perry, Buck Rodgers (COACH), Chris Sabo, Ryne Sandberg, Ozzie Smith, Darryl Strawberry, Robby Thompson, Andy Van Slyke, Bob Walk, Todd Worrell

VALUE: $275

1989 AMERICAN LEAGUE ALL-STAR TEAM - Harold Baines, Wade Boggs, Jose Canseco, Tony Fernandez, Chuck Finley, Julio Franco, Gary Gaetti, Mike Greenwell, Kelly Gruber, Mark Gubicza, Mike Henneman, Bo Jackson, Doug Jones, Tony LaRussa (MANAGER), Jeffrey Leonard, Don Mattingly, Mark McGwire, Mike Moore, Joe Morgan (COACH), Dan Plesac, Kirby Puckett, Doug Rader (COACH), Cal Ripken, Jeff Russell, Nolan Ryan, Steve Sax, Ruben Sierra, Terry Steinbach, Dave Stewart, Greg Swindell, Mickey Tettleton, Devon White

VALUE: $275

1989 NATIONAL LEAGUE ALL-STAR TEAM - Bobby Bonilla, Tim Burke, Will Clark, Vince Coleman, Eric Davis, Glenn Davis, Mark Davis, Andre Dawson, John Franco, Pedro Guerrero, Tony Gwynn, Von Hayes, Orel Hershiser, Jay Howell, Howard Johnson, Barry Larkin, Tom Lasorda (MANAGER), Jack McKeon (COACH), Kevin Mitchell, Tony Pena, Willie Randolph, Rick Reuschel, Buck Rodgers (COACH), Ryne Sandberg, Benito Santiago, Mike Scioscia, Ozzie Smith, John Smoltz, Darryl Strawberry, Rick Sutcliffe, Tim Wallach, Mitch Williams,

PLAYERS WHO WERE REPLACED: Mike Schmidt, Mike Scott

NOTES: Schmidt retired before the All-Star Game.

VALUE: $275

1990 AMERICAN LEAGUE ALL-STAR TEAM - Sandy Alomar Jr., George Bell, Wade Boggs, Ellis Burks, Jose Canseco, Roger Clemens, Dennis Eckersley, Cecil Fielder, Chuck Finley, Julio Franco, Ken Griffey Jr., Kelly Gruber, Ozzie Guillen, Ricky Henderson, Brook Jacoby, Randy Johnson, Doug Jones, Tony LaRussa (MANAGER), Jim Lefebvre (COACH), Mark McGwire, Gregg Olson, Dave Parker, Lance Parrish, Kirby Puckett, Cal Ripken, Frank Robinson (COACH), Bret Saberhagen, Steve Sax, Dave Stieb, Bobby Thigpen, Alan Trammell, Bob Welch

VALUE: $275

1990 NATIONAL LEAGUE ALL-STAR TEAM - Roberto Alomar, Jack Armstrong, Barry Bonds, Bobby Bonilla, Jeff Brantley, Will Clark, Roger Craig (MANAGER), Andre Dawson, Rob Dibble, Shawon Dunston, Lenny Dykstra, John Franco, Tony Gwynn, Neal Heaton, Barry Larkin, Jim Leyland (COACH), Dennis Martinez, Ramon Martinez, Kevin Mitchell, Randy Myers, Greg Olson, Chris Sabo, Ryne Sandberg, Mike Scioscia,

Dave Smith, Ozzie Smith, Darryl Strawberry, Frank Viola, Tim Wallach, Matt Williams, Don Zimmer (COACH)

PLAYERS WHO WERE REPLACED: Benito Santiago

VALUE: $275

A team ball for the 1990 American League All-Stars is worth $275.

1991 AMERICAN LEAGUE ALL-STAR TEAM - Rick Aguilera, Roberto Alomar, Sandy Alomar, Harold Baines, Wade Boggs, Joe Carter, Roger Clemens, Dennis Eckersley, Cecil Fielder, Carlton Fisk, Julio Franco, Cito Gaston (COACH), Ken Griffey Jr., Ozzie Guillen, Bryan Harvey, Dave Henderson, Rickey Henderson, Tom Kelly (COACH), Jimmy Key, Mark Langston, Tony LaRussa (MANAGER), Jack McDowell, Paul Molitor, Jack Morris, Rafael Palmeiro, Kirby Puckett, Jeff Reardon, Cal Ripken, Scott Sanderson, Ruben Sierra, Danny Tartabull

NOTES: Rod Carew was an honorary captain.

KEY SIGNATURES: R. Henderson, Puckett, Boggs, Clemens, Ripken.

VALUE: $150

1991 NATIONAL LEAGUE ALL-STAR TEAM - George Bell, Craig Biggio, Bobby Bonilla, Tom Browning, Brett Butler, Ivan Calderon, Will Clark, Andre Dawson, Rob Dibble, Tom Glavine, Tony Gwynn, Pete Harnisch, Art Howe (COACH), Howard Johnson, Felix Jose, John Kruk, Barry Larkin, Jim Leyland (COACH), Dennis Martinez, Ramon Martinez, Mike Morgan, Eddie Murray, Paul O'Neill, Lou Piniella (MANAGER), Chris Sabo, Juan Samuel, Ryne Sandberg, Benito Santiago, John Smiley, Lee Smith, Ozzie Smith, Darryl Strawberry, Frank Viola

NOTES: Hank Aaron was an honorary captain.

KEY SIGNATURES: O. Smith, Sandberg, Murray, Dawson, Gwynn.

VALUE: $150

Single-Signature Baseballs

$1,860

$2,520

$2,880

No element of the hobby has grown as fast as autographed single-signature baseballs. Driven by the popularity of collecting one autographed baseball for each Hall of Famer, this specialized area of collecting has shown astonishing increases in value. This task, which many experts believe is impossible, is still pursued with vigilance by each new collector entering the market.

Prices for single-signed baseballs of Hall of Famers have increased so dramatically that the average price for such an item is just under $2,000. A complete collection, if one was available in the market, could bring close to $500,000.

****

SINGLE-SIGNATURE BASEBALLS

Members of the Baseball Hall of Fame

Source: the Sports Collectors Digest Baseball Autograph Handbook, second edition

Player	Estimated Value
Cap Anson	$12,760
John Ward	$8,385
Sam Thompson	$8,000
Charles Radbourn	$7,600
Addie Joss	$7,375
Joe Kelley	$7,290
Dan Brouthers	$7,260
Tim Keefe	$7,200
Rube Waddell	$7,000
Mike Kelly	$6,785
Amos Rusie	$6,700
Jack Chesbro	$6,600
Roger Connor	$6,185
Christy Mathewson	$6,140
Al Spalding	$6,100
Morgan Bulkeley	$6,000

Many collectors believe prices in this niche of the market are inflated, while almost all agree that the task is beyond the scope of the average collector. Many think the market has lost its perspective and may experience a price correction. To better illustrate this point the following chart is included:

AUTOGRAPH VALUES

Item	Estimated Value
A cut signature of Abraham Lincoln	$2,700
A document signed by Thomas Jefferson	$5,000
A signed picture of Alexander Graham Bell	$1,400
A Branch Rickey single-signed baseball	$1,100
A cut signature of Benjamin Franklin	$1,600
A document signed by Napoleon I	$2,800
A cut signature of Wolfgang A. Mozart	$2,500
A signed picture of Charles Lindbergh	$1,400
A Bill McKechnie single-signed baseball	$1,460
A cut signature of Daniel Boone	$1,700
A Billy Evans single-signed baseball	$1,900

Source: These prices are averages compiled from a variety of ads and autograph price guides.

****

In a recent study I compared the autograph values of current and past stars by medium type. The study included no deceased players or Hall of Famers. The goal was to get a market value perspective of autographed single-signature baseballs versus cut signatures, autographed 3-by-5-inch index cards, and signed photographs or baseball cards.

Medium	Average Price	percent value vs. baseball
Cut signature	$3.24	n/a
Single-signed baseball	$27.56	11.7
3-by-5-inch index card	$6.76	24.5
Photograph/baseball card	$15.92	57.7

The market for single-signature baseballs is so strong that autographs of deceased Hall of Famers, in this form, will generally reduce the value comparison ratio of the three other types of medium listed, by a minimum of 50 percent. In other words, after a Hall of Famer's death a collector can expect the greatest level of autograph value appreciation to be in the form of single-signature baseballs.

****

Despite the skepticism, the market for autographed single-signature baseballs continues to flourish. Most new collectors begin collecting single-signed baseballs, a facet they believe is very rewarding. However, collectors choosing this niche for investment purposes should do so with extreme caution; the market can show volatile price changes. During the fall recession of 1990 a Babe Ruth single-signature baseball plummeted to $2,100, less than half the market value from six months before.

****

Some ball holders include cases for displaying cards.

AUTOGRAPH VALUES OF CURRENT AND PAST STARS

Single-signed Official League baseballs

Player	Estimated Value	Player	Estimated Value	Player	Estimated Value
Hank Aaron	$36	Jim Palmer	$26	Ken Griffey Jr.	$30
Ernie Banks	$26	Gaylord Perry	$22	Rickey Henderson	$33
Johnny Bench	$20	Pee Wee Reese	$24	Bo Jackson	$40
Yogi Berra	$24	Brooks Robinson	$21	Reggie Jackson	$32
Lou Brock	$20	Frank Robinson	$24	Roger Maris	$270
Rod Carew	$29	Enos Slaughter	$21	Billy Martin	$81
Joe DiMaggio	$235	Duke Snider	$26	Don Mattingly	$34
Bob Feller	$18	Warren Spahn	$20	Mark McGwire	$30
Whitey Ford	$23	Willie Stargell	$21	Thurman Munson	$540
Bob Gibson	$21	Billy Williams	$21	Dale Murphy	$23
Catfish Hunter	$21	Ted Williams	$55	Eddie Murray	$21
Fergie Jenkins	$22	Carl Yastrzemski	$21	Phil Niekro	$22
Al Kaline	$21	Wade Boggs	$32	Cal Ripken Jr.	$26
Harmon Killebrew	$22	George Brett	$35	Pete Rose	$28
Ralph Kiner	$21	Jose Canseco	$36	Nolan Ryan	$45
Sandy Koufax	$30	Steve Carlton	$29	Ryne Sandberg	$31
Mickey Mantle	$60	Will Clark	$34	Mike Schmidt	$37
Eddie Mathews	$21	Roger Clemens	$31	Tom Seaver	$33
Willie Mays	$37	Andre Dawson	$23	Ozzie Smith	$19
Willie McCovey	$21	Carlton Fisk	$26	Darryl Strawberry	$30
Joe Morgan	$25	Steve Garvey	$22	Dave Winfield	$24
Stan Musial	$42	Dwight Gooden	$28	Robin Yount	$27

Source: from the Sports Collectors Digest Baseball Autograph Handbook, second edition

Hall of Fame Roster

Hank Aaron
Grover Alexander
Walter Alston
Cap Anson
Luis Aparicio
Luke Appling
Earl Averill
Frank Baker
Dave Bancroft
Ernie Banks
Al Barlick
Edward Barrow
Jake Beckley
Cool Papa Bell
Johnny Bench
Chief Bender
Yogi Berra
Jim Bottomley
Lou Boudreau
Roger Bresnahan
Lou Brock
Dan Brouthers
Mordecai Brown
Morgan Bulkeley
Jesse Burkett
Roy Campanella
Rod Carew
Max Carey
Alexander Cartwright
Henry Chadwick
Frank Chance
Happy Chandler
Oscar Charleston
Jack Chesbro
Fred Clarke
John Clarkson
Roberto Clemente
Ty Cobb
Mickey Cochrane
Eddie Collins
Jimmy Collins
Earle Combs
Charles Comiskey
Jocko Conlan
Thomas Connolly
Roger Connor
Stan Coveleski
Sam Crawford
Joe Cronin
Candy Cummings
Kiki Cuyler
Ray Dandridge
Dizzy Dean
Ed Delahanty
Bill Dickey
Martin Dihigo
Joe DiMaggio
Bobby Doerr
Don Drysdale
Hugh Duffy
Billy Evans
Johnny Evers
Buck Ewing
Red Faber
Bob Feller
Rick Ferrell
Rollie Fingers
Elmer Flick
Whitey Ford
Rube Foster
Jimmie Foxx
Ford Frick
Frankie Frisch
Pud Galvin
Lou Gehrig
Charlie Gehringer
Josh Gibson
Bob Gibson
Warren Giles
Lefty Gomez
Goose Goslin
Hank Greenberg
Clark Griffith
Burleigh Grimes
Lefty Grove
Chick Hafey
Jesse Haines
Billy Hamilton
Will Harridge
Bucky Harris
Gabby Hartnett
Harry Heilmann
Billy Herman
Harry Hooper
Rogers Hornsby
Waite Hoyt
Cal Hubbard
Carl Hubbell
Miller Huggins
Catfish Hunter
Monte Irvin
Travis Jackson
Fergie Jenkins
Hugh Jennings
Ban Johnson
Judy Johnson
Walter Johnson
Addie Joss
Al Kaline
Tim Keefe
Wee Willie Keeler
George Kell
Joe Kelley
George Kelly
Mike Kelly
Harmon Killebrew
Ralph Kiner
Chuck Klein
Bill Klem
Sandy Koufax
Nap Lajoie
Kenesaw Landis
Tony Lazzeri
Bob Lemon
Buck Leonard
Freddie Lindstrom
John Lloyd
Ernie Lombardi
Al Lopez
Ted Lyons
Connie Mack
Larry MacPhail
Mickey Mantle
Heinie Manush
Rabbit Maranville
Juan Marichal
Rube Marquard
Eddie Mathews
Christy Mathewson
Willie Mays
Joe McCarthy
Tom McCarthy
Willie McCovey
Joe McGinnity
John McGraw
Bill McKechnie
Ducky Medwick
Johnny Mize
Joe Morgan
Stan Musial
Kid Nichols
James O'Rourke
Met Ott
Satchel Paige
Jim Palmer
Herb Pennock
Gaylord Perry
Eddie Plank
Charles Radbourn
Pee Wee Reese
Sam Rice
Branch Rickey
Eppa Rixey
Robin Roberts
Brooks Robinson
Frank Robinson
Jackie Robinson
Wilbert Robinson
Edd Roush
Red Ruffing
Amos Rusie
Babe Ruth
Ray Schalk
Red Schoendienst
Tom Seaver
Joe Sewell
Al Simmons
George Sisler
Enos Slaughter
Duke Snider
Warren Spahn
Al Spalding
Tris Speaker
Willie Stargell
Casey Stengel
Bill Terry
Sam Thompson
Joe Tinker
Pie Traynor
Dazzy Vance
Bill Veeck
Arky Vaughan
Rube Waddell
Honus Wagner
Bobby Wallace
Ed Walsh
Lloyd Waner
Paul Waner
John Ward
George Weiss
Mickey Welch
Zack Wheat
Hoyt Wilhelm
Billy Williams
Ted Williams
Hack Wilson
George Wright
Harry Wright
Early Wynn
Tom Yawkey
Carl Yastrzemski
Cy Young
Ross Youngs

Autographed Commemorative Baseballs

As the hobby matures, collector interest tends to shift toward a more creative approach to collecting. One such facet is collecting autographed commemorative baseballs. These baseballs typically acknowledge a particular event or milestone relevant to an individual's career, the game or a particular event. For example:

* Commemorative baseball relevant to an individual's career

  A baseball autographed by Jim Palmer and dated 5/16/65, the date of his first major league win.

* Commemorative baseball relevant to the game

  A baseball signed by all the living players who hit more than 500 home runs in their major league career.

* Commemorative baseball relevant to an event

  A baseball signed by Bobby Thomson and Ralph Branca, dated 10/3/51. "The Shot Heard 'Round the World"

Additionally, commemorative baseballs can acknowledge some of the anomalies of the game, such as combination baseballs signed by Johnny Roseboro and Juan Marichal; Pete Rose and Bart Giamatti; Willie Mays, Mickey Mantle and Duke Snider; and Moose Skowron, Catfish Hunter, Ducky Medwick and Rabbit Maranville. Commemorative baseballs can also be limited editions, actually being numbered by the signer in recognition of the particular format and its production.

Typically, however, commemorative collectors tend to center their collecting around items that have a greater significance to the game, such as autographed combination baseballs of "300 Game Winners," "MVP Award Winners," and players with "3,000 Hits" or "500 Home Runs." Although

Oscar Wilde once said, "Consistency is the last refuge of the unimaginative," he never tried to sell a baseball autographed by Roseboro and Marichal.

Numerous checklists of recognized game milestones and prestigious awards have been provided to assist those collectors of commemorative baseballs.

LIFETIME LEADERS - BATTING

Players with lifetime BATTING AVERAGE of .300 or higher
(Minimum of 10 major league seasons and 4,000 At Bats)

PLAYER	B.A.
1 Ty Cobb	.366
2 Rogers Hornsby	.358
3 Joe Jackson	.356
4 Pete Browning	.347
5 Ed Delahanty	.346
6 Willie Keeler	.345
7 Wade Boggs	.345
8 Billy Hamilton	.344
9 Ted Williams	.344
10 Tris Speaker	.344
11 Dan Brouthers	.342
12 Jesse Burkett	.342
13 Babe Ruth	.342
14 Harry Heilmann	.342
15 Bill Terry	.341
16 George Sisler	.340
17 Lou Gehrig	.340
18 Nap Lajoie	.339
19 Riggs Stephenson	.336
20 Al Simmons	.334
21 Cap Anson	.333
22 Paul Waner	.333
23 Eddie Collins	.333
24 Sam Thompson	.332
25 Stan Musial	.331
26 Heinie Manush	.330
27 Hugh Duffy	.329
28 Honus Wagner	.329
29 Rod Carew	.328
30 Tony Gwynn	.328
31 Tip O'Neill	.327
32 Jimmie Foxx	.325
33 Earle Combs	.325
34 Joe DiMaggio	.325
35 Babe Herman	.324
36 Joe Medwick	.324
37 Danny Lyons	.323
38 Edd Roush	.323
39 Sam Rice	.322
40 Ross Youngs	.322
41 Joe Kelley	.321
42 Kiki Cuyler	.321
43 Charlie Gehringer	.320
44 Chuck Klein	.320
45 Pie Traynor	.320
46 Mickey Cochrane	.320
47 George Van Haltren	.319
48 Ken Williams	.319
49 Roger Connor	.318
50 Earl Averill	.318
51 Arky Vaughan	.318
52 Roberto Clemente	.317
53 Chick Haley	.317
54 Zack Wheat	.317
55 Lloyd Waner	.316
56 Frankie Frisch	.316
57 Goose Goslin	.316
58 Elmer Flick	.315
59 Fred Clarke	.315
60 Bibb Falk	.314
61 Cecil Travis	.314
62 Mike Tiernan	.314
63 Hank Greenberg	.313
64 Hughie Jennings	.313
65 Jack Fournier	.313
66 Elmer Smith	.313
67 Bill Dickey	.313
68 Cupid Childs	.312
69 Jim O'Rourke	.312
70 Johnny Mize	.312
71 Joe Swell	.312
72 Barney McCosky	.312
73 Bing Miller	.312
74 George Brett	.311
75 Fred Lindstrom	.311
76 Jackie Robinson	.311
77 Baby Doll Jackson	.311
78 Rip Radcliff	.311
79 Ginger Beaumont	.311
80 Irish Meusel	.310
81 Luke Appling	.310
82 Bobby Veach	.310
83 John Stone	.310
84 Jim Bottomley	.310
85 Sam Crawford	.309
86 Bob Meusel	.309
87 Jake Beckley	.309
88 Jimmy Ryan	.309
89 Ted Larkin	.309
90 Jack Tobin	.309
91 Spud Davis	.308
92 George Brett	.308
93 Richie Ashburn	.308
94 Steve Brodie	.308
95 Stuffy McInnis	.308
96 Joe Vosmik	.307
97 Harry Stovey	.307
98 King Kelly	.307
99 Frank Baker	.307
100 Buck Ewing	.307
101 George Burns	.307
102 Matty Alou	.307
103 Hack Wilson	.307
104 Johnny Pesky	.307
105 Chick Stahl	.307
106 George Kell	.306
107 Dixie Walker	.306
108 Ernie Lombardi	.306
109 Ralph Garr	.306
110 Hank Aaron	.305
111 Bill Madlock	.305
112 Billy Herman	.304
113 Tony Oliva	.304
114 Patsy Donovan	.304
115 Mel Ott	.304
116 Cy Seymour	.304
117 Ed McKean	.304
118 Curt Walker	.304
119 Deacon White	.304
120 Charlie Jamieson	.303
121 Al Oliver	.303
122 Jake Daubert	.303
123 Pete Rose	.303

PLAYER	B.A.	PLAYER	B.A.	PLAYER	B.A.
124 Buddy Myer	.303	132 Carl Reynolds	.302	140 Paul Hines	.300
125 Harvey Kuenn	.303	133 Tommy Holmes	.302	141 Wally Berger	.300
126 George Gore	.303	134 Willie Mays	.302	142 Ethan Allen	.300
127 Pedro Guerrero	.302	135 Jack Doyle	.302	143 Enos Slaughter	.300
128 Paul Molitor	.302	136 Joe Cronin	.302	144 Hardy Richardson	.300
129 Hal Trosky	.302	137 Stan Hack	.301	145 Billy Goodman	.300
130 George Grantham	.302	138 Oyster Burns	.301		
131 Ben Chapman	.302	139 Mike Griffin	.300		

PLAYERS WITH 2,000 or more HITS

PLAYER	HITS	PLAYER	HITS	PLAYER	HITS
1 Pete Rose	4256	39 Lou Gehrig	2721	77 Dwight Evans	2446
2 Ty Cobb	4190	40 Rusty Staub	2716	78 Pie Traynor	2416
3 Hank Aaron	3771	41 Bill Buckner	2715	79 Mickey Mantle	2415
4 Stan Musial	3630	42 Dave Parker	2712	80 Stuffy McInnis	2406
5 Tris Speaker	3515	43 Billy Williams	2711	81 Enos Slaughter	2383
6 Honus Wagner	3430	44 Doc Cramer	2705	82 Edd Roush	2377
7 Carl Yastrzemski	3419	45 Fred Clarke	2703	83 Andre Dawson	2354
8 Eddie Collins	3311	46 Dave Winfield	2697	84 Orlando Cepeda	2351
9 Willie Mays	3283	47 George Davis	2683	85 Joe Judge	2350
10 Nap Lajoie	3251	48 Luis Aparicio	2677	86 Bily German	2345
11 Paul Waner	3152	49 Max Carey	2665	87 Joe Torre	2342
12 Rod Carew	3053	50 Nellie Fox	2663	88 Jake Daubert	2326
13 Lou Brock	3023	51 Harry Heilmann	2660	89 Dave Concepcion	2326
14 Cap Anson	3022	52 Ted Williams	2654	90 Eddie Mathews	2315
15 Al Kaline	3007	53 Jimmie Foxx	2646	91 Jim Bottomley	2313
16 Roberto Clemente	3000	54 Lave Cross	2645	92 Hugh Duffy	2313
17 Sam Rice	2987	55 Rabbit Maranville	2605	93 Bobby Wallace	2306
18 Sam Crawford	2964	56 Steve Garvey	2599	94 Carlton Fisk	2303
19 Willie Keeler	2955	57 Ed Delahanty	2593	95 Jim O'Rourke	2300
20 Frank Robinson	2943	58 Reggie Jackson	2584	96 Charlie Grimm	2299
21 Jake Beckley	2930	59 Ernie Banks	2583	97 Kiki Cuyler	2299
22 Rogers Hornsby	2930	60 Richie Ashburn	2574	98 Dan Brouthers	2288
23 Al Simmons	2927	61 Willie Davis	2558	99 Biddy McPhee	2287
24 Zack Wheat	2884	62 George Van Haltren	2558	100 Joe Cronin	2285
25 Frankie Frisch	2880	63 Heinie Manush	2524	101 Patsy Donovan	2266
26 Robin Yount	2878	64 Jimmy Ryan	2524	102 Darrell Evans	2362
27 Mel Ott	2876	65 Joe Morgan	2517	103 Jimmy Dykes	2256
28 Babe Ruth	2873	66 Buddy Bell	2514	104 Ron Santo	2254
29 Jesse Burkett	2872	67 Eddie Murray	2502	105 Jose Cruz	2251
30 George Brett	2863	68 Mickey Vernon	2495	106 Bert Campaneris	2249
31 Brooks Robinson	2848	69 Bill Dahlen	2478	107 Tommy Corcoran	2248
32 Charlie Gehringer	2839	70 Ted Simmons	2472	108 Joe Kelley	2245
33 George Sisler	2812	71 Joe Medwick	2471	109 Fred Tenney	2239
34 Vada Pinson	2757	72 Harry Hooper	2466	110 Mike Schmidt	2234
35 Luke Appling	2749	73 Roger Connor	2460	111 Willie Stargell	2232
36 Al Oliver	2743	74 Lloyd Waner	2459	112 Joe Sewell	2226
37 Goose Goslin	2735	75 Jim Rice	2452	113 Graig Nettles	2225
38 Tony Perez	2732	76 Red Schoendienst	2449	114 Joe DiMaggio	2214

PLAYER	HITS
115 Joe Kuhel	2212
116 Willie McCovey	2211
117 Bill Terry	2193
118 Stan Hack	2193
119 Cecil Cooper	2192
120 Larry Bowa	2191
121 Keith Hernandez	2182
122 Pee Wee Reese	2170
123 Sherry Magee	2169
124 Dick Bartell	2165
125 Billy Hamilton	2157
126 Hal Chase	2156
127 Yogi Berra	2150
128 Ed Konetchy	2146
129 Tommy Leach	2144
130 Ken Griffey Sr.	2143
131 Ken Boyer	2143
132 Herman Long	2142
133 Willie Randolph	2138
134 Wally Moses	2138
135 Dick Groat	2138
136 Don Baylor	2135
137 Maury Wills	2134

PLAYER	HITS
138 Buddy Meyer	2131
139 Monte Ward	2122
140 Tommy Davis	2122
141 Duke Snider	2116
142 Chris Chambliss	2109
143 Arky Vaughan	2103
144 Felipe Alou	2102
145 Clyde Milan	2099
146 Jimmy Sheckard	2097
147 Garry Templeton	2096
148 Dale Murphy	2095
149 Harvey Kuenn	2092
150 Hal McRae	2091
151 Al Dark	2089
152 Cesar Cedeno	2087
153 Paul Molitor	2086
154 Harmon Killebrew	2086
155 Ed McKean	2079
156 George Burns	2077
157 Chuck Klein	2076
158 Dummy Hoy	2067
159 Dixie Walker	2064
160 Bobby Veach	2064

PLAYER	HITS
161 Del Ennis	2063
162 Bob Elliott	2061
163 George Kell	2054
164 Bob Johnson	2051
165 Johnny Bench	2048
166 Bobby Doerr	2042
167 Willie Wilson	2038
168 Jack Glascock	2038
169 Lee May	2031
170 Ken Singleton	2029
171 Alan Trammell	2022
172 Earl Averill	2020
173 Reggie Smith	2020
174 Amos Otis	2020
175 George Burns	2018
176 Bill Mazeroski	2016
177 Johnny Mize	2011
178 Gary Matthews	2011
179 Brian Downing	2010
180 Bill Madlock	2008
181 Tony Taylor	2007
182 Frank White	2006
183 Dave Bancroft	2004

LIFETIME LEADERS - BATTING

Players with 300 or more HOME RUNS

	PLAYER	HR
1	Hank Aaron	755
2	Babe Ruth	714
3	Willie Mays	660
4	Frank Robinson	586
5	Harmon Killebrew	573
6	Reggie Jackson	563
7	Mike Schmidt	548
8	Mickey Mantle	536
9	Jimmie Foxx	534
10	Ted Williams	521
11	Willie McCovey	521
12	Eddie Mathews	512
13	Ernie Banks	512
14	Mel Ott	511
15	Lou Gehrig	493
16	Stan Musial	475
17	Willie Stargell	475
18	Carl Yastrzemski	452
19	Dave Kingman	442
20	Billy Williams	426

	PLAYER	HR
21	Darrell Evans	414
22	Duke Snider	407
23	Dave Winfield	406
24	Al Kaline	399
25	Eddie Murray	398
26	Dale Murphy	396
27	Graig Nettles	390
28	Johnny Bench	389
29	Dwight Evans	385
30	Frank Howard	382
31	Jim Rice	382
32	Orlando Cepeda	379
33	Tony Perez	379
34	Andre Dawson	377
35	Norm Cash	377
36	Rocky Colavito	374
37	Carlton Fisk	372
38	Gil Hodges	370
39	Ralph Kiner	369
40	Joe DiMaggio	361

This ball has signatures of all the living players who hit 500 or more homers in their careers.

	PLAYER	HR
41	Johnny Mize	359
42	Yogi Berra	358
43	Lee May	354
44	Dick Allen	351
45	George Foster	348
46	Ron Santo	342
47	Dave Parker	339
48	Boog Powell	339
49	Don Baylor	338
50	Joe Adcock	336
51	Jack Clark	335
52	Bobby Bonds	332
53	Hank Greenberg	331
54	Willie Horton	325
55	Gary Carter	319
56	Roy Sievers	318
57	Ron Cey	316
58	Reggie Smith	314
59	Al Simmons	307
60	Greg Luzinski	307
61	Fred Lynn	306
62	Lance Parrish	304
63	Rogers Hornsby	300
64	Chuck Klein	300

LIFETIME LEADERS - PITCHING

Pitchers with 200 or more WINS

	PLAYER	WON	LOSS	PCT.
1	Cy Young	511	313	.620
2	Walter Johnson	416	279	.599
3	Christy Mathewson	374	187	.667
4	G.C. Pete Alexander	373	208	.642
5	Warren Spahn	363	245	.597
6	Kid Nichols	361	208	.634
7	Pud Galvin	361	309	.539
8	Tim Keefe	341	224	.604
9	Steve Carlton	329	244	.574
10	John Clarkson	327	176	.650
11	Eddie Plank	325	193	.627
12	Don Sutton	324	256	.559
13	Phil Niekro	318	274	.537
14	Nolan Ryan	314	284	.525
15	Gaylord Perry	314	265	.542
16	Tom Seaver	311	205	.603
17	Mickey Welch	309	209	.597
18	Old Hoss Radbourn	308	191	.617
19	Lefty Grove	300	141	.680
20	Early Wynn	300	244	.551
21	Tommy John	288	231	.555
22	Tony Mullane	286	213	.573
23	Robin Roberts	286	245	.569
24	Ferguson Jenkins	284	226	.557
25	Jim Kaat	283	237	.544
26	Bert Blyleven	279	238	.540
27	Red Ruffing	273	225	.548
28	Burleigh Grimes	270	212	.560
29	Jim Palmer	268	152	.638
30	Bob Feller	266	162	.621

San Francisco Giants pitcher/catcher duo Juan Marichal and John Roseboro signed this baseball.

	PLAYER	WON	LOSS	PCT.
31	Gus Weyhing	266	229	.537
32	Eppa Rixley	266	251	.515
33	Jim McCormick	264	214	.562
34	Ted Lyons	260	230	.531
35	Red Faber	254	212	.545
36	Carl Hubbell	253	154	.622
37	Bob Gibson	251	174	.591
38	Joe McGinnity	248	144	.633
39	Amos Rusie	248	170	.593
40	Vic Willis	248	203	.550
41	Jack Quinn	248	219	.531
42	Jack Powell	248	255	.493
43	Juan Marichal	243	142	.631
44	Herb Pennock	240	161	.599
45	Three Finger Brown	239	127	.653
46	Waite Hoyte	237	182	.566
47	Whitey Ford	236	106	.690
48	Clark Griffith	235	143	.622
49	Charlie Buffington	230	151	.604
50	Luis Tiant	229	172	.571
51	George Mullin	229	192	.544
52	Sad Sam Jones	228	216	.514
53	Will White	227	167	.576
54	Catfish Hunter	224	166	.574
55	Jim Bunning	224	184	.459
56	Mel Harder	223	186	.545
57	Paul Derringer	223	212	.513
58	Jerry Koosman	222	209	.515
59	Joe Niekro	221	204	.520
60	Hooks Dauss	221	182	.548

	PLAYER	WON	LOSS	PCT.
61	Frank Tanana	220	208	.514
62	Jerry Reuss	220	191	.535
63	Earl Whitehill	218	185	.541
64	Bob Caruthers	217	101	.682
65	Freddie Fitzsimmons	217	146	.596
66	Mickey Lolich	217	191	.532
67	Jack Morris	216	162	.571
68	Stan Coveleski	216	143	.602
69	Wilbur Cooper	216	178	.548
70	Jim Perry	215	174	.553
71	Rick Reuschel	214	189	.531
72	Billy Pierce	211	169	.555
73	Bobo Newsom	211	222	.487
74	Chief Bender	210	128	.621
75	Jesse Haines	210	158	.571
76	Eddie Cicotte	209	149	.584
77	Milt Pappas	209	164	.560
78	Don Drysdale	209	166	.557
79	Vida Blue	209	161	.565
80	Carl Mays	207	127	.620
81	Bob Lemon	207	128	.618
82	Hal Newhouser	207	150	.580
83	Silver King	206	152	.575
84	Jack Stivelts	205	128	.616
85	Adonis Terry	205	197	.510
86	Lew Burdette	203	144	.585
87	Al Orth	203	183	.526
88	Charlie Root	201	160	.557
89	Rube Marquard	201	177	.532
90	George Uhle	200	166	.546

Pitchers with 2,000 or more STRIKEOUTS

	PLAYER	SO		PLAYER	SO		PLAYER	SO
1	Nolan Ryan	5511	15	Bob Feller	2581	29	Lefty Grove	2266
2	Steve Carlton	4136	16	Frank Tanana	2566	30	Eddie Plank	2246
3	Tom Seaver	3640	17	Jerry Koosman	2556	31	Tommy John	2245
4	Bert Blyleven	3631	18	Tim Keefe	2521	32	Jim Palmer	2217
5	Don Sutton	3574	19	Christy Mathewson	2502	33	G.C. Pete Alexander	2199
6	Gaylord Perry	3524	20	Don Drysdale	2486	34	Vida Blue	2175
7	Walter Johnson	3509	21	Jim Kaat	2461	35	Camilo Pascual	2167
8	Phil Niekro	3342	22	Sam McDowell	2453	36	Jack Morris	2143
9	Ferguson Jenkins	3192	23	Luis Tiant	2416	37	Charlie Hough	2096
10	Bob Gibson	3117	24	Sandy Koufax	2396	38	Bobo Newsom	2082
11	Jim Bunning	2855	25	Robin Roberts	2357	39	Dazzy Vance	2045
12	Mickey Lolich	2832	26	Early Wynn	2334	40	Dennis Eckersley	2025
13	Cy Young	2803	27	Rube Waddell	2316	41	Rick Reuschel	2015
14	Warren Spahn	2583	28	Juan Marichal	2266	42	Catfish Hunter	2012

Several MVP Award winners, including 1974 National League winner Steve Garvey, have signed this ball.

AWARDS

M.V.P. AWARDS

Selected by the Baseball Writers Association of America

AMERICAN LEAGUE		Year	NATIONAL LEAGUE	
Lefty Grove-Phil.	p	1931	Frankie Frisch-St. L	2b
Jimmie Foxx-Phil.	1b	1932	Chuck Klein-Phil.	of
Jimmie Foxx-Phil.	1b	1933	Carl Hubbell-N.Y.	p
Mickey Cochrane-Det.	c	1934	Dizzy Dean-St. L.	p
Hank Greenberg-Det.	1b	1935	Gabby Hartnett-Chi.	c
Lou Gehrig-N.Y.	1b	1936	Carl Hubbell-N.Y.	p
Charlie Gehringer-Det.	2b	1937	Joe Medwick-St. L.	of
Jimmie Foxx-Bos.	1b	1938	Ernie Lombardi-Cinn.	c
Joe DiMaggio-N.Y.	of	1939	Bucky Walters-Cinn.	p
Hank Greenberg-Det.	1b	1940	Frank McCormick-Cinn.	1b
Joe DiMaggio-N.Y.	of	1941	Dolph Camilli-Bkn.	1b

AMERICAN LEAGUE		Year	NATIONAL LEAGUE	
Joe Gordon-N.Y.	2b	1942	Mort Cooper-St. L.	p
Spud Chandler-N.Y.	p	1943	Stan Musial-St. L.	of
Hal Newhouser-Det.	p	1944	Marty Marion-St. L.	ss
Hal Newhouser-Det.	p	1945	Phil Cavarretta-Chi.	1b
Ted Williams-Bos.	of	1946	Stan Musial-St. L.	1b
Joe DiMaggio-N.Y.	of	1947	Bob Elliott-Bos.	3b
Lou Boudreau-Cleve.	ss	1948	Stan Musial-St. L.	of
Ted Williams-Bos.	of	1949	Jackie Robinson-Bkn.	2b
Phil Rizzuto-N.Y.	ss	1950	Jim Konstanty-Phil.	p
Yogi Berra-N.Y	c	1951	Roy Campanella-Bos.	c
Bobby Shantz-Phil.	p	1952	Hank Sauer-Chi.	of
Al Rosen-Cleve.	3b	1953	Roy Campanella-Bkn.	c
Yogi Berra-N.Y.	c	1954	Willie Mays-N.Y.	of
Yogi Berra-N.Y.	c	1955	Roy Campanella-Bkn.	c
Mickey Mantle-N.Y.	of	1956	Don Newcombe-Bkn.	p
Mickey Mantle-N.Y.	of	1957	Hank Aaron-Mil.	of
Jackie Jensen.-Bos.	of	1958	Ernie Banks-Chi.	ss
Nellie Fox-Chi.	2b	1959	Ernie Banks-Chi.	ss
Roger Maris-N.Y.	of	1960	Dick Groat-Pitt.	ss
Roger Maris-N.Y.	of	1961	Frank Robinson-Cinn.	of
Mickey Mantle-N.Y.	of	1962	Maury Wills-L.A.	ss
Ellie Howard- N.Y.	c	1963	Sandy Koufax-L.A.	p
Brooks Robinson-Balt.	3b	1964	Ken Boyer-St. L.	3b
Zoilo Versalles-Minn.	ss	1965	Willie Mays-S.F.	of
Frank Robinson-Balt.	of	1966	Roberto Clemente-Pitt.	of
Carl Yastrzemski-Bos.	of	1967	Orlando Cepeda-St. L.	1b
Denny McLain-Det.	p	1968	Bob Gibson-St. L.	p
Harmon Killebrew-Minn.	1b-3b	1969	Willie McCovey-S.F.	1b
Boog Powell-Balt.	1b	1970	Johnny Bench-Cinn.	c
Vida Blue-Oak.	p	1971	Joe Torre-St. L.	3b
Dick Allen-Chi.	1b	1972	Johnny Bench.-Cinn.	c
Reggie Jackson-Oak.	of	1973	Pete Rose-Cinn.	of
Jeff Burroughs-Tex.	of	1974	Steve Garvey-L.A.	1b
Fred Lynn-Bos.	of	1975	Joe Morgan-Cinn.	2b
Thurman Munson-N.Y.	c	1976	Joe Morgan-Cinn.	2b
Rod Carew-Minn.	1b	1977	George Foster-Cinn.	of
Jim Rice-Bos.	of	1978	Dave Parker-Pitt.	of
Don Baylor-Cal.	of	1979	Willie Stargell-Pitt.	1b
			Keith Hernandez-St. L.	1b
George Brett-K.C.	3b	1980	Mike Schmidt-Phil.	3b
Rollie Fingers-Mil.	p	1981	Mike Schmidt-Phil.	3b
Robin Yount-Mil.	ss	1982	Dale Murphy-Atl.	of
Cal Ripken-Balt.	ss	1983	Dale Murphy-Atl.	of
Willie Hernandez-Det.	p	1984	Ryne Sandberg-Chi.	2b
Don Mattingly-N.Y.	1b	1985	Willie McGee-St. L.	of
Roger Clemens-Bos.	p	1986	Mike Schmidt-Phil.	3b
George Bell-Tor.	of	1987	Andre Dawson-Chi.	of
Jose Canseco-Oak.	of	1988	Kirk Gibson-L.A.	of
Robin Yount-Mil.	of	1989	Kevin Mitchell-S.F.	3b
Rickey Henderson-Oak.	of	1990	Barry Bonds-Pitt.	of
Cal Ripken-Balt	ss	1991	Terry Pendleton-Atl.	3b

TRIPLE CROWN WINNERS

1878	Paul Hines-Prov. (NL)	1933	Chuck Klein-Phil. (NL)
1894	Hugh Duffy-Bos. (NL)	1934	Lou Gehrig-N.Y. (AL)
1901	Nap Lajoie-Phil. (AL)	1937	Joe Medwick-St. L. (NL)
1909	Ty Cobb-Det. (AL)	1942	Ted Williams-Bos. (AL)
1912	Heinie Zimmerman-Chi. (NL)	1947	Ted Williams-Bos. (AL)
1922	Rogers Hornsby-St. L. (NL)	1956	Mickey Mantle-N.Y. (AL)
1925	Rogers Hornsby-St. L. (NL)	1966	Frank Robinson-Balt. (AL)
1933	Jimmie Foxx-Phil. (AL)	1967	Carl Yastrzemski-Bos. (AL)

CY YOUNG MEMORIAL AWARDS

Year	MAJOR LEAGUES
1956	Don Newcombe-Bkn. (N)
1957	Warren Spahn-Mil. (N)
1958	Bob Turley-N.Y. (A)
1959	Early Wynn-Chi. (A)
1960	Vern Law-Pitt. (N)
1961	Whitey Ford-N.Y. (A)
1962	Don Drysdale-L.A. (N)
1963	Sandy Koufax-L.A. (N)
1964	Dean Chance-L.A. (A)
1965	Sandy Koufax-L.A. (N)
1966	Sandy Koufax-L.A. (N)

AMERICAN LEAGUE	Year	NATIONAL LEAGUE
Jim Lonborg-Bos.	1967	Mike McCormick-S.F.
Denny McLain-Det.	1968	Bob Gibson-St.L.
Mike Cuellar-Balt.	1969	Tom Seaver-N.Y.
Denny McLain-Det. (tie)		
Jim Perry-Minn.	1970	Bob Gibson-St. L.
Vida Blue-Oak.	1971	Ferguson Jenkins-Chi.
Gaylord Perry-Cleve.	1972	Steve Carlton-Phil.
Jim Palmer-Balt.	1973	Tom Seaver-N.Y.
Catfish Hunter-Oak.	1974	Mike Marshall-L.A.
Jim Palmer-Balt.	1975	Tom Seaver-N.Y.
Jim Palmer-Balt.	1976	Randy Jones-S.D.
Sparky Lyle-N.Y.	1977	Steve Carlton-Phil.
Ron Guidry-N.Y.	1978	Gaylord Perry-S.D.
Mike Flanagan-Balt.	1979	Bruce Sutter-Chi.
Steve Stone-Balt.	1980	Steve Carlton-Phil.
Rollie Fingers-Mil.	1981	Fernando Valenzuela-L.A.
Pete Vuckovich-Mil.	1982	Steve Carlton-Phil.
LaMarr Hoyt-Chi.	1983	John Denny-Phil.
Willie Hernandez-Det.	1984	Rick Sutcliffe-Chi.
Bret Saberhagen-K.C.	1985	Dwight Gooden-N.Y.
Roger Clemens-Bos.	1986	Mike Scott-Hou.
Roger Clemens-Bos.	1987	Steve Bedrosian-Phil.
Frank Viola-Minn.	1988	Orel Hershiser-L.A.
Bret Saberhagen-K.C.	1989	Mark Davis-S.D.
Bob Welch-Oak.	1990	Doug Drabek-Pitt.
Roger Clemens-Bos.	1991	Tom Glavine-Atl.

Rookie of the Year Awards

AMERICAN LEAGUE		Year	NATIONAL LEAGUE	
Combined Selection		1947	Jackie Robinson-Bkn.	1b
Combined Selection		1948	Al Dark-Bos.	ss
Roy Sievers-St. L.	of	1949	Don Newcombe-Bkn.	p
Walt Dropo-Bos.	1b	1950	Sam Jethroe-Bos.	of
Gil McDougald-N.Y.	3b	1951	Willie Mays-N.Y.	of
Harry Byrd-Phil.	p	1952	Joe Black-Bkn.	p
Harvey Kuenn-Det.	ss	1953	Jim Gilliam-Bkn.	2b
Bob Grim-N.Y.	p	1954	Wally Moon-St. L.	of
Herb Score-Cleve.	p	1955	Bill Virdon-St. L.	of
Luis Aparicio-Chi.	ss	1956	Frank Robinson-Cinn.	of
Tony Kubek-N.Y.	inf-of	1957	Jack Sanford-Phil.	p
Albie Peason-Wash.	of	1958	Orlando Cepeda-S.F.	1b
Bob Allison-Wash.	of	1959	Willie McCovey-S.F.	1b
Ron Hansen-Balt.	ss	1960	Frank Howard-L.A.	of
Don Schwall-Bos.	p	1961	Billy Williams-Chi.	of
Tommy Tresh-N.Y.	of-ss	9162	Ken Hubbs-Chi.	2b
Gary Peters-Chi.	p	1963	Pete Rose-Cinn.	2b
Tony Oliva-Minn.	of	1964	Dick Allen-Phil.	3b
Curt Blefary-Balt.	of	1965	Jim Lefebvre-L.A.	3b
Tommie Agee-Chi.	of	1966	Tommy Helms-Cinn.	3b
Rod Carew-Minn.	2b	1967	Tom Seaver-N.Y.	p
Stan Bahnsen-N.Y.	p	1968	Johnny Bench-Cinn.	c
Lou Piniella-K.C.	of	1969	Ted Sizemore-L.A.	2b
Thurman Munson-N.Y.	c	1970	Carl Morton-Mont.	p
Chris Chambliss-Cleve.	1b	1971	Earl Williams-Atl.	c
Carlton Fisk-Bos.	c	1972	Jon Matlack-N.Y.	p
Al Bumbry-Balt.	of	1973	Gary Matthews-S.F.	of
Mike Hargrove-Tex.	1b	1974	Bake McBride-St.L.	of
Fred Lynn-Bos.	of	1975	John Montefusco-S.F.	p

AMERICAN LEAGUE		Year	NATIONAL LEAGUE	
Mark Fidrych-Det.	p	1976	Butch Metzger-S.D.	p
			Pat Zachry-Cinn. (tie)	p
Eddie Murray-Balt.	dh	1977	Andre Dawson-Mont.	of
Lou Whitaker-Det.	2b	1978	Bob Horner-Atl.	3b
Alfredo Griffin-Tor.	ss	1979	Rick Sutcliffe-L.A.	p
Joe Charboneau-Cleve.	of	1980	Steve Howe-L.A.	p
Dave Righetti-N.Y.	p	1981	Fernando Valenzuela-L.A.	p
Cal Ripken-Balt.	ss-3b	1982	Steve Sax-L.A.	2b
Ron Kittle-Chi.	of	1983	Darryl Strawberry-N.Y.	of
Alvin Davis-Seat.	1b	1984	Dwight Gooden-N.Y.	p
Ozzie Guillen-Chi.	ss	1985	Vince Coleman-St.L.	of
Jose Canseco-Oak.	of	1986	Todd Worrell-St. L.	p
Mark McGwire-Oak.	1b	1987	Benito Santiago-S.D.	c
Walt Weiss-Oak.	ss	1988	Chris Sabo-Cinn.	3b
Gregg Olson-Balt.	p	1989	Jerome Walton-Chi.	of
Sandy Alomar-Cleve.	c	1990	Dave Justice-Atl.	of
Chuck Knoblauch-Minn.	2b	1991	Jeff Bagwell-Hou.	3b

Autographed Game Baseballs

Sandy Koufax used this ball during his no-hitter June 4, 1964, against the Phillies.

Nolan Ryan used this ball during his seventh no-hitter, May 1, 1991, against Toronto.

Game-used baseballs, although extremely valuable due to their rarity and historical significance, are primarily sought only by specialized collectors. Because dozens of baseballs are generally used in a major league game and there are no definitive markings to separate a store-bought baseball from those actually used at the ballpark, it is impossible to authenticate a game ball.

This ball from July 15, 1988, is from the 2,000th game Bob Boone caught.

Game balls are generally presented to the prominent player of the event, often the pitcher, and only when there has been a major achievement or milestone associated with the event. Otherwise, the umpires usually end up stashing them away for future use, or giving them back to the home team for batting practice.

Nolan Ryan used this ball on victim #3,509, tying Walter Johnson in career strikeouts.

Indians pitcher Bob Feller used this ball for his third no-hitter, on July 1, 1951.

Pete Rose hit this ball to break the National League hit record.

The game's most eminent baseballs reside in the National Baseball Hall of Fame or in the personal collections of those directly associated with the game. Few game baseballs ever find their way into the market, unless they are purchased from the initial source. With authenticity always a factor, and a limited access to purchase these relics, few collectors venture into this hobby segment.

From left to right: the ball Yankee Hall of Famer Mickey Mantle hit for home run #522; a ball used by Brooklyn Dodger pitcher Carl Erskine in the third game of the 1953 World Series, when he struck out 14 New York Yankees; a 1909 ball, the last ball pitched by Hall of Famer Jack Chesbro.

Autographed Celebrity Baseballs

President Franklin D. Roosevelt throws out the first ball.

"It is a pastime which is worth any man's while, so banish the blues by going to a ball game and waking up with the enthusiasts of the bleachers who permit no man to be grouchy among them."

President William Howard Taft

It is often difficult to establish when a boy becomes a man, or when dawn becomes morning. It is equally puzzling to explain our fascination with baseball. Some anthropologists even suggest our fascination stems from the game's derivation from ancient religious rites. Others claim it is a testament to our youth. Regardless of baseball's origin, our fascination with it may simply be attributable to its parable — the objective of each team is to win by scoring more runs than the

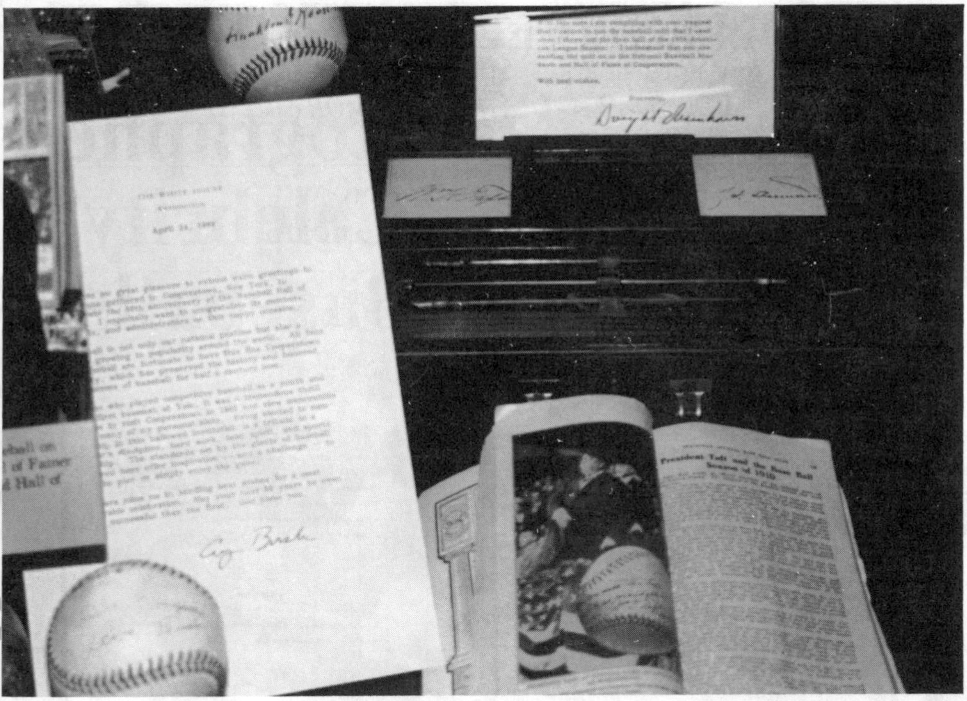

The Baseball Hall of Fame has a presidential showcase.

opponent, a goal that equates in concept to almost every objective in life.

Baseball is a game for men and women of all walks of life; a baseball can be a commemorative of their enthusiasm and achievements. President Taft once stated, "The game of baseball is a clean, straight game, and it summons to its presence everybody who enjoys clean, straight athletics. It furnishes amusement to thousands and thousands, and I like to go for two reasons — first, because I enjoy it myself, and second, because if by the presence of the temporary chief magistrate such a healthful amusement can be encouraged, I want to encourage it."

Presidents Ronald Reagan and George Bush signed the ball at left; President Jimmy Carter signed the ball at right.

COLLECTIBLES UNLIMITED

• New York's Largest Sports Memorabilia Store •

"A LEADER IN QUALITY MEMORABILIA"

718-507-2626 718-507-2626

An Opportunity To Own A Rare Piece Of * Americana *

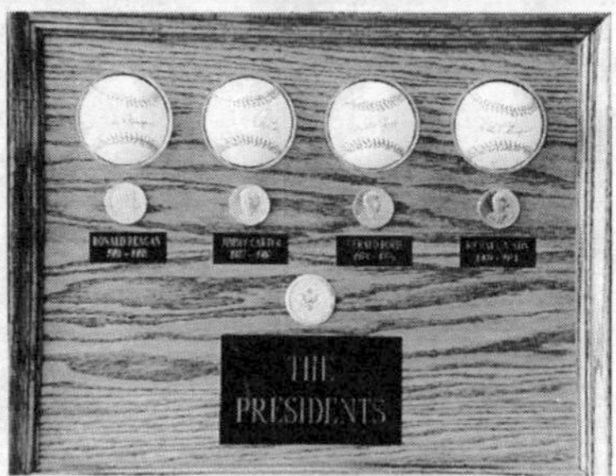

All 4 Living Past Presidents Reagan - Carter - Ford - Nixon.

It is exquisitely mounted & framed & includes Presidential commemorative coins with the Presidential Seal.

Limited Edition Of 12 Pieces.

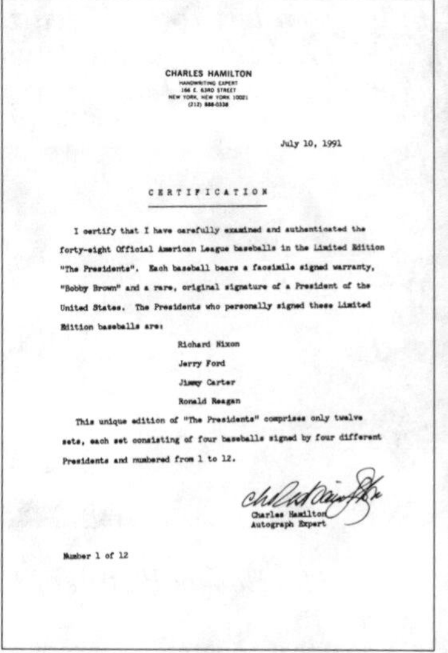

CHARLES HAMILTON
HANDWRITING EXPERT
166 E. 63RD STREET
NEW YORK, NEW YORK 10021
(212) 888-0338

July 10, 1991

CERTIFICATION

I certify that I have carefully examined and authenticated the forty-eight Official American League baseballs in the Limited Edition "The Presidents". Each baseball bears a facsimile signed warranty, "Bobby Brown" and a rare, original signature of a President of the United States. The Presidents who personally signed these Limited Edition baseballs are:

Richard Nixon
Jerry Ford
Jimmy Carter
Ronald Reagan

This unique edition of "The Presidents" comprises only twelve sets, each set consisting of four baseballs signed by four different Presidents and numbered from 1 to 12.

Charles Hamilton
Autograph Expert

Number 1 of 12

* Comes with a numbered letter of authencity from Charles Hamilton, autograph expert (Hitler Papers, Howard Hughes Will). "Charles Hamilton is the world's acknowledged authority on autographs" - Saturday Evening Post.

— AN INCREDIBLE INVESTMENT AT —
$2,995.00 PPD.

COLLECTIBLES UNLIMITED

63-48 Woodhaven Blvd.
Rego Park, NY 11374
718-507-2626

Add 5% Surcharge for Credit Cards.

Open 7 days
11 a.m. - 7 p.m.

This is an example of an ad from Sports Collectors Digest.

After throwing out the first baseball of the 1910 season, President Taft was later requested by Walter Johnson, the man who retrieved the ball, for his autograph. Taft complied and sent the ball back the very next day with the following inscription:
"For Walter Johnson, With the hope that he may continue to be as formidable as in yesterday's game. William H. Taft."

Baseball, as a popular medium for autographing, has spread to other occupational facets, too, including entrepreneurs, politicians, entertainers, and other sports figures. The Baseball Hall of Fame was even presented with an autographed baseball signed by the astronauts of the space shuttle "Atlantis" after their December 1988 mission. How about that?

Balls from left to right feature signatures of members of the Philadelphia Flyers hockey team; Olympic gold medalist skater Scott Hamilton; Secretary of State Henry Kissinger; and football great Joe Montana.

Presidents Dwight D. Eisenhower and John F. Kennedy

Boxing great Carmen Basilio

Boxing great Joe Frazier

Key Player/Individual Index

Includes name, years in the major leagues, teams played for, or associations.

Notes:

Players' names are those for which they are most widely known by during their careers.

Players' careers may have been interrupted due to military obligations (1940s) or injuries.

Some players may have also served as manager, or player/manager, during or following their careers.

Some players may have been on the roster but did not play.

Abbreviations: MVP = Most Valuable Player, HOF = Hall of Fame, Cy Young = Cy Young Award Winner, ROY = Rookie of the Year.

Members of the Baseball Hall of Fame have been included.

A

Aaron, Hank: 1954-76; Mil. 1954-65, Atl. 1966-74, Mil. 1975-76; MVP 1957, HOF.
Aase, Don: 1977-82; Bos. 1977, Cal. 1978-84, Balt. 1985-88, Mets 1989, L.A. 1990.
Abbott, Glenn: 1973-84; Oak. 1973-76, Seat. 1977-83, Det. 1983-84.
Abernathy, Ted: 1955-60, 1963-72; Wash. 1955-60, Cleve. 1963-64, Cubs 1965-66, Atl. 1967, Cinn. 1967-68, Cubs 1969-70, St.L. 1970, K.C. 1970-71.
Adair, Jerry: 1958-70; Balt. 1958-66, White Sox 1966-67, Bos. 1967-68, K.C. 1969-70.
Adams, Ace: 1941-46; N.Y. (N) 1941-46.
Adams, Bobby: 1946-59; Cinn. 1946-55, White Sox 1955, Balt. 1956, Cubs 1957-59.
Adams, Glenn: 1975-82; S.F. 1975-76, Minn. 1977-81, Tor. 1982.
Adams, Sparky: 1922-34; Cubs 1922-27, Pitt. 1928-29, St.L. 1930-33, Cinn. 1933-34.
Adcock, Joe: 1950-66; Cinn. 1950-52, Mil. 1953-62, Cleve. 1963, L.A. (A) 1964, Cal. 1965-66.
Agee, Tommie: 1962-73; Cleve. 1962-64, White Sox 1965-67, Mets 1968-72, Hou. 1973, St.L. 1973.
Aguayo, Luis: 1980-89; Phil. 1980-88, Yankees 1988, Cleve. 1989.
Aguirre, Hank: 1955-70; Cleve. 1955-57, Det. 1958-67, L.A. 1968, Cubs 1969-70.
Aikens, Willie: 1977-85; Cal. 1977-79, K.C. 1980-83, Tor. 1984-85.
Ainsmith, Eddie: 1910-24; Wash: 1910-18, Det. 1919-21, St.L. (N) 1921-23, Bro. 1923, N.Y. (N) 1924.
Aker, Jack: 1964-74; K.C. 1964-67, Oak. 1968, Seat. 1969, Yankees 1969-72, Cubs 1972-73, Atl. 1974, Mets 1974.
Alexander, Dale: 1929-33; Det. 1929-32, Bos. (A) 1932-33.
Alexander, Doyle: 1971 to present; L.A. 1971, Balt. 1972-76, Yankees 1976, Texas 1977-79, Atl. 1980, S.F. 1981, Yankees 1982-83, Tor. 1983-86, Atl. 1986-87, Det. 1987-present.
Alexander, Gary: 1975-81; S.F. 1975-77, Oak. 1978, Cleve. 1978-80, Pitt. 1981.
Alexander, Grover Cleveland: 1911-30; Phil. 1911-17, Cubs 1918-26, St.L. 1926-29, Phil. 1930; HOF.
Alexander, Matt: 1973-81: Cubs 1973-74, Oak. 1975-77, Pitt. 1978-81.

Allen, Bernie: 1962-73; Minn. 1962-66, Wash. 1967-71, Yankees 1972-73, Mont. 1973.
Allen, Dick: 1963-77; Phil. 1963-69, St.L. 1970, L.A. 1971, White Sox 1972-74, Phil 1975-76, Oak. 1977; ROY 1964, MVP 1972.
Allen, Ethan: 1926-38; Cinn. 1926-30, N.Y. (N) 1930-32, St.L. (N) 1933, Phil. (N) 1934-36, Cubs 1936, St.L. (A) 1937-38.
Allen, Johnny: 1932-44; Yankees 1932-35, Cleve. 1936-40, St.L. 1941, Bro. 1941-43, N.Y. (N) 1943-44.
Allen, Neil: 1979-89; Mets 1979-83, St.L. 1983-85, Yankees 1985, White Sox 1986-87, Yankees 1987-88, Cleve. 1989.
Alley, Gene: 1963-73; Pitt. 1963-73.
Allison, Bob: 1958-70; Wash. 1958-60, Minn. 1961-70; ROY 1959.
Almon, Bill: 1974-88; S.D. 1974-79, Mont. 1980, Mets 1980, White Sox 1981-82, Oak. 1983-84, Pitt. 1985-87, Mets 1987, Phil. 1988.
Alomar, Roberto: 1988 to present; S.D. 1988-90, Tor. 1991.
Alomar, Sandy: 1964-78; Mil. 1964-65, Atl. 1966, Mets 1967, White Sox 1967-69, Cal. 1969-74, Yankees 1974-76, Texas 1977-78.
Alomar, Sandy Jr.: 1988 to present; S.D. 1988-89, Cleve. 1990-present.
Alou, Felipe: 1958-74; S.F. 1958-63, Mil. 1964-65, Atl. 1966-69, Oak. 1970-71, Yankees 1971-73, Mont. 1973, Mil. 1974.
Alou, Jesus: 1963-79; S.F. 1963-68, Hou. 1969-73, Oak. 1973-74, Mets 1975, Hou. 1978-79.
Alou, Matty: 1960-74; S.F. 1960-65, Pitt. 1966-70, St.L. 1971-72, Oak. 1972, Yankees 1973, St.L. 1973, S.D. 1974.
Alston, Walter: manager 1954-76; Bro. 1954-57, L.A. 1958-76.; HOF.
Altman, George: 1959-67; Cubs 1959-62, St.L. 1963, Mets 1964, Cubs 1965-67.
Alvis, Max: 1962-70; Cleve. 1962-69, Mil. 1970.
Amaro, Ruben: 1958-69; St.L. 1958, Phil. 1960-65, Yankees 1966-68, Cal. 1969.
Amoros, Sandy: 1954-60; Bro. 1954-57, L.A. 1959-60, Det. 1960.
Andersen, Larry: 1975 to present; Cleve. 1975-79, Seat. 1981-82, Phil. 1983-86, Hou. 1986-90, Bos. 1990-present.
Anderson, Mike: 1971-79; Phil. 1971-75, St.L. 1976-77, Balt. 1978, Phil. 1979.
Anderson, Sparky: manager 1970 to present; Cinn. 1970-78, Det. 1979-present.
Andrews, Mike: 1966-73; Bos. 1966-70, White Sox 1971-73, Oak. 1973.
Andrews, Nate: 1937-46: St.L. (N) 1937, 1939, Cleve. 1940-41, Bos. (N) 1943-45, Cinn. 1946, N.Y. (N). 1946.
Andujar, Joaquin: 1976-88; Hou. 1976-81, St.L. 1981-85, Oak. 1986-87, Hou. 1988.
Anson, Cap: 1871-97; Rok. 1871, Ath. 1872-75, Cubs 1876-97; HOF.
Antonelli, Johnny: 1948-61; Bos. 1948-50; Mil. 1953, N.Y. (N) 1954-57, S.F. 1958-60, Cleve. 1961, Mil. 1961.
Aparicio, Luis: 1956-73; White Sox 1953-62, Balt. 1963-67, White Sox 1968-70, Bos. 1971-73; ROY 1956, HOF.
Appling, Luke: 1930-50; White Sox 1930-1950; HOF
Armas, Tony: 1976-89; Pitt. 1976, Oak. 1977-82, Bos. 1983-86, Cal. 1987-89.
Armstrong, Jack: 1988 to present; Cinn. 1988-1991.
Arnovich, Morrie: 1936-41, 1946; Phil. 1936-40, Cinn. 1940, N.Y. (N) 1941, N.Y. (N) 1946.
Arroyo, Luis: 1955-63; St.L. 1955, Pitt. 1956-57, Cinn. 1959, Yankees 1960-63.
Ashburn, Richie: 1948-62; Phil. 1948-59, Cubs 1960-61, Mets 1962.
Ashby, Alan: 1973-89; Cleve. 1973-76, Tor. 1977-78, Hou. 1979-89.
Aspromonte, Bob: 1956, 1960-71; Bro. 1956, L.A. 1960-61, Hou. 1962-68, Atl. 1969-70, Mets 1971.
Atwell, Toby: 1952-56; Cubs 1952-53, Pitt. 1953-56, Mil. 1956.
Auerbach, Rick: 1971-81; Mil. 1971-73, L.A. 1974-76, Cinn. 1977-80, Seat. 1981.
Averill, Earl: 1929-41; Cleve. 1929-39, Det. 1939-40, Bos. 1941.; HOF
Avila, Bobby: 1949-59; Cleve. 1949-58, Balt. 1959, Bos. 1959, Mil. 1959.

Ayala, Benny: 1974, 1976-86; Mets 1974, 1976, Balt. 1979-84, Cleve. 1985.
Azcue, Joe: 1960-72; Cinn. 1960, K.C. 1962-63, Cleve. 1963-69, Bos. 1969, Cal. 1969-72, Mil. 1972.

B

Backman, Wally: 1980 to present; Mets 1980-88, Minn. 1989, Pitt. 1990, Phil. 1991.
Bagby, Jim Sr.: 1912, 1916-23; Cinn. 1912, Cleve. 1916-22, Pitt. 1923.
Bagby, Jim Jr.: 1938-47; Bos. (A) 1938-40, Cleve. 1941-45, Bos. (A) 1946, Pitt. 1947.
Bagwell, Jeff: 1991-present; Hou. 1991-presnt; ROY 1991.
Bahnsen, Stan: 1966-82; Yankees 1966-71, White Sox 1972-75, Oak. 1975-77, Montreal 1977-81, Cal. 1982, Phil. 1982; ROY 1968.
Bailey, Bob: 1962-78; Pitt. 1962-66, L.A. 1967-68, Mont. 1969-75, Cinn. 1976-77, Bos. 1977-78.
Bailey, Ed: 1953-66; Cinn. 1953-61, S.F. 1961-63, Mil. 1964, S.F. 1965, Cubs 1965, Cal. 1966.
Bailor, Bob: 1975-85; Balt. 1975-76, Tor. 1977-80, Mets 1981-83, L.A. 1984-85.
Baines, Harold: 1980 to present; White Sox 1980-89; Texas 1989-90, Oak. 1990-present.
Bair, Doug: 1976-90; Pitt. 1976, Oak. 1977, Cinn. 1978-81, St.L. 1981-83, Det. 1983-85, St.L. 1985, Oak. 1986, Phil. 1987, Tor. 1988, Pitt. 1989-90.
Baker, Dusty: 1968-86; Atl. 1968-75, L.A. 1976-83, S.F. 1984, Oak. 1985-86.
Baker, Floyd: 1943-55: St.L. (A) 1943-44, White Sox 1945-51, Wash. 1952-53, Bos. (A) 1953-54, Phil. (N) 1954-55.
Baker, Frank: 1908-22; Phil. 1908-1914, Yankees 1916-22; HOF.
Baker, Gene: 1953-61; Cubs 1953-57, Pitt. 1957-61.
Balboni, Steve: 1981-90; Yankees 1981-83, K.C. 1984-88, Seat. 1988, Yankees 1989-90.
Bancroft, Dave: 1915-30; Phil. 1915-20, N.Y. (N) 1920-23, Bos. (N) 1924-27, Bro. 1928-29, N.Y. (N) 1930; HOF.
Bando, Chris: 1981-89; Cleve. 1981-88, Det. 1988, Oak. 1989.
Bando, Sal: 1966-81; K.C. 1966-67, Oak. 1968-76, Mil. 1977-81.
Banks, Ernie: 1953-71; Cubs 1953-71; MVP 1958, 1959, HOF.
Bannister, Alan: 1974-85; Phil. 1974-75, White Sox 1976-80, Cleve. 1980-83, Hou. 1984, Texas 1984-85.
Bannister, Floyd: 1977-89; Hou. 1977-78, Seat. 1979-82, White Sox 1983-87, K.C. 1988-89.
Barber, Steve: 1960-74; Balt. 1960-67, Yankees 1967-68, Seat. 1969, Cubs 1970, Atl. 1970-72, Cal. 1972-73, S.F. 1974.
Barfield, Jesse: 1981 to present; Tor. 1981-89, Yankees 1989-present.
Barker, Len: 1976-85, 1987; Texas 1976-78, Cleve. 1979-83, Atl. 1983-85, Mil. 1987.
Barlick, Al; umpire 1940-70; HOF.
Barnes, Jesse: 1915-27; Bos. (N) 1915-17, N.Y. (N) 1918-23, Bos. 1923-25, Bro. 1926-27.
Barrett, Marty: 1982-90; Bos. 1982-90.
Barrett, Red: 1937-40, 1943-49; Cinn. 1937-40, Bos. 1943-45, St.L. 1945-46, Bos. 1947-49.
Barrow, Ed: executive; HOF.
Bartell, Dick: 1927-43, 1946; Pitt. 1927-30, Phil 1931-34, N.Y. (N) 1935-38, Cubs 1939, Det. 1940-41, N.Y. (N), 1941-43, 1946.
Bass, Kevin: 1982 to present; Mil. 1982, Hou. 1982-89, S.F. 1990-present.
Battey, Earl: 1955-67; White Sox 1955-59, Wash. 1960, Minn. 1961-67.
Bauer, Hank: 1948-61; Yankees 1948-59, K.C. 1960-61.
Baumann, Frank: 1955-65; Bos. 1955-59, White Sox 1960-65.
Baumholtz, Frank: 1947-57; Cinn. 1947-49, Cubs 1949-55, Phil. 1956-57.
Baylor, Don: 1970-88; Balt. 1970-75, Oak. 1976, Cal. 1977-82, Yankees 1983-85, Bos. 1986-87, Minn. 1987, Oak. 1988; MVP 1979.
Bearden, Gene: 1947-53; Cleve. 1947-50, Wash. 1950-51, Det. 1951, St.L. 1952, White Sox 1953.
Beauchamp, Jim: 1963-65, 1966-73; St.L. 1963, Hou. 1964-65, Mil. 1965, Atl. 1967, Cinn. 1968-69, Hou. 1970, St.L. 1970-71, Mets 1972-73.
Beckert, Glenn: 1965-75; Cubs 1965-73, S.D. 1974-75.

Beckley, Jake: 1888-07; Pitt. 1888-96, N.Y. (N) 1896-97, Cinn. 1897-03, St.L. 1904-07; HOF.
Bedrosian, Steve: 1981 to present; Atl. 1981-85, Phil. 1986-89, S.F. 1989-90, Minn. 1991.
Belanger, Mark: 1965-82; Balt. 1965-81, L.A. 1982.
Bell, Beau: 1935-41; St.L. 1935-39, Det. 1939, Cleve. 1940-41.
Bell, Buddy: 1972-89; Cleve. 1972-78, Texas 1979-85, Cinn. 1985-88, Hou. 1988, Texas 1989.
Bell, Cool Papa: 1922-50; Negro Leagues; HOF.
Bell, Gary: 1958-69; Cleve. 1958-67, Bos. 1967-68, Seat. 1969, White Sox 1969.
Bell, George: 1981 to present; Tor. 1981-1990, Cubs 1991; MVP 1987.
Bell, Gus: 1950-64; Pitt. 1950-52, Cinn. 1953-61, Mets 1962, Mil. 1962-64.
Bell, Jay: 1986-present; Cleve. 1986-88, Pitt. 1989-present.
Belliard, Rafael: 1982-present; Pitt. 1982-90, Atl. 1991.
Bench, Johnny: 1967-83; Cinn. 1967-83; ROY 1968, MVP 1970, 1972; HOF.
Bender, Chief: 1903-17, 1925; Phil. 1903-1914, Balt. 1915, Phil. 1916-17, Chi. (A) 1925; HOF.
Benedict, Bruce: 1978-89; Atl. 1978-89.
Beniquez, Juan: 1971-88; Bos. 1971-75, Texas 1976-78, Yankees 1979, Seat. 1980, Cal. 1981-85, Balt. 1986, K.C. 1987, Tor. 1987-88.
Benzinger, Todd: 1987-present; Bos. 1987-88, Cinn. 1989-present.
Berenguer, Juan: 1978-present; Mets 1978-80, K.C. 1981, Tor. 1981, Det. 1982-85, S.F. 1986, Minn. 1987-present.
Berg, Mo: 1923-39; Bro. 1923, 1926-30, Cleve. 1931, Wash. 1932-34, Cleve. 1934, Bos. 1935-39.
Berger, Wally: 1930-40; Bos. 1930-37, N.Y. (N) 1937-38, Cinn. 1938-40, Phil 1940.
Bergman, Dave: 1975, 1977-90; Yankees 1975, 1977, Hou. 1978-81, S.F. 1981-83, Det. 1984-90.
Bernazard, Tony: 1979-87; Mont. 1979-80, White Sox 1981-83, Seat. 1983, Cleve. 1984-87, Oak. 1987.
Berra, Yogi: 1946-65; Yankees 1946-63, Mets 1965; MVP 1951, 1954, 1955; HOF.
Berry, Ken: 1962-75; White Sox 1962-70, Cal. 1971-73, Mil. 1974, Cleve. 1975.
Bevacqua, Kurt: 1971-85; Cleve. 1971-72, K.C. 1973, Pitt. 1974, K.C. 1974, Mil. 1975-76, Texas 1977-78, S.D. 1979-80, Pitt. 1981, S.D. 1982-85.
Biancalana, Buddy; 1982-87; K.C. 1982-87, Hou. 1987.
Bibby, Jim: 1972-84; St.L. 1972-73, Texas 1973-75, Cleve. 1975-77, Pitt. 1978-83, Texas 1984.
Bickford, Vern: 1948-54; Bos. 1948-52, Mil. 1953, Balt. 1954.
Biggio, Craig: 1988 to present; Hou. 1988-present.
Biittner, Larry: 1970-83; Wash. 1970-71, Texas 1972-73, Mont. 1974-76, Cubs 1975-80, Cinn. 1981-82, Texas 1983.
Billingham, Jack: 1968-80; L.A. 1968, Hou. 1969-71, Cinn. 1972-77, Det. 1978-80, Bos. 1980.
Black, Bud: 1981-present; Seat. 1981, K.C. 1982-88, Cleve. 1988-90, Tor. 1990, S.F. 1991.
Blackwell, Ewell: 1942, 1946-53, 1955; Cinn. 1942, 1946-52, Yankees 1952-53, K.C. 1955.
Blackwell, Tim: 1974-83: Bos. 1974-75, Phil. 1976-77, Mont. 1977, Cubs 1978-81, Mont. 1982-83.
Blair, Paul: 1964-80; Balt. 1964-1976, Yankees 1977-79, Cinn. 1979, Yankees 1980.
Blanchard, Johnny: 1955-65; Yankees 1955-65, K.C. 1965, Mil. 1965.
Blanks, Larvell: 1972-80: Atl. 1972-75, Cleve. 1976-78, Texas 1979, Atl. 1980.
Blanton, Cy: 1934-42; Pitt. 1934-39, Phil 1940-42.
Blasingame, Don: 1955-66; St.L. 1955-59, S.F. 1960-61, Cinn. 1961-63, Wash. 1964-66, K.C. 1966.
Blass, Steve: 1964-74; Pitt. 1964-74.
Blefary, Curt: 1965-72; Balt. 1965-68; Hou. 1969, Yankees 1970-71, Oak. 1971-72, S.D. 1972; ROY 1965.
Blomberg, Ron: 1969, 1971-76, 1978; Yankees 1969, 1971-76, White Sox 1978.
Blue, Vida: 1969-86; Oak. 1969-77, S.F. 1978-81, K.C. 1982-83, S.F. 1985-86; MVP 1971, Cy Young 1971.
Blyleven, Bert: 1970-1991; Minn. 1970-76, Texas 1976-77, Pitt. 1978-80, Cleve. 1981-85, Minn. 1985-88, Cal. 1989-91.
Boccabella, John: 1963-74; Cubs 1963-68, Mont. 1969-73, S.F. 1974.

Bochte, Bruce: 1974-86; Cal. 1974-77, Cleve. 1977, Seat. 1978-82, Oak. 1984-86.
Boddicker, Mike: 1980 to present; Balt. 1980-88, Bos. 1988-90, K.C. 1991.
Boggs, Wade: 1982 to present; Bos. 1982-present.
Bolling, Frank: 1954-66; Det. 1954-60, Mil. 1961-65, Atl. 1966.
Bonds, Barry: 1986 to present; Pitt. 1986-present; MVP 1990.
Bonds, Bobby: 1968-81; S.F. 1968-74, Yankees 1975, Cal. 1976-77, White Sox 1978, Texas 1978, Cleve. 1979, St.L. 1980, Cubs 1981.
Bonham, Ernie: 1940-49; Yankees 1940-46, Pitt. 1947-49.
Bonilla, Bobby: 1986 to present; White Sox 1986, Pitt. 1986-present.
Bonnell, Barry: 1977-86; Atl. 1977-79, Tor. 1980-83, Seat. 1984-86.
Boone, Bob: 1972-90; Phil. 1972-81, Cal. 1982-88, K.C. 1989-90.
Boone, Ray: 1948-60; Cleve. 1948-53, Det. 1953-58, White Sox 1958-59, K.C. 1959, Mil. 1959-60, Bos. 1960.
Borbon, Pedro: 1969-80; Cal. 1969, Cinn. 1970-79, S.F. 1979, St.L. 1980.
Borgmann, Glenn: 1972-80; Minn. 1972-79, White Sox 1980.
Borowy, Hank: 1942-51; Yankees 1942-45, Cubs 1945-48, Phil 1949-50, Pitt. 1950, Det. 1950-51.
Bosley, Thad: 1977-90; Cal. 1977, White Sox 1978-80, Mil. 1981, Seat. 1982, Cubs 1983-86, K.C. 1987-88, Cal. 1988, Texas 1989-90.
Bosman, Dick: 1966-76; Wash. 1966-71, Texas 1972-73, Cleve. 1973-75, Oak. 1975-76.
Boswell, Ken: 1967-77; Mets 1967-74, Hou. 1975-77.
Bottomley, Jim: 1922-37; St.L. (N) 1922-32, Cinn. 1933-35, St.L. (A) 1936-37; MVP 1928, HOF.
Boudreau, Lou: 1938-52; Cleve. 1938-50, Bos. 1951-52; MVP 1948, HOF.
Bouton, Jim: 1962-70, 1978; Yankees 1962-68, Seat. 1969, Hou. 1969-70, Atl. 1978.
Bowa, Larry: 1970-85; Phil. 1970-81, Cubs 1982-85, Mets 1985.
Boyd, Oil Can: 1982-present; Bos. 1982-89, Mont. 1990-91, Texas 1991.
Boyer, Clete: 1955-57, 1959-71; K.C. 1955-57, Yankees 1959-66, Atl. 1967-71.
Boyer, Ken: 1955-69; St.L. 1955-65, Mets 1966-67, White Sox 1967-68, L.A. 1968-69; MVP 1964.
Branca, Ralph: 1944-54, 1956; Bro. 1944-53, Det. 1953-54, Yankees 1954, Bro. 1956.
Bradford, Buddy: 1966-76; White Sox 1966-70; Cleve. 1970-71; Cinn. 1971, White Sox 1972-75, St.L. 1975, White Sox 1976.
Braggs, Glenn: 1986-present; Mil. 1986-90, Cinn. 1990-present.
Brandt, Jackie: 1956, 1958-67; St.L (N) 1956, N.Y. (N) 1956, S.F. 1958-59, Balt. 1960-65, Phil. 1966-67, Hou. 1967.
Braun, Steve: 1971-85; Minn. 1971-76, Seat. 1977, K.C. 1978-80, Tor. 1980, St.L. 1981-85.
Braxton, Garland: 1921-31, 1933; Bos. 1921-22, Yankees 1925-26, Wash. 1927-30, White Sox 1930-31, St.L. (A) 1931, 1933.
Bream, Sid: 1983-present; L.A. 1983-85, Pitt. 1985-90, Atl. 1991.
Brecheen, Harry: 1940, 1943-53; St.L. 1940, 1943-53.
Brenly, Bob: 1981-89; S.F. 1981-88, Tor. 1989, S.F. 1989.
Bresnahan, Roger: 1897, 1900-15; Wash. 1897, Chi. (N) 1900, Balt. 1901-02, N.Y. (N) 1902-1908, St.L. 1909-1912, Chi. (N) 1913-15; HOF.
Bressoud, Ed: 1956-67; N.Y. (N) 1956-57, S.F. 1958-61, Bos. 1962-65, Mets 1967, St.L. 1967.
Brett, George: 1973 to present; K.C. 1983-present; MVP 1980.
Brett, Ken: 1967-81; Bos. 1967-71, Mil. 1972, Phil 1973, Pitt. 1974-75, Yankees 1976, White Sox 1976-77, Cal. 1977-78, Minn. 1979, L.A. 1979, K.C. 1980-81.
Brewer, Jim: 1960-76; Cubs 1960-63, L.A. 1964-75, Cal. 1975-76.
Brewer, Tom: 1954-61; Bos. 1954-61.
Bridges, Rocky: 1951-61; Bro. 1951-52, Cinn. 1953-57, Wash. 1957-58, Det. 1959-60, Cleve. 1960, St.L. 1960, L.A. 1961.
Bridges, Tommy: 1930-46; Det. 1930-46.
Briles, Nelson: 1965-78; St.L. 1965-70, Pitt. 1970-73, K.C. 1974-75, Texas 1976-77, Balt. 1977-78.
Briggs, Johnny: 1964-75; Phil. 1964-71, Mil. 1971-75, Minn. 1975.

Brinkman, Ed: 1961-75; Wash. 1961-70, Det. 1971-74, St.L. 1975, Texas 1975, Yankees 1975.
Brock, Greg: 1982-present; L.A. 1982-86, Mil. 1987-present.
Brock, Lou: 1961-79; Cubs 1961-64, St.L. 1964-79; HOF.
Brohamer, Jack: 1972-80; Cleve. 1972-75, White Sox 1976-77, Bos. 1978-80, Cleve. 1980.
Brooks, Hubie: 1980 to present; Mets 1980-84, Mont. 1985-89, L.A. 1990-present.
Brouthers, Dan: 1879-96, 1904; Tro. 1879-80, Buf. 1881-85, Det. 1886-88, Bos. 1889-1891, Bro. 1892-93, Balt. 1894-95, Lou. 1895, Phil. 1896, N.Y. (N) 1904; HOF.
Brown, Bobby: 1946-54; Yankees 1946-54.
Brown, Chris: 1984-89; S.F. 1984-87, S.D. 1987-88, Det. 1989.
Brown, Jimmy: 1937-43; 1946; St.L. 1937-43; Pitt. 1946.
Brown, Larry: 1963-74; Cleve. 1963-71, Oak. 1971-72, Balt. 1973, Texas 1974.
Brown, Ollie: 1965-77; S.F. 1965-68, S.D. 1969-72, Oak. 1972, Mil. 1972-73, Hou. 1974, Phil. 1974-77.
Brown, Three Finger: 1903-16; St.L. 1903, Chi. (N) 1904-1912, Cinn. 1913, St.L. 1914, Bro. 1914, Chi. (F) 1915, Chi. (N) 1916.
Brunansky, Tom: 1981 to present; Cal. 1981, Minn. 1982-88, St.L. 1988-90, Bos. 1990-present.
Bruton, Bill: 1953-64; Mil. 1953-60, Det. 1961-64.
Bryant, Clay: 1935-40; Cubs 1935-40.
Bryant, Ron: 1967-75; S.F. 1967-74, St.L. 1975.
Brye, Steve: 1970-78; Minn. 1970-76, Mil. 1977, Pitt. 1978.
Buckner, Bill: 1969 to 1990; L.A. 1969-76, Cubs 1977-84, Bos. 1984-87, Cal. 1987-88, K.C. 1988-89, Bos. 1990.
Buechele, Steve: 1985-present; Texas 1985-91, Pitt. 1991.
Buford, Don: 1963-72; White Sox 1963-67, Balt. 1968-72.
Buhl, Bob: 1953-67; Mil. 1953-62, Cubs 1962-66, Phil. 1966-67.
Bulkeley, Morgan: executive; HOF.
Bumbry, Al: 1972-85; Balt. 1972-84, S.D. 1985; ROY 1973.
Bunning, Jim: 1955-71; Det. 1955-63, Phil. 1964-67, Pitt. 1968-69, L.A. 1969, Phil. 1970-71.
Burdette, Lew: 1950-67; Yankees 1950, Bos. (N) 1951-52, Mil. 1953-63, St.L. 1963-64, Cubs 1964-65, Phil. 1965, Cal. 1966-67.
Burgess, Smoky: 1949-67; Cubs 1949-1951, Phil. 1952-55, Cinn. 1955-58, Pitt. 1959-64, White Sox 1964-67.
Burgmeier, Tom: 1968-84; Cal. 1968, K.C. 1969-73, Minn. 1974-77, Bos. 1978-82, Oak. 1983-84.
Burke, Tim: 1985 to present; Mont. 1985-present.
Burkett, Jesse: 1890-05; N.Y. (N) 1890, Cleve. 1891-1898, St.L. (N) 1899-01, St.L. (A) 1902-04, Bos. (A) 1905; HOF.
Burks, Ellis: 1987 to present; Bos. 1987-present.
Burleson, Rick: 1974-87; Bos. 1974-80, Cal. 1981-86, Balt. 1987.
Burns, Britt: 1978-85; White Sox 1978-85.
Burns, George: 1914-29; Det. 1914-17, Phil. (A) 1918-20, Cleve. 1920-21, Bos. 1922-23, Cleve. 1924-28, Yankees 1928-29, Phil. (A) 1929; MVP 1926.
Burris, Ray: 1973-87; Cubs 1973-79, Yankees 1979, Mets 1979-80, Mont. 1981-83, Oak. 1984, Mil. 1985, St.L. 1986, Mil. 1987.
Burroughs, Jeff: 1970-84; Wash. 1970-71, Texas 1972-76, Atl. 1977-80, Seat. 1981, Oak. 1982-84, Tor. 1985; MVP 1974.
Busby, Jim: 1950-62; White Sox 1950-52, Wash. 1952-55, White Sox 1955, Cleve. 1956-57, Balt. 1957-58, Bos. 1959-60, Balt. 1960-61, Hou. 1962.
Busby, Steve: 1972-80; K.C. 1972-80.
Butler, Brett; 1981 to present; Atl. 1981-83, Cleve. 1984-87, S.F. 1988-90, L.A. 1991.
Byrd, Harry: 1950-57; Phil. 1950-53, Yankees 1954, Balt. 1955, White Sox 1955-56, Det. 1957; ROY 1952.

C

Cabell, Enos: 1972-86; Balt. 1972-74, Hou. 1975-80, S.F. 1981, Det. 1982-83, Hou. 1984-85, L.A. 1985-86.
Calderon, Ivan: 1984-present; Seat. 1984-86, White Sox 1987-90, Mont. 1991.
Caldwell, Mike: 1971-84; S.D. 1971-73, S.F. 1974-76, Cinn. 1977, Mil. 1977-84.
Callison, Johnny: 1958-73; White Sox 1958-59, Phil. 1960-69, Cubs 1970-71, Yankees 1972-73.
Camilli, Dolf: 1933-45; Cubs 1933-34, Phil. 1934-37, Bro. 1938-43, Bos. (A) 1945; MVP 1941.
Campanella, Roy: 1948-57; Bro. 1948-57; MVP 1951, 1953, 1955; HOF.
Campaneris, Bert: 1964-83; K.C. 1964-67, Oak. 1968-76, Texas 1977-79, Cal. 1979-81, Yankees 1983.
Campbell, Bill: 1973-87; Minn. 1973-76, Bos. 1977-81, Cubs 1982-83, Phil. 1984, St.L. 1985, Det. 1986, Mont. 1987.
Campbell, Bruce: 1930-42: White Sox 1930-32, St.L. (A) 1932-34, Cleve. 1935-39, Det. 1940-41, Wash. 1942.
Candelaria, John: 1975 to present; Pitt. 1975-85, Cal. 1985-87, Mets 1987, Yankees 1988-89, Mont. 1989, Minn. 1990, Tor. 1990, L.A. 1991.
Candiotti, Tom: 1983-present; Mil. 1983-84, Cleve. 1986-91, Tor. 1991.
Cannizzaro, Chris: 1960-65, 1968-74; St.L. 1960-61, Mets 1962-65, Pitt. 1968, S.D. 1969-71, Cubs 1971, L.A. 1972-73, S.D. 1974.
Canseco, Jose: 1985 to present; Oak. 1985-present; ROY 1986, MVP 1988.
Capra, Buzz: 1971-77; Mets 1971-73, Atl. 1974-77.
Carbo, Bernie: 1969-80; Cinn. 1969-72, St.L. 1973-73, Bos. 1974-76, Mil. 1976, Bos. 1977-78, Cleve. 1978, St.L. 1979-80, Pitt. 1980.
Cardenal, Jose: 1963-80; S.F. 1963-64, Cal. 1965-67, Cleve. 1968-69, St.L. 1970-71, Mil. 1971, Cubs 1972-77, Phil. 1978-79, Mets 1979-80, K.C. 1980.
Cardenas, Leo: 1960-75; Cinn. 1960-68, Minn. 1969-71, Cal. 1972, Cleve. 1973, Texas 1974-75.
Cardwell, Don: 1957-70; Phil. 1957-60, Cubs 1960-62, Pitt. 1963-66, Mets 1967-70, Atl. 1970.
Carew, Rod: 1967-85; Minn. 1967-78, Cal. 1979-85; ROY 1967, MVP 1977, HOF.
Carey, Max: 1910-29; Pitt. 1910-26, Bro. 1926-29; HOF.
Carlton, Steve: 1965-88; St.L. 1965-71, Phil. 1972-86, S.F. 1986, White Sox 1986, Cleve. 1987, Minn. 1987-88.
Carrasquel, Chico: 1950-59; White Sox 1950-55, Cleve. 1956-58, K.C. 1958, Balt. 1959.
Carroll, Clay: 1964-78; Mil. 1964-65, Atl. 1966-68, Cinn. 1968-75, Cubs 1976, St.L. 1977, White Sox 1977, Pitt. 1978.
Carter, Gary: 1974 to present; Mont. 1974-84, Mets 1985-89, S.F. 1990, L.A. 1991.
Carter, Joe; 1983 to present; Cubs 1983, Cleve. 1984-89, S.D. 1990, Tor. 1991.
Cartwright, Alexander: executive, HOF.
Carty, Rico: 1963-79, Mil. 1963-65, Atl. 1966-72, Texas 1973, Cubs 1973, Oak. 1973, Cleve. 1974-77, Tor. 1978, Oak. 1978, Tor. 1979.
Casanova, Paul: 1965-74; Wash. 1965-71, Atl. 1972-74.
Case, George: 1937-47; Wash. 1937-45, Cleve. 1946, Wash. 1947.
Cash, Dave: 1969-80; Pitt. 1969-73, Phil. 1974-76, Mont. 1977-79, S.D. 1980.
Cash, Norm: 1958-74; White Sox 1958-59, Det. 1960-74.
Castino, John: 1979-84; Minn. 1979-84; ROY 1979.
Castro, Bill: 1974-83; Mil. 1974-80, Yankees 1981, K.C. 1982-83.
Cater, Danny: 1964-75; Phil. 1964, White Sox 1965-66, K.C. 1966-67, Oak. 1968-69, Yankees 1970-71, Bos. 1972-74, St.L. 1975.
Caudill, Bill: 1979-87; Cubs 1979-81, Seat. 1982-83, Oak. 1984, Tor. 1985-86, Oak. 1987.
Cavarretta, Phil: 1934-55; Cubs 1934-55; MVP 1945.
Cedeno, Cesar: 1970-86; Hou. 1970-81, Cinn. 1981-85, St.L. 1985, L.A. 1986.
Cepeda, Orlando: 1958-74; S.F. 1958-66, St.L. 1966-68, Atl. 1969-72, Oak. 1972, Bos. 1973, K.C. 1974; ROY 1958, MVP 1967.

Cerone, Rick: 1975 to present; Cleve. 1975-76, Tor. 1977-79, Yankees 1980-84, Atl. 1985, Mil. 1986, Yankees 1987, Bos. 1988-89, Yankees 1990, Mets 1991.
Cerv, Bob: 1951-62; Yankees 1951-56, K.C. 1957-60, Yankees 1960, L.A. (A) 1961, Yankees 1961-62, Hou. 1962.
Cey, Ron: 1971-87; L.A. 1971-82, Cubs 1983-86, Oak. 1987.
Chadwick, Henry: writer; HOF.
Chalk, Dave: 1973-81; Cal. 1973-78, Texas 1979, Oak. 1979, K.C. 1980-81.
Chambliss, Chris: 1971-86, 1988; Cleve. 1971-74, Yankees 1974-79, Atl. 1980-86, Yankees 1988.
Chance, Dean: 1961-71; L.A. 1961-64, Cal. 1965-66, Minn. 1967-69, Cleve. 1970, Mets 1970, Det. 1971; Cy Young 1964.
Chance, Frank: 1898-14, Cubs 1898-12, Yankees 1913-14; HOF.
Chandler, Happy: commissioner; HOF.
Chandler, Spud: 1937-47; Yankees 1937-47; MVP 1943.
Chaney, Darrel: 1969-79; Cinn. 1969-75, Atl. 1976-79.
Chapman, Ben: 1930-41, 1944-46; Yankees 1930-36, Wash. 1936-37, Bos. 1937-38, Cleve. 1939-40, Wash. 1941, White Sox 1941, Bro. 1944-45, Phil. (N) 1945-46.
Chapman, Sam: 1938-51; Phil. (A) 1938-51, Cleve. 1951.
Charboneau, Joe: 1980-82; Cleve. 1980-82; ROY 1980.
Charleston, Oscar: Negro Leagues; HOF.
Chesbro, Jack: 1899-09; Pitt. 1989-02, Yankees 1903-09, Bos. 1909; HOF.
Christenson, Larry: 1973-83; Phil. 1973-83.
Cicotte, Eddie: 1905-20; Det. 1905, Bos. 1906-12, White Sox 1912-20.
Cimoli, Gino: 1956-65; Bro. 1956-57, L.A. 1958, St.L. 1959, Pitt. 1960-61, Mil. 1961, K.C. 1962-64, Balt. 1964, Cal. 1965.
Clancy, Jim: 1977 to present; Tor. 1977-88, Hou. 1989-91, Atl. 1991.
Clark, Horace: 1965-74; Yankees 1965-74, S.D. 1974.
Clark, Jack: 1975 to present; S.F. 1975-84, St.L. 1985-87, Yankees 1988, S.D. 1989-90, Bos. 1991.
Clark, Will: 1986 to present; S.F. 1986-present.
Clarke, Fred: 1894-11; Lou. 1894-1899, Pitt. 1900-1911; HOF.
Clarkson, John: 1882-94; Wor. 1882, Chi. (N) 1883-87, Bos. 1888-92, Cleve. 1892-94; HOF.
Clear, Mark: 1979-88, 1990; Cal. 1979-80, Bos. 1981-85, Mil. 1986-88, Cal. 1990.
Clemens, Roger: 1984 to present; Bos. 1984-present; MVP 1986, Cy Young 1986, 1987, 1991.
Clemente, Roberto: 1955-72; Pitt. 1955-72; MVP 1966, HOF.
Clendenon, Don: 1961-72; Pitt. 1961-68, Mont. 1969, Mets 1969-71, St.L. 1972.
Cleveland, Reggie: 1969-81; St.L. 1969-73, Bos. 1974-78, Texas 1978, Mil. 1979-81.
Clift, Harlond: 1934-45; St.L. (A) 1934-43, Wash. 1943-45.
Clines, Gene: 1970-79; Pitt. 1970-74, Mets 1975, Texas 1976, Cubs 1977-79.
Cloninger, Tony: 1961-72; Mil. 1961-65, Atl. 1966-68, Cinn. 1968-71, St.L. 1972.
Cobb, Ty: 1905-28; Det. 1905-1926, Phil. 1927-28; MVP 1911, HOF.
Cochrane, Mickey: 1925-37; Phil. (A) 1925-33, Det. 1934-37; MVP 1928, 1934, HOF.
Colavito, Rocky: 1955-68; Cleve. 1955-59, Det. 1960-63, K.C. 1964, Cleve. 1965-67, White Sox 1967, L.A. 1968, Yankees 1968.
Colbert, Nate: 1966-76; Hou. 1966-68, S.D. 1969-74, Det. 1975, Mont. 1975-76, Oak. 1976.
Colborn, Jim: 1969-78; Cubs 1969-71, Mil. 1972-76, K.C. 1977-78, Seat. 1978.
Coleman, Jerry: 1949-57; Yankees 1949-57.
Coleman, Joe: 1942-55; Phil (A) 1942-53, Balt. 1954-55, Det. 1955.
Coleman, Joe Jr.: 1965-79; Wash. 1965-70, Det. 1971-76, Cubs 1976, Oak. 1977-78, Tor. 1978, S.F. 1979, Pitt. 1979.
Coleman, Vince: 1985 to present; St.L. 1985-90; Mets 1991; ROY 1985.
Collins, Dave: 1975-90; Cal. 1975-76, Seat. 1977, Cinn. 1978-81, Yankees 1982, Tor. 1983-84, Oak. 1985, Det. 1986, Cinn. 1987-89, St.L. 1990.
Collins, Eddie: 1906-30; Phil. (A) 1906-14, White Sox 1915-26, Phil (A) 1927-30; HOF.

Collins, Jimmy: 1895-08; Bos. (N) 1895-00, Bos. (A) 1901-07, Phil. (A) 1907-08; HOF.
Collins, Ripper: 1931-38, 1941; St.L. (N) 1931-36, Cubs 1937-38, Pitt. 1941.
Combs, Earle: 1924-35; Yankees 1924-35; HOF.
Comiskey, Charles: 1882-94; St.L. 1882-89, Chi. (P) 1890, St.L. 1891, Cinn. 1892-94; HOF.
Concepcion, Dave: 1970-88; Cinn. 1970-88.
Cone, David: 1986 to present; K.C. 1986, Mets 1987-present.
Conigliaro, Tony: 1964-71, 1975; Bos. 1964-70, Cal. 1971, Bos. 1975.
Conlan, Jocko: umpire; HOF.
Conley, Gene: 1952, 1954-63; Bos. 1952, Mil. 1954-58, Phil. 1959-60, Bos. 1960-63.
Connolly, Tom: umpire; HOF.
Connor, Roger; 1880-97; Tro. 1880-82, N.Y. (N) 1883-89, N.Y. (P) 1890, N.Y. (N) 1891, Phil. (N) 1892, N.Y. (N) 1893-94, St.L. (N) 1894-97; HOF.
Consuegra, Sandy: 1950-57; Wash. 1950-53, White Sox 1953-56, Balt. 1956-57, N.Y. (N) 1957.
Coombs, Jack: 1906-18, 1920; Phil. 1906-1914, Bro. 1915-18, Det. 1920.
Cooney, Johnny: 1921-30, 1935-44; Bos. (N) 1921-30, Bro. 1935-37, Bos. (N) 1938-42, Bro. 1943-44, Yankees 1944.
Cooper, Cecil: 1971-87; Bos. 1971-76, Mil. 1977-87.
Cooper, Mort: 1938-47, 1949; St.L. (N) 1938-45, Bos. (N) 1945-47, N.Y. (N) 1947, Cubs 1949; MVP 1942.
Cooper, Walker: 1940-57; St.L. (N) 1940-45, N.Y. (N) 1946-49, Cinn. 1949-50, Bos. (N) 1950-52, Mil. 1953, Pitt. 1954, Cubs 1954-55, St.L 1956-57.
Cooper, Wilbur: 1912-26; Pitt. 1912-24, Cubs 1925-26, Det. 1926.
Corbett, Doug: 1980-87; Minn. 1980-82, Cal. 1982-86, Balt. 1987.
Coscarat, Pete: 1938-46; Bro. 1938-41, Pitt. 1942-46.
Coveleski, Stan: 1912, 1916-28; Phil. 1912, Cleve. 1916-24, Wash. 1925-27, Yankees 1928; HOF.
Covington, Wes: 1956-66; Mil. 1956-61, White Sox 1961, K.C. 1961, Phil. 1961-65, Cubs 1966, L.A. 1966.
Cowens, Al: 1974-86; K.C. 1974-79, Cal. 1980, Det. 1980-81, Seat. 1982-86.
Cramer, Doc: 1929-48; Phil. 1929-35, Bos. 1936-40, Wash. 1941, Det. 1942-48.
Crandall, Del: 1949-66; Bos. (N) 1949-50, Mil. 1953-63, S.F. 1964, Pitt. 1965, Cleve. 1966.
Crawford, Sam: 1899-17; Cinn. 1899-02, Det. 1903-17; HOF.
Crawford, Willie: 1964-77; L.A. 1964-75, St.L. 1976, Hou. 1977, Oak. 1977.
Cromartie, Warren: 1974, 1976-83, 1991. Mont. 1974, 1976-83, K.C. 1991.
Cronin, Joe: 1926-45; Pitt. 1926-27, Wash. 1928-34, Bos. 1935-45; HOF.
Crosetti, Frank: 1932-48; Yankees 1932-48.
Crowder, General: 1926-36; Wash. 1926-27, St.L. (A) 1927-30, Wash. 1930-34, Det. 1934-36.
Crowe, George: 1952-53, 1955-61; Bos. 1952, Mil. 1953, 1955, Cinn. 1956-58, St.L. 1959-61.
Crowley, Terry: 1969-83; Balt. 1969-73, Cinn. 1974-75, Atl. 1976, Balt. 1976-82, Mont. 1983.
Cruz, Jose: 1970-88; St.L. 1970-74, Hou. 1975-87, Yankees 1988.
Cruz, Julio: 1977-86; Seat. 1977-83, White Sox 1983-86.
Cuccinello, Tony: 1930-40, 1942-45; Cinn. 1930-31, Bro. 1932-35, Bos. (N) 1936-40, N.Y. (N) 1940, Bos. (N) 1942-43, White Sox 1943-45.
Cuellar, Mike: 1959, 1964-77; Cinn. 1959, St.L. 1964, Hou. 1965-68, Balt. 1969-76, Cal. 1977; Cy Young 1969.
Cullenbine, Roy: 1938-47; Det. 1938-39, Bro. 1940, St.L. (A) 1940-42, Wash. 1942, Yankees 1942, Cleve. 1943-45, Det. 1945-47.
Culp, Ray: 1963-73; Phil. 1963-66, Cubs 1967, Bos. 1968-73.
Cummings, Candy: 1872-77; Mut. (N) 1872, Bal. (N) 1873, Phi. (N) 1874, Har. (N) 1875-76, Cinn. (N) 1877; HOF.
Cunningham, Joe: 1954-66; St.L. 1954-61, White Sox 1962-64, Wash. 1964-66.
Curtis, Jack: 1970-84; Bos. 1970-73, St.L. 1974-76, S.F. 1977-79, S.D. 1980-82, Cal. 1982-84.
Cuyler, Kiki: 1921-38; Pitt. 1921-27, Cubs 1928-37, Bro. 1938; HOF.

D

D'Acquisto, John: 1973-82; S.F. 1973-76, St.L. 1977, S.D. 1977-80, Mont. 1980, Cal. 1981, Oak. 1982.

Dahlgren, Babe: 1935-46; Bos. (A) 1936-36, Yankees 1937-40, Bos. (N) 1941, Cubs 1941-42, St.L. 1942, Bro. 1942, Phil. 1943, Pitt. 1944-45, St.L. 1946.

Daley, Buddy: 1955-64; Cleve. 1955-57, K.C. 1958-61, Yankees 1961-64.

Dalrymple, Clay: 1960-71; Phil. 1960-68, Balt. 1969-71.

Dandridge, Ray: 1933-49; Negro Leagues; HOF.

Danning, Harry: 1933-42; N.Y. (N) 1933-42.

Dark, Alvin: 1946-60; Bos. (N) 1946-49, N.Y. (N) 1950-56, St.L. 1956-58, Cubs 1958-59, Phil. 1960, Mil. 1960; ROY 1948.

Darling, Ron: 1983 to present; Mets 1983-91, Mont. 1991, Oak. 1991.

Darwin, Danny: 1978-present; Texas 1978-84, Mil. 1985-86, Hou. 1986-90, Bos. 1991.

Daubert, Jake: 1910-24; Bro. 1910-18, Cinn. 1919-24.

Dauer, Rich: 1976-85; Balt. 1976-85.

Davalillo, Vic: 1963-74, 1977-80; Cleve. 1963-68, Cal. 1968-69, St.L. 1969-70, Pitt. 1971-73, Oak. 1973-74, L.A. 1977-80.

Davenport, Jim: 1958-70; S.F. 1958-70.

Davis, Alvin: 1984 to present; Seat. 1984-present; ROY 1984.

Davis, Chili; 1981 to present; S.F. 1981-87, Cal. 1988-90, Minn. 1991.

Davis, Curt: 1934-46; Phil. 1934-36, Cubs 1936-37, St.L. 1938-40, Bro. 1940-46.

Davis, Eric: 1984 to present; Cinn. 1984-present.

Davis, Glenn: 1984 to present; Hou. 1984-90, Balt. 1991.

Davis, Jody: 1981 to present; Cubs 1981-88, Atl. 1988-present.

Davis, Mark: 1980-81, 1983 to present; Phil. 1980-81, S.F. 1983-87, S.D. 1987-89, K.C. 1990-present; Cy Young 1989.

Davis, Ron: 1978-88; Yankees 1978-81, Minn. 1982-86, Cubs 1986-87, L.A. 1987, S.F. 1988.

Davis, Tommy: 1959-76; L.A. 1959-66, Mets 1967, White Sox 1968, Seat. 1969, Hou. 1969-70, Cubs 1970, Oak. 1970-71, Cubs 1972, Balt. 1972-75, Cal. 1976, K.C. 1976.

Davis, Willie: 1960-76, 1979; L.A. 1960-73, Mont. 1974, Texas 1975, St.L. 1975, S.D. 1976, Cal. 1979.

Dawley, Bill: 1983-89; Hou. 1983-85; White Sox 1986, St.L. 1987, Phil. 1988, Oak. 1989.

Dawson, Andre: 1976 to present; Mont. 1976-86, Cubs 1987-present; ROY 1977, MVP 1987.

Dean, Dizzy: 1930-41, 1947; St.L. 1930-37, Cubs 1938-41, St.L. (A) 1947; MVP 1934, HOF.

Dean, Paul: 1934-41, 1943; St.L. (N) 1934-39, N.Y. (N) 1940-41, St.L. (A) 1943.

DeCinces, Doug: 1973-87; Balt. 1973-81, Cal. 1982-87, St.L. 1987.

Deer, Rob: 1984-present; S.F. 1984-85, Mil. 1986-90, Det. 1991.

Delahanty, Ed: 1888-03; Phil. (N) 1888-89, Cleve. (P) 1890, Phil. (N) 1891-01, Wash. 1902-03; HOF.

DeLeon, Jose: 1983 to present; Pitt. 1983-86, White Sox 1986-87, St.L. 1988-present.

DeMaestri, Joe: 1951-61; White Sox 1951, St.L. (A) 1952, Phil. 1953-54, K.C. 1955-59, Yankees 1960-61.

Demaree, Frank: 1932-44; Cubs 1932-38, N.Y. (N) 1939-41, Bos. (N) 1941-42, St.L. (N) 1943, St.L. (A) 1944.

Dempsey, Rick: 1969 to present; Minn. 1969-72, Yankees 1973-76, Balt. 1976-86, Cleve. 1987, L.A. 1988-90, Mil. 1991.

Denny, John: 1974-86; St.L. 1974-79, Cleve. 1980-82, Phil. 1982-85, Cinn. 1986; Cy Young 1983.

Dent, Bucky: 1973-84; White Sox 1973-76, Yankees 1977-82, Texas 1982-83, K.C. 1984.

Dernier, Bob: 1980-89; Phil. 1980-83, Cubs 1984-87, Phil. 1988-89.

Derringer, Paul: 1931-45; St.L. 1931-33, Cinn. 1933-42, Cubs 1943-45.

Diaz, Bo: 1977-89; Bos. 1977, Cleve. 1978-81, Phil. 1982-85, Cinn 1985-89.

Dickey, Bill: 1928-43, 1946; Yankees 1928-43, 1946; HOF.

Dickson, Murry: 1939-59; St.L. (N) 1939-48, Pitt. 1949-53, Phil. 1954-56, St.L. 1956-57, K.C. 1958, Yankees 1958, K.C. 1959.

Dierker, Larry: 1964-77; Hou. 1964-76, St.L. 1977.

Dietz, Dick: 1966-73; S.F. 1966-71, L.A. 1972, Atl. 1973.

Dihigo, Martin: Negro Leagues; HOF.

Dillinger, Bob: 1946-51; St.L. (A) 1946-49, Phil. 1950, Pitt. 1950-51, White Sox 1951.

Dilone, Miguel: 1974-85; Pitt. 1974-77, Oak. 1978-79, Cubs 1979, Cleve. 1980-83, White Sox 1983, Pitt. 1983, Mont. 1984-85, S.D. 1985.

DiMaggio, Dom: 1940-53; Bos. (A) 1940-53.

DiMaggio, Joe: 1936-51; Yankees 1936-51; MVP 1939, 1941, 1947; HOF.

DiMaggio, Vince: 1937-46; Bos. (N) 1937-38, Cinn. 1939-40, Pitt. 1940-44, Phil. 1945-46, N.Y. (N) 1946.

DiPino, Frank: 1981-90; Mil. 1981, Hou. 1982-86, Cubs 1986-88, St.L. 1989-90.

Doak, Bill: 1912-24, 1927-29; Cinn. 1912, St.L. (N) 1913-24, Bro. 1924, Bro. 1927-29.

Dobson, Joe: 1939-54; Cleve. 1939-40, Bos. (A), 1941-50, White Sox 1951-53, Bos. 1954.

Dobson, Pat: 1967-77; Det. 1967-69, S.D. 1970, Balt. 1971-72, Atl. 1973, Yankees 1973-75, Cleve. 1976-77.

Doby, Larry: 1947-59; Cleve. 1947-55, White Sox 1956-57, Cleve. 1958, Det. 1959, White Sox 1959.

Doerr, Bobby: 1937-51; Bos. (A) 1937-51; HOF.

Donohue, Pete: 1921-32; Cinn. 1921-30, N.Y. (N) 1930-31, Cleve. 1931, Bos. (A) 1932.

Donovan, Dick: 1950-52, 1954-65; Bos. 1950-52, Det. 1954, White Sox 1955-60, Wash. 1961, Cleve. 1962-65.

Dotson, Richard: 1979-90; White Sox 1979-87, Yankees 1988-89, White Sox 1989, K.C. 1990.

Downing, Al: 1961-77; Yankees 1961-69, Oak. 1970, Mil. 1970, L.A. 1971-77.

Downing, Brian: 1973 to present; White Sox 1973-77, Cal. 1978-90, Texas 1991.

Drabek, Doug: 1986 to present; Yankees 1986, Pitt. 1987-present; Cy Young 1990.

Drago, Dick: 1969-81; K.C. 1969-73, Bos. 1974-75, Cal. 1976-77, Balt. 1977, Bos. 1978-80, Seat. 1981.

Dravecky, Dave: 1982-89; S.D. 1982-87, S.F. 1987-89.

Driessen, Dan: 1973-87; Cinn. 1973-84, Mont. 1984-85, S.F. 1985-86, Hou. 1986, St.L. 1987.

Dropo, Walt: 1949-61; Bos. (A) 1949-52, Det. 1952-54, White Sox 1955-58, Cinn. 1958-59, Balt. 1959-61; ROY 1950.

Drysdale, Don: 1956-69, Bro. 1956-57, L.A. 1958-69; Cy Young 1962, HOF.

Duffy, Frank: 1970-79; Cinn. 1970-71, S.F. 1971, Cleve. 1972-77, Bos. 1978-79.

Duffy, Hugh: 1888-01, 1904-06; Chi. (N) 1888-89, Chi. (P) 1890, Bos. (A) 1991, Bos (N) 1892-00, Mil. 1901, Phil. 1904-06; HOF.

Duncan, Dave: 1964, 1967-76; K.C. 1964, K.C. 1967, Oak. 1968-72, Cleve. 1973-74, Balt. 1975-76.

Dunston, Shawon: 1985 to present; Cubs 1985-present.

Duren, Ryne: 1954, 1957-65; Balt. 1954, K.C. 1957, Yankees 1958-61, L.A. (A) 1961-62, Phil. 1963-64, Cinn. 1964, Phil. 1965, Wash. 1965.

Durham, Leon: 1980-89; St.L. 1980, Cubs 1981-88, Cinn. 1988, St.L. 1989.

Durocher, Leo: 1925, 1928-45; Yankees 1925, Yankees 1928-29, Cinn. 1930-33, St.L. 1933-37, Bro. 1938-45.

Dwyer, Jim: 1973-90; St.L. 1973-75, Mont. 1975-76, Mets 1976, St.L. 177-78, S.F. 1978, Bos. 1979-80, Balt. 1981-88, Minn. 1988-89, Mont. 1989, Minn. 1990.

Dykes, Jimmy: 1918-39; Phil. (A) 1918-32, White Sox 1933-39.

Dykstra, Lenny: 1985 to present; Mets 1985-1989, Phil. 1989-present.

E

Early, Jake: 1939-49; Wash. 1939-46, St.L. (A) 1947, Wash. 1948-49.

Earnshaw, George: 1928-36; Phil. (A) 1928-33, White Sox 1934-35, Bro. 1935-36, St.L. 1936.

Easler, Mike: 1973-87; Hou. 1973-75, Cal. 1976, Pitt. 1977-83, Bos. 1984-85, Yankees 1986, Phil. 1987, Yankees 1987.
Easterly, Jamie: 1974-79, 1981-87; Atl. 1974-79, Mil. 1981-83, Cleve. 1983-87.
Eastwick, Rawly: 1974-81; Cinn. 1974-77, St.L. 1977, Yankees 1978, Phil. 1978-79, K.C. 1980, Cubs 1981.
Eckersley, Dennis: 1975-present; Cleve. 1975-77, Bos. 1978-84, Cubs 1984-86, Oak. 1987-present.
Edwards, Bruce: 1946-56; Bro. 1946-51, Cubs 1951-54, Wash. 1955, Cinn. 1956.
Edwards, Johnny: 1961-74; Cinn. 1961-67, St.L. 1968, Hou. 1969-74.
Elliott, Jumbo: 1923, 1925-34; St.L. (A) 1923, Bro. 1925-30, Phil. 1931-34, Bos. 1934.
Ellis, Dock: 1968-79; Pitt. 1968-75, Yankees 1976-77, Oak. 1977, Texas 1977-79, Mets 1979, Pitt. 1979.
Ellis, John: 1969-81; Yankees 1969-72, Cleve. 1973-75, Texas 1976-81.
Ellis, Sammy: 1962, 1964-69; Cinn. 1962, Cinn. 1964-67, Cal. 1968, White Sox 1969.
Ellsworth, Dick: 1958-71; Cubs 1958-66, Phil. 1967, Bos. 1968-69, Cleve. 1969-70, Mil. 1970-71.
Elston, Don: 1953, 1957-64; Cubs 1953, Bro. 1957, Cubs 1957-64.
Engle, Dave: 1981-89; Minn. 1981-85, Det. 1986, Mont. 1987-88, Mil. 1989.
English, Woody: 1927-38; Cubs 1927-36, Bro. 1937-38.
Ennis, Del: 1946-59; Phil. 1946-56, St.L. 1957-58, Cinn. 1959, White Sox 1959.
Epstein, Mike: 1966-74; Balt. 1966-67, Wash. 1967-71, Oak. 1971-72, Texas 1973, Cal. 1973-74.
Erskine, Carl: 1948-59; Bro. 1948-57, L.A. 1958-59.
Estrada, Chuck: 1960-67; Balt. 1960-64, Cubs 1966, Mets 1967.
Etchebarren, Andy: 1962, 1965-78; Balt. 1962, Balt. 1965-75, Cal. 1975-77, Mil. 1978.
Etten, Nick: 1938-47; Phil. 1938-42, Yankees 1943-46, Phil. (N) 1947.
Evans, Billy: 1906-27; umpire, HOF.
Evans, Darrell: 1969-89; Atl. 1969-76, S.F. 1976-83, Det. 1984-88, Atl. 1989.
Evans, Dwight: 1972 to present; Bos. 1972-1990, Balt. 1991.
Evers, Hoot: 1941-56; Det. 1941-52, Bos. 1952-54, N.Y. (N) 1954, Det. 1954, Balt. 1955, Cleve. 1955-56, Balt. 1956.
Evers, Johnny: 1902-17, 1922, 1929; Cubs 1902-13, Bos. 1914-17, Phil. 1917, White Sox 1922, Bos. (N) 1929; MVP 1914, HOF.
Ewing, Buck: 1880-97; Tro. 1880-82, N.Y. (N) 1883-89, N.Y. (P) 1890, N.Y. (N) 1891-92, Cleve. 1893-94, Cinn. 1895-97; HOF.

F

Faber, Red: 1914-33; White Sox 1914-33; HOF.
Face, Roy: 1953-69; Pitt. 1953-68, Det. 1968, Mont. 1969.
Fain, Ferris: 1947-55; Phil. (A) 1947-52, White Sox 1953-54, Det. 1955, Cleve. 1955.
Fairly, Ron: 1958-78; L.A. 1958-69, Mont. 1969-74, St.L. 1975-76, Oak. 1976, Tor. 1977, Cal. 1978.
Falcone, Pete: 1975-84; S.F. 1975, St.L. 1976-78, Mets 1979-82, Atl. 1983-84.
Farmer, Ed: 1971-74, 1977-83; Cleve. 1971-73, Det. 1973, Phil. 1974, Balt. 1977, Mil. 1978, Texas 1979, White Sox 1979-81, Phil. 1982-83, Oak. 1983.
Farrell, Dick: 1956-69; Phil. 1956-61, L.A. 1961, Hou. 1962-67, Phil. 1967-69.
Feller, Bob: 1936-56, Cleve. 1936-56; HOF.
Fernandez, Sid: 1983 to present; L.A. 1983, Mets 1984-present.
Fernandez, Tony: 1983 to present; Tor. 1983-90, S.D. 1991.
Ferrell, Rick: 1929-47; St.L. 1929-33, Bos. (A) 1933-37, Wash. 1937-41, St.L. (A) 1941-43, Wash. 1944-47; HOF.
Farrell, Wes: 1927-41; Cleve. 1927-33, Bos. (A) 1934-37, Wash. 1937-38, Yankees 1938-39, Bro. 1940, Bos. (N) 1941.
Felder, Mike: 1985-present; Mil. 1985-90, S.F. 1991.
Ferguson, Joe: 1970-83; L.A. 1970-76, St.L. 1976, Hou. 1977-78, L.A. 1978-81, Cal. 1981-83.
Ferriss, Boo: 1945-50; Bos. 1945-50.

Fidrych, Mark: 1976-80; Det. 1976-80; ROY 1976.
Fielder, Cecil: 1985-88, 1990 to present; Tor. 1985-88, Det. 1990-present.
Figueroa, Ed: 1974-81; Cal. 1974-75, Yankees 1976-80, Texas 1980, Oak. 1981.
Fingers, Rollie: 1968-85; Oak. 1968-76, S.D. 1977-80, Mil. 1981-85; MVP 1981, Cy Young 1981.
Finley, Chuck: 1986 to present; Cal. 1986-present.
Finney, Lou: 1931-47; Phil. (A) 1931-39, Bos. (A) 1939-45, St.L. 1945-46, Phil. (N) 1947.
Fischlin, Mike: 1977-87; Hou. 1977-80, Cleve. 1981-85, Yankees 1986, Atl. 1987.
Fisk, Carlton: 1969 to present; Bos. 1969-80, White Sox 1981-present; ROY 1972.
Fitzmorris, Al: 1969-78; K.C. 1969-76, Cleve. 1977-78, Cal. 1978.
Flanagan, Mike: 1975 to present; Balt. 1975-87, Tor. 1987-present; Cy Young 1979.
Flannery, Tim: 1979-89; S.D. 1979-89.
Fletcher, Elbie: 1934-49; Bos. (N) 1934-39, Pitt. 1939-47, Bos. (N) 1949.
Flick, Elmer: 1898-10; Phil. (N) 1898-02, Cleve. 1902-10; HOF.
Flood, Curt: 1956-71; Cinn. 1956-57; St.L. 1958-69, Wash. 1971.
Flynn, Doug: 1975-85; Cinn. 1975-77, Mets 1977-81, Texas 1982, Mont. 1982-85. Det. 1985.
Foiles, Hank: 1953-64; Cinn. 1953, Cleve. 1953-56, Pitt. 1956-59; K.C. 1960, Cleve. 1960, Det. 1960, Balt. 1961, Cinn. 1962, L.A. 1963-64.
Foli, Tim: 1970-85; Mets 1970-71; Mont. 1972-77, S.F. 1977, Mets 1978-79, Pitt. 1979-81, Cal. 1982-83, Yankees 1984, Pitt. 1985.
Fonseca, Lew: 1921-25, 1927-33; Cinn. 1921-24, Phil. (N) 1925, Cleve. 1927-31, White Sox 1931-33.
Foote, Barry: 1973-82; Mont. 1973-77, Phil. 1977-78, Cubs 1979-81, Yankees 1981-82.
Ford, Dan: 1975-85; Minn. 1975-78, Cal. 1979-81, Balt. 1982-85.
Ford, Whitey: 1950-67; Yankees 1950-67; Cy Young 1961; HOF.
Fornieles, Mike: 1952-63; Wash. 1952, White Sox 1953-56, Balt. 1956-57, Bos. 1957-63, Minn. 1963.
Forsch, Bob: 1974-88; St.L. 1974-88, Hou. 1988-89.
Forsch, Ken: 1970-86; Hou. 1970-80, Cal. 1981-86.
Forster, Terry: 1971-86; White Sox 1971-76, Pitt. 1977, L.A. 1978-82, Atl. 1983-85, Cal. 1986.
Fosse, Ray: 1967-79; Cleve. 1967-72, Oak. 1973-75, Cleve. 1976-77, Seat. 1977, Mil. 1979.
Foster, George: 1969-86; S.F. 1969-71, Cinn. 1971-81, Mets 1982-86, White Sox 1986; MVP 1977.
Foster, Rube: Negro Leagues; HOF.
Fournier, Jack: 1912-18, 1920-27; White Sox 1912-17, Yankees 1918, St.L. 1920-22, Bro. 1923-27.
Fox, Nellie: 1947-65; Phil. (A) 1947-49, White Sox 1950-63, Hou. 1964-65; MVP 1959.
Fox, Pete: 1933-45; Det. 1933-40, Bos. 1941-45.
Foxx, Jimmie: 1925-42, 1944-45; Phil. (A) 1925-35, Bos. 1936-42, Cubs 1942, 1944, Phil. (N) 1945; MVP 1932, 1933, 1938, HOF.
Franco, John: 1984 to present; Cinn. 1984-89, Mets 1990-present.
Franco, Julio: 1982 to present; Phil. 1982, Cleve. 1983-88, Texas 1989-present.
Francona, Terry: 1981-90; Mont. 1981-85, Cubs 1986, Cinn. 1987, Cleve. 1988, Mil. 1989-90.
Francona, Tito: 1956-70; Balt. 1956-57, White Sox 1958, Det. 1958, Cleve. 1959-64, St.L. 1965-66, Phil. 1967, Atl. 1967-69, Oak. 1969-70, Mil. 1970.
Frankhouse, Fred: 1927-39; St.L. (N) 1927-30, Bos. (N) 1930-35, Bro. 1936-38, Bos. (N) 1939.
Frazier, George: 1978-87; St.L. 1978-80, Yankees 1981-83, Cleve. 1984, Cubs 1984-86, Minn. 1986-87.
Freehan, Bill: 1961-76; Det. 1961-76.
Fregosi, Jim: 1961-78; L.A. (A) 1961-64, Cal. 1965-71, Mets 1972-73, Texas 1973-77, Pitt. 1977-78.
French, Larry: 1929-42; Pitt. 1929-34, Cubs 1935-41, Bro. 1941-42.
Frey, Lonny: 1933-48; Bro. 1933-36, Cubs 1937, Cinn. 1938-46, Cubs 1947, Yankees 1947-48, N.Y. (N) 1948.
Frick, Ford: commissioner; HOF.
Friend, Bob: 1951-66; Pitt. 1951-65, Yankees 1966, Mets 1966.

Frisch, Frankie: 1919-37; N.Y. (N) 1919-26, St.L. 1927-37; MVP 1931, HOF.
Frisella, Danny: 1967-76; Mets 1967-72, Atl. 1973-74, S.D. 1975, St.L. 1976, Mil. 1976.
Fryman, Woodie: 1966-83; Pitt. 1966-67, Phil. 1968-72, Det. 1972-74, Mont. 1975-76, Cinn. 1977, Cubs 1978, Mont. 1978-83.
Fuentes, Tito: 1965-78; S.F. 1965-74, S.D. 1975-76, Det. 1977, Oak. 1978.
Furillo, Carl: 1946-60; Bro. 1946-57, L.A. 1958-60.

G

Gaetti, Gary: 1981 to present; Minn. 1981-90, Cal. 1991.
Gagliano, Phil: 1963-74; St.L. 1963-70, Cubs 1970, Bos. 1971-72, Cinn. 1973-74.
Galan, Augie: 1934-49; Cubs 1934-41, Bro. 1941-46, Cinn. 1947-48, N.Y. (N) 1949, Phil. (A) 1949.
Galarraga, Andres: 1985 to present; Mont. 1985-present.
Galvin, Pud: 1875, 1879-92; St.L. 1875, Buff. 1879-1885, Pitt. (A) 1885-86, Pitt. (N), 1887-89, Pitt. 1890 (P), Pitt. (N) 1891-92, St.L. 1892; HOF.
Gamble, Oscar: 1969-85; Cubs 1969, Phil. 1970-72, Cleve. 1973-75, Yankees 1976, White Sox 1977, S.D. 1978, Texas 1979, Yankees 1979-84, White Sox 1985.
Gantner, Jim: 1976-present; Mil. 1976-present.
Garagiola, Joe: 1946-54; St.L. (N) 1946-51, Pitt. 1951-53, Cubs 1953-54, N.Y. (N) 1954.
Garber, Gene: 1969-88; Pitt. 1969-72, K.C. 1973-74, Phil. 1974-78, Atl. 1978-87, K.C. 1987-88.
Garcia, Damaso: 1978-89; Yankees 1978-79, Tor. 1980-86; Atl. 1988; Mont. 1989.
Garcia, Kiko: 1976-85; Balt. 1976-80, Hou. 1981-82, Phil. 1983-85.
Garcia, Mike: 1948-61; Cleve. 1948-59, White Sox 1960, Wash. 1961.
Gardner, Billy: 1954-63: N.Y. (N) 1954-55, Balt. 1956-59, Wash. 1960, Minn. 1961, Yankees 1961-62, Bos. 1962-63.
Garland, Wayne: 1973-81; Balt. 1973-76, Cleve. 1977-81.
Garms, Debs: 1932-35, 1937-45; St.L. (A) 1932-35; Bos. (N) 1937-39, Pitt. 1940-41, St.L. 1943-45.
Garner, Phil: 1973-88; Oak. 1973-76, Pitt. 1977-81, Hou. 1981-87, L.A. 1987, S.F. 1988.
Garr, Ralph: 1968-80; Atl. 1968-75, White Sox 1976-79, Cal. 1979-80.
Garrelts, Scott: 1982 to present; S.F. 1982-present.
Garrett, Wayne: 1969-78: Mets 1969-76, Mont. 1976-78, St.L. 1978.
Garver, Ned: 1948-61; St.L. (A) 1948-52, Det. 1952-56, K.C. 1957-60, L.A. 1961.
Garvey, Steve: 1969-87; L.A. 1969-82, S.D. 1983-87; MVP 1974.
Gaston, Cito: 1967-78; Atl. 1967, S.D. 1969-74, Atl. 1975-78, Pitt. 1978.
Gedman, Rich: 1980 to present; Bos. 1980-90, Hou. 1990-91, St.L. 1991.
Gehrig, Lou: 1923-39; Yankees 1923-39; MVP 1927, 1936, HOF.
Gehringer, Charlie: 1924-42; Det. 1924-42; MVP 1937, HOF.
Gentile, Jim: 1957-66; Bro. 1957, L.A. 1958, Balt. 1960-63, K.C. 64-65, Hou. 1965-66, Cleve. 1966.
Geronimo, Cesar: 1969-83; Hou. 1969-71, Cinn. 1972-80, K.C. 1981-83.
Giamatti, A. Bartlett; commissioner.
Gibson, Bob: 1959-75; St.L. 1959-75; MVP 1968, Cy Young 1968, 1970, HOF.
Gibson, Josh: Negro Leagues; HOF.
Gibson, Kirk: 1979 to present; Det. 1979-87, L.A. 1988-90, K.C. 1991.
Giles, Warren: executive; HOF.
Gilliam, Jim: 1953-66; Bro. 1953-57, L.A. 1958-66.
Giusti, Dave: 1962-77; Hou. 1962-68, St.L. 1969, Pitt. 1970-76, Oak. 1977, Cubs 1977.
Gladden, Dan: 1983-present; S.F. 1983-86; Minn. 1987-present.
Glavine, Tom: 1987 to present; Atl. 1987-present; Cy Young 1991.
Gleaton, Jerry Don; 1979-85, 1987-present: Texas 1979-80, Seat. 1981-82, White Sox 1984-85, K.C. 1987-89, Det. 1990-present.
Goltz, Dave: 1972-83; Minn. 1972-79, L.A. 1980-82, Cal. 1982-83.
Gomez, Lefty: 1930-43; Yankees 1930-42, Wash. 1943; HOF.
Gonzalez, Tony: 1960-71; Cinn. 1960, Phil. 1960-68, S.D. 1969, Atl. 1969-70, Cal. 1970-71.

Gooden, Dwight: 1984 to present, Mets 1984-present; ROY 1984, Cy Young 1985.
Goodman, Billy; 1947-62; Bos. 1942-57, Balt. 1957, White Sox 1958-61, Hou. 1962.
Goodman, Ival: 1935-44; Cinn. 1935-44.
Gordon, Joe: 1938-50; Yankees 1938-46, Cleve. 1947-50; MVP 1942.
Gordon, Sid: 1941-55; N.Y. (N) 1941-49, Bos. 1950-52, Mil. 1953, Pitt. 1954-55, N.Y. (N) 1955.
Gordon, Tom: 1988 to present; K.C. 1988-present.
Goslin, Goose: 1921-38; Wash. 1921-30, St.L. (A) 1930-32, Wash. 1933, Det. 1934-37, Wash. 1938; HOF.
Gossage, Goose: 1972-89, 1991 to present; White Sox 1972-76, Pitt. 1977, Yankees 1978-83, S.D. 1984-87, Cubs 1988, S.F. 1989, Yankees 1989; Texas 1991.
Grabarkewitz, Billy: 1969-75; L.A. 1969-72, Cal. 1973, Phil. 1973-74, Chi. 1974, Oak. 1975.
Grace, Mark: 1988 to present; Cubs 1988-present.
Grant, Mudcat: 1958-71; Cleve. 1958-64, Minn. 1964-67, L.A. 1968, Mont. 1969, St.L. 1969, Oak. 1970, Pitt. 1970-71, Oak. 1971.
Gray, Ted: 1946-55; Det. 1946-54, White Sox 1955, Cleve. 1955, Yankees 1955, Balt. 1955.
Green, Dallas: 1960-67; Phil. 1960-64, Wash. 1965, Mets 1966, Phil. 1967.
Greenberg, Hank: 1930-47; Det. 1930-46, Pitt. 1947; MVP 1935, 1940, HOF.
Greenwell, Mike: 1985 to present; Bos. 1985-present.
Grich, Bobby: 1970-86; Balt. 1970-76, Cal. 1977-86.
Griffey, Ken Jr.: 1989 to present; Seat. 1989-present.
Griffey, Ken Sr.; 1973 to present; Cinn. 1973-81, Yankees 1982-86, Atl. 1986-88, Cinn. 1988-90, Seat. 1990-present.
Griffin, Alfredo: 1976 to present; Cleve. 1976-78, Tor. 1979-84, Oak. 1985-87, L.A. 1988-present.
Griffin, Tom: 1969-82; Hou. 1969-76, S.D. 1976-77, Cal. 1978, S.F. 1979-81, Pitt. 1982.
Griffith, Clark: executive; HOF.
Grim, Bob: 1954-60, 1962; Yankees 1954-58, K.C. 1958-59, Cleve. 1960, Cinn. 1960, St.L. 1960, K.C. 1962; ROY 1954.
Grimes, Burleigh: 1916-34; Pitt. 1916-17, Bro. 1918-26, N.Y. (N) 1927, Pitt. 1928-29, Bos. 1930, St.L. 1930-31, Cubs 1932-33, St.L. 1933-34, Pitt. 1934, Yankees 1934; HOF.
Grimm, Charlie: 1916, 1918-36; Phil. (A) 1916, St.L. 1918, Pitt. 1919-24, Cubs 1925-36.
Grimsley, Ross: 1971-80, 1982; Cinn. 1971-73, Balt. 1974-77, Mont. 1978-80, Cleve. 1980, Cleve. 1982.
Grissom, Lee: 1934-41; Cinn. 1934-39, Yankees 1940, Bro. 1940-41, Phil. 1941.
Grissom, Marv: 1946, 1949, 1952-59; N.Y. (N) 1946, Det. 1949, White Sox 1952, Bos. (A) 1953, N.Y. (N) 1953-57, S.F. 1958, St.L. 1959.
Groat, Dick: 1952-67; Pitt. 1952-62, St.L. 1963-65, Phil. 1966-67, S.F. 1967; MVP 1960.
Groh, Heinie: 1912-27; N.Y. (N) 1912-13, Cinn. 1913-21, N.Y. (N) 1922-26, Pitt. 1927.
Gross, Greg: 1973-89; Hou. 1973-76, Cubs 1977-78, Phil. 1979-88, Hou. 1989.
Gross, Kevin: 1983 to present; Phil. 1983-88, Mont. 1989-90, L.A. 1991.
Gross, Wayne: 1976-86; Oak. 1976-83, Balt. 1984-85, Oak. 1986.
Grote, Jerry: 1963-78, 1981; Hou. 1963-64, Mets 1966-77, L.A. 1977-78, K.C. 1981, L.A. 1981.
Groth, Johnny: 1946-60; Det. 1946-52, St.L. 1953, White Sox 1954-55, Wash. 1955, K.C. 1956-57, Det. 1957-60.
Grove, Lefty: 1925-41; Phil. (A) 1925-33, Bos. (A) 1934-41; MVP 1931, HOF.
Grubb, Johnny: 1972-87; S.D. 1972-76, Cleve. 1977-78, Texas 1978-82, Det. 1983-87.
Gruber, Kelly: 1984 to present; Tor. 1984-present.
Guante, Cecilio: 1982-90; Pitt. 1982-86, Yankees 1987-88, Texas 1988-89, Cleve. 1990.
Gubicza, Mark: 1984 to present; K.C. 1984-present.
Guerrero, Pedro: 1978 to present; L.A. 1978-88, St.L. 1988-present.
Guidry, Ron: 1975-88; Yankees 1975-88; Cy Young 1978.
Guillen, Ozzie: 1985 to present; White Sox 1985-present; ROY 1985.
Gullett, Don: 1970-78; Cinn. 1970-76, Yankees 1977-78.

Gullickson, Bill: 1979-87, 1990-present; Mont. 1979-85, Cinn. 1986-87, Yankees 1987, Hou. 1990, Det. 1991.
Gumpert, Randy: 1936-38, 1946-52; Phil. 1936-38, Yankees 1946-48, White Sox 1948-51, Bos. (A) 1952, Wash. 1952.
Gura, Larry: 1970-85; Cubs 1970-73, Yankees 1974-75, K.C. 1976-85, Cubs 1985.
Gustine, Frankie: 1939-50; Pitt. 1939-48, Cubs 1949, St.L. (A) 1950.
Gwynn, Tony: 1982 to present; S.D. 1982-present.

H

Haas, Bert: 1937-38, 1942-43, 1946-49, 1951; Bro. 1937-38, Cinn. 1942-43, 1946, Phil. (N) 1948-49, N.Y. (N) 1949, White Sox 1951.
Haas, Moose: 1976-87; Mil. 1976-85, Oak. 1986-87.
Haas, Mule: 1925, 1928-38; Pitt. 1925, Phil. 1928-32, White Sox 1933-37, Phil. (A) 1938.
Hack, Stan: 1932-47; Cubs 1932-47.
Haddix, Harvey: 1952-65; St.L. (N) 1952-56, Phil. 1956-57, Cinn. 1958, Pitt. 1959-63, Balt. 1964-65.
Hadley, Bump: 1926-41; Wash. 1926-31, White Sox 1932, St.L. (A) 1932-34, Wash. 1935, Yankees 1936-40, N.Y. (N) 1941, Phil. (A) 1941.
Hafey, Chick: 1924-37; St.L. 1924-1931, Cinn. 1932-37; HOF.
Haines, Jesse: 1918, 1920-37; Cinn. 1918, St.L. (N) 1920-37; HOF.
Hairston, Jerry: 1973-77, 1981-89; White Sox 1973-77, Pitt. 1977, White Sox 1981-89.
Hall, Dick: 1952-71; Pitt. 1952-59, K.C. 1960, Balt. 1961-66, Phil. 1967-68, Balt. 1969-71.
Hall, Jimmie: 1963-70; Minn. 1963-66, Cal. 1967-68, Cleve. 1968-69, Yankees 1969, Cubs 1969-70, Atl. 1970.
Hall, Tom: 1968-77; Minn. 1968-71, Cinn. 1972-75, Mets 1975-76, K.C. 1976-77.
Hallahan, Bill: 1925-38; St.L. 1925-36, Cinn. 1936-37, Phil. 1938.
Haller, Tom: 1961-72; S.F. 1961-67, L.A. 1968-71, Det. 1972.
Hamilton, Billy: 1888-01; K.C. (A) 1888-89, Phil. 1890-95, Bos. (N) 1896-01, HOF.
Hamilton, Dave: 1972-80; Oak. 1972-75, White Sox 1975-77, St.L. 1978, Pitt. 1978, Oak. 1979-80.
Hammaker, Atlee: 1981 to present; K.C. 1981, S.F. 1982-1990, S.D. 1990-present.
Hamner, Granny: 1944-59, 1962; Phil. (N) 1944-59; Cleve. 1959, K.C. 1962.
Hands, Bill: 1965-75, S.F. 1965, Cubs 1966-72, Minn. 1973-74, Texas 1974-75.
Haney, Larry: 1966-78; Balt. 1966-68, Seat. 1969, Oak. 1969-73, St.L. 1973, Oak. 1974-76, Mil. 1977-78.
Hansen, Ron: 1958-72; Balt. 1958-62, White Sox 1963-67; Wash. 1968, White Sox 1968-69, Yankees 1970-71, K.C. 1972; ROY 1960.
Harder, Mel: 1928-47; Cleve. 1928-47.
Hargan, Steve: 1965-77; Cleve. 1965-72, Texas 1974-76, Tor. 1977, Texas 1977, Atl. 1977.
Hargrave, Bubbles: 1913-15, 1921-28, 1930; Cubs 1913-15, Cinn. 1921-28, Yankees 1930.
Hargrove, Mike: 1974-85; Texas 1974-78, S.D. 1979, Cleve. 1979-85; ROY 1974.
Harnisch, Pete: 1989-present; Balt. 1989-90, Hou. 1991.
Harper, Brian: 1979, 1981-present; Cal. 1979, 1981, Pitt. 1982-84, St.L. 1985, Det. 1986, Oak. 1987, Minn. 1988-present.
Harper, Tommy: 1962-76; Cinn. 1962-67, Cleve. 1968, Seat. 1969, Mil. 1970-71, Bos. 1972-74, Oak. 1975, Cal. 1975, Balt. 1976.
Harrah, Toby: 1969, 1971-86; Wash. 1969, 1971, Texas 1972-78, Cleve. 1979-83, Yankees 1984, Texas 1985-86.
Harrelson, Bud: 1965-80; Mets 1965-77, Phil. 1978-79, Texas 1980.
Harrelson, Ken: 1963-71; K.C. 1963-66, Wash. 1966-67, K.C. 1967, Bos. 1967-69, Cleve. 1969-71.
Harridge, Will: executive; HOF.
Harris, Bucky: 1919-29, 1931; Wash. 1919-28, Det. 1929, 1931; HOF.

Harris, Greg: 1981 to present; Mets 1981, Cinn. 1982-83, Mont. 1984, S.D. 1984, Texas 1985-87, Phil. 1988-89, Bos. 1989-present.

Harris, Mickey: 1940-52; Bos. (A) 1940-49, Wash. 1949-52, Cleve. 1952.

Hart, Jim Ray: 1963-74; S.F. 1963-73, Yankees 1973-74.

Hartnett, Gabby: 1922-41; Cubs 1922-40, N.Y. (N), 1941; MVP 1935, HOF.

Hassey, Ron: 1978 to present; Cleve. 1978-84, Cubs 1984, Yankees 1985-86, White Sox 1986-87, Oak. 1988-90, Mont. 1991.

Hassler, Andy: 1971, 1973-85: Cal. 1971, 1973-76, K.C. 1976-78, Bos. 1978-79, Mets 1979, Pitt. 1980, Cal. 1980-83, St.L. 1984-85.

Hatcher, Mickey: 1979-90; L.A. 1979-80, Minn. 1981-86, L.A. 1987-90.

Hatton, Grady: 1946-56, 1960; Cinn. 1946-54, White Sox 1954, Bos. (A) 1954-56, St.L. (N) 1956, Balt. 1956, Cubs 1960.

Hayes, Frankie: 1933-47; Phil. (A) 1933-42, St.L. 1942-43, Phil. (A) 1944-45, Cleve. 1945-46, White Sox 1946, Bos. 1947.

Hayes, Jackie: 1927-40; Wash. 1927-31, White Sox 1932-40.

Hayes, Von: 1981 to present; Cleve. 1981-82, Phil. 1983-present.

Healy, Fran: 1969, 1971-78; K.C. 1969, S.F. 1971-72, K.C. 1973-76, Yankees 1976-78.

Hearn, Jim: 1947-59; St.L. 1947-50, N.Y. (N) 1950-56, Phil. (N) 1957-59.

Heath, Jeff: 1936-49; Cleve. 1936-45; Wash. 1946, St.L. (A) 1946-47; Bos. (N) 1948-49.

Hebner, Richie: 1968-85; Pitt. 1968-76, Phil. 1977-78, Mets 1979, Det. 1980-82, Pitt. 1982-83, Cubs 1984-85.

Heep, Dan: 1979-90; Hou. 1979-82, Mets 1983-86, L.A. 1987-88, Bos. 1989-90.

Hegan, Jim: 1941-50; Cleve. 1941-57, Det. 1958, Phil (N) 1958-59, S.F. 1959, Cubs 1960.

Hegan, Mike: 1964-67, 1969-77; Yankees 1964-67, Seat. 1969, Mil. 1970-71, Oak. 1971-73, Yankees 1973-74, Mil. 1974-1977.

Heilmann, Harry: 1914-30, 1932; Det. 1914-29, Cinn. 1930, 1932; HOF.

Heise, Bob: 1967-77; Mets 1967-69; S.F. 1970-71, Mil. 1971-73, St.L. 1974, Cal. 1974, Bos. 1975-76, K.C. 1977.

Helms, Tommy: 1964-77; Cinn. 1964-71, Hou. 1972-75, Pitt. 1976-77, Bos. 1977; ROY 1966.

Hemsley, Rollie: 1928-44, 1946-47; Pitt. 1928-31, Cubs 1931-32, Cinn. 1933, St.L. (A) 1933-37, Cleve. 1938-41, Cinn. 1942, Yankees 1942-44, Phil. (N) 1946-47.

Hemus, Solly: 1949-59; St.L. (N) 1949-56, Phil. 1956-58, St.L. (N) 1959.

Henderson, Dave: 1981 to present; Seat. 1981-86, Bos. 1986-87, S.F. 1987, Oak. 1988-present.

Henderson, Rickey: 1979 to present; Oak. 1979-84, Yankees 1985-89, Oak. 1989-present; MVP 1990.

Henderson, Steve: 1977-88; Mets 1977-80, Cubs 1981-82, Seat. 1983-84, Oak. 1985-87, Hou. 1988.

Hendrick, George: 1971-88; Oak. 1971-72, Cleve. 1972-76, S.D. 1977-78, St.L. 78-84, Pitt. 1985, Cal. 1985-88.

Hendricks, Ellie: 1968-79; Balt. 1968-72, Cubs 1972, Balt. 1973-76, Yankees 1976-77, Balt. 1978-79.

Henke, Tom: 1982 to present; Texas 1982-84, Tor. 1985-present.

Henneman, Mike: 1987 to present; Det. 1987-present.

Henrich, Tommy: 1937-50; Yankees 1937-50.

Henry, Bill: 1952-1955, 1958-69; Bos. (A) 1952-55, Cubs 1958-59, Cinn. 1960-65, S.F. 1965-68, Pitt. 1968, Hou. 1969.

Herbert, Ray: 1950-66; Det. 1950-54, K.C. 1955-61, White Sox 1961-64, Phil. 1965-66.

Herman, Babe: 1926-37, 1945; Bro. 1926-31, Cinn. 1932, Cubs 1933-34, Pitt. 1935, Cinn. 1935-36, Det. 1937, Bro. 1945.

Herman, Billy: 1931-47, Cubs 1931-41, Bro. 1941-46, Bos. (N) 1946, Pitt. 1947; HOF.

Hernandez, Keith: 1974 to present; St.L. 1974-83, Mets 1983-89, Cleve. 1990-present; MVP 1979.

Hernandez, Willie: 1977-89; Cubs 1977-83, Phil. 1983, Det. 1984-89; MVP 1984, Cy Young 1984.

Herndon, Larry: 1974, 1976-88; St.L. 1974, S.F. 1976-81, Det. 1982-88.

Herr, Tom: 1979-91; St.L. 1979-88, Minn. 1988, Phil. 1989, Phil. 1990, Mets 1991, S.F. 1991.
Herrmann, Ed: 1967-78; White Sox 1967-74, Yankees 1975, Cal. 1976, Hou. 1976-78, Mont. 1978.
Hershberger, Mike: 1961-71; White Sox 1961-64, K.C. 1965-67, Oak. 1968-69, Mil. 1970, White Sox 1971.
Hershiser, Orel: 1983 to present; L.A. 1983-present; Cy Young 1988.
Herzog, Whitey: 1956-63; Wash. 1956-58, K.C. 1958-60, Balt. 1961-63.
Hickman, Jim: 1962-74; Mets 1962-66, L.A. 1967, Cubs 1968-73, St.L. 1974.
Higbe, Kirby: 1937-50; Cubs 1937-39, Phil. (N) 1939-40, Bro. 1941-47, Pitt. 1947-49, N.Y. (N) 1949-50.
Higgins, Pinky: 1930, 1933-46; Phil. (A) 1930, 1933-36, Bos. (A) 1937-38, Det. 1939-46, Bos. 1946.
High, Andy: 1922-34; Bro. 1922-25, Bos. 1925-27, St.L. (N) 1928-31, Cinn. 1932-33, Phil. 1934.
Higuera, Ted: 1985 to present; Mil. 1985-present.
Hildebrand, Oral: 1931-40; Cleve. 1931-36, St.L. 1937-38, Yankees 1939-40.
Hill, Marc: 1973-86; St.L. 1973-74, S.F. 1975-80, Seat. 1980, White Sox 1981-85.
Hiller, John: 1965-80; Det. 1965-80.
Hinton, Chuck: 1961-71; Wash. 1961-64, Cleve. 1964-71.
Hisle, Larry: 1968-71, 1973-82; Phil. 1968-71, Minn. 1973-77, Mil. 1978-82.
Hoak, Don: 1954-64; Bro. 1954-55, Cubs 1956, Cinn. 1957-58, Pitt. 1959-62, Phil. 1963-64.
Hobson, Butch: 1975-82; Bos. 1975-80, Cal. 1981, Yankees 1982.
Hodges, Gil: 1943-63; Bro. 1943-57, L.A. 1958-63.
Hodges, Ron: 1973-84; Mets 1973-84.
Hoeft, Billy: 1952-66; Det. 1952-59, Bos. 1959, Balt. 1959-62, S.F. 1963, Mil. 1964, Cubs 1965-66, S.F. 1966.
Hoerner, Joe: 1963-64, 1966-77; Hou. 1963-64, St.L. 1966-1969, Phil. 1970-72, At.L. 1972-73, K.C. 1973-74, Phil. 1975, Texas 1976, Cinn. 1977.
Hoffman, Glenn: 1980-87, 1989; Bos. 1980-87, L.A. 1987, Cal. 1989.
Hogsett, Chief: 1929-38, 1944; Det. 1929-36, St.L. 1936-37, Wash. 1938, Det. 1944.
Holland, Al: 1977-87; Pitt. 1977, S.F. 1978-82, Phil. 1983-85, Pitt. 1985, Cal. 1985, Yankees 1986-87.
Hollingsworth, Al: 1935-46; Cinn. 1935-38, Phil. 1938-39, Bro. 1939, Wash. 1940, St.L. 1942-46, White Sox 1946.
Holmes, Tommy: 1942-52; Bos. (N) 1942-51, Bro. 1952.
Holt, Jim: 1968-76; Minn. 1968-74, Oak. 1974-76.
Holtzman, Ken: 1965-79; Cubs 1965-71, Oak. 1972-75, Balt. 1976, Yankees 1976-78, Cubs 1978-79.
Honeycutt, Rick: 1977 to present; Seat. 1977-1980, Texas 1981-83, L.A. 1983-87, Oak. 1987-present.
Hooper, Harry: 1909-25; Bos. (A) 1909-1920, White Sox 1921-25; HOF.
Hooton, Burt: 1971-85; Cubs 1971-75, L.A. 1975-1984, Texas 1985.
Hopp, Johnny: 1939-52; St.L. 1939-45, Bos. (N) 1946-47, Pitt. 1948-49, Bro. 1949, Pitt. 1949-50, Yankees 1950-52, Det. 1952.
Horlen, Joe: 1961-72; White Sox 1961-71, Oak. 1972.
Horner, Bob: 1978-86, 1988; Atl. 1978-86, St.L. 1988; ROY 1978.
Hornsby, Rogers: 1915-37; St.L. 1915-26, N.Y. (N) 1927, Bos. (N) 1928, Cubs 1929-32, St.L. (N) 1933, St.L. (A) 1933-37; MVP 1925, 1929, HOF.
Horton, Willie: 1963-80; Det. 1963-77, Texas 1977, Cleve. 1978, Oak., 1978, Cleve. 1978, Tor. 1978, Seat. 1979-80.
Hough, Charlie: 1970 to present; L.A. 1970-80, Texas 1980-1990, White Sox 1991.
Houtteman, Art: 1945-57; Det. 1945-53, Cleve. 1953-57, Balt. 1957.
Howard, Elston: 1955-68; Yankees 1955-67, Bos. 1967-68; MVP 1963.
Howard, Frank: 1958-73; L.A. 1958-64, Wash. 1965-71, Texas 1972, Det. 1972-73; ROY 1960.
Howe, Art: 1974-82, 1984-85; Pitt. 1974-75, Hou. 1976-82, St.L. 1984-85.

Howe, Steve; 1980-85, 1987, 1991; L.A. 1980-85, Minn. 1985, Texas 1987, Yankees 1991; ROY 1980.
Howell, Jay: 1980-present; Cinn. 1980, Cubs 1981, Yankees 1982-84, Oak. 1985-87, L.A. 1988-present.
Howell, Roy: 1974-84; Texas 1974-77, Tor. 1977-80, Mil. 1981-84.
Howser, Dick: 1961-68; K.C. 1961-63, Cleve. 1963-66, Yankees 1967-68.
Hoyt, LaMarr: 1979-86; White Sox 1979-84, S.D. 1985-86; Cy Young 1983.
Hoyt, Waite: 1918-38; N.Y. (N) 1918, Bos. (A) 1919-20, Yankees 1921-30, Det. 1930-31, Phil. (A) 1931, Bro. 1932, N.Y. (N) 1932, Pitt. 1933-37, Bro. 1937-38; HOF.
Hrbek, Kent: 1981 to present; Minn. 1981-present.
Hubbard, Cal: 1937-51; umpire; HOF.
Hubbard, Glenn: 1978-89; At.L. 1978-87, Oak. 1988-89.
Hubbell, Carl: 1928-43; N.Y. 1928-43; MVP 1933, 1936, HOF.
Hubbs, Ken: 1961-63; Cubs 1961-63; ROY 1962.
Hudson, Sid: 1940-54; Wash. 1940-52, Bos. (A) 1952-54.
Huggins, Miller: 1904-16; Cinn. 1904-09, St.L. 1910-16; HOF.
Hughson, Tex: 1941-49; Bos. (A) 1941-49.
Hume, Tom: 1977-87; Cinn. 1977-85; Phil. 1986-87, Cinn. 1987.
Hundley, Randy: 1964-77; S.F. 1964-65; Cubs 1966-73, Minn. 1974, S.D. 1975, Cubs 1976-77.
Hunt, Ron: 1963-74; N.Y. (N) 1963-66, L.A. 1967, S.F. 1968-70, Mont. 1971-74, St.L. 1974.
Hunter, Billy: 1953-58; St.L. (A) 1953, Balt. 1954, Yankees 1955-56, K.C. 1957-58, Cleve. 1958.
Hunter, Catfish: 1965-79; K.C. 1965-67, Oak. 1968-74, Yankees 1975-79; Cy Young 1974, HOF.
Hurdle, Clint: 1977-87; K.C. 1977-81, Cinn. 1982, Mets 1983-85, St.L. 1986, Mets 1987.
Hurst, Bruce: 1980 to present; Bos. 1980-88, S.D. 1989-present.
Hurst, Don: 1928-34; Phil. (N) 1928-34, Cubs 1934.
Hutchinson, Fred: 1939-53; Det. 1939-53.
Hutton, Tommy: 1966, 1969, 1972-81: L.A. 1966, 1969, Phil. 1972-77, Tor. 1978, Mont. 1978-81.

I

Incaviglia, Pete: 1986-present; Texas 1986-90, Det. 1991.
Iorg, Dane: 1977-86; Phil. 1977, St.L. 1977-84, K.C. 1984-85, S.D. 1986.
Iorg, Garth: 1978-87; Tor. 1978-87.
Irvin, Monte: 1949-56; N.Y. (N) 1949-55, Cubs 1956; HOF.
Ivie, Mike: 1971, 1974-83; S.D. 1971, S.D. 1974-77, S.F. 1978-81, Hou. 1981-82. Det. 1982-83.

J

Jablonski, Ray: 1953-60; St.L. 1953-54, Cinn. 1955-56, N.Y. (N) 1957, S.F. 1958, St.L. 1959, K.C. 1959-60.
Jackson, Bo: 1986 to present; K.C. 1986-90; White Sox 1991.
Jackson, Danny: 1983 to present; K.C. 1983-87, Cinn. 1988-90, Cubs 1991.
Jackson, Grant: 1965-82; Phil. 1965-70, Balt. 1971-76, Yankees 1976, Pitt. 1977-81, Mont. 1981, K.C. 1982, Pitt. 1982.
Jackson, Larry: 1955-68; St.L. 1955-62, Cubs 1963-66, Phil. 1966-68.
Jackson, Randy: 1950-59; Cubs 1950-55, Bro. 1956-57, L.A. 1958, Cleve. 1958-59, Cubs 1959.
Jackson, Reggie: 1967-87; K.C. 1967, Oak. 1968-75, Balt. 1976, Yankees 1977-81, Cal. 1982-86, Oak. 1987; MVP 1973.
Jackson, Ron: 1975-84; Cal. 1975-78, Minn. 1979-81, Det. 1981, Cal. 1982-84, Balt. 1984.
Jackson, Sonny: 1963-74; Hou. 1963-67, Atl. 1968-74.
Jackson, Travis: 1922-36; N.Y. (N) 1922-36; HOF.
Jacobson, Baby Doll: 1915, 1917-27; Det. 1915, St.L. (A) 1915, 1917-26, Bos. (A) 1926-27, Cleve. 1927, Phil. (A) 1927.
Jacoby, Brook: 1981, 1983 to present; Atl. 1981, 1983, Cleve. 1984-91, Oak. 1991.

Jamieson, Charlie: 1915-32; Wash. 1915-17, Phil. (A) 1917-18, Cleve. 1919-32.
Jansen, Larry: 1947-54, 1956; N.Y. (N) 1947-54, Cinn. 1956.
Javery, Al: 1940-46; Bos. (N) 1940-46.
Javier, Julian: 1960-72; St.L. 1960-71, Cinn. 1972.
Jay, Joey: 1953-66; Mil. 1953-60, Cinn. 1961-66, Atl. 1966.
Jefferson, Jesse: 1973-81; Balt. 1973-75, White Sox 1975-76, Tor. 1977-80, Pitt. 1980, Cal. 1981.
Jenkins, Fergie: 1965-83; Phil. 1965-66, Cubs 1966-73, Texas 1974-75, Bos. 1976-77, Texas 1978-81, Cubs 1982-83; Cy Young 1971, HOF.
Jennings, Hughie: 1891-1903, 1907, 1909, 1912, 1918; Lou. (A) 1891, Lou (N) 1892-93, Balt. 1893-98, Bro. 1899, Balt. 1899, Bro. 1899-00, Phil. 1901-02, Bro. 1903, Det. 1907, 1909, 1912, 1918; HOF.
Jethroe, Sam: 1950-52, 1954; Bos. (N) 1950-52, Pitt. 1954; ROY 1950.
John, Tommy: 1963-89; Cleve. 1963-64, White Sox 1965-71, L.A. 1972-78, Yankees 1979-82, Cal. 1982-85, Oak. 1985, Yankees 1986-89.
Johnson, Alex: 1964-76; Phil. 1964-65; St.L. 1966-67, Cinn. 1968-69, Cal. 1970-71, Cleve. 1972, Texas 1973-74, Yankees 1974-75, Det. 1976.
Johnson, Ban: executive; HOF.
Johnson, Billy: 1943-53; Yankees 1943-51, St.L. 1951-53.
Johnson, Bob: 1933-45; Phil. (A) 1933-42, Wash. 1943, Bos. (A) 1944-45.
Johnson, Cliff: 1972-86; Hou. 1972-77, Yankees 1977-79, Cleve. 1979-80, Cubs 1980, Oak. 1981-82, Tor. 1983-84, Texas 1985, Tor. 1985-86.
Johnson, Davey: 1965-78; Balt. 1965-72, Atl. 1973-75, Phil. 1977-78, Cubs 1978.
Johnson, Deron: 1960-76; Yankees 1960-61, K.C. 1961-62, Cinn. 1964-67, Atl. 1968, Phil. 1969-73, Oak. 1973-74, Mil. 1974, Bos. 1974, White Sox 1975, Bos. 1975-76.
Johnson, Howard: 1983 to present; Det. 1982-84, Mets 1985-present.
Johnson, Judy: 1921-38: Negro Leagues; HOF.
Johnson, Ken: 1958-70; K.C. 1958-61, Cinn. 1961, Hou. 1962-65, Mil. 1965, Atl. 1966-69, Mets 1969, Cubs 1969, Mont. 1970.
Johnson, Lamar: 1974-82; White Sox 1974-81, Texas 1982.
Johnson, Roy: 1929-38; Det. 1929-32, Bos. (A) 1932-35, Yankees 1936-37, Bos. 1937-38.
Johnson, Si: 1928-38, 1940-43, 1946-47; Cinn. 1928-36, St.L. (N) 1937-38, Phil. (N) 1940-43, 1946, Bos. (N) 1946-47.
Johnson, Syl: 1922-40; Det. 1922-25, St.L. (N) 1926-33, Cinn. 1934, Phil. 1934-40.
Johnson, Walter: 1907-27; Wash. 1907-27; MVP 1913, 1924, HOF.
Johnstone, Jay: 1966-85; Cal. 1966-70, White Sox 1971-72, Oak. 1973, Phil. 1974-78, Yankees 1978-79, S.D. 1979, L.A. 1980-82, Cubs 1982-84, L.A. 1985.
Jones, Cleon: 1963-76; Mets 1963-75, White Sox 1976.
Jones, Doug: 1982, 1986 to present; Mil. 1982, Cleve. 1986-present.
Jones, Mack: 1961-71; Mil. 1961-65, Atl. 1966-67, Cinn. 1968, Mont. 1969-71.
Jones, Nippy: 1946-52, 1957; St.L. (N) 1946-51, Phil. (N) 1952, Mil. 1957.
Jones, Randy: 1973-82; S.D. 1973-80, Mets 1981-82; Cy Young 1976.
Jones, Ruppert: 1976-87; K.C. 1976, Seat. 1977-79, Yankees 1980, S.D. 1981-83, Det. 1984, Cal. 1985-87.
Jones, Sam: 1951-52, 1955-64; Cleve. 1951-52, Cubs 1955-56, St.L. 1957-58, S.F. 1959-61, Det. 1962, St.L. 1963, Balt. 1964.
Jones, Willie: 1947-61; Phil. 1947-59, Cleve. 1959, Cinn. 1959-61.
Joost, Eddie: 1936-55; Cinn. 1936-42, Bos. (N) 1943, 1945, Phil. (A) 1947-54, Bos. (A) 1955.
Jorgensen, Mike: 1968, 1970-85; Mets 1968, 1970-71, Mont. 1972-77, Oak. 1977, Texas 1978-79, Mets 1980-83, Atl. 1983-84, St.L. 1984-85.
Josephson, Duane: 1965-72; White Sox 1965-70, Bos. 1971-72.
Joshua, Von: 1969-80; L.A. 1969-74, S.F. 1975-76, Mil. 1976-77, L.A. 1979, S.D. 1980.
Joss, Addie: 1902-10; Cleve. 1902-10; HOF.

Joyner, Wally: 1986 to present; Cal. 1986-present.

Judd, Oscar: 1941-48; Bos. (A) 1941-45, Phil. (N) 1945-48.

Judge, Joe: 1915-34; Wash. 1915-32, Bro. 1933-34.

Jurges, Billy: 1931-47; Cubs 1931-38, N.Y. (N) 1939-45, Cubs 1945-47.

Justice, Dave: 1989-present; Atl. 1989-present.

K

Kaat, Jim: 1959-83; Wash. 1959-60, Minn. 1961-73, White Sox 1973-75, Phil. 1976-79, Yankees 1979-80, St.L. 1980-83.

Kaline, Al: 1953-74; Det. 1953-74; HOF.

Kamm, Willie: 1923-35; White Sox 1923-31, Cleve. 1932-35.

Kasko, Eddie: 1957-66; St.L. 1957-58, Cinn. 1959-63, Hou. 1964-65, Bos. 1966.

Kaufmann, Tony: 1921-31, 1935; Cubs 1921-27, Phil (N) 1927, St.L. (N) 1927-31, 1935.

Keefe, Tim: 1880-93; Tro. (N) 1880-82, N.Y. (A) 1883-84, N.Y. 1885-89, N.Y. (P) 1890, N.Y. (N) 1891, Phil. 1891-93; HOF.

Keegan, Bob: 1953-58; White Sox 1953-58.

Keeler, Willie: 1892-10; N.Y. (N) 1892-93, Bro. 1893, Balt. 1894-98, Bro. 1899-02, Yankees 1903-09, N.Y. (N) 1910; HOF.

Kell, George: 1943-57; Phil. (A) 1943-46, Det. 1946-52, Bos. (A) 1952-54, White Sox 1954-56, Balt. 1956-57; HOF.

Keller, Charlie: 1939-52; Yankees 1939-49, Det. 1950-51, Yankees 1952.

Kelley, Joe: 1891-08; Bos. (N) 1891, Pitt. 1892, Balt. 1892-98, Bro. 1899-01, Balt. 1902, Cinn. 1902-06, Bos. (N) 1908; HOF.

Kellner, Alex: 1948-59; Phil. (A) 1948-54, K.C. 1955-58, Cinn. 1958, St.L. 1959.

Kelly, George: 1915-17, 1919-30, 1932; N.Y. (N) 1915-17, Pitt. 1917, N.Y. (N) 1919-26, Cinn. 1927-30, Chi. 1930, Bro. 1932; HOF.

Kelly, King: 1878-93; Cinn. 1878-79, Chi. (N) 1880-86, Bos. (N) 1887-90, Cinn. 1891, Bos. (A) 1891, Bos. (N) 1891-92, N.Y. (N) 1893; HOF.

Kelly, Pat: 1967-81; Minn. 1967-68, K.C. 1969-70, White Sox 1971-76, Balt. 1977-80, Cleve. 1981.

Keltner, Ken: 1937-50; Cleve. 1937-49, Bos. (A) 1950.

Kemp, Steve: 1977-88; Det. 1977-81, White Sox 1982, Yankees 1983-84, Pitt. 1985-86, Texas 1988.

Kendall, Fred: 1969-80; S.D. 1969-76, Cleve. 1977, Bos. 1978, S.D. 1979-80.

Kennedy, Terry: 1978 to present; St.L. 1978-80, S.D. 1981-86, Balt. 1987-88, S.F. 1989-present.

Kennedy, Vern: 1934-45; White Sox 1934-37, Det. 1938-39, St.L. 1939-41, Wash. 1941, Cleve. 1942-44, Phil. 1944-45, Cinn. 1945.

Keough, Matt: 1977-83, 1985-86; Oak. 1977-83, Yankees 1983, St.L. 1985, Cubs 1986, Hou. 1986.

Kern, Jim: 1974-86; Cleve. 1974-78, Texas 1979-81, Cinn. 1982, White Sox 1982-83, Phil. 1984, Mil. 1984-85, Cleve. 1986.

Kerr, Buddy: 1943-51; N.Y. (N) 1943-49, Bos. 1950-51.

Kessinger, Don: 1964-79; Cubs 1964-75, St.L. 1976-1977, White Sox 1977-79.

Key, Jimmy: 1984 to present; Tor. 1984-present.

Killebrew, Harmon: 1954-75; Wash. 1954-60, Minn. 1961-74, K.C. 1975; MVP 1969, HOF.

Kiner, Ralph: 1946-55; Pitt. 1946-53, Cubs 1953-54, Cleve. 1955; HOF.

Kingman, Dave: 1971-86; S.F. 1971-74, Mets 1975-77, S.D. 1977, Cal. 1977, Yankees 1977, Cubs 1978-80, Mets 1981-83, Oak. 1984-86.

Kirkpatrick, Ed: 1962-77; L.A. (A) 1962-64, Cal. 1965-68, K.C. 1969-73, Pitt. 1974-77, Texas 1977, Mil. 1977.

Kison, Bruce: 1971-85; Pitt. 1971-79, Cal. 1980-84, Bos. 1985.

Kittle, Ron: 1982-present; White Sox 1982-86, Yankees 1986-87, Cleve. 1988, White Sox 1989-90, Balt. 1990, White Sox 1991; ROY 1983

Klein, Chuck: 1928-44; Phil. (N) 1928-33, Cubs 1934-36, Phil. (N) 1936-39, Pitt. 1939, Phil. (N) 1940-44; MVP 1932, HOF.

Klem, Bill: 1905-40; umpire; HOF.
Kline, Ron: 1952, 1955-70; Pitt. 1952, 1955-59, St.L. 1960, L.A. 1961, Det. 1961-62, Wash. 1963-66, Minn. 1967, Pitt. 1968-69, S.F. 1969, Bos. 1969, Atl. 1970.
Klippstein, Johnny: 1950-67; Cubs 1950-55, Cinn. 1956-58, L.A. 1958-59, Cleve. 1960, Wash. 1961, Cinn. 1962, Phil. 1963-64, Minn. 1964-66, Det. 1967.
Kluszewski, Ted: 1947-61; Cinn. 1947-57, Pitt. 1958-59, White Sox 1959-60, L.A. 1961.
Knepper, Bob: 1976 to present; S.F. 1976-80, Hou. 1981-89, S.F. 1989-90.
Knight, Ray: 1974, 1977-88; Cinn. 1974, 1977-81, Hou. 1982-84, Mets 1984-86, Balt. 1987, Det. 1988.
Knoop, Bobby: 1964-72; L.A. 1964, Cal. 1965-69, White Sox 1969-70, K.C. 1971-72.
Knowles, Darold: 1965-80; Balt. 1965, Phil. 1966, Wash. 1967-71, Oak. 1971-74, Cubs 1975-76, Texas 1977, Mont. 1978, St.L. 1979-80.
Konstanty, Jim: 1944, 1946, 1948-56; Cinn. 1944, Bos. (N) 1946, Phil. (N) 1948-54, Yankees 1954-56, St.L. 1956; MVP 1950.
Koosman, Jerry: 1967-85; Mets 1967-78, Minn. 1979-81, White Sox 1981-83, Phil. 1984-85.
Koslo, Dave: 1941-55; N.Y. (N) 1941-53, Balt. 1954, Mil. 1954-55.
Koufax, Sandy: 1955-66; Bro. 1955-57, L.A. 1958-66; MVP 1963, Cy Young 1963, 1965, 1966, HOF.
Kralick, Jack: 1959-67; Wash. 1959-60, Minn. 1961-63, Cleve. 1963-67.
Kranepool, Ed: 1962-79; Mets 1962-79.
Krause, Lew: 1961, 1964-74; K.C. 1961, 1964-67, Oak. 1968-69, Mil. 1971-72, Bos. 1972, St.L. 1973, Atl. 1974.
Kreevich, Mike: 1931, 1935-45; Cubs 1931, White Sox 1935-41, Phil. 1942, St.L. 1943-45, Wash. 1945.
Kremer, Ray: 1924-33: Pitt. 1924-33.
Krukow, Mike: 1976-89; Cubs 1976-81, Phil. 1982, S.F. 1983-89.
Kubek, Tony: 1957-65; Yankees 1957-65; ROY 1957.
Kubiak, Ted: 1967-76; K.C. 1967, Oak. 1968-69, Mil. 1970-71, St.L. 1971, Texas 1972, Oak. 1972-75, S.D. 1975-76.
Kuenn, Harvey: 1952-66; 1952-59, Cleve. 1960, S.F. 1961-65, Cubs 1965-66, Phil. 1966; ROY 1953.
Kuhel, Joe: 1930-47; Wash. 1930-37, White Sox 1938-43, Wash. 1944-46, White Sox 1946-47.
Kuhn, Bowie: commissioner.
Kuiper, Duane: 1974-85; Cleve. 1974-81, S.F. 1982-85.
Kurowski, Whitey: 1941-49; St.L. (N) 1941-49.

L

Laabs, Chet: 1937-47; Det. 1937-39, St.L. (A) 1939-46, Phil. (A) 1947.
Labine, Clem: 1950-62; Bro. 1950-57, L.A. 1958-60, Det. 1960, Pitt. 1960-61, Mets 1962.
LaCock, Pete: 1972-80; Cubs 1972-76, K.C. 1977-80.
LaCoss, Mike: 1978 to present; Cinn. 1978-81, Hou. 1982-84, K.C. 1985, S.F. 1986-present.
Lacy, Lee: 1972-87; L.A. 1972-76, Atl. 1976, L.A. 1976-78, Pitt. 1979-84, Balt. 1985-87.
LaGrow, Lerrin: 1970, 1972-80; Det. 1970, 1972-75, St.L. 1976, White Sox 1977-79, L.A. 1979, Phil. 1980.
LaHoud, Joe: 1968-78; Bos. 1968-71, Mil. 1972-73, Cal. 1974-76, Texas 1976, K.C. 1977-78.
Lajoie, Nap: 1896-16; Phil. (N) 1896-00, Phil. (A) 1901-02, Cleve. 1902-14, Phil. 1915-16; HOF.
Lamp, Dennis: 1977-present; Cubs 1977-80, White Sox 1981-83, Tor. 1984-86, Oak. 1987, Bos. 1988-present.
Landis, Jim: 1957-67; White Sox 1957-64, K.C. 1965, Cleve. 1966, Det. 1967, Bos. 1967, Hou. 1967.
Landis, Kenesaw Mountain: commissioner; HOF.
Landreaux, Ken: 1977-87; Cal. 1977-78, Minn. 1979-80, L.A. 1981-87.
Landrum, Tito: 1980-88; St.L. 1980-83, Balt. 1983, St.L. 1984-87, L.A. 1987, Balt. 1988.

Langford, Rick: 1976-86; Pitt. 1976, Oak. 1977-86.
Langston, Mark: 1984 to present; Seat. 1984-89, Mont. 1989, Cal. 1990-present.
Lanier, Max: 1938-53; St.L. 1938-51, N.Y. (N) 1952-53, St.L. (A) 1953.
Lansford, Carney: 1978-present; Cal. 1978-80, Bos. 1981-82, Oak. 1983-present.
LaPoint, Dave: 1980-present; Mil. 1980, St.L. 1981-84, S.F. 1985, Det. 1986, S.D. 1986, St.L. 1987, White Sox 1987-88, Pitt. 1988, Yankees 1989-90, Phil. 1991.
Larker, Norm: 1958-63; L.A. 1958-61, Hou. 1962, Mil. 1963, S.F. 1963.
Larkin, Barry: 1986 to present; Cinn. 1986-present.
LaRoche, Dave: 1970-83; Cal. 1970-71, Minn. 1972, Cubs 1973-74, Cleve. 1975-77, Cal. 1977-80, Yankees 1981-83.
Larsen, Don: 1953-67; St.L. 1953, Balt. 1954, Yankees 1955-59, K.C. 1960-61, White Sox 1961, S.F. 1962-64, Hou. 1964-65, Balt. 1965, Cubs 1967.
Lary, Frank: 1954-65; Det. 1954-64, Mets 1964, Mil. 1964, Mets 1965, White Sox 1965.
Lary, Lynn: 1929-40; Yankees 1929-34, Bos. (A) 1934, Wash. 1935, St.L. (A) 1935-36, Cleve. 1937-39, Bro. 1939, St.L. (N) 1939, St.L. (A) 1940.
Latman, Barry: 1957-67; White Sox 1957-59, Cleve. 1960-63, L.A. 1964, Cal. 1965, Hou. 1966-67.
Lau, Charlie: 1956, 1958-67; Det. 1956, 1958-59, Mil. 1960-61, Balt. 1961-63, K.C. 1963-64, Balt. 1964-67, Atl. 1967.
Laudner, Tim; 1981-89; Minn. 1981-89.
Lavagetto, Cookie: 1934-47; Pitt. 1934-36, Bro. 1937-47.
LaValliere, Mike: 1984 to present; Phil. 1984, St.L. 1985-86, Pitt. 1987-present.
Lavelle, Gary: 1974-87; S.F. 1974-84, Tor. 1985, 1987, Oak. 1987.
Law, Vance: 1980-89, 1991; Pitt. 1980-81, White Sox 1982-84, Mont. 1985-87, Cubs 1988-89, Oak. 1991.
Law, Vern: 1950-67; Pitt. 1950-67; Cy Young 1960.
Lazzeri, Tony: 1926-39; Yankees 1926-37, Cubs 1938, Bro. 1939, N.Y. (N) 1939; HOF.
Lea, Charlie: 1980-88; Mont. 1980-87, Minn. 1988.
Leach, Rick: 1981-90; Det. 1981-83, Tor. 1984-88, Texas 1989, S.F. 1990.
Leary, Tim: 1981, 1983-present; Mets 1981, 1983-84, Mil. 1985-86, L.A. 1987-89, Cinn. 1989, Yankees 1990-present.
Lee, Bill: 1969-82; Bos. 1969-78, Mont. 1979-82.
Lee, Bill: 1934-47; Cubs 1934-43, Phil. (N) 1943-45, Bos. (N) 1945-46, Cubs 1947.
Lee, Thornton: 1933-48; Cleve. 1933-36, White Sox 1937-47, N.Y. (N) 1948.
LeFlore, Ron: 1974-82; Det. 1974-79, Mont. 1980, White Sox 1981-82.
Leiber, Hank; 1933-42; N.Y. (N) 1933-38, Cubs 1939-41, N.Y. (N) 1942.
Leibrandt, Charlie: 1979-present: Cinn. 1979-82, K.C. 1984-89, Atl. 1990-present.
Lemanczyk, Dave: 1973-80; Det. 1973-76, Tor. 1977-80, Cal. 1980.
Lemaster, Denny: 1962-72; Mil. 1962-65, Atl. 1966-67, Hou. 1968-71, Mont. 1972.
LeMaster, Johnnie: 1975-85, 1987; S.F. 1975-85, Cleve. 1985, Pitt. 1985, Oak. 1987.
Lemon, Bob: 1941-58; Cleve. 1941-58; HOF.
Lemon, Chet: 1975-90; White Sox 1975-81, Det. 1982-90.
Lemon, Jim: 1950, 1953-63; Cleve. 1950, 1953, Wash. 1954-60, Minn. 1961-63, Phil. 1963, White Sox 1963.
Leonard, Buck: 1933-50; Negro Leagues, HOF.
Leonard, Dennis: 1974-86; K.C. 1974-86.
Leonard, Dutch: 1913-25; Bos. (A) 1913-1918, Det. 1919-1925.
Leonard, Jeffrey: 1977-90; L.A. 1977, Hou. 1978-81, S.F. 1981-88, Mil. 1988, Seat. 1989-90.
Lerch, Randy: 1975-84, 1986; Phil. 1975-80, Mil. 1981-82, Mont. 1982-83, S.F. 1983-84, Phil. 1986.
Lewis, Buddy: 1935-49; Wash. 1935-49.
Lezcano, Sixto: 1974-85; Mil. 1974-80, St.L. 1981, S.D. 1982-83, Phil. 1983-84, Pitt. 1985.
Lindblad, Paul: 1965-78; K.C. 1965-67, Oak. 1968-71, Wash. 1971, Texas 1972, Oak. 1973-76, Texas 1977-78, Yankees 1978.

Lindell, Johnny: 1941-50, 1953-54; Yankees 1941-50, St.L. (N) 1950, Pitt. 1953, Phil. (N) 1953-54.
Lindstrom, Freddie: 1924-36; N.Y. (N) 1924-32, Pitt. 1933-34, Cubs 1935, Bro. 1936.
Litwhiler, Danny: 1940-51; Phil. (N) 1940-43, St.L. (N) 1943-46, Bos. 1946-48, Cinn. 1948-51.
Linzy, Frank: 1963, 1965-74; S.F. 1963, 1965-70, St.L. 1970-71, Mil. 1972-73, Phil. 1974.
Lloyd, Pop: 1905-31; Negro Leagues; HOF.
Locker, Bob: 1965-73, 1975; White Sox 1965-69, Seat. 1969, Mil. 1970, Oak. 1970-72, Cubs 1973, 1975.
Lockman, Whitey: 1945-60; N.Y. (N) 1945-56, St.L. 1956, Yankees 1957, S.F. 1958, Balt. 1959, Cinn. 1959-60.
Lockwood, Skip: 1969-80; Seat. 1969, Mil.1970-73, Cal. 1974, Mets 1975-79, Bos. 1980.
Loes, Billy: 1950-61; Bro. 1950-56, Balt. 1956-59, S.F. 1960-61.
Logan, Johnny: 1951-63; 1951-52, Mil. 1953-61, Pitt. 1961-63.
Lolich, Mickey: 1963-76, 1978-79; Det. 1963-75, Mets 1976, S.D. 1978-79.
Lollar, Sherm: 1946-63; Cleve. 1946, Yankees 1947-48, St.L. 1949-51, White Sox 1952-63.
Lombardi, Ernie: 1931-47; Bro. 1931, Cinn. 1932-1941, Bos. 1942, N.Y. (N) 1943-47; MVP 1938, HOF.
Lonborg, Jim: 1965-79; Bos. 1965-71, Mil. 1972, Phil. 1973-79; Cy Young 1967.
Long, Dale: 1951, 1955-63; Pitt. 1951, St.L. (A) 1951, Pitt. 1955-57, Cubs 1957-59, S.F. 1960, Yankees 1960, Wash. 1961-62, Yankees 1962-63.
Lopat, Ed: 1944-55; White Sox 1944-47, Yankees 1948-55, Balt. 1955.
Lopata, Stan: 1948-60; Phil. (N) 1948-58, Mil. 1959-60.
Lopes, Davey: 1972-87; L.A. 1972-81, Oak. 1982-84, Cubs 1984-86, Hou. 1986-87.
Lopez, Al: 1928-47; Bro. 1928-35, Bos. (N) 1936-40, Pitt. 1940-46, Cleve. 1947; HOF.
Lopez, Aurelio: 1974, 1978-87; K.C. 1974, St.L 1978, Det. 1979-85, Hou. 1986-87.
Lopez, Hector: 1955-66; K.C. 1955-59, Yankees 1959-66.
Lowenstein, John: 1970-85; Cleve. 1970-77, Texas 1978, Balt. 1979-85.
Lowrey, Peanuts: 1942-55; Cubs 1942-49, Cinn. 1949-50, St.L. 1950-54, Phil. (N) 1955.
Lucas, Red: 1923-38; N.Y. (N) 1923, Bos. (N) 1924-25, Cinn. 1926-33, Pitt. 1934-38.
Lum, Mike: 1967-81; Atl. 1967-75, Cinn. 1976-78, Atl. 1979-81, Cubs 1981.
Lumpe, Jerry: 1956-67; Yankees 1956-59, K.C. 1959-63, Det. 1964-67.
Luque, Dolf: 1914-15, 1918-35; Bos. (N) 1914-15, Cinn. 1918-1929, Bro. 1930-31, N.Y. (N) 1932-35.
Luzinski, Greg: 1970-84; Phil. 1970-80, White Sox 1981-84.
Lyle, Sparky: 1967-82; Bos. 1967-71, Yankees 1972-78, Texas 1979-80, Phil. 1980-82, White Sox 1982; Cy Young 1977.
Lynn, Fred: 1974-90; Bos. 1974-80, Cal. 1981-84, Balt. 1985-88, Det. 1988-89, S.D. 1990; ROY 1975, MVP 1975.
Lyons, Ted: 1923-46; White Sox 1923-46; HOF.

M

Mack, Connie: manager 1894-50; HOF.
MacPhail, Larry: executive; HOF.
Maddox, Elliott: 1970-80; Det. 1970, Wash. 1971, Texas 1972-73, Yankees 1974-76, Balt. 1977, Mets 1978-80.
Maddox, Garry: 1972-86; S.F. 1972-75, Phil. 1975-86.
Maddux, Greg: 1986 to present; Cubs 1986-present.
Madlock, Bill: 1973-87; Texas 1973, Cubs 1974-76, S.F. 1977-79, Pitt. 1979-85, L.A. 1985-87, Det. 1987.
Maglie, Sal: 1945, 1950-58; N.Y. (N) 1945, 1950-55, Cleve. 1955-56, Bro. 1956-57, Yankees 1957-58, St.L. 1958.
Magrane, Joe: 1987 to present; St.L. 1987-present.
Mahler, Rick: 1979-90; Atl. 1979-88, Cinn. 1989-90.

Maldonado, Candy: 1981-present; L.A. 1981-85, S.F. 1986-89, Cleve. 1990, Mil. 1991, Tor. 1991.
Malone, Pat: 1928-37; Cubs 1928-34, Yankees 1935-37.
Maloney, Jim: 1960-71; Cinn. 1960-70, Cal. 1971.
Malzone, Frank: 1955-66; Bos. 1955-65, Cal. 1966.
Mancuso, Gus: 1928-45; St.L. (N) 1928-32, N.Y. (N) 1933-38, Cubs 1939, Bro. 1940, St.L. 1941-42, N.Y. 1942-44, Phil. 1945.
Manning, Rick: 1975-87; Cleve. 1975-83, Mil. 1983-87.
Mantilla, Felix: 1956-66; Mil. 1956-61, Mets 1962, Bos. 1963-65, Hou. 1966.
Mantle, Mickey: 1951-68; Yankees 1951-68; MVP 1956, 1957, 1962, HOF.
Manush, Heinie: 1923-39; Det. 1923-27, St.L. (A) 1928-30, Wash. 1930-35, Bos.. 1936, Bro. 1937-38, Pitt. 1938-39; HOF.
Maranville, Rabbit: 1912-35; Bos. (N) 1912-20, Pitt. 1921-24, Cubs 1925, Bro. 1926, St.L. 1927-28, Bos. (N) 1929-35; HOF.
Marberry, Firpo: 1923-36; Wash. 1923-32, Det. 1933-35, N.Y. (N) 1936, Wash. 1936.
Marichal, Juan: 1960-75; S.F. 1960-73, Bos. 1974, L.A. 1975; HOF.
Marion, Marty: 1940-50, 1952-53; St.L. (N) 1940-50, St.L. (A) 1952-53; MVP 1944.
Maris, Roger: 1957-68; Cleve. 1957-58, K.C. 1958-59, Yankees 1960-66, St.L. 1967-68; MVP 1960, 1961.
Marquard, Rube: 1908-25; N.Y. (N) 1908-15, Bro. 1915-20, Cinn. 1921, Bos. (N) 1922-25; HOF.
Marshall, Mike: 1981 to present; L.A. 1981-89, Mets 1990, Bos. 1990-present.
Marshall, Mike: 1967, 1969-81; Det. 1967, Seat. 1969, Hou. 1970, Mont. 1970-73, L.A. 1974-76, Atl. 1976-77, Texas 1977, Minn. 1978-80, Mets 1981; Cy Young 1974.
Marshall, Willard: 1942, 1946-55; N.Y. (N) 1942, 1946-49, Bos. (N) 1950-52, Cinn. 1952-53, White Sox 1954-55.
Martin, Billy: 1950-61; Yankees 1950-57, K.C. 1957, Det. 1958, Cleve. 1959, Cinn. 1960, Mil. 1961, Minn. 1961.
Martin, Jerry: 1974-84; Phil. 1974-78, Cubs 1979-80, S.F. 1981, K.C. 1982-83, Mets 1984.
Martin, Pepper: 1928-44; St.L. (N) 1928-44.
Martinez, Buck: 1969-86; K.C. 1969-77, Mil. 1978-80, Tor. 1981-86.
Martinez, Dennis: 1976 to present; Balt. 1976-86, Mont. 1986-present.
Martinez, Ramon: 1988 to present; L.A. 1988-present.
Martinez, Tippy: 1974-86, 1988; Yankees 1974-76, Balt. 1976-86, Minn. 1988.
Masi, Phil: 1939-52; Bos. (N) 1939-49, Pitt. 1949, White Sox 1950-52.
Masterson, Walt: 1939-53, 1956; Wash. 1939-49, Bos. (A) 1949-52, Wash. 1952-53, Det. 1956.
Mathews, Eddie: 1952-68; Bos. 1952, Mil. 1953-65, Atl. 1966, Hou. 1967, Det. 1967-68; HOF.
Mathewson, Christy: 1900-16; N.Y. (N) 1900-16, Cinn. 1916; HOF.
Matlack, Jon: 1971-83; Mets 1971-77, Texas 1978-83; ROY 1972.
Matthews, Gary: 1972-87; S.F. 1972-76, Atl. 1977-80, Phil. 1981-83, Cubs 1984-87, Seat. 1987; ROY 1973.
Mattingly, Don: 1982 to present; Yankees 1982-present; MVP 1985.
Maxvill, Dal: 1962-75; St.L. 1962-72, Oak. 1972-73, Pitt. 1973-1974, Oak. 1974-75.
Maxwell, Charlie: 1950-64; Bos. (A) 1950-54, Balt. 1955, Det. 1955-62, White Sox 1962-64.
May, Carlos: 1968-77; White Sox 1968-76, Yankees 1976-77, Cal. 1977.
May, Dave: 1967-78; Balt. 1967-70, Mil. 1970-74, Atl. 1975-76, Texas 1977, Mil. 1978, Pitt. 1978.
May, Lee: 1965-82; Cinn. 1965-71, Hou. 1972-74, Balt. 1975-80, K.C. 1981-82.
May, Milt: 1970-84; Pitt. 1970-73, Hou. 1974-75, Det. 1976-79, White Sox 1979, S.F. 1980-83, Pitt. 1983-84.
May, Pinky: 1939-43; Phil. 1939-43.
May, Rudy: 1965-83; Cal. 1965-74, Yankees 1975-76, Balt. 1976-77, Mont. 1978-79, Yankees 1980-83.
Mayberry, John: 1968-82; Hou. 1968-71, K.C. 1972-77, Tor. 1978-82, Yankees 1982.
Maye, Lee: 1959-71; Mil. 1959-65, Hou. 1965-66, Cleve. 1967-69, Wash. 1969-70, White Sox 1970-71.

Mays, Carl: 1915-29; Bos. (A) 1915-19, Yankees 1920-23, Cinn. 1924-28, N.Y. (N) 1929.
Mays, Willie: 1951-73; N.Y. (N) 1951-57, S.F. 1958-72, Mets 1972-73; ROY 1951, MVP 1954, 1965, HOF.
Mazeroski, Bill: 1956-72; Pitt. 1956-72.
Mazzilli, Lee: 1976-89; Mets 1976-81, Texas 1982, Yankees 1982, Pitt. 1983-86, Mets 1986-89, Tor. 1989.
McAuliffe, Dick: 1960-75; Det. 1960-73, Bos. 1974-75.
McBride, Bake: 1973-83; St.L. 1973-77, Phil. 1977-81, Cleve. 1982-83; ROY 1974.
McCarthy, Joe: manager 1926-50; HOF.
McCarthy, Tommy: 1884-96; Bos. (U) 1884, Bos. (N) 1885, Phil. 1886-87, St.L. (A) 1888-91, Bos. (N) 1892-95, Bro. 1896; HOF.
McCarver, Tim: 1959-80; St.L. 1959-69, Phil. 1970-72, Mont. 1972, St.L. 1973-74, Bos. 1974-75, Phil. 1975-80.
McCaskill, Kirk: 1985-present; Cal. 1985-present.
McCatty, Steve: 1977-85; Oak. 1977-85.
McClure, Bob: 1975-present; K.C. 1975-76, Mil. 1977-86, Mont. 1986-88, Mets 1988, Cal. 1989-present.
McCormick, Frank: 1934, 1937-48; Cinn. 1934, 1937-45, Phil. 46-47, Bos. (N) 1947-48; MVP 1940.
McCormick, Mike: 1956-71; N.Y. (N) 1956-57, S.F. 1958-62, Balt. 1963-64, Wash. 1965-66, S.F. 1967-70, Yankees 1970, K.C. 1971; Cy Young 1967.
McCovey, Willie: 1959-80; S.F. 1959-73, S.D. 1974-76, Oak. 1976, S.F. 1977-80; ROY 1959, MVP 1969, HOF.
McCraw, Tom: 1963-75; White Sox 1963-70, Wash. 1971, Cleve. 1972, Cal. 1973-74, Cleve. 1974-75.
McCullough, Clyde: 1940-56; Cubs 1940-48, Pitt. 1949-52, Cubs 1953-56.
McDaniel, Lindy: 1955-75; St.L. 1955-62, Cubs 1963-65, S.F. 1966-68, Yankees 1968-73, K.C. 1974-75.
McDougald, Gil: 1951-60; Yankees 1951-60; ROY 1951.
McDowell, Jack: 1987 to present; White Sox 1987-present.
McDowell, Roger: 1985-present; Mets 1985-89, Phil. 1989-present.
McDowell, Sam: 1961-75, Cleve. 1961-71, S.F. 1972-73, Yankees 1973-74, Pitt. 1975.
McGee, Willie: 1982 to present; St.L. 1982-90, Oak. 1990-present; MVP 1985.
McGinnity, Joe: 1899-08; Balt. 1889, Bro. 1900, Balt. 1901-02, N.Y. (N) 1902-08; HOF.
McGlothen, Lynn: 1972-82; Bos. 1972-73, St.L. 1974-76, S.F. 1977-78, Cubs 1978-81, White Sox 1981, Yankees 1982.
McGlothin, Jim: 1965-73; Cal. 1965-69, Cinn. 1970-73, White Sox 1973.
McGraw, John: 1891-06; Balt. (A) 1891, Balt. (N) 1892-99, St.L. (N) 1900, Balt. (A) 1901-02, N.Y. (N) 1902-06; HOF.
McGraw, Tug: 1965-84; Mets 1965-74, Phil. 1975-84.
McGregor, Scott: 1976-88; Balt. 1976-88.
McGriff, Fred: 1986 to present; Tor. 1986-90, S.D. 1991.
McGwire, Mark: 1986 to present; Oak. 1986-present; ROY 1987.
McKechnie, Bill: 1907, 1910-18, 1920; Pitt. 1907, 1910-12, Bos. (N) 1913, Yankees 1913, Ind. (F) 1914, New (F) 1915, N.Y. (N) 1916, Cinn. 1916-17, Pitt. 1918, 1920; HOF.
McLain, Denny: 1963-72; Det. 1963-70, Wash. 1971, Oak. 1972, Atl. 1972.
McLish, Cal: 1944, 1946-49, 1951, 1956-64; Bro. 1944, 1946, Pitt. 1947-48, Cubs 1949, 1951, Cleve. 1956-59, Cinn. 1960-61, Phil. 1962-64.
McMahon, Don: 1957-74; Mil. 1957-62, Hou. 1962-63, Cleve. 1964-66, Bos. 1966-67, White Sox 1967-68, Det. 1968-69, S.F. 1969-74.
McManus, Marty: 1920-34; St.L. (A) 1920-26, Det. 1927-31, Bos. (A) 1931-34.
McMillan, Roy: 1951-66; Cinn. 1951-60, Mil. 1961-64, Mets 1964-66.
McMullen, Ken: 1962-77; L.A. 1962-64, Wash. 1965-70, Cal. 1970-72, L.A. 1973-75, Oak. 1976, Mil. 1977.

McNally, Dave: 1962-75; Balt. 1962-74, Mont. 1975.
McQuinn, George: 1936, 1938-48; Cinn. 1936, St.L. (A) 1938-45, Phil. (A) 1946, Yankees 1947-48.
McRae, Hal: 1968, 1970-87; Cinn. 1968, 1970-72, K.C. 1973-87.
McWilliams, Larry: 1978-90; Atl. 1978-82, Pitt. 1982-86, Atl. 1987, St.L. 1988, Phil. 1989, K.C. 1989-90.
Meadows, Lee: 1915-29; St.L.(N) 1915-19, Phil. (N) 1919-23, Pitt. 1923-29.
Medich, Doc: 1972-82; Yankees 1972-75, Pitt. 1976, Oak. 1977, Seat. 1977, Mets 1977, Texas 1978-82, Mil. 1982.
Medwick, Joe: 1932-48; St.L. (N) 1932-40, Bro. 1940-43, N.Y. (N) 1943-45, Bos. (N) 1945, Bro. 1946, St.L. (N) 1947-48; MVP 1937, HOF.
Meine, Heinie: 1922, 1929-34; St.L. (A) 1922, Pitt. 1929-34.
Melton, Bill: 1968-77; White Sox 1968-75, Cal. 1976, Cleve. 1977.
Menke, Denis: 1962-74; Mil. 1962-65, Atl. 1966-67, Hou. 1968-71, Cinn. 1972-73, Hou. 1974.
Merritt, Jim: 1965-75; Minn. 1965-68, Cinn. 1969-72, Texas 1973-75.
Messersmith, Andy: 1968-79; Cal. 1968-72, L.A. 1973-75, Atl. 1976-77, Yankees 1978, L.A. 1979.
Metzger, Butch: 1974-78; S.F. 1974, S.D. 1975-77, St.L. 1977, Mets 1978; ROY 1976.
Metzger, Roger: 1970-80; Cubs 1970, Hou. 1971-78, S.F. 1978-80.
Meusel, Bob: 1920-30; Yankees 1920-29, Cinn. 1930.
Meusel, Irish: 1914, 1918-27: Wash. 1914, Phil. (N) 1918-21, N.Y. (N) 1921-26, Bro. 1927.
Meyer, Dan: 1974-85; Det. 1974-76, Seat. 1977-81, Oak. 1982-85.
Meyer, Russ: 1946-57, 1959; Cubs 1946-49, Phil. 1949-52, Bro. 1953-55, Cubs 1956, Cinn. 1956, Bos. 1957, K.C. 1959.
Michaels, Cass: 1943-54; White Sox 1943-50, Wash. 1950-52, St.L. (A) 1952, Phil. (A) 1952-53, White Sox 1954.
Milbourne, Larry: 1974-84; Hou. 1974-76, Seat. 1977-80, Yankees 1981-82, Minn. 1982, Cleve. 1982, Phil. 1983, Yankees 1983, Seat. 1984.
Millan, Felix: 1966-77; Atl. 1966-72, Mets 1973-77.
Miller, Bob: 1957, 1959-74; St.L. 1957, 1959-61, Mets 1962, L.A. 1963-67, Minn. 1968-69, Cleve. 1970, White Sox 1970, Cubs 1970-71, S.D. 1971, Pitt. 1971-72, S.D. 1973, Mets 1973, Det. 1973, Mets 1974.
Miller, Eddie: 1936-50; Cinn. 1936-37, Bos. 1939-42, Cinn. 1943-47, Phil. (N) 1948-49, St.L. (N) 1950.
Miller, Rick: 1971-85; Bos. 1971-77, Cal. 1978-80, Bos. 1981-85.
Miller, Stu: 1952-68; St.L. (N) 1952-56, Phil. (N) 1956, N.Y. (N) 1957, S.F. 1958-62, Balt. 1963-67, Atl. 1968.
Milner, John: 1971-82; Mets 1971-77, Pitt. 1978-81, Mont. 1981-82, Pitt. 1982.
Mincher, Don: 1960-72; Wash. 1960, Minn. 1961-66, Cal. 1967-68, Seat. 1969, Oak. 1970-71, Wash. 1971, Texas 1972, Oak. 1972.
Minoso, Minnie: 1949, 1951-64, 1976, 1980; Cleve. 1949, 1951, White Sox 1951-57, Cleve. 1958-59, White Sox 1960-61, St.L. 1962, Wash. 1963, White Sox 1976, 1980.
Minton, Greg: 1975-90; S.F. 1975-87, Cal. 1987-90.
Mirabella, Paul: 1978-90; Texas 1978, Yankees 1979, Tor. 1980-81, Texas 1982, Balt. 1983, Seat. 1984-86, Mil. 1987-90.
Mitchell, Dale: 1946-56; Cleve. 1946-56, Bro. 1956.
Mitchell, Kevin: 1984 to present; Mets 1984, 1986, S.D. 1987, S.F. 1987-present; MVP 1989.
Mitterwald, George: 1966, 1968-77; Minn. 1966, 1968-73, Cubs 1974-77.
Mize, Johnny: 1936-53; St.L. (N) 1936-41, N.Y. (N) 1942, 1946-49, Yankees 1949-53; HOF.
Mizell, Vinegar Bend: 1952-62; St.L. (N) 1952-53, 1956-60, Pitt. 1960-62, Mets 1962.
Molitor, Paul: 1978 to present; Mil. 1978-present.
Moffitt, Randy: 1972-83; S.F. 1972-81, Hou. 1982, Tor. 1983.
Monboquette, Bill: 1958-68; Bos. 1958-65, Det. 1966-67, Yankees 1967-68, S.F. 1968.
Monday, Rick: 1966-84; K.C. 1966-67, Oak. 1968-71, Cubs 1972-76, L.A. 1977-84.

Money, Don: 1968-83; Phil. 1968-72, Mil. 1973-83.
Monge, Sid: 1975-84; Cal. 1975-77, Cleve. 1977-81, Phil. 1982-83, S.D. 1983-84, Det. 1984.
Montanez, Willie: 1966, 1970-82; Cal. 1966, Phil. 1970-75, S.F. 1975-76, Atl. 1976-77, Mets 1978-79, Texas 1979, S.D. 1980, Mont. 1980-81, Pitt. 1981-82, Phil. 1982.
Montefusco, John: 1974-86; S.F. 1974-80, Atl. 1981, S.D. 1982-83, Yankees 1983-86; ROY 1975.
Moon, Wally: 1954-65; St.L. 1954-58, L.A. 1959-1965; ROY 1954.
Moore, Charlie: 1973-87; Mil. 1973-86, Tor. 1987.
Moore, Donnie: 1975-88; Cubs 1975-1979, St.L. 1980, Mil. 1981, Atl. 1982-84; Cal. 1985-88.
Moore, Jo-Jo: 1930-41; N.Y. (N) 1930-41.
Moore, Mike: 1982 to present; Seat. 1982-88, Oak. 1989-present.
Moore, Ray: 1952-53, 1955-63; Bro. 1952-53, Balt. 1955-57, White Sox 1958-60, Wash. 1960, Minn. 1961-63.
Moore, Terry: 1935-48; St.L. (N) 1935-48.
Moose, Bob: 1967-76; Pitt. 1967-76.
Morales, Jerry: 1969-83; S.D. 1969-73, Cubs 1974-77, St.L. 1978, Det. 1979, Yankees 1980, Cubs 1981-83.
Moreland, Keith: 1978-89; Phil. 1978-81, Cubs 1982-87, S.D. 1988, Det. 1989, Balt. 1989.
Moreno, Omar: 1975-86; Pitt. 1975-82, Hou. 1983, Yankees 1983-85, K.C. 1985, Atl. 1986.
Morgan, Joe: 1963-84; Hou. 1963-71, Cinn. 1972-79, Hou. 1980, S.F. 1981-82, Phil. 1983, Oak. 1984; MVP 1975, 1976, HOF.
Morgan, Mike: 1978-79, 1982-present; Oak. 1978-79, Yankees 1982, Tor. 1983, Seat. 1985-87, Balt. 1988, L.A. 1989-present.
Morris, Jack: 1977 to present; Det. 1977-90, Minn. 1991.
Morrison, Jim: 1977-88; Phil. 1977-78, White Sox 1979-82, Pitt. 1982-87, Det. 1987-88, Atl. 1988.
Morrison, Johnny: 1920-30; Pitt. 1920-27, Bro. 1929-30.
Moseby, Lloyd: 1980 to present; Tor. 1980-89, Det. 1990-present.
Moses, Jerry: 1965, 1968-75; Bos. 1965, 1968-70, Cal. 1971, Cleve. 1972, Yankees 1973, Det. 1974, S.D. 1975, White Sox 1975.
Moses, Wally: 1935-51; Phil. (A) 1935-41, White Sox 1942-46, Bos. (A) 1946-48, Phil. (A) 1949-51.
Moss, Les: 1946-58; St.L. (A) 1946-51, Bos. (A) 1951, St.L. 1952-53, Balt. 1954-55, White Sox 1955-58.
Mossi, Don: 1954-65; Cleve. 1954-58, Det. 1959-63, White Sox 1964, K.C. 1965.
Mota, Manny: 1962-80, 1982; S.F. 1962, Pitt. 1963-68, Mont. 1969, L.A. 1969-80, 1982.
Mueller, Don: 1948-59; N.Y. (N) 1948-57, White Sox 1958-59.
Mueller, Ray: 1935-40, 1943-51; Bos. (N) 1935-38, Pitt. 1939-40, Cinn. 1943-49, N.Y. (N) 1949-50, Pitt. 1950, Bos. (N) 1951.
Mulcahy, Hugh: 1935-47; Phil. 1935-46, Pitt. 1947.
Mullin, Pat: 1940-53; Det. 1940-53.
Mulliniks, Rance: 1977-present; Cal. 1977-79, K.C. 1980-81, Tor. 1982-present.
Mumphrey, Jerry: 1974-88; St.L. 1974-79, S.D. 1979, Yankees 1981-83, Hou. 1983-85, Cubs 1986-88.
Munger, George: 1943-52, 1956; St.L. 1943-52, Pitt. 1952, 1956.
Mungo, Van Lingle: 1931-45; Bro. 1931-41, N.Y. (N) 1942-45.
Munson, Thurman: 1969-79; Yankees 1969-79; ROY 1970, MVP 1976.
Murcer, Bobby: 1965-83; Yankees 1965-74, S.F. 1975-76, Cubs 1977-79, Yankees 1979-83.
Murphy, Dale: 1976 to present; Atl. 1976-90, Phil. 1990-present; MVP 1982, 1983.
Murphy, Dwayne: 1978-89; Oak. 1978-87, Det. 1988, Phil. 1989.
Murphy, Johnny: 1932-47; Yankees 1932-46, Bos. 1947.
Murphy, Tom: 1968-79; Cal. 1968-72, K.C. 1972, St.L. 1973, Mil. 1974-76, Bos. 1976-77, Tor. 1977-79.
Murray, Dale: 1974-85; Mont. 1974-76, Cinn. 1977-78, Mets 1978-79, Mont. 1979-80, Tor. 1981-82, Yankees 1983-85, Texas 1985.

Murray, Eddie: 1977 to present; Balt. 1977-88, L.A. 1989-present; ROY 1977.
Muser, Tony: 1969, 1971-78; Bos. 1969, White Sox 1971-75, Balt. 1975-77, Mil. 1978.
Musial, Stan: 1941-63; St.L. 1941-1963; MVP 1943, 1946, 1948, HOF.
Myer, Buddy: 1925-41; Wash. 1925-27, Bos. 1927-28, Wash. 1929-41.

N

Narleski, Ray: 1954-59; Cleve. 1954-58, Det. 1959.
Neal, Charlie: 1956-63, Bro. 1956-57, L.A. 1958-61, Mets 1962-63, Cinn. 1963.
Nehf, Art: 1915-29; Bos. 1915-19, N.Y. (N) 1919-26, Cinn. 1926-27, Cubs 1927-29.
Nelson, Dave: 1968-77; Cleve. 1968-69, Wash. 1970-71, Texas 1972-75, K.C. 1976-77.
Nelson, Gene: 1981-present; Yankees 1981, Seat. 1982-83, White Sox 1984-86, Oak. 1987-present.
Nettles, Graig: 1967-88; Minn. 1967-69, Cleve. 1970-72, Yankees 1974-83, S.D. 1984-86, Atl. 1987, Mont. 1988.
Newcombe, Don: 1949-60; Bro. 1949-57, L.A. 1958, Cinn. 1958-60, Cleve. 1960; ROY 1949, MVP 1956, Cy Young 1956.
Newhouser, Hal: 1939-55; Det. 1939-53, Cleve. 1954-55; MVP 1944, 1945.
Newman, Jeff: 1976-84; Oak. 1976-82, Bos. 1983-84.
Newsom, Bobo: 1929-30, 1932-48, 1952-53; Bro. 1929-30, Cubs 1932, St.L. (A) 1934-35, Wash. 1935-37, Bos. (A) 1937, St.L. (A) 1938-39, Det. 1939-41, Wash. 1942, Bro. 1942-43, St.L. (A) 1943, Wash. 1943, Phil. (A) 1944-46, Wash. 1946-47, Yankees 1947-48, Wash. 1952, Phil. 1952-53.
Nichols, Chet: 1951, 1954-64; Bos. 1951, Mil. 1954-56, Bos. 1960-63, Cinn. 1964.
Nichols, Kid: 1890-01, 1904-06; Bos. (N) 1890-01, St.L. (N) 1904-05, Phil. 1905-06; HOF.
Nicholson, Bill: 1936, 1939-53; Phil. (A) 1936, Cubs 1939-48, Phil. (N) 1949-53.
Niekro, Joe: 1967-88; Cubs 1967-69, S.D. 1969, Det. 1970-72, Atl. 1973-74, Hou. 1975-85, Yankees 1985-87, Minn. 1987-88.
Niekro, Phil: 1965-87; Mil. 1964-65, Atl. 1966-83, Yankees 1984-85, Cleve. 1986, Tor. 1987, Cleve. 1987, Atl. 1987.
Nokes, Matt: 1985 to present; S.F. 1985, Det. 1986-90, Yankees 1990-present.
Nolan, Gary: 1967-77; Cinn. 1967-77, Cal. 1977.
Noren, Irv: 1950-60; Wash. 1950-52, Yankees 1953-56, K.C. 1957, St.L. 1957-59, Cubs 1959-60, L.A. 1960.
Norman, Fred: 1962-80; K.C. 1962-63, Cubs 1964-67, L.A. 1970, St.L. 1970-71, S.D. 1971-73, Cinn. 1973-79, Mont. 1980.
Norris, Mike: 1975-83, 1990; Oak. 1975-83, Oak. 1990.
Northrup, Jim: 1964-75; Det. 1964-74, Mont. 1974, Balt. 1974-75.
Nuxhall, Joe: 1944, 1952-66; Cinn. 1944, 1952-60, K.C. 1961, L.A. 1962, Cinn. 1962-66.

O

Oberkfell, Ken: 1977-present; St.L. 1977-84, Atl. 1984-88, Pitt. 1988-89, S.F. 1989, Hou. 1990-present.
Odom, Blue Moon: 1964-76; K.C. 1964-67, Oak. 1968-75, Cleve. 1975, Atl. 1975, White Sox 1976.
O'Donoghue, John: 1963-71; K.C. 1963-65, Cleve. 1966-67, Balt. 1968, Seat. 1969, Mil. 1970, Mont. 1970-71.
Oester, Ron: 1978-90; Cinn. 1978-90.
O'Farrell, Bob: 1915-35; Cubs 1915-25, St.L. 1925-28, N.Y. 1928-32, St.L. (N) 1933, Cinn. 1934, Cubs 1934, St.L. (N) 1935; MVP 1926.
Office, Roland: l972, 1974-83; Atl. 1972, 1974-79, Mont. 1980-82, Yankees 1983.
Oglivie, Ben: 1971-86; Bos. 1971-73, Det. 1974-77, Mil. 1978-86.
Ojeda, Bob: 1980-present; Bos. 1980-85, Mets 1986-90, L.A. 1991.
Oliva, Tony: 1962-76; Minn. 1962-76; ROY 1964.

Oliver, Al: 1968-85; Pitt. 1968-77, Texas 1978-81, Mont. 1982-83, S.F. 1984, Phil. 1984, L.A. 1985, Tor. 1985.

Olson, Gregg: 1988 to present; Balt. 1988-present; ROY 1989.

Orosco, Jesse: 1979, 1981 to present; Mets 1979, 1981-87, L.A. 1988, Cleve. 1989-present.

O'Rourke, Jim: 1872-93, 1904; Man. (N) 1872, Bos. (n) 1873-75, Bos. (N) 1876-78, Pro. 1879, Bos. 1880, Buff. 1881-84, N.Y. (N) 1885-89, N.Y. (P) 1890, N.Y. (N) 1891-92, Wash. 1893, N.Y. (N) 1904; HOF.

Orta, Jorge: 1972-87; White Sox 1972-79, Cleve. 1980-81, L.A. 1982, Tor. 1983, K.C. 1984-87.

Osteen, Claude: 1957-75; Cinn. 1957-61, Wash. 1961-64, L.A. 1965-73, Hou. 1974, St.L. 1974, White Sox 1975.

Otis, Amos: 1967, 1969-84; Mets 1967, 1969, K.C. 1970-83, Pitt. 1984.

O'Toole, Jim: 1958-67; Cinn. 1958-67.

Ott, Ed: 1974-81; Pitt. 1974-80, Cal. 1981.

Ott, Mel: 1926-47; N.Y. (N) 1926-47; HOF.

Owen, Mickey: 1937-45, 1949-51, 1954; St.L. (N) 1937-40, Bro. 1941-45, Cubs 1949-51, Bos. (A) 1954.

Owen, Spike: 1983-present; Seat. 1983-86, Bos. 1986-88, Mont. 1989-present.

P

Paciorek, Tom: 1970-87; L.A. 1970-75, Atl. 1976-78, Seat. 1978-81, White Sox 1982-85, Mets 1985, Texas 1986-87.

Pafko, Andy: 1943-59; Cubs 1943-51, Bro. 1951-52, Mil. 1953-59.

Pagan, Jose: 1959-73; S.F. 1959-65, Pitt. 1965-72, Phil. 1973.

Page, Joe: 1944-50, 1954; Yankees 1944-50, Pitt. 1954.

Pagliarulo, Mike: 1984-present; Yankees 1984-89, S.D. 1989-90, Minn. 1991.

Paige, Satchel: 1926-1965; Negro Leagues, Cleve. 1948-49, St.L. (A) 1951-53, K.C. 1965; HOF.

Palmeiro, Rafael: 1986 to present; Cubs 1986-88, Texas 1989-present.

Palmer, David: 1978-89; Mont. 1978-85, Atl. 1986-87, Phil. 1988, Det. 1989.

Palmer, Jim: 1965-84; Balt. 1965-84; Cy Young 1973, 1975, 1976, HOF.

Pappas, Milt: 1957-73; Balt. 1957-65, Cinn. 1966-68, Atl. 1968-70, Cubs 1970-73.

Parker, Dave: 1973 to present; Pitt. 1973-83, Cinn. 1984-87, Oak. 1988-89, Mil. 1990, Cal. 1991, Tor. 1991; MVP 1978.

Parker, Wes: 1964-72; L.A. 1964-72.

Parnell, Mel: 1947-56; Bos. (A) 1947-56.

Parrish, Lance: 1977 to present; Det. 1977-86, Phil. 1987-88, Cal. 1989-present.

Parrish, Larry: 1974-88; Mont. 1974-81, Texas 1982-88, Bos. 1988.

Pascual, Camilo: 1954-71; Wash. 1954-60, Minn. 1961-66, Wash. 1967-69, Cinn. 1969, L.A. 1970, Cleve. 1971.

Passeau, Claude: 1935-47; Pitt. 1935, Phil. (N) 1936-39, Cubs 1939-47.

Patek, Freddie: 1968-81; Pitt. 1968-70, K.C. 1971-79, Cal. 1980-81.

Pattin, Marty: 1968-80; Cal. 1968, Seat. 1969, Mil. 1970-71, Bos. 1972-73, K.C. 1974-80.

Pearson, Albie: 1958-66; Wash. 1958-59, Balt. 1959-60, L.A. 1961-64, Cal. 1965-66; ROY 1958.

Pearson, Monte: 1932-41; Cleve. 1932-35, Yankees 1936-40, Cinn. 1941.

Peckinpaugh, Roger: 1910-27; Cleve. 1910-1913, Yankees 1913-21, Wash. 1922-26, Chi. 1927; MVP 1925.

Pena, Alejandro: 1981 to present; L.A. 1981-89, Mets 1990-91, Atl. 1991.

Pena, Tony: 1980 to present; Pitt. 1980-86, St.L. 1987-89, Bos. 1990-present.

Pendleton, Terry: 1984 to present; St.L. 1984-90, Atl. 1991; MVP 1991.

Pennock, Herb: 1912-34; Phil. (A) 1912-15, Bos. 1915-22, Yankees 1923-33, Bos. (A) 1934; HOF.

Pepitone, Joe: 1962-73; Yankees 1962-69, Hou. 1970, Cubs 1970-73, Atl. 1973.

Perez, Pascual: 1980 to present; Pitt. 1980-81, Atl. 1982-85, Mont. 1987-89, Yankees 1990-present.

Perez, Marty: 1969-78; Cal. 1969-70, Atl. 1971-76, S.F. 1976, Yankees 1977, Oak. 1977-78.

Perez, Tony: 1964-86; Cinn. 1964-76, Mont. 1977-79, Bos. 1980-82, Phil. 1983, Cinn. 1984-86.
Perry, Gaylord: 1962-83; S.F. 1962-71, Cleve. 1972-75, Texas 1975-77, S.D. 1978-79, Texas 1980, Yankees 1980, Atl. 1981, Seat. 1982-83, K.C. 1983; Cy Young 1972, 1978, HOF.
Perry, Gerald: 1983 to present; Atl. 1983-89, K.C. 1990, St.L. 1991.
Perry, Jim: 1959-75; Cleve. 1959-63, Minn. 1963-72, Det. 1973, Cleve. 1974-75, Oak. 1975; Cy Young 1970.
Pesky, Johnny: 1942, 1946-54; Bos. (A) 1942, 1946-52, Det. 1952-54, Wash. 1954.
Peters, Gary: 1959-72; White Sox 1959-69, Bos. 1970-72; ROY 1963.
Peterson, Fritz: 1966-76; Yankees 1966-74, Cleve. 1974-76, Texas 1976.
Petralli, Geno: 1982-present; Tor. 1982-84, Texas 1985-present.
Petrocelli, Rico: 1963, 1965-76; Bos. 1963, 1965-76.
Petry, Dan: 1979 to present; Det. 1979-87, Cal. 1988-89, Det. 1990, Bos. 1991.
Pettis, Gary: 1982 to present; Cal. 1982-87, Det. 1988-89, Texas 1990-present.
Phelps, Babe: 1931, 1933-42; Wash. 1931, Cubs 1933-34, Bro. 1935-41, Pitt. 1942.
Phelps, Ken: 1980-90; K.C. 1980-81, Mont. 1982, Seat. 1983-88, Yankees 1988-89, Oak. 1989-90, Cleve. 1990.
Philley, Dave: 1941, 1946-62; White Sox 1941, 1946-51, Phil. (A) 1951-53, Cleve. 1954-55, Balt. 1955-56, White Sox 1956-57, Det. 1957, Phil. (N) 1958-60, S.F. 1960, Balt. 1960-61, Bos. 1962.
Phillips, Tony: 1982-present; Oak. 1982-89, Det. 1990-present.
Pierce, Billy: 1945, 1948-64; Det. 1945, 1948, White Sox 1949-61, S.F. 1962-64.
Piersall, Jimmy: 1950, 1952-67; Bos. (A) 1950, 1952-58, Cleve. 1959-61, Wash. 1962-63, Mets 1963, L.A. 1963-64, Cal. 1965-67.
Piniella, Lou: 1964, 1968-84; Balt. 1964, Cleve. 1968, K.C. 1969-73, Yankees 1974-84; ROY 1969.
Pinson, Vada: 1958-75; Cinn. 1958-68, St.L. 1969, Cleve. 1970-71, Cal. 1972-73, K.C. 1974-75.
Pipgras, George: 1923-24, 1927-35; Yankees 1923-24, 1927-33, Bos. 1933-35.
Pipp, Wally: 1913, 1915-28; Det. 1913, Yankees 1915-25, Cinn. 1926-28.
Pizarro, Juan: 1957-74; Mil. 1957-60, White Sox 1961-66, Pitt. 1967-68, Bos. 1968-69, Cleve. 1969, Oak. 1969, Cubs 1970-73, Hou. 1973, Pitt. 1974.
Plank, Eddie: 1901-17; Phil. (A) 1901-1914, St.L. 1915-17; HOF.
Plesac, Dan: 1986 to present; Mil. 1986-present.
Plummer, Bill: 1968, 1970-78; Cubs 1968, Cinn. 1970-77, Seat. 1978.
Pocoroba, Biff: 1975-84; Atl. 1975-84.
Podres, Johnny: 1953-67, 1969; Bro. 1953-57, L.A. 1958-66, Det. 1966-67, 1969.
Pollet, Howie: 1941-42, 1946-56; St.L. (N) 1941-43, 1946-51, Pitt. 1951-53, Cubs 1953-56, Pitt. 1956.
Porter, Darrell: 1971-87; Mil. 1971-76, K.C. 1977-80, St.L. 1981-85, Texas 1986-87.
Porterfield, Bob: 1948-59; Yankees 1948-51, Wash. 1951-55, Bos. 1956-58, Pitt. 1958-59, Cubs 1959, Pitt. 1959.
Post, Wally: 1949, 1951-64; Cinn. 1949, 1951-57, Phil. (N) 1958-60, Cinn. 1960-63, Minn. 1963, Cleve. 1964.
Powell, Boog: 1961-77; Balt. 1961-74, Cleve. 1975-76, L.A. 1977; MVP 1970.
Power, Vic: 1954-65; Phil. (A) 1954, K.C. 1955-58, Cleve. 1958-61, Minn. 1962-64, L.A. 1964, Phil. (N) 1964, Cal. 1965.
Presley, Jim: 1984 to present; Seat. 1984-89, At. 1990, S.D. 1991.
Puckett, Kirby: 1984 to present; Minn. 1984-present.
Puhl, Terry: 1977 to present; Hou. 1977-90, K.C. 1991.

Q

Quinn, Jack: 1909-33; Yankees 1909-12, Bos. (N) 1913, Balt. 1914-15, White Sox 1918, Yankees 1919-21, Bos. (A) 1922-25, Phil. (A) 1925-30, Bro. 1931-33.

Quirk, Jamie: 1975-present; K.C. 1975-76, Mil. 1977, K.C. 1978-82, St.L. 1983, White Sox 1984, Cleve. 1984, K.C. 1985-88, Yankees 1989, Oak. 1989, Balt. 1989, Oak. 1990-present.
Quisenberry, Dan: 1979-90; K.C. 1979-88, St.L. 1988-89, S.F. 1990.

R

Radatz, Dick: 1962-67, 1969; Bos. 1962-66, Cleve. 1966-67, Cubs 1967, Det. 1969, Mont. 1969.
Radbourn, Charles: 1880-91; Buff. 1880, Prov. 1881-85, Bos. (N) 1886-90, Cinn. 1891; HOF.
Radcliff, Rip: 1934-43; White Sox 1934-39, St.L. 1940-41, Det. 1941-43.
Rader, Dave: 1971-80; S.F. 1971-76, St.L. 1977, Cubs 1978, Phil. 1979, Bos. 1980.
Rader, Doug: 1967-77; Hou. 1967-75, S.D. 1976-77, Tor. 1977.
Raffensberger, Ken: 1939-54; St.L. 1939, Cubs 1940-41, Phil. (N) 1943-47, Cinn. 1947-54.
Raines, Tim: 1979 to present; Mont. 1979-90, White Sox 1991.
Ramirez, Rafael: 1980 to present; Atl. 1980-87, Hou. 1988-present.
Ramos, Pedro: 1955-70; Wash. 1955-60, Minn. 1961, Cleve. 1962-64, Yankees 1964-66, Phil. 1967, Pitt. 1969, Cinn. 1969, Wash. 1970.
Randolph, Willie: 1975 to present; Pitt. 1975, Yankees 1976-88, L.A. 1989-90, Oak. 1990, Mil. 1991.
Raschi, Vic: 1946-55; Yankees 1946-53, St.L. 1954-55. K.C. 1955.
Rassmussen, Dennis: 1983-present; S.D. 1983, Yankees 1984-87, Cinn. 1987-88, S.D. 1988-present.
Rawley, Shane: 1978-89; Seat. 1978-81, Yankees 1982-84, Phillies 1984-88, Minn. 1989.
Ray, Johnny: 1981 to 1990; Pitt. 1981-87, Cal. 1987-90; ROY 1982.
Reardon, Jeff: 1979 to present; Mets 1979-81, Mont. 1981-86, Minn. 1987-89, Bos. 1990-present.
Redus, Gary: 1982-present; Cinn. 1982-85, Phil. 1986, White Sox 1987-88, Pitt. 1988-present.
Reed, Ron: 1966-84; Atl. 1966-75, St.L. 1975, Phil. 1976-83, White Sox 1984.
Reese, Pee Wee: 1940-42, 1946-58; Bro. 1940-42, Bro. 1946-57, L.A. 1958; HOF.
Regan, Phil: 1960-72; Det. 1960-65, L.A. 1966-68, Cubs 1968-72, White Sox 1972.
Reichardt, Rick: 1964-74; L.A. (A) 1964, Cal. 1965-70, Wash. 1970, White Sox 1971-73, K.C. 1973-74.
Reiser, Pete: 1940-42, 1946-52; Bro. 1940-42, Bro. 1946-50, Pitt. 1951, Cleve. 1952.
Reitz, Ken: 1972-82; St.L. 1972-80, Cubs 1981, Pitt. 1982.
Remy, Jerry: 1975-84; Cal. 1975-77, Bos. 1978-84.
Renko, Steve: 1969-83; Mont. 1969-76, Cubs 1976-77, White Sox 1977, Oak. 1978, Bos. 1979-80, Cal. 1981-82, K.C. 1983.
Repulski, Rip: 1953-61; St.L. 1953-56, Phil. (N) 1957-58, L.A. 1959-60, Bos. 1960-61.
Rettenmund, Merv: 1968-80; Balt. 1968-73, Cinn. 1974-75, S.D. 1976-77, Cal. 1978-80.
Reuschel, Rick: 1972 to present; Cubs 1972-81, Yankees 1981, Cubs 1983-84, Pitt. 1985-87, S.F. 1987-present.
Reuss, Jerry: 1969-90; St.L. 1969-71, Hou. 1972-73, Pitt. 1974-78, L.A. 1979-87, Cinn. 1987, Cal. 1987, White Sox 1988-89, Mil. 1989, Pitt. 1990.
Reynolds, Allie: 1942-54; Cleve. 1942-46, Yankees 1947-54.
Reynolds, Craig: 1975-89; Pitt. 1975-76, Seat. 1977-78, Hou. 1979-89.
Reynolds, Harold: 1983 to present; Seat. 1983-present.
Rhem, Flint: 1924-36; St.L. (N) 1924-32, Phil. 1932-33, St.L. 1934, Bos. 1934-35, St.L. (N) 1936.
Rhoden, Rick: 1974-89; L.A. 1974-78, Pitt. 1979-86, Yankees 1987-88; Hou. 1989.
Rice, Del: 1945-61; St.L. (N) 1945-55, Mil. 1955-59, Cubs 1960, St.L. (N) 1960, Balt. 1960, L.A. 1961.
Rice, Jim: 1974-89; Bos. 1974-89; MVP 1978.
Rice, Sam: 1915-34; Wash. 1915-33, Cleve. 1934; HOF.
Richard, J.R.: 1971-80; Hou. 1971-80.
Richardson, Bobby: 1955-66; Yankees 1955-66.

Richert, Pete: 1962-74; L.A. 1962-64, Wash. 1965-67, Balt. 1967-71, L.A. 1972-73, St.L. 1974, Phil. 1974.

Rickey, Branch: 1905-14; executive; HOF.

Riddle, Elmer: 1939-49; Cinn. 1939-47, Pitt. 1948-49.

Righetti, Dave: 1979 to present; Yankees 1979-90, S.F. 1991; ROY 1981.

Ripken, Cal Jr.: 1981 to present; Balt. 1981-present; ROY 1982, MVP 1983, 1991.

Rivera, Jim: 1952-61; St.L. (A) 1952, White Sox 1953-61, K.C. 1961.

Rivers, Mickey: 1970-84; Cal. 1970-75, Yankees 1976-79, Texas 1979-84.

Rixey, Eppa: 1912-33; Phil. (N) 1912-20, Cinn. 1921-33; HOF.

Rizzuto, Phil: 1941-42, 1946-56; Yankees 1941-42, 1946-56; MVP 1950.

Roberts, Dave: 1972-82; S.D. 1972-78, Texas 1979-80, Hou. 1981, Phil. 1982.

Roberts, Leon: 1974-84; Det. 1974-75, Hou. 1976-77, Seat. 1978-80, Texas 1981-82, Tor. 1982, K.C. 1983-84.

Roberts, Robin: 1948-66; Phil. (N) 1948-61, Balt. 1962-65, Hou. 1965-66, Cubs. 1967; HOF.

Robertson, Bob: 1967, 1969-76, 1978-79; Pitt. 1967, 1969-76, Seat. 1978, Tor. 1979.

Robinson, Bill: 1966-69, 1972-83; Atl. 1966, Yankees 1967-69, Phil. 1972-74, Pitt. 1975-82, Phil. 1982-83.

Robinson, Brooks: 1955-77; Balt. 1955-77; MVP 1964, HOF.

Robinson, Eddie: 1942, 1946-57; Cleve. 1942, 1946-48, Wash. 1949-50, White Sox 1950-52, Phil. (A) 1953, Yankees 1954-56, K.C. 1956, Det. 1957, Cleve. 1957, Balt. 1957.

Robinson, Frank: 1956-76; Cinn. 1956-65, Balt. 1966-71, L.A. 1972, Cal. 1973-74, Cleve. 1974-76; ROY 1956, MVP 1961, 1966, HOF.

Robinson, Jackie: 1947-56; Bro. 1947-56; ROY 1947, MVP 1949, HOF.

Robinson, Wilbert: 1886-02; Phil. (a) 1886-90, Balt. (a) 1890-91, Balt. (N) 1892-99, St.L. 1900, Balt. 1901-02; HOF.

Rodriguez, Aurelio: 1967-83; Cal. 1967-70, Wash. 1970, Det. 1970-79, S.D. 1980, Yankees 1980-81, White Sox 1982, Balt. 1983, White Sox 1983.

Rodriguez, Ellie: 1968-76; Yankees 1968, K.C. 1969-70, Mil. 1971-73, Cal. 1974-75, L.A. 1976.

Roe, Preacher: 1938, 1944-54; St.L. 1938, Pitt. 1944-47, Bro. 1948-54.

Roenicke, Gary: 1976, 1978-88; Mont. 1976, Balt. 1978-85, Yankees 1986, Atl. 1987-88.

Rogers, Steve: 1973-85; Mont. 1973-85.

Rogovin, Saul: 1949-57; Det. 1949-51, White Sox 1951-53, Balt. 1955, Phil. 1955-57.

Rojas, Cookie: 1962-77; Cinn. 1962, Phil. 1963-69, St.L. 1970, K.C. 1970-77.

Rolfe, Red: 1931-42; Yankees 1931-42.

Rollins, Rich: 1961-70; Minn. 1961-68, Seat. 1969, Mil. 1970, Cleve. 1970.

Romano, Johnny: 1958-67; White Sox 1958-59, Cleve. 1960-64, White Sox 1965-66, St.L. 1967.

Romero, Eddie: 1977, 1980-90; Mil. 1977, 1980-85, Bos. 1986-89, Atl. 1989, Mil. 1989, Det. 1990.

Rommel, Ed: 1920-32; Phil. (A) 1920-32.

Roof, Phil: 1961, 1964-77; Mil. 1961, 1964, Cal. 1965, Cleve. 1965, K.C. 1966-67, Oak. 1968-69, Mil. 1970-71, Minn. 1971-76, White Sox 1976, Tor. 1977.

Rooker, Jim: 1968-80; Det. 1968, K.C. 1969-72, Pitt. 1973-80.

Root, Charlie: 1923, 1926-41; St.L. (A) 1923, Cubs 1926-41.

Rosar, Buddy: 1939-51; Yankees 1939-42, Cleve. 1943-44, Phil. (A) 1945-49, Bos. (A) 1950-51.

Rose, Pete: 1963-86; Cinn. 1963-78, Phil. 1979-83, Mont. 1984, Cinn. 1984-86; ROY 1963.

Roseboro, Johnny: 1957-70; Bro. 1957, L.A. 1958-67, Minn. 1968-69, Wash. 1970.

Rosen, Al: 1947-56; Cleve. 1947-56; MVP 1953.

Roush, Edd: 1913-29, 1931; Chi. (A) 1913; Ind. (F) 1914, New. (F) 1915, N.Y. (N) 1916, Cinn. 1916-26, N.Y. (N) 1927-29, Cinn. 1931. HOF.

Rowe, Schoolboy: 1933-43, 1946-49; Det. 1933-42, Bro. 1942, Phil. 1943, 1946-49.

Royster, Jerry: 1973-88; L.A. 1973-75, Atl. 1976-84, S.D. 1985-86, White Sox 1987, Yankees 1987, Atl. 1988.

Rudi, Joe: 1967-82; K.C. 1967, Oak. 1968-76, Cal. 1977-80, Bos. 1981, Oak. 1982.

Rudolph, Dick: 1910-27; N.Y. 1910-11, Bos. (N) 1913-27.
Ruffing, Red: 1924-47, Bos. 1924-30, Yankees 1930-46, White Sox 1947; HOF.
Ruhle, Vern: 1974-86; Det. 1974-77, Hou. 1978-84, Cleve. 1985, Cal. 1986.
Runnels, Pete: 1951-64; Wash. 1951-57, Bos. (A) 1958-62, Hou. 1963-64.
Rush, Bob: 1948-60; Cubs 1948-57, Mil. 1958-60, White Sox 1960.
Rusie, Amos: 1889-98, 1901; Ind. (N) 1889, N.Y. (N) 1890-98, Cinn. 1901; HOF.
Russell, Bill: 1969-86; L.A. 1969-86.
Russell, Jack: 1926-40; Bos. (A) 1926-32, Cleve. 1932., Wash. 1933-36, Bos. (A) 1936, Det. 1937, Cubs 1938-39, St.L. (N) 1940.
Russell, Jeff: 1983 to present; Cinn. 1983-84, Texas 1985-present.
Ruth, Babe: 1914-35; Bos. (A) 1914-19, Yankees 1920-34, Bos. (N) 1935; HOF.
Ruthven, Dick: 1973-86; Phil. 1973-75, Atl. 1976-78, Phil. 1978-83, Cubs 1983-86.
Ryan, Connie: 1942-54; N.Y. (N) 1942, Bos. (N) 1943-50, Cinn. 1950-51, Phil. 1952-53, White Sox 1953, Cinn. 1954.
Ryan, Nolan: 1966 to present; Mets 1968-71, Cal. 1972-79, Hou. 1980-88, Texas 1989-present.
Ryan, Rosy: 1919-26, 1928, 1933; N.Y. (N) 1919-24, Bos. (N) 1925-26, Yankees 1928, Bro. 1933.

S

Saberhagen, Bret: 1984 to present; K.C. 1984-present; Cy Young 1985, 1989.
Sabo, Chris: 1988 to present; Cinn. 1988-present; ROY 1988.
Sadecki, Ray: 1960-77; St.L. 1960-66, S.F. 1966-69, Mets 1970-74, St.L. 1975, Atl. 1975, K.C. 1975-76, Mil. 1976, Mets 1977.
Sain, Johnny: 1942, 1946-55; Bos. (N) 1942, 1946-51, Yankees 1952-55, K.C. 1955.
Sakata, Lenn: 1977-87; Mil. 1977-79, Balt. 1980-85, Oak. 1986, Yankees 1987.
Salazar, Luis: 1980-90; S.D. 1980-84, White Sox 1985-86, S.D. 1987, Det. 1988, S.D. 1989, Cubs 1989-present.
Sambito, Joe: 1976-87; Hou. 1976-84, Mets 1985, Bos. 1986-87.
Sample, Bill: 1978-86; Texas 1978-84, Yankees 1985, Atl. 1986.
Samuel, Juan: 1983 to present; Phil. 1983-89, Mets 1989, L.A. 1990-present.
Sandberg, Ryne: 1981 to present; Cubs 1981-present; MVP 1984.
Sanders, Ken: 1964, 1966, 1968, 1970-76: K.C. 1964, Bos. 1966, K.C. 1966, Oak. 1968, Mil. 1970-72, Minn. 1973, Cleve. 1973-74, Cal. 1974, Mets 1975-76, K.C. 1976.
Sanderson, Scott: 1978-present; Mont. 1978-83, Cubs 1984-89, Oak. 1990, Yankees 1991.
Sanford, Jack: 1956-67; Phil. 1956-58, S.F. 1959-65, Cal. 1965-67, K.C. 1967; ROY 1957.
Sanguillen, Manny: 1967-80; Pitt. 1967-76, Oak. 1977, Pitt. 1978-80.
Santiago, Benito: 1986 to present; S.D. 1986-present; ROY 1987.
Santo, Ron: 1960-74; Cubs 1960-73, White Sox 1974.
Sauer, Hank: 1941-42, 1945, 1948-59; Cinn. 1941-42, 1945, 1948-49, Cubs 1949-55, St.L. 1956, N.Y. (N) 1957, S.F. 1958-59; MVP 1952.
Sax, Steve: 1981 to present; L.A. 1981-88, Yankees 1989-present; ROY 1982.
Schaal, Paul: 1964-74; L.A. (A) 1964, Cal. 1965-68, K.C. 1969-74, Cal. 1974.
Schalk, Ray: 1912-29; White Sox 1912-28, N.Y. (N) 1929; HOF.
Schang, Wally: 1913-31; Phil. (A) 1913-17, Bos. (A) 1918-20, Yankees 1921-25, St.L. (A) 1926-29, Phil. (A) 1930, Det. 1931.
Scarborough, Ray: 1942-43, 1946-53; Wash. 1942-43, Wash. 1946-50, White Sox 1950, Bos. (A) 1951-52, Yankees 1952-53, Det. 1953.
Schatzeder, Dan: 1977-90; Mont. 1977-79, Det. 1980-81, S.F. 1982, Mont. 1982-86, Phil. 1986-87, Minn. 1987, Cleve. 1988, Minn. 1988, Hou. 1989-90, Mets 1990.
Scheinblum, Richie: 1965, 1967-69, 1971-74; Cleve. 1965, 1967-69, Wash. 1971, K.C. 1972, Cinn. 1973, Cal. 1973-74, K.C. 1974, St.L. 1974.
Schiraldi, Calvin: 1984-90: Mets 1984-85, Bos. 1986-87, Cubs 1988-89, S.D. 1989-90.

Schmidt, Bob: 1958-65; S.F. 1958-61, Cinn. 1961, Wash. 1962-63, Yankees 1965.
Schmidt, Mike: 1972-89; Phil. 1972-89; MVP 1980, 1981, 1986.
Schmitz, Johnny: 1941-42, 1946-56; Cubs 1941-42, 1946-51, Bro. 1951-52, Yankees 1952, Cinn. 1952, Yankees 1953, Wash. 1953-55, Bos. 1956, Balt. 1956.
Schoendienst, Red: 1945-63; St.L. 1945-56, N.Y. (N) 1956-57, Mil. 1958-60, St.L. 1961-63; HOF.
Schofield, Dick: 1983-present; Cal. 1983-present.
Schrom, Ken: 1980, 1982-87; Tor. 1980, 1982, Minn. 1983-85, Cleve. 1986-87.
Schulte, Frank: 1904-18, Cubs 1904-16, Pitt. 1916-17, Phil. 1917, Wash. 1918; MVP 1911.
Schulte, Fred: 1927-37; St.L. (A) 1927-32, Wash. 1933-35, Pitt. 1936-37.
Schumacher, Hal: 1931-46; N.Y. (N) 1931-46.
Schwall, Don: 1961-67; Bos. (A) 1961-62, Pitt. 1963-66, Atl. 1966-67; ROY 1961.
Scioscia, Mike: 1980 to present; L.A. 1980-present.
Score, Herb: 1955-62; Cleve. 1955-59, White Sox 1960-62; ROY 1955.
Scott, Everett: 1914-26; Bos. (A) 1914-21, Yankees 1922-25, Wash. 1925, White Sox 1926, Cinn. 1926.
Scott, George: 1966-79; Bos. 1966-71, Mil. 1972-76, Bos. 1977-79, K.C. 1979, Yankees 1979.
Scott, Jack: 1916-29; Pitt. 1916, Bos. (N) 1917-21, Cinn. 1922, N.Y. (N) 1922-26, Phil. (N) 1927, N.Y. (N) 1928-29.
Scott, Mike: 1979-91; Mets 1979-82, Hou. 1983-91; Cy Young 1986.
Scott, Tony: 1973-75, 1977-84; Mont. 1973-75, St.L. 1977-81, Hou. 1981-84, Mont. 1984.
Seaver, Tom: 1967-86; Mets 1967-77, Cinn. 1977-82, Mets 1983, White Sox 1984-86, Bos. 1986; ROY 1967, Cy Young 1969, 1973, 1975.
Segui, Diego: 1962-75, 1977; K.C. 1962-65, Wash. 1966, K.C. 1967, Oak. 1968-72, St.L. 1972-73, Bos. 1974-75, Seat. 1977..
Seitzer, Kevin: 1986 to present; K.C. 1986-present.
Selkirk, George: 1934-42; Yankees 1934-42.
Seminick, Andy: 1943-57; Phil. (N) 1943-51, Cinn. 1952-55, Phil. 1955-57.
Severeid, Eric: 1911-26; Cinn. 1911-13, St.L. (A) 1915-25, Wash. 1925-26, Yankees 1926.
Sewell, Joe: 1920-33; Cleve. 1920-30, Yankees 1931-33; HOF.
Sewell, Luke: 1921-39, 1942; Cleve. 1921-32, Wash. 1933-34, White Sox 1935-38, Cleve. 1939, St.L. (A) 1942.
Sewell, Rip: 1932, 1938-49; Det. 1932, Pitt. 1938-49.
Shannon, Mike: 1962-70; St.L. 1962-70.
Shantz, Bobby: 1949-64; Phil. 1949-54, K.C. 1955-56, Yankees 1957-60, Pitt. 1961, Hou. 1962, St.L. 1962-64, Cubs 1964, Phil. 1964; MVP 1952.
Shaw, Bob: 1957-67; Det. 1957-58, White Sox 1958-61, K.C. 1961, Mil. 1962-63, S.F. 1964-66, Mets 1966-67, Cubs 1967.
Shawkey, Bob: 1913-27; Phil. 1913-15, Yankees 1915-27.
Shea, Spec: 1947-49, 1951-55; Yankees 1947-49, 1951, Wash. 1952-55.
Shelby, John: 1981-present; Balt. 1981-87, L.A. 1987-90, Det. 1991.
Shirley, Bob: 1977-87; S.D. 1977-80, St.L. 1981, Cinn. 1982, Yankees 1983-87, K.C. 1987.
Shocker, Urban: 1916-28; Yankees 1916-17, St.L. 1918-24, Yankees 1925-28.
Short, Chris: 1959-73; Phil. 1959-72, Mil. 1973.
Show, Eric: 1981-present; S.D. 1981-90, Oak. 1991.
Siebern, Norm: 1956, 1958-68; Yankees 1956, 1958-59, K.C. (A) 1960-63, Balt. 1964-65, Cal. 1966, S.F. 1967, Bos. 1967-68.
Siebert, Dick: 1932, 1936-45; Bro. 1932, 1936, St.L. (N) 1937-38, Phil. (A) 1938-45.
Siebert, Sonny: 1964-75; Cleve. 1964-69, Bos. 1969-73, Texas 1973, St.L. 1974, S.D. 1975, Oak. 1975.
Sierra, Ruben: 1986 to present; Texas 1986-present.
Sievers, Roy: 1949-65; St.L. 1949-53, Wash. 1954-59, White Sox 1960-61, Phil. 1962-64, Wash. 1964-65; ROY 1949.

Simmons, Al: 1924-44; Phil. 1924-32, White Sox 1933-35, Det. 1936, Wash. 1937-38, Bos. (N) 1939, Cinn. 1939, Phil. (A) 1940-41, Bos. (A) 1943, Phil. (A) 1944; HOF.
Simmons, Curt: 1947-67; Phil. 1947-60, St.L. 1960-66, Cubs 1966-67, Cal. 1967.
Simmons, Ted: 1968-88; St.L. 1968-80, Mil. 1981-85, Atl. 1986-88.
Simpson, Wayne: 1970-77; Cinn. 1970-72, K.C. 1973, Phil. 1975, Cal. 1977.
Sims, Duke: 1964-74; Cleve. 1964-70, L.A. 1971-72, Det. 1972-73, Yankees 1973-74, Texas 1974.
Singer, Bill: 1964-77; L.A. 1964-72, Cal. 1973-75, Texas 1976, Minn. 1976, Tor. 1977.
Singleton, Ken: 1970-84; Mets 1970-71, Mont. 1972-74, Balt. 1975-84.
Sisler, Dick: 1946-53; St.L. 1946-47, Phil. (N) 1948-51, Cinn. 1952, St.L. 1952-53.
Sisler, George: 1915-30; St.L. 1915-27, Wash. 1928, Bos. (N) 1928-30; MVP 1922, HOF.
Sisti, Sibby: 1939-42, 1946-54; Bos. (N) 1939-42, 1946-52, Mil. 1953-54.
Sizemore, Ted: 1969-80; L.A. 1969-70, St.L. 1971-75, L.A. 1976, Phil. 1977-78, Cubs 1979, Bos. 1979-80; ROY 1969.
Skinner, Bob: 1954, 1956-66; Pitt. 1954, 1956-63, Cinn. 1963-64, St.L. 1964-66.
Skowron, Bill: 1954-67; Yankees 1954-62, L.A. 1963, Wash. 1964, White Sox 1965-77, Cal. 1977.
Slaton, Jim: 1971-86; Mil. 1971-77, Det. 1978, Mil. 1979-82, Cal. 1983-86, Det. 1986.
Slaughter, Enos: 1938-59; St.L. 1938-53, Yankees 1954-55, K.C. 1955-56, Yankees 1956-59, Mil. 1959; HOF.
Smalley, Roy Jr.: 1975-87; Texas 1975-76, Minn. 1976-82, Yankees 1982-84, White Sox 1984, Minn. 1985-87.
Smith, Al: 1934-45; N.Y. (N) 1934-37, Phil. (N) 1938-39, Cleve. 1940-45.
Smith, Al: 1953-64; Cleve. 1953-58, White Sox 1959-62, Balt. 1963, Cleve. 1964, Bos. 1964.
Smith, Bob: 1923-37; Bos. (N) 1923-30, Cubs 1931-32, Cinn. 1933, Bos. (N) 1933-37.
Smith, Bryn: 1981-present; Mont. 1981-89, St.L. 1990-present.
Smith, Dave: 1980 to present; Hou. 1980-1990, Cubs 1991.
Smith, Hal: 1956-61, 1965; St.L. 1956-61, Pitt. 1965.
Smith, Jack: 1915-29; St.L. (N) 1915-26, Bos. (N) 1926-29.
Smith, Lee: 1980 to present; Cubs 1980-87, Bos. 1988-90, St.L. 1990-present.
Smith, Lonnie: 1978 to present; Phil. 1978-81, St.L. 1982-85, K.C. 1985-87, Atl. 1988-present.
Smith, Ozzie: 1978 to present; S.D. 1978-81, St.L. 1982-present.
Smith, Reggie: 1966-82; Bos. 1966-73, St.L. 1974-76, L.A. 1976-81, S.F. 1982.
Smith, Willie: 1963-71; Det. 1963, L.A. 1964, Cal. 1965-66, Cleve. 1967-68, Cubs 1968-70, Cinn. 1971.
Smoltz, John: 1988 to present; Atl. 1988-present.
Snider, Duke: 1947-64; Bro. 1947-57, L.A. 1958-63, S.F. 1964; HOF.
Snyder, Cory: 1986-present; Cleve. 1986-90, Tor. 1991.
Snyder, Frank: 1912-27; St.L. (N) 1912-19, N.Y. (N) 1919-26, St.L. (N) 1927.
Snyder, Russ: 1959-70; K.C. 1959-60, Balt. 1961-67, White Sox 1968, Cleve. 1968-69, Mil. 1970.
Soderholm, Eric: 1971-80; Minn. 1971-75, White Sox 1977-79, Texas 1979, Yankees 1980.
Sorensen, Lary: 1977-88; Mil. 1977-80, St.L. 1981, Cleve. 1982-83, Oak. 1984, Cubs 1985, Mont. 1987, S.F. 1988.
Soto, Mario: 1977-88; Cinn. 1977-88.
Southworth, Billy: 1913, 1915, 1918-27, 1929; Cleve. 1913, 1915, Pitt. 1918-20, Bos. (N) 1921-23, N.Y. (N) 1924-26, St.L. (N) 1926-27, 1929.
Spahn, Warren: 1942, 1946-65; Bos. (N) 1942, 1946-53, Mil. 1953-64, Mets 1965, S.F. 1965; Cy Young 1957, HOF.
Spalding, Al: 1871-78; Boston (n) 1871-75, Chi. (N) 1876-78; HOF.
Spangler, Al: 1959-71; Mil. 1959-61, Hou. 1962-65, Cal. 1965-66, Cubs 1967-71.
Speaker, Tris: 1907-28; Bos. (A) 1907-15, Cleve. 1916-26, Wash. 1927, Phil. 1928; MVP 1912, HOF.
Speier, Chris: 1971-89; S.F. 1971-77, Mont. 1977-84, St.L. 1984, Minn. 1984, Cubs 1985-86, S.F. 1987-89.

Spence, Stan: 1940-49; Bos. (A) 1940-41, Wash. 1942-47, Bos. (A) 1948-49, St.L. (A) 1949.
Spencer, Jim: 1968-82; Cal. 1968-73, Texas 1973-75, White Sox 1976-77, Yankees 1978-81, Oak. 1981-82.
Spencer, Roy: 1925-38; Pitt. 1925-27, Wash. 1929-32, Cleve. 1933-34, N.Y. (N) 1936, Bro. 1937-38.
Spikes, Charlie: 1972-80; Yankees 1972, Cleve. 1973-77, Det. 1978, Atl. 1979-80.
Spillner, Dan: 1974-85; S.D. 1974-78, Cleve. 1978-84, White Sox 1984-85.
Splittorff, Paul: 1970-84; K.C. 1970-84.
Squires, Mike: 1975-85; White Sox 1975-85.
Staley, Gerry: 1947-61; St.L. 1947-54, Cinn. 1955, Yankees 1956-56, White Sox 1956-61, K.C. 1961, Det. 1961.
Stanhouse, Don: 1972-80, 1982; Texas 1972-74, Mont. 1975-77, Balt. 1978-79, L.A. 1980, Balt. 1982.
Stanky, Eddie: 1943-53; Cubs 1943-44, Bro. 1944-47, Bos. (N) 1948-49, N.Y. (N) 1950-51, St.L. (N) 1952-53.
Stanley, Bob: 1977-89; Bos. 1977-89.
Stanley, Mickey: 1964-78; Det. 1964-78.
Stapleton, Dave: 1980-86; Bos. 1980-86.
Stargell, Willie: 1962-82; Pitt. 1962-82; MVP 1979, HOF.
Staub, Rusty: 1963-85; Hou. 1963-68, Mont. 1969-71, Mets 1972-75, Det. 1976-79, Mont. 1979, Texas 1980, Mets 1981-85.
Stearns, John: 1974-84; Phil. 1974, Mets 1975-84.
Stein, Bill: 1972-85; St.L. 1972-73, White Sox 1974-76, Seat. 1977-80, Texas 1981-85.
Steinbach, Terry: 1986 to present; Oak. 1986-present.
Stengel, Casey: 1912-25; Bro. 1912-17, Pitt. 1918-19, Phil. 1920-21, N.Y. (N) 1921-23, Bos. (N) 1924-25; HOF.
Stennett, Rennie: 1971-81; Pitt. 1971-79, S.F. 1980-81.
Stephens, Gene: 1952-64; Bos. (A) 1952-60, Balt. 1960-61, K.C. 1961-62, White Sox 1963-64.
Stephens, Vern: 1941-55; St.L. 1941-47, Bos. 1948-52, White Sox 1953, St.L. (A) 1953, Balt. 1954-55, White Sox 1955.
Stephenson, Riggs: 1921-34; Cleve. 1921-25; Cubs 1926-34.
Stewart, Dave: 1978, 1981 to present; L.A. 1978, 1981-83, Texas 1983-85, Phil. 1985-86, Oak. 1986-present.
Stewart, Sammy: 1978-87; Balt. 1978-85, Bos. 1986, Cleve. 1987.
Stieb, Dave: 1979 to present; Tor. 1979-present.
Stigman, Dick: 1960-66; Cleve. 1960-61, Minn. 1962-65, Bos. 1966.
Stillwell, Kurt: 1986-present; Cinn. 1986-87, K.C. 1988-present.
Stinson, Bob: 1969-80; L.A. 1969-70, St.L. 1971, Hou. 1972, Mont. 1973-74, K.C. 1975-76, Seat. 1977-80.
Stirnweiss, Snuffy: 1943-52; Yankees 1943-50, St.L. (A) 1950, Cleve. 1951-52.
Stone, Dean: 1953-63; Wash. 1953-57, Bos. 1957, St.L. (N) 1959, Hou. 1962, White Sox 1962, Balt. 1963.
Stone, Steve: 1971-81; S.F. 1971-72, White Sox 1973, Cubs 1974-76, White Sox 1977-78, Balt. 1979-81; Cy Young 1980.
Stoneman, Bill: 1967-74; Cubs 1967-68, Mont. 1969-73, Cal. 1974.
Stottlemyre, Mel: 1964-74; Yankees 1964-74.
Stratton, Monty: 1934-38; White Sox 1934-38.
Strawberry, Darryl: 1983 to present; Mets 1983-90, L.A. 1991; ROY 1983.
Stuart, Dick: 1958-69; Pitt. 1958-62, Bos. 1963-64, Phil. 1965, Mets 1966, L.A. 1966, Cal. 1969.
Stubbs, Franklin: 1984-present; L.A. 1984-89, Hou. 1990, Mil. 1991.
Suhr, Gus: 1930-40; Pitt. 1930-39, Phil. (N) 1939-40.
Sullivan, Billy: 1931-33, 1935-42, 1947; White Sox 1931-33, Cinn. 1935, Cleve. 1936-37, St.L. 1938-39, Det. 1940-41, Bro. 1942, Pitt. 1947.
Sullivan, Frank: 1953-63; Bos. (A) 1953-60, Phil. 1961-62, Minn. 1962-63.

Summers, Champ: 1974-84; Oak. 1974, Cubs 1975-76, Cinn. 1977-79, Det. 1979-81, S.F. 1982-83, S.D. 1984.
Sundberg, Jim: 1974-89; Texas 1974-83, Mil. 1984, K.C. 1985-86, Cubs 1987-88, Texas 1988-89.
Sutcliffe, Rick: 1976, 1978 to present; L.A. 1976, 1978-81, Cleve. 1982-84, Cubs 1984-present; Cy Young 1984.
Sutherland, Gary: 1966-78; Phil. 1966-68, Mont. 1969-71, Hou. 1972-73, Det. 1974-76, Mil. 1976, S.D. 1977, St.L. 1978.
Sutter, Bruce: 1976-88; Cubs 1976-80, St.L. 1981-84, Atl. 1985-88.
Sutton, Don: 1966-88; L.A. 1966-80, Hou. 1981-82, Mil. 1982-84, Oak. 1985, Cal. 1985-87, L.A. 1988.
Swan, Craig: 1973-84; Mets 1973-84, Cal. 1984.
Swift, Bill: 1932-41, 1943; Pitt. 1932-39, Bos. 1940, Bro. 1941, White Sox 1943.
Swift, Bob: 1940-53; St.L. (A) 1940-42, Phil. (A) 1942-43, Det. 1944-53.
Swindell, Greg: 1986 to present; Cleve. 1986-91.
Swisher, Steve: 1974-82; Cubs 1974-77, St.L. 1978-80, S.D. 1981-82.
Swoboda, Ron: 1965-73; Mets 1965-70, Mont. 1971, Yankees 1971-73.

T

Tabler, Pat: 1981 to present; Cubs 1981-82, Cleve. 1983-88, K.C. 1988-90, Mets 1990-91, Tor. 1991, K.C. 1991.
Tanana, Frank: 1973 to present; Cal. 1973-80, Bos. 1981, Texas 1982-85, Det. 1985-present.
Tapani, Kevin: 1989-present; Minn. 1989-present.
Tartabull, Danny: 1984 to present; Seat. 1984-86, K.C. 1987-present.
Taveras, Frank: 1971-82; Pitt. 1971-79, Mets 1979-81, Mont. 1982.
Taylor, Tony: 1958-76; Cubs 1958-60, Phil. 1960-71, Det. 1971-73, Phil. 1974-76.
Taylor, Zack: 1920-35; Bro. 1920-25, Bos. (N) 1926-27, N.Y. (N) 1927, Bos. (N) 1928-29, Cubs 1929-33, Yankees 1934, Bro. 1935.
Tebbetts, Birdie: 1936-42, 1946-52; Det. 1936-42, 1946-47, Bos. 1947-50, Cleve. 1951-52.
Tekulve, Kent: 1974-89; Pitt. 1974-85, Phil. 1985-88, Cinn. 1989.
Temple, Johnny: 1952-64; Cinn. 1952-59, Cleve. 1960-61, Balt. 1962, Hou. 1962-63, Cinn. 1964.
Templeton, Garry: 1976 to present; St.L. 1976-81, S.D. 1982-91, Mets 1991.
Tenace, Gene: 1969-83; Oak. 1969-76, S.D. 1977-80, St.L. 1981-82, Pitt. 1983.
Terrell, Walt: 1982-present; Mets 1982-84, Det. 1985-88, S.D. 1989, Yankees 1989, Pitt. 1990, Det. 1990-present.
Terry, Bill: 1923-36; N.Y. (N) 1923-36; HOF.
Terry, Ralph: 1956-67; Yankees 1956-57, K.C. 1957-59, Yankees 1959-64, Cleve. 1965, K.C. 1966, Mets 1966-67.
Tettleton, Mickey: 1984 to present; Oak. 1984-87, Balt. 1988-90, Det. 1991.
Thomas, Derrel: 1971-85; Hou. 1971, S.D. 1972-74, S.F. 1975-77, S.D. 1978, L.A. 1979-83, Mont. 1984, Cal. 1984, Phil. 1985.
Thomas, Frank: 1951-66; Pitt. 1951-58, Cinn. 1959, Chi. 1960-61, Mil. 1961, Mets 1962-64, Phil. 1964-65, Hou. 1965, Mil. 1965, Cubs 1966.
Thomas, Frank: 1990 to present; White Sox 1990-present.
Thomas, Gorman: 1973-86; Mil. 1973-83, Cleve. 1983, Seat. 1984-86, Mil. 1986.
Thomas, Tommy: 1926-37; White Sox 1926-32, Wash. 1932-35, Phil. (N) 1935, St.L. (A) 1936-37, Bos. (A) 1937.
Thompson, Danny: 1970-76; Minn. 1970-76, Texas 1976.
Thompson, Jason: 1976-86; Det. 1976-80, Cal. 1980, Pitt. 1981-85, Mont. 1986.
Thompson, Sam: 1885-98, 1906; Det. 1885-88, Phil. 1889-98, Det. 1906; HOF.
Thomson, Bobby: 1946-60; N.Y. (N) 1946-53, Mil. 1954-57, N.Y. (N) 1957, Chi. 1958-59, Bos. 1960, Balt. 1960.
Thon, Dickie: 1979 to present; Cal. 1979-80, Hou. 1981-87, S.D. 1988, Phil. 1989-present.

Thornton, Andre: 1973-87; Cubs 1973-76, Mont. 1976, Cleve. 1977-87.
Throneberry, Marv: 1955, 1958-63; Yankees 1955, 1958-59, K.C. 1960-61, Balt. 1961-62, Mets 1962-63.
Tiant, Luis: 1964-82; Cleve. 1964-69, Minn. 1970, Bos. 1971-78, Yankees 1979-80, Pitt. 1981, Cal. 1982.
Tidrow, Dick: 1972-84; Cleve. 1972-74, Yankees 1974-79, Cubs 1979-82, White Sox 1983, Mets 1984.
Tinker, Joe: 1902-16; Cubs 1902-13, Chi. (F) 1914-15, Cubs 1916. HOF.
Tobin, Jack: 1914-27; St.L. (F) 1914-15, St.L. (A) 1916-25, Wash. 1926, Bos. (A) 1926-27.
Tobin, Jim: 1937-45; Pitt. 1937-39, Bos. (N) 1940-45, Det. 1945.
Tolan, Bobby: 1965-77, 1979; St.L. 1965-68, Cinn. 1969-73, S.D. 1974-75, Phil. 1976-77, Pitt. 1977, S.D. 1979.
Tomlin, Dave: 1972-86; Cinn. 1972-73, S.D. 1974-77, Cinn. 1978-80, Mont. 1982, Pitt. 1983-85, Mont. 1986.
Torgeson, Earl: 1947-61; Bos. (N) 1947-52, Phil. 1953-55, Det. 1955-57, White Sox 1957-61, Yankees 1961.
Torre, Joe: 1960-77; Mil. 1970-65, Atl. 1966-68, St.L. 1969-74, Mets 1975-77; MVP 1971.
Torrez, Mike: 1967-84; St.L. 1967-71, Mont. 1971-74, Balt. 1975, Oak. 1976-77, Yankees 1977, Bos. 1978-82, Mets 1983-84, Oak. 1984.
Tovar, Cesar: 1965-76; Minn. 1965-72, Phil. 1973, Texas 1974-75, Oak. 1975-76, Yankees 1976.
Trammell, Alan: 1977 to present; Det. 1977-present.
Travers, Bill: 1974-81, 1983; Mil. 1974-80, Cal. 1981, 1983.
Travis, Cecil: 1933-41, 1945-47; Wash. 1933-41, 1945-47.
Traynor, Pie; 1920-37; Pitt. 1920-37; HOF.
Tresh, Mike: 1938-49; White Sox 1938-48, Cleve. 1949.
Tresh, Tom: 1961-69; Yankees 1961-69, Det. 1969; ROY 1962.
Trevino, Alex: 1978-90; Mets 1978-81, Cinn. 1982-84, Atl. 1984, S.F. 1985, L.A. 1986-87, Hou. 1988-90, Mets 1990, Cinn. 1990.
Triandos, Gus: 1953-65; Yankees 1953-54, Balt. 1955-62, Det. 1963, Phil. 1964-65, Hou. 1965.
Trillo, Manny: 1973-87; Oak. 1973-74, Cubs 1975-78, Phil. 1979-82, Cleve. 1983, Mont. 1983, S.F. 1984-85, Cubs 1986-88, Cinn. 1989.
Trosky, Hal: 1933-41, 1944, 1946; Cleve. 1933-41, White Sox 1944, 1946.
Trout, Dizzy: 1939-52, 1957; Det. 1939-52, Bos. 1952, Balt. 1957.
Trout, Steve: 1978-89; White Sox 1978-82, Cubs 1983-87, Yankees 1987, Seat. 1988-89.
Trucks, Virgil: 1941-58; Det. 1941-52, St.L. 1953, White Sox 1953-55, Det. 1956, K.C. 1957-58, Yankees 1958.
Tucker, Thurman: 1942-51; White Sox 1942-47, Cleve. 1948-51.
Tudor, John: 1979-90; Bos. 1979-83, Pitt. 1984, St.L. 1985-88, L.A. 1988-89, St.L. 1990.
Turley, Bob: 1951, 1953-63; St.L. (A) 1951, 1953, Balt. 1954, Yankees 1955-62, L.A. 1963, Bos. 1963.
Turner, Jerry: 1974-83; S.D. 1974-81, White Sox 1981, Det. 1982, S.D. 1983.
Turner, Jim: 1937-45; Bos. (N) 1937-39, Cinn. 1940-42, Yankees 1943-45.
Twitchell, Wayne: 1970-79; Mil. 1970, Phil. 1971-77, Mont. 1977-78, Mets 1979, Seat. 1979.
Tyson, Mike: 1972-81; St.L. 1972-79, Cubs 1980-81.

U

Ueberroth, Peter: commissioner 1984-89.
Uecker, Bob: 1962-67; Mil. 1962-63, St.L. 1964-65, Phil. 1966-67, Atl. 1967.
Uhle, George: 1919-36; Cleve. 1919-28, Det. 1929-33, N.Y. (N) 1933, Yankees 1933-34, Cleve. 1936.
Underwood, Tom: 1974-84; Phil. 1974-77, St.L. 1977, Tor. 1978-79, Yankees 1980-81, Oak. 1981-83, Balt. 1984.

Unser, Del: 1968-82; Wash. 1968-71, Cleve. 1972, Phil. 1973-74, Mets 1975-76, Mont. 1976-78, Phil. 1979-82.
Upshaw, Willie: 1978, 1980-88; Tor. 1978, 1980-87, Cleve. 1988.
Uribe, Jose: 1984-present; St.L. 1984, S.F. 1985-present.

V

Valentine, Bobby: 1969, 1971-79; L.A. 1969, 1971-72, Cal. 1973-75, S.D. 1975-77, Mets 1977-78, Seat. 1979.
Valentine, Ellis: 1975-83, 1985; Mont. 1975-81, Mets 1981-82, Cal. 1983, Texas 1985.
Valenzuela, Fernando: 1980-91; L.A. 1980-90, Cal. 1991; ROY 1981, Cy Young 1981.
Valo, Elmer: 1940-61; Phil. (A) 1940-54, K.C. 1955-56, Phil. (N) 1956, Bro. 1957, L.A. 1958, Cleve. 1959, Yankees 1960, Wash. 1960, Minn. 1961, Phil. 1961.
Van Slyke Andy: 1983 to present; St.L. 1983-86, Pitt. 1987-present.
Vance, Dazzy: 1915, 1918, 1922-35; Pitt. 1915, Yankees 1915, Yankees 1918, Bro. 1922-32, St.L. 1933, Cinn. 1934, St.L. 1934, Bro. 1935; MVP 1924, HOF.
Vander Meer, Johnny: 1937-43, 1946-51; Cinn. 1937-43, 1946-49, Cubs 1950, Cleve. 1951.
Vaughan, Arky: 1932-43, 1947-48; Pitt. 1932-41, Bro. 1942-43, 1947-48; HOF.
Veach, Bobby: 1912-25; Det. 1912-23, Bos. (A) 1924-25, Yankees 1925, Wash. 1925.
Veale, Bob: 1962-74; Pitt. 1962-72, Bos. 1972-74.
Veeck, Bill: executive; HOF.
Velez, Otto: 1973-83; Yankees 1973-76, Tor. 1977-82, Cleve. 1983.
Venable, Max: 1979-present; S.F. 1979-83, Mont. 1984, Cinn. 1985-87, Cal. 1989-present.
Ventura, Robin: 1989-present; White Sox 1989-present.
Vernon, Mickey: 1939-60; Wash. 1939-48, Cleve. 1949-50, Wash. 1950-55, Bos. (A) 1956-57, Cleve. 1958, Mil. 1959, Pitt. 1960.
Versalies, Zoilo: 1959-71; Wash. 1959-60, Minn. 1961-67, L.A. 1968, Cleve. 1969, Wash. 1969, Atl. 1971.
Veryzer, Tom: 1973-84; Det. 1973-77, Cleve. 1978-81, Mets 1982, Cubs 1983-84.
Vincent, Fay: commissioner.
Viola, Frank: 1982 to present; Minn. 1982-89, Mets 1989-present; Cy Young 1988.
Virdon, Bill: 1955-68; St.L. (N) 1955-56, Pitt. 1956-68; ROY 1955.
Virgil, Ozzie Jr.: 1980-90; Phil. 1980-85, Atl. 1986-88, Tor. 1989-90.
Voiselle, Bill: 1942-50; N.Y. (N) 1942-47, Bos. (N) 1947-49, Cubs 1950.
Vosmik, Joe: 1930-41, 1944; Cleve. 1930-36, St.L. 1937, Bos. (A) 1938-39; Bro. 1940-41, Wash. 1944.
Vuckovich, Pete: 1975-86; White Sox 1975-76, Tor. 1977, St.L. 1978-80, Mil. 1981-86; Cy Young 1982.

W

Waddell, Rube: 1897-10; Lou. 1897, 1899, Pitt. 1900-01, Chi. (N) 1901, Phil. (A) 1902-07, St.L. (A) 1908-10; HOF.
Wagner, Honus: 1897-17; Lou. 1897-99, Pitt. 1900-17; HOF.
Wagner, Leon: 1958-69; S.F. 1958-59, St.L. 1960, L.A. (A) 1961-63, Cleve. 1964-68, White Sox 1968, S.F. 1969.
Waitkus, Eddie: 1941, 1946-55; Cubs 1941, 1946-48, Phil. (N) 1949-53, Balt. 1954-55, Phil. (N) 1955.
Walberg, Rube: 1923-37; N.Y. (N) 1923, Phil. (A) 1923-33, Bos. (A) 1934-37.
Walk, Bob: 1980 to present; Phil. 1980, Atl. 1981-83, Pitt. 1984-present.
Walker, Bill: 1927-36; N.Y. (N) 1927-32, St.L. 1933-36.
Walker, Dixie: 1931, 1933-49; Yankees 1931, 1933-36, White Sox 1936-37, Det. 1938-39, Bro. 1939-47, Pitt. 1948-49.

Walker, Gee: 1931-45; Det. 1931-37, White Sox 1938-39, Wash. 1940, Cleve. 1941, Cinn. 1942-45.
Walker, Harry: 1940-43, 1946-51, 1955; St.L. (N) 1940-43, 1946-47, Phil. 1947-48, Cubs 1949, Cinn. 1949, St.L. (N) 1950-1951, 1955.
Walker, Jerry: 1957-64; Balt. 1957-60, K.C. 1961-62, Cleve. 1963-64.
Walker, Luke: 1965-74; Pitt. 1965-73, Det. 1974.
Wallace, Bobby: 1894-18; Cleve. 1894-98, St.L. (N) 1899-01, St.L. (A) 1902-16, St.L. 1917-18; HOF.
Wallach, Tim: 1980 to present; Mont. 1980-present.
Walling, Denny: 1975-90; Oak. 1975-76, Hou. 1977-88, St.L. 1988-90.
Walsh, Ed: 1904-17; White Sox 1904-16, Bos. (N) 1917; HOF.
Walters, Bucky: 1934-48, 1950; Phil. (N) 1934-38, Cinn. 1938-48, Bos. (N) 1950; MVP 1939.
Walton, Jerome: 1989 to present; Cubs 1989-present; ROY 1989.
Wambsganss, Bill: 1914-26; Cleve. 1914-23, Bos. (A) 1924-25, Phil. (A) 1926.
Waner, Lloyd: 1927-45; Pitt. 1927-41, Bos. (N) 1941, Cinn. 1941, Phil. (N) 1942, Bro. 1944, Pitt. 1944-45; HOF.
Waner, Paul: 1926-45; Pitt. 1926-40, Bro. 1941, Bos. (N) 1941-42, Bro. 1943-44, Yankees 1944-45; MVP 1927, HOF.
Ward, Duane: 1986-present; Atl. 1986, Tor. 1986-present.
Ward, Gary: 1979-90; Minn. 1979-83, Texas 1984-86, Yankees 1987-89, Det. 1989-90.
Ward, John Montgomery: 1878-94; Pro. (N) 1878-82, N.Y. (N) 1883-89, Bro. (P) 1890, Bro. 1891-92, N.Y. (N) 1893-94; HOF.
Warneke, Lon: 1930-43, 1945; Cubs 1930-36, St.L. (N) 1937-42, Cubs 1942-43, 1945.
Warstler, Rabbit: 1930-40; Bos. (A) 1930-33, Phil. (A) 1934-36, Bos. (N) 1936-40, Cubs 1940.
Washburn, Ray: 1961-70; St.L. 1961-69, Cinn. 1970.
Washington, Claudell: 1974-90; Oak. 1974-76, Texas 1977-78, White Sox 1978-80, Mets 1980, Atl. 1981-86, Yankees 1986-88, Cal. 1989-90, Yankees 1990.
Washington, U.L.: 1977-87; K.C. 1977-84, Mont. 1985, Pitt. 1986-87.
Wathan, John: 1976-85; K.C. 1976-85.
Watson, Bob: 1966-84; Hou. 1966-79, Bos. 1979, Yankees 1980-82, Atl. 1982-84.
Weaver, Earl: manager 1968-82, 1985-86.
Webster, Mitch: 1983-present; Tor. 1983-85, Mont. 1985-87, Cubs 1988, Mont. 1988, Cubs 1989, Cleve. 1990-present.
Weiss, George: executive; HOF.
Weiss, Walt: 1987 to present; Oak. 1987-present; ROY 1988.
Welch, Bob: 1978 to present; L.A, 1978-87, Oak. 1988-present.
Welch, Mickey: 1880-92; Tro. 1880-82, N.Y. (N) 1883-92; HOF.
Wert, Don: 1963-71; Det. 1963-70, Wash. 1971.
Wertz, Vic: 1947-63; Det. 1947-52, St.L. (A) 1952-53, Balt. 1954, Cleve. 1954-58, Bos. 1959-61, Det. 1961-63, Minn. 1963.
West, Sammy: 1927-42; Wash. 1927-32, St.L. (A) 1933-38, Wash. 1938-41, White Sox 1942.
Westlake, Wally: 1947-56; Pitt. 1947-51, St.L. (N) 1951-52, Cinn. 1952, Cleve. 1952-55, Balt. 1955, Phil. 1956.
Westrum, Wes: 1947-57; N.Y. (N) 1947-57.
Wheat, Zack: 1909-27; Bro. 1909-26, Phil. 1927; HOF.
Whitaker, Lou: 1977 to present; Det. 1977-present; Tigers, ROY 1978
White, Bill: 1956, 1958-69; N.Y. (N) 1956, S.F. 1958, St.L. 1959-65, Phil. 1966-68, St.L. 1969.
White, Devon: 1985 to present; Cal. 1985-1990, Tor. 1991.
White, Frank: 1973-90; K.C. 1973-90.
White, Roy: 1965-79; Yankees 1965-79.
White, Sammy: 1951-62; Bos. (A) 1951-59, Mil. 1961, Phil. 1962.
Whitehill, Earl: 1923-39; Det. 1923-32, Wash. 1933-36, Cleve. 1937-38, Cubs 1939.
Whitfield, Terry: 1974-80, 1984-86; Yankees 1974-76, S.F. 1977-80, L.A. 1984-86.
Whitney, Pinky: 1928-39; Phil. (N) 1928-33, Bos. (N) 1933-36, Phil. (N) 1936-39.

Whitson, Ed: 1977 to present; Pitt. 1977-79, S.F. 1979-81, Cleve. 1982, S.D. 1983-84, Yankees 1985-86, S.D. 1986-91.
Whitt, Ernie: 1976 to present; Bos. 1976, Tor. 1977-89, Atl. 1990-91, Balt. 1991.
Wilcox, Milt: 1970-86; Cinn. 1970-71, Cleve. 1972-74, Chi. 1975, Det. 1977-85, Seat. 1986.
Wilfong, Rob: 1977-87; Minn. 1977-82, Cal. 1982-86, S.F. 1987.
Wilhelm, Hoyt: 1952-72; N.Y. (N) 1952-56, St.L. (N) 1957, Cleve. 1957-58, Balt. 1958-62, White Sox 1963-68, Cal. 1969, Atl. 1969-70, Cubs 1970, Atl. 1971 L.A. 1971-72; HOF.
Williams, Billy: 1959-76; Cubs 1959-74, Oak. 1975-76; ROY 1961, HOF.
Williams, Cy: 1912-30; Cubs 1912-17, Phil. (N) 1918-30.
Williams, Davey: 1949, 1951-55; N.Y. (N) 1949, 1951-55.
Williams, Earl: 1970-77; Atl. 1970-72, Balt. 1973-74, Atl. 1975-76, Mont. 1976, Oak. 1977; ROY 1971.
Williams, Ken: 1915-16, 1918-39; Cinn. 1915-16, St.L. (A) 1918-27, Bos. (A) 1928-29.
Williams, Matt: 1987 to present; S.F. 1987-present.
Williams, Mitch: 1986-present; Texas 1986-88, Cubs 1989-90, Phil. 1991.
Williams, Stan: 1958-72; L.A. 1958-62, Yankees 1963-64, Cleve. 1965-69, Minn. 1970-71, St.L. 1971, Bos. 1972.
Williams, Ted: 1939-42, 1946-60; Bos. 1939-42, 1946-60; MVP 1946, 1949, HOF.
Williams, Walt: 1964, 1967-75; Hou. 1964, White Sox 1967-72, Cleve. 1973, Yankees 1974-75.
Wills, Bump: 1977-82; Texas 1977-81, Cubs 1982.
Wills, Maury: 1959-72; L.A. 1959-66, Pitt. 1967-68, Mont. 1969, L.A. 1969-72; MVP 1962.
Wilson, Don: 1966-74; Hou. 1966-74.
Wilson, Earl: 1959-70; Bos. 1959-66, Det. 1966-70, S.D. 1970.
Wilson, Glenn: 1982 to present; Det. 1982-83, Phil. 1984-87, Seat. 1988, Pitt. 1988-89, Hou. 1989-90.
Wilson, Hack: 1923-34; N.Y. (N) 1923-25, Cubs 1926-31, Bro. 1932-34, Phil. 1934; HOF.
Wilson, Jack: 1934-42; Phil. (A) 1934, Bos. (A) 1935-41, Wash. 1942, Det. 1942.
Wilson, Jim: 1945-46, 1948-49, 1951-58; Bos. (A) 1945-46, St.L. 1948, Phil 1949, Bos. 1951-52, Mil. 1953-54, Balt. 1955-56, White Sox 1956-58.
Wilson, Jimmy: 1923-40; Phi. (N) 1923-28, St.L. (N) 1928-33, Phil. (N) 1934-38, Cinn. 1939-40.
Wilson, Mookie: 1980-present; Mets 1980-89, Tor. 1989-present.
Wilson, Willie: 1976-present; K.C 1976-90, Oak. 1991.
Winfield, Dave: 1973 to present; S.D. 1973-80, Yankees 1981-90, Cal. 1990-present.
Wise, Rick: 1964, 1966-82; Phil. 1964, 1966-71, St.L. 1972-73, Bos. 1974-77, Cleve. 1978-79, S.D. 1980-82.
Witt, Bobby: 1986 to present; Texas 1986-present.
Witt, Mike: 1981 to present; Cal. 1981-90, Yankees 1990-present.
Wockenfuss, Johnny: 1974-85; Det.1974-83, Phil. 1984-85.
Wohlford, Jim: 1972-86; K.C. 1972-76, Mil. 1977-79, S.F. 1980-82, Mont. 1983-86.
Wood, Wilbur: 1961-78; Bos. 1961-64, Pitt. 1964-65, White Sox 1967-78.
Woodeshick, Hal: 1956, 1958-67; Det. 1956, Cleve. 1958, Wash. 1959-61, Det. 1961, Hou. 1962-65, St.L. 1965-67.
Woodling, Gene: 1943, 1946-62; Cleve. 1943, 1946, Pitt. 1947, Yankees 1949-54, Balt. 1955, Cleve. 1956-57, Balt. 1958-60; Wash. 1961-62.
Worrell, Todd: 1985-89; St.L. 1985-89; ROY 1986.
Worthington, Al: 1953-60, 1963-69; N.Y. (N) 1953-57, S.F. 1958-59, Bos. (A) 1960, White Sox 1960, Cinn. 1963-64, Minn. 1964-69.
Wright, Clyde; 1966-75; Cal. 1966-73, Mil. 1974, Texas 1975.
Wright, George: 1871-82; Bos. (n) 1871-75, Bos. (N) 1876-78, Pro. 1879, Bos. (N) 1880-81, Pro. 1882; HOF.
Wright, Harry: 1871-77; Bos. (n) 1871-75, Bos. (N) 1876-77; HOF.
Wyatt, John; 1961-69; K.C. 1961-66, Bos. 1966-68, Yankees 1968, Det. 1968, Oak. 1969.
Wyatt, Whit: 1929-45; Det. 1929-33, White Sox 1933-36, Cleve. 1937, Bro. 1939-45, Phil. (N) 1946.

Wynegar, Butch: 1976-88; Minn. 1976-82, Yankees 1983-86, Cal. 1987-88.
Wynn, Early: 1939-63; Wash. 1939-48, Cleve. 1949-57, White Sox 1958-63; Cy Young 1959, HOF.
Wynn, Jimmy: 1963-77; Hou. 1963-73, L.A. 1974-75, Atl. 1976, Yankees 1977, Mil. 1977.
Wynne, Marvell: 1983-90; Pitt. 1983-85, S.D. 1986-89, Cubs 1989-90.
Wyrostek, Johnny: 1942-43, 1946-54; Pitt. 1942-43, Phil. (N) 1946-47, Cinn. 1948-52, Phil. (N) 1952-54.

Y

Yastrzemski, Carl: 1961-83; Bos. 1961-83; MVP 1967, HOF.
Yawkey, Tom: executive; HOF.
Yeager, Steve: 1972-86; L.A. 1972-85, Seat. 1986.
York, Rudy: 1934, 1937-48; Det. 1934, 1937-45, Bos. (A) 1946-47, White Sox 1947, Phil. (A) 1948.
Yost, Eddie: 1944-62; Wash. 1944-58, Det. 1959-60, L.A. 1961-62.
Young, Cy: 1890-11; Cleve. 1890-98, St.L. (N) 1899-00, Bos. (A) 1901-08, Cleve. 1909-11, Bos. (N) 1911; HOF.
Young, Curt: 1983-present; Oak. 1983-present.
Young, Matt: 1983-present; Seat. 1983-86, L.A. 1987, Oak. 1989, Seat. 1990, Bos. 1991.
Youngblood, Joel: 1976-89; Cinn. 1976, St.L. 1977, Mets 1977-82, Mont. 1982, S.F. 1983-88, Cinn. 1989.
Youngs, Ross: 1917-26; N.Y. (N) 1917-26; HOF.
Yount, Robin: 1974 to present; Mil. 1974-present; MVP 1982, 1989.

Z

Zachry, Pat: 1976-85; Cinn. 1976-77, Mets 1977-82, L.A. 1983-84, Phil. 1985; ROY 1976.
Zahn, Geoff: 1973-85; L.A. 1973-75, Cubs 1975-76, Minn. 1977-80, Cal. 1981-85.
Zarilla, Al: 1943-53; St.L. (A) 1943-49, Bos. (A) 1949-50, White Sox 1951-52, St.L. 1952, Bos. (A) 1952-53.
Zernial, Gus: 1949-59; White Sox 1949-51, Phil. (A) 1951-54, K.C. 1955-57, Det. 1958-59.
Zimmer, Don: 1954-65; Bro. 1954-57, L.A. 1958-59, Cubs 1960-61, Mets 1962, Cinn. 1962, L.A. 1963, Wash. 1963-65.
Zisk, Richie: 1971-83; Pitt. 1971-76, White Sox 1977, Texas 1978-80, Seat. 1981-83.

Top 25
Most Valuable Autographed Team Baseballs

1. **1927 New York Yankees - $10,000:** Huggins, Gehrig, Lazzeri, Ruth, Combs, Meusel, Hoyt, Moore, Pennock.
2. **1932 New York Yankees - $5,500:** McCarthy, Gehrig, Lazzeri, Sewell, Ruth, Combs, Dickey, Ruffing, Allen, Pennock.
3. **1928 New York Yankees - $4,000:** Huggins, Gehrig, Lazzeri, Koenig, Ruth, Combs, Dickey, Pipgras, Hoyt, Pennock, Coveleski.
4. **1926 New York Yankees - $4,000:** Huggins, Gehrig, Lazzeri, Ruth, Combs, Meusel, Pennock, Hoyt.
5. **1924 New York Yankees - $3,750:** Huggins, Ruth, Dugan, Meusel, Combs, Gehrig, Pennock, Hoyt.
6. **1931 New York Yankees - $3,600:** McCarthy, Gehrig, Lazzeri, Sewell, Ruth, Combs, Chapman, Dickey, Ruffing, Gomez, Pennock.
7. **1925 New York Yankees - $3,475:** Huggins, Gehrig, Ruth, Hoyt, Pennock.
8. **1933 New York Yankees - $3,475:** McCarthy, Gehrig, Lazzeri, Sewell, Ruth, Combs, Chapman, Dickey, Gomez, Allen, Ruffing, Pennock.
9. **1929 New York Yankees - $3,400:** Huggins, Gehrig, Lazzeri, Ruth, Combs, Dickey, Wells, Hoyt, Pennock.
10. **1930 New York Yankees - $3,400:** Gehrig, Lazzeri, Chapman, Ruth, Combs, Dickey, Ruffing, Pennock, Hoyt, Gomez.
11. **1934 New York Yankees - $3,250:** McCarthy, Gehrig, Lazzeri, Ruth, Dickey, Combs, Gomez, Ruffing, Grimes.
12. **1923 New York Yankees - $3,125:** Pipp, Ruth, Witt, Meusel, Gehrig, Pennock, Hoyt, Huggins.
13. **1927 Philadelphia (AL) - $2,750:** Mack, Dykes, Hale, Cobb, Simmons, French, Cochrane, Collins, Wheat, Foxx, Grove.
14. **1921 New York Yankees - $2,700:** Huggins, Ward, Baker, Meusel, Ruth, Mays, Hoyt.
15. **1920 New York Yankees - $2,700:** Pratt, Ruth, Mays, Shawkey, Huggins.
16. **1923 New York Giants - $2,625:** Kelly, Frisch, Bancroft, Youngs, Jackson, Stengel, Terry, Wilson, Ryan, McGraw.
17. **1922 New York Yankees - $2,550:** Pipp, Meusel, Ruth, Schang, Baker, Bush, Shawkey, Hoyt, Huggins.
18. **1928 Philadelphia (AL) - $2,500:** Mack, Bishop, Hale, Cobb, Miller, Simmons, Cochrane, Foxx, Speaker, Collins, Grove, Quinn.
19. **1921 New York Giants - $2,400:** Kelly, Bancroft, Frisch, Youngs, Meusel, Snyder, Stengel, Nehf, McGraw.
20. **1922 New York Giants - $2,350:** Kelly, Bancroft, Frisch, Youngs, Meusel, Snyder, Stengel, Nehf, Jackson.
21. **1924 New York Giants - $2,300:** Kelly, Frisch, Jackson, Youngs, Wilson, Snyder, Terry, Lindstrom, Bentley, McGraw.
22. **1925 New York Giants - $2,250:** McGraw, Terry, Kelly, Jackson, Lindstrom, Youngs, Meusel, Frisch, Wilson.
23. **1927 New York Giants - $2,250:** McGraw, Terry, Hornsby, Jackson, Lindstrom, Harper, Roush, Ott, Grimes.
24. **1926 New York Giants - $2,150:** McGraw, Kelly, Frisch, Jackson, Lindstrom, Youngs, Terry, Ott.
25. **1920 Chicago White Sox - Uncertain:** E. Collins, Risberg, Weaver, Leibold, Felsch, Jackson, Schalk, Faber, Williams, Kerr, Cicotte.

Top All-Star Balls

1. 1933 American League - $8,000: Mack, Collins, Gehrig, Ruth.
2. 1934 American League - $7,000: Gehrig, Ruth, Foxx.
3. 1936 American League - $6,000: Foxx, Gehrig, DiMaggio.
4. 1938 American League - $5,500: Foxx, DiMaggio, Gehrig.
5. 1939 American League - $5,000: Foxx, DiMaggio, Gehrig.
6. 1937 American League - $5,000: Foxx, DiMaggio, Gehrig.
7. 1935 American League - $5,000: Foxx, Gehrig, Hornsby.
8. 1933 National League - $2,800: McGraw, Traynor, Waner, Frisch.
9. 1934 National League - $2,500: Ott, Traynor, Vaughan, Waner.
10. 1937 National League - $1,800: Frisch, Ott, Vaughan.

Can You Identify These Team Baseballs?

A.

B.

C.

A. 1941 New York Yankees
B. 1965 San Francisco Giants
C. 1954 New York Yankees
D. 1965 New York Mets
E. 1964 New York Mets

D.

E.

Can You Identify These Team Baseballs?

F.

G.

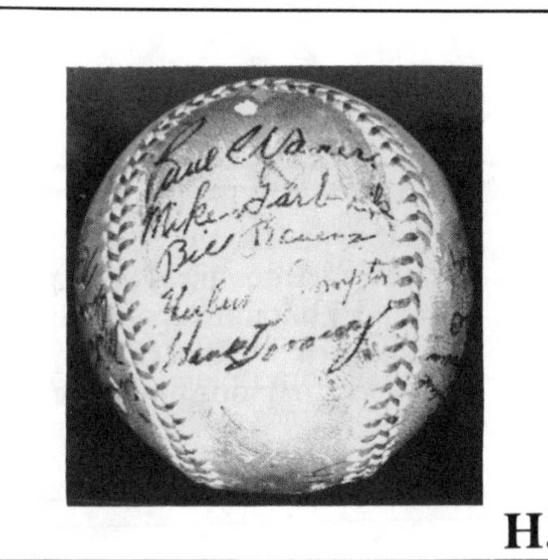

H.

F. 1978 New York Yankees
G. 1961 New York Yankees
H. 1945 New York Yankees
I. 1949 New York Yankees
J. 1960 New York Yankees

I.

J.

Can You Identify These Team Baseballs?

K.

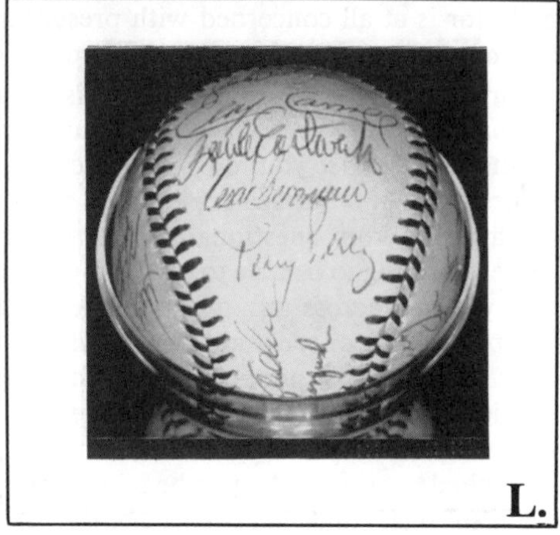

L.

M.

K. 1949 Brooklyn Dodgers
L. 1975 Cincinnati Reds
M. 1963 Brooklyn Dodgers
N. 1960 Pittsburgh Pirates
O. 1955 Brooklyn Dodgers

N.

O.

Suggestions

The acquisition of autographed baseball memorabilia should be handled with care if the collector is at all concerned with preserving the value and integrity of his collection. Here are some suggestions that are reinforced by other chapters in this book:

☆ Buy your material from an established and reputable dealer or obtain them in person. Qualify dealers yourself, by first purchasing small amounts of material easily verified for authenticity. Use your own judgement in determining whether a dealer is reputable; taking the advice of other dealers is a risk.

☆ Stay away from questionable material. If you can't explain the anomalies of a piece, how are you going to be able to sell it when such a time arises?

☆ If you run across any questionable material at a dealer's table, and you feel a need to express your concerns, do so in private.

☆ Do not make any public claims of forgery, unvalidated or unsubstantiated, that could lead to legal ramifications. If an item does not look good don't buy it.

☆ Usually, the more expensive the autographed item, the less likely it is a forgery. An autographed bat is less likely to be fake versus the same signature on a postcard.

☆ Try to collect material that can be dated, such as baseballs and cards.

☆ Stay away from signatures in pencil, unless you consider yourself an expert.

☆ Do not be intimidated as a dealer or collector. Have faith in your own ability to make an accurate judgement based on your knowledge.

☆ If you experience a bad transaction with another dealer or collector simply don't deal with him anymore.

☆ Quality will vary from one dealer to the next, and so will expertise. Try to deal with individuals who specialize in the areas you are collecting.

☆ Maintain an up-to-date clip file of authentic signatures for comparison.

☆ If you find an expensive item that you want to purchase, it may be worth spending a few dollars to have it authenticated by an expert.

☆ Cautiously inspect all autographed material over 30 years old before making a purchase. Material from members of the Hall of Fame inducted in the last 30 years, with the exception of those deceased prior to induction, is generally available and abundant in a variety of forms. You will find a lot more forged Babe Ruth signatures than those of Ted Williams.

☆ Meticulously study older signature samples. A person's signature can vary extensively with age and health.

☆ Always be familiar with a dealer's return policy prior to a purchase.

☆ Don't immediately discount the authenticity of unusual items; there are many unique items in this market.

The threat of forgery is not unique to autograph collecting, it is a concern to anyone who deals with any type of valuable merchandise. It is a threat that can be dissipated by education and following the suggestions of those who have made mistakes in the past. With a thorough knowledge of the characteristics of forgeries and genuine signatures, the expert can determine the authenticity of virtually all the materials examined. There will always be a small percentage that exemplify both characteristics; that fact must be accepted by both the collector and the hobby. Baseball autograph collecting is a wonderful way to cherish the memory of an individual, and, with the commitment of everyone in the hobby to educate themselves on forgery detection, it will continue to be an enjoyable pursuit.

Materials analysis — Chart I

Players who couldn't have signed in fountain pen (1884).
* — denotes unlikely (limited time) ** — very unlikely

Alexander Cartwright (1892)*	Mike Kelly (1894)*	Harry Wright (1895)*

Materials analysis — Chart II

Players who couldn't have signed in ballpoint pen (1944)
* — denotes unlikely (limited time) ** — very unlikely

Cap Anson (1922)
Jacob Beckley (1918)
Roger Bresnahan (1944)**
Dan Brouthers (1932)
Morgan Bulkeley (1922)
Alexander Cartwright (1892)
Henry Chadwick (1908)
Frank Chance (1924)
Jack Chesbro (1931)
John Clarkson (1909)
James Collins (1943) **
Charles Comiskey (1931)
Roger Connor (1931)
Candy Cummings (1924)
Ed Delahanty (1903)
Buck Ewing (1906)
Rube Foster (1930)
Pud Galvin (1902)
Lou Gehrig (1941)
Bill Hamilton (1940)
Miller Huggins (1929)
Hugh Jennings (1928)
Ban Johnson (1931)
Addie Joss (1911)
Tim Keefe (1933)
Willie Keeler (1923)
Joe Kelley (1943)**
King Kelly (1894)
Judge Landis (1944) **
Christy Mathewson (1925)
Tom McCarthy (1922)
Joe McGinnity (1929)
John McGraw (1934)
James O'Rourke (1919)
Ed Plank (1926)
Hoss Radbourn (1897)
Wilbert Robinson (1934)
Amos Rusie (1942)
Al Spalding (1915)
Sam Thompson (1922)
Rube Waddell (1914)
John Ward (1925)
Mickey Welch (1941)
George Wright (1937)
Harry Wright (1895)
Ross Youngs (1927)

Materials analysis — Chart III

Players who couldn't have signed in felt tip pen (1964).
* — denotes unlikely (limited time) ** — very unlikely

Cap Anson (1922)
Frank Baker (1963) **
Ed Barrow (1953)
Jacob Beckley (1918)
Chief Bender (1954)
James Bottomley (1959)
Roger Bresnahan (1944)
Dan Brouthers (1932)
Mordecai Brown (1948)
Morgan Bulkeley (1922)
Jesse Burkett (1953)
Alexander Cartwright (1892)
Henry Chadwick (1908)
Frank Chance (1924)
Oscar Charleston (1954)
Jack Chesbro (1931)
Fred Clarke (1960)
John Clarkson (1909)
Ty Cobb (1961)
Mickey Cochrane (1962)
Eddie Collins (1951)
James Collins (1943)
Charles Comiskey (1931)
Tom Connolly (1961)
Roger Connor (1931)
Candy Cummings (1924)
Kiki Cuyler (1950)
Ed Delahanty (1903)
Hugh Duffy (1954)
Bill Evans (1956)
John Evers (1947)
Buck Ewing (1906)
Rube Foster (1930)
Pud Galvin (1902)
Lou Gehrig (1941)
Josh Gibson (1947)
Clark Griffith (1955)
Bill Hamilton (1940)
Harry Heilmann (1951)
Rogers Hornsby (1963) **
Miller Huggins (1929)
Hugh Jennings (1928)
Ban Johnson (1931)
Walter Johnson (1946)
Addie Joss (1911)
Tim Keefe (1933)
Willie Keeler (1923)
Joe Kelley (1943)
King Kelly (1894)
Chuck Klein (1958)
Bill Klem (1951)
Nap Lajoie (1959)
Judge Landis (1944)
John Lloyd (1965) **
Connie Mack (1956)
Rabbit Maranville (1954)
Christy Mathewson (1925)
Tom McCarthy (1922)
Joe McGinnity (1929)
John McGraw (1934)
Kid Nichols (1953)
James O'Rourke (1919)
Mel Ott (1958)
Herb Pennock (1948)
Ed Plank (1926)
Hoss Radbourn (1897)
Eppa Rixey (1963) **
Wilbert Robinson (1934)
Amos Rusie (1942)
Babe Ruth (1948)
Al Simmons (1956)
Al Spalding (1915)
Tris Speaker (1958)
Sam Thompson (1922)
Joe Tinker (1948)
Dazzy Vance (1961)
Arky Vaughan (1952)
Rube Waddell (1914)
Honus Wagner (1955)
Bobby Wallace (1960)
Ed Walsh (1959)
Paul Waner (1965) *
John Ward (1925)
Mickey Welch (1941)
Hack Wilson (1948)
George Wright (1937)
Harry Wright (1895)
Cy Young (1955)
Ross Youngs (1927)

Hints for acquiring autographs through the mail

☆ Always include a self-addressed stamped envelope (SASE) for convenient response. Please be sure that the enclosed envelope is of proper size to house the returned material, and that proper postage is affixed.

☆ Be brief, personal and sincere with your request. Exhibit in a few sentences your genuine interest in, and knowledge of, a player's career. Courtesy is paramount.

☆ Avoid form letters. In addition to being inpersonal and unflattering, the letters typically have a low response rate.

☆ To avoid confusion and disappointing responses, requests should be succinct and specific. If personalization is desired, please clearly indicate it in your request.

☆ Be conscious of a player's time by including no more than one or two items to be autographed.

☆ Be reasonable with your expectations. Some players receive hundreds of requests a day and have little time to read a request, let alone respond to it.

☆ Don't risk sending expensive items through the mail. Although I am astounded by the accuracy and promptness exhibited by the U.S. Postal Service, most collectors are not in position to replace lost merchandise.

☆ Be creative with your request. Prior to sending out your letter collectors should ask themselves these questions: What is unique about my request that will make a player want to respond? Will my request stand out among the hundreds of others he receives? What would be my reaction to such a request?

Baseball autograph acquisition evaluation

This chart/scoring system was developed to aid the collector in determining his acquisition risk for a particular piece of autographed baseball memorabilia.

Question	Score	Possible Points
1.) How would you rate the scarcity of the item autographed? 5 4 3 2 1 (Abundant) (Scarce)	____	5
2.) Can the autographed item be dated? (Yes = 5, No = 1)	____	5
3.) Rate the value of the autographed item: 5 4 3 2 1 (High) (Low)	____	5
4.) Does the autographed item show any signs of alteration or variation from known characteristics? (Yes = 1, No = 10)	____	10
5.) Does the writing instrument used conform in origin to the signee's lifetime? (Yes = 5, No = 1)	____	5

6.) Was the material obtained through a reputable source? (Yes = 10, Unsure = 5, No = 1) ______ 10

7.) Is the source you obtained the item from willing to provide any guarantees, return policy, letter of authenticity, etc? (Yes = 10, No = 1) ______ 10

8.) Signature characteristics: (Score each) (Yes = 10, Unsure = 2, No = 0)

— Does the capitalization conform to known examples? ______ 10

— Does the signature size conform to known examples? ______ 10

— Does the character formation conform to known examples? ______ 10

— Does the signature slant conform to known examples? ______ 10

— Does the style (flamboyance) conform to known examples? ______ 10

Note: A "no" answer to any question after #5 should make you reconsider your purchasing plans.

Scoring:

7-60 high risk 60-80 moderate risk 80-100 little risk

Collector's checklist for mail ordering

Is there a minimum order?
What are the postage and handling costs?
What types of payments are accepted — VISA, MasterCard, etc.?
Is there a minimum credit card order?
What amount of sales tax is required?
Can items be reserved?
Does the dealer ship to post office boxes?
What are the proper insurance costs?
Are there volume discounts available?
Do I have to include a SASE (self-addressed stamped envelope) with the order?
Can items be shipped outside the continental United States?
Can I be added to the dealer's mailing list?
Does the dealer accept COD (cash on delivery) orders?
If CODs are accepted, what type of payment does the dealer prefer?
If I pre-order an item and change my mind at a later date, can I be refunded?
Can items be sent on approval?
Are foreign funds accepted?
Are all sales final?
What is the dealer's return policy?
When should I expect delivery?
How is the item being delivered?
Is there a money-back guarantee?

Common mail bid auction rules

- ☆ Postage and insurance are typically added to the invoice.
- ☆ Most auctions do not allow "buy" or unlimited bids. A "buy" is when the auctioneer is told by a bidder to buy the lot for a reasonable cost mutually determined, commonly 10 percent above previous bid.
- ☆ Commonly lots are not to be broken into individual items, therefore bidders are requested to bid by lot.
- ☆ The highest bid should represent the maximum selling price of the lot; no additional charges beyond postage and handling should be added to the total.
- ☆ Invoicing by seller should commence within 10 days after closing date of the sale. Payment upon receipt of invoice is expected promptly. Included with the invoice, and provided by the seller, should be a SASE (self-addressed stamped envelope) as a courtesy to the highest bidder.
- ☆ Mail bid sales commonly close two weeks from date of auction publication, unless otherwise stated by seller.
- ☆ As a guarantee that the highest bidder will honor his bid, seller may require a deposit. This deposit is typically not returned if high bidder fails to honor his bids, it shall however be applied as partial payment against the bid made by the highest bidder. Any deposit requested by seller must be clearly stated in the catalog or advertisement. Any deposits being held by seller from unsuccessful bidders must be returned promptly following the close of the auction.
- ☆ Any item not properly described — condition or grading, year, manufacturer — by the seller may be returned by the highest bidder. All items should be guaranteed authentic by the seller.
- ☆ A seller should allow a grace period of up to two weeks upon receipt of buyer for returns from highest bidder.
- ☆ A seller has the right to reject a bid for any reason whatsoever.
- ☆ A bidder is obligated to honor any and all bids submitted.
- ☆ Any unusual exception to common mail bid rules for an auction must be clearly stated by the seller in the auction catalog or advertisement.
- ☆ A pre-registration procedure may be requested in order to simplify bidding procedure on the final day of the auction.
- ☆ A seller should be accessible during specific times during the auction's duration in order to answer questions from bidders.
- ☆ A seller may request minimum bid increases over previous bid.

About the author

Mark Allen Baker has a bachelor's degree from the State University of New York. He has been published in various books and more than 20 periodicals, including Computer Graphics World, Byte, Computer Pictures, CFO, Public Relations Journal, Computer Graphics Review, Personal Computing, Topps Magazine and Sports Collectors Digest. During his career Baker has worked in a variety of finance, marketing, sales and executive management positions for the General Electric Corp., Genigraphics Corp. and Pansophic Systems Inc.

Formal museum studies, including training in paper preservation and conservation, have proven particularly helpful during Baker's 20 years of autograph collecting. Baker has also been involved in designing and manufacturing computer-based image processing systems that can be used for autograph authentication purposes.

Additional biographical data can be found in numerous professional directories, including "Who's Who in the East."

Other books by the author:

* Sports Collectors Digest Baseball Autograph Handbook, 1990, Krause Publications
* Sports Collectors Digest Baseball Autograph Handbook, second edition, 1991, Krause Publications

Acknowledgements

I would like to thank everyone at Krause Publications, especially Pat Klug, Mary Sieber, Mark Larson, Bob Lemke, Steve Ellingboe, Chris Williams, Gretchen Laatsch, Wendy Liter, Laureen Gagnow and Judy Floistad.

A special thanks to the National Baseball Hall of Fame, particularly William J. Guilfoile, and Bill Deane.

To Max Patkin, thanks for showing everyone that baseball is still just a game.

To my "ad hoc" production team (Alison Morrissey and Julie Ziele) for its diligent commitment to my task, and sincerest support.

To my brother Matthew Baker and my wonderful parents, Mr. and Mrs. Ford Baker, thank you for helping me make it through the most difficult period of my life, and giving me hope for the days ahead.

Additional source material and notes

( ) = page

Foreword

Prepared exclusively for this book by Max Patkin, Sept. 28, 1991.

(6) Photograph courtesy of Orion Pictures Corp. Copyright 1988; via Max Patkin.

Chapter 1

(10) "Baseball is the very symbol..." quoted from a transcript of a speech given by Mark Twain in 1889 in New York City

(10) "Baseball is not life itself..." from Season Ticket, by Roger Angell, Houghton Mifflin Co. 1988, Boston, Mass.

(11) Photograph courtesy of the National Baseball Library, Cooperstown, N.Y.

(15) Richard Nixon photograph courtesy of the National Baseball Library, Cooperstown, N.Y.

(16) 1924 Monarchs photograph courtesy of the National Baseball Library, Cooperstown, N.Y.

Chapter 2

(See Bibliography)

Sports Collectors Digest — "Starting an Autographed Baseball Collection," by Mark Allen Baker, March 10, 1989.

The Sporting News —"Set The Standard," March 4, 1905.

The New York Times — "From Spalding to Reach to Aaron — There's Only One Baseball," by Reginald Stuart, April 8, 1974.

The *Daily Press* (Utica) — "The National Pastime Is a Losing Proposition for Baseball Maker," by Murray Olderman, March 30, 1972.

Springfield Republican — "Baseballs 'Farmed Out' to Haiti," March 18, 1973.

The Sporting News — "Official Baseball Rules," 1988 (Reference Only).

Chicago Tribune — "Manufacturing baseballs is no game to Rawlings officials," April 26, 1987.

Chapter 3

(See Bibliography)

"Sharpie" is a registered trademark of the Sanford Corp. of Bellwood, Ill.

Nation's Business — "Mighty Battle of the Pens," November 1946.

(23) Photograph courtesy of the National Baseball Library, Cooperstown, N.Y.

(24) "A pen formed of a piece..." quoted from a 1890 U.S. patent.

(24) Photograph courtesy of Parker Pens.

Additional source material provided by Parker and Paper Mate, a division of the Gillette Co.

Chapter 4

(See Bibliography)

Chapter 5

(32) Photograph courtesy of Bleachers, Liverpool, N.Y.

(39) "In the market, if people..." from a conversation with Fay Vincent, June 1991 in Cooperstown, N.Y.

Chapter 6

(See Bibliography)

Chapter 7

(53) "Illegible Signatures" is a subjective analysis.

Chapter 12

(481) Rose photograph courtesy of the National Baseball Library, Cooperstown, N.Y.

Chapter 13

(482) Photograph courtesy of the National Baseball Library, Cooperstown, N.Y.

(482) "It is a pastime..." from the Spalding Official Baseball Guide, 1911.

(483) Showcase photograph courtesy of the National Baseball Library, Cooperstown, N.Y.

(483) "The game of baseball is a clean, straight game..." from the Spalding Official Baseball Guide, 1911.

(485) Eisenhower and Kennedy photographs courtesy of the National Baseball Library, Cooperstown, N.Y.

The National Baseball Hall of Fame and Museum and National Baseball Library supplied many of the baseballs for illustration throughout this book.

Selected bibliography and recommended reading

Angell, Roger. Season Ticket. Boston, Mass.: Houghton Mifflin Co., 1988.

Astor, Gerald and the National Baseball Hall of Fame and Museum Inc., the National Baseball Library. The Baseball Hall of Fame 50th Anniversary Book. New York: Prentice Hall Press, 1988.

Baker, Mark A. Sports Collectors Digest Baseball Autograph Handbook, Iola, Wis.: Krause Publications Inc., 1990.

Baker, Mark A. Sports Collectors Digest Baseball Autograph Handbook, second edition. Iola, Wis.: Krause Publications Inc., 1991.

Beckett, James and Dennis W. Eckes. The Sports Americana Baseball Memorabilia and Autograph Price Guide. Lakewood, Ohio: Edgewater Book Co. Inc., 1982.

Benjamin, Mary A. Autographs: A Key to Collecting. New York: R.R. Bowker, 1946; revised edition, 1963.

Berkeley, Edmund, editor, and Herbert Klingelhofer and Kenneth Rendell, co-editors. Autographs and Manuscripts: A Collector's Manual. New York: Charles Scribner's Sons, 1978.

Bowden, Glen. Collectible Fountain Pens. Glenview, Ill. Glen Bowden Communications

Carter, Craig, editor. The Sporting News — The Complete Baseball Record Book. St. Louis: The Sporting New Publishing Co., 1988.

Carvalho, David N. Forty Centuries of Ink, or a Chronological Narrative Concerning Ink and Its Background. New York: Banks Law Publishing Co., 1904.

Clapp, Anne F. Curatorial Care of Works of Art on Paper. Oberlin: Intermuseum Conservation Association, 1973.

Cohen, Richard and David S. Neft. The Sports Encyclopedia — Baseball — 11th Edition. New York, N.Y.: St. Martin's Press, 1991.

Doloff, Francis W., and Roy L. Perkinson. How to Care for Works of Art on Paper. Boston: Museum of Fine Arts, 1971.

Eckes, Dennis and R.J. Smalling. The Sport Americana Baseball Address List, No. 5. Cleveland: Edgewater Book Co. Inc., 1988.

Einstein, Charles, editor. The Fireside Book of Baseball. New York: Simon and Schuster, 1956.

Harrison, Wilson R. Suspect Documents: Their Scientific Examination. London: Sweet and Maxwell, 1958.

James, Bill. Historical Abstract of Baseball. New York: Villard Books, 1986.

Kathpalia, Yash Pal. Conservation and Restoration of Archive Materials. Paris: UNESCO, 1973.

Nickell, Joe. Pen, Ink, & Evidence. Lexington, Ky.: The University Press of Kentucky, 1990.

Lanigan, Ernest. The Sporting News Record Book for 1939. St. Louis: Charles C. Spink and Son, 1939.

Lawrence, Cliff. Official P.F.C. Pen Guide. Dunedin, Fla.

Maginnis, James P. Reservoir, Stylographic, and Fountain Pens. Cantor Lectures. London: William Trounce, 1905.

Osborn, Albert S. Questioned Documents, second edition. Montclair, N.J.: Patterson Smith, 1978.

Panati, Charles. The Browser's Book of Beginnings. Boston: Houghton Mifflin, 1984.

Reach Official Baseball Guide(s), edited by Francis Richter. Philadelphia: A.J. Reach Sporting Goods Co.

Reichler, Joseph, editor. The Baseball Encyclopedia, sixth edition. New York: Macmillian Publishing Co. Inc., 1985.

Reidenbaugh, Lowell. Take Me Out To The Ball Park. St. Louis: The Sporting News Publishing Co., 1983.

Reidenbaugh, Lowell. Baseball's Hall of Fame, Cooperstown, Where Legends Live Forever. New York: Arlington House Inc., 1986.

Rogosin, Donn. Invisible Men — Life in Baseball's Negro Leagues. New York: Antheneum, 1983.

Rosen, Alan. Insider's Guide To Investing in Baseball Cards and Collectibles. New York, N.Y.: Warner Books Inc., 1991

Spalding Official Baseball Guide. New York: American Sports Publishing Co., 1890-1941.

Thorn, John and Pete Palmer. Total Baseball, second edition. New York, N.Y.: Warner Books Inc., 1991.

Thorn, John. The Game for All America. St. Louis, Mo.: The Sporting News Publishing Co., 1988.

Webster's 9th New Collegiate Dictionary. Springfield: Miriam-Webster Inc., 1986.

Periodicals

John Raybin's Baseball Autograph News, 527 Third Ave., New York, N.Y. 10016

Sports Collectors Digest: Krause Publications Inc., 700 East State St., Iola, Wis. 54990

Street & Smith's Baseball: Conde Nast Publications Inc., Street & Smiths Sports Group, 304 East 45th St., New York, N.Y. 10017.

The Autograph Collector's Magazine, P.O. Box 55328, Stockton, Calif. 95205.

The Autograph Review, 305 Carlton Road, Syracuse, N.Y. 13207.